ASIMOV'S
GUIDE TO
THE BIBLE
TWO VOLUMES IN ONE

ASIMOV'S GUIDE TO THE BIBLE

TWO VOLUMES IN ONE
THE OLD AND NEW TESTAMENTS

ISAAC ASIMOV

Maps by Rafael Palacios

AVENEL BOOKS

NEW YORK

This book was previously published in two volumes as
Asimov's Guide to the Bible: Volume One, The Old Testament and
Asimov's Guide to the Bible: Volume Two, The New Testament

This edition is published by Avenel Books,
distributed by Crown Publishers, Inc., 225 Park Avenue South,
New York, New York 10003,
by arrangement with Doubleday & Company, Inc.
r q p o n m l
AVENEL 1981 EDITION

Manufactured in the United States of America

Library of Congress Cataloging in Publication Data

Asimov, Isaac, 1920–
Asimov's Guide to the Bible.

Reprint. Originally published in 2 v.: Garden
City, N.Y. : Doubleday, 1968-1969.
Includes indexes.
1. Bible—History of Biblical events.   2. Bible
—Criticism, interpretation, etc.   I.   Title.
II. Title: Guide to the Bible.
BS635.2.A8   1981   220.9′5   81-3537
ISBN 0-517-34582-X   AACR2

CONTENTS

Volume One

Volume Two

INTRODUCTION

The most influential, the most published, the most widely read book in the history of the world is the Bible. No other book has been so studied and so analyzed and it is a tribute to the complexity of the Bible and the eagerness of its students that after thousands of years of study there are still endless books that can be written about it.

I have myself written two short books for young people on the earlier books of the Bible* but I have long wanted to take on a job of more ambitious scope; one that I can most briefly describe as a consideration of the secular aspects of the Bible.

Most people who read the Bible do so in order to get the benefit of its ethical and spiritual teachings, but the Bible has a secular side, too. It is a history book covering the first four thousand years of human civilization.

The Bible is not a history book in modern sense, of course, since its writers lacked the benefit of modern archaeological techniques, did not have our concept of dating and documentation, and had different standards of what was and was not significant in history. Furthermore, Biblical interest was centered primarily on developments that impinged upon those dwelling in Canaan, a small section of Asia bordering on the Mediterranean Sea. This area makes only a small mark on the history of early civilization (from the secular viewpoint) and modern histories, in contrast to the Bible, give it comparatively little space.

Nevertheless, for most of the last two thousand years, the Bible has been virtually the only history book used in Western civilization. Even today, it remains the most popular, and its view of ancient history is still more widely and commonly known than is that of any other.

So it happens, therefore, that millions of people today know of Nebuchadnezzar, and have never heard of Pericles, simply because Nebuchadnezzar is mentioned prominently in the Bible and Pericles is never mentioned at all.

Millions know of Ahasuerus as a Persian king who married Esther, even though there is no record of such an event outside the Bible. Most of those same millions never suspect that he is better known to modern historians as Xerxes and that the most important event in his reign was an invasion of Greece that ended in utter defeat. That invasion is not mentioned in the Bible.

* *Words in Genesis* and *Words from the Exodus.*

Millions know certain minor Egyptian Pharaohs, such as Shishak and Necho, who are mentioned in the Bible, but have never heard of the great conquering Pharaoh, Thutmose III, who is not. People whose very existence is doubtful, such as Nimrod and the queen of Sheba, are household words because they are mentioned in the Bible, while figures who were colossal in their day are sunk in oblivion because they are not.

Again, small towns in Canaan, such as Shechem and Bethel, in which events of the Bible are described as taking place, are more familiar to us today than are large ancient metropolises such as Syracuse or Egyptian Thebes, which are mentioned only glancingly in the Bible, or not at all.

Moreover, usually only that is known about such places as happens to be mentioned in the Bible. Ecbatana, the capital of the Median Empire, is remembered in connection with the story of Tobit, but its earlier and later history are dim indeed to most people, who might be surprised to know that it still exists today as a large provincial capital in the modern nation of Iran.

In this book, then, I am assuming a reader who is familiar with the Bible, at least in its general aspects, but who knows little of ancient history outside the Bible. I assume a reader who would be interested in filling in the fringe, so to speak, and who would expect much of the Bible to become easier to understand if some of the places and people mentioned in it are made less mysterious. (After all, those places and people were well known to the original readers of the Bible, and it would be sad to allow so important a book to grow needlessly murky with the passing of the centuries because the periphery has grown dim and indistinct.)

I am attempting to correct this, in part at least. I will, for instance, speculate on who Nimrod might have been, try to define the time in which Abraham entered Canaan, place David's kingdom in its world setting, sort out the role played by the various monarchs who are only mentioned in the Bible when they fight against Israel and Judah, and work out the relationships among the Herods encountered by Jesus and the Apostles.

I am trying, in short, to bring in the outside world, illuminate it in terms of the Biblical story and, in return, illuminate the events of the Bible by adding to it the non-Biblical aspects of history, biography, and geography.

In doing so, there will be the constant temptation (born of the modern view of history) to bring in dates though few can be definitely assigned to individual events in the Bible. It will be convenient then to make use of a more or less arbitrary set of "periods" which will chop history into sections that will make for easy reference.

The period from the beginning of the earliest civilizations, say 4000 B.C. to 100 A.D., can be lumped together as "the Biblical period." Of this the period to 400 B.C. is "the Old Testament period," from 400 B.C. to 4 B.C. is the "inter-Testamental period," while the A.D. section is "the New Testament period."

The Biblical period can be broken down into smaller sections as follows:

4000 B.C. to 2000 B.C. — The Primeval period
2000 B.C. to 1700 B.C. — The Patriarchal period
1700 B.C. to 1200 B.C. — The Egyptian period
1200 B.C. to 1000 B.C. — The Tribal period
1000 B.C. to 900 B.C. — The Davidic kingdom

Thereafter, it is most convenient to name periods after the peoples who did, in fact, dominate western Asia. Thus:

900 B.C. to 600 B.C. — The Assyrian period
600 B.C. to 540 B.C. — The Babylonian period
540 B.C. to 330 B.C. — The Persian period
330 B.C. to   70 B.C. — The Greek period
 70 B.C. to 100 A.D. — The Roman period

During the last century of the Greek period, the Jews won a brief independence under the Maccabees, so that the century from 170 B.C. to 70 B.C. might be called "the Maccabean period."

I cannot pretend that in writing this book I am making any significant *original* contribution to Biblical scholarship; indeed, I am not competent to do so. All that I will have to say will consist of material well known to students of ancient history. (There will, however, be a few places where I will indulge in personal speculation, and label it as such.)

Nevertheless, it is my hope that this material, well known though it may be in separate bits, will now be presented in a newly useful way, since it will be collected and placed within the covers of a moderately sized book, presented in one uniform manner, and in a style and fashion which, it is hoped, will be interesting to the average reader of the Bible.

I intend to be completely informal in this book, and to adhere to no rigid rules. I won't invariably discuss a place or person at its first appearance in the Bible, if it seems to me I can make more sense out of it by bringing the matter up in a later connection. I will not hesitate to leave a discussion incomplete if I plan to take it up again later on. I will leave out items toward which I don't feel I can contribute anything either useful or interesting, and I will, without particular concern, allow myself to digress if I feel that the digression will be useful.

Again, since this book is not intended to be a scholarly compendium, I do not plan to burden its pages with such extraneous appurtenances as footnotes giving sources. The sources that I use are, after all, very general and ordinary ones.

First of all, of course, are various versions of the Bible:

a) The Authorized Version, originally published in 1611 and familiarly known as the "King James Bible." This is the Bible used in the various Protestant churches. It is the version which is most familiar to most Americans and it is from this version that I quote, except where otherwise indicated.

b) The Revised Standard Version, Thomas Nelson & Sons, 1946, 1952, and 1959.

c) Saint Joseph "New Catholic Edition," Catholic Book Publishing Co., 1962.

d) The Jerusalem Bible, Doubleday and Co., Inc., 1966.

e) The Holy Scriptures according to the Masoretic text, The Jewish Publication Society of America, 1955.

f) I have leaned particularly heavily on those volumes of the Anchor Bible (Doubleday) so far published, since these represent some of the latest and most profound thinking on the Bible.

Much of the Apocrypha is contained in the "New Catholic Edition" and, in addition, I have made use of the King James Version and the Revised Standard Version of these books.

I have also consulted, quite steadily, A New Standard Bible Dictionary, Third Revised Edition, Funk and Wagnalls Company, 1936, The Abingdon Bible Commentary, Abingdon Press, 1929, and "Dictionary of the Bible" by John L. McKenzie, S.J., Bruce Publishing Company, 1965.

In addition, I have turned to general encyclopedias, dictionaries, histories, geographies, and any other reference books available to me which could in any way be useful to me.

The result—well, the result can begin to be seen when you turn the page.

VOLUME ONE
THE OLD TESTAMENT

The Empire of
DAVID and SOLOMON

David's Kingdoms of Judah and Israel

Territory Conquered by David

Boundaries of the Empire of David and Solomon

0   Miles   50

palacios

BASHAN

ISRAEL

AMMON

MOAB

GILEAD

JABBOK R.

Mahanaim
Adamah
Rabbeth-ammon
Heshbon
Medeba
Dibon
Aroer
ARNON R.
Kir-mab

JORDAN R.

Jericho
Gilgal
Jabesh-gilead

Shechem

Beth-shan
Megiddo

JUDAH

Bethlehem
Hebron
Beth-shemesh
Lachish
Ziklag
Gerar
Beersheba

SALT SEA
(DEAD SEA)

Tamar

VERED R.

EDOM

Bozrah
Punon
Sela (Petra)

PHILISTIA

Joppa
Gezer
Ekron
Gath
Askalon
Ashkelon
Gaza

Raphia

AMALEKITES

Kadesh-barnea

Ezion-geber

EGYPT

RIVER OF EGYPT

To
Lawrence P. Ashmead
who has faith

1. GENESIS

Genesis

The Bible begins at the logical place—the beginning. The very
first verse starts:

Genesis 1:1. *In the beginning . . .*

The phrase "In the beginning" is a translation of the Hebrew word
bereshith. In the case of several of the books of the Bible, the first
word is taken as the title of the whole (much as Papal bulls are
named for the two Latin words with which they begin.) The Hebrew
name of the first book is, there, *Bereshith*.

The Bible was first translated into another language in the course of
the third century B.C. and that other language was Greek. This Greek
version was, according to tradition, based on the work of seventy
learned scholars, and it is therefore known as the Septuagint, from a
Latin word meaning "seventy."

In the Septuagint, the various books of the Bible were, naturally

The Nations of Genesis

enough, given Greek names. The Hebrew habit of using the first words as the name was not followed, and descriptive names were used instead.

The first book was named "Genesis," which means, literally, "coming into being." It implies a concern with births and beginnings which is appropriate for a book that begins with the creation of heaven and earth.

By ancient tradition, the first five books of the Bible were written by Moses, the folk hero who, according to the account given in the second through fifth books, rescued the Israelites from Egyptian slavery. Modern scholars are convinced that this theory of authorship is not tenable and that the early books of the Bible are not the single work of any man. Rather, they are the combined and carefully edited version of a number of sources. Despite this, the full name of the first book of the Bible as commonly given in English translation remains "The First Book of Moses, Called Genesis."

The first five books of the Bible give not only the traditional history of the ancestors of the Israelite people, but also describe a legal code as having been given to Moses by God and by Moses to the Israelites generally. Because of Moses' traditional role in what was, in actual fact, a set of laws that developed slowly over the centuries, the whole is termed the "Mosaic law" or, more simply still, "the Law." The Hebrew word for the first five books is "Torah," which is the Hebrew word for "law."

The Greek word for the first five books is "Pentateuch" ("five books"). In recent times, it has been recognized that the sixth book of the Bible is closely connected with the first five and is derived from similar sources. All six books may be referred to as the "Hexateuch" ("six books").

God

The Bible centers about God, and God is brought into the tale at once:

Genesis 1:1. *In the beginning God created the heaven and the earth.*

The Hebrew word, translated here as God, is "Elohim" and that is a plural form which would ordinarily (if tradition were defied) be translated "gods." It is possible that in the very earliest traditions on which the Bible is based, the creation was indeed the work of a plurality of gods. The firmly monotheistic Biblical writers would carefully have eliminated such polytheism, but could not perhaps do anything with the firmly ingrained term "Elohim." It was too familiar to change.

Some hints of polytheism seem to have survived the editing. Thus, after the first created man disobeys God's injunction not to eat of the tree of knowledge, God is quoted as saying:

> Genesis 3:22. . . . *Behold, the man is become as one of us, to know good and evil* . . .

Then, too, still later, when God is concerned over mankind's arrogance in attempting to build a tower that would reach to heaven, He is quoted as saying:

> Genesis 11:7. *Go to, let us go down, and there confound their language* . . .

It is possible to argue that this is not true evidence of early polytheism. God might be viewed as using the royal "we"; or as speaking to an angelic audience; or even, in the Christian view, as speaking in the persons of the Trinity.

Nevertheless, as far as we know the history of religion outside the Bible, early beliefs were always polytheistic and monotheism was a late development in the history of ideas.

The Seventh Day

Carefully and sparely, and with great vigor and beauty, the first thirty-four verses of the Bible tell the story of creation. Six acts of creation are described as taking place on six successive days:

> Genesis 2:2. *And on the seventh day God ended his work* . . . *and* . . . *rested* . . .
>
> Genesis 2:3. *And God blessed the seventh day, and sanctified it* . . .

This marks the traditional establishment of the Sabbath—a day separated from the ordinary days of the week and dedicated to God.

The role played by the Sabbath in Judaism was quite small at first, and quite enormous in the end. The dividing line comes at one of the great watersheds in Jewish history—the Babylonian Exile. This took place in the sixth century B.C. and will be dealt with extensively later in the book. It is that sixth-century dividing line to which I will refer when I say something is pre-Exilic or post-Exilic.

In pre-Exilic times the Sabbath is barely mentioned and seems to have been of little consequence among the Israelites. In post-Exilic times, its observance was of the greatest importance and Jews died rather than violate that observance.

It is tempting to suppose that the Sabbath was Babylonian in origin, and that it gained new significance to the Jews in exile (see page 576). Nor can one fairly use the first chapters of Genesis as evidence for the great antiquity of the Sabbath in its holiest form, since it is widely accepted these days that the creation tale received its present shape after the Babylonian Exile and was, in fact, a version of the Babylonian creation myth, purified of polytheism and grossness, and put into the loftiest and most abstract terms of which the Jewish priesthood was capable.

The creation tale is typical of those portions of the first few books of the Bible that were put into final form by priestly hands soon after the time of the Exile. Such portions are part of the "Priestly document" and are usually designated as P by Biblical scholars. The Priestly document is characterized by impersonality and by a heavy reliance on statistics and genealogies.

The Lord God

Once the P version of creation is ended, a new version begins:

Genesis 2:4. *These are the generations of the heavens and of the earth when they were created, in the day that the Lord God made the earth and the heavens.*

The distinctive feature here is the sudden use of the term "Lord God," where throughout the first thirty-four verses the Deity had been referred to as simply "God."

The Hebrew word, here translated as "Lord," is made up of four Hebrew letters, which can be written in English as YHVH, and which are expressed, traditionally but mistakenly, as "Jehovah" for reasons to be given later (see page 135). Modern scholars believe "Yahveh" is the more accurate presentation.

Where "god" is a general term for any deity, and where the capitalized form "God" expresses the one Deity of the Bible, Yahveh is the specific name of that specific Deity. Names were of considerable importance to ancient man, for they were considered an extension of personality. To be able to pronounce the name was to be able (according to folklore) to control the being named. Names were therefore tools of magic and Jews of post-Exilic times disapproved of magic, not because they did not believe in its reality, but because the magic was usually performed in the names of heathen idols.

The name of God came to be avoided on principle, therefore. When it did occur in some of the traditional sources of the early books of the Bible or in the writings of the prophets of pre-Exilic times, pious Jews took to saying *Adonai* ("Lord") instead. This euphemism was accepted in English translation and what might have been given as "the God, Yahveh" is given as "the Lord God" instead.

The use of the term "the Lord God" ("Yahveh Elohim") in place of God ("Elohim") is characteristic of a particular early strand of tradition which was incorporated into the Hexateuch. This strand is known as the "J document" because of its characteristic use of "Jehovah" ("Yahveh") in connection with God.

There is another strand of early tradition which like the P document uses simply Elohim for God, and it is the "E document." Both J and E are much more personal than P, tell stories with circumstantial detail and do not greatly interest themselves in the more formal aspects of the matter.

The J document may have been put into written form as early as the ninth century in the more southerly of the two kingdoms into which the Israelites were then divided. This was the kingdom of Judah. The E document was put into written form a century later in the northern kingdom of Israel.

The dominant tribe in the northern kingdom was Ephraim and that was sometimes used as a poetic synonym for Israel. There is thus the interesting coincidence that the J document can stand for

Judah as well as Jehovah, and the E document for Ephraim as well as Elohim.

The northern kingdom was destroyed toward the end of the eighth century B.C. and the priests of Judah incorporated E into their own J tradition. This made the primitive history of their ancestors more complete, but also introduced occasional duplications, with the same tale told twice, once with a northern orientation and once with a southern. Despite the careful dovetailing of verses, such duplicate versions can be dissected and identified.

During and after the Babylonian Exile, the priesthood took this combined JE version, added P material of their own, and produced Genesis as we have it now. It is not my purpose, in this book, to untwine Genesis and identify the source of each verse (something that is done in the Anchor Bible, for instance) but it is well to know that different sources do exist.

Man

In J's tale of creation (more primitive than that of P) God does not call human beings into existence by spoken command alone. Rather, he shapes them out of clay as a sculptor might:

> Genesis 2:7. *And the Lord God formed man of the dust of the ground, and breathed into his nostrils the breath of life; and man became a living soul.*

The word "man" is a translation of the Hebrew word *adam*, which is a general expression rather akin to what we mean when we say "mankind." (The Hebrew word for an individual man is *ish*.)

The word *adam*, used in reference to this first created man, came to be a proper name, Adam. The King James version slips into this usage later in the chapter:

> Genesis 2:19. . . . *the Lord God formed every beast . . . and every fowl . . . and brought them unto Adam . . .*

Actually, the Hebrew does not seem to make use of Adam as a proper name until the beginning of the fifth chapter:

> Genesis 5:1. *This is the book of the generations of Adam . . .*

and the Jerusalem Bible, for instance, is careful to translate *adam* as "man" up to that very point.

After forming man, God breathes life into him, a reminder that in primitive times, the breath was often equated with life for what seemed obvious reasons.

Dead creatures no longer breathed, and breath was invisible and impalpable and therefore seemed a fitting representation of that mysterious something that left the body at the moment of death. Indeed, the word "soul" used in Genesis 2:7 is a translation of the Hebrew *nephesh*, which means "breath."

Eden

Having formed man, God also prepares a dwelling place for him and that involves the mention of the first definite place name in the Bible:

> Genesis 2:8. *And the Lord God planted a garden eastward in Eden . . .*

Notice that it is not the garden itself that is named Eden. One cannot speak of "Eden" as though it were synonymous with the garden, any more than one can speak of "California" as though it were synonymous with Yosemite Park.

The garden is planted somewhere in a land called Eden and the location of that land is "eastward"; eastward, that is, from Canaan, which is the focal point of reference of the Biblical story and the home of both the writers and the original readers of Genesis.

The question, then, is: Where is Eden?

There have been numerous answers to this question, some of them exceedingly farfetched, and no definite answer acceptable to all is possible. And yet, if we were to try the simplest and most direct possible line of thought, a reasonable solution will offer itself.

In the first place, suppose we consider the geography of the region not as it was at the time the ancient Jews believed creation to have taken place (roughly 4000 B.C. by modern dating convention) but as it was in the much later time when the material in the Book of Genesis was reduced to writing.

Genesis is based, to some extent, on very ancient traditions, but these

The Garden of Eden

traditions were not reduced to writing until the ninth century B.C. at the earliest. Some strands of the book were not written until several centuries later and the whole was not unified and put together into the form we now have until the fifth century B.C.

The geographical references in Genesis must therefore refer to the situation as it was from the ninth to the fifth centuries B.C. (the Assyrian period and somewhat later) if they were to have meaning to the writer and reader.

Thus, if someone were to write a book, today, about the fourteenth-century American Indians, he might well write of "the Indian tribes that inhabited what is now the United States." To save space, he might speak elliptically of "the Indians of the United States," taking it for granted that the readers would realize the United States did not actually exist in the fourteenth century and would not be confused. In ancient times, when every copy of a book was produced by hand and not by the printing press, the need to be economical with words was far greater. It was not to be expected that anyone would write, "And the Lord God planted a garden eastward in the land which we now call Eden."

So we must ask ourselves where Eden was during the Assyrian period; and the Bible tells us that quite plainly. It refers to Eden several times— not as a mystical primeval site of a garden in which Adam and Eve roamed, but as a prosaic everyday land which was conquered by the Assyrians in the eighth century B.C.

Thus, when the Assyrian hosts of Sennacherib were laying siege to Jerusalem in 701 B.C., they sent a message to the men guarding the walls of the city, warning them not to rely on their God for salvation, as the gods of other nations had not saved those nations from conquest by the Assyrians:

> 2 Kings 19:12. *Have the gods of the nations delivered . . . Gozan, and Haran and Rezeph, and the children of Eden which were in Thelasar?*

Thelasar ("Tel-assar" in the Revised Standard Version) is the name of an Assyrian province, mentioned as "Til-asuri" in Assyrian inscriptions. It extended on both sides of the middle reaches of the Euphrates River and so was, indeed, "eastward" from Canaan—about four hundred miles due east, in fact.

And yet, even so, it is not necessary to suppose that the Biblical writer intended the specific, relatively small, area of Eden in the province of Thelasar. Place names have a tendency to broaden out and grow diffuse with time. Thus "Asia," which originally referred to the western section of what is now the nation of Turkey, spread out to include an entire vast continent, while "Africa," originally signifying the northern portion of the modern nation of Tunisia, spread out to include a continent almost as vast.

Consequently, Eden might well have been used not only as a specific geographical term, but also as a rather general one for the entire valley of the Euphrates River. This makes sense, too, for if the Bible makes Eden the original home of the human race, archaeology has revealed that on the banks of the Euphrates River there arose one of the earliest (if not *the* earliest) of civilizations.

By 3000 B.C., powerful cities dotted the banks of the Euphrates, an elaborate network of irrigation canals was in use, writing had been invented, and, in general, man as a civilized being was in existence.

The Euphrates River

By the time the Book of Genesis was being reduced to writing in its final form, the editor who was arranging the various source materials

The Tigris and Euphrates Rivers

must have realized that "Eden" had become a vague term and he set about defining the location of the garden more precisely in terms that undoubtedly made sense at the time, but that have become much less clear with the passage of over two thousand additional years.

He set up his definition by placing Eden and its garden at or near the junction of important rivers:

> Genesis 2:10. *And a river went out of Eden to water the garden; and from thence it was parted, and became into four heads.*
>
> Genesis 2:11. *The name of the first is Pison: that is it which compasseth the whole land of Havilah, where there is gold;*

Genesis 2:12. *And the gold of that land is good: there is bdellium and the onyx stone.*

Genesis 2:13. *And the name of the second river is Gihon: the same is it that compasseth the whole land of Ethiopia.*

Genesis 2:14. *And the name of the third river is Hiddekel: that is it which goeth toward the east of Assyria. And the fourth river is Euphrates.*

The rivers are listed in order of increasing familiarity to the writer so that the fourth river, the Euphrates, is merely mentioned. No need is felt to locate it by describing the regions it traverses. This is understandable since the Euphrates was familiar to the Jews of the Assyrian period and before and parts of it were not very distant. Indeed, in the time of David, when the Jewish kingdom was at its most extensive and powerful, its northern boundary lay on the upper Euphrates.

The Euphrates was known to the Assyrians as "Pu-rat-tu" from a still earlier term which meant "great river." The Hebrew term used in the Bible is "Perath," clearly a form of the Assyrian name, and our word "Euphrates" originated with the Greeks, who converted the strange Assyrian syllables into a set that made more sense to their own ears.

(The English Bible has reached us, to a large extent, from the Hebrew, via first Greek, then Latin. Many Hebrew names reach us in Graeco-Latin form therefore. In general, the Catholic version of the Bible clings more closely to the Graeco-Latin, where the King James Version and even more the Revised Standard Version tend to return to the original Hebrew.)

The Euphrates is indeed a "great river." It is the longest river in southwestern Asia, flowing for seventeen hundred miles. Two streams rise in eastern Turkey, the more northerly only seventy-five miles south of the Black Sea. They flow west separately for about two hundred miles, then join to form the Euphrates. Flowing south now, the river approaches within a hundred miles of the Mediterranean Sea, enters Syria and turns southeast, leaving Syria and passing through Iraq until it finally pours its waters into the Persian Gulf. Though rising and passing so closely to seas that open into the Atlantic Ocean, the river reaches the Indian Ocean at last.

It is a sluggish river that is navigable for quite a distance. During the spring the melting of snow in the mountainous source area causes its level to rise in a slow, potentially useful flooding. Properly controlled, this water supply can be used to turn the nearby land into a garden of fertility and productivity, and throughout the Biblical period irrigation canals were used in this manner.

The third river of Eden is the Hiddekel, which is the Hebrew version of the Assyrian "i-di-ik-lat." It is described in Genesis 2:14 as going "toward the east of Assyria"; that is, forming the eastern boundary of Assyria, and this assuredly was not so. Assyria was an extensive domain in the centuries when Genesis was written and lay on both sides of the river. However, Assyria is the Greek form of the Hebrew "Ashur," which applied not only to the nation, but to its original capital city. It is the city that is meant here and the Hiddekel does indeed skirt the city on the east.

The Hiddekel is not as long as the Euphrates, but its length is quite respectable just the same—1150 miles. It is more turbulent than the Euphrates and is not really navigable except for small boats and rafts. It is perhaps because of the savage danger of its turbulence that the Greeks gave it the name "Tigris" ("tiger"), the name by which we know it today.

The fact that the Biblical description of the rivers of Eden mentions "a river [that] . . . was parted, and became into four heads" might lead one to think that the Tigris and Euphrates (along with the other two rivers mentioned) must have a single source. This is almost so. One of the sources of the Tigris River is a lake in eastern Turkey that lies only a dozen miles south of one of the streams that go to make up the Euphrates.

There might therefore be a strong temptation to attempt to locate the garden of Eden specifically in eastern Turkey, except that there is no need to suppose that the writers of Genesis felt obliged to make use of our modern geographical conventions.

When we say that a river parts into two or more streams, we take it for granted that we are imagining ourselves to be moving downstream. But suppose two rivers join as they move downstream. If you follow the joined river upstream you will find it will part into the two rivers.

Let's see how this applies to the Euphrates and the Tigris. The two rivers flow southeastward in almost parallel fashion. At one point, about 350 miles from the Persian Gulf, they approach within twenty-five miles of each other, then move apart before approaching again.

In the time of the earliest civilizations that rose in the region, the Euphrates and the Tigris entered the Persian Gulf by separate mouths, that of the Tigris being almost a hundred miles east of that of the Euphrates.

At that time, however, the Persian Gulf extended about 175 miles further northwestward than it now does. The rivers, flowing southwestward from the Turkish mountains, carried mud and silt with them, slowly forming a delta that filled in the upper end of the narrow Persian Gulf, moving the seacoast 175 miles southeastward in six thousand years.

The Tigris and Euphrates had to continue flowing over the new land as it formed. As it happened, the Tigris flowed south and the Euphrates east. Eventually they met to form a single joined river, now known as the Shatt-al-Arab, which is 120 miles long.

At the time the Book of Genesis was reduced to writing, the Tigris and the Euphrates had already joined to form the common stream and surely the reference in Genesis 2:10 is to the parting (working upstream) of the Shatt-al-Arab into the Tigris and the Euphrates. The reference to the garden of Eden would then be, specifically, to the lower stretches of those two rivers, near where they come together and as it happens, it was precisely there (in the days before the two rivers had yet come together) that civilization arose.

That leaves the first and second rivers of the garden, the Pison and the Gihon. Neither river can be identified, though glamorous guesses have been made for each. Thus, the Pison ("Pishon," in the Revised Standard Version) "compasseth the whole land of Havilah, where there is gold . . . bdellium and the onyx stone." (The Anchor Bible has "lapis-lazuli" in place of the onyx stone.)

Havilah is thus pictured as a land of wealth, where one can find gold and other precious material. In searching for a fabled land of wealth that will represent Havilah, later Europeans had a tendency to fix upon India with its proverbial "wealth of the Indies." In that case, the Pison (or Pishon) might be the Indus River, the long river—as long as the Euphrates—that drains what is now Pakistan, flowing into the Arabian Sea.

As for the Gihon, that seems to be clearly described as compassing "the whole land of Ethiopia." Ethiopia was, in ancient times, a land to the south of Egypt, and a nation bearing that name is still located about five hundred miles south of Egypt nowadays. A tributary of the Nile River rises in Ethiopia and it seems logical to suppose, then, that the Gihon is the Nile River.

If we go no farther in our reasoning, then, the four rivers of Eden would be the Indus, the Nile, the Tigris, and the Euphrates, in that order. This is an intriguing guess. There are only two civilizations, as far as is known, that compete in age with that in the Tigris-Euphrates region. One arose on the banks of the Nile and the other on the banks of the Indus.

And yet the picture cannot be correct. Neither the Indus nor the Nile comes anywhere near the Tigris and Euphrates. The closest approach of the Indus to the Tigris-Euphrates is twelve hundred miles and the closest approach of the Nile is nine hundred, and this certainly does not gibe with the Biblical statement that the four rivers all come together. (While not everything in the Bible can be taken literally, it must certainly be supposed that the Biblical writers could tell when four rivers came together in a region of the world known to them.)

Let's consider the land of Havilah first. Whatever it is, it can't be India, since a word for India does occur in the Book of Esther and, in Hebrew, it is "Hoddu." Havilah itself is mentioned elsewhere, notably in Genesis 25:18 where it is described as part of the region in which the descendants of Ishmael live:

> Genesis 25:18. *And they dwelt from Havilah unto Shur, that is before Egypt, as thou goest toward Assyria* . . .

It is reasonably certain that the Ishmaelites were tribes of the Arabian borderland, southeast of Canaan and southwest of the Tigris-Euphrates and so, without trying to pin it down too carefully, we can suppose that Havilah was somewhere south of the Euphrates River.

If this is so, then the Pison (Pishon) may have been a tributary of the Euphrates, flowing into its lower stretches from Havilah to the south and west. It may not have been an important stream and, in the gradual desiccation of the area that has taken place in recent ages, it may have disappeared. (It may even have been a man-made canal, confused by the Biblical writer with a natural stream.)

And what about Ethiopia? That is far off in Africa. The Hebrew word, which is here translated as Ethiopia in the King James Version, is "Cush." Undoubtedly, there are occasions in the Bible where Cush does indeed refer to the region south of Egypt and where it is justifiably translated as Ethiopia. Very likely, this is not one of those places. Indeed, in the Revised Standard Version, the Gihon is described as flowing around the "land of Cush." The word is left in its Hebrew form and no attempt is made to equate it with Ethiopia.

More often than not, the Biblical Cush refers to some Arabian tribe.

There is a reasonable possibility that the word "Cush" in Genesis 2:13 refers to the land of the people whom the ancient Greek geographers spoke of as the Kossaeans, and whom modern historians refer to as the Kassites. They dwelt east of the Tigris and had a period of greatness in the centuries before the rise of Assyria, for between 1600 and 1200 B.C., the Kassites controlled the great civilization of the Tigris-Euphrates.

If this is so, then the Gihon may have been a tributary (now gone) of the Tigris, flowing in from the east—or, possibly, another man-made canal.

We are thus left with the following situation. The Pison (Pishon) joins the Euphrates near its ancient mouth and the Gihon joins the Tigris near its ancient mouth. The two double rivers then join in the new land gradually formed afterward. The four rivers all come together over a reasonably small area and the very ancient civilization that rose in that area may represent the historical kernel within the story of the garden of Eden.

This region was called, in the primeval period, by a name which we now render as "Sumer" or "Sumeria." In the Sumerian language, the word *eden* means "plain." No one knows where, exactly, the Sumerians came from, but if, as seems likely, they originally entered the area from the hilly regions to the east, they may well have thought of themselves as coming "to Eden"; that is, "to the plain."

If so, then the term "Eden" may point specifically at Sumeria, and its identification with the later Eden farther up the Euphrates may be accidental (even though it pointed us in the right direction).

In Hebrew, *eden* means "delight" or "enjoyment," which seems appropriate for the garden, but this is, in all likelihood, merely a fortunate etymological accident since Hebrew and Sumerian are not related languages. (In fact, Sumerian is not related to any known language.) Nevertheless, the accidental Hebrew meaning helped crystallize the feeling that Eden might be a mystical term without actual geographic meaning and that the place originally inhabited by mankind was merely "the garden of delight" with no place name at all.

One more speculation is possible. By 2500 B.C., centuries before Abraham was born, the Sumerians had already passed their peak. New tribes from the north, the Akkadians, took over "the plain" and harder times must have come for the Sumerians, who were now a conquered people. They must have looked back nostalgically to the great days of "the plain."

Can the Biblical tale of the glorious garden of Eden, lost forever, have been a reflection, at least in part, of the Sumerian longing for a past that had vanished?

The Serpent

After Adam is settled in the garden of Eden, God grants him the right to full enjoyment of its delights, with one exception. He says:

> Genesis 2:17. *But of the tree of the knowledge of good and evil, thou shalt not eat* . . .

God creates a woman as a companion for Adam, forming her out of the man's rib. Presumably the two might have lived in the garden in eternal happiness as long as they respected God's prohibition. There was, however, a spoiler in the garden:

> Genesis 3:1. *Now the serpent was more subtil than any beast of the field* . . .

The serpent is portrayed as able to speak and as maneuvering the naïve woman into eating the forbidden fruit in defiance of God's prohibition. The woman then encouraged Adam to eat it as well.

As told here, the serpent's evil is motiveless or, at best, arises out of mere delight in mischief. The Jews of post-Exilic times made this seem more reasonable, however, by equating the serpent with Satan, who is the spirit of Evil as God is the spirit of Good. (This notion was derived from Persian religious thought—see page 409.)

Actually, the tale of the serpent is quite un-Biblical in atmosphere. Only here and in one other case (that of Balaam's ass, see page 184) do the Hebrew scriptures mention talking animals. It seems quite likely that the tale of the serpent is extremely primitive and represents a remnant of nature myth (see page 175).

Eve

Because of the disobedience of the man and woman, who ate of the fruit of the tree despite prohibition, God drives them out of Eden. They may no longer live easily by food gathering but are condemned to the heavy labor of agriculture.

Several thousand years before the dawn of recorded history, agriculture had been invented somewhere in southwestern Asia. Agriculture gave man a more plentiful and more dependable food supply and made possible a large increase in population in those areas where it was practiced. Because crops were immobile and had to be cared for, farmers had to remain in one place. For mutual protection, they gathered in villages which gradually became cities and thus arose "civilization" (from a Latin word for "city-dweller").

Despite the material benefits brought to man by agriculture, it is quite likely that those who were used to the free wandering irresponsibility of hunting and food gathering (a life that probably seemed a great deal more fun in retrospect than in reality) could not help but view agriculture as a kind of detestable slavery.

Might it not be, then, that a second strand of historical significance to the tale of the expulsion from Eden includes a dim memory of the unfavorable aspects of the changeover to agriculture?

Once the man and his wife took up their life outside the garden, the man gave his wife a name:

> Genesis 3:20. *And Adam called his wife's name Eve; because she was the mother of all living.*

At the time these traditions were being reduced to writing, it was customary for Jews to give names with straightforward Hebrew meanings (usually with religious significance.) Thus, Jehoshaphat means "Yahveh has judged"; Ezekiel means "God strengthens"; Hananiah means "Yahveh is gracious" and so on.

The names of the men and women in the earliest traditions were often not in Hebrew and, therefore, were not of clear significance. The Biblical writers, searching for the meaning they felt ought to be in all names, would spot a resemblance to some Hebrew word or phrase and invent an explanation around it.

Thus the Hebrew name equivalent to our own Eve is Havvah, which has a similarity of sound to *hayah*, meaning "to live." (Actually, the initial "h" is a guttural sound not found in our language but similar to the German "ch.") Since Eve is regarded as the mother of the human race, it is tempting to equate Havvah and *hayah* and say that she received the name because she was the mother of all living. This is an example of "folk etymology," in which the Bible abounds. The real meaning of Havvah or Eve is, of course, unknown.

Cain and Abel

Adam and Eve had children:

> Genesis 4:1. And . . . Eve . . . bare Cain, and said, I have gotten a man from the Lord.
>
> Genesis 4:2. And she again bare his brother Abel. And Abel was a keeper of sheep, but Cain was a tiller of the ground.

The name Cain ("Kayin" in Hebrew) is usually taken to mean "smith." In the early days of civilization, the use of metals was introduced and the new material became exceedingly important both in ornamentation and in the manufacture of weapons for hunting and warfare. Men who could prepare the metals and work them into the necessary shapes were important and highly regarded artisans. To be a smith and be called one was a matter of honor, and to this day "Smith" is a common surname among the English and Americans.

This meaning of Cain seems clearer in a later use of the word, in the same chapter, as part of the name of a descendant of Cain:

> Genesis 4:22. And Zillah . . . bare Tubal-cain, an instructor of every artificer in brass and iron . . .

"Tubal-cain" means "smith of Tubal," where Tubal is a district in Asia Minor. In the centuries immediately preceding the period during which the legends in Genesis were reduced to writing, the techniques for obtaining iron from its ore were worked out in Asia Minor. The smiths of Tubal would therefore have become famous for producing iron weapons superior to anything that had been seen before, and the smiths of Tubal, "Tubal-cain," might well have entered legend as the founders of metallurgy.

Nevertheless, during the Exilic period, some clearly Hebrew meaning for the word was sought for and found in the similarity of kayin to kanah, meaning "to get." Eve was therefore made to say "I have gotten a man of the Lord" and to name her son something that was reminiscent of her first words on learning of his birth. Thus, the etymology was set.

Cain and Abel seem to represent the farmer and the herdsman (or nomad) respectively. The early histories are written from the standpoint of the farmers, the settled city-men, and in them the nomads are viewed as barbaric raiders, ruthless and bloodthirsty.

It was the farmers who multiplied, however, and it was civilization that spread. Nomads could triumph when internal dissensions weakened the city-men, but in the long run, civilization had the men, organization, and the advanced weapons that could be produced in quantity only by an elaborate technology. (Cain was not only a farmer, he was also a smith.)

In the end, civilization won completely, and that eventual and inevitable victory must have been foreseen long before it came to pass. The tale (briefly and obscurely told) of how Cain grew jealous of Abel and killed him may be, in part, a remnant of some nomadic lament over the all-encroaching tentacles of settled civilization.

In fact, the very name Abel ("Hebel" in Hebrew) means "a puff of air," seeming to imply the briefness and instability of the nomadic way of life against the steady push of the farmer. (We experienced a similar period in American history toward the end of the nineteenth century when the nomadic "cowboy" of the West had to give way, at last, to the plodding farmer and his barbed-wire fences.)

The name Abel may also be related to the Babylonian *aplu*, meaning "son." This would indicate a possible Sumerian origin for the tale.

Nod

After Cain murders Abel, he is driven away:

> Genesis 4:16. *And Cain went out from the presence of the Lord, and dwelt in the land of Nod, on the east of Eden.*

No one has tried to identify the "land of Nod" with any actual specific region and it is usually taken to be a metaphorical expression. The Hebrew word "Nod" is related to the term meaning "wanderer"; therefore to dwell in the land of Nod is taken to mean that one takes up a wandering life and becomes a nomad.

Here we seem to have a second strand incorporated into the ancient tale. Now we are dealing not with Cain the farmer and smith, but with Cain the nomad.

If Eden is taken to be Sumeria, then the region "east of Eden" would be that known as Elam. Elam, in what is now southwestern Iran, developed a civilization quite early, borrowing no doubt from the Sumerians. Its early history is very dim but there seems to have been intermittent warfare between Elam and whatever power ruled the Tigris-Euphrates for three thousand years.

Is it possible, then, that the story of Cain and Abel might be a combination of a villainous Elam attacking a blameless Sumeria (as told by the Sumerians) and a villainous farmer attacking a blameless nomad (as told by the nomads)?

Enoch [of Cain]

In Nod (despite its name) Cain seems to have settled down. He married, had a son:

Genesis 4:17. . . . *and he builded a city, and called the name of the city, after the name of his son, Enoch.*

Perhaps this is a dim reference to the ancient transition of a pastoral Elam to the ways of civilization. There is no record of any city named Enoch, but it is conceivable that this might be the city that eventually became known to later history as Susa. This dates back to the Stone Age and for thousands of years was the chief city of Elam.

The remainder of the fourth chapter deals quickly with the succeeding descendants of Cain, including Tubal-cain. The book of Genesis then returns to Adam to follow the line of descent that leads to the Israelites.

Seth

Adam has a third son:

Genesis 5:3. *And Adam lived an hundred and thirty years, and begat a son . . . and called his name Seth.*

This chapter is a portion of P again, and as generation after generation is given, the statistical data is carefully included. The age of each individual is given at the time of the birth of his first son, and at the time of his death.

Genesis 5:5. *And all the days that Adam lived were nine hundred and thirty years: and he died.*

These ages were legendary, reflecting parts of earlier Babylonian tales picked up by the Jews during the Exile and modified by the priesthood according to some unknown principle of their own. Nevertheless, those who feel every word of the Bible to be literally true have tried to make use of these figures (and of others given here and there in the Bible) to calculate the year in which Adam was born, and the universe created.

The Jews of the Middle Ages calculated the date of the creation to have been October 7, 3761 B.C., and this is still used in calculating the number of the year in the Jewish calendar. Thus, September 1968 A.D. is the beginning of the year 5729 by that calendar.

Christian theologians have come up with a variety of dates for the creation. The most familiar of these is one worked out by James Ussher, an Anglican archbishop of Armagh, Ireland. In 1654, he decided that the creation had taken place in 4004 B.C. (at 9 A.M. of October 23 of that year, according to some). The date 4004 B.C. is often found at the head of the first pages of the Bible in editions of the King James version.

Actually 4004 B.C. isn't a bad date for the establishment of historic times. Man began to have a history in the proper sense only after writing had been invented, and writing was invented a little before 3000 B.C. However, the first cities had been organizd as early as 8000 B.C. and prehistoric man (or creatures recognizably similar to man) have left remains that are well over a million years old.

The earth itself is some five billion years old and the universe as a whole perhaps fifteen billion years old.

Enoch [of Seth]

The descendants of Adam, through Seth, are then listed through eight generations (ten, counting Adam and Seth themselves) somewhat less hastily than those of Cain were mentioned. As a group, these are the antediluvian patriarchs. (A patriarch is the head of a tribe and by "antediluvian" is meant "before the Flood.")

The names of the line of Seth are suspiciously like those of the line of Cain, however. Both include an Enoch and a Lamech, and other names, if not identical, are very similar. It is possible that the two lines represent the same legendary material, one given by J and the other by P.

The antediluvian patriarchs are notable for their ages. Several, including Adam himself, lived nearly a thousand years. The record holder is Methuselah (whose name has become a byword for age) who attained the age of 969 years.

These patriarchs cannot be associated with any historical personages and nothing is known of them beyond this bare Biblical mention. They seem, however, to be a reflection of Sumerian legend. At least, the Sumerians had lists of nine or ten kings who reigned before the Flood, each of them living for many thousands of years. One was listed as having reigned nearly 65,000 years. The writer of this portion of Genesis, far from imposing on credibility by making use of extended life spans, apparently took legendary material and did his best to cut those ages down to reasonable size.

What's more, throughout the Hexateuch, the writers kept steadily reducing the ages attained by the chief figures in the tales though even at the end these were still boasting life spans somewhat in excess of a hundred years.

Of the antediluvian patriarchs, one attains an age markedly different from the others. This is Enoch, the father of Methuselah.

Genesis 5:23. *And all the days of Enoch were three hundred sixty and five years:*

Genesis 5:24. *And Enoch walked with God: and he was not; for God took him.*

The fact that Enoch is described as living 365 years, whereas his father Jared lived 962 years and his son Methuselah lived 969 years, seems odd. Is it a coincidence that there are 365 days in a year; that is, in the complete circuit of the sun across the skies? Is it possible that the verses given over to Enoch are all that remains of some Babylonian sun myth?

What is meant by saying that Enoch walked with God and was not is uncertain, but later traditions made it clear that the usual interpretation was that he was taken up alive into heaven as a reward for unusual piety.

It was supposed by the Jews of post-Exilic times that in heaven, Enoch was able to see the past and future of mankind. Between 200 B.C. and 50 B.C., several books were written purporting to have come from the pen of Enoch, describing this past and future. They are purely legendary and are a form of "religious fiction" which was fairly common in the post-Exilic period. (Some of it, as we shall see, found its way into the Bible.)

The books attributed to Enoch did not gain entry into the Bible, but there is a mention of them in the New Testament. In the Epistle of Jude, the writer says:

Jude 1:14. *And Enoch also, the seventh from Adam, prophesied of these* . . .

Ararat

If one adds up the ages of the antediluvian patriarchs at the time of the births of their respective sons, one finds that Noah, the great-great-great-great-great-great-great-grandson of Adam was born 1056 years after the creation or (accepting Ussher's figures) about 3000 B.C. When he was six hundred years old, that is, about 2400 B.C., there came the Flood.

This, according to the Bible, was a world-wide deluge, but there is no record of any such phenomenon, of course. The Egyptian civilization, for instance, was in a particularly flourishing state at this very time and was building its pyramids. Nor do the Egyptian records speak of any floods other than the annual overflow of the Nile, as far as we know.

This is not to say, however, that the Biblical story of the Flood was not based on some actual, but local, flood in Sumerian history.

Sumeria was a flat land between two large rivers. As is true of any large river (we have only to think of our own Missouri and Mississippi) unusual rises will bring about flooding conditions. In a country as flat as Sumeria, it would not take much of a flood to cover large portions of the entire region.

A particularly bad flood would live on in the memory of later generations, and particularly bad floods undoubtedly occurred. In 1929, the English archaeologist Sir Charles Leonard Woolley reported finding water-deposited layers as much as ten feet thick in his excavations near the Euphrates. Such deposits were not found everywhere in the region and Sumerian culture showed no over-all break. Nevertheless, the evidence exists that somewhere about 3000 B.C. there were indeed drastic floods of at least a local nature.

With time, as the story is told and retold it is dramatically inevitable that a flood which spreads out over parts of Sumeria and neighboring regions with great loss of life will be said to have covered "all the world," meaning the entire region. It is further inevitable that later genera-

The Flood and the Kingdom of Urartu (Ararat)

tions, with a much broader knowledge of geography, would accept the phrase "all the world" literally and reduce themselves to needless speculations on the impossible.

(A well-known example of this is the statement frequently met with among the ancient historians that Alexander the Great "conquered the world" and then wept for "other worlds to conquer." What was meant was merely that Alexander had conquered a large part of those sections of the world which were well known to the Greeks of the time. Actually, Alexander conquered only 4 or 5 per cent of the earth's land surface and had plenty of room in which to extend those conquests.)

The people of Sumeria and of Akkadia (lying to the northwest of

Sumeria) told and retold the tale of one particular flood, which may have been produced by unusually heavy rains on the region. Some people suspect the flood to have been too serious to be accounted for by rain alone and think there may have been a sudden rise in the water level of the Persian Gulf, leading to a disastrous influx from the sea.

It has occurred to me recently that a possible explanation for such an invasion of the sea would be the unlucky strike of a large meteorite in the nearly landlocked Persian Gulf. The splash that would result would take the form of a huge wave that might move inland catastrophically, sweeping away everything in its path.

The invasion of water from the sea (for whatever reason) is, indeed, involved in the Biblical description of the Flood:

> Genesis 7:11. *In the six hundredth year of Noah's life . . . were all the fountains of the great deep broken up, and the windows of heaven were opened.*

A tidal wave plus rain, in other words.

In 1872, an English archaeologist, George Smith, deciphered ancient tablets from the remains of a royal Assyrian library and found a description of a flood in which one man saves himself, his family, and samples of animal life on board a ship. The story is based on still older tales dating back to Sumerian times.

The hero of this tale is Gilgamesh, king of the Akkadian town of Erech. He is in search of eternal life and finds Ut-Napishtim, who has the secret. Ut-Napishtim tell his story. It appears that he was king of a Sumerian city at the time of the Flood and rode it out in a large ship. Gilgamesh obtained the secret of eternal life from him, nearly obtained the necessary conditions, and through misadventure lost it.

The details of this Sumerian flood story are very similar in a number of points to the story in the Bible. It seems quite likely that the Biblical story of the Flood is a version of this much earlier tale.

In the Biblical story, Noah's ark floats on the floodwaters for months. The waters slowly recede—

> Genesis 8:4. *And the ark rested . . . upon the mountains of Ararat.*

Notice that a specific mountain peak is not named. There is no mention of a "Mount Ararat." Instead the Bible clearly states "the mountains of Ararat," implying Ararat to be a region or nation within which there was a mountain range on which the ark came to rest. The Anchor Bible translates the phrase as "the Ararat range."

If further Biblical evidence is needed that Ararat is a region and not a mountain, it can be found in the fifty-first chapter of Jeremiah. The prophet is reporting God's promise to destroy Babylon, which at that time was on the point of conquering Judah:

Jeremiah 51:27 . . . *call together against her* [Babylon] *the kingdoms of Ararat, Minni, and Ashchenaz* . . .

But where and what was Ararat? Remember that in searching for it one must consider geography as it was known to those who reduced Genesis to writing and not necessarily as it was known in the time of the Sumero-Akkadians.

In Assyrian times there was a kingdom among the mountains in which the Tigris and Euphrates rose, in what is now eastern Turkey. It centered about Lake Van (a salt lake about the size and shape of our own Great Salt Lake) and is sometimes called the "kingdom of Van" in consequence. This kingdom extended from the lake to the Caucasus Mountains, and in Assyrian inscriptions is referred to as the kingdom of Urartu—of which name Ararat is clearly a version.

The kingdom of Urartu was greatly weakened by Assyrian attack and by 612 B.C. it had ceased to exist, at a time when Assyria itself was also being destroyed. In the area in which it had existed, new tribesmen arrived and a new name (of Persian origin) was given to the land, which became Armenia.

In those sections of the Bible which were reduced to writing after the end of Urartu, the term Armenia is used instead. Thus, in the Second Book of Kings, there is the tale of the assassination of the Assyrian king, Sennacherib, by his two sons, in 681 B.C., and of their rapid flight thereafter:

2 Kings 19:37. . . . *and they escaped into the land of Armenia* . . .

What is really meant, of course, is Urartu, since Armenia did not yet exist, and in the Revised Standard Version, the phrase is indeed changed to "the land of Ararat."

The tradition that the ark came to rest in Ararat some six hundred miles northwest of Sumeria again speaks in favor of the tidal-wave theory of the Flood. Ordinary river flooding would sweep floating objects downstream—southeastward into the Persian Gulf. A huge tidal wave would sweep them upstream—northwestward toward Ararat.

Despite all evidence, most people insist on thinking of Ararat as the name of a definite mountain peak and indeed the name Ararat was eventually applied to one. Mount Ararat is a mountain in the easternmost region of Turkey about seventy miles northeast of Lake Van. It has two peaks, Great Ararat and Little Ararat, the former being the higher, reaching 16,873 feet (3.2 miles) above sea level. The tradition remains firmly fixed that Noah's ark came to rest somewhere on Great Ararat and every once in a while there are expeditions there to find traces of it.

Ham

Once the Flood story is done, the writers of Genesis turn to the task of giving the names of the descendants of Noah. These, in almost every case, represent tribes or nations. It was common for ancient tribes to call themselves after the name of an ancestor (real or mythical). In fact, if a tribe was known by some name, it was assumed that it was because the members were descended from an ancestor of that name. (An ancestor from whom a tribe receives its name is an eponym of that tribe.)

Related tribes could be described as descending from eponyms who were brothers, and whose father was a still broader eponym. The Greeks, for instance, called themselves Hellenes and recognized themselves to exist as groups of related tribes called Aeolians, Dorians, Achaeans, and Ionians. They therefore supposed themselves all to be descended from a man named Hellen. Hellen was described as having two sons named Aeolus and Dorus, and a third son, Xuthus, who had twin sons named Ion and Achaeus.

In this spirit, the Book of Genesis describes the immediate descendants of Noah:

> Genesis 9:18. And the sons of Noah . . . were Shem, and Ham, and Japheth: and Ham is the father of Canaan.

The three sons of Noah represent the three great divisions of the peoples known to the ancient writers of the Bible.

In general, the descendants of Shem are pictured as occupying the Arabian peninsula and the regions adjoining it to the north, including the Tigris-Euphrates region, which is the center of interest in the early

The Hamites

portions of Genesis. Since this includes the Hebrews themselves, Shem is given the post of honor and is made the eldest son of Noah. At least, he is mentioned first.

It is for this reason that the languages of the people dwelling in this region are referred to as "Semitic." ("Sem" is the Graeco-Latin form of Shem.) These languages include Hebrew, Assyrian, Aramaean, and, as the most important living example, Arabic.

The descendants of Ham are described as inhabiting chiefly the corner of Africa adjacent to Asia. For this reason the original languages of the peoples of northeastern Africa are called "Hamitic." This includes Coptic (derived from the ancient Egyptian), the Berber languages of North Africa, and some of the languages of Ethiopia, such as Amharic.

The descendants of Japheth are described as inhabiting the regions to the north and east of the Tigris-Euphrates. Sometimes "Japhetic" is used to describe certain obscure languages in the northern mountainous regions of the Caucasus. Occasionally, it is used more broadly to include ancient Persian, for example. Since the language of the Persians is related to those spoken in India and in Europe, this book is (in the broader sense) being written in a Japhetic language. However, the importance of Europe is such (modern students of comparative philology being European in culture) that the broad classification gave way to the more geographically intelligible "Indo-European."

It is a mistake, though, to suppose that the writers of Genesis were influenced by language. Modern notions of philology are strictly modern. Rather, the Biblical writers were guided by political connections and by geographic propinquity. Such connections often did bespeak racial relatedness so that terms such as Semitic and Hamitic did turn out to make much sense, linguistically, but this was not true in every case.

A prime example is the case of Canaan. The people inhabiting the land (Canaanites) at the time the Hebrews moved in spoke a Semitic language and had a culture related to that of the Tigris-Euphrates region. By modern terminology, the Canaanites were distinctly Semites.

However, Genesis 9:18 goes out of its way to specify that "Ham is the father of Canaan." The reason for that is a simple one. Some three centuries prior to the Hebrew occupation of Canaan, the land had been conquered by Egyptian armies and for a long time formed part of the Egyptian Empire. Since Egypt was the most important of the Hamitic nations it seemed reasonable, according to the standards of the time, to describe Canaan as a son of Ham.

The end of the ninth chapter of Genesis relates a tradition in which

Noah, offended by his second son, Ham, curses him and condemns him and his son, Canaan, to servitude to his brothers. This reflects the fact that at the time Genesis was being reduced to writing, the Canaanites were indeed reduced to servitude to the Israelites, who were descendants of Shem.

Some moderns seem to think that Ham represents the Negro peoples and that this chapter can be used to justify Negro slavery. This is the purest piffle. Neither Ham, Canaan, nor any of their named descendants were viewed as Negroes by the Biblical writers.

Japheth

The Greeks, it seems, must be considered—in Biblical terms—to be among the descendants of Japheth. The writers of Genesis may even in this respect have been influenced by Greek traditions, reaching them dimly from the west.

For instance, Japheth himself has been identified by some with the Titan Iapetus in the Greek myths. (Since the initial "J" in Hebrew names is pronounced like a "Y" in Hebrew, as is the initial "I" in Greek names, the similarity between Japheth and Iapetus is greater than it appears to be in print.) According to the Greek myths, Iapetus was the father of Prometheus who, in turn, fathered the human race by molding them out of clay. For this reason, Iapetus was considered by the Greeks to be the ancestor of mankind; and, to the Hebrews, Japheth was the ancestor of that portion of mankind to which the Greeks belonged.

The sons and grandsons of Japheth are listed in the tenth chapter of Genesis:

Genesis 10:2. *The sons of Japheth; Gomer, and Magog, and Madai, and Javan, and Tubal, and Meshech, and Tiras.*

Genesis 10:3. *And the sons of Gomer; Ashkenaz, and Riphath, and Togarmah.*

Genesis 10:4. *And the sons of Javan; Elishah, and Tarshish, Kittim, and Dodanim.*

We must remember that such genealogies reflect the geographic and political situation of the Assyrian period, when the various parts of Genesis were reduced to writing.

Of the sons of Japheth, Gomer seems to be identical with the people who, in Assyrian inscriptions, were the "Gimirrai" and these in turn were the people known in Latin spelling as the Cimmerians. In earlier times they lived north of the Black Sea but in the seventh century B.C., pushed on by new bands of barbarians in the rear, they invaded Asia Minor and met the Assyrians there in earth-shaking battles. They were eventually defeated, to be sure, but Assyria was badly wounded in the process. The Cimmerians would certainly be in prominent view at the time the tenth chapter was being written and their eponym, Gomer, would, very reasonably, be viewed as the first-born of Japheth.

As for Magog, that may represent "the land of Gog" where Gog is the ruler known to us from the Greek historians as Gyges. He was king of the Lydians, a people in western Asia Minor, and was one of the important adversaries of the invading Cimmerians. In fact, he died in battle against them about 652 B.C.

Madai is supposed to refer to the Medes, who inhabited the territory east of Assyria, and who were soon to be among the final conquerors of Assyria. Tubal, Meshech, and Tiras are all thought to represent minor tribes of Asia Minor. The name Tiras bears some similarities to the Greek "Tyrsenoi," which was applied to a people who, it was thought, dwelt originally in Asia Minor but migrated to Italy. If so, Tiras could represent the Etruscans.

The most interesting of the sons of Japheth is Javan. This name is almost certainly identical with an archaic form of the Greek "Ion," who was the eponym of the Ionian Greeks. The Ionians had, about 1000 B.C., migrated eastward to occupy the islands of the Aegean Sea and the coasts of Asia Minor. Of the various Greek tribes they were the nearest to Canaan and would be best known to the Israelites of Assyrian times. Their tribal name would be naturally applied to the Greeks generally.

Of Gomer's sons, Ashkenaz may be identical with the name "Ashguza" found among Assyrian inscriptions. This seems to refer to the peoples known to the Greeks, and therefore to ourselves, as the Scythians. The Scythians were nomadic tribes who entered Europe from somewhere in central Asia some time before 1000 B.C. It was their pressure southward against the Cimmerians that drove the Cimmerians into Asia Minor. The Scythians took their place in the steppelands north of the Black Sea, and from that standpoint, Ashkenaz (Scythia) might well be considered the eldest son of Gomer (Cimmeria).

For some reason, the later Jews viewed Ashkenaz as the ancestor of the Teutonic people. For this reason German-speaking Jews were called "Ashkenazim" as contrasted with the Spanish-speaking "Sephardim."

It would be expected that the sons of Javan listed in Genesis 10:4 would refer to those Greek-speaking regions closest to Israel. Elishah seems to be similar to the "Alashiyah" found in Assyrian documents and this refers to the island of Cyprus. This had already been colonized by Greeks in Assyrian times, and it was the closest of all Greek-speaking lands to Canaan, being only two hundred miles to the northeast.

Indeed, Cyprus is mentioned twice, for Kittim surely represents Kition (Citium in Latin), a city on the southern coast of the island, the name of which was often used for the entire island.

Dodanim is widely thought to be a misprint for Rodanim; in fact, it is given as Rodanim in some early copies of the Bible. If the name is Rodanim then it is tempting to equate it with the island of Rhodes, two hundred miles west of Cyprus.

Tarshish, on the basis of references later in the Bible, is usually taken to represent a city in Spain. However, it occurs to me that in this one instance, it might represent Tarsus, an important Greek town, a hundred miles north of Cyprus, on the southern coast of Asia Minor. It was an important city in Assyrian times and might represent the Greeks of Asia Minor generally.

Cush

The most notable confusion in this tenth chapter, describing the nations of the Near East, occurs in connection with Cush, which I said earlier (see page 29) could be used to represent the Ethiopians, south of Egypt, and also the Kossaeans, east of the Tigris.

Genesis 10:6. *And the sons of Ham; Cush, and Mizraim, and Phut, and Canaan.*

Genesis 10:7. *And the sons of Cush; Seba, and Havilah . . .*

In Genesis 10:6, Cush clearly means the Ethiopians, south of Egypt, who, indeed, speak a Hamitic tongue. Phut (better, "Put," as given in the Revised Standard Version) is usually thought to represent the

peoples west of Egypt whom the Greeks called Libyans. These also
spoke a Hamitic language.

Mizraim is the Hebrew word for "Egypt," so he is the eponym
of that nation. Wherever else it occurs in the Bible, Mizraim is translated into "Egypt" (a term of Greek origin). If such translations
were done here, the verse might read: "And the sons of Ham; Ethiopia,
and Egypt, and Libya, and Canaan," which would accurately reflect
the area dominated by Egypt in the days of her greatness.

In the very next verse, however, Cush is described as the father of
Seba, Havilah, and a series of other sons, all of whom are clearly
eponyms of Arabian tribes. This Cush must be the one representing
the Kossaeans, and not the Hamitic Cush of Ethiopia.

Nimrod

This confusion of Cushes leads to a section of obviously Semitic
ethnology being included under Ham:

> Genesis 10:8. And [the Semitic] Cush begat Nimrod: he began
> to be a mighty one in the earth.
> Genesis 10:9. He was a mighty hunter . . .
> Genesis 10:10. And the beginning of his kingdom was Babel, and
> Erech, and Accad, and Calneh, in the land of Shinar.
> Genesis 10:11. Out of that land went forth Asshur, and builded
> Nineveh, and the city Rehoboth, and Calah,
> Genesis 10:12. And Resen between Nineveh and Calah . . .

Nimrod is the only name in Chapter 10 of Genesis who is clearly
an individual and not an eponym. Who, then, is Nimrod? Can he
be identified at all and equated with any historic personage? Or is he
lost forever in the primeval mists?

There is no question but that whoever he was, he is described
as ruling over the Tigris-Euphrates region, for that is where all the
cities named are known (where they are known at all) to have been
located. Furthermore the "land of Shinar" is accepted as being the
Biblical term used for what we would call "Sumeria."

Genesis 10:10 appears, then, to make Nimrod an important king
of the Tigris-Euphrates region, with his power based on the four cities

The Empire of Nimrod

of Babel, Erech, Accad, and Calneh. The location of Calneh is unknown
and there is general agreement now that its inclusion is an error and
that the word is not the name of a city but is Hebrew for "all of
them." The verse is made to read in the Revised Standard Version:
"The beginning of his kingdom was Babel, Erech, and Accad, all of
them in the land of Shinar."

The three cities that remain are no mystery. Erech corresponds to
the city known as "Uruk" in the ancient inscriptions of the region.
The city was first excavated in the 1850's and showed every sign of
having once been an extensive metropolis, with large temples and a
library. It dates back to 3600 B.C. at least. It was located on the
Euphrates River about forty miles from its ancient mouth. The Euphrates River has since changed its course somewhat and the ruins
of Erech are now several miles east of the present course of the river.

The mythical Gilgamesh (see page 40) was king of this city and this city was also ruled by a historical conqueror. This was Lugal-Zaggisi, king of Erech, who ruled shortly after 2300 B.C. He conquered other Sumerian city-states and was the first individual we know of to govern a sizable empire in the Tigris-Euphrates. His realm may even have reached the Mediterranean. His triumph was short-lived, however, thanks to another conqueror, associated with Accad, the second of the cities mentioned in Genesis 10:10.

Accad, or Akkad, is, in the ancient inscriptions, Agade. Its exact site is unknown but it was probably also on the Euphrates, about 140 miles upstream from Erech. The city gave its name to the upper portion of the Tigris-Euphrates region, which became known as Akkad.

The Akkadians who inhabited these upstream regions were not identical with the Sumerians, although they adopted the Sumerian culture. The Akkadians spoke a Semitic language, for instance, while the Sumerian language was non-Semitic (and, indeed, had no known linguistic affiliations).

The Akkadians were at first under Sumerian domination but about 2280 B.C., a man named Sharrukin ("righteous king" in Akkadian) came to power and established his capital in the city of Agade. That king has become Sargon of Agade to us. About 2264 B.C., he defeated Lugal-Zaggisi and founded an Akkadian Empire. Sargon's grandson, Naram-Sin, extended the empire even farther and about 2180 B.C. it was at its height.

About 2150 B.C., however, soon after Naram-Sin's death, barbarians from the eastern mountains invaded and conquered the Tigris-Euphrates region and brought the Akkadian Empire to an end. After a century of barbarian domination, the Sumerians won their freedom and, about 2000 B.C., experienced a last period of power. After that, the remaining city mentioned in Genesis 10:10 comes in.

The town of Babel was located on the Euphrates River about 40 miles downstream from Agade. It existed as a small and unremarkable place for over a thousand years while the Sumerian city-states still further downstream flourished and the Akkadian Empire rose and fell.

While the Sumerians were in their final period of glory, however, another group of peoples from the middle Euphrates, the Amorites, seized control of Babel about 1900 B.C., and made it the capital of an expanding empire.

Under the sixth king of the Amorite dynasty, Hammurabi, who reigned about 1700 B.C., Babel became a world metropolis and remained so for two thousand years, despite the fact that it was frequently conquered and ravished. Indeed, it was the glamor city of the East throughout Old Testament times and is best known to us by the Greek version of its name—Babylon. The entire Tigris-Euphrates region is commonly known as Babylonia after this city.

Under Amorite domination, the Sumerians finally broke and declined rapidly, losing their identity, though their culture remained to be inherited and elaborated by conqueror after conqueror. The language died out as a living vehicle for communication but remained as part of religious liturgy (like Latin in the modern Catholic Church) for some 1500 years, not dying out completely till 300 B.C.

The Amorites did not long survive the glories of Hammurabi. About 1670 B.C. the Kassites or Kossaeans invaded Babylonia from the East and established a "dark age" that lasted for nearly five hundred years.

With southern Babylonia thus in eclipse, the cities of the far northern reaches of the river valley had their chance to gain prominence. Whereas Genesis 10:10 concerns itself with southern Babylonia, verse 10:11 turns to the north.

The King James Version begins the verse by saying "Out of that land went forth Asshur." This is now generally accepted as a mistranslation of the Hebrew. The Revised Standard Version has the verse begin: "Out of that land he [Nimrod] went forth into Asshur."

Asshur is the region along the upper courses of the Tigris River, in what is now northern Iraq. The town of Asshur (or Ashur), which gave its name to the region, was located on the Tigris River about 230 miles north of Babylon and was founded (by Sumerian colonists, perhaps) as early as 2700 B.C. Asshur is far better known by the Greek version of its name—Assyria.

Assyria was part of the Akkadian Empire and then later part of the Amorite Empire. The Assyrian inhabitants of that region, however, maintained their identity and had periods of great prosperity. The capital of the region was moved from Ashur to cities further upstream on the Tigris, first to Calah, then finally to Nineveh. (The site of the town of Resen, described in verse 10:12 as lying between these two cities, is not known, but the word, like "Calneh," may not signify a town at all.)

The turning point in Assyrian history may have come during the reign of Shalmaneser I, about 1250 B.C. He is reputed to have built Calah and he may have witnessed the introduction into Assyria of the

art of smelting iron from Asia Minor, where it seems to have been
developed.

The use of iron weapons gives an army a great advantage over
one that is armed only with bronze weapons. Iron can be made harder
than bronze and iron edges are sharper and less easily blunted. Shalmaneser's son, Tukulti-Ninurta I, used his iron-armed warriors to make
himself the first of Assyria's conquering monarchs.

Despite occasional setbacks, Assyria grew stronger and stronger, displaced the Kassites, and established their rule over all of Babylonia,
then spread far beyond. By the time the traditions of Genesis were
being reduced to writing, Assyria was the most powerful nation the
world had yet seen.

It would appear, then, that the verses 10:8–12 are a brief résumé
of 2500 years of the history of the Tigris-Euphrates region, from the
period of the Sumerian city-states, through the Akkadian Empire, the
Amorite Empire, and, finally, the Assyrian Empire.

And where in this long history are we to find Nimrod?

The Biblical passage concerning him seems to telescope the deeds
of Lugal-Zaggisi, Sargon of Agade, Hammurabi, and Shalmaneser I (and
perhaps even Gilgamesh) and to make his single person reflect the
greatness of the Sumerians, Akkadians, Amorites, and Assyrians.

And yet to the writers of Genesis, the Assyrians were the latest and
greatest of the empires of the Tigris-Euphrates and their glory tended
to dim the memory of what had gone before. To the first conquering
king of Assyria might then go the credit not only for establishing
Assyrian might, but of performing all the deeds of the preceding
kingdoms as well. (It is as though a child receiving some garbled
notice of America's early history but understanding full well that George
Washington was the first President of the United States would then
write: "George Washington crossed the Atlantic Ocean in the May-
flower, discovered America, conquered Mexico, built Washington, D.C.,
and became first President of the United States.")

The first Assyrian conqueror of note was, as I have said, Tukulti-
Ninurta I. It seems very likely that he served as the original inspiration
for the Greek legend of Ninus. ("Ninurta" with a few letters dropped
and the Greek final -s, almost invariably used in their own names,
becomes "Ninus.") In the Greek legend, Ninus singlehandedly founds
Nineveh, conquers all of Babylonia and Armenia (Urartu), and the
nomadic regions to the east as well, founding the Assyrian Empire.

It seems quite possible that, in analogous fashion, "Ninurta" became "Nimrod" to the editors of Genesis. Indeed, the short picture of Nimrod in these few Biblical verses seems to point to an Assyrian monarch in particular. Assyrian art was powerful and cruel and one of the favorite objects of portrayal was that of the Assyrian kings in pursuit of big game. Hunting was undoubtedly a favorite and well-publicized sport of those monarchs and this is undoubtedly the reason for describing Nimrod as "a mighty hunter."

Then, too, the Assyrians succeeded the Kassites (Cush) as the dominant power in Babylonia, which makes it natural to have Nimrod described as the son of Cush.

Aram

With Nimrod out of the way, the writers of Genesis go on to complete the genealogy of Ham, by giving the descendants of Ham's sons, Mizraim [Egypt] and Canaan. Some of these have no particular interest and others will be more conveniently dealt with later.

Genesis then goes on to discuss the line of Shem:

> Genesis 10:22. *The children of Shem; Elam, and Asshur, and Arphaxad, and Lud, and Aram.*
>
> . . . .
>
> Genesis 10:24. *And Arphaxad begat Salah; and Salah begat Eber.*

The first two sons of Shem are Elam and Asshur, the eponyms of the Elamites and the Assyrians, which at the time that Genesis was reduced to writing were the most powerful nations of the "Semitic" world. I put "Semitic" in quotes because actually Elam was not Semitic in the modern sense; its language being of uncertain affiliation, and certainly not Semitic. However, its propinquity to Semitic Babylonia and Assyria and its long connection with both (if only through perennial war) fulfilled the Biblical criterion of the word. Almost to the very end of the Assyrian period, Elam was the great unconquered adversary of Assyria, so that it deserved being listed as an independent son of Shem. And since it was clearly the more ancient it deserved being listed as the eldest.

The other three sons of Shem might conceivably represent other areas at the borders of the Assyrian Empire, still unconquered in the eighth century B.C.

Aram is clearly the eponym of the Aramaean tribes. These emerged from northern Arabia about the twelfth century B.C., and infiltrated the fertile regions round about. Aramaean raids helped weaken the Assyrian Empire after its first round of conquests under Tukulti-Ninurta I, and Tiglath-Pileser I, the latter of whom died about 1100 B.C. For two centuries thereafter, the Assyrian Empire remained almost in a state of suspended animation. Western Asia was given a respite and smaller states were allowed to establish themselves.

Even when the Assyrian Empire had recovered and, after 900 B.C., began expanding again, an independent Aramaean kingdom nevertheless maintained itself north of Canaan until 732 B.C. To the writers of Genesis, then, it deserved notice as an independent son of Shem.

Lud is much more controversial. The similarity of sound gives rise to the thought that Lud is the eponym of Lydia, already mentioned in connection with Magog (see page 46). Lydia, in western Asia Minor, maintained its independence against Assyria although it paid tribute at times.

That leaves the two small kingdoms of Israel and Judah, which, at the time that Genesis was reduced to writing, also maintained a precarious independence. Surely, since it was in Israel and Judah that the two chief strands of Genesis were compiled, these would be noticed as independent sons of Shem.

In a way they were. Arphaxad (better, "Arpachsad," as the Revised Standard Version has it) is a complete puzzle linguistically and does not even seem to be a Semitic name. However, Genesis 10:24 states that Arphaxad was the grandfather of Eber and Eber is the eponym of the Hebrew people, which would include the inhabitants of both Israel and Judah (as well as certain other related peoples).

Babel

With the genealogies taken care of, the Book of Genesis goes on to relate one last tale centered about Babylonia.

While the descendants of Noah were still a relatively small group, all speaking a single language, they came to Shinar (Sumeria) and decided to build a huge tower there, with which to "reach unto Heaven."

However, God defeated their purpose by giving each man a different language, making it impossible for them to understand each other.

Unable to continue their complex building activities, they had to leave off, and this tale is used to explain the name of the city in which the tower was built:

Genesis 11:9. *Therefore is the name of it called Babel; because the Lord did there confound the language of all the earth* . . .

In other words, the writers of Genesis derived "Babel" from the Hebrew word *balal*, meaning "mixed," "confused," or "confounded." This derivation is, however, a false one, for in the Babylonian language, the name of the city is "Bab-ilu," meaning "gate of God." From this is derived the Hebrew "Babel" and the Greek "Babylon."

There was, as it happens, a tower in Babel; indeed, there were towers in most Sumerian and Babylonian cities. The temples to the gods in these cities took the form of stepped pyramids which were ascended by inclined planes about the outside. These were called ziggurats.

A large ziggurat in Babylon was begun by a Sumerian king and was left unfinished perhaps as a result of the disorders involved in the southward march of Sargon of Agade. For many centuries, the ziggurat remained incomplete and perhaps gained fame because of its shortcoming (as does the Leaning Tower of Pisa or Schubert's Unfinished Symphony). It served as the model, one might assume, for the Biblical tale of the unfinished tower in Babel.

However, in the sixth century B.C., Nebuchadnezzar, king of Babylon, finished the largest ziggurat ever built. It was formed in seven diminishing stages (one for each of the planets). The bottommost stage was 300 feet by 300 feet and the whole structure reared 325 feet into the air.

This would scarcely make a respectable skyscraper now, and it was much smaller than the tremendous pyramids built by the Egyptians. It was, however, the largest structure in southwestern Asia and, more remarkable still, it was what is now so familiar to us as the "tower of Babel"—finished at last.

Ur of the Chaldees

The eleventh chapter of Genesis concludes with a quick listing of the descendants of Shem and Arphaxad. Again the age of each postdiluvian patriarch is given at the time of the birth of the successor. The years he lived after this birth are also given. The total age given for these patriarchs gradually decreases. The age of Shem at the time of his death is given as 602 years (itself a fall-off from Methuselah's 969), but Terah, eight generations later, lives only 205 years, and his immediate descendants have lifetimes of less than 200 years.

If we add up the ages, it would seem that Abram, the son of Terah, was born 292 years after the Flood, or, roughly, 2100 B.C There is no way of checking this from any source outside the Bible, but it would better fit the dates of the later events of the Bible if his birth were placed a bit later in history—perhaps soon after 2000 B.C.

It is impossible, now, to tell whether Abram and his immediate descendants represent actual individuals or, as in the case of Nimrod, a telescoping of several. If we take the Biblical story at its face value, however, he is an individual and a well-depicted individual, too. Genesis makes him *sound* historical whether he is or not.

Abram (whose name was later altered to the now better-known Abraham) is the first of the patriarchs from whom the later Jews traced their descent not only physically but spiritually. The importance of Abraham over those that came before him, if we follow the Biblical story, was that he was the first to travel to Canaan and, according to legends which do not appear in the Bible, that he publicly abandoned the worship of idols and became a staunch monotheist. (The legends explain that his father, Terah, was a manufacturer of idols and that Abram broke them in anger.)

The tale of Abram begins in the Tigris-Euphrates region which has been the focus of the first eleven chapters of the Bible:

> Genesis 11:27. . . . *Terah begat Abram, Nahor, and Haran; and Haran begat Lot.*
> Genesis 11:28. *And Haran died before his father Terah in the land of his nativity, in Ur of the Chaldees.*

Ur, therefore, can be taken as the home of Abram's family, and the birthplace of Abram himself.

Ur was a Sumerian city, founded no later than 3500 B.C. and possibly much earlier. It was located on the right bank of the Euphrates River about 140 miles southeast of Babylon and right at what was then the coastline of the Persian Gulf. It was an important city in Sumerian days, a center of worship of the moon-god, Sin, possessor of an impres-

Ur of the Chaldees

sive ziggurat, and probably enriched by an important seagoing commerce, situated as it was on the seacoast.

About 2500 B.C., Ur experienced a period of considerable power under its "first dynasty." This, however, came to an end after two and a half centuries, when Ur fell under the triumphant armies of Lugal-Zaggisi and, later, Sargon of Agade.

The inhabitants and historians of Ur must have viewed these conquerors in a harshly unfavorable light. If it is true that Nimrod represents a dim memory of Lugal-Zaggisi and Sargon, among others, then it is interesting that in Jewish legend Nimrod is represented as king of Babylonia at the time of Abram's birth and is described as having sought, unsuccessfully, to kill Abram.

After the fall of the Akkadian Empire, Ur entered another period of greatness and commercial prosperity under its "third dynasty." This final period of Sumerian power lay between 2050 B.C. and 1950 B.C. and it was during that period that Abram was born.

Ur continued to exist throughout Old Testament times and it is mentioned in documents as late as 324 B.C. However, by the time Genesis was being reduced to writing, Ur was nothing but a decayed and obscure village. The writers of Genesis, in mentioning a town which, thanks to the birth of Abram there, was of surpassing interest to their readers, felt called upon to identify it somewhat. They therefore called it "Ur kasdim," which is translated as "Ur of the Chaldees" or, better, "Ur of the Chaldeans," as in the Revised Standard Version.

The Chaldeans were an Arabian tribe who pressed into Babylonia from the south, on the heels of the Aramaeans (see page 54), about 1150 B.C. It was not until nearly a thousand years after Abraham's time, then, that Ur really became part of the Chaldean territory. Nevertheless, during the Assyrian period, the Chaldeans were the most important tribal component of the Babylonian population, and "Ur of the Chaldees" was the most economical way of identifying the town, regardless of the anachronism of the phrase.

Haran

The period of Ur's prosperity was coming to an end during Abram's youth, however. The silting-up of the mouths of the Tigris and Euphrates meant that Ur could maintain its maritime prosperity only by constant labors. The continuing struggles among the Sumerian cities, however, sapped its energies and helped ruin Ur as a seaport. Furthermore, the rising might of the Amorite rulers of Babylon was gradually bringing all the Sumerian city-states to a common end.

It is not surprising, then, that Abram's family could see little future in remaining in Ur and left Sumeria altogether.

Genesis 11:31. . . . *they went forth . . . from Ur of the Chaldees . . . and they came unto Haran, and dwelt there.*

In doing this, the family was following the normal trade routes from Sumeria to the Mediterranean. The Mediterranean lies five hundred miles due west of Ur, but if one were to travel due west one would have to cross the northern reaches of the Arabian desert, and that would be impractical. Instead, one would follow the rivers to the northwest and then turn south, marking out a great crescent that would carry one over a distance of over a thousand miles. The greater distance is made up for by the fact that one travels over fertile, settled territory and can rely on obtaining food and supplies for men and animals over the route. Indeed, the regions traversed by Abram make up what is familiarly termed "the Fertile Crescent."

Abram and his family stopped at Haran, at the northern peak of the crescent, and remained there for several years. Haran is located on the eastern bank of the Balikh River, which flows south into the upper Euphrates, sixty miles away. Haran is about 170 miles east of the northeastern corner of the Mediterranean and is located in what is now southeastern Turkey, just north of the Syrian border.

It was, in Abram's time, an important commercial center and therefore a good place to settle down, at least for a while, and catch one's breath. Like Ur, it was a center of the worship of the moon-god, Sin.

The Anchor Bible points out certain difficulties in accepting the phrase "Ur of the Chaldees" and wonders if it might not possibly be better given as "land of the Chaldees." In that case, Haran itself might be the place of birth of Abram's family, rather than Ur, and the two might have been confused through the common moon-worship.

Birth in Haran rather than Ur would make Abram an Aramaean (or at least the native of a region that later became Aramaean) rather than a Sumerian. This would square with the description in the Book of Deuteronomy of the ancestor of the Israelites, presumably Abraham.

In the Revised Standard Version, this reads: "A wandering Aramaean was my father."

It might seem at first glance that it is significant that Abram's younger brother, who had died early, was named Haran. It cannot be taken, however, that he could possibly have been named for the city, for the two names are alike only in English. In Hebrew, the name of the city does not really begin with the sound represented by out "H" but by that represented by the German "Ch."

But it is not likely that this view will win out. The birth of Abram at Ur is not only firmly embedded in tradition, but has its attractive features as well.

Ur is one of those places in which excavation reveals thicknesses of silt resulting from a severe flood. It may be that emigrants from Ur, with Abram prominent among them, brought tales of this flood to Canaan, where it entered the traditional story of early man and remained there. Other Sumerian legends, such as that of the garden of Eden, of Cain and Abel, of the tower of Babel, may also have arrived with them.

The city of Haran enters into history as more than merely a place of which one might say "Abram slept here." It is the site of three dramatic battles. It was an important bastion of the Assyrian Empire and when that empire fell, it was at Haran that its forces made their last stand—and were destroyed. To the Romans, Haran was known as Carrhae. There, in 53 B.C., a Roman army under Crassus was defeated by the Parthians, a crucial check to the expanding empire. In 296 A.D., the Roman Emperor Galerius was defeated there by the Persians in another dramatic battle.

Canaan

Abram's father, Terah, died in Haran, and it was time for Abram to move on.

Genesis 12:5. *And Abram took Sarai his wife, and Lot his brother's son . . . and into the land of Canaan they came.*

Canaan is the name of that section of the Mediterranean coast of Asia that lies south of Asia Minor. The use of the name in that sense is found in Egyptian inscriptions dating back to 1800 B.C.

Canaan was the center of a late Stone Age civilization with distinct towns by 4000 B.C. By 3200 B.C., metalworking had been introduced and it entered the Bronze Age.

People speaking a Semitic language entered Canaan as early as 3000 B.C. and for the next thousand years, they benefited from contact with the expanding culture of the Tigris-Euphrates region and by renewed immigration. By the time of Abram's arrival, then, Canaan already had a long history of civilization and was occupied by a mixture of peoples, lumped together in the Bible as the "Canaanites."

Despite the Bible's characterization of Canaan as a son of Ham (see page 44) because of Egyptian domination of the land, most Canaanites not only spoke a Semitic language, they actually spoke Hebrew. The Israelites who eventually conquered the land spoke or adopted the language of the people they overcame but—and this is the essence of Israel's importance in history—made and, in the end, held to their own values in religion.

Egypt

While Abraham had gone on a thousand-mile journey, he had, in a sense, never left home, for the culture that had originated in Sumeria filled all the Fertile Crescent in his day. Canaan, however, represented the western limit of that culture. When Abram traveled southwestward out of Canaan, he emerged into a new world altogether.

Genesis 12:10. *And there was a famine in the land* [Canaan]: *and Abram went down into Egypt to sojourn there . . .*

This was natural enough, for Egypt depended upon the annual flooding of the Nile for its fertility and this rarely failed. Consequently the famines that plagued semi-arid lands whenever the rainfall dipped below normal usually left Egypt untouched.

Egypt shares with Sumeria the honor of being the earliest home of human civilization. By 3000 B.C., civilization was well advanced, writing had been developed (borrowed from Sumeria, most likely), art and literature flourished.

Egypt benefited by its location. In all directions it was isolated by desert or by sea and it could develop its own way without interference. Whereas western Asia saw a succession of different cities or tribes rise

The Egyptian Kingdom

to dominance and fall to ruin, with prosperity and disaster alternating, Egyptian history was comparatively calm.

On the other hand, Egypt suffered in its earliest age from that same geography. Egypt is a long, thin nation, a veritable thread of a country. Only the immediate banks of the Nile receive the life-giving water of the flood and the Egyptians found themselves cultivating some 550 miles of riverside with an average width of just about twelve miles. This linearity and lack of regional compactness meant that the country naturally broke itself into isolated fragments.

Toward the end of the fourth millennium B.C. these had coalesced into two portions. In the north, where the Nile approached the Mediterranean, it built up a delta (as the Tigris and Euphrates did) and into this delta the Nile poured, breaking up into a series of sluggish streams that fertilized an area in the rough shape of an equilateral triangle about one hundred miles on each side. (The Greek letter "delta" in its capital form is an equilateral triangle and it is that which gave the Nile delta, and, eventually, all river deltas whatever their shape, its name.) This Nile delta made up "Lower Egypt."

South of the delta is the river itself with its thin strip of fertile land along either bank. That is "Upper Egypt."

About 3100 B.C., a ruler of upper Egypt named Narmer, but better known by the Greek version of his name, Menes, made himself king over both Egypts and established his capital at Memphis, just about fifteen miles south of the beginning of the delta. The site of the capital was probably selected deliberately because it was nearly at the point of junction of the two earlier kingdoms, so that neither appeared to be dominating.

Menes was the first king of the 1st dynasty (where a dynasty signifies a ruling family with members following each other in, usually, unbroken succession) of united Egypt. Eventually, thirty dynasties were recorded as ruling Egypt, though some of the later ones represented foreign conquerors.

Egypt's first period of high prosperity is referred to as the "Old Kingdom." It endured during the 3rd to the 6th dynasties inclusive, from 2664 B.C. to 2181 B.C., a period of nearly five hundred years that neatly brackets the traditional date of the Flood. The first ruler of the 3rd dynasty was Zoser and, according to tradition, it was in his reign that the first pyramid was built.

The pyramids were large stone structures that were intended as vast tombs for the ruler. The Egyptian religion was strongly death-centered and it was felt that the route to eternal life lay in the physical preservation of the body. A vastly complicated system of embalming was developed and the production of mummies (some of which have survived many centuries into our own time) was carried through with care. The mummy of the ruler was buried with vast riches (to serve him in the next world) and care had to be taken to prevent sacrilegious thieves from rifling the tombs. The pyramids were attempts to prevent such thievery by sheer bulk and strength, together with hidden exits and cunningly contrived passages. These failed, almost entirely, although in 1922, the British archaeologists, the Earl of Carnarvon and Howard Carter, discovered the unrifled tomb of Tutankhamen, a ruler who died in 1343 B.C., and created a sensation.

The pyramid madness reached its peak in the 4th dynasty with Khufu, the second king of that dynasty (better known by the Greek version of his name, Cheops). He ruled from 2590 B.C. to 2568 B.C., just a trifle earlier than the first dynasty of Ur. He constructed what is now known as the "Great Pyramid," a monster of an edifice built from a square base 756 feet on each side and rising to a point 481½ feet above the level of the base. It is built out of huge granite blocks averaging 2½ tons in weight, and 2,300,000 such blocks went into the structure. According to Herodotus, it took 100,000 men thirty years to build the structure. Maybe that's not too exaggerated. Relative to the technology of the time, the Great Pyramid is the most ambitious project of man with the possible exception of the Great Wall of China; and it is certainly the most useless, without exception.

After the end of the 6th dynasty, a period of virtual anarchy followed. Egypt fell apart into separate segments as a result of the slow decline of central authority during the later years of the Old Kingdom and the steady rise to power of the feudal lords of the various towns and regions. During a century and a quarter five different dynasties ruled, overlapping perhaps. It was only Egypt's isolation that allowed it the luxury of this anarchy; otherwise it would certainly have fallen prey to some outside enemy.

It was not until 2052 B.C. that central authority under the 11th dynasty began to make itself felt again. By 1991 B.C. (about the time of Abram's birth), Amenemhet I, first king of the 12th dynasty, came to the throne. This initiated the "Middle Kingdom," a second period of high civilization and culture. It was then that Abram entered.

Pharaoh

In Egypt, Abram eventually found himself in an uncomfortable position when the beauty of his wife attracted unwelcome attention:

> Genesis 12:15. The princes . . . of Pharaoh saw her . . . and the woman was taken into Pharaoh's house.

The name "Pharaoh," uniformly used as a title of respect for the Egyptian ruler, comes from the Egyptian *pero*, meaning "great house"; that is, the ruler's palace. (One might similarly speak obliquely of "the White House" when one means the American President, or of the "Kremlin" when one means the Soviet ruling body.)

The difficulty of this respectful practice is that it makes it quite impossible to tell which Pharaoh is being referred to very often. If one asks which Pharaoh it was that tried to add Abram's wife to his harem, we can only answer that while we might guess, we can never know.

I would like to suggest that it was Sesostris I, the second king of the 12th dynasty, who ruled from 1971 B.C. to 1928 B.C. He extended Egypt's power to the south and west and under him Egypt experienced a prosperity that might have seemed very attractive to a "wandering Aramaean."

In fact, Abram did well in Egypt. If, eventually, he got into trouble with Pharaoh and received back his wife only after considerable unpleasantness, and if he decided it was the better part of valor to return to Canaan, he at least did so as a rich man.

Jordan River

On his return to Canaan, Abram found his herds so multiplied that there was insufficient forage for both them and the herds of his nephew, Lot. It seemed reasonable to separate and generously, he allowed Lot first choice of territory.

> Genesis 13:10. *And Lot lifted up his eyes, and beheld all the plain of Jordan, that it was well watered everywhere, before the Lord destroyed Sodom and Gomorrah, even as the garden of the Lord, like the land of Egypt . . .*
> Genesis 13:11. *Then Lot chose him all the plain of Jordan . . .*
> Genesis 13:12. . . . *and pitched his tent toward Sodom.*

Canaan is largely a semi-arid country and the one place where water was (and is) unfailingly available was in the valley of the Jordan River. The fertility is described in this verse as being like that of the land of the two great river civilizations: Sumeria ("the garden of the Lord," that is, Eden) and Egypt.

For its size, the Jordan River is certainly the most famous river in the world, thanks entirely to its Biblical associations. It rises from the mountains that run along the line where the modern states of Lebanon, Syria, and Israel meet, and flows directly south about 135 miles, flowing into an inland sea without an outlet. The waters of the Jordan never reach the ocean. The river winds and meanders so, however, that its full length if straightened out would be 250 miles.

In one respect, the Jordan River is quite unusual. Its level descends rapidly and, in its relatively short length, that level drops from source to mouth about three thousand feet, or well over half a mile. In fact, it is sometimes suggested that the name of the river is derived from this fact and from a Hebrew word meaning "to go down." This, however, may be mere coincidence and the name may arise from pre-Semitic sources.

The result of this descent is that the water level in the river, over

The Jordan River

the lower two thirds of its course, is actually below sea level. As far as is known, this is true of no other river in the world.

The reason for this is that the Jordan River occupies the northern tip of the Great Rift Valley, a gigantic downfaulted block in the earth's crust which continues southward past the mouth of the Jordan River, into the long, narrow Red Sea (which fills that section of the rift), and in a large arc through eastern Africa. The deep and narrow lakes: Rudolf, Albert, Tanganyika, and Nyasa, fill sections of the African portion of the rift. All told, the Great Rift Valley is some four thousand miles long.

Despite Lot's opinion, the Jordan is not a very attractive river. It is not navigable and it is steaming hot in the summer, with temperatures not uncommonly reaching 110° in the shade. The general unattractiveness of the Jordan valley is recognized in Genesis 13:10, which carefully explains that Lot's estimate was before the destruction of Sodom and Gomorrah (the story of which is told later in Chapter 19).

In modern times, the Jordan has gained new kinds of importance. First, it is a national boundary. After World War I, what had once been Canaan was freed from Turkish control and was set up as a separate area, Palestine, under British control. The Jordan River served as part of its eastern boundary and to the east was another region, Trans-Jordan, ("beyond the Jordan") also under British control.

Trans-Jordan became an independent kingdom in 1946. Then in 1948, a portion of Palestine was set up as an independent Jewish state, which adopted the name of Israel. There was war at once between Israel and the surrounding Arab states. Trans-Jordan occupied and annexed a portion of the land to the west of the Jordan River and changed its own name to Jordan. (That portion of Jordan west of the river was occupied by Israel after the Six-day War of 1967.)

Hebron

After Lot left, Abraham contented himself with the less fertile and apparently less desirable region southwest of the Jordan.

Genesis 13:18. Then Abram removed his tent, and came and dwelt in the plain of Mamre, which is in Hebron . . .

Actually, "plain of Mamre" is a mistranslation and, in the Revised Standard Version, it is "oaks of Mamre" with a footnote to the effect that it might be "terebinths of Mamre." In either case, the reference is, apparently, to a sacred grove of trees located (according to tradition) about two miles north of Hebron.

Hebron itself is twenty miles south of Jerusalem and is one of the oldest towns in Canaan. Although it is called Hebron here, that being its name at the time Genesis was placed in final form, it was apparently called Kirjath-arba in Canaanite times (as stated later in Genesis 23:2):

> Genesis 23:2. . . . *Kirjath-arba; the same is Hebron* . . .

Hebron still exists and has a population of about twenty-five thousand. Its Arabic name is "El-Khalil" ("the friend") in honor of Abraham, "the friend of God." Various ancient oaks in its vicinity are pointed out as the "oaks of Mamre" but it is not possible that any of them are really four thousand years old.

Amraphel

After the separation of Abraham and Lot, the "cities of the plain" with which Lot had cast his lot were subjected to invasion by armies from the east. The heads of the invading force are named:

> Genesis 14:1. . . . *Amraphel king of Shinar, Arioch king of Ellasar, Chedorlaomer king of Elam, and Tidal king of nations;*

This seems to picture the situation as it existed in the days of the final decay of Sumeria.

Elam, the constant enemy of Sumeria (see page 35) now has the upper hand. It had been conquered by Sargon of Agade and for centuries had remained more or less under Sumero-Akkadian rule. After Ur's final gasp of power had faded away, however, Elam moved in. In fact, Elamite onslaughts may have helped bring Ur to final ruin. (I would like to imagine that the news of this reached Abram in Haran or Canaan. If so, it might have seemed as though Cain were slaying Abel at last—see page 34—and helped fix that legend in the mind of those who traced their descent from Ur.)

Ellasar may well be the city referred to in Babylonian records as Larsa. This was a city on the Euphrates about twenty miles upstream from Ur. Ur's decline meant its temporary rise. Tidal is sometimes identified with Tudhaliya I, the ruler of some Hittite tribe. (I will have more to say about the Hittites later.)

The ruler mentioned in this verse who has received the lion's share of attention from Biblical scholars is, however, Amraphel king of Shinar. At this time—about 1900 B.C.—the Amorites (see page 50) had taken over Babylon. Eventually, they were to take over all of Sumeria, so that Amraphel, possibly a local ruler and no more, is already called, a little prematurely, the king of Shinar.

The greatest ruler of the Amorite line was, as I have said earlier, Hammurabi, who ruled about 1700 B.C. and is best known for the code of laws issued in his reign. A copy was discovered in modern times on a diorite stele eight feet high. Hammurabi eventually conquered Larsa, which, under its powerful king Rim-Sin, had made things hot for him for a while. He also conquered Elam. (Nevertheless, Elam had its recurrent periods of power later. The column on which the code of Hammurabi was inscribed was found in Susa, the Elamite capital, where it may have been taken after a successful Elamite raid on Babylon during one of the periods of weakness of the latter city.)

It has long been customary to say that Amraphel was Hammurabi, but this seems quite out of the question. Hammurabi reigned some centuries after the events of this chapter of Genesis must have taken place. The Biblical story has Chedorlaomer of Elam the leading element of the coalition (even though Amraphel is mentioned first in 14:1) and this would be unthinkable in Hammurabi's reign.

The picture, then, is of a Sumeria on the decline, with Babylon and Larsa acting as a pair of city-states under the domination of Elam, with whom some Hittite elements are allied (or are perhaps serving as mercenaries).

Apparently, Elam, having secured the Tigris-Euphrates, is now reaching westward for the rest of the Fertile Crescent, which for some centuries has been under the domination of whatever power had ruled in the east.

The Vale of Siddim

Against the invaders stood the forces of what were then the most populous and prosperous cities of Canaan, the five "cities of the plain":

Sodom, Gomorrah, Admah, Zeboiim, and Zoar, concerning which there will be more to say later.

Apparently, they had paid tribute for twelve years but now they refused further payment and prepared to resist.

> Genesis 14:3. *All these were joined together in the vale of Siddim, which is the salt sea.*

The "salt sea" is the inland sea into which the Jordan empties and a most unusual body of water it is. It is not large in size, only about forty-seven miles long and not more than ten miles wide. Its area is 370 square miles, which makes it only slightly larger than the five boroughs of New York City.

The descending Jordan River is at 1286 feet below sea level when it finally enters the "salt sea," the shores of which are thus lower than any other land area in the world.

If the depression in which the salt sea rests could be filled to sea level, it would form a much larger inland sea some two hundred miles long and twenty miles wide, almost as large as the state of Connecticut.

The reason why the salt sea does not fill the depression is simple. The amount of water it receives—that of the Jordan River carrying to it the rainfall upon the mountains in southern Syria and Lebanon—is small. Its temperature is high (readings of up to 140° F. are recorded in its neighborhood) and the loss of water by evaporation is high. The salt sea represents a puddle, so to speak, which has partly dried.

The water brought in by the Jordan River is fresh but it does contain small amounts of chemicals dissolved from the soil it passes over and the banks it passes between. These chemicals accumulate in the salt sea. If the salt sea had an opening to the ocean the chemicals would be washed out as fast as they came in and the waters of the sea would remain fresh. But there is no opening and the sea loses water only by evaporation. The chemicals do not evaporate and remain behind; more is constantly being added and none is removed. As a result, the sea is now from 23 to 25 per cent dissolved chemicals, mostly sodium chloride (common salt) and magnesium chloride, plus smaller quantities of a variety of other substances. It is rightly named the salt sea.

So heavy is the salt concentration (seven times that of the ocean) that nothing can live in the waters of the sea. For that reason, the Greek geographers took to calling it the Dead Sea, and it is by that name that it is best known to us. The name Dead Sea does not, however, occur in the Bible.

Despite the fact that the Dead Sea is a partly dried puddle resting at the bottom of a depression, we must not get the idea that it is almost all gone and that another little push will cause it to disappear altogether in a final burst of evaporation. Remember that the water of the Dead Sea fills part of the Great Rift Valley. This allows the Dead Sea, low though its level has fallen, to be one of the deepest lakes in the world. Its average depth is 1080 feet and its greatest depth is 1310 feet. The volume of water it contains is considerably greater than that in some apparently much larger lakes (in terms of surface area) which are very shallow. The Dead Sea contains about twelve times as much water, for instance, as does our own Great Salt Lake, although the latter, in terms of area, is four times as large.

The Dead Sea is a major source of chemicals and indeed plants now exist in its neighborhood for the extraction of potassium chloride from its waters. Chemicals that kill life in too great a concentration can act as fertilizers in proper dosage. Nowadays, the Dead Sea lies between the nations of Jordan and Israel.

The Dead Sea is divided into two unequal parts by a small peninsula that extends into it from the eastern shores. The northern part, making up about two thirds of the whole area, is the deep portion. The southern part, making up the remaining third, is quite shallow, with depths of from three to thirty feet. It is possible that the "vale of Siddim" mentioned in Genesis 14:3 refers to the neighborhood of this southern portion of the Dead Sea particularly.

Rephaims

The army of Chedorlaomer, on its way down the western half of the Fertile Crescent, quickly subdued the regions east and south of the Dead Sea:

> Genesis 14:5. . . . *Chedorlaomer, and the kings that were with him, . . . smote the Rephaims . . . and the Zuzims . . . and the Emims . . .*

The use of the expression "Rephaims," by the way, is an example of a false plural. The "-im" suffix is itself the Hebrew plural, and to add a further "-s" is superfluous. The Revised Standard Version speaks, therefore, of the Rephaim, Zuzim, and Emim. (The Zuzim are often identified with the "Zamzummim" mentioned later in the Book of Deuteronomy.)

These people predated those who arrived six or seven centuries after the time of Abraham—the Israelites and related tribes. The tradition is strong that the pre-Israelite inhabitants of Canaan, the Rephaim in particular, were giants. Indeed, the tradition of the one-time existence of giants, with sizes that are magnified as the tales are passed on from generation to generation, are very common in the folklore of all nations. The Bible states flatly in one much-discussed passage:

Genesis 6:4. *There were giants in the earth in those days . . .*

However, the Hebrew term here translated as "giants" is *Nephilim* and there is no way of being certain that giants is what is actually meant. It may simply have meant a race of mighty warriors, without particular reference to gigantic physical size. The Revised Standard Version evades the issue by leaving the Hebrew word untranslated and saying "The Nephilim were on the earth in those days."

Again in the Book of Numbers, in retailing the report of the spies sent into Canaan by Moses, the Bible has them say:

Numbers 13:33. *And there we saw the giants, the sons of Anak, which come of the giants . . .*

Here also the term is *Nephilim* and the Revised Standard Version reads: "And there we saw the Nephilim (the sons of Anak, who come from the Nephilim) . . ."

At least one reason for the persistent tales of giants may rest in the wonder felt by barbarian invaders at the sight of the works of the civilizations they replaced. Thus, when the Dorian Greeks invaded the Peloponnesus they were struck with astonishment at the thick walls of towns such as Mycenae and Tiryns, which had been strong-holds of the defeated Mycenaean civilization. Viewing the tremendous stone blocks that made up those walls, the Dorians decided that they could only have been built by giants and the Greek myths do indeed say that the huge one-eyed Cyclopes built those walls. (And such walls, made up of large stone blocks, held by their own weight without cement or mortar, are still called "cyclopean walls.")

Similarly, the Israelite invaders of 1200 B.C., viewing the elaborate fortifications of the Canaanite cities, may have felt they were fighting giants. The term must have been used metaphorically at first, as a dramatic expression of the technological advancement of the enemy. Thus, the verse in Numbers already cited goes on to say:

Numbers 13:33. . . . *and we were in our own sight as grasshoppers, and so we were in their sight.*

which is about how an unarmed man might feel facing a man with a loaded rifle, or how the latter might feel facing a man in a tank.

Nevertheless, all such expressions came to be accepted literally and in later rabbinical legends, the Rephaim, Emim, Zuzim, Zamzummim, Nephilim, and Anakim all became giants of absolutely tremendous size. It would certainly be strange if they were, however, since they were easily defeated by Chedorlaomer and also by the later Israelite invasion.

It is almost needless to say that archaeologists have come across no traces of giant races in historic times. To be sure, there are a very few fossil remains, mostly teeth, indicating the one-time existence of a manlike being even larger than the modern gorilla. These must, however, have lived a hundred thousand years ago and more, and it is unlikely in the extreme that any existed as recently as Abraham's time.

Salem

Chedorlaomer's army then turned the southern flank of the Dead Sea region, fell upon the forces of the cities of the plain, and defeated them. The city of Sodom was sacked and Lot, Abram's nephew, was one of those who were carried off to enslavement.

Abram (pictured in Chapter 14 of Genesis as a powerful desert sheik), on hearing of this, immediately gathered his men and set off in pursuit. He defeated a contingent of the army of Chedorlaomer and liberated Lot, together with much of the taken loot.

As Abram returned from this victorious raid:

Genesis 14:18. . . . *Melchizedek king of Salem brought forth bread and wine:* . . .

Genesis 14:19. *And he blessed him, and said Blessed be* Abram . . .

Melchizedek is Hebrew for "righteous king" and is thus the Canaanite equivalent of the Akkadian name "Sargon." Nowhere else in the Bible is Melchizedek mentioned except in reference to this single incident.

Naturally, there has been considerable speculation as to where Salem might be located. The later Jews decided that Salem (a Hebrew word meaning "peace") was a shortened form of Jerusalem. In the 76th Psalm, for instance, this shows up:

> Psalm 76:2. *In Salem also in his* [God's] *tabernacle, and his dwelling place in Zion.*

As is the fashion in Hebrew poetry, the same thing is said twice, so that Salem must be synonymous with Zion. Zion is a poetic way of referring to Jerusalem and therefore it seems very likely that Salem must be another reference to that city.

There have been objections to this interpretation on the grounds that before the Israelite conquest, Jerusalem was the home of a Canaanite tribe called the Jebusites and that the city itself was called Jebus.

Yet references in Egyptian chronicles dating back to well before the Israelite conquest refer to a city called "Urusalim" which seems almost certainly to be Jerusalem. It would seem then that Jerusalem is indeed a very ancient name (of which the derivation is unknown despite the correspondence of the last two syllables to the Hebrew word for "peace") and that Jebus is actually a late derivation from Jebusite.

If Salem is indeed Jerusalem, as seems most likely, it is the first appearance of that city, later so famous as the seat of the Temple, in the Bible. In fact, one reason the legend may have been retained and recorded in Genesis was to show that Abram himself paid tithes at the future site of the Temple.

Damascus

Abram's great sorrow at this time was the lack of a son and heir; a terrible situation in a family-centered tribal society. He bemoaned the fact that only some servant, not part of his bloodline, could inherit his accumulated property:

Genesis 15:2. . . . *I go childless, and the steward of my house is this Eliezer of Damascus.*

Damascus had already been mentioned earlier in the previous chapter as a place name used to describe the extent of Abraham's northward raid in pursuit of Chedorlaomer:

Genesis 14:15. . . . *he . . . pursued them unto Hobah, which is on the left hand of Damascus.*

In Genesis 14:15, the reference might be merely to a place where later the city of Damascus was built, but Genesis 15:2 refers to an actual city, one with native sons. And, indeed, Damascus was in existence at the time of Abraham and even a thousand years earlier perhaps. It is believed to be the oldest continuously occupied city in the world.

It is about 150 miles north of Jerusalem, centered in a verdant, well-watered area. Indeed, its name ("Dammesek" in Hebrew) is derived, apparently, from the Aramaic phrase *di masqya*, meaning "having water resources." It is an important city even today. It is the capital of the modern nation of Syria and has a population of about 475,000.

The Hittites

Nevertheless, God promises Abram a son and also promises him that his descendants shall inherit the land of Canaan and that the people then, or soon to be, living in the land shall be displaced. (This promise is repeated on several occasions in the Book of Genesis.) The tribes dwelling in Canaan are then enumerated, as they are to be enumerated on a number of occasions later in the Bible. They were also enumerated in the "Table of Nations" in the tenth chapter of Genesis, as children of Canaan. The details of the enumeration change from place to place. Here it is given as:

Genesis 15:19. *The Kenites, and the Kenizzites, and the Kadmonites,*
Genesis 15:20. *And the Hittites, and the Perizzites, and the Rephaims,*

The Hittite Kingdom

Genesis 15:21. *And the Amorites, and the Canaanites, and the Girgashites, and the Jebusites.*

There is wide variety in these names. The Kenites, Kenizzites, and Kadmonites are all desert tribes of the south and southeast. The Jebusites are the inhabitants of Jerusalem and its environs. Virtually nothing is known of the Perizzites and Girgashites, except that they are mentioned among the inhabitants in several of the lists. The Rephaim I have discussed earlier (see page 72).

The Canaanites are, obviously, a general term for the inhabitants of Canaan and the Amorites are used as an almost synonymous general term. This may be because in Abraham's time, the Amorites had become the most important of the west Semitic tribes. They had taken over Babylon and were on the way to the control of all the Tigris-Euphrates (see page 50).

By far the most interesting of the groups listed, however, is the Hittites.

The Hittites are sometimes referred to as the "sons of Heth" and Heth (the eponym of the tribe) is referred to in the tenth chapter of Genesis as the second son of Canaan:

Genesis 10:15. *And Canaan begat Sidon his firstborn, and Heth . . .*

Because the Hittites are invariably mentioned in the Bible as among the tribes of Canaanites, the feeling arose that they were a minor people, no more important than, let us say, Girgashites, who have never been heard of outside those few verses in the Bible in which they are mentioned. And yet the fact that Heth is Canaan's second-born bespeaks a certain importance.

The old Egyptian and Babylonian records do speak of the "Kheta" and the "Khatti" respectively (quite similar to "Heth") as a powerful people north of Canaan and the thought grew that these might be the Biblical Hittites and that they might not be an unimportant group of Canaanites after all. Archaeological findings in the nineteenth century seemed to point to a hitherto unknown empire that had once flourished in Syria and Asia Minor.

Finally, in 1906, a German archaeologist, Hugo Winckler, uncovered a store of cuneiform tablets near the village of Bogazkoy in central Turkey, about ninety miles east of the present Turkish capital, Ankara.

It turned out that the tablets were found on the site of the capital of what had indeed been a Hittite Empire.

Further investigation showed that the Hittites had ruled a powerful realm, had introduced the use of iron and of horse-drawn chariots (something which the Assyrians were later to improve on), and, for a few centuries, had disputed the mastery of western Asia with Egypt when the latter kingdom was at her most powerful.

How then could this great empire go unnoticed in the Bible and be mentioned only as an unimportant tribe?

Actually, this is an accident of history. In the time of Abraham and his immediate descendants, the Hittites had not yet reached the fullness of their strength. Indeed, Tidal, an early Hittite leader, is mentioned only as a confederate of Chedorlaomer (see page 68) and as of no more importance than a Sumerian city-state.

It was not until 1750 B.C., well after Abraham's time, that the Hittite "Old Kingdom" was founded and that a conquering Hittite king spread its power outside Asia Minor. And by that time, Abraham's descendants were on their way into Egyptian bondage and the focus of the Bible moves away for some centuries from Canaan.

After a century of Hittite decline between 1500 and 1400 B.C., there followed a period of even greater power, and the Hittite "New Kingdom" was established. Under Shubbiluliu, who reigned from 1390 B.C. to 1350 B.C., the Hittites reached the peak of their power and for a moment seemed on the point of establishing their dominion over all the civilized world. In the end, however, a long war with Egypt wore them out; they declined first slowly and then more rapidly, and by 1200 B.C. the Hittite Empire came to a final end.

When the Israelites invaded Canaan and the Biblical focus was restored to that land, the remnant of the Hittites remaining here and there in Canaan and to the north could be viewed as an unimportant tribe.

In short, the Bible talks of Canaan before the Hittites rose to power and after the Hittites fell from power, but never while the Hittites were in their full glory. And since the Bible was, until the nineteenth century, the chief source of historical knowledge concerning the ancient East, the great Hittite Empire vanished from sight. Only with Winckler's work did archaeological finds in the Middle East restore it to the knowledge of man.

Ishmael

At the suggestion of his wife, Sarai, Abram takes her servant, Hagar, as his concubine.

Genesis 16:15. *And Hagar bare Abram a son: and Abram called his son's name . . . Ishmael.*

Ishmael is the eponym of a group of tribes, collectively known as Ishmaelites in the Bible, who dwelt on the border of the Arabian desert south and southeast of Canaan. The Israelites recognized the kinship of these Arabian tribes to themselves by tracing the descent of those tribes from Abraham. It was a descent through a concubine, however, indicating the view (from the standpoint of the writers of Genesis) that the Ishmaelites were of subordinate importance in the scheme of things.

The Arabians in later centuries came under the influence of Judaism and even after the establishment of Islam in the seventh century A.D. accepted many parts of the Bible and embroidered the legendary material of Genesis in their own fashion. They considered themselves to be descended from Abram and Ishmael and the Arabic versions of those names, Ibrahim and Ismail, remain favorites among Moslems. According to Moslem legend, both Hagar and Ishmael are buried in Mecca.

Circumcision

Ishmael is not, however, the son through whom the descendants will arise to whom Canaan is promised. God now renews the promise, entering into a covenant with Abraham; something that in human terms would be a legal, binding agreement.

In return for the divine right to Canaan, Abraham, in his own name and that of his descendants, agrees to accept God as the national deity. God says:

Genesis 17:7. *And I will establish my covenant between me and thee and thy seed after thee . . . to be a God unto thee, and to thy seed after thee.*

As his "signature" to this agreement, Abram (now renamed Abraham—a change in name to signify the new situation) agrees to accept the rite of circumcision. (The Hebrew term for it is *berith*, meaning "covenant.") God says:

> Genesis 17:10. *This is my covenant, which ye shall keep* . . . *Every man child among you shall be circumcised.*

Circumcision is the removal of the foreskin of the penis; a loss which in no way hampers the sex act, and does not result in any inconvenience at all.

The custom is, actually, far older than Abraham and its origins are lost in prehistoric antiquity. It was practiced by the Egyptians and by the Canaanites, who were under the political and cultural domination of Egypt in Abraham's time. The rite was not practiced in the Tigris-Euphrates region, and the tale of Abraham's circumcision may represent a memory of the adoption of certain phases of Egyptian and Canaanite culture by the westward-wandering nomads.

Circumcision does not seem to have been particularly important among the pre-Exilic Jews. It was practiced, of course, and uncircumcised people (such as the Philistines) were looked down upon, but the overwhelming religious significance of the rite seemed to arise during the Exile.

When the Jews in Babylon were trying to maintain their national existence and to keep themselves separate from the overwhelming numbers of the Babylonians, circumcision grew important. It marked off the Jews from the uncircumcised Babylonians.

It was comforting, further, to interpret that mark of separation as the legal witness that the Promised Land, from which the Jews had been torn by the Babylonian conquerors, was Jewish by divine agreement, and would therefore be theirs again someday. The Book of Genesis, which was being put into its final form at the time, was naturally so edited as to stress this point.

The land was indeed restored and the importance and prestige of circumcision was thus fixed. Through all the Greek and Roman period, it continued to be the fundamental rite marking the entry of the infant (or the adult convert) into Judaism. It was partly over the rite of circumcision that Christianity and Judaism parted company in the time of the Apostle Paul.

Although many people nowadays attempt to interpret the operation as a measure intended for the purpose of hygiene or cleanliness, it is likely that to primitive man (innocent of our modern notions of hygiene) the act had magical overtones. It may, for instance, have been intended to ensure fertility.

Sodom and Gomorrah

But while the promised heir is awaited, the focus shifts again to the outside world.

Abraham learns that the cities of the plain—of which Sodom and Gomorrah were the most important—are to be destroyed in a great catastrophe. It had been in Sodom that Lot had chosen to live (see page 65) and it had been Sodom that had led the rebellion against Chedorlaomer (see page 70).

Sodom and Gomorrah

Abraham intercedes on behalf of those of the inhabitants of the cities who might be righteous and his nephew Lot is allowed to escape in time to the smallest of the cities of the plain, Zoar (although Lot's wife is lost, being turned into a pillar of salt, according to the story).

Genesis 19:23. . . . *Lot entered into Zoar.*

Genesis 19:24. *Then the Lord rained upon Sodom and upon Gomorrah brimstone and fire . . .*

Genesis 19:25. *And he overthrew those cities, and all the plain, and all the inhabitants of the cities, and that which grew upon the ground.*

The description of the catastrophe could match that of a volcanic eruption, combined with an earthquake; or, conceivably, a large meteorite strike. Certainly such events have proved catastrophic enough even in recent times. In 1883, a volcanic eruption on the island of Krakatoa in the strait between the Indonesian islands of Java and Sumatra killed 36,000 people in Java.

The question is, though, where Sodom and the other cities of the plain might have been located before the destruction. The "plain" seems to refer to the entire depression occupied by the Jordan River and the Dead Sea, which, according to Genesis 13:10, was "well watered everywhere."

Certainly the shores of the Dead Sea are bleakly infertile now but conceivably that might have been the result of the very catastrophe described here.

The most interesting possibility follows from certain signs that indicate that in Abraham's time, the level of the Dead Sea may have been some feet lower than it is today. It might therefore have been that the Dead Sea was at that time confined only to its deep portion, the northern two thirds (see page 71). The shallow, southern third might have been the dry, or perhaps marshy, plain on which Sodom and its sister cities were located, with a fresh-water table that kept the area fertile as it drained northward into the Dead Sea. This area might, indeed, have been the very "vale of Siddim" referred to in Genesis 14:3.

It might then have been that the catastrophe which overwhelmed Sodom and the other cities, whether a volcano or earthquake or meteorite strike, led to a slight subsidence of the land, so that the waters of the Dead Sea flooded southward; and this flood might have been made the worse as the result of a rise (for some reason) of the general water-level of the Sea. If all this were so, what was left of the cities (and considering the size and make-up of Canaanite cities of 1900 B.C., it wouldn't be much) would be covered by the waters of the Dead Sea.

It is only fair to say, however, that no extra-Biblical evidence of such a catastrophe is known and there are no reports of any remains of civilization buried under the waters of the southern end of the Dead Sea.

Although not mentioned here, two of the other cities of the plain were also destroyed, according to Deuteronomy:

> Deuteronomy 29:23. . . . *like the overthrow of Sodom, and Gomorrah, Admah, and Zeboim, which the Lord overthrew in his anger* . . .

Zoar, the last city of the plain, and the refuge of Lot, was spared. In the Book of Jeremiah, the prophet inveighs against Moab, mentioning Zoar among its cities:

> Jeremiah 48:33. *And joy and gladness is taken from the* . . . *land of Moab;* . . .
> Jeremiah 48:34. . . . *from Zoar even unto Horonaim* . . .

From the known location of Moab, this would place Zoar, most likely, southeast of the Dead Sea, perhaps nearly at the edge of the present shore, just far enough from the other cities to have escaped the catastrophe and inundation. No trace of Zoar remains in modern times.

During medieval times, by the way, when few Europeans ever saw the Dead Sea, impressions of it, arising out of the nineteenth chapter of Genesis, were most horrible. Its waters were thought to be black; the vapors above it poisonous; birds could not fly over it. None of this is true, of course. Its climate is miserable and its waters are bitter and contain no life, but it is not poisonous externally, and men can swim in it if they choose. (Such swimming is a remarkable experience, for the salt concentration makes the water unusually dense and one cannot sink in it even if one tries.)

Moab and Ammon

Lot's two daughters escaped with him from the destruction of Sodom. While hiding in a cave near Zoar, the daughters, at least, are depicted as convinced that the destruction had been universal. Feeling themselves to be the only possible mothers of future humanity, they made use of the only man available, their father, after making him drunk.

Genesis 19:37. *And the firstborn bare a son, and called his name Moab: the same is the father of the Moabites unto this day.*

Genesis 19:38. *And the younger, she also bare a son, and called his name Ben-ammi: the same is the father of the children of Ammon unto this day.*

The Moabites and Ammonites were peoples related to the Israelites in terms of language and culture, and the Biblical writers recognized this relationship by having them descended from Lot, the nephew of Abraham.

The Moabites and Ammonites descended upon Canaan from the eastern desert some five centuries after Abraham's time and perhaps a century before the Israelites themselves did. The Bible says this in its own fashion by placing the time of birth of the eponyms of Moab and Ammon before the time of birth of the eponym of Israel.

The actual origins of the names Moab and Ammon are not known, but they can be twisted to imply incestuous origin. "Moab" may mean "from father" and "Ben-ammi" seems to mean "son of my people." If this is taken to read "from [my own] father" and "son of my [own] people" nothing more is needed. Since for centuries after the Israelite conquest of Canaan, Moab and Ammon remained perennial enemies of the Israelites, the writers of Genesis were probably only too pleased to record the folk tale of their scandalous origin.

Gerar

After the destruction of Sodom, Abraham apparently felt the need of moving away from unpleasant associations and of making a new start.

Genesis 20:1. *And Abraham journeyed from thence . . . and sojourned in Gerar.*

Gerar is about forty miles west of Hebron and a little to the south. It is only about ten miles from the Mediterranean coast and not more than twenty miles northeast of what would now be considered the boundary of Egypt.

The writer of Genesis speaks of Gerar as being in Philistine territory for its king, on returning to his city, is recorded as having:

Genesis 21:32. *. . . returned into the land of the Philistines.*

Canaan in the Time of the Patriarchs

Again, at the end of the description of happenings during Abraham's stay at Gerar, a summary, as follows, is presented:

Genesis 21:34. *And Abraham sojourned in the Philistines' land many days.*

This should not be taken to mean that the Philistines actually occupied the territory of Gerar in Abraham's time. Gerar was in the area which eventually became Philistine, to be sure, some five centuries immediately preceding the time that Genesis was reduced to writing so it was best identified in that fashion. The anachronism was similar in nature to that involved in "Ur of the Chaldees" (see page 58).

Beersheba

While Abraham was in southern Canaan, a son was finally born to him and his wife, Sarah, and he was named Isaac.

In order that there might be no confusion as to who was to be Abraham's heir, Hagar, Abraham's concubine, and her son, Ishmael, were, at Sarah's insistence, cast out.

> Genesis 21:14. . . . *and she* [Hagar] *departed, and wandered in the wilderness of Beersheba.*

Wilderness is a term referring to uninhabited territory and presumably the city itself had not yet been founded. Its founding is attributed in the same chapter to Abraham, who is recorded as having dug a well in the area. He established the ownership of that well by coming to a formal agreement with the king of Gerar, an agreement involving an oath rendered inviolate by the ritual sacrifice of seven lambs.

> Genesis 21:31. *Wherefore he called that place Beersheba . . .*

The name of the town can be said to mean either "well of the oath" or "well of the seven" or, perhaps, "seven wells." In any case it is the water supply that marks the importance of the place. In the semi-arid land of Canaan, a reliable well or wells is essential for a permanent community and Genesis therefore deals in some detail with traditions concerning the digging of wells.

Beersheba, about twenty-eight miles southwest of Hebron, is about as far south as one can go and expect to find a reliable water supply. It is therefore the southernmost sizable town in Canaan and is usually taken by the Biblical writers as representing the southern boundary of the land. Farther south is the desert, or Negev (which is simply a Hebrew word for "south").

When Palestine was under Turkish rule prior to World War I, Beersheba was a small village with the Arabic name of Bir-es-saba. Some of its wells were still in existence and the largest was called the "Well of Abraham." In 1917, the British invaded Palestine from Egypt and won a victory over the Turks at Beersheba, one which led to the rapid conquest of Palestine.

Beersheba is now part of Israel, has a population of about 32,000, and is still the southernmost sizable town in the land (except for Elath, the Red Sea port). Its present importance depends upon the fact that it is an industrial and manufacturing center, thanks in part to its nearness to the chemicals produced at the Dead Sea, a little over thirty miles to the east.

Paran

Ishmael, after being cast out, made his home in the desert regions south of Canaan:

> Genesis 21:21. *And he dwelt in the wilderness of Paran: and his mother took him a wife out of the land of Egypt.*

Paran is an ill-defined area usually marked on the maps as including the northern portion of the triangular peninsula of Sinai, which lies between Canaan and Egypt. The nomadic tribes wandering there, and in the portions of Arabia neighboring it, are the Ishmaelites par excellence.

The region, thanks to its closeness to Egypt, would be under Egyptian influence even when Canaan itself was free, so that the fact that Ishmael had an Egyptian mother and an Egyptian wife seems to express the geographical and political situation in the personal terms appropriate for an eponym.

Moriah

There follows then the well-known story of Abraham's rocklike faith and his readiness to offer his son, Isaac—his long-awaited son—as a human sacrifice at God's order. At the last minute, however, Abraham is held back from the deed, and a ram is sacrificed in Isaac's place.

The place of the near sacrifice of Isaac is not closely specified. God's instructions are:

> Genesis 22:2. . . . . *get thee into the land of Moriah; and offer him* [Isaac] *there for a burnt offering upon one of the mountains . . .*

There seems no way of determining where the land of Moriah might be. It is not mentioned elsewhere in the Bible or anywhere outside the Bible. It is over two days' journey from Beersheba for Abraham sighted it on the third day, but the direction in which he was traveling is not given.

Among the later Jews, the tradition grew that the place of the near sacrifice of Isaac was destined to be the very place at which the Temple of Solomon was to be built. This place is referred to as Zion in every Biblical reference but one. The exception is a late-written reference:

2 Chronicles 3:1. *Then Solomon began to build the house of the Lord at Jerusalem in mount Moriah . . .*

Actually, the chance that the place of Isaac's ordeal and that of Solomon's Temple are the same may be flattering to later Jewish nationalism but is not at all likely to be true. Even in Abraham's time, the hill in Jerusalem was occupied and was within a well-fortified city. Abraham would not have had entry into it without careful negotiation that Genesis would surely have detailed.

Aram and Chesed

Meanwhile, Abraham's brother Nahor was back in Haran and news concerning him was brought to Abraham:

Genesis 22:20. . . . *Milcah . . . hath also born children unto thy brother, Nahor;*
Genesis 22:21. *Huz his firstborn, and Buz his brother, and Kemuel the father of Aram,*
Genesis 22:22. *And Chesed, and Hazo, and Pildash, and Bethuel.*
Genesis 22:23. *And Bethuel begat Rebekah . . .*

These are eponyms, of course, and the most important are Aram and Chesed. Aram is the eponym of the Aramaeans and, earlier in Genesis, is presented as a son of Shem. This apparent contradiction may be the result of the effort of the final editors of Genesis to keep each of two well-known traditions.

The two separate births of Aram also serve two separate functions if Aram is viewed as an eponym representing a people, rather than as an individual human being. In the tenth chapter, Aram is presented as a son of Shem to indicate that the Aramaeans were independent of Assyria at the time Genesis was reduced to writing (see page 23). Here, in the twenty-second chapter, Aram is presented as a son of Nahor, brother of Abraham, to indicate the kinship of the Aramaeans to the Israelites.

As for Chesed, he is probably the eponym of the Chaldeans ("Kasdim" in Hebrew). This is rather appropriate historically, since the Aramaeans and Chaldeans emerged from the desert into the Fertile Crescent at nearly the same time (see page 58).

The other names mentioned undoubtedly represent various Aramaean or Chaldean tribes and speculation about them is fruitless now. Huz (better "Uz" as in the Revised Standard Version) and Buz are of some interest with respect to the Book of Job, a matter which will be taken up in the appropriate place.

This short genealogy is also of direct interest to the Israelite readers of Genesis since Rebekah is listed as a daughter of Bethuel, who is himself first cousin to Isaac. Since Rebekah is later to marry Isaac, she is one of the ancestresses of the Israelites.

Machpelah

Eventually, Abraham's wife, Sarah, died at a time when she and Abraham were living in Hebron once more (referred to here at first by its Canaanite name of Kirjath-arba). Abraham bought a burial plot of "the children of Heth." This is usually interpreted as meaning "Hittite" though there is some argument about that which is not easily resolved. The transaction is carefully detailed.

Genesis 23:19. *And after this, Abraham buried Sarah . . . in the cave of the field of Machpelah before Mamre . . .*

Eventually, Abraham himself was buried in the cave (Genesis 25:9) as well as Isaac and his wife, and Isaac's younger son and one of his wives (Genesis 49:30–31; 50:13), all direct forebears of the Israelites.

By New Testament times, a tradition had arisen that a particular spot in Hebron represented the Cave of Machpelah. The Moslems (who were to be in occupation of Hebron for thirteen hundred years) respect the tradition and improve on it. The traditional site is enclosed in stone walls like a fortress and the enclosure is called the "Haram" (the "forbidden" place). One end is taken up by a mosque and the whole is treated with the deepest awe.

Mesopotamia

The time had now come for Abraham to be concerned over finding a wife for Isaac. Proud of his ancient lineage, he did not wish to have Isaac intermarry with any of the Canaanite peoples among whom he lived. He decided, therefore, to send his steward to Haran where his brother, Nahor, and his family still lived. A wife was to be selected from among that family.

> Genesis 24:10. *And the servant . . . arose, and went to Meso-potamia, unto the city of Nahor.*

The word "Mesopotamia" is Greek and not Hebrew. It is used as a translation of the Hebrew term "Aram-Naharaim" with reference to the country surrounding Haran. The Revised Standard Version retains "Mesopotamia" but the Catholic and Jewish versions in my possession use "Aram-Naharaim" without translation, as does the Anchor Bible.

Of course, Aram-Naharaim is rather an anachronism as the use of the term "Philistine" was earlier (see page 85). The Aramaeans were not actually in possession of that region for some centuries after the time of Abraham.

Mesopotamia means "between the rivers" and was applied by the Greeks to the land between the Tigris and Euphrates, at first only to the portions north of Babylonia and then to the whole region. In that sense, Haran, and all of Aram-Naharaim (which means "Aram on the rivers"), is in Mesopotamia. The term "Mesopotamia" remained popular in the west down to World War I, and was the most used name for what I have been calling the Tigris-Euphrates region, and Babylonia.

Prior to World War I, Mesopotamia was a possession of Turkey. It was taken from Turkey after World War I and became a British mandate. At that time, the native name of the land, Iraq, came into favor and is now used exclusively. In 1932, Iraq was recognized as an independent nation. Although Iraq includes most of the ancient Meso-potamia, it is not quite extensive enough to include Haran within its borders.

Syria

A bride was indeed found for Isaac. She was Rebekah, earlier mentioned as the daughter of Bethuel and granddaughter of Nahor (see page 89). She had also a brother, Laban, with whom the negotiations for marriage were carried on, and who was to play an important part later in Genesis.

The matter is summarized:

> Genesis 25:20. *And Isaac was forty years old when he took Rebekah to wife, the daughter of Bethuel the Syrian of Padan-Aram, the sister to Laban the Syrian.*

Padan-Aram (or "Paddan-Aram" in the Revised Standard Version) is clearly a term synonymous with Aram-Naharaim.

The term "Syrian" is the Greek version of "Aramaean" and throughout the King James Version, the terms "Aram" and "Aramaean" are translated as "Syria" and "Syrian" respectively. The Revised Standard Version speaks of "Bethuel the Aramaean" and "Laban the Aramaean" in this verse—although even to call them Aramaeans is anachronistic.

The term "Syria" stems back to a Babylonian word, "Suri," for a district along the upper Euphrates. In later times, the Greeks, pushing eastward, encountered this portion of the Aramaean lands first. The name Syria (in Latin spelling) came to apply to the eastern shores of the Mediterranean generally.

In the Bible, once that was translated into Greek, Syria came to be applied, in particular, to the region north of Canaan, which retained its independence of Assyria in the ninth and eighth centuries B.C. This became the Syria, with Damascus as its capital, which plays so important a role in the First and Second Books of Kings.

The region north of Canaan has remained Syria ever since, through Greek, Roman, and Moslem occupation. After World War I, Syria was freed of Turkish rule and was put under French mandate. In 1945, after World War II, the French also left and Syria became an independent republic, again with Damascus as its capital. It includes Haran near its northern border.

Midian

Before Genesis turns to a consideration of Isaac's descendants, however, it clears up the matter of the various Abrahamic lines through
concubines. Thus:

> Genesis 25:1. *Then again Abraham took a wife, and her name was
> Keturah.*
> Genesis 25:2. *And she bare him . . . Midian . . . and Shuah.*

Other descendants, over a dozen, are listed, but most are names
only. All are eponyms, one would assume, of various Arabian tribes,
of whom Midian is by far the best known. Midian is the eponym of the
Midianites who ranged over the land of Midian. This is usually marked
on the maps as occupying the northwest corner of Arabia, separated
from Sinai by a narrow arm of the sea, and thus quite close to the
"wilderness of Paran" occupied by the Ishmaelites. Indeed, the Midianites and Ishmaelites are used almost synonymously in the Bible.

Shuah is of some interest in connection with the Book of Job, a matter
which will be taken up later.

The descendants of Ishmael are given later in the chapter, all of whom
are now only names. Twelve of them are given, representing twelve
tribes, analogous perhaps to the twelve tribes of Israel. One of the tribal
eponyms is Massa, a name with some significance when the time comes
to take up the Book of Proverbs.

Abraham is recorded, then, as dying at the age of 175, and as being
buried in the cave at Machpelah by Isaac and Ishmael. A half century
later, Ishmael died at the age of 137 and now with all loose ends carefully knotted, Genesis turns to Isaac and his descendants.

Edom

Isaac and Rebekah have twin sons, Esau and Jacob. The characters
of the two are contrasted: Esau is a rough hunter, an unsubtle man
of the outdoors, loved and admired by his father. Jacob is a quiet,
shrewd man living at home and the favorite of his mother.

Esau is the elder by a few minutes and is therefore entitled to the birthright; that is, to the inheritance of the main portion of his father's property. He is also entitled to a father's blessing as his chief heir and such a blessing had great legalistic value in the society of that time.

Jacob managed, however, to outmaneuver his older brother. At one point, when Esau was returning faint and weary from a hunt, he asked for some of the soup of red lentils which Jacob was preparing.

Genesis 25:30. . . . *Feed me, I pray thee, with that same red pottage; for I am faint: therefore was his name called Edom.*

Jacob allowed him to eat but only after demanding the cession of the birthright in exchange, and receiving it.

The writer of Genesis thus gives Esau the alternate name of Edom ("red"), connecting that with the soup of red lentils that he desired. This made Esau (Edom) the eponymous ancestor of the Edomites, who, in centuries to come, were to occupy the territory south of Moab.

On the other hand, Jacob, who later in Genesis is given the alternate name of Israel, is the eponymous ancestor of the Israelites.

Throughout Old Testament times, there was continuing enmity between the Israelites and the Edomites. This is reflected backward into an enmity between the eponymous twin brothers.

Such enmity arose not only over the enforced sale of the birthright, but also as a result of a second successful deceit on the part of Jacob. Isaac, now blind and awaiting death, decided to give Esau the final blessing. To forestall this, Jacob dressed himself in Esau's clothes and put goatskins on his arms to imitate Esau's hairiness, and, pretending to be Esau, obtained his father's blessing.

Both these tales show a younger brother achieving hereditary dominance over an older. This forecast the actual historic situation—well established at the time Genesis was reduced to writing. The Israelites entered Canaan only after the Edomites had become well established on the outskirts, so that the Israelites were the "younger brother." On the other hand, through the centuries that followed the rise of David, the Israelites ruled over the Edomites.

Bethel

To prevent the possible murder of Jacob by a naturally resentful older brother, Rebekah decided to send her younger son away, at least temporarily. She persuaded Isaac to order him to Haran to get a wife for himself from the descendants of Nahor (as had been done in the case of Isaac himself).

On his nearly five-hundred-mile journey northward, Jacob slept at a certain place and dreamed of a ladder extending to heaven, with angels ascending and descending. He determined this to be a vision of God's dwelling place and decided that the ground on which he was standing was holy. (The Anchor Bible suggests that the vision of a ladder was really that of a ziggurat, which is built with steps working up along its outer walls.)

Genesis 28:19. *And he called the name of that place Bethel* . . .

The name "Bethel" means "house of God," an obvious reference to a temple, or even a ziggurat, which may have stood on the site quite early in Canaanite times.

The sacred traditions of Bethel were to have important consequences in the days of the divided kingdom a thousand years later, and to be a source of heresy among the Israelites. The city itself is located about fifty miles northeast of Beersheba and about eleven miles north of Jerusalem. It is now represented, according to general belief, by a village named Beitin.

Reuben and His Brothers

Jacob reached Haran safely and obtained not one wife, but two: Leah and Rachel, the daughters of Laban, who was the brother of his mother Rebekah. The girls were therefore his first cousins.

Carefully, the writers of Genesis record the birth of his children, beginning with his first:

Genesis 30:32. *And Leah conceived and bare a son, and she called his name Reuben* . . .

Jacob went on to have thirteen children listed by name: seven by Leah, two by Rachel, two by one concubine, Bilhah, and two by another concubine, Zilpah. Of these, twelve were born during his twenty-year stay with Laban and one was born after his return to Canaan.

These may be listed as follows:

Leah: Reuben, Simeon, Levi, Judah, Issachar, Zebulun, Dinah;
Rachel: Joseph, Benjamin;
Bilhah: Dan, Naphtali;
Zilpah: Gad, Asher.

All of these were sons, except for the one daughter, Dinah. It was Benjamin, the youngest child, who was born after Jacob's return to Canaan.

Each of the twelve sons was the eponym of a tribe of Israelites, though Joseph was, to be more accurate, the ancestor of two tribes, of which his sons were the eponyms.

It is sometimes tempting to interpret this in terms of a confederation of tribes uniting for the purpose of conquering Canaan and continuing to form a loose union (at times very loose) afterward. The tradition of descent from a single man, Jacob, would then be a way of marking off that confederation (binding it legally, in the family sense) as opposed to other related tribes—those of Edom, Moab, and Ammon, for instance—who did not join the confederation or even opposed it.

Furthermore, the division into four groups according to the maternal ancestress might indicate closer interrelationships. The "Leah tribes" may have formed the initial confederation, to which a pair of "Rachel tribes" later joined and the others still later.

However, such interpretations must remain guesswork. The only information we have concerning the early history of the Israelite tribes is what can be found in the Bible and this is not enough for the purpose.

It is interesting, though, that most of the sons of Jacob remain only names in the Book of Genesis. The only two who really appear as individuals are Judah and Joseph, the former eventually playing the chief role among the Leah tribes and the latter the chief role among the Rachel tribes. Moreover, when the Israelite kingdom was divided, the Joseph tribes (there were two of them) dominated the northern kingdom, while the tribe of Judah dominated the southern kingdom.

Genesis is built up chiefly of a pair of traditions, one developed in the northern kingdom, with tales of Joseph prominent; the other developed in the southern kingdom, with tales of Judah prominent.

While members of all twelve tribes are Israelites, it is the members of the tribe of Judah only that are, strictly speaking, Judeans, or Jews.

Seir

Jacob prospered in Haran and finally, after long-drawn-out quarreling with his father-in-law, Laban, left with his wives, his children, his cattle, and his goods. His next problem was to face his estranged brother, Esau. He had to prepare the way for such a meeting:

Genesis 32:3. *And Jacob sent messengers before him to Esau his brother unto the land of Seir, the country of Edom.*

Esau is pictured as already dwelling in the area which, centuries later, was to be occupied by the Edomites. Seir is an alternate name of the land which is more usually called Edom.

More specifically, Seir is the name given to the range of mountains that covers much of Edom. This range runs in a north-south direction from the Dead Sea to the Gulf of Aqaba, the northeastern arm of the Red Sea. Directly to the west of this range is a deep, narrow depression, which is now called Wadi el-Arabah, a continuation of the Great Rift Valley.

The Wadi el-Arabah starts below sea level at the Dead Sea, but rises, and at its highest point, just about halfway between the Dead Sea and the Gulf of Aqaba, it rises to some seven hundred feet above sea level, though even at that point it is flanked by considerably higher ground, east and west.

Sometimes the name Seir is applied specifically to the highest mountain peak of the Seir range, which is known as Mount Seir. It is located about thirty miles south of the Dead Sea and is about 4400 feet high.

An alternate name of Mount Seir is Mount Hor. This reflects the fact that prior to the occupation of the land by the Edomites, it was occupied by a group of people called Horites. Thus, in the description of the peoples defeated by Chedorlaomer, the account includes:

Genesis 14:6. *And the Horites in their Mount Seir . . .*

The Horites were, apparently, a non-Semitic people related to the Hittites. It was only a relatively small segment of these that had found their way so far south. Their main concentration was farther north and they are more frequently called "Hurrians." (The Horites to the south may, however, have been a distinct people with a name that only coincidentally resembled that of the Hurrians of the north.)

Like the Hittites, the Hurrians (Horites) had not yet reached the period of their greatness in patriarchal times. About 1475 B.C., however, they formed the kingdom of Mitanni along the northern Euphrates, taking up the area referred to in the Bible as Aram-Naharaim. For a while, Mitanni was one of the great powers of western Asia and held out against a conquering Egypt. A century later, however, it was over-shadowed by the Hittite New Kingdom and by 1275 B.C. it was defeated and absorbed by the Assyrians.

When the Israelites were conquering Canaan, the great days of Mitanni were over. Like the Hittites, they had flourished during the interval when the Bible's attention is absent from Canaan, and their deeds are therefore not recorded.

The Hurrians had, apparently, more of an influence over the early customs of the patriarchal period than had been expected. The Anchor Bible painstakingly analyzes the tales of the marriages of the patriarchs, of the position of concubines, of questions concerning birthright, and so on, and finds that much that would otherwise be puzzling in the stories of Abraham, Isaac, and Jacob becomes clear in the light of Hurrian custom.

Earlier I had explained that the Anchor Bible expressed doubt as to whether Abraham's origins were in Ur or in Haran (see page 59) and whether the Israelites could trace their ancestry to Sumerians or to Aramaeans. If Haran were the origin, it would perhaps be at a point in time before the coming of the Aramaeans but not before the coming of the Hurrians (or the people from whom the Hurrians had borrowed their culture). Perhaps one might properly have the Israelites say: "A wandering Hurrian was my father." The fact that the Hurrians were not Semitic is not a crucial argument against this theory. It seems clear that the Israelites adopted the Canaanite language when they occupied Canaan; who can tell what their language might have been earlier. It might have had strong Hurrian components.

Israel

Esau came to meet Jacob and the two approached each other east of the Jordan. Jacob made ready for the meeting in considerable fear. His company, including his wives and children, were most vulnerable. The mere act of traveling with them, of getting the company across rivers, for instance, was difficult.

Genesis 32:22. *And he rose up that night . . . and passed over the ford Jabbok.*

The Jabbok River is a tributary of the Jordan, flowing into it from the east at a point about twenty-five miles north of the Dead Sea.

After Jacob had supervised the crossing of the Jabbok on the part of his company and while he yet remained alone on the other side "there wrestled a man with him until the breaking of the day." In the morning, Jacob's adversary said:

Genesis 32:28. *. . . Thy name shall be called no more Jacob, but Israel . . .*

and thus he became the eponym of the Israelites. The descendants of Jacob are regularly called "the children of Israel" in the Bible. Once the Israelites conquered Canaan, it becomes the "land of Israel." When the kingdom of David and Solomon breaks up, the northern part, which is the greater in area, population, and power, is called Israel.

Finally, when the modern Jewish state was established in Palestine in 1948, it took the name Israel.

Shechem

Fortunately, Esau seemed to hold no grudge against Jacob, but treated him graciously and generously. Nevertheless, Jacob, not completely trusting the good will of his brother, managed to persuade Esau to return to Seir and to leave him and his family to their own devices.

Jacob then settled down in Canaan:

Genesis 33:18. *And Jacob came to Shalem, a city of Shechem . . . and pitched his tent before the city.*

Shalem is not mentioned, as a city, elsewhere in the Bible. It is the Hebrew word for "peace" and the passage as it stands in the King James Version is clearly a mistranslation. The Revised Standard Version has it: "And Jacob came safely to the city of Shechem." In other words he did not come to Shalem, a city of Shechem; he came "in peace" to the city of Shechem.

THE GREAT SEA
(Mediterranean Sea)

The City of Shechem

Shechem is about thirty miles north of Jerusalem and is considerably farther north than the areas where Abraham and Isaac dwelt. It was more than a hundred miles north of Seir, and no doubt Jacob felt that this was the sort of comfortable distance he wanted between himself and Esau.

Shechem is located in a narrow valley, not more than a hundred yards wide, between two mountains; a most strategic position, for it controls the road from the Jordan River to the sea, and from southern Canaan to northern. Through much of Biblical times, therefore, it was the most important city north of Jerusalem.

For forty years after the division of the Davidic kingdom, Shechem served as the capital of the northern kingdom. After that, when the capital of the northern kingdom was moved to Samaria, five miles northwest of Shechem, the importance of the older city began to decline.

After the destruction of Judea by Rome, the Emperor Vespasian initiated the rebuilding of a town near the site of what had once been Shechem, renaming it Neapolis ("new city"). This has been distorted into Nablus, its present name. It has a popultion of about 42,000.

Shechem was an important religious center, too. The first altar built by Abraham after he entered Canaan was near Shechem:

> Genesis 12:6. *And Abram passed through the land unto the place of Sichem* [Shechem] . . .
> Genesis 12:7. . . . *and there builded he an altar unto the Lord* . . .

All through Biblical times, Shechem retained its sacred character and it served as a rival at times even to the Temple at Jerusalem.

Hamor the Hivite

Jacob's stay in Shechem was, however, marked by tragedy:

> Genesis 34:1. *And Dinah, the daughter of Leah . . . went out to see the daughters of the land.*
> Genesis 34:2. *And when Shechem the son of Hamor the Hivite, prince of the country, saw her, he took her . . . and defiled her.*

The inhabitants of Shechem are here spoken of as Hivites. These are mentioned chiefly in connection with Shechem in the present instance and, in the Book of Joshua, as inhabiting Gibeon, a city some twenty-five miles south of Shechem. It is usual, therefore, to consider the Hivites another petty Canaanite tribe, concentrated in central Canaan. The Anchor Bible suggests, however, that the Hivites are a Hurrian people. Indeed, there may be some confusion, here and there in the Bible, between Horites, Hivites, and Hittites, and it is not really practical to try to untangle the matter completely.

Shechem wanted to marry Dinah after the rape, but the sons of Jacob agreed to permit this only if Shechem and all the males of the city would agree to be circumcised. (The lack of circumcision would seem to indicate that the Shechemites were not Semitic and this is a point in favor of the Hurrian theory.) After the circumcision, while the Shechemites were sore and uncomfortable, the sons of Jacob struck at them to avenge the rape.

> Genesis 34:25. . . . *Simeon and Levi, Dinah's brethren . . . came upon the city boldly, and slew all the males.*

This chapter of Genesis breaks into the personal story of Jacob and his sons and seems to describe a bit of early tribal history. It is not likely that two individual human beings would attack a city. Rather, this is a war of tribes, represented by their eponyms. Even Shechem, the rapist, is an eponym.

What may have happened is that three tribes in alliance attempted an assault on central Canaan prior to the general Israelite conquest of the land. The tribe of Dinah was defeated at Shechem and virtually destroyed and was then avenged by the tribes of Simeon and Levi, who themselves however, must have suffered badly and retired greatly weakened, eventually to join the Israelite confederacy when it gathered to assault Canaan.

That this is so is suggested by the fact that during the tribal period during and after the conquest of Canaan, Simeon and Levi were among the weakest of the tribes. Simeon occupied land in the far south and was absorbed by Judah soon after the conquest. Levi was never even assigned any coherent district but merely held certain isolated towns. The Levites in later times served a priestly function and were never again noted as warriors.

That the assault on Shechem was really a failure is indicated by the fact that Jacob is recorded as protesting bitterly against the raid and as finding himself forced to leave the area for fear of reprisal.

Nevertheless, the stay of Jacob in the area brought on certain patriarchal associations with Shechem. A mile and a half east of the city is still to be found "Jacob's Well," and a bit farther east, the tomb of Joseph. Indeed, the tradition arose in New Testament times that all of Jacob's sons were buried near Shechem.

Ephrath

Jacob and his family, after the troubles at Shechem, traveled southward about forty miles, passing through Bethel with its awe-inspiring memories for Jacob and then on to a point somewhere between Jerusalem and Hebron.

En route, the caravan had to stop for Rachel was giving birth to her second son, Benjamin, Jacob's youngest and the only son to be born in Canaan. With this birth, however, came tragedy again, for Rachel did not survive.

Genesis 35:19. *And Rachel died, and was buried in the way to Ephrath, which is Bethlehem.*

This is the first mention of Bethlehem in the Bible, Ephrath being its earlier, Canaanite name, or perhaps being the name of the tract of land in which the town itself was located.

Bilhah

While Jacob and his family dwelt in the region between Bethlehem and Hebron, still another variety of unpleasantness took place.

Genesis 35:22. *And it came to pass, when Israel dwelt in that land, that Reuben went and lay with Bilhah his father's concubine: and Israel heard it . . .*

Nothing further is said about this, as though the writers of Genesis found the matter too repulsive to pursue.

And it may be that this, too, reflects early tribal history. The tribe of Reuben must have been quite powerful at first. Since Reuben is listed as the oldest son of Israel, it may have been the leader of the confederacy when it was first formed.

The episode described above, may mirror an attempt by Reuben to make its leadership absolute. (One of the methods by which a usurper attempted to dramatize and legitimize his position in Old Testament times was to take over the harem of his predecessor. Absalom did this when he rebelled against David, his father.) There may have followed a civil war ("Israel heard it") in which Reuben was defeated. Certainly, Reuben's primacy was lost and when the Israelites conquered Canaan, Reuben played a minor role. Nor did the tribe survive long afterward.

Amalek

Before going on with the tale of Jacob's sons, the writers of Genesis again pause to tie up some loose ends. The death of Isaac at the age of 180 is described, and then the genealogy of Esau is given and disposed of. Notably:

Genesis 36:10. These are the names of Esau's sons; Eliphaz . . .

Genesis 36:11. And the sons of Eliphaz were Teman . . .

Genesis 36:12. And Timna was concubine to Eliphaz . . . and bare . . . Amalek . . .

Eliphaz and Teman are of interest in connection with the Book of Job and this will be discussed when that book is taken up.

As for Amalek, he is the eponym of the Amalekites, a tribe apparently considered by the Israelites to be related to the Edomites, since they lived south of Canaan near the Edomite territory.

Amalek is the last of the eponyms of the non-Israelite nations. Genesis has mentioned up to this point a number of tribes as having descended from Terah. All of these may, in a very general sense, be classified as Hebrews, since all are descended from Eber, the great-great-great-grandfather of Terah. The relationships can be made clear from the accompanying simplified genealogical table.

Seir the Horite

The Book of Genesis then goes on to make a quick list of the rulers of Edom. They list first the Horite rulers who preceded the Edomites:

Genesis 37:20. These are the sons of Seir the Horite . . .

Seir is the Horite eponym of the nation as Edom is the Hebrew eponym. It is very likely, of course, that the Edomites did not replace the Horites root and branch, but, as is customary in the case of such conquests, settled among them and intermarried with them.

Thus, although Esau is earlier described as having married "daughters of Heth" (Genesis 26:34), one of his wives is, in this present chapter, described as "Adah the daughter of Elon the Hittite," and another as:

Genesis 36:2. . . . Aholibamah the daughter of Anah the daughter of Zibeon the Hivite.

(The second "daughter" in the verse is changed to "son" in the Revised Standard Version.)

By Hivite, here, is probably meant Horite. For that matter, it is not entirely beyond the bounds of possibility that by "Elon the Hittite" is

THE RELATIONSHIP OF THE VARIOUS "HEBREW" TRIBES AS PRESENTED IN GENESIS

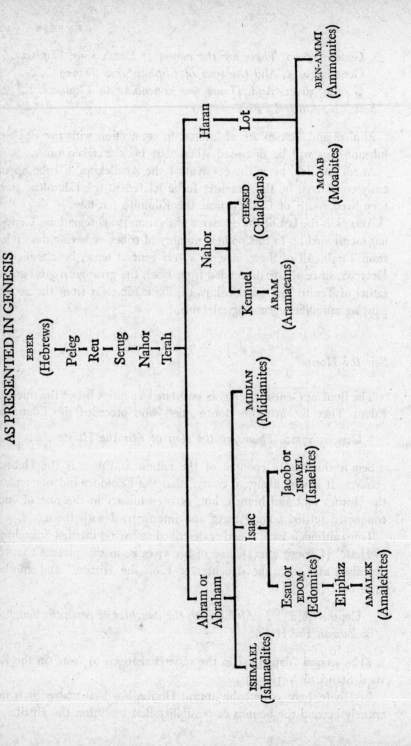

meant Elon, the Horite. As I said earlier, the Hittite-Hivite-Horite situation is hopelessly confused at times. It seems very likely, however, that these passages of the Bible indicate an intermingling of the Edomite invaders with the Horites already dwelling in the land.

Bela and Jobab

The chapter ends with a list of the successive kings that reigned over Edom before the kingship had been established in Israel. The Edomite kingship was not hereditary, since each new king seems to be unrelated to the one before, so that an elective monarchy may have been evolved.

The first two kings are of interest.

> Genesis 36:32. *And Bela the son of Beor reigned in Edom* . . .
> Genesis 36:33. *And Bela died, and Jobab* . . . *reigned in his stead.*

Bela the son of Beor is sometimes equated with Balaam the son of Beor, who shows up in the Book of Numbers as an adversary of the Israelites, while Jobab is sometimes equated with Job, the hero of the book of that name.

The first identification is very unlikely and arises only through the probably accidental similarity of names. The second identification may also be unlikely, but it is a more attractive one for there are other connections between this chapter of Genesis and the Book of Job. For instance, among the names given in the Horite genealogy is one reminiscent of Job's native land, Uz.

> Genesis 36:28. *The children of Dishan are these; Uz, and Aran.*

Potiphar

Genesis now enters its last section and deals with the story of Joseph, who is described as Jacob's favorite son and who is more than a little spoiled by the fact. He earns the hatred of his brothers by acting as a talebearer against them and by telling of dreams he has had which seem to foreshadow a day when he will be supreme over the family.

One day, Jacob sent Joseph to inquire after the welfare of his brothers, who were grazing the family's flocks in the neighborhood of Shechem (another reason for patriarchal associations—particularly that of Joseph and his brothers—with that city).

They had left Shechem by the time he arrived and had passed on to Dothan, a town about fifteen miles farther north. Joseph followed them there. The brothers spied him from the distance and conspired to kill him. At the intervention of Reuben or Judah (there are two traditions here, one stemming from the northern tribes and the other from the southern, and both are included by the final editors of Genesis) he is not killed but is sold to passing nomads. Jacob is then told Joseph was killed by wild beasts and the old father goes into deep mourning.

Joseph is carried southward, then westward to Egypt:

> Genesis 37:36. And the Midianites sold him into Egypt unto Potiphar, an officer of Pharaoh's . . .

Except for the short episode of Abraham's stay in Egypt (see page 64) this is the first appearance of this land as the scene of the Biblical story. Where Abraham's stay involves no details except for the mention of Pharaoh and his harem, the description of Joseph's stay is much more circumstantial. It begins immediately with the mention of the name of an Egyptian which, indeed, is a thoroughly Egyptian name. Potiphar is the shortened form of "Potiphera" meaning "he whom Ra gave." (This is analogous to the name "Theodore" in our own Western world.)

Pharez and Zarah

In view of the overwhelming importance of Judah among the tribes in later history, the writers of Genesis felt it necessary to incorporate some Judean genealogy. This seemed to them to be the logical point—Joseph had disappeared and the lapse of time could be emphasized by a shift in focus.

In circumstantial detail, it is told how Judah was tricked into consorting with Tamar, a woman who had originally been married to two of his sons, each of whom had died young and childless. Tamar then gave birth to twins, presenting them as new heirs to Judah.

During the childbirth, one of the twins began to emerge and the midwife tied a scarlet thread about the finger, declaring him to be the first-born. However:

Genesis 38:29. . . . *he drew back his hand* . . . [and] *his brother came out: and* . . . *his name was called Pharez.*

Genesis 38:30. *And afterward came out his brother* . . . *and his name was called Zarah.*

The two brothers are called Perez and Zerah in the Revised Standard Version and these names are preferable.

The twin brothers are eponyms who mark the two chief clans of the tribe of Judah, the Zerahites (or Zarthites) and the Perezites (or Pharzites). The tale told here undoubtedly reflects some early tribal history.

Apparently, within the tribe of Judah, the Zerahites achieved early dominance after two clans, represented by Judah's older sons, had died out. Therefore Zarah (Zerah) is listed here as technically the first-born. In time, however, the Perezites achieved the leadership, as is indicated by the fact that Zarah drew back and allowed his twin the actual primacy of birth.

If the importance of the Perezite clan needed reinforcement in the eyes of the later Jews, it is only necessary to point out that the great hero-king, David, and therefore all the subsequent Judean kings were Perezites, a fact made clear in the Book of Ruth.

Pharaoh [of Joseph]

In Egypt, Joseph, through his diligence and intelligence, prospers and is made steward of Potiphar's household. However, Potiphar's wife attempts to seduce the young man and, on failing, accuses him to her husband of having tried to rape her. Joseph is cast into prison.

There, again by his diligence and intelligence, he gains the favor of the jailer. He also gains the respect of his fellow prisoners by showing himself to be an ingenious interpreter of dreams. In particular, Pharaoh's butler, temporarily imprisoned, is gratified by Joseph's dream interpretation and promises to mention the matter to Pharaoh, but forgets.

Nor is it only the prisoners who dream:

Genesis 41:1. *And it came to pass* . . . *that Pharaoh dreamed, and behold, he stood by the river.*

Pharaoh dreamed that seven fat cows emerged from the river, but that seven lean cows emerged after them, ate the fat cows but remained as lean as before. He woke, then fell asleep and dreamed similarly about seven good ears of grain and seven bad ones.

Pharaoh's wise men were unable to interpret the dream to the monarch's satisfaction. Now Pharaoh's butler finally remembered the Hebrew slave who had been in prison with him.

Joseph was called for and interpreted the dreams at once. The seven fat cows and seven good ears of grain, he said, meant seven prosperous years, while the seven lean cows and seven bad ears of grain represented seven years of famine to follow, years of famine that would consume the land. The grain of the good years should therefore be carefully preserved and stored against the bad years to come.

Pharaoh was struck favorably by the interpretation and suggestion and placed Joseph in complete charge. Quickly he became the all-powerful prime minister of Egypt.

The question is, then, who was this Pharaoh, who was so favorable to a Hebrew slave and who, later, was to be benevolent to the family of Jacob generally? He could not very well be the usual run of Pharaohs for Egypt had so long been isolated that they were quite xenophobic; hostile at worst and patronizing at best to foreigners. The Egyptian Pharaoh was considered as a god by the Egyptians and by Pharaoh himself and he was not likely to delegate power to Asian foreigners. —Unless he himself were an Asian foreigner.

If we turn to Egyptian history, we find that the Middle Kingdom of Abraham's time (see page 64) lasted for two hundred years, from 1991 B.C. to 1786 B.C., enduring through much of the patriarchal period.

When the Middle Kingdom decayed there followed a new period of anarchy in Egypt, with weak dynasties ruling different portions of the kingdom.

About 1730 B.C. Egypt's weakness made it possible for Asian invaders to begin moving into the land. The Semitic invaders who, for a century and a half, were to rule the Nile delta and, on occasion, parts of the upper reaches of the Nile also, are called the Hyksos, which seems to be derived from Egyptian words meaning "foreign kings."

The Hyksos, making up the 15th and 16th dynasties in the ancient (more or less mangled) lists of Egyptian kings, established their capital at the northeastern edge of the delta, the point closest to Asia.

There is little record of the Hyksos and their rule remaining today, for later Egyptian historians apparently found the story of Egypt's defeat and subjection too unpleasant to talk about. The only account we have is that to be found in a book by Josephus, a Jewish historian who lived in the first century A.D. and who quoted from Manetho, an Egyptian historian who lived three centuries before Josephus' time.

From this, we might judge that the Hyksos ruled not only over the Nile delta, but also over part of the western half of the Fertile Crescent. If so, this is important.

Until the story of Joseph, the Book of Genesis had ignored Egypt except for a ten-verse description of Abraham's visit there. This was natural. Canaan had been, from the time of Sargon of Agade at least, and perhaps even from the time of Lugal-Zagissi of Erech, under the influence of the Tigris-Euphrates region. For much of the period, indeed, the Fertile Crescent had been a single realm, politically. This meant that movement was free between all parts of the Fertile Crescent. Abraham had come from Ur; his servant, and later Jacob, had returned to Haran temporarily; Sodom and its allies fought against invading armies from the Tigris-Euphrates.

Egypt, however, was another civilization and another world and was separated from the Fertile Crescent by a more or less permanent political boundary. Beginning in 1730 B.C., however, that political boundary was erased and the same power—the Hyksos—ruled over Canaan and over Egypt. Travelers between the two regions could move freely and when the Midianites purchased Joseph in Canaan it was easy to sell him as a slave in Egypt.

The picture of the friendly and gracious Pharaoh of Joseph's time may therefore be that of one of the Hyksos rulers. He would find Joseph a fellow Semite and would consider it perfectly thinkable to place the Egyptians under a Semitic viceroy.

Even this much is conjecture, of course, although it is *reasonable* conjecture, for the Bible makes no mention of the Hyksos as such, and no historical source outside the Bible (or those derived from the Bible) makes any mention of Joseph or of the dramatic events described in Genesis concerning his stay in Egypt. And even if Joseph's Pharaoh were indeed one of the Hyksos kings, it seems, on the basis of present knowledge at least, to be beyond hope to pin down which particular one of the line he might be.

According to Josephus, the tale of the Hyksos is the Egyptian version of the coming of Joseph and, later, of his family, to Egypt The Hyksos, according to Josephus' views, *were* the Israelites, but this is not taken seriously by anyone nowadays.

The River [Nile]

In Genesis 41:1, when the description of Pharaoh's dream begins, it is stated "he stood by the river."

In Egypt, it was never necessary to describe what was meant by "the river." There was only one river and it virtually *is* Egypt. Egypt is a desert land where it virtually never rains. What water there is comes from the single river that threads its length from south to north. What communication and trade there was in Biblical times came through the boats that passed up and down the Nile; what population existed, lived by virtue of the food that could be grown in the land that was flooded each summer by the life-giving waters of the Nile. The Greek historian Herodotus, in a famous phrase, called Egypt "the gift of the Nile" and so it was.

(Modern Egypt is still the gift of the Nile today. Fully twenty-seven million people crowd the narrow banks of the river while the land to east and west is virtually empty.)

It is not surprising that in Pharaoh's dream, he imagined that:

Genesis 41:2. . . . *there came up out of the river seven well-favoured kine and fatfleshed . . .*

Cattle do not literally emerge from a river, but if these cattle represent seven years of good harvest, it is only fitting they come out of the Nile, for all harvests depended upon its water. And seven lean cows would emerge from the Nile, if the Nile floods fell below normal height as once in a while they disastrously did.

The word "Nile" is neither Egyptian nor Hebrew, but is a Greek word of unknown derivation. "Nile" does not occur anywhere in the King James Version of the Bible, although it is used in the Revised Standard Version, which has Pharaoh "standing by the Nile," for instance, in Genesis 41:1.

The Egyptian word for the Nile was "Hapi," a sacred name used to represent the god of the river. In ordinary usage, the Nile was simply "the river," a phrase which in Egyptian is "Yor" and in its Hebrew form "Yeor."

The Nile is about four thousand miles long, a hair longer perhaps

The Nile River

than the Missouri-Mississippi and the Amazon. That would make it the longest river in the world.

Its remotest headwaters are in Tanganyika, where the Kagera River rises and flows 429 miles (forming a bit of the western boundary of Tanganyika) and then discharges into Lake Victoria, which in terms of surface area is the second largest fresh-water lake in the world. (Our own Lake Superior is the largest.) From the northeastern corner of Lake Victoria emerges the White Nile, which flows northward through Kenya, the Sudan, and Egypt and into the Mediterranean at last.

The main tributary is the Blue Nile. This rises in Lake Tana in northern Ethiopia. It flows east to begin with but makes a huge circle, joining the White Nile, at last, in Khartoum, the capital of the Sudan. The stretch of river downstream from the junction of the White Nile and the Blue Nile is the Nile itself, unqualified by adjective.

Two hundred miles north of Khartoum, another smaller tributary joins the Nile from the east and thereafter the river flows a thousand miles to the sea without a single further tributary, flowing through a solid stretch of desert in doing so.

The Nile flood is derived from the annual rains that fall not in Egypt but in east central Africa far upstream. The flood waters carry rich muck from the Ethiopian and Kenyan highlands. The Blue Nile, though shorter than the White Nile, is the more important in this respect, contributing much more to the flood volume.

The great length of the Nile, stretching southward as far as Egyptian, Greek, or Roman eyes could see, presented the ancient world with a mystery. Where was the far-off source of the Nile? Occasional reports that the Nile had its origin in great lakes were spread by Greek and, later, by Arabic merchants, and this seems to have reflected successful exploring expeditions.

It was not, however, until the 1870's that the African expeditions of the Anglo-American explorer Henry Morton Stanley placed east Africa and its lakes on the map in the full light of day, and only then was the Nile traced completely from source to sea.

On

With Joseph now a high official, Pharaoh bestowed on him a high-born wife:

> Genesis 41:45. . . . *and he gave him to wife Asenath, the daughter of Potipherah priest of On . . .*

Joseph's new father-in-law bore the same name as his old master, but the two need not necessarily be one man. Different men do bear the same name.

On, or Anu, was a city of great religious importance to the Egyptians. It was located at the southern base of the delta just about six miles northeast of modern Cairo. It was an important center for the worship of the Egyptian sun-god, Ra, so that the Egyptians called it "Pa-ra" ("house of Ra"). In the Book of Jeremiah, a direct Hebrew translation of Pa-ra is used for the city. Jeremiah in thundering against Egypt warns of the destruction that will follow a Babylonian invasion and says:

Jeremiah 43:13. *He shall break also the images of Beth-she-mesh . . .*

where "Beth-shemesh" means "house of the Sun."

The Greeks also used a translation of Pa-ra as the name of the city, calling it Heliopolis ("city of the Sun") and it is by that name that it is best known to posterity. It remained a center of Egyptian religion and learning throughout Old Testament times. It was well known for its obelisks and the Revised Standard Version changes the passage in Jeremiah 43:13 and makes "images of Beth-shemesh" into "obelisks of Heliopolis." Cleopatra's Needles, two great obelisks, taken out of Egypt and erected, one in London and one in New York's Central Park, are from Heliopolis.

After 300 B.C., when the Macedonian dynasty, the Ptolemies, took over Egypt and made Alexandria (about 220 miles northwest of Heliopolis) their capital, Heliopolis declined. Only a few ruins remain.

Goshen

Joseph's rule over Egypt was successful. The produce of the seven good years was carefully stored against the coming famine and two sons, Manasseh and Ephraim, were born to him. Then, when the famine came, Egypt was prepared.

Canaan was not, however. Jacob and his sons suffered from lack of food and the sons were sent to Egypt to buy grain. Joseph used the occasion to test them. He treated them harshly and demanded they bring Benjamin (whom Jacob had solicitously kept at home) with them if they ever came for food again.

They did so and Joseph maneuvered matters so that he seemed to have a legitimate reason for taking Benjamin captive and putting him to death. Once before the brothers had been willing to sacrifice one of themselves, regardless of the pain they might cause their father. Had they changed? Apparently, they had. They refused to abandon Benjamin, and Judah, in one of the most touching speeches of literature, offers himself as a slave in place of Benjamin since otherwise "thy servants shall bring down the gray hairs of thy servant our father with sorrow to the grave."

And then Joseph finally revealed himself and there was a grand reconciliation.

Since Joseph was now Egypt's all-powerful viceroy and since his successful handling of the crisis of famine must have made him popular throughout the land, he had no hesitation in inviting his entire family into Egypt; nor had Pharaoh any hesitation in welcoming them.

The word Joseph sent to his father was:

Genesis 45:10. *And thou shalt dwell in the land of Goshen, and thou shalt be near unto me . . .*

Goshen is usually represented as being located on the eastern border of the Nile delta. This would be the first portion of Egypt reached by settlers from Canaan. Furthermore, if all this were indeed taking place during the period of Hyksos rule, the Egyptian capital of Tanis, where Joseph would be holding office, would be right at the western borders of the district. Jacob and his sons would thus indeed be "near unto" Joseph.

Jacob, transfigured with joy, prepares to obey. Genesis lists the males who accompany him to Egypt, his sons, grandson, and great-grandsons, and counts all the males of the company (including Joseph and his sons) at the round figure of seventy.

They arrive, are introduced to Pharaoh, and then:

Genesis 47:11. . . . *Joseph . . . gave them a possession in the land of Egypt . . . in the land of Rameses . . .*

By "land of Rameses" is meant Goshen. It is an anachronistic name for it refers to a city of the region which was not built in the Hyksos period but only some centuries later.

Ephraim and Manasseh

Jacob was 130 years of age when he entered Egypt and lived there seventeen years. Then came the time when he felt himself to be dying. In his last days he asked Joseph to bring his sons to him. Joseph brought his young sons for their grandfather's blessing, and Jacob adopted them as his own:

Genesis 48:5. *And now thy two sons, Ephraim and Manasseh . . . are mine; as Reuben and Simeon, they shall be mine.*

Joseph thus came to be the ancestor of two of the tribes of Israel, those of Ephraim and Manasseh, and sometimes they are lumped together as the "Joseph tribes."

Since Jacob had twelve sons and since one of them, Joseph, was the ancestor of two tribes, there turned out to be thirteen tribes altogether. However, the tribe of Levi never received any distinct tract of land in Canaan in later centuries, but formed a priestly caste that lived scattered through the land. The twelve tribes of Israel, as represented in a later age by definite pieces of Canaanite territory, were: Reuben, Simeon, Judah, Dan, Gad, Issachar, Zebulun, Asher, Naphtali, Benjamin, Ephraim, and Manasseh.

The fact that Joseph fathered two tribes while the rest only fathered one each indicates that he received the birthright (a double share of the inheritance) in place of Reuben, who would ordinarily have received it as the eldest son. Joseph's inheritance of the birthright is made plain, at least in the King James Version, when Jacob tells him:

Genesis 48:22. *Moreover I have given to thee one portion above thy brethren . . .*

This is not a clear verse, however. The Hebrew word *shekem*, translated here as "portion," usually means "shoulder" and therefore perhaps a mountain slope. In the Revised Standard Version, Jacob is made to say "Moreover I have given to you rather than to your brothers one mountain slope . . ." On the other hand, it might refer to the city of Shechem, and the Anchor Bible translates it, "I give you as the one above your brothers, Shechem . . ."

As a matter of fact, when Canaan was apportioned among the tribes, centuries later, Ephraim received one portion and Manasseh, the second Joseph tribe, received another portion—including Shechem and its environs.

When Jacob prepared to bless Ephraim and Manasseh, Joseph carefully arranged matters so as to have Manasseh, the first-born, within reach of Jacob's right hand, since the old man, like his father before him, was blind with old age and could not tell them apart, unaided.

Nevertheless, Jacob crossed his arms, placing his right hand upon the head of Ephraim, the younger.

This again probably reflects early tribal history and suggests a situation parallel to that involving Pharez and Zarah (see page 107). At the start, Manasseh may have been the dominating group within the Joseph tribes, so that tradition has him Joseph's first-born. At some later date, however, Ephraim obtained and kept the upper hand.

Judah

Jacob then ordered his sons to gather round his deathbed while he forecast the future of each to them. There follows the "Testament of Jacob," which seems to reflect the situation as it existed in the time of David, so that the forty-ninth chapter of Genesis probably received its final form in that time.

The language used is oracular and, while possibly easily understood as referring to known historical events by the men of the time, has become obscure to us with the passage of time.

The first three sons are dismissed quickly. Their early domination had faded completely by David's time:

Genesis 49:3. *Reuben, thou art my firstborn* . . .

Genesis 49:4. *Unstable as water, thou shalt not excel; because thou wentest up to thy father's bed* . . .

Genesis 49:5. *Simeon and Levi are brethren; instruments of cruelty are in their habitations.*

. . . .

Genesis 49:7. *Cursed be their anger* . . .

The traditional reasons for their failure are Reuben's seduction of Bilhah, and the attack by Simeon and Levi on Shechem (see pages 100 and 102).

Turning then to his fourth son, Jacob is depicted as becoming enthusiastic.

Genesis 49:8. *Judah, thou art he whom thy brethren shall praise* . . .

. . . .

Genesis 49:10. *The sceptre shall not depart from Judah, nor a lawgiver from between his feet* . . .

This reflects the fact that when a stable and powerful kingdom was established over the land of Israel, it was David of the tribe of Judah that established it. Israel had by then defeated all its enemies and had established its domination over the entire western half of the Fertile Crescent. It seemed to have brought the story of Israel to a triumphant climax, a kind of "happy ending" that suffuses this part of the Testament.

To be sure, less than a century after David's coming to power, the kingdom was split in two and the Judean dynasty of David retained only the lesser half. Presumably the forty-ninth chapter was placed in its final form before the split had taken place.

Of course, the kingship over the southern portion of the land remained in the Davidic line without real interruption until 586 B.C., so that at no time for over four centuries did the sceptre "depart from Judah."

The remaining brothers are, with one exception, noted briefly and cryptically, and, on the whole, favorably. The exception is, of course, Joseph, who is praised exuberantly and lengthily. This is a reflection of the importance of the tribes of Ephraim and Manasseh during the tribal period before the establishment of David's kingdom.

It might also have been a matter of diplomacy. The northern tribes did not take kindly to Judean dominance and indeed broke away quickly enough. It would not have been politic to withhold praise from their outstanding representative.

Jacob then died at the age of 147, and was brought back by his sons to Canaan that he might be buried in the Cave of Machpelah where were already buried his grandparents, Abraham and Sarah, his parents, Isaac and Rebekah, and one of his wives, Leah.

About half a century later, Joseph died too, at the age of 110, and with that the Book of Genesis comes to an end at a date which might be estimated to be 1650 B.C. The curtain drops over an Egypt in which the Hyksos are still in firm control and the Israelites are still welcome guests of the nation.

When the curtain rises again, with the opening of the next book, some four centuries have passed, and conditions have changed drastically.

2. EXODUS

EXODUS · EPHRAIM · PHARAOH [OF THE OPPRESSION] · PITHOM AND
RAAMSES · THE DAUGHTER OF PHARAOH · MOSES · MIDIAN · PHARAOH [OF
THE EXODUS] · HOREB · JEHOVAH · AARON · THE MAGICIANS OF EGYPT ·
PASSOVER · ABIB · THE RED SEA · PI-HAHIROTH · OMER · AMALEK · JOSHUA ·
CHERUBIM · THE URIM AND THE THUMMIM · THE MOLTEN CALF

Exodus

Between the first two books of the Bible there is a long chronological gap of some four centuries following the entry of Jacob and
his sons into Egypt. To bridge the gap, the second book begins with
a hasty summary, listing the names of the heads of families who
entered Egypt:

> Exodus 1:1. *Now these are the names of the children of Israel . . .*

The phrase "Now these are the names" is a translation of the
Hebrew *ve-elleh shemoth*. The Jews use that phrase as the name of
this second book, usually reducing the phrase to the single word
"Shemoth" ("names"). The Septuagint named the book "Exodos"
(or, in the Latin equivalent, "Exodus"), meaning "going out," because it deals with the departure of the Israelites from Egypt.

Ephraim

Though the sons of Jacob are listed at the beginning of Exodus,
the Bible makes no further mention of the eponymous patriarchs of
the tribes as individuals, with a single exception.

In the First Book of Chronicles, which quickly reviews the genealogies of early history as viewed by the Jews of the post-Exilic

The Exodus

period, there is a passing mention that some sons of Ephraim (Joseph's younger son) took part in a cattle raid against a city in southern Canaan and were slain in the process.

1 Chronicles 7:22. *And Ephraim their father mourned many days, and his brethren came to comfort him.*

It is not clearly stated that this passage refers to the period during which the Israelites were in Egypt and, indeed, it is improbable that it does. Egypt was then in a strong and settled period of its history and it is unlikely that cattle raids within its borders would be permitted. Then, too, the site of the raid is some 150 miles from Goshen and that is a long distance to go chasing cattle.

It may well be that this verse records an early passage in tribal history within Canaan some centuries after the period when Jacob's sons had been alive. Ephraim may here represent the tribe generally rather than the ancestor individually.

Except for this one reference, all else concerning Jacob's sons is extra-Biblical legend. Joseph is supposed to have been the first of the brethren to have died and Levi the last. About 100 B.C., a book entitled *"The Testament of the Twelve Patriarchs"* was written, containing what were purportedly the deathbed statements of each of the twelve sons of Jacob. Each son reviewed his own life, bewailed his shortcomings, and urged his children to avoid his sins and to practice virtue. Whatever moral and ethical values these lectures might have, they are valueless as history.

Pharaoh [of the Oppression]

In any case, Exodus records that after the deaths of Joseph and his brothers, the Israelites prospered, multiplied, and grew numerous. And then:

> Exodus 1:8. . . . *there arose up a new king over Egypt, which knew not Joseph.*

The new Pharaoh, unlike Joseph's kindly patron, had no sympathy for the Israelites but, rather, feared them as a possible source of danger in the land and, therefore, took stern measures against them.

If the Pharaoh of Joseph were, indeed, one of the early Hyksos kings, then it seems fairly clear what happened—

The Hyksos did not, after all, completely control Egypt. Their power was concentrated in the delta and, far to the south, native Egyptian forces held local power and gathered strength.

About 500 miles up the Nile was a city later known to the Greeks as Thebes and it was the most prominent city of upper Egypt. Under the Old Kingdom and the Middle Kingdom, its importance was masked by Memphis and the cities of the delta. In times of political disintegration, however, dynasties at Thebes sometimes ruled over a virtually independent south. The 11th dynasty, for instance, in the years preceding the establishment of the Middle Kingdom, ruled from Thebes.

Once the Hyksos conquered Egypt, Thebes had another chance. Throughout the Hyksos period, it maintained a precarious independence, and gradually learned those military techniques (the horse and chariot, an improved bow, the use of body armor) of which it had been ignorant and with which the Hyksos armies had conquered Egypt.

In 1570 B.C., Ahmose, the first king of a new dynasty, the 18th, came to power in Thebes and launched a firm attack against the Hyksos, now complacent and rather decadent. Ahmose defeated them, broke their power, and made himself Pharaoh over all Egypt— once more under a native dynasty after a century and a half of foreign rule.

Ahmose might well have been the "new king over Egypt, which knew not Joseph." As representative of the resurgent Egyptians, he could have nothing but dislike and suspicion for the Israelites, who had been brought in by the Hyksos and whom he might consider nothing more than a remnant of them. In any renewed invasion from Asia, Ahmose might well consider that the Israelites would join with the invaders, to whom they would be bound by ties of culture and language.

Ahmose's reign, though it may have marked the beginning of this downturn in Israelite fortunes, may not have seen it carried through to completion. This sort of thing feeds on itself. The Israelites, treated as second-class citizens and as objects of suspicion, become disaffected and this disaffection is itself the excuse for intensified oppression. The oppressor, rightly fearing the resentment of the oppressed, finds discrimination escalating into slavery almost automatically.

Exodus 1:13. *And the Egyptians made the children of Israel to serve with rigour:*

Exodus 1:14. *And they made their lives bitter with hard bondage . . .*

It is the particular Pharaoh (not necessarily Ahmose; indeed, almost certainly not Ahmose) under whom Israelite enslavement reached its peak who is termed the "Pharaoh of the Oppression."

In deciding, then, who the Pharaoh of the Oppression might be, let us turn to Egyptian history.

After the time of Ahmose, the Egyptians, with the new battle techniques they had learned from the Hyksos, entered the most militarily successful era of their history. This period is known as the "New Kingdom" or, because Egypt spectacularly extended its power over portions of adjoining Asia, the "Empire."

The great military events that attended the establishment and maintenance of the Egyptian Empire took place entirely during the period of Israelite enslavement in Egypt and therefore no whisper of it is retained in the Bible, whose writers concentrated entirely on the fate of the Israelites.

Under Thutmose I (1525–08 B.C.) and Thutmose III (1490–36 B.C.)—particularly the latter, sometimes called "Thutmose the Great" and "the Napoleon of Ancient Egypt"—victorious Egyptian armies scoured the western half of the Fertile Crescent. In 1479 B.C., Thutmose III won a great battle at Megiddo, a city of northern Canaan, about fifty miles north of Jerusalem. With that, Canaan and all the land northward, nearly to the Euphrates, became Egyptian. Under Amenhotep III (1397–70 B.C.) the empire rested upon a plateau of prosperity and success.

With the son of Amenhotep III, Amenhotep IV (1370–53 B.C.), a decline set in. The new king was a religious revolutionary. In a land of numerous gods, he was a monotheist, recognizing a single god, Aton, represented in nature by the sun. Since his own name Amenhotep means "Amen is content" and glorifies the god, Amen, the new Pharaoh rejected the name as idolatrous and called himself Ikhnaton ("Aton is satisfied"). He also established a new capital at a city he named Akhetaton ("the horizon of Aton") located about halfway between Thebes and the delta. On its site now stands the village of Tell el Amarna.

Ikhnaton tried to establish the new monotheism throughout Egypt by force, but the priests of the older gods fought him relentlessly and on their side was the innate conservatism of the Egyptian people. After Ikhnaton's early death and a short reign of only about seventeen years, his new religion fell apart. Under his young son-in-law Tutankhaton (1352–43 B.C.) the old priesthood won a complete victory. Akhetaton was abandoned and Tutankhaton was forced to change his name to Tutankhamon.

While Ikhnaton was absorbed in his religious revolution, the Asian dominions of the empire were under constant attack. In A.D. 1887, the ruins of Akhetaton yielded a large cache of letters from Egyptian viceroys in Asia. It is a melancholy tale of continuous incursions from the north and east and of useless pleas for help to Ikhnaton, who lacked the ability, or perhaps the will, to fight off the marauding bands from the desert.

A more formidable foe was arising in the north. The Hittite Old Kingdom (see page 78) had been weakened and rendered harmless by Thutmose III, but after that conqueror's death, the Hittites hardened once more into their New Kingdom. In Ikhnaton's time, the greatest of the Hittite kings, Shubbiluliu, was on the throne. He conquered Mitanni and beat back the Egyptian boundary to Canaan itself.

After Tutenkhamon's death (and it was his untouched tomb that was discovered in A.D. 1922; see page 63) the 18th dynasty quickly declined and petered out. In its place a new family succeeded to the throne. This was the 19th dynasty, and its first member, Rameses I, became Pharaoh in 1304 B.C. Under him, the Egyptian Empire experienced a new period of vigor.

This dynasty reached its peak under Rameses II ("Rameses the Great"), whose long reign stretched from 1290 to 1223 B.C., and during this time Egypt came into direct conflict with the Hittites. In 1288 B.C., a great battle was fought between the two empires at Kadesh, about eighty miles north of Damascus. The battle was indecisive, as was the entire war, which ended in a compromise peace by which the Hittites retained their conquests of the previous century. The effort to withstand Egypt had, however, fatally weakened the Hittite power and had seriously strained Egypt itself.

Rameses II is the most famous of all the Pharaohs. His long reign gave him ample time to indulge in all his grandiose notions. He beautified Thebes, which was at the height of its splendor during his reign. He covered Egypt with gigantic statues of himself, with self-glorifying inscriptions, and is reported to have had 160 children by numerous wives and concubines.

Rameses II contributed largely to the later legend of "Sesostris." When, eight centuries after Egypt's great days of empire, Herodotus, the Greek historian, visited the ancient land, the priests and antiquarians of Egypt gladly rehearsed the glorious past, with improvements. By Herodotus' time, Egypt was far in decline and had been conquered by two different Asian empires, the Assyrian and the Persian. It suited Egyptian pride therefore to recall a time, now dimly lost in the mists of the far past, when it had been Egypt that was the world empire.

The name Herodotus reports for the conqueror was Sesostris, the actual name of three Pharaohs of the 12th dynasty, the first of whom might conceivably have been Abraham's Pharaoh (see page 64). The Middle Kingdom had first carried Egypt's power beyond its borders into Ethiopia. These deeds were combined with the still greater ones of Thutmose III and Rameses II and the whole escalated to the point where "Sesostris" conquered all of Ethiopia, penetrated Asia far beyond the Euphrates, marched through Asia Minor and into Europe, subduing the plains beyond the Black Sea.

After Rameses II, there were no further grounds for dreaming of a Sesostris. Egypt began to decline and, with only occasional minor rallies, each less successful than the one before, continued to decline throughout Biblical times.

Where, then, in this long history would the Pharaoh of the Oppression be found?

Ikhnaton offers an attractive possibility. He was unique in the long line of Pharaohs; a rebel, a breaker of tradition, a monotheist. Could he have been the kindly Pharaoh, welcoming the monotheistic Jacob and his sons into Egypt? This is quite unlikely, unfortunately, as Ikhnaton's reign is considerably too late for that.

There is another possibility. Could Ikhnaton have been reigning at the close of the period of Israelite enslavement rather than its start? Could he have learned his monotheism from Moses or, as some have suggested, could Moses have learned it from Ikhnaton?

Could it be, in fact, that Ikhnaton's father, Amenhotep III, was the strong Pharaoh of the Oppression, and that under Ikhnaton's feeble and self-absorbed rule, the Israelites broke out of Egypt? In favor of this are the Tell el Amarna reports from Canaan of the onslaught of the desert tribes. Might not these be the Israelites themselves, now out of Egypt and driving hard to conquer Canaan?

This is unlikely on several counts. In the first place, Ikhnaton's reign is too early for the Israelite conquest of Canaan. Such an early conquest will not square with the better-known dates of later events in the Bible.

This is not to deny that Canaan was under assault from the desert under Ikhnaton but it is very likely that the assaulters at that time were the tribes who settled down along the borders of Canaan (having failed to penetrate its interior against Egyptian defenses) as the Edomites, Moabites, and Ammonites. After all, the Biblical story is quite clear on the point that when the Israelites themselves approached

Canaan, the Edomites, Moabites, and Ammonites were already established on the ground and in firm possession of the land to the east and south of the Dead Sea.*

To be sure, these earlier invaders were closely allied to the Israelites and it may even be that some of the tribes who were later to join in the Israelite confederacy were already attacking Canaan and were to be joined later by tribes emerging from Egypt. There are some who suggest that only the Joseph tribes, Ephraim and Manasseh, were enslaved in Egypt; and that after they left Egypt they joined a federation of tribes who were attacking Canaan directly from the desert.

Then, too, if the Israelites had emerged from Egypt and conquered Canaan during and after the reign of Ikhnaton, they would have been caught up in the gigantic campaigns of Rameses II that followed. The Bible could not very well have failed to capture even an echo of the mighty battle of Kadesh.

One must look later, then, for the Pharaoh of the Oppression and speculation inevitably alights on Rameses II himself. Why not? Rameses II was a vainglorious despot quite capable of making the most arbitrary use of his powers. He was engaged in a life-and-death struggle with an Asian power and he was bound to look upon the Asians within his own realm with the utmost suspicion. It is quite conceivable that the Hittites would try to make use of an Israelite insurrection to divert Egyptian power, that at least some Israelites would look with favor on such a scheme, and that Rameses would suspect them of complicity even if they did not. Intensified enslavement and even a program of genocide is possible.

Furthermore, the reign of Rameses II is followed by a decline during which the Israelites could have broken out of Egypt. What's more, the decline does not reverse itself. Egypt does *not* enter Asia with renewed power so that the Israelites can conquer and occupy Canaan without interference from Egypt.

It would seem then that Rameses II would have to be the Pharaoh of the Oppression, *if* there is any Pharaoh of the Oppression at all. This last reservation is made necessary by the fact that there is no record outside the Bible of Israelites in Egypt, of their enslavement,

---

* The letters at Tell el Amarna refer to the invaders as "Khabiri"; that is, "Hebrews." However, the men of Edom, Moab, and Ammon were as Hebrew as the men of Israel.

and of their escape. In particular, none of the events in Exodus are to be found anywhere in the Egyptian records uncovered by modern archaeologists.

Pithom and Raamses

One of the pieces of evidence that points to Rameses II as the Pharaoh of the Oppression is contained in the nature of the work done by the Israelite slaves.

> Exodus 1:11. . . . And they built for Pharaoh treasure cities, Pithom and Raamses.

(The phrase "treasure cities" is clearly a mistranslation. The Revised Standard Version has "store-cities" in its place; cities, that is, in which provisions were stored for the use of armies advancing into Asia.)

The name Raamses (which in the Hebrew requires a very small change to become Rameses) seems significant. The name Rameses does not occur at all among the Pharaohs of the first eighteen dynasties, but eleven Pharaohs of that name are to be found in the 19th and 20th dynasties. Of them, Rameses II is by far the most famous and successful; also the most self-glorifying and the most apt to name a city for himself.

The ruins of Pithom (pa-tum in Egyptian, meaning "house of the setting sun") were discovered in 1882 about twelve miles west of what is now the Suez Canal. It was on a canal which Rameses II had had built from an eastern branch of the Nile to the bodies of water then making up the northernmost reaches of the Red Sea—a kind of primitive Suez Canal. The ruins contain, among other things, a statue of Rameses II, indicating that the city may well have been built in his reign.

Pithom is located in Goshen (see page 114) and Raamses was probably built some miles west of Pithom. Conceivably, a case may be made here. Since Rameses II was planning his large expedition into Asia against the Hittites, he needed good supply depots to his rear. Pithom and Raamses on the northeastern frontier would suit his purpose exactly, and since the Israelites were settled on the spot, it was convenient to make use of their labor.

Although the Bible specifically describes the Israelites as having built cities, many casual readers of the Bible seem to have picked up the notion that the Israelite slaves built the pyramids. This is not so. The pyramids were built a thousand years before Joseph entered Egypt.

This also disposes of the feeling that the pyramids might be the storehouses built under Joseph's direction to store the grain of the seven plentiful years. The pyramids couldn't serve such a purpose anyway, even if they were built in Joseph's time, for they are virtually solid structures with tunnels and cavities only large enough to hold the sarcophagus of a Pharaoh. As a matter of fact, the pyramids— oddly enough—are nowhere mentioned in the Bible.

The Daughter of Pharaoh

Rameses II, according to the Biblical story, commanded all Israelite boy babies to be drowned. As a result, when a son was born to a woman of the tribe of Levi, she tried to save him by placing him in a small boat (or "ark") of bulrushes, daubed with pitch to make it waterproof, and setting that afloat on the Nile. (The bulrushes were papyrus reeds, which the Egyptians used in making light boats and the pith of which they used in making a writing material. Our word "paper" comes from papyrus, even though paper is made from other materials now.)

The small boat containing the baby was discovered:

Exodus 2:5. *And the daughter of Pharaoh came down to wash herself at the river . . . and . . . saw the ark among the flags . . .*

Who the "daughter of Pharaoh" might be is, of course, not known. She is not named in the Bible and, since Rameses II is supposed to have had something like fifty daughters, there seems no hope of ever identifying the young lady. To be sure, the ancient Jewish historian Josephus, who retells the story of the Bible, filling in the gaps with later legend, gives her name as Thermouthes, but no Egyptian princess of that name and period is known. One of the early Church fathers gave the name as Merris and the name "Meri" does occur in the inscriptions of the time. But that could be mere coincidence.

Moses

The Hebrew name of the child is Mosheh. In the Septuagint, the various Hebrew names of the Bible are changed into Greek equivalents. This involves some nearly inevitable changes. The Greek alphabet doesn't include a letter for the "sh" sound, which does not occur in Greek, so a simple "s" must be substituted. Then, since Greek names almost invariably end in "s," a final "s" must be added. In this way, Mosheh becomes Moses.

The English versions of the New Testament (almost all of which was originally written in Greek) usually contain Hebrew names in the Greek form. For instance, Jesus is the Greek form of the Hebrew "Joshua." English versions of the Old Testament, however, usually restore the Hebrew forms as far as possible. This was not possible at all in the case of Moses, since that particular Greek form had become too well known to the population generally to be altered.

The priestly editors of the Hexateuch saw in the word "Mosheh" a similarity to the Hebrew *mashah*, meaning "to draw out," and therefore gave that as the derivation of the name:

Exodus 2:10. . . . *Pharaoh's daughter . . . called his name Moses: and she said, Because I drew him out of the water.*

Now an Egyptian princess is scarcely going to turn to the Hebrew language for a name (even if she could be imagined as bothering to learn the slaves' language in the first place). Besides, Moses happens to have a much more straightforward and natural meaning in Egyptian. It means "son." (Thus Thutmose means "son of Thoth" and Rameses means "son of Ra," both Thoth and Ra being Egyptian gods.)

The legend surrounding Moses' infancy seems no more plausible than the Hebrew derivation given his name. Ancient legends are full of tales of children cast away for some reason or other who are miraculously saved and go on to become people of great importance. In the Greek legends, this is the case with Perseus, Oedipus, and Paris, for instance; in the Roman legends, with Romulus; in the Persian legends, with Cyrus.

Most significant of all is a legend told of Sargon of Agade (see page 50) who lived over a thousand years before the time of Moses. The legend of Sargon has been found on Babylonian tablets dating back to several centuries before the Exile. The priests in Babylon who were preparing the Hexateuch in its final form must have heard the legend, and it is very likely that they appropriated it.

Sargon of Agade is described as the illegitimate son of a noblewoman who bore him in shame and secrecy, and then exposed him. She did this by putting him in a small boat of reeds, daubed with pitch, and letting him drift down the river. The baby was rescued by a poor man who raised him as his own son.

The Biblical writers improved the tale, however. Moses was a legitimate son and was raised by a princess.

There are no Biblical details concerning Moses' youth, but the legends of later times fill those years with activity designed to magnify the glory of the future leader of the Israelites. Josephus tells, for instance, how invading Ethiopians had Egypt at their mercy when Moses took over leadership of the Egyptian army and utterly defeated the Ethiopians. There is no evidence in Egyptian annals, however, for the events described by Josephus.

Midian

As a grown man, Moses found himself sympathizing with the Israelite slaves, presumably out of humanity and possibly because he had learned of his own origins. In a fit of anger he killed an Egyptian overseer and, when this was found out, left Egypt hurriedly, to avoid execution at the orders of an angered Pharaoh.

Exodus 2:15. . . . *Moses fled from the face of Pharaoh and dwelt in the land of Midian . . .*

Midian, it seems quite likely, is located in northwestern Arabia, just east of the Red Sea, about two hundred miles southeast of Goshen. It represents the shortest distance Moses could have traveled and placed himself outside the boundaries of Imperial Egypt.

According to later tradition, Moses was forty years old at the time of his flight to Midian. This is too pat, for it divides Moses' Biblically allotted lifetime of 120 years into neat thirds. From birth to 40, he would be an Egyptian prince, from 40 to 80 an exile in Midian, and from 80 to 120 a leader of the Israelites.

Pharaoh [of the Exodus]

While Moses was in Midian, getting married and having a son, a crucial change took place in Egypt:

> Exodus 2:23. *And it came to pass in process of time, that the king of Egypt died* . . .

and that took place in 1223 B.C., if the Pharaoh of the Oppression was indeed Rameses II.

Succeeding Rameses II was the far weaker Merneptah, who is usually thought of as the Pharaoh of the Exodus, the Pharaoh under whom the dramatic events described in the rest of the Book of Exodus took place.

Since these events represent little less than a complete disaster for Egypt, it is to be expected that the reign of Merneptah might be listed in Egyptian annals as one filled with trouble.

And so it is. To be sure, the exact events described in Exodus are not to be found anywhere in the Egyptian records, but there was plenty of trouble of another sort and Merneptah's reign witnessed a time of troubles for the whole region rimming the eastern Mediterranean Sea.

Every once in a while, in the course of ancient history, there come times when nomad peoples seem to be on the move. One tribe drives against another which in turn pushes against the next and so on like a series of falling dominoes. The settled cities of the civilized areas of the world eventually meet the brunt of the force and since their peoples cannot easily move and yield to the pressure, civilizations often meet with disaster at such times.

The thirteenth century B.C. witnessed one of these troublesome mass migrations of peoples. The pressure of barbarian invasions was beginning to be felt in Greece and southeastern Europe generally. Under that pressure, raiding bands from Greece, Crete, and such areas spread out across the Aegean Sea and plunged their way, west, south, and east. They invaded Asia Minor, and the Trojan War may have been an item in that invasion.

As a result of the disorders that racked Asia Minor then, a native people, the Phrygians, rose to power and dealt the final blow to the Hittite Empire, which had been fatally wounded in its great war against Rameses II. As a result, the Hittites declined to a bare remnant, and appeared to the Israelites, when they finally conquered Canaan, as no more than another small tribe.

Then, too, some tribes leaving Asia Minor under the pressure of invasions may have traveled westward to found the Etruscan civilization in Italy.

The invaders from southeastern Europe landed as well on the coasts of Egypt. To the Egyptians, they were the "Peoples of the Sea." The Egyptians managed to fight them off but only at great cost and the damage done the nation undoubtedly contributed greatly to the decline of its vigor. In the disorders accompanying the invasion, it is not at all unreasonable that the Israelites may have seized the opportunity to depart.

Furthermore, for the first time since the reign of Thutmose I, three centuries before, the Egyptian hold on Canaan was broken. A contingent of the Peoples of the Sea invaded Canaan and established themselves as the Philistines on its southern coast. Egyptian armies were either defeated or, very likely, melted away when they were called home to defend the motherland itself. Egyptian power did not return to Canaan for nine centuries, and the Israelites, in their drive to conquer Canaan, had to face only the native Canaanites and *not* a powerful Egyptian army. Indeed, for centuries their most inveterate enemies were the Philistines who had entered Canaan from the west, while the Israelites had plunged in from the east.

It seems to make sense, therefore, to accept Merneptah as the Pharaoh of the Exodus, whether one accepts the actual details described in the Bible or not.

Horeb

Moses' task of leading the Israelites out of Egypt begins in Midian.

Exodus 3:1. *Now Moses kept the flock of Jethro his father in law . . . and he led the flock . . . to the mountain of God, even to Horeb.*

It is common to consider mountains as particularly sacred to divine beings; one need only consider the Greek gods and their home on Mount Olympus. Apparently, the Bible has reference here to a mountain which was considered in the old Israelite traditions to be sacred to God.

Mount Horeb (Sinai)

The mountain is called Horeb here, but in other places in Exodus it is called Sinai. Both names are accepted as referring to the same mountain but it is the latter name which is much better known. It is not located in Canaan—everyone agrees on that—so it must represent an ancient tradition of holiness indeed, one that preceded the entry of the Israelites into Canaan. It is a holiness, moreover, which is not associated with the patriarchal age, for Sinai is never mentioned in the Book of Genesis.

Indeed, the holiness may trace back to Sumerian mythology for the name Sinai could refer back to the moon-god, Sin, who was an important object of worship both in Ur and in Haran (see page 59). In that case, though, one might wonder why there was no association of Sinai with Abraham, who lived in both Ur and Haran.

Some scholars believe that Mount Sinai is to be found somewhere on the Arabian side of the Red Sea, because that is where Moses was at the time. If Sinai were really connected with Sumerian mythology, that, too, would bespeak a location reasonably close to the Fertile Crescent. Then too, in several poetic passages of the Bible, Sinai is associated with mountains south of Canaan. For example, in a passage of Deuteronomy, commonly called the "Song of Moses," we have:

> Deuteronomy 33:2 . . . *The Lord came from Sinai, and rose up from Seir . . .*

Indeed, considering the parallelism of Hebrew poetry, and its trick of saying the same thing twice with slight variation, one might even be tempted to argue that Mount Sinai *is* Mount Seir (also called Mount Hor).

However, in early Christian times the tradition arose that the mountain was located on the triangular peninsula that lies on the boundary between Africa and Asia and that is now, in consequence, known as Sinai.

The Sinai Peninsula, about 140 miles long, is bounded on the north by the Mediterranean Sea and on the south by the Red Sea. The northern end of the Red Sea divides into two narrow arms, like the eyestalks of a snail, which bound Sinai on the southwest and southeast. The western horn, which is the longer and wider, is the Gulf of Suez; the eastern, the Gulf of Aqaba.

When Egypt was powerful, Sinai was part of its realm, as during the Middle Kingdom and during the Empire. After the invasion of the Peoples of the Sea, the ebbing of Egyptian power left Sinai to its own nomadic inhabitants. (Nowadays, Sinai forms part of modern Egypt but was occupied by Israel after the Six-day War of 1967.)

In southern Sinai is a range of mountains among which Mount Sinai is supposed to be located. By a tradition dating back to the sixth century A.D. it is identified particularly with the tallest peak, which is about 7400 feet, or nearly one and a half miles high. This peak bears the Arabic name of Jebel Musa ("Mount of Moses").

Jehovah

On Mount Horeb, Moses becomes aware of a bush that is burning steadily but is not consumed. He approaches and God, speaking to him out of the bush, commands him to return to Egypt and to lead the Israelites out of slavery.

In the process, God reveals his personal name:

> Exodus 3:14. *And God said unto Moses, I AM THAT I AM . . .*

The phrase, capitalized as a gesture of respectful awe, is translated I AM WHO I AM in the Revised Standard Version, with a footnote giving alternate readings of I AM WHAT I AM and I WILL BE WHAT I WILL BE.

Apparently the name of the Lord is here connected with some form of the word "to be," either in the present or future tense, as though the primary nature of God is external existence.

Moses returns to Egypt along with his elder brother, Aaron, but his first efforts fail to impress Pharaoh. The Egyptian monarch sharpens the oppression so that the Israelites themselves, who had first hailed Moses, turn against him. God reassures Moses and pronounces his name once more, this time in a briefer version:

> Exodus 6:3. . . . *I appeared unto Abraham, unto Isaac, and unto Jacob, by the name of God Almighty, but by my name JEHOVAH was I not known to them.*

The name here given for God is the YHVH I mentioned earlier (see page 20).

In later history, the Jews grew increasingly reluctant to articulate the actual name of God and it became a habitual gesture of respect with them to substitute for the four consonants wherever they occur the respectful title of "the Lord," which in Hebrew is *Adonai*.

In both the King James Version and the Revised Standard Version this procedure is followed and YHVH is consistently translated as "Lord." Exodus 6:3 is the one place where the King James Version abandons caution and actually makes use of the name of God. The Revised Standard Version does not do so but remains consistent and translates the clause in Exodus 6:3 as "but by my name the

Lord I did not make myself known to them." (The translation from the Masoretic text gives the Hebrew consonants themselves, untranslated, with a footnote directing that it be read "the Lord.")

The name Jehovah is almost universally accepted by English-speaking Christians as the manner of pronouncing YHVH, but that arose by mistake.

It seems that as the centuries passed and the Jews of later history spread throughout the east and began to speak Aramaic, Babylonian, and Greek, in preference to Hebrew, there grew up the danger that the proper pronunciation of the Biblical language would be forgotten. The Jewish scholars therefore placed little diacritical marks under the Hebrew consonants, indicating the vowel sounds that went with them in each particular word.

For YHVH, however, they did not produce the proper diacritical marks since the name was not supposed to be pronounced anyway. Instead, they wrote the diacritical marks for Adonai, the word that was supposed to be pronounced. Sometime during the Middle Ages, a Christian scholar, supposing that the vowels of Adonai belonged with the consonants YHVH, wrote out the name in full as Jehovah. (The initial J in Latin is pronounced like an initial Y in English.)

This mistake has persisted and will probably continue to persist. Actually, modern scholars seem to have decided that the correct pronunciation of YHVH is Yahveh.

During the greater portion of Old Testament times it was by no means certain that the worship of Yahveh, according to the ritual set forth in the first five books of the Bible (which, according to long-accepted tradition, both Jewish and Christian, were written by Moses), would win out among the Israelites. I will, in this book, speak of those who believed in the worship of Yahveh (particularly in the exclusive worship of Yahveh as the only God) as Yahvists.

Aaron

Moses and his brother Aaron were of the tribe of Levi and in later generations the priesthood was to be confined to the descendants of Aaron, so that the expression "Levite" came to be virtually synonymous with "priest." In view of this, Exodus pauses here to give an account of the genealogy of Aaron.

Levi is described as having had three sons, of whom Kohath was second, while Kohath had four sons of whom the first two were Amram and Izhar. The age at the time of death is given for Levi, Kohath, and Amram as 137, 133, and 137 years respectively, so that there is still the echo, here, of the patriarchal age of moderately extended lifetimes.

> Exodus 6:20. And Amram took him Jochebed . . . to wife; and she bare him Aaron and Moses . . .
> Exodus 6:21. And the sons of Izhar; Korah . . .

Korah, who was later to rebel against Moses and come to a bad end, is here described as Moses' first cousin. He is also the ancestor (despite his rebellion) of one of the guilds of Temple musicians, variously referred to in the Bible as the Korahites, Korhites, or Korathites, and who will be mentioned in connection with the Book of Psalms.

The line of Aaron is taken further:

> Exodus 6:23. And Aaron took him Elisheba . . . to wife; and she bare him Nadab, and Abihu, Eleazar and Ithamar.
>   . . . .
> Exodus 6:25. And Eleazar . . . took him one of the daughters of Putiel to wife; and she bare him Phinehas.

Nadab and Abihu died in the course of the Exodus but Eleazar and Ithamar survived to become the ancestors of the two chief priestly families of later times. Aaron was the first High Priest and he was succeeded by his son Eleazar and, eventually, by his grandson, Phinehas.

The Magicians of Egypt

After the Levite genealogy, the writers of Exodus return to the main current of its account.

Moses and Aaron approach Pharaoh once more and try to impress him by turning a rod into a serpent. Pharaoh, however, scorns what he considers a parlor trick and calls his own men to duplicate it.

> Exodus 7:11. . . . the magicians of Egypt . . . did in like manner with their enchantments.

The names of these magicians are not given. In the New Testament, however, in the second of Paul's Epistles to Timothy, there is the passage:

2 Timothy 3:8. . . . *Jannes and Jambres withstood Moses* . . .

There were a number who withstood Moses in the course of the passage of the Israelites from Egypt to Canaan. None of these had names that were anything like Jannes and Jambres, names which do not occur anywhere else in the Bible, in fact. The usual assumption, therefore, is that Paul was drawing upon some well-known legend which gave the names Jannes and Jambres to the Egyptian magicians who tried to duplicate the works of Moses and to show him up as a mere conjurer before Pharaoh. Indeed, some rabbinical legends have Jannes and Jambres so impressed by Moses that they eventually joined the Israelites, but died in the course of the Exodus.

The Red Sea

Passover

With Pharaoh scorning the first demonstration, Moses and Aaron bring, in swift succession, a series of disasters upon Egypt. These, involving visitations of frogs and insects, various pestilences, unusual weather such as hail or darkness, are generally referred to as "the ten plagues of Egypt."

Although these plagues, if they had taken place as described in the Bible, must have loomed large in any contemporary records or in later histories, no reference to them is to be found in any source outside the Bible. In 1950, Immanuel Velikovsky, in his book *Worlds in Collision* attempted to account for the plagues (and for some other events described in the Bible) by supposing that the planet Venus had undergone a near collision with the earth. The book created a moderate sensation among the general public for a while, but the reaction of astronomers varied from amusement to anger, and the Velikovskian theory has never, for one moment, been taken seriously either by scientists or by Biblical scholars.

The tenth plague was the crucial one. In its course, the first-born male of every house in Egypt was slain by divine action. The Israelites were spared. Each family was directed to eat a ceremonial meal and to place the blood of the lamb eaten in the course of that meal on the door of the house:

> Exodus 12:23. . . . *the Lord will pass through to smite the Egyptians: and when he seeth the blood . . . the Lord will pass over the door and will not . . . smite you.*

In commemoration of this awesome event, which marked the beginning of the escape from Egypt and the establishment of the Israelites as a nation, a ceremonial meal is eaten each year. The ceremony is named (according to the Bible) after the promise of God to "pass over" the Israelite houses. The original instructions refer to it thus:

> Exodus 12:11. . . . *it is the Lord's passover.*

The Hebrew word translated here as "passover" is *pesach* and the Biblical writers saw a similarity to the Hebrew word meaning "to pass over" and therefore wrote the passages in such a way as to stress that similarity. The real meaning of *pesach* is unknown.

In all probability, the Passover was an agricultural festival long ante-dating the time of Moses. Such festivals are common in all agricultural societies. (Americans have even invented one for themselves—Thanks-giving.) Usually such festivals, even among the early Israelites, were thoroughly pagan in inspiration.

The priestly writers of the Hexateuch could not revise the early traditions in too extreme a fashion. The various festivals were too popular and too deeply ingrained in tradition to be done away with. The best that could be done was to associate them firmly with some legendary event in Biblical history and divorce them from idolatry. Passover, the most important of the agricultural festivals, was associated with the most important event in the early legends—the Exodus.

(Such changed associations are common in the development of reli-gions. Thus, in the early history of Christianity, the pagan celebra-tion of the winter solstice—the Saturnalia—was converted into Christ-mas and made into the celebration of the birth of Jesus—something that will be discussed further in the second volume.

After the Exile, the Passover was one of the three festivals during which all pious Jews attempted to travel to Jerusalem and worship at the Temple. It was in the course of one of these Passovers that Jesus was crucified.

The anniversary of the resurrection of Jesus is still celebrated at the same time of the year as Passover, although never on the same day, for the Christian method of calculating the day differs from the Jew-ish method.

That anniversary is, in English, called "Easter" and this is another example of religious adaptation. The word comes from the name of an old Teutonic goddess of spring. A pagan spring festival was converted into the commemoration of the resurrection but its pagan name was kept to make the transition as easy as possible.

The word "Easter" is sometimes, quite wrongly, applied to Passover. This is done on one occasion in the King James Version. In the Book of Acts, it is described how the Apostle Peter was imprisoned at the time of the Passover, with the intention of bringing him to trial once the festival was over. The ruler is described as

Acts 12:4. . . . *intending after Easter to bring him forth to the people.*

The Revised Standard Version changes Easter to Passover in this case, of course.

Abib

The month in which the Exodus took place, and in which the Passover was celebrated, was Abib.

Exodus 13:4. *This day came ye out in the month Abib.*

Abib is an example of the names of the months used in pre-Exilic times. The word means "kernel of grain" and marks the time of the year when such kernels appeared.

Other such ancient names are mentioned here and there in the Bible. In connection with the building of the Temple under Solomon, for instance, the Bible records:

1 Kings 6:37. *In the fourth year was the foundation of the house of the Lord laid, in the month Zif:*
1 Kings 6:38. *And in the eleventh year, in the month Bul . . . was the house finished . . .*

The temple was then dedicated:

1 Kings 8:2. *And all the men of Israel assembled . . . at the feast in the month Ethanim . . .*

During the Babylonian Exile, however, the Jews made use of the Babylonian calendar and they kept that throughout their later history, down to the present day. The names of the months in the Jewish calendar are Babylonian now and are used in those Biblical books that are clearly post-Exilic, especially the books of Nehemiah and Esther. Thus, the month earlier known as Abid, in which Passover was celebrated, became Nisan:

Nehemiah 2:1. *And it came to pass in the month Nisan . . .*

The Red Sea

After the tenth plague, Pharaoh's resistance broke and he agreed to allow the Israelites to leave the land:

Exodus 12:37. *And the children of Israel journeyed from Rameses to Succoth . . .*

The location of Succoth is not agreed upon, but many people believe it to be located very close to Pithom (see page 126) or even to be identical with it. If so, the Israelites, upon leaving Egypt, headed east.

Had they borne northward, they could have reached and followed the coast, taking the most direct and shortest route into Canaan. That, however, would have led them into trouble.

The Peoples of the Sea were now invading various sections of the Egyptian realm. (This, in fact, may well have been the historical equivalent of the dramatic Biblical story of the plagues.) The Peoples of the Sea were establishing themselves on the very portion of the Canaanite coast that the Israelites would have reached first.

The Israelites, who were liberated slaves unused to war, were in no position to take on the well-armed, war-hardened invaders from the sea, soon to appear importantly in the Biblical story as the Philistines. The Israelites had to travel eastward, therefore, in order to flank the Philistine position and this brought them to the Red Sea.

Exodus 13:17. . . . *God led them not through the way of the land of the Philistines, although that was near; for God said, Lest peradventure the people repent when they see war, and they return to Egypt:*
Exodus 13:18. *But God led the people about, through the way of the wilderness of the Red Sea . . .*

The Red Sea is a long, narrow arm of the Indian Ocean, extending northwest and southeast in an almost straight line for 1450 miles. Its width is only between 150 and 200 miles, and from its shape one can guess that it is part of the Great Rift Valley.

The Red Sea is one of the most unpleasant parts of the ocean. It separates the African desert from the Arabian desert and receives little water in the form of rainfall, while the sun, baking as hotly as anywhere on earth, evaporates much water. For that reason, despite the fact that water constantly pours into the southern end of the sea, which is open to the main body of the Indian Ocean, the Red Sea manages to be saltier than any other part of the ocean. It is up to 4.1 per cent salt at the closed northern end, as compared to 3.5 per cent for the oceans generally.

The name "Red Sea" is of Greek origin and in Roman times, the name spread out into that portion of the Indian Ocean into which the sea opened—what we now call the Gulf of Aden, the Arabian Sea, and the Persian Gulf.

Why "Red"? There are several theories. The waters may turn red through some infestation of microscopic plants; the shells on the shore (or the rocks) may be red; the reflection of the setting sun as seen from Arabia may turn the waters red. You can take your pick. Perhaps none of these is the right reason; or perhaps there is no reason.

Pi-hahiroth

With the Israelites in the process of leaving Egypt, Pharaoh regretted having given permission for their departure. At the head of a detachment of cavalry he set out after them.

> Exodus 14:9. . . . *the Egyptians pursued after them . . . and overtook them encamping by the sea, beside Pi-hahiroth . . .*

The Bible then relates the story of the escape of the Israelites when the waters of the Red Sea miraculously parted for them, and then returned in time to drown the pursuing Egyptians.

Where did this parting take place? Presumably in the neighborhood of Pi-hahiroth, but the one great catch is that no one knows exactly where Pi-hahiroth might have been located.

We can eliminate the main body of the Red Sea at once. To imagine that the Israelites crossed the Red Sea proper, passing over 150 miles or so of emptied sea bottom which, in places, is something like a mile and a half deep, is unnecessary. Had they done so, they would have ended in the main portion of the Arabian peninsula and there is nothing in succeeding events, as described in the Bible, to make one think that happened. The succeeding events take place, rather, in the Sinai Peninsula and that is separated from Egypt by a northwestern extension of the Red Sea now known as the Gulf of Suez.

The Gulf of Suez is a miniature of the Red Sea; something of the same shape, but not as long, not as wide, and not as deep. It is two hundred miles long, nowhere more than thirty miles wide, and, at its northern end, it is only eighteen feet deep.

Even the Gulf of Suez, as it exists today, may not be the site of the Israelite "crossing of the Red Sea." The Hebrew name for the body of water that was crossed is *yam suph*. The phrase is translated as "Red Sea," but its literal meaning is "the sea of reeds."

In Exodus times (it is generally thought) the Gulf of Suez extended somewhat farther northward than it does today. In particular, it included two shallow bodies of brackish water called the Bitter Lakes. (These marshes are no longer on the map because they were filled in at the time the Suez Canal was built.)

In the Gulf of Suez extended up to and including the Bitter Lakes, this extension might have represented a shallow basin of sea water filled with reeds along its shores, and this might have been a Sea of Reeds in literal truth. The site of Pi-hahiroth may have been on the shores of this vanished extension of the Red Sea.

It would seem, from the Biblical account, that every one of the pursuing Egyptians was drowned. If a Pharaoh accompanied them, he was drowned, too. There are no records outside the Bible which indicate Merneptah, or any Pharaoh, to have drowned in the Red Sea. Nevertheless, if Merneptah died in this fashion, then the Exodus took place in 1211 B.C. by the best modern reckoning.

According to the Biblical reckoning:

Exodus 12:40. *Now the sojourning of the children of Israel, who dwelt in Egypt, was four hundred and thirty years.*

If this is accepted, then the entry of Jacob and his sons into Egypt took place in 1641 B.C. This date is neatly within the period of the Hyksos domination of Egypt as would be expected (see page 108).

Omer

The Israelites were fed, miraculously, by a food called manna dropping from the heavens. There have been attempts to advance a non-miraculous explanation. Some suggest the manna to have been the exudate of some particular tree. Others suggest it to have been a species of lichen. Whatever the nub of the account, however, it has been embroidered out of recognition by the Biblical writers.

The tale of the manna is from the P document as can be seen from the careful instructions given for the gathering of the manna and the warnings to observe the Sabbath. (This form of ritualism and meticulousness is characteristic of P.) It is therefore a late elaboration of some early legend, and there is no point in taking it literally.

Part of the instructions are:

> Exodus 16:16. . . . *Gather of it . . . an omer for every man . . .*

But how large is an omer? Even the editors of the Hexateuch seem to have been worried by that, for they added a definition:

> Exodus 16:36. *Now an omer is the tenth part of an ephah.*

Of course, if one doesn't know how large an ephah is that doesn't help. The trouble is that while strange units of measure are always difficult to put into familiar terms, there is particular confusion among the early Israelites.

Those of pre-Exilic times used Egyptian systems of measurement and those of post-Exilic times used Babylonian systems, and it is not always easy to tell them apart. The best estimate is that the omer is a little less than half a peck in our common units or about four liters in the metric system.

Amalek

After the crossing of the Red Sea, the Israelites headed for Mount Sinai, and the situation now changes radically. A weakened Egypt has been left behind and will not play a role as an adversary of the Israelites for fully three centuries. In its place are new enemies, the Semitic peoples who had, within the past century, settled down in the areas surrounding Canaan, displacing the earlier inhabitants. These, naturally, resisted the later influx of the Israelites.

The first of these mentioned as encountering the Israelites were Amalekites:

> Exodus 17:8. *Then came Amalek and fought with Israel in Rephidim.*

The location of Rephidim is unknown. If Mount Sinai is located in its traditional place near the southern apex of the Sinai Peninsula, then Rephidim would have to be located somewhere in the southern portion of the peninsula and it becomes a matter of wonder that the Amalekites were to be found there. References elsewhere in the Bible seem to place the Amalekites chiefly to the immediate south of Canaan and to make them neighbors, or even a branch, of the Edomites. This was recognized by the Biblical writers themselves since the eponym, Amalek, was described as a grandson of Esau/Edom (see page 103).

If the Israelites had reached the region south of Canaan on their way to Mount Sinai that would be a point in favor of those who would identify Mount Sinai with Mount Seir (see page 133). Or perhaps the story is displaced and the battle with Amalek in Rephidim did not take place en route to Mount Sinai but long afterward when the Israelites had left the mountain and were indeed in the region south of Canaan.

Putting such questions to one side, the Israelites maintained a strong tradition of continuing an undying enmity with the Amalekites; more so than with their other enemies. This may be because the Amalekites were the first to make war upon the Israelites, when they were least equipped to fight back, or because they did so in what seemed to the Israelites to be a peculiarly unfair and frustrating manner. Later, in the Book of Deuteronomy, Moses, in summarizing the events following the Exodus, is quoted:

Deuteronomy 25:17. *Remember what Amalek did unto thee by the way, when ye were come forth out of Egypt;*
Deuteronomy 25:18. *How he met thee by the way, and smote the hindmost of thee, even all that were feeble behind thee, when thou wast faint and weary . . .*

The Amalekites seemed strong to the Israelites, and in a prophecy described as having been uttered later in their progress toward Canaan, by Balaam, a non-Israelite prophet, they are described grandiloquently:

Numbers 25:20. . . . *Amalek was the first of the nations . . .*

and this is usually taken to mean that they were the most powerful of the nations of the region.

Perhaps they were, temporarily. Nomadic groups sometimes rise to tremendous local power as a result of sudden raids upon unprepared or decadent enemies and then vanish almost entirely after a comparatively short time. The outstanding example of this in history is the career of the Mongols, who, in the thirteenth century A.D., nearly conquered the world—then faded away.

The Amalekites could have anticipated the Mongolian feat only in the smallest way and over a very restricted area for neither the Egyptian nor the Babylonian records mention any people that can be identified with the Amalekites. The Bible is our only source concerning them.

The first pitched battle between the Amalekites and the Israelites ended in complete victory for the latter. War between them continued, however, until two centuries later, when Saul, Israel's first king, was to end the task, wiping out the Amalekite power and leaving only remnants, about which little further is heard.

Joshua

In this first battle with the Amalekites, a new military leader makes his appearance.

> Exodus 17:9. *And Moses said unto Joshua, Choose us out men, and go out, fight with Amalek . . .*

The fact that Joshua is introduced without warning or identification is one reason for thinking that this passage concerning the Amalekites is misplaced and actually describes something that took place near the end of the Exodus rather than near the beginning.

Later Joshua is mentioned as Oshea (Hoshea, in the Revised Standard Version) and is identified as the son of Nun and as a member of the tribe of Ephraim. Oshea ("salvation") was apparently his original name and Moses changed it to one more in line with Yahvism:

> Numbers 13:16. . . . *And Moses called Oshea the son of Nun Jehoshua.*

Jehoshua, of which Joshua is a shortened form, means "Yahveh is salvation."

Joshua remained Moses' military aide throughout the Exodus and eventually succeeded Moses as leader of the Israelites generally. This is the first indication of the military pre-eminence of the tribe of Ephraim, a pre-eminence they were to hold throughout the tribal period.

In later Old Testament times, it became more common to abbreviate Jehoshua as Jeshua. In Greek, the sound "sh" (not present in the Greek alphabet) was replaced by "s" and the usual Greek name-ending of "-s" was added so that Jeshua became Jesus.

Indeed, the New Testament (originally written in Greek) refers to Joshua, Moses' general, as Jesus on two occasions—at least in the King James Version. Thus, in the Book of the Acts of the Apostles, when Stephen summarizes Old Testament history for his audience, he refers to the tabernacle built under Moses' direction in the wilderness:

> Acts 7:45. *Which also our fathers that came after brought in [to Canaan] with Jesus . . .*

In the Revised Standard Version, the name in Acts 7:45 is given as Joshua. It is, of course, quite impossible for any version to change the name of Jesus Christ back to the Hebrew Joshua. That name is too fixed in human consciousness in its Greek form.

Cherubim

After the battle with the Amalekites, the Israelites reached Mount Sinai. There Moses ascended the mountain to receive instructions concerning various moral precepts (including the Ten Commandments) as well as the details of the structures to be built for the worship of God, the clothing of the High Priest, various rites, and so on.

Most sacred of the structures described was the "ark of the covenant," a simple chest which was to contain the tablets on which the Ten Commandments were inscribed, and over which the very presence of God was supposed to hover.

The ark was covered by a slab of gold called the mercy seat and—

> Exodus 25:18. *And thou shalt make two cherubims of gold . . . in the two ends of the mercy seat.*
> . . . .
> Exodus 25:20. *And the cherubims shall stretch forth their wings on high, covering the mercy seat with their wings, and their faces shall look one to another . . .*

(Actually, "cherubims" is a false plural. In Hebrew, the singular is *cherub*, the plural *cherubim*. The Revised Standard Version substitutes the simple "cherubim.")

It is not really certain what the cherubim might be. During the Assyrian period, the readers of the Biblical writings seem to have been expected to know what was meant by the word without the necessity of description or explanation. Thus, when Adam and Eve were driven out of Eden, God is described as placing guardians about the garden to prevent any return by man:

> Genesis 3:24. . . . *he placed at the east of the garden of Eden Cherubims, and a flaming sword which turned every way* . . .

The verse simply says "Cherubims" without description or explanation.

In connection with the ark of the covenant, the wings are mentioned, but not in order to explain the appearance of the cherubim for nothing else is described. The verses merely take pains to describe the exact position of the wings, which the readers are otherwise taken to be quite familiar with.

Centuries later, when Solomon built his Temple, he too made use of cherubim in appropriately enlarged scale:

> 1 Kings 6:23. And . . . *he made two cherubims of olive tree, each ten cubits high.*
> 1 Kings 6:24. And *five cubits was the one wing of the cherub and five cubits the other* . . .

Again, the mere fact of wingedness is all that is mentioned.

It might be simple to think that cherubim were merely human figures with wings, such as we usually visualize angels to be. Indeed, in later Jewish legends, the cherubim figured as among the higher orders of angels. (Moderns often apply the term to the winged Cupids depicted in sweetly sentimental paintings with the result that the term has come to be applied to children.)

On the other hand, the cherubim were guardians of objects particularly holy and unapproachable, and they might well have been fearsome in shape. The Assyrians, for instance, built at the gateways of their palaces and temples monstrous creatures meant to guard kings and gods. These were large representations of bulls, with the head

of a man and wings of an eagle. Other types of composite creatures
are also familiar in the various mythologies. For instance, there are
the Greek sphinxes, which had the head of a woman, the wings of
an eagle, and the body of a lion.

There is nothing in the Bible that would eliminate the possibility
that it was winged bulls or winged lions, rather than winged men,
that crouched on the mercy seat.

In favor of the cherubim as composite creatures is the initial
vision in the Book of Ezekiel. Here, the prophet describes beings
(later referred to by him as cherubim) which are clearly composite.

> Ezekiel 1:6. . . . *every one had four faces, and every one had*
> *four wings.*
>
> Ezekiel 1:7. . . . *and the sole of their feet was like the sole of*
> *a calf's foot . . .*
>
> . . . .
>
> Ezekiel 1:10. . . . *they four had the face of a man, and the face*
> *of a lion, on the right side; and they four had the face of an ox*
> *on the left side; they four also had the face of an eagle.*

The description, as we now have it, may be mangled and distorted with the passing of the years, and there is much dispute
over the vision, but the cherubim as envisioned by the ancient
Israelites must have been more than simply a winged human figure.

The Urim and the Thummim

Even more puzzling than the cherubim are objects which enter into
the meticulous and detailed description of the garments of the High
Priest. The ephod, a kind of linen vest, was partly covered by a
breastplate bearing twelve jewels, one for each of the tribes, and
carrying upon it some sort of pocket:

> Exodus 28:30. *And thou shalt put in the breastplate of judg-*
> *ment the Urim and the Thummim . . .*

Nobody knows what the Urim and Thummim are. The words are
Hebrew, but translating them is of no help, for they mean "lights"
and "perfections" respectively.

The most frequent guess is that the Urim and Thummim represent a form of lot used for guidance in determining the will of God. There might be one type of object indicating "yes" and another indicating "no" and if yes-no questions are put, the answers are given by the type of object which pops out of the pouch. It is even possible that a blank object was also included, one which signified neither yes nor no, indicating that divine guidance was refused.

The Bible certainly indicates that in early Israelite history, divine guidance was expected to make itself manifest in some sort of chance event. When King Saul was searching for the individual who had committed a sin, he set the Israelites generally on one side (letting them, perhaps, be represented by one of the lot-objects) and himself and his son Jonathan on the other (letting them be represented by the other lot-objects).

1 Samuel 14:41. *Therefore Saul said unto the Lord God of Israel, Give a perfect lot. And Saul and Jonathan were taken: but the people escaped.*

However, in this and other cases, in the King James Version, where casting lots is used to obtain divine guidance, the Urim and Thummim are not specifically mentioned. And usually when the Urim and Thummim are mentioned, the nature of their use is not described. There is only one place where the two combine and that is in the days before King Saul's final battle, when he sought for guidance and found none:

1 Samuel 28:6. *And when Saul inquired of the Lord, the Lord answered him not, neither by dreams, nor by Urim, nor by prophets.*

The Revised Standard Version, however, accepts a version of 1 Samuel 14:41 which is fuller than that found in the King James and which, indeed, makes matters explicit: "Therefore Saul said, 'O Lord God of Israel, why hast thou not answered thy servant this day? If this guilt is in me or in Jonathan my son, O Lord, God of Israel, give Urim; but if this guilt is in thy people Israel, give Thummim.' And Jonathan and Saul were taken, but the people escaped."

This sort of guidance by lot passed out of use before the end of the Old Testament period.

The Molten Calf

Moses' stay on Mount Sinai continued for so long that the Israelites back in the camp began to fear that he might never return. This encouraged those among them who felt uncomfortable with an invisible God. It is very common to desire some visible manifestation of the deity (nowadays as well as in ancient times) and the pressure increased on Aaron to supply one.

Aaron asked for gold:

> Exodus 32:4. *And he . . . fashioned it with a graving tool, after he had made it a molten calf: and they said, These be thy gods, O Israel . . .*

The choice of image is not as surprising as it might sound to modern ears. Primitive man did not differentiate as carefully between men and animals as we do. Before the rise of modern technology, wild carnivores were a continuing terror and menace and it was by no means certain that some animals, at least, might not be equal or superior to man. Then, too, many peoples believed that the souls of men might be reborn in animal form and that one particular species of creature might have close ties of subtle kindred with their own particular tribe. Others felt that since some animals were a necessary source of food, a representation of these creatures had somehow to be honored and propitiated.

Animal worship has, therefore, in one way or another, attracted man throughout history. Nowadays, it is most common in India, where among the Hindus cattle may not be killed, much less eaten, despite the endemic starvation in the land. This practice gives rise to the well-known phrase "sacred cow" for any belief rigidly held beyond reason.

In ancient times, animal worship was most widespread in Egypt. As an example, the city of Memphis paid special reverence to a sacred bull, Hapi, (known to the Greeks as Apis). The bull was considered a manifestation of the god Osiris and was given divine honors. Everything about it was surrounded with ritual and its every action was supposed to have great significance.

One might suppose that it was the Egyptian example that inspired the Israelites at the foot of Mount Sinai, but that is not necessarily so. To people who depend on cattle for meat, milk, and labor, the bull is bound to be considered an important figure indeed, because on his fertility all depended. Bulls would therefore play an important part in the ritual of many groups of people. The early Cretans, during the time when the Israelites were in Egypt, had long observed religious rituals in which bulls played a key role. Two thousand years later, the rites of Mithraism, a religion of Persian origin, also involved bulls. The Assyrians had their winged bulls and the other peoples of the Fertile Crescent also held bulls in varying degrees of reverence.

The Israelites, therefore, were not at all likely to see anything strange in bull worship, and the "calf" Aaron formed was undoubtedly a young bull. Indeed, if the cherubim were, as I myself suspect, winged bulls (see page 149), then the transition from an invisible presence resting between the cherubim on the ark of the covenant, to the cherubim themselves, could be an easy one. It might not even represent a full retreat from Yahvism since the golden figure might be taken for Yahveh made manifest.

This section of the Book of Exodus is thought to be based on legends that arose primarily among the Joseph tribes in northern Canaan. It may be that in very early tribal history some special association was made between the Joseph tribes and bulls. Thus, Moses, shortly before his death, is described as blessing each of the tribes separately, and when it is the turn of Joseph, part of the blessing is:

Deuteronomy 33:17. *His glory is like the firstling of his bullock . . .*

This shows up more specifically when, three centuries after the Exodus, the kingdom of Solomon splits into two halves. Since Jerusalem, which had been the center of worship under David and Solomon, remained with the southern half, it seemed politically dangerous to the king of the northern kingdom to allow such worship to continue. This king was Jeroboam of the tribe of Ephraim, one of the Joseph tribes, and he turned naturally, it would appear, to the bull, the ancient animal symbol of his tribe.

1 Kings 12:28. *Whereupon the king . . . made two calves of gold, and said unto them, It is too much for you to go up to Jerusalem: behold thy gods, O Israel . . .*

The use of the bull as a manifestation of God continued in the northern kingdom to the end of its history. However, it never obtained a foothold in the southern kingdom, and it is from the southern kingdom that the history of later Judaism and Christianity descends.

While the Israelites were celebrating the image of the young bull, Moses descended from the mountain. A brief civil war followed, with the Levites ranging themselves on Moses' side. The ringleaders among the bull-worshipers were slaughtered, and Moses' authority was reaffirmed.

With that done, Moses continued with his task of instituting the rituals of Yahvism, and the Book of Exodus ends with a careful accounting of how the ark of the covenant, the clothing of the High Priest, and other items are prepared in exact fulfillment of the instructions earlier given.

3. LEVITICUS

Leviticus

The third book of the Bible begins:

Leviticus 1:1. *And the Lord called unto Moses* . . .

The first word in Hebrew is V*ayikrah* ("And he called") and that is
the Hebrew title of the book.

The book is virtually one long section of the P document, given
over to ritualistic detail, so that it is easily the dullest book in the Bible
to the casual reader.

Its instructions are of primary interest to the priesthood, who are
drawn from among the descendants of Aaron, who was himself of the
tribe of Levi. Aaron and his descendants are therefore Levites, and the
word became synonymous with "priest."

The translators of the Septuagint, mindful of the book's involvement with the priesthood, called it "Levitikon" ("the Levitical book")
and we make use of the Latin equivalent, "Leviticus."

Leaven

One of the instructions concerning the ritual of sacrifice ordains
the avoidance of the use of leaven in objects offered to God:

Leviticus 2:11. *No meat offering which ye shall bring unto the
Lord, shall be made with leaven* . . .

Originally, the flour used in making bread was simply baked into flat, hard cakes that had the virtue of remaining fit to eat for long periods of time.

Dough which had, however, been left standing, would sometimes pick up microorganisms from the air and begin to ferment. The process of fermentation produced carbon dioxide which formed bubbles in the thick dough and puffed it up. Bread made from such fermented dough was light and fluffy. It would not keep as well as bread made from unfermented dough, but would tend to get dry and moldy, but it was still pleasant to eat when fresh.

A key step in bread manufacture must have taken place (in prehistoric times) when it was discovered that there was no need to wait for dough to ferment spontaneously. A small piece of already fermented dough would hasten the fermentation of large batches of fresh dough. This became proverbial, and the Apostle Paul, for instance, in speaking of the pervasive influence of evil says:

1 Corinthians 5:6. . . . *Know ye not that a little leaven leaveneth the whole lump?*

The word "leaven" (from a Latin word meaning "to raise") is a translation of the Hebrew word *hametz*, meaning "to be sour," something that is often characteristic of fermenting material. Our own equivalent word, "yeast," is traced back to a Sanskrit word meaning "to boil," which is a reference to the bubbles of carbon dioxide formed.

To the Israelites, fermentation seemed a form of corruption, and however pleasant leavened bread might be to eat, there was still the stigma of corruption and impurity about it. Bread to be offered on the altar to God must be pure and uncorrupt and must, therefore, be unleavened.

On Passover, because of the holiness of the season, only unleavened bread might be eaten and no trace of leaven must be found anywhere in the house. Indeed, a synonym for Passover is "the feast of unleavened bread."

Exodus 23:15. *Thou shalt keep the feast of unleavened bread . . . in the time appointed of the month Abib; for in it thou camest out from Egypt . . .*

The Last Supper of Jesus and his disciples took place at the time
of Passover. The bread broken by Jesus was therefore unleavened,
and the wafer used in the Catholic Mass, in commemoration of that
event, is unleavened too.

Undoubtedly the use of unleavened bread in ritual is extremely
ancient, dating back to long before the Exodus. The priestly editors of
the Hexateuch had to find some circumstance in the flight from Egypt
that made the eating of unleavened bread particularly appropriate
as a way of commemorating the Exodus. They found this in the haste
in which the Israelites left; a haste so great that the relatively slow
process of fermentation could not be waited for:

> Exodus 12:33. *And the Egyptians were urgent upon the people,
> that they might send them out of the land in haste . . .*

Unclean

Much of Leviticus deals with the clean and unclean:

> Leviticus 5:2. . . . *if a soul touch any unclean thing . . .*

To us, clean and unclean tends to be a hygienic matter. Something
is unclean if it is dirty, or has an offensive smell, or is laden with
dangerous bacteria. The Biblical use of the term involves religious
ritual.

Something is clean if it may be offered as a sacrifice to God, or if
it may stand in the presence of God. Something that may not be
offered as a sacrifice is unclean. People who, because of some deformity
or disease, or because they have touched an unclean thing or performed a forbidden act, are themselves unclean and cannot approach
the altar until the uncleanness has been removed.

In Leviticus, the items of food that are clean and may be eaten, and
those that are unclean and may not be eaten, are listed in detail.
For instance:

> Leviticus 11:3. *Whatsoever parteth the hoof, and is clovenfooted,
> and cheweth the cud, among the beasts, that shall ye eat.*
>
> . . . .
>
> Leviticus 11:7. *And the swine, though he divide the hoof, and be
> clovenfooted, yet he cheweth not the cud; he is unclean unto you.*

The basis on which animals are divided into clean and unclean is not known. Some say it is a matter of pragmatic rules of hygiene, some bring in primitive notions of totemism, some find in it a desire to forbid practices common to surrounding idolatry. Perhaps the chief thing in the mind of the priesthood that prepared the book of Leviticus was to work out a code of behavior that would serve to keep the Jews distinct and their religion intact from the attractions of surrounding cultures.

If so, the priesthood succeeded, for these sections of Leviticus were the basis of the dietary laws which became so important to the post-Exilic Jews. The dietary laws were so intricate and compulsive as to prevent pious Jews from eating with non-Jews, since the food prepared by non-Jews could never meet the standards of ceremonial cleanness.

And while many different foods were considered unclean, swine somehow represented the epitome of uncleanness—perhaps because it was so common a part of the diet of the surrounding Gentiles that its absence in the Jewish dietary was particularly conspicuous.

The disputes recorded in the New Testament over the matter of cleanness, between Jesus and his followers on the one hand and the orthodox Jews on the other, must be understood only in the ritualistic sense, of course, never in the hygienic.

The Day of Atonement

Leviticus is concerned with how to cancel out the consequences of sin, too, as well as of uncleanness. To sin—that is, to disobey the commandments of God, as Adam and Eve did in eating the fruit of the tree (the "original sin")—involves separation from God. To cancel sin according to a prescribed ritual is to restore one's self to the presence of God, to make one's self once more "at one" with God. The sinner must "atone" therefore, or make "atonement."

The High Priest can atone for the entire nation by means of appropriate rituals, and this is done on a particular day:

Leviticus 23:27. . . . *on the tenth day of this seventh month there shall be a day of atonement . . . and ye shall afflict your souls . . .*

"Day of atonement" is a translation of the Hebrew *Yom Kippur.* Yom Kippur is now the holiest day of the Jewish calendar and a strict day-long fast is involved ("ye shall afflict your souls"). Nevertheless, there is no record of the holiday having been observed until post-Exilic times.

Azazel

Yet if the Day of Atonement is itself a post-Exilic development, some of the rites associated with it must be old indeed. As part of the ritual two goats must be selected:

Leviticus 16:8. *And Aaron shall cast lots upon the two goats, one lot for the Lord, and the other lot for the scapegoat.*

The goat upon whom the Lord's lot fell (and here one might expect the Urim and Thummim would be used) would be sacrificed to the Lord as atonement for the sins of the nation. The other would be led off into the wilderness bearing with it all those sins, so that punishment might befall it rather than the nation of Israel and its people. Because the second goat escapes into the wilderness and is not sacrificed, the King James Version refers to it as a "scapegoat" ("escaped goat"). It is for this reason that the word has come to be applied to any person or object who, himself innocent, suffers vicariously for the deeds of another.

However, the Hebrew word that is translated as "scapegoat" in the King James Version is actually *Azazel.* The Revised Standard Version does not translate the word but makes the verse read: "And Aaron shall cast lots upon the two goats, one lot for the Lord and the other lot for Azazel."

Azazel is mentioned nowhere else in the Bible save for this one chapter, but it seems quite likely that it is the name of a demon thought of as dwelling in the wilderness. It might be pictured as an evil spirit that is the source of sin. In sending the second goat into the wilderness, the sins it carries could be viewed as returning to their source.

Later legends elaborated on Azazel. He was supposed to be one of the fallen angels, exiled from Heaven because he would not accept

newly created man as superior. An alternative suggestion involves a
rather obscure passage in the Book of Genesis:

> Genesis 6:2. . . . *the sons of God saw the daughters of men
> that they were fair; and they took them wives of all which they
> chose.*
>
> . . . .
>
> Genesis 6:4. . . . *and they bare children to them, the same became
> mighty men which were of old, men of renown.*

This remnant of primitive mythology, lingering on in the Bible,
was interpreted literally by the later Jews. They thought the angels,
deliberately rebelling against God, chose to corrupt themselves with
mankind out of lust for women and that this act helped bring on the
Flood. Some versions of this legend made Azazel the chief of these
angels.

Devils

Another relic of the past is contained in the next chapter, which
commands centralized worship under the guidance of the priesthood,
and forbids older, more independent rites:

> Leviticus 17:7. *And they shall no more offer their sacrifice unto
> devils . . .*

The word "devil" is from the Greek *diabolos*, which means
"slanderer." The name applies to evil spirits that slander God in
men's ears, urging them on to disobedience and sin. They can also be
viewed as slandering human beings to God, as Satan, in the Book of
Job, is pictured as slandering Job.

In this particular verse, "devils" is a translation of the Hebrew
word *sairrim*, which, literally, means "wild goats." There is a widespread tendency to think of goats as lustful animals personifying the
wild, fructifying force of nature. The Greeks visualized the woods to
be full of nature spirits in the shape of men with the horns, tail, and
hindquarters of goats, always in a state of sexual heat. They called
them "satyrs" and the word has entered the modern psychiatric
vocabulary to represent men suffering from insatiable sexual desires.

To the Yahvists, with their strait-laced sexual mores, such fertility gods were nothing more than evil spirits.

The Revised Standard Version recognizes the specific similarity of the satyrs to the sairrim and has Leviticus 17:7 read: "So they shall no more slay their sacrifices for satyrs . . ."

The popular conception of Satan today, with his horns, tail, and cloven hoof, shows that he is still pictured as a satyr.

Blood

The eating of blood is strongly forbidden:

> Leviticus 17:10. . . . *I will even set my face against that soul that eateth blood, and will cut him off from among his people.*
> Leviticus 17:11. *For the life of the flesh is in the blood . . .*

Blood is considered to contain the principle of life, as is reasonable, seeing that long-continued bleeding will kill a man who seems otherwise unharmed. Life, as the creation of God, cannot be appropriated by man, and man cannot, therefore, eat blood.

This prohibition was pronounced before the revelation at Sinai, for even Noah, after the Flood, is cited as having received such instructions. God tells Noah what he may eat:

> Genesis 9:3. *Every moving thing that liveth shall be meat for you . . .*
> Genesis 9:4. *But flesh with the life thereof, which is the blood thereof, shall ye not eat.*

This was interpreted by the later Jews as meaning that even those who did not receive the revelation at Sinai were still required to refrain from eating blood.

Thus, when a controversy arose in the early Christian church as to whether Gentile converts were required to accept the dietary regulations of the Mosaic law, the decision was that they were not so required. Nevertheless, their freedom was not absolute, for the conservative leaders of the church at Jerusalem insisted:

> Acts 15:20. . . . *that we write unto them that they abstain from pollutions of idols, and from fornication, and from things strangled, and from blood.*

Familiar Spirits

There are prohibitions of all sorts in the Book of Leviticus. There are lists of foods that one might not eat, and lists of sexual practices that one must not tolerate. Unethical behavior of various sorts are forbidden. In addition, some practices are forbidden by the Mosaic law which seem to be harmless enough. Thus:

Exodus 23:19. . . . *Thou shalt not seethe a kid in his mother's milk.*

and:

Leviticus 19:27. *Ye shall not round the corners of your heads, neither shalt thou mar the corners of thy beard.*

Presumably, this was designed to warn against practices that were particularly associated with heathens and idolatry. The Egyptian priesthood, for instance, shaved the hair from head and face.

Later Jews made elaborate deductions from such verses. The prohibition against boiling meat in milk, for instance, was built up into complicated avoidance of eating meat and dairy dishes at the same meal, or even preparing them or serving them, at different times, in the same utensils.

Another prohibition is:

Leviticus 19:31. *Regard not them that have familiar spirits, neither seek after wizards . . .*

A wizard is a "wise man," presumably one who knows how to bend supernatural forces to his will. He would be one who could govern spirits, and make servants of them. A "familiar spirit" is a "servant-spirit," from the Latin word *famulus,* meaning "servant."

The Bible does not say that such spirits do not exist, or that wizards do not have the power to which they pretend. The objections rests on the fact that the rites practiced by wizards are idolatrous.

The feminine version of the word "wizard" is "witch" and the Bible judges them harshly in one of the shortest and most influential of the Biblical verses:

Exodus 22:18. *Thou shalt not suffer a witch to live.*

Many unnecessary persecutions and cruelties have been visited on women (especially old women) as a result of this verse.

(It must be remembered, however, that ancient pagan practices endured, under cover, throughout the centuries of Christian Europe. Fighting witchcraft was sometimes Christianity's way of fighting an older and competing religion.)

Molech

The Book of Leviticus inveighed particularly against one particular form of idolatry.

To be sure, the Bible denounces all forms of idolatry; all forms of worship in which divine beings were represented in the form of some tangible likeness of a man, an animal, or a composite creature. It is possible to argue that the idol is not the god worshiped but only a visible representation of an invisible, divine essence, but even if this were so, the tendency of the ordinary worshiper would be to consider the visible object as the god.

The Yahvists thought this danger to be so great that increasingly, through Biblical times, they set their face against any image at all and grew more and more firm on that subject. —And one particular idol roused them to enormous rage.

Leviticus 20:2. . . . *Whosoever he be of the children of Israel, or of the strangers that sojourn in Israel, that giveth any of his seed unto Molech; he shall surely be put to death . . .*

Molech is, in this case, almost certainly a version of *melech* ("king"). It is a way of referring to the god of the people, similar to "the lord." The Biblical writers grew increasingly unable, as the centuries passed, to speak of idols as kings or lords and avoided this by pronouncing the word *bosheth* ("shame") whenever they came to such a reference to an idol. When diacritical marks (see page 135) were added to the words, *melech* received the marks for *bosheth*. In that way, *melech* became Molech.

The worship of Molech involved the sacrifice of children. Primitive men felt that the dearer and more loved the object sacrificed to a god, the more impressed the god would be and the more apt to answer the prayer. In times of dire distress, then, children would be sacrificed, even perhaps the child of the king.

In the later days of the Israelite kingdoms, when affairs were frequently desperate, such child sacrifice was performed. One suggestion is that living children were burnt to death in a fire built within the brazen idol, but it may be that the children were slain first and then sacrificed in some more ordinary fashion.

One of the later kings of Judah, Ahaz, sacrificed his son in this fashion:

> 2 Kings 16:3. *But he* [Ahaz] . . . *made his son to pass through the fire, according to the abominations of the heathen* . . .

Undoubtedly, many men of the period applied the word *melech* to Yahveh, and assumed themselves to be sacrificing to God in an approved manner as Abraham was ready to do in sacrificing Isaac. Of course, those who disapproved of human sacrifice must have been quick to point out that the sacrifice of Isaac was prevented. Even so, the prophets had to go to special pains to state, specifically, that Yahveh did not approve. The verses in Leviticus were made firm and strong and Jeremiah, in rehearsing the complaints of God against the Jews, has Him say:

> Jeremiah 7:31. *And they . . . burn their sons and their daughters in the fire; which I commanded them not, neither came it into my heart.*

Jubile

A special festival is mentioned in Leviticus, which seems to have been a priestly ideal that was never put thoroughly into practice:

> Leviticus 25:8. *And thou shalt number . . . seven times seven years . . .*
> Leviticus 25:9. *Then shalt thou cause the trumpet of the jubile to sound . . . in the day of atonement . . .*
> Leviticus 25:10. *And ye shall hallow the fiftieth year . . .*

The land was to remain fallow during the year; land which had been leased out was to be restored to the original owners; slaves were to be freed. In a way, it was a method of starting things fresh every half century so as to prevent the accumulation of economic injustice. It was a beautiful idea, but impractical.

Nevertheless, the word "jubile" (usually spelled "jubilee" and derived from the Hebrew word for trumpet) has come to represent a fiftieth anniversary.

About 100 B.C., a book was written by some unnamed Jew or Jews purporting to detail the primitive history of humanity. It modeled itself on Genesis but added a great many legendary details that had been built up since Genesis had reached its final form some three centuries before. It includes much detail concerning angels, for instance, and traces late customs back to the earliest times. Because it gives the history in a series of chapters, each dealing with a fifty-year period, it is called the "Book of Jubilees."

4. NUMBERS

Numbers

The fourth book of the Bible begins:

Numbers 1:1. *And the Lord spake unto Moses in the wilderness* . . .

The Hebrew name is taken from that first verse for it is "Bemidbar" meaning "in the wilderness."

The translators of the Septuagint were, however, impressed by the fact that the book includes the results of two censuses of the fighting men of the Israelite tribes. They therefore named the book "Arithmoi" ("Numbers"). The name of this book, unlike those of the first three, is translated into English, and is called "Numbers."

The Sum of the Congregation

The first census is recorded at the very start of the book:

Numbers 1:2. *Take ye the sum of all the congregation* . . .
Numbers 1:3. *From twenty years old and upward, all that are able to go forth to war* . . .

The second census was carried out forty years afterward, shortly before the entry into Canaan:

Numbers 26:2. *Take the sum of all the congregation . . . from twenty years old and upward . . . all that are able to go to war* . . .

The figures presented by the Book of Numbers are as follows:

Tribe	First Census	Second Census
Reuben	46,500	43,730
Simeon	59,300	22,200
Gad	45,650	40,500
Judah	74,600	76,500
Issachar	54,400	64,300
Zebulun	57,400	60,500
Ephraim	40,500	32,500
Manasseh	32,200	52,700
Benjamin	35,400	45,600
Dan	62,700	64,400
Asher	41,500	53,400
Naphtali	53,400	45,400
Total	603,550	601,730

These are only the adult males, of course. If one counts in the women and children and the "mixed-multitude" or half-breed hangers-on to whom the Bible occasionally refers, one gets the picture of some two million people wandering about the Sinai Peninsula. This seems implausibly large, considering this is more than the number of Israelites in the Davidic kingdom at its height. One suspects that the numbers represent a later tradition of questionable accuracy.

Regardless of the accuracy of the figures, however, two points can be made which reflect later history. First, the most populous tribes were pictured as Judah and Joseph. (If Ephraim and Manasseh are taken together, the Joseph tribes have 72,700 in the first census, almost the figure for Judah; and 85,200 in the second census, surpassing the figure for Judah.) This seems to reflect the situation four centuries later when the Davidic kingdom had split in two, with the Joseph tribes dominating the northern kingdom and Judah the southern.

Secondly, the most startling change in numbers is that of Simeon, which, between the first and second census, loses more than three fifths of its numbers. No other tribe is pictured as suffering anywhere near such losses and there is nothing in the actual events of Numbers to account for it. This, apparently, is an indication that at the time of the conquest of Canaan, Simeon was already considerably weakened, and this helps account for the fact that it played no great role in later Israelite history. This may be the result of a disastrous early attack on Shechem by Simeon and Levi, described in Genesis (see page 100) and made to appear there as though it were a victory of patriarchal times.

The tribe of Levi was not numbered with the other tribes for they were not to be among the warriors. Their task was to perform the priestly functions. Therefore, all the males were counted and not merely those above twenty years. The figure in the first census came to 22,273 and in the second to 23,000. Levi is thus made to seem smaller than any of the other tribes and this too may be a reflection of the attack on Shechem.

The Ethiopian Woman

The Israelites set out on their march toward Canaan and along the way, Moses had to contend with various types of disaffection. Even within his own family there was dissension, for his sister, Miriam, and his brother, Aaron, entered into an intrigue against him:

Numbers 12:1. *And Miriam and Aaron spake against Moses because of the Ethiopian woman whom he had married . . .*

From this verse one might picture, as many people do, a Negro woman as Moses' wife, since "Ethiopian" is used frequently nowadays as a euphemistic synonym for "Negro." However, there is no reason to think that a Negro woman was involved, or even an Ethiopian woman in the modern sense. The Hebrew word here translated as "Ethiopian" is "Cushi" and in the Revised Standard Version, Moses' wife is described as "the Cushite woman."

As I explained earlier (see page 19), a Cushite might indeed be an Ethiopian. According to legend, Moses served as an Egyptian general in his youth and led his troops in a victorious campaign in Ethiopia and might, conceivably, have picked up a wife or concubine there. However, there is no Biblical evidence of this and the legend of Moses' Ethiopian adventures is probably based on nothing stronger than this single verse.

Against this view is the fact that the Cushites are also Arabian peoples (see page 20).

Only one woman is specifically mentioned in the Bible as being married to Moses. Moses' marriage took place during his flight into Midian, in Arabia, and his stay at the home of a desert priest (see page 129):

Exodus 2:21. *And Moses was content to dwell with the man: and he gave Moses Zipporah his daughter.*

Zipporah may very well have been the Cushite woman referred to in Numbers 12:1. She could be resented by Miriam out of generalized intrafamilial jealousy, or, specifically, because she *was* a "Cushite woman"; that is, a Midianite and a foreigner, and not an Israelite.

In any case, Moses faced down his brother and sister and won out over dissent as he did on numerous other occasions in the course of the Exodus.

Caleb

Having reached the wilderness of Paran (see page 87) south of Canaan, Moses took the cautious step of sending spies into the land in order to observe the situation. Their reports might then serve as a ground for a rational distribution of forces and an efficient plan of campaign.

Twelve spies were selected, one from each tribe, but of these only two were of importance. One was Oshea of Ephraim, whom Moses renamed Jehoshua, or Joshua (see page 146). The other was a Judean:

Numbers 13:6. *Of the tribe of Judah, Caleb the son of Jephunneh.*

The career of Caleb is, in many respects, parallel to that of Joshua. Where Joshua was a hero of legends originating with the northern tribes, Caleb was the analogous hero of the southern ones.

In this verse, Caleb is treated as though he were simply a Judean, but in the Book of Joshua he is referred to more fully:

Joshua 14:6. . . . *Caleb the son of Jephunneh the Kenezite . . .*

A Kenezite or ("Kenizzite," as in the Revised Standard Version) is a descendant of Kenaz, who is listed in Genesis as a son of Eliphaz, the first-born of Esau. The Kenizzites, therefore, are an Edomite clan, who must have been adopted into the Judean tribe. This is not the only indication that the tribe of Judah contained non-Israelite elements. In Chapter 38 of Genesis, Judah is described as making an alien marriage:

Genesis 38:2. *And Judah saw there a daughter of a certain Canaanite . . . and he took her . . .*

This may be an indication that the tribe of Judah, located in southern Canaan, was at least partly Canaanite and Edomite in nature. It is even possible that in the early tribal period, Judah was not felt to be part of Israel, for in certain key portions of the book, Judah is conspicuously ignored. Even in Davidic times, when Judah was not only an integral part of Israel but supplied it with a ruling dynasty, there was a continuing lack of sympathy between it and the northern tribes. This was exacerbated into downright enmity and ended finally in civil war and schism.

Zin

From Paran, the spies traveled northward:

Numbers 13:21. *So they went up, and searched the land from the wilderness of Zin unto Rehob . . .*

Numbers 13:22. *And they . . . came unto Hebron; where . . . the children of Anak were. (Now Hebron was built seven years before Zoan in Egypt.)*

Numbers 13:23. *And they came unto the brook of Eshcol, and cut down from thence a branch with one cluster of grapes, . . . and they brought of the pomegranates and of the figs.*

Verse 21 indicates the thoroughness of the search for "the wilderness of Zin" is taken to be the northern edge of Paran, and therefore the desert area just south of Beersheba, while Rehob (exact location unknown) is a site in the extreme north of Canaan. The effect is that of saying that the United States has been searched "from Maine to California."

This may be hyperbole and the chief attention was concentrated on Hebron, the southernmost of the large, well-fortified cities of Canaan. It was formidable enough to allow the metaphoric description of its inhabitants as giants—a description later accepted literally (see page 73).

The parenthetical phrase makes Hebron's legendary ancientness specific by stating it to be seven years older than Zoan. Zoan is the Semitic name for the town called Tanis by the Greeks. It was the capital of the Hyksos kingdom and is used as a comparison because it was the nearest to Canaan of the notable cities of Egypt and therefore, perhaps, the best known.

The ancientness of Egyptian civilization was the proud boast of Egypt and was acknowledged with awe by its neighbors. There was no better way of testifying to the extreme age of a city than by claiming it to be older than an Egyptian city.

While Canaan would not seem an absolute garden spot to someone from California or the Nile, it would certainly seem so to tribes invading from the desert. Well-watered oases such as that in which Hebron was situated would seem particularly fertile and would justify the well-known description of Canaan used in several places in the early books of the Bible. Thus, in God's first interview with Moses, he promises to bring the Israelites out of Egypt:

> Exodus 3:8. . . . *unto a good land and a large, unto a land flowing with milk and honey . . .*

The produce of Eshcol, a district of orchards near Hebron, was brought back to the waiting Israelite host as proof that the description was justified.

Kadesh

The report of the spies was brought back to the place where the Israelites had established a semipermanent station:

> Numbers 13:26. *And they went and came to . . . the children of Israel, unto the wilderness of Paran to Kadesh . . .*

Kadesh means "holy" and probably received its name because it had some sacred associations for the pre-Israelite inhabitants of the

Kadesh-barnea

area. It is identified with a place called Ain Kadis today, located about fifty miles south of Hebron and in the northeastern corner of the Sinai Peninsula.

Despite the fertility of the Hebron area, the spies returned with an utterly pessimistic majority report. They felt the Canaanite cities were entirely too strong to be taken by assault and predicted disaster for any invasion attempt. Only Joshua and Caleb presented a minority report in favor of an immediate assault and they were nearly stoned as a result.

The disheartened Israelites considered a return to Egypt but Moses held them in place and for the next thirty-eight years, Kadesh remained the Israelite capital, while Moses and Joshua organized their forces for the task that lay ahead.

Korah, Dathan, and Abiram

The stay at Kadesh was bound to be a difficult one for Moses. Year after year of inactivity, with Canaan at hand but inaccessible, seemed to make a mockery of the Exodus and to cast doubt upon Moses' capacity as a leader. Serious disaffection appeared:

> Numbers 16:1. Now Korah, the son of Izhar . . . and Dathan
> and Abiram . . . sons of Reuben took men:
>
> . . . .
>
> Numbers 16:3. And they gathered themselves together against
> Moses and against Aaron . . .

Apparently, this chapter combines into one account what were actually two separate rebellions against Moses, one by Korah, and one
by the Reubenites.

The rebellion by Korah was specifically a religious schism. Moses
and Aaron were the sons of Amram, while Korah was the son of
Amram's younger brother, Izhar (see page 136). Since Moses assigned
the lion's share of the priestly duties to Aaron and the Amramites,
Korah felt unjustly discriminated against.

Korah's rebellion was put down, but perhaps not without a compromise being reached. At least Numbers points out later that, despite
the destruction of Korah and his band:

> Numbers 26:11. Notwithstanding the children of Korah died not.

In fact, the Korahites survived to become a hereditary guild of Temple
musicians, a concession they might have received in the case of a
Levite civil war, the memory of which forms the basis of the sixteenth
chapter of Numbers.

The Reubenite rebellion of Dathan and Abiram seems to have been
purely political. At some early point in tribal history, Reuben must
have held the leadership because the tradition is firm that Reuben is
the oldest son of Israel. In the course of the Exodus, the Reubenites
must have witnessed with dismay the shift in the religious leadership
to the tribe of Levi (Moses and Aaron) and the military leadership
to the tribe of Ephraim (Joshua). The tale of Dathan and Abiram
must be based on the memory of some attempt of Reuben to regain
its leadership and this attempt may also echo in the cryptic verse in
Genesis which describes Reuben as committing incest with his father's
concubine (see page 102).

The Reubenite rebellion was also crushed and never again in Israelite history did the tribe of Reuben play a significant role.

The Pit

The particular punishment of the rebellious Reubenites, according to the Biblical description, was that of being swallowed alive by the earth:

Numbers 16:32. *And the earth opened her mouth, and swallowed them up . . .*
Numbers 16:33. *They . . . went down alive into the pit . . .*

The Hebrew word, here translated as "the pit" is *Sheol*, and in the Revised Standard Version, Sheol is left untranslated. Sheol was visualized by the early Israelites as an underground world to which the souls of the dead departed. It was thought of at first as a dim place where there was no particular torture, but where there was an absence of joy. Nor was there any distinction between good and evil; all human beings went there upon death except those few who, like Enoch and Elijah, were taken alive to Heaven.

The picture is like that of other such places imagined by early men. The Greeks had such a world ruled by a god, Hades, and in the early Nordic myths there was such a world ruled by a goddess, Hel. Sheol is therefore replaced by "Hell" in some places in the Bible, and in the New Testament, which was originally written in Greek, it was translated as "Hades."

The moralization of Sheol, its conversion into a place of torture for the wicked, while the good go elsewhere, came later in history, toward the end of Old Testament times.

Mount Hor

The old generation was passing away, and few remained of those who were adults at the time of the Exodus. Miriam, Moses' sister, died at Kadesh, for instance.

The time came when some move had to be made. A direct assault from the south against Hebron seemed to be still out of the question and the alternative was to flank Hebron by traveling northeastward. Canaan could then be attacked from the more vulnerable east.

In order to travel directly northeastward, however, the territory of Edom would have had to be traversed. The Edomites were recognized as a Hebrew people related to the Israelites and the use of force against them was therefore ruled out. Permission was requested by Moses to pass through their territory peacefully, but this was refused. In later years, this refusal was used as a grievance against Edom and as a cause for enmity.

It was therefore necessary to outflank Edom's fortified areas, so the Israelites traveled southeastward:

> Numbers 20:22. *And the children of Israel . . . journeyed from Kadesh, and came unto Mount Hor.*

Mount Hor is often identified with the highest peak in the Seir mountain range (see page 96). Aaron died at this time and was buried on Mount Hor and the peak which is now identified with it is called Jebel Harun ("Mount Aaron") in Arabic.

Some statistics concerning Aaron's death are given later:

> Numbers 33:38. *And Aaron . . . died there, in the fortieth year after the children of Israel were come out of the land of Egypt.*
> Numbers 33:39. *And Aaron was an hundred and twenty and three years old . . .*

If the Exodus took place in 1211 B.C., then the death of Aaron took place in 1171 B.C. That must also have been the year of the death of Moses and of the entry into Canaan, for events now follow quickly although the Bible continues to interrupt those events with long speeches by Moses and others.

If we accept Aaron's age at his death, he must have been born in 1294 B.C., while Moses, who was three years younger, was born in 1291 B.C. (This last is an interesting date for it virtually coincides with the beginning of the reign of Rameses II, the Pharaoh of the Oppression; see page 125.)

The Serpent of Brass

When the period of mourning for Aaron was done, the Israelites continued their outflanking march, by traveling southward to the tip of the Gulf of Aqaba, around Edomite territory and then north again.

Here there occurs an event which was to have continuing traditions later.

A plague of serpents harassed the Israelites, the Bible explains:

> Numbers 21:9. *And Moses made a serpent of brass, and put it upon a pole, and it came to pass, that if a serpent had bitten any man, when he beheld the serpent of brass, he lived.*

This is an example of "sympathetic magic," the belief that like effects like, which is common among primitive people. (The most familiar example we have today is the voodoo belief that sticking pins in images will bring pain and sickness to the person represented by the image.) The use of the serpent, as described in this verse, is rather similar to the principles of homeopathic medicine, which follows the "hair of the dog that bit you" sort of reasoning.

The serpent is a particularly important animal in religious ritual, whether for good or evil. The fact that a serpent moves in so quiet and hidden a fashion and strikes so suddenly and so unexpectedly with so poisoned a fang, makes it an obvious representation of cunning and evil. It is such a representation of cunning evil in the story of the garden of Eden, for instance:

> Genesis 3:1. *Now the serpent was more subtil than any beast of the field . . .*

Something that is dangerous and evil is to be feared, and something that is feared had better be treated well and propitiated, so that serpents could be worshiped even while dreaded.

Then, too, the serpent is looked upon as symbolizing immortality because of its ability to shed its skin. Any primitive man, observing the process by which a serpent sheds an old, dull skin and emerges in a new, brightly colored one, might be excused if he assumed the serpent had undergone a process of rejuvenation. (We ourselves also shed our skin but we do so continuously, and little by little, here and there, so that the process is quite unnoticeable.)

Thus, in the Gilgamesh legend (see page 40), when the hero finally gains the plant that brought immortality, he has it stolen from him by a serpent, which then becomes immortal. (In the garden of Eden, it is the serpent who steals immortality from Adam and Eve, although it is not itself made immortal as a result, but is punished.)

The immortal serpent, victor over death, can thus be considered the particular associate of the medical profession, which labors to stave off, if not to conquer, death. Serpents were sacred to Asklepios, the Greek god of medicine, and even today the Medical Corps of the U. S. Army has as its insignia the caduceus, a staff about which two serpents are encircled.

In later Israelite history, however, as Yahvism grew stronger and more uncompromising, the serpent of brass, worshiped by the people, came under sharper and sharper disapproval. The fact of the association with Moses did not save it. The end came in the reign of Hezekiah, king of Judah, some five centuries after the Exodus:

> 2 Kings 18:4. He [Hezekiah] . . . brake in pieces the brasen serpent that Moses had made: for unto those days the children of Israel did burn incense to it: and he called it Nehushtan.

Nehushtan is usually translated as "a piece of brass." The impression one gets from the final clause of this verse, as given in the King James Version, is that when Hezekiah destroyed the serpent, he countered the shock of the populace by contemptuously labeling the object as of no ritual value at all but as nothing more than a piece of brass.

However, Nehushtan is related not only to the Hebrew word for "brass" but also to the word for "serpent." Nehushtan may have been the name of the object without any connotation of contempt. Indeed, the Revised Standard Version translates the final clause of 2 Kings 18:4 as "it was called Nehushtan," a matter-of-fact statement of information without interpretation.

Sihon

Even the circling of Edom did not remove all difficulties. East of Canaan lay the two kingdoms of Moab and Ammon. Of these two, Moab was the more southerly, occupying the eastern shores of the Dead Sea, while Ammon, to the north, lay east of the Jordan River.

Both were recognized by the Israelites to be Hebrew peoples, descendants of Terah by way of Lot and therefore (according to the interpretation of the Biblical writers), like Edom, immune to attack. Both Moab and Ammon had, presumably, established themselves at the borders of Canaan a century and a half before, in the time of Ikhnaton (see page 124).

THE GREAT SEA

(Mediterranean Sea)

Route of the Exodus
Route of the Conquest

0   Miles   25

Moab and Ammon

Just before the Israelites had arrived, however, the kingdoms—Moab in particular—had had to withstand the shock of another onslaught.

> Numbers 2:26. . . . Sihon the king of the Amorites . . . had fought against the former king of Moab, and taken all his land out of his hand, even unto Arnon.

The Amorites had, some seven centuries before, been a powerful people and had ruled most of the Fertile Crescent (see page 50). They had fallen before the onslaughts of the Hittites and of Imperial Egypt and were now either in subjection or, in places, maintained themselves precariously in patchwork principalities. At the time of the Exodus, there were, presumably, Amorite principalities in Canaan, and Sihon may have been the ruler of one. His attack against the Moabites may have represented the last successful action of the Canaanites against the remorseless pressure of the various Hebrew tribes.

Before Sihon's onslaught, Moab controlled the territory up to the Jabbok River. This is described elsewhere in this chapter as the southern boundary of Ammon and Sihon, therefore, conquered the stretch of land from the Jabbok down to the Arnon.

The Arnon, by the way, is a small river, flowing westward into the Dead Sea, reaching that body of water just about midway along its eastern shore. In later Biblical history it remained the northern boundary of Moab. Its modern name is Wadi Mojib, "Mojib" being a clear echo of "Moab."

Chemosh

In connection with the brief account of the victory of Sihon over Moab, a fragment of a victory ode exulting over the defeat of the Moabites is included. In part, it reads:

> Numbers 22:29. Woe to thee, Moab! thou art undone, O people of Chemosh . . .

Chemosh was the national god of Moab and it was natural to speak of Moab, in those days of wide acceptance of local gods, as the "people of Chemosh."

Only a few thinkers in those primitive times recognized a universal God. Generally, the feeling was that each bit of land had its own god, and that over its own bit of land each god had godlike power. It was even felt that the god was tied to the land; that if one traveled elsewhere it became necessary to worship the god of *that* land unless one carried his own god. Thus, when Rachel left the house of her father Laban, she took Laban's idols with her:

> Genesis 31:19 . . . *and Rachel had stolen the images that were her father's.*

and Laban was more distressed at this than at the loss of his daughters and the goods and cattle that Jacob had carried off:

> Genesis 31:30. . . . *though thou wouldest needs be gone . . . wherefore hast thou stolen my gods?*

The manner in which the Israelites carried the ark of the covenant with them during their travels in the wilderness had a little of the flavor of carrying God with them. Otherwise, one suspects, they might have felt it necessary always to travel back to Sinai to commune with Him.

In the religious thought of that day, there was no necessary feeling of antagonism toward the gods of other tribes, provided no actual war was going on and the enemy was not calling upon his god for help in your destruction (as you were calling upon yours for help in his destruction). The situation might be much the same as in our own feeling for the flags of foreign nations. If we are at peace with a foreign nation, international usage requires that we treat its flag with decent respect even in our own land. It would be even more a matter of elementary courtesy to treat the flag of a foreign nation with respect while inside the borders of that nation.

In later times, however, as a consciousness of the universality of Yahveh grew among the Israelites, and as the feeling deepened that there was only one God, not only for the Israelites but for all the world—that there was one *only* God—the attitude of the Yahvists toward the gods of other tribes hardened. The foreign gods were not only potential enemies; they were no gods at all. At most, they were demons who imposed their worship on the ignorant, unenlightened, or wicked. As a result, when Chemosh was referred to in later books of the Bible, it was as something shameful:

> 1 Kings 11:7. . . . *Chemosh, the abomination of Moab . . .*

Heshbon

The conflict between Sihon and Moab presented a wonderful opportunity for the Israelites. Whereas Moab and Ammon were related tribes, according to the Biblical interpretation of events, and therefore untouchable, Sihon was a non-Hebrew and might be attacked. Or, to put it in less idealistic fashion, Moab and Ammon were settled kingdoms with well-fortified borders that it might be difficult to attack. Thus the chapter states:

Numbers 21:24. . . . *the border of the children of Ammon was strong.*

(It may be, however, that this verse is mistranslated and that the Hebrew word translated as "strong" refers to the town of Jazer, defining it as the boundary of Ammon.)

It would seem reasonable, though, that the region conquered by Sihon would be in a state of confusion and weakness. The strong points, overthrown and broken down by the Amorites, might not yet have been restored; and although the Amorites had cowed Moab into submission they might be in no condition now to face a new, fresh foe.

This proved, indeed, to be the case. Israel demanded passage through the land, something Sihon could not allow. When passage was refused, the Israelites attacked, and defeated the Amorites,

Numbers 21:24. . . . *and possessed his land from Arnon unto Jabbok . . .*

Numbers 21:25. *And Israel . . . dwelt in all the cities of the Amorites, in Heshbon . . .*

Heshbon was the chief city of the region and was located about twenty miles east of the northern tip of the Dead Sea. It is still there as a town in Jordan, with the Arabic name of Hesban.

Bashan

The Israelites had now established themselves firmly on the eastern bank of the Jordan and had a base from which to launch the conquest of Canaan itself. That base, however, had to be broadened as widely as possible. Assuming that Moab and Ammon must remain inviolate, there was still the fertile pastures north of Ammon. These were attractive to the Israelites.

Numbers 21:33. *And they turned and went up by the way of Bashan: and Og the king of Bashan went out against them . . . to the battle at Edrei.*

The exact borders of Bashan are uncertain but it was, in general, located to the east of the Sea of Galilee. It was for a long time a prosperous, fertile region, so much so that the quality of its cattle became proverbial in Biblical times—and through the Bible in our own times, too. In the 22nd Psalm, its cattle are used metaphorically to represent the intensity of woes besetting the psalmist:

Psalm 22:12. *Many bulls have compassed me: strong bulls of Bashan have beset me round.*

And the prophet Amos uses them to represent the prosperous and self-satisfied aristocrats of the nation:

Amos 4:1. *Hear this word, ye kine of Bashan . . .*

Bashan was also famous for its oaks. The prophet Ezekiel, in ironically listing the glories of the merchant city of Tyre before going on to prophesy its utter fall, describes the excellence of its ships by saying, in part,

Ezekiel 27:5. *Of the oaks of Bashan have they made thine oars . . .*

Bashan remained prosperous under shifting tides of political change until it was taken over by the Arabs in the seventh century A.D. After that, decline was rapid. Nowadays, the territory that was once Bashan makes up the southwestern corner of Syria, bordering Jordan to its south and Israel to its west. Edrei, the sight of the battle between Og and the Israelites, exists now as the town of Deraa, right on the Jordanian border, with a population of about four thousand.

The territory is now largely occupied by the Druses, a Mohammedan sect which, since its establishment about A.D. 1000, has managed to maintain its existence even against the far superior power of the Turks before World War I, or the French after it.

The conquest of Bashan was one of the events in early Israelite military history that most impressed the later writers, both Biblical and post-Biblical. Part of the reason is that Og, king of Bashan, was reputed to be a giant. This is based upon a statement in the Book of Deuteronomy, where Moses is pictured as reviewing the events following the Exodus:

> Deuteronomy 3:11. *For only Og king of Bashan remained of the remnant of giants; behold, his bedstead was a bedstead of iron . . . nine cubits was the length thereof and four cubits the breadth of it . . .*

Judging from measurements made on the ruins of the Temple at Jerusalem (whose measurements in cubits we know), it would seem that a cubit is equal to about seventeen and a half inches. In that case, Og's bed was about thirteen feet long and six feet wide.* A large bed, to be sure, though it need not be taken that Og's body had to fill it top to bottom and side to side.

Later rabbinical writers expanded on Og's size and made him the last of the Nephilim who lived before the Flood (see page 72). To survive the Flood, however, Og would have had to be in Noah's ark, into which he could not fit. The legendmakers have it, then, that he sat astride the ark and was fed by Noah till the waters fell.

This association of Og and the Flood (concerning which there is no Biblical evidence whatever) may have been helped along by the fact that the Greek myths had an ancient King Ogyges who reigned during a great deluge. It might have seemed reasonable (to legendmakers) to suppose that Og and Ogyges were different forms of the same name.

The manner of Og's legendary death is also dramatic. He raised a huge mountain to hurl at the Israelites and tripped and fell in the attempt. Thereupon, Moses himself leaped at him and killed him. It is very likely that this last picture of Og is borrowed from the semicomic Greek myth of the revolt of the giants against Zeus and the Olympians. Those giants hurled mountains (one of the mountains crashed into the sea, according to the tale, and became Sicily) but were slain anyway.

---

* There are large, iron-gray stones of basalt placed over primitive graves in the area east of Jordan, about the size indicated in the verse. If this is considered, metaphorically, as the final resting place or "bed" of a ruler or warrior, that might account for the rise of the legend of Og's gianthood.

Balaam

The fact that the Israelites had conquered Heshbon and Bashan was quite sufficient to alarm Moab. Even though its own territory had not been attacked, it had no assurance it was not next on the list. Besides, Moab could scarcely have failed to consider Heshbon, the recent conquest of Sihon, as its own territory, and the Israelites, having conquered it in turn, were certainly not planning to restore it to Moab.

Balak, the king of Moab, decided to weaken the Israelites by the more subtle means of the supernatural, rather than by outright attack.

Numbers 22:5. *He sent messengers therefore unto Balaam . . . to Pethor . . . saying . . .*

Numbers 22:6. *. . . curse me this people . . . for . . . he whom thou blessest is blessed, and he whom thou cursest is cursed.*

Apparently, Balaam was a well-known sorcerer or magician of his time, one who was believed to know the rites whereby supernatural help or harm could be called down and who had demonstrated his knowledge and skill, at least to the satisfaction of common report.

Balaam's fame in this respect can be regarded as widespread for his town of Pethor is usually accepted as being on the Euphrates, some four hundred miles north of Moab. It is identified with a town called "Pitru" in the Assyrian records and "Pedru" in the Egyptian records. (Some consider this distance too great to be plausible and suggest that the verse has undergone some distortion and that Balaam was really an Ammonite living only a few dozen miles north of Moab.)

Balaam's power was accepted even by the Israelites and nowhere in the Bible is Balaam's power to bless and curse derided. It is rather treated as a fortunate miracle that God chose to make Balaam's curses come to nothing.

Indeed, belief can be sufficient. If the Moabites were convinced of the efficacy of Balaam's curse on the Israelites, they would fight with more confidence and spirit in the battle that followed. And if the Israelites were likewise convinced, they would have been correspondingly disheartened and might well have been defeated and driven away by the Moabites.

According to the later view, Balaam served for hire and bestowed his blessing and curses not necessarily as inspired to do so by God, but in response to the fees he was offered by those who wished to employ him. Thus, in the book of Jude in the New Testament, Jude says:

> Jude 1:11. *Woe unto them! for they . . . ran greedily after the error of Balaam for reward . . .*

For this reason the expression "Balaamite" is used to describe someone who uses religion primarily as a money-making device.

Baal

Balak had to send several times for Balaam, who was reluctant to accept the commission. (The several-times-repeated journey is a point in favor of those who feel that Balaam's home was not very far removed from Moab. The story of the missions is not entirely self-consistent and was probably derived from two separate and somewhat conflicting sources.)

Eventually Balaam did saddle up for the journey to Moab and on that journey occurred the famous incident of his talking ass. An angel blocked the way; an angel that the ass carrying Balaam could see but Balaam himself could not. When the ass balked, Balaam beat him and the ass spoke up in its own defense. This is one of the two incidents in the Bible in which an animal is depicted as speaking. (The serpent in Eden is the other.) The miraculous nature of this incident is such that later legends described the ass's mouth as one of the objects specially created in the initial week of creation for use in later history.

Once Balaam arrived in Moab, Balak hastened to place him where his curses might be most effective; in the mountain heights near Heaven where the gods might best hear him and where the power of his words could best fan out over the Israelites whom he was to curse:

> Numbers 22:41. . . . *Balak took Balaam and brought him up into the high places of Baal, that thence he might see . . . part of the* [Israelite] *people.*

The phrase "high places of Baal" is a translation of the Hebrew *Bamoth-Baal*, which later, in the Book of Joshua, is mentioned as a town in Moab. The town was located in the highlands, however, and was named in honor of Baal because the site was associated with important religious rites. The effect is therefore the same whether one speaks of "Bamoth-Baal" or of "the high places of Baal."

The word *baal* meant, in the various Semitic languages, "master" or "owner," sometimes in a very mundane sense. In the Book of Exodus, one finds:

> Exocus 21:28. . . . *the owner of the ox shall be quit.*

and "owner" is here the translation of the Hebrew word *baal*.

"Baal" was also used as a common title for Semitic deities with the precise connotation of the English "Lord." It was never used as the specific name of any idol. Indeed, the Israelites used the word as a title for Yahveh at least up through the time of David. Thus, one of the sons of King Saul (who was always depicted as a sincere Yahvist) was named Ishbaal or "man of the Lord," and one of his grandsons, Merib-baal or "hero of the Lord."

The word *baal* was so frequently used for idols, however, that the later Biblical writers could not look upon it as simply "Lord" or apply it, under any circumstance, to Yahveh. The term *Adonai* for "Lord" succeeded *baal* and in time, it became even disgraceful to use the earlier term. When the name Ishbaal had to be written, for instance, Ishbosheth was used instead:

> 2 Samuel 2:8. . . . *Abner . . . took Ish-bosheth the son of Saul, and brought him over to Mahanaim;*

Bosheth meant "shame" and was used to indicate what was considered a shameful word. The effect is the same as our own habit of sometimes using asterisks to fill out an improper word. It is as though we were to write "Ishbaal" as "Ish****."

Pisgah

Unfortunately, for the Moabites, Balaam found himself unable to curse the Israelites. Under the direct inspiration of God, according to the Biblical account, his attempts to curse were converted into blessings. Balak desperately sought other posts which might prove more efficacious:

> Numbers 23:14. *And he* [Balak] *brought him* [Balaam] . . . *to the top of Pisgah* . . .
>
> . . . .
>
> Numbers 23:28. *And Balak brought Balaam unto the top of Peor* . . .

Mount Pisgah is nowadays identified with a peak only six miles southwest of Heshbon and perhaps twelve miles east of the northern end of the Dead Sea. It is twenty miles north of the Arnon River and if the identification is correct, it makes it obvious that Moabite forces were edging into the territory recently conquered by the Israelites—perhaps while the main force of the latter was occupied in Bashan.

Mount Pisgah is 2644 feet high, or just about half a mile. Mount Peor, which has no certain identification, was probably somewhat north of Pisgah, so that although Peor was not quite as high a peak as Pisgah, it was closer to the enemy. An alternate name of Pisgah is Nebo and under the latter name it is most famous as the place of burial of Moses.

Unicorn

Balaam's inability to curse continued at all stations. From Mount Pisgah, Balaam praised God, saying:

> Numbers 23:22. *God brought them out of Egypt; he* [Israel] *hath as it were the strength of an unicorn.*

The Bible mentions the unicorn on several other occasions, notably in the Book of Job:

> Job 39:9. *Will the unicorn be willing to serve thee, or abide by thy crib?*

The Hebrew word represented in the King James Version by "unicorn" is *re'em*, which undoubtedly refers to the wild ox (*urus* or *aurochs*) ancestral to the domesticated cattle of today. The *re'em* still flourished in early historical times and a few existed into modern times although it is now extinct. It was a dangerous creature of great strength and was similar in form and temperament to the Asian buffaloes.

The Revised Standard Version translates *re'em* always as "wild ox." The verse in Numbers is translated as "they have as it were the horns of the wild ox," while the one in Job is translated "Is the wild ox willing to serve you?" The Anchor Bible translates the verse in Job as "Will the buffalo deign to serve you?"

The wild ox was a favorite prey of the hunt-loving Assyrian monarchs (the animal was called *rumu* in Assyrian, essentially the same word as *re'em*) and was displayed in their large bas-reliefs. Here the wild ox was invariably shown in profile and only one horn was visible. One can well imagine that the animal represented in this fashion would come to be called "one-horn" as a familar nickname, much as we might refer to "longhorns" in speaking of a certain breed of cattle.

As the animal itself grew less common under the pressure of increasing human population and the depredations of the hunt, it might come to be forgotten that there was a second horn hidden behind the first in the sculptures and "one-horn" might come to be considered a literal description of the animal.

When the first Greek translation of the Bible was prepared about 250 B.C. the animal was already rare in the long-settled areas of the Near East and the Greeks, who had had no direct experience with it, had no word for it. They used a translation of "one-horn" instead and it became *monokeros*. In Latin and in English it became the Latin word for "one-horn"; that is, "unicorn."

The Biblical writers could scarcely have had the intention of implying that the wild ox literally had one horn. There is one Biblical quotation, in fact, that clearly contradicts that notion. In the Book of Deuteronomy, when Moses is giving his final blessing to each tribe, he speaks of the tribe of Joseph (Ephraim and Manasseh) as follows:

Deuteronomy 33:17. *His glory is like the firstling of his bullock, and his horns are like the horns of unicorns . . .*

Here the word unicorn is placed in the plural since the thought of a "one-horn's" single horn seems to make the phrase "horns of a unicorn" self-contradictory. Still, the original Hebrew has the word in the singular so that we must speak of the "horns of a unicorn," which makes it clear that a unicorn has more than one horn. In addition, the parallelism used in Hebrew poetry makes it natural to equate "unicorn" and "bullock," showing that the unicorn is something very much resembling a young bull. The Revised Standard Version has, in this verse, the phrase "the horns of a wild ox."

And yet the fact that the Bible speaks of a unicorn seemed, through most of history, to place the seal of divine assurance upon the fact that a one-horned animal existed. The unicorn is therefore commonplace in legends and stories.

This is especially so since travelers in Greek times spoke of a one-horned beast that existed in India, and assigned great powers to the single horn of that animal. For instance, a cup made out of the horn of such a beast rendered harmless any poisonous liquid that might be poured into it.

There is, indeed, a one-horned beast in India (as well as in Malaya, Sumatra, and Africa) and this is the rhinoceros (from Greek words meaning "nose-horn"). The horn on its snout is not a true horn but is a concretion of hair; nevertheless, the concretion looks like a horn and fulfills the purpose of one. It is very likely that the rhinoceros is the Greek unicorn, although its horn scarcely possesses the magic qualities attributed to it in legend.

Since the rhinoceros is one of the largest land animals still alive, and is possessed of enormous strength, it might be thought to fit the description in the Bible. Some Latin translations of the Bible therefore convert the Greek *monokeros* into "rhinoceros." But this is farfetched. It is very unlikely that the Biblical writer knew of the rhinoceros and they certainly knew of the wild ox.

The unicorn entered European legend without reference to the rhinoceros, which was as unknown to the medieval Westerner as to the Biblical Israelite. The shape of the unicorn was, to the European, whatever fancy pleased to make it, and it is most familiar to us now as a rather horselike creature with a single long horn on its forehead. In this shape, two unicorns were depicted as supporting the royal arms of Scotland. When Scotland and England were combined under the House of Stuart in 1603, the Scottish unicorns joined the English lions on the coat of arms of what now became Great Britain.

The old enmity between the two nations is reflected in the nursery rhyme "The lion and the unicorn were fighting for the crown." The fact that it is an English rhyme and that England usually won the wars, though never conclusively, is signified by the second line, "The lion beat the unicorn all around the town."

The most distinctive feature of this modern unicorn is its horn, which is long, thin, slowly tapering, and a straight helix. It has precisely the shape and dimensions, in fact, of the single tooth of the male of a species of whale called the narwhal. This tooth takes the shape of a tusk, sometimes twenty feet long.

Undoubtedly, sailors occasionally obtained such tusks and then sold them to landlubbers for great sums by claiming each to be the horn of a unicorn with all the magical virtue of that object.

The Daughters of Moab

Though neither force nor enchantments had removed the Israelite danger from Moab, mere propinquity seemed on the point of becoming sufficient for the purpose. The Israelites, with their years of wandering through wilderness, had not been able to develop elaborate rituals and they found themselves fascinated by the enticing rites of the more sophisticated religions of settled city-dwellers:

> Numbers 25:1. And Israel . . . began to commit whoredom with the daughters of Moab.
> Numbers 25:2. And they [the Moabite women] called the people unto the sacrifices of their gods . . .
> Numbers 25:3 And Israel joined himself unto Baal-Peor . . .

where Baal-Peor ("the Lord of Mount Peor") was, presumably, Chemosh.

The apostasy of the Israelites is, according to the Biblical story, punished by a plague, and by firm measures on the part of Moses, who ordered the slaughter of the idolaters. Equating national gods with something of the emotions borne by national flags today, the horror of the Biblical writers at this event might be compared to our own feelings if we discovered a sizable segment of our own population gathering in time of war to salute the enemy flag and to sing the enemy anthem.

Nor was this trespass with respect to Chemosh considered an accident. It was supposed to be a deliberate policy on the part of the Moabites (following the advice of Balaam) to use their women for the purpose of seducing the Israelites to apostasy. Thus, Moses, in a later verse, is described as saying of foreign women:

> Numbers 31:16. *Behold, these caused the children of Israel, through the counsel of Balaam, to commit trespass against the Lord* . . .

The memory of this incident strengthened the position of the more intransigeant Yahvists in later history against intermarriage with foreign women.

Gilead

After the episode of Balaam and the incident of the seduction of the Israelites by Moab, it might be expected that war between Moab and Israel would be described. Instead, it is Midian that is attacked by Israel. The Midianite tribes of the eastern desert are described as having been in alliance with Moab against Israel, as having participated in the call to Balaam, and the Midianite women are also described as seducing Israelites.

This tale of war against the Midianites has its difficulties, however, and it is commonly thought to be unhistorical. It may perhaps be a pious invention of later times to mask an actual war fought inconclusively against Moab. After all, Moab remained in being and in control of the territory east of the Dead Sea for centuries. By failing to mention any war with Moab the Biblical writers could continue to maintain the position that the Israelites did not attack any Hebrew tribe.

Yet even with Moab in existence, the Israelites remained in occupation of most of the area east of the Jordan River and the Sea of Galilee. Part of this was Ammonite territory but the Bible is silent as to the fate of the Ammonites in this period. The Israelites are not described as attacking the Ammonites, a Hebrew people, yet their territory was soon to be settled by Israelite tribes. Indeed, part of the confederacy was eying the territory even in Moses' lifetime while the projected conquest of Canaan proper had not yet begun:

> Numbers 32:1. *Now the children of Reuben and the children of Gad had a very great multitude of cattle: and when they saw . . . the land of Gilead . . . behold, the place was a place for cattle;*

The boundaries of Gilead are indefinite but at its broadest, it covers the whole of the area east of the Jordan River; the "Trans-Jordan" we might call it.

Gilead had appeared earlier in the Biblical account. When Jacob had left Laban to return to Canaan, Laban pursued him and caught up with him in Gilead for a final interview:

> Genesis 31:23. *And he* [Laban] *. . . pursued after him* [Jacob] *seven days journey; and . . . overtook him in the mount Gilead.*

Mount Gilead could refer to the range of highlands running down the eastern side of the Jordan, or to a particularly prominent peak in that range just south of the Jabbok River and about twelve miles east of the Jordan. It is some 3600 feet high.

The tribes requesting the land had first to convince Moses that they were not proposing to quit the confederacy. They would participate in the conquest of Canaan and would return to their Trans-Jordanian holdings only after that conquest was assured. Once that was made plain, Moses permitted the allotment.

Gilead was, in consequence, divided among the cattle-owning tribes of Reuben and Gad. Reuben took the area south of Heshbon and north of Moab, while Gad had virtually the entire east bank of the Jordan. Bashan fell to the lot of part of the tribe of Manasseh (another portion of which occupied territory in Canaan proper).

In one sense, the Trans-Jordan was a good location, for the area was described as rich and desirable. It was, however, also exposed. Reuben was under the perpetual shadow of Moab and quickly faded out of Israelite history, probably through absorption into Moabite culture. Gad and Manasseh were exposed to raids from the Ammonites and the Midianites, and later had to bear the first brunt of the more serious assaults of the Syrian and Assyrian armies in the latter days of the Israelite kingdom.

The name Gilead may be a corruption of Gad (which occupied much of it) or vice versa. On the other hand, the Biblical genealogies have Gilead a grandson of Manasseh:

> Numbers 26:26. *Of the sons of Manasseh: . . . Machir . . . and Machir begat Gilead . . .*

There may be some connection between this eponymous ancestor of the body of men known as "Gileadites," the land itself, and the fact that a portion of the tribe of Manasseh occupied part of Gilead.

Just as Bashan was particularly known for its cattle, so Gilead was famous for the resinous products of some of its trees and shrubs; products which could be turned into soothing, fragrant ointments and used as skin softeners, cosmetics, perfumes, and incense.

This balsam, or balm, of Gilead was highly valued. When Joseph's brothers were planning to sell him for a slave it was to a party of traders to whom they sold him and they:

> Genesis 37:25. . . . *came from Gilead with their camels bearing spicery and balm and myrrh, going to carry it down to Egypt.*

When the prophet Jeremiah pleads with the people to return to the Lord, pointing out that the remedy to all their evils is in their midst only waiting for them, he makes use of the metaphorical (and rhetorical) question:

> Jeremiah 8:22. *Is there no balm in Gilead . . .*

The question is intended to have the obvious answer, yes! So, reasons Jeremiah, is God present for the relief of His people.

5. DEUTERONOMY

Deuteronomy

The fifth book of the Bible begins:

> Deuteronomy 1:1. *These be the words which Moses spake* . . .

In Hebrew, the opening phrase is *Elleh haddebarim* and that, or the
briefer form "Debarim" ("words") is the Hebrew name of the book.

The book does not advance Israelite history but purports to be the
record of a series of addresses given by Moses on the eve of his death
and of the Israelite entry into Canaan. These addresses recapitulate
the events of the Exodus and restate key portions of the law as it was
received from Sinai.

One might suppose that it was for this reason that the Greek-speaking
translaters of the Septuagint named the book "Deuteronomion" (which
became our own Deuteronomy) or "second law."

Actually, however, the Greek name arose through a misapprehension.
In the course of his discourses, Moses enjoins strict obedience to the
law on the part of the future kings of Israel:

> Deuteronomy 17:18. . . . *when he* [the king] *sitteth upon the
> throne of his kingdom* . . . *he shall write him a copy of this law* . . .
> Deuteronomy 17:19. *And it shall be with him, and he shall read
> therein* . . . *that he may learn* . . . *to keep all the words of this
> law* . . .

The phrase in verse 18, "a copy of this law" was incorrectly translated
in the Septuagint as *deuteronomion* ("a second law") and it is from
this that our name derives.

Canaan Before the Conquest

The bulk of Deuteronomy is neither J, E, nor P, but represents a fourth major source of the Hexateuch. It seems quite likely that Deuteronomy is the one book of the Hexateuch that existed in essentially its present fashion before the Exile.

At least, Deuteronomy, or part of it, is usually identified with "the book of the law" discovered in the Temple in 621 B.C. during the reign of King Josiah:

> 2 Kings 22:8. *And Hilkiah the high priest said unto Shaphan the scribe, I have found the book of the law in the house of the Lord* . . .

This came at a time when there was periodic strife between the temporal and spiritual power in the kingdom and when there had been two recent reigns that were disastrous for the Yahvists. On the other hand, there was now an impressionable young king on the throne, Josiah.

Perhaps it occurred to some among the priesthood to prepare an organized exposition of the laws which, in Yahvist eyes, ought to govern the king and the people, writing into it a clear spiritual supremacy. This writing, as the "book of the law" was then providentially "discovered" in the Temple and brought to the king. The doctrine, placed in the mouth of Moses, treated as of great antiquity, and put forward most eloquently, was bound to impress the king.

It did, and the priestly plan succeeded in full. Until then, Yahvism had been a minority sect, often persecuted, and sometimes in danger of being wiped out altogether. Now, for the first time, it assumed an ascendancy, and, thanks to the enthusiastic co-operation of Josiah, it was made the official religion of the land.

There was backsliding after Josiah's death, but Yahvism had been made powerful enough to meet the challenge of the Exile, which followed soon after. The Yahvistic priests, during the Exile, as they edited the old traditions and codified the laws, incorporated Deuteronomy virtually intact into the Hexateuch.

After the Exile, Yahvism, the minority sect, had become Judaism, the national religion of the people. Through its daughter religions, Christianity and Islam, Yahvism came to dominate the religious life of well over a billion people in the time that has passed since then. If Deuteronomy is dealt with briefly in this book because it is not primarily concerned with history, that does not mean it may not be the most important part of the Bible in some ways; or even the most important piece of writing in the world.

Lebanon

Moses begins his recapitulation of events at Sinai with God's instructions that the Israelites leave for Canaan. The boundaries of Canaan as assigned to them by God are given, and these are the ideal boundaries which, in the north particularly, were only very temporarily achieved at Israel's brief peak of power two centuries after the conquest:

> Deuteronomy 1:7. . . . *unto Lebanon, unto . . . the river Euphrates.*
> Deuteronomy 1:8. *Behold, I have set the land before you . . .*

Lebanon referred originally to two mountain ranges north of Canaan running parallel to the Mediterranean coast; one about twenty miles inland and the other about forty miles inland, each about a hundred miles long. These are higher than the highlands of Canaan, and have some peaks up to two miles high. The Lebanese mountains are therefore more notable for their snowy peaks than are any of the heights in Canaan and it is from that, apparently, that the mountain ranges and the land in which they are found get their names. "Lebanon" is from the Hebrew word for "white."

The Greeks distorted the name somewhat and called the mountain range nearer the sea the "Libanus" and the one farther inland the "Anti-Libanus." Between is a valley, about ten miles wide, which the Greeks called "Coele-Syria." Literally, this is "hollow Syria" and means, in freer translation, "the valley of Syria."

In post-Biblical times, the area around the Lebanese ranges was the home of a Christian sect, the Maronites, which persisted (under severe persecution at times) through the long centuries of Mohammedan domination. When the area was freed of Turkish rule, the French (who took over Syria as a mandate under the League of Nations) established Lebanon as a district separate from the rest of Syria, thanks to its difference in religion. In 1944, when independence came to the mandate, the region became a separate and independent state, the Lebanese Republic.

Modern Lebanon is a small nation, about twice as large as Delaware, and has a population of about 2,200,000. It lies directly north of modern Israel and the two are the only non-Moslem powers in a sea of Arabic states.

Just as Bashan was known for its bulls and oaks, and Gilead for its balm, Lebanon was known for its forests of cedar. Cedarwood is fragrant and makes excellent building material. Solomon built much of the Temple and of his palace out of cedar:

> 1 Kings 7:2. *He built also the house* [his palace] *of the forest of Lebanon . . . upon four rows of cedar pillars, with cedar beams upon the pillars.*

The cedar tree was looked upon as a particularly stately and magnificent tree, rivaling the oak as king of the forest.

During the time of the judges, Jotham, the lone survivor of a massacred family, addressed those who had helped conduct the massacre in a fable intended to imply that the worst people were now ruling the land. These he represented by the bramble, and he went on to point out that such a lowly object in its vainglory would not hesitate to attack the highest and best. He has the bramble say:

> Judges 9:15. . . . *and if not, let fire come out of the bramble, and devour the cedars of Lebanon.*

Similarly, Isaiah, in warning the proud and haughty to beware God's judgment (in "the day of the Lord"), uses both the cedars of Lebanon and the oaks of Bashan as metaphors for haughty pride.

> Isaiah 2:12. *For the day of the Lord . . . shall be upon every one that is proud and lofty . . .*
> Isaiah 2:13. *And upon all the cedars of Lebanon . . . and upon all the oaks of Bashan,*

The beauty and fragrance of the cedars and of their wood, and the use of cedar in temples and palaces, lent a glamorous glow to Lebanon generally, and this is made full use of in the Song of Solomon.

> Song of Solomon 4:8. *Come with me from Lebanon, my spouse . . .*
> Song of Solomon 4:11. . . . *the smell of thy garments is like the smell of Lebanon.*

And the loved one is described as:

> Song of Solomon 4:15. *A fountain of gardens, a well of living waters, and streams from Lebanon.*

The Island of Caphtor

Caphtor

Moses goes on to describe the route followed by the Israelites from Sinai to the Jordan, then pauses to tell something of the prehistory of Canaan. He describes the tribes that were evicted from their territory by the invading Edomites, Moabites, and Ammonites (presumably in the period of Ikhnaton.) The pre-Hebrew tribes are described, in accordance with later legends, as giants (see page 72).

In the list, however, are the Avim, who were displaced by a non-Hebrew people:

Deuteronomy 2:23. *And the Avims which dwelt in Hazerim, even unto Azzah, the Caphtorims, which came forth out of Caphtor, destroyed them, and dwelt in their stead.*

The district spoken of is the southern portion of the seacoast of Canaan. The town Azzah is taken to be Gaza, for instance, and that is near the southern edge of what, in the next stage of Israelite history, was to be Philistine territory. The Philistines did take the area at the time of the Exodus or shortly before and they ruled there in the centuries afterward. It seems certain then that by Caphtorim are meant the Philistines.

For further Biblical evidence, we find that the prophet Amos makes the identification when he quotes God as saying:

Amos 9:7. . . . *Have not I brought up . . . the Philistines from Caphtor . . .*

and Jeremiah does the same when he says:

Jeremiah 47:4. . . . *the Lord will spoil the Philistines the remnant of the country of Caphtor.*

The question then is: Where is Caphtor?

Unlike the other groups who established kingdoms over sections of Canaan and surrounding regions at this time, the Caphtorim (Philistines) established themselves on the seacoast. They, it would seem, invaded from the sea, rather than from Arabia. Indeed, it seems almost inevitable to conclude that they were part of the Peoples of the Sea who, in Merneptah's reign, were raiding the Egyptian coast. This may be an important hint as to the identity of Caphtor, since the Peoples of the Sea were, in part at least, of Greek origin.

This is borne out by the fact that the Israelites always spoke of the Philistines, particularly, as being "uncircumcised." Circumcision was a rite that was by no means confined to the Israelites. It was practiced among the ancient Egyptians and among most of the Semites of the western portion of the Fertile Crescent (the latter, perhaps, through Egyptian cultural influence.)

Abraham is described as not having been circumcised until he was well advanced in years:

Genesis 17:24. *And Abraham was ninety years old and nine, when he was circumcised . . .*

but, according to the Biblical story, Abraham was an east-Semite by birth. His circumcision can be viewed as the adoption of a west-Semitic rite.

The Philistines remained uncircumcised and it is tempting to think of them, then, as being neither Egyptian nor west-Semitic in culture and that leaves the strong possibility of their being Greek.

What, then, was the situation of the Greek world at the time of the Exodus, and before?

About 2000 B.C., in the time of Abraham, the Greeks entered the peninsula which is now called Greece. They found to the south, on the island of Crete (about sixty miles off the southeastern tip of Greece), an already advanced civilization. This was the Minoan civilization, named for the legendary King Minos of Crete.

The Greeks occupied the Greek peninsula and absorbed the Minoan culture, building strong cities of their own on that peninsula. These early Greeks may be referred to as Mycenaeans because one of their chief cities was Mycenae.

The Mycenaeans expanded vigorously at the expense of the declining Minoan culture and by 1400 B.C., shortly before the time of Ikhnaton, the original Minoans no longer formed a separate and distinct people. Even in Crete itself, the Greek language prevailed.

The Mycenaeans, soon after 1400 B.C., were beginning to feel the push of new waves of barbarians from the interior, including less civilized tribes of Greek-speaking peoples, and were themselves in increasing turmoil. Armed bands, seeking new homes after their old ones were ravaged, or merely seeking to carve out new dominions in place of a growingly insecure home base, made up strong contingents of the Peoples of the Sea.

The Mycenaeans of the Greek mainland were close to Asia Minor and they invaded that peninsula. The tale of the war against Troy seems to be a distant memory of that invasion. The Trojan War may have initiated (or been part of) the general turmoil on that peninsula that led to the final destruction of the Hittite Empire.

Could it be then that armed bands from Crete fanned southward to Egypt and eastward to Canaan, and that Caphtor refers to the island of Crete? Most Biblical scholars are content to think so.

Of course, not everything about the Philistines is Greek. In language and customs they are largely Semitic. The names of their cities, their kings, and their gods are Semitic words. This may represent a certain assimilation of west-Semitic culture after the invasion, but it may also indicate that the original invasion was at least partly Semitic to begin with.

Is this possible? Yes, it is, even if Caphtor was Crete. Greek myths make the Cretan king, Minos, the son of Europa, a princess from a portion of the Canaanite coast called by the Greeks Phoenicia. The Canaanite princess had been brought to Crete by Zeus in the guise of a bull.

This may be the mythical reminiscence of the days when trade and cultural exchange between the Minoan and Canaanite civilizations was rich and full. The Minoan civilization might even have stemmed in part from the older Canaanite civilization.

Nor was this fusion long-distance only. Both Minoans and Canaanites were in those days a seagoing people. At the height of Minoan power, the Cretan navy dominated the eastern Mediterranean and Cretan ships brought Minoan products and Minoan culture to the island of Cyprus, 350 miles to the east, and to the southern regions of the Asia Minor coast, which in spots is only fifty miles north of Cyprus. Canaanite (Phoenician) colonies were also established on Cyprus and throughout Biblical times, Cyprus remained part Greek and part Canaanite in culture.

Could it be, then, that the Israelites and Greeks, both heir to a kind of fused Minoan-Canaanite culture, are first cousins culturally speaking? Some archaeologists feel themselves attracted to this rather startling possibility.

Can it also be that the Caphtorim who invaded the southern coast of Canaan were not raiders from distant Crete, but from the much closer Cyprus and its environs? In that case Caphtor would be Cyprus and the raiders might have a Minoan-Canaanite culture, fusing Semitic language with a lack of circumcision.

Tiny, uncertain clues come from the fact that in Egyptian inscriptions, the term "Kafto" is used for a region that seems to include the southern coast of Asia Minor. Arguing on the other side, however, is the fact that the name for the inhabitants of Cyprus, as given in the Old Testament, seems to be "Chittim" or "Kittim."

This name seems to be derived from Kition (Citium, in Latin), a city on the southeastern coast of Cyprus and the chief center of

Canaanite (Phoenician) culture on the island. It is possible that a name meant for the chief city eventually spread out to include the entire island, displacing the older name of Caphtor.

Mount Hermon

Moses then describes the manner in which the Israelites conquered the district about Heshbon, and defeated Og of Bashan:

> Deuteronomy 3:8. *And we took . . . the land . . . from the river of Arnon unto Mount Hermon.*

Mount Hermon makes a good landmark for the northern edge of Canaan, so that to say "unto Mount Hermon" is like saying "to the northern limits of Canaan." Mount Hermon, about forty miles north of the Sea of Galilee, is a peak in the Anti-Libanus range; indeed, the highest peak, being 9232 feet high. Its modern name is Jebel esh Sheikh and it is on the border between Lebanon and Syria, about fifteen miles northeast of the northern border of modern Israel.

Rabbath

In telling of the crowning victory over Og, mention is made of Og's giant bedstead (see page 182):

> Deuteronomy 3:11. . . . *his bedstead was a bedstead of iron; is it not in Rabbath of the children of Ammon? . . .*

This city is sometimes referred to as Rabbath-ammon, to differentiate it from other cities of the same name elsewhere (as we would say Portland, Maine, to distinguish it from Portland, Oregon). An alternate spelling is Rabbah.

Rabbath was an important city of the trans-Jordan area, and lay about fifteen miles northeast of Heshbon. It was the chief city of the Ammonites and in that city the memory of the Ammonites survives although the tribe itself has long since vanished. The town, under the name of Amman, survives today as the capital of Jordan and has a population of some 250,000.

Mount Gerizim

After enumerating again the laws delivered from Mount Sinai, Moses warns the Israelites that there is both a blessing and a curse involved; a blessing if they are obedient to the law and a curse if they are not. Once they enter Canaan, they are to accede to this fact by solemn ritual in a specific spot:

> Deuteronomy 11:29. . . . *thou shalt put the blessing upon mount Gerizim and the curse upon mount Ebal.*

Gerizim and Ebal were the two mountains that flanked the narrow valley in which Shechem was located (see page 99), Gerizim on the south and Ebal on the north. They are not high mountains, the former being a bit less than 3000 feet high, the latter a bit more than 3000.

Later in Deuteronomy, in the twenty-seventh chapter, Moses describes in detail how, after the conquest of Canaan, the tribes shall distribute themselves on Mount Gerizim and Mount Ebal, one group to pronounce blessings and the other to pronounce curses. No doubt this reflects the religious importance of the area of Shechem in pre-Israelite days and marks the aura of sanctity that lingered over the area even after the Israelite conquest. This was true particularly of Mount Gerizim, which was associated with the blessings.

Among the later Jews, all holy places were gradually subordinated to and eventually swallowed by the Temple at Jerusalem, but Mount Gerizim continued as *the* sacred mountain to the sect of the Samaritans prominent in the region in New Testament times.

Belial

Moses goes on to warn the Israelites against the dangers of false prophets and of those who would worship other gods. He warns against:

> Deuteronomy 13:13. . . . *children of Belial . . . saying, Let us go and serve other gods . . .*

The word *belial* means, literally, "not profitable." Something that is *belial* is worthless and empty; "children of Belial" are people whose views and opinions are worthless and empty, and therefore not to be listened to.

It is a short step from considering something worthless to considering it wicked. We have a similar case in English. The word "naughty" originally meant worthless or empty, or something that "contained or was worth naught," but came to mean wicked (although today it has degenerated to the point where it merely describes troublesome children).

The use of *belial* untranslated, especially if it is left capitalized, as in the King James Version, tempts one into thinking of Belial as a spirit of evil, perhaps as the devil himself. This is avoided in the Revised Standard Version, which substitutes "base fellows" for "children of Belial."

Nevertheless, it is not only moderns who come to consider Belial the name of a demon. By New Testament times, the Jews had come to do just this and Belial had become a synonym for Satan. Thus, in the Second Epistle to the Corinthians, the Apostle Paul asks:

> 2 Corinthians 6:15. *And what concord hath Christ with Belial?* . . .

Saints

The last words ascribed to Moses in Deuteronomy make up a poem containing short comments on each of the tribes, praising them, or giving some intimation of the role they were to play in the time of the kingdoms. The poem ("the blessing of Moses") begins with an invocation of God:

> Deuteronomy 33:2. *And he* [Moses] *said, The Lord came from Sinai, and rose up from Seir* . . . *he shined forth from mount Paran, and he came with ten thousands of saints* . . .

The word "saint" is from the Latin *sanctus*, meaning "holy." That which is sanctified or holy is reserved for God and is withdrawn from worldly uses. The word "saints" in the verse just quoted is a translation of the Hebrew word *kadesh* but that can mean either a "holy person" or a "holy place." Thus, the town at which the Israelites camped for many years was Kadesh-barnea ("the holy place of Barnea").

It may be, then, that, with the parallelism of Hebrew poetry, the verse names the place at which God appears (the mountains south of Canaan) in slightly different ways: Sinai, Seir, Paran, and finally Meri-bath-Kadesh (some region near Kadesh-barnea). This is not in the least farfetched for there is such a place, mentioned only four verses earlier, with a slightly different spelling:

Deuteronomy 32:51. . . . *ye* [Moses] *trespassed against me* [God] *among the children of Israel at the waters of Meribah-Kadesh.*

The translation of the place name into "ten thousands of saints" thus gives an erroneous picture.

In the Psalms, the expression "saints" usually refers to godly, pious people, very much in the modern manner, and is a translation of *hasid* ("pious"). Thus:

Psalm 31:23. *O love the Lord, all ye his saints . . .*

In the time of the persecution of the Jews by the Seleucid king Antiochus IV, in 170 B.C. and afterward, the beleaguered Jews began to picture themselves as a people devoted to God and surrounded by hordes of evil idolaters. All believing Jews were *kadesh* and could be referred to in translation as "saints." When Daniel predicts that the Jews will eventually be secure, and glory in an ideal kingdom set up by God, he says:

Daniel 7:18. *But the saints of the most High shall take the king-dom . . .*

In the New Testament, Paul commonly takes the same view of the beleaguered early Christians. To him, writing in Greek, they are *oi hagioi* ("the holy ones" or "the saints"). Thus:

Philippians 1:1. *Paul and Timotheus . . . to all the saints . . . which are at Philippi . . .*

The Blessing of Moses

Like the earlier blessing of Jacob (see page 116), the blessing of Moses seems to be a collection of traditional sayings, assigned in retrospect to an early personage. Of the two, the blessing of Moses seems to be the later, and is appropriately ascribed, therefore, to the later personage.

For one thing the reference to Joseph in the blessing of Jacob makes no reference to the separate tribes of Ephraim and Manasseh. The blessing of Moses does, however, speaking of:

> Deuteronomy 33:17. . . . *the ten thousands of Ephraim, and the thousands of Manasseh.*

The fact that Joseph and Levi receive the longest and most glowing blessing would indicate that the sayings were collected and put into final form by priestly hands in the northern kingdom of Israel, which was dominated by the Joseph tribes and, in particular, by the "ten thousands" of the more populous Ephraim. In that case, this would have had to be done before the destruction of the northern kingdom in 722 B.C.

This is further indicated by the fact that the tribe of Judah is given brief and rather cool notice:

> Deuteronomy 33:7. . . . *let his hands be sufficient for him; and be thou an help to him from his enemies.*

No mention is made of Judah's kingship. This is natural if the sayings were collected in the northern kingdom after it had split away from Judean domination and would certainly not recognize the validity of the Davidic kingship. In the blessing of Jacob, however, much is made of the Judean kingship, which would indicate that that collection dated back to the time of the undivided kingdom—about 950 B.C. perhaps.

The blessing of Moses indicates further the decline of the tribes of Reuben and Simeon, of which signs are present even in the earlier blessing of Jacob.

Simeon is not mentioned at all in the blessing of Moses. The tribe has lost its tribal identity, has been absorbed into Judah, and is completely dismissed by the northern sources. Of Reuben, all that can be said is:

> Deuteronomy 33:6. *Let Reuben live, and not die; and let not his men be few.*

But even this palliates the actual situation for the word "not" was added by the pious translators of the King James Version, who would not let Moses say something that sounded like a curse. However, the word "not" is not present in the original Hebrew.

Catholic versions translate the verse: "May Ruben live and not die out, but let his men be few." This represents the actual situation in early tribal times and by the time of the kingdoms, Reuben *did* die out, having been absorbed by Moab.

—With the conclusion of the speeches in the book of Deuteronomy, Moses is taken to the top of Mount Nebo/Mount Pisgah, views Canaan, which he is not to be allowed to enter, dies, and is buried. His eventful life thus comes to its close.

6. JOSHUA

JOSHUA · JERICHO · GILGAL · THE WALL [OF JERICHO] · AI · GIBEON ·
AJALON · MEROM · ZIDON · THE PHILISTINES · THE TRIBES · MOUNT
EPHRAIM

Joshua

To the Jews, the first five books of the Bible ("The Law") make up
the first of the three grand divisions of the Old Testament. The second division includes twenty-one books that together make up "the
Prophets." Of these, the first six, which are primarily historical, are "the
early Prophets" and, the Book of Joshua, named for the general
whose actions dominate the events it describes, is the first.

However, Joshua is made up of the same sources as the five books of
the Law, was put into final written form at the same time, apparently,
by the same priestly groups, and brings the theme of the first five
books to a climax. There is thus plenty of justification in treating the
first six books (the Hexateuch) as a unit. (The rabbinical tradition
that Joshua himself wrote the book can be ignored.)

The Book of Joshua describes an idealized version of the conquest
of Canaan—a conquest that brings to a triumphant climax God's promise of Canaan to the descendants of Abraham, as described in Genesis.

The Israelite army, under unified leadership, is pictured as conquering the entire land in a brilliant set of campaigns. Actually, as would
appear from other evidence in the Bible itself, the conquest was far
more disorganized, gradual, and imperfect than that. Still, the key
incidents in Joshua, though made neat and glossy by priestly piety at
the time of the Exile (some seven centuries after the events described
in Joshua), may well reflect traditions that in turn represent actual
events.

The Conquest of Canaan

Jericho

The Book of Joshua begins at the moment of the death of Moses, with Joshua ben Nun, who, until then, had been Moses' military aide, promoted to commander in chief. It is after Joshua that the book is named, of course.

The City of Jericho

At once, Joshua made preparations to launch an offensive into Canaan.

> Joshua 2:1. *And Joshua . . . sent out of Shittim two men to spy secretly, saying, Go view the land, even Jericho . . .*

Jericho was a fortified town in the Jordan valley, five miles west of the Jordan itself and some fifteen miles northeast of Jerusalem. It is situated 850 feet below sea level and shares the semitropical temperatures of the Jordan valley generally.

Jericho is a very ancient populated site and there are signs of a town having existed there prior to 5000 B.C. The city faced by Joshua may have been the third located on the site; the first two each having in its turn been destroyed.

City-dwelling is one of the key symptoms of what we might call civilization (the very word "civilization" comes from the Latin word for "city-dweller"; that is, "citizen"). To build a city, even a simple one out of dried mud that takes up no more room all told than a modern city block, requires a certain level of technology and social co-operation. It is awesome to think that Canaan had already seen three thousand years of civilization at least at the time that Abraham entered.

It may have been much more than that. Older cities have been found in the Fertile Crescent. In 1966, archaeologists from the University of Toronto reported finding a site in the region of the upper Euphrates containing houses that must have been built as long ago as 8500 B.C. In comparison with such a date, the pyramids are modern structures, and Abraham almost a contemporary.

The Jericho that Joshua faced was well fortified indeed; the ruins believed to be Canaanite Jericho have walls twelve to fourteen feet thick. The spies, however, discovered morale within the town to be disastrously low. They had no trouble finding refuge with a harlot named Rahab who was willing to betray the town in exchange for safety during the inevitable sack. She reported:

> Joshua 2:9. . . . *your terror is fallen upon us, and . . . all the inhabitants of the land faint because of you.*

When this news was brought back to Joshua, he must have felt confident that with the defenders disheartened and with a "fifth column" within the town, he had only to attack. He made ready to do just that.

Gilgal

Joshua ordered the Israelite army out of Shittim, an encampment some five miles east of Jordan. Marching westward, he crossed the Jordan (which parted for him, according to the Biblical story, as the Sea of Reeds did for Moses). Joshua ordered that twelve stones be taken up from the temporarily dry bed of the Jordan.

> Joshua 4:19. *And the people . . . encamped in Gilgal in the east border of Jericho.*
> Joshua 4:20. *And those twelve stones, which they took out of the Jordan, did Joshua pitch in Gilgal.*

The word *gilgal* means "a circle of stones" and there are several places with that name mentioned in the Bible. A circle of large stones had religious significance to the men of the Stone Age, and such circles can be found in many places. The most famous and largest such circle still surviving—at least in part—is at Stonehenge in England. The Stonehenge circle is believed now to have served as a primitive calendar for the dating of such phenomena as lunar eclipses, but such is the close connection between astronomy and religion in primitive cultures that it is easy to believe that it served a religious purpose at the same time.

The best-known Gilgal in Canaan is this one mentioned in Joshua 4:19, and it is usually located a few miles from Jericho in the direction of Jordan. It is quite likely that the circle of stones that gave the area its name dated back to Canaanite times and played a role in Canaanite religion. The aura of sancity that lingered over it even after the conquest would have been highly repugnant to Yahvism if it had not been somehow assimilated to the priestly view of history. (This ability to assimilate earlier notions is characteristic of successful religions. Islam assimilated the Kaaba and the holiness of Mecca from the pagan past and Christianity assimilated the Christmas celebration from pagan rites centering about the winter solstice.)

In this case, the circle of stones was associated with Joshua's crossing of the Jordan. Nor does the fact that there were twelve stones necessarily reflect the twelve tribes of Israel and therefore point to Israelite origin. Through an astronomic accident, the cycle of seasons is nearly twelve times as long as the cycle of the moon's phases; i.e., the year is made up of twelve months. For this reason, the number twelve could have enormous significance to an agricultural society. For instance, the twelve signs of the zodiac are arranged to mark off the twelve months as the sun makes its circuit of the sky in the course of a year. Indeed, some try to relate the twelve tribes of Israel (why exactly twelve?) to the twelve signs of the zodiac, but this may be going a bit far. Some leeway must be allowed to coincidence, surely.

The Wall [of Jericho]

The siege of Jericho, as described in the Bible, was accompanied by ritualistic parades about the city by armed men, with priests also circling the city, bearing the ark of the covenant and blowing on trumpets. This was repeated for six days and on the seventh day the city was circled seven times (an indication of the small size of the city by modern standards). When that was done

> Joshua 6:20. . . . *the people shouted with a great shout, that the wall fell down flat . . .*

If the Biblical account is taken literally, this is a miracle, but those who seek natural explanations often suggest that it was an earthquake that did the trick. If so, it was a most fortunately timed earthquake.

Actually, it is easy to suppose that the circling of the city had a carefully designed tactical purpose. In the first place, it served to dishearten the city's defenders still further, for the people of Jericho would be nervous indeed at the somber and majestic spinning of a supernatural net about the city. To the religiously devout of those days, the invaders were calling on a perhaps powerful God who might be expected to do almost anything. The rulers of the city must have had much trouble to keep the populace from surrendering on the spot.

Secondly, while the defenders watched in fascination at the slow parading about the city, and listened to the awesome sound of the trumpets, they might not have had time to see and hear the very mundane activity of Joshua's sappers slowly undermining the city's walls.

So Jericho fell. The city was sacked and, it was intended, destroyed for all time.

> Joshua 6:26. *And Joshua* [said] . . . *Cursed be the man . . . that riseth up and buildeth this city Jericho . . .*

It has happened many times that cities have been destroyed and their sites cursed by inveterate enemies. The best-known case outside the Bible is that of Carthage, the largest and strongest Canaanite town in history (it was a Phoenician colony). Carthage had been engaged in three colossal wars with Rome, spaced out over more than a century, and at one point had come within a hairbreadth of defeating Rome. When Rome finally took Carthage in 146 B.C., it utterly destroyed the town and made provision that it never be rebuilt.

However, towns aren't built for no reason; they are usually placed at the site of a sea harbor or river crossing, or in some position where they control trade routes. The men of a properly positioned city become prosperous indeed and it is unlikely that such a position can be allowed to stand empty forever, whatever the curse resting upon it.

Thus, a little over a century after its destruction, Carthage was built again after all. Roman Carthage flourished for six centuries, almost as long as the original Canaanite town had existed.

In the same way, the time came when Jericho was rebuilt, almost upon the cursed site. In the reign of King Ahab, three centuries after Joshua, a new Israelite Jericho arose and this survived and flourished through New Testament times. This new Jericho was destroyed in the course of invasions of Persians and Arabs in the seventh century A.D. and still another Jericho was built by the Crusaders four centuries after that.

This last Jericho still exists today, its Arabic name being the recognizable Eriha. Its present population is about 2000.

Ai

After the fall of Jericho, Joshua continued the advance westward into the heart of central Canaan.

> Joshua 7:2. And Joshua sent men from Jericho to Ai, which is . . . on the east side of Bethel.

Ai was twelve miles northwest of Jericho and two miles further still to the northwest was Bethel, the important city associated with Jacob's dream of a ladder (see page 94). The two cities were either under common rule or acted in alliance against the Israelites.

The invaders, overconfident at first, attacked with too few numbers and were beaten off. Joshua therefore placed a contingent of men in ambush, then made a more careful attack. This time, he pretended defeat and ordered his men to break and run. The men of Ai and Bethel, overconfident in their turn, incautiously left their defenses to engage in hot pursuit. At an appropriate moment, the Israelites turned to fight and when the Canaanites attempted to return to their cities they found those cities occupied by the Israelites who had been in ambush. Ai was sacked, burned, and destroyed. Unlike Jericho, it was never rebuilt.

(After this, the Bible recounts how the Israelites ascended Mount Gerizim and Mount Ebal to perform the rituals of blessings and

curses that Moses had called for before his death. It is not likely that
this could have been done at so early a stage of the conquest but only
after Canaan was under more or less complete control. However, the
Deuteronomist writers were anxious to show the manner in which the
Israelites had obeyed the dictates of Moses to the utmost—as an example to their own times. They inserted the passage, therefore, at the
very earliest opportunity.)

Gibeon

The two victories of the Israelites over Jericho and over Ai put all
of Canaan into a state of urgent alarm. This was particularly true of
the city of Gibeon:

Joshua 9:3. *And when the inhabitants of Gibeon heard what
Joshua had done unto Jericho and to Ai,*
Joshua 9:4. *They did work wilily . . .*

One could scarcely blame Gibeon. The city is located about seventeen miles west of Jericho and five miles south of Ai, so it was very
likely to be the next target of the Israelite army.

(Gibeon was a large city for its time but is now represented only
by a small village, with the recognizable Arabic name of El Jib. The
people of Gibeon were Hivites, one of the tribes routinely mentioned
in the early books of the Bible as destined to conquest by the Israelites.
The Hivites had also controlled Shechem in patriarchal times; see page
100.)

The Gibeonites worked "wilily" by putting on worn clothes and
taking moldy provisions with them. When they appeared before Joshua
at his camp in Gilgal, they represented themselves as ambassadors
from a far country. A treaty of peace was made with them and later,
when the deception was discovered, the treaty was honored and
Gibeon was not destroyed, nor were its people slaughtered. The
Gibeonites are described as having been reduced to slavery but this
may not actually have come to pass until Solomon's time three centuries later.

It is difficult to see how the Gibeonites could have fooled Joshua in
this manner, or to believe that the fierce Israelite invaders would have
honored a treaty secured by deception. However, the writers of the

Book of Joshua, while describing an ideal and complete conquest of Canaan, had to account for the known fact that some Canaanite cities maintained a reasonable degree of independence into the time of David and Solomon. The tale of the trickery of Gibeon was one way of doing so without detracting from Joshua's military glory.

Ajalon

The defection of Gibeon to the Israelites was another serious blow to the Canaanites. The petty kingdoms of the south, under the leadership of the large towns of Jerusalem and Hebron, formed a confederacy against the common foe and marched against Gibeon in order to force it back into the Canaanite ranks.

Joshua and his forces moved quickly to the relief of Gibeon and in a great battle scattered and destroyed the Canaanites. It was during this battle that one of the best known of the events described in the Bible took place:

> Joshua 10:12. *Then spake Joshua . . . Sun, stand thou still upon Gibeon; and thou, Moon, in the valley of Ajalon.*
> Joshua 10:13. *And the sun stood still, and the moon stayed . . . So the sun . . . hasted not to go down about a whole day.*
> Joshua 10:14. *And there was no day like that before it or after it . . .*

Ajalon was a town about ten miles west of Gibeon.

The Bible describes this miraculous lengthening of the day to have been carried through for the purpose of allowing the Israelites to complete their victory. Interpreting them literally, men used these verses twenty-five centuries after the time of Joshua to fight the Copernican theory that the sun stood still and the earth moved about it. After all, if Joshua has to order the sun "stand thou still" it must imply that ordinarily the sun is moving. (This difficulty disappears if one understands the principle of "relative motion," but it is not the purpose of this book to consider the relationship of the Bible to science and we will pass on.)

Following that battle, the Bible rapidly describes Joshua's sweep through southern Canaan, in which he captures a series of cities in the territory that was later to make up the territory of the tribe of

Judah. Hebron itself was taken but no mention is made of Jerusalem
—and no wonder, for Jerusalem remained independent and Canaanite
until the days of David.

Merom

It was next the turn of the cities of northern Canaan to form a league
against Joshua.

Joshua 11:5. *And when all these kings were met together, they
came and pitched together at the waters of Merom, to fight against
Israel.*

The Jordan River, in its course, passes through or flows into three
enclosed bodies of water. The southernmost and largest is, of course,
the Dead Sea (see page 71). Some sixty-five miles north of the Dead
Sea is the Sea of Galilee, and about a dozen miles still farther north is
Lake Huleh. It is Lake Huleh which is usually taken to be the "waters
of Merom." It is the smallest of the three bodies of water associated
with the Jordan; it is only four miles long and three and a half miles
wide.

Zidon

At Merom, Joshua won another great victory and is described as leading the pursuit far (improbably far, in fact) to the north.

Joshua 11:8. *And the Lord delivered them into the hand of Israel,
who smote them, and chased them unto great Zidon . . .*

Zidon, or Sidon, is a city on the Mediterranean shore about 130
miles north of Jerusalem. The area about Zidon (Sidon), which nowadays makes up the coastal region of modern Lebanon, was inhabited by
Canaanites who were never conquered by the Israelites. Even at the
time of Israel's greatest power, the Canaanite cities of the Lebanese
shore, though in alliance with Israel, were not subjected to it.

At the time of the Israelite conquest of Canaan, the largest and
most powerful of these north-Canaanite cities was Zidon (Sidon) and
the people of the entire region were therefore referred to in the Bible
as Zidonians or Sidonians.

The City of Zidon

The people of the region were famous for their manufacture of a purple-red dye and made use of it in their own clothing to such an extent that the color gave a name to the people and the land. It is sometimes stated that the word "Canaan" is derived from an old Semitic word meaning "purple." That may or may not be so but it is quite clear that the Greek name for the region is derived from the color of the dye. The Greek name is "Phoenicia" from their word meaning "purple-red." It is as Phoenicians that the people are almost invariably known nowadays, though the word is not used in the Bible. Nor should the familiar term "Phoenician" be allowed to obscure the fact that the people we call Phoenicians were racially and culturally indistinguishable from the Canaanites to the south.

At the time of Joshua, the Phoenicians may already have made their greatest single contribution to culture—the invention of the alphabet. Writing itself seems to have been invented in a number of different places independently—in Sumeria, in China, in Central America. In all these cases, however, the symbols used were pictures of objects or abstract markings representing words or concepts.

As far as we know the Phoenicians were the first (at some dim period in their ancient history) to hit upon the idea of taking a few markings and letting each stand for a single consonant. By putting such markings (letters) together any word whatever could be produced; and even an unfamiliar word could then be pronounced by sounding the letters. The Phoenician alphabet was adopted by the various Hebrew tribes, including the Moabites and Israelites.

The Greeks adopted the Phoenician alphabet, too, allowing some of the letters to stand for vowel sounds. (Greek myths clearly state that the letters were introduced by the Phoenician prince, Cadmus, who migrated to Greece and founded the Greek city of Thebes.)

Indeed, it is usually accepted that the alphabet (as distinct from writing in general) was invented only once, and that all modern alphabets, however odd some of them seem, are more or less distorted versions of the original Phoenician alphabet.

In the centuries immediately after the Israelite conquest, the importance of Sidon declined. The greatest days of Phoenicia were still ahead; these, indeed, coinciding with the greatest days of Israel. In those great days, however, leadership would fall to other cities, not Sidon. Yet Sidon exists today as Saida, a Lebanese port with a population of about 25,000. Its once-excellent harbor is half silted up and is almost entirely useless. The town is surrounded by fruit orchards, however, and it is the Mediterranean terminus of an oil pipeline from Saudi Arabia.

The Philistines

Even under the idealized picture of the conquest as presented in the Book of Joshua, there was no denying that sections of Canaan remained unconquered. The chief of these included the section along the southern coast of Canaan:

Joshua 13:2. *This is the land that yet remaineth: all the borders of the Philistines . . .*

Joshua 13:3. *. . . . the Gazathites, and the Ashdothites, the Eshkalonites, the Gittites, and the Ekronites . . .*

Philistia

The term "Philistine," which replaces the older term "Caphtorim" (see page 199), may be the name the people of the region gave themselves. The Egyptian inscriptions speak of them as the "Pulesati." In Hebrew, this became "Pelishtim" and in Greek "Philistinoi."

In historical records outside the Bible, the Philistines are first heard of in the records of a new Egyptian dynasty, the 20th. After the death of Merneptah in 1211 B.C., the great 19th dynasty of Rameses II petered out with a few feeble Pharaohs of short reigns. The 20th dynasty began with the reign of Setnakht, in 1192 B.C.

In 1190 B.C., Rameses III came to the throne and began a reign of over thirty years. He was the last powerful native monarch of Egypt. Under him the Peoples of the Sea were finally driven off and a certain order and strength came back to Egypt. His influence was strong in Asia but even he could not reverse the flow of history, and events in Canaan continued without actual military interference on the Pharaoh's part. The Israelite conquest of Canaan seems to have taken place in his reign.

Furthermore, his archives refer to the coming of the "Pulesati."

They may have been a final contingent of the Peoples of the Sea, driven out of Egypt proper by Rameses' armies, and forced to turn to the Canaanite coast. Thus, the Philistines conquered the coast even as the Israelites were conquering the interior. The two great adversaries of the next several centuries had entered the land simultaneously.

The center of Philistine power was a sixty-mile stretch of the southern shore of Canaan, a region which can be referred to as "Philistia." The name persisted long after the great days of Philistine power had passed. Herodotus, the Greek historian, writing in the fifth century B.C., referred to the region as "Palaistina" and the name was eventually applied by the Romans to all of Canaan. Even today, "Palestine" has been used in naming the entire region once known as Canaan.

Philistia was composed of the five cities whose inhabitants are listed in Joshua 13:3—Ekron, Ashdod, Ashkelon, Gath, and Gaza. They seem to have been city-states, after the Greek fashion, with considerable independence, but capable of joining on occasion to fight a common enemy.

The northernmost of the cities was Ekron. This was about twenty-five miles west of Jerusalem and some nine miles from the sea. It still exists as a village named Akir.

Twelve miles southwest of Ekron, and three miles from the sea, is Ashdod, which was known as Azotos to the Greeks and survives today as the village of Esdud with a population of about 3500. In Philistia's prime, however, Ashdod was probably the most powerful of the five cities.

Another twelve miles southwest is Ashkelon, the only one of the five to be an actual seaport. The greatest event in its history came at the time of the Crusades (when it was known as Askalon to Europeans). In A.D. 1099, it was the site of a great victory of the Crusaders over the Egyptians. In 1270, however, it was destroyed by the Egyptian sultan of the time and it is a desolate site now.

Twelve miles east of Ashkelon is Gath, the most inland of the Philistine cities. Its inhabitants are "Gittites." It is most famous for the fact that it was the home city of the giant Goliath, whom the young David slew in single combat. However, it is the most thoroughly vanished of the Philistine cities and its exact site is uncertain.

Twelve miles south of Ashkelon and three miles from the sea is Gaza, the most southerly of the Philistine cities. Of the five, it has survived best and has had the most colorful history. It fell to Alexander the Great (eight centuries after the time of Joshua) after a long and desperate siege. It was an early Christian center and then a Moslem center. Battles were fought over it by the Turks and by Napoleon.

It gained contemporary notoriety as a result of the war between Israel and Egypt that followed the granting of independence to the former in 1948. Egyptian forces occupied Gaza and have maintained that occupation ever since. The Palestinian coast from Gaza to Egypt, about twenty-five miles long and an average of five miles deep, came to be known as the "Gaza strip." It was filled with Arab refugees from Israel, who were not resettled but kept in place as a political maneuver in order that enmity between Israel and the Arab world be exacerbated. Gaza's normal population is about 80,000 but with the addition of the refugees, well over 200,000 people filled it. The Gaza strip was taken by Israel in the course of the Six-day War in 1967.

The Tribes

Despite the admitted incompleteness of the conquest, the Book of Joshua goes on to describe the allotment of land in Canaan to each of the tribes, according to the instructions Joshua is recorded as having received from God.

Joshua 13:7. *Now therefore divide this land for an inheritance unto the nine tribes, and the half tribe of Manasseh.*

Almost all the rest of the Book of Joshua is given over to a painstaking account of the division of the land. It makes for very dull reading but it takes the place of a map in modern books and undoubtedly represents the situation as it arose out of the numerous frictions and settlements between the tribes in the days before the monarchy when they were in uneasy alliance, or in even uneasier strife.

Two of the tribes, Reuben and Gad, together with part of the tribe of Manasseh, had already received grants east of the Jordan (see page 191). West of the Jordan, in Canaan proper, Judah received the southernmost portion, its territory stretching as far north as Jerusalem. South of Judah were some desert hamlets that made up the allotment of the disappearing tribe of Simeon.

The Twelve Tribes

Across central Canaan, centered in Shechem, was the remainder of Manasseh. Between Manasseh and Judah lay Dan on the coast, and Ephraim and Benjamin inland. Benjamin included Jericho and Gibeon. North of Manasseh was Asher along the coast and, inland, Issachar, Zebulun, and Naphtali, going from south to north.

It is important to realize the small size of the allotments. Benjamin, the smallest of the tribes, occupied a territory of about three hundred square miles. This is about as large as the area of the five boroughs of New York City, and considerably smaller than the area of the city of Los Angeles.

All these tribal boundaries were idealized versions referred back in time from the situation as it existed in the period of the monarchy. They could not have existed in the form given at the time of the conquest. Jerusalem was assigned to Judah, for instance, but that town was not conquered by Israelites until the time of David. Philistia was divided between Judah and Dan, but Philistia was not conquered until David's time, too. The tribe of Asher was awarded much of the Phoenician coast which it never, in actual fact, controlled.

The tribe of Levi received no actual land grant. Its central role was that of serving as a priesthood and for that purpose it was considered enough that its members be granted a number of towns scattered through the various tribal areas.

Mount Ephraim

The Book of Joshua ends with the death of the secular and religious leaders of the Israelites of the period: Joshua and Eleazar (the latter being the son of Aaron and the nephew of Moses).

> Joshua 24:30. *And they buried him* [Joshua] *in . . . mount Ephraim . . .*
>
> . . . .
>
> Joshua 24:33. *And Eleazar, the son of Aaron died; and they buried him in a hill . . . in mount Ephraim.*

There is a line of hills running down the length of Canaan between the coastal plain and the plain of the Jordan. That portion which lies in the territory of Ephraim is called Mount Ephraim. The reference does not seem to be to a particular peak but, as we would perhaps say today, to "the Ephraim hills," or "the Ephraim highlands."

With the end of the Book of Joshua, we can consider Canaan as essentially Israelite territory, even if not completely so. Instead of Canaan, the territory will now be referred to as Israel.

7. JUDGES

Judah and Simeon

The Book of Judges, which describes the history of Israel immediately after the conquest, is rather miscellaneous in nature and is apparently a collection of ancient documents, not necessarily very closely related to each other. Although signs of editing are clear, the tale is not smoothed into a unified and pretty whole as in the Book of Joshua. So much is left that is unedifying and unflattering to Israel that one is forced to trust the Book of Judges to be a more accurate reflection of secular history than the Book of Joshua can be.

The first chapter of Judges deals with the conquest from a viewpoint entirely different from that in Joshua. Here there is no single army under unified command sweeping to a quick, complete victory. Rather, there is the picture of disunited tribes, each struggling alone against the enemy and not doing too well at it, in many cases.

Thus, no mention is made of Joshua's strenuous campaign through the south. Instead, the conquest of the area about Hebron is the task of the tribe of Judah in alliance with Simeon:

> Judges 1:3. And Judah said unto Simeon his brother, Come up with me into my lot, that we may fight against the Canaanites; and I likewise will go with thee into thy lot . . .

Although the forces of Judah (the weak tribe of Simeon probably did not make a significant contribution) are described as uniformly

The Twelve Tribes

successful, taking even Jerusalem and the Philistine cities of Gaza, Ashkelon, and Ekron, the victories were nevertheless limited. The highland areas, more sparsely settled, were abandoned to the Israelites. In the sense that these areas were previously under the domination of cities such as Jerusalem and Gaza, territory appertaining to those cities were annexed and the cities might then be glowingly described as having been conquered. The actual cities themselves and the tightly controlled lowland areas about them could not be taken, however, and the Bible makes the reason for that clear:

Judges 1:19. . . . *he* [Judah] *drave out the inhabitants of the mountain; but could not drive out the inhabitants of the valley, because they had chariots of iron.*

Until 3500 B.C. mankind used for its tools only those materials it could find at hand; materials that did not require sophisticated chemical treatment—bone, hide, wood, and stone, for instance. Stone has survived best through the ages and we know most about the stone tools used in ancient times. We refer to the period therefore as the "Stone Age."

Small nuggets of metals which occur free in nature (gold, silver, copper, meteoric iron) were occasionally found, and perhaps used as ornaments. It was not till about 3500 B.C. that the Egyptians learned how to smelt appropriate ores and obtain copper in quantity. By 3000 B.C. copper was in widespread use throughout the Fertile Crescent.

Copper itself is not hard enough to serve well as tools or weapons. It was soon discovered, however, that if tin ores were added to copper ores, a copper-tin alloy called bronze could be produced and this is much harder than copper.

By 2500 B.C. bronze weapons were coming into use and the Fertile Crescent was entering the "Bronze Age." A bronze spearpoint was sharper and tougher than one made of flint and could penetrate leather shields with no trouble. Bronze shields could, on the other hand, easily turn and blunt stone weapons. A bronze-armored army could, without difficulty, defeat a larger army fighting with stone and leather.

By 2000 B.C. the Bronze Age was penetrating Europe, and the battles of the Trojan War, as carefully described by Homer, were fought by warriors with bronze armor, bronze shields, and bronze weapons.

Bronze was an expensive material, however. Copper ores were rare, though sufficient quantities could at first be obtained from the Sinai Peninsula and from Cyprus. (Indeed, the word "copper" is supposed to be derived from "Cyprus.") Tin ores were even rarer. Phoenician trading vessels ventured long distances for the tin ores needed to manufacture bronze and reached the "Tin Islands." This is usually supposed to be the peninsula of Cornwall in southwestern England, together with some islands off its coast. It is interesting to think that Canaanites were in England thousands of years before the Romans.

Iron is much more common than either copper or tin and, under the proper treatment, is much harder than bronze. Iron, in other words, is at once cheaper and better than bronze. Why was it not used? The answer to that is that iron ores are not as easily smelted as are copper and tin ores; iron ores require hotter fires and more complicated metallurgical processes.

The first successful method for smelting iron ore was developed somewhere in or near Hittite territory about 1400 B.C. (while the Israelites were in Egyptian slavery). The new technique, which gave birth to the "Iron Age," did not come in time to save the Hittites but it survived the destruction of the Hittite Empire. It spread slowly through the Fertile Crescent and into Europe.

At the time of the Israelite conquest of Canaan, the use of iron in restricted quantities had come to the more sophisticated towns, but desert tribes were still innocent of its use. The Israelites, therefore, entered Canaan at the dividing line between the Bronze Age and the Iron Age, and had to fight iron with bronze. What they could do by sheer numbers and energy, they did. But anyone fighting iron with bronze reaches a quick limit to conquest. The men of Judah found this out the hard way.

So, apparently, did the men of the other Israelite tribes. Through the rest of the chapter, the failure of each tribe to complete the conquest by capturing the larger cities in their regions is carefully detailed. The tribe of Benjamin did not take Jerusalem; the tribe of Manasseh did not take Bethshea; the tribe of Ephraim did not take Gezer; the tribe of Zebulun did not take Kitron; the tribe of Asher did not take Zidon; and so on.

The Judges

Under the circumstances, the Israelite occupation of Canaan could scarcely have served as the opening of an immediate period of prosperity. Clinging precariously to the highlands, disunited, technologically backward, it was inevitable that the Israelites remain in subjection to one foreign power after another.

Only occasionally could one tribe or another gain a degree of freedom through the action of some competent military leader.

Judges 2:16. *Nevertheless the Lord raised up judges, which delivered them out of the hand of those that spoiled them.*

The word "judge" is here used in the sense of a "ruler" since in early cultures, the chief function of a tribal ruler in peacetime was that of judging disputes and reaching, it was to be hoped, some just decision. This had the crucial purpose of preventing internal feuds and disputes that would weaken the entire population in the face of some always waiting outer enemy.

Twelve judges are considered to have held sway over the tribes between the conquest of Canaan and the establishment of the monarchy. This number is arrived at rather shakily, but it has the significance of matching the number of Israelite tribes so that later tradition clung to it.

It was often customary in the past to suppose that each judge held sway over all Israel and that the periods of their power followed one another. If we assume this and carefully follow the references to periods of time (usually expressed in round numbers that are clearly not intended to be exact), the period of time covered by the Book of Judges works out to be 410 years.

The period ends with the accession of Saul to the throne and that event can be dated with fair confidence at 1028 B.C. The 410-year period for the Book of Judges would then place the conquest of Canaan around 1440 B.C. and the Exodus about 1480 B.C.

This is quite impossible. The Exodus and conquest could not conceivably have taken place in the fifteenth century B.C.

Instead, we must place the most likely date for the Exodus at about 1200 B.C. and the death of Joshua at about 1150 B.C. This means that the period of time covered by the Book of Judges cannot be more than 125 to 150 years.

To account for this short period, one need only assume that the judges did not rule all Israel and did not serve consecutively. The Book of Judges is a collection of sagas produced by each tribe separately with some editor or editors weaving them together into a single tale without bothering to detail the chronology. Under such circumstances, it would seem reasonable that the various judges ruled over single tribes or small groups of tribes and that two or three might flourish simultaneously.

At this low point in Israelite history—from 1150 to 1028 B.C.—it was all the Israelites could do to fight off the petty powers of the western half of the Fertile Crescent. They were fortunate indeed in that they had to face no great empires. Against a man like Thutmose III or Hammurabi, their judges would not have saved them.

In Egypt, Rameses III, the last of the strong native Pharaohs, died in 1158 B.C., almost simultaneously with Joshua. His successors were eight Pharaohs, all named Rameses, who were weak and of little importance. In 1075 B.C., the 21st dynasty began to rule and these consisted of the high priests in the distant city of Thebes. During the entire period of the judges, Egypt might as well have been on another planet.

In the east, the nation of Assyria was slowly gathering strength. The region of Assyria, on the upper Tigris, had developed a civilization in the earliest times. It had been part of the empire of Sargon of Agade (see page 50) but in later times, when the Tigris-Euphrates region was fragmented into city-states and Sumeria was dying, it went through a period of prosperity and strength. In the patriarchal period, Assyria was a land of wealthy merchants.

It fell under the domination of Hammurabi, but recovered its independence and by 1500 B.C. formed one of the group of states contending for control of the Fertile Crescent. These rivals were the Egyptian Empire, the Hittite Empire, the Mitannian Empire, and the Assyrian Empire. The Hittites badly weakened Mitanni and were in turn badly weakened by Egypt. When Egyptian power in Asia began to decay under Ikhnaton, Assyria became the strongest nation in the area.

In 1235 B.C., Tukulti-Ninurta I became king of Assyria and he was still reigning at the time of the Exodus. Under cover of the havoc being

created by the barbarian migrations of the time, Assyria absorbed what
was left of Mitanni and then conquered Babylonia, extending its power
to the Persian Gulf. Tukulti-Ninurta became extolled in legend as
the first conquering Assyrian king and serves as the model for the
Biblical Nimrod (see page 52) and the Greek Ninus in consequence.

However, Assyria was not yet ready for the domination of the entire
Fertile Crescent. Tukulti-Ninurta was followed by weak successors
under whom Babylonia regained its independence. The Assyrian king
Tiglath-Pileser I, who reigned from 1116 to 1093 B.C., again pushed
the land toward a period of power, but he too was followed by weak
successors who had to contend with the onslaughts of a new group of
nomads, the Aramaeans, from the north.

In other words, during the period of the judges, the day of Egypt
was over, and the day of Assyria had not yet quite come. In the
gap of time between the two, the Israelites were able to develop against
the opposition of only such enemies as they could (just barely) handle.

Ashtaroth

The later editor of the Book of Judges must have found it hard to
account for sufferings and defeats of the Israelites in view of the
tradition of divine providence that surrounded the tales of the Exodus
and conquest under Moses and Joshua.

His pious explanation of the later events was that defeat and enslavement were punishments visited upon the Israelites for succumbing to the lure of Canaanite religious rites.

> Judges 2:11. *And the children of Israel did evil . . . and served*
> *Baalim.*
>
> . . . .
>
> Judges 2:13. . . . *and Ashtaroth.*

The "-im" suffix is the regular Hebrew plural so that "Baalim"
should be translated "Baals" (and *is* so translated in the Revised
Standard Version). Ashtaroth, like Baalim, is also a plural. The singular
form in this case is Ashtoreth and this is the feminine equivalent of a
Baal. Just as Baal ("Lord") is the general title for a male Semitic deity,
so Ashtoreth ("Lady") is the general title for a female Semitic deity.

Ashtoreth is, actually, a distortion of the correct name, Ashtarte. The distortion is caused by pious editors who later substituted the vowel sounds of *bosheth* ("shame") into the name; doing as they had done in converting "Melech" to "Molech" (see page 162).

The most famous Ashtarte was the one worshiped in Tyre, the chief Phoenician city in the time of the monarchy. Her worship was to have an important influence on the kingdom of Israel. The version of her name used in Greek mythology is Astarte. The chief of the Babylonian goddesses bore another version of the name—Ishtar.

Othniel

Over and over again, the refrain of the Book of Judges is sounded. The Israelites serve other gods and are punished by subjection to a foreign tyrant. They repent and a judge arises to free them.

The first case arises almost immediately after the conquest.

Judges 3:7. *And the children of Israel did evil . . . and served Baalim and the groves.*

Judges 3:8. *. . . [and] the Lord . . . sold them into the hand of Chushan-rishathaim king of Mesopotamia . . .*

Judges 3:9. *And when the children of Israel cried unto the Lord, the Lord raised up a deliverer . . . Othniel the son of Kenaz, Caleb's younger brother.*

The Hebrew word translated in Judges 3:7 as "groves" is *asheroth*, the plural form of the word *asherah*. The term is left untranslated in the various modern versions of the Bible, for Asheroth is another term used to refer to female Canaanite deities. The confusion arises from the fact that the word is also used to indicate a pole or wooden pillar—a relic of ancient tree worship, perhaps—which was considered sacred to the goddess. From a pole to a tree to a grove is not a difficult progression. It may be that Asherah originated as still another form of Ashtarte.

"Mesopotamia" is the translation of "Aram-Naharaim," the district where Haran is located, so that the invasion may be viewed as coming from the north. There is no chance of locating the region specifically for Chushan-rishathaim (or Cushan-rishathaim) means, in Hebrew, "the Cushite of double wickedness." This was undoubtedly not the true name of the individual, but rather a scornful title given him by the Biblical writers. Who he might really be is therefore impossible to tell.

If the invasion came from the north, one must wonder why it is Othniel who leads the reaction to it. Othniel is a folk hero of Judah and the conqueror of Hebron according to Judges 1:13, and therefore a dweller in the extreme south. Either Chushan-rishathaim conquered all of Canaan down to Judah, or else Othniel acted as commander in chief of the united tribes. Neither seems very likely. Possibly the confusion is the result of a telescoping of two traditions, a northern and a southern.

Ehud

The next invasion, after the Israelites had again fallen prey to strange gods, is less puzzling.

> Judges 3:12. . . . *Eglon the king of Moab* . . .
> Judges 3:13. . . . *gathered unto him the children of Ammon and Amalek, and went and smote Israel, and possessed the city of palm trees.*

The picture is that of a federation of Trans-Jordanian Hebrew tribes formed under the leadership of Moab. These then repeated Joshua's tactic of striking across the Jordan River in the direction of Jericho ("the city of palm trees"). Jericho itself no longer existed but the confederacy occupied the surrounding area, which now formed the territory of the tribe of Benjamin.

The tide was turned when Ehud, a left-handed Benjamite, sent to Eglon with tribute, managed to stab him to death. (Presumably the left-handed use of a dagger hidden on the right side, rather than on the customary left, caught the king by surprise.) In the confusion that followed, an Israelite attack succeeded in driving the Moabites back across the Jordan.

Hazor

Othniel and Ehud are the first and second judges, and following the tale of Ehud is the barest mention of a third judge, Shamgar, who apparently won a victory over the Philistines. Following that comes a circumstantial tale of a major danger.

Judges 4:2. *And the Lord sold them* [the Israelites] *into the hand of Jabin . . . that reigned in Hazor; the captain of whose host was Sisera, which dwelt in Harosheth . . .*

Hazor

Judges 4:3. . . . *he had nine hundred chariots of iron; and twenty years he mightily oppressed the children of Israel.*

Hazor is located in far northern Canaan, in the territory assigned to the tribe of Naphtali. It is about four miles southwest of Lake Huleh. Harosheth is some forty miles southwest, near the sea, in the territory of Zebulun.

One gets the picture of a league of northern Canaanite cities, unconquered thanks to their iron-equipped armies, laying tribute on the northern Israelite tribes.

This situation clearly indicates the manner in which the account given in the Book of Joshua is a heavily idealized version of the conquest. It had been a King Jabin of Hazor who, according to the Book of Joshua, had led the northern coalition against the Israelites, and had been disastrously defeated by the waters of Merom (see page 217). Joshua followed up that victory energetically:

> Joshua 11:10. . . . Joshua . . . took Hazor and smote the king thereof with the sword . . .
> Joshua 11:11. And they smote all the souls that were therein, utterly destroying them . . . and he burnt Hazor with fire.

Could Joshua have actually won so great a victory? If so, how account for the phenomenal comeback of Hazor, which within a few decades was back in existence under another King Jabin and strong enough to control northern Israel. Or was the Canaanite defeat, to be described a bit later, anachronistically pushed back into Joshua's time?

Deborah

For a period of time after the conquest, Ephraim maintained its position as the leading tribe. Even if the over-all leadership of Joshua of Ephraim was a later idealization, it can nevertheless be taken that he won important victories even if he only led the Ephraimites. The glamour of Joshua's victories would extend forward over the generations and give Ephraim a jealously guarded claim to military pre-eminence.

In any united action of the tribes it would be taken for granted that Ephraim would supply the initiative and leadership; and failure on the part of other tribes to recognize this would result in civil war, as actually happened on at least one important occasion. (This is rather similar to the experience in Greece five or six centuries later, when any united action by the Greek city-states was almost automatically undertaken only under the leadership of Sparta.)

Ephraimite hegemony must have been most marked over the neighboring tribes of Benjamin to the south and Manasseh to the north. This may be reflected in the tradition that all three were descended from those sons of Jacob who had Rachel for a mother (Joseph and Benjamin). Ephraim, in other words, headed the close alliance of the

"Rachel tribes," and exerted its influence more informally beyond that central nucleus.

The term "Mount Ephraim" can be applied specifically to the hill country of Ephraim, but it can, in view of this, also be applied more loosely to the extension of the highland area north and south of Ephraim's immediate territory. This is all the more reasonable since the Book of Judges was put into final form after the time of the existence of the northern kingdom of Israel, which was so dominated by the tribe of Ephraim that Ephraim was used, poetically, as the name of the kingdom. "Mount Ephraim" would therefore naturally be used sometimes for the highlands of the north tribal area generally.

Thus, after Ehud the Benjamite had assassinated Eglon of Moab, he retired to the Israelite strongholds in the hills:

> Judges 3:27. . . . *he blew a trumpet in the mountain of Ephraim, and the children of Israel went down with him from the mount . . .*

It is not necessary to conclude that Ehud had to move into the territory of Ephraim proper in order to send out messages to rally troops. He could have done so from the western section of Benjamin. Nevertheless, it is natural to suppose that the Ephraimites must have joined him.

As is often the case when one member of a loose confederation is the recognized military leader, aggression is allowed to continue as long as the territory of that leader is not directly threatened. Thus, in Greece, it was often difficult to get Sparta to take action as long as the Peloponnesus was not invaded. Similarly, Ephraim was slow to act against the Moabites as long as it was only Benjamite territory that was occupied, and they were equally slow to act as long as Jabin of Hazor and his general Sisera confined their activity to placing the northern tribes of Naphtali and Zebulun under tribute.

There may at this time have been some sort of internal difficulties in Ephraim that we have no knowledge of, for the Rachel tribes seem to be led by a woman—a most unusual situation.

> Judges 4:4. *And Deborah, a prophetess . . . judged Israel at that time.*
> Judges 4:5. *And she dwelt . . . between Ramah and Bethel in mount Ephraim . . .*

The area between Ramah and Bethel was Benjamite territory and here is an example of the broader use of the term "mount Ephraim."

Mount Tabor

But as Canaanite hegemony in the north grew more menacing (or as the political situation within Ephraim became more settled), Deborah prepared to take action:

> Judges 4:6. And she sent and called Barak . . . of Kedesh-naphtali and said unto him . . . Go and draw toward mount Tabor, and take with thee ten thousand men of . . . Naphtali and . . . Zebulun
>
> Judges 4:7. And I will draw unto thee to the river Kishon Sisera, the captain of Jabin's army . . .

Kedesh, seven miles northwest of Hazor, was the most important Israelite town in Naphtali (and was called Kedesh-naphtali to differentiate it from other towns of the name). Presumably, it was the center of Israelite resistance and Barak was a guerrilla leader keeping the hopes of Israel alive. Now Deborah was urging him to combine the forces available to him and risk it in a pitched battle on Mount Tabor.

Mount Tabor is located at the southern border of Naphtali, where it meets the borders of Zebulun and Issachar. It is about twenty-five miles southwest of Hazor, forming a convenient rallying point for troops from several tribes, and an easily defensible area where they might gather and prepare. (Mount Tabor is only about five miles southeast of Nazareth, which over a thousand years later was to be the home of Jesus.)

The Kishon River, about fifty miles long, flows northwestward through northern Palestine, through the territory of Issachar and Zebulun, into what is now called the Bay of Acre. A northern tributary has its origin just west of Mount Tabor.

Barak was reluctant to risk his forces in the uncertainty of a pitched battle without assurance of firm Ephraimite support (just as the Greek city-states in later centuries were reluctant to oppose some foreign enemy without assurance of Spartan help).

Judges 4:8. *And Barak said unto her, If thou wilt go with me,
then I will go; but if thou wilt not go with me, then I will not go.*

Deborah gave the necessary assurance and at the head of the largest
alliance and the strongest Israelite army since the time of Joshua,
Barak defeated Sisera. Sisera was killed in flight by a woman to whom
he turned for help, and the Israelite army continued the war against
Jabin until Hazor was taken and destroyed, this time for good.

The Song of Deborah

The fifth chapter of the Book of Judges is notable for the "Song
of Deborah," considered one of the most ancient portions of the
Bible:

Judges 5:1. *Then sang Deborah and Barak . . . on that day . . .*

It was a paean of triumph at the victory over Sisera and in it
Deborah lists the tribes of the coalition that took part in the victory.
Ephraim and its satellites, Benjamin and Manasseh, are, of course,
listed first:

Judges 5:14. *Out of Ephraim was there a root of them . . . ;
after thee, Benjamin, among thy people; out of Machir came down
governors, and out of Zebulun they that handle the pen of the
writer.*
Judges 5:15. *And the princes of Issachar were with Deborah . . .*
. . . .
Judges 5:18. *Zebulun and Naphtali were a people that jeoparded
their lives . . .*

Machir is, apparently, an alternate name for Manasseh. Perhaps
the tribe of Manasseh is actually the union of two tribes, one of
which was called Machir (a term more often used for that portion of
the tribe that held territory east of the Jordan). The Bible solves the
problem by making Machir a son of Manasseh.

Genesis 50:23. *. . . . the children also of Machir, the son of
Manasseh were brought up upon Joseph's knees.*

Here the implication is that Machir was the only son of Manasseh, so that both Manasseh and Machir could serve as eponymous ancestors for the entire tribe.

Six of the tribes, then, took part in the battle: Ephraim, Benjamin, Manasseh, Zebulun, Issachar, and Naphtali, forming a solid bloc along the interior of northern Canaan.

Four of the tribes are singled out for contempt at not having joined:

Judges 5:15. . . . *For the divisions of Reuben, there were great thoughts of heart.*

Judges 5:16. *Why abodest thou among the sheepfolds, to hear the bleatings of the flocks? . . .*

Judges 5:17. *Gilead [Gad] abode beyond Jordan: and why did Dan remain in ships? Asher continued on the sea shore . . .*

The abstentions were reasonable after all. Asher on the northern shore facing the Phoenicians, and Dan on the southern shore facing the Philistines may well have had ample troubles at home without looking for enemies elsewhere. Reuben, which stood irresolute and finally decided to remain at home, was having similar trouble with Moab. Indeed, this chapter is the last in the Bible to mention Reuben as a tribe, so it had not long to endure. Gad was the only strong tribe that might have joined but didn't, and it may have felt secure behind the river and saw no need to risk lives.

Notice that the tribe of Judah, and its satellite Simeon, are not mentioned. It is quite possible that during the period of the judges, Judah was not part of the Israelite coalition and may not even have been recognized as part of Israel.

Indeed, it was only for a century, under the kings Saul, David, and Solomon, that Judah was united with Israel. Under Saul (an Israelite), Judah was in rebellion; and under David and Solomon (Judeans), Israel was restive. After Solomon, the two portions of the land fell apart and remained apart for the rest of their history.

Jezreel

In addition to the Canaanite enemy within the land, the Israelites were subjected to periodic raids by the nomads from beyond the Jordan—the Midianites and Amalekites. The tribe of Manasseh, which bordered on the central Jordan, suffered particularly from these raids into Israel, and the defense against the nomads was undertaken by Gideon, a member of that tribe. His opportunity came with the next raid:

Jezreel

Judges 6:33. *Then all the Midianites and the Amalekites . . . gathered together, and went over, and pitched in the valley of Jezreel.*

A river flows into the Jordan from the west about fifteen miles south of Lake Galilee and cuts through the line of hills that runs down the center of Israel. That is the valley of Jezreel and it represents a natural opening into the heart of northern Israel for raiders from the east.

The valley of Jezreel is in the territory of Issachar but Gideon did not intend to let Issachar fight alone:

Judges 6:35. *And he sent messengers throughout all Manasseh . . . and . . . unto Asher, and unto Zebulun, and unto Naphtali; and they came up to meet them.*

It was almost the same confederacy that fought the Hazorites under Sisera, but with the vital omission of Ephraim.

We can only guess why Gideon omitted Ephraim, but perhaps it was something like this. If Ephraim joined the coalition it would only be as the leader and they, in their military pride, would insist on a direct frontal attack. Gideon had what he thought was a better plan and to carry it through he needed to retain control in his own hands—which meant omitting Ephraim. His plan, he felt, would work against a nomad host, stronger in numbers than in discipline and organization.

He led a small band by night to the heights overlooking the Midianite encampment and attacked suddenly, with noise and lights, rather than with arms. Roused, shaken, not knowing what was going on, convinced that a formidable host had surrounded them, the Midianites fled in panic back to the Jordan, where the main army was waiting to destroy them at the fords.

Ephraim, having been notified with deliberate tardiness by Gideon and directed to the fords, participated in the battle at the Jordan, but it was plain to them that the successful strategy was Gideon's.

They were humiliated and angered. Not only had Gideon deliberately failed to recognize Ephraim's leadership, but he had then gone on to head a coalition and win a victory without them. Civil war was threatened between those who followed Gideon and an annoyed and jealous Ephraim:

> Judges 8:1. And the men of Ephraim said unto him [Gideon], Why hast thou served us thus, that thou calledst us not, when thou wentest out to fight with the Midianites? And they did chide with him sharply.

Smoothly, Gideon suggested that the crucial point of the battle came at the fords of the Jordan, where Ephraim had captured a number of the Midianite leaders. His own role, a mere raid, he dismissed as quite minor. The offended Ephraimites allowed themselves to be soothed and civil war was averted.

Succoth

Gideon pursued the remnant of the Midianite army east of the Jordan, in order to complete the victory. Partly, too, the pursuit of the enemy was a matter of private vengeance, for Zebah and Zalmunna, two Midianite leaders still at large, had been responsible (as it turned out) for the death of Gideon's brothers.

In the course of the pursuit, Gideon passed through the territory of the tribe of Gad, which was continuing its policy of isolation. It had not joined the coalition against Jabin and Sisera and it had not joined the coalition against the Midianites. (Since the Midianites would have had to pass through Gadite territory to reach the Jordan on their way into Israel, there is a strong possibility that Gad was worse than neutral; that it did not oppose the Midianites and paid them tribute in order that they might remain in peace while devastation fell on the land west of the Jordan.)

Even after Gideon's victory, they temporized and sought the safety of neutrality. When Gideon entered Succoth, on the Jabbok River perhaps four miles east of the Jordan, and asked for supplies, he was refused:

Judges 8:6. . . . *the princes of Succoth said, Are the hands of Zebah and Zalmunna now in thine hand, that we should give bread unto thine army?*

In other words, Gideon might yet be defeated and Succoth was not going to risk retaliation by the Midianites. The nearby town of Penuel (where Jacob had once wrestled with an angel) took the same attitude.

Gideon could do nothing about this at the time; the Midianites came first. He caught up with the nomads at Karkor, the exact site of which is unknown, but which may be some thirty miles east of the Jordan (a deep eastward penetration for an Israelite army of the time). Again Gideon won a complete victory, capturing the Midianite leaders and eventually executing them.

He then took reprisal against the Gadites, destroying the fortifications of Penuel, and executing the leading men of Succoth.

Gideon and Abimelech

The victories of Gideon had been sufficiently dramatic to give him the prestige required for kingship; that is, for hereditary rule.

Judges 8:22. *Then the men of Israel said unto Gideon, Rule thou over us, both thou, and thy son, and thy son's son also . . .*

Judges 8:23. *And Gideon said unto them, I will not rule over you . . . The Lord shall rule over you.*

This response was in accord with the views of the time at which the Book of Judges reached its final form; that is, after the time of the monarchy. The kings of Israel (and, to a lesser extent, of Judah) were all too often strongly anti-Yahvist. The Yahvists were, in turn, anti-monarchic, and this shows up in several places in the Bible.

Nevertheless, the chances are that Gideon *did* accept the kingship, if not "of Israel" then at least of Manasseh. He certainly ruled as judge in his lifetime and, after his death, the crucial test is whether his power was hereditary. Apparently it was, for his sons succeeded him to power. Again the power was just over Manasseh for only places in Manasseh are mentioned in this portion of the Book of Judges.

The advantage of hereditary rule lies in the fact that the succession can be made automatic, that it will pass from father to son (or to some other close relative) according to some fixed rule. The land is therefore not plunged into broils and civil war with the death of each ruler.

For this to work well, those relatives who do not inherit the kingdom should stand aside with good grace, but this did not always happen in ancient monarchies. With royal polygamy practiced, there would be large numbers of sons born of different mothers. The wives of the harem would intrigue for the succession of their own sons and the sons themselves would seek factions within the kingdom. The result would often be broils and civil wars anyway.

This was to be most clearly shown in Biblical history in the case of Israel's greatest king, David, but a little foretaste is given now. Gideon was a polygamist, and a fruitful one:

Judges 8:30. *And Gideon had threescore and ten sons of his body begotten; for he had many wives.*

Judges 8:31. *And his concubine that was in Shechem, she also bare him a son whose name he called Abimelech.*

It is interesting that "Abimelech" means "my father is king." The "king" might be a reference to a god rather than to Gideon, so perhaps it should not be taken too literally.

The question was which of Gideon's sons was to succeed him. In this connection, Abimelech may have felt like an outsider. Shechem was still essentially a Canaanite city, worshiping a Canaanite god, Baal-berith ("Lord of the covenant") and Abimelech as the son of a Canaanite woman may have been scorned and rejected by his brothers.

In any case, he made a virtue of necessity and intrigued with his mother's clan in Shechem, pointing out that they would fare better under one of their own as king. They saw the point and financed his next step, which was to hire a private army and use it to attack and slaughter the other sons. Left in power, Abimelech assumed the kingship but retained it for only a short while before trouble started:

> Judges 9:22. *When Abimelech had reigned three years over Israel,*
> Judges 9:23. . . . *an evil spirit* [arose] *between Abimelech and the men of Shechem* . . .

The Shechemites, disenchanted with Abimelech for some reason, rebelled against him. Abimelech bloodily suppressed the Shechemite rebellion and then went on to subdue other disaffected cities of Manasseh. He marched against Thebez (which is thought to be represented nowadays by a village named Tubas), about twelve miles northeast of Shechem. He took the city but was killed in the process.

Thus ended the house of Gideon and the first brief attempt at establishing a monarchy in Israel.

Mizpeh

Deborah and Gideon may be counted as the fourth and fifth of the judges, respectively. Two more, Tola and Jair (the sixth and seventh), are briefly mentioned in a verse apiece and soon thereafter the scene shifts to the Trans-Jordan.

While the tribe of Gad (Gilead) remained aloof from the troubles of Israel proper, it did not dwell in complete peace, even if the momentary irruption of Gideon's Manassite army is discounted.

When the tribe of Gad had settled in its territory, it had displaced the Ammonites, pushing them away from the Jordan valley and toward the east. This was not accomplished peacefully, of course, and there was continuing war between the Gadites and the Ammonites. The climax of that war is described:

Mizpeh

Judges 10:17. *Then the children of Ammon were gathered together, and encamped in Gilead. And the children of Israel assembled themselves together, and encamped in Mizpeh.*

The exact site of Mizpeh is uncertain but it may have been some
twenty miles southeast of the town of Succoth, earlier mentioned in
connection with Gideon's raid across the Jordan. It was near the eastern border of Gadite territory.

At the head of the Gadite army was Jephthah, who, in his eagerness
to win, vows, in case of victory, to sacrifice to God the first living thing
that emerges from his house upon his return home. Jephthah wins a
complete victory over the Ammonites and, on his return home, it is his
daughter and only child who emerges to greet him. Jephthah is forced,
in agony, to sacrifice her.

This tale of human sacrifice is so at odds with the rituals of Yahvism
that it is a matter of surprise that the later editors of the Book of
Judges allowed it to remain without some sign of disapproval. It is
often suggested that the tale is left unvarnished in an attempt to as-

similate into Yahvism the ritual of a pagan festival. The story concludes:

> Judges 11:39. . . . . And it was a custom in Israel,
> Judges 11:40. That the daughters of Israel went yearly to lament
> the daughter of Jephthah the Gileadite four days in a year.

There were well-known rites all over the ancient world celebrating
the death and subsequent rebirth of a god. This represented the annual
agricultural cycle: the death of crops in the winter and their rebirth in
the spring. It would be customary for women to bewail the death of
the god with great ceremony each year, and then to rejoice at the news
of the rebirth.

To deprive the women of their long-established custom would have
been difficult; to transfer it from a heathen god to the daughter of an
Israelite hero might have been easier.

Shibboleth

The victory of Jephthah displeased the Ephraimites, as Gideon's
victory had displeased them. The tribe of Gad, it seemed to Ephraim,
was attempting to take over the headship of Israel. Jephthah did not
succeed, as Gideon had, in mollifying the Ephraimites and this time
there was civil war.

The Ephraimite forces, with the self-confidence of a tribe considering
itself militarily supreme among the Israelites, promptly invaded Gad,
crossing the Jordan to do so.

Jephthah, in all probability, faded away before them, luring them
deeper into the country and farther from their bases, while he sent
contingents to occupy the fords of the Jordan and cut off their retreat.
In a sharp battle, he then defeated the Ephraimites and when the
beaten army fled, they found their way across the Jordan barred:

> Judges 12:5. . . . when those Ephraimites which were escaped said,
> Let me go over; . . . the men of Gilead said unto him, Art thou
> an Ephraimite? If he said, Nay;
> Judges 12:6. Then said they unto him, Say now Shibboleth: and
> he said Sibboleth: for he could not frame to pronounce it right. Then
> they took him, and slew him . . .

The word *shibboleth* meant "stream" but it had no significance in itself; it merely supplied the "sh" sound that was missing in the Ephraimite dialect. As a result of this passage, the word "shibboleth" is used in English to represent any catchword that serves to distinguish one group of men from another.

Forty-two thousand Ephraimites are recorded as having died in this civil war. That figure is undoubtedly exaggerated but the defeat was serious enough to end the Ephraimite hegemony over Israel. When the day came that a king finally arose over Israel, it was not from the tribe of Ephraim that he was taken.

Nazarite

Jephthah may be counted as the eighth judge and, after the conclusion of his story, three more are briefly mentioned in a verse or two apiece. These are Ibzan, Elon, and Abdon, the ninth, tenth, and eleventh judges respectively.

And now again there is a shift in scene; this time westward, to the southern coast, where the great enemy was the Philistines. The tribe that suffered most seriously from them was Dan, whose territory lay in the northern section of Philistia, which was dominated by the Philistines throughout the period of the judges.

Around the struggles between Danites and their Philistine overlords there arose tales of a folk hero, Samson. Samson is not a leader of an army, like Barak, Gideon, or Jephthah. He is, instead, a kind of Robin Hood or Superman, conducting a one-man campaign against the enemy and winning his way by brute strength, rather than by skill or intelligence.

It is uncertain how much of a nubbin of historical truth lies behind the undoubtedly exaggerated stories concerning him, for much of the Samson story can be made to fit into the type of solar myths common in ancient times: in which the life of a hero reflects the course of the sun through the heavens.

Samson's life is miraculous from the start, for his birth is announced to his mother beforehand by an angel:

> Judges 13:5. *For, lo, thou shalt conceive, and bear a son; and no rasor shall come on his head; for the child shall be a Nazarite unto God from the womb . . .*

The word "Nazarite" means "one who is separate"; that is, one who marks himself off from ordinary human beings and devotes himself to the spiritual life. The Nazarite in ancient Israel has some of the flavor of the monk in Christendom.

Nazarites must have been fairly common in the later monarchy and the rules for becoming one were written into the Book of Numbers and thus made part of the law of Moses:

Numbers 6:2. . . . When either man or woman shall . . . vow a vow of a Nazarite, to separate themselves unto the Lord:

Numbers 6:3. He shall separate himself from wine and strong drink . . .

. . . .

Numbers 6:6. . . . he shall come at no dead body.

Samson is the first person in the Bible to be recorded as a Nazarite, but he certainly was not an edifying one. Nothing about his life indicated any spiritual uplift, or even any moral sense. Nor did he fulfill the barest minimum of the Nazarite vows since he did come into contact with dead bodies and he participated at feasts where there must have been much drinking.

Only his unshaven head and long hair remain of the Nazarite way of life, and this is an essential part of a solar myth since long hair represents the rays of the sun. It may well be that it is merely to account for the long hair in a non-idolatrous fashion that the later editors of the Book of Judges made him a Nazarite and put him in a role he fit so poorly.

Zorah

Samson was born:

Judges 13:24. And the woman bare a son, and called his name Samson: and the child grew . . .

Judges 13:25. . . . in the camp of Dan between Zorah and Eshtaol.

Zorah, the home of Manoah, Samson's father, is located in the eastern section of Danite territory, about fifteen miles west of Jerusalem. Eshtaol is a couple of miles to its east.

Zorah

The very name Samson ("Shimshon" in Hebrew) bears a striking resemblance to the word *shemesh*, meaning "sun." Only two miles south of Zorah was the town of Beth-shemesh ("house of the sun") believed to be a center of sun-worship.

Delilah

From the beginning, Samson displayed a penchant for Philistine girls:

> Judges 14:1. And Samson . . . saw a woman in Timnath of the daughters of the Philistines.
> Judges 14:2. And he . . . told his father and his mother, and said . . . get her for me to wife.

(Timnath was a town about six miles west of Zorah.)

Samson did not marry her in the end but in the course of the courtship and engagement, Samson performed typical feats. He killed a lion with his bare hands; he killed thirty Philistines in anger over having lost a wager; he tied torches to the tails of foxes and turned them loose in Philistine grainfields.

Later, he breaks loose from binding ropes and singlehandedly slaughters large numbers of Philistines; he escapes from a city which has locked its gates on him, by lifting the gates bodily and carrying them away, and so on. None of these feats do Israel any good or the Philistines any serious harm, and many of them can be shown to fit solar myths commonly told in ancient times.

But then Samson meets his match in the form of another Philistine girl:

> Judges 16:4. *And it came to pass afterward, that he loved a woman in the valley of Sorek, whose name was Delilah.*

The Sorek River flows westward from the neighborhood of Jerusalem to the sea. It forms the southern boundary of Danite territory and cuts through Philistia south of Ekron and north of Ashdod. It is a natural route for eastward invasion of Philistine armies into central Israel.

Delilah is bribed by her Philistine compatriots to find out from Samson the secret of his strength. After several evasions, he tells her:

> Judges 16:17. . . . *There hath not come a rasor upon mine head . . . if I be shaven, then my strength will go from me, and I shall become weak, and be like any other man.*
>
> . . . .
>
> Judges 16:19. *And she* [Delilah] *made him* [Samson] *sleep upon her knees; and she called for a man, and she caused him to shave off the seven locks of his head; . . . and his strength went from him.*

There is nothing in the Nazarite ritual that implies that it is the purpose of the long hair to give unusual strength to a man. This is clearly mythological and fits in with the sun motif.

Delilah's name is closely akin to the Hebrew *lilah* ("night") so apparently the tale tells of night overcoming the sun and depriving it of its rays as it sets toward the horizon and becomes ruddy and dim.

Dagon

Now at last the Philistines could take Samson. They blinded him (the sun, which may be viewed as the eye of the heavens, is removed and vanishes from the sky with the coming of night) and put him to hard labor in prison. Then, in celebration

> Judges 16:23. . . . *the lords of the Philistines gathered them together for to offer a great sacrifice unto Dagon their god . . .*

Very little is known about the nature of Dagon for the rites to this god of the Philistines of Gaza and Ashdod died out after Old Testament times. Because the word "Dagon" resembles *dag*, the Hebrew word for "fish," the idol has often been supposed to represent a fish-god and even to be in the form of a merman, man above the waist and fish below. This is the form in which Milton describes Dagon in *Paradise Lost* when he calls the roll of the fallen angels.

Since the Philistines were a coastal people, to whom fish and fishing could have been important, this seemed reasonable. However, the name of the god is even closer to *dagan*, the Hebrew word for "grain," and it is therefore even more reasonable to suppose that Dagon was an agricultural god, a very common type of deity.

The one other important mention of Dagon in the Bible gives some hint of the appearance of the idol. In later years, the Philistines capture the ark of the covenant and take it into the temple of Dagon with drastic results for their idol:

> 1 Samuel 5:4. *And when they arose early on the morrow, behold, Dagon was fallen upon his face . . . and the head of Dagon and both . . . hands were cut off . . . ; only the stump of Dagon was left to him.*

In the Revised Standard Version, the final phrase is given as "only the trunk of Dagon was left to him."

If the bottom half of the idol had been that of a fish, it seems very difficult to believe that the Biblical writers would not have said "only the tail of Dagon was left to him." The weight of the evidence would seem to lie, then, despite Milton, in favor of Dagon as a grain-god.

In any case, the name Dagon is clearly Semitic and is a good example of how Philistine culture was Semitized after their arrival in Canaan (if not before).

The feast to celebrate the capture of Samson did not end well for the Philistines. They brought out the blinded Samson in order to make their enjoyment of the occasion the keener.

> Judges 16:22. *Howbeit the hair of his head began to grow again after he was shaven.*

Again the sun myth can be seen here, for although the eye of the day is blinded and the sun disappears, it invariably appears again. It rises once more in the east, with its rays weak and dim, yes, but growing brighter and stronger as it climbs in the sky.

In a last display of strength, Samson pushes apart the pillars supporting the roof of the large house in which they feasted. He himself, and many Philistines, died in the collapse that followed. In this way, a story which had many of the aspects of farce ended with a touch of tragic dignity. Samson is the twelfth judge, the last in the Book of Judges.

Dan

Dan and the Danite Migration

The Book of Judges does not end with the twelfth judge. The last five chapters add two supplementary narratives which are placed in this book because they belong in its particular historical period. The writer specifies this:

Judges 18:1. *In those days there was no king in Israel . . .*

Unlike the earlier accounts in this book, however, these final incidents are not associated with the feats of any specific judge.

The first account deals with the tribe of Dan, which found itself unbearably oppressed by the overpowering might of the Philistines, who occupied most of the region theoretically assigned to Dan at the conquest and dominated the rest.

> Judges 18:2. . . . *in those days the tribe of the Danites sought them an inheritance to dwell in; for unto that day all their inheritance had not fallen unto them . . .*

"In those days" merely specifies the period of the judges; it does not tell us certainly whether it comes before or after the feats of Samson. If it is assumed that because the incident follows the tales of Samson, it therefore occurs later in time and is good evidence that Samson's activities did not seriously weaken the Philistines or help the Danites.

The Danites decided, therefore, to seek for an area far away from the powerful Philistines, and sent a group of five men to reconnoiter the far north. Eventually

> Judges 18:7. . . . *the five men . . . came to Laish, and saw the people that were therein, how they dwelt careless, after the manner of the Zidonians . . . and they were far from the Zidonians and had no business with any man.*

In other words, they found a Phoenician (Canaanite) city, thirty miles inland, which could not easily be rescued by the main Phoenician power centers on the coast. Furthermore, it had lived in peaceful isolation, without having formed military alliances that might serve to make an assault against the city expensive and subject to retaliation.

The scouts reported this on returning home, whereupon a body of six hundred men were sent northward to secure the place. In passing through the territory of the bordering tribe of Ephraim, they calmly appropriated an idol built by Micah, an unoffending Ephraimite who had been hospitable to the spies on their earlier trip. They also took with them the Levite who had served as private chaplain to the Ephraimite. When Micah objected, the Danites threatened to kill him into the bargain.

> Judges 18:26. *And the children of Dan went their way: and when Micah saw that they were too strong for him, he turned and went back unto his house.*

This is an example of the anarchy of the times and the disunity of the tribes. Danites felt no compunction, presumably, in stealing from

Ephraimites. (From the fact that no Ephraimite force advanced to oppose the marauding Danites, it might be supposed that this happened after Ephraim's catastrophic defeat at the hands of Jephthah.)

Nor were the Danites the only offenders in this respect. They were offended against as well. When Samson, a Danite, was conducting his harassment of the Philistines, a band of men of Judah (neighboring Danite territory to the south and southeast), fearing general Philistine reprisals, acted to remove the troublemaking Samson:

> Judges 15:12. . . . *they said unto him, We are come down to bind thee, that we may deliver thee into the hand of the Philistines* . . .

They fulfilled their threat, too (though Samson later escaped the Philistines by means of his superstrength). Apparently, the men of Judah did not hesitate to sacrifice a Danite to what we would consider the common enemy.

As it is put in the final verse of the Book of Judges:

> Judges 21:25. *In those days there was no king in Israel: every man did that which was right in his own eyes.*

This lack of law and order, this feeling that might was the only right, goes far to explain the eventual Israelite clamor for a king and is something even the general anti-monarchic attitude of the final editors of the Book of Judges cannot hide.

But to return to the migrating Danite band—

They reached Laish and attacked it as consciencelessly as they had robbed the Ephraimite and with as great a success. They destroyed Laish and built a new city in its place.

> Judges 18:29. *And they called the name of the city Dan* . . .

The site of Dan is usually identified with the Arab town Tell el Kady, located on the upper Jordan, nearly thirty miles north of the Sea of Galilee. ("Dan" and "Kady" both mean "judge.")

Dan represented the farthest northern reach of any purely Israelite territory (although Israelite dominion in the greatest days of the monarchy extended much farther north over areas occupied by non-Israelites). The phrase "from Dan to Beersheba" can therefore be taken to mean "all Israel" since Beersheba was the southernmost Israelite town of any consequence. The distance from Dan to Beersheba is about

150 miles, which is equal to the distance from Albany to New York, a respectable distance in Old Testament times.

The site of Dan still stands at the northernmost edge of modern Israel, though Beersheba is far from the southern edge. Modern Israel controls a 120-mile stretch of desert (the Negev) south of Beersheba. Israel now extends over an extreme length of 270 miles.

Dan's position made it as isolated and exposed in its new role as an Israelite city as it had been in its earlier role as a Phoenician city. Not long after the death of Solomon, it was taken by a Syrian army from the north and that was the end of it. Its span of existence was two centuries.

Gibeah

The next account, the one with which the Book of Judges ends, is an even more distressing story, one which even more clearly indicates the state of anarchy and lawlessness that prevailed in Israel before the kingship was established.

It concerns a man of Ephraim who was traveling northward from Judah with his concubine, intending to cross the intervening territory

Gibeah

of Benjamin. The day was drawing to a close when he and his party reached Jerusalem, which lies on the boundary dividing the territory of

Judah from Benjamin. He might have stayed there for the night, but Jerusalem was then under the control of the non-Israelite Jebusites and the man of Ephraim preferred to find a nearby Israelite city in which to stay.

> Judges 19:12. . . . *We will not turn aside hither into the city of a stranger . . . ; we will pass over to Gibeah.*

(Gibeah lay five miles north of Jerusalem and was an important Benjamite center.) There he managed to find a night's lodging with an old man, who happened to be a fellow Ephraimite. That night, however, a gang of Benjamite toughs besieged the old man's house, and seizing the concubine, abused and eventually killed her.

Again, it would seem, tribal disunity exacerbated the situation. One cannot help thinking that the Benjamites would not have acted with such disregard of humanity if they had not been dealing with Ephraimites, members of another tribe, and therefore strangers.

The irony of it is that if the Ephraimite and his concubine had slept over in Jerusalem, the "city of a stranger" which he would not enter, he would probably have been safe.

The "outrage at Gibeah" is the city's only claim to a very dubious fame, and it was held up in later centuries as the very epitome of sinfulness, a standard against which to measure disgrace. Thus, the prophet Hosea, writing some four centuries later of his own generation, said:

> Hosea 9:9. *They have deeply corrupted themselves as in the days of Gibeah* . . .

Mizpeh [Benjamin]

The account of the events following the outrage of Gibeah is a puzzling one, for in several ways it seems inconsistent with other parts of Biblical history. When news of the outrage was spread among the tribes:

> Judges 20:1. . . . *all the children of Israel went out, and the congregation was gathered together as one man, from Dan even to Beersheba, with the land of Gilead, unto the Lord in Mizpeh.*

The Mizpeh here is not the one in Gadite territory where Jephthah's troops gathered before the battle with the Ammonites. Rather it was a town in Benjamin, near its border with Ephraim. In the period of the judges, this was used as a tribal meeting place on several occasions.

We need not literally suppose, of course, that "all the children of Israel" assembled there; but rather that representatives of all the tribes were there, including even those from beyond the Jordan.

The gathering is pictured as being horrified at the event and unanimously deciding on united action against Gibeah.

Judges 20:11. *So all the men of Israel were gathered against the city, knit together as one man.*

And yet this seems so unlikely. Throughout the period of the judges, the tribes of Israel did not unite even under the most pressing of dangers. They did not all unite against Sisera or against the Midianites or against the Ammonites. Indeed, Manasseh's fight against the Midianites nearly provoked civil war with Ephraim, and Gad's fight against the Ammonites did provoke such a civil war. Therefore it seems quite unbelievable that a united front could be set up on this occasion.

Perhaps the later editors idealized the situation. Could it be that what actually happened was that all Ephraim, rather than all Israel, united against Benjamin in defense of the manhandled Ephraimites?

If one were to search for historic justification, however, one might suppose that the Book of Joshua was accurate and that at the time of the conquest and perhaps immediately afterward the Israelite tribes *were* taking common action. Might then the outrage at Gibeah have happened right at the start of the period of the judges, despite its position at the end of the book?

After all, when in the war that followed, Israel suffered initial defeats, they turned to the ark of the covenant for advice and the Bible pauses in its account to say:

Judges 20:28. *And Phinehas, the son of Eleazar, the son of Aaron, stood before it in those days . . .*

But Eleazar was contemporary with Joshua, so that events occurring in the lifetime of Eleazar's son must be taking place immediately after the conquest, and while united action was still, presumably, part of the Israelite tradition.

The war finally turned against Benjamin. The Israelites were victorious, Gibeah was sacked, and the entire Benjamite territory devastated. Indeed, the Benjamite population was almost wiped out.

Judges 20:47. *But six hundred men turned and fled . . . unto the rock Rimmon.*

The "rock Rimmon" is sometimes identified with a wild, hilly region five miles north of Gibeah.

Only these six hundred men, the Biblical story indicates, remained of the Benjamites. Even if we assume an exaggeration, the story, if it has a foundation of historical truth at all, must indicate a serious and even devastating defeat of Benjamin. If so, it could not have happened toward the end of the period of the judges, for Benjamin was prosperous then. It was from Benjamin, in fact, that a king of Israel was soon to be drawn. On the other hand, the picture of a greatly weakened Benjamin early in the period of the judges might be considered consistent with the Moabite invasion that put Benjamin under enemy occupation and provoked the counteraction of Ehud (see page 234).

Jabesh-gilead

The story goes on to say that Israel repented the destruction of Benjamin and was unwilling to see a tribe disappear. The six hundred survivors might serve as a nucleus for repopulation but the Israelites had sworn to give them no wives. They looked therefore for some city or group that had not been represented in the war against Benjamin and that had therefore not participated in the oath.

Judges 21:8. . . . *And behold, there came none to the camp from Jabesh-gilead . . .*

Jabesh-gilead was a Gadite city, located east of the Jordan River about fifteen miles north of Succoth.

The Israelites proceeded to sack Jabesh-gilead and obtain a supply of wives for the Benjamites. In this way, Benjamin survived. Again, if this happened at all it could not have happened late in the period

Jabesh-gilead

of judges for in the time of King Saul, which followed hard after, Jabesh-gilead was a flourishing town.

(I can't resist the personal speculation that some Israelite writer in the early period of the monarchy decided to write what we would today call a historical romance centering about the affair at Gibeah. He filled it with violence and action and did not hesitate to adjust history to the dramatic needs of the story. And then, somehow, the tale was taken seriously by the priestly editors who later drew together the various tribal traditions into the Book of Judges. It was therefore included, but was placed at the end because it seemed to fit nowhere. Now, there it is, a puzzle for Biblical scholars to try to decipher.)

8. RUTH

THE BOOK OF RUTH · BETHLEHEM-JUDAH · MAHLON AND CHILION · RUTH · DAVID

The Book of Ruth

Following the Book of Judges, in the various versions of the Bible used by Christians, is a short book of four chapters, titled Ruth after its heroine. It is set in the time of the judges:

> Ruth 1:1. *Now it came to pass in the days when the judges ruled . . .*

Judah and Moab

One might almost think it was another of the tales of the time. Something to add to the accounts of the wars of Gideon and Jephthah, the exploits of Samson, the migration of the Danites, the outrage at Gibeah. Why then is it not made a part of the Book of Judges?

The answer is that it is not just another of the tales of the time. The material in the Book of Judges is uniformly bloody, primitive, and at times even repulsive, as is to be expected of stories based on the contemporary chronicles of a crude, barbaric era. The story of Ruth, on the other hand, is a charming pastoral idyl, written as though by someone looking back at a period from a long distance, and seeing it in the light of the "good old days," a time of simplicity and peace and good will—which the time certainly was not.

In short, the Book of Ruth was composed in the fifth century B.C. in all likelihood, after the return of the Jews from exile and some seven centuries after the time it purports to describe. And even though its central thesis is based on historic tradition, perhaps the details surrounding it are fictional.

The Jews recognized this by including the book only in the third division of the Bible—"The Writings." The books in this section were considered by them to be literature, rather than history.

Nevertheless, the historic point it makes is so important to the Christian scheme of things, that it has been drawn forward into the historic section of the Bible and placed in its appropriate position in the story—immediately after the Book of Judges.

Bethlehem-judah

The tale begins with a famine that drives a family of Israelites out of their home in Judah:

> Ruth 1:1. . . . *And a certain man of Bethlehem-judah went to sojourn in the country of Moab, he, and his wife, and his two sons.*

Bethlehem-judah is so called to distinguish it from Bethlehem-zebulun, about seventy-five miles northward. Bethlehem-judah is so much the more famous for reasons that will soon be made plain that any reference simply to Bethlehem may be taken to mean Bethlehem-judah.

In fact, the only mention of Bethlehem-zebulun in the Bible is thought to be in connection with Ibzan, one of the minor judges (the ninth in order) glancingly mentioned in the Book of Judges:

Judges 12:8. *And after him* [Jephthah] *Ibzan of Bethlehem judged Israel.*

Bethlehem-judah, located about six miles south of Jerusalem, apparently bore an earlier name of Ephrath (see page 102). Even in the time of David, the men of Bethlehem could be called Ephrathites:

1 Samuel 17:12. *Now David was the son of that Ephrathite of Bethlehem-judah, whose name was Jesse* . . .

and the writer of Ruth follows that custom in connection with the family entering Moab:

Ruth 1:2. *And the name of the man was Elimelech, and the name of his wife Naomi, and the name of his two sons Mahlon and Chilion, Ephrathites of Bethlehem-judah* . . .

Bethlehem had until now been mentioned in the Bible only in unhappy connections. Rachel had died near it, giving birth to Benjamin. The Danites migrating northward to consummate a bloody aggression took with them a Levite who was from Bethlehem-judah. The concubine who was brutally outraged and killed in Gibeah was of Bethlehem-judah.

Now, however, Bethlehem begins to take on a new and unique importance through its association with this family and what is to follow.

Mahlon and Chilion

In Moab, Elimelech dies, but his sons marry Moabite girls:

Ruth 1:4. *And they took them wives of the women of Moab; the name of the one was Orpah, and the name of the other Ruth: and they dwelled there about ten years.*

Ruth 1:5. *And Mahlon and Chilion died also both of them* . . .

Since "Mahlon" means "sickness" and "Chilion" means "wasting," they don't seem to be the type of names anyone would give children. Further, from the early death of the two sons, the names appear entirely too appropriate. The use of such appropriate names is, however, often characteristic of fiction.

Ruth

Naomi, bereft of her husband and sons, decides to return to Bethlehem and assumes that her daughters-in-law will not wish to go with her into a strange land. Orpah does indeed part from her, but the other daughter-in-law, Ruth, refuses flatly:

> Ruth 1:16. *And Ruth said, Intreat me not to leave thee . . . for whither thou goest, I will go; and where thou lodgest, I will lodge; thy people shall be my people, and thy God my God;*

and the two go to Bethlehem.

In Bethlehem, Ruth meets Boaz, a rich relative of Naomi's, who is attracted to the girl despite the fact that she is a foreigner, and is grateful to her for the love and care she is showing Naomi. Naomi shrewdly arranges matters so that Boaz ends by offering to marry Ruth in full, traditional style.

The marriage is made and eventually a son is born, which comforts Naomi and consoles her for her own losses. Ruth, her loyal daughter-in-law, although a Moabitess, is now considered a fully assimilated member of the community and the Israelite women praise her:

> Ruth 4:14. *And the women said unto Naomi . . .*
> Ruth 4:15. *. . . thy daughter in law, which loveth thee, . . . is better to thee than seven sons . . .*

She has remained ever since, to all men, one of the most attractive women in the Bible.

David

But now comes the real point of the story:

> Ruth 4:17. *And the women . . . gave it* [Ruth's son] *a name . . . Obed: he is the father of Jesse, the father of David.*

Ruth, in other words, was the great-grandmother of Israel's hero-king David.

The purpose of the book seems clear. It was written at the time when the Jews, like Naomi, were returning from exile. The exiles were bitterly anxious to purify the land from the strangers who had been settled on it during the Exile. Their leaders established a rigid and narrow racial policy by which all intermarriage with foreigners was forbidden and all who had already married foreign wives must put them away.

But there must have been many among the Jews who were appalled at the pettiness of such a policy and at the heartlessness with which it would have to be enforced. One of them wrote the Book of Ruth as a clarion call for universality and for the recognition of the essential brotherhood of man.

In writing the tale, the author might have been inspired by the existence of an actual tradition to the effect that David was part Moabite in ancestry. Certainly, at one period in his life when he was in peril and it seemed to him that not only he but his entire family was in danger of slaughter, David brought his parents to Moab for safety:

> 1 Samuel 22:3. *And David . . . said unto the king of Moab, Let my father and my mother . . . be with you, till I know what God will do for me.*

At the time, it may have been good policy for Moab's king to support David, who was then rebelling against Saul, since in that way Israel could be weakened. Nevertheless, David's confidence in Moab at this juncture may also have arisen from a realization of kinship.

If there was such a tradition, the writer of the Book of Ruth made superb use of it, and whether the details he added are fictional or not is of little moment as far as the book's deeper meaning is concerned.

By making the heroine a Moabitess, the writer sharpened the point of the story, for Moabite women were the traditional corrupters of Israelite men, thanks to the well-known story told in the Book of Numbers (see page 189). And yet this foreign woman was the ancestress of David.

The point could not have been made stronger. Not only could a foreigner be assimilated into Judaism and prove a worthy addition to it, but the foreigner might be the source of the highest good. Ought one to forbid foreign marriages as was done after the return from exile? Why, if Boaz's foreign marriage had been forbidden, there would have been no David.

To Christians, the importance went even further. Through David, Ruth was an ancestress of Jesus, and therefore the tale tends to reinforce the Christian view of the Messiah; that he is for all mankind and not for the Jews alone.

9. 1 SAMUEL

SHILOH · APHEK · KIRJATH-JEARIM · MIZPEH · SAUL · JABESH-GILEAD ·
JONATHAN · MICHMASH · AGAG · THE PROPHETS · BETHLEHEM · DAVID ·
GOLIATH · DAVID AND JONATHAN · NOB · ADULLAM · ZIKLAG · GILBOA ·
BETH-SHAN

Shiloh

We now move into a period of increasingly reliable history. The next group of books tells of the establishment of the monarchy, and of its progress, first as a single kingdom of Israel, then as two smaller kingdoms, until the final destruction of one and the temporary destruction of the other.

Originally this history was detailed in two books. The former was called "Samuel" because it dealt with the prophet and judge of that name, and with the first two kings of Israel, both of whom were anointed by that prophet. The second was called "Kings" for obvious reasons.

Since both books were rather long, and therefore inconvenient to handle in the days when books were printed on long rolls, the Jewish scholars in Egypt, who prepared the first Greek translation of the Bible about 250 B.C., divided each book into two parts. Thus, we now have 1 Samuel, 2 Samuel, 1 Kings and 2 Kings. Since all four books deal with the monarchy it would also be reasonable to call them 1 Kings, 2 Kings, 3 Kings, and 4 Kings. This, in fact, is what is done in the Catholic versions of the Bible. Nevertheless, I will follow the convention of the King James Version.

The book of 1 Samuel begins with Samuel's parents:

1 Samuel 1:1. *Now there was a certain man of Ramathaim-zophim, of mount Ephraim, and his name was Elkanah . . .*

The Kingdom of Saul

Ramathaim-zophim is also referred to as Ramathaim, or even as Ramah (but is then to be distinguished from the better-known Ramah in Benjamin). The site is not certain but the consensus seems to place it in western Ephraim about ten miles east of the modern

Shiloh

city of Tel Aviv. In New Testament times, it is to appear once again, but under the Greek version of the name—Arimathea.

Elkanah was an Ephraimite. His genealogy is traced back to his great-great-grandfather, who is identified as

1 Samuel 1:1. . . . *Zuph, an Ephrathite.*

This, however, is an error. The Revised Standard Version, as well as the New Catholic Edition and the Masoretic Edition all identify Zuph as "an Ephraimite." It is a small point, but if Samuel is viewed as having been descended from an Ephrathite, that is, from a man of Bethlehem-judah, his later relationship to David of Bethlehem may be misconstrued.

On the other hand, although Elkanah and his son Samuel are Ephraimites in the sense that they live in Ephraim, they are described in later records as being Levites by descent.

> 1 Chronicles 6:33. . . . *Of the sons of the Kohathites:* . . . *Shemuel,*
> 1 Chronicles 6:34. *The son of Elkanah* . . .

The Kohathites are the descendants of Kohath, second son of Levi. (Shemuel is but the Hebrew form of the name we call Samuel, and it is given as Samuel in this verse in the Revised Standard Version.) The tale continues, with reference to Elkanah:

> 1 Samuel 1:3. *And this man went* . . . *yearly to worship* . . . *in Shiloh* . . .

Shiloh, located in the hill country in the center of Ephraim, was the spiritual nucleus of the region. To it, Israelites traveled to sacrifice at appropriate times of the year, as, over a century later, they were to travel to the Temple at Jerusalem.

The history of Shiloh as the site of a religious shrine sacred to Israel dates back, according to tradition, to the time of Joshua:

> Joshua 18:1. *And* . . . *Israel assembled together at Shiloh, and set up the tabernacle of the congregation there.*

This tabernacle had been constructed at Mount Sinai, as described in the final third of the Book of Exodus, and it included the ark of the covenant, which was considered the resting place of God Himself. Eli, serving as High Priest at Shiloh at this time, was also an Ephraimite, who according to later tradition was a Levite, and a descendant of Ithamar, fourth and youngest son of Aaron.

Elkanah's wife, Hannah, had no children, and at Shiloh, she vowed that if she were granted a child, he would be raised as a Nazarite and devoted to the Lord. She later had a child, named him Samuel, and eventually sent him to Eli to serve at the temple.

The story is rather similar to that told of Samson and it may be that the story here has been, rather unaptly, cast back into the Book of Judges in order to explain Samson's long hair in a non-mythological fashion.

Aphek

In the interval since the Israelites had entered Canaan, matters had settled down in some ways. The Canaanites in the north had been crushed in the battle against Sisera. The various competing peoples across the Jordan—the Moabites, Ammonites, Midianites, and Amalekites—had been held off and beaten back through the activity of men such as Ehud, Gideon, and Jephthah.

But that left the Philistines, the most technologically advanced, best organized, and hence most dangerous of the early enemies of Israel. They were strong in the north, controlled the coastal area completely, and were dominant over the territory of Judah in the southern portion of Israel. This is indicated by the statement of the men of Judah who came to bind Samson and deliver him to the Philistines:

Judges 15:11. . . . [The] *men of Judah . . . said to Samson, Knowest thou not that the Philistines are rulers over us?*

The core of Israelite resistance to the Philistines was the centrally located Rachel tribes, headed by Ephraim. These had been weakened in the war against the Trans-Jordanian tribes under Jephthah, so it was a good time for the Philistines to make their advance, and the scene was set for a great, perhaps a climactic battle:

1 Samuel 4:1. . . . *Now Israel went out against the Philistines to battle, . . . and the Philistines pitched in Aphek.*

The site of Aphek is not certain, but there seems reason to think that the later town of Antipatris (mentioned in the New Testament) was built on its site. Aphek was, in that case, at the western edge of Ephraimite territory (perhaps five miles north of Samuel's home town of Ramathaim) and at the northern edge of Philistine territory (about twenty miles north of Ekron, the most northerly member of the Philistine federation).

After a preliminary defeat, the Israelites thought to alter matters by bringing the ark of the covenant into the camp, in the belief that the physical presence of God would ensure victory. The Philistines themselves accepted the validity of this view and are pictured as in deep consternation over the effect of the presence of the God of the Israelites. They nerved themselves to a desperate fight.

In a great battle, the Israelites were totally defeated; the two sons of Eli, who were with the army, were slain, and the ark of the covenant was taken. At hearing the news, the old High Priest, Eli, died of shock.

This battle, which may have taken place about 1080 B.C., marks the end of Shiloh as a religious center, less than a century after Joshua had established it as such by moving his headquarters there. Its actual fate is not described in the Bible because of the eventual overriding concern with Jerusalem as *the* religious center of the nation, references to earlier shrines are reduced to a minimum.

Still there are hints, as when the prophet Jeremiah threatens the king of Judah with destruction, quoting God's words as:

> Jeremiah 26:6. *Then will I make this house like Shiloh* . . .

It seems very likely that in the aftermath of the battle, the Philistines plundered deep into Israelite territory, destroying Shiloh. For a period of about half a century thereafter, Philistine domination extended, more or less loosely, over all of Canaan. The period from 1080 to 1030 B.C. may be taken as the peak of Philistine power.

Kirjath-jearim

Although Shiloh was gone, the ark of the covenant remained, albeit in enemy hands. The Biblical writers could not allow themselves to lose sight of the ark (which was eventually to grace the Temple at Jerusalem) and they devote two chapters to tracing its progress through Philistine territory.

The Philistines, who thoroughly accepted the ark as representing the physical presence of an enemy God, were in awe of it, and quite ready to see in any misfortune that befell themselves the angry work of that God. Ashdod, where the ark was first placed, experienced misfortunes, passed it on to Gath, which suffered equally, and passed it on to Ekron. The Ekronites indignantly refused it.

It was decided, therefore, after the ark had remained among the

Kirjath-jearim

Philistine cities for some seven months, to send the dangerous object into the interior so that distance might lend security. The ark left Philistia proper and passed into the land of Judah, which was then under tight Philistine control.

The first stopping place was Beth-shemesh (see page 250), which also suffered misfortunes, and the ark was sent still further on to a place where it was to remain for several decades:

> 1 Samuel 7:1. *And the men of Kirjath-jearim came, and fetched up the ark of the Lord* . . .
> 1 Samuel 7:2. *And . . . while the ark abode in Kirjath-jearim . . . the time was long . . . and . . . Israel lamented after the Lord.*

Kirjath-jearim is usually identified with a site about ten miles northwest of Jerusalem. It was at the extreme edge of the area directly controlled by the Philistines. In other words, it was as far distant as they could manage from their own population centers and yet not so far distant that the Ephraimites could repossess it. In point of fact, the Ephraimites never did. When the ark once more became the object of a centralized worship, it was the men of Judah who obtained it.

Mizpeh

What resistance the Rachel tribes could offer after the disaster at
Aphek centered about the person of Samuel. His association, as a child,
with the destroyed shrine at Shiloh gave him standing in later years
as a priest, and he did not flinch in the emergency:

> 1 Samuel 7:5. And Samuel said, Gather all Israel to Mizpeh.

This is the Mizpeh referred to in connection with the aftermath of
the outrage of Gibeah (see page 257). Its use in the Book of
Judges, in what may have been a fictional account, was probably
drawn from the more historic association with Samuel and its use as a
rallying point for what forces could be gathered from among the
shattered Israelites. The modern site of Mizpeh is occupied by a
village known to the Arabs as Nebi Samwel ("the prophet Samuel"),
and it is there that the traditional site of his grave is located.

The Bible goes on to make it appear that the Philistines were
massively defeated under Samuel, but this is doubtful. If it were so,
the desperate battle of Saul against the Philistines in succeeding years
would be difficult to explain. More likely, the anti-monarchic bias of
some of the priestly records incorporated into 1 Samuel (as in Judges)
is evident here and the feats of Saul and David are pushed backward
in time and given to Samuel the priest. Samuel's position is perhaps
more accurately presented in the picture of the geographical extent
of Samuel's power:

> 1 Samuel 7:16. And he [Samuel] went from year to year in
> circuit to Bethel, and Gilgal, and Mizpeh, and judged Israel in all
> those places.

Gilgal is not the town mentioned earlier in connection with the
advance of Joshua across the Jordan (see page 211) but is thought
to be another of the same name located about midway between
Samuel's home town Ramah (Ramathaim-zophim) and the destroyed
Shiloh. Bethel is ten miles south of Gilgal and Mizpeh is about eight
miles southwest of Bethel.

The picture one gets, then, is that of a twenty-mile strip of hill country in Ephraim and Benjamin, resolutely maintaining the apparently lost cause of Israel, and engaged in a more or less successful guerrilla war against the Philistines.

Saul

Whatever successes Samuel was able to achieve served only to keep in being a rather unsatisfactory state of affairs. Samuel kept matters from growing worse, but there seemed to be no signs that they would grow better. The Philistines had to be beaten and not merely held off. For this reason, particularly after Samuel had grown old, the clamor grew among the Israelites for a king. A half century had passed since the disaster at Aphek and it was time.

Samuel is pictured as warning the people against a monarchy, describing the burdens that would be placed upon them by a king. Here, once again, the anti-monarchism of the priestly historian shows itself. But whether Samuel objected or not, he set about searching for a suitable candidate for the kingship. This he found in the form of a young Benjamite:

1 Samuel 9:1. *Now there was a man of Benjamin, whose name was Kish* . . .

1 Samuel 9:2. *And he had a son, whose name was Saul, a choice young man, and a goodly* . . .

Saul, apparently, had been kept aloof from the problems of the day, and was not involved in the guerrilla fighting against the Philistines for, as it turned out, he did not even know of Samuel. (This seems puzzling, but perhaps the matter is not as strange as it appears. A guerrilla leader can scarcely find it safe to publicize himself too much. He is most secure and his operations most successful if he remains out of the limelight.)

Saul's encounter with Samuel came when he was trekking through the hills in search of three asses his father had lost. They passed near Samuel's station of the moment and Saul's servant, who had heard of Samuel, but only as a kind of magician, urged that they avail themselves of his services. For a piece of silver, Samuel might consent to do the equivalent of looking into a crystal ball and locating the asses.

Samuel, however, had his mind on something far more important. On seeing Saul he had the inspiration of making him king. Saul is described as extremely tall and good-looking and it might have occurred to Samuel that such a man would look every inch the king and by his appearance alone rally the people about him. Samuel may have thought further that it would not be difficult to dominate the young man and remain at his side as the all-powerful prime minister. He therefore anointed Saul as king:

> 1 Samuel 10:1. *Then Samuel took a vial of oil, and poured it upon his [Saul's] head, and kissed him, and said . . . the Lord hath anointed thee . . .*

The act of anointing probably originated as an act of cleansing. In the days before soap, scented oils would serve to remove grime and leave a pleasant fragrance behind. One would naturally anoint one's self when about to go before a superior; how much more so when about to go before God.

Therefore, when something was to be dedicated to God or presented before Him, the act of anointing was usually involved and it became symbolic of a divine grace being conferred upon the object or person anointed.

Thus, when Jacob dreamed of the ladder in Bethel, he took the stone he had rested his head upon, set it up as a pillar:

> Genesis 28:18. . . . *and poured oil upon the top of it.*

Again, when Aaron was formally made High Priest by Moses:

> Leviticus 8:12. *And he [Moses] poured of the anointing oil upon Aaron's head, and anointed him, to sanctify him.*

Now the device was used by Samuel to imply the special spiritual character of the kingship. Indeed, it came to be accepted that no one was really a king until he had gone through the careful ritual of anointing, so that the phrase "the anointed one" came to be synonymous with "the king."

Samuel next called a council at Mizpeh and carefully arranged matters so that Saul was chosen by lot, making use, presumably, of the Urim and Thummim (see page 150). Saul, who had already been secretly anointed, was now proclaimed king openly by the shouts of the representatives gathered at the council. This is believed to have taken place in 1028 B.C.

Jabesh-gilead

It was one thing to demand a king and quite another to rally round a particular individual chosen as king. To take up arms against

Jabesh-gilead

the Philistines was a serious thing and it required an experienced and able general. Saul was not yet tested in this respect.

1 Samuel 10:27. *But the children of Belial said, How shall this man save us? And they despised him . . .*

The test came soon enough:

1 Samuel 11:1. *Then Nahash the Ammonite came up and encamped against Jabesh-gilead . . .*

Jabesh-gilead, six miles east of the central Jordan, was, like all the Trans-Jordan, subjected to periodic Ammonite raids from the east. The greatest crisis had come in the time of Jephthah, but the great Ammonite defeat then had merely abated the danger. It had not ended it.

Jabesh-gilead, expecting no help from an Israel which was treading softly in the shadow of the Philistine power, made ready to surrender, but the terms of Nahash were brutal and sadistic—he insisted that the population of the city submit to having each their right eye put out. The people of Jabesh-gilead asked for a seven-day period of grace before submitting even to this and sent, in desperation, for a help they still dared not expect.

1 Samuel 11:4. *Then came the messengers to Gibeah of Saul, and told the tidings . . .*

Saul, however, rose to the occasion, sounding the call to arms and rallying an army behind him.

1 Samuel 11:7. *. . . And . . . the people . . . came out with one consent.*
1 Samuel 11:8. *And . . . he numbered them in Bezek . . .*

Bezek is in the hills of Manasseh, five miles north of Thebez, where Abimelech died (see page 245). It was due west of where Jabesh-gilead lay on the other side of the Jordan.

The numbers given of the troops that gathered on that occasion represent a late tradition and are impossibly high (300,000 men of Israel and 30,000 men of Judah) and anachronistically assume a divided kingdom, something that lay a century in the future. In actuality, Saul probably was able to gather merely the men from the areas of the Rachel tribes, and obtained a much smaller number—but enough to do the job. He marched across the Jordan and defeated the Ammonites. Jabesh-gilead was saved.

The enthusiasm of Israel for Saul was now great indeed. A general to lead Israel against the Philistines had been found. Saul was crowned king a second time at Gilgal, amid wild celebration.

(Of course, this double crowning of Saul may well represent the imperfect fusion of two traditions. The first would be a priestly anti-monarchic tradition in which the great judge of Israel, Samuel, anoints and crowns an unknown, bashful youth. The second would be a Benjamite tradition in which a tribal hero, Saul, accomplishes a great feat of arms and is acclaimed king in a triumph with which Samuel had nothing to do. The story of Samuel himself may represent a similar fusion of two traditions; one in which he is the warlike judge who rules all Israel and one in which he is an obscure seer with no more than a local reputation.)

Notice that Saul established his capital at Gibeah in Benjamin: the town of the "outrage." The Bible has occasion to tell later of the gratitude of the people of Jabesh-gilead to Saul. The Jabeshites remained loyal, in fact, when Saul and his house had sunk low in defeat.

Now the spirit of loyalty between two regions—in disaster as well as in prosperity—always strikes a romantic note in history if only because such disinterest on a regional scale is hard to find. In Greek history there is the friendship of Plataea and Athens, a friendship in which Plataea persevered to the death, for instance.

It was perhaps this well-known and romantic relationship between Gibeah of Saul and Jabesh-gilead that was in the mind of the writer of the possibly fictional tale of the consequences of the outrage at Gibeah. In that tale, Jabesh-gilead is pictured as the one Israelite town refusing to fight against Gibeah and as being destroyed in consequence.

Jonathan

With the Rachel tribes under a war hero, intensified conflict with the Philistines is inevitable; and at this point, Saul's son Jonathan is suddenly introduced:

> 1 Samuel 13:1. *Saul reigned one year; and when he had reigned two years over Israel,*
> 1 Samuel 13:2. *Saul chose him three thousand men of Israel; whereof two thousand were with Saul . . . and a thousand were with Jonathan . . .*

When Saul was introduced in the tale of his search for his father's asses, he was described as a young man, and yet he might even so have been a father of little children. To suppose, however, that two years after his anointing he is the father of a grown man capable of conducting men in war is difficult. The problem here rests with 1 Samuel 13:1, which is not actually a translation of the Hebrew but merely an attempt to make sense out of the original words. Literally translated, the Hebrew clause that begins the verse reads: "Saul was one year old when he began to reign."

It seems that something has been lost and the Revised Standard

Version has the verse read "Saul was . . . years old when he began to reign; and he reigned . . . and two years over Israel." It explains in a footnote that the gaps represent missing material.

It may well be that 1 Samuel 13:1 is actually a summarizing chronological verse that might say, for instance, "Saul was twenty-five years old when he began to reign; and he reigned twenty-two years over Israel." Saul himself probably didn't reign that long but the house of Saul, that is, he himself and one of his sons, reigned together that long.

In that case, we needn't suppose that the introduction of Jonathan comes two years after the start of Saul's reign. It might have come at any time; well toward the end of it, perhaps. Jonathan might therefore have been a boy at the time his father became king and a warlike young man at the time of the events in this chapter and the next.

As to what happened in the interval after the victory at Jabesh-gilead had settled Saul on the throne, we can easily suppose that the time was filled with a slow strengthening of Saul's kingdom. Quite obviously, Saul was starting from scratch:

> 1 Samuel 13:19. Now there was no smith found throughout all the land of Israel: for the Philistines said, Lest the Hebrews make them swords or spears:

The ill-armed Israelites might skulk in their fastnesses and emerge for hit-and-run raids but if Saul was to lead them into pitched battle they would simply have to be well armed. Undoubtedly, it took time to get the arms, capture them, buy them, or, perhaps, develop the skills necessary to make them. This dull interval of slow strengthening is slurred over in the Bible.

Michmash

Jonathan launched an attack:

> 1 Samuel 13:3. And Jonathan smote the garrison of the Philistines that was in Geba . . .
>
> . . . .
>
> 1 Samuel 13:5. And the Philistines gathered themselves together to fight with Israel . . . and pitched in Michmash . . .

Michmash

The Philistine outpost of Geba may really refer to the much larger and more important town of Gibeon, five miles west of Saul's capital, Gibeah. (Gibeon is the town that once deceived Joshua at the time of the conquest—see page 215.)

The Philistines, reacting to this provocation, advanced on Geba at once and reached Michmash, two miles northeast of Geba. (The town still exists and is known to the Arabs as Mukhmas.) The Israelite population scattered and hid before the advancing Philistines and Saul held back his small army and refused to give battle. Jonathan, however, conducted another raiding party against the Philistines, guiding his men over the hills to attack the Philistine camp from unexpected quarter. The Philistines, keyed up for an Israelite onslaught, mistook the relatively small attacking party for the main force of the enemy, and in a moment of panic, fled.

Jonathan had acted without orders and, indeed, probably against orders. Saul was angered, therefore, and undoubtedly jealous at the vast acclaim that greeted his son, and ordered Jonathan's execution. (The Bible advances a ritualistic explanation for the order.) The army refused to permit the execution, however, and a certain coldness must have remained thereafter between father and son. (It is not uncommon in monarchies, down to modern times, for rivalry and even hatred to exist between the king and the heir apparent.)

The Philistine defeat at Michmash was important. The Philistines temporarily fell back to their coastal and southern strongholds and Saul was given greater room for maneuver.

Agag

With the respite from the Philistine menace, Saul was able to turn southward to secure the desert border and lay the groundwork for a possible outflanking maneuver against the Philistine coast. The chosen target was the Amalekites, with whom the Israelites are described as having a traditional enmity dating back to the time of Moses.

> 1 Samuel 15:7. *And Saul smote the Amalekites* . . .
> 1 Samuel 15:8. *And he took Agag the king of the Amalekites alive* . . .

Agag, the ruler of a petty Amalekite tribe, cannot have been particularly powerful or renowned, and would not be considered so were it not for a remark in one of Balaam's blessings (see page 186). Speaking of Israel's future, Balaam says:

> Numbers 24:7. . . . *his king shall be higher than Agag* . . .

as though Agag were a standard symbol of great power.

Most scholars agree that the mention of Agag in this verse is a copyist's error. The name may originally have been Og. This would make sense, for the story of Balaam is placed at a time when Og of Bashan had been the mightiest monarch yet faced by the Israelites (see page 182). To say that the future king of Israel would be greater than Og would have been appropriate to the occasion, and the accidental change of Og to Agag is not a difficult one to imagine.

The Prophets

And yet while Saul was establishing and securing his kingdom, there were internal frictions. Saul the king and Samuel the kingmaker were at odds.

From the start, Samuel had kept his hand on the wheel of state for at the very time of Saul's anointing we hear for the first time of bands of prophets. When Saul was returning home from his encounter with Samuel:

> 1 Samuel 10:10. . . . *behold, a company of prophets met him* . . .

These prophets were groups of men who devoted themselves to ecstatic devotions. They would play instruments, sing, dance, put themselves into wild trances, and fall down in frenzy. They rather resembled certain orders of dervishes of later Islamic times, and if the word were here given as "dervishes" rather than "prophets," the picture would be clearer.

In their trances and ecstasies, these prophets or dervishes were believed to be divinely possessed, to have access to more than human knowledge, to be able to pronounce oracles, and so on. The very word "prophet" is from Greek words meaning "to speak forth"; that is, to relate and interpret the will of God as made manifest to the prophet during his trance or ecstasy.

In the time of Saul, the companies of prophets were by no means completely edifying. They may, indeed, have been hang-overs of paganism. Samuel, as the spiritual leader of the time, seems to have attempted to guide their energies into the path of Yahvism, but it is difficult to say how much success he might have had.

Yet the prophets were an excellent tool. They had the capacity to stir and influence the people and they tended to be strongly nationalistic, ready always to serve as the backbone of resistance against foreign oppression. Samuel, as their head, could direct them to meet and join Saul. It was the support of the bands of prophets that was Samuel's practical contribution to the establishment of Saul's kingship:

1 Samuel 10:26. *And Saul . . . went home to Gibeah; and there went with him a band of men, whose hearts God had touched . . .*

Undoubtedly, Samuel maintained his grip on Saul through the prophetic bands and yet Saul, after his victory at Jabesh-gilead, must have been increasingly irked at prophetic interference in his policies and must have attempted on several occasions to establish his independence.

The crisis came over the battle with the Amalekites. In rousing the people against the tribesmen, Samuel demanded that the Amalekites be exterminated entirely; a kind of "destroy the infidel" outlook. Saul, more humane or more practical, took Agag alive and kept the herds and other spoil from useless destruction. Samuel was enraged at this, executed Agag with his own hands, and told Saul:

1 Samuel 15:23. . . . *Because thou hast rejected the word of the Lord, he hath also rejected thee from being king.*

Bethlehem

Samuel, having moved into the opposition, needed someone to put up against Saul, and turned to the tribe of Judah:

1 Samuel 16:4. *And Samuel . . . came to Bethlehem . . .*

Prior to the time of Saul, the tribe of Judah is almost ignored in the Bible; so much so that there is strong suspicion that Judah was not considered part of Israel up to that time.

In the Book of Judges, Caleb and Othniel appear early as conquerors of southern Canaan, where later the tribe of Judah was to be. They are not Israelites, however, but members of Edomite clans. The tribe is not mentioned in the Song of Deborah, or in the course of the warlike deeds of Gideon or Jephthah.

In connection with the adventures of Samson, Judah's role is a completely inglorious one. Judah is subject to the Philistines and makes no move to throw off the yoke. Instead, to avoid trouble, the men of Judah hand Samson over to the Philistines.

Judah is mentioned in connection with Saul's battle at Jabesh-gilead, and is said to have supplied 10 per cent of the army. This, however, may be a later and non-historical addition, intended to show Judah as being involved in the national revival.

However, Saul in fighting the Amalekites, who inhabited the desert south of Judah, would have had to pass through Judah. It may be, then, that one of the consequences of the Philistine defeat at Michmash was the revolt of parts of Judah against the Philistines and their formation of an alliance with Saul.

And yet Judah's allegiance to Saul would have to be relatively weak. To the men of Judah, Saul would be a foreigner, and a Judean would therefore be more likely to be a suitable instrument for Samuel than would a member of the northern tribes who were becoming increasingly loyal to their hard-working, if not quite brilliant, king.

Then, too, Judah throughout its history was more strongly Yahvistic than the remainder of Israel was. The populous cities of the Canaanites had been in central and northern Canaan and it was there that the religious influence of the Canaanites had more successfully diluted the simpler desert rituals of Yahvism. Judah, closer always to the desert, might be more influenced by Samuel's Yahvistic point of view.

(It is interesting to compare Judah with Macedon. In ancient Greece, Macedon was a border area, Greek in culture and language but rather more primitive, and looked upon as semibarbaric by the Greeks themselves. At the time the Greeks were fighting their national war against Persia, Macedon remained under Persian domination, but the time was to come when Macedon defeated Persia more thoroughly than Greece ever did, and was to rule, briefly, over all of Greece.

In the same way, Judah was a border area of Israel, Israelite in culture and language but rather more primitive and looked upon, in all probability, as semi-Canaanite by the Israelites themselves. At the time the Israelites were fighting their national war against the great Philistine enemy, Judah remained under Philistine domination, but the time was to come when Judah defeated the Philistines more thoroughly than Israel ever did, and was to rule, briefly, over all of Israel.)

David

In Bethlehem, Samuel visited Jesse, the grandson of Boaz and Ruth (see page 264) and a man of wealth and substance. An appropriate member of his family would command widespread support throughout Judah. Jesse had eight sons and Samuel was most impressed with the youngest, David:

> 1 Samuel 16:12. . . . *he was ruddy,* . . . *and goodly to look to*
> . . .

> 1 Samuel 16:13: *The Samuel took the horn of oil and anointed him in the midst of his brethren* . . .

Once again, Samuel had chosen a handsome young man to make into a king.

Meanwhile, Saul, knowing that Samuel and the prophets had turned against him, and suspecting they would rouse rebellion, had grown, rather understandably, moody and suspicious. The courtiers suggested music as therapy and one of them (it is very tempting to suspect he was in Samuel's pay) suggested that a certain David, whom he praised as a skilled harpist, be brought to court.

Judah in David's Time

1 Samuel 16:21. *And David came to Saul, . . . and he became his armourbearer.*

. . . .

1 Samuel 16:23. *And . . . when the evil spirit . . . was upon Saul, . . . David took an harp, and played . . . so Saul was refreshed and was well . . .*

With David at court, gaining the confidence of Saul, and serving his apprenticeship in war under him, Samuel's plan was working well.

Goliath

There follows a second tale describing the introduction of David to Saul's court, one that is inconsistent with the first. Both are included, without any attempt to enforce consistency, as though the Biblical writers were saying, "On the other hand, some say this . . ."

The second tale begins with a confrontation between the Philistines and the Israelites:

1 Samuel 17:1. *Now the Philistines gathered together their armies to battle . . . at Shocoh . . .*

Shocoh is a town in Judah, about thirteen miles west of Bethlehem. If it is correct to assume that Saul's battle against the Amalekites was made possible by his alliance with a Judah that was rebelling against the Philistines, then it is reasonable to suppose that the Philistines would strive to restore Judah to the yoke by force, and that Saul's troops would be sent south to support the new ally.

At Shocoh, the armies faced each other in stalemate, each waiting for some favorable moment or condition to attack and, during the wait, a man of Gath challenged any member of the Israelite army to single combat, suggesting that victory for the entire army rest with the winner of the duel. He is described as a giant:

> 1 Samuel 17:4. . . . *Goliath of Gath, whose height was six cubits and a span.*

Accepting the cubit as roughly seventeen inches, and the span as nine inches, that would make his height just over nine feet. (The dramatic nature of this story, by the way, has so impressed later generations that "Goliath" has entered the English language as a term used for anything of monstrous size.)

Jesse's three oldest sons were serving with the army, and Jesse sent his youngest son, David, with supplies for his soldier brothers. The youngster heard the challenge and was indignant that it remained unaccepted. David offered to fight Goliath and faced him, unarmored, bearing only a sling. With a smooth stone, whirled speedily from the sling and aimed unerringly, he killed the giant and the Philistines fled.

This is one of the most famous stories in the Bible, so much so that any unequally matched contest is considered a "David-and-Goliath battle."

But the very drama of the story makes it suspect. In any real battle, would either army risk the outcome on a single combat? The circumstances surrounding the fight seem to be the deliberate creation of a skilled writer, intended to produce a profound emotional effect. Goliath's height and armor are stressed and exaggerated, as is David's youth and unarmed courage.

Then, after the battle, it turns out that neither Saul nor his general know the lad, and that it is only through his great fame as the slayer of Goliath that David gains entry into the court. This is a direct contradiction to the more believable story in the previous chapter.

Actually, the Bible contains a hint as to how the story of David and Goliath may have come to be written. Later, when the Bible lists some of the important warriors fighting in David's armies and tells of their feats of arms, we find:

2 Samuel 21:19. . . . *Elhanan . . . a Bethlehemite, slew the brother of Goliath the Gittite . . .*

Since "Gittite" means "a man of Gath" the verse seems clear. Goliath had a brother and he, too, was killed by a native of Bethlehem. But the phrase "the brother of" was added by the translators of the King James Version, who followed a similar verse in another book of the Bible.

In the Book of 1 Chronicles, which retells the history given in the Books of 1 Samuel and 2 Samuel, but which was written some centuries later, we have:

1 Chronicles 20:5. . . . *and Elhanan . . . slew Lahmi the brother of Goliath the Gittite . . .*

Lahmi is not mentioned elsewhere in the Bible and it is at least possible that it is an accidental spelling of "Bethlehemite." The writer of this verse may have assumed that to leave out the phrase "the brother of" would make the verse inconsistent with the well-known story that David killed Goliath, so he put it in. The translators of the King James Version followed suit in the original verse in 2 Samuel.

Nevertheless, there is no certainty that anything dropped out of the verse in 2 Samuel, and the Revised Standard Version gives 2 Samuel 21:19 as simply: ". . . Elhanan . . . the Bethlehemite, slew Goliath the Gittite . . ."

It might be, then, that the otherwise unknown Elhanan killed Goliath in the course of some battle and that a panegyricist in later years wrote a little historical tale filled with romantic and edifying detail, in which he ascribed the feat to Israel's great hero-king. Like the story of George Washington and the cherry tree, it caught on and came to be accepted as history. The telltale verse in 2 Samuel remained, however, and had to be patched up in 1 Chronicles—and in the King James translation.

David and Jonathan

In whatever fashion David came to court, whether as a harpist or as a war hero, he met Jonathan the heir apparent there:

> 1 Samuel 18:1. . . . *the soul of Jonathan was knit with the soul of David, and Jonathan loved him as his own soul.*

The intensity and disinterest of this friendship is such that the phrase "David and Jonathan" has become a byword for deep friendship, like the equivalent "Damon and Pythias" drawn from Greek history.

The Bible takes pains to show David innocent of all wrongdoing with respect to Saul, but even accepting the Biblical account, one wonders if the innocence was complete. David had been anointed by Samuel and therefore knew he was king, in the eyes of the priestly faction at least. How innocent toward Saul could he be?

Saul himself could eye David only with deep suspicion as time went on and as David's charm and his skill in war gained popularity for him. Even leaving the anointing episode to one side, we must remember that a popular general is always dangerous to a king.

Furthermore, Saul was probably suspicious of his own son as an aftermath of the battle of Michmash. To watch the popular heir apparent join forces with the popular general could lead to only one thought in the mind of any prudent king—they were plotting a coup.

> 1 Samuel 18:9. *And Saul eyed David from that day and forward.*

Nob

David could not remain unaware of the gathering coldness of the suspicious Saul and when Jonathan warned him of the danger to his life, David left court and joined those he felt to be sympathetic toward him:

> 1 Samuel 19:18. *So David fled, and escaped and came to Samuel to Ramah . . .*

If anything was needed to convict David in Saul's eyes, this was it, of course. Saul sent an armed contingent to take David, who eventually eluded them.

1 Samuel 21:1. *Then came David to Nob to Ahimelech the priest* . . .

The actual location of Nob is uncertain. The best Biblical evidence for that location comes from the Book of Isaiah. The prophet is describing the advance of the Assyrian army against Jerusalem and the climax comes:

Isaiah 10:32. *As yet shall he* [Assyria] *remain at Nob that day: he shall shake his hand against* . . . *Jerusalem.*

Since the Assyrian is advancing from the north that would make it seem as though Nob were on a height not far from Jerusalem in that direction, and in fact its site is traditionally identified with a hill in Benjamite territory two miles north of that city.

The City of Nob: Dashed line indicates David's flight

David must logically have been striving to reach the safety of Judah where his fellow tribesmen might rally round him. Saul must, equally logically, have foreseen this and kept men watching the routes toward Judah. David's doubling back into Benjamite territory and getting help under the nose of the king succeeded through its unexpectedness.

Nob seems to have represented the remnant of the old Shiloh-worship. Ahimelech is described as the son of a man who is elsewhere described as the grandson of Eli, the last High Priest at Shiloh, and it may have been to Nob that the survivors of the Philistine sack of the earlier holy city had fled.

Saul, angered at David's having eluded him, breaks out into reproaches against his courtiers, accusing all of them of conspiracy and making it quite clear he considers David merely a tool of Jonathan:

> 1 Samuel 22:8. . . . *my son hath made a league with the son of Jesse . . . my son hath stirred up my servant . . .*

One of the men about him, Doeg (identified as an Edomite), had seen David in Nob and so informed Saul. The furious king jumped at once to the conclusion that the priests were conspiring with David (although the Biblical version shows Ahimelech to have helped David under the impression that David was on state business for the king). Saul had felt it impolitic to move directly against the influential Samuel, but the relatively weak contingent of prophets and priests under Ahimelech seemed fair game.

Saul marched against Nob, took and destroyed the city, then ordered the eighty-five priests slaughtered. No Israelite dared perform the task, but Doeg the Edomite did it. One son of Ahimelech, Abiathar, escaped, however, and eventually joined David. He was the last survivor of the old line of Shiloh, the great-great-grandson of Eli.

Adullam

Meanwhile, David had finally made his way to Judah and was joined by members of his tribe:

> 1 Samuel 22:1. *David . . . escaped to the cave Adullam: and . . . all his father's house . . . went down thither to him.*
>
> 1 Samuel 22:2. *And every one that was in distress . . . in debt . . . discontented, gathered themselves unto him; . . . there were with him about four hundred men.*

Adullam is in the Judean hill country about fifteen miles from Bethlehem and only two miles southeast of the place where David is described as having killed Goliath. In that stronghold he fortified himself and became the leader of a guerrilla band. What followed was virtually war between David and Israel.

In this war, Israel was much the stronger and David survived only by skillful evasion tactics, moving from place to place and remaining always one step ahead of the vengeful and remorseless Saul. David fully realized that war as conducted in those days (and sometimes in our own) extended death to the families of the enemy, so he took his parents for safekeeping to Moab. (This tends to reflect the possibility that David was part Moabite by ancestry; see page 265.)

Ziklag

A number of tales are told of the futile hunt of Saul after David, and the Biblical writer takes obvious delight in the cleverness of David in eluding the pursuit.

Nevertheless, it seemed clear to David that he could not count on his luck holding forever. Sooner or later, a misstep would leave him surrounded by overwhelming forces. He decided, under this pressure, to join the Philistines as the only way of securing adequate protection:

> 1 Samuel 27:2. *And David . . . passed over with . . . six hundred men . . . unto Achish . . . king of Gath.*

Achish could only be pleased to take into his service a tried captain with a desperate band of men who could be viewed as deadly enemies of Saul. In a sense, Judah, having allied itself with Saul against the Philistines, was now allying itself with the Philistines against Saul.

Achish as part of the bargain gave David what would, in medieval times, have been called a fief of his own:

> 1 Samuel 27:6. *Then Achish gave him Ziklag that day . . .*

Ziklag was a city at the southern border of Judah, in what had once been counted as Simeonite territory, but which was now still under Philistine domination. Its exact site is unknown, but the best guess seems to be that it was about twenty miles southwest of Gath and a dozen miles from the sea.

David's role as a mercenary leader in the service of the Philistines was acutely embarrassing to the Biblical writers. They take pains to assure the reader that while Achish thought David was raiding Israelite outposts in Judah, David was *really* raiding the Amalekites and other nomad tribes of the desert. It seems unlikely that Achish could possibly have been fooled in this manner. It is reasonable to suppose, rather, that if David was serving as a mercenary, he did what he was hired to do.

It is interesting that in the course of his Philistine service, David is nowhere referred to by the Philistines as the slayer of Goliath. This is rather suggestive of the non-historical nature of that famous duel.

Mount Gilboa

Gilboa

The Philistines saw their chance now. Judah was alienated from Saul over the matter of David, and the priestly party had been offended past repair, thanks to the slaughter at Nob. The time was ideal for a renewed attack on Israel.

1 Samuel 28:4. *And the Philistines gathered themselves together, and came and pitched in Shunem; and Saul gathered all Israel together, and they pitched in Gilboa.*

Mount Gilboa, a mountain ridge about ten miles long, with its highest point about 1700 feet above sea level, is in northern Israel about seven miles west of the Jordan River, and some forty miles north of Gibeah.

Shunem, where the Philistines were encamped, lay some ten miles to the northwest. It is only five miles south of Mount Tabor, where Barak had once gathered the forces of northern Israel against Sisera.

Saul feared the worst and turned for advice to the priests. They would not help him and Samuel, who might in this time of national emergency have had the greatness to be reconciled, was recently dead. Saul, in desperation, sought out a practitioner of the older Canaanite cults. Upon inquiring, he was told:

> 1 Samuel 28:7. . . . *Behold, there is a woman that hath a familiar spirit at En-dor.*

A familiar spirit is one who serves the human being calling upon it (the Latin *famulus* means "servant"). Saul sought to obtain advice from Samuel by having this spirit bring him from the dead.

This woman with the familiar spirit is the well-known "witch of Endor." The town of Endor is about two miles from Shunem, midway between the latter town and Mount Tabor. Its only importance in history or in the Bible is its connection with the witch in this one chapter.

To get to the witch of Endor, Saul had to disguise himself and pass through the enemy lines. It served him nothing, however. The witch's magical rites resulted in a prophecy of disaster (as was logical, considering the obvious desperation and despair of Saul) and that prophecy further intensified the despair. Saul and the Israelite army was broken in morale before ever the fight began.

The Biblical narrator pauses here to explain in considerable detail that David (Israel's national hero) did not take part in the disastrous battle that followed. David offered to fight with the Philistine armies, but the Philistine leaders would not have it. They feared that in the heat of the battle, David might attempt to improve his own situation by defecting to Saul. David was forced to return to Ziklag and there he was soon fully engaged in reversing a temporary victory of the Amalekites.

The Philistines then attacked the Israelite encampment on Gilboa and won a complete victory. Jonathan was killed and Saul committed suicide. The battle of Gilboa and the death of Saul are thought to have taken place in 1013 B.C. Saul, therefore, had reigned fifteen years.

Beth-shan

At one blow, all the hard-won gains of Saul were destroyed. The Philistines were again in control of virtually all Israelite territory west of the Jordan. The Rachel tribes, which had been the core of the national revival, were prostrate.

The extent of the Philistine victory is symbolized by the manner in which the victors displayed Saul's corpse as a means of expressing their contempt for the beaten king and destroying what remained of Israelite morale:

1 Samuel 31:10. . . . *and they* [the Philistines] *fastened his body to the wall of Beth-shan.*

Beth-shan was an important Canaanite center about six miles northeast of Mount Gilboa. It had been a Philistine outpost ever since the battle of Aphek and was probably the center of Philistine power in the regions to the north of the Rachel tribes; a power Saul had never been able to break. (It is very probable that Saul was never really king over more than the Rachel tribes of Benjamin, Ephraim, and Manasseh, at the most. To the north and west lay the Philistines, to the south Judah.)

But there was the east, too. The Trans-Jordanian tribes had been allied with Saul since the battle against the Ammonites at Jabesh-gilead. Jabesh-gilead, which lay about a dozen miles southeast of Beth-shan, remembered Saul's service to them particularly, and now repaid it in the only way they could. They mounted an attack against Beth-shan, rescued Saul's body, and buried it with all due honor.

And thus, with the death of Saul and with honor, at least, saved, though all else seemed lost, the Book of 1 Samuel comes to an end.

The Empire of David and Solomon

10. 2 SAMUEL

HEBRON · MAHANAIM · MICHAL · ZION · TYRE · VALLEY OF REPHAIM ·
BAALE · MOAB · AMMON · MEPHIBOSHETH · URIAH THE HITTITE · ABSALOM ·
KIDRON · SHIMEI · HUSHAI · SHEBA · ARAUNAH

Hebron

Hebron

With the death of Saul and the smashing defeat of Israel, the
Philistines controlled all of Canaan west of the Jordan. There wasn't
even, for the moment, a nucleus of resistance in the hill country
of the Rachel tribes where, for so many years before the coming
of the monarchy, Samuel had kept alive the hopes of Israel.

There was David, to be sure, but he was a man of Judah who
had been leading a guerrilla war against Saul and the kingdom of

Israel, and was therefore not a man to whom patriotic Israelites could easily turn. Besides, at the moment of Saul's death, David was actually a Philistine vassal.

Yet it was not as a mere Philistine vassal that David viewed himself. His first step was to establish his clear leadership over Judah at least:

> 2 Samuel 2:3. *And his men that were with him did David bring up . . . and they dwelt in the cities of Hebron.*
> 2 Samuel 2:4. *And the men of Judah came, and there they anointed David king over the house of Judah . . .*

David reigned as king of Judah in Hebron from 1013 to 1006 B.C.

David's assumption of the kingship would not have been possible before the battle of Gilboa, for Saul would quite naturally have viewed an independent Judah under a strong king as a threat to himself and would have taken steps to crush David.

As it was, David was free not only from Israelite interference but even from Philistine hostility. Presumably the Philistines felt him to be a safe puppet and considered his kingship a device to distract and further divide the subject peoples over whom they now ruled.

David, however, in choosing Hebron for his capital had selected a well-fortified town in a thoroughly defensible hill area in the center of Judah. He would not be easily dislodged if it came to war between himself and the Philistines.

To prepare for that war—which David knew to be inevitable, if the Philistines did not—David set about winning over the followers of the dead Saul and the remnant of those who still cherished the hope of an independent Israel. David aspired to leadership of the Hebrew tribes generally.

Mahanaim

Yet the Israelite kingdom was not quite wiped out, either. Saul had had four sons. The three oldest had died at Gilboa:

> 1 Samuel 31:2. . . . *and the Philistines slew Jonathan, and Abinadab, and Malchishua, Saul's sons.*

but there remained the fourth son, Ish-bosheth. Abner, Saul's general in chief, who had survived the battle of Gilboa, fled with Ish-bosheth to safety across the Jordan:

Mahanaim

2 Samuel 2:8. . . . *Abner . . . took Ish-bosheth the son of Saul, and brought him over to Mahanaim;*

2 Samuel 2:9. *And made him king . . .*

The Trans-Jordanians might be expected to be fiercely loyal to the house of Saul in memory of that king's vigorous rescue of Jabesh-gilead. Since the Philistines apparently saw no profit to be gained by extending their lines of communication in a perilous advance across the Jordan (something that had once served to destroy Ephraim; see page 247), Ish-bosheth and Abner were momentarily safe.

The exact location of Mahanaim in the Trans-Jordan is not known. Some place it south of the Jabbok River and others north. One guess is that it was located at a point some four miles east of Jabesh-gilead.

Michal

David, the new king of Judah, began a course of difficult negotiation with Abner in an attempt to establish a united kingdom. Unfortunately, David's general in chief, Joab, was a war hawk who felt that only outright conquest was the course to pursue. He forced a war in which the Israelite army was defeated.

The weakening kingdom of Ish-bosheth held out, however, and David's purposes were blunted. He did not want to rule by right of conquest, with the certainty of rebellion afterward. He hoped, rather, for a legal accession to power in the hope of founding a permanently united kingdom.

Fortunately for David, Abner quarreled with Ish-bosheth and began to dicker with David behind his own monarch's back. David, sensing the coming of victory, set his price. In return for peace and, presumably, for a high post for Abner in the united kingdom, David said:

> 2 Samuel 3:13. . . . *Thou shalt not see my face, except thou first bring Michal Saul's daughter . . .*
> 2 Samuel 3:14. . . . *which I espoused . . .*

Michal had married David in the days when Saul was firm on his throne and David had served as a successful military leader under him. After David's flight from court, Michal had been given in marriage to someone else.

David's intent here is clear. As husband to Michal and son-in-law to the dead Saul, he would gain a kind of legal right to the succession to the throne of Israel. If, in particular, he were to have a son by Michal, that son would represent the fusion of the houses of Saul and of David and he could eventually be expected to reign over both kingdoms in peace and legality.

Michal was delivered to David by an Ish-bosheth too weak to dare refuse and Abner proceeded to make his alliance with David. The implacable Joab, however, sought out Abner and killed him. This threatened to upset the apple cart for Abner was highly regarded by the Israelites. David avoided disaster only by a public act of contrition.

Some at Ish-bosheth's court could now see the inevitable and two of the army leaders assassinated the king and brought his head to David. David quickly disassociated himself from this crime, too, executing the assassins.

But no grown son of Saul remained and the despairing Israelites could see that their only safety lay now in the hands of the shrewd king of Judah:

> 2 Samuel 5:3. So *all the elders of Israel came to the king to Hebron; and king David made a league with them . . . and they anointed David king over Israel.*

The united kingdom over which David thus came to rule in 1006 B.C. is called Israel in the Bible, but the kingdom was never really single. The two halves of the nation were never truly amalgamated. Israel remained conscious of its greater sophistication and wealth as compared to the rustic Judah and resented being governed by a dynasty of Judah. It might be best to consider David, and his son after him, to be kings of a dual monarchy, Israel-Judah.

Zion

Having achieved legal rule over Israel as well as Judah, David wanted to cement that rule in the will of the people generally. To gain that, David realized he would have to give up Hebron as his capital, for that city was far too closely identified with Judah. David could not afford to have himself considered nothing more than a man of Judah. Nor could he transfer his government into Israel itself, for if that gained the approval of the Israelites, it might lose him Judah, and Judah was the core of his strength.

But between the territory of Judah and Israel, and belonging to neither, was the city of Jerusalem. If that were David's capital it could satisfy both parts of the dual monarchy since it would represent a kind of neutral territory.

Furthermore, it was still occupied by a Canaanite tribe, the Jebusites, so that its existence represented an inconvenient barrier between the two halves of the kingdom, while its conquest would be a national victory hailed by both halves alike.

Finally, Jerusalem held an extremely strong position, as was evidenced by the fact that the Jebusites had kept their ground steadily

Zion and the City of David

against all efforts on the part of the Israelites to dislodge them. If David could take it, it would prove an equally sure stronghold for him.

For all these excellent reasons of state, Jerusalem was therefore placed under siege:

> 2 Samuel 5:6. *And the king and his men went to Jerusalem unto the Jebusites, the inhabitants of the land . . .*

The course of the siege is not clearly given in the following verses, but the outcome is certain. David won, and the magnitude of his victory raised his stature as a military leader in Israel as well as Judah, ensuring his kingship on a wave of national pride.

> 2 Samuel 5:7. . . . *David took the strong hold of Zion: the same is the city of David.*

Zion was the fortified height (about 2440 feet high) within the town—the place where the defenders could hold out longest. It was the equivalent of the Athenian Acropolis, for instance. When Zion was taken, Jerusalem was taken. Since it was upon Zion that David built his palace, it became the "city of David." Later, David's son, Solomon, was to build the Temple on Zion, so that the hill became the military, political, and religious center of Israel.

As such, it came to symbolize (especially in poetic language) all of Jerusalem, or even all of Israel. In the last century, the movement to restore a Jewish homeland in Palestine has been called "Zionism" as a result.

There seems no doubt that Zion in located in the southeastern portion of what is now called the "Old City" of Jerusalem. In Christian times, the tradition arose that Zion lay on a ridge about half a mile to the west, but this is no longer taken seriously.

The modern city of Jerusalem was divided between Jordan and Israel in 1948. All of the "Old City," which is on the site of ancient Jerusalem, including Zion, became part of Jordan then.

The "New City" built to the west of the "Old City" was begun in 1860 thanks to the money and drive of the British-Jewish philanthropist Sir Moses Haim Montefiore. It is now much larger than the "Old City," with a population three times as numerous. The "New City" serves as the capital of modern Israel, but it is the "Old City" that contains the holy relics of the past.

As a result of the Six-day War of 1967, Israel took all of Jerusalem and declared its determination never to yield any part of it again.

Tyre

The Israelites under David were still largely a pastoral and agricultural people. If David wanted to build an elaborate palace for himself on his new stronghold of Zion, he had to seek help among the relatively sophisticated inhabitants of the Canaanite cities.

2 Samuel 5:11. *And Hiram king of Tyre sent messengers to David, and cedar trees, and carpenters, and masons: and they built David an house.*

Tyre is a Phoenician city situated on the Mediterranean coast about twenty miles south of Zidon (Sidon). According to Herodotus, the Tyrians maintained that their city had been founded as far back as 2750 B.C., but undoubtedly local pride was imposing itself on the eager

Greek tourist. From mention (or lack of mention) in the old Egyptian records it would seem that Tyre was not founded until 1450 B.C. and in the beginning was a colony of the still older Zidon.

Originally, Tyre may have been located on the mainland, but its greatness came when it shifted to a rocky island offshore, making itself almost immune from conquest and, while its fleet remained in being, from enforced starvation. Indeed, its name ("Zor" in Hebrew) means "rock." Nowadays, the old rock upon which Tyre built its greatness has joined the mainland, thanks to the silting up of the sea between. The site is now a peninsula on the coast of modern Lebanon, and is occupied by a town, Souro, with a population of about eight thousand.

Tyre's merchants penetrated the western Mediterranean and even passed outward into the Atlantic Ocean. As a result of gaining a monopoly on trade with what was then the far west, Tyre grew rich and powerful. During the time of the judges, it had been Zidon that had been the most important of the Phoenician cities (see page 217), but sometime during the reign of Saul, Tyre began to move ahead. From then on, till the end of Phoenician history, Tyre remained the leading city of the region.

The first king of Tyre of whom there is a reliable record is Abibaal, who came to the throne about 1020 B.C., when Saul reigned in Israel. He remained on the throne through David's reign. His son, Hiram, was, in turn, a contemporary of David's son, Solomon. It was Hiram whose artisans built Solomon's Temple. The importance of Hiram's role in connection with this supremely important structure sent its shadow backward in time so that his artisans are reported as having built David's palace, too, though that was certainly built during the reign of Hiram's father.

Valley of Rephaim

By now it must have become clear to the Philistines that David had grown too strong to serve as a safe puppet. His accession to the kingship of Israel, over and above that of Judah, had undoubtedly taken place without Philistine permission and must automatically have meant a break with them:

2 Samuel 5:17. . . . *when the Philistines heard that they had anointed David king over Israel, all the Philistines came up to seek David* . . .

2 Samuel 5:18. . . . *and spread themselves in the valley of Rephaim.*

It would have been wise for the Philistines to have struck at once, but perhaps the various cities, never firmly united, could not bring themselves to act until David had captured Jerusalem and by then it was really too late.

The valley of Rephaim lies between Jerusalem and Bethlehem and very likely the Philistines placed Jerusalem under siege. That this is so appears from the further statement:

2 Samuel 5:16. . . . *David . . . went down to the hold.*

The hold (stronghold) is almost certainly Jerusalem and within that nearly impregnable fortress, David could allow the Philistines to blunt their armor uselessly while armies gathered elsewhere in Israel and he planned his counterattack.

In two separate battles, he defeated them handily. The erstwhile puppet had become a conqueror and the Philistines fell back upon their coastal cities. They were never again to control the interior and David had become undisputed master of the territory of the twelve tribes of Israel and Judah.

Baale

David realized that it was insufficient to have Jerusalem as the political center only of the dual monarchy. Among the differences separating Israel and Judah were variations in religious customs and traditions. It would be wise, therefore, to take measures to centralize and unify the religion of the new nation, focus it on Jerusalem, and build a bridge between the north and south in the form of a common ritual.

A marvelous opportunity presented itself in connection with the ark of the covenant, the central object of worship of the Rachel tribes in the days of the judges. It had been taken from Israel by the Philistines (see page 272) and ever since had been kept at the city of Kirjath-jearim on the northern boundaries of Judah, about ten miles west of Jerusalem. Why not bring it to Jerusalem, and establish it as a center of worship? The object was Israelite, the place was Judean, and both parts of the nation would be satisfied.

2 Samuel 6:2. *And David arose, and went with all the people* . . . *from Baale of Judah to bring up from thence the ark of God* . . .

Baale (or Baale-judah) is used here as an alternate name for Kirjath-jearim.

Moab

Master in his own land, David's next step was to cast his eyes abroad for imperial conquests—the common attitude of rulers of the time (and of our time as well).

The conquest began with Moab, which he reduced to a tributary nation. Considering David's earlier friendly relations with the Moabites and his traditional descent from a Moabite woman (see page 265), we would be curious to know what caused the war, but the Bible gives no clue:

2 Samuel 8:2. *And he* [David] *smote Moab, and . . . the Moabites became David's servants and brought gifts.*

This event bears a relation to one of the oracles traditionally assigned to Balaam (see page 186). He had been hired by the king of Moab to curse Israel and it seemed ironically just to the Biblical writers that he was forced, in his trance, to curse Moab instead:

Numbers 24:17. . . . *there shall come a Star out of Jacob, and a Sceptre shall rise out of Israel, and shall smite the corners of Moab* . . .

This verse has been taken by many Christians to represent a Messianic prophecy, and to forecast the coming of Jesus and the defeat by him of idolatry and evil. It is for this reason that the words "Star" and "Sceptre" are capitalized in the King James Version (but not in the Revised Standard Version).

A more prosaic possibility is that the oracle (reduced to writing only in the time of the kingdoms) is a triumphantly nationalistic reference to David and his Moabite conquest.

Ammon

One by one the neighboring principalities fell before David, whose foreign wars were uniformly successful.

When a new king acceded to the throne of Ammon, David sent messages of congratulations as a routine courtesy. The new king, suspecting the messengers of intended espionage, treated them with scornful disrespect, shaving half their beards and cutting off parts of their garments. This amounted to a declaration of war.

David treated it as such and the Ammonites formed an alliance with the Aramaean (Syrian) cities to the north, who also viewed with alarm the sudden rise of the new kingdom of Israel-Judah.

2 Samuel 10:6. . . . *the children of Ammon sent and hired the Syrians of Beth-rehob, and the Syrians of Zoba . . .*

The Aramaeans had entered the area north of Israel (an area called Syria by the Greeks and retaining that name to this day) after the fall of the Hittite Empire, mingling, as they did so, with the remnants of the Hittite people. Their coming was part of the same restless movement that had brought the Philistines and the Hebrew tribes into Canaan.

The united forces were defeated by David and his general, Joab. The Ammonites and Syrians were both conquered, and the Edomites in the south as well, and by 980 B.C., David ruled an empire that stretched from the Red Sea to the upper Euphrates. It took up all the eastern border of the Mediterranean, except for part of the actual shore which remained in the possession of the Phoenician cities. These retained their independence but were careful to remain on friendly terms with David.

David's realm was not large as empires go, covering, at its peak, an area of only thirty thousand square miles—about the size of the state of Maine. It was feeble and small compared to the Egyptian and Hittite Empires that preceded it, or the Assyrian, Babylonian, and Persian Empires that were to succeed it. Indeed, it existed at all only because of the accident of history that placed David in the midst of a short and rare period when there happened to be no great empires in Asia.

Nevertheless, David's empire remained a period of glory for Israel, when compared with the centuries before and after, and was looked back upon with pride and nostalgia by all the later generations that followed David.

Mephibosheth

If David was extending his sway externally, he had to be at least equally careful and vigorous in establishing his power internally. He must have been perfectly aware that Israel was bound to remain restive under a Judean dynasty and that this restiveness might find a rallying point about someone of the old Israelite dynasty of Saul.

It was customary in ancient monarchies (and in some comparatively modern ones, too) to remove all remaining members of displaced dynasties for the sake of the security of the reigning king, or, if one wanted to express matters more idealistically, for the peace and good order of the realm.

To murder Saul's descendants in cold blood would have been bad politically, possibly provoking the civil war David was trying to prevent. The opportunity to do so safely eventually came, however:

2 Samuel 21:1. *Then there was a famine in the days of David three years, year after year* . . .

That was David's chance. In the general anxiety to end the famine, people would assent to actions that might otherwise be strongly disapproved—if those actions were taken as being designed to propitiate an angry Deity. The blame for the famine was therefore carefully placed by the priesthood:

2 Samuel 21:1. . . . *It is for Saul, and for his bloody house, because he slew the Gibeonites.*

The occasion upon which Saul slew the Gibeonites is not specifically mentioned in the Bible. Such an action on the part of Saul was a serious violation of the treaty of peace between the Israelites and the Gibeonites, a peace which, according to tradition, had been made in the days of Joshua (see page 215). To the Gibeonites, such a violation would seem to have well deserved the anger of God.

It is also just barely possible that this is a reference to Saul's slaughter of the priests at Nob (see page 290). Abiathar had been the sole survivor of the massacre and now served as a high priestly official under David. His own rather understandable animus against the house of Saul would, in that case, have made him more than willing to co-operate with David in this respect.

For the official purpose of appeasing the Gibeonites, then, David hanged seven of the male descendants of Saul, including two sons (by a concubine) and five grandsons. The rains, of course, eventually came (they always do) and that seemed to justify the act. To inhibit the chance of second thoughts on the part of the Israelites once the famine was over, David labored to keep their good will by paying somber respects to those who had been executed, burying them with honor in their ancestral tomb, and transferring the bodies of Saul and Jonathan to that tomb also.

The male members of the house of Saul seemed done with, but David was not entirely certain:

2 Samuel 9:1. *And David said, Is there yet any that is left of the house of Saul, that I may shew him kindness* . . .

This verse appears in the Bible a dozen chapters before the execution of the seven descendants of Saul, so that the irony is lost. This event, however, must have come after the executions or David would not have been forced to search so hard for "any that is left of the house of Saul."

One member of that house remained. This was Mephibosheth, the son of Jonathan. He had been five years old at the time of Saul's final and fatal battle on Mount Gilboa. At the news that Saul and Jonathan were dead and the army lost, there was wild confusion in the palace at Gibeah. A nurse fled with Jonathan's youngster and dropped him. His legs were damaged and he was crippled for the rest of his life.

Mephibosheth was in hiding during David's reign (a course of action rendered prudent by the executions) but his whereabouts were betrayed to David, who found that he could not, in this case, readily solve matters by another execution. First, Mephibosheth was a son of Jonathan, with whom he had once sworn a compact of friendship. Then, to consider matters more practically, the young man was a cripple and not likely to attract the loyalty of a rebel force, seeing that he was in no position to lead an army.

And yet, David did not abandon caution entirely. He allowed Mephibosheth to live, but he kept him at court and under his eye:

2 Samuel 9:13. *So Mephibosheth dwelt in Jerusalem; for he did eat continually at the king's table* . . .

Uriah the Hittite

Another domestic affair related in detail was the manner in which David came to make an addition to his harem. The importance of this lay in the fact that it was a son of David by this new woman who eventually succeeded to the throne of Israel.

David first saw her bathing on the roof of her house. Much taken by her appearance, he sent to find out her identity and was told:

2 Samuel 11:3. . . . *Is not this Bathsheba, the daughter of Eliam, the wife of Uriah the Hittite?*

It had been two centuries, now, since the Hittite Empire had disappeared, but their culture lingered. They had been driven out of Asia Minor, a region in which the Phrygians were now dominant, but Hittite principalities had been established southward in what is now Syria. There, mingled with the Aramaeans, the Hittites maintained themselves for two more centuries until the entire region—Hittites, Aramaeans, Israelites together—went under the heel of the Assyrian Empire.

But we are still in David's reign. David, in his northward drive of conquest, had absorbed these Hittite city-states and it is not surprising that a number of their soldiers, including Uriah, had entered his service. From the fact that Uriah is a Hebrew name ("the Lord is light") it may well be that Uriah had sought preferment by adjusting his religious beliefs to those of the king and had changed his name to suit.

In any case, he received a poor reward. David appropriated Uriah's wife and then sent him out to battle (the war against the Ammonites was proceeding at the time) with instructions to Joab to arrange for Uriah's death. This was done.

Although the Biblical writers praise David all they can, they cannot praise this. David is blamed and denounced by Nathan, a religious leader of the time. The courage of the reproof and the manner in which David accepted that reproof is one of the more moving passages in the Bible. There are few enough occasions in history, both before David and since, when an absolute monarch bowed before someone who clearly set forth the difference between good and evil.

Absalom

David's cautious eye on the house of Saul kept matters safe in that direction, but when trouble came, it came from an unexpected quarter, the royal family itself.

Unfortunately, civil wars based on family rivalries were all too common in the ancient monarchies, and the reasons are not hard to find. Chiefly, they stemmed from the institution of polygamy, which was quite widespread at the time, even among the Israelites.

A harem served the king's pleasure and it was also a matter of status, for the power and glory of the king, and therefore of the people he ruled, was held to be reflected by the luxury and richness of his way of life. But polygamy also ensured a large supply of sons and in an age of high infant mortality, a large supply was required in order to make it likely that at least one or two might grow to healthy manhood and lead the nation after the death of the old king.

The value of this was largely negated, however, by the fact that there was usually no rigorous rule of descent. Of the royal house, the strongest, most decisive, or most unscrupulous might seize the throne by rapid action at the time of the king's death.

To prevent this, and the civil war that often took place thereafter, the old king might choose a successor, a choice that would carry great weight with the officialdom of the realm and with the people. To attain such a royal seal of approval, the different women of the harem would intrigue endlessly.

Sometimes an overeager son, either not certain of the father's blessing, or overcertain of his backing, would try to settle matters by striking *before* the death of the old king. It was this which happened in David's reign.

David's oldest son was Amnon, born while David was still merely king of Judah and reigning in Hebron. Under ordinary circumstances, he might be expected to have been the heir. David's second son was

Chileab, who is not mentioned after the verse recording his birth and may, therefore, have died young. His third son was Absalom.

Both Amnon and Absalom were full-grown men in the latter part of David's reign; both in the prime of life; and both, undoubtedly, with their eye on the succession. They were half brothers only, being the sons of different mothers. Under harem conditions, this meant there was bound to be no feeling of brotherhood between them.

The open break came in connection with Tamar, the full sister of Absalom and the half sister of Amnon. Amnon brutally raped Tamar, who fled in shame to the house of Absalom. Absalom, feeling now he would have popular opinion on his side, waited his chance to catch Amnon off guard.

Two years passed, during which, no doubt, Amnon felt the danger had passed, the memory of his crime dimmed. Absalom arranged a festival to which Amnon and the other princes were invited. Amnon was deliberately allowed to get drunk and when merriment was at its height, Absalom had his men strike and Amnon was killed.

That broke up the party, of course, and Absalom, uncertain of his father's reaction, quickly left the country.

2 Samuel 13:37. *But Absalom fled, and went to Talmai . . . king of Geshur.*

Talmai was his mother's father, and Geshur was one of the city-states to the north. It is usually placed just east of the Sea of Galilee.

Absalom was, however, the oldest surviving son of David and it was dangerous to leave him in exile. Enemies of Israel could easily invade the country on the pretext of placing Absalom on the throne and many in Israel might side with him. The country would then be divided against an essentially foreign invasion. This may have been in the mind of Joab, the realistic commander in chief of David's army. He maneuvered Absalom's return after three years, and his formal reconciliation with David after two more years.

Absalom was not satisfied, however. He was now David's logical heir, but could he count on David's blessing? Would not David, mindful of the killing of Amnon, choose another of his sons for the kingship?

Absalom determined to take no chance, but to prepare for action on his own. He was popular with the people, because he was good-looking and because of the natural sympathy he must have gained as the aggrieved party in the affair with Amnon. More than that, Absalom initiated a careful and deliberate campaign to ingratiate himself with the people by display of affability and graciousness and by a studied appearance of concern for their problems.

2 Samuel 15:6. . . . *so Absalom stole the hearts of the men of Israel.*

After four years (the King James Version says "forty" but this is widely considered a mistake and the Revised Standard Version says "four") he felt the time had come. He received permission to visit Hebron on what seemed a harmless pretext and once there, he had himself declared king and raised the standards of rebellion.

Undoubtedly, he had paved the way in Hebron and many were prepared, in advance, to back him. It is interesting that it was in Hebron, the Judean center, that Absalom made his first open move. Apparently, Absalom had strong Judean backing. Why this should be so the Bible does not specifically say. One might guess, however, that David throughout his reign had been concerned to win over the good will of the Israelites and had leaned over backward to avoid favoring his own Judeans. And there might well have been a strong Judean party which resented this and which would have preferred a king under whom a straightforward Judean hegemony over the empire might have been arranged.

Amasa, a Judean and, in fact, a cousin of Joab and a somewhat more distant relative of David himself, served as Absalom's general. Ahithophel, a native of the Judean city of Giloh, also defected to Absalom. He had been a member of David's council and had a formidable reputation for wisdom.

Later in the book, when the more eminent of David's soldiers are listed, mention is made of:

2 Samuel 23:34. . . . *Eliam the son of Ahithophel the Gilonite.*

This Eliam might conceivably be the same Eliam earlier mentioned as the father of Bathsheba. It might therefore be that Ahithophel was the grandfather of the woman who turned out to be David's favorite wife, and the great-grandfather of the man who turned out to be David's successor. It doesn't seem likely that in that case, he would defect to a son of David who was no relative of his own. On the other hand, he might have had no expectation that his own descendant would someday be king and he might have experienced humiliation at the highhanded manner in which David had brought his grand-daughter into the royal harem. There is no way of deciding this.

Kidron

Valley of the Kidron

David reacted at once. Absalom had prepared his net carefully and Jerusalem was unsafe. The old king's one chance was to get out into the open and across the Jordan where he might gather an army. Time could be on his side if he could snatch time. The people might grow disenchanted with Absalom; they might quail at the thought of at-tacking David if David did not at once succumb; they might even remember that the old king had found Israel and Judah in the grip of the Philistines and had raised them to empire, and might grow ashamed of their rebellion.

With his household, then, his staff and his armed bodyguard, he left the city:

2 Samuel 15:23. . . . *and all the people passed over: the king also himself passed over the brook Kidron . . . toward the way of the wilderness.*

Jerusalem is bounded on the east by the Kidron valley, which is now dry but which, in Biblical times, was the bed of a small stream, the brook Kidron, which flowed south into the Dead Sea.

Having crossed the Kidron, David and his retinue mounted the line of hills to the east.

2 Samuel 15:30. *And David went up by the ascent of Mount Olivet . . .*

Mount Olivet, or, as it is better known, the Mount of Olives, is a ridge about two and a half miles long, running north and south about half a mile east of Jerusalem and separated from that city by the Kidron valley. The highest part of Mount Olivet, due east of Zion, is about half a mile high.

Shimei

Dangers multiplied, for it was not merely a question of David's replacement by Absalom, but of the disintegration of the barely established empire. On Mount Olivet, David was overtaken by the servant of Mephibosheth, the son of Jonathan and only living direct descendant of Saul. According to the servant, Mephibosheth was remaining in Jerusalem in the hope of being called to the throne. After all, if, with Judean support, Absalom gained the throne, it might be the throne of Judah only, and Israel, regaining its independence, might turn to its older dynasty.

The extent of this danger was made plainer in Bahurim (a town whose exact site is unknown but which lay somewhere between Jerusalem and the Jordan). Shimei lived there, a Benjamite, a collateral relative of Saul, and presumably a man of influence in the area:

2 Samuel 16:5. . . . *Shimei . . . came forth, and cursed still as he came.*

2 Samuel 16:6. *And he cast stones at David . . .*

2 Samuel 16:7. *And thus said Shimei . . .*

2 Samuel 16:8. *The Lord hath returned upon thee all the blood*

of the house of Saul, in whose stead thou hast reigned; and the Lord hath delivered the kingdom into the hand of Absalom thy son: and behold thou art taken in thy mischief, because thou art a bloody man.

It sounds very much as though Shimei is referring to the execution of Saul's descendants (not described till several chapters later). The soldiers with David offered to kill Shimei, but David did not allow that. Shimei's curses were doing him little harm but what Shimei now had the courage to say in David's adversity, others might be thinking, and an unnecessary outrage against Shimei might simply serve to swell Absalom's army with Benjamites.

Hushai

What strength David possessed now lay in the fact that the core of his army, his elite troops, remained faithful and were with him. They were few in number but they could be counted on to give a good account of themselves.

Ahithophel, however, advised Absalom to attack David at once, even while the king was retiring in disorder toward the Jordan and before he could cross the river and begin organizing an army. Move now, while David is off balance, he urged in effect; strike while the iron is hot.

Now Absalom made his fatal mistake.

2 Samuel 17:5. *Then said Absalom, Call now Hushai . . . and let us hear likewise what he saith.*

Hushai was another of David's counselors, but was not a Judean. He was of the city of Archi, which was included in the territory of Ephraim. Unlike Ahithophel, he had not defected to Absalom but had been directed by David to remain in Jerusalem as what we would today call a "double agent."

Hushai gave the advice calculated to give David the one thing he needed—time. Hushai warned Absalom that a hasty attack on David might lead to a preliminary defeat by David's hardened warriors. The defeat might be minor and of no military significance but to the people it would prove that David was still the invincible conqueror and they would lose heart and melt away from Absalom. Therefore, said Hushai, do not attack till you have built up a large army.

Absalom took Hushai's advice and waited to build up his large army and that was his end. David got safely over the Jordan, where the Trans-Jordan tribes rallied round him as they had rallied round Ishbosheth, the son of Saul, a generation earlier. Ahithophel, deciding that victory for Absalom was now impossible, killed himself.

David's newly organized army, under his veteran officers, then struck back across the Jordan, meeting Absalom's hastily raised and poorly led levies, and utterly defeated them. Absalom was taken, and although David had ordered that he be unharmed, the practical Joab thought otherwise. A rebel left alive was one who would rebel again someday, and so he had Absalom killed.

David now returned to Jerusalem and resumed the undisputed kingship. Shimei, the Benjamite who had cursed David, came quickly to make his submission, while Mephibosheth came also, maintaining that he had been slandered, and that no thought of assuming the kingship had ever occurred to him.

David, aware that the victory did not necessarily wipe out the sources of disaffection, was careful to take no revenge. Shimei was allowed to live; Mephibosheth was taken back into favor. This was intended to appease the Israelite nationalists. As a measure of reconciliation with the Judean nationalists, he accepted Amasa, who had served as Absalom's general, as commander in chief in place of Joab. (Presumably, David did not forget Joab's action in killing Absalom against orders.)

Sheba

David's mildness was of no help. Certain factions among the Israelites, disappointed at the re-establishment of the Judean dynasty over the united kingdom, revolted. Their leader was Sheba, a Benjamite and therefore of the tribe of Saul. He rallied Israel about him on a purely nationalistic slogan:

2 Samuel 20:1. . . . *and he blew a trumpet, and said, We have no part in David, neither have we inheritance in the son of Jesse: every man to his tents, O Israel.*

Once again David's army had to take the field. The resourceful
and unscrupulous Joab found, in this renewed war, an opportunity to
gain his generalship once more. He assassinated Amasa and took over
the army, leading it northward. Sheba retreated hastily but was caught
and trapped in Abel of Beth-maacah, a city in the north, just across
the Jordan River from Dan. The inhabitants of the city killed Sheba
in order to prevent the otherwise inevitable sack, and the rebellion
came to an end.

Araunah

The tale of David's reign is now essentially over. The Book of 2
Samuel concludes with a summarizing list of David's heroes and of
some of their exploits, with a couple of psalms attributed to David,
and with one final tale included in the last chapter of 2 Samuel because
of its connection with the chief accomplishment of David's successor.
This last tale begins with a census:

2 Samuel 24:1. *And again the anger of the Lord was kindled
against Israel, and he moved David against them to say, Go, number
Israel and Judah.*

Why a census is treated, in this chapter, as a sin, is uncertain. Twice,
a census was supposed to have taken place in the wilderness before the
entry into Canaan (see page 165) and neither time was this described
as a sin. Moses himself had, according to the Biblical story, instituted
it.

Of course, in ancient times, a census was not a regular procedure
designed to provide the statistical data necessary to help guide the
destinies of a nation. It was rather a course of procedure taken at
irregular periods for one of two specific reasons: a reorganization of
the military draft, or a reorganization of the system of taxation.

The former purpose is indicated by the fact that in the census
described at the end of the Book of 2 Samuel only men of military
age were counted:

2 Samuel 24:9. . . . . *and there were in Israel eight hundred thousand valiant men that drew the sword; and the men of Judah were
five hundred thousand.*

This estimate (a very rough one, for methods of enumeration in ancient times are by no means to be compared with those of today) may be rather exaggerated for it indicates a total population of about four million, or very nearly the combined population of Israel and Jordan today.

That a census might also be used for taxation is best indicated in the famous chapter in the Gospel of St. Luke which begins:

Luke 2:1. And . . . there went out a decree from Caesar Augustus that all the world should be taxed.

and this involved first of all an enrollment of individuals, or what amounts to a census. The verse in the Revised Standard Version is given as "a decree went out from Caesar Augustus that all the world should be enrolled," while the New Catholic Edition translates the verse as "a decree went forth from Caesar Augustus that a census of the whole world should be taken."

In either case, whether for a military draft or for taxation, a census was bound to be unpopular and, if any natural disaster followed, those who opposed it would be sure to point to that as evidence of divine displeasure.

In this case the disaster was a pestilence that is recorded as killing seventy thousand men. The Biblical writers describe the occasion dramatically by having God stop the angel of death when Jerusalem was on the point of being destroyed. The exact position of the angel at the time of the order to halt is given:

2 Samuel 24:16. . . . And the angel of the Lord was by the threshingplace of Araunah the Jebusite.

2 Samuel 24:17. And David . . . saw the angel that smote the people . . .

David therefore purchased that threshing place and built an altar upon it. His son Solomon was later to build the Temple upon this same site, and it is tempting to think that the story of David and the census was embroidered with supernatural detail by the later writers in order to supply additional sanctification of the ground upon which the Temple stood.

11. 1 KINGS

ADONIJAH · THE PHARAOH [OF SOLOMON] · TIPHSAH · THE HOUSE OF THE
LORD · OPHIR · SHEBA · TARSHISH · HADAD THE EDOMITE · REZON · AHIJAH ·
SHISHAK · REHOBOAM · JEROBOAM · BEN-HADAD · SAMARIA · JEZEBEL ·
ELIJAH · ZAREPHATH · MOUNT CARMEL · JEZREEL · BEN-HADAD II · APHEK ·
NABOTH · RAMOTH-GILEAD

Adonijah

The First Book of Kings opens in the year 973 B.C., the fortieth
and last year of the reign of David. The old king had clearly only a
short time to live and the matter of the succession came up again.
Now that the three oldest sons of David were dead, the fourth,
Adonijah, seemed (to himself, certainly) the natural successor.

1 Kings 1:5. *Then Adonijah . . . exalted himself, saying, I will
be king . . .*

To be sure, David had not indicated him as successor, but then
neither had he indicated anyone else—at least not openly. Adonijah
made sure of the support of the army and of the priesthood by en-
listing on his side Joab, the commander in chief, and Abiathar, the
survivor of the slaughter at Nob and the last priest of the house of
Eli.

Both Joab and Abiathar were now old men, however, and their
power was on the decline. In opposition to Joab was the younger
soldier Benaiah, captain of the king's bodyguard, and in opposition to
Abiathar was the younger priest Zadok.

The younger men had their own candidate, Solomon, the son of
Bathsheba, who had retained her influence over David and who was
willing to take the chance of facing the old king concerning this matter.
On their side, also, was Nathan, head of the prophetic party.

The Empire of David and Solomon

David was not proof against such pressures and it might well have been his own intention to appoint Solomon his successor. In any case, he was forced to act now, and Solomon was anointed king with all the necessary ritual and trapping and, most important of all, with the official blessing of David.

Upon news of this event, the feast being given by Adonijah to celebrate *his* accession to the throne broke up at once. In the face of David's will, there was no further argument, and popular support shifted at once to Solomon.

Once David actually died and Solomon sat upon the throne, the new king took action to make sure that no chance of civil war over the succession remained. Adonijah and Joab were both killed at Solomon's orders. Shimei, who still represented the remnant of those who harked back to the dynasty of Saul (see page 315) was first confined to Jerusalem and, when he left on some apparently innocent occasion, was taken and executed.

Abiathar was exiled to his home city of Anathoth in Benjamin, and Zadok was made High Priest in his place. The descendants of Zadok remained the head of the Jerusalem priesthood through the history of the kingdom thereafter. In this way, Solomon was seated firmly on the throne.

> 1 Kings 2:46. . . . *And the kingdom was established in the hand of Solomon.*

The Pharaoh [of Solomon]

Israel had now reached a peak of power and prestige which enabled Solomon to take his place as a monarch of the first rank. In gathering a harem, he need not confine himself to local girls and to minor princesses only, but could aspire to those of the highest prestige.

> 1 Kings 3:1. *And Solomon made affinity with Pharaoh king of Egypt, and took Pharaoh's daughter and brought her into the city of David . . .*

This is the first mention of any Pharaoh since the one who drowned in the Red Sea and as usual no name is given.

The social prestige of marriage into the family of Pharaoh is great and at the time it must have made a triumphant impression. The

slaves who had fled Egypt centuries before now had grown so powerful that their king was worthy of a marriage alliance with Pharaoh.

The show was much more than the actuality, however, for Egypt
was by no means the Egypt it had been. The 20th dynasty, which had
vegetated along under its line of Rameses (see page 220) while the
judges dominated Canaan, came to an end about 1075 B.C. in the lifetime of Samuel and a hundred years before the accession of Solomon.

Since then, Egypt had disintegrated. The Pharaohs of the 21st
dynasty ruled only the Nile delta, while upper Egypt was under the
domination of the priests of Ammon, who ruled as virtual monarchs
from Thebes, the capital of the conquering monarchs of the great
18th dynasty.

The Egyptian capital under the 21st dynasty was Tanis or Zoan,
the city which, seven centuries earlier, had served as the capital of the
Hyksos. About the time of David's death, Psusennes II ascended
the Egyptian throne. His position as Pharaoh of the delta was not
enviable. He had to face the constant hostility of the Theban priests
and, in addition, there was a growing pressure from the desert tribes
to the west.

No doubt he felt that an alliance with Solomon, via the usual route
of a dynastic marriage, might secure his eastern flank and give him some
dependable military help if this was needed. He was willing to pay for
it, too, for he sent an expedition to capture a Canaanite city, Gezer,
in Philistine territory and gave it to Solomon as a dowry with his
daughter. It is the single recorded territorial annexation of Solomon's
reign.

Solomon's army was not, in actual fact, called upon, but the then
high prestige of Israel might have helped, for Psusennes retained his
shaky throne for well over thirty years, almost to the end of Solomon's
reign.

Tiphsah

The two Books of Kings reached their final form four centuries after
the great days of Solomon, at a time when Jerusalem had been ruling
over sharply restricted territory for a long time and when its very life
seemed at the mercy of powerful empires to the east. The reign of
Solomon, at the time in which Jerusalem's sway over surrounding

territory was at its maximum, is looked back upon with rhapsodic delight. The extent of Solomon's kingdom is given:

> 1 Kings 4:24. . . . *he had dominion over all the region on this side the river, from Tiphsah even to Azzah [Gaza], over all the kings on this side the river: and he had peace on all sides round about him.*

The river is clearly the Euphrates; no one doubts that. Tiphsah (meaning "ford") is commonly identified as the city known to the Greeks as Thapsacus, which is some three hundred miles northeast of Jerusalem. There is indeed a ford at that spot and since it controlled the most convenient place for crossing the middle Euphrates, it flourished and was, in Greek times, a sizable and prosperous city.

No doubt, Solomon's hold that far north was quite tenuous, and represented nothing more than the fact that the cities of Syria paid him tribute and were otherwise undisturbed in their local rule.

Nevertheless, the boundaries of Solomon's kingdom, from Tiphsah to Gaza, remained the ideal boundary in the eyes of the later historians. (Each nation seems to consider its "rightful boundaries" those it happened to hold at the peak of its power. Naturally, there is overlapping in every direction with the "rightful boundaries" of every neighboring power.)

In a way, the reign of Solomon is the climax of early Biblical history. The promise of Canaan is fulfilled. The escaping slaves from Egypt have made their way to Canaan, conquered it, held it, built it into an empire and now finally, under Solomon:

> 1 Kings 4:25. . . . *Judah and Israel dwelt safely, every man under his vine and under his fig tree, from Dan even to Beersheba . . .*

One might almost be tempted to heave a sigh of relief at such happiness after so many tribulations and to let it stand as a "they lived happily ever after" ending, except that there are no endings in history. Life goes on and a plateau of power will recede.

The House of the Lord

If Solomon's reign was the climax of early Israelite history, the building of the Temple was the climax of Solomon's reign in the

The House of the Lord

eyes of the Biblical writers. David had planned a Temple but his reign had been too stormy to give him the required years of peace it would have taken to build it. Solomon had those years of peace.

What Solomon needed were the necessary raw materials and skilled artisans and for both of these he could turn to Phoenicia. Hiram had just become king of Tyre in 969 B.C., four years after Solomon had ascended the throne and he, too, was ready for a large project. (Hiram was so famous to the Biblical writers in connection with the Temple that he was anachronistically placed on the throne of Tyre in David's time—see page 304.)

1 Kings 5:2. *And Solomon sent to Hiram, saying . . .*
. . . .

1 Kings 5:5. *. . . behold, I purpose to build an house unto the name of the Lord my God . . .*
. . . .

1 Kings 6:1. *And it came to pass . . . in the fourth year of Solomon's reign . . . that he began to build the house of the Lord.*

Undoubtedly, Hiram, a shrewd businessman, was well aware that his neighbor's ambitious plans would redound to the profit of Tyre, for he would supply the necessary timber and workmen at his own price and it would be a high one:

> 1 Kings 5:7. *And it came to pass, when Hiram heard the words of Solomon, that he rejoiced greatly* . . .

There is nothing wrong, in itself, in a building program. Fitted to the economy of a nation, it supplies employment and builds national pride. Unfortunately, the temptation is always present to go too far and Solomon (like many other monarchs before and after— as, for example, Rameses II of Egypt and Louis XIV of France) went too far.

For one thing, the building of the Temple meant the lavish use of forced labor:

> 1 Kings 5:13. *And king Solomon raised a levy out of all Israel; and the levy was thirty thousand men.*
> 1 Kings 5:14. *And he sent them to Lebanon* . . .

The Revised Standard Version translates the verse, "King Solomon raised a levy of forced labor out of all Israel."

Later it is stated that it was the remaining Canaanites only who were thus enslaved in fulfillment of the curse recorded as having been pronounced on Ham (see page 45).

> 1 Kings 9:22. *But of the children of Israel did Solomon make no bondmen* . . .

This last, however, sounds like a defense against the list of grievances presented by the Israelites who broke away from the Davidic dynasty. It seems much more likely that the labor gangs were formed from all available sources, from Israelites as well as Canaanites. The same might be said for taxes, which, Solomon saw to it, were collected efficiently.

The amount by which Solomon overextended his resources in his building program is indicated by the fact that he could not pay Hiram all the accumulated debt in either cash or goods but had to cede land as well. Once the building program was complete:

> 1 Kings 9:11. . . . *king Solomon gave Hiram twenty cities* . . .

The cities thus ceded were part of the tribal holdings of Naphtali in Israel. This could not help but be offensive to Israelite pride and was another item in the gathering score against the Davidic dynasty.

The building of the Temple is such a key fact to the Biblical writers that they give its date not only in terms of Solomon's reign but in terms of the greater sweep of Israelite history as well:

> 1 Kings 6:1. *And it came to pass in the four hundred and eightieth year after the children of Israel were come out of the land of Egypt . . . that he* [Solomon] *began to build the house of the Lord.*

This cannot be right. Four hundred eighty years before the beginning of the building of the Temple was 1449 B.C. and that was in the midst of the conquering reign of Thutmose III, Egypt's most victorious monarch. To have the Exodus take place then is unthinkable.

The Biblical writers frequently show themselves to be very number conscious and, indeed, in Greek and Roman times an almost mystical number lore grew up among them. This was called "gematria" (a corruption of the Greek, *geometria*) and it was by no means unique to the Jews. Numbers have a fascination for all peoples and mystical associations and combinations of numbers are to be found in all cultures. Even the rational Greeks were not immune and the great philosopher Pythagoras founded a school that simultaneously did great work in mathematics and foolishly wandered astray after number mysticism.

The 480-year period may in part have been suggested by counting the various judges as having ruled consecutively (see page 230) instead of, in part, concurrently, and the exact figure may have been suggested by the fact that 480 is equal to 12 multiplied by 40. After all, forty years can be considered the length of a full generation, and twelve has the mystical value of being the number of tribes (or, for that matter, the numbers of signs of the zodiac). What the writers are saying then is that the Temple was built a dozen generations after the Exodus.

Actually, 480 years is just about double the most likely figure. Counting from 1211 B.C., the death of Merneptah (see page 143), the beginning of the building of the Temple turns out to be 242 years after the Exodus.

Seven years were spent in building the Temple, which was therefore finished and dedicated in 962 B.C. and into which the ark of the covenant was then placed. Solomon also built a palace for himself and one for his Egyptian queen as well as fortifications for various towns.

Before leaving the subject, one item in the description of the Temple furnishings has attached to it an odd bit of mathematical curiosa. This involves one of the items described as having been made by a Tyrian metalworker:

> 1 Kings 7:23. And he made a molten sea, ten cubits from the one brim to the other . . . and a line of thirty cubits did compass it round about.

The exact function of the "molten sea" is not stated, though it seems most likely that it was a container for water used in the various rituals. The interesting point is that its upper rim seems to be circular in shape with a diameter of ten cubits and a circumference of thirty cubits. This is impossible, for the ratio of the circumference to the diameter (a ratio called "pi" by mathematicians) is given here as 30/10 or 3, whereas the real value of pi is an unending decimal which begins 3.14159 . . . If the molten sea were really ten cubits in diameter it would have to be just under thirty-one and a half cubits in circumference.

The explanation is, of course, that the Biblical writers were not mathematicians or even interested in mathematics and were merely giving approximate figures. Still, to those who are obsessed with the notion that every word in the Bible is infallible (and who know a little mathematics) it is bound to come as a shock to be told that the Bible says that the value of pi is 3.

Ophir

Solomon used Hiram's help also in building a navy for Israel and in supplying it with Tyrian sailors, then the best in the world. With it, Solomon was able to engage in sea trade:

> 1 Kings 9:28. And they came to Ophir, and fetched from thence gold . . . and brought it to king Solomon.

Ophir and Tarshish

Where Ophir might be is completely unknown but the puzzle of its whereabouts has never ceased to fascinate Biblical scholars, partly because of the aura of wealth that lay about it. There are not many places that serve as sources of gold, after all, and the gold of Ophir was accounted so fine and high in quality that the proverbial association became inevitable, like the cedars of Lebanon, the balm of Gilead, and the bulls of Bashan.

Thus, Job, in praising wisdom above all else and speaking of how impossible it is to find a price for it, says:

Job 28:16. *It cannot be valued with the gold of Ophir . . .*

The one clear hint as to the location of Ophir is given two verses before this first mention in connection with Solomon's sea trade.

1 Kings 9:26. *And king Solomon made a navy of ships in Ezion-geber, which is beside Eloth, on the shore of the Red sea, in the land of Edom.*

Ezion-geber and Eloth (or Elath) stood at the northern tip of the Gulf of Aqaba (see page 133). Since the independence of modern Israel, Elath has been built up again and is once more the nation's Red Sea port.

We might argue then that Ophir was located somewhere that could be reached by way of the Red Sea. This still leaves the matter rather wide open. India can be reached by way of the Red Sea and in after-times, Ophir was located still farther afield, in places which became famous for riches and wealth—the Far East, even Peru.

And yet the ships of the tenth century B.C. were not fit for long ocean voyages. The closer Ophir can be located to Israel, the more likely the location.

The one other place which the Biblical writers pause to describe as a source of fine gold is Havilah (see page 28). The location of Havilah is also uncertain but some scholars place it somewhere in southern Arabia and it seems reasonable to suppose that Ophir is also to be located there, perhaps on the site of what is now the kingdom of Yemen. This is the more probable because the mention of Ophir is followed by the mention of another kingdom (almost by reflex association, as it were) which is more surely located in that area.

Sheba

The penetration of Israel southward brought a return visit from a monarch of the south:

1 Kings 10:1. *And when the queen of Sheba heard of the fame of Solomon . . . she came to prove him with hard questions.*

The location of Sheba is by no means mysterious. In southwestern Arabia, on the site of what is now Yemen, there was a kingdom known to the Arabs as Saba and to the Greeks and Romans as Sabaea. There seems little doubt that this is the Biblical Sheba. And it might be that Ophir represents a district of Sheba, for the queen is pictured as wealthy:

1 Kings 10:2. *And she came to Jerusalem with a very great train, with camels that bare spices, and very much gold, and precious stones . . .*

(Sabaea was so prosperous that Romans called the area Arabia Felix —"fortunate Arabia"—in comparison with other parts of the peninsula, which contained one of the most unpleasant deserts in the world.)

However prosaically definite we may be about Sheba itself, there is little to be said about the queen. There is no record of any particular queen of Sheba, or of any such visit to Jerusalem, outside the Bible. Nor is the queen as much as given a name in the Bible. The later Arabs evolved the myth that her name was Balkis, and she is mentioned by that name in the Koran.

The modern Ethiopians have a tradition that queen Balkis was actually the queen of their own nation. This is not as completely odd as it might sound. Modern Ethiopia is just across the Red Sea from Sheba (or Yemen) at a point where that sea narrows down to a width of twenty miles or so. There is rather easy communication between the two nations and there have been times when Ethiopia dominated sections of southwestern Arabia. To be sure, this was some twelve centuries after Solomon but the connection is there to be remembered with the usual distortion.

The Ethiopians maintain that queen Balkis had a son by Solomon, and name that son Menelik. From Menelik is supposed to be descended the present ruling line of the emperors of Ethiopia. One of the traditional titles of the Ethiopian emperor, even today, is "Lion of Judah" in reference to this supposed Judean ancestry.

Tarshish

Solomon's commerce stretched out in another direction as well:

1 Kings 10:22. . . . *the king had at sea a navy of Tharshish with the navy of Hiram: once in three years came the navy of Tharshish, bringing gold, and silver, ivory, and apes and peacocks.*

Tharshish, more commonly referred to in the Bible as Tarshish, is sometimes considered as synonymous with Ophir. It is then suggested that Ophir must be three years journey from Israel and must thus be someplace distant like the Far East. However, it seems clear that two different fleets are here being described. There is the "navy of Hiram" and the "navy of Tharshish"; Solomon has one "with" (together with, or in addition to) another. The men of Hiram bring goods from Ophir, and the men of Tarshish bring goods from elsewhere.

Actually, the whereabouts of Tarshish is almost as mysterious as that of Ophir. There is no hint in the Bible of its location. It is very frequently equated with the district known to the Greeks and Romans as Tartessus. The chief evidence for this is the similarity in names and the fact that it is sufficiently far from Jerusalem to make the three-year term for the round trip and the period of trading seem reasonable.

Tartessus was the name given by the Greeks to that portion of Spain west of Gibraltar. Its capital city (of the same name) was at the mouth of the Guadalquivir River, about seventy-five miles northwest of Gibraltar. It was founded by the Phoenicians about 1200 B.C.; that is, at the time of the Exodus. It was at the height of its commercial prosperity in Solomon's reign. (Eventually, though, all of the commerce of the western Mediterranean was brought under the control of Carthage, the most successful of the Phoenician colonies. About 480 B.C., Carthage, then at the height of its power, destroyed Tartessus.)

There might be some question as to whether "ivory, and apes and peacocks" might be found in Spain, but why not? The Barbary ape (not a true ape) is still to be found in Gibraltar and in ancient times it must have been more widely spread. As for ivory, there were elephants in north Africa in ancient times.

Hadad the Edomite

The strength of the land (which Solomon poured freely into his building projects and his efforts at imperial luxury) declined and this made it more difficult to retain the hold over the increasingly restless subject peoples.

Solomon did possess a certain imperial responsibility and attempted to retain popularity with these peoples through an enlightened religious policy. He not only allowed them freedom of worship but tried to demonstrate himself to be king over all his subjects and not over the Judeans and Israelites alone. He added women of the subject nations to his harem (intended, and accepted, as an honor) and allowed temples to be built to their gods for their convenience.

This was undoubtedly good policy (it fits in with our modern notions of religious freedom) but it was viewed with dislike and hostility by the prophetic party. That hostility grew in the course of the later centuries and the Biblical writers expressed their opinion of Solomon's course of action unmistakably:

> 1 Kings 11:5. *For Solomon went after . . . Milcom the abomination of the Ammonites.*
>
> . . . .
>
> 1 Kings 11:7. *Then did Solomon build an high place for Chemosh, the abomination of Moab . . .*

That Solomon's attempts at placating the peoples of the realm were not unnecessary is shown by the fact that there were rebellions here and there, marring the idyllic picture of the reign which was drawn in the earlier chapters. Edom gave trouble from the beginning of Solomon's reign:

> 1 Kings 11:14. *And the Lord stirred up an adversary unto Solomon, Hadad the Edomite . . .*

Hadad was a member of the old Edomite royal house, who had survived the slaughter following Joab's conquest of Edom during David's reign. He had found sanctuary in Egypt but once David was dead, he made his way back to Edom. Exactly how he played his part as "adversary" against Solomon we are not told, but it seems quite reasonable to suppose he declared himself king of Edom and carried on a continuing guerrilla war with the royal army.

Rezon

There were similar troubles in the north:

1 Kings 11:23. *And God stirred him* [Solomon] *up another adversary, Rezon the son of Eliadah* . . .
1 Kings 11:24. *And he gathered men unto him* . . . *and they went to Damascus, and dwelt therein* . . .

The Syrian city-states had been placed under tribute by David, but Solomon's less warlike hand did not suffice to keep them in subjection. Rezon, gathering a guerrilla band about him, seized Damascus, and established himself there as an independent power.

Ahijah

Israel's greatest danger, however, was from within. The hostility between Judah and Israel had never died but was merely sleeping—with one eye open. That open eye consisted of the prophetic party.

Even in the days of Saul, Israel's first king, there had been the clash between the royal power and that of the prophets under the leadership of Samuel (see page 283).

Under David and Solomon, with the power, prestige, and glory of the monarchy at an all-time high, the role of the prophets sank accordingly and they made comparatively little impingement upon history. Nathan the prophet, however, did not hesitate to beard David and denounce him to his face in the matter of Uriah the Hittite (see page 310)—and was able to survive the encounter, too, and force the mighty king to do penance. It was the support of Nathan and the prophetic party that might have swung the balance to Solomon and against Adonijah when David lay dying.

Solomon's policy of religious toleration alienated the prophetic party, particularly those who were of Israelite (rather than Judean) origin. The prophets of Israel may not even have entirely approved the centralization of worship at Jerusalem and the consequent lessening of importance of the various Israelite shrines. For them, religious feelings went hand in hand with nationalism.

Ahijah, an Israelite prophet of Shiloh in Ephraim (which, in Eli's time a century before, had been the home of the most important shrine in Israel), must have been one of these prophet-nationalists. He had his eye on Jeroboam, also an Ephraimite, one who held high office under Solomon and who seemed to have the qualities of leadership.

1 Kings 11:29. . . . *when Jeroboam went out of Jerusalem . . . the prophet Ahijah the Shilonite found him . . .*

1 Kings 11:30. *And Ahijah caught the new garment that was on him, and rent it . . .*

1 Kings 11:31. *And he said to Jeroboam . . . thus saith the Lord . . . Behold I will rend the kingdom out of the hand of Solomon . . .*

With the backing of the prophetic party and of many disgruntled Israelites, Jeroboam rose in rebellion.

Shishak

The rebellion failed—for the while—and Jeroboam had to flee, but he had made himself an Israelite hero and Israel did not forget him.

1 Kings 11:40. . . . *And Jeroboam arose and fled into Egypt, unto Shishak king of Egypt, and was in Egypt until the death of Solomon.*

Egypt had had its own increasing troubles. The 21st dynasty which ruled the delta came to an end with the death of Solomon's father-in-law in 940 B.C. Anarchy increased further then, as rival generals seized at power. One of these was Sheshonk (the Biblical Shishak), who was a member of a tribe occupying the regions west of the Nile valley.

The whole northern coast of Africa west of Egypt was called Libya by the Greeks (a name of unknown origin). To the Greek writers on Egyptian history, therefore, Shishak was a Libyan, and the 22nd dynasty, which he founded, was the "Libyan dynasty."

Shishak's power extended only over the delta; upper Egypt continued under the rule of the priests of Thebes. Shishak was the only member of the dynasty who displayed any vigor at all. After him came a series of rulers who lorded it over separate sections of the delta and quarreled among themselves.

Even Shishak could not have been very impressive, for the Bible nowhere refers to him as "Pharaoh," but merely as "king." The impression is that he was not considered a legitimate Egyptian monarch, but merely a usurping general. He is the first ruler of Egypt, by the way, to whom the Biblical writers give an actual name.

Shishak was shrewd enough to recognize that Jeroboam might be a useful tool in combating or even destroying the power of his neighbor to the northeast and he offered him ready asylum, as a predecessor had once offered asylum to Hadad the Edomite.

Rehoboam

Solomon, like his father, reigned forty years, dying in 933 B.C. (These forty-year reigns of David and Solomon are suspiciously even. Each king reigned a full "generation." Still, the acceptance of Biblical chronology in this instance gives rise to no inconsistencies and there is no good reason to suggest any alternative.)

Solomon must have had many sons but there is no talk of any problems of succession. Only one son is mentioned and he becomes the third king of the Davidic dynasty.

> 1 Kings 11:43. . . . *and Rehoboam his* [Solomon's] *son reigned in his stead.*

His crowning made him king of Judah only. To become king of Israel as well, he had to undergo a similar rite at the old holy Ephraimite city of Shechem:

> 1 Kings 12:1. *And Rehoboam went to Shechem: for all Israel were come to Shechem to make him king.*

(Perhaps David and Solomon had to do the same but that is not mentioned in the Bible. It is mentioned in Rehoboam's case because of the events that now transpired.)

The Israelites did not come to the crowning in any compliant mood. It was not their intention to crown Rehoboam and make him legitimate

THE
GREAT SEA

(Mediterranean Sea)

Sidon
Zarephath
Tyre
Aecho
MT. LEBANON
Damascus
MT. HERMON
Dan
PHOENICIA
Hazor
ARAM
(SYRIANS)
SEA OF
CHINNERETH
Ashtaroth
BASHAN
YARMUK R.
Edrei
KISHON R.
Megiddo
Beth-shan
Ramoth-gilead
Mahanaim
ISRAEL
Jabesh-gilead
JORDAN R.
Tirzah
Shechem
JABBOK R.
Shiloh
GILEAD
AMMON
Joppa
Bethel
Rabbath-ammon
Jerusalem
Ashdod
Bethlehem
Madeba
SALT
SEA
Ashkelon
Gath
Diben
Gaza
PHILISTIA
Hebron
(DEAD
SEA)
Raphia
MOAB
Beersheba
Kir-moab
JUDAH
ZERED R.
RIVER OF EGYPT
EDOM
Kadesh-barnea

N

0   Miles   25

Israel and Judah During Rehoboam's Time

king of Israel unless he would in turn guarantee some relief from repression. They said to him:

1 Kings 12:4. *Thy father made our yoke grievous: now therefore make thou the grievous service . . . lighter, and we will serve thee.*

The young Rehoboam, with deplorable lack of judgment, scorned gentle speech. He threatened to make the yoke heavier still, and Israel revolted in an explosion of nationalist fury.

It was Rehoboam's intention to subdue the rebellion by force, but its strength and violence was surprising. Furthermore, the prophetic party even in Judah was apparently not entirely unhappy over the split. A weakening of the royal power meant a strengthening of the prophets. The Judean prophet Shemaiah counseled against attempting to reunite the kingdom by force:

1 Kings 12:24. . . . *Ye shall not go up, nor fight against your brethren the children of Israel . . .*

The rebellion was successful, therefore, and the split was permanent. Rehoboam was left the king of Judah only, though, ironically, the territory of the tribe of Benjamin (which had given the first royal line to Israel) remained with Judah, since the prosperity of the Benjamites now depended on Judah's one metropolis, Jerusalem, which lay right at the Benjamite borders.

The united kingdom of Israel-Judah had endured for only three quarters of a century, from 1006 B.C. to 933 B.C., and under two monarchs only. Now there were two sister kingdoms, Israel to the north and Judah to the south. (They are sometimes called the northern kingdom and southern kingdom respectively)

Nor did Rehoboam's troubles end once he had bowed to the inevitable and accepted the secession of Israel. Aside from the fact that bad blood and border warfare remained between the two kingdoms, Shishak of Egypt seized the opportunity offered him by the chaos on his borders to attack the divided and weakened nation in the fifth year of Rehoboam's reign (928 B.C.). He laid siege to Jerusalem, or perhaps occupied it, and in either case carried off much loot.

1 Kings 14:26. *And he [Shishak] took away the treasures of the house of the Lord, and the treasures of the king's house; he . . . took away all . . .*

Not only had Solomon's kingdom broken in two but Solomon's material glory was gone. The Temple in its original golden splendor (if we accept the description given by the Bible) lasted just forty years.

Jeroboam

Jeroboam had returned from exile as soon as word of Solomon's death reached him. It was he who led the Israelite party that demanded concessions of Rehoboam; it was he who led the rebellion that followed Rehoboam's refusal; and it was he who was made the first king of the re-established kingdom of Israel:

> 1 Kings 12:20. . . . *when . . . Israel heard that Jeroboam was come again . . . they . . . made him king over all Israel . . .*

Israel thus regained its independence, which it had lost after the death of Ish-bosheth. Jeroboam established his capital at Shechem at first, then at the more centrally located Tirzah, twelve miles to the northeast.

Having regained political independence for Israel, Jeroboam felt it necessary to regain religious independence as well for he reasoned:

> 1 Kings 12:27. *If this people go up to do sacrifice in the house of the Lord at Jerusalem, then shall the heart of this people turn again . . . unto Rehoboam.*

Jeroboam therefore set up sanctuaries at the northern and southern limits of his new kingdom, at Dan and Bethel, and there all Israelites were to sacrifice. The schism was complete.

Undoubtedly, this action of Jeroboam's was popular with the Israelites, who might well have looked upon the Temple at Jerusalem as a radical (and therefore irreligious) innovation, built on foreign soil by a foreign dynasty through forced labor.

Nevertheless, the new policy did not suit the prophetic party. Probably they would have preferred a closer adherence to ancient tradition, a reactivation of the shrines at places like Shechem and Shiloh, and a High Priesthood like that of Eli re-established. And this, precisely, was what Jeroboam probably didn't want; he wanted a ritual tied in with the new monarchy that would strengthen his dynasty. Then, too, Jeroboam had compromised with the desires of those people less capable of worshiping an abstract deity by placing the images of bulls in his sanctuary, symbolizing the fructifying element in nature.

Ahijah, the prophet, quickly disenchanted with the king he had helped to the throne, inveighed against him and delivered what he proclaimed to be God's word of doom:

> 1 Kings 14:9. . . . *thou hast . . . made thee other gods, and mol-*
> *ten images . . .*
> 1 Kings 14:10. *Therefore, behold, I will bring evil upon the house*
> *of Jeroboam . . .*

Indeed, Jeroboam's dynasty was not to endure long, but the new kingdom of Israel was to persevere under several different dynasties for over two centuries. The kingdom of Judah, while always less prosperous and powerful than its northern sister, remained under the Davidic dynasty throughout and endured for three and a half centuries.

It is very common to speak of Israel as consisting of ten tribes, since there were traditionally twelve tribes in Israel and only Judah and Benjamin remained under Rehoboam. However, the tribal system had faded under David and Solomon, and in any case Reuben and Simeon had disappeared by the time of the schism. At best, then, the kingdom of Israel consisted of eight tribes.

Rehoboam died in 917 B.C. after having reigned sixteen years. Jeroboam died in 912 B.C., having reigned twenty-one years.

Ben-hadad

The division of the kingdom of David and Solomon made a continuation of any policy of imperial conquest virtually impossible. Neither half by itself had the strength to be a conquering nation, particularly since the energies of each were absorbed by a smolderingly continuous hostility between them. Each nation, furthermore, sought allies among the neighbors and enemies of the other and each labored to enfeeble the other by any means.

In Judah, Abijam, the son of Rehoboam, began his reign in 917 B.C., and he was succeeded by his son Asa in 915 B.C. They were the fourth and fifth kings of the Davidic dynasty.

In Israel, Jeroboam's son Nadab began his rule in 912 B.C. A rebellion against him by one of his generals, Baasha, succeeded. Nadab was slain and Baasha ascended the throne in 911 B.C. As a measure of prudence, to prevent a counter-revolt, he did as was often customary in these cases and had all the male members of Jeroboam's family executed. Jeroboam's dynasty thus survived Jeroboam's death by just one year.

Both Asa of Judah and Baasha of Israel had long reigns, the former reigning for forty years to 875 B.C. and the latter twenty-three years to 888 B.C. War between Israel and Judah continued in those years, and Asa, getting the worst of it, sought help abroad:

1 Kings 15:18. *Then Asa took . . . silver and . . . gold . . . and sent them to Ben-hadad . . . king of Syria, that dwelt at Damascus, saying,*

1 Kings 15:19. *There is a league between me and thee . . .*

Ben-hadad was the third member of the dynasty founded by Rezon (see page 334). In less than half a century, Damascus, from a small principality precariously maintaining its independence against Solomon, had grown to take over the leadership of the other Aramaean regions so that one could speak of Ben-hadad as a "king of Syria." And where David had crushed the Syrian towns and extorted tribute from them, the great-great-grandson of David paid tribute to them in order to gain their help.

Syria was now at least the equal of Israel in strength. It accepted the alliance of Judah and attacked Israel's northern frontier, sacking the city of Dan, for instance, and apparently destroying it permanently, for it is not further mentioned in the Bible. Baasha was forced to make peace and for the next century and a half, Syria, rather than Judah, was Israel's chief enemy.

Samaria

The history of Israel continued to be troubled with dynastic problems. Baasha's son Elah succeeded in 888 B.C. and then history repeated itself. In a palace revolution, Zimri, a leader among Elah's bodyguard, killed Elah and all the family of Baasha. He did not, however, survive to establish a new dynasty.

The general of Israel's armed forces, Omri, was then engaged in

Samaria

besieging a Philistine city. He was acclaimed king of Israel by his troops and marched on Tirzah. Zimri died in the fiery ruins of his palace; another contender for the throne, Tibni, was also defeated and killed; and by 887 B.C. Omri held the throne firmly, the first member of Israel's third dynasty.

The capital city of Tirzah had now seen two dynasties brutally wiped out; the first having endured only twenty-two years, the second twenty-four years. That in itself was enough to make it an uncomfortable place for the new king. He cast about for a suitable site for a new capital, one that could be firmly identified with the new dynasty.

> 1 Kings 16:24. And he bought the hill Samaria of Shemer . . . and built on the hill . . . the city . . . Samaria.

The Hebrew name of the city, Shomron, is derived from Shemer, the name of the clan, or the individual, who owned the land before Omri's purchase. Samaria is, of course, the Greek version of the name.

Samaria lay about six miles northwest of Shechem, about midway between the Jordan River and the Mediterranean. It was centrally located in the kingdom and had considerable potentiality for defense since it was located on an isolated hill. It remained the capital of Israel through the remaining history of the kingdom (though its kings had favorite residences elsewhere on occasion, notably at Jezreel) and was sufficiently important to make Samaria a frequently used synonym for the entire kingdom.

The energetic Omri reigned for only a dozen years but in that time, secure in his new capital, he made Israel respected among her neighbors. To counter the danger of Syria, he made an alliance with the Phoenician cities and so stabilized the kingdom that his son could reign in peace after him—the first time that had happened in Israel's troubled history since the schism.

Such was the reputation of the king that in Assyrian inscriptions, Israel is referred to as the "land of Omri."

Jezebel

Omri was succeeded by his son Ahab in 875 B.C. with the royal power strengthened by the Phoenician alliance. At about the time that Omri had come to the throne, the dynasty of Hiram (see page 325) had been wiped out by Ithobaal (the Biblical "Ethbaal"), a priest of Ashtoreth, who then succeeded to the throne. By Ahab's time. Ithobaal's seat on the throne was clearly secure and Ahab felt safe in committing himself not only to an alliance but to the reinforcing cement of a dynastic marriage.

1 Kings 16:31. . . . *he [Ahab] took to wife Jezebel the daughter of Ethbaal king of the Zidonians . . .*

It was customary for kings in that time of religious inclusiveness to allow foreign queens their own religious rites, as Solomon had done for his own numerous wives.

Jezebel, however, was a dominating woman who wanted not merely to pursue the worship of her own particular "baal" (Melkart, a specific name which does not appear in the Bible) but labored to establish its worship throughout Israel generally. This may have been more than religious fervor; it may have been a device on her part to tie Israel more firmly to the Phoenician cities for the benefit of both.

It apparently suited Ahab's purposes to encourage her in this, for the prophetic party with its attempts to limit royal power and to dictate foreign policy along supernationalist lines could, in his eyes, well stand being weakened.

> 1 Kings 16:30. *And he [Ahab] reared up an altar for Baal in the house of Baal which he had built in Samaria.*

Elijah

It was the good fortune of the prophetic party that it now found itself in the hands of a strong leader, Elijah, the most dominating prophetic figure since Samuel. In the face of persecution, Elijah and his followers hardened their own stand and became increasingly intolerant of other worship.

Because of the deadly battle that followed, which was, in the long run, won by the Yahvists, Jezebel has become the very byword of a wicked, idolatrous woman, whereas Elijah was remembered by later generations with a veneration second only to Moses'.

Elijah enters the Biblical story as the forecaster of a drought that was to take place as punishment for the policies of Jezebel.

> 1 Kings 17:1. *And Elijah the Tishbite, who was of the inhabitants of Gilead, said unto Ahab . . . there shall not be dew nor rain these years . . .*

Elijah was from Tishbi, a town in Gilead, east of the Jordan. Its site is uncertain but it has been identified with a small village just west of Mahanaim.

Zarephath

Elijah's bearding of Ahab made it necessary for the prophet to remain in hiding thereafter, first in the Jordan valley and then far north in Phoenicia itself (the very home of the religious enemy where, perhaps, it was least likely that the royalist forces would look for him).

> 1 Kings 17:10. . . . *he arose and went to Zarephath . . .*

THE
GREAT SEA

(Mediterranean Sea)

Sidon

Zarephath

MT. LEBANON

LEONTES R.

MT. HERMON

Tyre

Dan

P H O E N I C I A

A R A M
(SYRIA)

Hazor

JORDAN R.

Accho

SEA OF
CHINNERETH

Aphek

KISHON R.

I S R A E L
(SAMARIA)

MT. CARMEL

YARMUK R.

VALLEY
OF JEZREEL

GILEAD

Dor

Jezreel

JORDAN R.

0   Miles   25

Zarephath and Mount Carmel

Zarephath is on the Phoenician seacoast, nearly twenty miles north of
Tyre (Jezebel's home city) and eight miles south of Sidon. The modern Arabic town of Sarafand stands near the place. Among the ruins of
the ancient town there stands a church on the traditional site of the
house in which Elijah lodged during his stay there.

Back in Israel, the state of the prophetic party worsened. Only those
remained alive who escaped Jezebel's harsh hand by flight or by going
into hiding. Thus, Obadiah, a high official of Ahab's court and a secret
Yahvist, helped some to live:

> 1 Kings 18:4. . . . *when Jezebel cut off the prophets of the Lord
> . . . Obadiah took an hundred prophets, and hid them . . . and fed
> them . . .*

Mount Carmel

After three years, however, Elijah took the chance of facing Ahab once more to foretell the imminent ending of the drought and to propose a direct contest between Yahveh and Melkart.

> 1 Kings 18:19. *Now therefore send, and gather to me all Israel unto Mount Carmel . . .*

There, Elijah proposed, eight hundred and fifty worshipers of Melkart and other Phoenician deities were to gather and attempt to light the fire under a sacrifice by means of their rites, while he alone and by himself was to try to do the same by calling on Yahveh.

Carmel is a mountainous ridge, about fifteen miles long, running northwest-southeast, just south of the Kishon River (see page 238). Its Hebrew name means "garden" or "vineyard" and, in ancient times particularly, it was well wooded and attractive. The maximum height, at about the middle of the ridge, is 1732 feet. Where it meets the sea, it forms a promontory called Cape Carmel. At the sea, just north of the ridge is the city of Haifa. The whole area is now part of the modern nation of Israel and Haifa is its second largest city. In ancient times, however, the site of Haifa carried no town of any importance.

The most important event in the history of Mount Carmel was the competition between Elijah and the worshipers of Melkart. Partly because of this and partly because it made for a pleasant retreat, it was a haunt for anchorites in early Christian times. When Palestine was temporarily in the hands of the Crusaders in the twelfth century A.D., a monastery was built there and an order of Carmelites was founded, an order which still flourishes.

The competition at Mount Carmel, which the Bible relates with loving detail, ended in a complete victory for Elijah. The wood caught fire at Elijah's word, after all the hundreds of competing priests found themselves unable to do a thing.

Ahab, witnessing the feat, was awed and impressed and allowed Elijah to order the massacre of the Baalists at the Kishon River.

Jezreel

For the moment, the towering figure of Elijah dominated King Ahab, all the more so as the drought ended at this time. Together, king and prophet left Mount Carmel:

> 1 Kings 18:45. . . . And Ahab rode, and went to Jezreel.
> 1 Kings 18:46. And . . . Elijah . . . ran before Ahab to the entrance of Jezreel.

The city of Jezreel was located in the valley of Jezreel (see page 241) about twenty-five miles southeast of Carmel and an equal distance north of Samaria. It was a favorite residence of Ahab and Jezebel.

Ahab must have told Jezebel of Elijah's deed with great enthusiasm but Jezebel was not impressed. She undoubtedly knew how the priests of Melkart arranged miracles when they wished to impress the populace, and she must have been certain that Elijah had merely managed to outsmart her own group in chicanery, nothing more.

We can well imagine that under her withering scorn, Ahab's new-found enthusiasm for the prophets faded. He allowed Jezebel to take over the reins of the religious policy once more and again Elijah was forced into exile, traveling southward this time through Judah to Mount Sinai, the traditional home of Yahveh.

It seemed to him that only the complete overthrow of the house of Omri would save Yahvism and he began long-range plans in this direction. Aware that the consummation of those plans might outlast his own time, he selected a successor to himself, one strong enough, in his estimation, to carry on the fight:

> 1 Kings 19:19. So he departed thence, and found Elisha . . . who was plowing . . . and Elijah passed by him, and cast his mantle upon him.

Ben-hadad II

Meanwhile Ahab had his hands full with the Syrian problem. Ben-hadad, who had defeated Israel badly in Baasha's time several decades before had been succeeded by his son Hadad-ezer, who is referred to in the Bible as another Ben-hadad, and who can therefore be called Ben-hadad II. (Hadad was a storm-god, well known over southwestern Asia and particularly popular at Damascus. He served as the national god of the Syrians and his name was therefore commonly incorporated into the royal name. Ben-hadad means the "son of Hadad.")

Ben-hadad II continued the firm, anti-Israel policy of his father:

> 1 Kings 20:1. *And Ben-hadad the king of Syria gathered all his host together . . . and he went up and besieged Samaria . . .*

Samaria held out but was hard pressed indeed and, for a while, was minded to surrender even under harsh terms. At this sign of weakness, however, Ben-hadad raised the price for surrender and Ahab was forced into continued warfare. He decided to risk everything on a pitched battle and retorted to a threat of destruction sent him by Ben-hadad with an aphorism that, in one form or another, is famous:

> 1 Kings 20:11. *And the king of Israel answered and said, Tell him, Let not him that girdeth on his harness boast himself as he that putteth it off.*

In other words, "Don't boast at the start of a battle as you would at the end of a victorious one." Or, in its most common form to us: "Don't count your chickens before they are hatched."

And Ahab proved his meaning well, for the Israelites fought with the fury of despair and the overconfident Syrian army was forced to flee after many casualties.

Aphek

A second battle was fought the next year.

> 1 Kings 20:26. *And it came to pass at the return of the year, that Ben-hadad numbered the Syrians and went up to Aphek, to fight against Israel.*

This is not the Aphek that figured in the wars against the Philistines two centuries earlier (see page 271), but is rather a town that is identified with the modern village of Fik, about three miles east of the Sea of Galilee, and roughly midway between Samaria and Damascus.

It was a measure of the size of the victory of the previous year that Ahab, who had then been besieged in his capital, could now meet the foe at the frontier.

This time the victory was again Israel's to an extent even greater than the first. Ben-hadad was forced to surrender, relinquish his father's conquests, and allow Israel commercial privileges in Damascus. Israel was stronger now than at any time since the schism with Judah.

In Ahab's wars against Syria, the prophetic party was on his side. Whatever the quarrels between prophets and monarch within the land, they closed ranks against the foreigner. Thus, it was a prophet who encouraged Ahab before the relief of Samaria:

> 1 Kings 20:13. And . . . there came a prophet unto Ahab . . . saying, Thus saith the Lord, Hast thou seen all this great multitude? behold, I will deliver it into thine hand this day . . .

But Ahab's relatively mild peace with the Syrians bitterly displeased the ultranationalist prophetic party and intensified their opposition to the throne.

Yet Ahab seems to have been statesmanlike in this respect. A living Syria, allied with Israel, and unembittered by unnecessary destruction and harsh oppression, could be a useful friend, particularly since a new enemy to both loomed to the north.

Assyria, of which much more will be said later, was under a strong king, Shalmaneser III, and was spreading its domination over the Fertile Crescent. According to Assyrian documents a battle was fought in 854 B.C. at Karkar (or Qarqar), a city located about a hundred miles north of Damascus, between Shalmaneser and an allied army led by Ben-hadad and Ahab in alliance. The Assyrians claim a victory but that is routine in the chronicles of the time. The fact is that the Assyrians annexed no territory and were therefore held to a draw at the least.

This stand against Assyria saved both Syria and Israel and gave each over a century of additional life and that certainly vindicated Ahab's policy of not fighting Syria to exhaustion so that both might fall helplessly into the Assyrian throat.

Oddly enough, there is no mention of the battle of Karkar in the

Bible. It may be that the Biblical writers were not willing to report so clear an indication that the prophetic party was wrong and Ahab right.

Naboth

Indeed, the Bible passes directly from the Syrian victory to the darkest deed of Ahab's reign as though to neutralize his military prowess by reference to his moral shortcomings.

Near Ahab's palace in Jezreel, there was a vineyard owned by a man named Naboth, which Ahab would have liked to have for his own.

> 1 Kings 21:2. *And Ahab spake unto Naboth saying, Give me thy vineyard . . . and I will give thee for it a better vineyard . . . or . . . the worth of it in money.*

Naboth refused to sell his ancestral holdings, however, and Ahab was helpless. Jezebel, however, was not. She bribed two men to swear that Naboth had committed treason and blasphemy and Naboth, thus framed, was executed. His vineyard, naturally, was confiscated by the throne, as was routine for the property of traitors.

The deed was very much like that in which David had arranged the death of Uriah and the "confiscation" of Uriah's wife. As Nathan had then denounced David to his face, so now Elijah appeared to denounce Ahab. Once more, the prophetic party placed itself on record as favoring the liberties of the people against royal oppression.

Ramoth-gilead

Israel was strong enough now, in the last years of Ahab's reign, to exert a clear domination over Judah, as well as over Syria. In 875 B.C., the same year in which Ahab had succeeded to the throne of Israel, Asa of Judah had died and his son Jehoshaphat (the sixth king of the Davidic dynasty) had succeeded. The continuing war with Israel had brought little good to Judah, and Jehoshaphat discontinued it and sought instead alliance and friendship with Ahab. He turned his eyes southward for expansion, maintaining the old grip on Edom

THE GREAT SEA
(Mediterranean Sea)

A R A M
(S Y R I A)

Ramoth-gilead

and trying to reinstate Solomon's old trade on the Red Sea, Judah's only gateway to the wide world outside. Here he was unsuccessful as Judah lacked the necessary experience with seagoing. An offer of help by Ahab was refused, for Jehoshaphat, though willing to be friends with Ahab, was not willing to give Ahab too much power in Judah.

The war with Syria had not been brought to a completely successful conclusion in Ahab's eyes, however, for one important piece of Israelite territory remained in Syrian hands. Ahab proposed to Jehoshaphat a united campaign against Syria for the recovery of the territory:

1 Kings 22:4. *And he [Ahab] said unto Jehoshaphat, Wilt thou go with me to battle to Ramoth-gilead?* . . .

Ramoth-gilead is another of the Trans-Jordan cities. Its exact location is unknown but it is usually considered to be somewhere north of Mahanaim.

There is an indication here that Yahvism was stronger in Judah than in Israel. Before the battle, Ahab consulted the prophets (at

Jehoshaphat's suggestion) but chose four hundred prophets of the Phoenician deities. They predicted victory, but Jehoshaphat would not accept that:

> 1 Kings 22:7. *And Jehoshaphat said, Is there not here a prophet of the Lord besides, that we might inquire of him?*

Reluctantly, Ahab produced one, who promptly predicted defeat and was placed in prison for his pains.

The battle took place. It was long and bloody and might indeed have gone to the Israelites, but a chance arrow struck Ahab and wounded him seriously. Though he fought on, death came by evening and the Israelites broke off the battle.

With the death, in 853 B.C., of Ahab, after a reign of twenty-two years, the First Book of Kings comes to an end.

12. 2 KINGS

MOAB · BAALZEBUB · ELISHA · MESHA · NAAMAN · JEHORAM OF JUDAH ·
HAZAEL · JEHU · JEHOASH · BEN-HADAD III · AMAZIAH · JEROBOAM II · PUL ·
REZIN · SHALMANESER V · SO · HABOR · SAMARITANS · SENNACHERIB ·
TIRHAKAH · ESARHADDON · BERODACH-BALADAN · MANASSEH · JOSIAH ·
PHARAOH-NECHOH · NEBUCHADNEZZAR · GEDALIAH · EVIL-MERODACH

Moab

The death of a strong king is bound to be followed by disorders,
as subject peoples seize the chance to rebel, and as surrounding independent nations take the opportunity to attack. Moab struck as soon
as news reached it of Ahab's death:

> 2 Kings 1:1. *Then Moab rebelled against Israel after the death
> of Ahab.*

The schism between Israel and Judah had made it almost impossible
for either nation to do much more than hold its own territory. Judah
maintained a precarious hold on Edom, and Israel held the Trans-
Jordan. Syria in the north of Israel was permanently independent
and when it was strong, its power tended to stretch out over the
Trans-Jordan.

Similarly, when Israel was strong, its armies pressed south from
Gilead and controlled Moab. This happened in the reign of Omri
when that capable monarch (much underrated in the Bible) took
Moab about 880 B.C. Ahab held it through his own stormy reign, but
with his death Moab rose.

Israel and Judah

Baalzebub

Ahab's son Ahaziah succeeded to the throne (the first time an Israelite dynasty survived to be represented by a third member) and found himself faced with the Moabite insurrection. Unfortunately, he sustained a bad fall, lay seriously ill, and was unable to lead the army.

2 Kings 1:2. . . . *and he* [Ahaziah] *sent messengers and said unto them, Go, inquire of Baalzebub the god of Ekron whether I shall recover of this disease.*

Baalzebub (more familiar in the New Testament version of the spelling, Beelzebub) means "Lord of the Flies."

This sounds odd at first and there are at least two explanations of its meaning. One is that the actual name was Baalzebul, meaning "Lord of the House," that is, "Lord of the Temple," a natural title for people to give their chief god. It would then seem that the Biblical writers, unable to bring themselves to give an idol a title which seemed to them to belong only to Yahveh, converted it to Baalzebub by the change of a letter.

A second explanation is that Baalzebub really did mean "Lord of the Flies" and that this was a legitimate title of the chief god of the Philistine city of Ekron, for it meant he had the power to bring or prevent insect plagues, which were great and fearful realities in the ancient world. It is not unlikely that the ancients noticed the rise in disease incidence where flies were plentiful and a "Lord of the Flies" might be, in general, a god with special powers in the field of health and medicine. This would explain why Ahaziah in his extremity should seek out Baalzebub in particular even though (as he must have known) this would enrage the prophetic party in Israel. And this it did, for Elijah arrived at once to denounce the action.

For some reason, Baalzebub grew to receive particular attention from the later Jews as the idolatrous god par excellence. Thus, when the reports of Jesus' ability to heal men spread, some said skeptically:

Matthew 12:24. . . . *This fellow doth not cast out devils, but by Beelzebub the prince of the devils.*

By "prince" we mean leader or chief so that Beelzebub (the New Testament spelling) was considered the chief devil, the being more familiarly known to us as Satan. In *Paradise Lost*, John Milton makes use of a whole hierarchy of fallen angels and therefore has Satan and Beelzebub as separate beings, but he makes Beelzebub second only to Satan.

To return to Ahaziah— His appeal to Baalzebub was of no help to him. He died after reigning two years and his younger brother, Jehoram, also referred to as Joram, fourth member of the dynasty of Omri, ascended the throne in 852 B.C.

Elisha

Elijah, the great leader of the prophetic party, did not long survive Ahaziah. The Bible recounts the legend that he was taken up alive into heaven:

> 2 Kings 2:11. . . . *there appeared a chariot of fire, and horses of fire, . . . and Elijah went up by a whirlwind into heaven.*

His lieutenant, Elisha, remained behind to inherit his position and his aims. This is indicated by a physical action that has entered into the language as a metaphor:

> 2 Kings 2:13. *He* [Elisha] *took up . . . the mantle of Elijah that fell upon him, and went back . . .*

From this point on, to his death a half century or more later, Elisha headed the prophetic party and kept it in vigorous life.

Elijah lived on, however, in the awed memory of later generations. His bold stand against a powerful king and queen in favor of Yahvism, his courageous denunciation of tyranny and absolutism, was infinitely impressive and must have led to the feeling that nothing less than a living translation into heaven could do for so holy a man. This, in turn, encouraged the thought that someone taken alive into heaven might someday return alive from heaven.

In later generations when the kingdom of Israel and Judah had both been destroyed and when the surviving Jews looked forward with mingled hope and dread to the day when the Lord would set up a new order on earth, it was felt that Elijah would then play a key role. Thus, the prophet Malachi, writing four centuries after Elijah, states God's promise as:

Malachi 4:5. *Behold, I will send you Elijah the prophet before the coming of the great and dreadful day of the Lord.*

In the New Testament, in which the view is taken that the new order on earth has been brought by Jesus, the forecoming of Elijah is accepted. Jesus is quoted as saying:

Matthew 17:12. *But I say unto you, That Elias [Elijah] is come already . . .*

Matthew 17:13. *Then the disciples understood that he spake unto them of John the Baptist.*

Mesha

Moab was still in successful rebellion at the time of Jehoram's accession to the throne of Israel, and the fact is noted once more, this time with the name of the Moabite ruler:

2 Kings 3:4. *And Mesha king of Moab . . .*
2 Kings 3:5. *. . . rebelled against the king of Israel.*

Israel under Jehoram was still allied with Jehoshaphat of Judah and this fact offered the Israelite monarch a strategic opportunity. Rather than attack Moab from the north in a straight head-to-head clash, a combined Israelite-Judean army could move southward through Edom (a Judean dependency) and around the southern edge of the Dead Sea. Moab could then be attacked along her unprepared southern frontier. The march, however, was a difficult one. The heat and lack of water must have badly damaged soldier morale and led Jehoram to fear either an ignominious retreat or a disastrous defeat.

Jehoshaphat at this point (as several years before with Ahab) suggested that a prophet be consulted. (This is good policy since if the prophet predicts victory, soldier morale shoots upward and this may indeed suffice to produce victory.) This time it was Elisha that stood before the monarchs and again it is clear that the prophetic party

Mesha's Kingdom

was closer at heart to rustic Judah than to citified Israel, for Elisha says contemptuously to Jehoram:

2 Kings 3:14. . . . *were it not that I regard the presence of Jehoshaphat . . . I would not look toward thee, nor see thee.*

Elisha predicts victory and, indeed, victories of the combined kings over the Moabites are recorded. But then, in one cryptic verse, the whole is nullified and Moab is left free and independent.

2 Kings 3:27. *Then he* [Mesha of Moab] *took his eldest son . . . and offered him for a burnt offering upon the wall. And there was great indignation against Israel: and they* [the allied forces] *departed from him, and returned to their own land.*

To understand this, we must remember that Moab's cultural and religious level was much like that of Israel and Judah. In 1869, a German missionary, F. A. Klein, discovered a memorial inscription on a piece of black basalt, three and a half feet high and two feet wide. It was found in the ruins of Dibon, a Moabite city about twelve miles east of the Dead Sea and some four miles north of the Arnon River.

It turned out to be an inscription in ancient Hebrew (the oldest lengthy inscription in that writing now extant) and it had been set up by Mesha to commemorate the events of his reign. It is called the "stone of Mesha" or the "Moabite stone."

The language used has a Biblical sound except that the Moabite god, Chemosh, replaces the Israelite God, Yahveh. Thus, the stone says: "Omri, King of Israel, afflicted Moab for many days, because Chemosh was angry with his land." Also, "Chemosh said unto me, Go, take Nebo against Israel" and "Chemosh drave him out from before me," and so on.

To many at this time it must have seemed that there was a rough kind of democracy among gods, each having its own territory within which it might ordinarily be supreme, until such time as one god might develop greater strength than another so that the human agents of one would then be able to invade the land and defeat the human agents of the other. This view, "henotheism," was that of the vast majority of ancient peoples.

It is very likely that even the Yahvists were at this time henotheists, though this is hard to tell from the Bible, for the later writers, whose views of Yahveh were considerably more exalted, would have been embarrassed by such evidence as they might find in the traditional legends and chronicles and would have modified them. Verse 3:27 in 2 Kings is a case in point.

If a god is angry with his people, he may be propitiated by a sacrifice; the more valued the object sacrificed the more certain the propitiation. The sacrifice of a human would be better than that of any animal and the sacrifice of the heir to the throne would be best of all. The Biblical writers are firm in their insistence that Yahveh was not like the gods of other nations and abhorred human sacrifice, but Abraham's near sacrifice of Isaac, and Jephthah's actual sacrifice of his daughter are traces of a more primitive view.

Certainly Chemosh did not disapprove of human sacrifice and Mesha, driven to despair by the victorious advance of the allied army, sacrificed his son. This could well be a useful act in a henotheistic society. The Moabite army, aware of the sacrifice, would be certain that Chemosh would now be fighting on their side. Since the battle was on Moabite territory and Chemosh was supreme in Moab, they could fight with the assurance of victory.

The allied army, equally aware of the sacrifice, would feel Yahveh to be weak on alien soil and would fight in equal expectation of defeat. With the Moabites sure of winning and the Israelites sure of losing there could only be one outcome.

The phrase "there was great indignation against Israel" is given in the Revised Standard Version as "there came great wrath upon Israel," and it seems very likely that the indignation or wrath here spoken of was that of Chemosh. It is possible that the earliest form of the verse was "there came the great wrath of Chemosh upon Israel," and the Biblical writers, unwilling to make it appear that Chemosh was a real god who could display effective wrath, or was anything more than a false idol, eliminated the mention of his name.

Naaman

The early chapters of 2 Kings include a number of wonder tales concerning Elisha, and the best developed of these involves a Syrian general who, according to Jewish legend (but *not* according to anything in the Bible) had been the one whose arrow had slain Ahab:

> 2 Kings 5:1. Now Naaman, captain of the host of the king of Syria, was . . . a mighty man in valour, but he was a leper.

A young Israelite maidservant, taken captive in the wars with Israel, suggested that Naaman consult the wonder-working Elisha in Israel. Naaman followed this advice and was instructed to wash himself seven times in the Jordan River. Despite Naaman's initial nationalistic indignation at the suggestion that the Jordan had greater curative powers than the rivers of Syria, he did as he was told and was cured.

This, naturally, convinced Naaman of the power of Yahveh:

> 2 Kings 5:17. And Naaman said, Shall there not . . . be given to thy servant two mules' burden of earth? for thy servant will henceforth offer neither burnt offering nor sacrifice unto other gods, but unto the Lord.

Henotheistically, he required the earth, for in sacrificing to Yahveh, he would have to stand on the soil of Israel, or it would do no good. By bringing some Israelite soil to Damascus he would create for himself a little island over which Yahveh would have power.

Israel and Syria (Aram)

Naaman also recognized that he could not carry his private worship too far or make it too exclusive, and he said to Elisha:

2 Kings 5:18. In this thing the Lord pardon thy servant, that when my master goeth into the house of Rimmon to worship there, and he leaneth on my hand, and I bow myself in the house of Rimmon . . .

Elisha's answer was a simple:

2 Kings 5:19. . . . Go in peace . . .

which was the equivalent of consent. Perhaps the earliest versions of the story gave the consent more explicitly, for Elisha (who is not recorded as objecting to Naaman's assumption that only on Israelite soil could Yahveh be worshiped) might have been more of a henotheist himself than the later Biblical writers were willing to allow.

Rimmon, by the way, seems to be an alternate name for Hadad, the national god of Damascus. Hadad was a storm-god and "Rimmon" seems to mean "the Thunderer." (This was precisely the epithet often given to the Greek storm-god, Zeus.)

As a result of verse 5:18, the expression "to bow to Rimmon" has come to mean the act of conforming to a social custom one knows to be wrong merely in order to avoid trouble.

Jehoram of Judah

Judah continued her policy of careful subservience to Israel. When, in 851 B.C., Jehoshaphat of Judah died, after having reigned for twenty-four years:

> 2 Kings 8:16. . . . *Jehoram the son of Jehoshaphat . . . began to reign.*

Jehoram (or Joram) of Judah, the seventh king of the Davidic dynasty, happened to have the same name as that of the contemporary king of Israel. Another link was in the form of a dynastic marriage, for Jehoram of Judah was married to Athaliah, the daughter of Ahab and Jezebel, and was therefore brother-in-law, as well as namesake, to Jehoram of Israel.

While Jehoshaphat had been alive, Yahvism was in the ascendant in Judah at least, but Jehoram of Judah was, apparently, as much under the influence of Athaliah as Ahab of Israel had been under the influence of Jezebel:

> 2 Kings 8:18. *And he* [Jehoram of Judah] *walked in the way of . . . the house of Ahab: for the daughter of Ahab was his wife.*

Then, too, just as after the death of Ahab, Moab had revolted against Israel, so now after the death of Jehoshaphat, Edom revolted against Judah.

Jehoram died in 844 B.C. and his son Ahaziah, the eighth king of the Davidic dynasty, came to the throne. (To add further to the confusion of those trying to keep these names straight, Ahaziah, the son of Jehoram of Judah, was the namesake of Ahaziah, the elder brother of Jehoram of Israel.)

Ahaziah of Judah was a young man of twenty-two, completely under the thumb of his mother Athaliah. Judah seemed doomed to be absorbed by Israel.

Hazael

That this did not happen was due, partly, to Israel's continuing troubles with Syria.

About the time that Ahaziah became king of a shrunken and tottering Judah, a palace revolution took place in Damascus. When Ben-hadad II of Syria fell sick, one of his courtiers, Hazael, hastened the death of the old king:

> 2 Kings 8:15. . . . *he* [Hazael] *took a thick cloth, and dipped it in water, and spread it on his* [Ben-hadad's] *face so that he died: and Hazael reigned in his stead.*

Hazael turned out to be a vigorous ruler and under him, in fact, Syria rose to the peak of its power.

The war over Ramoth-gilead, where Ahab had received his fatal wound a dozen years before, was renewed now. In the course of the war, Jehoram of Israel was wounded and forced to retire to Jezreel, leaving the army under the command of his general, Jehu.

While Jehoram remained in Jezreel, recuperating, his ally (and nephew) Ahaziah of Judah came to Jezreel, as an assurance, presumably, of his loyalty. Jezebel was still alive, and in Jezreel, and it might well have been a source of pride to her to see the two kings together; one her son and the other her grandson. Disaster, however, was close at hand.

Jehu

Jehoram's wound gave the prophetic party its opportunity. A disabled king was useless in time of war and the people might welcome the opportunity to place a vigorous general on the throne instead. Such a general was Jehu, who was either a Yahvist or was willing to become one to gain the throne.

Elisha sent to assure him of the support of the prophetic party and urged him to assume the kingship. His fellow officers were enthusiastically willing:

2 Kings 9:13. . . . *they hasted . . . and blew with trumpets, saying, Jehu is king.*

Jehu marched instantly on Jezreel with the intention of laying it under siege and establishing his kingship by executing Jehoram. Jehoram and Ahaziah, the two kings, came out to meet Jehu's army and did so, according to the Biblical writer, in the very vineyard that had once belonged to Naboth (see page 350). There Jehu killed Jehoram and when Ahaziah attempted to escape, had him pursued and killed likewise.

Jezebel, her son and grandson dead, retained her pride and courage to the end.

2 Kings 9:30. *And when Jehu was come to Jezreel, Jezebel heard of it; and she painted her face, and tired her head, and looked out at a window.*

That is, she put on eye make-up (the Revised Standard Version renders the phrase "she painted her eyes and adorned her head") to hide any signs of grief and to show herself even at this last moment a queen. Posterity, unwilling to give the old queen credit for any virtue, even that of courage, uses the term "painted Jezebel" to signify not bravery in the face of disaster, but merely to signify wickedness—usually sexual wickedness, of which there is no Biblical ground for accusing Jezebel.

From the window, Jezebel taunted Jehu with being another Zimri, who had killed a king but who had lived to rule only seven days before giving way to Omri, the founder of the house which Jehu was now destroying (see page 342).

Jehu did not allow himself to be disturbed by the comparison. He had Jezebel thrown from the window and killed. Having done that, he proceeded to take the usual dynastic precautions:

2 Kings 10:11. *So Jehu slew all that remained of the house of Ahab in Jezreel, and all his great men, and his kinsfolks, and his priests, until he left him none remaining.*

The house of Omri, Israel's third dynasty, had thus lasted forty-four years, and had seen four kings: Omri, Ahab, Ahaziah, and Jehoram. Now, in 843 B.C., the line was at an end and Jehu founded the fourth dynasty of Israel.

The worship of the Phoenician god, Melkart, was so intimately entwined with the house of Omri that it was good policy for Jehu to destroy the cult. He killed its priests and desecrated its temples and restored Yahvism to its wonted supremacy. However, it was Yahvism after the fashion of Jeroboam, with its bull-worshiping sanctuaries. To the more advanced of the prophetic party, this was insufficient.

Moreover, the civil war in Israel was Hazael's opportunity. The army in Ramoth-gilead could scarcely stand before him while Israel itself was convulsed in political and religious revolution.

2 Kings 10:32. *In those days . . . Hazael smote them in all the coasts of Israel;*

2 Kings 10:33. *From Jordan eastward, all the land of Gilead . . .*

Israel, its Trans-Jordanian territories lost, was penned between the Jordan and the sea.

Jehu had to find help. None could be received from Phoenicia after Jehu's actions against the Tyrian princess Jezebel and all that she had represented. Nor could any be expected from Judah, which was, temporarily, in the grip of Jezebel's vengeful daughter, Athaliah.

Jehu therefore turned to the one remaining source of help—Assyria. That powerful nation was still under the rule of Shalmaneser III, who, nearly fifteen years before, had been withstood by the united forces of Syria and Israel. Now the new king of Israel paid tribute to Assyria in 841 B.C. and acknowledged Assyrian overlordship in return for Assyrian help against Syria, thus helping to hasten the day when Syria and Israel alike would fall prey to the Assyrian power.

The fact of Jehu's tribute to Assyria is known from Assyrian inscriptions; it is not mentioned in the Bible. The Assyrian records call Jehu by the then usual title used by them for the kings of Israel—the "son of Omri." This, despite the fact that Jehu, far from being a descendant of Omri, had just killed every such descendant he could find. Jehu reigned for twenty-eight years, dying in 816 B.C.

Jehoash

The house of Omri still remained in Judah in the person of· Ahaziah's mother, Athaliah, the daughter of Ahab and Jezebel. She

Syria at Its Height

seized power at the news of the slaying of her son Ahaziah by the usurper, Jehu. To keep herself in power, she destroyed all the males of the house of David she could find.

2 Kings 11:2. *But Jehosheba, the daughter of king Joram* [Jehoram of Judah], *sister of Ahaziah, took Joash the son of Ahaziah, and stole him from among the king's sons which were slain; and they hid him . . . from Athaliah, so that he was not slain.*

2 Kings 11:3. *And he was with her hid in the house of the Lord six years. And Athaliah did reign over the land.*

If Jehosheba was the daughter of king Jehoram and the sister of Ahaziah, she must also have been the daughter of Athaliah, unless she was the daughter of Jehoram by a concubine. The Bible does not make that clear. It seems difficult to believe that Athaliah would kill her own grandsons and it may be that the "king's sons" referred to are the various male members of the house of David, the sons and grandsons of Jehoram by various concubines.

The hiding of Jehoash (or Joash) might conceivably have been intended not so much to save him from death, but to save him from an upbringing according to Athaliah's religious views.

In 837 B.C., Jehoiada the High Priest (and husband of Jehosheba) felt the time was right. He displayed the person of the boy-king to the Judean generals and allowed the mystic aura of descent from David to do its work.

The army was won over and Athaliah was killed. The cult of Melkart which she had established in Jerusalem was wiped out, and Jehoash reigned as the ninth king of the Davidic dynasty.

It is interesting to note, though, that Jehoash was the grandson of Athaliah and the great-grandson of Ahab and Jezebel. Through all future kings of Judah ran the blood not only of David but also of Jezebel.

The reign of Jehoash had its share of disasters. Hazael of Syria, having swept up the Trans-Jordan, circled the Dead Sea, laid siege to and conquered the Philistine city of Gath, and was then ready to march against Jerusalem itself. The city was saved only when Jehoash used the treasures of the Temple as tribute to Hazael, bribing him, in effect, to leave Jerusalem in peace.

This humiliated the army leaders, of course, and enraged the priesthood. In 797 B.C., Jehoash, having so narrowly escaped one palace revolution when a baby, fell prey to another, and was assassinated by disaffected conspirators. He had reigned thirty-nine years—forty-five, if the period of Athaliah's usurpation is added to the toll.

Ben-hadad III

After Jehu's death in 816 B.C., his son Jehoahaz succeeded to the throne and continued to wage a losing fight against the formidable Hazael of Syria. Jehoahaz, after a sixteen-year reign, died in 800 B.C. and was succeeded by his son Jehoash. (Again the reigning monarchs of Israel and Judah were, for a few years, namesakes.)

The Syrian tide was beginning to ebb, however. In 810 B.C., the Syrian conqueror had died:

> 2 Kings 13:24. . . . *Hazael king of Syria died: and Ben-hadad his son, reigned in his stead.*

This was Ben-hadad III, whose proper name, apparently, before he adopted the royal cognomen, was Mari. Israel's temporary salvation lay not so much in its own efforts as in the fact that Syria was at this time being pounded hard by Assyria.

Assyrian power was in a period of rapid decline after the death of Shalmaneser III in 824 B.C. (while Jehu was still king of Israel) but in a brief flash of effort under Adadnirari III, it managed to besiege Damascus in 805 B.C. and inflict serious punishment.

Assyria's weakness prevented her from completing the conquest of Syria, but the hand of Ben-hadad III had been permanently enfeebled and Israel in three campaigns under Jehoash was able to recover the territories lost to Hazael.

The Israelite monarch was supported in these campaigns by the ultranationalist prophetic party, of course. In the course of these campaigns, Elisha died and a sorrowing Jehoash was at his bedside.

Elisha was not succeeded by anyone of similar force, and the prophetic party in Israel declined and was not an important factor in the final three quarters of a century of Israel's existence.

Amaziah

The fortunes of Judah also seemed to take a temporary upturn. In the reign of Amaziah, Edom, which had retained its independence for fifty years since the death of Jehoshaphat, was retaken:

2 Kings 14:7. *He* [Amaziah] *slew of Edom . . . ten thousand . . .*

Amaziah, heartened by this victory, attempted then to break the subservient alliance that the kings of Judah had maintained with the kings of Israel for eighty years. Unfortunately, he was not that strong. He might beat Edom but in battle with Israel he lost. Jerusalem was taken by Jehoash of Israel, part of its fortifications were destroyed, and the Temple was sacked.

Amaziah, as a result of this military humiliation, met the same fate as his father. In 780 B.C., after a seventeen-year reign, Amaziah was assassinated and his son Azariah sat on the throne as the eleventh king of the Davidic dynasty.

Jeroboam II

In 785 B.C. Jehoash of Israel died and was succeeded by his son Jeroboam II, the fourth monarch of the line of Jehu. He reigned for forty years till 744 B.C. and under him Israel reached the height of prosperity and power.

Syria's desperate wounding by Assyria combined with the Assyrian period of weakness that intensified afterward and left a power vacuum to the north. Jeroboam II filled it:

2 Kings 14:25. *He restored the coast of Israel from the entering of Hamath unto the sea of the plain.*

Hamath is a town in northern Syria and the sea of the plain is the Dead Sea. By this verse is meant then that Israel was in control of all of Syria, probably in the sense that the cities of Syria were forced to pay tribute to Jeroboam. (Syrian home rule continued, however, and there was still a ruler in Damascus who might be called the king of

The Kingdom of Jeroboam II

Syria.) Judah, as a result of its defeat during the previous reign, was probably also a tributary, so that for the space of a few decades at least, the empire of David and Solomon seemed restored.

It was but a brief bit of Indian summer, however, that could endure only until giant Assyria was on its feet again. It lasted the time of Jeroboam II, but scarcely any more.

When Zachariah, the son of Jeroboam II, ascended the throne of Israel in 744 B.C., he represented the fifth generation of the line of Jehu, whose great-great-grandson he was. The dynasty had endured an unprecedented (for Israel) hundred years—but the end was at hand. Zachariah had been reigning only six months when he was unseated and murdered by a palace conspiracy, and after a month of confusion, an army officer named Menahem forced his own acceptance as the new king.

Pul

Menahem's hold on the throne was insecure and, as is not uncommon in such cases, he sought foreign help:

2 Kings 15:19. *And Pul the king of Assyria came against the land: and Menahem gave Pul a thousand talents of silver, that his hand might be with him to confirm the kingdom in his hand.*

Assyria had had prior contacts with Israel (see pages 349 and 365) but until now it had been Syria that was the prime danger. Now it was Assyria itself and so although the Biblical writers had ignored Assyria before, they can do so no longer. In this verse, contact between Assyria and Israel is mentioned for the first time, and it might be well here to review Assyria's history.

Assyria had been a wealthy and prosperous merchant realm in Abraham's time and this period of its history is sometimes referred to as the "Old Assyrian Empire." In the next few centuries, however, Assyria was hard put to it to survive under the pressures of the great powers of the age: Egypt, the Hittites, and the Mitanni.

It was only after the destruction and anarchy that followed upon the coming of the Peoples of the Sea that Assyria was to have its chance again. With the Hittite and Mitanni realms virtually destroyed and with Egypt weakened and driven out of Asia, Assyria stepped forward.

About 1200 B.C., while the Israelites were making their way toward Canaan, the Assyrian king Tukulti-Ninurta (the Biblical Nimrod— see page 53) conquered Babylonia, introducing a period sometimes called the "Middle Assyrian Empire." The Middle Empire reached the height of its power under Tiglath-Pileser I, who ruled from 1116 to 1078 B.C., during the period of the judges in Israel.

Tiglath-Pileser I carried his conquests westward and was the first Assyrian monarch to reach the Mediterranean, doing so in the region north of Canaan.

The Assyrian hold at that distance was still light and after the death of Tiglath-Pileser there was a decline. The Aramaean tribes, advancing southward and eastward from Asia Minor, threw back the Assyrians and put an end to their Middle Empire. It was as a result of the gap that followed in Assyrian power that David was able to establish his own empire over the western half of the Fertile Crescent.

The Aramaeans occupied Syria and were themselves subjected by David, but in Solomon's time they established the kingdom of Damascus that was to cost Israel so much in the days of Ahab and his successors.

Once again, Assyria revived. In 883 B.C., when Omri was king of Israel, a strong Assyrian monarch, Ashurnasirpal, came to the throne, and founded the "Late Assyrian Empire." He reorganized the Assyrian army and made maximum use of iron weapons and armor. These were much cheaper than bronze weapons and made it possible for the Assyrians to equip a mass army of infantry that could smash through the lighter and more specialized chariot-led armies of their foes.

Ashurnasirpal also introduced a policy of extreme cruelty. The inhabitants of captured cities were fiendishly tortured to death. This may have resulted from the king's innate sadism or as part of a deliberate policy for weakening the will of the enemy through terror. If the latter was the case, it succeeded, and Ashurnasirpal re-established the empire of Tiglath-Pileser I, which again reached the Mediterranean.

His son Shalmaneser III succeeded to the throne in 859 B.C. during the reign of Ahab, and Assyrian force, firmly established to the north, turned southward against Syria and Israel. The battle of Karkar in 854 B.C. (see page 349) blunted that drive for the while.

Nevertheless, Assyria's giant strength hovered remorselessly over the two kingdoms and both, at various times, were forced to pay tribute to her. The case of Jehu has been mentioned (see page 365).

Shalmaneser died in 824 B.C. and once again, Assyria was governed by incompetent rulers and the threat of her armies receded, as she found herself fighting for her life against the growing might of the new kingdom of Urartu to the northwest (see page 41). It was in this interval that first Hazael of Syria and then Jeroboam II of Israel were able to enjoy brief periods of illusory power.

In 745 B.C., just before the death of Jeroboam II, an Assyrian general deposed the feeble Assyrian monarch of the moment and placed himself on the throne as the first of a new dynasty of Assyrian kings. For a final period of a century and a half Assyria grew great again—greater than it had ever been before.

The new king is the Biblical "Pul," and this may be a form of his real name, "Pulu," by which he is listed in the Babylonian annals. A usurper needs to pile about himself all the emotional values he can manage and so Pul adopted the glorious name (to Assyrians) of Tiglath-Pileser and became the third to be so called.

It was Pul, or Tiglath-Pileser III, who checked the career of the kingdom of Urartu, defeating it in 743 B.C. And it was to Tiglath-Pileser III that Menahem paid tribute.

Rezin

Worse was to follow. In 738 B.C., Menahem's son Pekahiah, the second king of Israel's fifth dynasty, succeeded to the throne and carried on his father's pro-Assyrian policy (actually the only safe and logical one for the times). This did not suit the more rabid war hawks, however, and the general in chief, Pekah, initiated a conspiracy and killed him, becoming king in 737 B.C. The fifth dynasty had lasted only seven years.

Pekah then set about forming an anti-Assyrian alliance like that which had been at least reasonably successful a little over a century before at Karkar. He allied himself with Rezin of Damascus for that purpose and they endeavored to bring in Judah as a third member.

Judah had just come through a comparatively prosperous period in her history. In 780 B.C., Azariah, the eleventh king of the Davidic

line, had succeeded his father Amaziah. In a forty-year reign he led
a Judah which remained quietly in the shadow of Jeroboam II, and
experienced a reasonable peace and prosperity.

In later life, Azariah developed leprosy and his son Jotham became
regent about 750 B.C., succeeding to the throne as twelfth king of the
Davidic line in 740 B.C.

Jotham was not ready to join the anti-Assyrian alliance, suspecting,
and quite rightly, that the alliance would not succeed and would
merely hasten the day it was intended to stave off. The kings of
Syria and Israel attempted to change Jotham's mind by force.

> 2 Kings 15:37. *In those days the Lord began to send against*
> *Judah, Rezin the king of Syria, and Pekah* [of Israel] . . .

Judah resisted and the war was still continuing when Jotham died
and was succeeded by his son Ahaz, thirteenth king of the Davidic
line, in 736 B.C.

The Syrian forces occupied Edom and besieged Jerusalem. In this
connection, the King James Version first makes use of the word "Jew"
as an alternate form of "Judean" or "man of Judah."

> 2 Kings 16:6. . . . *Rezin . . . recovered Elath . . . and drave the*
> *Jews from Elath* . . .

although the Revised Standard Version translates the phrase "and
drove the men of Judah from Elath."

Ahaz, seeing the inevitable defeat before him, took the truly desperate expedient of sending tribute to Tiglath-Pileser III as a token of
submission, and appealing to him for help.

The Assyrian monarch responded at once and with a strong hand:

> 2 Kings 15:29. *In the days of Pekah . . . came Tiglath-Pileser*
> . . . *and took . . . Gilead, and . . . all the land of Naphtali.*

Nor was Syria to be neglected:

> 2 Kings 16:9. . . . *the king of Assyria went up against Damascus*
> *and took it . . . and slew Rezin.*

In 732 B.C. the Syrian kingdom came to an end after an existence
of two and a half centuries. Damascus has remained an important and
flourishing city ever since but it came under foreign rule in 732 B.C.

and remained under foreign rule in unbroken fashion for over twenty-six hundred years. Not until A.D. 1941 did Damascus again become the capital of a native Syrian nation (although it has in times past become the capital of a large empire under a foreign dynasty).

Thus only thirteen years after the death of Jeroboam II, Israel was virtually confined to the district surrounding Samaria.

Shalmaneser V

With Syria crushed and Israel chastened, all attempts at resistance in the western end of the Fertile Crescent came, at least temporarily, to an end. Tiglath-Pileser III could turn to the eastern end and crush a rebellion in Babylonia. (Babylonia was in a state of perennial revolt against Assyria but all the revolts were crushed—except the last one.)

Meanwhile, another palace revolution—the last one—had upset the throne of Israel. Pekah, whose reign had been unsuccessful and who had led his kingdom into disaster against the Assyrians, was assassinated as a result of a conspiracy led by a man named Hoshea. Hoshea became king in 732 B.C. According to the Assyrian records, Hoshea was appointed by Tiglath-Pileser III or, at least, did not become king until he had received Assyrian approval.

While Tiglath-Pileser lived, Hoshea remained submissive to Assyria. When Tiglath-Pileser died, in 726 B.C., there was an instant stirring. As stated earlier, the death of a strong king calls forth prompt rebellions on the chance that his successor will be a weakling and that the confusion of an interregnum will last long enough to make the rebellion successful.

Tiglath's son and successor, Shalmaneser V, took quick action, however. Hoshea was one of those who placed himself in rebellion on the death of the old king and Shalmaneser turned on him.

2 Kings 17:3. *Against him* [Hoshea] *came up Shalmaneser king of Assyria; and Hoshea became his servant, and gave him presents.*

In other words, Hoshea acknowledged Assyrian domination and Israel became a tributary kingdom. Even so, Hoshea would not have gotten off so lightly, in all probability, if Shalmaneser had not had pressing problems elsewhere.

So

At the first opportunity after the departure of Shalmaneser's army, Hoshea judged that various complications would keep the Assyrian busy indefinitely, and rebelled again. He sought further assurance by sending for help from abroad:

> 2 Kings 17:4. . . . he . . . sent messengers to So king of Egypt, and brought no present to the king of Assyria . . .

Again Egypt makes a shadowy appearance in the Bible. The Libyan dynasty of Sheshonk (the Biblical Shishak) was petering out into the usual final whimper at about this time. In the delta, a pair of native kings (the 24th dynasty) ruled briefly, and a line of kings from Ethiopia in the south also seized power, forming the 25th dynasty.

This is the first impingement of Ethiopia upon Israel, if one eliminates the highly dubious case of the queen of Sheba (see page 331).

The main core of ancient Ethiopia was located northwest of the modern kingdom of that name. It was to be found just south of Egypt in the territory now occupied by the Sudan. Under the conquering Pharaohs of the 18th dynasty, Ethiopia was conquered by Egypt and remained a subject province for four centuries.

About 1100 B.C., toward the end of Egypt's 20th dynasty and well after the death of her last powerful Pharaoh, Rameses III, Ethiopia gained her independence and formed an increasingly powerful state centered about the city of Napata. This was located on the upper Nile, near the fourth cataract, quite close to the modern city of Merowe in northern Sudan.

This kingdom, consistently called Ethiopia in the English version of the Bible (and Cush in the Hebrew original) is sometimes called Nubia to distinguish it from the modern Ethiopia.

By 736 B.C. Ethiopia was beginning to turn the tables on Egypt and while Assyria was destroying Syria and Israel, the Ethiopians took over parts of the Nile delta.

It was to the aggressors on the south that Hoshea turned for salvation from the aggressors of the north. So, king of Egypt, is referred to as Shab'i in the Assyrian records and it is just possible he may represent Shabaka of the 25th dynasty.

Egypt's motivation is clear. She could not help but view the continuing growth of Assyrian strength with alarm and she did everything she could to encourage rebellions among the Assyrian vassal states. Unfortunately, she had virtually no power of her own, and although she could subsidize and bribe, she could not support. Those nations which listened to Egyptian blandishments and accepted Egyptian gold invariably found that at the crucial moment, when they faced the Assyrian army, Egyptian help was nowhere to be found or was, at best, inadequate.

In the end it was disaster for everybody—including Egypt.

Habor

Shalmaneser reacted vigorously again at the news of the renewed rebellion. He marched against Israel, laid it waste, captured and deposed Hoshea, and then, in 725 B.C., laid siege to Samaria.

With the courage of despair, Samaria, isolated and hopeless, managed to continue its resistance for three years. Perhaps this resistance exasperated the Assyrians generally and Shalmaneser was made the scapegoat. In any case, Shalmaneser died in 722 B.C., possibly through assassination, since a usurper (possibly the conspirator who arranged the assassination) came to the throne and served as the first monarch of Assyria's last and most spectacular dynasty.

The usurper again chose a glorious name intended to shed a glow of honored tradition about himself. He went far, far back to the days of Sargon of Agade (see page 50) seventeen centuries before, for the purpose. Since there was an earlier Sargon in the list of Assyrian kings, this new one is known as Sargon II.

It was Sargon II who completed Shalmaneser's work and brought the siege of Samaria to a quick and successful conclusion, even though the Bible does not take note of the change in monarch but refers to him only as "the king of Assyria."

2 Kings 17:6. *In the ninth year of Hoshea, the king of Assyria* [Sargon] *took Samaria and carried Israel away into Assyria, and placed them in Halah and in Habor by the river of Gozan, and in the cities of the Medes.*

Habor (Khabur), the River of Gozan

Thus, in 722 B.C., there came to a permanent end the kingdom of Israel, which had existed for a little over two hundred years since the successful rebellion led by Jeroboam. To those interested in coincidences, it might be noted that Israel entered Canaan four and a half centuries before under a Hoshea (Joshua) and now left under another Hoshea.

Sargon adopted a procedure introduced by Tiglath-Pileser III. Instead of pacifying a territory by wholesale murder and destruction, which made it less profitable thereafter to its Assyrian masters, the same end was attained by deporting the leading citizens of a nation to another portion of the empire, while new colonists were brought in. In this way, the ties and tradition that bound peoples to the land were broken—an important matter to a henotheistic people who felt themselves deserted by their god—and the will to resist and rebel atrophied.

In this case, some twenty-seven thousand Israelites were deported. This obviously did not represent the entire population of Israel but it probably included virtually all the ruling classes: the landowners and leaders.

They were never heard of again, and they have long been known to tradition as the "Ten Lost Tribes" of Israel.

Later generations found it difficult to believe that the tribes to whom God had made so many promises could really be wiped out even though the Bible ascribes the destruction of those tribes to the fact that they had abandoned Yahvism and worshiped idols.

Many people believed legends to the effect that the Ten Tribes still existed in some remote fastness of Asia or Africa, that they had established a powerful kingdom, and that they would someday emerge, glowing with true religion, to rescue the downtrodden Jews (or Christians, depending on who was devising the legends) from their oppressors.

The Jewish historian Josephus, writing eight centuries after the destruction of Israel, reported that the Ten Tribes still existed beyond the Euphrates and were a powerful nation. After that the stories grew wilder and wilder. The Ten Tribes were supposed to form a powerful kingdom in Ethiopia, or in Mongolia, or even in America.

Some even believed that existing modern nations might be the descendants of the Ten Tribes. In the nineteenth century, the notion grew in some circles that the Ten Tribes somehow became the Scythians, living north of the Black Sea in Greek times, that these became the Saxons ("Isaac's sons"), and, since these invaded Britain, that the English people are therefore the descendants of the Ten Tribes. Surely it is hard to imagine anything more silly than these beliefs of the so-called "British-Israelite" cult.

What really happened to the Ten Tribes? The apparent truth is completely unromantic. The Second Book of Kings says, in a slightly garbled verse, that they were deported to "Halah and in Habor by the river of Gozan, and in the cities of the Medes."

Habor is almost certainly the river now known as Khabur, which is a tributary of the Euphrates, flowing into it from the north. The Khabur River rises in southeastern Turkey and flows generally southward for about two hundred miles through what is now northeastern Syria. It enters the Euphrates about thirty miles south of the Syrian provincial town of Deir ez Zor. Gozan and Halah are cities on the

Khabur. They are referred to as the "cities of the Medes" not because they were in Median territory at the time, but because they had come under Median domination a century and a half later when the material in the Second Book of Kings reached its final form.

What it amounts to, then, is that the Israelites were moved about 450 miles northeastward to the top of the Fertile Crescent. They were indeed only about sixty miles east of the city of Haran where Abraham had sojourned on his way to Canaan (see page 59).

And what happened to the Ten Tribes on the Khabur River? Nothing very startling. They undoubtedly intermarried with the people of the region, adopted the gods and customs of the region, and "vanished" by assimilation.

This is what usually happens to tribes who come to be isolated from "home base." What happened to the Vandals who had once invaded and conquered North Africa? To the Alans, who had once conquered Hungary? To the Khazars, who once controlled the Ukraine?

To be sure, two centuries later, the inhabitants of Judah were deported and did *not* assimilate themselves into the new surroundings. Because the Jews survived (and there were reasons for it), one wonders why the Israelites did not. That, however, is the reverse of the real problem. One should accept the fact that the Israelites did not survive, and wonder why the Jews did!

Samaritans

To eke out the depleted population of Israel, Sargon brought in colonists from other parts of the Assyrian Empire.

> 2 Kings 17:24. *And the king of Assyria brought men from Babylon . . . and placed them in the cities of Samaria instead of the children of Israel . . .*

It is these colonists and their descendants that in later books of the Bible are referred to as "Samaritans."

At first the immigrants tried to maintain their own religious traditions, but henotheistic feelings were strong and when natural disaster struck the blame was placed on the fact that:

Samaria and Surrounding Lands

2 Kings 17:26. . . . *they know not the manner of the God of the land.*

One of the deported priests was therefore returned.

2 Kings 17:28. . . . *one of the priests . . . dwelt in Bethel, and taught them how they should fear the Lord.*

This did not, however, bring about friendly relations with the people of Judah. The Yahvism they were taught was admixed with what seemed to the Judeans to be all sorts of error.

2 Kings 17:33. *They feared the Lord, and served their own gods, after the manner of the nations* [from which they came] . . .
2 Kings 17:34. *Unto this day they do after their former manners* . . .

The Samaritan religion became, in effect, a kind of Yahvistic heresy, and the orthodox of Judah would by no means accept that and seemed more hostile at times to the heretics than to the outright pagan. (This kind of attitude also existed among Christians of later centuries, so it is not as puzzling as it might be.) Much of later Biblical history involves a running and irreconcilable feud between the Judeans and the Samaritans, an odd shadow of the original feud with a similar territorial basis between David and Saul and between Rehoboam and Jeroboam.

Sennacherib

Only Judah was left now. In 720 B.C., two years after the end of Israel, Ahaz died, and his son Hezekiah (the fourteenth king of the Davidic dynasty) came to the throne.

Under him for some years there was a period of peace and even of relative prosperity as he was careful to do nothing to offend Assyria. Under him also, the prophetic party achieved full domination. Isaiah, an important and influential spokesman of Yahvism, flourished in his reign, and no doubt the Judeans were impressed by the continual insistence on the part of the Yahvists that the reason Israel had come to a bad end was its addiction to idol worship.

Sargon meanwhile continued his victorious career, defeating Urartu

The Assyrian Empire under Sennacherib

to the north so badly that it entered a period of decline and played no significant part in history thereafter. He also managed to keep the turbulent Chaldean tribes, which now controlled Babylonia, under control, though they were a continual source of trouble for him.

However, in 705 B.C. Sargon died, and this was the signal for conspiracies and rebellions against Assyria. Hezekiah, encouraged by the nationalist prophetic party, was among those who stopped payment of tribute.

Sargon's son, however, had succeeded to the throne and was not to be trifled with. He had to tend to serious rebellions in Babylonia but eventually, in 701 B.C., he turned his attention to Judah:

> 2 Kings 18:13. Now . . . did Sennacherib king of Assyria come up against all the fenced cities of Judah, and took them.

Sennacherib is the Biblical version of the name of Sargon's son, which might, more accurately, be given as Sinakhe-erba.

Hezekiah at once gave in and offered tribute but Sennacherib was not to be so mollified. His army advanced and laid siege to Jerusalem.

Tirhakah

It would seem that if the Assyrian army had been allowed to concentrate its full efforts upon Jerusalem, the city must have fallen. However, that was not to be. Assyria's cruelties in establishing its empire brought its own nemesis in its wake for its subjects revolted at every possible chance and the last century of Assyria's existence was one long battle against rebellion with her monarchs scarcely able to draw a free breath between.

The Bible, unfortunately, is not entirely clear as to exactly what happened in this particular case, since attention is concentrated on the propaganda exchanges between the besiegers and besieged, rather than upon military events beyond Jerusalem. However, one can deduce that Sennacherib had to detach forces to take care of trouble farther west.

> 2 Kings 19:9. . . . he heard say of Tirhakah king of Ethiopia, Behold he is come out to fight against thee . . .

By the king of Ethiopia is meant one of the Ethiopian rulers of the Nile delta. The one in question may be Taharqa.

Tirhakah, or Taharqa, was badly defeated, but even the defeat distracted the Assyrians and helped Jerusalem, and in the end Sennacherib was forced to leave Judah without taking the capital.

The reasons for this are varied. The Bible attributes it to a plague which suddenly struck and killed 185,000 Assyrians in the army in one night.

The Greek historian Herodotus doesn't mention the siege of Jerusalem, but he does speak of Sennacherib's campaign against Egypt and he describes a sudden retreat of the Assyrians, too, explaining that it took place because a plague of mice had gnawed their arrows and quivers and the leatherwork of their shields.

As for the records of Sennacherib, they speak only of victories, of a besieged Jerusalem, of tribute sent him by Hezekiah.

The indisputable fact, however, is that while Jerusalem was besieged as Samaria had been besieged a quarter century earlier, Jerusalem survived, where Samaria did not. Judah retained its national identity where Israel had not.

On the other hand, the fact is just as indisputable that Judah sustained severe damage, that its land had been laid waste, that its capital had barely escaped destruction, and that the end was merely that Judah was still a tributary of Assyria.

Undoubtedly, although the Bible treats the episode as a great victory redounding to the credit of Isaiah and the prophetic party, the prophetic party lost much prestige. It was a victory that was hard to distinguish from a disaster.

Esarhaddon

Sennacherib came to a bad end, for he was assassinated while supervising at religious rites in 681 B.C. Two of his own sons were the assassins, but a third son defeated the parricides and drove them into exile, assuming the throne himself:

2 Kings 19:37. . . . *And Esarhaddon his son reigned in his stead.*

The Bible tells us nothing more of Esarhaddon (Assur-ah-iddin), but he was the third capable member of the line of Sargon II.

Esarhaddon recognized the fact that Assyria would never have rest until the rebellions that cropped up constantly here and there in the

The Assyrian Empire under Esarhaddon

realm ceased. He did not see that it was Assyrian policy itself that was responsible, but placed the blame on Egyptian gold.

He therefore decided to strike the poison at the source. He marched an army into the Nile delta, defeated the Egyptians in 671 B.C., and took over control of Egypt. For the space of a generation, the northern half of the kingdom was more or less under Assyrian control, though it remained restless and the native leaders still waited their chance in the south.

Berodach-baladan

There is no question but that one of the reasons for the survival of Judah lay in the fact that the Assyrian kings had always to concentrate on, first and foremost, Babylonia.

For three centuries, Babylonia had been more or less under the domination of Assyria. Conscious of a past history of over two thousand years and of great empires of their own, the Babylonians never entirely submitted but rose time and again.

In the last few decades, the rough Chaldean tribes that had emerged from the Arabian deserts south of Babylonia had been encroaching on Babylonia and by Sargon's time, they were in control of Babylon itself.

Sargon and Sennacherib were forced into chronic warfare with the Chaldean leader Marduk-apal-iddin, a name which, in the Bible, is distorted into Merodach-baladan and, in the Second Book of Kings, through a misprint which has been piously retained across the centuries, into Berodach-baladan.

The Chaldean sought for allies everywhere among the enemies outside the Assyrian Empire and the rebels within the empire. Among the latter was Hezekiah.

2 Kings 20:12. *At that time Berodach-baladan . . . king of Babylon, sent letters and a present to Hezekiah.*

It is not certain when this embassy took place. It may have occurred in the early days of Sennacherib's reign and may have been a direct cause of the campaign of that monarch against Jerusalem. Perhaps, too, it was action by Merodach-baladan that forced Sennacherib to lift the siege of Jerusalem.

Merodach-baladan was eventually defeated by Sennacherib, but while he occupied Assyrian energies, so much the less remained to be expended on Judah.

The prophetic party disapproved of dealings of this sort, for they were isolationists as well as nationalists. To the monarchs of the time, the combination of isolationism and nationalism seemed suicide. One either submitted to the ruling empire, or one sought and found allies before rebelling.

Manasseh

Hezekiah died in 693 B.C., and his twelve-year-old son Manasseh, the fifteenth king of the Davidic line, ascended the throne and ruled for fifty-five years.

Now the disastrous rebellion against Sennacherib came back to plague the prophetic party. Assyria continued strong and was simply not to be withstood. Undoubtedly, the prophets continued to preach singlehanded rebellion and trust in God, but Manasseh and his advisers would not have any of that.

The prophetic party was therefore suppressed with violence:

> 2 Kings 21:16. *Moreover Manasseh shed innocent blood very much . . .*

and tradition has it that Isaiah himself found a martyr's death in the course of this reign.

And yet, Manasseh's reward was that he secured for Judah peace and prosperity during a long fifty-five-year reign—the longest in Biblical annals. It might seem on the face of it that Manasseh and Judah were being rewarded by a pleased Deity but when the Yahvists gained control later on, Manasseh's memory was vilified. If he had statesmanlike motives for his actions, they were suppressed and forgotten.

Manasseh's system continued in the short reign of his son Amon, who ruled from 639 to 638 B.C. as the sixteenth king of the Davidic line.

Josiah

In 638 B.C., Amon's son Josiah, the seventeenth king of the Davidic line, ascended the throne as an eight-year-old boy, and now there came a mighty change.

For one thing, Assyria was suddenly, and quite unexpectedly, falling upon evil days. She was suppressing rebellions with clearly greater effort. The hopes of all the subject nations, including Judah, were rising. The vision of freedom was before their eyes and nationalist movements were gaining strength everywhere. In Judah, that nationalist movement was embodied in the prophetic party.

As the young Josiah matured, he proved to be susceptible to the regenerating nationalism and was sympathetic to Yahvism. The last strong king died in 625 B.C. when Josiah was twenty-one and the Assyrian Empire began to fall apart almost at once. By 620 B.C., things had matured to the point where the priesthood could safely suggest the appropriation of funds for the repair of the Temple. The Temple had, naturally, undergone considerable deterioration during the long period under which the anti-Yahvist kings Manasseh and Amon had been on the throne.

In the course of these repairs, a discovery was made:

> 2 Kings 22:8. And Hilkiah the high priest said unto Shaphan the scribe, I have found the book of the law in the house of the Lord.

The "book of the law" is usually identified by Biblical scholars as part of the Book of Deuteronomy. This may actually have been reduced to writing in 650 B.C. during the long and, for the Yahvists, horrible reign of Manasseh. The Yahvist tradition may well have seemed in danger of perishing and the secret commitment of that tradition to writing may have seemed the only way out. The book would then have been hidden in the Temple and been brought forth only when a new king, sympathetic to Yahvism, was on the throne.

Josiah, greatly impressed by the words of Deuteronomy, led Judah into a complete and thoroughgoing revival. Every scrap of idolatry was removed from the land. For instance:

> 2 Kings 23:10. And he defiled Topheth, which is in the valley of the children of Hinnom, that no man might make his son or his daughter to pass through the fire to Molech.

Manasseh had, according to the Bible, himself sacrificed his son to Molech (see page 163) and Topheth was the name given to the furnaces at which this was done.

The furnace used for the rites in Judah was located in the "valley of the children of Hinnom." The phrase "of Hinnom" is "Ge-Hinnom" in Hebrew. This valley curves past the southern end of Jerusalem and joins the valley of Kidron.

Such was the horror felt by the later Jews at the sort of religious rites that went on at the Topheth in Ge-Hinnom, and such the strong association with a kind of destructive fire, that both words (Tophet and Gehenna in English) became synonymous with Hell.

Josiah's reformation was complete and was climaxed by a celebration of the Passover:

> 2 Kings 23:22. *Surely there was not holden such a passover from the days of the judges that judged Israel, nor in all the days of the kings of Israel, nor of the kings of Judah.*

This was the final victory of Yahvism among the Judeans. Succeeding kings might backslide but the people did not. Military disaster seemed but to strengthen their beliefs. From this point on, then, Yahvism, which had earlier been merely one of the sects competing for a hold on the people of Israel and Judah, begins its transition to Judaism, the religion of the Jewish people.

Pharaoh-nechoh

But Josiah's fate was bound up with the great events taking place in the world beyond the narrow confines of Judah.

Esarhaddon's conquest of Egypt did not end rebellions in Assyria. Rather, it meant that Assyria had a new area of rebellion to worry about, for Egypt was itself seething with continual unrest. Indeed, when Esarhaddon died in 668 B.C., it was while he was marching toward Egypt to put down a rebellion.

He was succeeded by his son Asshurbanipal, the fourth king of the line of Sargon II and the last great king of Assyria, but one who is not mentioned in the Bible at all. Asshurbanipal was not a great conquering king, though he managed to put down rebellions and defend the empire against barbarian incursions. He is best known as a patron of culture and he collected the greatest library the world had yet seen.

Ever since the reign of Sargon II, the Cimmerians, barbarians from the north of the Black Sea (see page 46), had been pouring southward into Asia Minor and into Assyrian territory. Assyria had been able to defeat them only with great effort and at great cost. Asshurbanipal

Necho's Expedition

had to lead two expeditions into rebellious Egypt and fight two bitter campaigns against the Chaldeans in Babylonia. He had also to fight against the barbarian Medes to the east of Babylonia.

By main force, Assyria was held together, but more and more its strength was a matter of outer show only. The Assyrian Empire was like a hollow structure with the walls growing thinner and thinner. It looked well but one good, hard knock—

The subject nations sensed this and waited eagerly and, as mentioned earlier, nationalist movements grew stronger.

Asshurbanipal died in 625 B.C., five years before Josiah's reformation, and that was the signal for the final rebellion. The Chaldeans of Babylonia joined forces with the Medes and together they attacked the Assyrian homeland. The Assyrian army, finally stretched beyond endurance, broke. Nineveh, the Assyrian capital, was taken in 612 B.C. and the Assyrian Empire came to an end and the conquerors divided the spoil among themselves.

For a few years, however, a remnant of the Assyrian Empire, centered about Haran (see page 59), held out under a general named Ashur-uballit.

Meanwhile, important events were transpiring in Egypt, too. The rebellion that had been in progress there at the time of Esarhaddon's death was never properly repressed by Asshurbanipal, who found himself intensely busy elsewhere. Egypt could not be quieted.

Psamtik, an Egyptian general who ruled the delta as a viceroy for the Assyrians, took over in his own name and by 652 B.C. he controlled the country. He became Psamtik I, first Pharaoh of the 26th dynasty, and established his capital at Saïs, a city on a western branch of the Nile, near the Mediterranean, about 175 miles northwest of Memphis. For this reason, the period during which the 26th dynasty ruled is known as the Saitic period.

In 610 B.C., two years after the destruction of Nineveh, Psamtik I died and was succeeded by his son Necho, known in the Bible as Pharaoh-nechoh.

> 2 Kings 23:29. *In his* [Josiah's] *days Pharaoh-nechoh king of Egypt went up against the king of Assyria to the river Euphrates: and king Josiah went against him; and he* [Pharaoh-nechoh] *slew him* [Josiah] *at Megiddo, . . .*

The king of Assyria here referred to can only have been Ashur-uballit at Haran. Necho wanted his share of the Assyrian spoils, and to keep Chaldea from becoming too powerful, while Josiah was anxious to keep Necho out of Asia in order that he himself might control Syria as in the time of Solomon.

The armies met at Megiddo in Samaritan territory about fifty-five miles north of Jerusalem in 608 B.C. It was a spot where, over six centuries before, Thutmose III had fought a gigantic battle against the Canaanites (see page 122). Almost as though the days of the Egyptian Empire had returned, Necho won a victory, Josiah was killed, and Egyptian power was established in the southwest corner of Asia.

Josiah had reigned for thirty years and now he was succeeded by his son Jehoahaz, the eighteenth king of the Davidic line, but the choice did not please Necho. He carried off Jehoahaz to life imprisonment in Egypt and established Jehoiakim, another son of Josiah (and the nineteenth king of the Davidic line) in his place.

For a while Jehoiakim remained an Egyptian puppet, faithfully paying tribute to Necho. To do that, he had to recede from the Yahvist position of his father. He could not listen to the nationalist prophetic party which had brought death to Josiah when he fought Egypt without allies, in the approved prophetic fashion.

2 Kings 23:37. *And he* [Jehoiakim] *did that which was evil in the sight of the Lord* . . .

Nebuchadnezzar

Necho's adventure in imperialism did not last long.

The Chaldean leader who had mounted the successful campaign against the Assyrian Empire and who had taken the Assyrian capital at Nineveh was Nabopolassar, who, under Asshurbanipal, had served as viceroy of Babylonia.

Having accomplished that task of taking Nineveh, and spending some years in consolidating his victory, he then sent his forces westward against Necho, placing those forces under his son. The son's name was Nabu-kudurri-usur ("Nebo defend the boundary"), which comes out in the Bible as Nebuchadnezzar. The father died in 605 B.C. before the campaign was finished and the son ascended the throne as Nebuchadnezzar II (Nebuchadnezzar I had reigned five hundred years earlier over Babylonia).

The empire of Nabopolassar and Nebuchadnezzar is variously known as the "New Babylonian Empire," the "Neo-Babylonian Empire," and the "Chaldean Empire."

In the first year of his reign, Nebuchadnezzar met Necho at Carchemish. Carchemish had once been an important city of the Mitanni and, later, of the Hittites. It had been captured by Thutmose III for the Egyptian Empire, and by Sargon II for the Assyrian Empire. It was located on the upper Euphrates River on what is now the boundary between Syria and Turkey, about sixty miles west of Haran and nearly five hundred miles north of Jerusalem.

Nebuchadnezzar was completely victorious at Carchemish and Necho, his dreams of Asian glory forever gone, scuttled back to Egypt and remained there till his death in 593 B.C.

Meanwhile Nebuchadnezzar cleaned up the last pockets of Assyrian resistance at Haran by 601 B.C. He could then turn his attention in 600 B.C. to minor problems such as Judah.

The Sixth Century B.C.

2 Kings 24:1. . . . Nebuchadnezzar king of Babylon came up, and Jehoiakim became his servant three years: then he turned and rebelled against him.

Judah switched from being an Egyptian tributary to being a Babylonian one. Its rebellion in 597 B.C. was, of course, worse than useless. Jehoiakim died at its beginning after an eleven-year reign and his son Jehoiachin ascended the throne as the twentieth king of the Davidic line.

Jehoiachin only reigned for three months, for Nebuchadnezzar laid siege to the rebellious Jerusalem in 597 B.C., taking the city, stripping it of whatever he could find, and carrying off the king and the principal men to the number of ten thousand.

Jerusalem and Judah remained in being, however, and Nebuchadnezzar appointed Jehoiachin's uncle (the brother of Jehoiakim and the third son of Josiah to sit on the throne) to the throne. The new king, taking the name of Zedekiah, was the twenty-first king of the Davidic line—and the last.

He began as a docile puppet of the Chaldean monarch, but as once Hoshea had been lured into fatal revolt by promised help from So of Egypt that never materialized, so now Zedekiah was lured into a revolt just as fatal by an Egyptian promise just as false.

In 587 B.C. Zedekiah rose and the Babylonian army returned to the siege. After a year and a half, the city was taken. Zedekiah and a remnant of the army tried to flee but were smashed near Jericho.

Zedekiah was imprisoned and blinded, his sons were executed, and further deportations depopulated the land. The kingdom of Judah came to an end 427 years after the accession of David to the throne, and the Temple itself was destroyed.

Gedaliah

There remained Judeans in Judah, of course, even after the deportations, and Nebuchadnezzar appointed a governor to rule them.

2 Kings 25:22. . . . Nebuchadnezzar . . . over them . . . made Gedaliah the son of Ahikam, the son of Shaphan, ruler.

Gedaliah was the grandson of the scribe who, in the reign of Josiah, had received the news of the discovery of the Book of Deuteronomy and who had carried that news to Josiah. Now, thirty-four years after that discovery and the great Passover that had climaxed it, Judah was half empty and the scribe's grandson ruled over the remnant.

Gedaliah tried to build anew but the people, fearing further punishment from Nebuchadnezzar, assassinated him and many fled to Egypt. Judah was more desolate than ever.

Evil-merodach

The Jews in Babylonia might well have been assimilated and might have "disappeared" as the Israelites in Assyria had a century and a half before. As it turned out (with important consequences in world history) they did not. They survived to return to Judah and to carry on their traditions and their culture.

It is rather fitting, therefore, that the Second Book of Kings does not end with the destruction of Jerusalem and the Temple, the end of Judah, and the emptying of the land. Rather, it goes a little past that to show something that reads like the faint promise of a beginning of better days.

> 2 Kings 25:27. . . . *in the seven and thirtieth year of the captivity of Jehoiachin king of Judah . . . Evil-merodach . . . did lift up the head of Jehoiachin . . . out of prison.*

Nebuchadnezzar had died in 562 B.C. and was succeeded by his son Amel-Marduk ("man of Marduk"), which, in the Bible, becomes "Evil-merodach."

He apparently took a kindlier attitude toward the captive Jews, freeing Jehoiachin, who had been briefly king of Judah at the time of Nebuchadnezzar's first siege of the city.

He may have thought of re-establishing the Jews in their homeland but he did not reign long enough to carry that thought through, if he had it at all. In 560 B.C., he was killed in a palace conspiracy, and the Jews remained captive for another generation.

It is on this moment of renewed optimism, however, that the Second Book of Kings ends.

13. 1 CHRONICLES

ADAM • JUDAH • BOAZ • ZERUIAH • SOLOMON • JOSIAH • JOHANAN •
JECONIAH • LEVI • MERIB-BAAL • DAVID • SATAN

Adam

Following the Book of 2 Kings is a pair of books (1 Chronicles and 2 Chronicles) that, in a sense, recapitulate the whole of the Bible from the beginning to the fall of Jerusalem.

These books were written after the return from exile in Babylon. It was usual to suppose, earlier, that they were written as late as 300 or even 250 B.C., but more recent thinking on the subject seems to favor a date as early as 400 B.C.

The Hebrew title of the books is "Dibre Hayyamim" meaning "records of the times," for which "chronicles" is certainly an adequate translation. When the Bible was translated into the Greek, however, the translators found the books most significant in the sense that they supplied fuller information concerning the history of Judah than was contained in the Books of 1 and 2 Kings. For that reason they referred to the books as "Paraleipomenon" ("concerning things omitted"). This name is retained (in Latin spelling) in the Catholic translations of the Bible, where one can find 1 and 2 Paralipomenon in place of 1 and 2 Chronicles.

In the Hebrew Bible, the Books of 1 and 2 Chronicles are placed in the third and least esteemed division, "The Writings," because of their late composition. What's more, they are placed at the very end of the section, which makes them the last of all the books in the Hebrew canon.

In the Latin translation and in the various English versions that

The Empire of David and Solomon

stem from it, the Books of 1 and 2 Chronicles follow (more logically, perhaps) immediately after 1 and 2 Kings, so much of which they repeat.

The situation at the time the "Chronicler" was writing was one that was completely different from that prevailing while the kingdom of Judah existed. It was then only patriotic to believe that the kingdom and the Davidic line that ruled it would continue forever, and this belief is reflected in the Bible. Thus, Nathan the Prophet quotes the words of the Lord to David:

2 Samuel 7:16. *And thine house and thy kingdom shall be established for ever before thee . . .*

But the Chronicler and his generation knew well that the kingdom of Judah had come to an end in 586 B.C. and that no king of the line of David had reigned for nearly two centuries and that, moreover, there was no immediate prospect of the re-establishment of the kingdom under a Davidic monarch.

It became necessary to interpret history in another fashion, then, and to understand the words of God, as given in tradition, in another way. The Chronicler therefore set about writing a history that would yield that interpretation.

For his purposes, it was necessary to get through the very earliest ages in only the briefest possible way and this could be done through a list of genealogies. Not only would genealogies be the most economical way of reaching the essential moment at which he wanted to begin his history proper, but it would also be of devouring interest to the Jews.

The Exile had broken the chain of tradition that had marched down the centuries during the time of the kingdoms, and had wiped out many records. Family relationships may have become fuzzy and national pride had bitten the dust in the decades of imprisonment. Through an adequate listing of authentic genealogies, each returning Jew could place himself accurately in the tribal system and society could renew itself properly.

And so it comes about that the first word of 1 Chronicles is Adam:

1 Chronicles 1:1. *Adam, Sheth, Enosh,*

Judah

The first chapter suffices for the hasty recital of names that serves to take care of all the Biblical genealogies but those of Jacob (Israel). Beginning with Chapter 2, the genealogy of the twelve tribes of Israel can be given.

In the earlier books of the Bible, the tribes are treated in the traditional order of their seniority. Reuben comes first, then Simeon, then Levi, and only then Judah—the fourth-born. The Chronicler was aware of this:

> 1 Chronicles 5:1. . . . *the sons of Reuben the firstborn of Israel* . . .

Nevertheless, from the vantage point of 400 B.C., it is clear that *the* important tribe is Judah:

> 1 Chronicles 5:2. *For Judah prevailed above his brethren, and of him came the chief ruler* . . .

and therefore the genealogy of Judah was taken up first in defiance of birthright. It was, moreover, taken up in greater detail than that of any of the other tribes. In fact, the four tribes that made up the kingdom of Judah (Judah itself; Simeon, which had been amalgamated into Judah's tribal system before David; Benjamin; and Levi) are treated in a total of 258 verses, while the remaining tribes of the forever-vanished kingdom of Israel receive a total of fifty verses. And Judah itself has the lion's share—one hundred verses.

Boaz

As quickly as he can, the Chronicler proceeds to the ancestry of David and this goes in part:

> 1 Chronicles 6:11. . . . *and Salma begat Boaz,*
> 1 Chronicles 6:12. *And Boaz begat Obed* . . .

No mention is made of Boaz having begotten Obed by Ruth (see page 265). This is not because the Chronicler ignores women completely, for in listing the sons of Judah, he says:

> 1 Chronicles 2:4. *And Tamar his daughter in law bare him Pharez and Zerah* . . .

The Book of Ruth may have been written at about the time that the Chronicler was working on his own writings and it is not at all hard to believe that he was aware of its contents (for it had to be popular or it would not have gotten into the Hebrew canon).

Two possibilities suggest themselves, each with a certain plausibility. The Book of Ruth may, indeed, have been a piece of historical fiction and no such woman as Ruth may have appeared in the early records which the Chronicler used as his source material.

Or else, if the writer of the Book of Ruth made use of an authentic tradition then it may be that the Chronicler deliberately refused to use it. The Chronicler was on the side of those who favored a rigid exclusivism among the returning Jews, a putting away of foreign wives, and the Book of Ruth was written to present the other side (see page 265). The Chronicler might have preferred to ignore, therefore, the part-Moabite ancestry of David.

Zeruiah

When Jesse is reached, his children are listed, including David (his youngest son) and two sisters:

> 1 Chronicles 2:15. . . . *David* . . .
> 1 Chronicles 2:16. *Whose sisters were Zeruiah and Abigail* . . .

If the Chronicler is correct, then some of David's heroes are close relatives. Thus, Zeruiah had three sons: Abishai, Joab, and Asahel, who were all David's lieutenants in his early days as an outlaw. In particular, Joab rose to be commander in chief. All three were David's nephews. Again, Abigail was the mother of Amasa, who was Absalom's general (see page 313) and who briefly replaced Joab as commander in chief. He, too, was a nephew of David, which may help account for David's leniency after the crushing of Absalom's rebellion.

Solomon

The third chapter begins with a listing of David's sons. Nineteen of them are listed and the list is by no means exhaustive.

1 Chronicles 3:9. *These were all the sons of David, beside the sons of the concubines* . . .

Of these Solomon is the tenth listed so that there might possibly have been at least nine sons ahead of him in line for the throne. The deaths of the first and third (Amnon and Absalom) in the lifetime of David are described in 2 Samuel, and the fourth (Adonijah) lived to dispute the succession. Of the rest nothing is known.

There follows immediately the line of descent of Solomon, which includes only those who were kings of Judah:

1 Chronicles 3:10. *And Solomon's son was Rehoboam, Abia* [Abijam] *his son, Asa his son, Jehoshaphat his son,*
1 Chronicles 3:11. *Joram his son* . . .

Starting with David, son succeeded father as king of Judah down to Josiah, a list of seventeen generations, quite a remarkable record for any dynasty.

Josiah

With Josiah, there is for the first time more than one son listed:

1 Chronicles 3:15. *And the sons of Josiah were* . . . *Johanan* . . . *Jehoiakim* . . . *Zedekiah* . . . *Shallum.*
1 Chronicles 3:16. *And the sons of Jehoiakim: Jeconiah* . . .

Upon Josiah's death in the battle of Megiddo, one of his sons succeeded to the throne, Jehoahaz, and this one is not listed by that name in verse 3:15. In the Book of Jeremiah, however, that prophet (who lived at the time and witnessed the events) speaks of the matter:

Jeremiah 22:11. . . . *Shallum the son of Josiah* . . . *reigned instead of Josiah* . . .

Jeremiah 22:12. . . . *he shall die in the place whither they have led him captive.*

Jehoahaz was indeed taken captive by Pharaoh-nechoh and kept in captivity to his death (see page 392). It would seem, then, that Shallum was the personal name of the prince and Jehoahaz was his "throne name," assumed when he became king. It is not at all an uncommon practice for a person to change his name upon becoming king. Sometimes the name is changed in order to choose one that has associations with the throne, so that Mari of Syria became Ben-hadad upon becoming king (see page 368) and Pulu of Assyria became Tiglath-Pileser (see page 373). In modern times, the best-known case of systematic name-changing upon achieving high position is the case of the Popes at Rome: Achille Ratti became Pius XI in 1922; Eugenio Pacelli succeeded him as Pius XII in 1939; Angelo Roncalli succeeded him as John XXIII in 1958; and Giovanni Montini succeeded him as Paul VI in 1963.

Apparently Shallum/Jehoahaz was appointed king by popular acclaim despite the fact that he was the youngest of Josiah's sons:

2 Kings 23:30. . . . *And the people of the land took Jehoahaz . . . and made him king . . .*

It might be conjectured that this was because he was the most anti-Egyptian of Josiah's sons and therefore most popular. This may be why Necho had him removed at once and replaced with Jehoiakim, whom he may have considered more tractable and who was, in any case, the oldest surviving son of Josiah and therefore the one with the best claim to the throne anyway. (The eldest son, Johanan, of whom nothing more is heard, may have died in Josiah's lifetime.)

Jehoiakim is the first king of Judah to replace a brother rather than a father. In his case, the name by which he is listed in 1 Chronicles is already his throne name:

2 Kings 23:34. *And Pharaoh-nechoh made Eliakim . . . king . . . and turned his name to Jehoiakim.*

Jehoiakim was succeeded by his son Jehoiachin, whose name is given in 1 Chronicles as Jeconiah.

Jehoiachin (Jeconiah) was on the throne only a short while before being taken and carried off into lifelong captivity by Nebuchadnezzar (sharing the fate, if not the captor, of his uncle Jehoahaz).

In his place, Nebuchadnezzar put on the throne the one remaining son of Josiah; the prince whose name is given as Zedekiah in 3:15. This, too, is a throne name:

> 2 Kings 24:17. *And the king of Babylon made Mattaniah . . . king . . . and changed his name to Zedekiah.*

Zedekiah was the last reigning king of Judah.

Johanan

In a way, though, it is Johanan, Josiah's first-born (who probably died young) who bears the most interesting name. Johanan is a shortened version of Jehohanan, meaning "Yahveh is gracious."

The name "Johanan" appears only once in the Biblical books coming before 1 Chronicles and that once is at the very end of the book immediately preceding—2 Kings. The name was that of an army officer of the time of Gedaliah:

> 2 Kings 25:23. . . . *there came to Gedaliah . . . Johanan the son of Careah, . . .*

In the later books of the Bible, the name is mentioned more often. Remember, now, that the initial "J" in English versions of Biblical names is equivalent to the Hebrew letter "yodh," which represents the sound "y." The Greeks would start such a name with their letter "iota," which we write "I," and which also sounds like a "y" at the beginning of a word. It is natural, then, that the Greek version of "Johanan" would be "Ioannes" if we allow further for the absence of the "h" in the Greek alphabet and for the Greek habit of placing an "s" at the end of almost all names. This is easily seen to be equivalent to the German "Johannes," and this, in turn, is easily shortened to the English "John."

In other words, however strange the name "Johanan" may appear to us when we come across it in the Old Testament, it is the same name that we find as "John" in English versions of the New Testament, and is the name that in one form or another is most common of all among Europeans and men of European ancestry.

Jeconiah

The last part of the third chapter traces the line of David through the Exile. It begins with Jeconiah (Jehoiachin), the grandson of Josiah, who was briefly king of Judah in 597 B.C. and who was carried off to exile by Nebuchadnezzar. He remained alive and even survived to be well treated by Amel-Marduk (Evil-merodach) after Nebuchadnezzar's death (see page 396).

1 Chronicles 3:17. *And the sons of Jeconiah; Assir, Salathiel . . .*

Eight sons are listed, but the first, Assir, is not really a son. It means "captive" and the Revised Standard Version translates verse 3:17 (using an alternate version of Salathiel's name): "and the sons of Jeconiah, the captive: Shealtiel."

The sons of Pediah, Jeconiah's third son, are given, and then those of Zerubbabel the oldest son of Pediah, and so on.

In the volume of the Anchor Bible which deals with 1 Chronicles, the following approximate birth years are given:

Pedaiah	595 B.C.
Zerubbabel	570 B.C.
Hananiah	545 B.C.
Shechaniah	520 B.C.
Shemaiah	495 B.C.
Neariah	470 B.C.
Elioenai	445 B.C.
Hodaviah	420 B.C.

Hodaviah, according to the genealogy, is the eighth generation after Jeconiah and the twenty-sixth generation after David.

Hodaviah was the eldest son of Elioenai and he had six younger brothers, of whom Anani was the youngest. The Anchor Bible estimates that the birth date of the youngest son was about 405 B.C.

Thus, the line of David is followed through for nearly two centuries after the end of the kingdom and the fact that the record ends with Anani is one indication that the Chronicler might have been writing about 400 B.C.

The careful manner in which the Chronicler details the genealogy might be taken as a reasonable indication of the fact that the Chronicler does not consider the kingdom of Judah or the Davidic line to have come to an irrevocable end.

Nevertheless, one gets the distinct impression that the Chronicler is not sanguine about the Davidic line. As the history he is about to write will demonstrate, there is something he considers an alternate to the kingdom and its monarch—and that is the Temple and its High Priest. The Temple had, indeed, been restored in the Chronicler's day and as the supremacy among the tribes passed from Reuben to Judah, so it might conceivably be that the promise of external existence would pass from kingdom to Temple.

Levi

Thus, when the Chronicler reaches the tribe of Levi, he gives it a detailed genealogy second only to that of Judah, for it is from that tribe that the priesthood is drawn:

1 Chronicles 6:1. *The sons of Levi . . .*

The list of High Priests is given during the time of the kingdom, ending with:

1 Chronicles 6:15. *And Jehozadak went into captivity . . . by the hand of Nebuchadnezzar.*

Jehozadak was the twelfth in descent from Zadok, who had become High Priest at the beginning of the reign of Solomon (see page 322). Zadok himself is the ninth in descent from Eleazar, the son of Aaron.

Merib-baal

The genealogies of the remaining tribes are then run through, more or less quickly, until the last—Benjamin—is reached. Benjamin is, of course, the youngest son of Jacob according to tradition, but there are other possible excuses for its position. Saul, whom David replaced as king, was a Benjamite, and if David's tribe Judah is considered first, it is rather neat to consider Saul's tribe Benjamin last. Besides, it is through Benjamin that one approaches the genealogy of Saul and it is with the death of Saul that the Chronicler intends to begin his history proper.

> 1 Chronicles 8:33. . . . *Saul begat Jonathan* . . .
> 1 Chronicles 8:34. *And the son of Jonathan was Merib-baal; and Merib-baal begat Micah.*

Merib-baal is an alternate name of Mephibosheth (see page 309) and through Micah, Saul's descendants are continued many generations, presumably to the time of exile. Apparently, the line of Saul (though reduced by David's policy to Mephibosheth alone) managed to flourish. Referring to the later members of the line:

> 1 Chronicles 8:40. *And the sons of Ulam . . . had many sons, and sons' sons, an hundred and fifty.*

It is interesting to note, though, that at no time past David's reign is there a record of any attempt to restore the line of Saul.

David

David, the human hero of the Chronicler's history, is not a hero in his capacity as a human being, but rather as an ideal founder of Temple-worship. Of his life story only the central "Temple-core" is kept; that plus lists of names of genealogical interest. His youth, his adventures with Saul and Jonathan, the personal sins and problems of later life—all are eliminated. Even his conquests, when mentioned, are important only because the loot gained makes it possible for the Temple to be built, furnished, and ornamented.

Thus, Saul's death is described and then:

> 1 Chronicles 11:3. . . . *came all the elders of Israel . . . to Hebron . . . and they anointed David king over Israel . . .*

There is no mention of the seven years in which Ish-bosheth was king of Israel in the Trans-Jordan, of Abner's defection and of the political intrigues that followed (see page 300). One would suppose that in a single moment of exaltation, David was unanimously raised to the kingship.

Once David is king, the Chronicler moves on to the capture of

Jerusalem, so that we now have the man who initiates Temple-worship, and the place where it is initiated. The bringing of the ark of the covenant to Jerusalem is told in great detail, as is David's thwarted intention to build the actual Temple himself, and the preparation he makes to have his successor do so. Then we pass on to his death and the succession of Solomon to the throne. There is no mention of the dynastic dispute between Solomon and Adonijah (see page 320).

This picture of David's reign is, in our modern view, so limited and partial as to amount to a falsification of history. There was, however, undoubtedly no conscious attempt at falsification as such on the part of the Chronicler, who did not have our view of history. Rather, he was trying, according to his lights, to "truthify" history, so to speak. That is, he saw in the history of the Davidic monarchy a central thread which he wished to expose more clearly to all men. He therefore cut away what were to him obscuring irrelevancies and painted that central thread in brighter colors to make it more visible. The result is history which we might call "impressionistic" and its purpose, as with impressionistic art, is to make apparent what realism might hide.

Satan

Only once in the Chronicler's history does David appear less than ideal and that is in connection with his sin in taking a census. This item, however, must be included, for it is central to the theme. It was on the threshing floor where David, according to the legend, had seen the angel (see page 319) that the Temple was to be built. Yet, even so, the tale is told with an important difference.

In the pre-Exilic version of the story, it is stated:

> 2 Samuel 24:1. . . . *the anger of the Lord was kindled against Israel, and he moved David against them to say, Go, number Israel and Judah.*

God alone is here viewed as the source of all things and it is God who inspires David's evil impulse. By the time of the Chronicler, however, there had come to seem to be a flavor of blasphemy in supposing that God would punish Israel by first inspiring an evil act that he could then use as an excuse for the punishment. As the Chronicler tells the story, then:

1 Chronicles 21:1. *And Satan stood up against Israel, and provoked David to number Israel.*

The Hebrew word *satan* means "adversary"; that is, one who opposes. It does not necessarily have to have a supernatural sense, and is occasionally used in the Bible to represent an ordinary human adversary. The Hebrew word is then translated as simply "adversary." A case of this kind is in the Book of 1 Kings, where Rezon of Syria rebels against Solomon:

1 Kings 11:24. *And he was an adversary to Israel all the days of Solomon . . .*

Sometime after the Babylonian captivity, however, the notion arose that there was a supernatural Adversary; a being whose official duty it was to work for man's evil as God worked for man's good. This capital-S Satan was without power to force men to do evil, but he could tempt men to sin and turn against God, and it was by succumbing to such temptation that man brought evil into the world.

Such a concept was useful in that it helped explain the source of evil, for it is always difficult to explain the existence of evil and misery in the world and the frequent apparent triumph of bad over good in the face of the existence of an all-powerful, all-good God. Even if one explained that evil came as a punishment to sinning mankind, where came the evil within man that caused him to sin in the first place? Thus, the notion of a supernatural Satan pushing man toward sin was convenient.

And the concept came, very likely, by way of the Persians.

By 400 B.C., when the Chronicler was writing, the Persians had become the dominant nation in Asia, and Persian thought would be expected to be very influential among all nations which, like Judah, were under Persian rule. This was particularly so since Persian religion had just been systematized by a great prophet, Zarathustra (Zoroaster, in the Latinized form of the name), at about the time of the return from Babylonian captivity, and the earth rang, so to speak, with the new doctrine.

Zoroastrianism offered a dualistic view of the universe. There was a principle of good, Ahura-Mazda (or Ormuzd), and a principle of evil, Ahriman, which were viewed as virtually independent of each other and very nearly equal. The creation of the world, its development and history, were all incidents in the unending celestial warfare between these two principles, each at the head of a separate army of innumerable spirits.

There is a certain exciting drama to such a view of the universe, and Judaism was penetrated by it to a limited extent. A principle of evil, Satan, was conceived of, but never viewed as independent of God or equal to Him. Instead, Satan is considered to be as surely a creation of God as man himself is.

In later times, he was described as having been an angel originally, even the chief of the angels. Through pride, however, he refused to obey God and bow down to man at the time of the creation of Adam. He was therefore, with numerous followers, ejected from heaven. Once fallen, he became twisted with envy and infinite malice and took on the task of tempting mankind to fall from grace as he himself had.

Satan is not mentioned, as such, in any of the books of the Bible before 1 Chronicles, but the workings of evil found here and there could be reinterpreted in the new light. Most importantly, Satan was equated with the serpent who tempted Eve in the garden of Eden.

The tale of Satan, of his rebellion against God, and of his fall from heaven, forms the central framework of Milton's great epic poem *Paradise Lost*, which is based on the first chapters of Genesis.

Furthermore, Satan does not perform his evil task without remaining under the firm control of God. It is even possible to view Satan as fulfilling the necessary function of tempting mankind and of improving the nature of the soul by exercising it, so to speak; keeping it muscular by giving it temptations to overcome. Satan might then, too, act as a sieve separating the better souls from the worse.

It was part of Satan's function to carry an evil report of man to God, to slander them. (This shows itself best in the Book of Job.) The Greek word for "slanderer" is *diabolos* (literally "to throw across," since slanderous words are like obstacles thrown across the path to block progress) and from this comes our word "devil" and the adjective "diabolical." The word "devil" is used in places in the King James Version to refer to woodland fertility spirits, which are called "satyrs" in the Revised Standard Version (see page 159), but the capital-D Devil is Satan. Satan, the Adversary, is also the Devil, the Slanderer. The Mohammedans call the Adversary Eblis, also from *diabolos*.

In Zoroastrianism, the powers of evil who fight under the banner of Ahriman are the "devas," but this has nothing to do with "devil."

Quite the contrary! The same word occurs in Sanskrit and is given to the gods and the spirits of good in India.

This is not really surprising for the gods of one people are the demons of their neighbors. Undoubtedly, Indian religious thought was penetrating Persia in Zarathustra's time and in beating it back, the Persians stigmatized the alien gods as demons—as the Jews considered Canaanite gods to be abominations, and as the Christians later converted the Greek and Roman gods into evil spirits.

The word "deva" reaches us not through Persian but through Sanskrit and therefore retains its godlike aspect. From it we get the Greek *dios*, the Latin *deus*, and the French *dieu*, all meaning "God," as well as our English adjective "divine."

14. 2 CHRONICLES

JOPPA • MOUNT MORIAH • ARABIA • REHOBOAM • ABIJAH • ASA •
JEHOSHAPHAT • JEHOIADA • AMAZIAH • UZZIAH • AHAZ • HEZEKIAH •
MANASSEH • THE PRAYER OF MANASSES • JOSIAH • KING OF THE CHALDEES

Joppa

What interests the Chronicler concerning the reign of Solomon is
his building of the Temple and his wealth. Since, to the Chronicler,
material benefits accompany righteous action, and since no righteous
action is greater than the building of the Temple, Solomon's wealth is
described in terms of unbridled exaggeration.

Solomon arranges with Hiram of Tyre (here called Huram) for
the supplies needed for the Temple. Hiram agrees:

> 2 Chronicles 2:16. And we will cut wood . . . and . . . bring it
> to thee in floats by sea to Joppa; and thou shalt carry it up to
> Jerusalem.

Joppa (the modern Jaffa) is a port on the Mediterranean about
thirty-five miles northwest of Jerusalem. It was the nearest sizable harbor (though not a very good one) to the capital city and was the natural seaport to which to send material bound for Jerusalem.

It first enters history as one of the towns captured by Thutmose III
when that Egyptian conqueror established his empire in Asia. After
the decline of Egypt, Joppa came under Phoenician control. It is mentioned in the Book of Joshua as part of the idealized territory of the
tribe of Dan, but it never came under Israelite control at any time before David (none of the coastal strip did—that remained Philistine
to the south and Phoenician to the north). It is only now, therefore,
except for the mention in Joshua, that Joppa appears in the Bible.

Israel and Judah

As the seaport of Jerusalem, Joppa was of considerable importance at the time of the Crusades, changing hands between the Christians and Moslems several times, but eventually settling down to a long Turkish control.

In 1909, when Palestine was still part of the Ottoman Empire and when Joppa or Jaffa was a strongly Arabic town, the Jews of the city established a suburb of their own, three miles to the north, which they called Tel Aviv. After World War I, when Palestine became a British mandate, the Jewish town, thanks to immigration and financial help from abroad, quickly grew into a modern city designed along Western lines.

After Israel won its independence in 1948, Tel Aviv served as the interim capital until 1950, when the new city of Jerusalem took its place. In 1950, Tel Aviv was combined with Jaffa (from which most of the Arabs had departed) into a single municipality. Tel Aviv/Jaffa is now the largest city in Israel, with a population of about four hundred thousand.

Joppa bears the rather odd distinction of being one of the few Canaanite cities to play a role in a Greek myth. The hero Perseus had killed the monstrous Medusa in the far-off land of the Hyperboreans and was hurrying home when he spied a naked woman chained to a rock on a cliff outside the city of Joppa. This was Andromeda, being sacrificed to a sea monster by her father Cepheus and her mother Cassiopeia, who were the Ethiopian king and queen of Joppa. He rescued her, of course.

But why should the rulers of Joppa be described as Ethiopians? If it is not to be dismissed as merely the ignorance of geography on the part of the Greek mythmakers, we can speculate, perhaps, as follows—

While the Greek legends may have reached their later, relatively sophisticated, forms at the hands of Greek poets of the Golden Age, they were undoubtedly based on hoary old tales stretching back into the dim past. The legends are placed in Mycenaean times before the Trojan War—a time when Egypt was the greatest power in the world and the Pharaohs of the 18th and 19th dynasties controlled adjacent portions of Asia, including Canaan. Therefore, it was fair enough to speak of an Egyptian king of Joppa, meaning the governor who ruled under Pharaoh.

In the eighth century B.C., however, when Greece was becoming a colonizing land and when her ships were pushing out over the Mediterranean for the first time since the fall of the great kingdoms of Trojan times, she became aware of an Egypt that was then under an Ethiopian dynasty. It was easy to read this backward into time and replace the Egyptian "king" at Joppa by an Ethiopian one.

Mount Moriah

The building of the Temple is begun:

2 Chronicles 3:1. *Then Solomon began to build the house of the Lord at Jerusalem in Mount Moriah . . . in the place that David had prepared in the threshingfloor of Ornan the Jebusite.*

Thus, the place of the Temple is here tied in with two awesome episodes of the past, something that the description in 1 Kings did not do. At the threshingfloor of Ornan (called Araunah in 2 Samuel; see page 319) David had seen an angel, and in the land of Moriah, Abraham had nearly sacrificed Isaac (see page 87).

(The Samaritans, on the other hand, maintained that Abraham had nearly sacrificed Isaac on Mount Gerizim, since that was *their* sacred mountain.)

Arabia

Once the Temple is completed, the Chronicler tells of the visit of the queen of Sheba and continues to describe the wealth and glory of Solomon:

2 Chronicles 9:14. . . . *And all the kings of Arabia . . . brought gold and silver to Solomon.*

In the earlier books of the Bible, the tribes in the arid regions south and east of Canaan were named separately, so that there is mention of Ammonites, Moabites, Edomites, Amalekites, Midianites, and so on.

Only now is the general geographic term "Arabia" used. "Arabia" is the Latinized version of "Arab," which is the general Semitic term for the people of the desert beyond Canaan. The meaning of "Arab" is not certain. It might simply mean "nomad" for the word resembles the Hebrew *arabah*, meaning "steppe." It might also mean something self-glorifying like "man of the master race."

In any case, Arabia is now the name given to the large, mostly desert peninsula south of the Fertile Crescent, which is about one million square miles in area and has a population, nowadays, of about ten million.

Many people think of it as the original home of the peoples speaking Semitic languages. Since it is not a fertile territory, its population easily multiplies past the point where the land will support it and tribes will therefore wander northward into one portion or another of the Fertile Crescent. This tendency may well have been most marked in prehistoric times, when the trend to aridity was first making itself felt, but it has continued well into historic times, the most recent and, in some respects, greatest eruption coming in the seventh century A.D., when Arabs spread Mohammedanism across vast tracts in Asia and Africa.

The Akkadians may have emerged from Arabia to invade Sumeria at the dawn of history and give the area its conquering hero, Sargon. The various Canaanite groups may have come from Arabia, as may the later Aramaeans and Chaldeans, to say nothing of the Hebrew tribes themselves.

Rehoboam

For the period after Solomon's death, the Chronicler follows the history of Judah, and of Judah only. The history of Israel, except where it impinges on Judah, is ignored, for in the Chronicler's time it was clear that Israel had been a dead end and was gone. Even Elijah and Elisha are ignored. It was through Judah and Judah alone, the Chronicler was certain, that the eternal nature of God's promises were to be fulfilled.

The history of Judah is a history of the Temple and of the monarchy. The Temple is a great constant; the ideal place of worship and the true hero of the history. The monarchy, on the other hand, is a swinging pendulum. There are good kings who reform worship and bring it in line with the Temple ideal; there are bad kings who pervert worship and encourage idolatry. There are kings who are at times good and at times bad.

The Chronicler's thesis is that true religion and worldly prosperity go hand in hand; good kings prosper and bad kings suffer. To make that thesis clear, both prosperity and suffering are enormously exaggerated. Good kings win over vast hordes of enemies and are wealthy indeed; bad kings lose enormous battles. Repentance converts bad to good at once; apostasy as quickly converts good to bad, and at every stage of the game there is some prophet or priest to encourage the good and denounce the bad.

In the Book of 1 Kings, for instance, Rehoboam, the successor of Solomon, is briefly dealt with and is described as uniformly unfortunate. He brings about the schism between Israel and Judah through nothing less than criminal folly, and he suffers the invasion of Shishak of Egypt.

In the Book of 2 Chronicles, however, there is a pendulum swing. Immediately after the schism, the Levites in Israel are described as flocking to Judah:

2 Chronicles 11:13. *And the priests and the Levites that were in all Israel resorted to him* [Rehoboam] *out of all their coasts.*

The Book of 1 Kings does say that Jeroboam is setting up his shrines in Bethel and Dan appointed non-Levites as priests—

1 Kings 12:31. . . . *he . . . made priests of the lowest of the people, which were not of the sons of Levi.*

—so that it seems reasonable that Levites should emigrate to Judah where the Temple-worship and priestly honor would be open to them. This is not specified in 1 Kings, but it suits the Chronicler's purpose to emphasize this and possibly exaggerate it since it shows that only in Judah did true religion continue and that what religion remained in Israel was totally false.

Rehoboam and the Levites at first behaved themselves:

2 Chronicles 11:17. . . . *for three years they walked in the way of David and Solomon.*

and therefore Rehoboam prospered:

2 Chronicles 11:21. . . . *he took eighteen wives, and threescore concubines; and begat twenty and eight sons, and threescore daughters.*

But then he backslid:

2 Chronicles 12:1. . . . *Rehoboam . . . forsook the law . . . and all Israel with him.*
2 Chronicles 12:2. *And . . . Shishak king of Egypt came up against Jerusalem, because they had transgressed . . .*
2 Chronicles 12:3. *With twelve hundred chariots, and threescore thousand horsemen: and . . . people . . . without number . . . the Lubims, the Sukkiims, and the Ethiopians.*

The Chronicler exaggerates the size of the army, but the details are otherwise plausible. Shishak is the first of the Libyan dynasty and the "Lubims" are, without much question, the Libyan cohorts that served under him. The Ethiopians are mercenaries from the south. The Sukkiims are less easily identifiable but it may be a reference to Succoth (or Sukkoth), a town in the eastern portion of the Nile delta (see page 141). The Sukkiims may therefore be the native Egyptians of the delta.

As a result of the invasion, Rehoboam and the nation swung back in response to a warning by Shemaiah the prophet:

2 Chronicles 12:6. *Whereupon the princes of Israel and the king humbled themselves . . .*

In consequence of that, while Jerusalem and the Temple were looted, king and nation were not entirely destroyed.

Abijah

Succeeding Rehoboam was his son Abijah, which may be the throne name, where Abijam (the name used in 1 Kings) was the proper name.

The Chronicler usually gives the name of the king's mother at the time his accession is noted, since this is of genealogical interest. In the case of Abijam there seems to be some confusion in this respect.

> 1 Kings 15:2. . . . *his [Abijam's] mother's name was Maachah, the daughter of Abishalom.*
>
> 2 Chronicles 11:20. . . . *he [Rehoboam] took Maachah the daughter of Absalom, which bare him Abijah . . .*
>
> 2 Chronicles 13:2. . . . *His [Abijah's] mother's name . . . was Michaiah the daughter of Uriel of Gibeah . . .*

Absalom, David's rebel son, did have a mother named Maachah, and may have had a daughter (or granddaughter) of the same name, although she is never mentioned in the chapters dealing with Absalom. And who Uriel might be is unknown. There is no likelihood that the confusion can ever be straightened out but it is interesting that if Absalom is really Abijah's grandfather (or great-grandfather) then for all that his bid for the throne was lost, his blood flows in all the kings of the Davidic line after Rehoboam.

In 1 Kings, it is simply stated that Abijah (Abijam) of Judah and Jeroboam of Israel were at war, and no details are given. However, the stronger Israel did not manage to beat down the weaker Judah and the Chronicler uses that as a way of demonstrating his thesis. He describes a battle in which eight hundred thousand men of Israel fought four hundred thousand men of Judah. Abijah made a rousing pro-Temple speech to the enemy before the battle and even though the Israelites outnumbered the Judeans and surrounded them besides, the Judeans won a great victory and

> 2 Chronicles 13:17. . . . *there fell down slain of Israel five hundred thousand men*

so that Jeroboam was permanently enfeebled and soon died:

> 2 Chronicles 13:21. *But Abijah waxed mighty, and married fourteen wives . . .*

Asa

Asa, the son of Abijah, is described as a reforming king. Consequently, one can be confident that he has nothing to fear in the face of a new invasion—one that is not mentioned in 1 Kings:

> 2 Chronicles 14:9. *And there came out against them* [Judah] *Zerah the Ethiopian with an host of a thousand thousand and three hundred chariots and came unto Mareshah.*

The thought of a million-man army swarming into Judah (Mareshah is about twenty-five miles southwest of Jerusalem) in the ninth century B.C. rather staggers the imagination. The Chronicler, however, is just emphasizing the glory of Asa's eventual victory and the figure need not be taken seriously.

> 2 Chronicles 14:11. *And Asa cried unto the Lord* . . .
> 2 Chronicles 14:12. *So the Lord smote the Ethiopians before Asa* . . .
> 2 Chronicles 14:13. *And Asa* . . . *pursued them unto Gerar* . . .
> 2 Chronicles 14:14. *And they smote all the cities round about Gerar* . . .

The Chronicler may exaggerate and moralize but he does not, apparently, manufacture stories outright. Zerah and his invasion are not mentioned in 1 Kings, which, however, concentrates to a large extent on Israel, and it may well be that Zerah's attack was actually only a minor raid by a border chieftain.

Shishak, after his own successful raid, may have placed an army detachment at Gerar, south of Judah, and in Asa's time, an Ethiopian mercenary may have been in charge of that detachment. It would be his raid that was beaten off.

Asa reigned from 915 to 875 B.C. and in this period the second Pharaoh of the Libyan dynasty reigned. He was Osorkon I, who reigned from 919 to 883 B.C. It is not beyond the realm of the possible that Zerah was Osorkon.

In Asa's case, however, the pendulum swings back. He is pressed hard by Baasha of Israel and therefore makes an alliance with Syria. Such trust in worldly alliances rather than in the Lord offends the prophetic party, and the Chronicler hastens from that to an account of Asa's death through a disease of the feet. He puts in a further touch of disapproval in a pair of verses that are sometimes used in modern times as a jibe at the medical profession:

> 2 Chronicles 16:12. . . . *yet in his disease he sought not to the Lord but to the physicians.*
> 2 Chronicles 16:13. *And Asa slept with his fathers* . . .

Jehoshaphat

The next king, Jehoshaphat, is described by the Chronicler as a great reforming monarch, and his reign is therefore a time of peace and power:

2 Chronicles 17:12. And Jehoshaphat waxed great exceedingly . . .

The fact that Jehoshaphat was a loyal and even subservient ally of Ahab of Israel (the worldly reason for Judah's peace and prosperity at this time) is mentioned in connection with their combined war at Ramoth-gilead, during the course of which Ahab died (see page 352). Jehoshaphat is only mildly denounced for this, however.

His continuing reform policy leads to a great victory over the Moabites and Ammonites, but his continuing alliance with Israel is blamed for the failure of his trading fleet (see page 351).

Jehoiada

With Jehoram, the husband of Athaliah and therefore the son-in-law of Ahab and Jezebel (see page 362), and his son Ahaziah (the son also of Athaliah) there is a serious reaction. Under the influence of Athaliah, Phoenician cults are brought into Judah. Both monarchs came to a bad end, therefore. Under Jehoram, Jerusalem was taken and sacked by Philistines and Arabs and the king died soon after of an incurable disease of the intestines. As for Ahaziah, he was slain in Israel, in the course of the revolution of Jehu (see page 364).

Athaliah's usurpation and the saving of Joash is then taken up (see page 367) and here the hero is Jehoiada the High Priest and the husband of Jehoshabeath (Jehosheba), the royal infant's aunt.

Jehoiada organizes the conspiracy that kills Athaliah and places Joash on the throne, but does so with meticulous care that the Temple ritual be observed in all its details. He reinstates reform and as long as he lives all goes well. His death is recorded in a way that is reminiscent of Genesis:

2 Chronicles 24:15. But Jehoiada waxed old, and was full of days when he died; an hundred and thirty years old was he when he died.

Thereafter Joash backslid and when he is reproved for this by Zechariah, the son of Jehoiada, the king has Zechariah stoned to death in the court of the Temple:

> 2 Chronicles 24:22. *Thus Joash the king remembered not the kindness which Jehoiada . . . had done to him, but slew his son . . .*

As a result a small Syrian army invaded the land and defeated a larger Judean defending force; Joash was afflicted with disease and, finally, was assassinated by men of his court.

Amaziah

The next king, Amaziah, began his reign quite well. Having decided to reconquer Edom, which had rebelled after Jehoshaphat's death, he hired a hundred thousand Israelite mercenaries. When the prophetic party objected to this dependence on worldly help, Amaziah released them and forfeited the money with which he had hired them. As a result:

> 2 Chronicles 25:11. *And Amaziah . . . smote of the children of Seir ten thousand.*

Amaziah's victory led him into trouble, however, for he was attracted by the Edomite gods.

> 2 Chronicles 25:14. . . . *Amaziah . . . brought the gods of the children of Seir, and . . . bowed down . . . before them . . .*

It is this which the Chronicler finds to be the cause of Amaziah's subsequent defeat by Joash of Israel (see page 369) and his final assassination at the hands of conspirators.

Uzziah

Amaziah was succeeded by his son:

> 2 Chronicles 26:1. *Then all the people of Judah took Uzziah . . . and made him king . . .*

Uzziah is, apparently, the throne name of the king, while his proper name (used in 2 Kings) is Azariah. Uzziah was a reforming king and this accounted to the Chronicler for the fact that he defeated the Philistines and Ammonites, that he successfully reorganized the Judean army and strongly fortified Jerusalem.

2 Chronicles 26:15. . . . *And his name spread far abroad; for he was marvellously helped, till he was strong.*

In a worldly sense, Uzziah's prosperity was probably due to his careful subservience to the successful Jeroboam II of Israel. The prosperous Uzziah, however, overstepped the bounds and trespassed on the prerogatives of the priesthood. (David and Solomon had successfully done so, but the position of the priests had hardened since those days.)

2 Chronicles 26:16. . . . *when he* [Uzziah] *was strong, his heart was lifted up* . . . *and* [he] *went into the temple of the Lord to burn incense* . . .

He was promptly stricken with leprosy and remained a leper till he died.

Ahaz

The Chronicler's pendulum continues to swing. Jotham succeeds his father Uzziah and continues the reform policy. In consequence, he defeats the Ammonites.

Under Ahaz, the next king, there is a reaction and Judah is promptly defeated by the Syrians. And as Ahaz's idolatry is particularly heinous, the punishment described is extravagantly high:

2 Chronicles 28:6. *For Pekah* [of Israel] . . . *slew in Judah an hundred and twenty thousand in one day* . . . *because they had forsaken the Lord* . . .

Hezekiah

Ahaz's son Hezekiah is, however, the greatest reformer of all, in the Chronicler's view. Hezekiah is, indeed, exalted by him to a point of equality with the later king, Josiah. This makes sense from the

Chronicler's standpoint, since Hezekiah was victorious in battle and Josiah was defeated, so that the reforming deeds of the former must at least equal, if not surpass, those of the latter.

Hezekiah began by reopening and rededicating the Temple, which apparently had been closed during the disastrous reign of Ahaz. He then prepared and kept an extremely elaborate Passover and followed that by the destruction of all idolatrous altars in the kingdom.

Following all this righteous behavior, Sennacherib invaded Judah and laid siege to Jerusalem (see page 384), and to the Chronicler it seems perfectly natural that the Assyrian should retreat without being able to take the city.

> 2 Chronicles 32:27. *And Hezekiah had exceeding much riches and honour* . . .
>
> . . . .
>
> 2 Chronicles 32:30. . . . *And Hezekiah prospered in all his works.*

Manasseh

But following what to the Chronicler was the best of the kings of Judah in the days after Solomon, came his son Manasseh, who was the worst. He restored all the ways of his grandfather, Ahaz:

> 2 Chronicles 33:9. *So Manasseh made Judah and the inhabitants of Jerusalem to err, and to do worse than the heathen* . . .

Now the Chronicler is in a dilemma, for Manasseh reigned for fifty-five years and, as far as we can tell from 2 Kings, that reign was one of peace and quiet.

The Chronicler therefore brings disaster upon him; a disaster not mentioned in 2 Kings:

> 2 Chronicles 33:11. *Wherefore the Lord brought upon him the captains of the host of the king of Assyria, which took Manasseh* . . . *and bound him* . . . *and carried him to Babylon.*

Now the Chronicler may color heavily, but he does not, apparently, attempt outright invention. We may assume then that something happened in the reign of Manasseh which the Chronicler was able to interpret as captivity.

It is certain that Judah was an Assyrian tributary in the days of Manasseh and tributary kings were not uncommonly forced to visit the capital as an expression of loyalty or to engage in some administrative function or other. Assyrian records speak of two occasions on which Manasseh was present in the capital. One of these occasions was in 672 B.C. after Manasseh had been reigning for twenty years. Esarhaddon was then king of Assyria and was anxious to assure his son and heir, Asshurbanipal, a quiet succession. He therefore ordered the various vassal kings, including Manasseh, to Assyria to swear allegiance and vow loyalty.

Manasseh was not actually taken to Assyria by a conquering army but it is quite possible that he left in the company of an Assyrian military guard and the people (and even Manasseh himself) could not be quite sure that the dread Esarhaddon might not decide to keep him captive and replace him on the throne with someone else. Out of this, it was easy for the Chronicler to devise Manasseh's captivity and point the moral.

However, Manasseh returned from Assyria and ruled for another generation. That could not be denied and it had to be explained according to the Chronicler's system. The only way was to have Manasseh repent and then return to Jerusalem as a reforming king (something that is not mentioned in 2 Kings, nor in the words of the contemporary prophet Jeremiah).

2 Chronicles 33:12. *And when he [Manasseh] was in affliction, he besought the Lord . . . and humbled himself greatly . . .*
2 Chronicles 33:13. *And prayed unto him; and he [the Lord] . . . heard his supplication, and brought him again to Jerusalem . . .*

The Prayer of Manasses

Particular interest would naturally be centered about the prayer of Manasseh. Because Manasseh was so consummate and notorious a sinner, his redemption by prayer was a clear indication that all men might find forgiveness if properly penitent and this was a matter of great theological interest. Naturally, there was curiosity as to the nature of the prayer, particularly since the Chronicler says the prayer exists in the records, even though he does not give it himself.

2 Chronicles 33:18. *Now the rest of the acts of Manasseh, and his prayer unto his God . . . are written in the book of the kings of Israel.*

2 Chronicles 33:19. *His prayer also, and how God was intreated of him, . . . are written among the sayings of the seers.*

If, by "the book of the kings of Israel," the Biblical Book of 2 Kings is meant, the Chronicler errs, for the prayer is not to be found there (or is no longer to be found there, at any rate). As for the "sayings of the seers" in which the prayer is to be found, this is lost.

In later years, however, perhaps about 100 B.C., a prayer was written by an unnamed poet, a prayer designed for the use of sinners who craved mercy. It was a short prayer, only fifteen verses long, but was so beautiful that it became easy to believe that it was indeed the prayer that had been uttered by Manasseh in his Assyrian dungeon. It therefore came to be included in some editions of the Bible as that prayer.

In particular, it was included in the Greek translation of the Bible that circulated among the Greek-speaking Jews of the city of Alexandria, in Egypt.

This translation is called the Septuagint, from the Latin word for "seventy." According to legend, Ptolemy II, king of Egypt, was on good terms with his subjects, the Alexandrian Jews, and agreed to help them prepare a translation of their holy books. He brought in seventy-two scholars (altered by later legends to an even seventy) from Jerusalem at his own expense and had them translate the first five books of the Bible (the Pentateuch) into Greek. It was the first translation of any of the Biblical books into a foreign language. Over the next two centuries, additional books were translated and these eventually included the supposed prayer of Manasseh (which may, to be sure, have been written in Greek to begin with).

About 90 A.D., Jewish scholars gathered in a Judean town named Jamnia, about thirty miles west of Jerusalem. Twenty years before, the Romans had sacked Jerusalem and destroyed the Temple and the Jews were scattered abroad. Only the Bible and the tenets of Judaism which it contained could be counted on to hold them together. There had therefore to be one standard Bible for all Jews and the scholars had to decide of what books this Bible would consist.

The books they accepted now make up the Jewish Bible. In general, though, they did not accept those books, however edifying, that were written after about 150 B.C. Those were too clearly the work of men rather than of God. One of the books *not* accepted by the Jewish scholars was the prayer of Manasseh.

Some of the eliminated books nevertheless remained in the Septuagint. Christian scholars made use of the Septuagint, and when Latin translations were made, the books eliminated by the Jewish scholars were translated and kept. Some are still to be found in English-language Bibles used by Catholics today.

Jerome, who about A.D. 400 prepared the Vulgate, or the official Latin Bible now used by the Catholic Church, worked in Palestine, learned Hebrew, used the assistance of rabbis, and consulted Hebrew versions of the Bible as well as the Septuagint. He knew of the difference in the books they contained.

For those books contained in the Greek version and not in the Hebrew, Jerome used the word "Apocrypha." This word means "hidden" and, after all, some of the books in the Greek Bible had been withdrawn and, therefore, "hidden" from the reader who studied the Hebrew Bible. Thus, the prayer of Manasseh becomes one of the apocryphal books, or, to put the phrase in a slightly different form, part of the Apocrypha.

The Protestant versions of the Bible (including the King James) follow the Hebrew system and do not include the Apocrypha. For that reason, the prayer of Manasseh, is not to be found in the King James version of the Bible. Nevertheless, the apocryphal books were put into English by the translators of the King James Version and exist also in the Revised Standard Version. Since the translation was from the Greek, the Greek form of Manasseh is used and the final "-s" used in Greek names makes the book "The Prayer of Manasses." In the Revised Standard Version, however, it is "The Prayer of Manasseh."

Josiah

Amon, who follows Manasseh, is another backslider and is assassinated—but then comes Josiah.

Although the Chronicler has placed as much of the reforming credit as possible upon Hezekiah, there is no question but that after the reigns of Manasseh and Amon, reform is once again needed, and the tradition of Josiah's work is, in any case, too strong to be ignored. The tale is therefore repeated, complete with the discovery of the Book of Deuteronomy and the celebration of the great Passover.

Yet Josiah died in battle and the Chronicler had to explain that. Of course, the death was, in one sense, a blessing, for it meant that Josiah would not survive to see the destruction of the Temple and of the kingdom.

This is not, however, enough for the Chronicler, who needs a positive cause. Therefore, on the occasion of Josiah's fatal war against Necho of Egypt, the Chronicler adds something not present in 2 Kings. As the battle of Megiddo approaches, the Egyptian monarch sends ambassadors to the Judean, with the message:

> 2 Chronicles 36:21. . . . I come not against thee this day . . . God commanded me to make haste: forbear thee from meddling with God, who is with me . . .
> 2 Chronicles 36:22. Nevertheless Josiah . . . hearkened not unto the words of Necho from the mouth of God . . .

In other words, Josiah died because in this case he was disobedient to God.

King of the Chaldees

The reigns of the sons and grandson of Josiah, ending with Zedekiah, are hastened through briefly. All backslid as did the people and the priests:

> 2 Chronicles 36:14. Moreover all the chief of the priests, and the people, transgressed very much . . .

They were warned by prophets but that did no good:

> 2 Chronicles 36:16. But they [the people] mocked the messengers of God, and despised his words, and misused his prophets, until the wrath of the Lord arose against his people, till there was no remedy.
> 2 Chronicles 36:17. Therefore he brought upon them the king of the Chaldees [Nebuchadnezzar] . . .

So, ironically, history comes full circle. One wonders if the Chronicler, in using the phrase "king of the Chaldees" rather than the more natural "king of Babylon," does not deliberately stress the irony. After all, Abraham, to whom Canaan was first promised, reached that land from Ur of the Chaldees (see page 56) and now the Jews are carried out of that land by the king of the Chaldees.

15. EZRA

The Chronicler

The Chronicler did not complete his story with the downfall of
Zedekiah and the destruction of the Temple in 586 B.C. He was
writing, after all, about 400 B.C. at the earliest estimate and much
remained to be told.

The actual period of exile was of little interest to him, for the
Temple, the non-human hero of his history, did not then exist. He
therefore fills in that period with nothing more than genealogies like
that of the line of descent of Jeconiah in the third chapter of 1 Chronicles (see page 405).

A half century after Zedekiah's death, however, there begins a period
in which the project of the rebuilding of the Temple comes under
discussion and now the Chronicler's interest is aroused once more.
Immediately after his account of the end of the kingdom of Judah,
therefore, the Chronicler passes on to an account of a royal proclamation by the new king of a new nation; a proclamation which led to
the construction of a new Temple.

Because of this gap in time and the radically sudden change in
atmosphere from an established kingdom and a centuries-old Temple
to a band of impoverished returnees trying desperately to build a house
of worship, there was a tendency to divide the Chronicler's history
at this point. The earlier portion makes up 1 Chronicles and 2 Chron-

Jerusalem Restored

icles.* The later portion might be called the Book of Ezra, or perhaps the Book of Ezra and Nehemiah, because these two men, Ezra the scribe and Nehemiah the governor, played important roles in the reestablishment of the Temple and of the community.

In Jewish tradition, it was Ezra the scribe who wrote these books; who was the man I have been referring to as the Chronicler. There is no certainty about this, but, on the other hand, there is nothing implausible about it either.

The Jewish scholars who placed the Bible in its final form toward the end of the first century A.D. recognized that the Book of Ezra and Nehemiah, like 1 and 2 Chronicles, could appear only in "the Writings" because of its comparatively late date of composition. However, whereas 1 and 2 Chronicles duplicated, to a very large extent, the early historical books of the Bible, Ezra and Nehemiah added new material not present elsewhere. For that reason Ezra and Nehemiah was more useful and was placed ahead of 1 and 2 Chronicles, even though from the historical viewpoint it came afterward.

In order to make the historical connection clear despite this reversal of chronology, the verses at the dividing line are duplicated. The first three verses of Ezra are quoted virtually verbatim at the very end of the last chapter of 2 Chronicles.

In the various versions of the Bible used by Christians, 1 and 2 Chronicles are placed not at the end of the Old Testament but immediately after 1 and 2 Kings. Then, as an additional piece of logical arrangement, the Book of Ezra appears not before but *after* 1 and 2 Chronicles, so that the Chronicler's history can be read as a unit, with the only jog coming at the point where the verses ending 2 Chronicles are repeated at the beginning of Ezra. (The repetition is retained.)

It eventually became customary to divide the final part of the Chronicler's history into two parts, the Book of Ezra, and the Book of Nehemiah. In view of the belief that Ezra was the Chronicler and wrote both books, and since he appears in both books, it is also possible to call the books 1 Ezra and 2 Ezra. This is adhered to in Catholic versions of the Bible, which, however, make use of the Greek form of the name so that the books become 1 Esdras and 2 Esdras.

---

* These are handled as two separate books only for convenience sake, as in the case of 1 and 2 Samuel and 1 and 2 Kings, with full recognition that actually they form a single work.

The Sixth Century B.C.

ARABIAN SEA

INDIA

INDUS R.

Pattala

PERSIAN EMPIRE

SAKAE

MASSAGETAE

JAXARTES R.

ARAL SEA

Persian Empire

CHORASMIA

Oxus

Taxila

GANDARA

BACTRIA

Maracanda

SOGDIANA

Bactra

ARIANA

ARACHOSIA

PACTYANS

PARICANIANS

GEDROSIA

DRANGIANA

MEDIAN EMPIRE

ARIA

PARTHIA

CARMANIA

UTIANS

MARGIANA

Sagartians

Asada

PERSIS

Persepolis

Pasargadae

DAHAE

HYRCANIA

AMARDI

Ecbatana

Susa

ELAM

PERSIAN GULF

CASPIAN SEA

COLCHIS

CAUCASUS MTS.

Persian Empire

Trapezus

Sinope

Cabira

ARMENIA

Nineveh

TIGRIS R.

EUPHRATES R.

Babylon

NEW BABYLONIAN EMPIRE

PERSIAN EMPIRE

ARABIA

SCYTHIANS

BLACK SEA

BITHYNIA

KINGDOM OF LYDIA

CAPPADOCIA

Hatra

Carchemish

Sidon

Damascus

CILICIA

Tarsus

Ephesus

Sardis

Miletus

PISIDIA

LYCIA

CYPRUS

Megiddo

Jerusalem

JUDAH

RED SEA

THRACE

DANUBE R.

MACEDONIA

ILLYRIA

EPIRUS

GREECE

Athens

Sparta

CRETE

THE GREAT SEA (Mediterranean Sea)

Cyrene

LIBYANS

PERSIAN EMPIRE

Ammonium

Sais

Memphis

KINGDOM OF EGYPT

Thebes

NILE R.

ETHIOPIA

ARABIAN SEA

Miles

0   1000

Persian Empire c.500 B.C.

Median Empire 625–550 B.C.

New Babylonian Empire 625–539 B.C.

Cyrus, king of Persia

The Book of Ezra begins with the event that first initiated the rebuilding of the Temple and dates it in the fashion of ancient times:

Ezra 1:1. *Now in the first year of Cyrus king of Persia . . .*

In this way, the Chronicler skips lightly over a vast change that had come over the political complexion of western Asia.

The Chaldeans, in defeating the Assyrians and taking Nineveh, had been in alliance with the Medes, a people living to the north of Assyria and south of the Caspian Sea—a region known as Media. After the fall of Nineveh, the Chaldeans, ruling from Babylon, had taken control of the entire Fertile Crescent, while the Medes extended their rule over a vast stretch of land to the north and east.

The Median Empire was much the larger in area but it stretched over barbaric areas of nomad tribes. The Chaldeans, on the other hand, ruled the very cradle of civilization, a land of intensely irrigated, agriculturally rich land, full of large and luxurious cities. Under Nebuchadnezzar, who came to the throne of Chaldea in 605 B.C., Babylon was the largest, wealthiest, and most powerful city in the world and was capital of its mightiest empire.

Nebuchadnezzar died in 561 B.C. after a most successful rule of forty-four years, having survived the capture of Jerusalem by a full quarter century. The monarchs who followed him were, however, much weaker than he. His son Amel-Marduk (the Evil-merodach of the Bible; see page 396) succeeded him but was dethroned by a conspiracy in 560 B.C. After several years of instability, Nabonidus, who was not of the line of Nebuchadnezzar, ascended the throne in 556 B.C. He was a scholar rather than a soldier and left the rule of Babylon to others while he involved himself in antiquarian studies.

Media, the one great power which might have taken advantage of the weakness of the Babylonian kings, was not particularly warlike either. In 593 B.C., while Nebuchadnezzar was still comparatively new on the throne, Astyages became king of the Medes. He was still king when Nebuchadnezzar died and his long reign was peaceful. It happened, however, that within a decade of Nebuchadnezzar's death, the

Median Empire was shaken by war and a new tribe became dominant.

This tribe had been living under Median rule in a district now called Fars, which lies along the northern shores of the Persian Gulf. To the ancient inhabitants of the land, it was Parsa, and to the Greeks, Persis. It is from the last that we get our present words "Persia" and "Persian."

The Persians were closely akin to the Medes, with similar language and similar traditions, so that there was much confusion concerning the two among foreigners. Sometimes they were spoken of as "the Medes and the Persians." Sometimes, Jews and Greeks alike spoke of "Medes" when they really meant "Persians."

About 600 B.C., there was born to one of the leading Persian families a child they named Kurush. In Hebrew, this name became Koresh, and in Greek, Kuros. The last, in Latin spelling, is Cyrus, and it is by that name that we know him. Later, legends arose which made Cyrus the grandson of Astyages, and stated that the Median king had exposed the baby to certain death because an oracle had foretold that he would be killed and replaced on the throne by the infant once he had grown to manhood. Cyrus was suckled and kept alive by a dog and then taken care of by a shepherd till he was grown.

This legend can be dismissed. Similar stories are told of the founders of other nations—of Romulus, the legendary founder of Rome, for instance. Such a story has the ulterior purpose of serving to cast a mantle of legitimacy over a usurper and making him seem the lawful successor to the king he has replaced by force.

It is much more likely that Cyrus was exactly what he seemed: a Persian leader who was no member of the royal line at all. He rebelled against Astyages, and about 550 B.C. succeeded in placing himself upon the throne. What had been the Median Empire was now the Persian Empire.

Cyrus now entered upon a career of conquest. He took all of Asia Minor and extended the borders of his kingdom to the shores of the Aegean Sea. In 538 B.C. he took Babylon from its disorganized rulers and all the Fertile Crescent was in his hands. To the Jews in Babylon, this was the "first year of Cyrus king of Persia."

The Persian Empire, as put together by Cyrus, was the greatest realm that western Asia had yet seen. It encompassed all the Asian territory of Assyria, plus Asia Minor and large tracts to the east.

Jeremiah

Cyrus was completely unlike the conquerors who had flourished before him. He did not engage in wholesale killings and deportations. Rather he chose to treat the conquered peoples gently, allowing them their self-respect and even considerable home rule. The result was that the Persian Empire was an administrative success as well as a territorial one. It experienced revolts, to be sure, but it also enjoyed periods of peace over wide areas. The moral, for conquerors, would seem to be plain. The lighter the grip, the firmer the hold.

The Jews were one of the groups that benefited from Cyrus's policy. The Persian king found a group of them making up a rather prosperous colony in Babylon and he offered to allow them to return:

> Ezra 1:3. *Who is there among you of all his* [God's] *people?* . . . *let him go up to Jerusalem* . . . *and build the house of the Lord* . . .

The Chronicler points out that thus was fulfilled a prophecy of Jeremiah, something that is mentioned briefly here but more fully at the end of 2 Chronicles:

> 2 Chronicles 36:20. . . . *they* [the Jewish exiles] *were servants to him* [Nebuchadnezzar] *and his sons until the reign of Persia:* 2 Chronicles 36:21. *To fulfill the word of the Lord by* . . . *Jeremiah, until the land* . . . *lay desolate* . . . *threescore and ten years.*

The prophecy is recorded in the Book of Jeremiah, thus:

> Jeremiah 29:10. *For thus saith the Lord, That after seventy years be accomplished at Babylon I will visit you* . . . *causing you to return to this place.*

And yet the period of exile was not seventy years. From the destruction of the Temple in 586 B.C. to Cyrus's proclamation in 538 B.C. was a lapse of time of only forty-eight years.

Of course, Jeremiah and the Chronicler may not have thought of seventy years as representing a precise length of time. (Ancient historians were much less time conscious than we are.) Seventy years may merely have meant the "lifetime of a man" to them.

On the other hand, the seventy years that were accomplished at Babylon may refer to the duration of the Chaldean Empire, which from the accession of Nebuchadnezzar to that of Cyrus lasted sixty-seven years.

And again, the reference may be to the Temple itself rather than to the people, as I shall explain later in the chapter.

Sheshbazzar

There was a quick response to Cyrus's edict:

Ezra 1:5. *Then rose up the chief of the fathers of Judah and Benjamin, and the . . . Levites . . . to go up to build the house of the Lord . . .*

Ezra 1:6. *And all they that were about them strengthened their hands with . . . silver . . . gold . . . goods . . . beasts . . .*

The specific mention of the tribes of Judah, Benjamin, and Levi makes it clear that only the exiles of the kingdom of Judah are involved. The descendants of earlier exiles from the kingdom of Israel, carried off by Sargon of Assyria, would still be somewhere in the dominions of Cyrus and might conceivably have been included in the edict. However, it was now nearly two centuries since the Israelites had been carried off. By now, apparently, they had been absorbed and had lost all consciousness of being Israelites.

Even the Jews in Babylon had assimilated themselves to an extent. Not all went rushing back to Jerusalem. Some remained behind. The fact that they donated objects of value to help those who were planning to make the trip indicates that they were reasonably well-to-do and might have seen no point in leaving a place where they were prosperous and secure and where by now they felt at home. (This is precisely the situation in which modern American Jews find themselves. Many are prosperous and secure and see no reason to leave their homes and flock to Israel—though they are willing to make financial contributions.)

Cyrus is described as also contributing to the returnees, ordering that the various Temple furnishings, which had been carried off by Nebuchadnezzar, be returned:

Ezra 1:7. . . . *Cyrus . . . brought forth the vessels of the house of the Lord . . .*

Ezra 1:8. *Even those did Cyrus . . . bring forth by the hand of Mithredath . . . and numbered them unto Sheshbazzar, the prince of Judah.*

Mithredath is an interesting name. It means "given by Mithra," one of the important Persian deities on the side of Ormuzd and the forces of good (see page 409). A later version of the Persian religion, built about Mithra as a sun symbol, was known as Mithraism and, in the time of the Roman Empire, it vied with Christianity for supremacy. The Greek version of the name Mithredath is Mithridates. Rulers by this name reigned over the kingdoms of Parthia and of Pontus in Roman times. In particular, Mithridates VI of Pontus (sometimes known as Mithradates the Great) fought Rome nearly to a standstill in the first century B.C.

The name "Sheshbazzar" is a puzzle. Its meaning is unclear but it is certainly a Babylonian name and not a Hebrew one. Yet it is borne by someone who is "the prince of Judah." Presumably the Jews exiled in Babylon tended to adopt Babylonian names just as American Jews tend to adopt American names.

Since Sheshbazzar is "the prince of Judah," it is natural to look for him among those of the Davidic line listed earlier by the Chronicler. The sons of Jeconiah, the exiled king of Judah, are there given:

1 Chronicles 3:17. . . . *Salathiel his [Jeconiah's] son,*
1 Chronicles 3:18. *Malchiram also, and Pediah, and Shenazar . . .*

It is very tempting to identify Shenazar (itself apparently a Babylonian name) with Sheshbazzar. If so, Sheshbazzar would be the fourth son of Jeconiah. If the three older sons were dead or incapacitated, Sheshbazzar would be literally the prince of Judah, the legal king of the land. It is even conceivable that the difference between Shenazar and Sheshbazzar arises because the son of Jeconiah adopted the latter as a throne name once his leadership of Judah was thus officially recognized.

To be sure, Cyrus had no intention of restoring Judah as a political kingdom, whether independent or tributary, but merely wished to restore Jerusalem as the center of what seemed to him to be an unimportant cult.

Zerubbabel

Sheshbazzar led a party to Jerusalem and under him, apparently, the work began:

> Ezra 5:16. . . . *Sheshbazzar . . . laid the foundation of the house of God . . .*

However, if so, he was apparently only a titular head, cast in the role as (perhaps) the oldest living scion of the house of David and therefore lending an air of sanctity and legitimacy to the project. As the son of Jeconiah he must have been an old man at the time of this first return, and a younger man would have taken over after Sheshbazzar's ceremonial laying of the cornerstone, so to speak. Later on, it is only this younger man who is mentioned:

> Ezra 2:1. *Now these are the children . . . that went up out of the captivity . . .*
> Ezra 2:2. *Which came with Zerubbabel . . .*

Some suggest that Zerubbabel (also a Babylonian name, meaning "child of Babylon") is simply another name for Sheshbazzar, but nothing forces this assumption. Zerubbabel is a distinct individual also mentioned among the descendants of Jeconiah:

> 1 Chronicles 3:19. *And the sons of Pedaiah were, Zerubbabel, and Shimei.*

Elsewhere, to be sure, he is listed as the son of another:

> Ezra 5:2. *Then rose up Zerubbabel the son of Shealtiel . . .*

However, Shealtiel is commonly equated with Salathiel, listed in 1 Chronicles as Jeconiah's oldest son. In either case, Zerubbabel is the nephew of Sheshbazzar, the grandson of Jeconiah, and therefore the great-great-grandson of Josiah and the descendant, in the twentieth generation, of David.

Jeshua

Eventually, an altar was built upon which sacrifices might be performed:

> Ezra 3:2. *Then stood up Jeshua the son of Jozadak . . . and Zerubbabel . . . and builded the altar . . .*

The name Jeshua is a form of the earlier Joshua, which is itself a shortened form of Jehoshua. This form appears commonly in the Chronicler's history, and it has special interest because it is this name which, in the Greek form, is Jesus.

Jeshua is the son of Jozadak (Jehozadak), who is listed in the sixth chapter of 1 Chronicles as the High Priest at the time of the fall of the kingdom, the High Priest who went into Babylonian captivity (see page 406).

Now his son had returned to officiate at the altar. Thus, not only is the secular power unbroken in the line from Jeconiah to Sheshbazzar to Zerubbabel; but the priestly power is unbroken, too, from Jehozadak to Jeshua.

The Adversaries of Judah

But the returnees were not building the Temple in a vacuum. There were people living in what had once been the kingdoms of Israel and Judah. These included those who had never been exiled in the first place. Sargon of Assyria carried off only a small portion of the Israelites, and Nebuchadnezzar of Babylon only a small portion of the Judeans. In both cases, though, the exiles had been taken from the upper classes—the administrators, landowners, artisans, scholars, and intellectuals generally. Those who remained behind were the peasants and the unlettered.

Then, too, the Assyrian kings had resettled Israel with outsiders and these had undoubtedly intermarried with the remaining natives to form the Samaritans (see page 380). After the exile from Judah, these Samaritans had spread southward to take over parts of what had once been northern Judah, while the Edomites moved northward from their desert fastnesses into what had once been southern Judah.

The Jewish exiles in Babylon, on the other hand, had prospered and had further developed Judaism. As compensation for the loss of their land and freedom, they turned to that which alone distinguished them clearly from their neighbors—their sacred writings. The various traditions and law codes may have hardened and fused and the early books of the Bible may have approached their final form during the Exile. (It may be for this reason that so much of the first few chapters of Genesis has a marked tinge of Babylonic myth about it—see page 40.)

Then, too, important prophets helped develop the ideas of Judaism further, so that the Jews of Babylon had a religion advanced and etherealized in many respects beyond that which was held traditionally by the remaining inhabitants of Judah.

For these reasons the rebuilding of the Temple was bound to bring trouble. To the people living in the land about Jerusalem, the returnees were foreigners who came flooding into the land in a highhanded fashion, with strange religious ways and haughty speech. To the returnees, on the other hand, the people living on the land were strangers and foreigners, occupying usurped space, and practicing a debased religion only superficially resembling Judaism.

The situation was precisely the same as that in the twentieth century when Jews from Europe and America returned to an Israel they considered their ancestral home and found themselves face to face with Arab dwellers who considered them strangers and intruders. The apparently irreconcilable hostility of Israel and its Arab neighbors mirrors the hostility of the Jews and Samaritans in Persian times and later.

Ezra 4:1. . . . *the adversaries of Judah and Benjamin* [the Samaritans] . . .

Ezra 4:2. . . . *came to Zerubbabel . . . and said . . . let us build with you* . . .

Ezra 4:3 *But Zerubbabel . . . said unto them, You have nothing to do with us.*

There is nothing at this point to indicate that the offer of the Samaritans was insincere. Zerubbabel might have been more diplomatic, but, like Rehoboam four centuries before (see page 338), he was harsh and insulting, and the result was the same, enmity in place of possible co-operation.

Darius I

The Samaritans could not oppose the Jews directly since both alike were under the firm eye of the Persian kings. The Samaritans could, however, try to influence those kings by pointing out the possible dangers of allowing an exclusivistic religious group to come to power in a place as strategically situated as Jerusalem.

> Ezra 4:4. *Then the people of the land weakened the hands of the people of Judah, and troubled them in building.*
> Ezra 4:5. *And hired counsellors against them to frustrate their purpose all the days of Cyrus king of Persia, even until the reign of Darius king of Persia.*

Cyrus died in 530 B.C., eight years after his edict allowing the Jews to return to Jerusalem. Succeeding him was his son Cambyses, (Kambujiya, in Persian) who had been ruling Babylon while his father was off on his campaigns. In order to ensure his place on the throne, Cambyses had his brother Smerdis executed. He then set out to conquer Egypt, the one portion of the Assyrian Empire which had not yet been taken over by the conquering Persians.

In Egypt the 26th dynasty was still in power. Seventy years had passed since Necho (against whom Josiah of Judah had fought) had died and now the Pharaoh was Psamtik III. In 525 B.C. Cambyses marched against him and won an easy victory. Psamtik III was overthrown and later executed, so that Saitic Egypt came to an end. For over a century afterward, Persian kings were to rule as the 27th dynasty.

Cambyses attempted to extend his African dominions even more, with plans to attack Ethiopia to the south, or Carthage to the west, but the deserts were too hostile and his line of communications too long. Furthermore, a Zoroastrian priest, pretending to be Cambyses' dead brother Smerdis, was proclaiming himself king back in Persia and Cambyses had to hurry home. On the way back, in 521 B.C., he died, whether through natural causes, or as a result of assassination or suicide.

The Persian Empire

For some months thereafter, the usurper was in control of Persia, but opposition to him centered about Darius (Darayavaush, in Persian) who was a member of the younger branch of the Persian royal family. Gathering other noblemen about himself, he attacked the usurper, defeated him, and made himself king.

Darius faced rebellions in his turn almost at once, but he put them down with a sure hand and with great skill. He then proceeded to reorganize the kingdom, dividing it up into provinces (satrapies), establishing good roads and canals, arranging for a sound monetary system, and generally overseeing a strong and efficient government.

He also continued Persian conquests. He extended Persian control eastward over sections of northwestern India (the modern Pakistan) and, about 512 B.C., led an army across the Hellespont into Thrace (the region making up modern Bulgaria). It was the first time any Asian monarch had led an army into Europe and he brought his dominions up to the Danube River.

Darius is best remembered among Westerners for the events of the last decade of his thirty-five-year-long reign. The Greek cities on the Aegean coast of Asia Minor revolted in 500 B.C. and received help from Athens. The revolt was crushed and Darius set about punishing the Athenians. A Persian expeditionary force landed on Athenian territory near the village of Marathon in 490 B.C. and there, in one of the most famous battles of ancient times, was defeated. Darius died in 486 B.C. with Athens still unpunished.

This last defeat was a very minor one as far as the Persian Empire was concerned and should not be allowed to obscure the fact that Darius's reign was essentially one of great achievements both abroad and at home. Under him, Persia reached the peak of its power.

The short reign of Cambyses tends to be overshadowed by the greater achievements of Cyrus who preceded him and Darius who followed him, and the Book of Ezra moves straight from Cyrus to Darius, slurring over Cambyses. Indeed, Cambyses is nowhere mentioned in the Bible.

Ahasuerus

Before going into details concerning the results of the intrigues carried on by the Samaritans at the courts of Cyrus and Darius, the

Book of Ezra rounds off those intrigues by describing their continuation into the following reigns:

> Ezra 4:6. *And in the reign of Ahasuerus . . . wrote they unto him an accusation against the inhabitants of Judah and Jerusalem.*

After the death of Darius I in 486 B.C., his son Xerxes succeeded to the throne. Xerxes continued his father's plan of punishing the Greeks. He had to pause first, though, to suppress a serious revolt in Egypt and took several years; time used by the Greeks in desperate preparation for the coming Persian assault.

Finally, a mighty Persian army invaded Greece and an equally mighty Persian fleet (manned by Phoenicians, for the most part) swept the Aegean. Xerxes' navy was defeated in 480 B.C. in the battle of Salamis and his army was defeated on land the next year at Plataea. Xerxes gave up the plan to conquer Greece and retired to a life of ease with his harem.

The "Persian War" makes up the main body of the history of Herodotus, the first great history of Western tradition, and its events have made up a drama almost without parallel in all the twenty-five hundred years that have since elapsed. Those mighty events, however, cast no ripple in Biblical affairs for they did not affect the Jews, and no mention is made of them in the Bible.

It is generally accepted that Xerxes is the Ahasuerus referred to in Ezra 4:6. The names do not seem similar but "Xerxes" is, after all, only the Greek version of the king's name. To the Persians, Xerxes was Khshayarsha. Place an "A" in front and the change to Ahasuerus is not a difficult one to see.

Artaxerxes

The tale of Samaritan intrigues continues:

> Ezra 4:7. *And in the days of Artaxerxes . . .*

In 465 B.C., Xerxes was assassinated in a court intrigue and his son Artaxerxes I (Artakhshatra) succeeded. During Artaxerxes' forty-year reign, the Persian Empire held its own. It kept off the Greeks, not so much with armies as with money, encouraging them to fight among themselves. Rebellions flared here and there in the vast Persian dominions but they were easily put down and in the end Artaxerxes died in peace in 424 B.C.

Aramaic

To be sure, by the time of Xerxes and Artaxerxes, it was not the Temple that was in question; that had been completed in Darius's reign, as will be explained later, and was a dead issue. Rather, it was the fact that the Jews were also attempting to build walls about Jerusalem that was now in question.

This could easily be interpreted as a rebellious act, since the Jews might be planning to protect themselves by these walls against the Persian army. The Samaritans therefore wrote to Artaxerxes, pointing out that the Jews had once controlled large sections of the Fertile Crescent from Jerusalem and had a bad record as rebels against the Assyrians and Babylonians who had preceded the Persians. And, as the Bible says,

> Ezra 4:7. . . . *the letter was written in the Syrian tongue* . . .

In fact, in the original version of the Book of Ezra, this letter is quoted in Aramaic (Syrian).

Aramaic is a Semitic dialect, closely related to Hebrew but sufficiently different so that a person understanding one would have trouble understanding the other. The relationship is perhaps like that of German to Dutch, or French to Spanish.

Aramaic was more widely spread than Hebrew. At the time of the Exodus, the Aramaean tribes had drifted not only into Syria (Aram) but into many of the regions of the Fertile Crescent, including Babylonia. It followed that knowledge of Aramaic came to be widespread through the area. The Aramaeans prospered as merchants, traveled widely, and their language became a kind of lingua franca, a language in which most educated people could manage to make themselves understood, even though one might not understand the native language of the other.

Thus, at the time the Assyrians under Sennacherib were besieging Jerusalem, Assyrian emissaries shouted propaganda messages in Hebrew from outside the walls in order to dishearten the defenders. The Judean emissaries, hoping to stop this, asked humbly:

> 2 Kings 18:26. . . . *Speak, I pray thee . . . in the Syrian language; for we understand it . . .*

Both Assyrians and Judeans could meet on the common ground of the Aramaic tongue.

Presumably, the Jews in Babylon found it easy to get along with Aramaic until they learned Babylonian, so that Hebrew began to be almost foreign to them (as it is to most Jews outside Israel today). Furthermore, the mixed population in what had once been Israel and Judah probably found themselves drifting to Aramaic.

For that reason certain books written late in Biblical times, sections of the Book of Daniel in particular, were written in Aramaic. And in New Testament times, Aramaic was the language of the Jewish people generally. Thus, Jesus spoke in Aramaic rather than in Hebrew.

Asnapper

In the course of this letter in Aramaic, the original petitioners describe themselves by the cities they had inhabited before the Assyrian resettlement of peoples. The list concludes:

> Ezra 4:10. *And the rest of the nations whom the great and noble Asnapper brought over, and set in the cities of Samaria . . .*

Clearly, Asnapper must refer to some important Assyrian monarch who ruled after the destruction of the kingdom of Israel. There were four of these and the first three—Sargon, Sennacherib, and Esarhaddon—are mentioned by name in the Bible so that Asnapper is not likely to be one of them. That leaves the fourth—Asshurbanipal (see page 390)—and it is generally accepted that this is who is meant by Asnapper.

Achmetha

With the record of Samaritan obstructionism through the century following Cyrus's decree made clear, the story goes back to the first decades of work. Apparently Samaritan hostility at the start had interrupted work on the Temple itself:

> Ezra 4:24. *Then ceased the work of the house of God . . . unto the second year of the reign of Darius . . .*

The work was still in a state of suspended animation in 520 B.C., in other words, eighteen years after Cyrus's original edict. Under the verbal lash of enthusiasts such as Haggai and Zechariah, work started again:

> Ezra 5:2. *Then rose up Zerubbabel . . . and Jeshua . . . and began to build the house of God . . .*

But now there were new Persian governors over the area and some question arose as to what structure was being erected and by what right. The Jews referred to the edict under Cyrus, but Cyrus was dead, as was his successor, and the confusion of a civil war had just taken place. The matter had to be referred to Darius himself, and the records were successfully searched:

> Ezra 6:2. *And there was found at Achmetha, in the palace that is in the province of the Medes, a roll, and therein was a record . . .*

Achmetha is about 280 miles northeast of Babylon. Its name in the language of its ancient inhabitants was Hangmatana, which became Ecbatana to the Greeks and Hamadan to the modern inhabitants. Hamadan is now part of modern Iran, 180 miles west of the Iranian capital, Teheran, and possessing a population of over one hundred thousand.

Ecbatana, to use its most familiar ancient name, had its greatest political importance in the half century following the fall of Nineveh, for it was then the capital of the Median Empire. Cyrus took it in 550 B.C. and it lost its status as capital in favor of cities in Persia itself. However, its location among the mountains made it a good place for a summer residence so that it continued to serve as a kind of subsidiary royal center.

Darius, having located the decree, confirmed it, and ordered his local officials in Judea to hasten and encourage the building.

> Ezra 6:15. *And this house* [the Temple] *was finished . . . in the sixth year of the reign of Darius the king.*

Since Darius became king in 521 B.C. and that year counts as his first, the Temple was completed in 516 B.C. just twenty-two years after Cyrus's decree and just seventy years after the Temple had been destroyed by Nebuchadnezzar. It is certainly tempting to feel that the seventy years of exile referred to by Jeremiah can be interpreted as applying not to the physical exile of the Jews in Babylon so much as to their spiritual exile from the Temple.

Sometimes the rebuilt Temple is called the "second Temple." The first had endured from 923 to 586 B.C.—a stretch of 337 years. The second Temple was to do better. It was to endure 586 years until its destruction by the Romans in A.D. 70.

Ezra

There is now a lapse of at least half a century and Ezra appears on the scene. The name is a shortened form of Azariah, a common name carried by some two dozen people mentioned in the Bible, including that king of Judah who is also known by the throne name of Uzziah.

> Ezra 7:6. . . . *Ezra went up from Babylon* . . .
> Ezra 7:7. . . . *in the seventh year of Artaxerxes the king.*

If we assume that it is Artaxerxes I who is meant, he came to the throne in 465 B.C. and his seventh year would be 459–58 B.C. That would be the year, then, of Ezra's visit to Jerusalem.

If Ezra is considered the Chronicler, a point in favor is the fact that on introducing himself he proudly gives his pedigree, tracing it back to Aaron (but skipping a number of generations in doing so). He also describes his function:

> Ezra 7:6. . . . *he [Ezra] was a ready scribe in the law of Moses* . . .

A scribe is "one who writes," a secretary; and it was precisely during the Exile that scribes became particularly important. The legal, theological, and historical traditions of the Jews had to be reduced to writing and prepared in many copies now that the people were scattered; otherwise isolated groups would forget.

Ezra was one of the groups who copied and studied the books

and since these books contained the Jewish ritual law, he (and other scribes, too) was the equivalent of what we might today call a lawyer.

There is an important difference between a prophet and a scribe. A prophet speaks from inspiration and not only can, but often does, break new ground. A scribe is bound to the letter and, in fact, has a vested interest in the preservation of the letter since only by its exact knowledge does he fulfill his function. There is for that reason a certain aridity about scribes, a certain lack of flexibility which, in periods of stress and emergency, keeps them from moving with the times and forces them into what may prove unpopular and even untenable positions. In the New Testament, scribes are usually mentioned with disapproval.

One difficulty arises concerning the date 458 B.C. given above as the year of Ezra's arrival in Jerusalem. If Ezra is indeed the Chronicler then it might seem he would have to be alive at least as late as 400 B.C. since some of the genealogies in 1 Chronicles stretch that far. Yet Ezra had already obtained a reputation by the time of his visit to Jerusalem and could not have been a young man. If mature in in 458 B.C., could he still be alive in 400 B.C.?

It is possible, of course, that he might have written the history before 400 B.C. and that a disciple added the verses required to bring it up to date, so to speak. On the other hand, Ezra may have come to Jerusalem considerably later than 458 B.C.

Artaxerxes I was not the only king of his name to rule over Persia. After the death of Artaxerxes I in 424 B.C., one of his sons ruled under the name of Xerxes II and then another as Darius II. In 404 B.C., Darius II died, and his son, Artaxerxes II, came to the throne. If it is this second Artaxerxes to whom Ezra refers in 7:7, then Ezra came to Jerusalem in 398 B.C.

Unfortunately, there is no easy way of determining from the Biblical account which Artaxerxes is meant and of deciding whether Ezra arrived in 458 or 398 B.C.

Hattush

One possible hint lies with one of the heads of the families that are described as coming to Jerusalem with Ezra:

Ezra 8:2. . . . *of the sons of David; Hattush.*

Hattush is listed in the Davidic genealogy in the third chapter of 1 Chronicles:

> 1 Chronicles 3:19. . . . *and the sons of Zerubbabel; Meshullam and Hananiah* . . .
>
> . . . .
>
> 1 Chronicles 3:21. *And the sons of Hananiah . . . Shechaniah.*
> 1 Chronicles 3:22. *And the sons of Shechaniah; Shemaiah; and the sons of Shemaiah; Hattush* . . .

Hattush was thus the great-great-grandson of Zerubbabel, and a member of the twenty-fourth generation after David.

According to the Anchor Bible, Hattush's younger brother Neariah has an estimated birth year of 470 B.C. (see page 405). We might suppose then that Hattush was born in 475 B.C. If, then, Ezra had come to Jerusalem in 458 B.C., Hattush would have been seventeen years old; a fine age for the trip, but would he then be considered among those described by Ezra as:

> Ezra 8:1. *These are now the chief of their fathers* . . .

or, to use the phraseology of the Revised Standard Version, "These are the heads of their fathers' houses . . ."?

Surely a seventeen-year-old boy would scarcely be the head of the house of David. There would very likely be older members to serve that function.

Yet if Ezra had come to Jerusalem in 398 B.C., Hattush would be seventy-seven years old and would make a good patriarchal head of the royal house, but is it likely that a man of that age would decide to make the arduous trip to Jerusalem?

So one still stands irresolute as to which of the two dates to choose.

Regardless of the date, though, the line of David had lost its political significance. Even the nominal sovereignty of a Sheshbazzar or a Zerubbabel was gone. The Jewish community was become a theocracy and when Ezra arrived it was he, the scribe, and not Hattush, the prince, who was in charge.

He found that in the time that had elapsed since the rebuilding of the Temple, there had been much intermarrying between the returnees and those who had been in the land all along. Horrified, Ezra demanded and enforced the end of such marriages and the ejection of foreign wives and their children from the community.

This was thought of at the time as the only sure way in which Judaism could be preserved in pure form. Intermarriage was bound to be followed by a dilution of social custom and a distortion of ritual, it seemed. This may be so, in fact, but to those of us who now live in a pluralistic society and try to measure up to its ideals, Ezra's policy seems inhumane, narrow, and wrong. That there were those among the Jews themselves who also thought so, is evidenced by the fact that at about this time the beautiful little Book of Ruth was written (see page 265) and proved so popular that it was included in the Hebrew Bible despite the fact that its heroine was a Moabitess.

16. NEHEMIAH

SHUSHAN • SANBALLAT THE HORONITE • ELIASHIB • ASHDODITES • EZRA •
1 ESDRAS

Shushan

The events of the next book also deal with the period of the
restoration of the Temple and it begins at once with the identity of
the chief character:

> Nehemiah 1:1. *The words of Nehemiah* . . .

from which the name of the book is derived. Much of the book consists of the memoirs of Nehemiah, presumably quoted and edited into
a larger whole by the Chronicler (or Ezra, if that be he).

The date of the beginning of the events of the book is also given;
twice, in fact:

> Nehemiah 1:2. . . . *in the twentieth year, as I was in Shushan
> the palace* . . .

and, again:

> Nehemiah 2:1. . . . *in the twentieth year of Artaxerxes the
> king* . . .

If the king is Artaxerxes I, then his twentieth year is 446–45 B.C.;
if Artaxerxes II, it is 385–84 B.C. The second date is too late if we
are to accept the fact that the Chronicler was writing in 400 B.C.
Therefore we can place ourselves in the year 445 B.C., some seventy
years after the completion of the second Temple.

Jerusalem at the Time of Nehemiah

Nehemiah held an honorable post as cupbearer to the Persian king, which gave him the chance to talk to him personally:

Nehemiah 2:1. . . . *I took up the wine, and gave it unto the king . . .*

and such conversations could, apparently, take place in the presence of the queen:

Nehemiah 2:6. *And the king said unto me, (the queen also sitting by him) . . .*

Personal service in the presence of the queen would seem to mean, in an eastern court of the time, that Nehemiah was a eunuch. The Bible does not, however, make that clear.

Shushan, the scene in which we first find Nehemiah, is better known to us by the Greek version of its name, Susa. Susa is far more ancient than the Persian kingdom, since it was in its earliest history the capital of the kingdom of Elam, which lay northeast of Babylonia and northwest of Fars, the Persian homeland.

Elam was a rival of Babylonia even before the time of Abraham. It was conquered by Sargon of Agade (see page 50) and by Hammurabi (see page 69). When Babylon was weak, however, Elam had occasional periods of domination. Chedorlaomer (see page 68) was a king of Elam, for instance.

The most dramatic period of Elam's history, however, came in the time of Assyrian domination. Just as Egypt sought to save itself from Assyria by encouraging revolts against that land in Judah, Israel, and Syria, so Elam encouraged revolts in Babylon. Merodach-baladan (see page 387) managed to maintain himself against Assyria only with Elamite support. It was probably only because Assyria had its hands continually full with Elam that Judah managed to hang on to a nominal independence and survive to see Assyria destroyed.

Elam did not have Judah's good fortune, however. It did not survive. It fought Assyria in campaign after campaign for a century, coming back after defeat, always resolute, always defiant. It is a great epic of its sort, but because there is no Elamite literature that survives today that can compare with the historical books of the Bible, or with the writings of the Greeks, the Elamite struggle is carried on in soundless darkness and is all but vanished from modern consciousness. Finally, in 640 B.C., after several campaigns by Asshurbanipal, Elam was utterly destroyed and devastated and Susa was razed to the ground.

The best of what remained of the Elamite population was deported and some of them must have been added to the Samaritans for among the people represented by the letter to Artaxerxes (see page 446) are:

> Ezra 4:9. . . . the Susanchites . . . and the Elamites,
> Ezra 4:10. . . . whom . . . Asnapper brought over, and set in the cities of Samaria . . .

Here is the additional reason for considering Asnapper to be Asshurbanipal.

Elam played no further role in history but it had its posthumous revenge. The effort to crush Elam cost the last bit of strength Assyria could muster. It was exhausted and within a generation it fell before the combined might of the Chaldeans and the Medes, and was wiped out every bit as thoroughly as Elam had been.

Meanwhile, the Persians were able to expand northwestward from Fars into Elam, thereafter generally called Susiana, and make it an integral part of Persia. Susa was rebuilt by Darius I and made into the winter capital of the empire. Its site (in what is now southwestern Iran) is marked only by ruins and by a little village named Shush.

Sanballat the Horonite

At the time that the Book of Nehemiah opens, a party of Jews had arrived in Susa. Their business is not described but one can reasonably speculate that it might have been in connection with the letter to Artaxerxes sent by the Samaritans. The Jews of Jerusalem feared its consequences and might well have sent a deputation to Artaxerxes to present their own case. In doing so, they would have approached Nehemiah, as a Jew who had access to the ear of the king.

They informed Nehemiah that conditions in Jerusalem were bad and that the walls about the city had been destroyed, presumably by Samaritan enemies supported by the local Persian officials.

After several months, Nehemiah succeeded in approaching Artaxerxes and in persuading him to grant permission for the walls to be built and for Nehemiah to travel to Jerusalem to oversee the matter. According to the later Jewish historian Josephus, Nehemiah did not arrive in Jerusalem till 440 B.C.

In Jerusalem, Nehemiah faced opposition from the local governors. After he had surveyed the state of the walls, he proposed an immediate drive to rebuild them:

> Nehemiah 2:19. *But when Sanballat the Horonite, and Tobiah . . . the Ammonite, and Geshem the Arabian, heard it, they . . . said . . . will ye rebel against the king?*

Sanballat bears a Babylonian name (Sin-uballit, which means "Sin [the moon-goddess] has given life"). This does not necessarily mean that he was a moon-goddess worshiper, since he may just have been using a popular name of the period, just as a modern American might have Hannibal as a first name without any intention of showing himself to be a worshiper of the Carthaginian Baal. As a Horonite, Sanballat was a native of Beth-horon, a town ten miles northwest of Jerusalem. Presumably he was a Samaritan and perhaps even the local governor of Samaria.

Tobiah has a Hebrew name and is described, later in the book, as being connected to various Jews by marriage. He is called an Ammonite probably because he was the local governor of districts in the Trans-Jordan. It is quite likely that he was a Yahvist but was certainly not an orthodox Jew as orthodoxy was then viewed. Either he was a Samaritan, or a Jew who was in sympathy with the Samaritans.

Geshem the Arabian apparently was a Nabataean, a member of an Arabic tribe that now appears on the Biblical horizon. After the destruction of the kingdom of Judah, the Edomites moved northward into Judah and behind them came the Nabataeans, who occupied what had previously been Edom. Their capital was established at Petra, a city which had elaborate house and temple fronts carved out of the pink cliffside. It attained prosperity because it was an important crossing point for various trade routes. Its site is often equated with the Edomite city of Selah, which is mentioned in the Bible in connection with Amaziah's reconquest of Edom (see page 369):

2 Kings 14:7. He [Amaziah] ... took Selah by war ...

In the third century B.C. the Nabataeans were to form a prosperous kingdom. At the time the Romans were crushing the Jewish rebellion in A.D. 68, they also annexed the Nabataean kingdom. It became the province of Arabia Petraea. Nearly two centuries later, the province even gave an emperor to Rome, Philip "the Arabian."

Eliashib

The building of the walls began, with the High Priest initiating the proceedings:

Nehemiah 3:1. Then Eliashib the high priest rose up with his ... priests, and they builded the sheep gate ...

Eliashib continues the line of priests descending from Zadok, the High Priest under Solomon, for he is the grandson of Jeshua who returned with Zerubbabel (see page 440):

Nehemiah 12:10. And Jeshua begat Joiakim, Joiakim also begat Eliashib ...

The walls as built enclosed a tiny city indeed; the "city of David" in the south (that is, the rocky heights of Zion on which David had built his palace six centuries before) and the Temple and its environs to the north. The entire enclosure may have been seven modern city blocks long and an average of two city blocks wide.

Ashdodites

The Samaritans and other surrounding nations, annoyed at the progress of the wall, were prepared to take mob action against it.

In a very real sense, the little Judean enclave at Jerusalem was surrounded. There were Samaritans under Sanballat to the north; the Trans-Jordanian tribes under Tobiah to the east, and the Nabataeans under Geshem to the south. To complete the circle there was also an enemy to the west:

> Nehemiah 4:7. . . . *the Arabians, and the Ammonites, and the Ashdodites . . . were very wroth.*

The Ashdodites refer, in a narrow sense, to the inhabitants of the Philistine city of Ashdod (see page 221). The phrase has come to mean more than that in post-Exilic times.

The Philistines had been subdued by David and had formed part of the united kingdom first and then, later, of the kingdom of Judah, but they had continued to maintain their cultural identity. At various times they rebelled but under Uzziah they were reduced to submission again:

> 2 Chronicles 26:6. And he [Uzziah] . . . *warred against the Philistines, and brake down the wall of Gath . . . and the wall of Ashdod . . .*

However, the Philistines suffered with Judah in the days of Assyrian ascendance, for in 711 B.C.:

> Isaiah 20:1. . . . *Sargon the king of Assyria . . . fought against Ashdod and took it.*

The Assyrian governor who thenceforth ruled Philistine territory had his seat at Ashdod. The term "Ashdodite" came, therefore, to mean the Philistines generally, so that Nehemiah was facing the Philistines as seven centuries before Samson had faced them.

Nehemiah's answer was a resolute defense. Half the Jews built the walls and half patrolled the environs of the city, armed and ready for war. The builders themselves wore swords and the atmosphere was very much like that in the frontier villages of modern Israel, where farmers plow their fields with rifles strapped to their backs.

Presumably, the Samaritans were not ready to make actual war. That would get them in trouble with Persia since Nehemiah had the royal permission for the work. Since Nehemiah refused to be thwarted by the mere war of nerves involved in continuing threats and menacing scowls, the raising of the walls continued and, according to Josephus, they were completed in 437 B.C.

Nehemiah also labored to solve the economic difficulties of the tiny community and mentions a date still later, for at one point he says:

Nehemiah 6:14. . . . *from the time that I was appointed . . . governor . . . from the twentieth year even unto the two and thirtieth year of Artaxerxes . . .*

You might think that this ought to settle which of the Artaxerxes Nehemiah worked under since surely both would not have reigned for the comparatively long time of thirty-two years. However, through a coincidence, Artaxerxes I reigned forty-one years and Artaxerxes II reigned forty-six years. If, however, we still consider the king to have been Artaxerxes I, the year that Nehemiah now mentions as the thirty-second of the king is 433 B.C.

Ezra

Chapters 8, 9, and 10 of Nehemiah suddenly return to Ezra, who is described as reading to the population of Jerusalem out of the sacred writings:

Nehemiah 8:1. *And all the people gathered themselves together . . . and they spake unto Ezra the scribe to bring the book of the law of Moses . . .*

Nehemiah 8:2. *And Ezra . . . brought the law before the congregation . . .*

Nehemiah 8:3. *And he read therein . . . before the men and the women . . .*

Ezra then led a religious reform which was different from all those that had preceded. Now there was no longer merely the spoken word of a prophet, or even just the book found in the Temple in Josiah's time (which may have possessed only dubious authority in the eyes of many of the men of the time). There was now the whole body of the Torah, the first five books of the Bible, written, expounded, and interpreted by the scribes so that all men might now study, understand, and observe the very letter of the law.

The presence of the written law (to which the prophetic books and the "Writings" were later added to form the Bible) made it impossible for the Jews ever again to waver from Judaism. The Jews kept the faith thereafter, through exiles far more widespread, prolonged, and inhumanly cruel than that visited upon them by Nebuchadnezzar.

This episode of the reading of the law brings up once again the problem of the chronology of Ezra. Ezra appears in two places; first at the end of the Book of Ezra, where he breaks up the mixed marriages, and second at the end of the Book of Nehemiah, where he leads the religious reform. It would seem that these two sections belong together; that the breakup of the mixed marriages ought to be followed at once by the religious reform and that the interposition of the Nehemiah chapters is artificial.

The question then is whether the Ezra story, as a whole, comes before Nehemiah or after Nehemiah, and this again depends on which Artaxerxes is referred to in Ezra 7:7 (see page 449). If Nehemiah's work in Jerusalem took place from 445 to 433 B.C., then Ezra's work comes first if he really came to Jerusalem in 458 B.C. in the seventh year of Artaxerxes I. It comes afterward, on the other hand, if he came to Jerusalem in 398 B.C. in the seventh year of Artaxerxes II.

One additional verse can now be called upon to help make the decision. When Ezra arrived in Jerusalem and was shocked to discover the prevalence of mixed marriages:

> Ezra 10:6. *Then Ezra rose up . . . and went into the chamber of Johanan the son of Eliashib: and . . . did eat no bread, nor drink water: for he mourned . . .*

Is it possible that the Eliashib mentioned here is the Eliashib who was High Priest in Nehemiah's time (see pag 457)? Eliashib did have a son or grandson named Johanan:

Nehemiah 12:22. *The Levites in the days of Eliashib, Joiada, and Johanan* . . .

What's more, Johanan did serve as High Priest. The Jewish colony in Elephantine, a city in upper Egypt, addressed letters to him dated 408 B.C. and he is further mentioned in Josephus.

If the Johanan of Ezra 10:6 is this Johanan, it would be very strong evidence in favor of Ezra's arrival in Jerusalem in 398 B.C. in the seventh year of Artaxerxes II.

And yet not all doubt is removed. Neither Johanan nor Eliashib is described here as a High Priest or even as a priest and it is possible (though perhaps not likely) that Ezra's host for the night was just an ordinary individual with the increasingly common name of Johanan.

1 Esdras

The tale told by the Chronicler concerning the destruction and rebuilding of the Temple is told over again in another book, also attributed to Ezra. This one is considered apocryphal, however, and to distinguish it from the canonical Book of Ezra, use is made of the Greek equivalent of the name and it is called 1 Esdras (for there is another apocryphal book called 2 Esdras). To those who adhere to the Catholic system of referring to the Books of Ezra and Nehemiah as 1 Esdras and 2 Esdras, the apocryphal books are 3 Esdras and 4 Esdras.

Both 1 and 2 Esdras were included in some Greek versions of the Bible. At the Council of Trent in 1546, however, the Catholic Church decided officially which books it would consider canonical and these did not include the Prayer of Manasses (see page 425) or either of the Esdras books. These are apocryphal to Catholics as well as to Jews and Protestants.

1 Esdras was written no earlier than 150 B.C. and perhaps considerably later (though not later than A.D. 50 since Josephus refers to it). In general, 1 Esdras deviates from Ezra-Nehemiah only in unimportant details and its chief point of interest lies in the retelling of an old fable.

The fable is told as taking place in the reign of Darius, who, after a feast, retired to sleep. Three of his bodyguard pass the time by each stating what he thinks is the strongest. The first chooses wine, the second the king, and the third, women.

(In the original tale, it would have made more sense if the first chose the king—the obvious choice—the second wine, and the third women. The second can then point out that even the king succumbs to wine, and the third that even the king respects his mother and loves his wife. Both second and third are correct but since the third would undoubtedly please the women of the court he would be the sure winner.)

In 1 Esdras, the story is modified to suit the writer's purposes. The third guardsman chooses more than merely women:

1 Esdras 3:12. *The third wrote, Women are strongest: but above all things Truth beareth away the victory.*

Darius is told of the contest, is amused, and demands that each guardsman defend his point of view before the open court. The first and second speak in favor of wine and the king. Then the third guardsman is, for the first time, identified:

1 Esdras 4:13. *Then the third, who had spoken of women, and of the truth, (this was Zorobabel) began to speak.*

(Since the apocryphal books appear in the Greek and not in the Hebrew, proper names are given closer to the Greek than the Hebrew forms in the King James Version—unlike the situation in connection with the canonical books. Hence we have Zorobabel rather than Zerubbabel.)

Zerubbabel speaks of women, as in the old fable, but then launches into an impressive encomium on truth, ending:

1 Esdras 4:40. . . . *Blessed be the God of truth.*
1 Esdras 4:41. . . . *And all the people then shouted, and said, Great is Truth, and mighty above all things.*

Since Zerubbabel had won, Darius offered to grant him whatever he might wish, and Zerubbabel immediately asked him to confirm Cyrus's decree that the Temple be rebuilt. Thus, this fable is tied in with Jewish history.

It is unlikely in the extreme that anything like this ever happened, but it is a pretty story.

17. ESTHER

AHASUERUS · INDIA · VASHTI · MORDECAI · HAMAN · PUR · ZERESH · THE REST OF ESTHER

Ahasuerus

Following the historical books comes what can only be described as a piece of historical fiction, the Book of Esther.

Esther does not have the gentle charm of the Book of Ruth, the earlier book that seems to have fictional elements. It is, instead, a savage book. The Book of Esther is, in fact, the one book of the Bible in which the word "God" does not occur.

Esther may have been written as late as 130 B.C. and it breathes the air of nationalism one would expect of that period in which the Jews were finally living in an independent kingdom again after having undergone a period of savage persecution. It is probably the chauvinistic nationalism of the book that made it so popular among Jews as to force its inclusion in the Biblical canon.

The book begins by placing itself in time.

Esther 1:1. *Now it came to pass in the days of Ahasuerus* . . .

Ahasuerus is usually identified with Xerxes I (see page 445), who reigned from 486 to 465 B.C. At this period the Persian Empire was still apparently at the peak of its power, as it had been under Darius, but the downhill slide was already beginning. Xerxes is best known to history in connection with his great expedition against Greece, which failed so miserably.

The Persian Empire

India

A good indication of the late date of publication of the book is the fact that it is not enough to mention Ahasuerus. The monarch must be identified:

> Esther 1:1. . . . (this is Ahasuerus which reigned, from India even unto Ethiopia, over an hundred and seven and twenty provinces:)

This describes, accurately enough, the wide extent of the territory of the Persian Empire at its height. The verse is also remarkable for being the one place (except for a similar expression in another verse later in this same book) where India is mentioned in the Bible.

Nor can there be any doubt that the Hebrew word used in this place, "Hoddu," can mean anything but India. Not only did Ahasuerus (Xerxes) actually rule from Ethiopia to India, but the words "Hoddu" and "India" come from the same source.

Indian civilization dates far back indeed; farther back than modern archaeologists suspected early in this century. Since 1920, ruins along the Indus River have been excavated, yielding traces of unexpectedly large and well-planned cities near the sites of villages now known as Harappa and Mohenjo-Daro; cities that might date as far back as 3300 B.C. This Indus civilization was one of the three ancient ones of the dawn of city building, for it was contemporaneous with the Sumerian culture (see page 30) and with the Egyptian Old Kingdom (see page 63).

About 1200 B.C., the Indus valley was invaded by people whom we call "Aryans." They spoke an early form of the Indo-European group of languages, Sanskrit, so that one sometimes speaks of that group as the "Aryan languages." They came from what is now called Iran, the nation which lies to the west of the Indus valley. Indeed, Iran (and Iraq, too) are forms of the word "Aryan."

Aryan invasion came in the era in which there were vast movements of peoples everywhere, and it was part of the same unsettlement that brought the Philistines and Hebrews into Canaan.

What the name of the Indus River was before the Aryans came, we don't know. The Aryans, however, called it "Sindhu," which, in Sanskrit, simply means "river." The name was applied to the region traversed by the river and the area about the mouth of the river is still called "Sind."

Persia invaded the region of the Indus about 500 B.C. in the reign of Darius I. In Persian, Sind became "Hind" or "Hindu." The name gradually spread from the Indus valley through all the vast subcontinent, which became "Hindustan" ("the land of Hind"). We still speak of the natives as "Hindus," their religion as "Hinduism," and their chief language as "Hindi."

The Jews adopted the Persian word with a little distortion and "Hindu" became "Hoddu."

The Greeks also adopted the Persian word with a different sort of distortion and "Hindu" became "Indos." From this comes the English version of "Indus" for the river and "India" for the subcontinent, these being the Latin forms.

Ironically enough, in 1947, when the Indian subcontinent achieved independence, it was broken into two nations, and the area about the Indus River, the *original* India, lost the name and is now called Pakistan. It is the rest of the region that is called India.

Only from the time of Darius, to shortly after the death of Alexander the Great—500 to 300 B.C.—were the Indus valley and the Jordan valley under the control of a single political system. Before that period India was beyond the Biblical horizon and after that period it receded again (though never completely) until A.D. 1500, when Western civilization again impinged upon it, this time permanently.

Vashti

The tale of the Book of Esther begins in the third year of the reign of Ahasuerus (484 B.C.) with a tremendously elaborate feast in Shushan, a feast lasting half a year. (This was at a time when the real Xerxes had just crushed a rebellion in Egypt and another in Babylon, and was preparing a tremendous army for the ill-fated invasion of Greece.) At the end of the great feast, a more intimate, week-long feast for the officials of the kingdom was initiated.

> Esther 1:9. Also Vashti the queen made a feast for the women in the royal house . . .

Vashti is unknown to history and, indeed, goes unmentioned in the Bible outside the Book of Esther. Xerxes' real wife during the early portion of his reign was Amestris, the daughter of a Persian general, if we go by Herodotus.

Yet Vashti is not a purely made-up name. It has a definite source, the same source from which the names of all the chief characters of the book (aside from Ahasuerus) are drawn. This source is simply Babylonian mythology. Vashti is the name of an Elamite goddess.

Mordecai

Toward the end of this final feast, when Ahasuerus was quite drunk, he ordered Vashti to come to him in order that he might display her beauty. Vashti refused this indignity and Ahasuerus, in a fit of anger, had her deposed as queen. He then ordered that beautiful women be gathered together in order that out of them he might pick another queen.

Esther 2:5. *Now in Shushan the palace there was a certain Jew, whose name was Mordecai . . .*

Esther 2:6. *Who had been carried away from Jerusalem . . . with Jeconiah . . . whom Nebuchadnezzar . . . had carried away.*

Esther 2:7. *And he brought up Hadassah, that is, Esther, his uncle's daughter . . .*

Mordecai is here described as having been carried off with Jeconiah (Jehoiachin; see page 395), an event that took place in 597 B.C., and as still being alive in 484 B.C. This would imply that Mordecai, and Esther too, were centenarians at the time of this tale. This indicates the author of the book, who is living three and a half centuries after the events he describes, is *not* following ancient records but is inventing things and is uncertain of his chronology.

The name Mordecai is not Hebrew and, instead, seems to be suspiciously like that of the chief god of the Babylonians, Marduk, which, in its Hebrew form, is Merodach. As for Esther (the official throne name that came to be carried by Mordecai's cousin), that is even more clearly a form of Ishtar, the chief Babylonian goddess. Indeed, the Aramaic version of that goddess's name is indeed Esther. The name Hadassah, by which Esther was originally known within the family, is

closely related to a Babylonian word for "bride," which is used as a title
for Ishtar. And in Babylonian mythology Marduk and Ishtar are cousins, as are Mordecai and Esther in the Book of Esther.

It is very tempting to suppose that the writer of Esther is adapting
Babylonian mythology into a supposedly historical tale designed to
please the ears of his readers.

Be that as it may, the tale goes on to relate that Esther was included
among the maidens brought to Ahasuerus and that he preferred her
to the others and made her his queen.

> Esther 2:16. So Esther was taken unto king Ahasuerus . . . in the
> seventh year of his reign.
> Esther 2:17. And the king . . . made her queen instead of Vashti.

According to this tale, then, Esther became queen in 480 B.C., the
year of the battle of Salamis. To be sure, the name Esther is rather like
the name of Xerxes' queen, Amestris, but there is nothing about the
known facts concerning Amestris that in any way resembles what is
told in this book concerning Esther.

At the advice of her cousin Mordecai, Esther does not tell the king
that she is Jewish, but Mordecai remains in clandestine touch with her.
This turns out to be useful for when Mordecai learns of a palace intrigue against Ahasuerus, he informs Esther, who, in turn, warns the
king. The intriguers are hanged and Mordecai is officially commended
in the records.

Haman

Now the chief villain appears:

> Esther 3:1. After these things did king Ahasuerus promote Haman
> the son of Hammedatha the Agagite, and advanced him . . . above
> all the princes . . .

Haman is made the equivalent of prime minister, in other words. As
prime minister of Ahasuerus (Xerxes), one would expect that the
Greeks would have heard of him. He is not to be found in Herodotus,
however, or in any of the other Greek historians, nor is anyone to be
found with any similar name.

On the other hand, the chief male deity of the Elamites was named Hamman.

This introduces an interesting speculation. In the centuries before the establishment of the Persian Empire, Elam was at intermittent war with whichever nation ruled the Tigris-Euphrates region to the north-west. The final round in the struggle came under Asshurbanipal, when the Assyrians once and for all destroyed Elam (see page 455).

In a sense then, Babylonia replaced Elam in the city of Susa during the final decades of the Assyrian Empire; and according to the thinking of the time, the Babylonian gods replaced the Elamite gods. The chief Babylonian god, Marduk, replaced the chief Elamite god, Hamman, and the chief Babylonian goddess, Ishtar, replaced the Elamite goddess, Vashti. This is similar to the events in the Book of Esther, in which Esther replaces Vashti as queen in Shushan (Susa), and, as is recounted later in the book, Mordecai replaces Haman as prime minister.

Haman is identified as the son of an "Agagite." There is no mention of this tribe in secular history or, indeed, anywhere in the Bible outside this book. However, Agag is the name given in the Bible to the king of the Amalekites who was captured by Saul and killed by Samuel.

> 1 Samuel 15:32. *Then said Samuel, Bring ye hither to me Agag the king of the Amalekites* . . .
>
> 1 Samuel 15:33. *. . . And Samuel hewed Agag in pieces* . . .

It is to be assumed, then, that Haman is being described as an Amalekite.

This would have special significance to the readers of the book for the Amalekites were considered prototypes of the enemies of Israel; and with the Amalekites the Bible predicted nothing but unrelenting war. It seemed reasonable that a remaining individual of that anti-Jewish tribe would now set himself about destroying the Jews.

Furthermore, Mordecai's ancestry was described upon his introduction:

> Esther 2:5. *. . . Mordecai, the son of Jair, the son of Shimei, the son of Kish, a Benjamite.*

He was of the tribe of Saul then, and possibly even a descendant of Saul, who had once defeated and captured the ancestor of Haman. Thus, the conflict in the Book of Esther would echo the conflict in the First Book of Samuel.

Pur

Haman's hatred of the Jews is goaded on by the fact that Mordecai refused to bow before him when all others showed him the respect due a prime minister. The reason for Mordecai's refusal is not given but the usual explanation is that he was unwilling to give to a mere human the kind of reverence due only to God.

Haman is then depicted as turning to some ritualistic device for determining a fortunate day for the forthcoming massacre of the Jews.

> Esther 3:7. . . . *in the twelfth year of king Ahasuerus, they cast Pur, that is, the lot . . .*

In other words, the writer of the Book of Esther equates "Pur" ("Purim" in the plural) with lots, possibly like the Urim and Thummim (see page 150) used in ancient Yahvistic rituals. Later on, the events recounted in this book are made the occasion for a commemorative feast which the author names Purim because of this. This feast is still celebrated by Jews to this day.

Actually, it is quite uncertain that Purim really means "lots," or what the origin of the festival might be.

There are suggestions that Purim might actually be a Babylonian spring festival which involved some mythic tale of the seasons involving Marduk and Ishtar. This festival was adopted by the Jews in Babylon, just as Jews in America are unable to resist the gigantic social pressure of the season and adopt the secular aspects of the Christmas celebrations. It may have been one of the purposes of the writer of the Book of Esther to revise the Babylonian myth into Jewish history and convert a pagan festival into a patriotic Jewish observance.

Having established the day of reckoning (which turns out to be nearly a year in the future), Haman persuades Ahasuerus to give him carte blanche to destroy the Jews, who, Haman assures the king, do not consider themselves bound by the king's laws and are therefore rebels. Ahasuerus allows Haman his way.

Zeresh

Mordecai at once appeals to Esther to use her influence with the king to nullify the decree. Esther begins by requesting that Ahasuerus and Haman attend a banquet she will give. They agree and Haman in particular is in high spirits at this mark of royal favor.

Yet on seeing Mordecai, who still refuses to bow to him, he is enraged and frustrated. When he returns home, he recounts all his good fortune to his wife and family but admits that it all means nothing as long as Mordecai lives.

Esther 5:14. *Then said Zeresh his wife . . . Let a gallows be made . . . that Mordecai may be hanged thereon: then go thou . . . unto the banquet . . .*

Now in Elamite mythology, the chief god, Hamman, has as his wife the goddess Kirisha. This is suspiciously similar to Zeresh and is another point in favor of the mythological inspiration of this book.

The night before the banquet, the king, sleepless, has the records read to him and learns of Mordecai's part in frustrating the palace plot. He therefore calls in Haman to ask his advice on the method of honoring a man who deserved great gratitude from the king. Haman, feeling it is himself who is in question, describes an elaborate ceremony which is then, to Haman's infinite disgust, applied to Mordecai.

Then, at the banquet, Esther reveals herself to be Jewish and demands the life of Haman. Ahasuerus grants her request and Haman is hanged on the very gallows he had designed for Mordecai. Mordecai is made prime minister in Haman's place.

The decree that the Jews be slaughtered could not be rescinded for, as the book relates, the laws of the Medes and Persians cannot be altered. However, the Jews are allowed to defend themselves and there is a kind of civil war in which the Jews are victorious. (These last events are completely implausible and there is no record of such a civil war anywhere outside this book.)

The Rest of Esther

The Book of Esther, as it stands, however pleasing it might be to nationalistic Jews, was troublesome to others, if only because it made no reference to God. For that reason, a number of additions were made to supply the lack, together with circumstantial quotes from supposed documents (quotations that are so unrealistic as to detract still further from the possible historicity of the book).

The Jewish scholars did not accept these additions but they appear in the Septuagint. These additions, called "The Rest of Esther" by the translators of the King James Version, therefore make up part of the Apocrypha.

Jerome, in translating the Bible into Latin, recognized the apocryphal nature of the additions but did not eliminate them. Instead, he removed them from their proper place in the book and put them at the end as a series of supplements. This arrangement is to be found in Catholic versions of English Bibles.

The Rest of Esther contains a verse which seems to give the name of the translator of part (or perhaps all) of the Book of Esther into Greek:

> Esther 11:1. *In the fourth year of the reign of Ptolemeus and Cleopatra, Dositheus . . . brought this epistle . . . which they said . . . Lysimachus the son of Ptolemeus, that was in Jerusalem, had interpreted . . .*

All the kings of Egypt from 305 to 44 B.C. (Macedonian in extraction) were named Ptolemaios, or Ptolemy in the English version. A very common name for the Egyptian queens at this time was Cleopatra. In 116 B.C. Ptolemy VIII came to the throne and ruled in conjunction with his mother, Cleopatra III. If this is the Ptolemy and Cleopatra intended, then the fourth year of their reign would be 113 B.C.

As for Lysimachus, he must be an Alexandrian Jew living in Jerusalem. The Alexandrian Jews at the time would frequently have Greek names as American Jews today frequently have American names. That his father's name was Ptolemy would not make him a prince, either. No doubt many men carried the name who were by no means part of the royal family.

The Rest of Esther goes on to talk of Mordecai's dreams, and of the details of the plot against the king which he foils. Mordecai's prayers, and Esther's, are quoted. (In his prayer, Mordecai explains that it is not out of pride that he refuses to bow to Haman, but in order that he might not give to man what ought only to be given to God.) In addition, two letters are quoted which purport to be official orders from Ahasuerus, the first ordering that the Jews be exterminated and the second permitting the Jews to defend themselves and to live under their own laws.

One oddity in the last letter is a strange accusation against Haman:

> Esther 16:10. *For Aman* [Haman], *a Macedonian . . . a stranger from the Persian blood . . .*

For Ahasuerus (Xerxes) to denounce Haman as a Macedonian is a clear anachronism. The time was to come, a century and a half after the incidents in Esther were supposed to have happened, when the Macedonian conqueror Alexander the Great was to destroy the Persian Empire and make it his own, but in Xerxes' time, Macedon was a kingdom under Persian domination, not dangerous to anybody.

Still, at the time Esther was written it was the Macedonian kings of the Seleucid Empire, and not the ancient and nearly forgotten Amalekites, who were the great enemies of the Jews, and this verse can be considered a thrust at them.

18. JOB

JOB · UZ · SATAN · TEMAN · ORION · THE PLEIADES · ARCTURUS · BUZ · MAZZAROTH · BEHEMOTH · LEVIATHAN

Job

The Book of Job, which follows Esther, is a philosophic drama dealing with the problem of good and evil. It is so little concerned with secular history that the question of whether it describes events that really happened does not really arise. Its religious and ethical message would be the same even if it is the fiction it seems to be.

No one can say exactly when the book might have been written. Most scholars seem to conclude that the book as we now have it is post-Exilic, and was composed sometime during the Persian period. It begins:

Job 1:1. *There was a man . . . whose name was Job . . .*

No genealogy is given for Job, and no connection with Biblical history is attempted. Perhaps none was needed at the time of writing, for Job seems to have been the hero of a well-known legend; a legend describing a good man of superhuman patience who bore up under great misfortune without ever losing his faith in God.

The original legend must be ancient (there is even a form of it existing in Babylonian literature) and the writer of the Biblical Book of Job includes it as a prose introduction and a prose ending to the book. In between that beginning and ending, however, he inserts his own deep poetic probing of the relationship between God and man, allowing it to be carried like rich cargo within the simple and sturdy vessel of the well-known Job legend.

The Great Sea

(Mediterranean Sea)

Sidon
Zarephath
MT. LEBANON
HITTITE EMPIRE
Damascus
Tyre
MT. HERMON
Laish (Dan)
BASHAN
KINGDOM OF OG
Accho
Hazor
Chinnereth
Karnaim
Ashtaroth
SEA OF CHINNERETH
Madon
Dor
CANAANITES
Edrei
Megiddo
Beth-shan
Pella
Ramoth-gilead
Tirzah
Jabesh-gilead
Shechem
Succoth
Jacob's Well
Penuel
JABBOK R.
Joppa
HIVITES
Jazer
Rabbath-ammon
Lod
Bethel
KINGDOM OF SIHON
Ai
Jericho
Gezer Gibeon
Jerusalem
Gilgal
Heshbon
AMMON
Ashdod
(Jebus, Salem)
Ashkelon
Bethlehem
Medeba
Gath
JEBUSITES
SALT SEA
Jahaz
Guza
(Azzah)
Lachish
Mamre
Dibon
Eglon
Debir
Kirjath-arba
Aroer
Gerar
(Hebron)
(DEAD SEA)
ARNON R.
GERAR R.
Beersheba
Arad
Ar
Raphia
BESOR R.
Kir-moab
MOAB
AMALEKITES
Hormah
KENITES
Rehoboth
Zoar
ZERED R.
RIVER OF EGYPT
WILDERNESS OF ZIN
Oboth
Kadesh-barnea
Punon
ARABAH
EDOM

0   Miles   25

Canaan Before the Conquest

There is one Biblical reference that seems to deal with the original Job legend. This is to be found in the writings of the prophet Ezekiel, who lived during the Exile and therefore, very likely, before the Book of Job was written. When Ezekiel quotes God's warning that He will destroy idolators, it is specified that evildoers will not escape because of the merits of the pious among them.

> Ezekiel 14:13. . . . when the land sinneth against me . . . then will I . . . cut off man and beast from it:
> Ezekiel 14:14. Though these three men, Noah, Daniel, and Job were in it, they should deliver but their own souls . . .

Uz

Job's genealogy may not be given, but his home is.

> Job 1:1. There was a man in the land of Uz, whose name was Job . . .
> . . . .
> Job 1:3. . . . this man was the greatest of all the men of the east.

At once the question arises: Where was Uz? As far as the essential point of the book is concerned, the question need not be asked, for the great problem dealt with in the Book of Job transcends time and space. But here we are devoting ourselves to the secular side of the Bible and the "land of Uz" must have had some significance to the original readers of the book. What was that significance?

The fact that Job is characterized as "the greatest of all the men of the east" would seem to imply that he was a wealthy sheik, dwelling to the east of Canaan on the border of the desert.

If, however, we turn back to the genealogical lists of Genesis, we find:

> Genesis 10:22. The children of Shem; . . . Aram.
> Genesis 10:23. And the children of Aram; Uz . . .

The names in these early genealogies stand for eponymous ancestors, and individuals are said to be related when the areas or tribes they represent are neighboring. If the individual Uz is said to be a son of

Aram, it is reasonable to suppose that the land of Uz is a district in Aram (that is, Syria) and that Uz is therefore north of Canaan. Indeed, Assyrian inscriptions speak of a district called "Ussai" in Syria.

Yet, on the other hand, the prophet Jeremiah at one point lists the kingdoms slated to meet God's wrath and works his way up the Mediterranean coast from Egypt to Phoenicia:

> Jeremiah 25:19. *Pharaoh king of Egypt* . . .
> Jeremiah 25:20. *. . . and all the kings of the land of Uz, and all the kings of the land of the Philistines* . . .

This would seem to place Uz between Egypt and Philistia and, therefore, to the south of Canaan.

An even clearer indication of this is to be found in a verse in the Book of Lamentations. In that book, the writer, bewailing the fate of Jerusalem after its destruction by Nebuchadnezzar, bursts out into a sarcastically bitter denunciation of Edom, which he pictures as rejoicing over Jerusalem's fall:

> Lamentations 4:21. *Rejoice and be glad, O daughter of Edom, that dwellest in the land of Uz* . . .

There are thus Biblical reasons for supposing Uz to be either east, north, or south of Canaan, and this is certainly an unsatisfactory state of affairs.

Still, when the descendants of Esau are given in Genesis, Uz crops up again among them:

> Genesis 36:28. *The children of Dishan are these; Uz* . . .

A few verses later on the rulers of Edom are listed:

> Genesis 36:31. *And these are the kings that reigned in the land of Edom before there reigned any king over* . . . *Israel.*
> Genesis 36:32. *. . . Bela the son of Beor reigned in Edom* . . .
> Genesis 36:33. *And Bela died and Jobab* . . . *reigned in his stead.*

Could Jobab have been Job? Could the writer of the book have viewed Job as a king in Edom while the Israelites were still struggling to establish themselves in Canaan? Certainly, the later rabbis seemed to think that Uz was in Edom and that Job was a wealthy Edomite who lived during the time when the Israelites were enslaved in Egypt.

(Because the story was placed at this time, rabbinic tradition had it that the Book of Job was written by Moses, something modern scholars do not accept, of course.)

Satan

With Job introduced, the scene switches to heaven:

> Job 1:6. . . . *there was a day when the sons of God came to present themselves before the Lord, and Satan came also among them.*

This mention of Satan, whose name is not to be found in any of the books based on pre-Exilic records, is one of the reasons for supposing the book to be post-Exilic.

The Persian influence is shown in the picture of God as the head of a numerous court of assisting spirits. The difference from the Persian view rests in the fact that Satan is not the coequal head of a band of evil spirits but is merely a single spirit, as much subject to God as are the others. Satan has, apparently, the important and useful role of testing human beings to see whether their faith in God is staunch, or merely superficial. In this role, he acts only with God's permission and only as far as God permits.

Teman

God praises Job's piety to Satan, who at once points out that it is easy for a wealthy and fortunate man to be grateful for the rewards he receives. God therefore gives Satan permission to visit Job with misfortune in order to demonstrate that Job will remain pious.

Job's flocks and goods are destroyed; his sons and daughters are killed; he himself is afflicted with boils. At no time, however, does Job allow any blasphemous expression to cross his lips. He remains pious and continues to praise God.

Three friends then come to Job:

> Job 2:11. . . . *Eliphaz the Temanite and Bildad the Shuhite and Zophar the Naamathite: . . . to mourn with him and to comfort him.*

Eliphaz the Temanite is certainly intended to be considered an Edomite:

> Genesis 36:4. *And Adah bare to Esau Eliphaz* . . .
> . . . .
> Genesis 36:11. *And the sons of Eliphaz were Teman* . . .

Teman (a word meaning "south" in Hebrew) seems to have been the name of a district in Edom (an alternate name for Esau; see page 93). In several places in the Bible, Teman is used as a poetic synonym for all of Edom. Thus, in the Book of Jeremiah, the prophet says:

> Jeremiah 49:7. *Concerning Edom, thus saith the Lord of hosts; Is wisdom no more in Teman?* . . .

If we say then "Eliphaz the Temanite," we might as well say "Eliphaz the southerner" or "Eliphaz the Edomite." Perhaps the writer even meant Eliphaz the son of Esau. In all likelihood, the original readers of the book took him to be either this Eliphaz or a near descendant of him.

Bildad the Shuhite is, apparently, a descendant of Shuah:

> Genesis 25:2. *And she* [Keturah] *bare him* [Abraham] . . . *Shuah.*

Abraham's sons by Keturah apparently serve as the eponymous ancestors for the various Arabian tribes, Midian being the best known. The Shuhites, Bildad among them, would be Arabians then, living to the south or southeast of Edom.

Zophar the Naamathite was an inhabitant of the town of Naamah. There was a town in Judah by that name but no one thinks that town was meant. Presumably, it was another town of that name farther to the south.

Even if the case of Zophar is omitted, the probable locations of Eliphaz and Bildad make it seem all the more likely that the writer viewed Job as dwelling south of Canaan and that he was probably considered an Edomite.

In the original story, the constancy of Job was rewarded by a return of his prosperity and a growth of new happiness—as is, indeed, recorded at the end of the book. Between the beginning just described and that ending, however, the writer has put in a series of speeches by Job and answers by his friends (plus a final answer by God) that hold the meat of the book. In these speeches, Job is anything but patient and uncomplaining, and seriously questions the justice of God. Nevertheless, this has not, for some reason, altered the common conception of Job as a patient, uncomplaining man.

Orion

Most of the brilliantly poetical give-and-take of the Book of Job involves ethical and theological questions not the concern of this volume. Yet amid the flow of metaphor some interesting material objects are mentioned. Most of the few specific astronomical references to be found in the Bible, for instance, are here in Job.

Job reasons that misfortunes have fallen upon him undeservedly and that God is acting as a capricious tyrant. He lists the great accomplishments of God, accomplishments which prove Him to be far beyond the reach of mere man and make His presumed tyranny impossible to challenge. Job includes among God's accomplishments:

> Job 9:9. . . . [God] *maketh Arcturus, Orion, and Pleiades, and the chambers of the south.*

The Hebrew word translated here as Orion is *kesil* which means "fool." How do we go from "fool" to "Orion"? Let's begin with Orion.

By all odds, the most spectacular constellation of the heavens, particularly in the winter when nights are longest and casual observation of the sky most likely, is Orion. No other constellation contains so many bright stars.

The seven brightest stars are arranged in a particularly suggestive manner. Two are on top, two on bottom, while the remaining three form a closely spaced line between. It is not very difficult to see in this arrangement a large man. The two upper stars represent the shoulders, the two lower stars the legs, and the three middle stars the waistline or belt. If fainter stars are added there are three stars in a vertical line suspended from the belt, making a kind of sword, and there are stars above one shoulder which can be pictured as representing an arm and a club. There are even stars beyond the other shoulder that can, without stretching matters too badly, represent some sort of shield.

It is almost inevitable, then, that the constellation be interpreted as representing either a giant warrior or a giant hunter. In the Greek myths, Orion was a giant hunter whose deeds are reminiscent of the better-known Hercules. According to one version, he was beloved by Artemis, the goddess of the hunt (naturally, a great hunter would be). His boasting and conceit offended the other gods, however, and Apollo paid him back by playing on Artemis' vanity. He dared her to shoot at a target she could barely see, expressing doubt of her ability to hit it. In vainglorious display, she shot at it accurately and when she raced for the target to retrieve her kill she found it had been Orion and she had slain him. In grief, she placed him in the sky.

However, the early Greeks borrowed most or all of their astronomy from the Babylonians; and among them this concept of a giant in the sky. The Babylonians pictured the constellation as a bound giant; bound presumably for some act of rebellion against the gods. The Jews in the course of the Exile would naturally pick up Babylonian astronomy. They might easily have viewed the bound giant as Nimrod, punished for his presumption in attempting to erect the Tower of Babel (itself a Babylon-inspired legend; see page 55). Clearly, any man who tried to defy God was a fool and to the Jews it would be natural, then, to refer to the constellation we call Orion as "The Fool."

The chains binding Orion are mentioned later in the Book of Job, when God challenges man to match the divine powers:

Job 38:31. *Canst thou . . . loose the bands of Orion?*

The Pleiades

A second constellation mentioned in Job 9:9 is *kimah*. This is taken to mean a closely bound group of stars, and the best known of all closely bound groups is a small cluster of medium-bright stars called the Pleiades. The notion of a close-bound cluster arises from the later verse just mentioned, of which the first part is:

Job 38:31. *Canst thou bind the sweet influences of Pleiades . . .*

The "sweet influences" are the forces of attraction holding the stars of the Pleiades together and the Revised Standard Version has the verse read, "Can you bind the chains of the Pleiades . . ."

In Greek mythology, the Pleiades were seven sisters whom, in life, Orion the hunter chased. They were rescued by the gods, who changed them into doves, then placed them in the heavens. However, they are not far to one side of the constellation Orion, who seems still to be pursuing them across the skies.

Arcturus

The third constellation mentioned in Job 9:9 is *ash*. It is translated as "Arcturus" in the King James Version but this is the least certain of the three translations. Arcturus is not a constellation (that is, a group of apparently connected stars) but a single star; one of the brightest in the heavens, to be sure.

It is referred to again in God's speech questioning man's powers:

> Job 38:32. *Canst thou . . . guide Arcturus with his sons?*

The reference to "sons" makes little sense in connection with Arcturus. However, if we search for another constellation in the skies as notable as Orion or as unusual as the Pleiades, we must consider Ursa Major, the Great Bear. Its most noticeable feature is the group of seven stars we know as the "Big Dipper." Not only are these stars quite bright and eye-catching, but they are so near the north celestial pole that they never set in North Temperate latitudes at any time of night or year. Even today, people who know nothing else about the night sky will point out the Big Dipper without trouble.

If one considers *ash* to signify the Great Bear, then the "sons" might refer to the three stars in the handle of the Big Dipper (often pictured as an incongruously long tail to the bear). The cup of the Dipper would be part of the constellation proper, and the three stars of the handle would be the sons tagging along in polite single file.

The Revised Standard Version therefore translates Job 9:9 as "Who made the Bear and Orion, the Pleiades, and the chambers of the south" and translates Job 38:32 as "Can you . . . guide the Bear with its children?"

As for the fourth object mentioned in Job 9:9—*khadre teman*—its significance is completely lost. It is translated literally as "chambers of the south" in the King James Version, in the Revised Standard Version and in the Anchor Bible. Further than that no one can go.

Buz

Eventually, Job's eloquence in his own defense confounds his three friends and Job's accusations against God, which have been mounting in intensity and fervor, demand a divine answer. This is delayed six chapters, however, when a fourth friend is suddenly introduced. He is described as being angry that Job's view of God as a tyrant had seemingly prevailed.

Job 32:2. *Then was kindled the wrath of Elihu the son of Barachel the Buzite, of the kindred of Ram . . .*

Here, too, arises the question of a Syrian versus an Edomite scene for the story. As a Buzite, Elihu may be considered a descendant of someone named Buz, or as an inhabitant of a land named Buz. Buz appears in Genesis among the descendants of Nahor, the brother of Abraham. These are listed as:

Genesis 22:21. *Huz his firstborn, and Buz his brother . . .*

Since Nahor was living in Haran at the time, well north of Canaan, a northern or Syrian locale for Buz might be indicated. This is particularly interesting since "Huz" might more accurately be rendered "Uz" and is so rendered in the Revised Standard Version and in the Anchor Bible. Both Uz, the home of Job, and Buz, the home of Elihu's father, are indicated to be in the north. This is made more pointed by the statement that Elihu was "of the kindred of Ram" for some feel that Ram is a misprint for "Aram" or Syria.

Against all this is the fact that Jeremiah, in listing the nations being warned by God (see page 477), mentions Buz as follows:

Jeremiah 25:23. *Dedan and Tema, and Buz . . .*

Now in the Book of Genesis, Dedan is listed as a grandson of Abraham by Keturah:

Genesis 25:1. . . . *Abraham took a wife, and her name was Keturah.*
Genesis 25:2. *And she bare him . . . Jokshan . . .*
Genesis 25:3. *And Jokshan begat . . . Dedan . . .*

while Tema is a son of Ishmael:

> Genesis 25:13. . . . *these are the names of the sons of Ishmael . . .*
> . . . .
> Genesis 25:15. *Hadar, and Tema.* . . .

Since Dedan and Tema are thus shown to be Arabic clans, Jeremiah's grouping of Buz with these two would mean that Buz also was an Arabic clan, and the southern scene for Job is again indicated.

The long speech of Elihu that follows his introduction seems to be a late interpolation. At least, Elihu adds nothing particularly new to previous arguments, he is not answered by Job, nor is he mentioned later in the book.

Mazzaroth

At the conclusion of Elihu's speech, God is suddenly introduced, and personally answers Job, contrasting divine omnipotence with human limitations. He points out, for instance, that man is unable to order the heavens. He introduces one astronomical object not mentioned earlier in the book:

> Job 38:32. *Canst thou bring forth Mazzaroth in his season?*

Mazzaroth occurs only in this one verse of the Bible and is a transliteration of the Hebrew word. The connection of Mazzaroth with seasonal progression (it is brought forth "in his season") rouses some speculation that it might mean the zodiacal constellations as a group. Each of these reaches the zenith at a different month of the year so that the whole acts as a primitive calendar of the year's seasons. There is also the possibility that Mazzaroth means "the planets," whose paths follow a much more complicated pattern against the sky and which therefore require much greater virtuosity to govern and regulate.

Behemoth

God goes on to describe further the wonders of nature which have been divinely created, guided, and regulated and which mankind is incompetent to cope with.

Job 40:15. Behold now behemoth, which I made with thee; he eateth grass as an ox.

The Hebrew word *behemoth* is the plural of *behemah*, meaning "beast." The word is placed in the plural to imply, apparently, that the behemoth is many beasts in size and strength; it is the greatest of beasts.

We have here a description of a huge herbivorous creature of powerful strength, and it would be natural to equate behemoth with the elephant, which is the largest land animal alive today and which "eateth grass as an ox."

Further verses, however, rather spoil this notion:

Job 40:21. He lieth . . . in the covert of the reed, and fens.
Job 40:22. . . . the willows of the brook compass him about.

This gives the impression of a river animal and turns the attention to the hippopotamus, the second largest land animal. It, too, is herbivorous.

In ancient times, the hippopotamus was quite common along the Nile and it is to be expected that the writer of the Book of Job was familiar with it. (Indeed, might not the writer have lived in Egypt and been a little hazy about Palestinian geography, thus giving rise to some of the uncertainties concerning the geographic setting of the book?)

Nevertheless, as the Anchor Bible points out, the behemoth seems to be larger and stronger than even a hippopotamus or elephant. Instead, it bears a mythological character, especially in the later rabbinical tales, and in some of the Apocrypha, where the behemoth is pictured as unimaginably colossal and as designed to be killed in the Messianic age to feed all the righteous at once. The Anchor Bible suggests that it might be a hang-over from a Mesopotamian myth of the great bull killed by Gilgamesh.

Leviathan

God, having described behemoth at some length, goes on at even greater length to describe another creature.

Job 41:1. Canst thou draw out leviathan with an hook?

The leviathan is obviously a sea creature and is described as the largest and most fearsome of them. Most Biblical commentators consider Leviathan, at least in this passage, to represent the deadly man-eating crocodile of the Nile, a fit companion piece for the hippopotamus of the Nile.

Very commonly, in poetic imagery, the term is applied to a sea creature which far surpasses the crocodile in size—the whale. The largest whale, the blue whale of Antarctic waters, is up to a hundred feet long and weighs as much as 150 tons. It is not only the largest animal now alive, but the largest animal that *ever* lived, the dinosaurs and other extinct animals of aeons past included.

But again there seem to be strong mythological components to Leviathan, as to behemoth. In many mythologies, the supreme god, shortly after his birth, or his coming into being, is described as defeating some huge monster. Often, he creates the universe out of the remnants of that monster. This can be taken as symbolizing the victory of order over disorder; of cosmos over chaos.

In Babylonian mythology, Marduk, the chief god, destroys the monster Tiamat and creates the universe out of it. Tiamat is supposed to be the symbolic representation of the sea, and Marduk's creation of the universe thus parallels the creation of civilization by the Sumerians. To create a settled agricultural society, the Sumerians had to tame the rivers in order that floods might be prevented and orderly irrigation ensured.

This Babylonian myth representing the origin of civilization can be traced very shadowily into the Bible. At the very start of Genesis, the creation is described:

> Genesis 1:2. *And the earth was without form and void; and darkness was upon the face of the deep* . . .

"The deep"—that is, the chaotic and unorganized sea—is a translation of the Hebrew *tehom*, which is rather similar to Tiamat.

God does not fight the deep or kill it, but by the sheer force of divine command creates the world. Nevertheless, this version may be a late one, superimposed by a more sophisticated priesthood upon an earlier and more primitive version of the creation that hewed closer to the common mythological notions.

For instance, in the 74th Psalm, the power of God is described as follows:

Psalms 74:13. *Thou didst divide the sea by thy strength: thou brakest the heads of the dragons in the waters.*

Psalms 74:14. *Thou brakest the heads of leviathan in pieces . . .*

This is often taken as a symbolic description of God's punishment of the Egyptians (represented as "leviathan" and as a "dragon") prior to the Exodus, and of his feat in parting the Red Sea. This is a reasonable interpretation, since it could easily be considered poetically appropriate to represent Egypt as a crocodile, just as today we represent the United States by an eagle and the Soviet Union by a bear. But it is also possible that this is a reference to a primitive myth in which God is pictured as bringing about the creation by destroying the monster representing the chaotic sea.

Leviathan can also represent the forces of evil in the world, to be slain (symbolically) by God at the end of days in order to create a new world of righteousness and good, just as it was slain at the beginning of days to create the world that now exists. Thus, in the words of the prophet Isaiah:

Isaiah 27:1. *In that day the Lord . . . shall punish leviathan the piercing serpent . . . and he shall slay the dragon that is in the sea.*

At the end of God's speech, Job realizes divine omnipotence and understands the folly of trying to penetrate God's plans and purposes with the limited mind of a human being. He repents and is then restored to more wealth than he originally had. He has a new set of sons and daughters and dies in happiness after a long life.

19. PSALMS

DAVID * THE SON * SELAH * NEGINOTH * SHEOL * CHERUB * AIJELETH SHAHAR *
ACROSTICS * SIRION * MASCHIL * ABIMELECH * JEDUTHUN * THE SONS OF
KORAH * THE DAUGHTER OF TYRE * SOLOMON * SYNAGOGUES * RAHAB *
MOSES * HALLELUJAH * MINE   ANOINTED * HAM * MELCHIZEDEK * SONG
OF DEGREES * THE RIVERS OF BABYLON

David

The Book of Psalms consists of 150 devotional poems, intended to
be chanted. The Hebrew name of the book is "Tehillim," meaning
"praises," since a great many of them praise God. The expression
"psalm" is from a Greek word meaning "to pluck at strings," a clear
indication of the musical instruments intended to accompany the
chanting. *Psalterion* is the Greek word for a stringed instrument and
the collection of psalms is called the "Psalter."

Traditionally, the authorship of most of the psalms is attributed
to king David, so that the book is sometimes referred to as "The
Psalms of David." Fully 101 of the psalms have captions that state
the name of the author and in seventy-three cases he is given as
David, sometimes with details as to the circumstances under which
the psalm was written.

Nevertheless, there is no way of proving the authorship of any
individual psalm. The Psalter is a collection of five separate anthologies
of psalms and may not have reached its present form till 150 B.C.
Some of the psalms clearly indicate their post-Exilic origin, although
it is quite possible that others may date back to quite early times,
even to David's.

The temptation to attribute psalms to David is a natural one. He
is stated in the historical books to be a skilled harpist. When Saul
was troubled with melancholia, the monarch sought surcease in music:

1 Samuel 16:17. *And Saul said . . . Provide me now a man that can play well, and bring him to me.*

1 Samuel 16:18. *Then answered one of the servants and said, Behold, I have seen a son of Jesse . . . that is cunning in playing . . .*

And when David was brought to court:

1 Samuel 16:23. *. . . David took an harp, and played with his hand: so Saul was refreshed . . .*

Furthermore, poetic works are introduced into the Second Book of Samuel and attributed to David. The most notable is the dirge over Saul and Jonathan, supposed to have been composed by David after the disastrous battle of Gilboa; a dirge that begins:

2 Samuel 1:19. *The beauty of Israel is slain upon thy high places: how are the mighty fallen!*

Outright psalms are attributed to him, too:

2 Samuel 23:1. *Now these be the last words of David. David . . . the sweet psalmist of Israel, said,*

It might be natural, then, to attribute any particularly good, or particularly popular, psalm to the sweet psalmist of Israel.

The Son

Psalm 2 is an example of one that sounds as though it could be pre-Exilic. It is clearly written in celebration of the coronation of a new king, and from the archaic nature of the language, it is generally placed in the time of the monarchy.

The psalm visualizes subject peoples planning rebellion and enemies planning to attack (as was but too often customary in the unsettled times when a new king was ascending the throne). Then the new king himself speaks and pictures God as standing behind him and as promising him dominion and power:

Psalm 2:7. *. . . the Lord hath said unto me, Thou art my Son; this day have I begotten thee.*

The kings of the ancient monarchies of the Middle East customarily considered themselves to be the adopted sons of the national god,

and the day of the coronation was the day on which they were "begotten" as such sons. The Jews were not entirely free of this view.

Thus, when the prophet Nathan informs David that God does not
wish him, as a man of war, to build the Temple, he nevertheless adds
that God will establish David's line upon the throne and take particular care of the dynasty:

> 2 Samuel 7:13. . . . *I will stablish the throne of his* [David's]
> *kingdom for ever.*
> 2 Samuel 7:14. *I will be his father, and he shall be my son . . .*

Later Christian thought saw more to it than this, however. Jesus,
as the Messiah, was considered as bearing a special relationship to
God; a relationship that was most easily expressed in the word "son."
This psalm was therefore considered to have Messianic significance, and
even if it were written with a particular earthly king in mind, it never-
theless had a further, deeper meaning, and applied to the Messiah.
It is for this reason that the King James Version capitalizes the word
"Son" in the twelfth verse of the psalm. The Revised Standard
Version, which is less concerned with Messianic prophecies, puts the
word in the lower case.

Selah

The 3rd Psalm is the first to have a title:

> Psalm 3: *A Psalm of David, when he fled from Absalom his*
> *son.*

The Hebrew could mean either "A Psalm Written by David" or
"A Psalm Concerning David" and it is to be noted that the phrase
"A Psalm of David" can also have either of these two meanings in
English. However, the traditional assumption is that it means "written
by."

The psalm contains an odd word at the end of three of the verses:

> Psalm 3:2. *Many there be which say of my soul, There is no*
> *help for him in God. Selah.*

The expression "Selah" occurs seventy-one times altogether in the
Book of Psalms, almost always at the end of a verse, and usually at

the end of a natural pause in the thought. Presumably, it gives some direction to those chanting the psalm, but what that direction might be, nobody knows.

Neginoth

Other directions involving the musical accompaniment of the psalms are sometimes given in the titles.

> Psalm 4. *To the chief Musician on Neginoth* . . .
> Psalm 5. *To the chief Musician upon Nehiloth* . . .

Neginoth means "stringed instruments," while *nehiloth* means "pipes" or "wind instruments." In the Revised Standard Version, the title to Psalm 4 is given as "To the choirmaster, with stringed instruments," while that to Psalm 5 is given as ". . . for the flutes . . ." The title of Psalm 6 is less easily interpreted:

> Psalm 6. *To the chief Musician on Neginoth upon Sheminith* . . .

Sheminith means "the eighth" and this could mean an eight-stringed instrument. It could also refer to an octave, and means perhaps that the psalm is to be sung in two voices an octave apart. The title of Psalm 7 is more puzzling still:

> Psalm 7. *Shiggaion of David, which he sang unto the Lord, concerning the words of Cush the Benjamite.*

The meaning of *shiggaion* is unknown and, out of desperation, it is usually considered as simply meaning "psalm." And if that were not puzzle enough, the reference to Cush the Benjamite is likewise mysterious, for no reference to this incident occurs elsewhere in the Bible.

It also seems useless to attempt to interpret the titles of the next two psalms:

> Psalm 8. *To the chief Musician upon Gittith* . . .
> Psalm 9. *To the chief Musician upon Muthlabben* . . .

Gittith is, presumably, some sort of musical instrument, but no one can say what. *Muthlabben* might be dismissed in similar fashion but it seems to mean "death of" and that cannot be right. Either it also means something else, or it is the result of a copyist's error, and the original meaning can no longer be salvaged.

Psalm 9 contains still another mysterious word:

> Psalm 9:16. . . . *the wicked is snared in the work of his own hands. Higgaion. Selah.*

Higgaion means "meditation" and perhaps it directs a pause during which the singers may meditate on what has been chanted.

The title of Psalm 16 is:

> Psalm 16. *Michtam of David.*

Michtam has been connected with the Hebrew word for gold, and it is conceivable that the 16th Psalm is estimated by the anthologists who gathered this group as a particularly good one; a "golden psalm," in other words.

Sheol

The 18th Psalm, one of the longer ones, has a title to suit:

> Psalm 18. . . . A *Psalm of David* . . . *in the day that the Lord delivered him from the hand of all his enemies, and from the hand of Saul* . . .

This particular psalm is quoted in the twenty-second chapter of 2 Samuel after the description of the rebellions of Absalom and of Sheba are done with (see page 318). David has indeed been delivered from the hand of all his enemies but it is puzzling why Saul, the enemy disposed of a generation earlier, should be singled out for mention.

One possibility (accepted by the Anchor Bible) is that "Saul" is a copyist's error for Sheol, the afterworld (see page 173). The psalm would then be one of gratitude for the psalmist's escape from death. This seems to fit in with the subject matter of the psalm:

> Psalm 18:4. *The sorrows of death compassed me* . . .
> Psalm 18:5. *The sorrows of hell* [Sheol] *compassed me about* . . .

Even in the immediate post-Exilic period, the picture of Sheol is still that of a shadowy existence, like that of the Greek Hades rather than of the later notions of Hell. The word is usually associated with existence underground, as is indicated by the common use of the term "pit" for Sheol:

Psalm 28:1. . . . I become like them that go down into the pit . . .

There are synonyms for Sheol that indicate something worse than more shadowy non-existence. Thus, in the Book of Job, Job describes his own misery as creating a visible Hell for him while he is yet alive:

Job 26:6. Hell [Sheol] is naked before him, and destruction hath no covering.

And in the Book of Psalms:

Psalm 88:11. Shall thy lovingkindness be declared in the grave? or thy faithfulness in destruction?

In both these verses, the parallelism of Hebrew poetry makes "destruction" a synonym of the grave, or of Sheol. "Destruction" is a direct translation of the Hebrew word Abaddon. This is left untranslated in the Revised Standard Version to make it clearer that a place is meant and not an abstract process.

The fact that Abaddon means "destruction" or "ruin" carries a more dreadful aura about it than is achieved by the comparatively neutral word "Sheol." The Anchor Bible translates Abaddon as "Perdition" in Job 26:6. This word comes from a Latin term meaning "ruin" or "loss," again emphasizing the worse aspects of Sheol and illustrating the growing concept of Hell as a place of torture and eternal punishment.

Gradually, Abaddon changed from a place to a fiend in charge of that place. Abaddon became the evil spirit of Hell's tortures, a kind of infernal Torquemada. Abaddon is mentioned in this guise in the Book of Revelation in the New Testament:

Revelation 9:11. . . . the angel of the bottomless pit, whose name in the Hebrew tongue is Abaddon, but in the Greek tongue hath his name Apollyon.

Apollyon (from a Greek word meaning "to destroy completely") is one of the allegorical elements in John Bunyan's book The Pilgrim's Progress, published in the 1680's. The extreme popularity of Bunyan's book has made Apollyon familiar in the guise of a fiend armed with fiery arrows.

Cherub

At least parts of the 18th Psalm may be very old, for Yahveh is pictured as a storm-god, in the fashion of the archaic Song of Deborah (see page 239).

Psalm 18:10. *And he* [the Lord] *rode upon a cherub and did fly: yea, he did fly upon the wings of the wind.*

The cherubim are usually pictured anthropomorphically as powerful supernatural winged creatures (see page 148), but here one gets a glimpse beyond, to the natural phenomena that inspired the thought. This passage of the psalm describes the terrific natural catastrophes— earthquakes, volcanoes, hail, thunderstorms—that seem to bear direct witness to the overwhelming power of God. The cherub may represent the storm blast, the terrifyingly destructive power of the invisible air.

Aijeleth Shahar

The title of the 22nd Psalm is:

Psalm 22. *To the chief Musician upon Aijeleth Shahar.*

Aijeleth Shahar is translated "The Hind of the Dawn" in the Revised Standard Version. It is possible that this is the name (or the first phrase) of some well-known melody to which the psalm was supposed to be sung. If so, the same may be true in several other cases:

Psalm 46. . . . *A Song upon Alamoth.*
Psalm 56. *To the chief Musician upon Jonath-elemrechokim . . .*
Psalm 57. *To the chief Musician, Al-taschith . . .*
Psalm 60. *To the chief Musician upon Shushan-eduth . . .*

In the Revised Standard Version, *Jonath-elemrechokim* is translated as "The Dove on Far-Off Terebinths." As for *Alamoth* and *Shushan-eduth*, these are left untranslated in the Revised Standard Version, but seem to mean "The Young Maidens" and "Lily of the Testimony."

Al-taschith means "do not destroy." Can this, too, be the first words of a well-known melody of the times? Or did some copyist make a hasty note to ensure the safety of a copy he had just prepared and did the little notation then get frozen into the Biblical canon?

Acrostics

The 25th Psalm has a structure that is completely lost in English translation. Each line begins with a different letter of the Hebrew alphabet, in order. The first line begins with *aleph*, the second with *beth*, the third with *gimmel*, and so on.

Such an arrangement, in which the initial letters of successive verses (or final letters, or both) give the alphabet in order, or spell out words, are called "acrostics," from a Greek expression meaning "the ends of verses."

The 25th Psalm is by no means the only acrostic psalm. The 34th is another example. The 119th Psalm is a particularly complicated one for it consists of twenty-two parts, each of which contains eight lines. Each part is headed by a successive letter of the alphabet, and each of the eight lines of that part begins with that letter.

Biblical acrostics are found outside the Book of Psalms, too. The last section of the last chapter of Proverbs is an anacrostic poem praising the virtuous woman. Again, each of the first four chapters of Lamentations is an acrostic poem.

Acrostics have their uses. By starting each line with a letter in alphabetic order, an aid to memory is granted the reciter. Then, too, it is pleasant for a poet to display his virtuosity by writing an attractive poem within the limits of an artificial convention. On the other hand, the limits so set often force a writer to settle for less than the best, and acrostic poems in the Bible tend to display a certain illogicality in sequence. A line has to be written to fit the new initial rather than to carry on the previous thought.

Sirion

The 29th Psalm describes the might of God in terms of nature images:

> Psalm 29:5. *The voice of the Lord breaketh the cedars* . . .
>
> Psalm 29:6. *He maketh them also to skip like a calf; Lebanon and Sirion like a young unicorn.*

Sirion, here, is the Phoenician term for Mount Hermon (see page 202) in Lebanon. This is stated specifically in Deuteronomy:

> Deuteronomy 3:9. (*Which Hermon the Sidonians call Sirion; and the Amorites call it Shenir;*)

The use of a Phoenician name is no accident. Apparently, this psalm is a Yahvistic adaptation of an older Canaanite hymn to the storm-god. The parallelism in verse 6 between "calf" and "young unicorn" again shows the unicorn to be a wild ox (see page 186). The Revised Standard Version has the verse read, "He makes Lebanon to skip like a calf, and Sirion like a young wild ox."

Maschil

The 32nd Psalm has the title:

> Psalm 32. *A Psalm of David. Maschil.*

The word *Maschil* is left untranslated in both the Revised Standard Version and the Anchor Bible, here and in the title of several other psalms, but seems to carry the connotation of "instruction." Perhaps the psalms so denoted were supposed to carry special occult meanings apparent only to the initiated, but this is just a guess.

Abimelech

The 34th Psalm has a circumstantial title:

> Psalm 34. *A Psalm of David, when he changed his behaviour before Abimelech* . . .

This must surely refer to the episode in David's life when, as a fugitive from Saul, he sought refuge in the court of Achish, king of Gath. Fearing that the Philistines would kill him or give him up to Saul, he feigned madness in order to ensure his release:

1 Samuel 21:13. *And he* [David] *changed his behaviour before them* [the Philistines], *and feigned himself mad* . . .

It is usual to suppose that the reference to Abimelech in the title of the 34th Psalm is a copyist's mistake for Achish. However, it is just possible that Abimelech was a general title for Philistine kings. In Genesis, Abimelech, king of Gerar, is mentioned in two different tales. The Genesis tales refer to a time before the coming of the Philistines, to be sure, but the title may have lingered on, as Egyptian kings were called Pharaoh regardless of their name or dynasty.

Jeduthun

The 39th Psalm seems to be dedicated to an individual:

Psalm 39. *To the chief Musician, even to Jeduthun* . . .

There were, apparently, three chief clans devoted to the musical service of the Temple. The Chronicler traced back the ancestry of these clans to the time of David:

1 Chronicles 25:1. *Moreover David* . . . *separated to the service of the sons of Asaph, and of Heman, and of Jeduthun, who should prophesy with harps, with psalteries, and with cymbals.*

What the title may really mean is that the psalm is "after the manner of Jeduthun"; that is, in the style made use of by the clan. Or perhaps it had been composed by members of the clan, despite the routine ascription of the psalm to David.

One psalm is ascribed to Heman:

Psalm 88. . . . *Maschil of Heman the Ezrahite.*

(where Ezrahite should really be Zerahite; see page 107).

Quite a number are ascribed to Asaph:

Psalm 50. *A Psalm of Asaph.*

The eleven psalms from 73 to 83 inclusive are all attributed to Asaph and they may represent a collection used by the Asaphic clan.

The Sons of Korah

The 41st Psalm ends with a verse praising God:

> Psalm 41:13. *Blessed be the Lord God of Israel from everlasting,
> and to everlasting. Amen, and Amen.*

This is not considered part of the psalm but is, rather, a ritualistic
formula of praise which serves to end a collection of psalms. Such
praise of God is called a "doxology," from a Greek word meaning
"giving praise."

Psalms 1 to 41 inclusive are considered to be the first of the five
collections making up our Book of Psalms. All of the psalms of this
first collection are ascribed to David, or in a few cases are left un-
ascribed. The 42nd Psalm, however, which is the first of the second
collection, has a title, but does not include David's name.

> Psalm 42. *To the chief Musician, Maschil, for the sons of Korah.*

Although Korah is pictured as a rebellious Levite during the time
of the Exodus (see page 172), and as one who was destroyed by
Moses, his family remained and survived to form an important group
in the Temple ritual:

> 1 Chronicles 9:19. . . . *the Korahites, were over the work of the
> service, keepers of the gates of the tabernacle . . .*

The Daughter of Tyre

The 45th Psalm is rather secular. Its title includes a significant
phrase:

> Psalm 45. . . . *A song of loves.*

It is written, apparently, in honor of a royal marriage and is what
the Greeks would call an *epithalamion* ("at the bridal chamber").
The bride is a foreign princess:

> Psalm 45:12. *And the daughter of Tyre shall be there with a
> gift . . .*

The natural assumption might be that the wedding being described is that between Ahab of Israel and Jezebel of Tyre, or between Jehoram of Judah and Athaliah, the daughter of Jezebel (see page 362). It has also been suggested, with perhaps less likelihood, that it celebrates the wedding of Solomon and the Egyptian princess, or of Jeroboam II (see page 369) and some foreign princess.

Solomon

Psalm 72 is one of two in the Book of Psalms that mention Solomon in the title. (The other is the 127th Psalm.)

Psalm 72. *A Psalm for Solomon.*

It is a prayer that the reigning king, probably newly come to the throne, reign long and justly; that he be rich and powerful. The notion that Solomon in particular is concerned arises naturally out of the mention of nations that were traditionally involved with his trading ventures (see page 332).

Psalm 72:10. *The kings of Tarshish and of the isles shall bring presents: the kings of Sheba and Seba shall offer gifts.*

Sheba and Seba are intended to describe two different sections of Arabia. Thus, in the listing of the nations in the tenth chapter of Genesis, both are mentioned in a related fashion:

Genesis 10:7. *And the sons of Cush; Seba . . . and Raamah: and the sons of Raamah; Sheba . . .*

Psalm 72 is the last psalm of the second book. It ends with a doxology and then with a final verse:

Psalm 72:20. *The prayers of David the son of Jesse are ended.*

And so they are as far as this second collection is concerned.

The first two collections of psalms are not entirely independent. As might be expected of different anthologies, there are some duplications. Thus, the 14th Psalm in the first collection is virtually identical with the 53rd Psalm in the second book. Then again, the 70th Psalm in the second book is virtually a repeat of the last five verses of the 40th Psalm in the first book.

Synagogues

The 74th Psalm pictures a land in ruins, with the enemy triumphant. Unless one pictures David speaking in allegories or in prophetic vision, it becomes impossible to ascribe it to him or, in
fact, to any period in the history of the kingdoms. At the earliest it
must be after the destruction of the Temple by Nebuchadnezzar:

> Psalm 74:7. *They have cast fire into thy sanctuary, they have
> defiled by casting down the dwelling place of thy name to the
> ground.*

Indeed, the psalm might possibly be dated later still, for the very
next verse goes on to say:

> Psalm 74:8. *They said in their hearts, Let us destroy them to-
> gether: they have burned up all the synagogues of God in the
> land.*

The word "synagogue" is from the Greek expression meaning "an
assembling together" and is precisely analogous to the Latin-derived
"congregation" or the Anglo-Saxon-derived "meeting place." The Revised Standard Version uses the Anglo-Saxon equivalent and translates
the verse: "they burned all the meeting places of God in the land."

The synagogue did not become prominent until the time of the
Exile. With the Temple destroyed and the ritualistic paraphernalia of a
centralized worship gone, something had to be improvised if Judaism
were to survive. Worship came to be centered about the written books
being produced by the scribes. Groups of Jews gathered at meeting
places, or synagogues, to study the books, read them aloud, sing the
hymns, and so on.

Even after the return and the rebuilding of the Temple, the new
habit persisted. Not all Jews had returned, after all, and even those
who were back in the land had become used to the relatively informal
gatherings and continued them. By Greek times, the synagogue had
grown important indeed, and it was only then, during the Seleucid
persecution, that one might say "they have burned up all the synagogues." It is for this reason that suggestions are made that the 74th

Psalm, or at least the version we now possess, may be among the latest ones and may have been composed in 165 B.C.

Rahab

The 87th Psalm lists the heathen nations surrounding Judea, and predicts that all will turn to God and Jerusalem eventually. (Or perhaps the reference is to the Jews who were scattered abroad among the surrounding nations even after the rebuilding of the Temple, with the psalm containing the hope that all would eventually return.) The list of nations contains one strange name, however:

> Psalm 87:4. *I will make mention of Rahab and Babylon . . . behold Philistia, and Tyre, with Ethiopia . . .*

Rahab seems to be another name for the mythical monster destroyed by God at the beginning of time to create the world:

> Psalm 89:10. *Thou hast broken Rahab in pieces, as one that is slain . . .*

or:

> Isaiah 51:9. *Awake, awake, put on strength, O arm of the Lord . . . Art thou not it that has cut Rahab, and wounded the dragon?*

Rahab, like Leviathan (also used as the name for the primitive monster; see page 487), seems to make reference to a nature myth. Where Leviathan is the chaotic sea tamed by the forces of order, so Rahab (meaning "storm") would seem to be the howling of the elements; elements that had to be subdued by the forces of order before they subverted the universe.

But Rahab, like Leviathan, could be used as a symbolic representation of Egypt; and talk of breaking or cutting or wounding could then be equated with God's punishment of Egypt at the time of the Exodus.

The representation of Egypt as a monstrous dragon is a rather appropriate one. Egypt is, essentially, the banks of the Nile River, the ever-fertile ribbon through the desert that saw the growth of a mighty civilization and was the richest portion of the world for thousands of years. The river wound like a great snake or dragon across the land, and Ezekiel uses this metaphor very effectively when he quotes God as saying to Egypt:

> Ezekiel 29:3. . . . *Behold, I am against thee, Pharaoh king of Egypt, the great dragon that lieth in the midst of his rivers . . .*
> Ezekiel 29:4. . . . *I will put hooks in thy jaws . . . and I will bring thee up out of the midst of thy rivers . . .*

Here the language that might be appropriate for the battle between the God of order and the monster of chaos is made into a metaphoric description of a battle between God and Egypt.

Ezekiel wrote during the Exile, and by post-Exilic times, Rahab had apparently become an accepted synonym for Egypt. In the 87th Psalm, it seems clearly to be used in this manner.

Moses

The 89th Psalm, a sad one apparently composed during the Exile, ends the third collection and closes with a doxology. The 90th Psalm, the first of the fourth collection, is the only one in the Book of Psalms that is attributed to none other than Moses:

> Psalm 90. *A Prayer of Moses the man of God.*

This may be because it speaks of the creation—the peculiar province of Genesis, a book traditionally written by Moses.

> Psalm 90:1. *Lord, thou hast been our dwelling place . . .*
> Psalm 90:2. *Before . . . ever thou hadst formed the earth . . .*

Hallelujah

The 104th Psalm ends:

> Psalm 104:35. . . . *Bless thou the Lord, O my soul. Praise ye the Lord.*

The 105th Psalm, immediately afterward, ends also with "Praise ye the Lord." In fact, "Praise ye the Lord" occurs at the beginning or end (or both beginning and end) of fifteen different psalms in the last two collections of the Book of Psalms. In Hebrew, the expression is "Hallelujah" ("praise Yah").

The Greek form of the word is "Alleluia" and that occurs in Revelation:

> Revelation 19:1. . . . I heard a great voice of much people in heaven, saying, Alleluia . . .

Mine Anointed

The 105th Psalm has a curiously influential verse. The care of God for those who follow him is detailed; as in the Patriarchal Age, when he cared for Abraham and his few descendants, precariously existing in a hostile land:

> Psalm 105:14. He suffered no man to do them wrong: yea, he re-proved kings for their sakes;
> Psalm 105:15. Saying, Touch not mine anointed, and do my proph-ets no harm.

The reference seems to be to the passage in Genesis when God re-proves Abimelech, king of Gerar, in a dream, after Abimelech has taken Abraham's wife, Sarah, into his harem. God says:

> Genesis 20:7. Now therefore restore the man his wife; for he is a prophet . . . and if thou restore her not, know thou that thou shalt surely die . . .

This passage in the 105th Psalm served as a kind of shield for the priesthood against the secular power. In the middle ages, it was used to protect priests from being tried by secular courts, since the king must do God's prophets (a term extended, liberally, over the clergy gener-ally) no harm. This was valuable for the clergy, since the clerical courts did not pronounce the death sentence, and this was called "benefit of clergy."

This was eventually extended to all who could read (since literacy was virtually confined to the clergy in the middle ages). If a person convicted of murder could read a passage from the Bible, he was ex-empt from execution but was merely branded on the hand. A second murder, however, would mean execution. Literacy meant one murder free, so to speak, but no more. Soon after 1800, this practice was ended. Perhaps too many people were learning to read.

Ham

The 105th Psalm recalls the days of Egyptian slavery, too, and the Exodus that followed:

Psalm 105:23. Israel also came into Egypt; and Jacob sojourned in the land of Ham.

The parallelism of Hebrew poetry shows that "land of Ham" is a name for Egypt. Ham is that son of Noah from whom the nations of northeastern Africa are descended, according to the genealogical lists in Genesis:

Genesis 10:6. And the sons of Ham; Cush, and Mizraim . . .

Mizraim is the Hebrew word for Egypt, so that what is really being said is that Egypt is the son of Ham, and Ham can therefore be used poetically to represent Egypt as well as Mizraim can.

Indeed, Ham is the better name of the two, since the ancient Egyptians' name for their own land was a word very like Ham. The word was usually taken to mean "black" as a reference to the black fertile land bordering the Nile, in contrast to the arid yellow sands of the desert on either side.

Melchizedek

The 106th Psalm ends with a doxology and the 107th begins the fifth and last collection incorporated into the Book of Psalms. The 110th Psalm is another one of those which praises a king, perhaps on the occasion of his coronation, promising him greatness and power. More than that, he is promised priesthood:

Psalm 110:4. The Lord hath sworn, and will not repent, Thou art a priest for ever after the order of Melchizedek.

This might well be a reference to the struggle between king and High Priest for control of the Temple ritual. This struggle appears most prominently in the Bible in connection with the tradition that Uzziah was struck with leprosy as punishment for attempting to lead the Temple rites (see page 423). The priestly position was that only Levites of the line of Zadok could properly conduct them. The king, a member of the tribe of Judah and a descendant of David, could have nothing to do with them.

The Psalm recalls, however, that there was a king of Jerusalem named Melchizedek (see page 73). This was a priest so acceptable to God that Abraham himself did him reverence. The capacity for priesthood might therefore be viewed as adhering to the king in Jerusalem from earliest times, well before the birth of Levi himself. If the king were considered as inheriting that priesthood by virtue of his office, he was a priest "after the order of Melchizedek."

Song of Degrees

Psalms 120 to 134 inclusive bear titles such as:

Psalm 120. A Song of degrees.

"Degrees" means "steps." One might picture such psalms being sung as a priestly procession moves up one of the stairways associated with the Temple. For that reason, the title is given as "A Song of Ascents" in the Revised Standard Version.

On the other hand, these psalms might have been used by pilgrims going to the Temple for one of the great festivals. They would "go up" to Jerusalem in stages—or "ascend by degrees." The possibility of pilgrim usage is strengthened by the fact that the writer of the 120th Psalm bemoans the fact that he lives among the heathen:

Psalm 120:5. *Woe is me, that I sojourn in Mesech, that I dwell in the tents of Kedar.*

Mesech, or Meshech, is described in the genealogies of Genesis as being a son of Japheth.

Genesis 10:2. *The sons of Japheth; . . . Tubal, and Meshech, and Tiras.*

while Kedar is a son of Ishmael:

> Genesis 25:13. . . . *The sons of Ishmael . . . Nabajoth; and Kedar, and Adbeel . . .*

These two terms, Mesech and Kedar, are used poetically here to signify non-Jewish societies in general.

The Rivers of Babylon

The 137th Psalm is clearly of Exilic origin:

> Psalm 137:1. *By the rivers of Babylon, there we sat down, yea, we wept, when we remembered Zion.*

Babylon is, of course, on the Euphrates River and the Tigris River is about forty miles to the east. The exiled Jews, spread over the region, might, conceivably, have been referring to these two as the rivers of Babylon.

However, Babylonia was an irrigated land and the reference is much more likely to be to the numerous intersecting canals. We would get a truer picture if we were to read the phrase, "By the canals of Babylon . . ." Indeed, the Revised Standard Version avoids making use of the misleading "rivers" and translates the phrase, "By the waters of Babylon . . ."

20. PROVERBS

SOLOMON · HEZEKIAH · SPARE THE ROD · AGUR · LEMUEL

Solomon

The Book of Proverbs gets its name from its first phrase:

Proverbs 1:1. *The proverbs of* . . .

This phrase, in Hebrew, is "Mishli," which is the title of the book in Hebrew. The word *mishli* might more accurately be translated as "the wise sayings of," as is done in the Anchor Bible.

"Proverb" is a narrow term, for it is not only a "wise saying," but it is also a "folk saying," a pithy one, usually, that has arisen out of the experience of people generally. It is usually of unknown origin and frequently used in everyday speech.

The Book of Proverbs is a heterogeneous collection that includes proverbs in this narrow sense, and more elaborate "wise sayings" as well. It is an example of the "wisdom literature" that was gathered by writers of many ancient nations: the teachings of experience, usually with a strong moralistic or religious bent.

In the case of the Jews, most wisdom literature was ascribed to Solomon almost as a matter of course, for he was, traditionally, the wisest of men:

1 Kings 4:30. *And Solomon's wisdom excelled the wisdom of all the children of the east country, and all the wisdom of Egypt.*
1 Kings 4:31. *For he was wiser than all men* . . .
1 Kings 4:32. *And he spake three thousand proverbs* . . .

Two sections of the Book of Proverbs are indeed made up of a group of short aphorisms which are specifically ascribed to Solomon.

The Empire of David and Solomon

The first extends from Chapter 10 through the first half of Chapter 22 and begins:

Proverbs 10:1. *The proverbs of Solomon* . . .

The second collection covers chapters 25 through 29 and begins:

Proverbs 25:1. *These are also proverbs of Solomon* . . .

There is no doubt but that many of the proverbs are ancient indeed and could have reached back to Solomon's time and even earlier. There is nothing impossible in Solomon having collected a group of proverbs or even having put them into literary form. Still, much of the atmosphere of the book seems to make it almost certainly belong to a period considerably later than Solomon's time, and the final form of the collection, including the two lists of proverbs assigned to Solomon, may not have reached its present form till post-Exilic times, say about 300 B.C. At that time, the general ascription must have been placed at the beginning to cover the entire book:

Proverbs 1:1. *The proverbs of Solomon the son of David, king of Israel.*

Hezekiah

The Book of Proverbs itself implies that at least some of the material in it underwent editing well after the time of Solomon. Thus, in introducing the second collection of Solomonic proverbs:

Proverbs 25:1. *These are also proverbs of Solomon, which the men of Hezekiah king of Judah copied out.*

Hezekiah ruled two centuries after Solomon and was a firm Yahvist. Apparently, he patronized a school of scribes, one of whose tasks was the collection and organization of the Yahvist literature of the past.

Spare the Rod

Some of the Solomonic proverbs are indeed household expressions, in one form or another, even today:

Proverbs 13:24. *He that spareth his rod hateth his son: but he that loveth him chasteneth him betimes.*

This is almost invariably cited as "Spare the rod and spoil the child." More apt to be correctly quoted is:

Proverbs 15:1. *A soft answer turneth away wrath . . .*

Then there is:

Proverbs 16:18. *Pride goeth before destruction, and an haughty spirit before a fall.*

which is almost universally condensed to "Pride goes before a fall."

Agur

The thirtieth chapter of the book begins with a completely obscure line; at least in the King James Version:

Proverbs 30:1. *The words of Agur the son of Jakeh, even the prophecy: the man spake unto Ithiel, even unto Ithiel and Ucal.*

The phrase "even the prophecy" seems to be the translation of the Hebrew word *massa* and, apparently, this should not be translated, for it is meant here as the name of a locality. The first line should speak of "Agur the son of Jakeh of Massa."

In the Book of Genesis, Massa is mentioned in the genealogical tables:

Genesis 25:13. . . . *the sons of Ishmael . . .*
Genesis 25:14. *And Mishma, and Dumah, and Massa,*

Massa might therefore be assumed to be found in Ishmaelite territory in northern Arabia.

The reference to Ithiel and Ucal makes no sense as such, for these do not seem to be proper names. The Anchor Bible translates the verse as: "The words of Agur ben Jakeh of Massa. The man solemnly affirmed, 'There is no God! There is no God, and I can[not know anything].'"

It would seem, then, that the verse in question describes the statement of an agnostic, which the chapter then goes on to counter.

Lemuel

The first half of the last chapter of Proverbs is assigned to a king other than Solomon; or at least, it appears to be:

Proverbs 31:1. *The words of king Lemuel, the prophecy that his mother taught him.*

Here again "prophecy" might be an unnecessary translation of a place name, and the Revised Standard Version has it: "The words of Lemuel, king of Massa."

There has been some tendency in the past to assume that Lemuel was another name for Solomon, but this is not at all likely. In fact, the Anchor Bible wipes out Lemuel altogether by supposing it to be a copyist's error for a very similar Hebrew word which, when translated, would make the first verse, "Words [of advice] to a king acting foolishly, A solemn injunction which his mother lays on him:"

The last half of this last chapter consists of an acrostic poem in praise of the industrious housewife that begins with the well-known:

Proverbs 31:10. *Who can find a virtuous woman? for her price is far above rubies.*

21. ECCLESIASTES

THE PREACHER • VANITY • THE WISDOM OF SOLOMON • ECCLESIASTICUS

The Preacher

Following the Book of Proverbs is a second item coming under the heading of "wisdom literature." This begins:

Ecclesiastes 1:1. *The words of the Preacher . . .*

"Preacher" is a translation of the Hebrew word *koheleth*, which is of uncertain meaning. Usually, it is associated with the word *kahal*, meaning "an open assembly," so that *koheleth* might be one who convenes such an assembly or addresses it. If the assembly is gathered together for the purpose of religious instruction, then its addresser would be a preacher.

The Greek word for an assembly is *ekklesia* and one who addresses it would be *ekklesiastes*. In Latin spelling that is *ecclesiastes* and this is the title to the book.

The Preacher announces his identity as:

Ecclesiastes 1:1. *The words of the Preacher, the son of David, king in Jerusalem.*

This seems to be a clear indication that it is Solomon talking, and has often been taken as such. However, this is merely the common ascription of almost any piece of wisdom literature to Solomon. Actually, the book seems to be post-Exilic and to have been written, at the best guess, between 300 and 200 B.C.

The Empire of David and Solomon

Vanity

The book opens with the author's general thesis:

> Ecclesiastes 1:2. *Vanity of vanities, saith the Preacher, vanity of*
> *vanities; all is vanity.*

The Hebrew word translated here as "vanity" implies something as insubstantial as air, so that the Anchor Bible translates the verse "A vapor of vapors! . . . All is vapor."

The word "vanity" comes from a Latin term meaning "empty." The expression "vanity of vanities" in Hebrew idiom implies a kind of maximum vanity, just as "song of songs" is the greatest song and "king of kings" is the greatest king.

Perhaps, then, the verse, in modern terms, could be translated "All is nothing . . . Nothing means anything."

That, in effect, is the central thesis of the book—the emptiness of earthly things.

In order to impress this fact, the Preacher maintained that life was empty not only for the poor and weak, but for the rich and powerful as well. He therefore continues his role as king.

> Ecclesiastes 1:12. *I the Preacher was king over Israel in Jerusalem.*
> Ecclesiastes 1:13. *And I gave my heart to seek and search out by*
> *wisdom concerning all things that are done under heaven . . .*

Here it seems even clearer than before that the Preacher is impersonating Solomon. Yet this impersonation continues only through the first two chapters of the book and it would appear to be merely a literary device. Even the most magnificent and happiest of all kings (in Jewish eyes), Solomon himself, is pictured as being unable, in the long run, to find anything meaningful in life.

In the end the Preacher feels all that can be done is to seize the temporary and ephemeral joys that come along and to remain unconcerned for anything more lasting:

> Ecclesiastes 8:15. . . . *a man hath no better thing under the sun,*
> *than to eat, and to drink, and to be merry . . .*

And in the end he returns to his original thesis:

Ecclesiastes 12:8. *Vanity of vanities, saith the preacher, all is vanity.*

Another writer, apparently appalled at the pessimism of the Preacher, added an addendum to the book; an addendum which came to be included in the canon. Its nub is:

Ecclesiastes 12:13. . . . *Fear God, and keep his commandments . . .*

The Wisdom of Solomon

Not all wisdom literature succeeded in being admitted to the Jewish canon, even though ascribed to Solomon. This happened when the books supposedly written by Solomon were actually composed after the approximate cutoff date of 150 B.C. A case in point is that of a book apparently written by an Alexandrian Jew sometime between 100 and 50 B.C.

The writer, himself unknown, assumes the personality of Solomon in order to dramatize his praise of a personified Wisdom. For this reason the book is known as "The Wisdom of Solomon."

The author's personification of Solomon is clearest in the seventh chapter:

Wisdom of Solomon 7:7. *Wherefore I prayed, and understanding was given me: I called upon God, and the spirit of wisdom came to me.*

This clearly refers back to the passage in the First Book of Kings in which Solomon is described as seeing God in a dream and being offered anything he wishes. Solomon, in the dream, replies:

1 Kings 3:9. *Give . . . thy servant an understanding heart to judge thy people, that I may discern between good and bad . . .*

Since Solomon is, however, certainly *not* the author, this apocryphal book is often called more appropriately "The Book of Wisdom" and it is by that name that it appears in the Catholic versions of the Bible.

Ecclesiasticus

Another piece of wisdom literature is notable for bearing within it the name of the author, speaking in his own right and making no attempt to ascribe his words to an ancient worthy.

Ecclesiasticus 50:27. *Jesus the son of Sirach of Jerusalem hath written in this book the instruction of understanding and knowledge.*

For this reason, the title of the book is given as "Wisdom of Jesus, Son of Sirach." The name is here presented in Greek form. In Hebrew it would be "Joshua ben Sira." This book was composed too late to qualify for the Jewish canon and was consigned to the Apocrypha. It is, however, to be found in the Catholic version of the Bible.

Because of the high caliber of its ethical teachings, the book was much used as a source of texts for sermons and was closely associated with churchly preaching from quite early times. Cyprian, the bishop of Carthage, took to calling this book "Ecclesiasticus" ("the church book") as early as A.D. 250 and the custom has continued ever since.

Something about the date at which the book was written may be deduced from a reference toward the end of the book. The writer begins

Ecclesiasticus 44:1. *Let us now praise famous men, and our fathers that begat us.*

He goes on to call the list of notables from Biblical history: Enoch, Noah, Abraham, Isaac, Jacob, Moses, Aaron, Phinehas, Joshua, Caleb, Samuel, Nathan, David, Solomon, Elijah, Elisha, Hezekiah, Isaiah, Josiah, Jeremiah, Ezekiel, Zerubbabel, and Nehemiah.

Having gone through the list, he then proceeds to reach a natural climax by praising a recent spiritual leader of the people—carrying his brief review of history to what was then the contemporary era:

Ecclesiasticus 50:1. *Simon the high priest, the son of Onias, who in his life repaired the house again, and in his days fortified the temple:*

The trouble is that there were two High Priests by the name of Simon in the early Greek era. The first, whom we might call Simon I, was High Priest about 300 B.C., while the second, Simon II, was High

Priest about 200 B.C. What's more, both had fathers who were named Onias. It is much more likely, though, that Simon II is the one being referred to, for if the book had been written in 300 B.C. or shortly thereafter it would, very likely, have entered the canon.

Backing this view is a reference in the preface to the book—

Ecclesiasticus was originally written in Hebrew. This Hebrew version was lost and, throughout Christian times, the book was known only in Greek and Aramaic, and in translations from manuscripts in those languages. The fact that the Hebrew version did exist, however, was assumed from the statement of a grandson of the writer. He came to Egypt, where the Jews spoke Greek, and in a preface that is usually included with the book, he explains (with becoming modesty) that he labored to prepare a Greek translation from the Hebrew. As for his time of arrival in Egypt, that was "in the eight and thirtieth year . . . when Euergetes was king."

The thirteen Macedonian kings of Egypt, who ruled from 305 to 44 B.C., each took the name Ptolemy, but each added a second name (or had it added by sycophantic courtiers), usually of self-praise. The name "Euergetes" means "benefactor," for instance. There were two Ptolemies so named. One was Ptolemy III, who reigned from 246 to 221 B.C., and the other was Ptolemy VII, who reigned from 145 to 116 B.C. The former reigned twenty-five years and the latter reigned twenty-nine years, so that neither could be said to have an "eight and thirtieth year."

In the case of Ptolemy VII, however, the 145 to 116 B.C. stretch covers only the period in which he was sole ruler. His older brother had begun to rule in 181 B.C. as Ptolemy VI but his record was wretched. In 170 B.C., he had shown himself so incompetent a war leader that public opinion forced him to associate his younger brother with him on the throne. Ptolemy VII might therefore be said to have begun to reign in 170 B.C. and his "eight and thirtieth year" would then be about 132 B.C.

If we assume the translator's grandfather to have written the book half a century before, that would make the date of Ecclesiasticus about 180 B.C.

The existence of a Hebrew version of Ecclesiasticus was confirmed in 1896 when portions of Hebrew manuscripts were found which contained about two thirds of the book. Still older scraps of Ecclesiasticus were found among the Dead Sea Scrolls.

22. THE SONG OF SOLOMON

SOLOMON • EN-GEDI • SHARON • THE VOICE OF THE TURTLE • TIRZAH • SHULAMITE

Solomon

The third of the canonical books to be attributed to Solomon is The Song of Solomon. Its first verse is its title:

Song of Solomon 1:1. *The song of songs, which is Solomon's.*

By "song of songs" the Hebrew idiom expresses a maximum. It is the best or most beautiful song to have been written by Solomon. In the Catholic version of the Bible, the book is known as "The Canticle of Canticles," from the Latin title "Canticum Canticorum" ("Song of Songs"). The Hebrew title is "Shir Ha-shirim," also meaning "Song of Songs."

As in the case of Ecclesiastes, the author of this book is surely not Solomon. The book is post-Exilic and seems to have been written about 300 B.C. or even later. It is attributed to Solomon because of the latter's traditional literary ability:

1 Kings 4:32. *And he [Solomon] spake three thousand proverbs: and his songs were a thousand and five.*

The Song of Solomon is a love poem, frankly erotic, apparently composed to celebrate a wedding. This, too, is appropriate, for Solomon had numerous wives and was, presumably, an experienced lover:

1 Kings 11:3. . . . *he had seven hundred wives . . . and three hundred concubines . . .*

The Empire of David and Solomon

Because of the erotic nature of the book, it has been customary to find allegorical values in it that would make more of it than a description of bodily passion. In the guise of the portrayal of the love of a man and a woman, Jews would have it speak of the love between Yahveh and Israel; Catholics of the love between Christ and the Church; Protestants of the love between God and man's soul.

However, if we simply accept the words as they stand, the book is a human love poem and a very beautiful one.

Interpreting the book literally, it would seem to be a kind of poetic drama, in which a number of different characters speak: the bridegroom, the bride, a chorus of women, and perhaps others. Since the book, as it appears in the Bible, gives no hint as to when one character stops speaking and another starts, or which character says what, the sorting out of the speeches presents a difficult problem but one which, fortunately, need not concern us.

Some speeches are, of course, transparent enough. Surely, it is the bride who says:

> Song of Solomon 1:5. *I am black, but comely . . . as the curtains of Solomon.*
> Song of Solomon 1:6. . . . *I am black, because the sun has looked upon me . . .*

The adjective "black" does not mean that the bride is a Negress for the blackness is the result of exposure to the sun. She is tanned. The Revised Standard Version has the fifth verse read "I am very dark," and the sixth verse, "I am swarthy."

There might be a tendency to think of her as the Egyptian princess who married Solomon, since she might be expected to be dark in coloring. Or else it might be the queen of Sheba; a swarthy Arabian woman. Yet that is only forced upon us if we imagine the poem to be written literally by or about Solomon. Viewed simply as a love poem in the tradition of Solomon, the bride is probably a peasant girl:

> Song of Solomon 1:6. . . . *my mother's children . . . made me the keeper of the vineyards . . .*

En-gedi

The bride speaks of her lover:

Song of Solomon 1:14. *My beloved is unto me as a cluster of camphire in the vineyards of En-gedi.*

En-gedi is a site midway along the western shores of the Dead Sea. It would seem an unlikely place for anything but desolation, yet it is an oasis, thanks to the presence of natural spring water. The name "En-gedi" means "spring of the kid." The site was famous in Jewish history as one of the places in which David found refuge from the pursuing Saul:

1 Samuel 23:29. *And David . . . dwelt in strongholds at En-gedi.*

The expression "camphire," by the way, is a transliteration of the Hebrew *kopher.* By it is meant henna, a shrub with fragrant white flowers. The Revised Standard Version translates it "My beloved is to me a cluster of henna blossoms."

Sharon

The bride describes herself again:

Song of Solomon 2:1. *I am the rose of Sharon, and the lily of the valleys.*

Sharon is a coastal plain lying between Jaffa and Mount Carmel, about fifty miles long and six to twelve miles wide. It doesn't figure often in the Bible for through much of Biblical history it was occupied by the Phoenician and Philistine power.

It passed into Israelite hands under David. He owned flocks of cattle that grazed there under a native herdsman:

1 Chronicles 27:29. *And over the herds that fed in Sharon was Shitrai the Sharonite . . .*

The Voice of the Turtle

The Song of Solomon is full of beautiful nature imagery but one image rings false in modern ears through no fault of its own. The bride describes her beloved as pleading with her to come with him for it is springtime:

Song of Solomon 2:12. *The flowers appear on the earth; the time of the singing of birds is come, and the voice of the turtle is heard in our land.*

The phrase "voice of the turtle" seems odd, for to us the turtle is an ugly, slow-moving, shelled reptile that is voiceless, that is not associated with spring, and that certainly doesn't bear association with the beauties of flowers and birds.

It is we, however, who are wrong, and not the verse. There is a type of bird we call a dove, deriving that name from an old Teutonic word that may make reference to its dull, rather dark plumage. It makes a cooing sound which to some ears may sound like tur-tur-tur-tur. The Hebrew word for it, imitating this sound, is *tur*, and the Latin word is *turtur*. By substituting "l" for "r" at the end, this becomes "turtle." The "voice of the turtle" refers to the cooing of this migratory dove which reaches Jerusalem in the springtime.

However, there is also the shelled reptile earlier mentioned. This is called a tortoise, perhaps (but not certainly) from a Latin word meaning "crooked" because of its curved legs. To the ears of English-speaking sailors, "tortoise" seemed an odd-sounding word and they substituted for it the more familiar "turtle," thus giving the ugly reptile the name of a pleasant bird.

In order to distinguish the bird from the reptile, it became necessary to call the bird a "turtledove." It is so spoken of elsewhere in the King James Version, but not here in the Song of Solomon. The Revised Standard Version removes the apparent anomaly by having the clause read "and the voice of the turtledove is heard in our land."

Tirzah

The pangs of love temporarily lost and the thrills of love regained are described and at one point the bridegroom says to the bride:

Song of Solomon 6:4. *Thou art beautiful, O my love, as Tirzah, comely as Jerusalem . . .*

The parallelism of Hebrew poetry forces the writer to seek a synonym or analogy for Jerusalem. He might have used Zion, but was searching for something less routine, perhaps, and chose Tirzah. As Jerusalem was the capital of the southern kingdom, so Tirzah was the capital of the northern kingdom from the time of Jeroboam I to Omri, about 900 to 880 B.C. (see page 339). This is an indication that the poem had to be written after the time of Solomon, for Tirzah was in no way analogous to Jerusalem in the reign of a king ruling over a united kingdom.

On the other hand, we cannot use this verse as evidence that the poem was necessarily written before the time of Omri, when Samaria displaced Tirzah as the capital of Israel. To have made use of Samaria as an analogue of Jerusalem in post-Exilic times would have seemed blasphemous for by then Samaria was the center of the hated and heretical Samaritans. The writer was thus forced to reach back beyond Samaria to Tirzah, which had no impossible associations.

Shulamite

The bride is addressed by her native town, either by the bridegroom or by a chorus:

Song of Solomon 6:13. *Return, return, O Shulamite . . .*

It is usually supposed that Shulamite is a copyist's error for Shunammite, a woman of the town of Shunam, which is about three miles north of Jezreel.

Finally the book reaches its climax in a passionate declaration of the strength of true love:

Song of Solomon 8:7. *Many waters cannot quench love, neither can the floods drown it: if a man would give all the substance of his house for love, it would utterly be contemned.*

In other words, love cannot be destroyed if present; but cannot be bought if absent.

23. ISAIAH

ISAIAH · AMOZ · SERAPHIM · SHEAR-JASHUB · IMMANUEL · THE BRANCH ·
COCKATRICE · LUCIFER · APOCALYPSE OF ISAIAH · ARIEL · LILITH · THE
MARTYRDOM OF ISAIAH · SECOND ISAIAH · CYRUS · THE SERVANT OF THE
LORD · BEL · BEULAH

Isaiah

The Old Testament books that follow the Song of Solomon in the Christian versions of the Bible record the work of sixteen named prophets who were supposed to have flourished during the three-century period from 750 to 450 B.C.

These books are not placed entirely in chronological order. They are divided into two sections on the basis of length. Fully two thirds of the material in these prophetic books is to be found in the first three, dealing with the prophets Isaiah, Jeremiah, and Ezekiel. These are the "major prophets" and they, at least, are placed in chronological order. The Book of Isaiah, dealing with the period of Assyrian ascendancy, comes first.

From a strictly historical and secular viewpoint the Book of Isaiah presents many confusions. Isaiah is not likely to have systematically written down his utterances. Rather, his sayings were, presumably, written down by his disciples and followers, with what changes and additions we can only guess. These made up separate collections which some later editor put together, not necessarily in chronological order but rather in that order which he thought would produce the greatest effect.

What's more, as time passed, additional material was added to the book and made to seem the product of Isaiah. The later portions of the book are certainly not Isaiah's work but are the product of a man (possibly two men) living centuries later. The Book of Isaiah may not

THE
GREAT SEA
(Mediterranean Sea)

N

Sidon
Tyre
Accho
Dor
Joppa
Gaza
Raphia

PHOENICIA
MT. LEBANON
MT. HERMON
Damascus
Dan
DAMASCUS
ASSYRIAN
EMPIRE
QARNINI
BASHAN
Ashtaroth
SEA OF
GALILEE
Aphek
HAURAN
YARMUK R.
Edrei
Ramoth-gilead
Mahanaim
GILEAD
JABBOK R.
AMMON
Rabbath-ammon
Heshbon
Medeba
Dibon
MOAB
Kir-moab
ZERED R.
ARABS

GALILEE
PLAIN OF
MEGIDDO
Megiddo
Beth-shan
PLAIN OF SHARON
DURU
Samaria
Shechem
SAMARIA
Shiloh
Bethel
Jerusalem
Gath
Bethlehem
SALT
SEA
Hebron
(DEAD
SEA)
Beersheba
JUDAH
PHILISTIA
EDOM
KINGDOM
OF EGYPT
JORDAN R.

0   Miles   25

Judah in the Time of Hezekiah

have been put into its present form until as late as 350 B.C., or well over three centuries after Isaiah's death.

The general period in which Isaiah carried out his prophetic mission is given in the first verse of the book:

> Isaiah 1:1. *The vision of Isaiah . . . which he saw . . . in the days of Uzziah, Jotham, Ahaz, and Hezekiah, kings of Judah.*

Since Uzziah came to the throne in 780 B.C. and Hezekiah died in 692 B.C., this at once makes Isaiah a man of the eighth century B.C.

For the actual year of the beginning of his mission, there is more information later in the sixth chapter, a chapter which should, if the final editors of the book had been following a chronological scheme, have come first. Isaiah recounts the miraculous manner in which he became a prophet, and begins his description of the event with a date:

> Isaiah 6:1. *In the year that king Uzziah died . . .*

Uzziah died in 740 B.C. and that, therefore, can be taken as the date when Isaiah began his work. Presumably, he was a relatively young man at the time, for he was still active during Sennacherib's siege of Jerusalem nearly forty years later. If we consider Isaiah to have been a young man of twenty when he saw his vision, he would have been born in 760 B.C. at a time when the fortunes of Israel and Judah were flourishing.

In 760 B.C. Jeroboam II of Israel had extended Israel's borders to their broadest extent since the time of Solomon, and under Uzziah, Judah, too, was prosperous and content (see page 423). The men of the kingdoms must have been contented, foreseeing no evil.

In 745 B.C., however, Jeroboam II died and almost at once Israel began to fall prey to dynastic disorders. In that same year, the strong Tiglath-Pileser III became king of Assyria, and that nation entered on its last and mightiest period of aggression. Israel had less than a quarter century of life left it.

Apparently, Isaiah could clearly see, by 740 B.C., that the good days were gone and the evil times had come and he said so in the manner made necessary by the way of thought of the time. He announced the judgment of Yahveh upon a sinful people.

Amoz

The name of Isaiah's father is given:

Isaiah 1:1 *The vision of Isaiah the son of Amoz . . .*

Absolutely nothing is known concerning Amoz, for he is not mentioned in the Bible except as the father of Isaiah in this verse and in a few others like it. He is to be carefully distinguished from Amos, a prophet who was an older contemporary of Isaiah. (The two names, Amoz and Amos, are less similar in Hebrew than in English.)

There is a rabbinic tradition (based on no more, perhaps, than a similarity in names) that Amoz was a brother of king Amaziah, who was Uzziah's father. If this were so, Isaiah would be a member of the royal family and a first cousin to king Uzziah. He and Uzziah would both be grandsons of Joash, who had been saved as an infant in Athaliah's time (see page 367).

If so, Isaiah is rather unusual, for it would seem natural for prophets of his sort to have been drawn from among the poor, since the prophets were spokesmen of protest. The prophets were, generally, the radicals of their day, frequently standing in opposition to the formal priesthood, which (as long as their prerogatives were preserved) acted in coalition with the monarchy.

The priesthood then, as always, was primarily interested in the minutiae of ritual. This was something that could easily be followed by anyone and generally presented no difficulties. It might be a tedious way of gaining God's favor, but it was not really painful.

The prophets, however, were likely to disdain ritual and to insist, instead, on a high ethical code of behavior, something that could present serious difficulties. After all, it is not only often difficult to perform the ethical good; it is sometimes puzzling to determine what the ethical good might be.

Isaiah, himself, put it this way:

Isaiah 1:11. *To what purpose is the multitude of your sacrifices unto me? saith the Lord . . .*

. . . .

Isaiah 1:13. *Bring no more vain oblations; incense is an abomination to me . . .*

Isaiah 1:14. *Your new moons and your appointed feasts my soul hateth . . .*

. . . .

Isaiah 1:16. *Wash you, make you clean; put away the evil of your doings . . .*

Isaiah 1:17. *Learn to do well; seek judgement, relieve the oppressed, judge the fatherless, plead for the widow.*

Furthermore, there was a tendency for the prophets to denounce the rich and powerful, for these were apt to be the most worldly, most satisfied to let ritual (if anything) serve as religion. Isaiah speaks against the tendency of these rich to squeeze out the poor farmer and to multiply their own holdings, polarizing society into a few large landowners and many tenant farmers or slaves. (This is a development that tends to affect societies generally, and not ancient Judah alone.) Isaiah says:

Isaiah 5:8. *Woe unto them that join house to house, that lay field to field, till there be no place, that they may be placed alone in the midst of the earth.*

And yet scholars judge from Isaiah's style of writing that he did indeed belong to the upper classes and certainly there are cases in history where aristocrats have lived and fought on behalf of the dispossessed of the world and against, as the saying has it, their own class. The example of the Russian novelist Count Leo Tolstoy springs to mind, for instance.

Seraphim

Isaiah describes his call in terms of a vision of God experienced by him within the Temple:

Isaiah 6:1. *In the year that king Uzziah died I saw also the Lord sitting upon a throne, high and lifted up, and his train filled the temple.*

Isaiah 6:2. *Above it stood the seraphims: each one had six wings;*

with twain he covered his face, and with twain he covered his feet, and with twain he did fly.

Isaiah 6:3. *And one cried unto another and said, Holy, holy, holy, is the Lord of hosts: the whole earth is full of his glory.*

"Seraphim" is the Hebrew plural of *seraph*, so that the word "seraphims" in the King James Version is a double plural, the English form grafted on to the Hebrew. In the Revised Standard Version, the final "s" is dropped.

The seraphim are mentioned only here in the Bible, and they are taken to be winged manlike creatures rather similar to the cherubs described in connection with other visions of God.

In later times, the seraphim were included among the complicated celestial hierarchy worked out by mystical writers. The best-known such hierarchy was produced about A.D. 450, perhaps, by an unknown writer whose work was ascribed to an earlier worthy named Dionysius the Areopagite, and who is himself referred to, in consequence, as the "pseudo-Dionysius."

According to the system of the pseudo-Dionysius there were nine classifications of beings between man and God and of these the angels were lowest and archangels next to the lowest. Above these, in order, came principalities, powers, virtues, dominations, thrones, cherubim, and seraphim. Because the cherubim and seraphim were described in prophetic visions as being in immediate attendance upon God, they naturally rated highest.

In our present age, less wedded to such speculation, a seraph has become merely another word for an angel.

The word "seraph" is related to the Hebrew word *saraph*, meaning "to burn." The seraphim may therefore be spoken of in English as "the Burning Ones." This may refer to the gleaming radiance issuing from them, or the burning ardor with which they serve God.

On the other hand, the word is used elsewhere in the Bible, where it refers not to angelic beings but to "fiery serpents" (as the word is then translated), the adjective presumably referring to the agonizing burning of their poisonous bite.

Numbers 21:6. *And the Lord sent fiery serpents among the people . . .*

If the image of a "fiery serpent" is taken literally, one can scarcely avoid thinking of the lightning. If the earliest view of Yahveh was that of a storm-god, as one would suspect from the Song of Deborah (see page 239) and some of the Psalms (see page 494) then it is thoroughly natural that His manifestation be accompanied by a fearsome display of lightning and by the scudding of the dark storm blast.

By the time of the prophets, however, the lightning had apparently been personified into the winged seraphim, as the storm blast had become the cherubim (see page 494).

Shear-jashub

Already, as Isaiah had received his call, the times were growing manifestly turbulent. Israel and Syria were attempting to organize a coalition against the power of Assyria. When Jotham, who had succeeded Uzziah to the throne of Judah, preferred to remain outside the coalition (judging, rightly, that it was doomed to disastrous failure), the allied forces of Israel and Syria invaded Judah (see page 374). The war continued through 735 B.C., when Jotham died and his son Ahaz succeeded to the throne.

The new king, young and irresolute, required strengthening:

Isaiah 7:3. *Then said the Lord unto Isaiah, Go forth now to meet Ahaz, thou, and Shear-jashub thy son . . .*

The fact that Isaiah could, on a moment's notice, approach the king is usually taken as another indication of his position in the royal family.

Shear-jashub, the name of Isaiah's son, was chosen deliberately by the father for its meaning in connection with the prophetic message. Isaiah says as much:

Isaiah 8:18. . . . *the children whom the Lord hath given me are for signs . . . from the Lord . . .*

The meaning of "Shear-jashub" is "a remnant shall return." This reflects the feeling, common to Isaiah and the prophets generally, that an evil time at hand was to be succeeded eventually by better times. If the nation is left desolate and the population carried off into exile, nevertheless "a remnant shall return" and the nation shall live again.

Perhaps Isaiah's son was born shortly after the prophet's call and was four or five years old at the time of the meeting with Ahaz.

Immanuel

Isaiah assures Ahaz that he need not fear Israel or Syria, for destruction is almost upon them. All Judah need do is to hold out resolutely.

Viewed secularly, we can see reason behind Isaiah's point of view. The energetic Tiglath-Pileser of Assyria must have known that Israel and Syria were attempting to establish a coalition against him and it was certain that he would attack the coalition before they could complete their plans. It was also certain that Assyria would smash the small western nations. Judah, for its safety, need only remain neutral and wait.

Ahaz, however, did not feel it safe to do nothing but hold on. Neutrality in times of great conflict laid one open to the enmity of both sides and Tiglath-Pileser, even if victorious, might consider Judah's neutrality to be a sign of secret enmity. Ahaz felt it politically wise to declare himself on the Assyrian side and accept Assyrian overlordship.

This Isaiah opposed vehemently. He may well have felt that Assyrian overlordship would mean the ascendancy of Assyrian religious practices and the persecution of the nationalistic Yahvists (as in fact came to pass a half century later in the reign of Manasseh) and he argued hard for a go-it-alone policy, promising God's help.

> Isaiah 7:11. *Ask thee a sign of the Lord . . .*
> Isaiah 7:12. *But Ahaz said, I will not ask, neither will I tempt the Lord.*

The word "tempt" is translated as "test" in the Revised Standard Version. Ahaz, in refusing to ask God to meet some test, is technically correct since the Bible on more than one occasion makes it plain that it is not for man to imagine he can make God jump through hoops on demand. Besides, Ahaz has undoubtedly made up his mind and is anxious to end the interview.

Isaiah is annoyed, however, and proceeds to advance a sign anyway:

> Isaiah 7:14. . . . *Behold, a virgin shall conceive, and bear a son, and shall call his name Immanuel.*
>
> . . . .
>
> Isaiah 7:16. . . . *before the child shall know to refuse the evil, and choose the good, the land thou abhorrest shall be forsaken of both her kings.*

In other words, in two or three years, before the time when a child, born in the near future, becomes old enough to exert even the simplest judgment, the attacking kings shall be defeated. And if this happens, Ahaz will be forced to realize that Isaiah sees clearly and speaks truly. (And, indeed, three years later, in 732 B.C., Tiglath-Pileser III took Damascus, executed the Syrian king and permanently destroyed the Syrian kingdom, while Israel, rendered powerless, was allowed a limping life for ten more years; see page 375.)

The most interesting part of Isaiah's "sign," however, is the identity of the child who was to be called Immanuel.

To Christians generally, this is a reference to the virgin birth of Jesus, but that rests, of course, upon the word translated in the King James Version as "virgin." In the Hebrew, the word so translated is *almah* and this is actually used to refer to a young woman who might or might not be a virgin. The Hebrew language has a specific word (*bethulah*) for "virgin" but that is not used here. The Revised Standard Version therefore translates Isaiah 7:14 as "Behold, a young woman shall conceive and bear a son . . ."

But let us leave the Messianic aspect of the verse to one side. Whatever the merits or demerits of the traditional Christian interpretation of the verse, it must have a more immediate meaning. Isaiah could scarcely offer to Ahaz, as a sign for the present predicament, the birth of a child more than seven centuries later.

But what child of his own time can Isaiah be referring to? The name Immanuel means "God is with us" and this has symbolic meaning in connection with Isaiah's message of the moment. God is with Judah and will not allow it to be destroyed by Syria and Israel. No child named Immanuel is, however, recorded as having been born in that period of history, or anywhere in the Bible, for that matter. Still, if the name is symbolic, any other name of equal symbolism might do.

Sometimes it is suggested that the reference may be to Ahaz's own son, Hezekiah, who was to come to the throne eventually. Since he was to be one of the three great Yahvistic kings of Judah (the other two being Jehoshaphat and Josiah) later interpreters tended to apply flattering verses to him. However, Hezekiah became king in 720 B.C. and was already an adult at that time:

> 2 Kings 18:1. . . . *Hezekiah the son of Ahaz . . . began to reign.*
> 2 Kings 18:2. *Twenty and five years old was he when he began to reign . . .*

This means he was born in 745 B.C. and at the time of the interview between Ahaz and Isaiah must have been ten years old and had already reached an age at which he was capable of making judgments. Hezekiah is not, therefore, a reasonable choice for Immanuel.

Indeed, if we seek for the simplest and most straightforward solution to the problem, what seems more likely than that Isaiah's reference to a young woman is a reference to his own wife. (Isaiah was only twenty-five at the time and his wife may well have been little more than twenty.) In fact, immediately after the description of the meeting with Ahaz, Isaiah records the birth of a second son:

> Isaiah 8:3. . . . *Then said the Lord to me, Call his name Maher-shalal-hash-baz.*
> Isaiah 8:4. *For before the child shall have knowledge to cry, My father, and my mother, the riches of Damascus and the spoil of Samaria shall be taken away before the king of Assyria.*

The name "Maher-shalal-hash-baz" means "haste-spoil, speed-booty." The reference is to Syria and Israel, which are hastening onward to become spoil and booty for the Assyrians. And before the child is old enough to say "mama," the end will come for the northern kingdoms.

Thus, Isaiah says precisely the same things for the predicted child Immanuel and for the actual child Maher-shalal-hash-baz. The names are the obverse sides of the coin for Immanuel refers to Judah's good fortune and Maher-shalal-hash-baz to Syria's and to Israel's bad fortune. The names are different but the symbolism is the same and that is what counts.

It seems perfectly reasonable, then, to suppose Isaiah's own son is the predicted Immanuel.

Nevertheless, Ahaz followed his own judgment as to the proper course and became tributary to Assyria. Isaiah had failed to swing the king to the Yahvist way of thinking, and nothing is heard of the prophet in connection with specific political events until the Assyrian siege of Jerusalem a generation later.

The Branch

Some of the writings in the Book of Isaiah expand the prophet's notion that after some disaster of the future, a remnant of the faithful would return and build anew. This remnant, purged of the sins that brought about the disaster, would be ruled by an ideal king:

> Isaiah 9:6. *For unto us a child is born, unto us a son is given; and the government shall be upon his shoulder: and his name shall be called Wonderful, Counseller, The mighty God, The everlasting Father, The Prince of Peace.*
> Isaiah 9:7. *Of the increase of his government and peace there shall be no end . . .*

It may be that such rhapsodic praises of an ideal king might have grown out of odes written in honor of a coronation. In Isaiah's time, such praises might have been sung in honor of Hezekiah's coming to the throne in 720 B.C. The phrase "unto us a child is born, unto us a son is given" would refer to the coronation process by which a king becomes an adopted son of the national god (see page 490). The flattering names given the king and the promise of a reign of perfect happiness would be the lavish poetic license usually taken on such an occasion.

Or, alternatively, the ode might have been written in honor of Josiah, who ascended the throne nearly a century later, in 638 B.C. The ode might then, because of its poetic beauty, have been placed within the Isaianic collection.

However, even if the verses originally referred to a specific king such as Hezekiah or Josiah, the later Jews could not have been satisfied to read no further meaning into them. Neither Hezekiah nor Josiah had had truly successful reigns. Hezekiah had survived the siege of Jerusalem but only just barely and Judah had been devastated. Josiah died in battle and a generation after his death, the Jewish kingdom was destroyed.

More and more, therefore, the references were taken to stand for some ideal king who had not yet arisen, who was to come at some vague time in the future.

The king, of course, would be of the Davidic dynasty; nothing else seemed possible for only the line of David had ever ruled over Judah, and it had been promised eternal kingship in the Bible:

> Isaiah 11:1. *And there shall come forth a rod out of the stem of Jesse, and a Branch shall grow out of his roots:*
>
> Isaiah 11:2. *And the spirit of the Lord shall rest upon him . . .*

Again this might be the routine flattery applied to a new king such as Hezekiah or Josiah. The new king is always a flourishing new growth; the old king always a decayed old one. If, however, the reference is shifted to an ideal king of the future, the Davidic dynasty might be viewed as cut down (a stem, or more properly translated, a stump, is all that is left) and a new and flourishing growth arises out of it.

In the reign of the ideal king all of creation is restored to the kind of absolute peace one might envision as having originally been found in the garden of Eden:

> Isaiah 11:6. *The wolf also shall dwell with the lamb, and the leopard shall lie down with the kid; and the calf and the young lion and the fatling together; and a little child shall lead them.*

Another such glowing picture of an ideal future, and one even more frequently quoted, occurs near the beginning of the Book of Isaiah:

> Isaiah 2:2. *And it shall come to pass in the last days, that the mountain of the Lord's house shall be . . . exalted . . . and all nations shall flow into it.*
>
> . . . .
>
> Isaiah 2:4. . . . *and they shall beat their swords into plowshares and their spears into pruninghooks: nation shall not lift up sword against nation, neither shall they learn war any more.*

This vision of an ideal future may have begun to grow before the eyes of Jews despondent over the reality of a triumphant Assyria in Isaiah's time. It grew stronger as the disasters of the Babylonian Exile, the disappointments of the return from exile, and the horrors of the

Seleucid persecution overtook the Jews. By New Testament times, this orientation to the future had become the dominant note in Judaism and was, indeed, responsible for the events of the New Testament and for the great turning point in human history heralded by those events.

The ideal future centered about the king of David's line who was to arise. Kings are anointed with oil as part of the religious ceremony that makes them king. Therefore kings can be referred to as "the anointed" and are indeed so referred to in the Bible. Thus, when David had come upon Saul sleeping and had cut off a portion of Saul's robe, his conscience forbade him to do more, although self-interest alone might have counseled a quick assassination:

> 1 Samuel 24:6. . . . *the Lord forbid that I should . . . stretch forth mine hand against him, seeing he is the anointed of the Lord.*

Nor need the term be restricted to kings anointed according to Yahvistic ritual. Cyrus of Persia is referred to in this manner in the later portions of the Book of Isaiah:

> Isaiah 45:1. *Thus saith the Lord to his anointed, to Cyrus . . .*

The Hebrew word for "anointed" is *mashiakh*, which is given in transliterated English as "messiah." More and more, as time passed, and as the Jewish vision was fixed with increasing fervor on the ideal king of the future, the term was confined to him. We can therefore speak of the ideal king as (with a capital) the Messiah.

According to Christian thought, of course, the Messiah is Jesus, and the word "Branch" in Isaiah 11:1 is taken as a reference to Jesus and is therefore capitalized in the King James Version. In the Revised Standard Version, the word is not capitalized.

Cockatrice

In the description of the ideal Messianic kingdom, several ways of indicating the total absence of danger or harm are to be found. In each, the trick is to combine the utterly helpless with the completely harmful. The climax is reached when infants are mingled with serpents.

> Isaiah 11:8. *And the sucking child shall play on the hole of the asp, and the weaned child shall put his hand on the cockatrice' den.*

The two parts of the verse contain the parallelism that is the essence of Hebrew poetry, and it may be taken that the Hebrew words translated as "asp" and as "cockatrice" both signify some venomous serpent. The asp is, indeed, a small poisonous snake found in Egypt. (Cleopatra was supposed to have committed suicide by allowing an asp to bite her.)

The cockatrice, however, is something else again. The word may have originated in medieval times as a form of "crocodile." The crocodile, like the serpent, is a deadly reptile. It might almost be viewed as a gigantic, thick snake, with stubby legs. To Europeans, unfamiliar with the crocodile except by distant report, the snaky aspects of the creature could easily become dominant.

Moreover, once "cockatrice" is formed from "crocodile," the first syllable is suggestive, and the fevered imagination develops the thought that the monster originates in a cock's egg. This is itself a monstrous perversion of nature for, of course, cocks are male birds that do not lay eggs. The egg, thus perversely laid, must, moreover, be hatched by a serpent, and the product, then, is a creature with a snake's body and a cock's head.

The cockatrice is pictured as the ultimate snake. It kills not by a bite but merely by a look. Not merely its venom, but its very breath is fatal. Because the cockatrice is the most deadly snake and therefore the king of snakes, or because of the cock's comb which may be pictured as a crown, the cockatrice is also called a "basilisk" (from Greek words meaning "little king").

Of course, the Biblical passage in Isaiah (and there are a couple of other verses in this book and in that of Jeremiah which mention the cockatrice) cannot be used as evidence in favor of the reality of this completely imaginary creature. The Hebrew word, translated as "cockatrice" in the King James Version, signified no cock-headed serpent that can kill with a look; it signifies merely a poisonous snake.

In the Revised Standard Version, the word is translated as "adder," which is the name of a common European poisonous snake and, it should perhaps be noted, the only venomous snake to be found in the British Isles. "Adder" is a much less misleading translation of the Hebrew term than "cockatrice" is, but in actuality the adder is not likely to be the actual creature meant by Isaiah. Instead, the horned viper, a poisonous snake found in the Near East, is the most likely candidate.

Lucifer

It is not only Jerusalem and Judah that are warned in the Book of Isaiah concerning the wrath of God. The surrounding heathen nations are also warned of doom, and first in line is Babylon.

It is easy to suspect that chapters 13 and 14, in which the doom of Babylon is foretold with savage imagery, is not really Isaianic. In Isaiah's time, it was Assyria that was the conquering nation and Babylon lay under its thumb in more devastating fashion than Judah did. The paean of hatred and scorn should, it would be expected, be turned against Assyria and the new capital that Sennacherib had built at Nineveh.

On the other hand, a century after Isaiah's time, it was Babylon under Nebuchadnezzar that was the oppressor. It is reasonably likely, then, that this passage is of later origin and was possibly composed during the Exile at a time when Babylon seemed doomed to fall before the conquering armies of Cyrus the Persian.

Picturing Babylon as already fallen, the writer recites a taunting poem of sarcastic contempt for the mighty Babylonian monarch now brought low. In part, it goes:

> Isaiah 14:12. *How art thou fallen from heaven, O Lucifer, son of the morning!* . . .
> Isaiah 14:13. *For thou hast said in thine heart, I will ascend into heaven* . . .
> Isaiah 14:14. . . . *I will be like the most High.*
> Isaiah 14:15. *Yet thou shalt be brought down to hell* . . .

The Hebrew word here translated as "Lucifer" is *helel*. Literally, it means "The Shining One," and is thought to refer to the planetary body we call Venus.

Venus is the brightest of the planets in our sky and, next to the sun and the moon, the brightest object in the heavens. Because of the position of its orbit between the earth's orbit and the sun, it is always seen (from earth) to be fairly close to the sun. When it is in that part of its orbit that puts it to the east of the sun, it shines out most clearly after sunset, and sets never more than three hours afterward. It is then visible only in the evening and is called the evening star.

On the other side of its orbit, when Venus is to the west of the sun, the planet rises first and for a short period of time (never more than three hours), it shines in the eastern sky as dawn gradually breaks. It is then the morning star.

It is only natural that cultures unlearned in astronomy and not particularly observant of the heavens would consider the evening star and the morning star to be two separate bodies. In Isaiah's time, even the clever Greeks were of this opinion. It was not until two centuries after Isaiah's time that the Greek philosopher Pythagoras discovered the two to be the single body that the Greeks then came to call Aphrodite and the Romans (and ourselves) Venus. It is very likely that Pythagoras discovered this in the course of his travels in the East (tradition says he visited Babylonia and it was the Babylonians who were the great astronomers of ancient times).

Venus, in its morning star aspect, could be called the "daystar" for its rising heralds the coming of day. It is also the "son of the morning" for it is only as morning approaches that it is possible to see it. Thus, the Revised Standard Version translates verse 14:12 as "How art thou fallen from heaven, O day-star, son of the morning."

The Greeks, in the period when they thought Venus to be two bodies, called the evening star "Hesperos" and the morning star "Phosphoros." *Hesperos* means "west" and it is always in the west that the evening star appears. *Phosphoros* means "light-bringer" and it is therefore the essential equivalent of "daystar." By the Romans, the Greek terms were translated directly into Latin. The evening star became "Vesper" ("west") and the morning star became "Lucifer" ("light-bringer").

The Hebrew *helel* is therefore translated as Phosphoros in Greek versions of the Bible; and as Lucifer in Latin versions.

The use of the term "Lucifer" in connection with the overweening pride of the Babylonian king is an ironic thrust at the habit of applying fulsome metaphors for royalty. Flattering courtiers would think nothing of naming their king the Morning Star, as though to imply that the sight of him was as welcome as that of the morning star heralding the dawn after a long, cold winter's night. This habit of flattery is confined neither to the East nor to ancient times. Louis XIV of France, two and a half centuries ago, was well known as the Sun King.

The writer of the verses concerning Lucifer ironically described his fall from absolute power to captivity and death as the fall of the morning star from the heavens to Hell.

With time, however, these verses came to gain a more esoteric meaning. By New Testament times, the Jews had developed, in full detail, the legend that Satan had been the leader of the "fallen angels." These were angels who rebelled against God by refusing to bow down before Adam when that first man was created, using as their argument that they were made of light and man only of clay. Satan, the leader of the rebels, thought, in his pride, to supplant God. The rebelling angels were, however, hurled out of Heaven and into Hell. By the time this legend was developed the Jews had come under Greek influence and they may have perhaps been swayed by Greek myths concerning the attempts of the Titans, and later the Giants, to defeat Zeus and assume mastery of the universe. Both Titans and Giants were defeated and imprisoned underground.

But whether Greek-inspired or not, the legend came to be firmly fixed in Jewish consciousness. Jesus refers to it at one point in the Gospel of St. Luke:

> Luke 10:18. And he [Jesus] said . . . I beheld Satan as lightning fall from heaven.

It seemed natural to associate the legend with the Isaianic statement; indeed, that statement about Lucifer may even have helped give rise to the legend. In any case, the early Church fathers considered Isaiah's statement to be a reference to the eviction of the devil from Heaven, and supposed Lucifer to be the angelic name of the creature who, after his fall, came to be known as Satan. It is from this line of argument that our common simile "proud as Lucifer" arose.

Apocalypse of Isaiah

After oracles predicting disaster for a number of individual nations (Moab, Egypt, Tyre, etc.) are presented, there comes a four-chapter sequence (chapters 24 to 27 inclusive) in which extreme disaster for the earth generally is forecast.

These chapters are an example of what is called "apocalyptic" literature, from Greek terms meaning "to uncover"; that is, "to reveal."

Apocalyptic literature purported, in other words, to describe matters that could not be known to man except by inspired revelation. Subjects included in such revelation might be the machinery that controlled the movements of heavenly bodies; the details of the manner in which the universe was created; or, most commonly of all, the details of the fate to befall the earth in the future, particularly the story of the end of earthly history.

The study of the end of days is called "eschatology," from a Greek word meaning "last things." Much apocalyptic writing is eschatological in nature.

After 200 B.C. apocalyptic writing became very common among Jews. The situation seemed to call for it.

Before that time, there had been a tendency to consider the return from the Exile a sort of happy ending of the Biblical story. The Old Testament, as we have it, almost makes it seem so for the latest of the authentic historical books in the Jewish canon is Nehemiah, featuring the restoration of the walls of Jerusalem.

And yet the happy ending seemed to dissolve into nothing; into worse than nothing, for persecution under the Seleucid Empire rose to a high pitch after 200 B.C. and the condition of the Jews was suddenly more miserable than it had been even in the days of Nebuchadnezzar. The frustration was the greater since the new miseries seemed to be without cause.

In the time of the old kingdoms of Israel and Judah, the kings and the people had been periodic idolaters and had been constantly backsliding and were therefore viewed as having been properly punished. After the Exile, however, the Jews had been faithful monotheists, and had not sinned in the same fashion as the generations before the Exile had sinned. Why, then, did matters go so poorly and why was the Seleucid Empire (and, in later centuries, the Roman Empire) so triumphant in its pagan cruelty?

The theory developed that the earth as a whole had grown so wicked that, as in the days just before Noah's Flood, it was past saving, and that it was part of God's scheme to bring all the earth to a destruction from which only a few of the faithful would be saved.

The writers of such literature found a kind of recompense for present injustice in the view of a future in which the mighty tyrants of the earth would be properly punished while the oppressed faithful would be liberated and brought to joy. God would judge between the good and the evil in that final day of destruction; even the dead would come back to life if they were worthy; and there would be the final glorious rule of God.

In other words, if all were not right now, all would be made right in the future.

The writers of apocalyptic literature generally ascribed their writings to some ancient whose name would carry weight and who, for his holiness, would be considered to have had the whole scheme of history revealed to him by God. A number were ascribed to Enoch; others were ascribed to Moses, to Ezra, to Noah, and so on.

At least one rather early apocalypse must have been ascribed to Isaiah, and successfully so, for it appears in the Book of Isaiah, even though scholars agree it cannot have been written by him, but must have been composed some centuries after his death. Chapters 24 to 27 of the Book of Isaiah are commonly referred to as "The Apocalypse of Isaiah" and that is a good name if it is remembered that it refers to the book in which it is found rather than the person who uttered it.

The Apocalypse of Isaiah begins with a picture of destruction:

Isaiah 24:1. *Behold, the Lord maketh the earth empty, and maketh it waste, and turneth it upside down.*

It makes veiled allusions, as is common in apocalyptic literature. After all, since such writings are describing the fall of empires that are then in secure power, to be too plain in the description would be to invite an accusation of treason and the inevitable punishment that would follow. The veiled allusions would be clear enough to the initiated readers. Thus:

Isaiah 24:10. *The city of confusion is broken down . . .*
Isaiah 24:11. *. . . all joy is darkened . . .*
Isaiah 24:12. *In the city is left desolation . . .*

Which is the city of confusion? Clearly, whichever city was acting the part of tyrant at the time the passage was written. If it were written in the time of the Exile, it could only mean Babylon and all the readers would see that at once. Later on, it could be reinterpreted to mean Antioch, capital of the Seleucid kings, and still later, to mean Rome.

At every period the oppressed Jews of the time would have no doubt as to which was "the city of confusion" (or "city of chaos" as the Revised Standard Version has it), while the authorities, if made aware of the verse, would find it difficult to prove treason in it.

Another example of circumspect allusion is to be found in a reference to Moab:

Isaiah 25:10. . . . *Moab shall be trodden down . . . even as straw is trodden down for the dunghill.*

Moab is the traditional enemy of Israel from the time of Moses (see page 183) but it rarely had its independence, or served as a real danger, after the time of David. Nevertheless, it remained as a personification of all the enemies of the Jews and the readers of Isaiah would clearly see Moab as standing for Babylon, Antioch, or Rome, depending on the period in which the verse was read.

At the end of time, the powerful are punished:

Isaiah 24:21. . . . *in that day . . . the Lord shall punish . . . the kings of the earth . . .*
Isaiah 24:22. *And they shall be gathered together as prisoners . . . and shall be shut up . . .*

The oppressed faithful are uplifted:

Isaiah 25:8. . . . *the Lord God will wipe away tears . . . and the rebuke of his people shall he take away . . .*

The dead faithful shall be resurrected:

Isaiah 26:19. *Thy dead men shall live . . . and the earth shall cast out the dead.*

This verse is good evidence for the lateness of the apocalypse, for the doctrine of resurrection of the dead reaches its development in the post-Exilic period, certainly not as early as the lifetime of Isaiah.

God will then put an end to all evil and establish a new order:

Isaiah 27:1. *In that day the Lord . . . shall punish leviathan . . . and he shall slay the dragon that is in the sea.*

Jews will then return from exile (another sign that the passage is to be dated long after the time of Isaiah) to worship God:

ASIMOV'S GUIDE TO THE BIBLE

Isaiah 27:12. . . . *in that day . . . ye shall be gathered one by one,*
O ye children of Israel.

Isaiah 27:13. . . . *and shall worship the Lord in the holy mount of*
Jerusalem.

Ariel

After the apocalyptic chapters there is a return to clearly Isaianic
prophecies concerning the immediate problems of his time. Judah had
remained a loyal Assyrian tributary since 735 B.C. and had remained
secure while Sargon destroyed Israel and carried its leaders off into an
exile from which they never returned (see page 378).

But in 705 B.C., Sargon had died and his son Sennacherib had succeeded to the throne. The various provinces of the Assyrian Empire,
taking advantage of possible confusion, of the possible weakness of the
new king, rebelled at once. Hezekiah, the son of Ahaz, who was now
king of Israel, joined in this rebellion by refusing his tribute. For a
while, Judah could do this with impunity for Sennacherib was busy
with other, more important, portions of the Assyrian realm. Judah might
gamble further that Sennacherib might be defeated resoundingly and
that the Assyrian realm might be sufficiently weakened to secure Judah
against all retaliation. Such a thing had happened before.

Isaiah, however, did not think it would happen this time.

Isaiah 29:1. *Woe to Ariel, to Ariel, the city where David*
dwelt! . . .

Ariel is variously translated as "the lion of God," "the hearth of
God," or "the fireplace of God," but by whatever translation it is called
it is clearly Jerusalem. Since Jerusalem is the site of the Temple,
upon whose altar sacrifices are burnt (hence "hearth" or "fireplace"),
Ariel might perhaps be most fairly translated as the "altar of God."

Judah's rebellion was carried through partly at the instigation of
Egypt, which was still independent of Assyria, but which feared the
inevitable day when Assyria would attack and, probably, conquer. Only
by keeping the Assyrian realm in periodic turmoil could she hope to
stave off the evil day, and for that purpose, Egypt's wealth was always
ready to be handed out to those who determined policy among the

subject nations of Assyria. Egypt was also constantly ready to promise military assistance; a useless promise since this was a period in which Egypt was militarily weak.

Isaiah saw clearly that any reliance upon Egypt was bound to lead to disaster and (in the King James Version) pictured her, mockingly, as one who is barely strong enough to do anything.

Isaiah 30:7. *For the Egyptians shall help in vain and to no purpose: therefore have I cried concerning this, Their strength is to sit still.*

In this verse, the King James Version translates *Rahab* as "strength." The word might also be taken as the usual personification of Egypt, so that the Revised Standard Version leaves it untranslated and has the verse read: "For Egypt's help is worthless and empty, therefore I have called her 'Rahab who sits still.'"

The climax of the Judean rebellion, the siege of Jerusalem by Sennacherib, is described in four chapters of Isaiah (36 to 39 inclusive) which virtually repeat the history of that siege contained in three chapters (18 to 20) of the Second Book of Kings.

Lilith

In the course of this middle section of the Book of Isaiah, there is another piece of apocalyptic writing, describing the end of the old order and the coming of a new, ideal world. As part of the destruction, we have:

Isaiah 34:5. *For my sword . . . shall come down upon Idumea . . .*

Idumaea is the name given to Edom in Greek and Roman times, and the Revised Standard Version uses "Edom" in its place. Here again, as in the case of Moab earlier, Edom is not meant merely as itself but as a representation of heathen oppressors generally.

The desolation that is to befall Edom (the oppressing heathen empires) is described in savage terms. It is to be swept clear of humanity and given over to all the noxious forms of life from nettles to dragons. One passage, unnecessarily weakened in the King James Version, is:

Isaiah 34:14. . . . *the screech owl also shall rest there . . .*

The Hebrew word translated here as "screech owl" is *lilith* and that is the name given to a monster of the night. It is derived from *lilitu*, the name given it in Babylonian mythology and that is itself derived from the Semitic word for "night." The Revised Standard Version strengthens the verse by making it read: "there shall the night hag alight."

(The darkness has always been filled with fearsome things, both in reality, when mankind had to face the nocturnal predators, and in imagination, when things half-seen in dim moonlight took on menacing shapes, and sounds from objects unseen rent the soul with fright. We who now live in a world where artificial lighting has abolished the dark tend to forget just how frightening the night can be and how easy it is to people the night with monsters.)

The later rabbis personified the night hag and made her into Lilith, a beautiful woman who was Adam's wife before Eve was created. He could not endure her because she was so shrewish (or perhaps she could not endure him because he was so sober and grave) and they parted. She became a demon of the night who, according to some stories, joined with the serpent to bring about the fall of Adam and Eve, and who is of special danger to children ever since, perhaps because of her rage at her own childlessness.

The Martyrdom of Isaiah

Nothing is known of the life of Isaiah after the failure of Sennacherib's siege of Jerusalem. Since the first verse of the book mentions no king later than Hezekiah, it might easily be assumed that Isaiah died a natural death shortly after the siege and before 692 B.C. when Hezekiah himself died. This would be a natural event, for Isaiah would be in his sixties and men do die in their sixties.

Nevertheless, later tradition had it that he lived on into the reign of Manasseh and that is not impossible. If so, times must have grown dangerous for the prophet. If Sennacherib had not succeeded in actually taking and sacking Jerusalem, he had nevertheless taught Judah a painful lesson. In Manasseh's reign, Judah accepted a completely pro-Assyrian policy, paying its tribute and remaining a faithful puppet.

The Yahvists, as dangerous nationalists who would certainly bring ruin upon the nation (so Manasseh would be convinced) with their inflammatory calls for reliance upon God alone, were suppressed. No doubt many of the more intransigent were executed:

2 Kings 21:16. . . . *Manasseh shed innocent blood very much, till he had filled Jerusalem from one end to another . . .*

It is not specified that Isaiah was killed and it is rather unlikely that he would have been, without its being specifically mentioned. Besides, Manasseh was only twelve when he came to the throne and it might not have been till well on into his reign that his anti-Yahvist policies reached their extreme. Isaiah would have had to be quite old by that time.

But the tradition arose in later times that Isaiah was executed in Manasseh's time. The legend even goes into the gory detail that Isaiah, in trying to escape Manasseh's malignant wrath, hid in a hollow tree and that Manasseh ordered the tree, with Isaiah inside, to be sawed in two.

About A.D. 100 this legend was incorporated into a tale of Jewish origin called "The Martyrdom of Isaiah."

The legend was sufficiently well known even before its commitment to writing (at that there may have been earlier written versions that have not survived) to cast a reflection of itself into the New Testament.

Thus, in the Epistle to the Hebrews, the writer is listing the great deeds of Jewish history, and having reached the time of Joshua, merely summarizes the rest. In hastily listing the hard fates unflinchingly faced by the prophets, he says:

Hebrews 11:37. *They were stoned, they were sawn asunder, were tempted, were slain by the sword . . .*

The phrase "sawn asunder" is thought to be a reference to Isaiah.

Second Isaiah

The Book of Isaiah continues after the end of the Sennacherib chapters—but with a marked and sudden change. The language, style, and background all shift.

In the earlier chapters, Judah is a kingdom facing destruction and

The New Babylonian (Chaldean) Empire

it is castigated unsparingly by the harsh prophetic tongue. In the later chapters, Judah is in exile and despair and it is uplifted with lyric enthusiasm by a prophet promising rescue.

It begins at once:

> Isaiah 40:1. *Comfort ye, comfort ye my people, saith your God.*
> Isaiah 40:2. *Speak ye comfortably to Jerusalem . . .*

Furthermore, Isaiah speaks now not of Ahaz, Hezekiah, and Sennacherib, but of Cyrus of Persia, who ruled a century and a half after Sennacherib:

Isaiah 45:1. *Thus saith the Lord . . . to Cyrus, whose right hand I have holden, to subdue nations before him . . .*

It is possible to argue, if one is wedded to the literal word of the Bible, that the Isaiah of Hezekiah's time foresaw the period of the Exile in great detail, down to the name and deeds of the monarch who was to establish the Persian Empire and liberate the Jews, and that he spoke his vision in a style that was altered from what it had been.

This point of view, however, has no important advocates today. It is assumed instead that a prophet of the period of the Exile wrote under the honored name of Isaiah and that, since he was every bit as great a poet as Isaiah, if not actually greater, his work was included with that of the earlier prophet in the present Book of Isaiah.

So it comes to pass that the great prophet of the Exile, certainly one of the great influential voices of history, is doomed to complete anonymity forever (as far as we can now tell). He can be referred to only as the "Second Isaiah," or, using the Greek term for "second," as the "Deutero-Isaiah."

Cyrus

The Second Isaiah is convinced that the Exile is soon to be broken and he even sees the one whose worldly hands will be used by God to break that exile. Cyrus of Persia has, apparently, just taken Ecbatana, destroyed the Median Empire, and replaced it with the still more powerful Persian Empire. This is considered by the Second Isaiah to be the work of God:

Isaiah 41:2. . . . [God] *raised up the righteous man from the east, called him to his foot, gave the nations before him, and made him rule over kings?*

Cyrus's home province is Persia, which lies east of Babylonia. To the Jews in Babylonian Exile, he is therefore the "man from the east." Now that Cyrus has established himself in the royal seat of Ecbatana, he hovers to the north of Babylonia like a thundercloud and the Second Isaiah gladly waits his coming:

Isaiah 41:25. *I [God] have raised up one from the north, and he shall come . . .*

Cyrus conquered Media in 549 B.C. but it was not until 538 B.C. that he took Babylon. The writings of Second Isaiah seem to fall between these two dates and can be placed about 540 B.C., or just two centuries after the call of the First Isaiah.

We have in the views of the Second Isaiah a clear departure from henotheism (see page 359). The Second Isaiah seems to be certain that Yahveh is as powerful outside Judah as ever He was inside it. Nor does he imagine for a moment that the Babylonian gods are stronger than Yahveh just because the Babylonians had defeated and scattered Yahveh's people. Instead, he pictures a universal God. He thinks of Yahveh as not merely the supreme and only God of Israel, but the supreme and only God of the universe. If Judah was defeated and destroyed and the Jews were driven into exile that was the action of none other than God and served the divine purpose. And if the great heathen conqueror Cyrus appeared on the scene, he too was but another tool in the hand of Yahveh.

The Second Isaiah was even confident that the universality of the only God was something that eventually all people would acknowledge:

Isaiah 45:14. *Thus saith the Lord, the labour of Egypt and merchandise of Ethiopia and of the Sabeans . . . shall come after thee . . . and . . . they shall make supplication unto thee, saying, Surely God is in thee; and there is none else, there is no God.*

The Servant of the Lord

The anonymity of the Second Isaiah might be considered broken by certain passages in which, just conceivably, he may be speaking of himself. The Second Isaiah pictures Israel as particularly serving God's purposes for all the world. He quotes God as saying:

Isaiah 41:9. *But thou Israel art my servant . . .*

The servant may be meek and passive, but he will hold to God's law faithfully until all the world comes to accept it:

Isaiah 42:4. *He shall not fail nor be discouraged, till he have set judgement in the earth: and the isles shall wait for his law.*

But then, at the beginning of the forty-ninth chapter, the Servant is personified. The Second Isaiah speaks in the first person as though he himself represents the idealized Israel serving its God. He is discouraged at the fruitlessness of his efforts:

Isaiah 49:4. *Then I said, I have laboured in vain, I have spent my strength for nought, and in vain . . .*

God encourages him, informing him (in line with the Second Isaiah's views as to the universality of Yahveh) that his mission is not for Jews only:

Isaiah 49:6. *. . . I will also give thee for a light to the Gentiles, that thou mayest be my salvation unto the end of the earth.*

The Second Isaiah describes the Servant of the Lord as suffering for his labors; and if he is talking about himself (in an access of self-pity) it is easy to see that his advanced views on the nature of God might have been found unacceptable not only by the heathen but by most of the Jews of the time and that he would therefore have reason to feel rejected:

Isaiah 53:3. *He [the Servant] is despised and rejected of men; a man of sorrows, and acquainted with grief: . . . he was despised, and we esteemed him not.*

According to the later Christian view, the picture drawn by the Second Isaiah is a prophetic foretelling of the career of Jesus. This would be, by that interpretation, a new kind of Messianic prophecy. The Messiah is not pictured as the ideal king of the First Isaiah, who establishes his power with force and who reigns in glory; but rather as a prophet, beaten, bruised, and killed, who even in this fashion was, through apparent total defeat, fulfilling the will of God.

Bel

The Second Isaiah foresees the inevitable destruction of Babylon by Cyrus and rejoices at the downfall of its idols:

Isaiah 46:1. *Bel boweth down, Nebo stoopeth . . .*

Bel is the Babylonian word for "lord," the equivalent of the Phoenician "Baal." Originally, Bel was the name given particularly to the important Sumerian god En-lil, who was a god of the air and sky; a storm-god originally, like the Greek Zeus or the most primitive conceptions of Yahveh. The seat of En-lil's worship was in the Sumerian city of Nippur on the Euphrates, about fifty miles downstream from Babylon.

When Babylon became powerful and grew to dominate the land under Hammurabi (see page 69) its local god, Marduk (Merodach to the Jews) naturally grew, henotheistically, in importance. Marduk assimilated the attributes of En-lil and became the new Bel. (Nippur, however, remained an important center of worship long after it had lost its political importance. Religious ritual is just about the most conservative aspect of human culture.)

The importance of Marduk was emphasized by the creation myth that originated in Babylon. When Tiamat (the chaotic force of the sea) threatened the old Sumerian gods, they dared not battle the monster. It was Marduk, a second-generation god, the son of Ea (a Sumerian god worshiped particularly at Eridu, near what was then the mouth of the Euphrates), who dared venture forth into battle. He destroyed Tiamat and formed the universe out of its remains. With that deed, Marduk was promoted to supremacy over the older Sumerian pantheon, a reflection in heaven of the supremacy on earth of Babylon over the older Sumerian cities.

Of course, when Assyria dominated Babylon, they considered their own national god, Asshur, to have been the hero of the Tiamat story; but under Nebuchadnezzar, with Babylon again supreme, Marduk was also the great god once more. He was Bel-Marduk ("Lord Marduk") or just Bel.

This was understood by the Jews, for the prophet Jeremiah, in predicting the fall of Babylon, uses the two names of the god in poetic parallelism:

Jeremiah 50:2. . . . *Babylon is taken, Bel is confounded, Merodach is broken in pieces* . . .

Nebo (Nabu in Babylonian) was originally a Sumerian god, worshiped at Borsippa, just a couple of miles south of Babylon. He was viewed as a god of wisdom, who had, for instance, invented writing. When Babylon became supreme over Sumeria, Nebo was accepted into the Babylonian system of gods. Because of Borsippa's closeness to Babylon, Nebo may have been familiar to them and have been accepted as a near neighbor of Marduk, so to speak. He was therefore given an honored place in the pantheon, made the son of Marduk in the Babylonian mythology, and placed second in power to him. Nebo's name occurs in that of Nebuchadnezzar.

Beulah

The final eleven chapters of Isaiah seem to strike a lower note than those that went before and many suggest that the Second Isaiah ends with the fifty-fifth chapter. Those that follow, then, are thought to have been written by another and still later hand, the Third Isaiah, or the Trito-Isaiah.

In these final chapters the return from exile is no longer imminent, as it is with the Second Isaiah, but seems actually to have taken place. Where in the Second Isaiah the return is anticipated with jubilation and seen as the coming of an ideal state, there is disillusion with the actuality in the Third Isaiah. Idolatry is denounced; and the reference appears to be to the Samaritans, or to the Jews who had returned and who were falling in with the practices of those who inhabited the land. The leaders of the new community are denounced.

However, as is almost always the case in the prophetic books, there is hope for the future; there is always the idealized state on the horizon. A new and glorified Jerusalem is envisaged:

Isaiah 60:10. *And the sons of strangers shall build up thy walls . . .*

If this verse is taken literally then the walls of Jerusalem had not yet been rebuilt and the Third Isaiah must be writing about 450 B.C., before the coming of Nehemiah. His words would fall about a century after the Second Isaiah and nearly three centuries after the First.

The new, ideal land is described glowingly and, speaking to the personified Jerusalem, the writer says:

Isaiah 62:4. *Thou shalt no more be termed Forsaken; neither shall thy land any more be termed Desolate: but thou shalt be called Hephzi-bah, and thy land Beulah . . .*

Hephzibah means "My delight is in her" and Beulah means "Married." The picture is of God loving and marrying the land. God and His people will be united and inseparable. The Revised Standard Version translates the terms so that the end of the verse reads: ". . . your land . . . shall be called My delight is in her, and your land Married."

Because of this verse, the "land of Beulah" has come to mean something very close to heaven and in Bunyan's *The Pilgrim's Progress* it represents a kind of pleasant anteroom in which the pilgrims rest till they are invited into the Celestial City.

24. JEREMIAH

JEREMIAH · TAHAPANES · RAMAH · SHILOH · AHIKAM · SHESHACH · BARUCH · JEHOIAKIM · ZEDEKIAH · HANANIAH · THE LETTER OF JEREMIAH · ZEDEKIAH · NEBUZARADAN · GEDALIAH · ISHMAEL · JOHANAN · PHARAOH-HOPHRA

Jeremiah

The second of the major prophets, chronologically as well as in his position in the Bible, is Jeremiah ("Yahveh is exalted"). The book announces its authorship at once:

Jeremiah 1:1. *The words of Jeremiah the son of Hilkiah, of the priests that were in Anathoth in the land of Benjamin.*

Jeremiah 1:2. *To whom the word of the Lord came in the days of Josiah . . . in the thirteenth year of his reign.*

Jeremiah 1:3. *. . . unto the carrying away of Jerusalem captive . . .*

Since Josiah came to the throne in 638 B.C., the thirteenth year of his reign would be 626 B.C. and in that year, Jeremiah began a prophetic mission that was to carry him through more than forty years of tragedy, to the final fall of Jerusalem and a little beyond. It was a time of gathering doom, reaching a climax of total disaster, and this is reflected in Jeremiah's writings.

There was in Josiah's time a Hilkiah of importance. Indeed, he was no less than the High Priest whose discovery of the Book of Deuteronomy in the Temple crystallized the reforms of Josiah:

2 Kings 22:8. *And Hilkiah the high priest said unto Shaphan the scribe, I have found the book of the law in the house of the Lord . . .*

Judah and the Chaldean Empire

There might be an impulse to think of Jeremiah as the son of this High Priest, but this is completely unlikely. If he were, he would be high in the priestly hierarchy. Instead, the first verse makes it plain he is of provincial origin, a member of a priestly clan of the Benjamite town of Anathoth, some four miles northeast of Jerusalem.

As it happens, the Bible speaks earlier of a priest who had his holdings in Anathoth. This was Abiathar, the only survivor of the slaughter at Nob (see page 291) and the last representative of the house of Eli to hold an official position in the priesthood. After David's death, Abiathar had supported Adonijah for the succession (see page 320). When Solomon outmaneuvered Adonijah and established himself on the throne, Abiathar suffered the penalty for having guessed wrong:

> 1 Kings 2:26. *And unto Abiathar the priest said the king* [Solomon], *Get thee to Anathoth, unto thine own fields* . . .
> 1 Kings 2:27. *So Solomon thrust out Abiathar from being priest unto the Lord* . . .

Zadok, who had earlier been associated with Abiathar in the highest rank of the priesthood under David, now became sole High Priest, and from him the entire line of High Priests descended, down to the Exile and even beyond.

Far from being of the High Priestly Zadokite line, then, Jeremiah is very likely to have been a descendant of Abiathar and, through him, of Eli, a member of the line that had been displaced by Zadok and his descendants and that had lived in obscurity at Anathoth for three centuries as a result.

Jeremiah, like Isaiah, was presumably quite young when he first received his call. He implies this himself for in describing the call, he quotes himself as answering:

> Jeremiah 1:6. . . . *Ah, Lord God! behold, I cannot speak: for I am a child.*

This might be metaphorical; a modest claim to be only a child in understanding. However, if he remained an active prophet for forty years, he must have been a young man at the beginning. If he were twenty at the time, then he was born in 646 B.C., when idolatrous king Manasseh (see page 424) had been on the throne nearly half a century. It would make Jeremiah just about the same age as king Josiah, during whose reign the call had come.

The call came to Jeremiah at a crisis in history, as it had come to Isaiah. To Isaiah it came when the Assyrian menace suddenly rose and overshadowed all else. Now it came to Jeremiah at the time when the Assyrian Empire was beginning its astonishingly rapid collapse and all the Fertile Crescent was thrown into confusion.

In 626 B.C., the very year of Jeremiah's call, Asshurbanipal, the last strong Assyrian king, had died. Rebellions arose everywhere and the strength of the Assyrian army was no longer sufficient to cope with them. Invasions of the Cimmerian nomads from the north had kept Asia Minor in turmoil during Asshurbanipal's reign. They had finally been very largely destroyed but the effort had stretched Assyrian strength past its limits.

Now, with Asshurbanipal's death, the Cimmerians, in what proved to be a last gasp, were raiding southward again, and the distraught Assyrians, busied with revolts in Babylonia and elsewhere, could do nothing about it. It may have been to these Cimmerian raids that an early verse in Jeremiah refers:

Jeremiah 1:14. *Out of the north an evil shall break forth upon all the inhabitants of the land.*

However, the Cimmerians could not take fortified towns and their relatively undisciplined hordes were most suited to hit-and-run. Their threat was soon done. Other, far more dangerous threats were to follow.

Tahapanes

The chronology of the Book of Jeremiah is incredibly tangled. The Anchor Bible, in order to achieve a kind of chronological order, is forced to shuffle the chapters of Jeremiah, but even so, some passages which are not dated and which do not refer to events that can be dated remain puzzling as far as chronology is concerned.

In the second chapter, Jeremiah complains bitterly of Judah's apostasy: of its following after strange gods and its acceptance of idolatrous customs. This section may therefore come at the beginning of his ministry, before the reforms of Josiah. (The Book of Deuteronomy was found in the Temple five years after Jeremiah's call.)

At one point, in describing the misfortunes that befell Judah as a result of its apostasy, he says:

Jeremiah 2:16. *Also the children of Noph and Tahapanes have broken the crown of thy head.*

Egypt had regained its independence from Assyria in 664 B.C., a generation before Jeremiah's call, and as Assyria declined rapidly, Egypt's relative power increased. For the first time in five centuries it was to play an effective role in international affairs.

The 26th dynasty, which then ruled Egypt, had its power centered in the delta, in the city of Saïs, so that the nation in this period is spoken of as "Saitic Egypt." Noph is Memphis, the ancient capital of the delta (see page 63), so that "the children of Noph" makes a logical metaphorical representation of Egypt.

Tahapanes (spelled Tahpanhes later in Jeremiah, and Tehaphnehes in the Book of Ezekiel) was a frontier town in the northeast of Egypt, near the Mediterranean coast and just about at the site of what is now the Suez Canal. When Saitic Egypt began to face eastward and to dream of expansion into Asia, Tahapanes was fortified and converted into a strong base for military operations. It would be the nearest important Egyptian city to Judah, and the people in Jeremiah's time would be conscious of it as a representation of Egyptian might.

The verse is interpreted by some as referring to the defeat of Judah by Egypt in 608 B.C. when Josiah was killed. Surely the king of Judah might be referred to as "the crown of thy head" by someone addressing the men of Judah. If so, however, Jeremiah's strictures against apostasy would be out of place, for Josiah's reform was approved of, in general, by Jeremiah. Thus, Jeremiah, in addressing the son of Josiah rhetorically:

Jeremiah 22:15. . . . *did not thy father . . . do judgment and justice . . .*

Jeremiah 22:16. *He judged the cause of the poor and needy . . .*

If, then, the second chapter relates to a time before Josiah's reform, 2:16 cannot refer to Josiah's death and may merely have the general meaning of "even the Egyptians are now stronger than you," a scornful reference to the Egypt that had been weak for so long.

The Greeks called Tahapanes Daphne, and the Anchor Bible uses the Greek terms for both cities. "The men of Memphis and Daphne, They too have cracked your skull." Tahapanes is in ruins now but the mound under which it is buried is called Tel Defenneh, so that the name lives.

Ramah

Jeremiah might well have been conscious of his descent from the house of Eli, who had been High Priest at an Ephraimite shrine, for the northern kingdom of Israel seemed often to come to his mind. In fact, there is a sympathy for the lost and scattered Israel which would have been unusual in a Judean, for Judah and Israel were at war through much of their history. Could it be that some of Jeremiah's bitterness arose out of a sense of alienation, a feeling that he was a northerner lost among Judean strangers?

Thus, in his bitter denunciation of Judah (so bitter that such denunciatory speeches are referred to in the English language as "jeremiads") the prophet compares the land unfavorably to the northern kingdom. He defends Israel against the standard Judean argument that the northern kingdom had gone down to Assyrian destruction because it had drifted away from the Davidic line and the true worship at Jerusalem, and sacrificed instead at idolatrous altars in Dan and Bethel. Jeremiah says flatly:

> Jeremiah 3:11. *And the Lord said unto me, The backsliding Israel hath justified herself more than treacherous Judah.*

Again, in another passage he weeps over fallen Israel with moving sorrow:

> Jeremiah 31:15. . . . *A voice was heard in Ramah, lamentation and bitter weeping; Rahel [Rachel] weeping for her children refused to be comforted for her children, because they were not.*

Rachel was the ancestress of the three tribes of Ephraim, Manasseh, and Benjamin. Whether Jeremiah considered himself an Ephraimite through his descent from Eli, or a Benjamite through the site of his family's holdings, he would, in either case, have felt himself a descendant of Rachel.

There were two traditions as to the site of Rachel's grave. One had her buried in Judah, north of Bethlehem:

> Genesis 35:19. *And Rachel died, and was buried in the way to Ephrath, which is Bethlehem.*

Another had her buried in Benjamin. Thus, the prophet Samuel speaks of:

> 1 Samuel 10:2. . . . *Rachel's sepulchre in the border of Benjamin at Zelzah . . .*

The location of Zelzah is unknown, but Jeremiah clearly accepts the Benjamite tradition and Zelzah may be an alternative name for Ramah. Ramah is four miles northwest of Jeremiah's home town of Anathoth and it is there he places the tomb of his ancestress. He pictures her ghost as haunting the place and weeping constantly for the tribes carried off into permanent exile a century before.

Then, when Jeremiah begs the men of Judah to return to God and establish an ideal state, he describes such a state as including the returned exiles of Israel:

> Jeremiah 3:18. *In those days the house of Judah shall walk with the house of Israel, and they shall come together out of the land of the north . . .*

Shiloh

Jeremiah's consciousness of his northern origin makes him less apt to accept certain aspects of Josiah's reform. By wiping out all local religious altars and practices as heathen and idolatrous, Josiah had centered all worship at the Temple at Jerusalem and there were many who must have thought that this Temple had magic powers to protect the city and its people. To Jeremiah the Temple was an institution from which his own family had been barred, and in his mind was the memory of an older temple which, in its time, had been just as holy.

Jeremiah denounced the overimportance attached to Jerusalem in his so-called "Temple Sermon," which he delivered within the Temple itself. The Temple Sermon is given early in Jeremiah but is dated in a passage that is found considerably later in the book:

> Jeremiah 26:1. *In the beginning of the reign of Jehoiakim the son of Josiah . . . came this word from the Lord, saying . . .*
> Jeremiah 26:2. . . . *Stand in the court of the Lord's house, and speak unto all the cities of Judah . . .*

The sermon is then given, shortly after the death of Josiah in battle with Egypt in 608 B.C. The Egyptian armies controlled the land for the moment but they made no attempt to lay siege to Jerusalem and take it. It was sufficient for Egypt to rely on their puppet, Jehoiakim, whom their influence had placed on the throne. (Egypt was far more concerned with the gathering strength of the Chaldeans under Nabopolassar and his son Nebuchadnezzar. They had recently taken Nineveh and had established themselves as master of the Tigris-Euphrates.)

Undoubtedly, the nationalist element in Judah, ignoring the realities of the situation, felt that Jerusalem was safe under all circumstances and against all comers simply because of the existence of the Temple and of the purification of Temple-worship by the elimination of all competing cults.

Jeremiah, less impressed by the sanctity of the Temple, said:

> Jeremiah 7:4. *Trust ye not in lying words, saying, The temple of the Lord, The temple of the Lord, The temple of the Lord* . . .

He points out that it is not ritualistic worship and reform that will save Judah, but ethical reform, and quotes God as saying:

> Jeremiah 7:9. *Will ye steal, murder, and commit adultery, and swear falsely* . . .
> Jeremiah 7:10. *And come and stand before me in this house* . . . *and say, We are delivered* . . .

Then, out of his own background he recalls the case of an earlier temple, the sanctity of which did not keep it from destruction. Jeremiah quotes God as saying:

> Jeremiah 7:12. *But go ye now unto my place which was in Shiloh, where I set my name at the first, and see what I did to it for the wickedness of my people Israel.*

Ahikam

The Temple Sermon got Jeremiah into trouble. As a matter of fact, he was in continual trouble throughout his life. A prophet could not, like Jeremiah, constantly predict the most disastrous evils in the most violent language without making himself unpopular to a populace that wanted (like all populaces) comfort and reassurance. Jeremiah was an annoyance, a gadfly, and there must have been many who would have been willing to see his mouth shut by force. Unfortunately, the Book of Jeremiah gives us no detailed chronological account of the opposition, but there are occasional references in passing. At one point, Jeremiah quotes his enemies:

> Jeremiah 18:18. *Then said they, Come and let us devise devices against Jeremiah . . . let us smite him . . . and let us not give heed to any of his words.*

Jeremiah naturally incurred the wrath of the High Priestly officials, who, at times, did not hesitate to lay violent hands upon him:

> Jeremiah 20:1. *Now Pashur . . . who was . . . chief governor in the house of the Lord, heard that Jeremiah prophesied these things.*
> Jeremiah 20:2. *Then Pashur smote Jeremiah . . . and put him in the stocks . . .*

Jeremiah was as unpopular in his home town as in Jerusalem. The reason is not given but perhaps those at Anathoth were afraid that Jeremiah's unpopularity might spread to the people of his home town. They might have felt that by getting rid of him they would remove themselves from an unpleasant and dangerous spotlight. Jeremiah quotes God, warning the enemies of his own town:

> Jeremiah 11:21. . . . *thus saith the Lord of the men of Anathoth, that seek thy life, saying, Prophesy not in the name of the Lord, that thou die not by our hand:*
> Jeremiah 11:22. . . . *thus saith the Lord of hosts, Behold I will punish them . . .*

Jeremiah underwent a particularly dangerous moment, however, after his Temple Sermon, when in the very Temple itself he had warned Jerusalem of suffering the fate of Shiloh. This naturally outraged the worshipers, who viewed it as outright blasphemy. The people demanded he be executed at once. There was recent precedent for such an action:

> Jeremiah 26:20. . . . *there was . . . a man that prophesied in the name of the Lord, Urijah . . . who prophesied against this city . . .*
> Jeremiah 26:21. *And when Jehoiakim the king . . . sought to put him to death . . . Urijah . . . fled . . . into Egypt.*

Jeremiah 26:22. *And Jehoiakim . . . sent men into Egypt . . .*
Jeremiah 26:23. *And they fetched forth Urijah out of Egypt and brought him unto Jehoiakim . . . who slew him . . .*

Nevertheless, there were people of importance who, either because they agreed with Jeremiah, or feared the consequences of killing a prophet, pleaded against the execution. They cited the case of the prophet Micah, who had spoken much as Jeremiah had spoken back in the reign of Hezekiah a century earlier and who had been left completely unharmed. One man of influence in particular protected Jeremiah and kept him from harm:

Jeremiah 26:24. . . . *the hand of Ahikam the son of Shaphan was with Jeremiah, that they should not give him into the hand of the people to put him to death.*

Ahikam had been a high official under Josiah and had been one of those involved in the reforms under that king:

2 Kings 22:12. *And the king [Josiah] commanded Hilkiah the priest and Ahikam the son of Shaphan . . .*
2 Kings 22:13. *Go ye, inquire of the Lord . . . concerning the words of this book that is found . . .*

Sheshach

One can well imagine that Jeremiah is frustrated and in despair at the fact that his denunciations produce enmity and anger, rather than repentance.

Jeremiah 25:1. . . . *in the fourth year of Jehoiakim . . .*
Jeremiah 25:2. . . . *Jeremiah spake . . . saying*
Jeremiah 25:3. *From the thirteenth year of Josiah . . . even unto this day, that is the three and twentieth year . . . I have spoken unto you, . . . but ye have not hearkened.*

It is now 605 or 604 B.C. and a new crisis is upon Judah. The fall of Assyria is now complete, and the period of confusion that followed is almost over. The Chaldeans, ruling from Babylon, have emerged the winners. In 605 B.C. Nebuchadnezzar, son of Nabopolassar (who had taken Nineveh) defeated Pharaoh-nechoh at Carchemish. The Egyptian conqueror of Josiah was driven back to the Nile and Egypt's short foray into Asia was over. Egypt was not to become a conquering power for three more centuries. Then, in 604 B.C., Nabopolassar died and the victorious Nebuchadnezzar came to the throne.

Jeremiah judged that under Nebuchadnezzar's forceful leadership the Chaldeans would drive on toward the re-establishment of empire over the entire Fertile Crescent, under Babylon now rather than under Nineveh. Sinful Judah would be given over to the Babylonian conqueror by God.

> Jeremiah 25:8. *Thus saith the Lord of hosts; Because ye have not heard my words,*
> Jeremiah 25:9. *Behold, I will send ... Nebuchadrezzar ... against this land, and against the inhabitants thereof ... and will utterly destroy them ...*

(Nebuchadrezzar, as the Babylonian king is called here, is also referred to as Nebuchadnezzar in books written later and even in other parts of the Book of Jeremiah; as, for instance, in the reference:

> Jeremiah 29:1. ... *all the people whom Nebuchadnezzar had carried away captive ...*

It is the latter version, with the "n," that is more familiar to the average man, perhaps because it is to be found in the popular Book of Daniel, and which I am therefore routinely using myself. Nevertheless, it is the version with the "r" that is closer to the Babylonian original. The "n" undoubtedly arose through a copyist's error.)

Having predicted Nebuchadnezzar's conquest of Judah, Jeremiah goes on to predict that the people of Judah will go into exile for seventy years (see page 436), and to describe all the nations that are to fall to the conquering Babylonians. In this list, the climax comes with:

> Jeremiah 25:26. ... *and the king of Sheshach shall drink after them.*

Sheshach does not refer literally to any kingdom or region; it is rather an example of a simple code called "athbash" by which some dangerous reference is made which is clear to the initiated but which does not involve the writer in quite as much danger of execution for treason.

In this code, the letters of the Hebrew alphabet are reversed. The first letter of the alphabet is replaced by the last, the second letter by the next to the last, the third letter by the third from the last, and so on.

In Hebrew, the word "Sheshach" is spelled "shin-shin-caph," where "shin" is the second letter from the end and "caph" is the twelfth letter from the end. If we reverse this and take the second and twelfth letter from the beginning, we have "beth-beth-lamed," which is "Babel," or "Babylon." In short, Sheshach is the code word for Babylon and the prediction is that after Babylon conquers a long list of nations it is Babylon herself who will then be conquered in the end.

That this is so is all the more certain since in a later chapter, in describing the coming fall of Babylon, "Sheshach" is used as a synonym in poetic parallelism:

> Jeremiah 51:41. *How is Sheshach taken!* . . . *how is Babylon become an astonishment among the nations!*

Baruch

Jeremiah felt it necessary, however, to make a final attempt to persuade Judah to change its course from one that promised certain disaster. In the fourth year of Jehoiakim, therefore, he states that he was commanded by God to commit his various utterances to writing:

> Jeremiah 36:4. *Then Jeremiah called Baruch the son of Neriah: and Baruch wrote from the mouth of Jeremiah all the words of the Lord . . . upon a roll of a book.*

Baruch, Jeremiah's trusted secretary in the later part of the prophet's life, remained with Jeremiah till the fall of Jerusalem and after the fall traveled to Egypt with the prophet. According to one tradition, however, Baruch did not remain in Egypt but left it after Jeremiah's death and went to Babylon, where he died in 574 B.C. There is no Biblical evidence in favor of this, but there is nothing impossible about it, either.

Based on this tradition, there is an apocryphal book (accepted as canonical by the Catholics) entitled "The Book of Baruch" and purportedly written by him in Babylon:

Baruch 1:1. *And these are the words . . . which Baruch . . . wrote in Babylon.*

Baruch 1:2. *In the fifth year . . . what time as the Chaldeans took Jerusalem, and burnt it with fire.*

Since Jerusalem was sacked by the Babylonians in 586 B.C., the book is thus dated 582/581 B.C.

The first half of the book is in prose and consists of a confession of national sin, making the destruction of Jerusalem and the exile of the people a just punishment for that sin and now pleading for forgiveness. The second part of the book consists of two poems, one praising wisdom after the fashion of the Wisdom of Solomon (see page 515), and the second promising the consolation of return from exile after the fashion of the Second Isaiah (see page 548). It seems quite certain that the book was not written by Baruch but was written long after his time and is a composite work by different hands, reaching its final form as late as A.D. 100 perhaps.

Two apocalyptic books ascribed to Baruch were discovered in the nineteenth century. These are called the Syriac Apocalypse of Baruch and the Greek Apocalypse of Baruch, after the languages in which the manuscripts were written. They seem to be even later than the apocryphal Book of Baruch.

Jehoiakim

Once his words were committed to writing, Jeremiah was anxious to have them reach the king. Apparently, he did not have the easy entry into the royal presence that Isaiah had, so that he had to work his way through Temple officials who did have such entry. Unfortunately, after his Temple Sermon, Jeremiah was forbidden to enter the Temple grounds and he had to send Baruch.

Jeremiah 36:5. *And Jeremiah commanded Baruch saying . . . I cannot go into the house of the Lord:*

Jeremiah 36:6. *Therefore go thou, and read in the roll . . .*

The scroll was read to Temple functionaries, who anxiously told the king of the matter. The king sent an official for the scroll and had it read to him.

The men of the Temple seem to have been surprisingly anxious to forward Jeremiah's words to the king and there may be good secular reasons for this. The political situation at the moment was particularly ticklish and for once Jeremiah and the Temple may have been pulling in the same direction.

Ever since Necho of Egypt had slain Josiah at Megiddo, Judah had been tributary to Egypt, but now with Babylon in its turn triumphant over Egypt, there was a question as to whether Judah ought to remain faithful to Egypt, or to change sides and go over to Babylonia. Each alternative had its advocates and there was an Egyptian and a Babylonian party in the land. The Temple functionaries, approached by Baruch, may well have been convinced that Egypt was done, and could see that as a practical matter the only safe course was to submit to Nebuchadnezzar. Since Jeremiah was saying the same thing, his writings were eagerly forwarded to the king.

Jehoiakim, however, was apparently of the Egyptian party, and there seem to have been strong personal reasons for that.

After Josiah had been killed at Megiddo, the people of Judah acclaimed his youngest son, Shallum (throne name, Jehoahaz), as king:

> 2 Kings 23:30. . . . *And the people of the land took Jehoahaz the son of Josiah, and anointed him, and made him king . . .*

But Necho, who now controlled Judah, would not have this. He preferred his own candidate, one whom he could rely on, and who was perhaps bound to him by oaths, sworn in return for the kingship. The Egyptian monarch therefore deposed Shallum and put his older brother on the throne:

> 2 Kings 23:34. *And Pharaoh-nechoh made Eliakim the son of Josiah king . . . and turned his name to Jehoiakim, and took Jehoahaz away: and he [Jehoahaz] came to Egypt, and died there.*

Jehoiakim was thus beholden to the Egyptian Pharaoh for his throne. Even if he felt no compunctions at violating any oath of loyalty he had given, he would very likely have felt that if Nebuchadnezzar were to take over Judah, even through Judah's peaceful submission, the Babylonian king would be bound to consider Jehoiakim an Egyptian puppet and therefore untrustworthy. He would do as Necho had done and place his own man on the throne. Out of pure self-interest, then, and quite against the national good, Jehoiakim was of the Egyptian party.

Furthermore, Jehoiakim could not very well have felt kindly toward Jeremiah, since the prophet had inveighed against the king personally and in no polite terms, either. Among the prophet's utterances (which, presumably, were not included in the scroll to be handed the king, but which Jehoiakim must have known about) were:

Jeremiah 22:18. . . . *thus saith the Lord concerning Jehoiakim . . . They* [the people] *shall not lament for him . . .*
Jeremiah 22:19. *He shall be buried with the burial of an ass, drawn and cast forth beyond the gates of Jerusalem.*

Therefore, when a courtier named Jehudi read to Jehoiakim the fearful predictions of doom uttered by Jeremiah, Jehoiakim reacted at once with gloomy wrath.

Jeremiah 36:23. . . . *when Jehudi had read three or four leaves, he* [Jehoiakim] *cut it with the penknife, and cast it into the fire . . . until all the roll was consumed . . .*

Jeremiah had Baruch rewrite the scroll, but clearly the pro-Egyptian course was fixed as far as Jehoiakim was concerned. Even when he was finally forced to pay cautious lip service to Nebuchadnezzar he felt unsafe upon the throne and watched for the first opportunity to rebel.

Zedekiah

The opportunity came in 601 B.C. when Nebuchadnezzar suffered a local defeat at the hands of the Egyptians. At once Jehoiakim refused tribute. It took some time for Nebuchadnezzar's hands to be sufficiently free to deal with the situation in force, but by 597 B.C., the Babylonian army was besieging Jerusalem. Jehoiakim died in the course of the siege and his son Jehoiachin (also referred to in the Bible as Jeconiah and Coniah) reigned in his place.

Jerusalem was forced to capitulate, however, and then Nebuchadnezzar did to Jehoiakim's son what he would have done to Jehoiakim if that king had survived (and what Jehoiakim would have expected him to do). Nebuchadnezzar deposed the king and placed his own candidate on the throne. Jehoiachin was carried off into Babylonian captivity after a reign of only three months and with him was carried off much of the aristocracy and elite of the nation. What was left behind was placed under the rule of still another of Josiah's sons:

> 2 Kings 24:17. And the king of Babylon made Mattaniah . . . king . . . and changed his name to Zedekiah.

It is conceivable that Jeremiah might have indulged in the hope, in the early days of Zedekiah's accession to the throne, that now all would be well.

The nation, made aware of Babylon's overwhelming power, might settle down to a quiet subservience and experience peace and prosperity in the shadow of Nebuchadnezzar, as a century before, under Manasseh, they had experienced peace and prosperity in the shadow of Esarhaddon of Assyria. In Manasseh's time, however, king and nation had plunged deeply into idolatry. Now (so it might have seemed to Jeremiah), with the experience of Babylonian devastation, the nation would turn to God and cleanse itself. Then a mollified Yahveh would forgive His people, destroy Babylon, and establish an ideal state in Judah.

All this (just possibly) may have been in Jeremiah's mind in connection with the following verses:

> Jeremiah 23:5. Behold, the days come . . . that . . . a King shall reign and prosper . . .
> Jeremiah 23:6. In his days Judah shall be saved . . . and this is his name whereby he shall be called, the Lord Our Righteousness.

The Lord Our Righteousness is, in Hebrew, Yahveh-tsidkenu, whereas Zedekiah is, in Hebrew, "Tsidkiahu" and means "Righteous is Yahveh." One name is the inverse of the other.

These verses in Jeremiah are usually taken to be Messianic in nature and to speak of an ideal king in the indefinite future. Nevertheless, it is at least conceivable that the reference is to the new king, who had taken the throne name of "Righteous is Yahveh."

Hananiah

If Jeremiah had hopes of peace and recovery, they were quickly blasted. The Egyptian party in Jerusalem remained strong. At every word of disorder anywhere in the Babylonian dominions, their hopes rose and Zedekiah let himself be swayed by the public feeling against Babylon. Judah tried, foolishly, to form a coalition of neighboring states against Babylon, when all of them together were no match for Nebuchadnezzar. They further attempted to get promises of help from Egypt, a nation which always promised, but somehow never delivered.

In Egypt, Necho had died in 593 B.C. and had been succeeded by Psamtik II. Psamtik welcomed into the land various Jewish exiles who, in the unsettled times, felt it safer to flee westward. He even formed a contingent of Jewish soldiers to fight in his armies. Naturally he could not trust such a contingent on the northeastern front where they might have to fight other Jews and might therefore change sides.

Instead, he placed them on the southern frontier, notably on Elephantine, an island in the Nile River, just south of the first cataract (near the southern border of modern Egypt). There they would serve to guard against raiders striking northward from Ethiopia.

In 588 B.C. Psamtik II died and was succeeded by Pharaoh-hophra, whom the Greeks called Apries. It was this Pharaoh who intrigued with the Egyptian party in Judah and encouraged Zedekiah to make a stand against Nebuchadnezzar.

Jeremiah, to dramatize the absolutely suicidal nature of this policy, made a yoke for himself and wore it, telling everyone who would hear that Judah should patiently wear the Babylonian yoke as the only means of survival. Naturally, this seemed an unpatriotic and defeatist attitude and was not popular with the people, who persisted in their belief that Jerusalem and its Temple were inviolable, a belief supported by the announcements of many who claimed to be prophets of God. (The case of Sennacherib's failure actually to take Jerusalem over a century earlier and the failure of Nebuchadnezzar to sack the city after his first siege must undoubtedly have encouraged the prophets in this view.)

Jeremiah 28:1. . . . *in the beginning of the reign of Zedekiah . . . in the fourth year . . . Hananiah . . . spake . . . in the house of the Lord . . . saying,*

Jeremiah 28:2. *Thus speaketh the Lord . . . I have broken the yoke of the king of Babylon.*

Jeremiah 28:3. *Within two full years will I bring again into this place all the vessels of the Lord's house that Nebuchadnezzar . . . took away . . .*

Jeremiah 28:4. And I will bring again to this place Jeconiah . . . with all the captives of Judah . . .

And to dramatize this statement Hananiah broke Jeremiah's yoke to indicate how God would break the yoke of Babylon.

Undoubtedly, this speech, given in Zedekiah's fourth year (594 B.C.), must have been met with the wild approval of the populace. Even Jeremiah did not quite dare stand against it at that moment, for he would undoubtedly have been torn in pieces if he had. Instead, he went along with the jubilant crowd:

Jeremiah 28:6. Even the prophet Jeremiah said, Amen: the Lord do so: the Lord perform thy words . . .

It was only afterward, when the mob had dispersed, that Jeremiah could safely announce that Hananiah was a false prophet, pandering to the nationalist hopes of the people.

The Bible records that he predicted Hananiah's death for false prophecy and that Hananiah died within two months. Nevertheless, it is plain that the people of Judah preferred to believe the flattering, hopeful words of Hananiah rather than the doleful, hopeless words of Jeremiah.

The Letter of Jeremiah

The nationalist agitation within Judah had an echo in Babylon. Undoubtedly, numbers of the exiles believed that God was about to destroy Babylon, as some prophets were predicting, and were ready to rise in revolt. News of this agitated Jeremiah.

The exile of 597 B.C. had drawn off the leaders of Judah, its craftsmen, its intellectuals. Bitterly, Jeremiah had referred to this in a parable of figs:

Jeremiah 24:1. The Lord shewed me . . . two baskets of figs . . . after . . . Nebuchadrezzar . . . had carried away captive Jeconiah . . . and the princes of Judah, with the carpenters and smiths . . .
Jeremiah 24:2. One basket had very good figs . . . and the other basket had very naughty figs, which could not be eaten, they were so bad.

Jeremiah then likened the captives to the good figs and those that remained in Jerusalem to the bad. It is clear that he considered it would be fatal to have the Babylonian exiles rise in rebellion. They would only be slaughtered. To Jeremiah, they seemed the hope of the future. Even if Jerusalem were destroyed, the exiles, he felt, would someday return to start the nation anew.

Jeremiah therefore took the occasion of a mission to Nebuchadnezzar sent by Zedekiah (perhaps protesting his loyalty to Babylon) to send a message to the exiles:

Jeremiah 29:1. *Now these are the words of the letter that Jeremiah . . . sent from Jerusalem unto . . . all the people whom Nebuchadnezzar had carried away captive . . .*

. . . .

Jeremiah 29:5. *Build ye houses . . . and plant gardens . . .*
Jeremiah 29:6. *Take ye wives, and beget sons and daughters . . . that ye may be increased there, and not diminished.*
Jeremiah 29:7. *And seek the peace of the city . . .*

In Babylon, at least, Jeremiah's views won out. The exiles in Babylon did make new lives for themselves without abandoning Judaism. They were allowed to live in peace and in due time (actually less than the seventy years predicted by Jeremiah) those who wished to do so were allowed to return to Judah. What's more, those who remained in Babylon were sufficiently prosperous to lend considerable financial help to those who returned (see page 437).

Centuries later, in 100 B.C., a short tract was written which purported to be a copy of the letter that was sent by Jeremiah to the exiles. It is devoted largely to an argument against idol worship, trying to demonstrate by a variety of arguments that idols are useless, helpless, the mere work of men's hands, and so on. It was not accepted as canonical by the Jews but appears in some Greek and Syriac versions of the Bible as a sixth and final chapter to the Book of Baruch. It appears, in this fashion, in the Catholic versions of the Bible, and in the King James Version of the Apocrypha, where it is titled "The Epistle of Jeremy." In the Revised Standard Version of the Apocrypha it is presented as a separate book, made up of a single chapter and called "The Letter of Jeremiah."

Zedekiah

If the exiles in Babylon were kept in quiet and peace, not so the Jews in the homeland. By 589 B.C., the pressure of public opinion had forced Zedekiah into outright rebellion against Nebuchadnezzar and in 588 B.C., Jerusalem was placed under siege by the Chaldean armies, while the rest of the nation, with the exception of one or two strong points, was occupied.

Bitterly, Jeremiah predicted that the city would be destroyed if resistance continued and that the only safety lay in surrender. He actually urged individuals to surrender if the city as a whole did not do so:

> Jeremiah 21:9. *He that abideth in this city shall die by the sword, and by the famine, and by the pestilence: but he that goeth out, and falleth to the Chaldeans . . . shall live . . .*

Such a statement was naturally viewed by the patriots of Judah as treason. An advance by the Egyptian army forced Nebuchadnezzar to lift the siege temporarily and hurry westward to face the Egyptians, and Jeremiah's forebodings seemed to have been turned to nothing. Sennacherib, in his time, had had a similar problem (see page 384) and the siege of Jerusalem at that time had been permanently lifted. Surely this would happen again. Jeremiah warned the people that this would not be so. Nebuchadnezzar would return.

Yet Jeremiah seized the brief respite to attempt to make a trip to Benjamin to attend to his property. He was at once seized by men of the army and accused of trying to desert to the Chaldeans. He denied it vigorously but he was not listened to, and was put in prison.

Zedekiah, however, was by no means certain that Jeremiah was the false prophet he seemed at the moment when the Chaldean siege had been lifted. He apparently had a sneaking belief in Jeremiah's worth and consulted him even while he was in prison (but secretly, to avoid having the nationalists find out).

> Jeremiah 37:17. *Then Zedekiah the king sent, and took him [Jeremiah] out [of prison]; and the king asked him secretly . . . Is there any word from the Lord . . .*

But Jeremiah was obdurate. He predicted only disaster and he was put back into prison. According to one story, he was put into a dungeon without food or water, and would have died if Zedekiah had not been persuaded to take him out at the last minute. One way or another, however, Jeremiah remained in prison for the duration of the siege and never stopped predicting disaster and urging surrender.

Still, he held out a long-range hope, for while in prison, he ostentatiously arranged for the purchase of land in his home town as an indication that the day would yet come when Judah would be Jewish again, despite the Chaldean devastation; a day when such purchases as he now made would hold good.

> Jeremiah 32:15. *For thus saith the Lord . . . Houses and fields and vineyards shall be possessed again in this land.*

Nebuzaradan

The Chaldeans did return to the siege and in 587 B.C., the city was taken, sacked, and burned. The walls were broken down, and the Temple was destroyed. Zedekiah attempted flight but was taken. His children were executed and he himself was blinded. A second deportation of Jews was then ordered by Nebuzaradan, captain of Nebuchadnezzar's elite troops:

> Jeremiah 39:9. *Then Nebuzaradan . . . carried away captive into Babylon the remnant of the people that remained in the city . . .*
> Jeremiah 39:10. *But . . . left of the poor of the people, which had nothing . . . and gave them vineyards and fields.*

Thus, as a result of two successive deportations, one at the beginning of the reign of Zedekiah in 597 B.C. and one at the end in 586 B.C., the elite of the nation were carried off. In Babylon, the exiles retained the essence of Judaism and developed it further. The first five books of the Bible (the Pentateuch or Torah) were put into written form, and apparently the Book of Joshua as well.

Back in Judah, however, the poor who remained, lacking religious sophistication, kept up a form of Yahvism of a more primitive sort.

When, a half century later, Jews from Babylon began to return to Judah, they considered their own developed version of Yahvism to be the only true form, and despised and antagonized those already on the land. It was only with difficulty, therefore, that they managed to rebuild the Temple against local hostilities (see page 441).

The Jews never really returned from Babylon en masse. Even after the rebuilding of the Temple and the walls of Jerusalem, important communities of Jews remained in the cities of Babylonia. These persisted throughout Biblical times and well beyond. After the destruction of the second Temple by the Romans in A.D. 70, Babylonia became the center of Jewish intellectual life for a thousand years.

The Jewish community in Babylonia remained important through the period of renewed Persian domination which followed after the decline of the Seleucid Empire; and for additional centuries after the conquest of the area by the Mohammedan Arabs. Only in A.D. 1100, when the area was falling prey to continuing civil wars and to the dominating power of the comparatively uncivilized Turkish tribes, did the Babylonian centers of Jewish learning fade, while new centers appeared in Moslem Spain.

One must not, therefore, think of the Babylonian Exile as merely a hiatus and a temporary stage in Jewish history. It was of vital importance to the development of Judaism (and of the two religions that arose out of it, Christianity and Mohammedanism) and it was, in some respects, a permanent exile and the beginning of the Diaspora (a Greek word meaning "dispersion"). The Diaspora, a name given collectively to the Jewish communities dwelling outside Judah, continues to this day, twenty-five hundred years after Nebuchadnezzar's time, even despite the re-establishment in 1948 of a Jewish nation in the land that had once been Canaan.

Gedaliah

After the destruction of Jerusalem, Judah was reorganized into a Chaldean province and a native governor was put over what remained of its population:

> 2 Kings 25:22. And as for the people that remained in the land of Judah . . . over them he [Nebuchadnezzar] made Gedaliah the son of Ahikam, the son of Shaphan, ruler.

Gedaliah was the son of the same Ahikam who had on an earlier occasion saved Jeremiah's life (see page 564). A brother of Ahikam and his son (the uncle and cousin of Gedaliah) had been among those who had tried to bring Jeremiah's scroll to the attention of Jehoiakim (see page 567).

> Jeremiah 36:10. *Then read Baruch . . . the words of Jeremiah in the house of the Lord, in the chamber of Gemariah the son of Shaphan . . .*
>
> Jeremiah 36:11. *When Michaiah the son of Gemariah . . . had heard . . . all the words of the Lord,*
>
> Jeremiah 36:12. *Then he went down into the king's house . . .*

Apparently, the entire family of Shaphan was strongly pro-Babylonian and of Jeremiah's mind that only through submission to Nebuchadnezzar could Judah find safety. Gedaliah was therefore a natural choice as governor.

After the fall of Jerusalem, Jeremiah, as a well-known spokesman of the pro-Babylonian point of view, was to be taken care of:

> Jeremiah 39:11. *Now Nebuchadrezzar . . . gave charge concerning Jeremiah to Nebuzaradan . . . saying,*
>
> Jeremiah 39:12. *Take him, and look well to him, and do him no harm.*
>
> . . . .
>
> Jeremiah 39:14. *. . . they . . . took Jeremiah out of . . . prison, and committed him unto Gedaliah . . . that he should carry him home.*

Ishmael

Gedaliah attempted to re-establish order and to assure the inhabitants of Judah that they might live peaceably under Nebuchadnezzar. Unfortunately, there were elements in opposition to this:

> Jeremiah 40:13. *. . . Johanan the son of Kareah . . . came to Gedaliah . . .*
>
> Jeremiah 40:14. *And said unto him, Dost thou . . . know that Baalis the king of the Ammonites hath sent Ishmael the son of Nethaniah to slay thee? . . .*

The motives of the Ammonite king are uncertain. Perhaps it was merely the chance of completing the destruction of the Jewish kingdom in memory of the centuries of long hostility. Perhaps he was acting on behalf of Egypt. The fall of Jerusalem could only have doubled and redoubled the desperate intrigues of the Egyptians to keep the area in turmoil and the Chaldeans occupied.

As for Ishmael, he perhaps required no great urging. He is described as:

> Jeremiah 41:1. . . . Ishmael the son of Nethaniah the son of Elishama, of the seed royal . . .

As a member of the royal family, he might have envisaged the re-establishment of the kingdom, with Egyptian help, and his own anointment as king.

Gedaliah was apparently one of those high-minded men who can believe no evil, and he refused to credit the report. In consequence, he was assassinated after having remained in office only three months (or possibly one year and three months).

It was the last straw and after that there was no chance of any sort of Jewish community in the land.

Johanan

The assassination of Gedaliah had been accompanied by a general massacre of those faithful to him, and those Jews who escaped must have been certain that the criminal act of Ishmael would bring down the final installment of Chaldean vengeance.

This time, it seemed very likely, Nebuchadnezzar would not stop to distinguish guilty from innocent but would slaughter all alike, and there seemed no alternative but to flee to the one neighboring land where the Chaldean arm could not yet reach:

> Jeremiah 41:16. Then Johanan the son of Kareah . . . and the remnant of the people . . .
> Jeremiah 41:17. . . . departed . . . to go to enter into Egypt,
> Jeremiah 41:18. Because of the Chaldeans, for they were afraid of them . . .

On the way to Egypt, they passed the home of Jeremiah and asked his advice. Jeremiah did not depart from his pro-Babylonian policy. He felt that in Egypt there would be no more safety than in Judah, and he may even have thought that a flight into Egypt would be a provocation to Nebuchadnezzar; that it would look very much like what we would today call setting up a government-in-exile.

Against Jeremiah's advice, however, the group of Jews traveled on into Egypt. In fact, they forced Jeremiah and Baruch to accompany them.

This new departure of Jews into Egypt (like the legendary one under Jacob and Joseph twelve centuries earlier) had important consequences. The Elephantine colony (see page 571) was probably reinforced and a form of Yahvism was built up there, complete with a temple. The Jews of the colony worshiped Yahveh under the name of Yahu, and picked up elements of Egyptian religion as well. They apparently were not conscious of the manner in which their religious customs departed from those that were being developed in Babylon.

In 1903, papyri were discovered on the island and these revealed that at the time the Temple was being rebuilt in Jerusalem, Elephantine had fallen on bad days. Its temple had been destroyed by the Egyptians and in 407 B.C., they were asking permission of Persian authorities (who now controlled Egypt) to rebuild that temple. They had previously applied for help to the newly built Temple at Jerusalem but had received no answer, since to the Jews at Jerusalem there could be only one Temple. To them, the Jews at Elephantine were heretics and no more to be regarded than the Samaritans.

In Greek times, the entry of Jews into Egypt assumed floodlike proportions. By New Testament times, there were nearly a quarter of a million Jews along the Nile, and something like one third of Egypt's capital city, Alexandria, was Jewish.

In New Testament times, the Jews of Egypt were largely Greek in language and culture. The comparison between the Hellenized Jews of Egypt and those of Judea must have been something like the comparison today between the Americanized Jews of the United States and those of Israel.

Pharaoh-hophra

In Egypt, Jeremiah fought against the dilution of Yahvism by Egyptian practices. His denunciation ended with a thunderous:

Jeremiah 44:30. *Thus saith the Lord; Behold, I will give Pharaoh-hophra king of Egypt into the hand of his enemies and into the hand of them that seek his life . . .*

Pharaoh-hophra, who ruled Egypt at the time of the destruction of Jerusalem, managed to avoid destruction at the hands of Nebuchad-nezzar, but Jeremiah's prophecy came to pass just the same.

In 569 B.C., seventeen years after the fall of Jerusalem, Pharaoh-hophra tried to bring under his control a Greek colony established at Cyrene, on the north African coast, about five hundred miles west of the Nile. His troops revolted and acclaimed an officer named Aahmes (Amasis, to the Greeks) as Pharaoh. Troops loyal to Hophra were defeated by the rebels and Hophra was executed while Aahmes reigned in his place.

One wonders if Jeremiah was still alive to see the end of Pharaoh-hophra. He would have been seventy-seven years old then, a not-im-possible age. However, there is no way of telling. His denunciation of the Egyptian monarch is his last recorded utterance and there is no Biblical account of his death.

25. LAMENTATIONS

Jeremiah

The Book of Lamentations consists of five separate poems, each making up a separate chapter and all dealing with the central theme of the destruction of Jerusalem and its desolation thereafter. In the Jewish canon, it is considered part of the third division of the Bible, the Writings, and it is not included among the prophetic books. The Hebrew title is taken from the first word. The book begins:

> Lamentations 1:1. *How doth the city sit solitary, that was full of people* . . .

and the Hebrew name is therefore "Ekhah" ("how").

The tradition arose quite early, however, that Jeremiah was the author of Lamentations and for that reason, the book was placed immediately after the Book of Jeremiah in the Septuagint and in the various Christian versions that descended from that. The title of the book in the English versions is, in full, "The Lamentations of Jeremiah."

The case for authorship by Jeremiah rests, generally, in the fact that Jeremiah was the most prominent Biblical character to be in Jerusalem through the period of its great disaster. Then, too, Jeremiah is mentioned in the Bible in connection with the composition of lamentations, that form of poetry which bewails a tragedy. When the reforming king Josiah was brought back dead from the battle of Megiddo:

> 2 Chronicles 35:25. . . . *Jeremiah lamented for Josiah* . . .

This particular lamentation cannot be represented by the Book of Lamentations, of course. For one thing, Jerusalem was not destroyed until twenty-two years after Josiah's death. For another, Lamentations does not mention Josiah. The only reference in it to any king is:

> Lamentations 4:20. *The breath of our nostrils, the anointed of the Lord, was taken* . . .

The New Babylonian Empire

and it makes much more sense in the context of the book to suppose that this is a poetic reference to Zedekiah, Judah's last king.

But it is extremely unlikely that Jeremiah can have been the author of the book. The mere fact that it is not included in the prophetic canon in the Hebrew Bible would indicate it was composed rather late.

The five poems do not seem to be by the same hand, the third chapter in particular seeming different from the rest, and later. Furthermore, the first four poems are acrostics (see page 495), a highly artificial form, and it doesn't seem likely, somehow, that Jeremiah in his grief over Jerusalem would sit down to work out, slowly and painfully, a set of acrostic poems. That rather bears witness to a literary effort taken on later and in retrospect.

26. EZEKIEL

Ezekiel

Ezekiel ("God strengthens") was, apparently, a younger contemporary of Jeremiah, and it is therefore chronologically fitting that his utterances should follow those of Jeremiah.

> Ezekiel 1:1. *Now it came to pass in the thirtieth year . . . as I was among the captives . . . that . . . I saw visions of God.*
> Ezekiel 1:2. *In . . . the fifth year of king Jehoiachin's captivity.*

Ezekiel, then, had been carried off with Jehoiachin after Nebuchadnezzar's first siege of Jerusalem in 597 B.C. The book begins in the fifth year of that captivity; that is, in 593 B.C. At that time, the kingdom of Judah still existed, with Zedekiah as its king and with Jeremiah the prophet warning it, unheeded, of its coming fate.

If by "the thirtieth year" Ezekiel means that he is in the thirtieth year of his life (something that is not at all certain) then he was carried off to Babylon in his twenty-fifth year and he was born in 627 B.C., during the reign of Josiah. This would make him some twenty years younger than Jeremiah and, in fact, he would have been born the year before Jeremiah received his call. It is possible that, as some traditions have it, he may even have been a disciple of Jeremiah.

Ezekiel was a priest, presumably of the line of Zadok, since he shows himself greatly interested in the minutiae of the Temple service.

> Ezekiel 1:3. *The word of the Lord came . . . unto Ezekiel the priest . . . by the river Chebar . . .*

The New Babylonian Empire

The "river Chebar" is one of the larger canals that interlaced the Babylonian plains. Its name in the original Akkadian was "nar Kabari" ("Grand Canal") and it led from Babylon southeastward to Uruk (Erech). Somewhere on its shores there was the settlement of Jews of whom Ezekiel was a prominent and respected leader.

Tammuz

Ezekiel's call is attended by a mystical vision of God, something like that of Isaiah but attended by greater detail. The prophet is instructed to denounce the wickedness of Jerusalem and to proclaim the imminence of its siege and destruction. A year later, Ezekiel does so by describing visions of the idolatrous practices he claims are being practiced in the very Temple itself:

Ezekiel 8:14. *Then he* [God] *brought me to the door of the gate of the Lord's house which was toward the north; and behold, there sat women weeping for Tammuz.*

In ancient agricultural societies, it was common to personify the phenomenon of the death of vegetation in the winter (or in the acme of summer heat) and its rebirth in the spring (or with the coming of the rains). The personification took the form of a deity who died and was taken into the underworld, from which he was later rescued by another deity. It was customary for women to bewail the death of the deity at fixed times of the year and then to rejoice loudly over the rebirth and resurrection.

To modern Westerners, the most familiar form of this sort of tale is found among the Greek myths. This tale tells of Demeter, the Greek goddess of agriculture, and her daughter Persephone. Persephone is stolen by Hades, the god of the underworld, and Demeter seeks her all over the world. While she seeks, all vegetation dies and winter comes over the world. Eventually, Demeter finds Persephone and a compromise is reached. Persephone may stay with Demeter part of the year and with Hades the rest, and this explains the recurring cycle of growth and death and growth again.

The Babylonians have a myth of this sort, too; one that long antedates the Greek version, of course, and goes back, in fact, to Sumerian days before the time of Abraham. In the Sumerian myth, Dumu-zi (the name which later became Tammuz) is the brother and lover of Ishtar, the goddess of earth and sky. Tammuz is killed by a boar while hunting, or, perhaps, through some thoughtless act of Ishtar, and must descend into the underworld. Ishtar follows and ransoms him only with the greatest difficulty. It is for this Tammuz that the women first wail and then rejoice.

(The Babylonians called the month of the summer solstice Tammuz in honor of the god and the Jews borrowed the name. This heathen god, despite Ezekiel, is still honored in the Jewish calendar today, just as Western calendars contain the month of March, a name used freely by Jews and Christians alike though it honors the pagan god Mars.)

The Tammuz myth spread along with agriculture and always it was to the women that its rites particularly appealed. After all, in primitive societies it is the women who are most concerned with agriculture. In the western half of the Fertile Crescent Tammuz was called "Lord" (*Adonai*). This was "Adonis" in the Greek version of the name and Greek mythology adopted the tale of Tammuz when they told of Adonis, the young lover of Aphrodite, who was killed by a boar to the goddess's infinite distress. (And gave us the word "Adonis" to represent any extremely handsome young man.)

The Israelites undoubtedly worshiped Tammuz and these rites were popular with the women among them. Indeed, the writers of the final version of the Book of Judges probably tried to mask the idolatrous practices of the women by referring to their weeping for Tammuz as weeping for Jephthah's daughter (see page 246).

Nor has the practice died out completely even today, for the emotions surrounding the religious ritual in connection with the death and resurrection of Jesus—Good Friday followed by Easter—owes something to the millennia in which the god of vegetation died and was reborn every year.

Tyrus

The first half of the Book of Ezekiel is given over entirely to the denunciation of Judah and the prediction of disaster for it; all this, presumably, having been uttered in the near-decade period between the time of Ezekiel's call and the final destruction of Jerusalem.

Thereafter, Ezekiel turns upon those nations surrounding Judah who were to share in its destruction at the hands of the conquering Chaldeans:

> Ezekiel 26:1. . . . *in the eleventh year* . . . *the word of the Lord came unto me saying* . . .
>
> . . . .
>
> Ezekiel 26:7. . . . *Behold, I will bring upon Tyrus Nebuchadnezzar* . . .

Tyrus is the Greek form of the town we call Tyre (and the word appears as Tyre throughout in the Revised Standard Version).

Tyre shared in the troubles suffered by the peoples of the western half of the Fertile Crescent in the face of the advance of first the Assyrians and then the Chaldeans. Fortunately for itself, however, Tyre was on the coast, her citadel being on a rocky island offshore. As long as her ships controlled the sea she could not be starved out. For that reason, she could withstand longer sieges than cities like Damascus, Samaria, and Jerusalem, which could be completely invested. For that same reason, sieges of Tyre were likely to end in a compromise settlement, with Tyre retaining her integrity.

Thus, at the time Shalmaneser V was laying siege to Samaria (see page 375), he was also besieging Tyre. The city resisted firmly through a five-year siege, defeating the ships which the Assyrians used in an attempt to break her life line. In the end, Tyre agreed to pay tribute to Sargon, but it retained its self-government.

It continued to pay tribute to the nations which came to power after the fall of Assyria, but more reluctantly. They shared in the Egyptian-encouraged intrigues against Babylonia that led to Judah's destruction and it was quite obvious that Nebuchadnezzar intended to punish Tyre when he was done with Jerusalem.

Ezekiel's prophecy "in the eleventh year" took place in 587 B.C., when Jerusalem's fate was sealed and when the forthcoming siege of Tyre was a sure thing. Ezekiel goes on to predict Tyre's destruction as a result of this siege and in great detail describes the manner of its sacking. Indeed, throughout the passage Ezekiel glorifies the Chaldean armies as though he were a Babylonian patriot. Perhaps he had been "assimilated" into Babylonian life in this sense for there are no oracles among his utterances that are against Babylon, only against Babylon's enemies (including Judah).

This is not so strange a thought, really. As far as we can tell, the Jewish colonies in Babylonia were well treated; they were allowed the full practice of their religion; they were allowed to enter into the economic life of the nation and grow well-to-do. The proof of this is that when they were finally allowed to return to Judah and rebuild their Temple, many of them preferred to remain in Babylonia. It is not at all impossible to imagine a Jew retaining a profound loyalty to Judaism while feeling a secular patriotism toward a religiously alien but otherwise benevolent power. American Jews are precisely in that sort of position today.

Nevertheless, as it turned out, Ezekiel was overenthusiastic in his pro-Babylonian pride, for Nebuchadnezzar failed after all to sack Tyre. He maintained his siege for thirteen years, till 573 B.C. (three years longer than the renowned siege of Troy) and in the end had to come to a compromise arrangement.

Ezekiel himself had to recognize this hard fact:

> Ezekiel 29:17. *And it came to pass in the seven and twentieth year . . . the word of the Lord came unto me, saying,*
> Ezekiel 29:18. *. . . Nebuchadrezzar . . . caused his army to serve a great service against Tyrus . . . yet had he no wages, nor his army . . .*

This statement is dated 571 B.C., the twenty-seventh year of Ezekiel's captivity, and two years after the siege of Tyre had been lifted. It is the latest dated statement of the prophet and since his call came in the fifth year of his captivity, he was active over a period of at least twenty-two years. If he was thirty years old at the time of his call, he was fifty-two at the time of this statement.

Elishah

Yet before the passage of time enlightens Ezekiel to the true outcome of the siege, he composes a long dirge for supposed-fallen, or going-to-fall Tyre, and in it he recites those places that contribute to the merchant city's wealth and prosperity in a veritable orgy of geographical terms, some of which we can no longer surely identify. Thus:

> Ezekiel 27:7. *. . . blue and purple from the isles of Elishah was that which covered thee.*

There is the possibility that Elishah was a district in Cyprus, an island in the eastern Mediterranean which had been colonized by the Phoenicians. Another possibility, however, involves a farther Phoenician colony, on the northern coast of Africa.

Tradition has it that in 814 B.C., when Joash was on the throne of Judah, a party of Tyrians established a colony near the site of modern Tunis. Through the centuries, this colony, which came to be known as Carthage, from words originally meaning "new town," flourished. By

Ezekiel's time, it dominated north Africa and had established itself in Sicily.

The traditional leader of the original colonizing party had been a Tyrian princess named Dido in the Greek and Roman histories, but that seems to have been her throne name. Her earlier name, according to those same histories, was Elissa. Could it have been that this name actually reflects one of the names by which Carthage was known in the civilized centers of the Fertile Crescent? Is the "Elishah" referred to in this verse Carthage? If so, it is the only reference to Carthage in the Bible.

Again:

> Ezekiel 27:8. *The inhabitants of Zidon and Arvad were thy mariners . . .*

Zidon is, of course, Sidon (see page 217). Arvad is an island about two miles off the Syrian coast, some hundred miles north of Sidon. It was quite prosperous in Biblical times.

Gebal

Ezekiel goes on:

> Ezekiel 27:9. *The ancients of Gebal . . . were in thee thy calkers.*

Gebal (the modern town of Jubyl in Lebanon) is on the Phoenician seacoast about forty miles north of Sidon. In very ancient times, in the days when the pyramids were being built, Gebal may have been the most important of the Phoenician cities, but it was eventually eclipsed, first by Sidon and later by Tyre.

An inscription in the Phoenicians' alphabet (from which all other alphabets are believed to have descended) has been found in diggings in that city and has been dated back to before the time of the Exodus. It may conceivably have been in Gebal that the alphabet was invented.

In later centuries, Gebal was the center of trade in Egyptian papyrus, which was much valued for book production in Greek and Roman times. Rolls of papyrus came, therefore, to be called *biblia* from the Greek name of the city, which was Byblos. And since in

Christian times the rolls of papyrus on which the Scriptures were written came to be *the* books, they were the "Biblia" par excellence and to this day we call the holy writings of the Jews and Christians the "Bible."

And still more:

> Ezekiel 27:14. *They of the house of Togarmah traded in thy fairs with horses . . . and mules.*

Togarmah is equated with the "Tilgirimmu" mentioned in Assyrian inscriptions. These are taken to be in horse-breeding country in east-central Asia Minor.

The Prince of Tyrus

Ezekiel also inveighed against Tyre's ruler and here, at least, his prophecy did not entirely miss fire:

> Ezekiel 28:2. *Son of man, say unto the prince of Tyrus, Thus saith the Lord God . . .*
> . . . .
> Ezekiel 28:7. . . . *I will bring strangers upon thee . . .*
> Ezekiel 28:8. *They shall bring thee down to the pit and thou shalt die . . .*

The king of Tyre at the time of Nebuchadnezzar's siege was Ithobaal II. (Ithobaal I, ruling three centuries earlier, had been the father of Jezebel.)

Ithobaal II did suffer a personal defeat, for by the terms of the final agreement between Tyre and Nebuchadnezzar, Ithobaal was forced to abdicate and he and his family were taken off to exile in Babylon (but not killed, thus falsifying that part of Ezekiel's prediction). In Ithobaal's place, Baal II ruled an essentially independent Tyre that was nevertheless careful not to offend Babylon needlessly.

Tyre continued to exist in peace and prosperity under the Persians, who conquered and supplanted the Chaldeans. Indeed, it was not until two and a half centuries after Nebuchadnezzar's siege, when a far greater conqueror, Alexander the Great, laid siege to the city, actually took it, and sacked it, that Tyre's pride was finally broken. Never again would it be able to dispute with empires.

Syene

The New Babylonian Empire and Egypt

But it was Egypt which was the real enemy of Nebuchadnezzar. It had been the force behind the little nations that had tried to withstand the Chaldean might. Its gold, its encouragement, even on occasion its armies, had strengthened them. Now, it alone of the ancient centers of civilization remained outside the Chaldean Empire. Somehow, it continued to maintain its independence and Chaldean frustration seems to be mirrored in the lengthy invectives hurled against Egypt by Ezekiel:

> Ezekiel 29:1. *In the tenth year . . . the word of the Lord came to me, saying,*
> Ezekiel 29:2. *. . . . set thy face against Pharaoh . . . and prophesy against him and against all Egypt:*

The prophecy is dated 588 B.C., while Jerusalem was still holding out, and while Egypt's interference was delaying the fall of that city. (Ezekiel was certainly no nationalist or he would have been praising Egypt rather than denouncing it at this time.) Ezekiel's denunciation is savage:

> Ezekiel 29:10. . . . I [God] *will make the land of Egypt utterly waste and desolate, from the tower of Syene even unto the border of Ethiopia.*

The word "tower" is apparently an unnecessary translation of the word *Migdol*. Various fortified posts might be termed Migdol from the stone fortresses or towers that would be their most prominent feature. The Revised Standard Version therefore translates the clause as "from Migdol to Syene, as far as the border of Ethiopia."

Syene is the Greek name of the place called "Seveneh" in Hebrew. It is located on the Nile at just about the position of the First Cataract, with the island Elephantine (see page 571) in the river itself near there. Ethiopian invaders floating down the Nile in order to raid Egyptian cities would have difficulties negotiating the rapids at the First Cataract and might have to bypass it overland. A fortified Egyptian city at that point would be necessary to ensure Egypt's safety.

Syene and Elephantine mark the effective southern boundary of Egypt proper in ancient times. They are about 550 miles south of the Mediterranean. In modern times, Syene is called Aswan, and is notable for being the site of a huge dam that will back up the waters of the Nile into a long lake, serving to irrigate millions of acres of desert and produce much electric power as well. The southern boundary of modern Egypt lies about 150 miles south of Aswan.

Since Ezekiel's threat is that Egypt will be devastated from end to end, and since Syene represents its southern frontier, Migdol must be located on its northern frontier. One guess is that it refers to a town twelve miles south of the Mediterranean and a few miles east of what is now the Suez Canal, which the Greeks called Magadalos.

Pathros

Ezekiel predicts that the Egyptians will be scattered and dispersed through the nations but will experience a kind of partial restoration after forty years.

Ezekiel 29:14. *And I will . . . cause them* [the Egyptians] *to return into the land of Pathros . . . and they shall be there a base kingdom.*

Pathros is the name given to "upper Egypt," the portion of the land south of the delta. The implication is that a portion of Egypt will regain independence to form a weak nation, one that is no longer a great power.

To be sure, this had happened previously in Egyptian history. When the Hyksos controlled the delta, for instance, native Egyptian rulers maintained themselves in Thebes and controlled "Pathros" until they finally took over all of Egypt.

This did not, however, happen on this occasion. Nebuchadnezzar did not conquer Egypt; the Egyptians were not scattered and dispersed; there was no need for any restoration.

To be sure, in 568 B.C., shortly after the death of Pharaoh-hophra (see page 580) and the accession of the usurper Aahmes, Nebuchadnezzar tried to take advantage of the confusion in Egypt by invading the land. We know little of that episode but it could not have been the resounding Babylonian success that Ezekiel had confidently predicted. Egypt survived with no apparent damage.

Indeed, Aahmes survived to rule for another generation over a prosperous Egypt. He witnessed the death of Nebuchadnezzar, the decay of the Chaldean Empire under Nebuchadnezzar's successors, and the final fall of that empire to Cyrus the Persian. He did not die till 525 B.C., just before Egypt itself was to fall to Cambyses, the son of Cyrus.

Ezekiel's prophecies might almost be made to fit (if their virulence is softened) what did befall Egypt at the hands of Cambyses.

Ezekiel 30:15. *And I* [God] *will pour fury upon Sin, the strength of Egypt . . .*

Sin is usually identified with Pelusium, the Greek name for a city on the Mediterranean coast about seventy-five miles east of the Nile delta. It served as an Egyptian stronghold guarding against invasions from the east. When Cambyses marched against Egypt in 525 B.C., he defeated the Egyptian army at Pelusium and there was little resistance to him thereafter. The Revised Standard Version has the verse read "And I will pour my wrath upon Pelusium, the stronghold of Egypt."

But of course, Egypt was not destroyed even when the Persians did conquer it at last some half century after Ezekiel's threatenings, nor were the Egyptians carried off into exile.

Gog

The last third of the Book of Ezekiel is apocalyptic in nature, foretelling first a future invasion of Israel by the hordes of a mysterious ruler from the north; and of their complete defeat:

> Ezekiel 38:1. *And the word of the Lord came unto me, saying,*
> Ezekiel 38:2. *Son of man, set thy face against Gog, the land of*
> Magog . . . *and prophesy against him.*

The phrase "the land of Magog" may be an attempt of some later editor to identify the nation led by Gog. In the genealogical tables of Genesis, Magog is listed as the second son of Japheth and may simply mean "the land of Gog" (see page 46). It would make much more sense to say "set thy face against Magog, the land of Gog" and the reversal may be a copyist's error.

In either case, the question is: Who is Gog? It is often suggested that Gog represents Gyges, the founder of the Lydian monarchy, about a century before Ezekiel's time.

Gyges fell in battle against the hordes of nomad Cimmerians coming down from north of the Black Sea and devastating Asia Minor in the reign of Asshurbanipal of Assyria. For decades the nomads remained the terror of the Fertile Crescent and no doubt, for generations afterward, the thought of hordes from the north remained nightmarishly in the minds of men. Perhaps Gyges, the fighter against the Cimmerians, was confused with his foe, and Gog came to mean the nomadic invaders in general.

Eventually, "Gog, the land of Magog" was further distorted into the belief that there were two enemies, Gog and Magog, and that these would afflict the earth in the final days. They are mentioned in just this connection in the New Testament in the Book of Revelation:

> Revelation 20:7. . . . *Satan shall be loosed out of his prison,*
> Revelation 20:8. *And shall go out to deceive the nations . . . Gog*
> *and Magog, to gather them together to battle . . .*

In the Book of Ezekiel, written before the effect of Persian dualism on Jewish religious thought, only God is mentioned in connection with Gog. In Revelation, written long after Persian dualism had permeated Judaism, it is Satan who inspires them.

The euphony, perhaps, of the names Gog and Magog has caused them to live on in British legend as a pair of giants born of daughters of the Roman Emperor Diocletian (who reigned about nine hundred years after the time of Ezekiel). Greater-than-life statues called Gog and Magog have been kept in London. The latest of these, fourteen feet high, were constructed in 1708, and were destroyed in 1940 during the bombing of London by the Nazi Luftwaffe.

Following the defeat of Gog, the ideal Israel is established and in his description of this, Ezekiel launches into a meticulous description of the structure of the Temple and of the nature of its ritual. This has served almost as a constitution for the re-established Jewish community under the Persians, so that Ezekiel is sometimes called "the father of Judaism."

Ezekiel did not himself survive, in all probability, to witness the fall of Babylon (he would have had to live to be almost ninety to have done that), but men such as Ezra carried with them the new spirit of Ezekiel, and the second Temple was organized in Ezekiel's image.

27. DANIEL

DANIEL · JEHOIAKIM · BELTESHAZZAR · CHALDEANS · FEET OF CLAY · SHADRACH, MESHACH, AND ABEDNEGO · NEBUCHADNEZZAR · BELSHAZZAR · MENE, MENE, TEKEL, UPHARSIN · DARIUS THE MEDIAN · THE LITTLE HORN · THE ANCIENT OF DAYS · GABRIEL · SEVENTY WEEKS · MESSIAH THE PRINCE · MICHAEL · GRECIA · THE KING OF THE SOUTH · THE SHIPS OF CHITTIM · SUSANNA · BEL AND THE DRAGON

Daniel

In the various Christian versions of the Bible, Daniel is found after Ezekiel as a fourth major prophet. Since the events related in the book supposedly take place during the Babylonian Exile, in the reigns of Nebuchadnezzar and his successors, it comes, in chronological fitness, after the Books of Isaiah, Jeremiah, and Ezekiel.

In the Jewish canon, however, Daniel is not to be found among the prophets at all, but among the Writings. From this, it might be presumed that at the time that Daniel was written the collection of prophetic books had reached their final form and been closed. Since at least one of the prophetic books (Jonah) had been written as late as 300 B.C., it would seem to follow that Daniel was written after 300 B.C. and could not have been written by the individual who gave the book its name and who is the hero of its tales.

In fact, the Book of Daniel is probably among the last written of the Jewish canon and may date from as late as 165 B.C. A few decades later, and it might not have been allowed into the canon at all, but would have had to remain in the Apocrypha (where some might argue it really belongs anyway).

The evidence for this late authorship is manifold. Parts of the book are written in Aramaic, which seems to place it in a time when Aramaic had become so much the common speech of the people that Hebrew

The New Babylonian Empire

was understood only by the educated. Other subtle facets of the language used bespeak the Greek period rather than the time of the Exile.

Where Isaiah, Jeremiah, and Ezekiel make no anachronistic mistakes concerning the times supposed to be theirs, the Book of Daniel is replete with anachronisms as far as it deals with the period of the Exile. It treats, however, of the Greek period with easy correctness and while this might be explained by those dedicated to the literal acceptance of the Bible as a case of prophetic insight, it is odd that Daniel should be so correct in his view of what was to him the "future" and so hazy about his view of what was to him the "present." It is easier to believe that the writer was a man of Greek times, to whom the Exile was an event that had taken place four centuries earlier and concerning the fine details of which he was a bit uncertain.

There is nothing we can say about the Daniel on whom the book of that name is based except that he must have been a folk hero known for his wisdom and arcane knowledge. Ezekiel mentions him three times, in a way which seems to make him an ancient worthy.

Thus, in stressing the fact that God would save only the righteous out of a sinful city and that not one sinner would be saved for the sake of those righteous he has God say:

> Ezekiel 14:14. Though . . . Noah, Daniel, and Job, were in it, they should deliver but their own souls by their righteousness . . .

Daniel is here equated with Noah, who lived at the time of the Flood, and Job, who lived before the Exodus. Surely Daniel must be also ancient. It is always the ancient who are reverenced and it somehow seems implausible that Ezekiel should pass over such names as Isaiah and Jeremiah and even Elijah in order to mention a contemporary, and a younger contemporary at that.

Again, when denouncing Ithobaal of Tyre (see page 590), Ezekiel says sarcastically:

> Ezekiel 28:3. Behold, thou art wiser than Daniel; there is no secret that they can hide from thee:

Clearly, the legendary Daniel was renowned for his wisdom and can be used as a standard in that respect. Surely, he is not a younger contemporary of Ezekiel. He is an ancient, borrowed by the writer of the Book of Daniel, who needed someone who was of both exemplary piety and of unparalleled wisdom. He therefore took this Daniel and placed him in the period of the Exile.

We can even see why he was placed in that period. It was going to be the writer's purpose to denounce the Seleucid Empire, which in the second century B.C. was persecuting Judaism ferociously. To avoid charges of rebellion and treason, the writer had to refrain from attacking the Seleucids directly. By putting the book into a period of past disaster, he could attack them indirectly. He could make Babylon and Nebuchadnezzar surrogate villains for Syria and the Seleucids and his readers would know what he meant while the overlords might have trouble proving it.

Jehoiakim

The anachronisms of Daniel begin with the first verse:

Daniel 1:1. *In the third year of the reign of Jehoiakim . . . came Nebuchadnezzar . . . unto Jerusalem, and besieged it.*

Daniel 1:2. *And the Lord gave Jehoiakim . . . into his* [Nebuchadnezzar's] *hand, with part of the vessels of the house of God: which he carried into the land of Shinar . . .*

The third year of the reign of Jehoiakim would be 606 B.C., at which time Nebuchadnezzar was not yet king of Babylon. It was in 597 that Nebuchadnezzar took Jerusalem the first time (without actually destroying it). Jehoiakim had died by then and it was his son Jehoiachin who was given into the hand of the conqueror.

Then, too, "Shinar" is an archaism that no contemporary of Nebuchadnezzar would have used. That name (the equivalent of "Sumer") was used of the land in Abraham's time (see page 48). To the Hebrews of the Exile, it was Chaldea and the temptation was to push Chaldea into the past (and speak of Ur of the Chaldees, for instance; see page 56) rather than pull Shinar forward.

Finally, Nebuchadnezzar is always spelled with the incorrect "n" in Daniel; and never, as in Jeremiah and Ezekiel, which were really composed in the Exilic period, with an at least occasional "r" to make it the more nearly correct "Nebuchadrezzar."

Belteshazzar

From among the Jews carried away in this first exile (the same in which Ezekiel had been carried away; see page 595) a number of the young men were taken to be brought up with a Chaldean education in order that they might be given positions at court:

Daniel 1:6. *Now among these were . . . Daniel, Hananiah, Mishael, and Azariah:*

Daniel 1:7. *Unto whom the prince of the eunuchs gave names:*

*for he gave unto Daniel the name of Belteshazzar; and to Hananiah,
of Shadrach; and to Mishael, of Meshach; and to Azariah, of
Abednego.*

The Yahvistic names, in other words, were changed to those involving
the names of Babylonian deities. For instance, Daniel ("God is the
judge") becomes Belteshazzar ("Bel protect his life"), where Bel is
the great Babylonian god, Marduk (see page 552). Similarly, Azariah
("Yahveh helps") becomes Abednego, or, in proper spelling, Abednebo
("servant of Nebo").

Similarly, Hananiah ("Yahveh is gracious") becomes Shadrach
("Aku commands"), where Aku is, presumably, some lesser deity.
Mishael ("who is what God is") becomes Meshach, a word of doubtful
meaning, arising, perhaps, through the conversion by the writer of the
Hebrew name into one that sounds Babylonian to his ears.

The four Jews did well at court, were accepted into royal favor:

> Daniel 1:21. *And Daniel continued even unto the first year of
> Cyrus.*

Daniel, in other words, remained in favor till 538 B.C., some sixty
years after he went into exile. If Daniel were eighteen at the time of the
Exile, he would be seventy-eight years old at the fall of Babylon to
Cyrus—a not impossible situation. At least we do not have in this
book the impossibly condensed chronologies we find in Esther (see
page 467).

Chaldeans

Nebuchadnezzar, like Pharaoh in the time of Joseph over a thousand
years earlier, had a dream:

> Daniel 2:2. *Then the king commanded to call the magicians, and
> the astrologers, and the sorcerers, and the Chaldeans, for to shew
> the king his dreams . . .*
>
> . . . .
>
> Daniel 2:4. *Then spake the Chaldeans to the king in Syriack, O
> king . . . tell thy servants the dream, and we will shew the inter-
> pretation.*

The Babylonians, like the Egyptians, were renowned for their magical powers. Actually, civilization and technology were most highly developed in those two areas in pre-Greek times and to peoples less highly developed, the ability to build the pyramids or foretell lunar eclipses would naturally be taken as a sign of magical adeptness. Undoubtedly, the learned among the Egyptians and Babylonians were not in the least averse to allowing the reputation of magic to spread. It enhanced their own value.

In aftertimes, the very word "Chaldean" (or, as we would say today, "Babylonian") came to be synonymous with magician, sorcerer, wise man, or astrologer. Here in verse 2:2, four types of the learned in magical arts are named, with no feeling that one of them refers to a nationality rather than a pursuit.

The very use of the word in this sense is another anachronism. In the time of the Exile, a Chaldean was a mighty and dreaded warrior and the word is used in this sense in the Book of Jeremiah, for instance.

A later editor of the Book of Daniel may have inserted the phrase "in Syriack" (that is, "in Aramaic") to account for the fact that a large section of the book (from this verse on, in fact, to the end of Chapter 7) is in Aramaic. Actually, there is no reason why the court officials should speak Aramaic to the king rather than his native Babylonian; and if they did, there is no real reason why the writer needs to specify it. Then, too, even if he wanted to quote the wise men in Aramaic for greater authenticity, there would be no reason to go on for a number of chapters in that language. Actually, as I said earlier, the Aramaic is an indication of the late composition of the book and the inserted phrase is a completely ineffectual attempt to mask that.

Feet of Clay

Unfortunately for the wise men, Nebuchadnezzar could not recall the dream, and yet he demanded a quick interpretation on pain of death. Daniel, like a new Joseph, offered to first reconstruct the dream and then interpret it, and thus save the lives of the magicians. He said to Nebuchadnezzar:

Daniel 2:31. *Thou, O king, sawest, and behold a great image . . .*
Daniel 2:32. *This image's head was of fine gold, his breast and his arms of silver, his belly and his thighs of brass,*

Daniel 2:33. His legs of iron, his feet part of iron and part of clay.

Daniel 2:34. Thou sawest . . . that a stone . . . smote the image upon his feet that were of iron and clay, and brake them to pieces.

Daniel 2:35. Then was the iron, the clay, the brass, the silver, and the gold, broken to pieces . . . and the stone . . . became a great mountain, and filled the whole earth.

It is from the description of this dream that the common expression "feet of clay," meaning a weak point in an otherwise strong object, came into use.

Daniel's interpretation is that Nebuchadnezzar and the Chaldean Empire which he rules is the head of gold.

Daniel 2:39. And after thee shall arise another kingdom inferior to thee, and another third kingdom of brass, which shall bear rule over all the earth.

Daniel 2:40. And the fourth kingdom shall be strong as iron . . .

Daniel 2:41. And whereas thou sawest the feet and toes, part of potters' clay, and part of iron, the kingdom shall be divided . . .

Daniel 2:42. . . . the kingdom shall be partly strong, and partly broken.

Daniel 2:44. And in the days of these kings shall the God of heaven set up a kingdom, which shall never be destroyed . . .

If this were really said in the time of Nebuchadnezzar, it would be an example of divine prescience indeed; but since it was very likely said four centuries after the time of Nebuchadnezzar it represents a schematic description of known history.

The second kingdom "inferior to thee" was, presumably, the Median Empire, which the writer of Daniel assumes (as can be deduced from a later passage) to have followed the Chaldean Empire. Actually, it existed concurrently with the Chaldean, but, though larger in area, the Median Empire was smaller in wealth, civilization, and military power and was hence inferior.

The third kingdom "which shall bear rule over all the earth" was undoubtedly the Persian Empire, which conquered first the Medes and then the Chaldeans and eventually ruled a vast territory that included almost all the territories known to the Jews of the time.

Finally, the fourth kingdom "strong as iron" is the Macedonian

Empire established by Alexander the Great two and a half centuries after Nebuchadnezzar's time. The two legs of iron symbolize the fact that after Alexander's death his empire was broken up and that two of its large fragments particularly interested the Jews. These were Egypt under the Ptolemies, and western Asia under the Seleucids. The Ptolemaic and Seleucid Empires were at more or less constant war with each other and Judah was torn between them. From 300 to 200 B.C. Judah was mostly under the tolerant sway of the Ptolemies, but after 200 B.C. it came under the intolerant rule of the Seleucids.

It was in the time of terror and agony under the Seleucids that the Book of Daniel was written and the stone, a re-established ideal Judah, that would destroy the Seleucid Empire, consisting as it did of weak monarchs as well as strong ones (clay mixed with iron), was a reference to the Jewish revolt against the Seleucids that began in 168 B.C.

Shadrach, Meshach, and Abednego

The third chapter of Daniel tells another legend about Nebuchadnezzar. He had a huge statue built of himself to which all his subjects were to grant divine honors. Those who refused were to be burned alive and, of course, the loyal Jews, Shadrach, Meshach, and Abednego (Daniel is not mentioned in this chapter for some reason), refused. The indicated punishment was visited upon them:

> Daniel 3:23. *And these three men, Shadrach, Meshach and Abednego, fell down bound into the midst of the burning fiery furnace.*

The results were not as expected, however. Nebuchadnezzar, on surveying the situation, said:

> Daniel 3:25. . . . *Lo, I see four men loose, walking in the midst of the fire, and they have no hurt; and the form of the fourth is like the Son of God.*

As it stands in the King James Version, the final phrase, capitalized as it is, might seem a clear reference to Jesus, but the phrase is not quite correct. As given in the Revised Standard Version, it reads "the fourth is like a son of the gods," in other words, like an angel.

To explain this more clearly, perhaps, some later hand composed an additional section intended to be placed immediately after verse 3:23. It contained a prayer supposedly recited by Azariah (Abednego) within the furnace and a psalm of praise to God, chanted by the three. This additional section does not appear in the Jewish canon, but only in the Apocrypha. It is accepted as canonical in the Catholic Bible.

The section bears the title of "The Song of the Three Holy Children" in the King James Version, and "The Prayer of Azariah and the Song of the Three Young Men" in the Revised Standard Version.

A few prose verses are also included in the section;

> Three Holy Children 1:26. *But the angel of the Lord came down into the oven . . . and smote the flame of the fire out of the oven;*
> Three Holy Children 1:27. . . . *so that the fire touched them not at all, neither hurt nor troubled them.*

And it was this angel of the Lord, apparently, that the later writer introduced to make it quite plain that it was an angel that Nebuchadnezzar saw, an angel that had performed a miracle.

Clearly, this legend was meant to apply to the time of writing. It was the Seleucid monarchs, not Nebuchadnezzar, who claimed divine honors; and it was the Seleucid monarchs, not Nebuchadnezzar, who threatened the Jews with death for practicing their religion. The writer was assuring the readers of the ever-present and watchful eye of God.

Nebuchadnezzar

The fourth chapter deals with still another legend of Nebuchadnezzar. Again he has a dream and again Daniel interprets it. This time, the interpretation is that Nebuchadnezzar, unless he forswears his sins and reforms, is going to be condemned to lose his mind and eat grass like an ox.

At the end of a year, Nebuchadnezzar in a moment of pride is suddenly stricken:

> Daniel 4:33. *The same hour was the thing fulfilled upon Nebuchadnezzar: and he was driven from men, and did eat grass as oxen, and his body was wet with the dew of heaven, till his hairs were grown like eagles' feathers, and his nails like birds' claws.*

And he remained so until he repented.

Of course, there is no record in secular history of Nebuchadnezzar suffering from any such strange malady, and it is in the highest degree unlikely that he did. It remains only to decide where the writer got the idea that the great Chaldean conqueror browsed on grass.

One guess is particularly attractive. The Assyrians built statues in the shape of bulls with human heads and birds' wings to represent good-luck deities. They are the inspiration of the Biblical cherubim (see page 148). These were built in front of Sargon's palace and are as characteristic of Assyria as the pyramids are of Egypt and the pillared temples of the Greeks. Such figures, or tales of them, must have remained after the Assyrian Empire itself had been destroyed and in Greek times all kinds of fanciful tales must have been made up to account for these composite representations. The tale of a Chaldean monarch who was forced to eat grass like an ox till his hair grew like eagles' feathers is transparently based on such statues.

Belshazzar

The next incident described in Daniel takes place after the death of Nebuchadnezzar and, apparently, shortly before the fall of Babylon to the Persians:

> Daniel 5:1. *Belshazzar the king made a great feast . . . and . . .*
> Daniel 5:2. *. . . . commanded to bring the golden and silver vessels which his father Nebuchadnezzar had taken out of the temple which was in Jerusalem . . .*

Apparently, the writer of Daniel knew of only two kings of Babylon during the period of the Exile: Nebuchadnezzar the first and Belshazzar, supposedly his son, the second and last. A writer actually living in the Exilic period or shortly afterward could not have made that mistake.

Nebuchadnezzar died in 562 B.C., twenty-four years after the destruction of Jerusalem, and was succeeded by his son, Amel-Marduk (not Belshazzar). Amel-Marduk is referred to in the Bible as the "Evil-merodach" who lightened the captivity of Jehoiachin (see page 396).

In 560 B.C., Amel-Marduk was assassinated by his brother-in-law, Nergal-ashur-usur (whose name is slurred into Neriglissar by the

classical historians). For four years this son-in-law of Nebuchadnezzar sat on the throne and it is just barely possible that he is mentioned
in the Bible. Thus, in Jeremiah's description of the fall of Jerusalem,
a list of Nebuchadnezzar's generals is given:

> Jeremiah 39:2. . . . *the city was broken up.*
> Jeremiah 39:3. *And all the princes of the king of Babylon came in*
> . . . *even Nergal-sha-rezer, Samgar-nebo, Sarsechim* . . .

Is it possible that Nergal-sha-rezer is a misspelling of Nergal-ashur-
usur? Can it further be that Nebuchadnezzar bestowed one of his
daughters upon this general, who then, in later years, seized the throne
from his old ruler's weaker son?

Nergal-ashur-usur died in 556 B.C. and was succeeded by his son,
Labashi-Marduk, a grandson of Nebuchadnezzar, but there was opposition to him. The opposition proclaimed Nabu-naido ("Nabu is glorious"), who was no relative at all of Nebuchadnezzar. They won out
and Nabu-naido, better known to us as Nabonidus, the Greek version
of the name, sat on the throne as the last king of the Chaldean Empire.
He was to reign seventeen years.

Where, then, is Belshazzar?

Well, Nabonidus was the son of a priest and, apparently, had had a
scholarly upbringing. His chief interest was in religion and in antiquarian research. He restored old temples and built new ones. He
searched for old cylinders and inscriptions, dug them up carefully and
reproduced them (performing invaluable services for modern historians).

He was not at all interested in war and neglected the defenses of the
nation.

He therefore associated his oldest son with himself and made him a
kind of viceroy. The burdens of the defense of the empire sat upon that
son's shoulders. His name was Bel-shar-utsur ("Bel, protect the king")
and it is he who, in the Book of Daniel, is known as Belshazzar. He is
not the king but the crown prince, and he is not the son, or any other
relation, of Nebuchadnezzar.

The times were growing dark for Chaldea in the time of Nabonidus
and Belshazzar. It had been in 559 B.C., soon after the assassination of
Amel-Marduk, that Cyrus had inherited rule over the Persian tribes. In
550 B.C., after Nabonidus had been on the throne five or six years, Cyrus
defeated and absorbed the Median Empire and became a world power.

The Chaldean Empire faced an overwhelming danger only a dozen years after the death of Nebuchadnezzar.

The empire formed an alliance with Saitic Egypt and with the nation of Lydia in Asia Minor, but that didn't help. In 546 B.C., Lydia was crushed by Persia and all of Asia Minor passed over to Cyrus.

Chaldea was next.

Mene, Mene, Tekel, Upharsin

In the middle of Belshazzar's feast, at which the holy vessels of the Temple were being profaned:

> Daniel 5:5. . . . *came forth fingers of a man's hand, and wrote . . . upon . . . the wall of the king's palace . . .*

The words were unintelligible to the onlookers, so Daniel, the now aged interpreter of Nebuchadnezzar's dreams, was sent for. This was his interpretation:

> Daniel 5:25. *And this is the writing* . . . MENE, MENE, TEKEL, UPHARSIN.
> Daniel 5:26. *This is the interpretation* . . . MENE; *God hath numbered thy kingdom, and finished it.*
> Daniel 5:27. TEKEL; *Thou art weighed in the balances, and found wanting.*
> Daniel 5:28. PERES; *Thy kingdom is divided, and given to the Medes and the Persians.*

The actual meaning of Mene, Mene, Tekel, Upharsin is uncertain. The words are apparently Aramaean and may represent the names of weights. Mene is the "mina," which is roughly equivalent to the modern pound, and Tekel is the "shekel," which is one fiftieth of a mina, or a third of an ounce. Upharsin is more puzzling. The Revised Standard Version changes it to "parsin" and it may be a pun on "Parsa," the native word for what we call Persia. Some think that Upharsin is a form of a word that originally meant a half shekel.

In any case, an inscription made up of the names of weights might give the impression of God weighing the worth of Chaldea in comparison with Persia and finding Chaldea "wanting"—that is, the lighter of the two. This is reminiscent of the scenes in the Greek epic, the *Iliad*, in which Zeus consults the Fates by placing the lots of two fighters in separate balances of the scale to see which one outweighs the other. This may be the source of the vision of God weighing Belshazzar in the balance.

It is this dramatic incident that has given rise to the common phrase "the handwriting on the wall" to signify a certain indication of imminent disaster even amid apparent success.

Darius the Median

Certainly, what followed the episode was dramatic enough, according to the Book of Daniel:

> Daniel 5:30. *In that night was Belshazzar . . . slain.*
> Daniel 5:31. *And Darius the Median took the kingdom, being about threescore and two years old.*

It was in 538 B.C. that Gobryas, a general of Cyrus the Persian, led an army into the city of Babylon and Cyrus was indeed about sixty-two years old at the time. Babylon itself offered no resistance. Belshazzar, maintaining a last-ditch struggle at some point outside Babylon, was slain.

But what is this about Darius the Median? Who was he? No one, apparently. He arises, apparently, out of the conviction that the four great empires appeared consecutively: Chaldean, Median, Persian, Greek (see page 602); whereas actually Chaldean and Median existed together and both fell to the Persian. The writer's conviction of consecutive empires leads him to suppose that Babylon had to fall to a Mede and that it was only afterward that Cyrus supplanted the Mede.

As for the name Darius, given to the mythical Median conqueror of Babylon, this must be drawn from the Darius who came to the Persian throne in 521 B.C., seventeen years after the fall of Babylon, and the most capable and renowned of all the Persian monarchs.

The rest of the Book of Daniel dates itself sometimes in the reign of Cyrus, sometimes in the reign of Darius the Mede, and no useful purpose can be gained from trying to place actual dates to the chapters. The writer was not describing actual incidents and had no specific dates in mind.

At one point, he gives the name of the father of Darius the Mede:

Daniel 9:1. *In the first year of Darius the son of Ahasuerus, of the seed of the Medes . . .*

The father of the real Darius the Persian was Hystaspes. If Ahasuerus is Xerxes I of Persia (see page 463), then he was the son of Darius, not the father.

The famous story is then told of Daniel being thrown into a den of lions because he violated an edict (which Darius was tricked into signing) forbidding anyone to address any petition to anyone but himself. Daniel's open prayers to God were construed as a violation of this edict. Nevertheless, an angel was sent to protect him from the lions and he remained unharmed. Again, it is the Seleucid monarchs that are really meant and the reader is assured of God's care at all times.

Daniel 6:28. *So . . . Daniel prospered in the reign of Darius, and in the reign of Cyrus the Persian.*

Thus, Darius the Median is described as being followed by Cyrus the Persian in line with the writer's mistaken view of history.

The Little Horn

The remainder of the Book of Daniel is a series of apocalyptic visions, with the facts of human history (as the writer saw them) disguised in the form of mystic symbolism, presumably to avoid trouble with the authorities. The first vision described is that of four beasts, representing the four kingdoms, arising, in succession, out of the sea:

Daniel 7:4. *The first was like a lion, and had eagle's wings . . .*
Daniel 7:5. *. . . a second, like to a bear . . .*
Daniel 7:6. *. . . another, like a leopard . . . the beast had four heads . . .*
Daniel 7:7. *After this . . . behold a fourth beast, dreadful and terrible, and strong exceedingly; and it had great iron teeth . . . and it had ten horns.*
Daniel 7:8. *I considered the horns, and behold, there came up among them another little horn, before whom there were three of the first horns plucked up by the roots . . .*

The first beast is clearly the winged lion that gave rise to the notion that Nebuchadnezzar ate grass (see page 605) and represents the Chaldean Empire. The bear is the Median Empire, and the leopard the Persian Empire. The leopard's four heads are the four monarchs of the Persians whom the writer will mention again later in the book. The fourth beast is the Macedonian Empire set up by Alexander the Great, whose enormous feats of conquest astonished all beholders and have steadily remained a wonder of history through succeeding ages.

To the writer, that portion of Alexander's empire which came under the rule of his general Seleucus and his descendants is the important part, for it is under these Seleucids that the Jews were suffering persecution. The prime persecutor, in particular, was Antiochus IV, the eighth reigning monarch of the line, who came to the throne in 175 B.C.

The symbolism of the ten horns and the additional "little horn" seems clear. Each horn is a king of the Seleucid line and Antiochus himself is the little horn. He apparently became king only after a short civil war between rival factions. Antiochus was victorious, uprooting three horns, leaving seven, and making himself the eighth king.

The Ancient of Days

Daniel then saw the beasts slain before the judgment seat of God:

> Daniel 7:9. . . . the thrones were cast down, and the Ancient of days did sit, whose garment was white as snow, and the hair of his head like the pure wool . . .

The "Ancient of days" is, of course, God, visualized as an old man since he existed from the beginning of time and even before. The Revised Standard Version removes the effect of "Ancient" as a capitalized noun and has the phrase read: "one that was ancient of days took his seat."

In place of the destroyed beasts, a new kingdom was set up:

> Daniel 7:13. . . . behold, one like the Son of man . . . came to the Ancient of days . . .
> Daniel 7:14. And there was given him dominion, and glory, and a kingdom . . . which shall not pass away . . .

It is sometimes suggested that this is a Messianic utterance; that the fourth kingdom is the Roman Empire and that the Son of man represents Jesus. (That is why the King James Version capitalizes "Son"; the

Revised Standard Version does not.) It seems much more likely,
though, that what is meant here is that a new and eternal kingdom is
given to the ideal Jewish state, represented here in the likeness of a man
rather than in the likeness of the beasts that represented the various
heathen and idolatrous kingdoms.

Gabriel

The last five chapters of Daniel are in Hebrew. This may mean that
they were written by a different hand than those that wrote the six
preceding chapters. Or, perhaps, the shift to Hebrew is to further disguise the treasonable meaning of the visions described in those chapters.

Another vision is described. A ram with two horns (Media and Persia)
is destroyed by a goat with one large horn (Macedon under Alexander
the Great). The goat then develops several horns from among which a
little horn appears—again a reference to the Seleucid kings and to
Antiochus IV. The meaning of the vision was explained to Daniel
through supernatural means:

> Daniel 8:16. *And I heard a man's voice . . . which called, and said,*
> *Gabriel, make this man to understand the vision.*

Gabriel ("hero of God") is a product of the development of the
Jewish view of angels under Persian influence. Gabriel is one of the
four archangels (chief angels)—or of the seven, or twelve, or seventy,
depending on the writer who is working out the mystical interrelationships.

Perhaps because of his role in the Book of Daniel, Gabriel is usually
thought of as God's messenger, explaining divine meanings to selected
human beings. In the New Testament it is Gabriel who explains to
Mary that she is to bear Jesus, and in Mohammedan legends, it is
Gabriel who takes Mohammed to Heaven and dictates the Koran to
him.

In later Jewish legends, intended to fill out the details omitted in the
earlier Biblical books, it was the angel Gabriel who supposedly took on
the guise of a man and directed the young Joseph to the place where his
brethren were pasturing their sheep. Gabriel was also, according to
legend, one of those who buried Moses, and one of those who destroyed
the army of Sennacherib.

Daniel is the only book in the Jewish canon in which angels are given names. Elsewhere the names of the angels appear only in the Apocrypha and in the New Testament. This is another sign of the late composition of Daniel.

Seventy Weeks

The writer then represents Daniel as considering Jeremiah's prediction that the kingdom of Judah would be restored, presumably in ideal form, after seventy years from the time of the destruction of the Temple. In the time of Zerubbabel and Nehemiah, it must have seemed to Jews, generally, that the prophecy was coming true. After all, Jews again controlled Jerusalem and the second Temple was opened to worship just seventy years after the destruction of the first Temple (see page 449).

To later Jews, though, particularly to those living under the Seleucids, there must have seemed a bitter irony in the prediction. The restored state of Jerusalem had remained under the firm control of first the Persians, then the Ptolemies, then the Seleucids. Not only did it never become the ideal Israel dominating the world, but it was actually being threatened under the Seleucids with utter extinction. How could all this be squared with Jeremiah's prediction?

A modification of that prediction had to be made and the writer of Daniel turned to the mystic lore of numbers. The Jews, like many of the ancient peoples (even certain of the Greek philosophers), felt there were all sorts of hidden meaning in numbers and that special numbers had special characters.

Seven, for instance, was a number of peculiar significance. This might be traced back to the seventh day being the Sabbath, but this in turn seems to be of Babylonian origin, where the seven-day week rose from the fact that there were seven "planets" in the heavens. Each of the planets was in charge of a particular day of the week. We still have a remnant of this in Sunday (the sun), Monday (the moon), and Saturday (Saturn). In the Romance languages the other days are similarly identified. In French, for instance, Tuesday, Wednesday, Thursday, and Friday are *mardi* (Mars), *mercredi* (Mercury), *jeudi* (Jupiter), and *vendredi* (Venus).

But whatever the origin of the special characteristics of seven, to

Daniel seven was a sacred number. The seventy years of Jeremiah were really seven decades, and might not the sacred significance of that be increased further by an additional multiplication by seven? Instead of seventy years, there would be seventy weeks (seventy times seven) of years. Gabriel explains this to Daniel:

> Daniel 9:24. *Seventy weeks are determined upon thy people and upon thy holy city, to finish the transgression and to make an end of sins.*

The phrase "seventy weeks" is expanded to "seventy weeks of years" in the Revised Standard Version.

Seventy weeks of years, or 490 years, counting from the destruction of the first Temple in 586 B.C., would carry matters to 96 B.C., a date safely in the writer's future. (As it turns out, of course, the ideal Jewish state was not established in 96 B.C., either, and that date has no particular significance in Jewish history.)

Messiah the Prince

Daniel's vision goes into greater detail:

> Daniel 9:25. . . . *from the going forth of the commandment to restore and to build Jerusalem unto the Messiah the Prince shall be seven weeks, and threescore and two weeks: the street shall be built again . . .*
> Daniel 9:26. *And after threescore and two weeks shall Messiah be cut off . . .*

One might see in this a reference to Jesus, particularly since the King James Version capitalizes "Messiah" and "Prince." The Revised Standard Version does not, however. The phrase in 9:25 is rendered "an anointed one, a prince," and in 9:26, "an anointed one." And we must remember that the writer of Daniel is speaking obscurely, at least to us. His original readers would have had no trouble.

What the twenty-fifth verse seems to say is that seven weeks of years (forty-nine years) will pass from Jeremiah's prediction, or from the fall of the first Temple in 586 B.C. to the coming of an anointed king who will make it possible to rebuild. A passage of forty-nine years (seven times seven, a sacred number indeed) brings us to 537 B.C., which is indeed within a year of the time (538 B.C.) when Cyrus granted Jews permission to rebuild; and remember that Cyrus is specifically spoken of by the Second Isaiah as one whose hand God holds and therefore as an anointed king (see page 549).

It is completely reasonable, then, to understand "Messiah the Prince" to signify Cyrus of Persia. Following Cyrus are sixty-two weeks of years (434 years) during which Jerusalem exists as a city. At the end of that time, 104 B.C., "shall Messiah be cut off."

This can't be the same Messiah spoken of in the verse before. In the first place, four and a third centuries have passed, and in the second, the first is a prince, a secular leader, and the second is not. The second is merely "an anointed one"; that is, a High Priest.

As a matter of fact, there was a High Priest in the time that Daniel was probably written who was a champion of Judaism against the Seleucids and against those Jews who advocated a compromise with Seleucid views. He was Onias III, the son of that Simon II who was praised so highly by Jesus, son of Sirach (see page 516). Onias III became High Priest in 198 B.C. When Antiochus IV became king, Onias III was first deposed, then imprisoned, and finally, in 171 B.C., executed. This quickly led to the final crisis that brought on a Jewish revolt against the Seleucids. The killing of Onias III can therefore be looked upon as a turning point.

It may, therefore, be Onias III who is the Messiah that is cut off, although the date given in Daniel misses the actual date by sixty-six years. (However, no one has been able to make the dates given in Daniel's vision come out both significantly and accurately.)

The peak of persecution that follows on the death of Onias III is also described:

> Daniel 9:26. . . . *the prince that shall come shall destroy the city and the sanctuary . . .*
> Daniel 9:27. . . . *for one week: and in the midst of the week he shall cause the sacrifice and the oblation to cease, and for the overspreading of abominations he shall make it desolate . . .*

The language as the writer approaches his own time becomes more carefully obscure. Apparently, he speaks now of the final week—the seven-year period after the death of Onias III in which Seleucid persecution is at its height—from 171 to 165 B.C.

In the "midst of the week," or in 168 B.C., Antiochus IV took Jerusalem and pillaged it. He outlawed Judaism and ordered the Temple to be profaned and dedicated to Zeus. Swine were deliberately sacrificed on the altar in order to subject it to the most vile desecration possible in the eyes of pious Jews. Such sacrifices were "abominations" and the Temple was rendered so unclean that it had to be abandoned, or made "desolate" till it could be cleansed again by painstaking ritual. These idolatrous sacrifices are sometimes spoken of as "the abomination of desolation."

The final cleansing and rededication of the Temple did take place in 165 B.C. at the end of the week of years and Antiochus IV died in 163 B.C.

Michael

In Daniel's next vision, he is helped by a heavenly messenger who reaches him only after resistance from one angel and help from another:

Daniel 10:13. . . . *the prince of the kingdom of Persia withstood me one and twenty days: but, lo, Michael, one of the chief princes, came to help me* . . .

Here we have the late Jewish view that each nation had a guardian angel of its own (a kind of henotheism reduced to a subsidiary level). Michael ("who is like God?") is the guardian angel of Judah. The angel tells Daniel:

Daniel 10:20. . . . *now will I return to fight with the prince of Persia: and* . . . *lo, the prince of Grecia shall come.*
Daniel 10:21. . . . *there is none that holdeth with me in these things, but Michael your prince.*

Naturally, in his capacity as the guardian angel of Judah, Michael is considered by the Jews to be the greatest of the angels. In the legends concerning the fall of Satan from Heaven (see page 540), Michael is viewed as the leader of the loyal angels, fighting for God against the devil. This is mentioned in Revelation:

Revelation 12:7. *And there was war in heaven: Michael and his angels fought against the dragon: and the dragon* . . .
Revelation 12:8. . . . *prevailed not* . . .
Revelation 12:9. *And the great dragon was cast out* . . . *into the earth, and his angels were cast out with him.*

Another mention of Michael and the devil, contending on earth, is to be found in the New Testament Book of Jude:

> Jude 1:9. . . . *Michael the archangel . . . contending with the devil . . . about the body of Moses . . .*

Grecia

Daniel is told:

> Daniel 11:2. . . . *Behold there shall stand up . . . three kings in Persia; and the fourth shall be far richer than they all: and . . . shall stir up all against the realm of Grecia.*

The four kings of Persia are foreshadowed earlier by the leopard with four heads that represented that empire (see page 609). Presumably, the four kings of Persia are Cyrus, Cambyses, Darius, and Xerxes. That the fourth is Xerxes is indicated by the fact that his famous expedition against Greece is mentioned.

The King of the South

In guarded language, Daniel is told of the coming of Alexander the Great and of the breakup of Alexander's empire; then, of the history of the fragments of importance to Jewish history:

> Daniel 11:5. *And the king of the south shall be strong . . .*
> Daniel 11:6. . . . *the king's daughter of the south shall come to the king of the north to make an agreement . . .*

The two fragments of importance are Ptolemaic Egypt and the Seleucid Empire. Egypt lies to the south and west of Judah, and the Seleucid Empire to the north and east. The "king of the south" refers to the Ptolemies, and the "king of the north" to the Seleucids.

These verses and those that follow refer to the continuing wars between the Ptolemies and the Seleucids for the control of what had once been the land of Canaan. The early Ptolemies were victorious:

Kingdoms of the Ptolemies and the Seleucids

> Daniel 11:7. . . . *one . . . shall come with an army, and shall enter into the fortress of the king of the north . . . and shall prevail:*

This probably refers to Ptolemy III, who reigned from 246 to 221 B.C. and who defeated the Seleucids in what is called the Third Syrian War, taking all of Syria and even sections of Asia Minor. His reign represented the peak of Ptolemaic power.

After Ptolemy III, however, a series of weak kings ruled in Egypt:

> Daniel 11:15. *So the king of the north shall come . . . and take the most fenced cities: and the arms of the south shall not withstand . . .*

This very likely refers to Antiochus III, who ruled from 223 to 187 B.C. Under him the Seleucid Empire was at the peak of its power. Between 201 and 195 B.C., he fought the Fifth Syrian War with Egypt and took all the Asian coast, including Judah. With that, Judah passed from the Ptolemies to the Seleucids.

The Ships of Chittim

The rise of Antiochus IV is then described in the most insulting terms:

> Daniel 11:21. *And in his estate shall stand up a vile person . . . he shall . . . obtain the kingdom by flatteries.*

Antiochus IV became king in 175 B.C. and in 171 B.C. he launched another attack on Egypt, against the weak and cowardly Ptolemy VI. It may be that part of the cause of the Seleucid persecution of the Jews rested in the fact that the Jews, in all likelihood, were pro-Egyptian in their sympathies. They had been well treated, by and large, under the Ptolemies, and Alexandria, the capital of Ptolemaic Egypt, may well have contained more Jews (and certainly more prosperous Jews) than Jerusalem itself did. To Antiochus, the attack on Judaism may have seemed a political necessity. His execution of Onias III in 171 B.C. (page 614) may have been intended to remove a possible rallying point against the pro-Seleucid High Priests he had installed in Jerusalem, and to prevent a rising in his rear while he was busy in Egypt.

Antiochus won his war—but times had changed. There was a new power in the world now; that of Rome. The Roman Republic had no desire to see any eastern kingdom grow strong enough to dispute over-lordship of the Mediterranean world. They ordered the victorious Antiochus out of Egypt, and Antiochus, very much against his will, had to leave. He could beat the Egyptians but he knew he could not beat the Romans.

Daniel 11:30. *For the ships of Chittim shall come against him: therefore he shall be grieved, and return, and have indignation against the holy covenant . . .*

Chittim is Cyprus (page 201). The writer of Daniel is rather vague on the geography of the mysterious regions out past the Mediterranean shores and this would be his way of saying "the ships from the western islands." Of course, it is the Roman power that he means and this is the only reference to Rome in the Old Testament.

Antiochus IV, unbearably humiliated by this treatment from Rome, must have felt the need for some victory, however small, with which to save his face before his people and himself. No doubt, the Jews were openly jubilant at the way in which Antiochus had been made to crawl before the Romans, and this caused him to "have indignation against the holy covenant" and helped drive him on to occupy Jerusalem and profane the Temple.

Daniel 12:2. . . . *there shall be a time of trouble, such as never was . . .*
. . . .
Daniel 12:7. . . . *it shall be for a time, times, and an half . . .*
. . . .
Daniel 12:11. . . . *from the time that . . . the abomination that maketh desolate* [was] *set up, there shall be a thousand two hundred and ninety days.*

The reference to "time, times, and an half" is taken to mean one year plus two years plus half a year, or three and a half years. And, of course, 1290 days is also equal to about three and a half years, and it did take about that long after the profanation of the Temple before the Jewish rebels could retake and repurify it.

Susanna

The canonical Book of Daniel ends with the twelfth chapter, but there are, in addition, several short legends told of Daniel, stressing his wisdom and cleverness. Three of them are included in the Apocrypha and these are considered canonical by the Catholic Church.

The first is "The History of Susanna," which appears as the thirteenth chapter of Daniel in the Catholic versions of the Bible.

The book is titled after its heroine, whose name means "lily." It is what we would today call a detective story and, considering the time of its composition, it is an excellent one and has been sufficiently popular, as a result, to make the name Susanna and Susan common among young ladies even today.

The setting is in Babylon during the Exile:

Susanna 1:1. *There dwelt a man in Babylon, called Joacim:*
Susanna 1:2. *And he took a wife, whose name was Susanna . . .*

Quickly, the two villains are introduced:

Susanna 1:5. *The same year were appointed two of the ancients of the people to be judges . . .*

The "ancients," or elders, proved to be wicked, and Jewish tradition identified them, therefore, with two prophets denounced as false by Jeremiah:

Jeremiah 29:21. *Thus saith the Lord . . . of Ahab . . . and . . . Zedekiah . . . which prophesy a lie unto you in my name; Behold, I will deliver them into the hand of Nebuchadrezzar . . .*

But since Susanna is generally considered a work of fiction, such an identification need not be taken seriously.

The two elders lusted after Susanna and tried to seduce her. Her virtue was proof against their elderly charms and they conspired to accuse her of adultery, in order to punish her for her refusal. They stated they had seen her intimate with a young man whom they had not been strong enough to arrest. The assembly, impressed by the word of the elders, condemned Susanna to death.

At this point Daniel enters:

Susanna 1:45. . . . *when she was led to be put to death, the Lord raised up the holy spirit of a young youth, whose name was Daniel:*

Daniel's youth, at the time of this event, has led some old editions of the Bible to place this story at the beginning of the Book of Daniel rather than at the end. Certainly there is some sense to this.

Daniel demanded the right to cross-examine the elders separately before the council. He asked each the name of the tree under which he had seen the criminal intimacy take place. Each named a different tree and it was plain that they were lying. Susanna was freed and, presumably, lived happily ever after, while the elders were put to death for bearing false witness.

Bel and the Dragon

The two remaining legends of Daniel are combined under the title of "Bel and the Dragon." These are included as the fourteenth chapter of Daniel in the Catholic versions of the Bible. Both tales are designed to show the folly of idolatry.

The tales are laid in the time of Cyrus:

Bel and the Dragon 1:1. *And king Astyages was gathered to his fathers, and Cyrus of Persia received his kingdom.*

This apocryphal tale is more accurate, at this point, than the canonical Book of Daniel. Here there is no mention of "Darius the Median." Astyages was, indeed, the last king of the Medes. He was defeated by Cyrus, who ruled in his place and who then went on to conquer Lydia and Babylonia.

In the first short tale, Daniel got into trouble with Cyrus because he would not worship the idol Bel (or Marduk), to which every day the Babylonians devoted twelve bushels of flour, forty sheep, and fifty gallons of wine.

Daniel maintained that Bel was a false god, and Cyrus pointed out how much he ate and drank. Daniel therefore secretly arranged to have the floor of the room in which the idol stood covered with fine ashes and the doors sealed after the offerings had been made. The next morning, footsteps were found in the ashes and it turned out there was a secret room to which the priests of Bel, with their families, took the food and ate it. The priests were therefore killed and the temple destroyed.

As a matter of fact, the great Babylonian temple of Marduk was indeed destroyed by a Persian king, but for strictly secular reasons. It was Xerxes who razed it in punishment for a Babylonian rebellion against his rule, and as part of a general sack of the city.

In the second tale Cyrus orders Daniel to worship a dragon (probably a large snake). Daniel refuses, pointing out that the dragon can easily be killed, so that it is no god. He then proceeds to feed it a concoction that kills it.

The king was forced to hand over Daniel to the indignant Babylonians and they threw him into a lion's den. Here, as in the canonical book, Daniel is saved by divine intervention, but with an added feature, for another prophet is introduced.

Bel and the Dragon 1:33. *Now there was in Jewry a prophet, called Habbacuc . . .*

or, as the Revised Standard Version has it: "Now the prophet Habakkuk was in Judea."

There was indeed a prophet by that name in Judah, and he was the author of one of the canonical prophetic books. Undoubtedly, the writer of Bel and the Dragon meant this Habakkuk, but if so, he missed out a bit chronologically. Habakkuk was active in the reign of Josiah and shortly afterward, or over half a century before the time of Cyrus. He was not likely to be alive at the time of this tale.

But putting this small matter to one side, the prophet Habakkuk fed Daniel after he was miraculously transported from Judea to Babylon. Daniel was then freed unharmed and once again was triumphant over all his enemies.

28. HOSEA

Hosea

The final twelve canonical books of the Old Testament are twelve relatively short prophetic works, which, for convenience' sake, were combined into a single scroll in ancient times. One might therefore speak of a "book of the twelve."

Indeed, Jesus, son of Sirach, implies just that. In his memorial to the famous men of Biblical history (see page 516) he goes through the books of the Bible in order (and thus shows which were accepted as canonical in the Judea of his day). Having spoken of Isaiah, Jeremiah, and Ezekiel, the major prophets, he does not list the remaining prophets separately, but merely says:

Ecclesiasticus 49:10. *And of the twelve prophets let the memorial be blessed* . . .

(Be it noted that there is no mention of Daniel, a book very likely composed after his time.)

The twelve prophets are sometimes called the "minor prophets," not because their teachings are necessarily unimportant from a religious standpoint, but simply because their messages are much shorter than those included under the names of Isaiah, Jeremiah, and Ezekiel.

The twelve minor prophets do not occur in chronological order, though this may have been the original intention. Unfortunately, the traditional period of activity of the individual prophets does not always agree with the one determined by modern scholarship.

Hosea, who heads the list, is indeed one of the earlier ones of the twelve, but he is not the earliest. He is the only one of the twelve

Israel and Judah at the Time of Hosea

to be a man of Israel, a northerner, rather than a man of Judah. Indeed, although there were northern prophets who, in later times, were greatly honored by the Jews (Elijah, for instance), Hosea is the only northerner whose utterances are collected into a formal and separate book.

That Hosea is a northerner is not specifically stated, but it is deduced from the fact that virtually all his speeches are addressed to Israel rather than Judah. In addition, he refers to the Israelite monarch in a possessive that includes himself:

Hosea 7:5. *In the day of our king* . . .

The book begins by dating itself:

Hosea 1:1. *The word of the Lord that came unto Hosea . . . in the days of Uzziah, Jotham, Ahaz, and Hezekiah, kings of Judah, and in the days of Jeroboam, . . . king of Israel.*

This introductory verse is probably by the later hand of a Judean editor anxious to date the book in Judean terms.

Uzziah became king in 780 B.C. and Hezekiah died in 692 B.C. As for Jeroboam II, he ruled from 785 to 745 B.C. The book gives clear evidence of knowledge of the near anarchy that pervaded Israel in the quarter century between Jeroboam's death and the destruction of Israel by Assyria. If, then, we were to guess that various parts of the book represent utterances made between 750 and 720 B.C., Hosea would have preached from the last years of Jeroboam II to the destruction of Israel. In Judean terms, that would date him from the final years of Uzziah through the reigns of Jotham and Ahaz and into the beginning of the reign of Hezekiah. This would account for the dating of the first verse and would make Hosea an older contemporary of Isaiah.

The name Hosea, by the way, is a version of the more correct Hoshea, the name borne by the last king of Israel.

Jezreel

The first three chapters of Hosea are taken by most commentators to be autobiographical and to relate the story of Hosea's marriage. Hosea's wife proved unfaithful but the prophet found he loved her

anyway and took her back. In this, he discovered a symbolic reference
to God's love for Israel and God's willingness to forgive Israel her
transgressions.

As was true of Isaiah at roughly the same point in history, Hosea
gave his children symbolic names:

> Hosea 1:3. . . . *he went and took Gomer . . . which conceived,
> and bare him a son.*
> Hosea 1:4. *And the Lord said unto him, Call his name Jezreel;
> for yet a little while, and I will avenge the blood of Jezreel upon
> the house of Jehu . . .*

A century earlier, Jehu had overthrown the reigning house of Omri
and had established himself on the throne (see page 364). The prophetic party had justified this result, since it overthrew an idolatrous
line of kings who were attempting to introduce Tyrian worship, and
who were energetically persecuting the Yahvists. Nevertheless, even the
Yahvist editors of the material in the Second Book of Kings could not
hide the fact that the revolution had been carried through very bloodily
and that Jehu had remorselessly killed a large number of helpless
people.

The murder of an anointed king, regardless of the personal characteristics of that king, is bound to be looked upon with horror by
people taught to believe that the anointment represented the adoption
of the monarch by a deity. This quasi-holy character of the kingship
served to protect kings from assassination down to modern times, and
explains some of the horror produced in conservative minds by the
British execution of Charles I in 1649 and the French execution of
Louis XVI in 1793.

There is bound to be a feeling, therefore, that an act of regicide
will have its consequences, even though these may be delayed. Thus,
Shakespeare, in his historical plays, sees some of the disasters befalling
England in the fifteenth century as being the consequence of the forced
deposition and later murder of Richard II (even though Shakespeare
recognizes him as an unworthy king).

Similarly, there could well have been a feeling in Israel that the
horrors that Jehu carried through in Jezreel (where Jezebel was among
those killed) would come back to haunt his descendants. So far, Jehu,
his son, his grandson, and Jeroboam II, his great-grandson, had reigned

for a century of reasonable peace. Indeed, under Jeroboam II, Israel reached a peak of power. Nevertheless, Hosea foresees the coming disaster and with the king's death in 740 B.C., that disaster begins. Jeroboam's son Zachariah succeeds to the throne as the fifth member of the dynasty of Jehu, but he is assassinated almost at once and then comes the downward spiral.

The accession of Tiglath-Pileser III to the Assyrian throne in 745 B.C. and the quick evidences that here was a strong, warlike monarch who was sure to engage in westward aggressions must have made it clear to Hosea, as to Isaiah, that the time was running out for the little kingdoms.

Jareb

It seemed to Hosea that even submission to Assyria wound not cure the general decay sweeping over Israel and Judah:

> Hosea 5:13. *When Ephraim saw his sickness and Judah saw his wound, then went Ephraim to the Assyrian, and sent to king Jareb: yet could he not heal you, nor cure you of your wound.*

There is no Assyrian king named Jareb, so it must be a nickname. It is associated with a Hebrew word meaning "to strive" or "to fight." Perhaps it might be translated as "the fighting king" or "the warlike king" and in either case it is obviously Tiglath-Pileser III of Assyria. The Revised Standard Version translates "king Jareb" as "the great king," a common title for the king of the Middle Eastern empires of ancient times.

In the event, Hosea's judgment proved correct. Submission to Assyria did not save the kingdoms for each rebelled, until the former was finally crushed by Assyria and the latter by the successor kingdom of Chaldea.

Shalman

The disaster Hosea predicts is expressed in a number of ways, including the very familiar:

Hosea 8:7. *For they have sown the wind, and they shall reap the whirlwind . . .*

and the less poetic, but more specific:

Hosea 10:14. . . . . *all thy fortresses shall be spoiled, as Shalman spoiled Beth-arbel . . .*
Hosea 10:15. . . . *in a morning shall the king of Israel utterly be cut off.*

Neither Shalman nor Beth-arbel can be certainly identified, nor can the incident be pin-pointed. Some suggest that Shalman is a king of Moab, contemporary to Hosea (one such is referred to as Salamanu in Assyrian inscription) and to some local victory in the Trans-Jordan which he won just before the time of the prophet's utterance.

Another possibility is that the verse refers to Shalmaneser V, who succeeded Tiglath-Pileser III in 727 B.C. In this case, Hosea may be speaking as Shalmaneser is marching to the siege of Samaria and be referring to a victory won by him en route. It is this siege which led to the fall of Samaria and the destruction of Israel even though Shalmaneser V did not live to see its conclusion.

David

As is usually true of the prophets, however, Hosea sees beyond the immediate destruction to an ideal future:

Hosea 3:5. *Afterward shall the children of Israel return, and see the Lord their God, and David their king . . . in the latter days.*

This sounds as though it was uttered after Sargon's carrying off of the Israelites into captivity, but of course those exiles never returned. The mention of David himself rather than a descendant of his may be simply symbolic, but it may also reflect an early notion among the Jews, predating the development of the Messianic notion.

It is an attractive idea, for a nation which has experienced greater times in its past (or imagines it has) sometimes dreams that some powerful king, whom it magnifies in tradition, is not really dead. Thus, king Arthur sleeps in Avalon, waiting to return on some day when his country really needs him. Similarly, the twelfth-century German emperor, Frederick Barbarossa, sleeps under the Kyffhäuser mountain, likewise awaiting his country's call.

Perhaps, then, this verse is a reflection of a time when Jews expected the return of David himself.

Of course, it is odd to have a northerner say this. The northern kingdom had been only uneasily subject to David and Solomon at the best of times and had revolted from the Judean dynasty immediately after Solomon's death, showing no signs, thereafter, of any longing to return to its original allegiance. Would Hosea dream of the return of David, or could the verse be the addition of a later Judean hand?

29. JOEL

Joel

Joel ("Yahveh is God") is the first of the eleven minor prophets of Judah. The collection of his utterances bears no dates but begins merely:

Joel 1:1. *The word of the Lord that came to Joel . . .*

Since the book makes no mention of the Assyrian or Babylonian menace, it would seem that Joel either spoke before those menaces had made themselves plain or after they had passed. In other words, the book must be dated either before 750 B.C. or after 500 B.C.

At the time the Jewish canon was being established, it was the first alternative that seemed to attract the scribes, and for that reason Joel was placed early in the group of minor prophets.

This, however, is extremely unlikely and modern commentators seem certain that the book was written after the return from exile. There are, after all, no references to kings, or to the idolatries that were so prevalent during the kingdom. There is, on the other hand, mention of the deportation of the Jews and the scattering that followed the destruction of Jerusalem:

Joel 3:2. . . . *my people . . . whom they have scattered among the nations.*

There is even a reference to the Greeks, who did not come into the Jewish ken until well along in the Persian period:

Joel 3:6. . . . *the children of Jerusalem have ye* [Tyre and Sidon] *sold unto the Grecians . . .*

Judah at the Time of Joel

The reference here is undoubtedly to the lucrative slave trade carried on by the Phoenicians in ancient times.

Consequently, the Book of Joel is usually dated about 400 B.C.

The Day of the Lord

Joel begins by describing a plague of locusts and then moves on to consider this a disaster symbolizing a much more awful event that will strike the world as the equivalent many times over of the locust plague:

> Joel 1:15. . . . *for the day of the Lord is at hand, and as a destruction from the Almighty shall it come.*

The day of the Lord, to which Joel refers, is, of course, the apocalyptic final accounting (see page 543) at which the tyrants who oppress the Jews will be punished, while the Jews themselves will be compensated with an ideal state and eternal security.

Because the day of the Lord is viewed as a day on which the nations are judged, it has come to be called "Judgment Day."

The Valley of Jehoshaphat

God is quoted as describing the events of Judgment Day:

> Joel 3:2. *I will also gather all nations, and will bring them down into the valley of Jehoshaphat, and will plead with them there for my people . . . whom they have scattered among the nations . . .*

God is not pictured as pleading like a suppliant but rather like a prosecuting attorney and judge. The Revised Standard Version makes this clearer by translating this portion of the verse "I will enter into judgement with them there, on account of my people."

No one has succeeded in definitely identifying the valley of Jehoshaphat and it is probably not a real place. The word Jehoshaphat means "Yahveh has judged" and perhaps the verse does not refer to king Jehoshaphat of Judah but should be translated "and will bring them down into the valley of the judgment of the Lord."

Joel pictures the judgment as involving nations as a whole and the punishment as being made to fit the crime:

> Joel 3:4. . . . *what have ye to do with me, O Tyre and Zidon* . . .
> . . . .

> Joel 3:6. *The children* . . . *of Jerusalem have ye sold unto the Grecians* . . .

> Joel 3:7. *Behold, I will raise them out of the place whither ye have sold them, and will return your recompence upon your own head:*

> Joel 3:8. *And I will sell your sons and your daughters into the hand of the children of Judah, and they shall sell them* . . . *to a people far off.*

Gradually, this notion of judgment by nations was still further etherealized to the point where judgment became individual and personal. This is expressed, for instance, in the final verse of Ecclesiastes, a late addition to a book that is itself post-Exilic:

> Ecclesiastes 12:14. *For God shall bring every work into judgment, with every secret thing, whether it be good, or whether it be evil.*

The notion of individual judgment is also implied in the late-written Book of Daniel:

> Daniel 12:2. *And many of them that sleep in the dust of the earth shall awake, some to everlasting life, and some to shame and everlasting contempt.*

30. AMOS

Amos

The third of the twelve minor prophets is Amos and he seems to be, in actual fact, the oldest (chronologically) of the group. Indeed, he was the first example of a new phenomenon in the history of Judaism: the inspired visionary whose words were preserved in writing.

Amos and those who followed are generally called prophets, but there are many differences between the new breed and the old bands of prophets led by men such as Samuel and Elisha. The latter were ecstatics who in their fits were thought to be mystically close to God. Amos, on the other hand, was a lone wolf, who needed no fits or seizures but spoke in plain language on what he considered the important problems of the day. Indeed, on being questioned, he denies that he is a prophet (in the old sense):

> Amos 7:14. *Then answered Amos and said . . . I was no prophet, neither was I a prophet's son; but I was an herdman . . .*

The Book of Amos is dated in the first verse:

> Amos 1:1. *The words of Amos, who was among the herdmen of Tekoa . . . in the days of Uzziah king of Judah, and in the days of Jeroboam . . . king of Israel, two years before the earthquake.*

When the earthquake referred to might be is unknown. There is no mention of an earthquake in the reign of Uzziah or of Jeroboam in the Books of Kings or Chronicles. Rabbinic tradition states that it took place when Uzziah was stricken with leprosy for attempting to officiate

CYPRUS

THE
GREAT SEA
(Mediterranean Sea)

ASSYRIAN EMPIRE
HAMATH
Hamath

EUPHRATES R.

ORONTES R.

Arvad

Kadesh

Tadmor

Gebal
(Byblos)

Zedad
Hazar-enan

KINGDOM OF
DAMASCUS

Sidon

Damascus

Tyre

Dan

CONTROLLED BY ISRAEL

Accho

Hazor

Megiddo

ISRAEL

Edrei
Ramoth-gilead

Samaria

Joppa

Bethel

Rabbath-
ammon

CONTROLLED BY JUDAH

Ashkelon
PHILISTIA

Jerusalem
Tekoa

Gath

Gaza

Hebron

AMMON

CONTROLLED BY ISRAEL

N

Raphia

Beersheba

Kir-moab
MOAB

JUDAH

Kadesh-
barnea

EDOM
Punon

Under political or economic
control of JEROBOAM II

Sela

CONTROLLED BY JUDAH

KINGDOM
OF EGYPT

Elath

GULF OF
AQABA

0   Miles   100

Israel and Judah

at the Temple rites. This is merely legend, of course, but even if it were true, the exact year in which Uzziah was stricken is unknown. Some scholars find reason to believe that the leprosy struck eight years before Uzziah's death; that is, in 748 B.C. If that was the year of the earthquake, then Amos prophesied in 750 B.C. and, actually, that is the usual estimate of the date of Amos's discourses.

One of Amos's apocalyptic visions states:

> Amos 8:9. *And it shall come to pass in that day, saith the Lord God, that I will cause the sun to go down at noon, and I will darken the earth in the clear day.*

This seems to be a reference to a solar eclipse and such an eclipse was visible in Israel and Judah in 763 B.C. If Amos indeed prophesied in 750 B.C. then it is quite reasonable to expect he had witnessed the eclipse thirteen years earlier and that his impression of it colored this verse.

If this is so, Amos is a contemporary of Hosea and Isaiah, perhaps a little older than either.

Chiun

Amos was a Judean, a native of Tekoa, which was a village some ten miles south of Jerusalem. Nevertheless, although the book records brief warnings of destruction against the nations surrounding Judah, and even against Judah itself, Amos's chief target was Israel:

> Amos 7:15. . . . *the Lord took me as I followed the flock, and the Lord said unto me, Go, prophesy unto my people Israel.*

It was to Bethel he traveled: the southern outpost of Israel, twenty miles north of Tekoa. There he preached against the Israelite custom of worshiping at the shrines of Bethel and Dan (see page 339) and against the idolatrous manner of the worship there. For instance, he refers (rather obscurely) to some form of star-worship:

> Amos 5:26. . . . *ye have borne the tabernacle of your Moloch and Chiun your images, the star of your god.*

The Revised Standard Version clarifies this somewhat by leaving "tabernacle" untranslated and translating Moloch instead. The verse becomes: "You shall take up Sakkuth your king, and Kaiwan your star-god, your images." Apparently, then, Amos is referring to two idols, Sakkuth and Kaiwan (Chiun); or perhaps they are alternate names of the same deity, expressed in poetic parallelism. Neither is mentioned anywhere else in the Bible but Kaiwan may be a form of the Babylonian Kaiman, a deity representing the planet Saturn. If so, this is one of the only two references to the planets in the Bible; the other involves Lucifer, that is, Venus, in the Book of Isaiah (see page 538).

Amaziah

Amos also inveighed against the injustices in Israel, against the luxury of the few and the poverty of the many, against the harshness of the rich toward the poor. Like the later prophets Isaiah and Jeremiah he denounced mere ritual and demanded ethical behavior. He quotes God:

> Amos 5:21. *I hate, I despise your feast days* . . .
> Amos 5:22. *Though ye offer me burnt offerings* . . . *I will not accept them* . . .
> Amos 5:23. *Take thou away from me the noise of thy songs* . . .
> Amos 5:24. *But let judgment run down as waters, and righteousness as a mighty stream.*

With this view it is reasonable to suppose that Amos did not believe that the day of the Lord ("Judgment Day") could possibly be a day of great joy for all Jews alike; since he could not believe that all Jews alike would be saved by the mere existence of the Temple ritual. Righteousness was required and for those in whom it was absent all the ritual in the world would not help. Therefore he warned:

> Amos 5:18. *Woe unto you that desire the day of the Lord! to what end is it for you? the day of the Lord is darkness and not light.*

This seems to foreshadow the notion of individual judgment and salvation, rather than national judgment.

For the nation's failure to bring about a thoroughgoing moral reform, Amos quotes God as predicting certain disaster:

Amos 7:9. . . . *I will rise against the house of Jeroboam with the sword.*

Here, apparently, Amos went too far. He might denounce idolatry and demand justice all he wished and he could be dismissed as a mere dreamer and ranter. When he spoke of rising against the king, however, he was encouraging rebellion and was speaking treason. Amaziah, the Israelite priest officiating at Bethel, had no choice but to consider it that:

Amos 7:10. *Then Amaziah the priest of Bethel sent to Jeroboam king of Israel, saying, Amos hath conspired against thee . . .*

. . . .

Amos 7:12. *Also Amaziah said unto Amos, O thou seer, go, flee thee away into the land of Judah, and there eat bread, and prophesy there:*

Amos 7:13. *But prophesy not again any more at Bethel . . .*

Amos returned a spirited answer and predicted an evil end for Amaziah (whether such an end came to pass the Bible does not say). However, Amos presumably returned to Judah, for had he stayed in Israel he would very likely have been convicted of treason and executed and there is no tradition concerning his martyrdom.

31. OBADIAH

Obadiah

The Book of Obadiah is the shortest book in the Old Testament, consisting as it does of a single chapter made up of twenty-one verses. Nothing about its author is known for the book starts off with nothing more than the author's name:

Obadiah 1:1. *The vision of Obadiah . . .*

There are a dozen Obadiahs mentioned in the Bible outside this book, the most notable of whom appears in the First Book of Kings. This Obadiah was an important official in the palace of Ahab of Israel:

1 Kings 18:3. *And Ahab called Obadiah which was the governor of his house. (Now Obadiah feared the Lord greatly:*
1 Kings 18:4. *For . . . when Jezebel cut off the prophets . . . Obadiah took an hundred prophets, and hid them by fifty in a cave and fed them . . .*

Obadiah, for performing such a dangerous feat, in the very midst of a notoriously idolatrous court, was looked up to by later Jews, and the first-century Jewish historian Josephus maintained it was this Obadiah who was the prophet and who wrote the short book that goes by that name.

This, however, would date the book about 860 B.C., which seems to be impossible. In this book, Edom is anthematized for its crime in joining the invaders who destroyed Jerusalem:

The Great Sea
(Mediterranean Sea)

N

SIDON
Sidon
MT. LEBANON
LEONTES R.
Tyre
Damascus
PERSIAN EMPIRE
MT. HERMON
Dan
ARAMAEANS
BASHAN
Karnaim
KARNAIM
Accho
SEA OF GALILEE
RETURN OF THE BABYLONIAN EXILES
PHOENICIANS
YARMUK R.
KISHON R.
Dor
MT. CARMEL
Megiddo
Beth-shan
GILEAD
DOR
SAMARIA
JORDAN R.
Samaria
Shechem
JABBOK R.
Joppa
Ono
Lod
Hadid
Bethel
Rabbath-ammon
AMMON
Jericho
JUDAH
Jerusalem
Bethlehem
Ashdod
ASHDOD
Azekah
Tekoa
SALT SEA
PHILISTINES
Gaza
Hebron
En-gedi
(DEAD SEA)
MOAB
Beer-sheba
IDUMAEA
EDOMITES
Kir-moab
ARABS
ZERED R.
EGYPT
0   Miles   25

Judah

Obadiah 1:11. . . . *thou stoodest on the other side, in the day that the strangers carried away captive his [Judah's] forces, and foreigners entered into his gates, and cast lots upon Jerusalem, even thou wast as one of them.*

This, it is generally agreed, is a reference to the destruction of Jerusalem by Nebuchadnezzar in 586 B.C., so that it would seem that the book cannot be earlier than that.

It cannot be too late, either. In the final verses, Obadiah seems to expect a restoration of Israel as well as Judah:

Obadiah 1:20. . . . *the captivity . . . of the children of Israel shall possess . . . [the land] of the Canaanites . . . and the captivity of Jerusalem . . . shall possess the cities of the south.*

Since the Israelites never returned and did not participate in the reoccupation of the land, it may well be that the Book of Obadiah was written before the Return, or at least so early after the Return that the non-return of Israel had not yet been accepted. At a guess, the book may be dated 500 B.C.

Sepharad

The final verses also place the exiled Jews in a spot otherwise unmentioned in the Bible:

Obadiah 1:20. . . . *and the captivity of Jerusalem, which is in Sepharad . . .*

No one knows the locality which is here identified as Sepharad. It does not seem to fit the name of any place in Babylonia, where the Jews were in exile, and the word may be a corruption of an original which is now impossible to recover.

One speculation has been that the word refers to Sardis, the capital of Lydia, in western Asia Minor. There is, however, no reason to think that there was any notable Jewish colony in that city in Exilic times.

During the Middle Ages, Jews flourished in Moslem Spain and the rabbis of the day decided, quite without justification, that Sepharad was a reference to Spain. As a result the Jews of Spain and Portugal, together with their descendants down to the present day, are referred to as Sephardim, as opposed to the Ashkenazim (see page 47), which include the Jews from northern and eastern Europe.

These two groups remained distinct in certain aspects of ritual as well as in ancestry. The Sephardim inherited details of their ritual from the Babylonian school since Moslem rule extended over both Spain and Babylonia (or Iraq, as we now call it) and communications across the width of their empire remained possible and easy for many centuries. The Ashkenazim, however, were descendants of those Jews who, both before and after the Roman destruction of Jerusalem, had maintained themselves in Europe and, eventually, came under Christian rule. They had no contact with Babylonia and inherited the ritual of Judea.

The Sephardic Jews were evicted from Spain in 1492 and were scattered over North Africa and the Middle East. An important community of Sephardim remained in Salonika, Greece, and was not finally destroyed until 1941, when the Nazis occupied the land.

Some of the Sephardim found their way to Holland, England, and, eventually, the United States. The early Jewish migrants to the United States were Sephardim. Benjamin Disraeli, a Prime Minister of England in the 1870's, and Benjamin Cardozo, an American Supreme Court Justice of the 1930's, were of Sephardic origin.

The common language of the Sephardim is Ladino, a mixture of Hebrew and Spanish, whereas that of the Ashkenazim is Yiddish, closely related to medieval German. Each has its own rules for pronouncing Hebrew and the modern nation of Israel has adopted the Sephardic pronunciation, although the Sephardim make up only a small percentage (perhaps one sixth) of the total Jewish population of the world.

32. JONAH

JONAH • NINEVEH • THE GREAT FISH • THE GOURD

Jonah

The Book of Jonah is unlike any of the other prophetic books in that it is not primarily a record of the utterances of the prophet. Rather it is a short story, clearly fictional. The hallmarks of fiction rest in its anachronisms and its elements of fantasy.

It is included in the books of the prophets because its protagonist, Jonah, would seem to be a man who lived in the time of the kingdoms and who is mentioned in the reliable historical section of the Bible:

2 Kings 14:25. He [Jeroboam II] *restored the coast of Israel . . . according to the word of the Lord . . . which he spake by the hand of his servant Jonah, the son of Amittai . . . of Gath-hepher.*

Gath-hepher is a town in Israel, in the section which, by Roman times, had come to be called Galilee. Indeed, it is only about three miles northeast of Nazareth, and the traditional tomb of Jonah is still to be found there. The real Jonah might, therefore, like Hosea, be viewed as an Israelite rather than a man of Judah.

Jonah (the real man) flourished in the early part of the reign of Jeroboam II, for the verse records that he predicted the successful outcome of the king's plans for territorial expansion. That would make the prophet active about 780 B.C. Scholars agree that the book cannot be that early, so that it was not written by Jonah himself or even by one of his immediate disciples. The book makes use of the phraseology of some of the later psalms; its language shows similarities to that used in the time of Ezra and Nehemiah; and its teachings have particular meaning for the time of the return from exile.

The Mediterranean World in the time of Jonah

A reasonable guess is that the book was written about 300 B.C. by some anonymous Judean. The book, although dealing with an Israelite prophet, is not an Israelite production in the sense that the Book of Hosea is.

Nineveh

The Book of Jonah begins with God's instructions to Jonah:

Jonah 1:1. *Now the word of the Lord came unto Jonah, the son of Amittai, saying,*

Jonah 1:2. *Arise, go to Nineveh, that great city, and cry against it; for their wickedness is come up before me.*

Here is an anachronism. Nineveh is treated as "that great city," the capital of the Assyrian Empire; and, of course, so it was during the time when Judah, under Manasseh, was an Assyrian tributary. Then it was indeed "that great city," the most powerful and dreaded military center in the world.

However, the real Jonah was active about 780 B.C. and at that time Assyria was in a period of decay and was no threat to anyone. (How else could Jeroboam II have created his short-lived empire?) Moreover, Nineveh was then only a small provincial town. The capital of Assyria in Jonah's day was Calah, as it had been for five centuries, from the reign of Shalmaneser I in 1270 B.C.

It was Sennacherib who established the royal residence at Nineveh nearly a century after the time of the real Jonah, and Nineveh remained a world-conquering city for only about three quarters of a century. Its fame far outshadows that of Calah, partly because it was when Nineveh was capital that the Assyrian Empire reached its maximum extent; and partly because it was when Nineveh was capital that the Assyrian Empire was mistress over Judea, so that the city was rewarded by ample mention in the Bible.

Later in the book, the writer refers to Nineveh in the past tense:

Jonah 3:3. . . . *Now Nineveh was an exceeding great city . . .*

The use of the past tense is an indication that the book had been written (or at least reached its final form) not only after 612 B.C., when Nineveh was destroyed, but long after, so that even its memory had grown faint and could stand refreshing.

The Great Fish

Jonah was not willing to preach in Nineveh and perhaps we can sympathize with him in this. A Jew asked to preach repentance to the city of Berlin in the time of Hitler's ascendancy might have suffered similar pangs of reluctance.

Jonah therefore took passage in a ship to Tarshish at the western edge of the Mediterranean (see page 332). There is here a bit of henotheism on the part of Jonah, for his action can only be understood if he felt that God was not powerful outside Israel and that the greater the distance from Israel, the weaker the hand of God.

The writer himself is not, however, a henotheist, and he makes it plain that God cannot be escaped by mere physical distance. The ship is struck by a storm and the mariners attempt to save themselves by lightening the ship and throwing unnecessary cargo overboard. They also cast lots to find out who among them had angered the gods, and the lot fell upon Jonah, who was promptly thrown overboard. (Ever since, a person or object that is believed to cause bad luck to those about him has been called a "jonah." The slang equivalent, "jinx," is not derived from Jonah despite the common possession of "j" and "n.")

Once in the water, Jonah underwent a most unusual experience:

> Jonah 1:17. Now the Lord had prepared a great fish to swallow up Jonah. And Jonah was in the belly of the fish three days and three nights.

Since the book is fiction, it would be best to consider the "great fish" an element of fantasy, a mythological monster, and let it go at that. Nevertheless, the popularity of the tale and the long centuries during which it was considered to describe actual history have led to endless discussions of the creature.

Popularly, Jonah's fish is considered to have been a whale. Nor can one counter this by saying that the whale is not a fish, for this is the case only according to the classification schemes of modern biologists, who recognize the whale to be a mammal with warm blood and lungs, rather than a true fish with cold blood and gills. Before the rise of modern biology, however, fish (or the equivalent word in other languages) would be applied to any sea creature. We recognize this in such common words as "shellfish," "jellyfish," and "starfish," none of which represent what the modern biologist would consider a fish. In Biblical times, therefore, a great fish could very easily signify a whale.

The suggestion that the fish is a whale is strengthened in the minds of Christians by the fact that Jesus is quoted as referring to it as such:

> Matthew 12:40. . . . *Jonas* [Jonah] *was three days and three nights in the whale's belly* . . .

If it was a whale that swallowed Jonah, then we are left with the fact that the only type of whale with a throat large enough to swallow a man intact is the sperm whale—the largest of the toothed whales. (There are larger whales which have whalebone strands or "baleen" in their mouths. These strands serve to strain out the tiny creatures on which the huge whales feed. Such baleen whales have throats suited to the size of the creatures they eat and could not swallow a man's hand, let alone a man.)

Sperm whales are not found in the Mediterranean and, in the course of nature, it is completely unlikely that a man should be swallowed by one there, or, still further, survive three days and nights of such incarceration. All difficulties disappear, however, if it is remembered that the Book of Jonah is a fantasy.

The Gourd

Jonah repented and was cast out upon dry land by the fish. The order to go to Nineveh was now repeated and this time Jonah obeyed. Through the city he went, proclaiming that Nineveh would be destroyed in forty days.

Whereupon, to Jonah's surprise, apparently, all of Nineveh repented, from the king on downward. All sat in sackcloth and fasted. This, in itself, is as great a miracle as the three-day stay in the fish and, of course, there is no record of such a remarkable occurrence anywhere in secular history. Indeed, what is even more significant, there is no mention of such an unusual Yahvistic victory in the historical books of the Bible itself. Clearly this is another element of fantasy.

But to continue. As a result of Nineveh's mass repentance, God decided not to destroy Nineveh after all. The city was spared.

At this unexpected turn, Jonah was furious. He had not wanted to undertake the perilous mission but had tried to escape and been swallowed by a fish for his pains. Now, after all he had gone through, all had come to nothing. (One must assume he did not consider repentance an achievement, but only the city's destruction.) Presumably, though, he harbored hopes that God might destroy the city after all:

> Jonah 4:5. *So Jonah went out of the city, and sat on the east side . . . till he might see what would become of the city.*
> Jonah 4:6. *And the Lord God prepared a gourd, and made it to come up over Jonah, that it might be a shadow over his head . . .*

"Gourd" is the translation of the Hebrew word *kikayon* and is, it would seem, a poor translation. The Revised Standard Version satisfies itself with the more general "And the Lord God appointed a plant." The best guess is that by the *kikayon* is meant the castor-oil plant which is common in tropical countries and which can grow to tree size.

God, however, causes the gourd to die the next day, and Jonah, finding a sudden absence of shade, is furious once more. Then comes the climax and the moral of the tale:

> Jonah 4:10. *Then said the Lord, Thou hast had pity on the gourd, for the which thou hast not laboured, neither madest it grow . . .*
> Jonah 4:11. *And should not I spare Nineveh, that great city, wherein are more than sixscore thousand persons that cannot discern between their right hand and their left hand; and also much cattle.*

Jonah is thus taught a lesson in mercy and pity and the writer emphasizes the care of God for all His creatures and rebukes the narrow views of the nationalists. Even if the men of Nineveh are sinners, they have repented; and aside from that, there are children in Nineveh who are too young yet even to have learned to tell their right hand from their left and surely they cannot be considered sinners worthy of death. And in a final phrase Jonah is reminded of the innocent animals in the city—virtually the only place in the Bible where a love of animals is clearly displayed.

(This is the very reverse of the primitive conception of God as evidenced by Samuel's insistence on the complete extermination of the Amalekites down to their cattle and his denunciation of Saul for attempting to set limits to the destruction—see page 283.)

Clearly, the Book of Jonah, like that of Ruth, is the product of that school of Jewish thought which was universalist and which opposed the nationalist views of Ezra and his followers (see page 451). It is the universality of God and the attribute of divine mercy that are the lessons of Jonah. Those who think of the book as nothing more than the story of a man and a whale miss the whole point.

33. MICAH

MICAH • BETHLEHEM EPHRATAH • ISAIAH

Micah

The name Micah is a shortened form of Micaiah ("who is like Yahveh?"). The most important Micaiah in the Bible is a prophet of Ahab's time. Before the battle of Ramoth-gilead (see page 351) Ahab arranged to have his court prophets predict victory. His ally, Jehoshaphat of Judah, requested that a prophet of Yahveh also be consulted:

> 1 Kings 22:8. *And the king of Israel said unto Jehoshaphat, There is yet one man, Micaiah the son of Imlah, by whom we may inquire of the Lord: but I hate him; for he doth not prophesy good concerning me, but evil . . .*

Micaiah is called but he prophesies defeat and disaster. He is mocked by the other prophets and is ordered off into imprisonment.

There is no chance at all, of course, that this Micaiah is the author of the Book of Micah. Micaiah is an Israelite and the time of the battle of Ramoth-gilead is 854 B.C. As the first verse of the Book of Micah proclaims, the author is a Judean who preached over a century after the time of Ahab's death:

> Micah 1:1. *The word of the Lord that came to Micah the Morasthite in the days of Jotham, Ahaz and Hezekiah . . .*

Micah was thus the fourth of the great prophets of the eighth century B.C., a contemporary of Isaiah, Hosea, and Amos. Whereas Hosea was a northerner, and Isaiah an aristocrat of Jerusalem, Micah, like Amos, was a Judean provincial. His description as a Morasthite in-

Israel and Judah

dicates him to be a native of Moresheth-gath, a town about twenty-five miles southwest of Jerusalem, near the borders of Philistine territory.

The fact that Micah begins with a warning of the destruction of Samaria would indicate that the early passages of the book antedate the destruction of that city by Sargon in 722 B.C. Later, he denounces the corruption of the priesthood of Judah and quotes God as saying:

Micah 3:12. *Therefore shall Zion for your sake be plowed as a field, and Jerusalem shall become heaps . . .*

This verse was quoted, a century later, in the Book of Jeremiah, at the time when that prophet was in danger of being lynched for his Temple Sermon. Those who defended him pointed out that Micah, like Jeremiah, had predicted the destruction of Jerusalem and had not been executed.

Jeremiah 26:19. *Did Hezekiah . . . put him* [Micah] *. . . to death? did he* [Hezekiah] *not fear the Lord . . .*

Micah's prophecy, thus specified as having been in the time of Hezekiah, was probably uttered with reference to the forthcoming siege of Jerusalem by Sennacherib. If so, it was not entirely fulfilled, for Jerusalem was not destroyed. It may be that the use of the quotation at the time of Jeremiah's Temple Sermon also served the purpose of soothing the indignant people by reminding them that prophecies of doom need not be regarded too seriously.

Bethlehem Ephratah

After the visions of destruction, Micah passes on, as is customary for the prophets, to picture the ideal state of the future and to predict the coming of the Messiah. There are some suggestions that the Messianic chapters of Micah are later additions to the utterances of the prophet of the time of Hezekiah; and that the additions date from the time of the Exile a century and a half later. It was during the Exile, after all, that Messianic hope and longings grew intense.

One piece of evidence in favor of this is a mention of Babylon as a place of exile for "the daughter of Zion":

Micah 4:10. . . . *thou shalt go even to Babylon . . . there the Lord shall redeem thee . . .*

In Micah's time, it was Nineveh, not Babylon, that was the enemy. If this reference is not accepted as a divinely inspired prophetic vision of the future, then it must be taken to indicate, for that verse at least, a later origin than the time of Micah.

Micah refers to the Messiah in a verse that became famous in later centuries:

> Micah 5:2. *But thou, Beth-lehem Ephratah, though thou be little among the thousands of Judah, yet out of thee shall he come forth unto me that is to be ruler in Israel; whose goings forth have been from of old, from everlasting.*

If this verse is of Exilic origin then it may well be that Bethlehem Ephratah is deliberately used as a symbolic way of referring to the house of David by way of its ancestral town of origin. Any direct mention of the coming of a new king of the Davidic line might have brought down Babylonian suspicion of attempted treason. If so, this prediction would be one of an ideal king arising from the Davidic line, which had now, through dethronement and imprisonment, become "little among the thousands of Judah." (The Revised Standard Version has it read "little . . . among the clans of Judah.")

The "goings forth" which "have been from of old, from everlasting" would refer to the fact that the line was an ancient one, stretching back to the beginnings of the monarchy centuries earlier. The term "everlasting" gives one the impression of eternal existence, and, therefore, of a Messiah who existed coevally with God. However, "everlasting" seems to be a poor translation, and the Revised Standard Version has the passage read "whose origin is from of old, from ancient days" with no implication of a more-than-historic origin.

Despite the interpretation I suggest here, the fact is that Micah 5:2 came to be interpreted literally as describing the place where the Messiah was to be born. It came to be expected that the Messiah, like his ancestor David, was to be born in Bethlehem.

Isaiah

Micah, in his vision of the Messianic future, is quoted as predicting a time when swords would be beaten into plowshares and war would cease in almost the precise words Isaiah used (see page 535).

Since the two prophets are contemporaries, it is difficult to argue that Isaiah was quoting Micah or that Micah was quoting Isaiah. Perhaps the passage is the Exilic utterance of some anonymous person which later editors placed in the Bible in different manners; one attributing it to Isaiah and one to Micah, with the resulting discrepancy never having been smoothed out.

The Book of Micah, like that of Isaiah, denounced the injustices practiced by the rich upon the poor and upheld the view that religion is not essentially ritual. In a very famous passage, the Book of Micah defines what it considers to be the essence of true religion:

Micah 6:7. *Will the Lord be pleased with thousands of rams, or with ten thousands of rivers of oil? . . .*
Micah 6:8. *He hath shewed thee, O man, what is good; and what doth the Lord require of thee, but to do justly, and to love mercy, and to walk humbly with thy God?*

34. NAHUM

Nahum

This book of three chapters is devoted to a paean of joy over the forthcoming destruction of Nineveh:

> Nahum 1:1. *The burden of Nineveh. The book of the vision of Nahum the Elkoshite.*

(or, as the Revised Standard Version has it: "An oracle concerning Nineveh. The book of the vision of Nahum of Elkosh.")

The location of the town of Elkosh is unknown, though some have suggested it to be southwest of Jerusalem in the neighborhood of Moresheth-gath, the home town of Micah (see page 652).

The book, which treats Nineveh's fall as a matter of inevitability, was probably written not long before 612 B.C., when the city was taken by the allied forces of Chaldea and Media.

> Nahum 2:4. *The chariots shall rage in the streets* [of Nineveh] . . .
> . . . .
> Nahum 2:6. *The gates of the rivers shall be opened, and the palace shall be dissolved.*
> Nahum 2:7. *And Huzzab shall be led away captive* . . .

The meaning of Huzzab is uncertain. If it is not some sort of copyist's error, then it may be a symbolic name for Nineveh; or it may refer to some Assyrian goddess and idol; or even to the Ninevite queen. The Revised Standard Version has the passage read, ". . . the palace is in dismay; its mistress is stripped . . ."

The Assyrian Empire

35. HABAKKUK

Habakkuk

Nothing is known of the prophet, for the first verse of this book simply says:

Habakkuk 1:1. *The burden which Habakkuk the prophet did see.*

The reference to Habakkuk in Bel and the Dragon (see page 622) can be completely discounted, of course.

This brief book must, apparently, be dated shortly after that of Nahum, perhaps about 605 B.C. Nineveh has fallen for now it is the Chaldeans who represent the great danger and against whom the wrath of God is promised. This view rests, actually, upon a single verse. When Habakkuk complains to God about the evils being practiced in Judah, he is assured that there will be a punishment:

Habakkuk 1:6. *For lo, I raise up the Chaldeans . . .*

36. ZEPHANIAH

Zephaniah

Zephaniah is given the longest genealogy of any of the prophets:

> Zephaniah 1:1. *The word of the Lord which came unto Zephaniah, the son of Cushi, the son of Gedaliah, the son of Amariah, the son of Hizkiah . . .*

Hizkiah is a form of Hezekiah, and the name is given as Hezekiah in the Revised Standard Version. It is very tempting to suppose that the genealogy is stretched through four generations in order that it be made to reach a particularly important person. If so, it could be that by Hezekiah is meant the king of Judah, and that Zephaniah is therefore the great-grandson of that king.

This would fit, without distortion, the dating of the book, which is given as:

> Zephaniah 1:1. . . . *in the days of Josiah . . . king of Judah.*

Josiah is also the great-grandson of Hezekiah and it might be, then, that Zephaniah (like Isaiah; see page 527) is a member of the royal family and is, indeed, second cousin of the reigning king.

Zephaniah denounces idolatry and quotes God as saying:

> Zephaniah 1:4. . . . *I will cut off the remnant of Baal from this place . . .*

This passage, at least, would seem to be dated earlier than Josiah's reformation of 621 B.C. The utterances of Zephaniah must be viewed against the background of the beginning of Assyria's rapid fall and the quickly gathering anarchy that sweeps over western Asia, compounded, perhaps, by the final raids of the nomadic Cimmerians (see page 558).

Judah

The prophet sees in all this a foretaste of the coming day of the Lord and a sample of its nature:

Zephaniah 1:14. *The great day of the Lord is near* . . .

Zephaniah 1:15. *That day is a day of wrath, a day of trouble and distress, a day of wasteness and desolation, a day of darkness and gloominess, a day of clouds and thick darkness.*

37. HAGGAI

HAGGAI · ZERUBBABEL

Haggai

The Book of Haggai is dated quite specifically:

> Haggai 1:1. *In the second year of Darius . . . came the word of the Lord by Haggai the prophet unto Zerubbabel . . . governor of Judah, and to Joshua . . . the high priest . . .*

Darius ascended the throne of Persia in 521 B.C. and Haggai's message was therefore advanced in 520 B.C.

The Jewish exiles had returned to Jerusalem seventeen years earlier and yet the Temple had not been rebuilt (owing largely to the hostility of the people of the land; see page 441). It was Haggai's task, therefore, to spur on Zerubbabel and Joshua, the political and religious leaders of the returnees, to complete the task. With renewed vigor (and with the patronage of Darius; see page 448), the Jews bent to the task and the Temple was rebuilt.

Zerubbabel

The final short speech attributed to Haggai is Messianic in character. What's more, the Messiah is named, for Haggai quotes God as saying:

> Haggai 2:22. *. . . I will overthrow the throne of kingdoms . . .*
> Haggai 2:23. *In that day . . . will I take thee, O Zerubbabel, my servant . . . and will make thee as a signet: for I have chosen thee . . .*

Judah

Since Zerubbabel was of Davidic descent (see page 405) and since he was in charge of the Jewish community at the time of the restoration of the Temple, it would seem natural to consider him as a possible Messiah, but the hope came to nothing.

Haggai is not heard of after 520 B.C. and may well have died a natural death shortly after his emergence on the stage of Jewish history. There is, after all, some reason to consider him an old man for at one point he asks, with reference to the second Temple as it is under construction:

> Haggai 2:3. *Who is left among you that saw this house in her first glory: and how do ye see it now? is it not in your eyes in comparison of it as nothing?*

If one accepts the implication that Haggai did see the first Temple and could make the comparison (and was challenging other ancients to do the same), then he was of advanced age. Even if he were only fourteen at the time of the destruction of the Temple in 586 B.C., he would be eighty in 520 B.C. A natural death at that age would not be surprising.

Zerubbabel also disappears from history. It is reasonable to suppose that being made the object of Messianic prophecies was fatal to his usefulness as a Judean governor, at least as far as the Persians were concerned. After this time, in fact, the leader of the Jewish community was the High Priest alone. It was as though the Persians had decided it would be too dangerous to allow the Jews a secular ruler as well.

The Jews were to continue to remain without a secular ruler for four centuries thereafter, until the time of the Maccabees.

38. ZECHARIAH

ZECHARIAH • SATAN • THE BRANCH • HADRACH • THE SHEPHERDS

Zechariah

Zechariah is a contemporary of Haggai and the prophetic activity of
the two began in the same year, 520 B.C.

> Zechariah 1:1. *In the . . . second year of Darius, came the word
> of the Lord unto Zechariah . . .*

The two prophets are even mentioned together in the Book of Ezra:

> Ezra 5:2. *Then the prophets, Haggai . . . and Zechariah . . .
> prophesied unto the Jews that were in Judah . . .*

However, whereas Haggai's work ended the year it began, Zechariah
continued to prophesy at least as late as 518 B.C.:

> Zechariah 7:1. *And it came to pass in the fourth year of king
> Darius, that the word of the Lord came unto Zechariah . . .*

It was Zechariah, therefore, who (as possibly much the younger man
of the two) continued the task of encouraging the rebuilding of the
Temple after Haggai's voice had fallen mute.

Satan

Zechariah speaks of the sufferings and defeats of Judah and of the
coming restoration of the kingdom in a series of visions granted him by
an angel (rather like those in the later Book of Daniel). At one point,
the change in Judah's fortunes is described as follows:

Zechariah 3:1. And he shewed me Joshua the high priest standing before the angel of the Lord, and Satan standing at his right hand to resist him.

Zechariah 3:2. And the Lord said unto Satan, the Lord rebuke thee, O Satan . . .

Zechariah 3:3. Now Joshua was clothed with filthy garments . . .

Zechariah 3:4. And he [the Lord] . . . spake . . . saying, Take away the filthy garments. . . . I will clothe thee with change of raiment.

Joshua here represents, apparently, the Jewish nation, clothed in the sins of its fathers, but now rescued and promoted into grace and virtue (as symbolized by the new clothing).

The Jews of Babylonia had come under Persian influence only in 538 B.C. when Cyrus conquered Babylon, but already, less than twenty years later, Persian dualism had affected Judaism to the point where Satan began to play a part. Here Satan fulfills his early role (also shown in the Book of Job, which was written perhaps a century after Zechariah's time) as a kind of prosecuting attorney against mankind and, particularly, against the Jewish people.

The Branch

To Zechariah, as to Haggai, the prospect of the completion of the second Temple was a clear indication of the coming of the Messiah, the predicted scion of the Davidic line, who would rule over an ideal Jerusalem. Thus, after Joshua is attired in clean garments, he is told, in Zechariah's vision:

Zechariah 3:8. Hear now, O Joshua . . . behold, I will bring forth my servant the Branch.

Here, Isaiah's metaphor of the Messiah, as the fresh branch arising out of the withered stock of the Davidic line, is used.

Nor does the Branch, in this case at least, refer merely to some indefinite ideal king of the future. He is named:

*Zechariah 6:9. And the word of the Lord came unto me saying,
. . . .*

Zechariah 6:11. . . . *take silver and gold, and make crowns, and set them upon the head of Joshua . . . the high priest;*

Zechariah 6:12. *And speak unto him, saying . . . Behold the man whose name is The Branch; and he shall . . . build the temple of the Lord.*

Originally, this passage seems to have referred to two men, for Zechariah describes himself as being instructed to make "crowns" (in the plural), which would mean two of them at least. Rather than suppose that both were placed on Joshua's head, it would be more reasonable to suppose that one was set on Joshua and the other on a second person, and that this second person is introduced to Joshua as "The Branch." The Branch is described as someone who will "build the temple of the Lord" and this can only be Zerubbabel. Zechariah is thus, like Haggai, naming Zerubbabel as the Messiah.

He goes on:

Zechariah 6:13. *Even he [The Branch, or Zerubbabel] shall build the temple of the Lord and he shall bear the glory, and shall sit and rule upon the throne; and he [Joshua] shall be a priest upon his throne; and the council of peace shall be between them both.*

A later editor seems to have tampered with this passage by removing actual reference to Zerubbabel, since this portion of the prophecy was quickly shown to be untrue, and the secular rule vanished. On the other hand, the High Priesthood continued unbroken throughout the succeeding centuries, so that Joshua's name might be allowed to stay.

Hadrach

The last six chapters of this book do not appear to be from the hand of the Zechariah who is the author of the first eight. The style of the language alters; the background against which the language is spoken seems to have changed radically; and there are references to events that don't fit in with the time of the immediate return from exile.

This later section of the book begins:

Zechariah 9:1. *The burden of the word of the Lord in the land of Hadrach, and Damascus . . .*

This section of the book is not carefully dated, as is the earlier section (in two different places); nor is the prophet's name mentioned.

Hadrach, unmentioned elsewhere in the Bible, is apparently a town in northern Syria and the first verses of the ninth chapter describe the passage of a conquering army down the length of Syria and Philistia:

Zechariah 9:3. . . . *Tyrus did build herself a strong hold* . . .
Zechariah 9:4. *Behold, the Lord will cast her out* . . . *and she shall be devoured with fire.*
Zechariah 9:5. . . . *and the king shall perish from Gaza* . . .

It is tempting to see in this passage a reference to the career of Alexander the Great as he impinged upon that area of the world inhabited by the Jews. In 333 B.C., Alexander defeated Darius III of Persia at the battle of Issus at the northeastern corner of the Mediterranean Sea, some four hundred miles north of Jerusalem. He then proceeded to march southward, taking all of Syria (Hadrach and Damascus) without a fight. Phoenicia, all but Tyre, capitulated. Tyre, undoubtedly remembering its heroic defense against Nebuchadnezzar (see page 588) fortified itself and held out.

Alexander the Great, however, was a far more deadly opponent than Nebuchadnezzar. The siege lasted seven months of desperate attack and defense and in the end Alexander won and Tyre was destroyed, in 332 B.C. Alexander also reduced Gaza after a stubborn siege, executing its Persian governor.

Those astonishing victories over a Persian Empire which, for two centuries, the Jews must have considered invincible could not help but seem supernatural in character. Alexander must be a tool in the hand of God, overturning the great kingdoms of the earth in order to prepare the way for the coming of the Messianic kingdom. Certainly, the Jews did not attempt to join in any resistance against Alexander and the armies of that mighty conqueror moved harmlessly past them.

If it is indeed the career of Alexander the Great that inspires this passage, the writer might have taken the view that the great military power attributed to the Messiah by earlier prophets was fulfilled in the form of a heathen king. The true Messiah might now appear in quite other guise to bring about the state of ideal peace associated with him. With military affairs taken care of, the non-military aspect, the humility, the peaceful nature of the Messiah could be emphasized:

Zechariah 9:9. Rejoice greatly, O daughter of Zion; shout, O daughter of Jerusalem: behold, thy King cometh unto thee: he is just, and having salvation; lowly, and riding upon an ass, and upon a colt the foal of an ass.

Zechariah 9:10. . . . and he shall speak peace unto the heathen: and his dominion shall be from sea even to sea, and from the river even to the ends of the earth.

The Shepherds

If this peaceful picture arises in the immediate aftermath of Alexander's victory, it is followed at once by a series of strenuous and obscure passages that seem to date later still, from the period of Seleucid persecution, when the Jews rose in revolt against their Greek-speaking masters. Thus, immediately after the picture of the humble Messiah riding upon an ass, there is a picture of war:

Zechariah 9:13. . . . I have . . . raised up thy sons, O Zion, against thy sons, O Greece . . .

Again, there is hostility toward other nations, rather than the notion of a Messiah who "shall speak peace unto the heathen." Thus:

Zechariah 10:11. . . . . the pride of Assyria shall be brought down, and the sceptre of Egypt shall depart away.

The reference here seems to be to the two portions of Alexander's broken empire which were of particular interest to the Jews: Ptolemaic Egypt and the Seleucid kingdom. The latter was commonly known as Syria because its Syrian centers of power were nearest the Jews, and this Syria is here converted, presumably by a copyist's error, to Assyria.

There follow passages concerning shepherds which defy intrepreta-tion. The shepherds can well refer to the various High Priests of the Temple during the period of the Seleucid persecution, and to the struggle for power among them as some supported compromise with Greek culture while others held out for firm adherence to the principles of Judaism. The events of the time, known in full detail to the original readers of the passage, are known only sketchily to us and this leaves us confused. Thus:

Zechariah 11:8. Three shepherds also I cut off in one month . . .

This may be a reference to three High Priests deposed in a short space of time owing to the strife of contending factions, but the details are unknown.

The writer seems to be speaking of himself as one of the shepherds:

> Zechariah 11:4. *Thus saith the Lord my God; Feed the flock* . . . .
>
> Zechariah 11:7. . . . *and I fed the flock.*

For some reason not made plain to us, but probably clear to the original readers, the shepherd resigned from his position and asked for his wages:

> Zechariah 11:12. . . . *So they weighed for my price thirty pieces of silver.*
>
> Zechariah 11:13. . . . *And I took the thirty pieces of silver, and cast them to the potter in the house of the Lord.*

The shepherd considers this payment to be insultingly small and it may even have been meant as a deliberate insult, since thirty pieces of silver is set in the Mosaic law as the compensation for an injury to a slave:

> Exodus 22:32. *If the ox shall push a manservant or a maidservant; he* [the owner of the ox] *shall give unto their master thirty shekels of silver* . . .

The word "potter" seems to be a mistranslation of the Hebrew word, which really means "treasury." The Revised Standard Version has Zechariah 11:13 read "I took the thirty shekels of silver and cast them into the treasury in the house of the Lord." It is as though, disdaining to bother with so small a sum, the shepherd donated it to the Temple.

The book ends with an apocalyptic picture of the final battle of the heathen against Jerusalem, their defeat, and the establishment of the ideal Messianic kingdom.

39. MALACHI

Malachi

The author's name is given in the first verse of the book:

Malachi 1:1. The burden of the word of the Lord to Israel by Malachi.

The name Malachi means "my messenger" and it is possible that it does not represent the actual name of the author but arises out of a misunderstanding on the part of a later editor.

Later in the book there occurs the verse:

Malachi 3:1. Behold I [God] will send my messenger, and he shall prepare the way before me . . .

the messenger being one who prepares the world for the day of the Lord.

If the editor assumed that the messenger had come and was the author of the book, he would naturally place "my messenger" or, in Hebrew, Malachi, in the superscription.

But if this is indeed the origin of the reputed name of the author of the book, it would seem to be a mistake. Later in the book, there is mention again of someone to be sent to prepare the way, and this time the messenger is named:

Malachi 4:5. Behold I will send you Elijah the prophet before the coming of the great and dreadful day of the Lord:

It is difficult to tell when the book was written but the best estimate seems to be about 460 B.C. At that time, the second Temple had already been built but Jerusalem was still without walls and helpless, and the people were despondent and apathetic.

It could already be seen that the prophecies of Haggi and Zechariah, two generations earlier, had not come to pass, for Zerubbabel had faded out in most un-Messiahlike fashion. What's more, the inspiring presence of Nehemiah (see page 456) had not yet made itself felt. It was Malachi's task, therefore, to assure the despondent Jews (and threaten them, too) that the day of the Lord would nevertheless come and that they had better be ready for that coming.

VOLUME TWO
THE NEW TESTAMENT

To
Lawrence P. Ashmead
who still has faith

1. TOBIT

Tobit

Following the Book of Nehemiah in the Roman Catholic version of the Bible are two short historical books which are not found in either the Jewish or the Protestant canon. They are therefore part of the Apocrypha. First comes one that is set in the Assyrian period, roughly 700 B.C.; then one with a very confused chronology that speaks of Nebuchadnezzar, who was at the height of his power about 580 B.C.

These tales do not portray actual history, but seem to be what we would call today "historical romances." Their fictional nature does not prevent them from serving religious or ethical purposes, of course, but since in this book I am primarily interested in the secular aspects of the Bible, there will be a particular interest in trying to sort out the chronology.

The first of these tales is the Book of Tobit, which begins at once with the character for whom it is named:

Tobit 1:1. *The book of the words of Tobit . . .*

Tobit is a form of the Hebrew name Tobiah, which, in its Greek form, is Tobias. In the Catholic version, the Book of Tobit is termed the Book of Tobias.

The date at which the book was written is not known for certain, but it may be about 200 B.C. It is possible that the author lived in Alexandria, which at that time was the capital of Egypt. About 200 B.C., Judea passed from the friendly hands of the Macedonian rulers of Egypt (the Ptolemies) to the much harsher grip of the Macedonian rulers of Syria (the Seleucids). A new period of persecution of the

Jerusalem Restored

Jews began and the story of Tobit, dealing with the Assyrian persecution, five centuries before, reflects this.

The time in which the events described in Tobit are supposed to have happened are given:

> Tobit 1:2. . . . [Tobit] *in the time of Enemessar* [Shalmaneser] *king of the Assyrians was led captive . . .*

This makes Tobit alive in 722 B.C. when the city of Samaria, having been besieged by Shalmaneser of Assyria, was taken by Shalmaneser's successor Sargon (see page I-377).* Numbers of the Israelites were taken off into exile and Tobit with them.

Tobit, speaking in the first person, describes himself as of the tribe of Naphtali.

> Tobit 1:4. . . . *when I was . . . young, all the tribe of Nephthali* [Naphtali] *. . . fell from the house of Jerusalem . . .*

Apparently, Tobit is speaking here of the rebellion of Jeroboam which succeeded in founding an independent Israel in 933 B.C. Clearly, it is impossible for Tobit to have been alive both in the time of Jeroboam and in the time of Shalmaneser. Nor does the author intend to imply that Tobit was as long-lived as the antediluvian patriarchs, for at the time of a central event later in the book, Tobit is described as not too old a man.

> Tobit 14:2. *And he* [Tobit] *was eight and fifty years old . . .*

Rather, it is merely the chronological confusion we would expect of an author writing some five centuries after the events related; an author who had only a hazy notion of the order of events and no records to use as a reliable source. In short, it is what one would expect if Tobit were originally written as a piece of edifying fiction, telling what might have happened, rather than what did happen.

Rages

Tobit, however, remained faithful to Jerusalem, even when carried off to exile in Nineveh. He managed to obtain a high position at the

---

* Where page references to Volume I are given they will be preceded by "I", otherwise not. Thus "page I-123" will refer to page 123 of Volume I while "page 123" will refer to page 123 of Volume II, the one you are now holding.

Assyrian court, being placed in charge of the purchasing of provisions with government money, and having freedom of movement about the dominion.

> Tobit 1:14. And I went into Media, and left in trust with Gabael ... at Rages ... ten talents of silver.

This again is anachronistic, for though parts of Media were under the control of the Assyrian Empire, much of it (including the region about Rages) was not. It is very unlikely that Tobit could travel freely (as an official of the Assyrian court) outside the border, especially if he were carrying large quantities of government money. Nor is ten talents a mean sum of money. A talent would be equal to about $2000 in today's money.

In 200 B.C., however, the regions that had once been Assyria and Media were both under the domination of the Seleucid kings and formed part of a single realm. The writer of the Book of Tobit was thus reflecting the geography of his own time rather than that of the supposed time of the book.

Rages (also spelled Rhages) was an important city of Media, perhaps second only to Ecbatana (see page I-448). It was located about 150 miles northeast of Ecbatana, and its ruins are only five miles south of Teheran, the capital of modern Iran.

Rages' period of greatest glory came later, however, well after Biblical times. It was a capital of the Persian kingdoms that flourished in Roman times and before the coming of the Mohammedans it was the center of Zoroastrian religion. To the Persians, the city was known as Rai.

In Mohammedan times, it was the birthplace of Harun-al-Rashid, the Caliph of the Arabian Nights. It was also the birthplace of a great medieval physician who was known as "al-Razi" to the Persians, from his birthplace, and as Rhazes to Europeans.

Rages was devastated by the Mongol invaders in A.D. 1220 and never recovered.

Asmodeus

But misfortunes crowded upon Tobit. Once the Assyrian conqueror died, Sennacherib succeeded to the throne and he is pictured as a violent anti-Semite who ordered the killing of Jews and forbade their corpses to be buried.

It is considered a frightful thing in many cultures for a dead body to be left undisposed of, to be left deprived of appropriate religious rites. There are usually beliefs that the souls of such bodies must drift about aimlessly through shadows and cannot find rest until the bodies they once inhabited are appropriately cared for. The Greeks of Homer's time believed this, and so did the Jews.

In threatening a people with punishment, for instance, not only death is foretold but lack of burial. Thus, Jeremiah, quoting God's warning to Judea in the last years of the kingdom, says:

> Jeremiah 16:4. *They shall die of grievous deaths . . . neither shall they be buried . . .*

Sennacherib, then, is pictured as deliberately punishing Jews after death, as well as in life. Tobit engages in an act of piety by burying such bodies and gets into trouble with the authorities in consequence. He is forced to leave the country, and his property is confiscated.

Esarhaddon succeeds to the throne and appoints a relative of Tobit to high office. The relative intercedes for Tobit, who returns to Nineveh. But then, after once again burying a corpse, he is stricken with cataracts of the eyes and goes blind. His faith remains strong and he continues to praise God, but he longs for death.

Meanwhile, in Ecbatana, a girl named Sara, a niece of Tobit, is also longing for death—

> Tobit 3:8. *Because that she had been married to seven husbands, whom Asmodeus the evil spirit had killed, before they had lain with her . . .*

With seven husbands dead, each on the wedding night, she was being reproached as a husband-murderer.

Asmodeus, the real murderer, does not occur in any canonical book of the Bible. His name is a corruption of that of a demon in Persian mythology—"Aeshma deva," the demon Aeshma.

Partly because of this story in the Book of Tobit, Asmodeus was, in later centuries, taken to be the demon in charge of marital unhappiness. He played a role also in non-Biblical legends concerning Solomon and was sometimes held to be identical with Satan himself.

Raphael

But better days were coming for both Tobit and Sara, for their
devoutness and prayers had their effect. God heard them—

Tobit 3:17. *And Raphael was sent to heal them both . . .*

Under the influence of Persian religious thought (which postulated
vast armies of good and evil spirits), the Jews in the centuries after
the restoration had worked out an increasingly complex structure for
the celestial hierarchy. There were not merely angels, for instance, but
archangels ("chief angels") as well. Tradition eventually listed seven
such archangels, of whom only two, Gabriel and Michael, are to be
found anywhere in the books included in the King James Version.
In addition, Raphael is included here in the apocryphal Book of Tobit
and Uriel in the apocryphal 2 Esdras. Others are mentioned in non-
Biblical legends.

Mohammedan tradition lists four archangels. Mohammedans share
Gabriel and Michael with the Jews and Christians and add Azrael
and Israfel. Azrael is the angel of death, and Israfel sounds the trumpet
on the day of judgment and resurrection (the task which falls to
Gabriel in Christian tradition).

The choice of Raphael as the angel to heal Tobit and Sara is appropriate since Raphael means "God heals."

Azarias

Suddenly Tobit remembers the ten talents he had left in Rages and
decides to send his son, Tobias, to Rages to collect it. To strengthen
the son on his dangerous journey through heathen lands he gives him
a code of behavior to follow (as, in *Hamlet*, Polonius lectures his son,
Laertes, before the latter's trip to Paris). One of the maxims is:

Tobit 4:15. *Do that to no man which thou hatest . . .*

This is translated in the Revised Standard Version as "And what
you hate, do not do to any one." This is the negative version of what
is commonly called the Golden Rule—that of guiding your actions

by empathy; that is, by putting yourself in the place of the other person.

The Golden Rule is more familiar to us in its positive form; a form which advises us not merely to refrain from doing what is hateful, but to proceed to do what is desirable. The positive form is given in the course of Jesus' Sermon on the Mount:

> Matthew 7:12. Therefore all things whatsoever ye would that men should do to you, do ye even so to them . . .

or, as expressed in Luke:

> Luke 6:31. And as ye would that men should do to you, do ye also to them likewise.

One often hears the Golden Rule expressed as follows: "Do unto others as you would have others do unto you." This is not the form, however, in which the saying occurs in the Bible, either in the King James Version or the Revised Standard Version.

Tobias, in preparing for the journey, comes across Raphael in human guise, and Raphael offers to guide the young man to Rages. Tobias' father, Tobit, inquires carefully as to the identity of the guide:

> Tobit 5:12. Then he [Raphael] said, I am Azarias . . . and of thy brethren.

Azarias is the Greek form of the Hebrew Azariah, or Ezra, and the name is carefully chosen, for it means "Yahveh helps."

Tigris River

Tobias and the angel set out on their journey.

> Tobit 6:1. . . . they came in the evening to the river Tigris, and they lodged there.

Here one can see that the writer may well be an Alexandrian for he shows himself deficient in knowledge of Asian geography. It would seem he believes Nineveh to be a day's journey from the Tigris (referred to elsewhere in the Bible as Hiddekel, see page I-27), when actually the Assyrian capital was situated right on that river.

What's more, Nineveh was on the eastern bank of the river and since Rages was some five hundred miles east of Nineveh, one does not have to reach or cross the Tigris at all in going from one city to the other.

While washing in the river, Tobias catches a large fish and Raphael instructs him to keep the heart, liver, and gall. The heart and liver, he explains, can be used in combating demons, while the gall is a cure for cataracts.

Edna

Eventually they reach Ecbatana, still 150 miles short of their goal. There, Raphael proposes they stay with Raguel, the father of Sara, and that a marriage be arranged between the two young people. When they arrived at Raguel's house, the host noted the family resemblance of Tobias at once:

> Tobit 7:2. *Then said Raguel to Edna his wife, How like is this young man to Tobit my cousin!*

It is a mark of the popularity of the books of the Apocrypha that so many proper names in them have come into common use. Tobias is itself an example, both in that form, and in its English abbreviation, Toby.

Edna is another case, perhaps a surprising one. It does not sound like a Biblical name and, in fact, it does not occur in the canonical books. At first thought, one might guess that it is an Anglo-Saxon name since the prefix "Ed-" (from "Aed-" meaning "property" and hence a natural component of the names of propertied people) was a common feature among the Anglo-Saxon gentry. Examples are Edward, Edwin, Edmund, Edgar among males and Edith and Edwina among females.

Edna, however, is a Hebrew word, meaning "rejuvenation."

After this, all goes well. Tobias obtains leave to marry Sara, although he is duly warned of the death of seven previous husbands. Tobias, however, burns the fish's liver in the wedding chamber and the charm drives Asmodeus away. The marriage is consummated happily and there is a long wedding feast.

Raphael travels onward to Rages and collects the ten talents due

Tobit. All return home after this and there Tobias uses the fish's gall to cure his father's cataracts.

Raphael then reveals himself and everything ends in total happiness. The family enjoys wealth, long life, and many descendants. In a veritable orgy of anachronisms and twisted chronologies, Tobit, on his deathbed, advises Tobias to leave Nineveh, which is soon to fall. Tobias retires to Ecbatana, his wife's city, and survives long enough to see the destruction of Nineveh:

> Tobit 14:15. . . . *before he* [Tobias] *died he heard of the destruction of Nineve* [Nineveh], *which was taken by Nabuchodonosor* [Nebuchadnezzar] *and Assuerus* [Ahasuerus] . . .

Actually, it was taken by Nabopolassar, the father of Nebuchadnezzar, and by the Median king, Cyaxares. Ahasuerus (that is, Xerxes) did not reign until a century and a quarter after the fall of Nineveh.

However, it may have been the author's intention to use the destruction of Nineveh as an indication to his readers that the Seleucid Empire would also be destroyed. If so, and if the book was indeed written in 200 B.C., then the writer was a fairly good prophet. The Seleucid Empire was not utterly destroyed, to be sure, but its power over Judea was broken and the Jews entered a period of prideful independence once more. And that time came but a generation after the Book of Tobit was written (if we accept 200 B.C. as the date of writing), so that its first readers may have lived to see the breaking of the Seleucid grip, as Tobias lived to see Nineveh fall.

2. JUDITH

NABUCHODONOSOR • ARPHAXAD • RAGAU • HYDASPES • HOLOFERNES • JOACIM •
BETHULIA • JUDITH • BAGOAS

Nabuchodonosor

The historical romance following the Book of Tobit is the Book
of Judith, named after the heroine of the tale. The best guess as to its
date of authorship is somewhere about 150 B.C., shortly after the tyranny
of the Seleucids had been overcome. It was a period of great nationalistic fervor and tales telling of great deeds against impossible
odds must have been much in favor. Judith is an example.

Despite the fact that the Book of Judith lacks the supernatural
elements found in Tobit, Judith is even more clearly fictional. It deals
with a victory that is mentioned nowhere outside this book, with places
and people not to be found elsewhere, and its chronology is hopelessly
twisted. It is not included in the Jewish canon or in the King James
Version. Nevertheless it has been immensely popular for the sake of
the story it told.

It begins by dating itself:

Judith 1:1. *In the twelfth year of the reign of Nabuchodonosor*
[Nebuchadnezzar], *who reigned in Nineve* [Nineveh] . . .

If this date is to be taken soberly, then the Book of Judith begins
in 594 B.C. when Zedekiah is on the throne in Jerusalem and the
kingdom of Judah is tottering toward its fall.

However, the confusion has already started, for Nebuchadnezzar
reigned in Babylon over a Chaldean Empire and not in Nineveh over
an Assyrian one. Indeed, Nebuchadnezzar came to the throne only
after Nineveh had completely been destroyed.

Jerusalem Restored

Arphaxad

But the tale does not begin with Nebuchadnezzar only; it switches
to another monarch at once:

Judith 1:1. . . . *in the days of Arphaxad, which reigned over*
the Medes in Ecbatane,
Judith 1:2. *And built in Ecbatane walls round about* . . .

There is no record of anyone named Arphaxad, or anything like it,
among the kings of the Medes.

According to Herodotus, the first important king of the Medes was
Deioces, who came to the throne about 700 B.C. and reigned till 647 B.C.
Southern sections of Media were then under intermittent Assyrian
control after Sargon's conquering armies had invaded it in 710 B.C.

Under Deioces, however, Media regained a certain freedom of action. According to Herodotus, he built Ecbatana, by which is probably
meant that he fortified it and made it his capital city and royal residence. Undoubtedly he paid tribute to the Assyrian kings at Nineveh, but he founded a royal line that was to become great in the century after his death.

Deioces' son, Phraortes, reigned, according to Herodotus, from
647 B.C. to 625 B.C. and he extended Median power. Assyria was at
the time occupied with Elamite wars, Babylonian rebellions, Egyptian
intrigue, and incursions by the Cimmerian barbarians. With Assyria
thoroughly occupied, Phraortes could piece together the tribes north
and east of Assyria and put them together into an empire ruled from
Ecbatana—one which was soon to help destroy Assyria.

We can suppose, therefore, that the Arphaxad referred to in Judith
1:1 represents a telescoping of dim memories concerning Deioces and
Phraortes, and is mostly Phraortes.

Ragau

Phraortes' successes roused the concern of Assyria and eventually
there was war between the nations. This is reflected in the Book of
Judith:

Judith 1:5. *Even in those days king Nabuchodonosor made war with king Arphaxad . . . in the borders of Ragau.*

Ragau is the city termed Rages in the Book of Tobit (see page 18). It is deep within Median territory, so one must envisage a slashing Assyrian offensive.

In real history, Phraortes ruled when Asshurbanipal (the Asnapper of the Book of Ezra, see page I-447) was on the Assyrian throne. Asshurbanipal did attack Phraortes and, according to Herodotus, Phraortes was defeated by the Assyrian armies, and killed, in 625 B.C. —the last year of Asshurbanipal's reign.

The dim memory of this war could have been converted into the battle of Ragau in which Nebuchadnezzar of Assyria defeats Arphaxad of Media.

Hydaspes

The army which had been gathered by Nebuchadnezzar is described:

Judith 1:6. *And there came unto him all they that . . . dwelt by Euphrates, and Tigris, and Hydaspes, and the plain . . . of the Elymeans, and very many nations of the sons of Chelod.*

By and large this isn't bad as a description of the eastern half of the territory ruled over by the Assyrians (or by the real Nebuchadnezzar, for that matter). The sons of Chelod are the Chaldeans, who were subject to Assyria in the time of Asshurbanipal and who ruled over the entire Fertile Crescent in the time of Nebuchadnezzar. The Elymeans are the Elamites, whom Asshurbanipal conquered (see page I-455).

The one serious flaw is the mention of the Hydaspes River. This is one of five rivers which flow through the Pakistani province of Punjab (the very name of which means "five rivers"). Its modern name is the Jhelum River.

The Hydaspes was at or near the easternmost boundary of the Persian Empire and of the short-lived dominion of Alexander the Great that followed. Indeed, Alexander fought the fourth of his four great battles in Asia on the Hydaspes River in 326 B.C.

In attempting to explain that Nebuchadnezzar was drawing his army from the most distant corners of his empire, the writer of Judith mentioned the Hydaspes almost automatically, for that was the limits of an empire with which he was far more familiar than with the Assyrian.

Nebuchadnezzar also demanded troops from the nations west and south of Assyria. These are listed in full but, in summary, consist of Asia Minor, Syria, Israel, Judah, and Egypt. The western lands refused help and Nebuchadnezzar swore vengeance, then went on to defeat Arphaxad with the army he had on hand.

Holofernes

With Media conquered, Nebuchadnezzar was ready to turn west.

Judith 2:4. . . . *Nabuchodonosor . . . called Holofernes the chief captain of his army . . . and said unto him,*

Judith 2:5. . . . *thou shalt go forth from my presence . . .*

Judith 2:6. *And thou shalt go against all the west country because they disobeyed my commandment.*

Asshurbanipal had, in the course of his reign, actually campaigned in the west. This was in Egypt, which was in revolt at the time of his accessions (see page I-390). There is no record, though, that in the process he inflicted any particular damage upon Judah. During his reign, indeed, Manasseh (see page I-425) was king of Judah, and he was loyally pro-Assyrian and had a peaceful reign.

To be sure, the tradition arose that in Manasseh's reign there had been some trouble with Assyria, for in 2 Chronicles there is mention made of Manasseh having been imprisoned and taken off to Babylon (see page I-425). The writer of Judith may have had some vague notion of Asshurbanipal's western campaign and Manasseh's reputed imprisonment.

But who, then, was Holofernes? There is no mention of any such general anywhere in the records of Assyria or Babylon.

As it happens, three centuries after the reign of Asshurbanipal, there arose a situation which involved events of a similar nature. It was the Persian Empire that now ruled western Asia with a mighty hand, and the monarch on the throne was Artaxerxes III, who reigned

from 358 to 338 B.C. Just as Asshurbanipal was the last of the powerful
Assyrian monarchs, so Artaxerxes III was the last of the powerful
Persian monarchs.

Artaxerxes, like Asshurbanipal, had to conduct campaigns in Egypt,
for Egypt rebelled periodically against Persian rule. In fact in 404 B.C.,
after the death of the Persian king, Darius II, Egyptian rebellions had
succeeded to the extent where native kings held effective control of
Egypt. The traditional histories list three dynasties, the 28th, 29th,
and 30th, in this period of time. None of the native kings was particularly powerful and most ruled only briefly.

At the time Artaxerxes III came to the Persian throne, Nectanebo II,
last king of the 30th dynasty and, indeed, the last native king ever
to rule Egypt until medieval times, had just come to power. In 346 B.C.,
Artaxerxes III, after great preparations, sent an expedition westward
into Egypt. There followed five years of hard campaigning which
crushed Nectanebo II and re-established Persian rule.

And who was one of the generals who led the Persian host? Holofernes.

It seems reasonable, then, to suppose that the writer of Judith had
telescoped the Egyptian campaign of Artaxerxes with that of Asshurbanipal and made Holofernes, the Persian general, the leader of the
Assyrian hosts.

Joacim

The march of Holofernes is given in detail, with many geographical
names apparently made up out of thin air, for they cannot be identified
with anything on the surface of the Earth. One gathers, however, that
Holofernes struck northwestward from Nineveh, conquered Asia Minor,
then turned south to work his way down the coast, occupying or
devastating Syria, Phoenicia, and Philistia.

It was next the turn of Judea:

Judith 4:1. *Now the children of Israel, that dwelt in Judea, heard
all that Holofernes . . . had done . . .*

Judith 4:2. *Therefore they were exceedingly afraid . . . and were
troubled for Jerusalem, and for the temple . . .*

Judith 4:3. *For they were newly returned from the captivity.*

This now adds an additional element of anachronism. We have the Assyria of the seventh century B.C. under the rule of Nebuchadnezzar of the sixth century B.C., which sends its army under a general of the fourth century B.C. to attack a re-established Judea of the fifth century B.C. Not a century is left out.

Nor is the period of re-established Judea left with a mere mention. Some circumstantial evidence is introduced in the form of the identity of the high priest.

Judith 4:6. *Also Joacim the high priest . . . was in those days in Jerusalem . . .*

Joacim would, in Hebrew form, be Joiakim, and he is mentioned in the Book of Nehemiah.

Nehemiah 12:10. *And Jeshua begat Joiakim, Joiakim also begat Eliashib . . .*

In other words Joiakim was the son of Jeshua who had rebuilt the Temple with Zerubbabel (see page I-440) and the father of Eliashib who had rebuilt the city walls with Nehemiah (see page I-457). By this it would seem that the events of the Book of Judith fall just between those chronicled in the Book of Ezra and those in the Book of Nehemiah.

Bethulia

Judea girds itself for a despairing defense and sends messages to strategic places:

Judith 4:6. *. . . Joacim . . . wrote to them that dwelt in Bethulia . . .*
Judith 4:7. *Charging them to keep the passages of the hill country . . . and it was easy to stop them that would come up, because the passage was strait, for two men at the most.*

Bethulia is a name that does not occur elsewhere in the Bible. Some suppose that it might be Shechem for that is located in a narrow pass between two mountains (see page I-99).

However, one can see that the writer of Judith owes a certain debt to Herodotus. The writer's mythical Nebuchadnezzar brings the huge power of his empire to bear upon a tiny Judea, as the real Xerxes bore down upon a tiny Greece. Holofernes moves westward then southward, as Xerxes' general Mardonius did. The inexorable progress is halted by the tiny Judean army as the other progress was halted by the tiny Greek army. And the crucial battle is to come at a narrow pass where a small force can hold off a vast army.

It is useless then to seek Bethulia on the map of Judea; it is sooner to be found on the map of Greece, for Bethulia is really Thermopylae. Indeed, as events prove, it is to be a combined Thermopylae and Marathon.

Judith

Holofernes lays siege to the city of Bethulia and captures its water supply so that the inhabitants, in the extremity of thirst, are ready to surrender, a course of action which now comes to the attention of the heroine of this book.

Judith 8:1. *Now at that time Judith heard thereof . . .*

Judith is the feminine form of "Judah" and means "Jewish woman." It is the popularity of this book and the excitement of the story it tells, and, consequently, the number of times its climax has been used as an inspiration in art, that has made the name Judith so common among us.

Judith is given a genealogy that is clearly nonhistorical. The names cannot be identified and some of them have no parallel elsewhere in the Bible. She is described as a beautiful and pious widow, her husband having died three years before.

Bagoas

Judith is indignant at hearing of the news of projected surrender. She exhorts the elders to hold firm while she puts her own plan into operation. She dresses herself in all her finery and leaves the city as a defector. Her beauty assures her respectful treatment and she is brought to Holofernes. She tells him that the Jews in Bethulia are sinning and are therefore sure to be beaten. She offers to help Holofernes win, provided her own religious scruples are respected and she is allowed to retire each night to pray in private.

For three days she keeps up a fixed pattern of behavior, getting the sentries used to seeing her pass out of the camp late each night to pray.

By the fourth day Holofernes thought he would improve the situation by having Judith join him at dinner:

> Judith 12:11. *Then said he to Bagoas the eunuch . . . Go now, and persuade this Hebrew woman . . . that she come unto us, and eat and drink with us.*

Bagoas is the Greek form of a Persian name meaning "given by God" and was often used for eunuchs, so that the phrase "Bagoas the eunuch" was almost a cliché.

The most famous "Bagoas the eunuch" was a renegade Egyptian in the service of Artaxerxes III at the time of the latter's campaign against Egypt, the very campaign in which the real Holofernes figured. For a while, Bagoas was the power behind the throne and taxed and plundered the subject peoples (including the Jews) remorselessly.

Eventually he aspired to full power. As a eunuch he could not reign openly, but he might at least exert control over a thoroughgoing puppet. In 338 B.C. he arranged for the murder of Artaxerxes III plus all his children but the youngest. The youngest son, Arses, he placed on the throne and when Arses showed signs of independence, Bagoas had him and his children killed too, in 336 B.C.

A distant relative of the Persian royal line was then placed on the throne by Bagoas. The new king called himself Darius III and would have suffered the same fate as his two predecessors if he hadn't avoided that by killing Bagoas. This, however, was the only forceful action of Darius III. Soon he had to face Alexander the Great and the remainder of his life was one long disaster. He died in 330 B.C. as Persia's last king. With that, the Persian Empire that had been inaugurated by Cyrus two and a quarter centuries before came to an end.

The writer of Judith must certainly have known of the wickedness of the historical "Bagoas the eunuch" and it would be a natural name for him to give Holofernes' minion.

Judith accepts the invitation, encourages Holofernes to drink to excess. When the feast is over, all depart to allow Holofernes to have

Judith with him in private. By that time, however, Holofernes is in a drunken stupor and Judith cuts off his head with his own sword.

She wraps the head in the canopy of the bed and retires, apparently for private prayer, as she has done on previous nights. This time, however, she goes to Bethulia and displays the head. The Jews are heartened and the Assyrian army, on discovering the death of their commander, are driven into panic. They flee and are slaughtered by the pursuing Jews, who are thus (according to the tale) saved from Nebuchadnezzar forever.

3. 1 MACCABEES

1 Maccabees

With Malachi, the canonical books of the Old Testament (according to the arrangement in the Christian versions of the Bible) come to an end. The prophetic impulse, as the traditional Jewish view has it, faded out after the return from the Babylonian Exile, and with the rebuilding of the Temple and the walls of Jerusalem.

This does not seem actually to be so, since a number of the canonical books were written well after 430 B.C., when Jerusalem's walls were completed. In every such case, however, tradition insists on attributing authorship to a period well before that critical date. Thus, the Book of Jonah, written as a work of imagination in 300 B.C. or thereabouts, was attributed back in time to some near contemporary of the historical prophet, who was active about 780 B.C. Late psalms were attributed to David; late compilations of proverbs to Solomon, while apocalyptic writings composed in the Greek period were attributed to worthies of the period of Exile and Return, such as Daniel and Zechariah.

This meant that historical events after 430 B.C. could never be dealt with directly and inserted into the Bible. They had to be attributed to ancients to comply with strict Jewish tradition and therefore had

Palestine Under the Maccabees

to be presented in obscure, apocalyptic form, or else remain in the Apocrypha.

And yet Jewish history was eventful and interesting in the period between 200 B.C. and A.D. 100; more so in some ways than ever before. Once again an independent Jewish state was established as in the days of Saul and David. Once again a colossal catastrophe approached inexorably as in the days of Jeremiah. Once again prophets spoke out and changed the world as in the days of the Second Isaiah.

But in the Jewish canon, there is not a whisper of this. For knowledge concerning this period we must turn to the Apocrypha, to the New Testament, and to secular historians such as Josephus.

If we turn to the Apocrypha first, we encounter the books of the Maccabees (a name that will be explained later). There are five books grouped under this name, two of which are present in the Apocrypha since they were included in the Greek versions of the Bible. The first of these books, 1 Maccabees, is by far the better from the standpoint of historical value.

Its author is unknown but he was clearly a Jew of rationalist tendencies, for the book contains no miracles. It deals with a forty-year period, from 175 B.C. to 135 B.C., and (unless some of the final passages are later additions) must have been written some time between 135 B.C. and 100 B.C. by a Palestinian Jew.

It was originally written in Hebrew and a copy of that Hebrew version was seen as late as A.D. 400 by the Latin churchman, Jerome. The Hebrew version has not survived to our day, however. Our oldest versions are in Greek so that the King James Version of the translation (which I am using in my quotations) makes use of the Greek versions of the common names. The Revised Standard Version of the translation changes these, however, to conform with those used in translations from the Hebrew, as in the canonical books of the Old Testament.

Philip, the Macedonian

The Book of 1 Maccabees deals with the Jewish rebellion against overlords of Macedonian descent and the writer therefore begins with the foundation of Macedonian power over Asia.

The Macedonian conquest took place in the fourth century B.C., a

The Western Portion of the Empire of Alexander the Great

time when Judea was comparatively quiet. In fact, the history of the Jews under the Persians is virtually unknown to us—and this is probably a sign of the absence of disaster. (Thomas Carlyle said, "Happy the people whose annals are blank in history-books.")

Josephus mentions a Jewish rebellion against the Persians about 350 B.C. but Artaxerxes III, who was then the Persian king, quickly crushed it, and did so without much damage. Perhaps the Jews merely did not get out of the way fast enough when Artaxerxes III marched westward to put an end to an earlier Egyptian rebellion that had kept Egypt precariously independent for about fifty years. It is this event that may have inspired the Book of Esther and the Book of Judith. In this period, too, a final schism may have taken place between the Jews and the Samaritans, one that was never healed.

Yet while Jewish history was subsiding to a low murmur, great things were happening in Greece. After the Greeks had hurled back the attempt of Xerxes (Ahasuerus) to conquer their land, there followed a Golden Age that filled the fifth century B.C. Even while Jerusalem was painstakingly being rebuilt and while Nehemiah was struggling to give it walls again, the Greek city of Athens produced a culture that has been the pride of mankind ever since.

The culture went into decline by the end of the fifth century B.C., however, for a variety of reasons, among which the chief, perhaps, was the continuing and continual warfare between the Greek cities. By 350 B.C., when the Jews were rounding out a sleepy century after the time of Nehemiah and were stirring uneasily as Artaxerxes III marched past them toward Egypt, the Greek cities had ground themselves into virtual exhaustion. The time was ripe for some outside force to take over all of them and that force is named in the very first verse of 1 Maccabees:

> 1 Maccabees 1:1. . . . *Philip, the Macedonian* . . .

Macedon, or Macedonia, was a land just north of Greece, semi-barbarian at the time of Greece's golden age, but under strong Greek influence. Its people spoke a Greek dialect and its ruling classes were interested in Greek literature and culture. It remained without important influence in Greek history until the middle of the fourth century B.C. when two things happened at once. First, the Greek cities, as I said before, had exhausted themselves with warfare; and second, there came to rule over Macedon a most remarkable man, Philip II. It is he who is referred to in 1 Maccabees 1:1 as "Philip, the Macedonian" and who is often referred to in our own histories as "Philip of Macedon."

Philip seized power over Macedon in 359 B.C. at just about the time Artaxerxes III ascended the Persian throne. Philip at once began to reorganize his army, increase governmental efficiency, extend his power over surrounding barbarian powers, and engage in cautious warfare against the Greek cities.

In 338 B.C. Philip defeated the combined armies of the Greek cities of Athens and Thebes, and made himself the strongest power in Greece. At the battle, leading the charge which finally decided the outcome, was Philip's eighteen-year-old son, Alexander.

Once Philip had gained control of Greece, he forced the Greek cities to recognize him as the leader of a united force of Greeks and Macedonians which he intended to lead against Persia. In 336 B.C., however, almost at the very moment when he planned to cross the Aegean Sea, enter Asia Minor, and begin his Persian War, Philip was assassinated.

Alexander

Succeeding to the throne was Philip's son, now twenty years old, who ruled as Alexander III. In view of his amazing career, however, he is universally known as "Alexander the Great." Alexander began by re-establishing his father's power against revolts throughout his dominions, and once again defeated the Greeks. Then in 334 B.C. he left Greece for Asia.

> 1 Maccabees 1:1. *And it happened, after that Alexander son of Philip, the Macedonian, who came out of the land of Chettiim, had smitten Darius king of the Persians and Medes, that he reigned in his stead . . .*

Chettiim, or Kittim, is generally taken as being the island of Cyprus which contained the Greek city of Kition (see page I-47). Before the time of Alexander, Kition was the Greek city closest to Judea, and it was natural to broaden the name to include Greece generally.

Alexander found himself facing a weak adversary when he invaded the Persian Empire. Artaxerxes III, the last strong Persian monarch, had died in 338 B.C. and, after a couple of years of confusion, a gentle and unwarlike (even cowardly) individual succeeded to the throne under the title of Darius III. He did so just in time to receive the force of Alexander's invasion.

Alexander quickly won an initial victory over local Persian forces in northwestern Asia Minor. He then passed through the length of that peninsula before meeting the main Persian army in the southeast corner. There he won a great victory in 333 B.C., following which he marched southward through Syria and Judea (see page I-667).

He took Jerusalem without resistance. Josephus describes the high priest of Jerusalem emerging from the city in full priestly regalia to meet Alexander and protect the city. Alexander is then described as having said he had seen just such a man in a dream, so that he pro-

The Empire of Alexander the Great

ceeded to treat Jerusalem with respect. This may or may not be true; there is no evidence for it outside Josephus.

Alexander entered and took Egypt, also without resistance, and directed the establishment of the city of Alexandria (named for himself) in 332 B.C.

In 331 B.C. Alexander left Egypt and advanced eastward into Babylonia, where he defeated the Persians in a third great battle. That was the end of the Persian Empire. In 330 B.C., Darius III was assassinated by some of his own officials, exactly two centuries after the death of Cyrus (see page I-442) and Alexander ruled the vast land in his place.

The Macedonian conqueror spent seven more years marching and countermarching through the eastern stretches of what had been the Persian dominion, winning every battle he fought and eventually carrying his victorious troops into India.

Here they refused to go any farther and Alexander is supposed to have wept because there were no more worlds to conquer. In 324 B.C. he returned to Babylon.

Alexander's Servants

Alexander did not long survive his amazing victories. In 323 B.C., at the age of thirty-three, he died:

1 Maccabees 1:7. *So Alexander reigned twelve years, and then died.*

1 Maccabees 1:8. *And his servants bare rule every one in his place.*

1 Maccabees 1:9. *And after his death they all put crowns upon themselves; so did their sons after them* . . .

At Alexander's death, he left behind him a wife, an infant son, a shrewish mother, and a mentally retarded half brother. None of these could possibly withstand the ambitions of the powerful generals (Alexander's "servants" in the words of 1 Maccabees) who had been trained under Philip and Alexander.

The generals fought ceaselessly among themselves for mastery but none of them won a complete victory. By 301 B.C. it became obvious that Alexander's empire would never be reunited and that each general would have to be content with being king over but a portion of it.

Ptolemaic Egypt and Seleucid Asia

The first to settle down to this new realization was the general, Ptolemy, who had made himself governor of Egypt immediately after Alexander's death. He kept this post and, in 306 B.C., assumed the title of king of Egypt, a title which was to be retained by his descendants (the Ptolemies) for nearly three centuries. Egypt, in this period, is referred to as "Ptolemaic Egypt."

Another of Alexander's generals was Seleucus, who established himself as king of much of western Asia in 306 B.C. His descendants (the Seleucids) reigned for almost as long as the Ptolemies did and their dominions are usually referred to as the Seleucid Empire.

There were other kingdoms established upon the ruins of Alexander's Empire, but it was those of the Ptolemies and the Seleucids that concerned the Jews. In the initial partition of the empire, the eastern shores of the Mediterranean were divided evenly between the two kingdoms. The southern half, including Judea, was part of the Ptolemaic dominion, and the Jews remained under the Ptolemies for a century.

Syria, to the north of Judea, was part of the Seleucid power from the beginning. The Seleucids, at the start, reigned also over Babylonia and the stretches to the east which came to be called Parthia.

It was the Syrian portion of the Seleucid Empire which was closest to Judea. In later centuries, when much of the eastern portion of that empire had been lost, its power was centered in Syria, where its western capital, Antioch, was located. For this reason the Seleucid Empire is frequently referred to as "Syria," though there is no connection except a geographic one, between Seleucid Syria and the Syria that fought against Israel in the days of Ahab (see page I-348).

Antiochus the King

The writer of 1 Maccabees does not pause to detail the history of the Macedonian kingdoms after the death of Alexander (a history which would be reasonably well known, in outline at least, to his original readers) but skips a century and a half to get immediately to the point:

> 1 Maccabees 1:10. *And there came out of them a wicked root . . . son of Antiochus the king . . .*

In most of the Hellenistic kingdoms of the time, successive rulers were known by some one of a very few names, so that there were many Ptolemies in Egypt and many Antiochuses among the Seleucids. The modern fashion of numbering kings of the same name was not in use in ancient times. Instead, each ruler took, or was given, some surname, usually some very flattering one.

Here, for instance, are the surnames of the first five Ptolemies, who ruled over Judea as well as over Egypt:

Ptolemy I Soter ("savior"), 306–285 B.C. He was given this surname in 304 B.C. when he came to the aid of the island of Rhodes at a time when it was being besieged by another Macedonian general. He was succeeded by his son.

Ptolemy II Philadelphus ("loving his sister"), 285–246 B.C. He was so called because late in life, in deference to Egyptian custom, he married his full sister. The name was applied to the two of them, really. Under the patronage of Ptolemy Philadelphus, the Museum and Library at Alexandria made that city the world center of science and learning. Also under his patronage, the Bible was first translated into some language other than Hebrew and the Septuagint came into being. He was succeeded by his son,

Ptolemy III Euergetes ("benefactor"), 246–221 B.C. Under him, Ptolemaic Egypt reached the peak of its power. He fought the Seleucids and defeated them, marching victoriously into Babylonia, annexing much of Syria and even parts of Asia Minor. He was succeeded by his son,

Ptolemy IV Philopater ("loving his father"), 221–203 B.C. This surname was perhaps a bit of propaganda, for this Ptolemy definitely ordered the execution of other close members of his family, including his mother. Some suspect he may have had a hand in the death of his father, too. Egypt began to decline in his reign. He was succeeded by an infant son,

Ptolemy V Epiphanes ("god manifest"), 203–181 B.C. The meaning of this name reflects the fact that in the ancient monarchies the king was considered the adopted son of the national god and therefore was himself a sort of god. Of course, the primitive notion of "god" was not as exalted or abstract as the notions developed by the Jews and Christians, and the Egyptian view toward a monarch as "god manifest" might be no stronger than a Jewish view concerning the high priest or a Christian view concerning the Pope.

As for the Seleucid Empire, the following are its early monarchs:

Seleucus I Nicator ("conqueror"), 305–280 B.C., who was followed by his son,

Antiochus I Soter ("savior"), 280–261 B.C., who was in turn followed by his son,

Antiochus II Theos ("god"), 261–246 B.C. In his reign large stretches of the eastern portion of the Seleucid Empire gained their independence under native monarchs and the history of Parthia (a name that is actually a form of "Persia") begins. He was succeeded by his son,

Seleucus II Callinicus ("gloriously victorious"), 246–226 B.C. Despite his surname, he was deafeated by Ptolemy III Euergetes and the Seleucid Empire sank to a low ebb. Torn at by Parthians in the east and Egyptians in the west, his twenty-year disastrous reign closed with the succession of his son,

Seleucus III Ceraunus ("thunderbolt"), 226–223 B.C., who was assassinated in the course of a war with a small Macedonian kingdom in Asia Minor. His younger brother succeeded to the throne. This brother is Antiochus III and it is he who is referred to in 1 Maccabees 1:10 as "Antiochus the king."

Under Antiochus III, 223–187 B.C., the Seleucid Empire made a remarkable recovery. As a result of a series of wars, Antiochus III gradually extended Seleucid power over Asia Minor; he defeated the Parthian tribes and returned them to Seleucid control; and, finally, he tackled Egypt.

He fought two wars against Egypt. In the first of these, he was unsuccessful, losing an important battle at Egypt's borders. When the infant Ptolemy V Epiphanes came to the throne, Antiochus quickly tried again. With Egypt distracted by courtiers intriguing for control of the government, Antiochus was victorious by 198 B.C. As a result of this war, Judea was wrested from Egypt and passed under the domination of the Seleucids.

Rome

In a way, though, Antiochus III had been born too late. He gloried in his victories, which seemed, in his own eyes, to rival those of Alexander. He called himself therefore Antiochus III Magnus ("great") and is known in our own histories as Antiochus the Great.

The Roman World in Maccabean Times

If he had died in 198 B.C. the name might have been deserved, but he lived on and found himself entangled with Rome, with results hinted at in the book of 1 Maccabees:

> 1 Maccabees 1:10. *And there came out of them a wicked root, Antiochus surnamed Epiphanes, son of Antiochus the king, who had been an hostage at Rome . . .*

The city of Rome, according to Roman legend, had been founded in 753 B.C. This was when Jeroboam II was king of Israel and Uzziah king of Judah, when Amos and Hosea were prophesying and when Isaiah was about to receive his call.

Rome was a kingdom at first but in 509 B.C., shortly after the Second Temple was dedicated in Jerusalem, it evicted its seventh king, Tarquinius Superbus, and established the Roman Republic. Little by little, over the centuries, it increased its power until, by 270 B.C. when the Jews were under the mild and beneficent rule of Ptolemy II Philadelphus, the Romans had gained control over the entire Italian peninsula.

From 264 B.C. to 202 B.C., while the Ptolemies and Seleucids were continuing their endless wars, Rome fought two gigantic wars of her own with the North African city of Carthage and eventually won a complete victory. Her power was established over the large islands near Italy (Sicily, Sardinia, and Corsica) and over the coasts of Spain. She was the greatest power of the western Mediterranean and her growing shadow began to darken the east.

Some of the smaller Macedonian kingdoms began to form alliances with Rome and to seek her protection against the Seleucid Empire, which, under Antiochus III, seemed invincible. Indeed, even Egypt had a treaty of friendship with Rome that dated back to Ptolemy II, and she too called on Rome for help.

Antiochus III, however, felt no need to be concerned about distant Rome. He considered himself unbeatable and had no hesitation in moving against the small kingdom of Pergamum in western Asia Minor, a kingdom which was Rome's ally.

Rome's warning was disregarded and, in 192 B.C., Rome and Antiochus were at war. Antiochus III invaded Greece but found that defeating the Roman army was by no means the same as defeating the poorly led Egyptian armies or smashing the disorganized Parthian hordes in the east. In 191 B.C. Antiochus III was badly defeated by the

Romans in Greece. When the disillusioned Seleucid monarch retreated hastily to Asia Minor, the Romans followed grimly (setting foot in Asia for the first time) and defeated him again in 190 B.C.

Antiochus III was forced to make a disastrous peace in 189 B.C. He had to pay a large indemnity, lose his fleet, and give up Asia Minor. One of his younger sons—the Antiochus referred to in 1 Maccabees 1:10—was handed over as hostage to the Romans, this serving as a guarantee that the terms of the treaty would be fulfilled. (The Parthian sections of the empire seized their chance to break away again, this time permanently, and the Seleucid Empire was confined to Syria and Babylonia. This was still a sizable dominion, for it was just about the empire ruled over by Nebuchadnezzar.)

In order to pay the indemnity to Rome, Antiochus attempted to force various temples to give up their store of gold. In one city, in 187 B.C., where he was supervising the looting of the temple, he was killed by the inhabitants.

Antiochus Epiphanes

Antiochus III was succeeded by his oldest son, Seleucus IV Philopater, under whom the Seleucid Empire began a slow recovery. The Romans, to make sure he would cause no trouble, forced him, on his accession, to send his son Demetrius as a hostage to Rome. Seleucus was assassinated in 175 B.C. by one of his own ministers, who then attempted to make himself king.

Meanwhile, Seleucus' younger brother Antiochus, who had been sent a hostage to Rome, had been well treated there and had grown to admire Roman institutions. Just about the time that Seleucus was assassinated, Antiochus had been released (or had slipped away) and was making his way back to Antioch. He hastened his steps and managed to seize the throne from the usurper and to take over the kingship. He became Antiochus IV Epiphanes.

1 Maccabees 1:10. *And there came out of them a wicked root, Antiochus surnamed Epiphanes . . . and he reigned in the hundred and thirty and seventh year of the kingdom of the Greeks.*

Seleucus I, the founder of the Seleucid Empire, had begun the practice of counting the years from a victory he gained in 312 B.C., a victory that had enabled him to establish himself firmly in Babylon. He considered his empire to have been founded at that time and 312 B.C. is therefore the first year "of the kingdom of the Greeks" or, as we would say today, the year 1 of the Seleucid era. Therefore, 176/175 B.C. would be the year 137 of the Seleucid era and it is in that year that Antiochus IV gained the throne.

In later years the Jews commonly used the Seleucid era in the course of their business and commercial transactions at a time when every kingdom and almost every city had its own methods for counting the years. As the Jews were scattered widely over the east, their use of the Seleucid era together with the local systems offered later historians a useful method of knitting together the various chronologies.

The Seleucid era remained the most important and widespread manner of counting the years in the Greek-speaking world until the establishment of the Roman era; that is, the system of counting from the year of the legendary founding of the city of Rome. (Later still, the now nearly universal system of counting the years from the birth of Jesus was adopted.)

The Place of Exercise

Alexander the Great, in conquering the Persian Empire, did more than merely make himself king over vast tracts of land. He introduced Greek culture to the east. This culture has always been a very attractive one and it was widely adopted. All of Asia Minor became Greek in culture if not in race, and throughout Egypt and Babylonia tendrils of Greek culture extended. Even in Bactria (the region we now call Afghanistan) a semi-Greek kingdom was set up which survived for over a century, from 250 B.C. to 135 B.C.

The Jews were not immune to the attractiveness of Greek culture, any more than they were immune to Canaanite culture in the days of the judges and the kings, or to American culture today. In the time of the Seleucids, there were many among them who wanted to "assimilate," and to establish gymnasia after the Greek fashion—something at which the writer of 1 Maccabees, strongly anti-Greek, stands aghast:

> 1 Maccabees 1:11. *In those days went there out of Israel wicked men, who persuaded many, saying, Let us go and make a covenant with the heathen that are round about us . . .*
>
> . . . .
>
> 1 Maccabees 1:14. *Whereupon they built a place of exercise at Jerusalem according to the customs of the heathen:*
>
> 1 Maccabees 1:15. *And made themselves uncircumcised . . .*

At the gymnasia, the Greeks were accustomed to exercise and to engage in athletic contests in the nude. (The very word "gymnasium" is from a Greek word meaning "naked.") This in itself was horrifying to those Jews who clung to the old ways. Worse still, Jews who exercised in the nude could clearly be seen to be circumcised; to avoid this embarrassment, the custom arose of wearing false foreskins, thus making them "uncircumcised."

This development was, of course, welcomed by the Seleucid rulers. In the first place they, like all the Macedonian rulers, were seriously intent on spreading Greek culture, since they felt it to be far superior to all other cultures.

Then, too, people who clung to old non-Greek ways were more apt to revolt against the ruler in an effort to establish their independence so that they might then live their own way freely. This consideration might well apply particularly to the Jews, since they had only been under Seleucid domination for a quarter of a century and since many co-religionists remained under the Ptolemies, in Alexandria and elsewhere. It might well have seemed to Antiochus IV that the Jews would feel a natural bond to his traditional enemy, Egypt, unless they became Greek in culture and broke their ties with the well-treated Alexandrian Jews.

For this reason Antiochus IV did everything in his power to encourage the hellenization (the Greeks called themselves "Hellenes") of Judea. Nor must such behavior be considered as abnormal or unique to Antiochus. Rather it is common practice in most lands, then and now, to attempt to unify culture. Here in the United States, immigrants from lands of widely different language and culture have been encouraged to learn English and adopt American ways.

To be sure, such a program works best when it is conducted moderately, letting the dominant culture win its way by its own attractiveness and convenience, rather than attempting to impose it by naked force.

Ptolemy

Egypt had a new king too. When Ptolemy V died in 181 B.C., his son, Ptolemy VI Philometer ("loving his mother"), succeeded. He was a young man who was dominated by his mother, a fact that no doubt accounts for his nickname.

There remained bad blood between the Ptolemies and the Seleucids despite the overriding menace of Rome, for there was still the problem of Judea. Antiochus III had been defeated by Rome, but they had allowed him to retain Judea, which he had taken from the Ptolemies, and the Egyptians wanted it back.

Antiochus IV, however, felt no need to return territory that the Romans had let his father keep. He may even have felt that, in view of his own years of pleasant stay in Rome, the Romans would look upon him as one of their own, and favor his enterprises.

Ptolemy's mother remained a force for peace, but after she died, warfare broke out. It was Egypt, apparently, that struck the first blow, and in this she proved foolish, for Ptolemy VI was a weak and unwarlike king (though gentle and humane) while Antiochus IV was a capable general. Antiochus invaded Egypt in 170 B.C.

> 1 Maccabees 1:17. *Wherefore he* [Antiochus IV] *entered into Egypt with a great multitude . . .*
> 1 Maccabees 1:18. *And made war against Ptolemee king of Egypt: but Ptolemee was afraid of him, and fled . . .*

Antiochus pursued the retreating Egyptian king to the walls of Alexandria and actually captured him. The Egyptians, left without a king, promptly put Ptolemy's younger brother on the throne, as Ptolemy VII Euergetes II—note the repetition of the surname.

(Sometimes Ptolemy VII is reserved for the young son of Ptolemy VI, while the brother who now shared his throne is called Ptolemy VIII. However, there is no great chance of confusion here for the Ptolemy who was placed on the throne after the capture of Ptolemy VI is universally known in history not by number but as "Physcon" or "Pot-Belly" because he grew fat in the course of his long reign. It was this Ptolemy VII, or Physcon, by the way, who was referred to by the translator of Ecclesiasticus, see page I-517.)

Antiochus IV did not feel in a position actually to take Alexandria, for he was uncertain as to Rome's attitude if he went that far. He therefore released Ptolemy VI. He felt that with two Ptolemies quarreling over the throne, Egypt would fall into civil war and one side or another would call on his help. He would then take over the country under a show of legality.

The Egyptians, however, outmaneuvered him. The two Ptolemies decided to rule jointly and did so in peace. The angered Antiochus threw caution aside and invaded Egypt a second time in 168 B.C.

But now Rome had had enough. A Roman envoy from Alexandria faced the Seleucid monarch in front of his troops and ordered him to withdraw. Antiochus had to back down before this single representative of the distant Roman power and, utterly humiliated, march back to his own land.

Jerusalem

The Book of 1 Maccabees refers only to the first invasion of Egypt, the one that was glorious from the standpoint of Antiochus IV. Of course, even a victorious campaign consumes money and the Seleucids had been dreadfully short of that commodity ever since Rome had exacted its indemnity. One way out was to confiscate the hoarded wealth of temples—something that had been the death of Antiochus III—and Antiochus III's son, returning from Egypt, passed through Jerusalem and looted its Temple as a matter of course:

> 1 Maccabees 1:20. *And after that Antiochus had smitten Egypt,*
> *he returned again in the hundred forty and third year* [169 B.C.] ...
> 1 Maccabees 1:21. *And entered proudly into the sanctuary, and*
> *took away the golden altar* ...
> . . . .
> 1 Maccabees 1:23. *He took also the silver and the gold, and the*
> *precious vessels: also he took the hidden treasures which he found.*

The writer does not go on to tell of the second invasion of Egypt and of its humiliating end for Antiochus, but we needn't rely on secular history only to know of it. The incident is mentioned in the Book of Daniel (see page I-619):

Daniel 11:30. *For the ships of Chittim* [Rome] *shall come against him* [Antiochus IV]: *therefore he shall be grieved, and return, and have indignation against the holy covenant* . . .

It seems reasonable enough to suppose that Antiochus IV, half-maddened with frustration, would be anxious to vent his anger on some victim. The Jews were weak enough for the purpose and were not protected by Rome and it is possible, besides, that they angered him further by being incautiously jubilant over this shameful defeat of the king who had looted their Temple only two years before.

Antiochus took action:

1 Maccabees 1:29. . . . *the king sent his chief collector of tribute . . . who came unto Jerusalem with a great multitude,*

1 Maccabees 1:30. *And . . . fell suddenly upon the city, and smote it very sore . . .*

With Jerusalem taken and sacked, Antiochus further decided that Hellenization was to proceed with all possible speed:

1 Maccabees 1:41. *Moreover king Antiochus wrote to his whole kingdom, that all should be one people,*

1 Maccabees 1:42. *And every one should leave his laws . . .*

As a climax of the new policy, the Temple was profaned. Antiochus decided that Judaism should be brought into line with Hellenism by identifying Zeus and Yahveh and erecting a statue to Zeus-Yahveh in the Temple itself, supplying it, very likely, with his own royal face. To the orthodox Jews this was the greatest imaginable blasphemy:

1 Maccabees 1:54. *Now . . . in the hundred forty and fifth year* [167 B.C.], *they set up the abomination of desolation upon the altar . . .*

To enforce the new policy, Antiochus ordered copies of the Jewish Scriptures to be destroyed, forbade circumcision and the Jewish dietary regulations, then executed those caught clinging to the old ways. For a time it looked as though Judaism would be destroyed and that those who held out uncompromisingly against Antiochus IV would die as martyrs.

Mattathias

But now a remarkable family appears on the scene:

> 1 Maccabees 2:1. *In those days arose Mattathias . . . a priest . . .
> from Jerusalem, and dwelt in Modin.*

Mattathias is the Greek form of the Hebrew Mattathiah ("gift of
Yahveh"). This name is mentioned only once in the canonical books
of the Bible and then only in a post-Exilic incident:

> Nehemiah 8:4. *And Ezra the scribe stood upon a pulpit of wood,
> . . . and beside him stood Mattathiah . . .*

but it had grown popular in Seleucid times.

According to Josephus, the great-great-grandfather of Mattathias was
named Hashmon (or Asmon, in the Greek form) so that the family
may be called the Hasmonaeans or Asmoneans collectively. When
Jerusalem had been taken by Antiochus' forces, Mattathias and his
family moved to Modin (Modein in the Revised Standard Version),
a town some seventeen miles to the northwest.

Judas Maccabeus

Mattathias had five stalwart sons:

> 1 Maccabees 2:2. *And he had five sons, Joannan* [Johanan], *called
> Caddis:*
> 1 Maccabees 2:3. *Simon, called, Thassi:*
> 1 Maccabees 2:4. *Judas, who was called Maccabeus:*
> 1 Maccabees 2:5. *Eleazar, called Avaran: and Jonathan, whose sur-
> name was Apphus.*

Even among the Jews it was becoming customary to adopt surnames
to serve as identification. In this case, the surnames are of uncertain
meaning, except, possibly, for that of Mattathias' third son: Judas Maccabeus.

This surname is often considered a Greek version of the Hebrew
word "makkabi" ("the hammerer"). It is suggested that the third son

is Judas the Hammerer, so called because of the hammer blows he was soon to inflict upon the Seleucid army. On the other hand, there is some indication that he had this name before the battles were joined, and an alternate suggestion is that it is from the Hebrew "makab" ("to appoint"). He would then be Judas the Appointed; appointed, that is, by God to lead his people against the Seleucids.

Judas itself is, of course, the Greek form of Judah. It is very likely that the heroism of Judas Maccabeus made the name Judas [Judah] so popular among the Jews in the centuries following.

Because Judas Maccabeus is the hero of what was to follow, the family has come to be called, in English, the Maccabees—a name that is more familiar now than the more accurate Hasmonaeans. Similarly, the Jewish kingdom that was eventually established under their rule is called the "Maccabean kingdom," and the times the "Maccabean era." Jewish writings dealing with this period of time are lumped together as the various books of the Maccabees even when they have nothing directly to do with the family, and the first of these, the one with which I am now dealing, is 1 Maccabees.

Assideans

The spark that initiated the Jewish rebellion against the Seleucids was set off by an officer of Antiochus who came to Modin to enforce the new laws. He asked Mattathias, as a prominent Jewish leader, to set a good example and to carry through a sacrifice in the manner required by law. To Mattathias, this was idolatry and he refused.

However, there were other Jews who were not so insistent on the old ways. The Seleucid officer, in asking Mattathias to perform the sacrifice, pointed out that it was being done by the Jews generally:

1 Maccabees 2:18. . . . *fulfil the king's commandment, like . . . the men of Juda . . . and such as remain at Jerusalem . . .*

In this, he was probably telling the truth. In aftertimes, a successful revolution is looked back upon as the rising of a united nation or group, but most of that is the patriotic gilding of memory, and it is not so. In all revolutions, those who ardently pursue the fight to the death are in the minority and there are usually at least as many who are ardently anti-revolutionary, plus an actual majority that is apathetic and will go where they are led (in either direction), if necessary, but who best prefer to be left alone.

Our own Revolutionary War was conducted by a minority of Rebels who faced not only the British, but Tories who were at least equal in numbers to themselves. And most colonists did not incline strongly to either side. And today the Civil Rights movement among Negroes has, as one of its problems, the apathy of most Negroes.

So it must have been that the Jews in the time of Antiochus were by no means all bitterly anti-Seleucid. Many were willing to conform; perhaps even eager, in their pro-Greek views, to do so. Thus, when Mattathias refused the sacrifice, someone else quickly stepped up to perform it, either out of conviction or, perhaps, out of the thought that unless someone did, the entire town would be massacred.

> 1 Maccabees 2:23. . . . *there came one of the Jews in the sight of all to sacrifice on the altar . . . according to the king's commandment.*

At seeing this, Mattathias flew into a rage, slew the Jew and the Seleucid officer. That was the Lexington-and-Concord of the Jewish rebellion. Mattathias and his sons had to flee to the hills, and around them they began to collect other rebels.

In particular, Mattathias was joined by a party of fervid men whose adherence to the traditional Mosaic Law was absolute:

> 1 Maccabees 2:42. *Then came there unto him a company of Assideans, who were mighty men of Israel, even all such as were voluntarily devoted unto the law.*

The word Assideans (or Hasideans in the Revised Standard Version) is the Greek form of the Hebrew "Hassidim," meaning "the pious ones." Their sole concern lay in religion. They were uninterested in politics and it was only when the practice of Judaism was outlawed that they were willing to resort to violence.

They were stalwart fighters, but in some ways they were an embarrassment, for a truly uncompromising adherence to the letter of the law can create problems. The many prohibitions that had grown up concerning the Sabbath day made many pious men feel that it was unlawful to take even such worldly action on the Sabbath as was required for self-defense. Thus, Josephus says that when Ptolemy I, in the first few years after Alexander's death, marched into Judea to establish his dominance over the region, he was able to seize Jerusalem without resistance by attacking on the Sabbath. The Jews would not defend the walls on that day.

Similarly, a party of the ultra-pious, tracked down by Seleucid forces on the Sabbath, decided to let themselves be killed without resisting. They said:

> 1 Maccabees 2:37. . . . *Let us die all in our innocency: heaven and earth shall testify for us, that ye put us to death wrongfully.*

There is something impressive about such faith, but it is no way to fight a war. Mattathias and his friends mourned the dead, but they insisted on a new policy:

> 1 Maccabees 2:41. . . . *Whosoever shall come to make battle with us on the sabbath day, we will fight against him . . .*

Here was an example of adjusting the Law to fit the serious needs of men, something that was to play a part in the later development of Judaism and in the teachings of Jesus, too.

Beth-horon

Mattathias did not live long. He was old, and the exertions of the field took its toll:

> 1 Maccabees 2:70. *And he died in the hundred forty and sixth year* [166 B.C.] . . .
> 1 Maccabees 3:1. *Then his son Judas, called Maccabeus, rose up in his stead.*

But now the forces of the Seleucid Empire were moving to put down the revolt and, as is often the case, the government began by underestimating the seriousness of the trouble. It was, to begin with, left to the governor of Samaria, Apollonius, the local official on the spot:

> 1 Maccabees 3:10. *Then Apollonius gathered the Gentiles together, and a great host out of Samaria, to fight against Israel.*

Judas Maccabeus came out to meet him. Apollonius was, in all likelihood, overconfident and marched forward carelessly, convinced he could easily handle a few rebels. That was his mistake. Judas' men swarmed down upon him, probably out of ambush, and his army was defeated. Apollonius himself was killed and Judas took his sword and used it in later battles.

The Seleucids had to do better than that, and the next step involved the army itself and a general, Seron. Now it was not the local levies from Samaria, but the army itself.

> 1 Maccabees 3:16. *And when he* [Seron] *came near to the going up of Bethhoron, Judas went forth to meet him with a small company* . . .

Beth-horon is about twelve miles northwest of Jerusalem, near Mattathias' adopted town of Modin. Here, Judas and his men lay in ambush in the surrounding hills and once again a lightning attack caught a Seleucid army by surprise and destroyed it.

Persia

The Jewish victory at Beth-horon was sufficiently spectacular to raise the rebellion from a local tumult to an internationally observed matter. Clearly, the prestige of the regime now required that a major effort be put into the suppression of the rebels.

Unfortunately for Antiochus it was easier to see the need than to do something about it. The same old problem arose—lack of money. Furthermore, the empire was fading at the other end, too. If Judas and his army of irregulars were shaking the west, in the east whole provinces were falling away.

The Parthian rulers, who had been subservient to the Seleucids even as late as the reign of Antiochus III, were little by little enlarging their independence. In 171 B.C., a vigorous king, Mithridates I, ascended the Parthian throne and the last vestige of dependence on the Seleucids disappeared. Indeed, Mithridates extended his power in all directions and was making himself a major factor in central Asia.

It may be that if Parthia had remained quiet, Antiochus could have handled the Jewish rebellion. As it was, he found himself pulled in both directions. His prestige abroad, already badly shaken by his humiliation in Egypt, demanded that he not allow the Jews to remain unpunished. On the other hand, if he could but bring the eastern provinces back into the fold, he could collect all the money he needed in the form of a punitive tribute.

With prestige pulling one way and money the other, he made the worst possible decision. He decided to divide his forces and embark on a two-front war:

1 Maccabees 3:31. *Wherefore, being greatly perplexed in his mind, he [Antiochus IV] determined to go into Persia [Parthia], there to take the tributes of the countries, and to gather much money.*

1 Maccabees 3:32. *So he left Lysias, a nobleman, . . . to oversee the affairs of the king from the river Euphrates unto the borders of Egypt . . .*

Antioch

Antioch

Antiochus IV left his young son with Lysias, and half his army as well and his instructions were to wipe out the Jewish rebels.

1 Maccabees 3:37. *So the king took the half of the forces that remained, and departed from Antioch, his royal city, the hundred forty and seventh year [165 B.C.]; and . . . passed the river Euphrates . . .*

Antioch, the "royal city"—that is, the Seleucid capital—was, at this time, a comparatively young city.

When Alexander the Great died in 323 B.C., Babylon was still the gratest city of the east, and it was in Babylon that he died. Babylon remained a great prize for the generals who contended for the crown. It was captured by Seleucus I Nicator in 312 B.C. and that established him on the throne of Macedonian Asia and served to mark the date of the founding of the Seleucid Empire.

Yet the capture by Seleucus was the last important event in Babylonian history. Seleucus was a founder of cities and felt that his capital ought to be a new city, and not one as old and as hoary with non-Greek tradition as Babylon was. The year of his conquest of Babylon, Seleucus therefore began to build a new capital for himself on the Tigris River some twenty miles north of Babylon. He called the new city Seleucia, after himself.

As Seleucia grew, Babylon declined. The people left the old city for the new and the buildings of Babylon served as raw material for construction in Seleucia. By Maccabean times, the mighty Babylon of Hammurabi and Nebuchadnezzar was finished and sixteen centuries of histories closed with a whimper. The city that had carried off the Jews four centuries before was now a miserably dying village; and Jerusalem, which it had temporarily destroyed, was still alive after all and about to embark on a new period of independence.

However, Seleucia was not the only capital. To be sure, it was centrally located and it grew rich and prosperous. If the Seleucids had remained there and concentrated on the eastern portion of their empire they might have fused Greek and Persian into a combined society that would have lasted indefinitely.

Psychologically, though, the Seleucids were always drawn westward. The Greek core was to the west and the Seleucids were always aware of the enormous attraction of all things Greek. A few miles of Syria, or a stretch of the coast of Asia Minor, meant more to them than a thousand miles of central Asia. So they fought endless wars with Egypt while vast tracts of the east crumbled. And because of their concentration on the west, they needed a center there.

In 300 B.C., Seleucus had founded a city in northwest Syria near the Mediterranean. He named it Antiochea, in memory of his father, the Macedonian general, Antiochus, and we know it as Antioch. This city, near the Greek thick of things, was ideal as a western capital.

Through the succeeding reigns, each successive monarch enlarged and beautified Antioch. The center of gravity of the Seleucid Empire shifted westward and by the time of Antiochus IV, Antioch was the major city of the realm, and stood second only to Alexandria in the Greek world.

The Temple

While Antiochus IV, with half the army, had gone eastward to Parthia, Lysias was left with the other half to take care of the Jews. It was far easier for Lysias, however, to receive his instructions than to carry them out.

In the course of the next year, Lysias sent two armies into Judea and each was defeated. Judas Maccabeus had shown himself unbeatable and now he could count on a period of wary peace while the chastened Seleucids held back to recoup.

It was time, therefore, to rededicate the profaned Temple. Judas Maccabeus chose priests who had never compromised with the Seleucid authorities, tore down the profaned altar and buried the stones. A new altar was built and new vessels supplied, and finally:

> 1 Maccabees 4:52. . . . *in the one hundred forty and eighth year* [164 B.C.], *they rose up betimes in the morning,*
> 1 Maccabees 4:53. *And offered sacrifice according to the law upon the new altar* . . .
> . . . .
> 1 Maccabees 4:56. *And so they kept the dedication of the altar eight days* . . .
> . . . .
> 1 Maccabees 4:59. *Moreover Judas and his brethren* . . . *ordained, that the days of the dedication of the altar should be kept in their season from year to year by the space of eight days* . . .

The anniversary of the dedication of the Temple is celebrated to this day, by the Jews, as the eight-day feast of Hanukkah ("dedication").

Judas deliberately set the date of the dedication of the cleansed Temple, on the third anniversary of its profanation, and therefore three and a half years after the capture of Jerusalem by Antiochus IV.

This three-and-a-half-year interval is mentioned by the writer' of Daniel, who was apparently at work on it at this time. Since he placed the book in the time of the Exile four centuries earlier and had Daniel relate it as a prophecy, he was forced to use apocalyptic language:

> Daniel 7:25. *And he* [Antiochus IV] *shall speak great words against the most High, . . . and think to change times and laws: and they* [the Temple and the pious Jews] *shall be given into his hand until a time* [one year] *and times* [plus two years] *and the dividing of time* [plus half a year].

Idumea

Idumea

The Temple was rededicated and Judas fortified Mount Zion, but there was no opportunity to rest. The enthusiasm of the victories would have declined and faded, if the Jews now remained on the defensive; the élan and esprit would vanish, the forces disperse, and the revolt would wither away. Judas apparently decided to pass over to the offensive, and attack the areas bordering on Judea:

> 1 Maccabees 5:3. *Then Judas fought against the children of Esau in Idumea . . . and he gave them a great overthrow . . .*

This was not the first example of the rapid about-face of the Jews from a persecuted minority to an imperial power. Eight and a half centuries before, David had taken a nation of Philistine vassals and, in the course of a few years, not only won Israelite independence but established Israelite hegemony over the Philistines and other surrounding nations.

Here the case was more limited, for the Maccabean state never approached the physical dimensions or the comparative power of David's kingdom. Nevertheless, the victory of Judas was the first step toward the conquest of Edom (or Idumea, which is the Greek version of the name).

Perhaps the nationalists of the time felt they could justify warfare against Idumea not only as a matter of traditional enmity, traced all the way back to the legends of Jacob and Esau (see page I-93), but also because during the period of the Babylonian Exile, the Idumeans, under the pressure of the Nabatean Arabs (see page I-457), had been forced northward. What was called Idumea in Maccabean times had been southern Judah in the time of the monarchy, and the Jews may well have felt they were but retaking what was their own. (Similar arguments have served as excuse for any number of wars since.)

But it was more than mere conquest. The Maccabeans eventually enforced Judaism on the conquered Idumeans; doing as they would not be done by. The case of a religious minority that becomes an oppressor as soon as it is in power has been seen numerous times in history. Consider, for instance, the Puritans who fled oppression in England and came to America for the sake of religious liberty and who then proved most keen in refusing it to others than themselves. The usual excuse, in all times, is that the victors are merely exalting Truth over Falsehood, and are selflessly saving the souls of the losers. The losers, however, generally have trouble recognizing the good intentions of those who are so thoughtfully converting them at the point of the sword.

Galilee

The forces of Judas struck outward in all directions, not only toward the south against Idumea, but eastward against the Ammonites. There was trouble in the north, too. The Greeks in Gilead (east of the Jordan and north of Ammonite territory) gathered against the Jews who

Galilee

lived there and laid siege to them in one of the Gileadite cities. The besieged Jews sent letters to Judas and his brothers, pleading for help:

> 1 Maccabees 5:14. *While these letters were yet reading, behold, there came other messengers from Galilee . . . who reported on this wise,*
> 1 Maccabees 5:15. *. . . They of . . . all Galilee of the Gentiles, are assembled together against us . . .*

Galilee refers to the northernmost section of what had once been Israel; the territory which, in the time of the judges, was settled by the tribes of Naphtali and Zebulon.

This northern area was never firmly held by the Israelites. The Canaanites remained strong in the north long after Joshua's conquest, as is evidenced by the tales of the battle against Sisera (see page I-238).

Down to the time of David himself, the Phoenician coastal cities (inhabited by Canaanites, be it remembered) dominated the north.

To those at the center of Israelite power—farther south among the Rachel tribes of Ephraim, Manasseh, and Benjamin—the north could well be looked upon as *galil haggoyim*. This means, literally, "district of the nations" or "district of the [non-Israelite] tribes."

A Latin word for a tribe or clan was *gens* and members of the same tribe or clan were "gentiles." Therefore *galil haggoyim* could be translated as "district of the gentiles." *Galil* became *Galilaea* in Latin and "Galilee" in English, leaving us with "Galilee of the Gentiles."

The term Gentile, for non-Jew, is used steadily in 1 Maccabees, and has come down, in this sense, to modern times. Mormons, however, apply the word to non-Mormons, so that to a Mormon a Jew is a Gentile.

References to Galilee prior to the time of the Assyrian conquest and the destruction of the Northern Kingdom are not found in the Bible. Prior to that time, the lands of Naphtali and Zebulon are referred to instead. The turning point comes in Isaiah where the depredations of Assyria are described and both terms, pre-Assyrian and post-Assyrian, are used for the area:

> Isaiah 9:1. . . . *at the first he lightly afflicted the land of Zebulun and the land of Naphtali, and afterward did more grievously afflict her . . . in Galilee of the nations.*

By Maccabean times, Jewish colonists had begun to penetrate Galilee once more, but its population was still largely Gentile.

Ptolemais

In the face of this double danger, Judas divided his forces. He and his younger brother Jonathan, with the smaller army, advanced into Gilead. His older brother, Simon (another version of the name Simeon, by the way), led the larger army into Galilee. The division of forces proved, for once, not to be fatal. Both were victorious and both were able to evacuate the besieged Jews back to the safety of Judea:

> 1 Maccabees 5:21. *Then went Simon into Galilee, where he fought many battles with the heathen, . . .*

1 Maccabees 5:22. *And he pursued them unto the gate of Ptole-*
mais.

Ptolemais was a city on the Phoenician coast some twenty-five miles
south of Tyre—the southernmost of the Phoenician cities. Its older
name had been Accho and it lay in the territory theoretically assigned
to Asher. The northern tribes never did assert their theoretical supremacy over the Phoenician coast, of course; a fact recognized in the Bible:

Judges 1:31. *Neither did Asher drive out the inhabitants of Accho,*
nor the inhabitants of Zidon . . .

The early Ptolemies controlled the area and in 260 B.C., Accho was
renamed Ptolemais in their honor. It kept that name after the area
had been wrested from Egyptian hands by Antiochus III, and indeed
throughout the Roman period long after Ptolemies and Seleucids had
alike vanished.

It resumed its original name after the Moslem conquest in A.D. 638.
In the time of the Crusades, five centuries later, the city was known to
the Christians as St.-Jean-d'Acre or, more simply, Acre. It is now a city
of modern Israel, named Akko, and has a population of some thirty
thousand.

Antiochus V Eupator

The Maccabean attacks were successful, in part, because the Seleucid
Empire was more or less paralyzed by events in Parthia. Antiochus IV
was having no success there. The writer of Maccabees tells of the failure
of his attempt to loot a temple in Elymais and of his falling sick with
grief in consequence; a grief further exacerbated by the news of Lysias'
defeats in Judea.

The story of the temple-looting is undoubtedly a mistake. It is a
tale transferred from Antiochus III (see page 48) to his son, perhaps
through the writer's eagerness to have Antiochus IV sink into utter
failure. His sickness, it would seem from secular sources, was not grief,
but tuberculosis, something more likely to be fatal.

The despoiler of the Temple died in Gabae, a town now known as
Isfahan, in central Iran, nine hundred miles east of Jerusalem.

1 Maccabees 6:16. *So king Antiochus died there in the hundred*
forty and ninth year [163 B.C.].

1 Maccabees 6:17. *Now when Lysias knew that the king was dead, he set up Antiochus his son . . . to reign in his stead, and his name he called Eupator.*

Antiochus V Eupator ("of noble birth") was nine years old at the time of his accession. He was controlled by Lysias, who ruled the empire through him.

The accession of a young king was made to order for the Jewish rebels under Judas Maccabeus. There were bound to be dynastic squabbles and while the various candidates for the throne and for power behind it fought among themselves, the Jews could safely risk the offensive.

In 162 B.C., the year after the death of Antiochus IV, Judas even dared attack the citadel in Jerusalem; that is, the fortress within which the Seleucid garrison had retired at the time, over a year before, when the main city of Jerusalem had been taken and the Temple rededicated.

But that attack stirred Lysias, who decided to take a chance on dynastic troubles remaining in abeyance and mount a strong counterattack (something to which he was urged by parties of loyalist Jews —the "Tories" of the Maccabean rebellion).

A fresh Seleucid army advanced southward, stronger than any previous one, and armed with a new type of weapon not hitherto used against the rebels—elephants. Eleasar, one of the brothers of Judas, fought his way to one of the beasts, stabbed it in the abdomen, and killed it, but the elephant, in dying, fell upon Eleasar and killed him in turn. He was the first of the five sons of Mattathias to die.

Eleasar showed that elephants, too, were mortal, but the Jewish army was nevertheless facing odds that were too great for it. Fighting desperately, they were nevertheless slowly pushed toward the edge of exhaustion through famine.

But then Lysias' gamble failed. He was forced to face a dynastic problem. A nobleman who had been with Antiochus IV in the east had now made his way back with what was left of Antiochus' army and attempted to seize power. Lysias, faced with this threat to the very core of his policy, was forced to turn away from the trouble in the outskirts.

He therefore offered the Jews a compromise peace. Two points were involved, the religious liberty of the Jews and their political independence. Lysias felt that, under the circumstances, he could yield the first, if the Jews would yield the second. There were important elements in the rebel army, the Assideans, for instance, who were interested only in religious liberty, and Judas had to accept the compromise. At least, for the time.

Demetrius I Soter

Lysias returned to Antioch, now under the control of his competitor, defeated him and retook the city—but the situation remained unstable. There were other competitors in the field.

Seleucus IV Philopater, the predecessor and older brother of Antiochus IV, had sent a son, Demetrius, into Roman captivity (see page 48). That son of an older brother was, by modern standards, more deserving of the throne than the reigning monarch, Antiochus V, who was but the son of a younger brother. Demetrius, when he heard of the death of his uncle, Antiochus IV, at once petitioned the Roman Senate for permission to return to Antioch and assume the kingship. Rome, preferring a weak child on the Seleucid throne to a capable young man, refused permission and Demetrius promptly escaped and made his way to the Seleucid coast on his own.

> 1 Maccabees 7:1. *In the hundred and one and fiftieth year* [161 B.C.] *Demetrius the son of Seleucus departed from Rome, and came up with a few men unto a city of the sea coast, and reigned there.*

In the civil war that followed, Demetrius was a quick winner. Antiochus V and Lysias were captured and killed and the new king took the name of Demetrius I Soter. Rome accepted the reality of the situation and recognized Demetrius as king.

Demetrius attempted to retrieve the Seleucid position with respect to Judea, not so much by immediate military action as by first laying a careful foundation of support for himself among the Jewish "Tories" of whom there were many.

> 1 Maccabees 7:5. *There came unto him* [Demetrius] *all the wicked and ungodly men of Israel, having Alcimus, who was desirous to be high priest, for their captain:*
> 1 Maccabees 7:6. *And they accused the people* [the rebel forces] *to the king* . . .

With the Tories on the king's side and with the Assideans neutral, Demetrius felt it timely to send an army into Judea once more. At its head was Nicanor, a general who had been with the king in Rome and, according to Josephus, had escaped with him.

Judas, however, had not forgotten how to be a hammerer. Rallying his forces against a superior enemy yet once again, he met the Seleucid army at Beth-horon, some fourteen miles northwest of Jerusalem, and there he won the most remarkable victory of his career (and, as it turned out, the last). Nicanor himself was slain and once again the forces of the Seleucid Empire were forced to back off with burnt fingers.

The Romans

For five years now, Judas Maccabeus and his brothers had been facing superior forces and winning by rapid movement and surprise and by taking advantage of Seleucid preoccupation with other rebellions and with civil wars. But good luck, and even good management, cannot be expected to continue forever. What was needed was outside help, and at that time the smaller nations of the east found their friend in the new giant of the west, the giant who, in the end, would swallow them all:

1 Maccabees 8:1 *Now Judas had heard of the fame of the Romans . . .*

Even as late as the time of Alexander the Great, Rome had been merely another barbarian tribe of the hinterland as far as the Greeks were concerned. Possibly no Jew had as much as heard of the Roman name at the time.

It wasn't until 281 B.C., in fact, that Rome suddenly impinged upon the Greek world. At that time it was the Macedonian monarchs who seemed supreme. One of them, Ptolemy II Philadelphus, ruled over Egypt and under his mild sway Jews were translating the Bible into Greek. Another, Antiochus I Soter, ruled over the Seleucid kingdom. Other Macedonians ruled Greece itself and the districts to the north. In particular, a Macedonian named Pyrrhus ruled over Epirus, a region northwest of Greece. Of all the Macedonian rulers of his day, Pyrrhus was the most capable general.

The westernmost portion of the Greek world had, as its chief representatives, a number of wealthy cities on the coast of southern Italy. These cities had been settled five to six centuries before in the days

The Roman World

when Amos, Hosea, and Isaiah preached in Israel and Judah. These cities had always had their troubles with the poorly organized tribes of the interior and now the martial city of Rome had conquered all of Italy right down to the seacoast and the Greek cities were terrified.

They called in Pyrrhus to help. Pyrrhus eagerly responded and beat the Romans in two battles. The Romans persevered, however, and in the end beat Pyrrhus and by 270 B.C. had taken over every Greek city in southern Italy.

The Greek world ought to have grown alarmed at this point and united to defeat this strangely powerful newcomer. Unfortunately for themselves, they miscalculated. The western city Carthage measured its strength against Rome in two mighty wars, and the Macedonian kingdoms may have felt the two cities to be so evenly matched as to be certain to destroy each other.

The Macedonians relaxed therefore, let Rome and Carthage deal each other mighty blows, and amused themselves by interminable battling among themselves.

For a while it seemed that the Macedonians had calculated shrewdly indeed, for both Carthage and Rome came, each in its turn, to the very edge of disaster. In the end, however, it was not a stalemate but a complete and utter Roman victory and by 200 B.C. Rome was the strongest single power in the world.

Even then, the Macedonian kingdoms might have won out if they could have combined, but the rivalries that had grown up among them in a century of warfare were too powerful to bury.

The Galatians

Rome, therefore, continued to win victories, and these are summarized in this chapter of 1 Maccabees:

> 1 Maccabees 8:2. . . . *It was told him* [Judas Maccabeus] *also of their wars . . . among the Galatians, and how they had conquered them . . .*

The Galatians (or Gauls) had moved southward into Italy and taken Rome itself in 390 B.C. when that city was yet a small power, and when the Jews were vegetating peacefully under the Persians. Rome shook itself free, but the Gauls settled in the rich valley of the Po River. What is now northern Italy came to be called "Cisalpine Gaul" (Gaul on "this side of the Alps"—"this side" from the standpoint of the Romans).

As the Romans grew stronger, the Gauls grew weaker. In 295 B.C. the Romans inflicted a devastating defeat on the Gauls and by 222 B.C. they had annexed the whole region of Cisalpine Gaul and extended their power to the Alps.

This was the more remarkable to those easterners who had been watching the Roman advance, for even while the Romans were beating back the Gauls steadily, the Macedonian kingdoms were proving helpless against barbarians of the same kind.

In 280 B.C., even as Pyrrhus was fighting Rome in Italy, bands of Gauls raided southward into Macedon and for several years absolute terror and anarchy gripped that land, and Greece to the south as well.

In 278 B.C. the Gauls crossed over into Asia Minor and devastated that region. It wasn't until 235 B.C. that they were finally defeated and tamed. They were then forced to settle down in a region in central Asia Minor which came to be called Galatia. By that time they had become civilized and had adopted the Greek culture.

The ease with which the Romans had handled their Gauls could not but be noted and admired in the east.

Spain

The Romans had won victories outside Italy, too:

> 1 Maccabees 8:3. *And what they* [the Romans] *had done in the country of Spain . . .*

Even while the Romans had been defeating the Gauls, they had been fighting the first long war with Carthage to a successful conclusion. After that war, Carthage had tried to recoup by setting up a new empire in Spain, winning control of the Mediterranean region of that wild and, at that time, barbarous country.

In 219 B.C., then, shortly after the annexation of Cisalpine Gaul by Rome, Carthage was ready for a second war. This time the Carthaginian forces were led by Hannibal, one of the very greatest generals of all time. For sixteen years the Carthaginian managed to maintain himself in Italy, winning great victories and suffering not one real defeat.

Rome held on doggedly, however, sending its armies to fight outside Italy, even while Hannibal devastated their homeland. In particular, one of the Roman generals, Scipio, fought brilliantly in Spain, defeating the Carthaginians there and, in effect, annexing the land to Rome.

Scipio then went to Africa to attack Carthage itself. Hannibal returned to face him and in a final battle at the north African town of Zama in 202 B.C. Scipio and Rome won.

Philip and Perseus

The quick summary of Roman progress continues:

1 Maccabees 8:5. *Beside this, how they* [the Romans] *had discomfited in battle Philip, and Perseus, king of the Citims . . .*

This refers to happenings after the climactic battle of Zama. Of the Macedonian kingdoms, the one nearest to Rome was that of Macedon itself (referred to here as Citims, or more properly Kittim, see page I-47). Macedon was not the vigorous imperial power it had been under Philip II and Alexander the Great. The emigration of Macedonians to the conquered lands in the south and the east, the losses in war, and the havoc of the raids by the Gauls had reduced its power. Nevertheless, it was still strong enough to maintain control over Greece.

In 220 B.C., Philip V, an energetic and capable king, came to power over Macedon. He watched as Rome locked in deadly combat with Hannibal and attempted to give Hannibal support. For this, Rome never forgave him. Once Hannibal was defeated, Rome declared war upon Philip and, in 197 B.C., inflicted a decisive defeat upon him. Macedon lost its power over Greece and had to pay Rome a large indemnity. For the rest of his life, Philip kept cautiously out of trouble.

In 179 B.C., Philip died and was succeeded by his son, Perseus. Carefully Perseus prepared for revenge against Rome. His plans, however, miscarried. His allies betrayed him and he had to face the Roman army alone. He was beaten in battle in 168 B.C., the very year in which

Antiochus IV was profaning the Temple at Jerusalem. With that defeat the Macedonian monarchy was ended and Macedon was divided into four small republics.

Eumenes

If Rome could punish, it could also reward:

> 1 Maccabees 8:6. *How also Antiochus the great king of Asia . . . was discomfited by them* [the Romans];
>
> . . . .
>
> 1 Maccabees 8:8. *And the country of India, and Media, and Lydia, . . . they took of him, and gave to king Eumenes.*

The Antiochus referred to here as the "great king of Asia" was, of course, Antiochus III, whose victories, and whose subsequent defeats by the Romans, were described earlier in this chapter (see page 47–48).

The Eumenes referred to is a king in western Asia Minor. At the time when the Jews were in Babylonian Exile, western Asia Minor made up a kingdom ruled by people known to the Greeks as Ludoi. These were the Ludim of the Bible (see page I-54) and the kingdom is known to us as Lydia. It reached a peak of prosperity and power under its king, Croesus, who reigned from 560 to 546 B.C. In 546 B.C. Lydia was conquered by Cyrus the Persian and its name disappeared from history. After the time of Alexander the Great, its people were rapidly hellenized. The Lydian language disappeared and was replaced by Greek.

In 283 B.C., when Asia Minor was loosely connected to the newly founded Seleucid Empire, a certain Macedonian viceroy named Philetaeros ruled over the city of Pergamum, in what had once been Lydia. He managed to make himself independent of the Seleucids after the death of Seleucus I Nicator and thus was founded the kingdom of Pergamum.

The nephew of Philetaeros succeeded to the throne as Eumenes I in 263 B.C. Soon after his accession he defeated Antiochus I, the second Seleucid monarch, and confirmed the independence of Pergamum. At this time the Gauls were creating havoc in Asia Minor, so that independence was a doubtful boon.

Eumenes I was succeeded by his nephew, Attalus I, however, in

241 B.C. and he managed to defeat the Gauls decisively in 235 B.C. That ended the Gallic menace and raised the prestige of Pergamum sky-high. It prospered under enlightened rule and learning was encouraged to the point where the library in Pergamum was second only to Alexandria in size and excellence. (Indeed, the jealous Ptolemies refused to export papyrus to Pergamum, thus depriving them of the material on which to copy books. The Pergamese invented a method of treating animal skins for the purpose—more permanent but also more expensive—and this gave us "parchment," a word derived from "Pergamum.")

In 197 B.C., Attalus I died and his son, Eumenes II, became king. This is the Eumenes of 1 Maccabees 8:8.

Eumenes II found himself facing Antiochus III at the height of that monarch's success, and for a while it looked as though Antiochus would retake all of Asia Minor. Eumenes II appealed to Rome, which had just beaten Philip V of Macedonia.

Rome responded and after defeating Antiochus III (with the army of Eumenes fighting alongside the Roman legions) his Asia Minor conquests were handed over to Pergamum, which now reached the peak of its power.

The writer of 1 Maccabees lists Lydia, Media, and India as being handed over to Pergamum. This is overenthusiastic of him. Lydia, representing the western half of Asia Minor, did, to be sure, make up the kingdom of Pergamum after the defeat of Antiochus. Indeed, Pergamum was almost Lydia come back to existence—but a Greek-speaking Lydia.

India and Media were, however, not given to Pergamum. They were far to the east and not even Rome could give them to anybody. Nevertheless, as the direct consequence of Antiochus' defeat, India, Media, and other eastern sections of the Seleucid Empire regained a permanent independence. If Pergamum did not gain them, the Seleucid Empire lost them.

The Grecians

And finally:

1 Maccabees 8:9. *Moreover how the Grecians had determined to come and destroy them* [the Romans];

1 Maccabees 8:10. *And that they* [the Romans] *. . . fighting with them* [the Greeks] *slew many of them, and carried away captives . . .*

To say that the Greeks had "determined to come and destroy" the Romans is to give entirely too much credit to the poor Greeks. They were in no position at the time to destroy anyone but themselves, but the writer of 1 Maccabees was living at a time when the Jews were intensely anti-Greek and this is reflected in the verses.

Actually, the crime of the Greeks was that some of their cities (united in what was called the "Achaean League") had, in the eyes of Rome, not been sufficiently active in supporting the Romans against Perseus of Macedon. The Greeks could not at that time possibly resist the power of Rome, and for Rome, attacking the Achaean League was like snatching a rattle from a baby. A thousand leading Greeks were carried away captive to Rome in 168 B.C.

Bacchides

Rome's conquests, its loyalty to its friends, its republican form of government, and its civic virtue are all described with a kind of lyrical exaggeration. Certainly there seemed some justification for the Jewish hope (at this time) in Rome.

Her defense of Pergamum against the Seleucids, and her strengthening of Pergamum at Seleucid expense, were very impressive. Surely, if Judea formed an alliance with Rome, similar benefits would befall her. (Of course, Rome supported her allies for her own reasons and, in the end, absorbed them all, enemies and allies alike, but the writer of 1 Maccabees did not have the advantage of our hindsight.)

The writer describes the emissary sent by Judas to Rome and the treaty of alliance formed with Rome, but one can only wonder if such an alliance were really formed. Perhaps it was merely reported by the forces of Judas as a kind of "war of nerves" against the Seleucids, who had ample reason to be in dread of the very name of Rome.

If the alliance was merely a propaganda weapon, it failed; and if it was real, it was a dead letter. Demetrius proceeded to move again against the rebels and Rome did nothing to help Judas.

1 Maccabees 9:1. . . . *when Demetrius heard that Nicanor and his host were slain in battle, he sent Bacchides and Alcimus into the land of Judea the second time, and with them the chief strength of his host:*

. . . .

1 Maccabees 9:3. . . . *the first month of the hundred fifty and second year* [160 B.C.] *they encamped before Jerusalem:*

The forces of Judas had themselves suffered numerous casualties in the fight against Nicanor, and in the face of a fresh army of Seleucids and Tories the spirits of many quailed. There were massive desertions and Judas found himself with only eight hundred men left.

The sensible thing to do was to retreat, but if he did that he would have been left without an army. A brave battle and an inspiring death might be better in the long run. That was the path he chose. In the battle that followed, the small band of rebels fought desperately, but the sheer weight of the enemy was insurmountable and they were virtually wiped out.

Judas Maccabeus died, with the rest, in 160 B.C., seven years after his father had sounded the trumpet call of revolt.

With the death of Judas, the Seleucids were, for the moment, triumphant, and Judea was now completely in the hands of the pro-Seleucid Jews:

1 Maccabees 9:23. *Now after the death of Judas the wicked began to put forth their heads in all the coasts of Israel, and there arose up all such as wrought iniquity.*

. . . .

1 Maccabees 9:25. *Then Bacchides chose the wicked men, and made them lords of the country.*

1 Maccabees 9:26. *And they made enquiry and search for Judas' friends, and brought them unto Bacchides, who took vengeance of them* . . .

Yet the defeat was not total. Demetrius had learned by the mistake of Antiochus and the laws against Judaism were not revived; the Temple was not profaned once more. The revolt had been a political failure, but it seemed to be a religious success.

Or was it? Could it not be that where force had failed, gradual assimilation under the guidance of a Tory high priest might succeed?

Jonathan

Judea was not to have a chance to find out, however. Two of the sons of Mattathias were dead, fallen in war against the Seleucids. Three remained, John the eldest, Simon the second, and Jonathan, the fifth and youngest.

It was Jonathan, who had already displayed talent as a leader of men, to whom the surviving rebels turned in the dark days after Judas' death, when the Seleucid general, Bacchides, controlled the country through his puppet high priest, Alcimus.

> 1 Maccabees 9:28. *For this cause all Judas' friends came together, and said unto Jonathan,*
>
> . . . .
>
> 1 Maccabees 9:30. . . . *we have chosen thee this day to be our prince and captain* . . .
>
> 1 Maccabees 9:31. *Upon this Jonathan took the governance upon him . . . and rose up instead of his brother Judas.*

The arms of the rebels were indeed feeble at this time, however. They could scarcely make head against the powerful Bacchides without help. John, the eldest brother, was sent to the Nabatean Arabs for such help and he was treacherously slain by them in 159 B.C. Only Jonathan and Simon were left now.

Fighting desperately, they led their rebel band to temporary safety across the Jordan River into the wilderness of the Transjordan:

> 1 Maccabees 9:48. *Then Jonathan and they that were with him leapt into Jordan, and swam over unto the farther bank* . . .
>
> . . . .
>
> 1 Maccabees 9:50. *Afterward returned Bacchides to Jerusalem, and repaired the strong cities in Judea* . . .

But Jonathan, safe in the Transjordan, mounted perpetual raids against Judea, and defeated or eluded all parties sent out after him. Eventually the Seleucids grew weary of endless petty fighting that drained their energies and weakened them in other more vital directions. They came to agreement with Jonathan; let him rule Judea as long as he maintained the peace of the kingdom and recognized Seleucid overlordship.

Alexander Epiphanes

This was, perhaps, an unstable situation, but it did not last long. After Demetrius I Soter had ruled, with comparative ability, for ten years, dynastic squabbles once again upset the Seleucid monarchy:

> 1 Maccabees 10:1. *In the hundred and sixtieth year* [152 B.C.] *Alexander, the son of Antiochus surnamed Epiphanes, went up and took Ptolemais* . . .

Actually, this Alexander was an impostor of obscure origin, whose real name was Balas. He pretended to be a son of Antiochus IV, and therefore a brother of the young Antiochus V Eupator whom Demetrius I had had killed.

Fortunately for himself, this Balas (known to us most commonly as Alexander Balas) had powerful support abroad. The Egyptian king, Ptolemy VI Philometer (see page 51), and the new king of Pergamum, Attalus II, who had succeeded his older brother Eumenes II in 160 B.C., both favored Alexander Balas. This was not because they believed Balas' claim to be the legitimate king, but because they were willing to do anything that would weaken their old enemy, the Seleucid Empire.

Both Pergamum and Egypt were allies of Rome, and Rome remembered now, perhaps, that Demetrius had become king without their permission (see page 68). At any rate, Rome, too, lent its support to Alexander Balas.

Demetrius was desperate. His troops might easily desert to the rising star of the impostor and he needed some reliable men to fight on his side. What about the Jews fighting under Jonathan? He had the best evidence that they were fierce fighting men and they might be bought. It was with that in mind, perhaps, that Demetrius named Jonathan to the post of governor of Judea.

With that appointment in his hand, Jonathan was able to take up residence in Jerusalem and suppress the pro-Seleucid faction which had been in power since the death of Judas eight years before.

To compete with this, Alexander Balas promptly offered Jonathan the post of high priest. This was a departure from custom. Till now the Seleucids had merely confirmed high priests who had been appointed by the Jews; this, however, was a direct Seleucid appointment. Nevertheless, Jonathan did not stand too firmly on the fine points but accepted:

> 1 Maccabees 10:21. *So in the seventh month of the hundred and sixtieth year, at the feast of the tabernacles, Jonathan put on the holy robe . . .*

Jonathan may have chosen this time of the year deliberately to take psychological advantage of a Messianic prophecy. A century before certain prophetic writings had appeared which were attributed to the earlier prophet Zechariah (see page I-664). These spoke of the ideal king receiving worship from all at the feast of the tabernacles:

> Zechariah 14:18. . . . *the Lord will smite the heathen that come not up to keep the feast of tabernacles.*

Jonathan might be well aware that the rigorously pious could not help but disapprove of a high priest who was not of the direct line of earlier high priests and who was but the appointee of a heathen king. By using Zechariah's words, he might have answered such objections in the eyes of the people generally, and he inaugurated a new high-priestly line that was to continue for over a century.

Demetrius again raised the stakes and finally granted Judea independence, adding to it Samaria and Galilee. Jonathan, however, remained with Alexander Balas. Either his resentment against Demetrius as the conqueror of Judas and the oppressor of the Jews was too great or, as is more likely, his cool estimate of the situation was that Demetrius was going to lose and his promises would not be kept.

In 150 B.C., Demetrius and Alexander Balas finally met in battle. Alexander was completely victorious and Demetrius was slain on the field of battle after a twelve-year reign. Alexander Balas ascended the throne in Antioch as Alexander Epiphanes.

Alexander Balas remembered his allies, forming a marital alliance with Egypt by marrying Cleopatra, daughter of Ptolemy VI. The two kings met with much ceremony, in Ptolemais, and Jonathan was called to the city to meet with them, too. There he was confirmed in his rule over Judea.

Demetrius II Nicator

This interval of happy-ending-for-everyone was not to continue. The only thing, it seemed, that ever continued was dynastic rivalry. The dead king, Demetrius I, had a son, another Demetrius, who was abroad in exile. He now returned, and with him was a band of Cretan mercenaries:

> 1 Maccabees 10:67. . . . *in the hundred threescore and fifth year* [147 B.C.] *came Demetrius son of Demetrius out of Crete into the land of his fathers* . . .

The civil war was renewed and the Jews were deeply involved, for the new Demetrius was completely hostile to Jonathan, who, after all, had turned against his father and had supported the usurping Alexander. The Jews, however, as in the days of Judas, withstood Demetrius' general, Apollonius, and won a resounding victory.

Ptolemy VI of Egypt, observing the new civil war, could not resist interfering. To be sure, he had placed Alexander Balas on the throne and had given him his daughter in marriage, but why be satisfied with an ally when you can have the kingdom itself?

The Egyptian monarch therefore invaded the Seleucid dominions, taking advantage of the confusion of the renewed civil wars. He passed by Judea without incident and took Antioch, making himself, for the moment, ruler of the Seleucid realm as well as of Egypt.

Alexander Balas, who was in the northern provinces at the time, dealing with a local rebellion, hastened to Antioch and the two armies met and fought in 145 B.C. Alexander Balas was defeated and his five-year reign was ended. He fled to Arabia, where he was murdered. The victor, Ptolemy VI, had been wounded in battle, however, and died soon after.

This left Demetrius the only contender remaining in the field and by default he became king as Demetrius II Nicator ("conqueror").

> 1 Maccabees 11:19. *By this means Demetrius reigned in the hundred threescore and seventh year.*

Antiochus VI

By now, however, the everlasting dynastic minuet had had deadly results. Mithridates I (see page 58) was still king of Parthia, and all the while that the Seleucid kings had been fighting useless battles in the west and growing steadily weaker, he had been expanding his own power constantly. In 147 B.C., just when Demetrius II had landed on the Seleucid shores, the Parthians took Babylonia, driving the Seleucids from an area that had been theirs for a hundred and fifty years.

The great empire which had been two thousand miles wide even as late as the time of Antiochus III had, in a mere half century, shrunk to almost nothing. It had come to include little more than the province of Syria.

Demetrius at the head of a mere nubbin of what had once been the Seleucid Empire—a nubbin, moreover, bled white by continuing warfare—found himself short on funds. Desperately he tried to economize at the expense of his army. This is certainly the most effective means of economizing from a sheer dollars-and-cents point of view since the army is almost always the greatest swallower of funds, but as many rulers both before and after the time of Demetrius II have found out, such economy is virtually suicide when the army controls the government.

A discontented army is bound to be a tempting tool in the hands of any ambitious general; especially since the old king, Alexander Balas, still had a young son in exile, one who might serve as a useful rallying device:

> 1 Maccabees 11:39. . . . *there was one Tryphon, that had been of Alexander's part afore, who, seeing that all the host murmured against Demetrius, went to Simalcue the Arabian, that brought up Antiochus the young son of Alexander,*
> 1 Maccabees 11:40. *And lay sore upon him to deliver him this young Antiochus, that he might reign in his father's stead . . .*

Meanwhile Jonathan was trying to profit once again through Seleucid troubles and offered to strike a bargain with Demetrius. Jonathan had been besieging the citadel in Jerusalem, which was still, after all this time, in Seleucid hands, and was not succeeding. He offered therefore to help Demetrius against his disaffected army, in return for Seleucid evacuation of the citadel.

Demetrius gladly accepted a contingent of three thousand tough Jewish fighters and used them to put down disorders in Antioch. He would not, however, abandon the citadel, and the outmaneuvered Jonathan waited angrily for the chance to strike back.

The chance came soon enough. Tryphon had managed to talk Simalcue into releasing his ward and, returning with him, raised the standard of revolt:

1 Maccabees 11:54. *After this returned Tryphon, and with him the young child Antiochus, who reigned, and was crowned.*

This was in 143 B.C. and the new boy king reigned as Antiochus VI Epiphanes Dionysus. He was merely a puppet, of course. The real ruler was Tryphon.

This was Jonathan's chance. He promptly transferred his support to the young Antiochus.

Lacedemonians

Apparently Jonathan during this period strove further to strengthen his appearance by judicious alliances abroad. The writer of 1 Maccabees chooses to describe two such alliances in detail, but out of considerations of prestige only, for neither alliance ever helped Jonathan. The first was a renewal of the alliance with Rome, which (if it existed at all) had been ineffective so far and continued ineffective.

The other was still more useless:

1 Maccabees 12:2. *He [Jonathan] sent letters also to the Lacedemonians . . .*

The Lacedemonians are the people living in Lacedemon, a region more commonly known to us as Sparta. They are therefore the Spartans.

Sparta, a city in southern Greece, had had a great history. In the time of Nebuchadnezzar and the Jewish Exile in Babylon, Sparta had been the most powerful of the Greek cities and it maintained this position for two additional centuries. Together with Athens, Sparta had defeated the Persian invasion under Xerxes (Ahasuerus) in 479 B.C.

Sparta

Then, after a long war with Athens, Sparta emerged victorious in 404 B.C. and for thirty years controlled Greece.

In 371 B.C., however, the Spartans had been defeated by the army of the Greek city of Thebes and, at one blow, fell from power and never regained it.

Sparta retired into sulky isolation. They refused to join the armies of Alexander the Great in his conquest of Persia (the only mainland Greeks to refuse) for they insisted that only Spartans could lead such an army. They were defeated on several occasions by Macedonian armies thereafter and, by the time of the Maccabees, Sparta had been reduced to a complete nonentity. Her alliance was worth nothing except, perhaps, for the glow cast about her by the glamour of her name and past history.

The basis of this alliance between Jews and Spartans was made a matter of family relationship. The writer of 1 Maccabees quotes letters that were supposed to have passed between the two peoples a century and a half before. These were quoted as saying:

> 1 Maccabees 12:21. *It is found in writing, that the Lacedemonians and Jews are brethren, and that they are of the stock of Abraham . . .*

This is an odd tradition that could only have been inspired to encourage a political marriage of convenience. No one takes it seriously, even though some scholars now maintain that Hebrew and Greek civilizations may have had some strands of origin in common.

Tryphon

But Tryphon wearied of the indirection of possessing power under the cover of the boy Antiochus VI and decided he would prefer the role of king, undisguised:

> 1 Maccabees 12:39. *Now Tryphon went about to get the kingdom of Asia, and to kill Antiochus the king, that he might set the crown upon his own head.*

This, he feared, might alienate his strongest ally, Jonathan. In order to prevent that, he maneuvered the Jewish leader into a trap, inviting him to come to Ptolemais with a small escort. For once, Jonathan's shrewdness deserted him and he accepted the invitation.

> 1 Maccabees 12:48. *Now as soon as Jonathan entered into Ptolemais, they of Ptolemais shut the gates, and took him . . .*

With that done, Tryphon felt that there would be sufficient confusion and uncertainty in Judea to make invasion of the land easy. In the course of this invasion, he rid himself finally of his two encumbrances:

> 1 Maccabees 13:23. *And when he came near to Bascama, he slew Jonathan, who was buried there.*
>
> . . . .
>
> 1 Maccabees 13:31. *Now Tryphon dealt deceitfully with the young king Antiochus, and slew him.*
>
> 1 Maccabees 13:32. *And he reigned in his stead, and crowned himself king of Asia . . .*

This was in 142 B.C. Jonathan had led the Jewish forces for eighteen years with skill and ability and would be better known today if his career had not been overshadowed by the shorter but more glamorous one of his older brother, Judas.

Simon

But even now, one son of Mattathias was left alive; Simon, the second oldest. He was quickly elected the new leader:

1 Maccabees 13:8. *And they* [the people] *answered with a loud voice, saying, Thou* [Simon] *shalt be our leader instead of Judas and Jonathan thy brother.*

Simon attempted to ransom Jonathan but failed and when it was certain that Jonathan had been killed, he obtained the buried body and reburied him in Modein, the city where the Jewish revolt had broken out a quarter century before.

Simon prepared himself for renewed war:

1 Maccabees 13:33. *Then Simon built up the strong holds in Judea, and fenced them about . . . and laid up victuals therein.*

Furthermore, Simon now approached Demetrius II Nicator, who, all during the period of time when first Antiochus VI and then Tryphon had called themselves kings, had maintained an army and had insistently held on to his own claim. In return for Simon's offer of help, Demetrius now finally granted Judea formal independence:

1 Maccabees 13:41. *Thus the yoke of the heathen was taken away from Israel in the hundred and seventieth year* [142 B.C.].
1 Maccabees 13:42. *Then the people of Israel began to write in their instruments and contracts, In the first year of Simon the high priest, the governor and leader of the Jews.*

Independence was thus won a quarter century after the beginning of the revolt. The independence was symbolized by altering the system of dates. The year 142 B.C., which was Year 170 of the Seleucid era, became Year 1 of the "Era of the Maccabees."

Simon was religious and military leader of the Jews, having succeeded his brother as high priest and general. He did not call himself king, however. Perhaps he felt that, not being of the Davidic line, he could not be a true king of the Jews.

Soon after the gaining of their independence, the Jews successfully completed their long siege of the citadel in Jerusalem with its Seleucid garrison. The garrison, facing starvation, surrendered:

> 1 Maccabees 13:50. . . . *and when he* [Simon] *had put them* [the garrison] *out from thence, he cleansed the tower from pollutions:*
>
> 1 Maccabees 13:51. *And entered into it the three and twentieth day of the second month, in the hundred seventy and first year* [141 B.C.] . . .

And for the first time since Nebuchadnezzar's destruction of Jerusalem 445 years before, the land of Judah was completely free and the foot of no foreign soldier was to be found in Jerusalem. That freedom, alas, was to last no more than eighty years and was not to remain unbroken even in that short period.

Arsaces

Demetrius, having secured Jewish aid against Tryphon, attempted to strengthen himself in the east as well in preparation for the final showdown with the usurping general:

> 1 Maccabees 14:2. *But when Arsaces, the king of Persia and Media, heard that Demetrius was entered within his borders, he sent one of his princes* . . .
>
> 1 Maccabees 14:3. *Who went and smote the host of Demetrius, and took him, and brought him to Arsaces* . . .

Almost all the kings of Parthia (referred to here as Persia and Media) bore the throne-name of Arsaces, so that the entire dynasty is referred to as the Arsacids. The king who fought against Demetrius was the same Mithridates I who had come to the throne in the time of Antiochus IV and who was now approaching the end of his long reign of more than thirty years. His throne name was Arsaces V Epiphanes.

In 147 B.C., Mithridates I had taken Babylonia from the Seleucids and now, in 139 B.C., he capped his career by taking prisoner the

Seleucid monarch himself, the great-grandson of Antiochus the Great. Mithridates treated Demetrius kindly, however, and even gave him his sister's hand in marriage.

And meanwhile Simon ruled in peace over Judea and the power was made hereditary in his descendants.

Antiochus VII Sidetes

The imprisoned Demetrius had, abroad, a younger brother, Antiochus, who was now to make the attempt to seize the kingdom. He confirmed the independence of the Jewish state to avoid trouble in that direction, and then invaded the land:

> 1 Maccabees 15:10. *In the hundred threescore and fourteenth year* [138 b.c.] *went Antiochus into the land of his fathers: at which time all the forces came together unto him, so that few were left with Tryphon.*

Tryphon was eventually forced to flee the land and Antiochus was accepted as monarch, ruling as Antiochus VII Euergetes, although he is far better known as Antiochus VII Sidetes. The surname "Sidetes" is derived from the fact that he was brought up in the town of Side in southern Asia Minor.

Antiochus VII was the last vigorous monarch of the Seleucid line. Having gained the throne, he visualized the restoration of his kingdom to its former glories and broke with Simon. Once again (and for the last time) Judea found itself facing the threat of Seleucid invasion.

John Hyrcanus I

But Simon was growing old and was eager to transfer the responsibilities of government to younger men. He had three stalwart sons: Judas, John, and Mattathias:

> 1 Maccabees 16:2. *Wherefore Simon called his two eldest sons, Judas and John, and said unto them . . .*
> 1 Maccabees 16:3. *. . . I am old . . . be ye instead of me . . . and go and fight for our nation . . .*

Unfortunately, Simon had also a son-in-law, Ptolemy, who coveted power for himself. He therefore invited his father-in-law and brothers-in-law to a banquet.

1 Maccabees 16:14. . . . *in the hundred threescore and seventeenth year* [134 B.C.] . . .

Simon, Judas, and Mattathias came and, after they had drunk enough to be harmless, Ptolemy had them disarmed and murdered. Thus died Simon, the last of the five sons of Mattathias the priest, eight years after he had assumed the rule and thirty-three years after the beginning of the Jewish rebellion.

With the death of Simon, the Book of 1 Maccabees comes to an end. It is worth while, however, to add a short epilogue.

For a time it seemed that the early years of the rebellion had returned. Simon's remaining son, John (better known as John Hyrcanus), took to the hills with a guerrilla band to fight Ptolemy, who played the role of the Jewish Tories of the previous generation and called in Antiochus VII.

In 133 B.C. Antiochus invaded Judea and, after a prolonged siege, took Jerusalem. He accepted a large tribute, however, and left the land.

Then in 130 B.C., Antiochus VII, elated by his successes, turned to the east. Perhaps he could still win back the eastern provinces. The formidable Parthian king, Mithradates I, had died in 138 B.C. and had been succeeded by Phraates II (also called Arsaces VI Euergetes) and it may be that Antiochus felt the new king would be less vigorous than the old.

If so, he miscalculated. In 129 B.C. the Parthians won a great victory over Antiochus, who was killed. His brother, Demetrius II, was then released from Parthian imprisonment (that had endured ten years) and became the Seleucid king again. He remained so until 125 B.C., when he died and was succeeded by his son, Antiochus VIII.

However, with Antiochus VII had died every spark of Seleucid vigor. The kingdom was just a shadow now, destined to drag on in inglorious existence for another half century, but of no account whatever in international affairs.

Judea could ignore it and, under the rule of John Hyrcanus, it expanded its territories and entered into a half-century period of prosperity and glory. It was John Hyrcanus who felt himself strong enough to force the Idumeans to accept Judaism. He reigned till 104 B.C. and

his son succeeded and, finally, found the dynasty to be well enough
established to deserve the title of king.

For the first time since the destruction of the First Temple nearly
five centuries before, the Jews had a king—but not, of course, of the
line of David.

4. 2 MACCABEES

Jason of Cyrene

The second Book of Maccabees, written perhaps a century later than the first, is not a continuation of the first, but is rather a parallel history covering only the period to the death of Judas Maccabeus. Whereas 1 Maccabees is primarily secular in character, 2 Maccabees centers to a much greater extent on the story of the high-priestly factions and is primarily interested in religion.

It declares itself to be the abridgement of a much larger work:

> 2 Maccabees 2:23. *All these things, I say, being declared by Jason of Cyrene in five books, we will assay to abridge in one volume.*

Cyrene was a city on the north African coast about five hundred miles west of the Nile. It was founded by Greek colonists in 631 B.C. when Josiah ruled in Judah. It was at Cyrene that Pharaoh-hophra's soldiers rebelled and declared Aahmes to be their king (see page I-580). It was taken by Alexander the Great in 331 B.C. and it became part of Ptolemaic Egypt. Cyrene was second only to Alexandria as a Jewish center in Egypt.

Jason is, of course, a Greek name, but in the Greek period it was not unusual for Jews to adopt Greek names that were close to the Hebrew originals. Many a Joshua called himself Jason.

The original history of Jason of Cyrene is, unfortunately, lost. It was written in Greek and so was the abridgement we call 2 Maccabees.

The abridger begins by quoting a pair of letters that have nothing

Palestine Under the Maccabees

really to do with the subject matter of the book, but urge the Jews in Egypt to keep the new feast of Hanukkah, even though it was not part of the Mosaic commandments. Since the feast commemorated events in Judea that may have seemed beyond the horizon to the Egyptian Jews, there might well have been a lack of motivation among the latter to celebrate. There would, instead, have been the usual religious conservatism against all innovations.

The two letters are dated:

2 Maccabees 1:7. *What time as Demetrius reigned, in the hundred threescore and ninth year* [143 B.C.], *we the Jews wrote unto you in the extremity of trouble that came upon us in those years* . . .

. . . .

2 Maccabees 1:10. *In the hundred fourscore and eighth year* [124 B.C.], *the people that were at Jerusalem . . . sent greeting and health unto Aristobulus, king Ptolemeus' master* . . .

The earlier letter was sent in the time of Demetrius II, just about the time that Jonathan was captured and killed by the usurper Tryphon (see page 85), one of the dark moments of the Jewish rebellion.

By the time the second letter was sent, Demetrius had just died and his young son, Antiochus VIII, was on a powerless throne. John Hyrcanus I was ruling in peace in Jerusalem.

On the Egyptian throne was Ptolemy VII "Physcon" (see page 51). He had reigned first with his older brother, Ptolemy VI, and then alone, from 170 B.C. to 116 B.C., the longest reign in Ptolemaic history. Aristobulus is apparently a learned Jew who was one of the scholars patronized by Ptolemy and therefore considered Ptolemy's teacher (or "master").

Naphthar

The writer of 2 Maccabees, in quoting the letter to Aristobulus, stresses the continuity of Jewish ritual. The letter seeks to prove that it was unbroken by the Exile into Babylonia. (The letter speaks of Babylonia, erroneously, as Persia.)

Thus, the letter states that at the time of the Exile, some of the priests preserved the fire of the altar in the hollow of a dry cistern. A century and a half later, when Nehemiah was in Jerusalem, the fire was recovered:

> 2 Maccabees 1:20. . . . *Neemias* [Nehemiah] . . . *did send of the posterity of those priests that had hid . . . the fire: but . . . they found no fire, but thick water . . .*

The "thick water" (that is, a viscous fluid) was brought up, and used to help light a strong fire.

> 2 Maccabees 1:36. *And Neemias called this thing Nephthar, which is as much as to say, a cleansing . . .*

Naphthar or, as we would say, naphtha is a word that can be traced back to the Persian "naft" and further back still to the Babylonian "naptu." It is not surprising that Nehemiah, who had lived at the Persian court, should use a Persian word for a substance that was unfamiliar to the Jews.

Naphtha is a viscous organic fluid which is inflammable. It is an oil that issues forth from the rocks and its modern name is "petroleum" (from Latin words meaning "rock oil"). The Middle East is one of the great reservoirs of petroleum and even in ancient times there were places where petroleum seeped out to the surface. Such seepages, if set on fire, could give rise to "eternal flames," which would be of important religious significance to many of the ancients. This was particularly true in Persia, where such seepages were known and where fire was, in any case, worshipped as a manifestation of Ahura Mazda, lord of light (see page I-409).

Thus, when Nehemiah reported the find to the Persian monarch:

> 2 Maccabees 1:34. . . . *the king, inclosing the place, made it holy . . .*

It is doubtful that any historical value at all can be placed on this legend, but it does seem that the writer must be at least aware of the uses of natural naphtha seepage. And the passage is interesting as an early reference to petroleum.

Judaism

Having completed his letter-quoting, the writer then goes on to introduce his history concerning:

2 Maccabees 2:21. . . . *those that behaved themselves manfully to their honour for Judaism . . .*

This is the first known use of the term Judaism.

Onias

The historical section of 2 Maccabees begins with the picture of peace and quiet before the coming of Antiochus IV:

2 Maccabees 3:1. . . . *the holy city [Jerusalem] was inhabited with all peace, and the laws were kept very well, because of the godliness of Onias the high priest . . .*

Here is a reference to the last of the legitimate high priests, stretching in an unbroken line from Zadok, who served under Solomon when the First Temple was built (see page I-322). The continuity had been maintained even during the Babylonian Exile, and Zadokite high priests were in charge when the Second Temple was constructed.

In the Book of Nehemiah, the line of high priests is carried down to Jaddua:

Nehemiah 12:11. *And Joiada begat Jonathan, and Jonathan begat Jaddua.*

From passages in the histories of Josephus, the first-century Jewish historian, it is thought that this Jaddua was high priest at the time that Alexander the Great passed through Judea. It was Jaddua who, according to legend, confronted Alexander in his high-priestly regalia (see page 39).

Jaddua was high priest from about 350 B.C. to 300 B.C. Following him, according to the information given by Josephus, was Onias I, who held the office from 300 B.C. to 280 B.C. It was in his time that Ptolemy I took Jerusalem and began the century-long domination of Ptolemaic Egypt over Judea. He is also the Onias who, according to the dubious story in 1 Maccabees, first formed an alliance with Sparta (see page 83).

In the letter quoted there as having been written to Sparta in Maccabean times, it is stated:

1 Maccabees 12:7. *There were letters sent in times past unto Onias the high priest from Darius, who reigned then among you . . .*

(Of course, no Darius ever reigned over the Spartans. Elsewhere in the chapter the Spartan king is referred to as Areus. He reigned from 309 to 265 B.C.)

Onias I was succeeded by a son, Simon I, by another son, Eleazar, and about 276 B.C. by a brother, Manasseh. Then Onias II, a son of Simon I, became high priest in 250 B.C. It may have been under Onias II that the Greek translation of the Bible, the Septuagint, was produced in Egypt.

Onias II was eventually succeeded by his son, Simon II, who was mentioned by Jesus, son of Sirach (see page I-516), with great approval:

> Ecclesiasticus 50:1. *Simon the high priest, the son of Onias, who in his life repaired the house again, and in his days fortified the temple . . .*

Simon II, also called "Simon the Just," was high priest from about 219 B.C. to 196 B.C. It was in his time that Antiochus III the Great wrested Judea from the Ptolemies. The Jews did not participate in this war and Antiochus III left them in peace.

In 196 B.C. the son of Simon the Just, Onias III, succeeded to the office of high priest. He too is depicted as pious and holy, wedded to the conservative doctrines of Judaism. It is Onias III who is referred to in 2 Maccabees 3:1.

Seleucus

The felicity of the period is perhaps exaggerated by the historian in order to make a dramatic contrast with the horrors to follow. Even the Seleucid monarch himself is depicted as patronizing the Jewish rites:

> 2 Maccabees 3:3. . . . *Seleucus king of Asia of his own revenues bare all the costs belonging to the service of the sacrifices.*

The Seleucus here referred to is Seleucus IV Philopater, elder son of Antiochus the Great, who succeeded to the throne in 187 B.C. His generosity to the Temple seems most strange, for the Seleucid monarchy was virtually bankrupt at this time. The defeat of Antiochus III by Rome, just a few years before, had placed the load of a back-breaking indemnity upon the land. It could be paid only by rifling the various temples of their hoarded wealth. Antiochus III had died in a popular uprising when he attempted such rifling and his son was in no position to pay to a Temple when circumstances were much more likely to force him to steal from one.

Indeed, the book goes on at once to point out that this was actually the case.

Simon

As often happens, external trouble comes upon a land because internal trouble invites it:

> 2 Maccabees 3:4. . . . one Simon . . . , who was made governor of the temple, fell out with the high priest about disorder in the city.

During post-Exilic days, the high priest had been both the religious and the civil head of Judea, but this sound policy came to an end during the time of Onias II. This was when Judea was still under the control of Egypt and the strong king, Ptolemy III Euergetes, was on the throne.

For some reason Onias II refused to pay the annual tax laid upon the Temple. This was unwise and would have led to serious troubles had not Onias' nephew, Joseph, taken action. He persuaded Onias II to let him go to Egypt and there he managed to placate Ptolemy III. He also managed to win for himself the post of "governor of the temple." In other words, the prerogatives of Onias II were henceforth restricted to matters of religion and his civil powers were given to Joseph.

Now there were two lines of Zadokite officials in Jerusalem—a religious line and a civil line. Onias III was of the religious line and Simon (the son of Joseph) was of the civil line.

Naturally, when powers formally confined to one official come to be shared by two there are constant quarrels over jurisdiction. The fact that Onias III and Simon were second cousins did not make the quarrels less bitter.

In such quarrels, one or the other of the disputants is bound to appeal to some outside power. This Simon did. He reported to the Seleucid governor of the district that the Temple was filled with wealth that was being withheld from the king.

Seleucus IV, who needed money badly, sent an official named Heliodorus to investigate the matter.

The attempt of Heliodorus to investigate the Temple is described in the book as having been thwarted by supernatural means. Afterward, Heliodorus grew friendly with Onias. It is possible, however, if history is viewed cynically, to suppose that Onias bribed Heliodorus to "lay off" and that Heliodorus conceived the idea of gaining power for himself with, perhaps, the financial help of the Temple at Jerusalem.

In 175 B.C., Heliodorus assassinated Seleucus IV. He then made some sort of attempt to make himself king but Seleucus' younger brother, Antiochus, was returning from Roman captivity (see page 48) and he seized the throne as Antiochus IV Epiphanes.

Jason the brother of Onias

If Antiochus IV knew of (or suspected) any intrigue between the high priest and his brother's assassin, he would naturally have harsh feelings toward the former. As for Onias III, fearing reprisal, he would be bound to cast about for help to Egypt, a land with which Antiochus IV intended to go to war.

Antiochus IV could scarcely be expected to march against Egypt, leaving an enemy such as Onias III in his rear to rouse, perhaps, a Jewish rebellion that would negate any Egyptian victories he might gain.

Again, rivalries within the family of the high priest paved the way for infringing upon Jewish prerogatives. Onias had a brother, Joshua, who coveted the office of high priest. Joshua was a Hellenizer rather than a conservative and showed it by adopting the Greek name of Jason.

> 2 Maccabees 4:7. . . . when Antiochus . . . took the kingdom, Jason the brother of Onias laboured underhand to be high priest,
> 2 Maccabees 4:8. Promising unto the king . . . three hundred and threescore talents of silver, and of another revenue eighty talents:
> 2 Maccabees 4:9. Beside this, he promised to assign an hundred and fifty more, if he might have licence to set him up a place for exercise . . .

The desire to be high priest was not only a matter of honor and prestige. Whoever was high priest controlled the revenues of the Temple, which were considerable, and was therefore (if he were not scrupulously honest) on the highroad to wealth. Jason obviously planned to enrich himself through graft, particularly since he maneuvered to maintain what we would today call the "gymnasium concession" for himself as well. The aristocratic youth of Judea, eager to participate in the Greek way of life, would pay for the privilege and a good part of the money would stick to Jason's hands.

For all this, Jason was willing to share some of the loot with Antiochus IV for he needed the king's word to be made high priest. Since Antiochus IV needed money badly for his projected Egyptian war, the arrangement with Jason was made.

Now Antiochus could march off into Egypt.

Menelaus

When it came time to remit an installment of the promised payment to Antiochus IV, Jason sent an emissary:

> 2 Maccabees 4:23. . . . *Jason sent Menelaus, the aforesaid Simon's brother, to bear the money unto the king . . .*

It was a case of brothers all around. A few years before, Simon had coveted the post held by Onais III and had therefore intrigued with Seleucus IV. Now the brother of Simon coveted the post held by Jason, the brother of Onias III, and intrigued with Antiochus IV, the brother of Seleucus IV.

Simon's brother was named Onias but he took the Greek name of Menelaus, and once Jason was so incautious as to give him entry to Antiochus, Menelaus seized the chance at once. He offered Antiochus three hundred talents more than Jason had agreed to pay. This was fine as far as Antiochus IV was concerned. He was willing to sell the high priesthood to the highest bidder at any time. Jason was forced to flee across the Jordan and Menelaus became high priest.

Daphne

Meanwhile, Onias III, who was looked upon by all conservative Jews as the only legitimate high priest, was living in semi-imprisonment in Antioch. When the news of Menelaus' open-faced thievery reached Onias (Menelaus was reported to have used certain gold vessels of the Temple as bribes to Seleucid officials), the old high priest denounced the usurper:

> 2 Maccabees 4:33. . . . *Onias . . . reproved him* [Menelaus], *and withdrew himself into a sanctuary at Daphne, that lieth by Antiochia.*

Daphne was a suburb of Antioch, about five miles away, and undoubtedly Onias made use of a Greek temple, from which it would have been sacrilege, in Greek eyes, to remove him.

Menelaus, however, persuaded the Seleucid commander in the district (with bribes perhaps) to induce Onias to leave the sanctuary, by giving oath for his safety. Once Onias was out of the Temple, he was promptly murdered. This was in 170 B.C.

The murder at once became a *cause célèbre*. The Jews were on the verge of rebellion at this slaughter of the last legitimate high priest. Even many Greeks were horrified at the sacrilege committed against their own temple. Antiochus IV, returning from the suppression of a rebellion in part of his dominion in Asia Minor, was forced to quiet the populace by executing the officer who had committed the deed.

Scholars are quite certain that it is Onias III to whom the writer of the Book of Daniel refers in his passage about a Messiah, or "anointed one" (see page I-613); that is, a high priest:

> Daniel 9:26. *And after threescore and two weeks shall Messiah be cut off . . .*

After that, Antiochus IV made a second foray into Egypt, achieved complete success but was driven out by a Roman ultimatum (see page 52). He then turned against Jerusalem, which had been the scene of disorders between the factions of Jason and Menelaus, took the city, pillaged the Temple, and killed many Jews who resisted, all with the help and the official backing of Menelaus.

Eleazar

The Temple was then profaned and rededicated to Zeus, and Judaism was outlawed. The writer of 2 Maccabees gives details lacking in

1 Maccabees concerning the martyrdom of conservative Jews who would not give up their religious customs even under torture.

Since such stories are not told in the more reliable 1 Maccabees, one might wonder if they are not merely atrocity stories made up after the fact. However, the history of Nazi Germany has proved to all of us that atrocity stories are sometimes simple truth, and understatements at that.

In any case, the stories, whether strictly true or propaganda inventions, are told in grisly detail as edifying examples of loyalty to the death. These are the first martyr-tales in the Judeo-Christian tradition and formed a precedent for the many later such tales that formed so large a part of early Christian literature.

An example is that of Eleazar:

2 Maccabees 6:18. *Eleazar, one of the principal scribes, an aged man, . . . was constrained to . . . eat swine's flesh.*

2 Maccabees 6:19. *But he, choosing rather to die gloriously, . . . spit it forth, and came of his own accord to the torment.*

2 Maccabees 6:20. *As it behoved them to come, that are resolute to stand out against such things . . .*

Eleazar is described as dying on the rack, even though every attempt was made to persuade him to go through a nominal acquiescence to paganism. An even more gruesome tale is told of the torture and death of a woman and her seven sons.

Alcimus

Thereafter the tale passes on to the rebellion of the Jews under the leadership of Judas Maccabeus. The same story told in 1 Maccabees is repeated, though, it is generally thought, less reliably.

The deaths of the villains of the piece are given in considerable (but implausible) detail. Thus, Antiochus IV is described as dying in lingering torments from a loathsome disease, and as attempting to make up for his evils in order to recover—even vowing to become a Jew.

Menelaus was executed by the Seleucids themselves in the reign of Antiochus V Eupator. He was left to rot unburied (a supremely terrible fate in the eyes of the Jews of the time).

When Demetrius I Soter became king he was approached by still another representative of the Zadokite line:

> 2 Maccabees 14:3. *Now one Alcimus, who had been high priest, and had defiled himself wilfully in the times of their mingling with the Gentiles, . . .*
> 2 Maccabees 14:4. *Came to king Demetrius in the hundred and one and fiftieth year* [161 B.C.] . . .

Alcimus was accepted as high priest by Demetrius and led invasions into Judea, in the course of one of which there took place the battle in which Judas Maccabeus was killed.

For a while Alcimus ruled over Jerusalem as a Seleucid puppet. His end is not told in 2 Maccabees, which ends with Judas' last victory over Nicanor. It is, however, described in 1 Maccabees:

> 1 Maccabees 9:54. . . . *in the hundred fifty and third year* [159 B.C.], . . . *Alcimus commanded that the wall of the inner court of the sanctuary should be pulled down . . .*
> 1 Maccabees 9:55. *And as he began to pull down, even at that time was Alcimus plagued . . .*
> 1 Maccabees 9:56. *So Alcimus died at that time with great torment.*

That was the end of the Zadokites, if Alcimus was indeed one. Seven years later, Jonathan, brother of Judas Maccabeus, was made high priest (see page 80) and a new line, non-Zadokite in origin, was initiated.

3 Maccabees

There are other books dealing with the general period of the Maccabees that have never been considered canonical by any important group and are therefore not included even in the Apocrypha.

The Book of 3 Maccabees, the best known of these, is a work of fiction written probably by an Alexandrian Jew toward the end of the first century B.C., or even later, when Roman rule was becoming increasingly oppressive.

Just as the Book of Esther was written in Seleucid times to encourage Jews of that period with tales of miraculous rescues under a previous oppressor, so 3 Maccabees was written in Roman times for the same purpose through use of the same literary device.

The time of the incidents told in the book actually falls a generation before the Maccabean revolt and the Maccabees themselves play no part in it.

The book opens in the last decades of Ptolemaic control of Judea. Ptolemy IV Philometer of Egypt and Antiochus III of the Seleucid Empire are at war. Eventually Antiochus is to be the victor, but the book opens at a stage where Ptolemy has just won a victory in southern Judea (at Raphia, near Gaza), in 217 B.C.

Flushed with victory, Ptolemy enters Jerusalem and conceives a desire to enter the sanctuary of the Temple, where only the high priest might enter. (In later years, the Roman general, Pompey, entered the sanctuary and that incident might have helped inspire this story.) Ptolemy IV, unlike Pompey, is thwarted by the opposition of the high priest and the people and, according to the story, by divine intervention as well.

Ptolemy IV decides to seek revenge by having all the Jews of Alexandria killed. He plans to shut them into the hippodrome and have them trampled by five hundred elephants who are first maddened with wine. On three successive days, this plan is prevented by divine intervention and, eventually, angels turn the elephants back on the Egyptian army.

At once Ptolemy IV turns from persecuting the Jews to befriending them (as Ahasuerus does in the Book of Esther) and all ends in happiness and triumph.

As for 4 Maccabees, written about the same time as 3 Maccabees, that is essentially a sermon on the value of martyrdom. The martyr atones for the sins of others and achieves eternal blessedness in heaven. The author uses as his examples the cases of Eleazar and of the woman and her seven sons, which were described in 2 Maccabees.

Finally, 5 Maccabees is a sober history of the Maccabean period from beginning to end. However, its first part is based on 1 and 2 Maccabees and its remainder is based on Josephus, so it adds nothing to what is known from other sources.

5. MATTHEW

THE NEW TESTAMENT · THE GOSPEL ACCORDING TO ST. MATTHEW ·
MATTHEW · JESUS CHRIST · DAVID · RACHAB · THE WIFE OF URIAS ·
ZOROBABEL · THE HOLY GHOST · MARY · HEROD · WISE MEN FROM THE
EAST · KING OF THE JEWS · THE STAR · BETHLEHEM · THE CHILDREN . . .
IN BETHLEHEM · EGYPT · ARCHELAUS · NAZARETH · JOHN THE BAPTIST ·
ELIJAH · PHARISEES AND SADDUCEES · THE SON · SATAN · HERODIAS ·
ZABULON AND NEPHTHALIM · THE CARPENTER'S SON · JESUS' BRETHREN ·
CAPERNAUM · SIMON · JAMES · DECAPOLIS · THE LAW · PUBLICANS
· PATERNOSTER · MAMMON · THE DOGS · THE CENTURION · THE SON OF MAN
· GERGESENES · THE TWELVE APOSTLES · SIMON THE CANAANITE · JUDAS
ISCARIOT · SAMARITANS · THE DISCIPLES OF JOHN · THE PHARISEES · THE
SABBATH · JESUS' MOTHER AND BRETHREN · PARABLES · THE DAUGHTER OF
HERODIAS · BETHSAIDA · CAESAREA PHILIPPI · PETER · MOSES AND ELIAS ·
JAMES AND JOHN · THE MOUNT OF OLIVES · HOSANNA · THE TEMPLE · THE
SON OF DAVID · THE HERODIANS · ZACHARIAS SON OF BARACHIAS · THE
ABOMINATION OF DESOLATION · TALENT · CAIAPHAS · JUDAS ISCARIOT ·
GETHSEMANE · THE JUDAS KISS · CHRIST · PETER · PONTIUS PILATE · THE
POTTER'S FIELD · BARABBAS · PILATE AND PILATE'S WIFE · CRUCIFIXION ·
CYRENE · GOLGOTHA · VINEGAR AND GALL · ELI, ELI · JOSEPH OF ARIMATHEA
· THE FIRST DAY OF THE WEEK · MARY MAGDALENE

The New Testament

The books considered part of the Biblical canon by the Jews are
thirty-nine in number, and all have been considered in the first volume
of this book.

The central theme of the Bible, in Jewish eyes, is the contract or
covenant entered into between God and the Jewish people. The first
mention of this covenant is God's promise to give Canaan to the
descendants of Abraham.

> Genesis 15:18. *In the same day the Lord made a covenant with*
> *Abram [Abraham], saying, Unto thy seed have I given this land,*
> *from the river of Egypt unto the great river, the river Euphrates . . .*

The Dominions of Herod the Great

This promise was repeated several times in Genesis, and clearly there had to be some return made by Abraham and his descendants. This return was made through the Israelites' acceptance of the Law as pronounced at Mount Sinai, according to the Biblical tradition, and incorporated into the first five books of the Bible. The covenant was therefore specifically mentioned again when the Israelites were at Mount Sinai.

Exodus 34:27. *And the Lord said unto Moses, Write thou these words: for after the tenor of these words I have made a covenant with thee and with Israel.*

After the Israelites entered and occupied the "Promised Land," the covenant continued to hold. They were to remain God's special charge, a people "peculiar" to Him, and their stay in the land was to continue in peace and security, as long as they adhered to the Law and, therefore, to their end of the bargain. When Israel fell away from the Law, the people received the punishment due those who broke a solemn contract. Then, when the people repented and returned to the Law, they were always forgiven. This cycle of apostasy and punishment, repentance and forgiveness, is the constant theme of the Book of Judges (see page I-232).

Through the Biblical account of the centuries that follow the period of the judges, the covenant is broken on numerous occasions by the Israelites. Indeed, it would seem to have been adhered to by only a small, and often persecuted, minority until after the return from Babylonian Exile.

Thus, some of the pre-Exilic prophets conceived of God as growing weary of a covenant that seemed never to be kept. The prophet Hosea names his third son Lo-ammi ("not my people"), stating this to have been at God's direction:

Hosea 1:9. *Then said God, Call his name Lo-ammi: for ye are not my people, and I will not be your God.*

Again, in the eschatological visions recorded in the Book of Jeremiah, the prophet looks forward to a triumphant day when God would make a new start, so to speak, with his people; wipe the slate clean and begin again:

Jeremiah 31:31. *Behold, the days come, saith the Lord, that I will make a new covenant with the house of Israel, and with the house of Judah . . .*

The followers of Jesus came early to believe that in the teachings of Jesus was to be found exactly this new covenant; a new contract between God and man, replacing the old one with Israel that dated back to Sinai and even beyond that to Abraham.

Thus, in the Epistle to the Hebrews (traditionally written by the Apostle Paul), this is specifically stated.

Hebrews 8:6. . . . *he [Jesus] is the mediator of a better covenant, which was established upon better promises.*

The writer then goes on to quote from Jeremiah to show that the coming of such a new and better covenant was predicted.

The word "testament" is used in the Bible as a synonym for "covenant." Thus Jesus himself, shortly before his trial and conviction, is quoted as referring to a new covenant to which his death is to bear witness:

Matthew 26:27. *And he took the cup, and gave thanks, and gave it to them, saying, Drink ye all of it;*
Matthew 26:28. *For this is my blood of the new testament . . .*

(The adjective "new" was not present in the earliest versions but seems to have been added later to emphasize the fresh turn taken in the scheme of things with the advent of Jesus. The Revised Standard Version keeps the older word for testament and omits the adjective, making the passage read, "For this is my blood of the covenant," a reading with which the Jerusalem Bible agrees.)

The Jewish Scriptures, dealing with the older covenant, can therefore be referred to as the "Old Testament." The books written about Jesus and his earliest disciples are called the "New Testament."

The Christian versions of the Bible include both Old and New Testaments. Christians consider them equally inspired, but with the New Testament representing the fulfillment and climactic completion of the Old. The Jews, on the other hand, adhere to the original covenant only and to them the Old Testament is the whole of the Bible.

The Gospel According to St. Matthew

The New Testament opens with four different biographies of Jesus by, according to tradition, Matthew, Mark, Luke, and John, in that order. Each of these biographies is called a "gospel" and the second is specifically so named:

> Mark 1:1. *The beginning of the gospel of Jesus Christ, the Son of God . . .*

The word gospel is from the Anglo-Saxon "god spell" meaning "good news." In other words, the term refers not so much to the biography of Jesus as to the higher meaning of his life. The story of Jesus is the story of the coming of the Messiah, the initiation of the new covenant between God and man, the arrival of salvation—and this certainly must be considered good news.

The Greek form of the word is "evangelos" ("bringing good news") and the four biographers of Jesus are therefore called "the four evangelists."

Each of the evangelists is given the title "saint." This is from the Latin "sanctus" meaning "holy." In the Old Testament the term is used in the Book of Daniel to represent those Jews who are faithful to the Law despite the pressure of Seleucid persecution.

> Daniel 7:21. . . . *the same horn* [Antiochus IV] *made war with the saints, and prevailed against them . . .*

Among Christians, it means, in part, those pious and godly people who keep themselves from all corruption, are devoted to the teachings of Jesus, and are the object of God's particular love.

The first three gospels, those of Matthew, Mark, and Luke, are very similar (although they are by no means identical). They are therefore called the "synoptic gospels." The word "synoptic" is from Greek terms meaning "with one eye." The three gospels can be placed side by side, in other words, and viewed simultaneously with a single glance without the contents going badly out of focus.

Matthew is the first of the gospels in the New Testament because, according to early tradition, it was the first to be written. This, however, is now doubted by nearly everyone. The honor of primacy is generally granted to Mark, which is the second gospel in the Bible as it stands.

Matthew incorporates almost all of Mark and, in addition, includes material which is thought by some to belong to a still earlier collection of sayings of Jesus. This collection is now lost and its existence can be deduced only indirectly. It is usually termed Q for *Quelle*, the German word for "source."

There is some possibility that Matthew was written originally in Aramaic. At least a Christian writer of the second century, Papias, is quoted by a somewhat later writer as having referred to Matthew composing his work "in the Hebrew language." One would suppose Aramaic to have been meant by that since that was the common speech in the Judea of New Testament times (see page I-446). There is no certainty that Papias in referring to Matthew's gospel is referring to the one we now have and call by Matthew's name.

In any case, if Matthew was originally written in Aramaic, it was quickly translated into Greek and the Aramaic original (if it existed at all) was lost. The Jerusalem Bible speculates that the Aramaic version of Matthew was indeed the oldest of the gospels (could it have been Q?) and was the source used by Mark. Matthew was then translated into Greek (our present version) and Mark was used as an additional source.

Certainly Matthew is the only book of the New Testament that can possibly have been first written in Aramaic. It seems quite certain that all the other books of the New Testament were first written in Greek.

Little can be said as to the time when Matthew was written. From the references to the destruction of the Temple, which are found in various places in the gospel, it is often suggested that the book reached its present form shortly after the fateful year of A.D. 70.

Matthew

But who was Matthew? The name is associated with the first gospel by a tradition which seems to trace back to the reference by Papias, mentioned earlier, to a gospel written by Matthew.

Matthew is the English form of the Greek "Mattathias" or, in Hebrew Mattathiah ("the gift of God"). It is a name that grew common by New Testament times, partly because of the great pride of the Jews in the achievements of the Maccabean period. Mattathias is, of course, the name of the father of Judas Maccabeus and the heroic initiator of the revolt against the Seleucids (see page 54).

Matthew is also the name of one of the disciples chosen by Jesus, according to this gospel.

> Matthew 9:9. *And . . . Jesus . . . saw a man, named Matthew, sitting at the receipt of custom: and he saith unto him, Follow me. And he* [Matthew] *arose, and followed him.*

Christian tradition points to this particular Matthew as the author of this gospel, but there is no evidence beyond that tradition.

It is annoying that the gospels do not carry a clear statement of authorship in the modern fashion, but there are several possible reasons for anonymity. Holy books, in the Jewish tradition, rarely carried any notice of real authorship but were assigned to some ancient worthy. Indeed, there might be considered the very real force of the feeling that a truly holy book was inspired by God and that the worldly author acted only as a mouthpiece and deserved no credit.

On a more mundane level, the time of the writing of the gospels was a hard one for Christians. Jewish hostility was pronounced and so was Roman hostility. The sharp persecution by the Emperor, Nero, was not long in the past and, in the aftermath of the Jewish rebellion, the Jews that survived were resentful, indeed, of Christian failure to join the rebellion. It might well be that a gospel writer preferred to remain anonymous out of considerations of personal safety.

Jesus Christ

The notion of the coming of the Messiah must have had hard sledding in the Maccabean era. Judas Maccabeus had about him a heroism that might easily have been equated with the vision of the Messiah as a conquering king. And when he died, that vision might easily have been transferred to the first few of his successors, since under them the Jewish state briefly returned to a period of glory such as it had not known since the days of Solomon.

Certainly, if a comparatively feeble individual such as Zerubbabel could be greeted as the Messiah by Haggai (see page I-662), one of the heroic Maccabees might have been.

But it had been stressed over and over again in the prophetic books of the Old Testament that the Messiah would have to be an offspring of the line of David. Zerubbabel had indeed been such an offspring, but the Maccabees had not, and the Maccabees therefore could not include the Messiah among their number, in the view of pious Jews, no matter what other arguments there might be in favor of it.

The Messiah still belonged to the future, therefore, in the time of the Maccabees. While the Maccabean kingdom was prosperous, Messianic longings could be muted, but when the kingdom fell and Judea came under the domination of Rome, those longings sharpened again. Matthew begins his good news, or gospel, with the announcement of the coming of the Messiah:

Matthew 1:1. *The book of . . . Jesus Christ . . .*

The Hebrew word Messiah means "the anointed one." The Greek word "khrisma" is the oil used for anointing (our word "cream" traces back to "khrisma"). The Messiah, to whom such oil is applied would be "Khristos" in Greek, "Christus" in Latin, "Christ" in English. Since Jesus is the Greek form of the Hebrew name Joshua, the first verse of Matthew is equivalent to "The book of . . . Joshua the Messiah . . ."

David

To someone as steeped in the Jewish tradition as Matthew, it is obvious that the first task to be undertaken if the story of the Messiah is to be told is to demonstrate that he *is* the Messiah. And to do that, it must be shown, first of all, that the Messiah is a member of the line of David. Matthew therefore begins with a genealogy.

Matthew 1:1. *The book of the generation of Jesus Christ, the son of David, the son of Abraham.*

The genealogy begins with Abraham, who is by no means the first man, but is the one with whom God first made a covenant relating to the Jewish people who were to descend from him. From the Jewish interpretation of history as the tale of a covenant between man and God, a covenant to be fulfilled by the Messiah, one would naturally begin with Abraham, and Matthew with his deep-ingrained Jewishness does just this.

Matthew follows a highly artificial scheme in presenting this genealogy:

Matthew 1:17. . . . *all the generations from Abraham to David
are fourteen generations; and from David until the carrying away
into Babylon are fourteen generations; and from the carrying away
into Babylon unto Christ are fourteen generations.*

Why Matthew should feel it necessary to establish such symmetry is
not certain. Perhaps he felt that by pointing out the great events that
took place after two sets of fourteen generations, he made it reasonable
that one ought to expect the Messiah after a third set of fourteen
generations.

Or it may be that there is numerological significance now lost or that
Matthew was trying to set up some acrostic device that can no longer
be followed. In any case, in order to obtain his sets of fourteen,
Matthew was forced to distort the genealogy, and this can scarcely be
considered as adding to the plausibility of whatever argument he
might have had in mind.

Rachab

The first set of fourteen are: (1) Abraham, (2) Isaac, (3) Jacob, (4)
Judas [Judah], (5) Phares [Perez], (6) Esrom [Hezron], (7) Aram
[Ram], (8) Aminadab, (9) Naasson [Nahshon], (10) Salmon, (11)
Booz [Boaz], (12) Obed, (13) Jesse, and (14) David.

The names down to Perez are given in Genesis and the remainder
are given in Ruth.

Included in the list are three women, and, oddly enough, each of the
three is, in one way or another, tainted. The first appears as follows:

Matthew 1:3. *And Judas* [Judah] *begat Phares* [Perez] *and Zara*
[Zerah] *of Thamar* [Tamar] . . .

Zerah is mentioned because he was a twin brother of Perez and
both were born at the same time. However, it was through Perez that
David and, therefore, Jesus traced their descent. Tamar begot them of
Judah by a kind of deceit that was justified according to patriarchal
custom, but in doing so, she played the part of a harlot:

Genesis 38:15. *When Judah saw her, he thought her to be an
harlot; because she had covered her face.*

The other two women are mentioned shortly after:

> Matthew 1:5. *And Salmon begat Booz [Boaz] of Rachab [Rahab]; and Booz [Boaz] begat Obed of Ruth . . .*

Ruth was, of course, a Moabite woman, something which would make a strict Jew of New Testament times uneasy, even if she were an ancestress of David.

The real curiosity, however, is Rahab. The tale of both Tamar and Ruth are given in some detail in the Old Testament, but nothing at all is mentioned, at least in the canonical books, of any marriage between Salmon and Rahab.

Salmon is mentioned at the end of the Book of Ruth as part of the line of descent going from Perez to David, a passage which Matthew uses as reference. In Ruth, however, no wife is mentioned for Salmon.

In the Book of 1 Chronicles, a person with a name similar to Salmon is mentioned in the genealogical tables:

> 1 Chronicles 2:51. *Salma the father of Beth-lehem . . .*

If this Salma is the same as the Salmon who is David's great-great-grandfather, then the verse might signify that Salmon was the first of the family to settle in Bethlehem. He may even have led the contingent that took it from the Canaanities. But here too no wife is mentioned.

Who, then, is Rahab? There is a Rahab in the Old Testament, and she is the woman who sheltered Joshua's spies when they entered Jericho (see page I-211). This woman, however, did not merely play the part of a harlot, as Tamar did. According to the Biblical statement, she *was* a harlot.

> Joshua 2:1. *And Joshua . . . sent out . . . two men to spy . . . And they went, and came into an harlot's house, named Rahab, and lodged there.*

Can this be the Rahab referred to as Salmon's wife? Chronologically it is possible. If David was born in 1050 B.C. as the youngest son of Jesse, who might therefore himself have been born about 1100 B.C., it is quite possible that Jesse's grandfather might have been a warrior between 1200 B.C. and 1170 B.C., when Joshua's conquest might have taken place.

It is very likely that, in later Jewish tradition, Rahab was viewed as a convert to Judaism after the fall of Jericho, and as meriting a reward for her protection of the spies. If she were a convert, like Ruth, she might very well merit a part of the ancestry of David, as Ruth did.

Of course, one wonders how much significance to give to the term "harlot." She might, conceivably, have been the priestess of a Canaanite goddess and as such may have engaged in fertility rites. This would make her a harlot in the puritanical eyes of the Jewish Yahvists, but surely not an ordinary harlot in the modern sense.

Matthew may have mentioned these because each was involved in a colorful event taken note of in the Old Testament and probably popular among its Jewish readers and easily coated with legend. For this reason he may have fallen prey to the temptation of pedantry, and displayed his knowledge of and interest in the Scriptures. On the other hand, one might also reason that if Moabites and harlots are in the line of Jesus' ancestry, it might signify that Jesus arose from all kinds of people and therefore came to suffer for all kinds of people, the sinful as well as the saint, the Gentile as well as the Jew.

The Wife of Urias

The list of fourteen names following David, down to the Babylonian captivity, are: (1) Solomon, (2) Roboam [Rehoboam], (3) Abia [Abijam], (4) Asa, (5) Josaphat [Jehoshaphat], (6) Joram, (7) Ozias [Uzziah or Azariah], (8) Joatham [Jotham], (9) Achaz [Ahaz], (10) Ezekias [Hezekiah], (11) Manasses [Manasseh], (12) Amon, (13) Josias [Josiah], and (14) Jechonias [Jehoiachin].

A fourth woman is mentioned among this group:

> Matthew 1:6. . . . *David the king begat Solomon of her that had been the wife of Urias* [Uriah] . . .

This, of course, was Bathsheba, with whom David committed adultery (see page I-310). Again a woman is mentioned who is the subject of a dramatic story that involves a taint.

Matthew here lists fourteen kings who reigned after David, but in achieving what is to him a magic number of fourteen, he omits several. Thus, he states:

> Matthew 1:8. . . . *and Joram begat Ozias* [Uzziah] . . .

Bur Joram died in 844 B.C. and Uzziah began to reign in 780 B.C., leaving a sixty-four-year gap. This gap contained three kings of Judah, as well as a usurping queen. Joram was succeeded by his son, Ahaziah, who (after an interregnum in which Queen Athaliah reigned) was succeeded by his son, Joash, who was succeeded by his son, Amaziah. Uzziah then followed as Amaziah's son.

Ahaziah, the first of the omitted kings, was the son of Athaliah and therefore the grandson of Ahab of Israel and of his wife, Jezebel (see page I-362). One might almost suspect that Ahaziah and his immediate descendants were omitted in order to avoid mentioning this fact. Nevertheless, mentioned or not, it must follow from Matthew's genealogy that the wicked queens Jezebel and Athaliah are to be included among the ancestors of Jesus.

Still a fourth king is omitted from the line of succession:

Matthew 1:11. *And Josias* [Josiah] *begat Jechonias* [Jehoiachin] . . .

But Josiah was the father of Jehoiakim, who was, in turn, the father of Jehoiachin.

Zorobabel

The final portion of Matthew's genealogy includes the descendants of Jehoiachin after the Exile. The first two generations follow the genealogy given in the Book of 1 Chronicles (see page I-405):

Matthew 1:12. *And after they were brought to Babylon, Jechonias* [Jehoiachin] *begat* [1] *Salathiel* [Shealtiel]; *and Salathiel* [Shealtiel] *begat* [2] *Zorobabel* [Zerubbabel] . . .

After Zerubbabel, a list of names is given that is not found anywhere else in the Bible and which, if valid, we must assume to have been taken from genealogical listings no longer available to us. They are: (3) Abiud, (4) Eliakim, (5) Azor, (6) Sadoc, (7) Achim, (8) Eliud, (9) Eleazar, (10) Matthan, (11) Jacob, and (12) Joseph.

The climax of the genealogy is reached:

Matthew 1:16. *And Jacob begat Joseph the husband of Mary, of whom was born* [13] *Jesus, who is called Christ.*

The names in this third group are only thirteen in number, despite Matthew's statement there are fourteen. Since it is quite certain that Matthew could count we can only assume that somewhere in the early copyings of this list, a name in the third group dropped out and has been lost forever.

Attempts have been made to twist matters so that the magic number fourteen is reached with the list before us. Some have counted Jehoiachin in this list despite the fact that he is also counted in the middle third. Others have attempted to count Mary as a separate generation, since she is mentioned, but in that case one ought also to count Tamar, Rahab, Ruth, and Bathsheba.

No, the best that can be done is to state that, on the face of it, there are fourteen generations from Abraham to David, eighteen from David to the Exile, and thirteen from the Exile to Jesus. Fortunately, though, Matthew's little game with numbers is not really of importance and it isn't paid much mind, except as an interesting quirk in Matthew's system of thought.

The Holy Ghost

In chapter 1:16, Matthew clearly avoids concluding the list of "begats" by saying that Joseph begat Jesus. Rather he carefully identifies Joseph as merely the husband of Mary "of whom was born Jesus."

This paves the way for Matthew's account of Jesus having been born of a virgin:

> Matthew 1:18. *Now the birth of Jesus Christ was on this wise: When as his mother Mary was espoused to Joseph, before they came together, she was found with child of the Holy Ghost.*

The word "ghost" is of Anglo-Saxon origin and means "spirit" or "soul." Ghost, spirit, or soul—whatever it be called—represents something intangible which can be regarded as the essence of life, apart from the material body. It can be the essence of life within a body (a man's soul) or the essence of life in the absence of a body altogether (a supernatural being).

Primitive peoples, generally, consider the universe to be populated by myriads of spirits of all sorts; spirits capable of interfering with human activity and, in some cases, capable of taking possession of a human body in successful competition with its own proper spirit.

The monotheistic Jews also had their popular tales of evil spirits capable of taking possession of human bodies (as in the Book of Tobit, see page 19). Even at its most lofty, Judaism speaks of angels, though viewing them always as messengers of God, who are incapable of independent action. (The case of Satan and his rebellion against God is a rather late development in Jewish thought, adopted only after exposure to Persian dualism, see page I-409.)

Angels might be viewed as merely an extension of God; as representing the spirit of God manifesting itself on Earth in order to guide human action.

It was felt that whenever a man took decisive action and exhibited unusual traits of leadership, it was not so much the action of his own feeble spirit but that of the Spirit of God which entered into him and guided him. Thus:

> Judges 3:10. *And the Spirit of the Lord came upon him* [Othniel], *and he judged Israel, and went out to war . . .*

Or:

> Judges 6:34. *But the Spirit of the Lord came upon Gideon, and he blew a trumpet . . .*

Again, when Samson is described as performing a feat of more-than-human strength:

> Judges 14:6. *And the Spirit of the Lord came mightily upon him, and he rent him* [a lion] *as he would have rent a kid . . .*

The Spirit of God might well be called the Holy Spirit, to avoid using the term "God" (something the Jews of the New Testament period did avoid whenever possible—Matthew especially so). In the King James Version it is called the Holy Ghost, which is synonymous. However, the popular usage of "ghost," as signifying the spirits of the dead, has so robbed the word of its dignity that "Holy Ghost" seems odd to modern ears and Holy Spirit is preferable. The Revised Standard Version uses Holy Spirit throughout.

To say, then, that Mary "was found with child of the Holy Ghost" is to say that her pregnancy was the direct result of the working of the divine influence within her and had nothing to do with the usual manner of achieving pregnancy.

Mary

Joseph, finding that his betrothed is pregnant, assumes she has behaved improperly and feels that he cannot go through with the marriage. He is warned against this by an angel:

> Matthew 1:20. . . . *the angel of the Lord appeared unto him in a dream, saying, Joseph, thou son of David, fear not to take unto thee Mary thy wife: for that which is conceived in her is of the Holy Ghost.*

The name of Jesus' mother is, in Hebrew, Miriam (the name of Moses' sister). In Aramaic, the name became Mariam, and in Roman times it was easy to change this, by dropping the final letter, to Maria, the feminine version of the good Roman name, Marius. Maria is still the version of the name used in most European languages, though it becomes Marion or Marie in French, and Mary in English.

Because of the emphasis here on the fact that her pregnancy was the result of the action of the Holy Spirit and not of man, she is considered by Christians to have been a virgin even while pregnant and is therefore commonly called the "Virgin Mary" or just "the Virgin."

Matthew's emphasis on the virgin birth would seem to negate his earlier emphasis on the Davidic genealogy of Jesus. He shows that Joseph, the husband of Mary, was a descendant of David, but then goes on to show that this same Joseph was not the father of Jesus.

One might account for this by saying that Joseph was considered by the people of his time to be the father of Jesus, so that in the course of *ordinary* human affairs Jesus was of Davidic descent, thus fulfilling that qualification for Messiah-hood. Then, the line of argument might go, Jesus came to be recognized as the divine Son of God and this was so much greater a qualification for Messiah-hood that Davidic descent could be dismissed as an Earthly detail of only Earthly importance.

Another explanation is to suppose that while Matthew gives the genealogy of Joseph, Mary herself is of Davidic descent also, and Jesus is of that descent through his undoubted mother as well as through his merely reputed father. The gospels do not say this directly but the belief of the Davidic descent of Mary, as well as of Joseph, is firmly ensconced in Christian tradition.

And yet virgin birth is completely outside the Jewish tradition and is not demanded by any of the Old Testament prophecies concerning the Messiah. How, then, does Matthew come upon it? Being Matthew, he is bound to support the virgin birth by citing an Old Testament prophecy and he can find only one:

> Matthew 1:22. *Now all this was done, that it might be fulfilled which was spoken of the Lord by the prophet, saying,*
> Matthew 1:23. *Behold, a virgin shall be with child, and shall bring forth a son . . .*

This refers to a passage in Isaiah:

> Isaiah 7:14. . . . *Behold, a virgin shall conceive, and bear a son . . .*

but it is not a very useful passage in this connection. Matthew's use of the word "virgin" in his quotation is mistaken, though it has led early translations of the Bible, including the King James Version, to make use of the word "virgin" in the Isaiah passage as well. In fact, the Hebrew word used by Isaiah means "young woman" and can apply equally well to one who is not a virgin. And, in any case, whether "virgin" or "young woman," the passage from Isaiah is unlikely to have Messianic significance (see page I-532) and, but for these verses in Matthew quoting it, would never be taken to have it.

But then, why the tale of the virgin birth, told with such urgency, that a marginal Old Testament verse has to be searched for and found by Matthew to account for it?

Perhaps we can indulge in a little speculation here. That which was first known about Jesus must have been the tale of his ministry when disciples flocked about him. Presumably he was an obscure Galilean, until his preaching made him famous, and the details of his birth and childhood were not known. Mark, the oldest of the gospels, has nothing to say about his birth and childhood. Rather, Mark starts his tale of Jesus with Jesus as an adult, beginning his ministry.

After Jesus' death, tales of his birth and childhood arose. It is quite possible that many were legitimate reminiscences of those who had known him as a youngster or of members of his family. On the other hand, people being what they are, embroidery may have entered into the legends concerning so remarkable a person as the Messiah and the Son of God.

The sort of detail which individuals of completely Jewish background would expect of the Messiah would be a detailed genealogy that would connect him with David. Such a genealogy is given by Matthew and we have no reason to say that it is inaccurate (aside from the small discrepancies we have pointed out that arise out of Matthew's eagerness to attain the magic number of fourteen).

But the Jews were, in those days, surrounded by a vast world of Gentiles who had traditions of their own. It was quite customary and usual in Gentile legend (almost necessary, in fact) that any great hero, any wonder-worker be the son of a god. A virgin could be impregnated by a god in magical fashion—this would not be impossible in the Greek tradition.

And, as it happened, there were Jews not only in Judea, where Jewish thought was provincial and conservative, but in Alexandria and other places where the Greek influence was strong. Greek versions of the Bible used the Greek word for "virgin" in the Isaiah quotation, and it is quite possible that Matthew followed the Greek version rather than the Hebrew version in supporting the virgin birth, and that he did not deliberately misquote.

In Jesus' time, the possibility of virgin birth may have taken on added force. The Roman historian Livy, who died just a few years before the start of Jesus' ministry, had written a history of Rome that proved enormously popular. In it he retells the tale of the founding of Rome by the twin brothers Romulus and Remus. The interesting part of that legend is that Romulus and Remus are described by him as being of virgin birth. Their mother, Silvia, was a Vestal Virgin whose children were fathered by Mars.

Greek-speaking Jews would surely place no credence in that, and yet there might have been the impulse to feel that if a virgin birth could be used to exalt the founders of the pagan city of Rome, how much more could one rightly be used to exalt the founding of the kingdom of God.

One might wonder, then, if Matthew might not have been faced with two traditions concerning Jesus' birth, the strictly Jewish genealogy of Davidic descent, and the Greek-Jewish story of the virgin birth. And, although mutually exclusive, Matthew accepted both.

It is interesting that the tradition of the virgin birth is firmly and clearly stated only in this first chapter of Matthew. There are verses in Luke that can be made to support it, but not indisputably, and there are no other references to it at all anywhere else in the New Testament.

Herod

The general period of Jesus' birth is given:

Matthew 2:1. . . . *Jesus was born . . . in the days of Herod the king . . .*

The mention of Herod at once tells us that the day of the Maccabean kingdom is over. Much has happened in the century that passed between the ending of 1 Maccabees and the opening of Matthew.

1 Maccabees had ended with the assassination of Simon in 135 B.C. His second and sole surviving son established himself as John Hyrcanus I in 134 B.C., coming to a peaceful arrangement with Antiochus VII Sidetes (see page 88), the last Seleucid monarch of any consequence.

John Hyrcanus extended the boundaries of Judea by conquest. He established his rule over Samaria and Galilee to the north and he brought Idumea, to his south, under complete domination. The Samaritans retained their heretical religion, but orthodox Judaism was established in Galilee and in Idumea.

The Idumeans accepted Judaism (in some cases at the point of the sword) but the converts were not wholeheartedly accepted by the Jewish nationalists. Despite their observance of the proper religion, Idumeans were still viewed as Edomites, descendants of Esau, and therefore the hereditary enemies of the Jewish descendants of Jacob.

John Hyrcanus I died in 104 B.C. and was succeeded by an elder son, Aristobulus, who assumed the title of king, something the Seleucid kingdom, now under Antiochus VIII Grypus ("hook-nosed"), was powerless to prevent.

Aristobulus reigned only a year and, in 103 B.C., his younger brother, Alexander Jannaeus, succeeded. In the course of a twenty-seven-year-reign, Alexander raised Judea to the peak of its power. By the time he died, in 79 B.C., Judea was very much in the position of Israel in the time of Jeroboam II, six and a half centuries before (see page I-369).

Under Jeroboam II, Israel seemed great and prosperous, but its greatness was overshadowed by Assyria, a fact which became evident immediately after Jeroboam's death. In the case of Alexander Jannaeus, Judea's greatness was darkened by the even greater shadow of Rome.

The substance of that shadow was making its way onto the Judean stage after the death of Alexander Jannaeus, and its coming was hastened by dynastic squabbles that set various Maccabees at each other's throats.

Since the time of Jonathan, brother of Judas Maccabeus, the high priesthood had remained in the family of the Maccabees and Alexander Jannaeus was, for instance, at once king and high priest.

After Alexander's death, however, this combination of offices fell apart. The high priesthood went to Alexander's elder son, John Hyrcanus II, but the civil rule remained with Alexander's widow, Alexandra.

Alexandra died in 67 B.C. and one might have expected John Hyrcanus II to serve now as real king as well as high priest, but in this he was disputed by his younger brother, Aristobulus II. In the civil war that followed, John Hyrcanus II had the support of a very able man, Antipater, who had been governor of Idumea under Alexander Jannaeus. Antipater was an Idumean by birth, although Jewish by religion.

The civil war could not have come at a worse time, for Roman armies under General Gnaeus Pompeius (called Pompey in English) were cleaning up the east. The last of the various small powers that, a century before, had been brawling and squabbling on the international stage were now being swallowed, one by one.

In 64 B.C., Pompey entered Antioch and put an end to the Seleucid monarchy. A little over a century before, that monarchy had tyrannized over Judea, but now, under its last kings, it was a feeble patch of territory absorbed by Rome as the province of Syria.

Independent Judea survived the great Seleucid Empire as she had once survived the great Assyrian Empire—but not for long. Both sides in the Jewish civil war were appealing to Pompey for help, of course, and the Roman general, as was to be expected, agreed at once to move in. In 63 B.C. he invaded Judea and took Jerusalem after a three-month siege. Out of curiosity he invaded the Holy of Holies in the Temple but did it no harm otherwise.

Pompey ended by deciding in favor of John Hyrcanus II. He left him as high priest and carried off Aristobulus II and his two sons to Rome.

The Roman did not allow Hyrcanus any secular power, however. He gave that over to Antipater the Idumean in return for Antipater's services to the Roman cause. (It was good policy to do so. Antipater, an Idumean, could never be accepted wholeheartedly by the narrowly nationalistic Jews, and he would therefore always require Roman support to keep his position safe against his subjects. While he needed the Roman soldiers, he would naturally be loyal to the Roman cause.)

Thus, in 63 B.C., a little more than a century after the revolt of Mattathias and his sons, the Maccabean monarchy came to an end.

The fate of the last Maccabees was generally sad. Aristobulus II and his elder son, Alexander, escaped from Rome and made an attempt to regain the kingdom, but they were captured and both were killed in 49 B.C. The younger son, Antigonus Mattathias, survived. Before he died the elder son had married Alexandra, daughter of John Hyrcanus II, and by her had had a son, Aristobulus III.

There were thus, in 49 B.C., three male Maccabees left: (1) John Hyrcanus II, the high priest; (2) his nephew, Antigonus Mattathias; and (3) his grandson, Aristobulus III. The real ruler remained Antipater the Idumean.

But now it was Rome itself that was involved in a civil war. The general, Pompey, had gone to war with another and greater Roman general, Julius Caesar; and Pompey died in the course of the struggle. Antipater had made his way carefully among the contending factions and when Caesar emerged as victor, Antipater found himself still in favor, even though he had been Pompey's man to begin with.

But Caesar was assassinated in 44 B.C. and a new civil war erupted. Antipater the Idumean was assassinated in 43 B.C. and his sure ability to maneuver safely over slippery footing was removed.

Furthermore, Parthia, which ruled Babylonia and vast regions to the east, took advantage of the Roman civil wars to strike westward. For a while it was as though the times of Nebuchadnezzar were reborn, as conquering horsemen rode out of the east to take over Syria and Judea in 40 B.C.

The Jews welcomed the Parthians, though, as they had never welcomed the Chaldeans, for they saw the Parthians as rescuers from the Romans. Antipater's older son, Phasael, was killed in war against the invaders, and the high priest, John Hyrcanus II, was carried off into captivity. What's more, his ears were cut off so that, as a physically mutilated person, he could never serve as high priest again.

In place of the mutilated Hyrcanus, Antigonus Mattathias was made king and high priest. One might almost imagine the Maccabean king-

dom to have been restored but, of course, the new king served merely
as a Parthian puppet.

But Antipater the Idumean had a second son, Herodes (called
Herod in English). He was, like his father, Jewish in religion, though
an Idumean by descent. Under his father, he had served as governor of
Galilee. When the Parthians took Judea, Herod managed to escape
and made his way to Rome.

In Rome he persuaded the Roman general, Marcus Antonius (Mark
Antony), who was then in power, to declare him king of Judea and
to outlaw Antigonus Mattathias. Herod then returned to Judea and
found the Parthians already on the run before a Roman counterattack.
With the help of Roman arms, Herod invaded Judea and, after three
years, took Jerusalem itself in 37 B.C. Antigonus Mattathias was executed.

Now two Maccabees were left. John Hyrcanus II returned from
captivity in 36 B.C., but his cropped ears kept him permanently retired,
so his grandson, Aristobulus III, served as high priest.

Herod, although king now with the full support of the Romans,
could never feel secure while there were Maccabees alive about
whom a nationalist revolt might center.

He tried to neutralize the Maccabean attraction by entering into a
marriage alliance with the family. Aristobulus III had a sister, Mariamne
(still another version of the Hebrew name, Miriam), and Herod took
her as his second wife.

Even that did not erase his insecurity. He had Aristobulus III executed in 35 B.C. and the crop-eared Hyrcanus in 30 B.C. In a fit of
jealousy he killed his wife, Mariamne, in 29 B.C. and that was the end
of the Maccabees, except for Herod's own children by Mariamne.
(Herod, the Henry VIII of his time, married eight times after Mariamne's death, so that he had ten wives altogether, although only one
at a time.)

The birth of Jesus during the reign of Herod raises an interesting
point in chronology. The Romans dated events from the year in which,
according to legend, the city of Rome had been founded. That year
was 1 A.U.C., where the initials stand for *ab urbe condita* ("from the
founding of the city"). According to this scheme, Pompey took
Jerusalem in the year 690 A.U.C.

Unfortunately, however, none of the gospels date the birth of Jesus
according to this scheme or, for that matter, according to one of the

other schemes used in the Bible. The evangelists might have used the Seleucid era that was used in the books of the Maccabees, for instance. Or they might have named the number of the year of Herod's reign after the fashion of the dating in 1 and 2 Kings.

But no scheme was used. Matthew simply says "in the days of Herod the king" and anything closer than that must be worked out by deduction.

Some five hundred years after the time of Jesus, such deductions were made by a scholarly theologian and astronomer named Dionysius Exiguus, who lived in Rome. He maintained that Jesus had been born in 753 A.U.C., and this date for Jesus' birth was widely accepted.

Gradually, as the centuries passed, the old Roman system of counting the years was dropped. Instead, it became customary to count the years from the birth of Jesus. That year was A.D. 1, or "Anno Domini" ("the year of our Lord").

The years prior to the birth of Jesus were labeled B.C. ("before Christ"). Thus, if Jesus was born in 753 A.U.C., then Rome was founded 753 years before his birth, or 753 B.C. The entire system of dating used in this book (and, indeed, in any modern history book) follows this "Christian Era" or "Dionysian Era" in which A.D. 1 is equated with 753 A.U.C.

And yet scholarship in the centuries since Dionysius Exiguus has made a revision necessary. For instance, from sources outside the Bible it is quite clear that Herod ascended the throne in 716 A.U.C., that is, 37 B.C. He reigned for thirty-three years, dying in 749 A.U.C. or 4 B.C.

But if that is so, it is impossible for Jesus to have been born in 753 A.U.C. and still have been born "in the days of Herod the king," since Herod had died four years before. If Jesus were born in the time of Herod then he must have been born no later than 4 B.C. (four years "before Christ," which certainly seems paradoxical).

And even this is merely the latest he could have been born by that verse in Matthew. He could well have been born earlier, and some have suggested dates even as early as 17 B.C.

Wise Men from the East

The birth of Jesus was accompanied by remarkable circumstances, according to Matthew, who tells first of a pilgrimage to the place of Jesus' birth:

Matthew 2:1. *Now when Jesus was born in Bethlehem of Judaea in the days of Herod the king, behold, there came wise men from the east to Jerusalem . . .*

"Wise men" is a translation of the Greek "magoi," which has entered our language by way of the Latin as "magi." The word is derived from "magu," the name given to their priests by the Persian Zoroastrians.

Throughout ancient history, the priests were considered the repositories of important knowledge. Not only did they know the techniques for the propitiation of the gods, but—in Babylonia particularly—they studied the heavenly bodies and their influences upon the course of human affairs. The priests were therefore learned astrologers (who, in the course of their studies, picked up considerable legitimate astronomy as well).

The Jews had learned of the Babylonian priesthood in the time of the Exile, and in the Book of Daniel the word "Chaldean" is used as synonymous with "wise man." If the Jews had forgotten this, there was occasion to refurbish that knowledge during the brief Parthian supremacy over Judea. (The arcane powers of the "magi" are memorialized in our language, by the way, with the word "magic," which is derived from "magi.")

The tale of the wise men is short. They come to see the infant Jesus, they leave presents, and depart; their impact on legend is great, however. In the popular imagination, the wise men have been taken to be three in number and have become three kings and have even been given names: Melchior, Gasper, and Balthazar.

According to medieval legend, their bodies were taken by Helena (the mother of Constantine I, the first emperor to become Christian) to Constantinople. From there, they were eventually removed to Milan, Italy, and still later to Cologne, Germany. There, in Cologne Cathedral, they are supposed to be buried, so that they are sometimes referred to as the "Three Kings of Cologne."

King of the Jews

The wise men, having arrived in Jerusalem, had a simple question:

Matthew 2:2. . . . *Where is he that is born King of the Jews? . . .*

They were searching, in other words, for the Messiah.

There had been a decline in the passionate intensity of longing for a Messiah during the palmy days of the Maccabees, but the longing had not disappeared altogether. After all, the Maccabees did not set up a completely ideal state that ruled over all the world and, in any case, they were not of the Davidic line.

To be sure, the Maccabees realized that dreams of a Messiah would have to be directed against their own Levite dynasty, unless properly deflected, and they must have encouraged writings that would tend to do this.

During the Maccabean period, for instance, the apocryphal work "The Testaments of the Twelve Patriarchs" appeared. This purported to be a transcript of the last words of the twelve sons of Jacob as they lay on their deathbeds. Passages in it pointed clearly to a Levite Messiah. Psalm 110, with its mention of Melchizedek as both king and high priest (see page I-504) although not of Davidic lineage—having lived, in fact, nearly a thousand years before David—may have been used to support the Maccabees, too. (Indeed, some suspect the psalm may have been written in early Maccabean times and slipped into the canon at the last minute.)

All attempts, however, to set up a Levite Messiah must have failed to win any enthusiasm at all among the Jews generally. The prophetic writings were too clear on the point of the Davidic descent of the Messiah and the hallowed memory of David himself and of the empire he founded remained too sharp and clear. Messianic hopes may have ebbed under the Maccabees but what hope remained was for a Messiah of the line of David.

And then the Maccabees were gone. Despite the heroism of Judas Maccabeus and his brothers, despite the conquests of John Hyrcanus I and Alexander Jannaeus, the line had been a brief and, in the end, unsuccessful interlude in Jewish history. And those who piously awaited the Messiah might well have been pleased, rather than otherwise, at the Maccabean failure. After all, the Maccabees were not of the stock of David; how could they possibly have succeeded?

Now under the heavy hand of Herod, the alien from Idumea, and under the still heavier weight of the Roman arms that supported him, the Jews were growing increasingly restive. Surely it was time for the Messiah to come, establish himself as the ideal King of the Jews, bring the heathen oppressors to justice, and place all the world under his mild rule so that all peoples everywhere might finally come to Jerusalem to worship.

There is no reason to be surprised that the Messianic fervor in Judea made itself felt far outside the borders of the land. There were large colonies of Jews outside Judea, notably in Alexandria and in Babylonia. The three wise men from the east could, conceivably, have heard of such matters from the Jews in their land and been impressed by the tale.

The Star

But even if the wise men had heard of Jewish speculations as to the Messiah, what made them choose that moment to head for Jerusalem? It would have to be divine inspiration and Matthew casts that inspiration, quite fittingly, into the form of an astrological manifestation—something that would professionally interest the Babylonian priesthood:

> Matthew 2:2 . . . *Where is he that is born King of the Jews? for we have seen his star in the east, and are come to worship him.*

There is nothing in Old Testament prophecy to make a star the specific manifestation of the Messiah. To be sure, one of Balaam's oracles states:

> Numbers 24:17. . . . *there shall come a Star out of Jacob . . . and shall smite the corners of Moab . . .*

and this has been taken as a Messianic utterance by many. Nevertheless, modern scholars accept this as a reference to David, written into the oracle in the time of the kingdom and attributed to the legendary sage Balaam.

Then, too, there is a passage in Isaiah which goes:

> Isaiah 60:3. *And the Gentiles shall come to thy light, and kings to the brightness of thy rising.*

This refers to Isaiah's vision of an ideal Jerusalem, to arise after the return from exile, but it is easy to interpret it as referring also to the Messianic period and, specifically, to the manner in which the wise men of the east followed the light of the star to the birth of Jesus.

If, however, Matthew has this in mind, he does not quote the verse from Isaiah.

If Matthew had quoted that verse, it might be easier to accept the star as a miraculous manifestation of divine guidance visible only to the wise men and to no one else. But Matthew calmly refers to the star without reference to prophecy, as though it were a perfectly natural phenomenon (bent to the divine purpose, of course) and much effort and imagination has been expended to determine what that natural phenomenon might have been.

The most obvious solution would be that the star was a "nova"— a new star appearing suddenly in the heavens, possibly attaining startling brightness, and then fading out to invisibility after some months.

Such events have indeed been known to happen. Astronomers know that stars can sometimes explode and increase in brightness a millionfold or more for a short period of time. In the case of particularly tremendous explosions ("supernovae") among stars reasonably close to ourselves, the result may be the sudden appearance of a star that will grow as bright as the planet Venus in a spot where previously no star bright enough to be seen by the naked eye had been visible.

Three such supernovae have been known to have appeared in the last thousand years—one in 1054, one in 1572, and one in 1604. Could one also have appeared in Herod's time?

It seems doubtful. Surely such a supernova would have been noticed. Of course, the supernova of 1054 was not noticed by European astronomers, but this was during the Dark Ages, when astronomy in Europe was virtually nonexistent. It *was* observed by astronomers in China and Japan, and we have their records. (We know they were correct because in the spot where they located their "guest-star" there is now a cloudy ball of gas that is the clear remnant of an explosion.)

In Herod's time, Greek astronomy was still alive, however, even though past its greatest day, and a supernova would most certainly have been noted and referred to. It seems quite unlikely that such a reference would not have existed and survived to our time and so the chance of a supernova is generally dismissed.

Another possibility is that the star might have been the result of a close approach of two or more of the heavenly bodies, so that they would shine together with abnormal brightness for a short period of time. The only bodies in the skies that move independently against the starry background are the planets, and occasionally two or more approach fairly close to each other.

Astronomers understand these movements quite well now and can trace them back with considerable accuracy for thousands of years. They can tell, for instance, that in 7 B.C., Jupiter and Saturn approached each other quite closely.

The approach was not so close as to make it in the least possible that observers would mistake the two for a single unusually bright star. Still, there is no reason to suppose this would be necessary. The close approach of the two planets is a rare event (although a still closer approach of Jupiter and Saturn than that in 7 B.C. took place in 1941) and to astrologers there might have been significance in it. It is not inconceivable that the approach might in the minds of some have been associated with the coming of a Messiah.

And, finally, there is the possibility of a bright comet. Comets come and go erratically and, until a little over two centuries ago, there was no known method to predict those comings and goings. Comets were generally considered to presage disasters—plagues, wars, deaths of notable men—but to the wise men of the east perhaps a particular comet might have been associated with the coming of the Messiah.

Nowadays we can calculate the paths of a number of comets and can trace them backward in time. We can know of one comet that did appear in the reign of Herod. This was Halley's Comet, which made one of its returns of every seventy-six years to the inner Solar System in the year 11 B.C.

One might suppose then that in the decades following Jesus' death, when his disciples piously scraped together whatever records they could find of his life, some might remember the appearance of an unusual phenomenon in the heavens at about the time of his birth—either Halley's Comet or the close approach of Jupiter and Saturn. The Jews were not themselves astronomers (indeed, they eschewed astronomy, because the study of the stars in those days was invariably and notoriously associated with heathen idolatry) and would describe any such manifestation as simply "a star."

Matthew may well have picked up the story, with the miraculous associations that gathered about it, and included it in his gospel.

Bethlehem

The question of the wise men was a disturbing one:

> Matthew 2:3. *When Herod the king had heard these things, he was troubled, and all Jerusalem with him.*

Herod and "all Jerusalem" (that is, the ruling groups of the city, whose welfare was tied to the king and his court) might well be troubled by any rumor that a possible Messiah had arisen. For one thing, such a Messiah would be considered the rightful king of Judea, and Herod would suddenly be a usurper in the eyes of all pious Jews. It is a rare king who would willingly face the possibility of being removed from the kingship, without some attempt to protect himself. In fact, in all kingdoms, ancient and modern, any attempt by someone other than the king to declare himself the rightful king, or to be declared so by others, is considered treason and treated as such.

It might be argued that the concern of Herod and the aristocracy was not only for themselves, but for the nation as a whole, too. Herod is usually pictured as a bloody, cruel tyrant, but this is largely through the picture drawn of him by the Jews who opposed him and by this chapter of the New Testament. If this is disregarded, and if the excesses of his private life (which were horrible but not noticeably more so than those of other rulers of his time) are also discounted, then Herod seems to have been a capable ruler who made a considerable (though futile) effort to win the regard of the people he governed. Reports of Messiahs were indeed dangerous to everyone in Judea, from Herod's standpoint, more so to the people, in fact, than to Herod himself (who was old and was soon to be removed from his throne in the ordinary course of nature anyway).

The trouble was that to the more militant Jewish nationalists, there seemed no question but that the Messiah would prove a warrior-king, a super-David who would settle matters with the Romans, and make Judea what it should rightly be—the master of the world. This would happen because the Messiah would be filled with the Spirit of the Lord and God himself would fight on behalf of the nation as he had done so many times in the past.

Indeed, there was the example of the Maccabean revolt, of the courage and devotion of Judas Maccabeus and his brothers in turning back and defeating the powerful Seleucid kingdom.

It is not difficult to see that the glorious victories of Judas must have had, in the end, a disastrous influence on Jewish history, for it filled Judea with enthusiastic nationalists who discounted mere disparities of number and power. The Romans, to them, seemed as capable of being beaten by sheer determination, patriotic fervor, and trust in God, as the Seleucids had been.

Those Jews who were less blind to Earthly realities and less confident of divine support, understood the great strength of Rome and must have viewed nationalist agitation with absolute terror. They must have realized that there was the constant danger of a suicidal uprising; one that would be followed by the full exertion of Roman power, which would descend like a sledge hammer, crushing the state into extinction, nationalists and moderates alike. This was no idle fear, either, for at the time of Jesus' birth exactly such a tragic denouement was just seventy years in the future.

Herod might therefore be viewed as clearly feeling it to be his duty to nip all Messianic hopes in the bud—for the good of all. He therefore inquired of the chief priests and scribes (those best acquainted, that is, with Biblical lore) as to where the Messiah might be found.

> Matthew 2:5. *And they said unto him, In Bethlehem of Judea: for thus it is written by the prophet,*
>
> Matthew 2:6. *And thou Bethlehem, in the land of Juda* [Judah] *. . . out of thee shall come a Governor, that shall rule my people Israel.*

The reference is to a quotation from Micah (see page I-653). Thus, the "little town of Bethlehem," locally famous till then as the birthplace of David, entered a new career of world-wide fame as the reputed birthplace of Jesus.

Herod next instructed the wise men to go to Bethlehem and to bring him back news of the child that he might worship him too. There is no question, though, that his real intention was to do away with the supposed Messiah. This is so certain that Matthew doesn't even bother to specify it at that moment.

The wise men depart and:

> Matthew 2:9. *. . . the star, which they saw in the east, went before them, till it came and stood over where the young child was.*

Because of the association of the star with the place of birth of Jesus at Bethlehem, it is commonly called "the star of Bethlehem."

The Children . . . in Bethlehem

The wise men worshipped the child, left their gifts, and then— warned in a dream (a favorite device of Matthew's)—left without reporting back to Herod. Herod, lacking the knowledge he needed, desperately ordered a general killing of all the infants in Bethlehem, hoping to include among them the reputed Messiah:

> Matthew 2:16. *Then Herod . . . sent forth, and slew all the children that were in Bethlehem . . . from two years old and under . . .*
> Matthew 2:17. *Then was fulfilled that which was spoken by Jeremy* [Jeremiah] *the prophet, saying,*
> Matthew 2:18. *In Rama* [Ramah] *was there a voice heard, lamentation, and weeping, and great mourning, Rachel weeping for her children, and would not be comforted, because they are not.*

The reference is to a passage in Jeremiah (see page I-560) which refers to the carrying off of Israel into exile by Sargon. Rachel was the ancestress of the chief tribes of Israel, Ephraim, and Manasseh, and her weeping over "her children" is therefore metaphorically apt. The tribe of Benjamin was also descended from Rachel, and Jeremiah, brought up in Benjamite territory, would be sensitive to the thought of Rachel's weeping; Ramah being a town in Benjamin that was a tradi- tional site of Rachel's grave.

The application of the verse from Jeremiah to the "slaughter of the innocents" by Herod is far less apt. To be sure, such a slaughter would be well worth bewailing, but the fact remains that Leah, not Rachel, was the ancestress of the Judeans, and the children of Bethlehem were Judeans. Perhaps the use of the quotation was suggested to Matthew by the fact that there was a tradition that placed Rachel's grave close to Bethlehem:

> Genesis 35:19. *And Rachel died, and was buried in the way to . . . Beth-lehem.*

And yet this dreadful deed of Herod's seems very likely to be apocryphal. It is hard to believe that it ever happened. Not only is the slaughter not mentioned anywhere else in the New Testament, but it is not mentioned in any of the secular histories of the time, either. It is rather remarkable that such a deed would be overlooked when many more far less wicked deeds of Herod were carefully described.

Surely Matthew would not have accepted this tale of the killing of the infants merely because of his eagerness to introduce a not-very-apt quotation.

Perhaps something more is involved. Many heroes of pagan legend survived infancy only after a narrow escape from some king who tried to kill him. This is true of legends concerning Cyrus, who founded the Persian Empire, and Romulus, who founded Rome. Cyrus had a grandfather and Romulus a great-uncle who, in each case, were kings and had divine foreknowledge that the just-born child would someday depose them. Both children were exposed and left to die; both survived. In Jewish legend, Abraham, as an infant, miraculously survived the attempts of evil King Nimrod upon his life. It is not surprising that similar tales might arise concerning Jesus after his death.

Out of perhaps many such tales that were spread about, Matthew chose one he felt best suited the situation. The Biblical tale of Moses' infancy involves the child's suspense-filled escape after Pharaoh had ordered the indiscriminate slaughter of the Israelite children . . .

> Exodus 1:15. *And the king of Egypt spake to the Hebrew mid-wives* . . .
> Exodus 1:16. . . . *When ye do the office of a midwife to the Hebrew women* . . . *if it be a son, then ye shall kill him* . . .

Moses escaped Pharaoh's slaughter and Jesus escaped Herod's slaughter. It may have been this parallel that was in Matthew's mind. He seized upon this particular tale and buttressed it with the quotation from Jeremiah in order to present Jesus as a new and greater Moses.

Egypt

The infant Jesus escaped the slaughter because Joseph, like the wise men, was warned in a dream:

Matthew 2:13. . . . *Arise, and take the young child and his mother, and flee into Egypt* . . .

Matthew 2:14. *When he arose, he took the young child and his mother by night, and departed into Egypt:*

Matthew 2:15. *And was there until the death of Herod: that it might be fulfilled which was spoken . . . by the prophet, saying, Out of Egypt have I called my son.*

The reference is to the prophet, Hosea:

Hosea 11:1. *When Israel was a child, then I loved him, and called my son out of Egypt.*

On the face of it that verse in Hosea is a clear reference to the Exodus and it is only Matthew's quotation of it that would make anyone give it Messianic significance. Indeed, it might seem natural to wonder if the flight into Egypt was introduced only so that Matthew could indulge in his favorite exercise of quoting an Old Testament verse, for Jesus' stay in Egypt is not referred to in any other place in the New Testament.

One might speculate that here too, perhaps, Matthew adopted a tradition for inclusion in his gospel in order to make even clearer the parallel he was drawing between Moses and Jesus. Moses came out of Egypt—and so did Jesus.

Archelaus

Eventually Herod died (in 4 B.C., as stated earlier), perhaps not long after Jesus' birth:

Matthew 2:22. . . . *Archelaus did reign in Judaea in the room of his father Herod* . . .

Herod, with his many wives, had many children (fourteen all told) but few survived him. This was not only the results of the natural hazards of infancy, but because of Herod's own pathologically suspicious nature, particularly in later life. He was easily moved to anger by hints of possible conspiracies against him. It was this which led him to kill his beloved wife, Mariamne (the Maccabean), and to follow that, eventually, by the execution of the two sons she bore him. He had other sons also executed, including his oldest, Antipater.

Upon his death, however, he still had several sons surviving; including Archelaus, Antipas, and Philip. He divided his kingdom among them. (The family name, Herod, is often added to the names of these sons, so that we may speak of Herod Archelaus, Herod Antipas, and Herod Philip. The name Herod was almost a throne name for those descendants of Antipater the Idumean who ruled over parts of the land.)

Archelaus, the eldest survivor, was given control of the core of the realm: Judea, with Samaria, to the north and Idumea to the south. Herod tried to give him the title of king, too, but the Roman Emperor, who had to approve Herod's will, refused to allow it. Archelaus was given the lesser title of "ethnarch" (equivalent to "provincial governor") as though deliberately to lessen his prestige and power.

Antipas received Galilee for his share, as well as Perea, the district east of the Jordan River (which had once been called Gilead, (see page I-191). Philip received Iturea, the district east and north of the Sea of Galilee.

Antipas and Philip were both called "tetrarchs" ("ruler of a fourth part of a province"), which would have made literal sense if Herod's kingdom had been divided among four sons rather than three. However, it might be reasoned that Archelaus, as the eldest, received a double share and ruled two fourths of the kingdom while Antipas and Philip ruled one fourth each.

Nazareth

Once Herod died, it was safe for Joseph and his family to return, and he is so informed by an angel in terms which again reinforce the parallel between Moses and Jesus:

> Matthew 2:19. *But when Herod was dead, behold, an angel of the Lord appeareth in a dream to Joseph in Egypt,*
> Matthew 2:20. *Saying, Arise, and take the young child and his mother, and go into the land of Israel: for they are dead which sought the young child's life.*

The parallel is to the period when Moses fled into Midian after he had killed the Egyptian overseer (see page I-129). There he remained till Pharaoh's death, upon which he is told by God:

The Divisions of Herod's Kingdom

Exodus 4:19. . . . *Go, return into Egypt: for all the men are dead which sought thy life.*

But Matthew now faces a problem. He has reported the traditions that clustered about Jesus' birth at the Messianic city of Bethlehem and everything he says is consistent with the view that Bethlehem was the native town of the family; that they lived there as their ancestors had lived there before them. It would therefore be natural for them to return to Bethlehem after Herod's death, but this would not do.

Jesus, during his ministry, was considered a native of Galilee. He is constantly referred to as a Galilean and no reference is made, during his ministry, of his birth in Bethlehem.

It is therefore necessary for Matthew to explain how Joseph and his family, although natives of Bethlehem, came to live in Galilee—and very soon after Jesus' birth, too, so that his Bethlehem origin might not play much role in his adulthood.

Joseph is described, therefore, as indeed setting out for Bethlehem after Herod's death:

Matthew 2:22. *But when he* [Joseph] *heard that Archelaus did reign in Judaea . . . he was afraid to go thither: notwithstanding, being warned of God in a dream, he turned aside into the parts of Galilee . . .*

This is not unreasonable. Archelaus, the son of Herod, might have heard of the tale of the birth of the Messiah shortly before his father's death and he might be just as anxious to do away with the dangerous youngster. To be sure, Galilee was under the control of another son of Herod, but it may well be that Joseph judged Antipas to be the less dangerous of the two.

Certainly Archelaus, by his behavior, soon antagonized both the Jews and Samaritans under his rule to such an extent that, although they were bitter enemies who could virtually never agree, they did agree in their detestation of the new ruler. Both appealed desperately to Rome for relief, and such was the justice of their case that Archelaus was removed from office after he had ruled ten years. Herod Antipas, on the other hand, ruled for over forty years without too greatly antagonizing his subjects, a good sign perhaps that he was milder and more reasonable than his brother.

Matthew goes on to specify the town in Galilee to which Joseph brought his family:

> Matthew 2:23. *And he* [Joseph] *came and dwelt in a city called Nazareth . . .*

Nazareth, a town in southern Galilee, is not mentioned in the Old Testament. The modern city usually identified as Nazareth lies just halfway between the Mediterranean Sea and the southern edge of the Sea of Galilee, about twenty miles from each. It is some seventy miles due north of Bethlehem. Its population today is about twenty-six thousand. It is part of the modern nation of Israel, but most of its inhabitants are Christians.

Matthew goes on to explain the coming of Joseph and his family to Nazareth in terms of Old Testament prophecy:

> Matthew 2:23. *. . . . that it might be fulfilled which was spoken by the prophets, He shall be called a Nazarene.*

What quotation Matthew might have in mind here is uncertain. Certainly at no point in the Old Testament is the Messiah referred to as a Nazarene in the sense that he was to be living in Nazareth.

It could be that Matthew stumbles into a confusion with Nazarite here (see page I-248) and that the reference is to the passage where Samson's mother is warned by an angel of a forthcoming son who is to fulfull God's purpose. The angel says:

> Judges 13:5. *. . . . the child shall be a Nazarite unto God from the womb: and he shall begin to deliver Israel out of the hand of the Philistines.*

Another possibility is that what Matthew is referring to is the habit of calling the Messiah the "Branch"—that is, the new, flourishing growth from the decaying stump of the Davidic line. This first appeared in Isaiah:

> Isaiah 11:1. *And there shall come forth a rod out of the stem of Jesse, and a Branch shall grow out of his roots . . .*

As a result, prophets began to speak of the "Branch" as a covert way of referring to the Messiah, when an open mention might have been interpreted as treason. When Zechariah speaks of the Messiah, he says:

Zechariah 6:12. . . . *Behold the man whose name is The Branch*
. . .

The Hebrew word for "Branch" in this case is "netzer," and
Matthew may see a similarity here to "Nazarene."

In either case, whether Matthew is matching Nazarene and Nazarite,
or Nazarene and Netzer, he is indulging in, at best, a play on words,
and is not referring to any actual prophecy of the Messiah being an
inhabitant of Nazareth.

John the Baptist

Matthew now passes from the tales of Jesus' birth and childhood
and comes immediately to his adult work and what seems to be, in this
and the other synoptic gospels, the final year of his life. No date is
given in Matthew for this final year. It is merely stated:

Matthew 3:1. *In those days came John the Baptist, preaching in
the wilderness of Judaea* . . .

A more careful chronological note in the Gospel of St. Luke,
which will be discussed in time (see page 275), suggests the date is
A.D. 29, at which time Jesus must have been at least thirty-three years
old, very likely thirty-five, and just possibly even older.

John the Baptist is the first of several important individuals named
John in the New Testament. The Hebrew version of the name is
more closely represented as Johanan and it is in this form that it
appears in the Old Testament. The eldest son of Josiah was Johanan,
as was the eldest of the five Maccabean brothers.

The Greek version of Johanan is Ioannes and this eventually reached
English as John.

John the Baptist could be considered the last of the Hebrew
prophets of the old school. Like the prophets of the Old Testament, he
maintained that the day of the Lord was at hand and the final
establishment of the ideal world was imminent. The burden of his
preaching was:

Matthew 3:2. . . . *Repent ye: for the kingdom of heaven is at
hand.*

By "kingdom of Heaven" is meant "kingdom of God," with heaven substituted because Matthew shares the increasing reluctance of the Jews of the time to use any divine name. The expression "kingdom of God" is freely used in the New Testament outside Matthew.

What's more the establishment of the kingdom of God is to be preceded by a thorough winnowing of good from evil, saints from sinners, as had been promised by the earlier prophets too:

> Matthew 3:11. . . . he that cometh after me is mightier than I . . .
>
> Matthew 3:12. . . . he will throughly purge his floor, and gather his wheat into the garner; but he will burn up the chaff with unquenchable fire.

Those who came to John in repentance were baptized; that is, dipped in water ("baptize" is from a Greek word meaning "dip in water") in a symbolic washing away of sin and preparation for the new state of affairs.

Baptism was not a rite prominent in Jewish practice. Ezekiel speaks of the symbolic use of water to cleanse Jews after the profanation of their exile among the heathen and their exposure to heathen practices:

> Ezekiel 36:24. For I will take you from among the heathen, . . . and will bring you into your own land . . .
>
> Ezekiel 36:25. Then will I sprinkle clean water upon you, and ye shall be clean . . .
>
> Ezekiel 36:26. A new heart also will I give you, and a new spirit will I put within you . . .

And this was what John the Baptist claimed to be doing by means of the baptismal rite. He used the water of the Jordan River and we might wonder whether he was not influenced here by Elisha's words to the Syrian leper Naaman (see page I-360):

> 2 Kings 5:10. . . . Go and wash in Jordan . . . and thou shalt be clean.

Whatever use Jews may have put baptism to, however, circumcision remained the rite marking the true entry of the Gentile into the brotherhood of Judaism. In Christian practice, partly as a result of the work of John the Baptist, baptism replaced circumcision as the initiatory rite.

Elijah

One might assume from the words quoted by Matthew of the Baptist's teachings, that John was awaiting the imminent arrival of the divine fury of a warlike king of heaven and that the last chapter of Earthly history was at hand. In Christian tradition, however, he is the forerunner of Jesus, a Messiah who did not at all fit the imaginings of the Jewish nationalists.

Matthew characteristically interprets the Baptist's role in terms of an Old Testament verse:

> Matthew 3:3. *For this* [John] *is he that was spoken of by the prophet Esaias* [Isaiah], *saying, The voice of one crying in the wilderness, Prepare ye the way of the Lord, make his paths straight.*

This verse comes from the very beginning of the utterances of the Second Isaiah (see page I-547):

> Isaiah 40:3. *The voice of him that crieth in the wilderness, Prepare ye the way of the Lord, make straight in the desert a highway for our God.*

It is possible to interpret this verse, in view of its position, as a reference by the Second Isaiah to himself, almost as a title to his writings. In this view, the verse might represent something like "Utterances, by a Prophet that Crieth in the Wilderness." And yet, to be sure, even if this were the primary meaning of the verse, it might well seem applicable to some future precursor of the Messiah.

Certainly John the Baptist viewed himself as the precursor of the Messiah and even saw the precise role he was playing, for he seemed to model himself deliberately on Elijah:

> Matthew 3:4. *And the same John had his raiment of camel's hair, and a leathern girdle about his loins; and his meat was locusts and wild honey.*

Compare this with a description of Elijah in the Old Testament:

> 2 Kings 1:8. . . . *He was an hairy man, and girt with a girdle of leather about his loins . . .*

John's ascetic diet of food which one might gather in the desert (and the ascetic diet, with much fasting, that he imposed upon his disciples) called to mind the time that Elijah remained in the wilderness, eating nothing more than was brought to him, miraculously, by ravens:

1 Kings 17:6. *And the ravens brought him* [Elijah] *bread and flesh in the morning, and . . . in the evening; and he drank of the brook.*

The re-enactment of Elijah was not without its point. A late development in Jewish Messianic thinking had been that Elijah would return to Earth as a precursor of the Messiah. Indeed, the last passage of the last prophetic book of the Bible makes this statement:

Malachi 4:5. *Behold, I will send you Elijah the prophet before the coming of the great and dreadful day of the Lord . . .*

In the Christian versions of the Bible, Malachi is the last book of the Old Testament and there is a kind of neatness about the fact that the last book of the Old Testament ends with the promise of Elijah, and the first book of the New Testament opens with a prophet modeling himself on Elijah.

Matthew later quotes Jesus as confirming this identification of John the Baptist and Elijah:

Matthew 17:12. *But I say unto you, That Elias* [Elijah] *is come already, and they knew him not . . .*

Matthew 17:13. *Then the disciples understood that he spake unto them of John the Baptist.*

Pharisees and Sadducees

John's preaching was popular—he was what we would today call a successful revivalist. The fact of his popularity rests not only on Biblical evidence, but on that of Josephus, who mentions John the Baptist with approval.

Nor was it the nameless common herd alone that flocked to be baptized. Some of the leaders of the religious thought of the time came as well; perhaps sincerely, perhaps out of curiosity, perhaps a little of both.

Matthew 3:7. . . . *he* [John the Baptist] *saw many of the Phari-sees and Sadducees come to his baptism . . .*

The Pharisees and Sadducees are two of the Jewish religious sects of the period; sects that had their origin in the travail of the Seleucid persecution and the Maccabean rebellion.

There were Jews who were sympathetic to Hellenism and who did not take part in the rebellion; who even fought on the side of the Seleucids against the Maccabees (see page 67).

Even after the success of the rebellion, there were many Jews who felt some sympathy with Hellenism and were loath to expand Jewish ritual and make Jewish life more and more different from that of the rest of the world.

Naturally, these tended to be drawn from among the upper classes. These were more apt to have a knowledge of Greek and to have studied Hellenic culture. In particular (and almost paradoxically) they included the high priests and their circles. Indeed, the party called itself the "Zadokim," presumably from Zadok, the first of the high priests of the Temple of Solomon. The word Zadokim became Saddoukaioi in Greek and Sadducees in English.

The Sadducees accepted only the written law (there was no avoiding that) and refused all the embroidery that tradition and custom had added to it in the centuries since the Exile. They refused to accept the beliefs and legends of angels, spirits, and demons which had expanded in the Persian and Greek periods; nor did they accept the doctrines of resurrection and an afterlife of reward and punishment.

It seems odd to moderns to read of an important Jewish sect in Roman times denying the resurrection, but actually that doctrine did arise late. References to it appear in the Old Testament only in very late passages. The clearest reference is at the end of Daniel, just about the last book to be added to the canon:

Daniel 12:2. *And many of them that sleep in the dust of the earth shall awake, some to everlasting life, and some to shame and everlasting contempt.*

Opposed to the Hellenizers during the Maccabean revolt were the Assideans or, in Hebrew, Hasidim (see page 56), a word meaning "the pious ones." They were laymen and country folk who utterly rejected Hellenism and who held to a colorful variety of Judaism about which all sorts of traditions had grown. (This is not an unusual phenomenon. Compare today the subtle Christianity of the ministers of important urban congregations and the manner in which it accepts modern science and contemporary thought, with the fervor and traditionalism of those who accept the "old-time religion" in what is called the Bible Belt.)

After the revolt had succeeded, the Assideans developed into two groups. The smaller of the two were the Essenes, who never numbered more than a few thousand. The name is of unknown derivation but is sometimes traced back to a Hebrew word meaning "healers." They lived in isolated communities, practicing celibacy and asceticism, rather like Christian monks. They are not mentioned in the New Testament, but scholars speculate on the possibility that John the Baptist may have been influenced by Essene thought. The main groups of Essenes were concentrated on the northwestern shores of the Dead Sea, and the "Dead Sea scrolls," recently discovered, seem to have been the relics of an Essene-like community.

The greater portion of the Assideans developed into a more worldly group of pietists, ones less removed from society and taking an active part in the political developments of the time. They called themselves, in Aramaic, "Perishaiya," meaning apparently "the separated ones." Since the word "holy" carries the notion of being separated from worldly things and consecrated to God, to call one's self "separated" is not very far removed from calling one's self "holy." This carries a note of smug self-approval which was, perhaps, the least attractive facet of this party. The word "Perishaiya" became "Pharisaios" in Greek and "Pharisees" in English.

The Pharisees accepted not only the written Law itself but also the oral traditions that had grown up about it. They tended to be milder in practice than the Sadducees because oral tradition often softened the harsh letter of the Mosaic Law.

Indeed, Pharisaic teaching at its best very much resembles that of the New Testament. The Jewish teacher Hillel, who died about A.D. 10, taught a kindly religion of love and represents a kind of Jewish parallel to the doctrines of Jesus. Hillel was even, purportedly, of the line of David. However, no miracles are associated with Hillel's name nor did he (or anyone else on his behalf) ever claim Messiah-hood.

At its worst, though, the Pharisees evolved so many trivial rites as an adjunct to religion that no one without great study could be sure of mastering them all. The Pharisees tended to look down upon those who, for lack of leisure time or for lack of learning, did not or could not obey all the ritual, and this did not particularly endear them to the common people. The people in turn tended to adhere to more popular and dramatic teachers who gave them the consolation they needed and demanded a proper inner attitude rather than the mechanical adherence to a complicated set of rites. They turned to men like John the Baptist, and Jesus. In fact, Jesus' teaching might almost be considered as Pharisaic ethics without Pharisaic ritual.

The Sadducees and Pharisees took turns at being politically dominant in the Judea of Maccabean times. Immediately after the rebellion, the Pharisees were in control, for the Sadducees were tarred with the disgrace of having been what we would call, today, "Quislings."

However, although the Seleucid monarchy had been defeated, Hellenic culture remained as attractive as ever, and the Maccabean kings began to Hellenize and to take on the role against which their fathers had fought and died.

The Sadducees therefore regained control of the Temple under John Hyrcanus I and the Pharisees entered the opposition. (It was at this time they adopted their name. Perhaps a little self-praise helped ease the pain of having lost power.)

They were in open revolt under Alexander Jannaeus—a kind of Maccabean revolt against the Maccabees which was repressed bloodily. Later, Alexander's widow, Alexandra, made peace with the Pharisees and for a while things were quiet.

After her death, however, the civil war between her two sons, John Hyrcanus II and Aristobulus II broke out. The Pharisees supported the former and for a while were in control again. During the reign of Herod, and afterward, it was again the turn of the Sadducees to be in power and the Pharisees to be in the opposition.

When representatives of these two parties came to John for baptism he reviled them both, taking up the stand of the common man, so to speak, against those who, like the Sadducees, emptied Judaism of its content and those who, like the Pharisees, filled it too full.

Indeed, he took up a Jeremiah-like attitude. Jeremiah, in his Temple sermon (see page I-562), had warned that the mere existence of the Temple would not protect an ethically evil people. John warned that the mere fact of being Jewish would not serve as protection, either:

Matthew 3:9. *And think not to say within yourselves, We have Abraham to our father: for I say unto you, that God is able of these stones to raise up children unto Abraham.*

The Son

Now, finally, Jesus appears as an adult coming to John the Baptist in order to be baptized.

As it happens, Josephus, who mentions John the Baptist, does not mention Jesus. There is, to be sure, a paragraph in his history of the Jews which is devoted to Jesus but it interrupts the flow of the discourse and seems suspiciously like an afterthought. Scholars generally believe this to have been an insertion by some early Christian editor who, scandalized that Josephus should talk of the period without mentioning the Messiah, felt the insertion to be a pious act.

Nor, in fact, is there mention of Jesus in any contemporary or nearly contemporary record we have, outside the New Testament.

There have been those who have maintained, because of this, that Jesus never existed, but this seems going too far. The synoptic gospels do not bear the marks of outright fiction as do the books of Tobit, Judith, and Esther, for instance. The synoptic gospels are not filled with anachronisms but prove accurate when they discuss the background of their times. What they say of John the Baptist, for instance, jibes with what Josephus says. Moreover, they contain no incidents which seem flatly to contradict known historical facts.

To be sure, the synoptic gospels are full of miracles and wonder tales which are accepted, *in toto,* by many pious Christians. Still, if some of us, in this rationalist age of ours, wish to discount the miracles and the element of the divine, there still remains a connected, non-miraculous, and completely credible and sensible story of the fate of a Galilean preacher. We can try to trace this story as it is told in Matthew.

For instance, suppose we discount Matthew's tales of Jesus' birth and childhood, as after-the-fact traditions designed to accomplish two things: (1) show him to be a Bethlehem-born scion of the line of David, and therefore qualified to be the Messiah, and (2) demonstrate a similarity between his early career and that of Moses.

If we do this, then what we might call the "historic Jesus" enters the scene first as an adult Galilean, who has heard of the preaching of John the Baptist and has traveled to Judea to be baptized.

As a matter of fact, the gospel of St. Mark, the oldest of the four, starts exactly in this fashion. There is no mention in Mark of a virgin birth at Bethlehem, or of any of the tales of the first two chapters of Matthew. Mark starts with John the Baptist and the baptism of Jesus.

With his baptism the "historic Jesus" feels the impulse to become, himself, a preacher and prophet. In modern terms, he feels the "call to the ministry," but Matthew expresses it in a fashion appropriate to his own time.

> Matthew 3:16. And Jesus, when he was baptized, went up straight-way out of the water: and, lo, the heavens were opened unto him, and he saw the Spirit of God descending like a dove, and lighting upon him . . .

This, as described here, seems to be a vision which only Jesus experienced; the heavens were opened "unto *him*, and *he* saw." Un-doubtedly, there was a large crowd being baptized at this time, and there is no indication, in the synoptic gospels, at least, that this was an open manifestation visible to all.

The passage goes further than that, however. Jesus is portrayed as becoming conscious at this time of more than a mere call to preach:

> Matthew 3:17. And lo a voice from heaven, saying, This is my beloved Son, in whom I am well pleased.

The statement "This is my beloved Son" would seem to mean that at this moment Jesus knew himself to be the destined King; that is, the Messiah. Even non-Messianic kings of Judah were considered to be the adopted sons of Yahveh (see page I-489); how much more so the Messiah.

This, however, may be a matter of the gospel writer's pious inter-pretation of matters after the fact. If we try to follow the "historic Jesus" it would seem that the realization of Messiah-hood came con-siderably later.

(The phrase "the Son of God" is considered, in Christian thought, to signify something far more transcendental and subtle than the role assigned to the Messiah in Jewish thought. The later Christian view does not, however, appear clearly in the synoptic gospels. It does do so in the gospel of St. John.)

To Mark, the Spirit of God enters Jesus at the time of the baptism, and it is then and only then, apparently, that he enters his role as Messiah. In Matthew, however, things can't be that simple. The Spirit of God, according to him, entered Jesus at the moment of conception (see page 116), so that he was born the Messiah and could scarcely have need of baptism. Matthew, therefore, must have John the Baptist recognizing this fact. When Jesus came to be baptized:

Matthew 3:14. . . . *John forbad him, saying, I have need to be baptized of thee, and comest thou to me?*

Matthew 3:15. *And Jesus answering said unto him, Suffer it to be so now: for thus it becometh us to fulfil all righteousness . . .*

And yet this realization, on the part of John, of Jesus' role as Messiah, does not fit the tale of the "historic Jesus" as told in Matthew; for at a later period John is clearly revealed as quite uncertain as to the nature of Jesus' mission.

Satan

Once Jesus felt the desire and impelling drive to become a preacher, it is reasonable to suppose that he might have retired for a period of contemplation and decision. What kind of preacher was he to be? What would be his general approach? What would he try to accomplish?

Matthew, expanding on a verse in Mark, puts this into the vocabulary of the time by recounting how, after the baptism, Jesus retired to the wilderness, fasted, and was tempted by Satan to adopt the wrong approach in his ministry. It is characteristic of Matthew that he recounts the struggle between Jesus and Satan as a battle of Old Testament quotations.

Satan urged Jesus, in the first temptation, to satisfy his hunger after fasting by turning stones to bread, something God ought to be glad to do at the request of a devout and pious man. Jesus answers that with a quotation:

Matthew 4:4. *But he [Jesus] answered and said, It is written, Man shall not live by bread alone, but by every word that proceedeth out of the mouth of God.*

The quotation is from Deuteronomy:

> Deuteronomy 8:3. . . . . *man doth not live by bread only, but by every word that proceedeth out of the mouth of the Lord doth man live.*

This might be interpreted as representing Jesus' decision that his role was not to aim merely at an improved economy or a betterment of man's material lot, but to induce moral and ethical regeneration.

Satan next urges Jesus to demonstrate his powers by flinging himself from the top of the Temple and allowing angels to rescue him.

> Matthew 4:6. *And* [Satan] *saith unto him, If thou be the Son of God, cast thyself down: for it is written, He shall give his angels charge concerning thee: and in their hands they shall bear thee up, lest at any time thou dash thy foot against a stone.*

Here Satan is described as lending a metaphorical statement in the Psalms a literal interpretation:

> Psalm 91:11. . . . . *he shall give his angels charge over thee . . .*
> Psalm 91:12. *They shall bear thee up in their hands, lest thou dash thy foot against a stone.*

But Jesus retorted with another quotation:

> Matthew 4:7. *Jesus said unto him, It is written again, Thou shalt not tempt the Lord thy God.*

> (Deuteronomy 6:16. *Ye shall not tempt the Lord your God . . .*)

That is, God is not to be put to the test and made to perform tricks to satisfy the vanity or uncertainty of man. This answer might be interpreted as a decision by Jesus to reject spectacular methods in his mission; to win hearts, that is, by an exhibition of his goodness and not of his power. (Actually, the accounts of the evangelists combine the two aspects and have Jesus demonstrate God's power by miracles of kindliness—the healing of the sick, for the most part.)

In the final temptation, Satan offers him all the kingdoms of the world:

> Matthew 4:9. . . . . *All these things will I give thee, if thou wilt fall down and worship me.*

To which Jesus responds with a third quotation:

Matthew 4:10. . . . *Get thee hence, Satan: for it is written, Thou shalt worship the Lord thy God, and him only shalt thou serve.*

(Deuteronomy 6:13. *Thou shalt fear the Lord thy God, and serve him . . .*)

(Deuteronomy 6:14. *Ye shall not go after other gods . . .*)

Thus, apparently, Jesus rejects the traditional interpretation of the Messiah as a powerful and ideal king who overthrows the enemies of Israel by force and establishes his rule over all the world in the fashion of a super-Alexander.

This decision to be a Messiah of peace rather than one of war is crucial, apparently, to the tale of the "historic Jesus."

Herodias

Jesus' decision to devote his life to the ministry of God must have been sharpened by the news of the arrest of John the Baptist, since that increased the need for someone to take John's place and continue to spread his message:

Matthew 4:12. *Now when Jesus had heard that John was cast into prison, he departed into Galilee; . . .*

. . .

Matthew 4:17. *From that time Jesus began to preach, and to say, Repent: for the kingdom of heaven is at hand.*

Matthew does not, at this point, give the reason for the arrest of the Baptist, but he returns to the subject later.

Matthew 14:3. *For Herod had laid hold on John, and bound him, and put him in prison for Herodias' sake, his brother Philip's wife.*

Matthew 14:4. *For John said unto him, It is not lawful for thee to have her.*

The story behind this is a complicated one. To begin with we must consider the sons of Herod "the Great" (the king reigning at the time of Jesus' birth; see page 124). Three have been mentioned already as sharing Herod's dominion after his death. One of these, however,

Herod Archelaus, is now out of the picture, having been deposed in A.D. 6, a quarter century before the beginning of Jesus' ministry.

Of the other two, we have first, Herod Antipas, the tetrarch of Galilee and Perea. He was the son of Herod the Great by Malthace, Herod's sixth wife, who had been a Samaritan. Herod Antipas was, therefore, half Idumean and half Samaritan by birth and, consequently, doubly obnoxious to Jewish nationalists. He had been tetrarch ever since his father's death in 4 B.C. and, indeed, ruled altogether for forty-three years, a period which was for the most part one of peace and prosperity for the land.

Second, there is Herod Philip, a son of Herod the Great by his seventh wife, Cleopatra, a Judean woman (despite her name). Herod Philip was made tetrarch of Iturea on Herod's death and he may therefore be called "Philip the Tetrarch." He, too, was still ruling at the time of Jesus' ministry and seems to have been a model ruler.

But there appears to be still another son of Herod the Great, one who does not rule over any section of the kingdom and who, to the confusion of the narration, is also called Philip. We will call him simply "Philip" to distinguish him from Philip the tetrarch. He was Herod's son by Herod's fifth wife, Mariamne II. (She must be distinguished from Mariamne I, who was Herod's second wife.) Mariamne II was not of Maccabean descent and so Philip was in no way a Maccabean.

Finally, we have Herodias, who was the daughter of Aristobulus, who was in turn the son of Herod the Great by Mariamne I. Since it was Mariamne I who was a Maccabean, we can consider Herodias, the granddaughter of Herod the Great, a Maccabean through her grandmother. (Herodias' father, Aristobulus, had been excuted by *his* father, Herod, in 6 B.C., when the old king, sick and soon to die, had grown paranoid and was seeing conspiracies everywhere in his complicated family life.)

Herodias married Philip, her half uncle, while Herod Antipas married the daughter of Aretas, a king of the Nabatean Arabs.

Early in his reign, Herod Antipas tired of his wife and divorced her, taking, as his second wife, Herodias, who divorced Philip. Herodias had thus left one half uncle to become the wife of another half uncle.

As a result, Aretas, feeling the rejection of his daughter to be an insult, declared war on Herod Antipas and defeated him. He achieved nothing by this, however, except perhaps the soothing of his pride. The

Romans could not allow local wars to get too out-of-hand and they interfered, allowing Herod Antipas to keep both his tetrarchy and his new wife.

John the Baptist violently denounced this new marriage as incestuous, not so much because Herodias was Herod Antipas' half niece, but because she was his ex-sister-in-law.

Herod Antipas did not allow himself to be driven by this denunciation into giving up Herodias. Rather, he grew impatient with John the Baptist. He didn't mind John's theological doctrines—Judea was a land of constant and complicated theological dispute in those days—but he did object to any interference with his private life. Besides, he may well have suspected a political motivation behind the denunciation, and felt that John was in the pay of the Nabateans, and was attempting to stir up an internal revolt that would suit the purposes of the still-angry Aretas.

John was therefore imprisoned by Herod at Machaerus (according to Josephus), a fortified village on the southern border of Perea, east of the Dead Sea. Herod did not, however, dare take the logical step of executing John and closing his mouth once and for all, for he feared the unrest that might follow from John's numerous disciples. John therefore remained imprisoned for a period of time.

Zabulon and Nephthalim

Matthew sees Jesus' return to Galilee to begin his ministry as the fulfillment of a prophecy:

Matthew 4:14. *That it might be fulfilled which was spoken by Esaias* [Isaiah] *the prophet, saying,*

Matthew 4:15. *The land of Zabulon* [Zebulon], *and the land of Nephthalim* [Naphtali], *by the way of the sea, beyond Jordan, Galilee of the Gentiles;*

Matthew 4:16. *The people which sat in darkness saw great light; and to them which sat in the region and shadow of death light is sprung up.*

The quotation appears in the Old Testament as:

Isaiah 9:1. *Nevertheless the dimness shall not be such as was in her vexation, when at the first he lightly afflicted the land of*

Zebulun and the land of Naphtali, and afterward did more grievously afflict her by the way of the sea, beyond Jordan, in Galilee of the nations.

Isaiah 9:2. The people that walked in darkness have seen a great light: they that dwell in the land of the shadow of death, upon them hath the light shined.

The two verses in Isaiah do not, however, belong together. The first verse (9:1) belongs to the material in the eighth chapter, in which Isaiah is talking about the destruction, not long before, of Israel by the Assyrian forces under Sargon. The second verse (9:2) represents a complete change of subject and even a shift from prose to poetry. It starts a coronation hymn which might have been written, originally, to celebrate the anointing of a new king, possibly Hezekiah (see page I-423).

In the Hebrew Bible (and in the new Jerusalem Bible as well), Isaiah 9:1, with its reference to Naphtali and Zebulon, is to be found as the last verse of the eighth chapter (Isaiah 8:23), while what is Isaiah 9:2 in the King James Version begins the ninth chapter as Isaiah 9:1.

This is by far the more logical separation of the two chapters, and the combination of the two verses in the same chapter was undoubtedly influenced by their quotation together by Matthew, who was anxious to make it seem that the reference to the light in darkness referred particularly to Zebulon and Naphtali so that he might indulge in his hobby of making as much of Jesus' career as possible seem to have been predicted by the Old Testament.

The Carpenter's Son

It might be supposed that in returning to Galilee, Jesus would first of all go back to his own town. If he did, however, he remained there only a short while, something that Matthew skips over hurriedly:

Matthew 4:12. . . . *he [Jesus] departed into Galilee;*
Matthew 4:13. *And leaving Nazareth . . .*

What happened in Nazareth at this time, if anything, Matthew does not say, but later in the gospel, Matthew does recount the events that took place during a (presumably) later visit to Nazareth. These same events are recounted by Luke as having taken place during a visit to Nazareth near the start of his ministry, and it is tempting to wonder if perhaps it did not happen at the *very* start of that period of his life.

We could suppose, in tracing the "historic Jesus," that, filled with his new sense of mission, he returned to Nazareth and began to preach there first of all:

> Matthew 13:54. *And when he was come into his own country, he taught them in their synagogue, insomuch that they were astonished* . . .

But in doing so, he did not please his audience. They remembered him as a youngster who had grown to manhood in their town, and now he had the nerve, apparently, to set himself up as a preacher over them. Matthew quotes the audience as asking, resentfully:

> Matthew 13:54. . . . *Whence hath this man this wisdom* . . .
> Matthew 13:55. *Is not this the carpenter's son? is not his mother called Mary?* . . .
> Matthew 13:56. . . . *Whence then hath this man all these things?*

Both Jesus' father and mother are here mentioned, but his father, Joseph, never appears as a living person anywhere in the New Testament except in connection with the tales of Jesus' birth. It is usually assumed, therefore, that he died some time during Jesus' youth.

It would appear from these verses that Joseph was a carpenter, but what about Jesus? Luke, in telling the same incident, has the audience ask:

> Luke 4:22. . . . *Is not this Joseph's son?*

and there is no mention of carpentering.

Mark, on the other hand—author of the oldest of the gospels—records the incident and has the audience ask:

> Mark 6:3. *Is not this the carpenter, the son of Mary* . . .

Is it possible, then, that the "historic Jesus," before his baptism by John and his call to the ministry, was a carpenter in Nazareth and that his townspeople were highly offended that a common laborer with no theological education (the common people were notoriously unlearned in the Pharisaic complications of the Law in those days) should presume to set himself up as a preacher? And if he displayed knowledge of the Law, having learned it through intelligence and industry, that would not alter the fact that as a common laborer he ought to sit in the audience and listen to his "betters."

Both Luke and Matthew, writing later, when Jesus had grown mightier in the memory of his disciples, might indeed have felt reluctant to emphasize Jesus' position as a laborer. Matthew made Joseph the carpenter (though it is quite possible that father and son were both carpenters; that Jesus was brought up in his father's trade) while Luke drops the embarrassing word altogether.

In any case, Jesus assuages his disappointment by a thought similar to our own "Familiarity breeds contempt."

> Matthew 13:57. . . . *Jesus said unto them, A prophet is not without honour, save in his own country, and in his own house.*

The experience seems to have shown Jesus that if his mission were to be successful, it would have to be some place where he wasn't known so well that people would let themselves be influenced by the nature of his earlier trade or the state of his formal education.

Jesus' Brethren

The incident at Nazareth reveals something else about Jesus' family. The audience ironically recites the names of Jesus' relatives to show that they are not mistaken, that this upstart preacher is indeed the lowly carpenter they know and not some visiting dignitary. They mention not only his mother and father, but his brothers and sisters as well.

> Matthew 13:55. *Is not this the carpenter's son? is not his mother called Mary? and his brethren, James, and Joses, and Simon, and Judas?*
>
> Matthew 13:56. *And his sisters, are they not all with us?*

If one interpreted these verses in the simplest possible manner, one would come to the conclusion that the "historic Jesus" was the member of a large family, and that Joseph and Mary had five sons and several daughters.

Even if one were to accept Matthew's tale of the virgin birth of Jesus, this possibility is not eliminated. He says:

> Matthew 1:25. *And [Joseph]* knew her *[Mary]* not till she had brought forth her firstborn son: *and he called his name Jesus.*

Even if Mary remained a virgin till Jesus' birth, there is nothing in this verse which would force us to believe that Joseph had no relations with Mary *after* the birth of Jesus, and that Mary might not have borne a number of children in the normal manner who would then have been younger brothers and sisters to Jesus. One might even argue that a "firstborn" son implies at least a secondborn son and possibly others. It would have been easy to say "only son" or even "only child" if Mary had had no more children.

This picture of a normal home life, of Mary as a multiple mother, of Jesus with four younger brothers and several younger sisters, is, however, unacceptable to many Christians who believe firmly in the tradition of the perpetual virginity of Mary, and reasons have been advanced to make the apparently clear words of the verse mean other than they seem to mean.

One theory is that the individuals referred to as the brothers and sisters of Jesus were actually Joseph's children by a previous marriage and not the sons of Mary at all. They would then be Jesus' older half brothers and half sisters. Against that, is the fact that no such earlier marriage of Joseph is mentioned anywhere in the Bible.

A more tenable theory is that the men were not his brothers but relatives of another kind—say, cousins. The word "brother" is indeed used in the Bible to mean, on occasion, "kinsman." Thus Lot is Abraham's nephew, but:

> Genesis 13:8. *And Abram [Abraham]* said unto Lot, Let there be no strife, I pray thee, between me and thee, . . . *for we be* brethren.

Again Jacob is Laban's nephew, but:

> Genesis 29:15. *And Laban said unto Jacob, Because thou art my* brother, *shouldest thou therefore serve me for nought?* . . .

However, in such cases enough genealogical material is usually given to enable the exact relations of the individuals involved to be worked

out. This is not so in the case of Jesus' brethren, and those who argue
for a more distant relationship must seek indirect evidence.

Thus, Matthew speaks of several women witnessing the crucifixion:

> Matthew 27:56. *Among which was . . . Mary the mother of James
> and Joses . . .*

Names are frequently repeated from family to family, but here we
have a James and Joses who are the sons of Mary. Could these be the
James and Joses mentioned as Jesus' brothers, along with Simon and
Judas, here unmentioned? If so, they must be the sons of another
Mary, for if this Mary were Jesus' mother as well, surely Matthew
would have said so. In that case, who was this other Mary?

In an analogous verse in the gospel of St. John, we have:

> John 19:25. *Now there stood by the cross of Jesus his mother,
> and his mother's sister, Mary the wife of Cleophas . . .*

Could it be that the brothers mentioned in Matthew 13:55 are the
sons of Jesus' aunt Mary, rather than of his mother Mary, and are
therefore actually his first cousins?

However, many modern scholars do not seek roundabout explanations but accept Mary, the mother of Jesus, as being the mother of
others as well. Certainly, if we try to trace a "historic Jesus" in whom
the tale of the virgin birth is not involved, there is no reason to question
the fact that he had true brothers and sisters.

Capernaum

Leaving Nazareth, Jesus went to a larger city in Galilee, where he
might expect more success than in his small home town:

> Matthew 4:13. *And leaving Nazareth, he [Jesus] came and dwelt
> in Capernaum, which is upon the sea coast . . .*

Capernaum is about twenty miles northeast of Nazareth and, in the
time of Jesus, was an important town with a Roman garrison, a tax-
collection office, and a sizable synagogue. Its Hebrew name was
"Kapharnahum" ("village of Nahum"), which became "Kapharnaoum"
in Greek and "Capernaum" in English.

Despite the fame of Capernaum as the site of Jesus' preaching, it

Early Journeys of Christ

eventually faded away until, in modern times, there was even a dispute as to its location.

It was located "upon the sea coast" but that does not mean the Mediterranean Sea, as one might think, but upon the inland lake of fresh water that is found to the east of Galilee along the upper courses of the Jordan River.

The lake is pear-shaped with the broad end at the north. It is not large, only thirteen miles long and seven and a half miles wide at its broadest point. It has a surface area of only sixty-five square miles (three times the size of Manhattan Island).

The lake has had a variety of names, all taken from cities or districts along its western shores. For instance, a very early town near its southern end was named Chinnereth. It is mentioned in the records of the conquering Thutmose III of Egypt (see page I-122) long before the Exodus. It gave its name to the lake and to the western shores of that lake.

The lake is barely mentioned in the Old Testament, for the centers of population and power in Israel and Judah lay well to the south. When it is mentioned at all, it is usually brought in as part of a boundary delineation:

Numbers 34:11. . . . *and the border shall descend, and shall reach unto the side of the sea of Chinnereth eastward . . .*

The western shores of the lake are mentioned in connection with a Syrian invasion of about 900 B.C.

1 Kings 15:20. *So Ben-hadad* [of Syria] *. . . smote . . . Cinneroth* [Chinnereth], *with all the land of Naphtali.*

Modern Israel still uses the Old Testament name for the lake, calling it "Yam Kinneret," and on its shores is a town called Kinneret, with a population of about a thousand.

On the northwestern shores of the lake is a small plain, not more than two miles each way, where two small rivulets enter it. It was called Gennosar or Gennesarat, a name of uncertain origin. Perhaps it means "garden of Hazor," Hazor being the Canaanite ruler of the region in the time of the judges (see page I-235).

At any rate, that district gave its name to the lake also, and the names are used in the Bible, the Apocrypha, and in Josephus. Thus:

1 Maccabees 11:67. *As for Jonathan and his host, they pitched at the water of Gennesar . . .*

and, in the New Testament:

Luke 5:1. . . . *he* [Jesus] *stood by the lake of Gennesaret,*

In modern Israel a village stands on the northwest shore of the lake. It has a population of perhaps five hundred and its name is Ginnosar.

After the exodus when the northern reaches that had once made up the tribal territory of Naphtali and Zebulon became known as Galilee (see page 64), the lake became known as the Sea of Galilee:

Matthew 4:18. *And Jesus, walking by the sea of Galilee . . .*

That is perhaps the name by which it is best known to Christians ever since, but it is not the latest of its names. In Jesus' own time, still a newer name arose.

The largest and most modern city on the shores of the lake in Jesus' time was one that was built in A.D. 20 (less than a decade before Jesus began his ministry) by Herod Antipas. It was named Tiberias after the Roman Emperor then reigning and Antipas made it his capital. It was primarily a Gentile city and was looked upon by the Jews with horror, partly for that reason and partly out of superstition, for it was built on the site of an ancient cemetery.

The city is mentioned only once in the New Testament, and then only in the gospel of St. John, the latest and most Greek-oriented of the gospels:

John 6:23. (*Howbeit there came other boats from Tiberias . . .*)

That city, too, gave its name to the sea, a name also found in John:

John 6:1. *After these things Jesus went over the sea of Galilee, which is the sea of Tiberias.*

Tiberias still exists and is still the largest city on the shores of the lake. It has a population of about twenty-two thousand, and its name is still affixed to the lake, which is known in Arabic as "Bahr Tabariya" and in American geographies as "Lake Tiberias."

Simon

In Capernaum, Jesus rapidly attained the success and got the hearing that he was denied in Nazareth. He even began to collect disciples:

Matthew 4:18. *And Jesus, walking by the sea of Galilee, saw two brethren, Simon called Peter, and Andrew his brother, casting a net into the sea: for they were fishers.*
Matthew 4:19. *And he saith unto them, Follow me, and I will make you fishers of men.*
Matthew 4:20. *And they straightway left their nets, and followed him.*

Simeon is the form of the name used in the Old Testament, and in one place that form is used for Simon Peter:

Acts 15:14. *Simeon hath declared how God at the first did visit the Gentiles . . .*

There was a strong tendency, however, to shorten it to Simon, since that happened to be a perfectly good Greek name and there was a continuing tendency among even conservative Jews in this period to adopt or be given Greek names.

The Jews did not have our system of surnames and it was customary

to distinguish an individual from others of the same name by the use
of his father's name. Thus, at one point, Jesus says:

> Matthew 16:17. . . . *Blessed art thou, Simon Bar-jona . . .*

By Simon Bar-jona is meant, "Simon, son of Jona."

But this too might be insufficient, and it was common to add to a
man's name some nickname drawn from his personal appearance or
character, something that would be highly individual. This was noted in
the case of the sons of Mattathias, the priest who sparked the Maccabean rebellion (see page 54).

Simon, perhaps because of his size and strength, or because of his
firmness of will, or both, was called, in Aramaic, Simon Cephas (Simon,
the Rock). In Greek, "rock" is "petros" and in Latin it is "petrus."
This becomes "peter" in English and so Simon is frequently referred to
as Simon Peter.

The nickname can be used by itself if it is sufficiently distinctive
and becomes sufficiently well known. Thus, Paul, in his First Epistle to
the Corinthians, denounces the factionalism of the early Church, saying:

> 1 Corinthians 1:12. . . . *every one of you saith, I am of Paul; and
> I of Apollos; and I of Cephas . . .*

where Cephas is Simon. And we, of course, know him best simply as
Peter.

Andrew is not a name that occurs in the Old Testament. It is the
English version of the Greek "Andreas" meaning "manly." The final
"-ew" in the English version may have been influenced by the form of
Matthew.

Matthew's story makes it seem that Peter and Andrew were simply
called and they followed, unable to help themselves, attracted and
mesmerized by the divine in Jesus. And yet, if we are tracing the
"historic Jesus," it isn't at all unreasonable to assume that Peter and
Andrew first heard him preach, were attracted to his doctrines, and
then joined him.

James

Nor were the brothers, Peter and Andrew, the only disciples gained
in Capernaum. Another pair of brothers were quickly collected:

Matthew 4:21. *And going on from thence, he saw other two brethren, James the son of Zebedee, and John his brother, in a ship with Zebedee their father, mending their nets; and he called them.*

Matthew 4:22. *And they immediately left the ship and their father, and followed him.*

Zebedee, the name of the father of James and John, is the English version of the Greek "Zebedaios" which is, in turn, derived from the Hebrew Zebediah. A number of men of that name are mentioned in the Old Testament but none of importance.

John, son of Zebedee, is the second of the important Johns in the New Testament, the first being John the Baptist, of course.

James would seem, at first, to be a name distinct from any in the Old Testament, but that appears so only if we look upon the English version of the name. It comes from the Greek "Iakhobos" and the Latin "Jacobus," so that James is clearly equivalent to Jacob.

Decapolis

The fame of Jesus' preaching began to spread widely. In the Jewish kingdoms of that time, a skillful preacher, learned in the Law and ready to illustrate his points with interesting tales that pointed an analogy or a moral ("parables"), was bound to attract attention. Word concerning him would travel quickly, as one person excitedly told another, and many would come to see and hear the new attraction. The effect would be the same as that of a new philosopher in Athens, a new gladiator in Rome, or a new popular play in New York.

Concerning holy men of all ages, reports of miraculous cures have always been circulated. This has been true not only of the times before Jesus, but of the times since. The kings of England, few of whom were particularly holy, and some of whom were particularly unholy, were considered capable of curing a disease called scrofula simply by touching the sick individual; and the monarch touched for the "king's evil" into the eighteenth century. Even today there are any number of faith-healers who cure people by the "laying on of hands." Such is the complicated nature of disease and the important influence of mental attitude upon it that a patient who thoroughly believes a certain course of treatment will help him (even if it is only the casual touch of an indifferent king or of a backwoods healer) is indeed often helped.

Many tales of cures brought about by Jesus are recorded by the enthusiastic evangelists, and it is useless to try to suggest naturalistic explanations for each one. To the believing Christian, all the cures described are completely possible, having been brought about not by faith-healing or by a kind of primitive psychiatry, but by the direct intervention of divine power.

In the search for the "historic Jesus," however, it may be sufficient to say that many who accepted Jesus as a holy man believed he could help their illnesses and were indeed helped by him. The tales of his cures were spread abroad (and were exaggerated in the telling and retelling, as is invariably and inevitably the case in such situations). Such tales helped increase his fame further:

> Matthew 4:24. *And his fame went throughout all Syria . . .*
> Matthew 4:25. *And there followed him great multitudes of people from Galilee, and from Decapolis, and from Jerusalem . . .*

The mention of Decapolis ("ten cities") is particularly interesting. At the time of the conquests of Alexander the Great, Greek cities were planted everywhere that his armies trod; and this tendency continued under the Macedonian kings who fell heir to his dominions. Under the Seleucids, the region east of the Jordan River and the Sea of Galilee came to be studded with Greek towns.

At the height of the Maccabean monarchy, the area was conquered by Alexander Jannaeus, but when Pompey marched into Judea and reorganized the area, the Greek cities were freed. They formed a league among themselves and in the time of Jesus enjoyed considerable self-government. The ten cities that formed part of the league are given differently by different authorities, but apparently the northernmost was Damascus itself, sixty miles northeast of Capernaum. This is the same Damascus that had been the capital of the Syrian kingdom against which Ahab had fought.

If people came from the Decapolis to hear Jesus, they may have included some Gentiles. This is not specifically stated, but there is nothing impossible about it. Just as some Jews were strongly attracted to Greek culture, some Greeks would be strongly attracted to Judaism. Even if such Greeks stopped short of conversion, they might yet be sufficiently interested to go hear some outstanding preacher.

In view of the later history of Christianity, the fact that Jesus' preaching may early have spread among Greeks, and Gentiles generally, is of extreme importance.

The Law

At this point Matthew feels it appropriate to give a sampling of the doctrines that Jesus was preaching, and that attracted such wide attention. He does so in a sermon covering three chapters. Probably the passage as given by Matthew is not actually a single sermon spoken at one time, but is a collection of representative "sayings." The sermon is introduced thus:

> Matthew 5:1. *And seeing the multitudes, he [Jesus] went up into a mountain: and when he was set, his disciples came unto him:*
> Matthew 5:2. *And he opened his mouth, and taught them . . .*

In A.D. 394 the Christian bishop St. Augustine wrote a commentary on this sermon which he entitled "Concerning the Lord's sermon in the mountain" and since then these chapters of Matthew have been referred to as "The Sermon on the Mount."

There have been attempts to pick out some particular hill near Capernaum on which the sermon might have been delivered, but there seems no way of reaching a decision.

The Sermon on the Mount, as given in Matthew, is, as is to be expected, closely tied in with Old Testament teachings. Many phrases which we associate very strongly with the Sermon and with Jesus' teachings have close parallels in the Old Testament. Thus an often quoted passage appears in the early verses of the Sermon, verses that give blessings to various groups of individuals and are therefore called the "Beatitudes" from the Latin word for "happiness" or "blessedness." It goes:

> Matthew 5:5. *Blessed are the meek: for they shall inherit the earth.*

Compare this with:

> Psalm 37:11. *But the meek shall inherit the earth . . .*

Indeed, it might be supposed that one of the purposes of Matthew in recording the Sermon on the Mount is to support a particular point of view which he represents among the early Christians.

After Jesus had passed from the scene, his sayings survived only because they were remembered and repeated by word of mouth. There is no evidence that Jesus ever put his teachings into permanent written form.

Oral teaching that must be carried on by word of mouth can give rise to disputes. There were naturally many sayings quoted by one listener or another and in some cases a saying might be reported in one form by one person and in another form by someone else. The sayings might even be quoted in self-contradictory forms and could be used to support widely divergent theological points.

Perhaps the most basic of the early splits among Christians was between those who held the teachings of Jesus to be merely a refinement of Judaism, and those who held them to be a radical change from Judaism. The former would maintain the supremacy of the Mosaic Law even for Christians; the latter would deny it.

Matthew, the most Jewish of the evangelists, apparently believed in the supremacy of the Law, and in the Sermon on the Mount he quoted Jesus as being strenuously and unequivocally of that belief:

> Matthew 5:17. *Think not that I am come to destroy the law, or the prophets: I am not come to destroy, but to fulfil.*
>
> Matthew 5:18. *For verily I say unto you, Till heaven and earth pass, one jot or one tittle shall in no wise pass from the law, till all be fulfilled.*

Matthew follows that with another verse which seems aimed by him directly at the heads of those among the early Christians who took up the other point of view:

> Matthew 5:19. *Whosoever therefore shall break one of these least commandments, and shall teach men so, he shall be called the least in the kingdom of heaven . . .*

This extreme view, as quoted, is strengthened by a consideration of the meaning of "jot" and "tittle." Jot is the Hebrew letter "yodh," the smallest (little more than a fat dot) letter in the Hebrew alphabet. In Greek the letter is named "iota," and is the smallest in the Greek alphabet (so that one says "not an iota" meaning "not a bit"). In English the letter is "i" and it is the smallest in our alphabet.

A tittle is a translation of a Greek word meaning "little horn." It would be a small mark that would distinguish one Hebrew letter from another. The equivalent in English would be the small line that distinguishes a Q from an O.

The Revised Standard Version translates the verse: "For truly, I say to you, till heaven and earth pass away, not an iota, not a dot, will pass from the law until all is accomplished." Nothing, in other words, would change in the Law as a result of Jesus' coming, not even the smallest particle.

The interpretation of this passage depends on the phrase "till all be fulfilled." Matthew seems to imply that this is synonymous with "till heaven and earth pass." Other views are possible, however, and are stated in the Bible, as we shall see, and it was these other views that eventually won out.

It may very well be that the "historic Jesus" did indeed hold the view given here in Matthew, for in the synoptic gospels he is always pictured—despite his disputes with the Pharisees—as an orthodox Jew, adhering to all the tenets of Judaism.

Publicans

If anything, Jesus (as represented by Matthew) would strengthen the Law, rather than weaken it. Thus, in the Sermon on the Mount, Jesus is quoted as preaching the necessity for exceeding the letter of the Law in matters of morals and ethics. It is not sufficient to refrain from killing one's fellow man; one must refrain from even being angry with him, or expressing contempt for him. It is insufficient to refrain from committing adultery; one must not even allow one's self to entertain lustful feelings. It is insufficient to refrain from swearing false oaths; one should not swear at all, but simply tell the truth.

Although the Mosaic Law permitted retaliation in kind to personal injuries, Jesus held it better that there were no retaliation at all. One should return good for evil. After all, he points out, to return good for good is easy; that is a natural tendency that affects even the irreligious. Those who wish ethical perfection must do more than that:

> Matthew 5:46. *For if ye love them which love you, what reward have ye? do not even the publicans the same?*

The publicans are held up here as an extreme. If even the publicans can do this, anyone can. The Greek word used here is "telonai" which is translated into the Latin "publicani" and which becomes, in English, "publicans."

In Rome the publicani were originally the contractors who agreed, for appropriate payment, to perform public works and services. One of the most important of these public works and services was to collect taxes.

It was difficult to collect taxes in a realm the size of the Roman Empire in a day when modern means of transportation and communication did not exist, and when modern business procedures were unheard of. The mere fact that Arabic numerals did not exist, enormously multiplied the difficulties of regulating the Roman economy.

Roman financial procedures were always inefficient and wasteful and the burden of this was laid upon the people of the empire, particularly, in New Testament times, upon the people of the provinces.

The Roman government did not have the organization required to collect taxes, so what they did was to farm out permission to make such collections to rich men who had considerable cash available. These could, for a large sum, buy the right to collect the taxes of a certain province. The sum they paid would represent the tax collection as far as the government was concerned. The government would have the taxes it needed on the spot. It need take no further trouble for it.

The publicani, however, would now have to recoup their payment out of the taxes they collected, which they could then keep. It was as "tax collectors" that the people of the provinces best knew the publicani, and the word is translated as "tax collector" in the Revised Standard Version.

The trouble with this system was that if the publicani, or tax collectors, gathered less than they had paid out, they would suffer a loss, whereas if they could gouge out more than they had paid, they would make a profit. The more merciless the gouging, the higher the profit, so it was to the interest of the publicani to force payment of every cent they could get by the harshest application of the letter of the Law as interpreted most favorably to themselves.

No tax collector, however lenient and merciful, is actually going to be loved, but a "publican" of the Roman sort was sure to be hated above all men as a merciless leech who would take the shirt off a dying child. It is not to be wondered at, then, that the word "publican" is used as representing an extreme of wickedness in the Sermon on the Mount.

Of course, the men to whom Jesus referred were not the publicani themselves, not the wealthy businessmen in Rome who waxed fat on the misery of millions. They were merely the army of small employees who owned the actual outstretched hands and who then passed the money on to their superiors.

But in a way, these were even worse, for they were usually Jews who took the job as a means of making a living and, in this fashion, earned the hatred and contempt of their fellow Jews. There were numerous Jewish nationalists at this time who felt the Romans to be oppressors who must be fought against and overthrown in Maccabean fashion. To endure the presence of the Romans was bad enough, to pay taxes to them was worse, but to collect taxes for them was the limit and beyond the limit.

Paternoster

Jesus continues the Sermon on the Mount, denouncing ostentation in piety. He decries giving alms openly, praying in public, or deliberately exaggerating one's appearance of suffering while fasting, all in order to receive admiration and gain a reputation for piety. Jesus points out that if it is human acclaim that is wanted, then it is received and that is all the reward that is likely to come.

He also counsels against uselessly long or ritualistic prayers:

> Matthew 6:7. . . . *when ye pray, use not vain repetitions, as the heathen do: for they think that they shall be heard for their much speaking.*
>
> . . . .
>
> Matthew 6:9. *After this manner therefore pray ye: Our Father which art in heaven, Hallowed be thy name.*

and there follows the well-known "Lord's Prayer," so-called because it is the prayer recited by Jesus himself. In Latin the first words "Our Father" are "Pater noster," so that the prayer is sometimes called "the Paternoster."

Ironically enough, in view of Jesus' admonition in Matthew 6:7, it is often customary to repeat the Paternoster a number of times in a fast, mumbling sort of way—so that the word "patter" for such fast, mumbling speech is derived from "Paternoster."

Mammon

As is not unusual for preachers who gather their disciples from among the poor, Jesus had harsh words to say about wealth and the wealthy. The "historic Jesus" was himself a carpenter, his first four disciples were fishermen. Undoubtedly it was the poor and unlearned who followed him, while the aristocracy (the Sadducees) and the intelligentsia (the Pharisees) opposed him.

It is not surprising, then, that the gospels, and early Christian teaching in general, had a strong note of the social revolutionary about it. It may even have been this note that contributed greatly to the gathering of converts in the first couple of centuries after Jesus' death.

In the Sermon on the Mount, Jesus urged less care for gathering the material riches valued on Earth and more care for the gathering of the ethical riches valued in heaven. Indeed, to care too much for Earthly things meant, inevitably, that one would withdraw one's attention from the subtler values of heaven:

Matthew 6:24. *No man can serve two masters:* . . . *Ye cannot serve God and mammon.*

Mammon is, here, an untranslated Aramaic word meaning "wealth." Because of its use in this manner in this verse, it is very commonly supposed that mammon is an antithesis of God; that it is the name of some demon or heathen idol that serves as a god of wealth. Thus, John Milton, in his *Paradise Lost*, makes Mammon one of the fallen angels who followed Satan. In fact, he makes him the most despicable of the lot, for even in Heaven, before his fall, Milton pictures him as exclusively concerned with admiring the gold of Heaven's pavement.

It would get the meaning across more efficiently if the phrase were translated (as in the Jerusalem Bible) as "God and money."

In a way, this represented a shift from early Jewish thought. In the absence of a hereafter of reward and punishment, it was felt that the pious were rewarded on earth with wealth, health, and happiness, while the sinful were punished with impoverishment, sickness, and misery. It was this thought which sparked the intricate discussion concerning the attitude of God toward good and evil which is found in the Book of Job (see page I-479).

With reward and punishment reserved for the next life, the thought might naturally arise that people who had it "too good" on Earth would have to suffer for it in the hereafter just to even the score. There could well be some comfort in this view to those who were poor and oppressed and the evangelists sometimes quote Jesus in such a way as to make him appear to support this view.

Placing God and mammon in opposition, as in Matthew 6:24, is an example. An even more extreme example, which virtually damns rich men merely for being rich, is the familiar verse in which Jesus says:

> Matthew 19:24. . . . *It is easier for a camel to go through the eye of a needle, than for a rich man to enter into the kingdom of God.*

Once Christianity became widespread and popular enough to attract the rich and powerful, much effort had to be expended to explain away this verse. Thus, for example, it was sometimes pretended that "Needle's Eye" was the name of a narrow gate through the Jerusalem walls and that a full laden camel could not pass through until some of the load was removed. Therefore, the verse could be taken as meaning that a rich man could get into Heaven only after a suitable portion of his wealth had been given to charity—or the Church. However, it makes more sense to accept the verse as meaning just what it seems to mean —an expression of a savage feeling against the rich on the part of the poor who made up the early Christian congregations.

The Dogs

Toward the end of the Sermon on the Mount, a verse occurs that is not connected with what precedes or succeeds, but stands by itself:

> Matthew 7:6. *Give not that which is holy unto the dogs, neither cast ye your pearls before swine, lest they trample them under their feet, and turn again and rend you.*

Both dogs and swine were ritually unclean animals which were scavengers and therefore literally unclean as well. To apply either term to someone was a matter of high insult—and still is in many cultures. (Consider the German expletive "Schweinhund" or "pig-dog.")

The question is: What or whom are the dogs and swine being referred to in this verse? The verse might simply mean that one ought not to try to teach religious truths to inveterate scoffers or those utterly lost in sin, and yet that scarcely seems to be right. To whom ought one to teach the truth? To those who already believe?

Jesus himself refutes this, for when he is accused of associating with sinners, he is quoted as saying:

> Matthew 9:12. . . . *They that be whole need not a physician, but they that are sick.*

On the other hand, the reference to dogs and pigs may be a quotation selected by Matthew to support his own view of a Jewish-oriented Christianity. In other words, he might be saying that one ought not to make a great effort to spread the teachings of Jesus among the Gentiles. Perhaps it was Matthew's view that there was too great a danger of the Gentiles being offended by efforts at proselytization and indulging in forceful persecution of the Christians; they would "turn again and rend you" as, in fact, they actually did on occasion. He might also feel that those Gentiles who accepted Christianity without knowledge of the Mosaic Law would pervert the teachings of Jesus; they would "trample them under their feet."

That all this might indeed be so is supported by another passage in Matthew where the matter is stated quite plainly and where the meaning of the word "dog" is unmistakable.

During a stay north of Galilee, Jesus is accosted by a Canaanite woman who requests him to heal her sick daughter.

At first, Jesus does not answer her at all, but when she persists:

> Matthew 15:24. . . . *he answered and said, I am not sent but unto the lost sheep of the house of Israel.*
>
> . . . .
>
> Matthew 15:26. . . . *It is not meet to take the children's bread, and to cast it to dogs.*

Here Matthew clearly presents his version of a Jesus whose business lies entirely within the boundaries of Jewish nationalism. (To be sure, these verses are not the end of this particular passage; more of that shortly.) Furthermore the antithesis of "children" and "dogs" is clearly meant to represent that of "Jews" and "Gentiles." This shows a strong anti-Gentile bias on the part of some of the early Jewish Christians; a bias which, as we shall see in later gospels, was amply returned by some of the early Gentile Christians.

This view of Jesus' teachings—as pictured by Matthew—is also shown when Jesus' disciples are sent out to spread those teachings. They receive clear instructions:

> Matthew 10:5. . . . *Jesus . . . commanded them, saying, Go not into the way of the Gentiles, and into any city of the Samaritans enter ye not:*
>
> Matthew 10:6. *But go rather to the lost sheep of the house of Israel.*

The Centurion

And yet Matthew could not possibly present the situation too narrowly. At the time that the gospel was written, it was quite clear that most Jews were resolutely rejecting the Messiah-hood of Jesus and would never accept it, whereas a surprising number of Gentiles were asking admittance. Christianity could not close the door upon the Gentile or it would die. Even Matthew saw that.

He therefore pictures the Gentile as allowed to enter but, it must be said, sometimes does so rather grudgingly. Thus, consider again the case of the Canaanite woman who accosts Jesus with a request to heal her daughter and is told that the children's food is not to be cast to dogs. She accepts the analogy submissively:

> Matthew 15:27. *And she said, Truth, Lord: yet the dogs eat of the crumbs which fall from their masters' table.*

Whereupon Jesus accepts the justice of the remark (one might almost consider it a gentle reproof) and heals the woman's daughter. According to Matthew's view here, it would seem, the Gentile is accepted, if he enters humbly, with full knowledge of his inferior status.

A less grudging attitude is evidenced by an incident related of Jesus immediately after the Sermon on the Mount, one that not only welcomes Gentiles, but warns obdurate Jews.

> Matthew 8:5. . . . *when Jesus was entered into Capernaum, there came unto him a centurion, beseeching him,*

Matthew 8:6. *And saying, Lord, my servant lieth at home sick of the palsy* . . .

A centurion was an officer who commanded a hundred men, and the word is derived from the Latin "centum" meaning "a hundred men." He would be equivalent to a noncommissioned officer in our army. It is uncertain in this case whether the centurion was actually a member of the occupying Roman army or in the forces of Herod Antipas. In either case, he was not Jewish.

The centurion begs Jesus not to bother coming personally, but to say the healing word from a distance. Jesus does as the centurion asks, saying:

Matthew 8:10. . . . . *I have not found so great faith, no, not in Israel.*

Matthew 8:11. *And I say unto you, That many shall come from the east and west, and shall sit down with Abraham, and Isaac, and Jacob, in the kingdom of heaven.*

Matthew 8:12. *But the children of the kingdom shall be cast out into outer darkness* . . .

Matthew considers Jesus' miracles of healing to bear out an Old Testament prophecy:

Matthew 8:17. *That it might be fulfilled which was spoken by Esaias [Isaiah] the prophet, saying, Himself took our infirmities, and bare our sicknesses.*

This is from a verse in Second Isaiah in which the prophet describes the suffering servant (see page I-550):

Isaiah 53:4. *Surely he hath borne our griefs, and carried our sorrows* . . .

The Son of Man

Jesus is pictured in the synoptic gospels as careful, during this early part of his ministry, to avoid arousing the suspicion of the authorities with respect to his Messianic status. Both the religious and secular leaders would strike quickly at those they considered were falsely claiming to be the Messiah, since such false Messiahs would stir up revolts and do much damage.

Even if Jesus himself were discreet, his growing popularity might cause those who followed him to proclaim him the Messiah in too incautious a fashion, and this, apparently, he wished to avoid. He is therefore described as preferring that his miraculous cures not be too widely publicized. Thus, after curing a leper:

Matthew 8:4. . . . *Jesus saith unto him, See thou tell no man; but go thy way, shew thyself to the priest, and offer the gift that Moses commanded . . .*

In other words, the cured leper is to have himself declared ritually clean according to the Mosaic system, but he is not to say how it came about. Jesus showed the same discretion in references to himself. Thus, when a scribe offered to become his disciple, Jesus points out the hardships involved:

Matthew 8:20. *And Jesus saith unto him, The foxes have holes, and the birds of the air have nests; but the Son of man hath not where to lay his head.*

The phrase "Son of man" is a common way of saying simply "man." It is frequently used in the Book of Ezekiel, when God is quoted as addressing the prophet:

Ezekiel 2:1. *And he* [God] *said unto me, Son of man, stand upon thy feet, and I will speak unto thee.*

The phrase seems to emphasize the lowliness of man as compared to God; the infinite inferiority of the former to the latter. It is as though God addressed a man as "Mortal!"

Outside of Ezekiel, the phrase does not appear in the Old Testament except in the very late Book of Daniel. There it is used in one case precisely as in Ezekiel, when the angel Gabriel speaks to Daniel:

Daniel 8:17. . . . *he* [Gabriel] *said unto me, Understand, O son of man . . .*

But in the second place, Daniel is describing an apocalyptic vision (see page I-610):

Daniel 7:13. *I saw in the night visions, and, behold, one like the Son of man came with the clouds of heaven, . . .*

Daniel 7:14. *And there was given him . . . an everlasting domin-*
ion . . . and his kingdom . . . shall not be destroyed.

Daniel had previously symbolized a variety of heathen nations oppressing Israel in the form of wild beasts; now he symbolized the ideal
kingdom of a Messianic Israel in the form of a man, to show its
greater worth. "One like the Son of man" can be paraphrased, "a
figure in the shape of a man."

Because of this one passage, however, the phrase "son of man"
came to be used as a metaphoric way of speaking of the Messiah.
Perhaps this was useful at times when it was dangerous to be too openly
Messianic in one's hopes. By speaking of the "son of man" one could indicate the Messiah to those who were in sympathy; but before a judge
one might maintain that the phrase meant simply "man."

Jesus is quoted as referring to himself in this fashion on a number
of occasions. It is, indeed, the most frequent title he gives himself. We
might picture the "historic Jesus" as pleased by his own success and
beginning to think that his mission might be a great one indeed.
Cautiously he could begin to refer to himself as "son of man," a Messianic title which could always be defended as a form of humility
used after the fashion of Ezekiel.

Gergesenes

Jesus' successes at Capernaum encouraged him, apparently, to try
to extend his work beyond Galilee:

Matthew 8:18. *Now when Jesus saw great multitudes about him,*
he gave commandment to depart unto the other side.

By "the other side" is meant, of course, the eastern shore of the
Sea of Galilee. This eastern shore was outside the tetrarchy of Galilee
and was, rather, part of the Decapolis.

Matthew 8:28. *And when he was come to the other side into the*
country of the Gergesenes, there met him two possessed with
devils . . .

"Gergesenes" is apparently a copyist's error, as is the version
"Gadarenes" which appears elsewhere in the gospels. The best version

would be "Gerasenes," for the reference seems to be to a Greek town named Gerasa, a place which has been identified with the present village of Kersa on the east shore of Lake Tiberias, five miles across the water from Capernaum.

Jesus is described as casting out the demons who, at their own request, are transferred into a herd of swine who then dash into the Sea of Galilee and are drowned.

The Greek inhabitants of the place seemed unappreciative of this invasion of a prophet from Galilee and of the disturbances his revivalist preaching seemed to bring.

> Matthew 8:34. . . . the whole city came out to meet Jesus: and . . . besought him that he would depart out of their coasts.

The Twelve Apostles

The increasing numbers of those who flocked to him seem to have convinced Jesus that he would have to place more of the responsibility upon those among his disciples whom he considered most trustworthy and capable. (Perhaps he attributed the failure of his mission to Gerasa to the fact that the work he was attempting was too great for him to attend to properly, preventing him from achieving completely satisfactory results.) He therefore appointed deputies:

> Matthew 10:1. . . . he . . . called unto him his twelve disciples [and] . . . gave them power against unclean spirits . . .
> Matthew 10:2. Now the names of the twelve apostles are these; the first, Simon, who is called Peter, and Andrew his brother; James the son of Zebedee, and John his brother;
> Matthew 10:3. Philip, and Bartholomew; Thomas, and Matthew the publican; James the son of Alphaeus, and Lebbaeus, whose surname was Thaddaeus . . .

Of these ten, the calls of five—Peter, Andrew, James, John, and Matthew—were mentioned specifically. The others are here named for the first time.

The word "apostle" is from the Greek "apostolos" meaning "one who is sent away." In the New Testament it means, specifically, one who is sent away to preach, as now Jesus is sending away his disciples to do. The word "missionary" (one who is sent forth on a mission) is exactly synonymous.

The word is most frequently applied to the twelve men appointed by Jesus, but it can be used for any missionary. In fact, the most famous apostle is none of these twelve, but Paul who did not take up his mission till after Jesus' death, and who never saw Jesus during the latter's lifetime.

Simon the Canaanite

The eleventh name to be included is a rather startling one:

Matthew 10:4. *Simon the Canaanite . . .*

Can there be a Canaanite among the apostles?

Actually, the word is a mistranslation of the Greek "Kananaios." It should be "Simon the Cananaean" and is so given in the Revised Standard Version. A Cananaean has nothing to do with Canaan but comes from an Aramaic word "kannai" meaning "a zealous one."

In Luke this is made clearer, for in his list of apostles we have:

Luke 6:15. *Matthew and Thomas, James the son of Alphaeus, and Simon called Zelotes . . .*

In the Revised Standard Version, this phrase is given as "Simon who was called the Zealot."

The Zealots, mentioned in the Bible only on this occasion, made up an important and even fateful party among the Jews of Roman times. They were that branch of the Pharisees who demanded action against the Romans. Where the Pharisees, generally, were inclined to suffer foreign domination patiently as long as their religious views were respected, the Zealots were not.

They slowly gained power in Judea and Galilee and eventually their belligerency and intransigence, combined with Roman rapacity, forced the Jewish revolt in 66 B.C. The Zealots held out with a kind of superhuman obstinacy that forced the war to drag on for three years and killed off those same Zealots virtually to the last man.

Judas Iscariot

Just as Simon Peter is invariably placed first in all the lists of the apostles, Judas Iscariot is always placed last since it is he who, in the end, betrays Jesus:

Matthew 10:4. . . . *Judas Iscariot, who also betrayed him.*

Usually the word "Iscariot" is taken to mean "man of Kerioth." Kerioth, a city in Judea proper, is listed in the Book of Joshua among the cities in the territory assigned to Judah:

Joshua 15:25. *And Hazor, Hadattah, and Kerioth . . .*

It is often stated, then, that Judas was the only Judean in an assemblage of Galileans. One would then be entitled to wonder whether the feeling of being an "outsider" did not play a part in the eventual betrayal.

Actually, though, there is no indication anywhere in the gospels that Judas was a Judean rather than a Galilean—except for this very doubtful interpretation of the word "Iscariot." Actually, a more recent and much more interesting interpretation is that the word "Iscariot" arose out of a copyist's transposition of two letters and that it should more accurately be "Sicariot." If so, Judas would be a Galilean like all the other apostles, chosen by Jesus from the local citizens of Capernaum and environs.

But then, what is "Sicariot"? This can be someone who is a member of the party of the "Sicarii." These were so called from a Greek word meaning "assassins" because it refers to men carrying little knives, "sicae," under their robes. This was the name given to the most extreme Zealots who believed in outright assassination of Romans and pro-Romans as the most direct and effective means of fighting foreign domination.

Judas Iscariot might be called "Judas the Terrorist," and if we accept this version of the meaning of the name it helps give a useful interpretation to events in the career of the "historic Jesus."

Samaritans

Jesus sends the apostles to the Israelites only (see page 172):

> Matthew 10:5. . . . *Go not into the way of the Gentiles, and into any city of the Samaritans enter ye not* . . .

The Samaritans, who had established themselves as a distinct sect at the time the returning Jews had refused to allow them a share in the Second Temple (see page I-441), still survived. (In fact, a small number of them survive down to this very day.)

For a while, after the return from exile, the Jews and Samaritans progressed in parallel fashion. Under the Persians, both lived in peace and were protected from each other. To match the Jewish temple in Jerusalem, the Samaritans built one on their sacred Mount Gerizim (see page I-203) in 332 B.C. Both were persecuted by Antiochus IV and both the Jewish and the Samaritan temples were profaned.

After the Maccabean revolt, however, matters changed. Now the Jews were dominant. The Maccabeans conquered Samaria and, in 129 B.C., John Hyrcanus I destroyed the Samaritan temple.

The Samaritans survived the destruction of their temple and clung stubbornly to their beliefs (just as the Jews had). When the Romans established control over Judea, the Samaritans were liberated and allowed the free exercise of their religion. This was good policy for the Romans, who weakened the Jews by establishing an enemy in their midst and these made both of them easier to rule.

In New Testament times the hatred between Jew and Samaritan was particularly intense, as hatred often is between peoples with similar but not identical views, with histories of having inflicted wrongs upon each other. This hatred plays an important role in a number of gospel passages, as, for instance, in the one quoted above in which Samaritans are classed with Gentiles.

The Disciples of John

But Jesus' successes were attracting the attention not only of the plain people who came to hear him or to follow him, but also of many religious leaders.

For one thing, he attracted the attention of John the Baptist. John was in prison, of course, but his disciples were active. His disciples may even have looked with impatience and disapproval upon this new leader who, it might have seemed to them, was merely trying to strut in the borrowed feathers of their imprisoned leader.

They were ready to find faults and shortcomings in Jesus and his teachings and they picked on his greatest weakness (at least in the eyes of the orthodox of the times). That was his failure to adhere to the letter of the Law and the tradition, let alone go beyond it as a sign of particularly exemplary piety.

Matthew 9:14. *Then came to him the disciples of John, saying, Why do we and the Pharisees fast oft, but thy disciples fast not.*

Jesus answered by pointing out that while he was present with his disciples they had cause for rejoicing and therefore did not fast (fasting being a sign of mourning).

Perhaps this explanation was brought to John the Baptist, who pondered on the possible Messianic significance of such a reply. John had declared himself to be the immediate forerunner of the Messiah and, now that he was imprisoned, he must have been certain that the Messiah would momentarily appear. One could imagine him responding eagerly to any news that might be interpreted as Messianic and Jesus' suggestion that his very presence was cause for rejoicing might be significant. Could he be the Messiah?

Matthew 11:2. . . . *John . . . sent two of his disciples,*
Matthew 11:3. *And said unto him* [Jesus], *Art thou he that should come, or do we look for another?*

Jesus asked that the tales of his achievement be brought back to John, but he does not directly and specifically claim to be the Messiah.

The Pharisees

But John was in prison and even if he and his disciples refused to accept Jesus or were actively displeased with him, the harm they could do was small. Much more dangerous were the Pharisees, especially those among them who were entirely given over to the belief that salvation lay in the meticulous observation of all the precepts of the Law as interpreted in the most stringent manner. (The scribes, too, as students of the Law—see page I-450—tended to be wedded rather inflexibly to ritual. For this reason, the scribes and the Pharisees are often coupled in the gospels, as groups who separately and together opposed Jesus.)

Not all the Pharisees were like this, by any means, and at their best (see page 145) Pharisaic teachings were very like those in the New Testament. However, there were Pharisees whose regard for the minutiae of ritual was superstitious in intensity, or who actually welcomed the fact that so few people had the time, inclination, or learning to uphold the ritual to the last degree. When this was so, the few who could (these Pharisees themselves) might feel smugly superior to all the rest.

In a parable quoted in Luke, Jesus himself describes such a Pharisee, as praying after that fashion:

> Luke 18:11. . . . *God, I thank thee, that I am not as other men are* . . .

Of course, it sometimes happens that people who behave with great affectation of sanctity don't always live up to the ideals they profess. And it also happens that those who smart under the snubs of another's self-consciously superior sanctity rejoice in any shortcomings they discover in that sanctity. There is a tendency, therefore, to find some scribes and Pharisees to be hypocrites as well, and all three words are found together in various places in the gospels.

Indeed, in our own language, the word "pharisaical" is applied to a self-conscious and hypocritical sanctimoniousness.

While all this was undoubtedly true of some Pharisees, it was certainly not true of all. But it was the more narrow Pharisees who particularly opposed Jesus that were identified as *the* Pharisees—with no indication that there was any other kind—by the naturally hostile evangelists.

As Jesus' fame grew, then, the attention of the scribes and Pharisees was attracted, and they disapproved. Social prejudice may well have been involved. After all, Jesus was merely an unlearned carpenter from some small town.

This could not very well be used as an open argument against him, but it would predispose the scribes and Pharisees (proud of their learning) against him. They would then be all the readier to find fault with his laxity in observing ritual.

Thus, in treating a sick man, Jesus said:

> Matthew 9:2. . . . *Son, be of good cheer; thy sins be forgiven thee.*
> Matthew 9:3. *And, behold, certain of the scribes said within themselves, This man blasphemeth.*

After all, only God could forgive sins, so that Jesus seemed to be arrogating to himself Messianic, if not actually divine, powers.

Jesus also seemed to have no hesitation about subjecting himself to the social stigma of associating with disreputable people, including even publicans (see page 167). He actually accepted a publican as a disciple:

> Matthew 9:9. . . . *Jesus . . . saw a man, named Matthew, sitting at the receipt of custom: and he saith unto him, Follow me. And he arose, and followed him.*

The Pharisees, conscious of their own strict rectitude, questioned this disapprovingly.

> Matthew 9:11. *And when the Pharisees saw it, they said unto his [Jesus'] disciples, Why eateth your Master with publicans and sinners?*

Jesus pointed out in response that it was not the letter of the Law that was demanded by God and not correct ritual. What was demanded was ethical behavior.

> Matthew 9:12. . . . *Jesus . . . said unto them, . . .*
> Matthew 9:13. . . . *go ye and learn what that meaneth, I will have mercy, and not sacrifice . . .*

The quotation is from the prophet Hosea, who quotes God as making the same point:

> Hosea 6:6. *For I desired mercy, and not sacrifice; and the knowledge of God more than burnt offerings.*

The Pharisees could not very well deny the quotation or disown Hosea, but their disposition could scarcely be improved at having a "backwoods preacher" reading them lessons from the Scriptures. Antagonism continued to grow.

The Sabbath

What seems to have been the final break with the Pharisees arose over the question of Jesus' attitude toward the Sabbath:

> Matthew 12:1. *At that time Jesus went on the sabbath day through the corn; and his disciples were an hungred, and began to pluck the ears of corn, and to eat.*
> Matthew 12:2. *But when the Pharisees saw it, they said unto him, Behold, thy disciples do that which is not lawful to do upon the sabbath day.*

The origin of the Sabbath, the seventh day of the week, as a holy day to be devoted to God, is, according to Hebrew legend, placed in the epoch of the creation. God is described as creating the heaven and the earth in six days:

> Genesis 2:2. *And on the seventh day God ended his work . . . and he rested . . .*
> Genesis 2:3. *And God blessed the seventh day, and sanctified it . . .*

The name "Sabbath" is derived from a Hebrew word meaning "to break off" or "to desist." The worldly purpose of the Sabbath was to desist from work one day a week, to rest; as God had rested from His work.

Observance of the Sabbath was made one of the Ten Commandments received by Moses at Mount Sinai:

> Exodus 20:8. *Remember the sabbath day, to keep it holy.*
> Exodus 20:9. *Six days shalt thou labour, and do all thy work:*
> Exodus 20:10. *But the seventh day is the sabbath of the Lord thy God: in it thou shalt not do any work . . .*

But the Pentateuch, the first five books of the Bible, reached its final written form only during the Babylonian Exile, and it was not till then, perhaps, that the Sabbath received its present significance. There are, after all, but few and inconsiderable mentions of the Sabbath in the historical books dealing with the period before the Exile. It is not mentioned in the Psalms, in the Proverbs, or in the Book of Job. It is not mentioned in Deuteronomy, except for its listing in the Ten Commandments.

There is speculation that the Sabbath originated among the Babylonians as a full moon festival. The Babylonians called the fifteenth day of the month "sappatu," and in a lunar month that begins with the new moon the fifteenth day is the full moon.

The possibility that the Sabbath was a full moon festival complementary to the well-known new moon festival might be argued from various Biblical verses dated from before the Exile, verses in which the new moon and the Sabbath are mentioned together in complementary fashion.

Thus, when a woman wished to go to the wonder-working prophet Elisha after her son had died of sunstroke, her husband said to her:

> 2 Kings 4:23. . . . *Wherefore wilt thou go to him to day? it is neither new moon, nor sabbath.*

The prophet Hosea quotes God as threatening Israel:

> Hosea 2:11. *I will also cause all her mirth to cease, her feast days, her new moons, and her sabbaths . . .*

And Amos, characterizing the greediness of the merchants, eager to make unfair profits with false weights, pictures them sarcastically, with the parallelism characteristic of Hebrew poetry:

> Amos 8:5. . . . *When will the new moon be gone, that we may sell corn? and the sabbath, that we may set forth wheat . . .*

It may be that the Sabbath became more than just another lunar festival during the Exile, when the priests and scribes sought for ways to mark off Jewish thinking and keep Judaism alive. They would want to prevent the assimilation that had caused the men of the Northern Kingdom of Israel to disappear in the course of their Assyrian exile.

Ezekiel ("the father of Judaism") may have made the significant contribution of making observance of the Sabbath part of the fundamental contract between God and Israel, for Ezekiel quotes God as saying:

> Ezekiel 20:12. *Moreover also I gave them my sabbaths, to be a sign between me and them . . .*

By the time of the return from Exile, the Sabbath had definitely taken on the connotation it has borne among Jews ever since. Nehemiah, visiting the restored Jerusalem, is horrified at seeing work done on the Sabbath:

> Nehemiah 13:15. *In those days saw I in Judah some treading wine presses on the sabbath* . . .
> Nehemiah 13:16. *There dwelt men of Tyre also therein, which brought fish,* . . . *and sold on the sabbath unto the children of Judah* . . .
> Nehemiah 13:17. *Then I contended with the nobles of Judah, and said unto them, What evil thing is this that ye do, and profane the sabbath day?*

Increasing numbers of restrictions hedged about the Sabbath until, by the time of the Seleucid persecution, the observation of the Sabbath had become, among the conservative faction, the very touchstone separating the orthodox Jews from the Hellenizers. Indeed, the orthodox Assideans would not violate the Sabbath even to save their lives (see page 57). The Maccabees had to arrange a general understanding to allow at least self-defense on the Sabbath. Nevertheless, the more ritualistic factions among the Jews, and that included certain groups of Pharisees in particular, were particularly rigid about Sabbath behavior.

Jesus' disciples, by plucking ears of grain, removing the hulls, and eating the kernels, were involved in a form of harvesting and that was expressly forbidden on a Sabbath:

> Exodus 34:21. *Six days thou shalt work, but on the seventh day thou shalt rest: in earing time and in harvest thou shalt rest.*

Jesus' attitude, however, was one of scorn for legalistic positions that exalted the Sabbath at the expense of humanitarian considerations, a view expressed most succinctly in the Gospel of St. Mark:

> Mark 2:27. *And he* [Jesus] *said unto them* [the Pharisees], *The Sabbath was made for man, and not man for the sabbath* . . .

Jesus' Mother and Brethren

To the Pharisees, it must have seemed that Jesus was aiming to break down the very core of Judaism; the careful ritual that preserved it (as

though in amber) from the overwhelming numbers of the hostile outside world. Jesus had to be stopped.

> Matthew 12:14. *Then the Pharisees . . . held a council against
> him [Jesus], how they might destroy him.*

Presumably what the Pharisees wish to do is destroy his influence;
matters have not yet reached the stage where it would seem necessary to
bring about his death. Apparently, the strategy decided upon by the
Pharisees is to accuse him of black magic:

> Matthew 12:24. . . . *they [the Pharisees] said, This fellow doth
> not cast out devils, but by Beelzebub the prince of the devils.*

Jesus countered that by demanding to know how one devil could be
made to cast out another, since such a civil war in the ranks of devildom
would destroy them all:

> Matthew 12:25. . . . *Every kingdom divided against itself is
> brought to desolation; and every city or house divided against itself
> shall not stand . . .*

Nevertheless, there may well have been a falling away of his followers.
Many must have felt that if the learned Pharisees tabbed a man as a
demon-worshipper, they must know what they were talking about.

Indeed, it could well be argued that his family, too, was disturbed
at this. Undoubtedly, word of Jesus' successes must have been coming
back to Nazareth and the family would naturally be pleased. Once evil
reports started reaching them, however, they would be quite justified in
fearing for his safety—and they went in search of him.

At least it is at just about this point that Matthew mentions their
coming:

> Matthew 12:46. *While he [Jesus] yet talked to the people, behold,
> his mother and his brethren stood without, desiring to speak with him.*

Were they come to urge him to return home with them? Were they
hoping to persuade him to abandon his mission before incalculable
harm came to him?

Matthew doesn't say, but Mark's version of this same incident is
preceded (over not too great a distance) by what might well be
considered a most significant passage:

> Mark 3:21. . . . *his friends . . . went out to lay hold on him: for they said, He is beside himself.*

The word here translated as "friends" could mean "kinsfolk," and, indeed, the Jerusalem Bible says "his relatives" rather than "his friends."

This verse in Mark is not embarrassing for that evangelist. He makes no mention of Jesus' virgin birth or of the miracles attendant thereon, so he has no reason to suppose that Jesus' mother and brethren should more readily have faith in him than anyone else.

Matthew's account of the virgin birth, however, and of the unusual events accompanying it—the worship of the kings, Herod's search for the baby, the warning dream—present a situation in which Jesus' mother and, probably, other kinsmen as well couldn't help but have at least a strong suspicion of Jesus' Messianic mission. Matthew, therefore, couldn't very well include the verse about Jesus' relatives thinking he was out of his mind, without being inconsistent, so he omits it.

Nevertheless, if we are following the "historic Jesus" we are strongly tempted to believe that Jesus' family did fear for him and did come to take him home where they might keep him safe and sane. Matthew's account of Jesus' reaction to the coming of his relatives could, it might be argued, lend this view credence. If his mother and brothers had come for an ordinary friendly visit, surely Jesus would gladly have seen them and spoken to them. If, however, Jesus suspected they were coming to dissuade him from his mission, and if he placed his mission even above family ties, he would naturally react just as Matthew describes:

> Matthew 12:49. . . . *he [Jesus] stretched forth his hand toward his disciples, and said, Behold my mother and my brethren!*

Apparently, he refuses to see his family and, as a matter of fact, his family does not appear again in the remainder of Matthew. (They are mentioned a chapter later in the account of Jesus' failure to impress the people of Nazareth—but they do not appear.)

Parables

In the gospels, Jesus is often described as making his points by means of parables (from a Greek word meaning "comparison"). These are short tales which could be taken literally at face value, or could be compared point by point with an analogous message concerning the relationship of God and man.

And it is immediately after the account of the visit of Jesus' mother and brothers that Matthew chooses to present a collection of such parables:

> Matthew 13:3. *And he* [Jesus] *spake many things unto them* [his audience] *in parables* . . .

It is possible, of course, to miss the point of a parable and the disciples of Jesus are pictured as puzzled when their master seemed deliberately to remain parabolic and to refrain from plain speaking:

> Matthew 13:10. *And the disciples came, and said unto him, Why speakest thou unto them in parables?*

The explanation given is that the very murkiness of the parables acts to sift the hearts of men. Those who honestly want to enter the kingdom will make the effort to understand, while those who are insufficiently eager will not do so.

It is possible to interpret this, however, as a rational response to the gathering force of Jesus' enemies. For Jesus to speak directly concerning his unorthodox religious views might further enrage the Pharisees and perhaps even bring down upon his head political dangers. By speaking in parables, those unsympathetic to him could be fobbed off with the literal tale (it's just a story about a man planting wheat) while those who sympathized with Jesus would have no trouble seeing the point.

The Daughter of Herodias

And there was good reason for Jesus to speak cautiously and in parables, for dangers even beyond the Pharisees were lowering upon him. John the Baptist was dead!

Herod Antipas had hesitated to execute John, for fear of the political complications that might follow as a result of the anger and resentment of those who followed him. The vindictive Herodias, however, on whom the weight of John's denunciation had rested (see page 152), maneuvered Herod into a rash vow.

Matthew 14:6. . . . When Herod's birthday was kept, the daughter of Herodias danced before them, and pleased Herod.

Matthew 14:7. Whereupon he promised with an oath to give her whatsoever she would ask.

Matthew 14:8. And she, being before instructed of her mother, said, Give me here John Baptist's head in a charger.

Matthew 14:9. And the king was sorry: nevertheless for the oath's sake . . . he commanded it to be given her.

Matthew 14:10. And he sent, and beheaded John in the prison.

The girl who danced was Herodias' daughter by Philip, her first husband. She is not named in the Bible, but her name is given in the writings of Josephus as Salome (a feminine version of Solomon).

To complete the complexities of the Herodian family arrangement, this Salome later married her half great-uncle, Philip the tetrarch, so that she was at one and the same time the half great-niece, the step-daughter, and the half sister-in-law of Herod Antipas—and, through her mother, a descendant of the Maccabees as well.

Bethsaida

The death of John the Baptist did not result in serious trouble, after all, for Herod Antipas. Probably he gained courage from this fact and grew the more ready to take a stern stand against troublesome reformers. To him, Jesus seemed merely another John the Baptist.

Matthew 14:1. . . . Herod the tetrarch heard of the fame of Jesus,
Matthew 14:2. And said unto his servants, This is John the Baptist; he is risen from the dead . . .

Presumably, since Herod Antipas had had no repercussions from his execution of John, he would not hesitate to imprison and execute the new prophet who had stepped into John's shoes. Jesus decided not to give Herod Antipas the chance to do this.

Matthew 14:13. When Jesus heard of it, he departed thence by ship into a desert place apart . . .

Luke, in telling this incident, is more specific:

Luke 9:10. . . . *And he . . . went aside privately into a desert place belonging to the city called Bethsaida.*

By a desert place is meant a lonely place, an unfrequented one.

Bethsaida ("house of the fishers") is located just north of the Sea of Galilee, to the east of the place where the Jordan River enters. Since the Jordan River is the eastern boundary of Galilee, Bethsaida is not in Galilee but in Iturea. Thus, Jesus places himself outside the jurisdiction

The Galilee Mission

of Herod Antipas, and within that of the mild Philip the tetrarch from whom no violence was to be feared.

Bethsaida had been rebuilt by Philip the tetrarch about a quarter century before Jesus had begun his ministry and it had been renamed Julias, in honor of Julia, daughter of the then-reigning Roman Emperor.

Matthew tells of crowds following Jesus to his place of retreat and of numerous miracles which he performed. In particular, he tells of Jesus feeding five thousand men plus an indefinite number of women and children on five loaves and two fish, miraculously multiplied.

This miracle of feeding the multitude is quite unique for it is the only miracle that is described in similar terms in all four gospels. But even if we discount miracles, we can suppose that Jesus continued to preach in Bethsaida and gathered crowds of both the pious and the curiosity-seekers.

Perhaps Herod Antipas, chagrined at having Jesus slip out of his grasp, demanded that his brother Philip return the fugitive. And perhaps Philip, unwilling to do so, merely sent word to Jesus, suggesting he move on. Whatever the reason, Jesus did not stay in Bethsaida long.

> Matthew 15:39. *And he sent away the multitude, and took ship . . .*

That sounds as though he recrossed the Sea of Galilee and returned to the dominions of Herod Antipas. If he did, it was merely to accomplish some purpose before moving onward again, for soon he is to be back in Iturea.

Jesus may well have felt defeated at this time. The populace had not risen in defense of John the Baptist, or to avenge him, either. They had flocked to Jesus in numbers, but when things grew hard they fell away. They did not gather about him to protect him from the Pharisees and from Herod. Instead, he had to go into flight.

It may have seemed to him at this point that his entire Galilee mission was a failure as his initial attempt in Nazareth had been. He had lasted longer in Capernaum and had had enormous, if temporary, success—but in the end he had been driven out.

Possibly, it was now that he uttered a bitter denunciation of the cities in which he had been preaching:

> Matthew 11:20. *Then began he to upbraid the cities wherein most of his mighty works were done, because they repented not:*

Matthew 11:21. . . . *woe unto thee, Bethsaida!* . . .

Matthew 11:22. . . . *It shall be more tolerable for Tyre and Sidon at the day of judgment, than for you.*

Matthew 11:23. *And thou, Capernaum, which art exalted unto heaven, shalt be brought down to hell* . . .

Caesarea Philippi

Jesus, on leaving Bethsaida, must have felt himself abandoned. Only a group of his most faithful disciples were with him and he had left the scene of his Galilean triumphs far behind.

Matthew 16:13. . . . *Jesus came into the coasts of Caesarea Philippi* . . .

Caesarea Philippi was an Iturean city some thirty miles north of the Sea of Galilee. The town had grown in importance in Herodian times. Herod the Great had built a temple there and his son, Philip the tetrarch, had enlarged the city and renamed it Caesarea in honor of the family name of the Roman Emperor.

Since there were many Caesareas in the empire, this one was called Caesarea Philippi ("Philip's Caesarea") by way of identification.

Peter

Perhaps Jesus was seriously questioning the nature of his mission now that he found himself driven far from home. Was it a failure? Had the call he had felt on the day of his baptism by John been an illusion? He turns to his disciples:

Matthew 16:13. . . . *Whom do men say that I the Son of man am?*

In response to Jesus' question, the disciples told him that various people thought he was John the Baptist risen from the dead, or that he was Elijah or Jeremiah or some other prophet of the past. But Jesus pressed on. That was the opinion of those who had been casually exposed to him. What about the disciples themselves, who by now knew him very well?

Matthew 16:15. . . . *But whom say ye that I am?*
Matthew 16:16. *And Simon Peter answered and said, Thou art the Christ, the Son of the living God.*

This is the turning point of the gospel. Jesus greeted the assurance joyfully. After all, Peter's confidence in his Messiah-hood could not come from his mission's worldly success, which was, at the moment, nonexistent. It could only be inspired by heaven.

Matthew 16:17. *And Jesus answered . . . Blessed art thou, Simon Bar-jona: for flesh and blood hath not revealed it unto thee, but my Father which is in heaven.*

It was on this assurance of faith and confidence on the part of his disciples that Jesus felt he could continue and carry on to final success. In return for Peter's avowal, Jesus could appoint him "second in command," so to speak, and his successor:

Matthew 16:18. *And I say also unto thee, That thou art Peter, and upon this rock I will build my church; and the gates of hell shall not prevail against it.*
Matthew 16:19. *And I will give unto thee the keys of the kingdom of heaven . . .*

Jesus was punning here. Since "Peter" means "rock," he was saying: "You are Rock and on this rock . . ."

It was the most influential pun in all history. Peter, according to tradition, went to Rome in later life and became the first Bishop of Rome. It was believed that succeeding Bishops of Rome inherited this role as the rock upon which the Church was built and each continued to hold the keys of the kingdom of heaven.

It was the Bishop of Rome who came to be called the Pope (from the word "papa," a general term for priests) and thus began the doctrine of papal supremacy over the Church, and through the Church over all Christians. Not all Christians accepted this doctrine and there are still hundreds of millions who don't today—but there are also hundreds of millions who do.

Nevertheless, although Jesus now accepted the role of Messiah-hood, he did not lose all sense of caution:

Matthew 16:20. *Then charged he his disciples that they should tell no man that he was Jesus the Christ.*

Moses and Elias

The acceptance of Messiah-hood by Jesus and, on his behalf, by the disciples is then placed in miraculous terms. Jesus is described as taking his chief disciples, Peter, James, and John, to a high mountain—

Matthew 17:2 *And was transfigured before them: and his face did shine as the sun, and his raiment was white as the light.* Matthew 17:3. *And, behold, there appeared unto them* [the disciples] *Moses and Elias* [Elijah] *talking with him* [Jesus].

Then, too, it was unthinkable to the evangelists that Jesus could be the Messiah and yet not be able to foretell his own fate; or that this fate could come to him against his will and not have an important Messianic purpose. Jesus is therefore described not only as foreseeing his death and its purpose but as explaining it not once but several times to his disciples:

Matthew 16:21. *From that time forth began Jesus to shew unto his disciples, how that he must go unto Jerusalem, and suffer many things . . . and be killed, and be raised again the third day.*

In the search for the "historic Jesus" this pious view of the Evangelists must, however, be discounted. Despite their report of Jesus' plain speaking and of the overwhelming evidence of the "Transfiguration," there are various points later in the gospels where the disciples (Peter most of all) behave as though they had no premonition of disaster; and as though disaster, when it came, left them in despair and the abandonment of their belief in Jesus' Messiah-hood.

We can continue the story, therefore, on the assumption that Jesus and his disciples, now that they were secure in their feeling that they were carrying through the mission of the Messiah, were counting on a straightforward Messianic triumph.

James and John

Indeed, now that the disciples accepted the belief that Jesus was the Messiah, so far were they from understanding what the consequences were fated to be that two of them asked for positions of honor. Mark tells the incident most baldly:

> Mark 10:35. And James and John, the sons of Zebedee, come unto him [Jesus], saying . . .
>
> . . . .
> Mark 10:37. . . . Grant unto us that we may sit, one on thy right hand, and the other on thy left hand, in thy glory.

They were asking for high office in the Messianic kingdom, which, they felt, was about to be established; and doing so, moreover, behind the backs of the rest.

> Mark 10:41. And when the [other] ten heard it, they began to be much displeased with James and John.

and Jesus had to work hard to restore amity among his followers.

Matthew, in his version, softens it considerably by absolving James and John of sole responsibility for this exercise in intrigue, and placing at least part of the blame on the easy-to-forgive partiality of a mother:

> Matthew 20:20. Then came to him [Jesus] the mother of Zebedee's children with her sons . . .

According to Matthew, it was the mother who actually asked the favor of Jesus. But perhaps one might prefer Mark's version of the two apostles boldly asking for preference on their own responsibility, rather than hiding behind their mother's skirts to do so.

The restoration of peace among the disciples may well have come about through the promise of equal rank for all:

> Matthew 19:28. And Jesus said unto them, . . . ye which have followed me, in the regeneration when the Son of man shall sit in the throne of his glory, ye also shall sit upon twelve thrones, judging the twelve tribes of Israel.

Once again, Matthew interprets Jesus' Messianic mission in a strictly Jewish sense.

The Mount of Olives

Now that Jesus was determined to carry through his role as Messiah, he had to go to Jerusalem, for it was there that, according to all the prophecies, the Messianic kingdom would be established.

> Matthew 19:1. . . . *Jesus . . . departed from Galilee, and came into . . . Judaea beyond Jordan . . .*

Jesus crossed the Jordan to Jericho and then traveled westward toward Jerusalem, deliberately following the activities predicted of the Messiah's coming:

The Journey of Jesus to Jerusalem

> Matthew 20:29. *And as they departed from Jericho, a great multitude followed him.*

. . . .

Matthew 21:1. *And . . . they drew nigh unto Jerusalem, and were come to Bethpage, unto the mount of Olives . . .*

The Mount of Olives, a hill about half a mile high, is less than half a mile east of Jerusalem. Jesus did not select that route by accident. It was from the Mount of Olives, according to prophecy, that the Messiah would appear. Thus, Zechariah, in predicting the divine coming on the day of the Lord says:

Zechariah 14:4. *And his feet shall stand in that day upon the mount of Olives, which is before Jerusalem on the east . . .*

At Bethpage, a village on the mount, Jesus made his final preparations. The excitement among his disciples must have been extreme, for it is reasonable to suppose that they expected Messianic success to follow at once. At least, Jesus is quoted as having predicted this to his disciples shortly after he had undertaken his Messianic role in Caesarea Philippi.

Matthew 16:28. *Verily I say unto you, There be some standing here, which shall not taste of death, till they see the Son of man coming in his kingdom.*

This has been variously interpreted, but if this were said to the disciples, one could assume that it was accepted at face value and that the trip to Jerusalem was made in the assurance that the Messianic kingdom was about to be established.

With the establishment of the kingdom in mind, Jesus planned to enter Jerusalem mounted, in the traditional fashion of a king, and not on foot. Thus, when Solomon was acclaimed king, one of the symbolic forms this acclamation took was his mounting of the royal mule:

1 Kings 1:38. *So Zadok the priest, and Nathan the prophet, and Benaiah . . . caused Solomon to ride upon king David's mule . . .*

And yet the mount was not to be a royal one, for in one important prophesy the Messiah is recorded as destined to come into Jerusalem in humble fashion, riding upon an ass.

Zechariah 9:9. *Rejoice greatly, O daughter of Zion; . . . behold, thy King cometh unto thee: . . . riding upon an ass, and upon a colt the foal of an ass.*

In order to fulfill the prophecy, Jesus sent two disciples to get a young ass for him so that he might make his entry upon it. This is done, and he is described as entering Jerusalem upon an ass in all the gospels but that of Matthew.

Matthew, in his eagerness to quote the passage from Zechariah (which is not quoted in the other gospels) and to demonstrate its fulfillment to the letter, misses the point of Hebrew poetic parallelism. The phrase "riding upon an ass, and upon a colt the foal of an ass" describes the *same* act in two slightly different phrases.

Matthew assumes, instead, that two different animals are involved and has the disciples bring two, an ass and its colt:

Matthew 21:7. *And* [the disciples] *brought the ass, and the colt, and put on them their clothes, and they set him* [Jesus] *thereon.*

This gives us a rather odd picture of Jesus riding two animals at once.

Hosanna

As described by Matthew, Jesus had an important and large party enthusiastically on his side. Part may have come with him, drawn by his teachings; others may have been in Jerusalem but had heard tales of a wonder-working prophet coming to Jerusalem. In any case, his passage toward Jerusalem from the Mount of Olives is pictured as a triumph:

Matthew 21:8. *And a very great multitude spread their garments in the way; others cut down branches from the trees, and strawed them in the way.*

Matthew 21:9. *And the multitudes that went before, and that followed, cried, saying, Hosanna to the Son of David: Blessed is he that cometh in the name of the Lord; Hosanna in the highest.*

The word "hosanna" is a Greek version of a Hebrew phrase meaning "Save! We pray!" or, in ordinary language, "Please help us." The acclamation is a paraphrase from the Book of Psalms.

Psalm 118:25. *Save now, I beseech thee, O Lord: O Lord, I beseech thee, send now prosperity.*

Psalm 118:26. *Blessed be he that cometh in the name of the Lord . . .*

The twenty-fifth verse has "Hosanna" translated into "Save now, I beseech thee." Left untranslated, the verse would read, "Hosanna, O Lord: O Lord, hosanna . . ."

It was clear that Jesus was being acclaimed with a passage that was applied to God in the Psalms, and that he was therefore being called the Messiah. Indeed, the use of the term "Son of David" made that explicit.

The disciples led and guided the cheering, and there were those in the crowd who were horrified at the blasphemy involved in acclaiming a Galilean preacher as the Messiah. This is brought out in Luke:

Luke 19:39. *And some of the Pharisees from among the multitude said unto him, Master, rebuke thy disciples.*

Luke 19:40. *And he [Jesus] answered . . . I tell you that, if these should hold their peace, the stones would immediately cry out.*

It was no longer a matter of overenthusiastic disciples. Jesus himself was, if not actually proclaiming Messiah-hood in the full view of the people of Jerusalem, accepting such a claim by others.

The Temple

In his new role as ultimate authority, Jesus took drastic action in the very Temple itself:

Matthew 21:12. *And Jesus went into the temple of God, and cast out all them that sold and bought in the temple, and overthrew the tables of the moneychangers, and the seats of them that sold doves,*

Matthew 21:13. *And said unto them, It is written, My house shall be called the house of prayer; but ye have made it a den of thieves.*

Actually, the moneychangers and merchants performed an essential service for those who wished to perform those rites that required the donation of small sums and the sacrifice of small birds. Through laxness, however, commercialism seems to have been allowed to invade

0 Feet 1500

TO SHECHEM AND NORTH

THIRD NORTH WALL?

THIRD NORTH WALL?

Psephinus Tower?

BEZETHA

Pool of Bethesda

HADRIAN'S WALL

Fortress of Antonia

SECOND NORTH WALL

BEAUTIFUL ALTAR GATE?

Garden of Gethsemane

TO JOPPA AND WEST

Calvary (Church of the Holy Sepulchre)

SUBURB

Xystus (Market)

Solomon's Porch

Court of Women

TO BETHANY AND JERICHO

Pool of Amygdalon

Herod's Temple

Court of the Gentiles

Phasael Tower

GENNATH GATE

Hasmonaean Palace

Council House

Hippicus Tower

Mariamme Tower

HULDAH GATES

VALLEY OF THE KIDRON

TO BETHLEHEM AND SOUTH

Herod's Palace

UPPER CITY

Royal Porch

House of Caiaphas

TYROPOEON VALLEY

ACRA

Gihon Spring

Serpent's Pool

House of the Last Supper

LOWER CITY

PILATE'S AQUEDUCT

ESSENE GATE

Pool of Siloam Lower Pool

VALLEY OF HINNOM

Jerusalem

the sacred precincts of the Temple instead of being kept well outside. Perhaps, too, some of the merchants were not above sharp practice at the expense of ignorant and naïve pilgrims from the country districts. (It is quite possible that Jesus, in Galilee, heard indignant tales concerning the manner in which his neighbors were cheated on their visits to the Temple.)

Jesus' exercise of power within the Temple and his preachings there bitterly offended the Sadducees. They might have ignored fine doctrinal points and questions of ritual since they themselves rejected all the Pharisaic traditions that had grown up about the written

Law. The Temple, however, was their own preserve and they did not take lightly the forceful actions of outsiders within it. Furthermore, Jesus' quotation was an offensive one, for in referring to the Temple as "a den of thieves" he was making use of Jeremiah's Temple Sermon, which, of all passages in the Old Testament, must have been least pleasing to the priests of the Temple (see page I-561).

Jeremiah 7:11. *Is this house* [the Temple] . . . *become a den of robbers in your eyes? Behold, even I have seen it, saith the Lord.*

The reaction of the Temple priesthood is described:

Matthew 21:15. *And when the chief priests and scribes saw the wonderful things that he* [Jesus] *did, and the children crying in the temple, and saying, Hosanna to the Son of David; they were sore displeased* . . .

Nevertheless, Jesus' preaching, as well as his deeds, was gathering enthusiastic crowds about him and the Temple priests could hardly claim to be popular among the unlettered and impoverished multitude. They were at a loss for proper action:

Matthew 21:46. . . . *when they sought to lay hands on him, they feared the multitude, because they* [the multitude] *took him* [Jesus] *for a prophet.*

Nor could they take the opportunity to seize him at night when he was relatively alone, for Jesus was cautious enough not to remain in Jerusalem overnight.

Matthew 21:17. . . . *he* [Jesus] *left them, and went out of the city into Bethany; and he lodged there.*

Bethany was a suburb of Jerusalem, about a mile to the east and just on the other side of the Mount of Olives.

The Son of David

Jesus was greeted as the Son of David on his entrance into Jerusalem and is so addressed at various times in the gospel. The phrase is synonymous with "Messiah," since the Messiah was generally expected (on the basis of numerous Old Testament prophecies) to be of the line of David and therefore to be a son (that is, a descendant) of David.

In the first couple of chapters of Matthew (and of Luke as well), Jesus is considered to be literally a descendant of David and his line of descent is given, as well as the tale of his birth in Bethlehem. Nowhere else, however, is this taken into account. Jesus is always identified as being of Nazareth and nowhere is he reported as correcting the impression by declaring himself to be of Bethlehem.

Even when he was entering Jerusalem and being acclaimed as Messiah, he was identified as a Galilean:

> Matthew 21:10. *And when he* [Jesus] *was come into Jerusalem, all the city was moved, saying, Who is this?*
> Matthew 21:11. *And the multitude said, This is Jesus the prophet of Nazareth of Galilee.*

This was a serious bar to Jesus' claim to be the Messiah. Matthew cannot say so since he maintains that Jesus was indeed of the Davidic line. In the gospel of St. John, however, where the birth at Bethlehem and the Davidic descent play no part, the objection is stated:

> John 7:41. *Others said* [of Jesus], *This is the Christ. But some said, Shall Christ come out of Galilee?*

We could imagine, then, that the Pharisees of Jerusalem must have been outraged at this sight of a Galilean nobody coming into town and claiming to be the Messiah. The claim could easily have been scotched. They had only to face him and say, in effect, "You say you are the Messiah, and if so of whose descent must the Messiah be?" Jesus would have had to answer, "He is a descendant of David," and the Pharisees could then say, "Well, then, since you are not a descendant of David, how can you be the Messiah?"

If Matthew's tale of Jesus' Davidic descent is true, we might then expect that Jesus would win the argument by a shattering display of evidence as to his birth at Bethlehem and his descent from David.

Suppose, though, that Jesus were not born in Bethlehem and were not of Davidic descent—that these elements in Matthew are legends of comparatively late origin. In that case, Jesus would have had to counter the argument by demonstrating, somehow, that the Messiah did not have to be of Davidic descent; that it was impossible, in fact, that he be of Davidic descent.

In Matthew's account, Jesus does precisely this, disproving the Davidic descent of the Messiah, even though it goes squarely against Matthew's tale of Jesus' descent from the line of David.

In Matthew's account, however, it is Jesus who raises the point, for no clear reason:

> Matthew 22:41. *While the Pharisees were gathered together, Jesus asked them,*
>
> Matthew 22:42. *Saying, What think ye of Christ? whose son is he? They say unto him, The Son of David.*

Jesus then demonstrates that they are wrong by the clever use of an Old Testament verse. It is perhaps the neatness of his argument that made the tale so popular that it could not be left out of the gospel even though it was an embarrassing contradiction to Matthew's tale of Jesus' birth:

> Matthew 22:43. *He [Jesus] saith unto them, How then doth David in spirit call him Lord, saying,*
>
> Matthew 22:44. *The Lord said unto my Lord, Sit thou on my right hand, till I make thine enemies thy footstool?*
>
> Matthew 22:45. *If David then call him Lord, how is he his son?*

The reference here is to one of the Psalms:

> Psalm 110:1. *The Lord said unto my Lord, Sit thou at my right hand, until I make thine enemies thy footstool.*

Jesus is quoted as interpreting the second "Lord" as signifying the Messiah, something which, indeed, was a common interpretation among the Jews in Roman times and among Christians now. Therefore the writer of the Psalm (presumably David) speaks of the Messiah as "my Lord" and David, Jesus argues, would scarcely address his own descendant as a superior—so that the Messiah must be more than merely a descendant of David.

(Of course, the Psalm could be interpreted non-Messianically. It is thought to be a coronation psalm in which God is described as addressing the new king of Judah. The second "my Lord" is the common address of respect for the king and the verse could be translated as beginning "God said to the king . . .")

By having Jesus ask the original question, one might speculate that Matthew was trying to present the passage as a battle of wits between

Jesus and the Pharisees, in which Jesus by a clever bit of what we would today call "Talmudic" reasoning presents a thesis to the Pharisees and dares them to refute it. The thesis need not be true—that is not the issue—but the failure of the Pharisees to answer establishes Jesus' superiority over them. And they failed:

Matthew 22:46. *And no man was able to answer him a word . . .*

Nevertheless, it is tempting to suggest that the Pharisees proposed the original question and that Jesus calmly denied the necessity of Davidic descent, saving himself—to the Pharisees' surprise—from what they believed to be a crushing gambit, and that only Matthew's commitment to the Davidic descent prevented him from presenting it as such. The passage could then be considered as a glance at the "historic Jesus" who was a Galilean carpenter but insisted on being regarded as the Messiah despite that.

The Herodians

It grew increasingly clear to the Temple authorities that Jesus' claims would not easily be quashed. Galilean backwoodsman or not, he had a quick wit and a fund of ready quotations. Yet he had to be stopped just the same before Messianic fervor produced dangerous unrest all across the city. If Jesus' doctrinal views could not be used against him, what about his political views?

If Jesus could be forced to say something politically subversive, instead of merely doctrinally heretical, the Romans could be called in. Roman soldiers could act at once without having to stop to exchange Old Testament quotations:

Matthew 22:16. *And they [the Pharisees] sent out unto him their disciples with the Herodians, saying, Master, we know that thou art true . . . neither carest thou for any man . . .*

By this flattery, they hoped they would trick him into making some uncompromising statement regardless of whom it would offend. And just in case he did, they had the Herodians with them. These were civil officials who supported the Herodian dynasty. Presumably they worked constantly with the Romans, had entry to the Roman governor, and could report to him quickly of any subversive remark made by Jesus.

It seemed certain to those now questioning Jesus that anyone claiming to be the Messiah would have to hold out hopes for the overthrow of the Roman Empire and for the establishment of the ideal Jewish state. It was exactly this that the populace expected of a Messiah. A question that was bound, it seemed, to force Jesus either to advocate rebellion or to give up all Messianic pretenses was now fired at him:

> Matthew 22:17. *Tell us therefore, What thinkest thou? Is it lawful to give tribute unto Caesar, or not?*

("Caesar," of course, was the title given to the Roman Emperor. It harked back to Julius Caesar, who had been assassinated in 44 B.C., but whose grandnephew became Rome's first Emperor, fifteen years later.)

If, now, Jesus refused to answer, surely he would be despised as a coward by those in the audience who advocated resistance to Rome, and they must have represented the majority of those who eagerly acclaimed Jesus as the Messiah. If he advocated payment of tribute, that would be even worse. If, on the other hand, he advocated non-payment of tribute, that would give the Romans instant reason to intervene.

Jesus sought a way out. The coins used in paying tribute had the figure of Caesar on them. That made those coins unfit to be handled by Jews anyway, strictly speaking. The first of the Ten Commandments forbade the making of any representations of any living thing and Jewish monarchs, such as the various Herods, were usually careful to avoid stirring up the orthodox by putting their own portraits upon their coins. The idolatrous coin, which it was sinful for Jews to handle, might just as well be given to the man whose portrait was there. Jesus said:

> Matthew 22:21. . . . . *Render therefore unto Caesar the things which are Caesar's; and unto God the things that are God's.*

Jesus had thus found a safe path between the horns of what had seemed an insoluble dilemma. He had advocated tribute payment, which kept the Romans from interfering; but had done so for a thoroughly religious reason which was consistent with his role as Messiah.

And yet Jesus' enemies may have won a point here, too. One can easily picture the Zealots among Jesus' audience as waiting impatiently for his answer. They were fiercely anti-Roman and they wanted a Messiah who would lead them with divine force against the hated Romans.

Here, then, was the question. Shall we pay tribute?

The proper Messianic answer, in the Zealot view, was a thunderous "No!"

That would begin the rebellion at once; just as at one time, the refusal of Mattathias to participate in a heathen sacrifice had begun the rebellion of the Maccabees.

And instead, Jesus found refuge in an evasion. If the crowd in general applauded Jesus' clever retort, might it not be that some of the more extreme Zealots now fell away in contempt. This was not their man. This was not the Messiah they were waiting for.

And how must Judas Iscariot have felt? If it were indeed true that he was an extreme Zealot (see page 179) he may well have been filled with a wild anger at the failure of this man he had believed to be the Messiah. If this is so, it explains what was to follow.

Zacharias son of Barachias

But if Jesus was careful to avoid offending the Romans, he did not hesitate to strike back at the religious leadership. He is pictured by Matthew as preaching to the multitude, at this time, and in the course of his talk, denouncing the scribes and Pharisees unsparingly, as individuals whose piety was concerned entirely with ritual and not with substance, and who were therefore hypocrites.

He spoke ominously, furthermore, of the manner in which truly pious men in the past had been killed by an unappreciative people, and he warns of retribution:

> Matthew 23:35. . . . *upon you may come all the righteous blood shed upon the earth, from the blood of righteous Abel unto the blood of Zacharias son of Barachias, whom ye slew between the temple and the altar.*

This is generally believed to be a reference to the fate of Zechariah, the high priest in the time of Joash of Judah (see page I-422). Zechariah had berated the court for tolerating idolatry and had won the enmity of the king and his courtiers:

> 2 Chronicles 24:21. *And they conspired against him* [Zechariah], *and stoned him with stones at the commandment of the king in the court of the house of the Lord.*

This identification is the more convincing since it would make it seem that Jesus was deliberately including all the unjust murders of just men that had been mentioned from one end of the Bible to the other. In the Hebrew Bible, the books of Chronicles are placed at the end, and all the Old Testament books are divided (by modern usage) into a total of 929 chapters. The murder of Cain is the first to be mentioned and is found in the fourth chapter; that of Zechariah is the last and is in the 917th chapter.

It must be admitted, however, that the Zechariah spoken of in 2 Chronicles is differently identified as to his father's name:

> 2 Chronicles 24:20. *And the Spirit of God came upon Zechariah the son of Jehoiada* . . .

Why, then, Jesus should identify him as the "son of Barachias" is uncertain. Is a different individual being referred to after all? Or is the mention of Barachias a copyist's (mistaken) added identification, based on confusion with another Zechariah casually mentioned in Isaiah?

> Isaiah 8:2. *And I took unto me faithful witnesses to record, Uriah the priest, and Zechariah the son of Jeberechiah.*

The Abomination of Desolation

There follows, then, an apocalyptic passage in which Jesus describes the future. Some of it seems to deal quite specifically with the destruction of Jerusalem by the Romans that was to take place forty years after the gospel period.

> Matthew 24:15. *When ye therefore shall see the abomination of desolation, spoken of by Daniel the prophet, stand in the holy place* . . .

Matthew 24:16. *Then let them which be in Judaea flee into the mountains . . .*

The abomination of desolation was the statue of Zeus erected in the Temple by Antiochus IV, and could mean, more generally, the triumph of pagan forces over Jerusalem, something which happened in A.D. 70.

In the course of the Jewish rebellion against Rome, the followers of Jesus took the pacifist view and did not participate in the defense of Jerusalem, but fled into the hills. It may be, therefore, that these verses were added to the traditional apocalyptic discourse of Jesus, after the fact, and that this gospel (and the other synoptic gospels, as well) did not reach their completed present form till after A.D. 70.

After the reference to the fall of Jerusalem, there follows a general description of the future beyond, given in typical Old Testament terms of total destruction:

Matthew 24:29. *Immediately after the tribulation of those days shall the sun be darkened, and the moon shall not give her light, and the stars shall fall from heaven . . .*

Following that will be the appearance of the Messiah and the establishment of the ideal kingdom.

Matthew 24:30. *. . . . and they shall see the Son of man coming in the clouds of heaven with power and great glory.*

This, however, raises a problem. To those who believed that Jesus was the Messiah, the Messiah had already come. Apparently there would have to be a "second coming." This second coming was not to be long delayed:

Matthew 24:34. *Verily I say unto you, This generation shall not pass, till all these things be fulfilled.*

To be sure, it is usually now maintained that this verse refers to the fall of Jerusalem and not to the second coming, which is described immediately before. Nevertheless, this was not the view of the early Christians, who, in line with this verse, expected the second coming daily.

Still, Jesus refused to specify an exact time for the second coming.

Matthew 24:36. *. . . . of that day and hour knoweth no man, no, not the angels of heaven, but my Father only.*

Talent

One of Jesus' parables, quoted in connection with the suddenness and unexpectedness of the second coming, deals with a man who gives money into the care of servants, then returns suddenly and demands an accounting.

Matthew 25:15. *And unto one he gave five talents, to another two, and to another one; to every man according to his several ability . . .*

The "talent" was originally a Greek unit of measure, from a word meaning "a balance." This is a reference to the time when gold and silver were carefully weighed out on a balance before being used for payment—before the time (in the sixth century B.C.) when coins of standard weight, stamped with the portrait of the monarch as a guarantee of honest measure, came into use.

The talent was a large unit of money, especially for ancient times. The talent used in Judea in New Testament times was equal to six thousand shekels and that was undoubtedly the equivalent of several thousand dollars in modern money.

The use of the word in the verses above, in which each man receives a number of talents according to his abilities, has given rise to the use of the word as an expression of a particular ability possessed by an individual. In fact, in modern English, the use of the word as a unit of money has completely died out and the only meaning of "talent" of which most people are aware is that of a superior ability of some sort.

Caiaphas

To the Pharisees and to the Temple authorities, Jesus' final speeches must have seemed to represent an intolerable danger. The ignorant populace was being aroused into fury by Jesus' accusations against them. Anything might follow and the case was taken to the very highest religious authority among the Jews, the high priest himself:

Matthew 26:3. *Then assembled together the chief priests, and the scribes, and the elders of the people, unto the palace of the high priest, who was called Caiaphas . . .*

The office of the high priest was not what it once was. The true Zadokites had passed in the time of Antiochus IV. The Maccabean high priests had passed with the coming of Herod. The last of the Maccabean high priests, Aristobulus III, had been executed in 35 B.C. at the order of Herod. In the century that followed (the last century of the existence of the Temple) there had been numerous high priests set up by Herod or by the Roman authorities and these were chosen out of one or another of a few of the aristocratic Judean families.

The hold of these last high priests, without either Zadokite or Maccabean prestige, on the allegiance of the common people must have been slight indeed, but they controlled the Temple and grew rich and powerful because of that.

In A.D. 6, Annas ("Hanan" in Hebrew) was appointed high priest and remained in office until A.D. 15. He was then deposed by an incoming Roman official who, undoubtedly, felt he could use the bribes that would come his way if he were in a position to appoint a new high priest. For a while Simon, the son of Annas served and then, in A.D. 18, Caiaphas (his given name was Joseph, according to Josephus), the son-in-law of Annas, succeeded to the post. At the time of Jesus' stay in Jerusalem, Caiaphas had already been high priest for eleven years and was to remain high priest for seven more.

Caiaphas could see the seriousness of the situation for, in his position, he was bound to know the Romans well. He had to deal with them frequently and he undoubtedly obtained his office in the first place only through financial dickering with them.

The Judean of the countryside, or of the Jerusalem slums, or (even more so) the Galilean of the provinces could have little knowledge of the true strength of Rome. He could see only the few Roman soldiers who might have been present in a nearby garrison. The common people might believe the Romans could be beaten, especially if they felt that a miraculous Messiah was on their side.

However, Caiaphas knew that the Romans could *not* be beaten— not at this stage in their history—and forty years later this was proved tragically correct to the Jews.

To be sure, Jewish rebels of this period usually believed the Messiah to be with them, and at this particular moment the Jerusalem populace was hailing Jesus as the Messiah. Caiaphas, however, did not believe this. It is important to remember that, in the century after the fall of the Maccabees, many men with Messianic pretensions arose and that every one of them had some following. Concerning every one of them, there rose wonder tales of miraculous feats and cures, tales that grew in the telling.

Matthew quotes Jesus himself as witness to this in the apocalyptic discourse:

> Matthew 24:24. *For there shall arise false Christs, and false prophets, and shall shew great signs and wonders; insomuch that, if it were possible, they shall deceive the very elect.*

To Caiaphas, Jesus could only be one of these "false Christs." From his point of view Jerusalem was rumbling with excitement over a provincial preacher, who was rabble-rousing the populace to a dangerous pitch. In just a couple of days, the Passover was to be celebrated and pilgrims would be flocking into the city from all directions to worship at the Temple. Excitement would reach the fever point and, fortified by the certainty of Messianic help, someone would kill a Temple official or, worse still, attack a Roman soldier. Then all would be lost. There would be a rebellion and Judea would be crushed and wiped out. What Antiochus IV had failed to do, the Romans would succeed in doing.

Indeed, this point of view is made explicit in John where at this point of the story the following views of the priestly officials are quoted:

> John 11:48. *If we let him thus alone, all men will believe on him: and the Romans shall come and take away both our place and our nation.*
>
> John 11:49. *And one of them, named Caiaphas, being the high priest that same year, said unto them . . .*
>
> John 11:50. . . . *it is expedient for us, that one man should die for the people, and that the whole nation perish not.*

This last remark is often quoted as an example of appalling cynicism, but of course it is a principle that is used constantly by all nations both before and after the time of Caiaphas.

Nor can the high-priestly view be considered as overly pessimistic, since forty years later it all turned out as they had feared. The Romans did come and take away their place and their nation. It might even be argued that only because the authorities took action against Jesus were forty years of additional life given the nation.

Judas Iscariot

Not only did the authorities decide that Jesus must be apprehended and removed as a great danger to the nation, they felt also that it had to be done at once. In two more days it would be Passover and it might then be too late. The very act of trying to make the arrest on that most nationalistic of all Jewish holidays (when God had smitten the Egyptians) might stir passions to the point of revolt, even if revolt had not already broken out spontaneously:

> Matthew 26:4. And [the chief priests] consulted that they might take Jesus by subtilty, and kill him.
> Matthew 26:5. But they said, Not on the feast day, lest there be an uproar among the people.

It was clear, moreover, that the arrest had best be carried through at night, when the city was sleeping, so that there be no uproar at the very moment of arrest, and so that the city might be presented with a completed deed in the morning. Indeed, if the deed could be carried through without an immediate revolt, the mere success of it would prevent a revolt, since what kind of Messiah could be arrested by a few soldiers? To many, Jesus would then seem a false Messiah and there would be a vast falling-away from him.

But—and here was the problem—where was Jesus staying at night? The authorities would find him, but would they find him in time?

As it happened, Caiaphas found an unexpected ally. One of Jesus' chief disciples, Judas Iscariot, defected:

> Matthew 26:14. Then one of the twelve, called Judas Iscariot, went unto the chief priests,
> Matthew 26:15. And said unto them, What will ye give me, and I will deliver him unto you? . . .

In other words, he would point Jesus out to them in the quiet of night and make it possible for them to arrest him without fuss.

Judas' action here has made his name a byword for villainy through all ages since. To call someone "a judas" is to call him a traitor in the extreme.

But what was Judas' motive? Matthew implies that it was greed since he asked for money, "What will ye give me . . ."

In John, this view is sharpened, and it is implied that as treasurer of the group Judas was in charge of funds and helped himself to them:

> John 12:6. . . he [Judas] *was a thief, and had the bag, and bare what was put therein.*

Could it be that his defalcations had been detected and that he was forced into betrayal in a wild attempt to avoid disgrace?

But if it were greed that motivated Judas, it would seem that he profited very little. The priestly officials were in a position where they would have been willing to pay handsomely indeed for the service Judas was offering and yet Matthew reports:

> Matthew 26:15. . . . *And they covenanted with him for thirty pieces of silver.*

One can't help but wonder if Matthew's penchant for Old Testament prophecies hadn't gripped him here. This was the price mentioned by Zechariah in connection with his mysterious shepherd (see page I-669):

> Zechariah 11:12. *And I said unto them . . . give me my price; . . . So they weighed for my price thirty pieces of silver.*

Matthew must have had this verse in mind. Only Matthew of all the Evangelists mentions the specific sum paid for the betrayal, for only he feels it necessary to match Old Testament prophecy.

Could it be that the betrayal was only secondarily for money (if at all) and that the real motive was something else?

It is frequently mentioned (see page 179) that Judas was the only Judean among the apostles and that he was therefore less loyal to a Galilean preacher than were the other apostles, all of whom were Galileans.

Indeed, there have been strongly anti-Semitic individuals who have argued that only the Judeans were the true Jews in the modern sense and that Galileans were only converted Jews who were not really of Jewish descent. It follows, in their line of reasoning, that Galileans are virtuous and that Jews are wicked and that no further reason is needed to explain Judas' betrayal.

Such arguments are, of course, beneath contempt, even if Judas were indeed the only Judean. But was he? That view depends entirely on the thought that Iscariot means "man of Kerioth," a theory which has been accepted very widely for centuries but is doubtful nevertheless. If, indeed, Judas Iscariot is a misreading for Judas Sicariot ("Judas the Terrorist") then it is possible to view the betrayal in an entirely different light.

Suppose Judas was heart and soul one of those extremists who desired and demanded instant war against Rome. He may have attached himself to Jesus in the hope that this man might indeed be the Messiah whose coming would put an end to the hated Roman dominion at once. It may have been with a gathering excitement that he traveled with Jesus to Jerusalem, that he witnessed Jesus' triumphant entry, his cleansing of the Temple and his gathering popularity.

Judas may have felt sure that Passover would be the signal for the divine battle, so often foretold in detail by the prophets, in which all the forces of heathendom would be destroyed and the Son of David would be seated on the throne of the kingdom.

What changed things? It may well have been the matter of the Roman tribute and Jesus' retort that what was Caesar's would have to be given to Caesar (see page 206). To Judas, this may have seemed a disclaimer of any intention to oppose Rome politically and a declaration on Jesus' part that he was concerned with religious and ethical matters only. If so, that would have been a crushing blow to him.

Then, too, if Jesus did in fact preach the second coming, and if that passage (see page 209) is not an insertion by later hands after Jesus' death, then that could well have completed Judas' disillusionment. It was now that Judas wanted action—not having it postponed after the Messianic coming to a second coming.

What happened next might be explained in one of two ways. Judas might have been so sick with disillusionment as to have yearned for revenge. Feeling he had been made a fool of, he might have hastened, in a fit of rage, to get back at what he considered a deceiver by arranging to have him arrested and executed.

Or, it might be that Judas still felt Jesus to be the Messiah, but one who was, unaccountably, backing away from the final showdown. Per-

haps by placing him in danger of arrest, he could *force* Jesus to take
what Judas would have considered appropriate Messianic action.

All this, of course, is guesswork—nothing more than supposition.
Still, there is one more item that may be added.

While the priests were conferring, and while Judas was arranging
his betrayal, Jesus was spending his last night in Bethany. There a
woman pours a jar of expensive ointment over his head.

The disciples are pictured as annoyed at the waste, feeling that the
ointment might have been sold and the proceeds donated to the poor,
but Jesus consoles them with the observation that he was being
anointed for his forthcoming burial.

In John, however, it is only Judas who is recorded as complaining:

John 12:4. *Then saith . . . Judas Iscariot . . .*
John 12:5. *Why was not this ointment sold for three hundred
pence, and given to the poor?*

(It is at this point that John states that Judas said this not out of
regard for the poor but because he was a thief who was in charge of
the treasury.)

In John, it was after this event that Judas carried through his betrayal. If we consider John's account, might this not fit in with the
theory of Judas' disillusionment. Might he not have been irritated at
the act of anointment—the traditional rite of establishing the kingship? The physical action emphasized Jesus to be the Messiah, the
"Anointed One," and that must have sharpened Judas' sick feeling
that Jesus was betraying the Messiah-hood by refusing to lead a revolt
against Rome.

Gethsemane

On Passover Eve, Jesus and his disciples dined within Jerusalem.
This is the "last supper." Judas Iscariot was at this meal, but immediately afterward must have slipped away to consult with the priestly
officials.

Jesus and the remaining disciples then left but did not go far:

Matthew 26:36. *Then cometh Jesus with them unto a place called
Gethsemane . . .*

Jerusalem

Gethsemane was just outside Jerusalem on the western slopes of the Mount of Olives and, presumably, in an olive grove where once an oil press had stood. (The name "Gethsemane" means "oil press.") Judas knew Jesus would be there, something that is made specifically clear in John:

John 18:2. *And Judas . . . knew the place: for Jesus ofttimes resorted thither with his disciples.*

Interpreted from a rationalistic standpoint, the "historic Jesus" possibly expected the next day to be crucial and to be the day on which the city would rise in his favor so that, under the circumstances, he stayed as close to the city as possible.

Presumably, now that the moment of decision was at hand, a feeling of uncertainty gripped him. Was what he was doing really correct? Would he succeed? He is recorded as spending the time in an agony of prayer.

Matthew 26:39. And he . . . fell on his face, and prayed, saying, O my Father, if it be possible, let this cup pass from me: nevertheless not as I will, but as thou wilt.

One can, in this verse, see the "historic Jesus" shrinking from attempting the final test, uncertain of success, fearing the consequences, and yet feeling that there was no way out.

The Judas Kiss

The suspense was suddenly ended, however, with the arrival of the armed men sent by the priests. Judas had guided them to the place where Jesus was to be found—a place known to Judas but not to the authorities. It was now, in the quiet of night, that Jesus could be taken, and when Passover Day dawned the potential rebellion would be stymied because of the sudden lack of a leader—and the revelation that Jesus had been nothing but a deceiving and false Messiah.

The only possibility of failure now lay in the fact that, by mistake, a disciple might be arrested and Jesus might escape. There were three disciples with Jesus at this final scene of prayer at Gethsemane:

Matthew 26:37. And he [Jesus] took with him Peter and the two sons of Zebedee . . .

and any one of the three might be mistaken for Jesus. It was, after all, dark, and the armed men did not, presumably, know Jesus by sight.

Judas therefore had to identify Jesus unmistakably and he offered to do so:

Matthew 26:48. . . . he [Judas] . . . gave them a sign, saying, Whomsoever I shall kiss, that same is he: hold him fast.

To modern Americans, this seems to aggravate the treason; to betray with a kiss is peculiarly villainous. That is, in part, a reflection of our own social customs, in which kissing has been made a sign of particular intimacy and affection. In other cultures, however, a kiss between men on meeting can be quite common. It would be the normal greeting and of no greater significance than a handshake in our culture. The treason is, of course, bad enough even so.

Jesus is pictured by Matthew as surprised at Judas' coming and as unaware of the traitor's purpose:

> Matthew 26:49. . . . *he [Judas] came to Jesus, and said, Hail, master; and kissed him.*
> Matthew 26:50. *And Jesus said unto him, Friend, wherefore art thou come? Then came they [the armed men], and laid hands on Jesus, and took him.*

To be sure, this section of the gospel is full of indications that Jesus knew beforehand of Judas' treasons and the results thereof, as would be expected of the divine foreknowledge of a Messiah. And it is sometimes suggested that Jesus' question of Judas, "Wherefore art thou come?" is a metaphoric way of saying, "Do what you have come to do." That is, "Let's get this over with."

Nevertheless, if we consider the "historic Jesus" we might well consider him to have been surprised at Judas' sudden appearance and unaware, for just a moment, as to the significance of it. The question then makes sense at face value.

One of the disciples present offered a token resistance. He is unnamed here, but John states it to have been Peter:

> Matthew 26:51. . . . *one of them which were with Jesus stretched out his hand, and drew his sword, and struck a servant of the high priest's, and smote off his ear.*
> Matthew 26:52. *Then said Jesus unto him, Put up again thy sword . . .*

We might picture the "historic Jesus" as seeing that resistance was useless and unwilling to have his disciples killed for nothing. Perhaps he felt a sense of relief that the crisis of the revolt would not come. Or perhaps he still considered himself the Messiah and was certain that there would yet be a divine intervention on his behalf.

(The traditional Jesus, as accepted by virtually all Christians since then, knew what was to come, and that the trial, crucifixion, and resurrection were part of the divine scheme.)

The disciples at that point reacted, however, as though they were facing the arrest of the "historic Jesus" rather than that of a divine Messiah:

> Matthew 26:56. . . . . *Then all the disciples forsook him, and fled.*

Christ

It now became necessary for the priestly authorities to find some sort of crime for which Jesus could be convicted; one, if possible, that would carry the death penalty. If he were merely punished and released, or worse yet, acquitted, after all this trouble they had taken, the result would surely be told throughout Judea as an example of the divine protection of the Messiah and revolt would be a certainty.

And yet to convict Jesus on a matter of purely doctrinal dispute would be difficult:

> Matthew 26:59. *Now the chief priests . . . sought false witness against Jesus, to put him to death;*
> Matthew 26:60. *But found none . . .*

In desperation, they turned to the matter of Messiah-hood itself. Certainly, to claim, falsely, to be the Messiah, was the height of blasphemy and deserved death. And certainly, Jesus' disciples had openly claimed him to be the Messiah, and Jesus had implicitly accepted the role by refusing to rebuke them for doing so (see page 200).

This, however, was not enough. The claims of the disciples might be disowned; implicit acceptance of the claims might be explained away. If, however, Jesus could be maneuvered into an open avowal of Messiah-hood, under oath, in court, they would have him.

In fact, they would have everything they needed. The priesthood could not, at this time in history, pronounce and carry through a death sentence on their own. The approval of the Roman governor of Judea was needed. Such approval might not be obtained for a purely doctrinal matter (for such disputes the Roman rulers avoided involvement as a matter of policy—there was too much chance of sparking a troublesome revolt). However, if Jesus laid claim to Messiah-hood, he simultaneously laid claim to being the rightful and ideal King of the Jews. This, in turn, was a clear form of political revolt against Rome's authority, even if Jesus made not a single overt move against Rome. That meant the Roman authorities could be called in and a death sentence was sure of being carried out.

The crucial question was therefore asked under oath:

Matthew 26:63. . . . *the high priest . . . said unto him, I adjure thee by the Living God, that thou tell us whether thou be the Christ . . .*

Matthew 26:64. *Jesus saith unto him, Thou hast said: nevertheless I say unto you, Hereafter shall ye see the Son of man sitting on the right hand of power, and coming in the clouds of heaven.*

The phrase, "Thou hast said" is, in itself, evasive, meaning "This is something you have said," as though Jesus himself were careful neither to affirm nor to deny. Mark's version of the question and answer makes Jesus present his inquisitor with an open admission:

Mark 14:61. . . . *the high priest asked him, . . . Art thou the Christ . . .*

Mark 14:62. *And Jesus said, I am . . .*

However, even in Matthew's more cautious version of Jesus' answer, Jesus goes on to expand his view with a Messianic quotation. The remark concerning the Son of man is from the Book of Daniel:

Daniel 7:13. . . . *one like the Son of man came with the clouds of heaven . . .*

Daniel 7:14. *And there was given him dominion, and glory, and a kingdom . . .*

That was it. Jesus seemed to be making a clear comparison of himself with the figure in Daniel, one who was commonly accepted at the time as representing the Messiah (see page I-610). The high priest had what he wanted:

Matthew 26:65. *Then the high priest rent his clothes, saying, He hath spoken blasphemy; what further need have we of witnesses? . . .*

Matthew 26:66. *What think ye? They* [the court] *answered and said, He is guilty of death.*

Peter

If Jesus, even at this crisis, maintained a firm belief in his Messiah-hood, this was not so of his disciples. All had fled, and only one is recorded as being present, secretly, at the trial:

Matthew 26:58. . . . *Peter followed him* [Jesus] *afar off unto the high priest's palace, and went in, and sat with the servants, to see the end.*

After the end of the trial, Peter was recognized three different times as being one of the disciples of Jesus. It was Peter's chance to be as true to his mission as Jesus was, but he failed. Each time he denied knowing Jesus, the third time most emphatically:

Matthew 26:74. *Then began he* [Peter] *to curse and to swear, saying, I know not the man . . .*

Pontius Pilate

The priestly officials also had what they needed to bring Jesus before the Roman authorities:

Matthew 27:1. *When the morning was come, . . . the chief priests . . .*
Matthew 27:2. . . . *bound him* [Jesus], *. . . led him away, and delivered him to Pontius Pilate the governor.*

This is the first mention in Matthew of the secular ruler of Judea since the reference to Archelaus at the time of the return of Joseph and his family from Egypt (see page 135).

Archelaus, or Herod Archelaus, ruled as ethnarch over Judea, Samaria, and Idumea after the death of his father, Herod the Great, in 4 B.C. His rule, however, was harsh and oppressive and he succeeded in antagonizing both Jews and Samaritans. Both groups, in a rare exhibition of cooperation, appealed for relief to the Roman Emperor.

Rome was not in the least averse to strengthening its hold upon the unruly province, for Judea had an important strategic significance at the time. Immediately to Judea's east was the powerful kingdom of Parthia, and that kingdom was Rome's most dangerous enemy in New Testament times.

In 53 B.C., for instance, not long after Judea had passed under Roman domination, the Parthians had defeated a Roman army at Carrhae. (This was the Graeco-Roman name for Haran, the city where Abraham and his family had once dwelt. See page I-59.) Seven Roman legions had been destroyed, the worst Roman defeat ever suffered, up to that time, in the east, and a defeat that had not yet been avenged. Then again, in 40 B.C., the Parthians had taken advantage of civil wars in Rome to occupy large sections of Roman territory in the east. They had occupied Judea, which had cooperated with them willingly against Rome, and against the Roman puppet, Herod.

As long as Judea retained even the semblance of independence, then, she was a danger to Roman security for its ruler might at any time decide to intrigue with the Parthians.

Rome therefore took advantage of the complaints of the Jews and Samaritans to depose Herod Archelaus in A.D. 6, allowing him to live out the remaining twelve years of his life in exile.

Neither Judea nor Samaria got independence as a result, of course. Instead the area was made part of a Roman province, complete with a Roman ruler and a well-armed Roman garrison.

Judea, although made part of the province of Syria, was, because of its strategic importance, given special status. A governor was appointed by the emperor, one who was to be responsible directly to himself as well as to the provincial ruler of Syria. The Latin name for such an official was "procurator" ("caretaker"). In Greek, the name given the Roman officials over Judea was "hegemon" ("leader") and in the King James Version, and the Revised Standard Version too, this becomes "governor."

The first four procurators of Judea ruled quietly enough. In A.D. 26, however, Pontius Pilate was appointed. He was a man of obscure birth who owed his advancement to the fact that he was a protégé of Lucius Aelius Sejanus, who was then the leader of the Praetorian Guard (a contingent of soldiers which guarded Rome itself) and the most powerful man in the empire at the moment.

Sejanus was strongly anti-Jewish and Pilate probably took his job on the understanding that he was to keep the Jews in check, weaken them at every opportunity, and prevent them from ever serving as a Parthian cat's-paw against Rome.

Pilate set about this with a will. Where earlier procurators had made their headquarters at Caesarea, a city on the Samaritan coast, fifty miles northwest of Jerusalem, Pontius Pilate stationed troops in the capital itself. This meant the army, with its ensigns bearing the portrait of the emperor, moved into Jerusalem. The excited Jews considered such portraits to be a violation of the commandment against idolatry and protested violently. Eventually Pilate had to remove the objectionable portraits when it seemed that a revolt would be the inevitable result if he didn't. There was no question but that he could crush such a revolt, but disorders that might bring in the Parthians would look bad on his record if it seemed that he had deliberately provoked them.

Pilate may have made it a practice to be in Jerusalem during the Passover season, when the city was crowded, and dangerous emotions ran high. He was undoubtedly ready to take instant action in case such feelings became a revolt. He might even have welcomed the chance. He had already, on one recent occasion, showed no hesitation in slaughtering a Galilean mob that had begun proving disorderly during a festival:

> Luke 13:1. . . . some . . . told him [Jesus] of the Galilaeans, whose blood Pilate had mingled with their sacrifices.

He would have no hesitation in doing so again. The high priest must have known this and his treatment of Jesus must have had, as one of its motives, the desire to forestall this eventuality by any means, to deflect Pilate's anger from the Jews generally to a single man so that "one man should die for the people."

The Potter's Field

Judas Iscariot is pictured, meanwhile, as horrified at the consequences of his betrayal:

> Matthew 27:3. Judas, . . . when he saw that he [Jesus] was condemned, repented himself . . .

If he had planned to force Jesus into Messianic action, he felt now that that plan had failed and that he was going to be responsible for Jesus' death. If he had been seeking to punish Jesus for not being the kind of Messiah that Judas would have liked to see, then apparently he felt that the death penalty was more punishment than he had intended.

He attempted to return the thirty pieces of silver to the priestly officials and when they refused to accept it from his hands, he threw the money down and went off and hanged himself, so that he died on the same night as his betrayal. This remorse tends to relieve the traitor of some of the utter blackness that has gathered about his name.

Unfortunately, the plausibility of Matthew's dramatic tale of the end of Judas suffers from the suspicion that the evangelist was merely trying to introduce yet another Old Testament quotation. With reference to the thirty pieces of silver that Judas had cast aside, Matthew explains that the priests felt that the money, which was the price of treachery, could not be put back in the treasury. It carried a man's blood on it.

> Matthew 27:7. And they . . . bought with them the potter's field, to bury strangers in.
>
> Matthew 27:8. Wherefore that field was called, The field of blood, unto this day.
>
> Matthew 27:9. Then was fulfilled that which was spoken by Jeremy [Jeremiah] the prophet, saying, And they took the thirty pieces of silver . . .
>
> Matthew 27:10. And gave them for the potter's field . . .

The potter's field was, presumably, a place where one could obtain clay of a kind suitable for the making of pottery. From the verses just quoted, the phrase "potter's field" has come to mean any public burial place for use of the criminal, the homeless, the paupered—anyone who could not afford, or did not deserve, a better resting place.

Matthew's Old Testament quotation, however, is even more than usually unapt, in this case. For one thing, it is not from Jeremiah, but from Zechariah's cryptic tale of the shepherds. (The mistake may have come about because Jeremiah talks about buying a field at one point, see page I-575, and tells a parable about potters at another point, but it is a mistake just the same.)

In the Book of Zechariah, the shepherd who resigned received thirty pieces of silver for his wages (see page I-669)—

Zechariah 11:13. . . . And I took the thirty pieces of silver, and cast them to the potter in the house of the Lord.

But the "potter in the house of the Lord" is by no means the "potter's field." Indeed, the very word "potter" is a mistranslation and may appear in the Old Testament verse as a result of Matthew's misuse of the passage and its effect upon the piety of those who worked on the King James Version. The Revised Standard Version has the phrase read "the treasury in the house of the Lord."

In other words, the money was, in Zechariah, deposited in the Temple treasury, which is precisely what the priests refused to do with Judas' money. The two passages are therefore not parallel, as Matthew apparently felt, but, on the contrary, antithetical.

There is a competing tradition of Judas' death, given in the Acts of the Apostles:

Acts 1:18. Now this man [Judas] purchased a field with the reward of iniquity; and falling headlong, he burst asunder in the midst, and all his bowels gushed out.

Acts 1:19. And it was known unto all the dwellers at Jerusalem; insomuch as that field is called in their proper tongue [Aramaic], Aceldama, that is to say, The field of blood.

According to this competing tradition—which involves no Old Testament prophecies—Judas felt no remorse and committed no suicide. He lived long enough to carry through a business transaction designed to make him a landowner and died afterward of some sort of stroke.

Barabbas

Apparently, Pilate accepted Jesus' evasive answer to the high priest ("Thou hast said") as negative, or at least as not positive, and was therefore uncertain that he merited execution. Or perhaps Pilate wanted to disoblige the high priest, who, Pilate may well have felt, had his own ulterior motives for wanting Jesus dead, quite apart from his actual guilt or innocence:

Matthew 27:18. *For he* [Pilate] *knew that for envy they* [the priests] *had delivered him* [Jesus].

At any rate, he went over the head of the priestly party to the people themselves, and offered to release a prisoner in honor of the Passover festival.

Matthew 27:16. *And they* [the Romans] *had then a notable prisoner, called Barabbas.*
Matthew 27:17. *Therefore . . . Pilate said . . . Whom will ye that I release unto you? Barabbas, or Jesus which is called Christ?*

Barabbas is not further described in Matthew. Mark, however, says:

Mark 15:7. *And there was one named Barabbas, which lay bound with them that had made insurrection with him, who had committed murder in the insurrection.*

It might well be then that Barabbas had been one of the Sicarii, or terrorists, who had led a guerrilla band against the Romans, and had carried through the assassination of some Roman official. He might well therefore be a hero to the Zealots, the very ones who were disenchanted with Jesus for having backed away in the matter of the tribute.

Given their choice between a bandit leader who did not preach but fought against the Romans, and one who preached and called himself a Messiah but took no action and submitted tamely to capture, imprisonment, and trial, the populace (or at least the vocal Zealots among them) called for Barabbas—and got him.

Barabbas is not a proper name but is the Aramaic equivalent of a surname, meaning "son of the father." The word "Christ" or "Messiah" can also be termed as "son of the Father" (though with a capital letter). Oddly enough, tradition asserts that Barabbas' proper name was Joshua or, in Greek, Jesus. Consequently, what Pilate was asking the crowd was whether they wanted Jesus, son of the father, or Jesus, son of the Father.

There have indeed been those who suggested that Barabbas and Jesus are the same person and that the tale of a bandit leader and of a meek and peaceful Messiah somehow got entwined, that Jesus was tried before Pilate but was released as Barabbas, and that the tale

of the crucifixion and resurrection is the embroidery of later legend.
It is unlikely, however, that this view will ever gain many adherents.

Pilate and Pilate's Wife

Matthew emphasizes the reluctance of Pilate to give the order for
execution. Partly, he explains this through the use of his favorite device of a dream:

> Matthew 27:19. *When he* [Pilate] *was set down on the judgment
> seat, his wife sent unto him, saying, Have thou nothing to do with
> that just man: for I have suffered many things this day in a dream
> because of him.*

This is the only appearance of Pilate's wife in the New Testament,
but tradition has been busy with her. It is said that her name was
Claudia Procula and that she was, or later became, a secret Christian.
She is even canonized in the Greek Orthodox Church.

Having offered to release Jesus and having had to release Barabbas
instead, Pilate is faced with a shouted cry for the execution of Jesus.
Pilate protested:

> Matthew 27:23. *And the governor said, Why, what evil hath he
> done? . . .*
> Matthew 27:24. *When Pilate saw that he could prevail nothing,
> . . . he took water, and washed his hands before the multitude, say-
> ing, I am innocent of the blood of this just person . . .*

All the four gospels agree that Pilate was reluctant to order the
execution of Jesus, but only Matthew inserts this hand-washing—a
dramatic act that makes the English phrase "to wash one's hands of"
mean "to disclaim responsibility."

Possibly it was an act of Jewish ritual which the Roman Pilate would
not have performed, but it was one which Matthew, who knew a great
deal about Jewish ritual and very little about Roman ways, found
natural to include.

In the Book of Deuteronomy, it is stated that if a murdered body
be found and the murderer not be known, the people of the nearest
town go through a certain ritual, involving a heifer, for absolving
themselves of guilt:

Deuteronomy 21:6. *And all the elders of that city . . . shall wash their hands over the heifer . . .*

Deuteronomy 21:7. *And they shall . . . say, Our hands have not shed this blood . . .*

Since Pilate thus proclaims his innocence, Matthew has the impatient crowd accept the responsibility themselves, making use of the dramatic Old Testament idiom used for the purpose:

Matthew 27:25. *Then answered all the people, and said, His blood be on us, and on our children.*

This statement, which is found in none of the other gospels, and which may well have arisen merely out of Matthew's penchant for interpreting and describing everything in accordance with Old Testament prophecy, ritual, and idiom, has cost the Jews a fearful price in the two thousand years since Jesus' death.

As for Pilate, his later years are obscure. He remained as Procurator of Judea till A.D. 36, when he was finally recalled because his tactlessness continued to rouse revolts among the Jews and Samaritans.

The manner of his death is not known. Hostile tradition has him executed by the Roman Emperor, or committing suicide to avoid such execution. On the other hand, there are also legends concerning his later conversion to Christianity, based perhaps on the accounts of his reluctance to condemn Jesus. There are apocryphal writings, too, which no longer exist, but which are referred to by some of the early Christian writers. They were supposed to have represented his report concerning the trial and resurrection of Jesus. Pilate is even canonized as a saint in the Abyssinian church.

Crucifixion

Having disclaimed responsibility for Jesus' death, Pilate gave the order for execution:

Matthew 27:26. *Then released he Barabbas unto them: and when he had scourged Jesus, he delivered him to be crucified.*

Crucifixion was neither a Jewish nor a Greek method of execution. Among Jews, it was common to stone people to death; among the

Greeks, to force them to take poison. The Romans, however, used crucifixion as a punishment for treason. (So did other peoples, such as the Persians and Carthaginians.)

A person, nailed to a wooden cross, died slowly of exposure, hunger, and thirst. It was a cruel death; all the more so, since it was so public as to divest the dying man of every shred of dignity, exposing him to the jeers of heartless onlookers.

Yet, the fact remains that Jesus was not condemned to an unusual or uncommon death, but one that was routine by Roman law. In 72 B.C., about a hundred years before the execution of Jesus, a band of gladiators and slaves rebelled against Rome under the leadership of Spartacus. They were eventually defeated by the Roman general Marcus Licinius Crassus (a general who was to be defeated and killed fifteen years later by the Parthians at the battle of Carrhae; see page 223). Crassus captured some six thousand of the slaves and, according to the story, crucified them wholesale along the road from Rome to Capua, so that any traveler would find himself going miles and miles between a seemingly endless row of men slowly dying in painful torture. (Similarly, Darius I of Persia at one time crucified three thousand Babylonian rebels wholesale.)

Crucifixion, as a means of punishment, continued to be part of the Roman law till it was abolished by Constantine I, the Roman Emperor who first legalized the practice of Christianity.

Cyrene

It was customary for a man about to be crucified to carry the heavy cross, or part of it, to the place of execution. Jesus may have been unable to lift the cross after the events of the night and the mistreatment to which he had been subjected.

> Matthew 27:32. *And as they* [the escorting soldiers] *came out, they found a man of Cyrene, Simon by name: him they compelled to bear his* [Jesus'] *cross.*

Presumably, Simon had arrived in Jerusalem in order to attend the Passover festival, and found himself unexpectedly carrying a cross. Cyrene (see page 91) had a large Jewish colony in New Testament times. Jason, the historian of the Maccabean revolt, on whose works

2 Maccabees was based, was a man of Cyrene. In 117 B.C., Cyrene became independent of Egypt, and in 67 B.C. it was absorbed by Rome.

Golgotha

Jesus was next led to the place of execution:

Matthew 27:33. . . . *they were come unto a place called* [in Aramaic] *Golgotha, that is to say, a place of a skull* . . .

This is a grisly name indeed, deriving perhaps from the fact that some vaguely skull-shaped promontory was in the neighborhood, or from the existence of skulls of previous men executed there. (Both suggestions are mere guesses.)

In Luke the Latin equivalent of the name is given:

Luke 23:33. . . . *they were come to the place, which is called Calvary* . . .

The site of Golgotha/Calvary is not exactly known but it must have been just outside Jerusalem.

There Jesus was crucified, with the record of the crime set above his head, as was customary:

Matthew 27:37. *And set up over his head his accusation written,* THIS IS JESUS THE KING OF THE JEWS.

This is a version of the significance of the name "Jesus Christ" and is a record of the fact that Jesus was executed for the crime of treason against Rome—claiming to be a king without Roman approval.

Vinegar and Gall

Matthew is intent on demonstrating that every aspect of the crucifixion fulfills Old Testament prophecy. Thus, he describes a drink offered Jesus by the soldiers:

Matthew 27:34. *They gave him vinegar to drink mingled with gall* . . .

This sounds like an additional heartless torment inflicted upon a dying man. Actually, it is the reverse. Vinegar (which is derived from

French words meaning "sour wine") can, in this case, be taken literally as the sour wine that was the customary drink for the Roman soldiers. The passage is translated in the Revised Standard Version as "they offered him wine to drink, mingled with gall . . ."

Gall itself is exceedingly bitter, but what may be meant here is some form of deadening anesthetic. Mark, indeed, does not mention gall but describes the incident:

Mark 15:23. *And they gave him to drink wine mingled with myrrh . . .*

If Matthew bases his description on what is said in Mark, why does he change the humane wine and myrrh, clearly intended as a kindly attempt to anesthetize Jesus and deaden the pain he must suffer, into the heartless vinegar and gall, which sounds so like an additional torment? Why needlessly multiply the apparent sins of the crucifiers? Apparently Matthew introduces vinegar and gall to hark back to a passage in the Psalms where the psalmist describes his own distress with poetic exaggeration:

Psalm 69:21. *They gave me also gall for my meat; and in my thirst they gave me vinegar to drink.*

Eli, Eli

Death was not long delayed:

Matthew 27:46. *And about the ninth hour Jesus cried with a loud voice, saying, Eli, Eli, lama sabachthani? that is to say, My God, my God, why hast thou forsaken me?*

It might be suggested that this was the last cry of despair of the "historic Jesus"—the Galilean carpenter who felt the urge to preach, convinced himself at last that he was the Messiah, held to this faith to the last minute, and now—finally—had to realize he was not the Messiah after all and that the whole of his mission had but brought him to this horrible death.

Yet it is not likely that Matthew could possibly have thought this (or Mark, in whom also this dying cry is to be found). Rather, some Old Testament significance is to be sought.

The cry "My God, my God, why hast thou forsaken me?" is the opening of the 22nd Psalm:

Psalm 22:1. *My God, my God, why hast thou forsaken me? why art thou so far from helping me, and from the words of my roaring?*

It is a quotation that is particularly apt for the occasion, since the psalmist describes himself (in the King James Version) as in the extreme of despair and as suffering a fate very like crucifixion:

Psalm 22:16. *For dogs have compassed me: the assembly of the wicked have inclosed me: they pierced my hands and my feet.*

Psalm 22:17. *I may tell all my bones: they look and stare upon me.*

Psalm 22:18. *They part my garments among them, and cast lots upon my vesture.*

Matthew describes the literal fulfillment of the poetic description of the extremity of misfortune in the eighteenth verse and quotes that verse too, pointing to its fulfillment:

Matthew 27:35. *And they crucified him, and parted his garments, casting lots . . .*

The sharpest association of the passage with the crucifixion is the phrase "they pierced my hands and my feet." The Revised Standard Version, which keeps the phrase, points out in a footnote that in the original Hebrew the word which is translated as "pierced" in the Latin versions of the Bible, actually means "like a lion." In the Jewish version of the Bible, the sixteenth verse is given ". . . Like a lion, they are at my hands and my feet." The Jerusalem Bible gives it: ". . . they tie me hand and foot." One wonders if "pierced" was inserted in translation as a reference backward from Jesus' exclamation on the cross.

Joseph of Arimathea

After his death, Jesus was buried:

Matthew 27:57. *When the even was come, there came a rich man of Arimathaea, named Joseph, who also himself was Jesus' disciple:*

Matthew 27:58. *He went to Pilate, and begged the body of Jesus.*

Having obtained the body, he buried it in his own new tomb—dug into the rock—and placed a great stone in the opening.

The town of Arimathea, the birthplace of this disciple of Jesus, is not mentioned in the Bible elsewhere, but it is usually identified with Ramathaim-Zophim, the birthplace of the prophet Samuel (see page I-267).

Joseph of Arimathea does not appear in the Bible except for this one deed, and the reputed site of his tomb is now memorialized by the Church of the Holy Sepulchre in Jerusalem.

Joseph is, however, the subject of a much later legend. He was supposed to have been the custodian of the cup from which Jesus urged his disciples to drink in the course of the last supper:

> Matthew 26:27. *And he took the cup, and gave thanks, and gave it to them, saying, Drink ye all of it;*
> Matthew 26:28. *For this is my blood of the new testament . . .*

This cup came to be called the "Holy Grail." Its possession was supposed to have preserved Joseph of Arimathea through many years of imprisonment. Eventually he was supposed to have brought the cup to the town of Glastonbury in southwestern Britain and there it disappeared. (These legends were very much elaborated and encouraged by the monks at the Abbey of Glastonbury.)

Much of the cycle of legend that surrounded Britain's King Arthur and his knights dealt with the attempts to recover the Holy Grail.

The First Day of the Week

The story of the "historic Jesus" ends here with his burial, for if we are to eliminate the miraculous, then the tale of the resurrection must be put down to legend.

If the burial had really been the end in every way, however, it is very probable that Jesus' disciples would gradually have forgotten their old teacher, that no new disciples would have gathered in his memory, and that the history of the world would have been enormously different.

However, even if we take the rationalist view that there was no resurrection in reality, it cannot be denied that there was one in the belief of the disciples and, eventually, of hundreds of millions of men —and that made all the difference.

Matthew describes the priestly authorities as fearing a coup on the part of Jesus' disciples. They say so to Pilate:

> Matthew 27:63. . . . Sir, . . . that deceiver [Jesus] said, while he was yet alive, After three days I will rise again.
> Matthew 27:64. Command therefore that the sepulchre be made sure until the third day, lest his disciples come by night, and steal him away, and say unto the people, He is risen from the dead . . .

The priestly authorities presumably feared that Jesus, even though dead, might still be used as a rallying cry for a revolt against the Romans. A resurrection would be faked and used as proof of the divine Messiah-hood of Jesus. Pilate, also seeing the danger, granted a contingent of soldiers to guard the tomb.

The belief that Jesus would rise on the third day is given by Matthew, characteristically, in terms of an Old Testament analogy. At one point, when Jesus is asked for some sign that he is indeed a heaven-inspired preacher, Jesus refuses, except to point out one analogy (found spelled out only in Matthew):

> Matthew 12:40. For as Jonas [Jonah] was three days and three nights in the whale's belly; so shall the Son of man be three days and three nights in the heart of the earth.

Now the crucifixion had taken place on a Friday, according to all four gospels. Thus Matthew says:

> Matthew 27:62. Now the next day, that followed the day of preparation . . .

The "next day" was the day after the crucifixion and it followed the "day of preparation," which was therefore the day of the crucifixion. By the "day of preparation" is meant the day on which one prepares for the Sabbath. It is the day before the Sabbath (our Saturday) and, therefore, Friday.

It is for this reason that the crucifixion is commemorated by Christians on a Friday ("Good Friday").

Then comes the story of the sequel to the crucifixion:

Matthew 28:1. *In the end of the sabbath, as it began to dawn toward the first day of the week,*

Matthew 28:2. *. . . there was a great earthquake: for the angel of the Lord descended from heaven, and came and rolled back the stone from the door . . .*

Those guarding the tomb and those coming to mourn are alike astonished, but the angel addresses the latter:

Matthew 28:5. *. . . Fear not ye: for I know that ye seek Jesus, which was crucified.*

Matthew 28:6. *He is not here: for he is risen, as he said . . .*

With the crucifixion taking place on Friday and the resurrection on Sunday ("the first day of the week") one can suppose that Jesus remained "in the heart of the earth" three days (Friday, Saturday, Sunday). However, Matthew's comparison with Jonah's "three days and three nights" in the whale misses, as so many of Matthew's quotations do.

Jesus died on Friday at the ninth hour, shortly after he cried out, "My God, my God, why hast thou forsaken me?" (See page 232.)

This, counting the hours—in the fashion of the time—from sunrise to sunset, would be about 3 P.M. by the modern scheme of hours. If Jesus rose at dawn on Sunday, say 6 A.M., then while he was in the heart of the earth for parts of three different days, he was there for only two nights and one day.

The fact that the resurrection took place on the first day of the week (Sunday) gave that day a special significance to the followers of Christ. It was the "Lord's Day" to be treated with special significance.

At first, it was distinct from the Sabbath (the Seventh Day, or Saturday), which the early Christians celebrated in the usual manner. However, as hostility grew between Christians and Jews, and as the Christians gathered their numbers more and more from among the Gentiles, Sunday came to take on the attributes of a Sabbath and Saturday was abandoned by the Christians altogether.

The anniversary of the particular Sunday on which Jesus was resurrected is commemorated as Easter Sunday.

Mary Magdalene

Among the women who watched at the site of the crucifixion was one called Mary Magdalene:

> Matthew 27:55. *And many women were there beholding* [the crucifixion] *afar off, which followed Jesus from Galilee* . . .
> Matthew 27:56. *Among which was Mary Magdalene* . . .

She was also present at the grave at dawn on the Sunday following:

> Matthew 28:1. *In the end of the sabbath . . . came Mary Magdalene . . . to see the sepulchre.*

Mary Magdalene means Mary of Magdala, Magdala being a town on the west shore of the Sea of Galilee. Its exact location is uncertain, but it may have been a suburb of Tiberias.

The only reference to Mary Magdalene in the gospels, other than as a witness of the crucifixion and resurrection, is as a woman cured by Jesus:

> Mark 16:9. *Now when Jesus was risen early the first day of the week, he appeared first to Mary Magdalene, out of whom he had cast seven devils.*

This is said also by Luke, though not in connection with the resurrection, but with an earlier period while Jesus was still in Galilee:

> Luke 8:1. . . . *he* [Jesus] *went throughout every city and village, preaching . . . and the twelve were with him,*
> Luke 8:2. *And certain women, which had been healed of evil spirits and infirmities, Mary called Magdalene, out of whom went seven devils* . . .

Mary Magdalene has been considered, in tradition, to have been a prostitute and to have repented as a result of her meeting with Jesus. The seven devils might then be considered devils of lust.

This is probably so only because she is mentioned in Luke almost immediately after a tale about another woman. This one comes into Jesus' presence while he is dining with a Pharisee:

> Luke 7:37. *And, behold, a woman in the city, which was a sinner . . .*
>
> Luke 7:38. *. . . stood at his feet behind him weeping . . .*

This sinner was, indeed, a prostitute in all likelihood, but there is no direct identification, anywhere in the Bible, of this woman with Mary Magdalene. To be possessed by devils, as Mary Magdalene was, would be the sign of what we would today call mental illness, rather than anything else. We might much more reasonably consider Mary Magadalene a cured madwoman rather than a reformed prostitute.

Nevertheless, the term "magdalen" is now used to refer to a reformed prostitute, or to a house for reformed prostitutes. And, since Mary Magdalene, as a repentant sinner, is always shown in paintings with her eyes red and swollen with weeping, the word "maudlin" (the British pronunciation of "magdalen") has come to mean tearfully or weakly emotional.

The existence of Mary Magdalene may explain a puzzle concerning the resurrection—why it was believed, and yet not believed.

On the one hand, there seems no question that the disciples accepted the resurrection and that they continued to preach the doctrines of Jesus on that basis, so that their successors, after three centuries, won the empire.

On the other hand, if Jesus did indeed rise from the dead, why was this not the signal for a wild acclamation of the Messiah and a revolt against Rome, as the authorities feared?

One might reconstruct events something like this. Mary Magdalene was the first to see the risen Jesus:

> Mark 16:9. *Now when Jesus was risen early the first day of the week, he appeared first to Mary Magdalene, out of whom he had cast seven devils.*
>
> Mark 16:10. *And she went and told them that had been with him, as they mourned and wept.*
>
> Mark 16:11. *And they . . . believed not.*

Nevertheless, the tale of Mary Magdalene must eventually have carried conviction to the mourning disciples, who would, after all, have wanted fervently to believe that Jesus was indeed the Messiah and would rise from the dead.

Once Mary Magdalene's tale of an empty tomb and of a Jesus who appeared to her was believed, confirming tales would naturally arise in later times. There would come tales of Jesus having appeared to this disciple or that, under such circumstances or others, and a number of them would be recorded in the gospels when these came to be written. But all might conceivably have rested entirely upon the word of one witness, Mary Magdalene.

Yet Mary Magdalene had been possessed by "seven devils." She had been a madwoman or, in any case, seriously disturbed, and her behavior might have remained erratic enough to give her the reputation of being "touched." Even if she had shown marked improvement under Jesus' influence, the shock of the arrest, trial and crucifixion might well have unhinged her once more and made her an easy target for hallucination.

Aside from the disciples, who may have accepted her story only after a while, there might have been no one who would lend it credence. The people generally would have shrugged off anything she had to say as the ravings of a madwoman.

It would follow from this that though the disciples might believe (and more and more fervently as time went on), there would be no general acceptance of the tale by the people. And there were no disorders and certainly no revolt against Rome.

The view given in the gospels is, of course, that Jesus did rise, and he appeared not to Mary Magdalene alone but to a number of people on several different occasions, walking and talking with them. Matthew pictures the disciples as returning home after receiving the tale of the resurrection:

Matthew 28:16. *Then the eleven disciples went away into Galilee, into a mountain where Jesus had appointed them.*

. . . .

Matthew 28:18. *And Jesus came and spake unto them* . . .

To explain the disbelief of the Jews generally, Matthew advances a rather unlikely tale that is not found in the other gospels. He says the priestly authorities bribed the guardians of the tomb to say that they had fallen asleep and that while they slept, Jesus' disciples stole the body and that Jesus had not really risen.

What makes the tale unlikely is that sleeping while on patrol is a cardinal sin for soldiers at all times and it is unlikely that the guards would have let themselves be bribed into admitting such a thing. Even though the priests promised to protect them from the consequences if Pilate heard that they had slept on duty, it is doubtful that they would have taken the chance.

Nevertheless, that is what Matthew says and he concludes:

Matthew 28:15. *So they took the money, and did as they were taught* [instructed]: *and this saying is commonly reported among the Jews until this day.*

6. MARK

THE GOSPEL ACCORDING TO ST. MARK · MARK · JOHN THE BAPTIST ·
THE UNCLEAN SPIRIT · LEVI THE SON OF ALPHAEUS · ABIATHAR ·
BOANERGES · LEGION · TALITHA CUMI

The Gospel According to St. Mark

It is generally accepted that Mark is the earliest of the four gospels, and it is certainly the shortest.

It has been suggested that this first of the gospels was put into writing in order to circulate among Christians the story of the sufferings of Jesus and his steadfastness under affliction. Perhaps this was in order to encourage Christians at a time when they, generally, were undergoing persecution.

The first serious persecutions of Christianity were initiated in Rome by the Emperor Nero after the great fire of A.D. 64 and it is indeed likely that Mark's gospel may have been written shortly after.

From the fact that Jesus' apocalyptic discourse is included and the destruction of Jerusalem clearly indicated (see page 209), it is thought that it might not have been written till after A.D. 66, when the Jewish rebellion against Rome began. There are even those who feel the final form was attained only after A.D. 70 and the Roman destruction of the Second Temple. It could not, however, have been long after A.D. 70, for the gospel must have been in existence and circulating before Matthew and Luke came to be written—since the two latter borrowed extensively from Mark.

Mark's gospel seems to have been written for Christians of Jewish origin, but apparently not for those with extensive knowledge of Biblical lore. There is none of Matthew's Old Testament pedantry. Perhaps the writer of Mark was not himself a very educated man—at least the Greek of the gospel is not very polished.

Palestine in the Time of Christ

Mark

Papias, the second-century Christian bishop, stated that someone named Mark had composed a gospel, using information obtained from Simon Peter himself as his source. It is certain that it is this second gospel to which he refers.

Apparently Peter did have a younger associate named Mark (or Marcus, to use the fuller Latin form of the name). He refers to this man affectionately as one would a disciple or follower, in his first epistle:

1 Peter 5:13. *The church . . . saluteth you; and so doth Marcus my son.*

Nor, despite the Latin name, is Mark a Gentile. Mark appears to be only a surname added to the Jewish proper name of John (Johanan). Thus, in Acts:

Acts 12:12. *. . . he [Peter] came to the house of Mary the mother of John, whose surname was Mark . . .*

John Mark must have been quite young at the time of the crucifixion and he does not appear by name in the gospels. There is, however, one incident described in Mark but not in the other gospels which may indeed refer to Mark himself. It comes just after the arrest of Jesus, when his disciples fled. One unidentified person is described as remaining for a while:

Mark 14:51. *And there followed him a certain young man, having a linen cloth cast about his naked body; and the young men* [who had come to arrest Jesus] *laid hold on him:*

Mark 14:52. *And he left the linen cloth, and fled from them naked.*

Nothing follows from this event and the young man does not reappear. Tradition has it, though, that this young man is Mark himself, and that the evangelist could not resist mentioning his own presence at a key point in the story of Jesus.

John the Baptist

Mark begins his gospel with John the Baptist. He has nothing to say of the virgin birth in Bethlehem, of any marvels or miracles relating to Jesus' infancy. He does not even make mention of the descent from David. In this gospel, Jesus is referred to as the Son of God (that is, the Messiah) but rarely as the Son of David.

In fact, if we had only the gospel of St. Mark to guide us to the life of Jesus, we would have to assume that Jesus was born in Nazareth after the ordinary fashion of men, into a poor Galilean family of no royal pretensions.

Such an origin is so out of line with Old Testament prophecies concerning the Messiah that Matthew may have written *his* gospel primarily in order to assert such matters as the Davidic descent and the birth in Bethlehem. Only so could Jesus be defended against the claims of Jewish theologians that he could *not* be the Messiah because he was of Galilean birth and of non-royal lineage.

In Mark the first mention of Jesus is in connection with his baptism:

> Mark 1:9. . . . *in those days,* . . . *Jesus came from Nazareth* . . . *and was baptized of John in Jordan.*

and thereafter the Spirit of God descended upon him as in Matthew.

John the Baptist is described as the forerunner (as he is in all the gospels) and as knowing that to be his function:

> Mark 1:7. *And* [John the Baptist] *preached, saying, There cometh one mightier than I after me, the latchet of whose shoes I am not worth to stoop down and unloose.*

In Matthew at the time of Jesus' baptism, John is described as specifically recognizing Jesus as that mightier one, but there is none of this in Mark.

The Unclean Spirit

Following the baptism, Mark refers briefly to the episode of the temptation, but without details, certainly without the Old Testament quotations that Matthew introduced for the delectation of his learned audience.

Jesus then chooses his first four disciples and begins his preaching activity. Mark concentrates heavily on his activities as a miraculous healer. Thus, at Capernaum:

> Mark 1:23. . . . *there was in their synagogue a man with an unclean spirit . . .*
>
> . . . .
>
> Mark 1:25. *And Jesus* [said] . . . *come out of him.*
> Mark 1:26. *And . . . the unclean spirit . . . came out of him.*

Mark quotes the unclean spirit as crying out at the approach of Jesus:

> Mark 1:24. . . . *what have we to do with thee, thou Jesus of Nazareth? . . . I know thee who thou art, the Holy One of God.*

Mark uses the phrase "Jesus of Nazareth" since there is no indication in this gospel that Jesus was born anywhere but in Nazareth. The phrase was well enough known to be adopted in the other gospels, despite the tale of the birth at Bethlehem. Furthermore, Mark, who never mentions the Davidic descent, makes use of "Holy One of God" as a phrase signifying the Messiah, rather than "Son of David."

Levi the son of Alphaeus

Mark records Jesus as selecting a publican for a disciple:

> Mark 2:14. *And as he passed by, he saw Levi the son of Alphaeus sitting at the receipt of custom, and said unto him, Follow me. And he arose and followed him.*

Matthew tells the same story, but of the disciple Matthew (presumably the Evangelist himself), and says nothing of the publican being the son of Alphaeus.

In Matthew's list of the twelve apostles he lists two pairs of brothers:

> Matthew 10:2. . . . *Simon . . . Peter, and Andrew his brother; James the son of Zebedee, and John his brother . . .*

If Levi (or Matthew) were the son of Alphaeus, a third pair of brothers must be found among the apostles, for there is a second James, distinguished, as the son of Alphaeus, from James, son of Zebedee. Ought not Levi (or Matthew) be mentioned together with James the son of Alphaeus? In the list of apostles, Matthew includes:

> Matthew 10:3. . . . *Matthew the publican; James the son of Alphaeus, and Lebbaeus, whose surname was Thaddaeus.*

The pattern in Matthew is that the lesser known brother follows the better known (or, perhaps, the younger follows the older) and the father's name is mentioned only for the brother mentioned first. Now Lebbaeus is a Greek form of the name Levi, so that the verse 10:3 might almost seem to include James the son of Alphaeus and Levi, his brother. Yet there is no mention of the brotherhood; Matthew is placed on the other side of James; and Matthew seems to go out of his way to identify himself as "Matthew the publican."

In Mark's list of apostles, brotherhood is less important. Andrew, for instance, is not identified as the brother of Peter (although he is so identified at the time both were accepted as disciples). Andrew is not even placed next to Peter. Mark says:

> Mark 3:18. *And Andrew, and Philip, and Bartholomew, and Matthew, and Thomas, and James the son of Alphaeus, and Thaddaeus . . .*

Matthew is not identified. Yet why would Matthew claim to be a publican if he were not; the calling was a disgraceful one (see page 167). Or did Matthew wish to emphasize his rise to grace by blackening his position before that rise?

Abiathar

Mark begins early to describe the gathering dismay of the orthodox among the Jews at Jesus' doctrines; at his claim to have the power to forgive sins and at his cavalier attitude toward the Sabbath (see page 184).

In maintaining that the Sabbath might be broken, when necessary, for the good of men, Jesus pointed out an action of David himself as a precedent. When David was a fugitive from Saul, and suffering the pangs of hunger, the high priest at Nob allowed him to use the special hallowed bread, ordinarily reserved for priests only. Thus human necessity rose above ritual.

In giving this example, however, Mark made a factual error:

Mark 2:26. . . . *he* [David] *went into the house of God in the days of Abiathar the high priest, and did eat the shewbread* . . .

But it was not Abiathar who was high priest at the time this incident took place, but Abiathar's father, Ahimelech (see page I-290). It is an understandable slip, however, for Abiathar was the sole survivor of the slaughter of the priests at Nob as a result of their having fed David, and Abiathar was closely connected with David throughout the latter's subsequent reign. It would be almost second nature for a Jew of New Testament times to think of Abiathar in connection with King David.

Matthew and Luke both repeat this story, but neither mentions the name of the high priest, thus avoiding the slip.

Boanerges

In Mark's list of the twelve apostles, an interesting addition is a surname given to the sons of Zebedee:

Mark 3:17. *And James the son of Zebedee, and John the brother of James; and he* [Jesus] *surnamed them Boanerges, which is, The sons of thunder* . . .

Boanerges is a Greek transliteration of the Aramaic "benai regesh," which means "sons of anger." This may represent a tradition to the effect that James and John were fiery in temper and always ready to take angry action.

A clear example of this is to be found in Luke. There, when Jesus was rebuffed by Samaritans who would not allow him to enter one of their villages, James and John demand retaliation:

Luke 9:54. *And when his disciples James and John saw this, they said, Lord, wilt thou that we command fire to come down from heaven, and consume them, even as Elias* [Elijah] *did?*

The reference here is to a tale of Elijah, who, when fifty soldiers came to arrest him in the time of Ahaziah, king of Israel, used fire from heaven in his defense:

> 2 Kings 1:10. *And Elijah answered and said to the captain of fifty, If I be a man of God, then let fire come down from heaven, and consume thee and thy fifty. And there came down fire from heaven, and consumed him and his fifty.*

Jesus, however, rebuked his wrathful disciples:

> Luke 9:56. . . . *the Son of man is not come to destroy men's lives, but to save them . . .*

Legion

In Mark's telling of the casting out of devils in the country of the Gadarenes or Gergesenes (see page 176), he has Jesus speaking to the possessing devils:

> Mark 5:9. *And he* [Jesus] *asked him* [the possessing spirit], *What is thy name? And he answered, saying, My name is Legion: for we are many.*

Legion is capitalized in the King James Version, and in the Revised Standard Version as well, as though it were a proper name, the name of the inhabiting spirit.

Actually "legion" is the name given to the principal unit of the Roman army and is from a Latin word meaning "to gather together." A legion is a group of soldiers "gathered together." In New Testament times, a legion consisted of some six thousand soldiers, and the word could therefore be used to indicate a great number. The statement "My name is Legion: for we are many" is equivalent to saying, "There are thousands of us."

And, indeed, the spirits are then sent into thousands of swine:

> Mark 5:13. . . . *the unclean spirits . . . entered into the swine: . . . (they were about two thousand;) . . .*

Talitha cumi

Mark's account of Jesus' life and death is so like Matthew's in essentials that there remains little to say that has not been said in the previous chapter. One interesting point might be mentioned:

For all that Mark seems to have written in Greek, it is closer to the Aramaic even than Matthew. In fact, part of the imperfection of the Greek of this gospel seems to be that it contains numerous Aramaic forms of expression, literally translated, as though Mark were writing in Greek, but thinking in Aramaic.

Oftener than in the other gospels, Mark gives the actual Aramaic and then translates it, as in the case of "Boanerges." Another example arises in the case of the young daughter of a synagogue official—a girl whom Jesus raises from the dead. All three synoptic gospels tell of this miracle, but only Mark reports Jesus' words, on raising the girl, in the native Aramaic:

> Mark 5:41. *And he* [Jesus] *took the damsel by the hand, and said unto her, Talitha cumi; which is, being interpreted, Damsel, I say unto thee, arise.*

At another time, Mark reports Jesus' curing of a deaf man with a speech impediment:

> Mark 7:34. *And looking up to heaven, he* [Jesus] *sighed, and saith unto him, Ephphatha, that is, Be opened.*

And still again, at Gethsemane, when Jesus prays, addressing God as "Father," the Aramaic word is given first:

> Mark 14:36. *And he* [Jesus] *said, Abba, Father, all things are possible unto thee; take away this cup from me* . . .

7. LUKE

THE GOSPEL ACCORDING TO ST. LUKE * LUKE * THEOPHILUS * ZACHARIAS *
ELISABETH * MARY * JOHN THE BAPTIST * CAESAR AUGUSTUS * CYRENIUS *
BETHLEHEM * CHRISTMAS * SIMEON * THE DOCTORS * TIBERIUS CAESAR *
THE SON OF JOSEPH * JUDAS THE BROTHER OF JAMES * THE CENTURION *
THE GOOD SAMARITAN * LAZARUS THE BEGGAR * A FAR COUNTRY * HEROD
ANTIPAS * THE CRUCIFIXION

The Gospel According to St. Luke

The third and last of the synoptic gospels seems, like that of
St. Matthew, to have been based largely on the gospel of St. Mark,
but with additional matter included.

Luke is therefore certainly later than Mark, and is probably later
than Matthew as well. Scholars generally seem to agree that Luke
was written some time after the crucial year, A.D. 70, when Jerusalem
was taken and the Temple destroyed by the Romans. Some have
even suggested dates as late as A.D. 100, though A.D. 80 would be more
generally acceptable.

If Luke is later than Matthew, it nevertheless seems to have been
written independently. The additional matter included in Luke, beyond what is found in Mark, is for the most part quite different from
the additional matter found in Matthew.

Partly, this may have arisen out of a difference in intent.

Suppose we begin with the gospel of St. Mark, the earliest of
the synoptics, and view it for what it seems to be—the simple story
of a prophet and wonder-worker who is viewed by the author as the
Messiah, and who is wrongfully accused and executed but triumphantly
restored to life. The story as told by Mark is intended for the ordinary
Christian of Jewish background.

Matthew, in his rewriting of this gospel, added material designed

Palestine in the Time of Christ

(in his view) to fit it for the ears of those learned in Old Testament lore, by interlarding it with many references to Biblical prophecies and, for the purpose, making use of such legends concerning Jesus as were common at the time and would lend themselves to such prophecies.

Luke, on the other hand, rewrote Mark's gospel in a way to make it fit, particularly, for the ears of Gentiles who are sympathetic to Christianity and are considering conversion—or perhaps are already converted and wish to know still more concerning the background to their new religion. Old Testament prophecies are largely ignored by Luke as unessential and the Jews are cast more clearly in the role of villains than they are in Matthew and Mark. The Roman authorities are treated more gently than in the first two gospels, and Jesus himself is portrayed as far more sympathetic to Gentiles in Luke than in the other synoptic gospels.

Luke

It is widely considered that Luke was himself a Gentile, though none of the evidence is conclusive. His name is Roman, for Luke ("Loukas" in Greek and "Lucas" in Latin) is a shortened version of either Lucius or Lucanus, both good Roman names. This, in itself, settles nothing, of course, for Roman names were sometimes adopted by Jews in New Testament times. Paul is a Roman name, but the apostle Paul was certainly Jewish.

Then, too, the Greek in which Luke is written is judged to be of significantly greater literary value than that of either Matthew or Mark (and indeed the superiority of Luke seems evident to most even in English translation) so that the author is judged to have had a thorough Greek education. This increases the possibility that he was a Gentile, though it still doesn't make it certain.

We can search for more hints in the fact that the same author who wrote Luke almost certainly wrote the Acts of the Apostles as well, the book in which the events of the decades following the crucifixion are given, particularly matters concerning the travels of the Apostle Paul.

There are indications that the writer of Acts was actually a companion of Paul who accompanied him on his travels. Thus, at one point Paul is described as seeing the vision of a man in Macedonia crying for help:

Acts 16:10. *And after he had seen the vision, immediately we endeavoured to go into Macedonia . . .*

It may be that the writer of Acts has suddenly switched to a quotation from Paul's memoirs, without indicating the fact. (The conventions about the use of quotation marks are modern, of course.) It seems more reasonable, however, to suppose that the use of "we" means that the writer was one of Paul's entourage who tried with him to arrange for passage to Macedonia.

But who might this companion be? Persons particularly close to Paul are mentioned by him several times in his letters. Thus, in the Epistle to the Colossians, Paul brings his letter to a close by sending greetings from those around him:

Colossians 4:14. *Luke, the beloved physician, and Demas, greet you.*

It is usually assumed that Luke was Paul's personal doctor, and the nature of the post alone would assure a close connection of the two throughout Paul's arduous travels. In the Second Epistle to Timothy, Paul specifically states:

2 Timothy 4:10. *. . . Demas hath forsaken me, having loved this present world . . .*
2 Timothy 4:11. *Only Luke is with me . . .*

thus indicating the particular close fidelity of his physician. Luke is also mentioned in the closing of the Epistle to Philemon as one of those from whom greeting is sent.

The tradition is that it is this Luke who was author of both the third gospel and Acts. This tradition dates back to Irenaeus, a bishop who served in Gaul about A.D. 170.

That still doesn't help us decide whether Luke was Jewish or Gentile.

Yet the Book of Acts seems to deal with Antioch in a particularly detailed manner, as though the author were well acquainted with church matters there. The Christians at Antioch were largely of Gentile background (there were relatively few Jews there) and if Luke was a member of the church of that city, the chances are good that he was a Gentile. An early church father, Eusebius of Caesarea, wrote a history of the Church in A.D 324, and he considered Luke to have been a citizen of Antioch of Syrian extraction. This is the tradition generally accepted.

And yet there is a verse in Acts that lists some of the members of the church at Antioch:

> Acts 13:1. *Now there were in the church that was at Antioch certain prophets and teachers; as Barnabas, and Simeon that was called Niger, and Lucius of Cyrene* . . .

Can Lucius of Cyrene be the Luke of the Pauline epistles? This has been suggested by some. But Cyrene was an important Jewish center and if Luke were a native of Cyrene rather than of Antioch, the chance that he was Jewish is materially increased.

On the whole, the best evidence in favor of Luke's Gentile origin is his writing itself and its sympathetic attitude toward Gentiles.

Theophilus

Luke begins his gospel in approved Greek fashion by addressing the person for whom it is intended:

> Luke 1:3. *It seemed good to me also . . . to write unto thee in order, most excellent Theophilus,*
> Luke 1:4. *That thou mightest know the certainty of those things, wherein thou hast been instructed.*

This sounds as though Luke were attempting to further the conversion of some specific Greek. Absolutely nothing is known about this prospective convert, but it is usually supposed that he was of good family since Luke refers to him as "most excellent."

Some have suggested that Theophilus was an official of the Roman court that was trying the Apostle Paul, and that the gospel of St. Luke was in the nature of a brief for the defense, prepared by Paul's close friend and associate. It was intended to acquaint the court with the fact that Paul was not a traitor to Rome but a messenger from God.

There are also suggestions that Theophilus (the name means "one who loves God") was not a person at all but represented, allegorically, potential converts generally.

Zacharias

Luke was under no illusion that he was to write the first biography of Jesus, for he was well aware that a number of such biographies already existed. There was Mark, for one, and perhaps a number that were never accepted as canonical and have since been lost:

> Luke 1:1. *Forasmuch as many have taken in hand to set forth in order a declaration of those things which are most surely believed among us . . .*

It may well have been, though, that if he was not the first in the field, he intended to be most complete. Mark began with the baptism of Jesus by John, at a time when Jesus was already a grown man, and ends with the resurrection. Matthew goes back to Jesus' birth, but in Luke we go further back still to the birth of John the Baptist.

The purpose, here, may have been to make it perfectly clear that John was a subsidiary element, a forerunner, and one who clearly recognized his own role as a mere herald of the greater man to follow. This may have been particularly important in the light of the doctrinal disputes in decades immediately following the crucifixion, when the followers of John the Baptist maintained for some time a tradition that was apparently independent of the followers of Jesus. Thus, in Acts, a newcomer is introduced as follows:

> Acts 18:24. . . . *a certain Jew named Apollos . . . came to Ephesus.*
> Acts 18:25. . . . *knowing only the baptism of John.*

He was apparently a follower of the doctrines of John the Baptist who, however, knew of Jesus and quickly joined the followers of Jesus.

Luke, therefore, begins with Zacharias, the father of John the Baptist, an individual not mentioned elsewhere in the New Testament:

Luke 1:5. *There was in the days of Herod . . . a certain priest named Zacharias, of the course of Abia* [Abijah] *. . .*

The priesthood was divided into twenty-four divisions or "courses," each of which served a week at the Temple so that a given man served for one week at a time, twice each year. These twenty-four courses are each named for an ancestor of Aaronic descent and these are listed in 1 Chronicles. Among them are:

1 Chronicles 24:10. *The seventh to Hakkoz, the eighth to Abijah . . .*

Zacharias was thus a priest of the eighth course.

Elisabeth

The mother of John the Baptist is also introduced:

Luke 1:5. *. . . and his* [Zacharias'] *wife was of the daughters of Aaron, and her name was Elisabeth.*

Elisabeth ("Eleisabet" in Greek) is a good Aaronic name, since it is equivalent to the Hebrew "Elisheba," which was the name of Aaron's wife:

Exodus 6:23. *And Aaron took him Elisheba . . . to wife . . .*

The couple were childless and, as they were advanced in years, it seemed as though that state might be permanent. Elisabeth shared this fate with a number of women in the Old Testament: Sarah, the wife of Abraham; Rachel, the wife of Jacob; the unnamed wife of Manoah; and Hannah, the wife of Elkanah. In each of the cases mentioned, the barrenness was ended through divine intervention and a notable son was born: Isaac, Joseph, Samson, and Samuel, respectively. The story of Elisabeth follows these earlier models.

Zacharias takes his turn at service in the Temple, in a year not specified. The angel Gabriel appears to him, just as an angel appeared to the wife of Manoah. Zacharias is told he will have a son in terms that echo, in part, the words of the earlier tale concerning the wife of Manoah. Shortly thereafter, Elisabeth did indeed become pregnant.

Mary

The story now shifts to the future mother of Jesus:

> Luke 1:26. *And in the sixth month* [of Elisabeth's pregnancy] *the angel Gabriel was sent from God unto a city of Galilee, named Nazareth,*
> Luke 1:27. *To a virgin espoused to a man whose name was Joseph, of the house of David; and the virgin's name was Mary.*
> Luke 1:28. *And the angel . . . said . . .*
> . . . .
> Luke 1:31. . . . . *behold, thou shalt conceive in thy womb, and bring forth a son, and shalt call his name JESUS.*

Luke stresses the fact that Mary is a virgin, but this is by no means as clear a statement of the virgin birth as is to be found in Matthew. Mary, although a virgin at the time of this "annunciation," was engaged to be married, and Gabriel's words might be taken as meaning that she would conceive after her marriage with Joseph had been consummated, and in the ordinary manner of conception.

To be sure, the story goes on:

> Luke 1:34. *Then said Mary unto the angel, How shall this be, seeing I know not a man?*

It is an odd question, considering that she is about to be married, unless, as some commentators suggest, she intends to be a perpetual virgin, even if she marries. (However, Luke doesn't say so.) Another possibility is that Mary conceived at the instant of the annunciation and therefore while she was still a virgin. Yet Gabriel in answering Mary's question uses the future tense:

> Luke 1:35. *And the angel answered . . . , The Holy Ghost shall come upon thee . . .*

Though it is hard to say that Luke declares the virgin birth unequivocally and—if Luke is read *alone*—it is easy to argue that a virgin birth is not intended, still Christians generally accept Luke's tale of the annunciation as signifying Jesus' birth of a virgin.

Gabriel also told Mary the news concerning Elisabeth:

Luke 1:36. And, behold, thy cousin Elisabeth, she hath also con-
ceived a son in her old age: and this is the sixth month with
her . . .

Mary hastened to visit her cousin ("the visitation"). When she entered the house of Zacharias, Elisabeth greeted her at once:

Luke 1:42. And she [Elisabeth] spake out with a loud voice,
and said, Blessed art thou among women, and blessed is the fruit of
thy womb.

The first part of her greeting is a duplicate of the last part of the
greeting given Mary by Gabriel:

Luke 1:28. And the angel . . . said, Hail, thou that art highly
favoured, the Lord is with thee: blessed art thou among women.

In the Revised Standard Version, the greeting of Gabriel begins
"Hail, O favored one" and in the Catholic version, "Hail, full of
grace."

There is a tendency to think that the phrase "blessed art thou
among women" was accidentally transferred from Elisabeth to Gabriel
in the copying process. It is for this reason that the Revised Standard
Version omits it in Gabriel's greeting.

By combining the two greetings and adding the name of the person
greeted and the name of the child who is to be the fruit of Mary's
womb, we have "Hail, Mary, full of grace, the Lord is with thee.
Blessed art thou among women, and blessed is the fruit of thy womb,
Jesus." The first two words of this greeting, in Latin, are "Ave, Maria"
and this greeting is the famous prayer of that name which is so
prominent in the liturgy of the Roman Catholic Church.

Elisabeth's reference to the fruit of Mary's womb is in the present
tense, which may mean that the evangelist considers Mary to be already pregnant. If so, this is the strongest evidence for the virgin
birth in Luke.

Yet one can't help but wonder if the legend of the visitation was
not chosen by Luke for inclusion in his gospel primarily because it
offered a chance to demonstrate that John the Baptist recognized Jesus'
priority and transcendent importance even in the womb. He has
Elisabeth say to Mary:

Luke 1:44. . . . *as soon as the voice of thy salutation sounded in mine ears, the babe leaped in my womb for joy.*

This would be a strong point for the followers of Jesus and against the competing followers of John.

In the course of the visit of Mary to Elisabeth, Mary chants a hymn of praise to God which begins:

Luke 1:46. *And Mary said, My soul doth magnify the Lord . . .*

The hymn is very much like that ascribed to Hannah on the occasion of her giving birth to Samuel, and is widely considered to be inspired by it.

Actually, it is Elisabeth, rather than Mary, whose case was like Hannah's. It was Elisabeth who, like Hannah, was barren for many years despite marriage, and it was Elisabeth who, like Hannah, had been blessed with conception by God and with vindication in a society that considered barrenness a punishment for sin.

It is to be expected, then, that the hymn, which follows immediately after Elisabeth's greeting to Mary, should be intoned by Elisabeth rather than Mary. In some old manuscripts, indeed, Luke 1:46 reads, "And she said, My soul doth magnify the Lord," where "she" might refer to Elisabeth as easily as to Mary. Perhaps the transfer of the prayer from Elisabeth to Mary is part of the victory of the disciples of Jesus over those of John in the decades when the gospels were written.

The first phrase of the song is, in Latin, "Magnificat anima mea Dominum" and it is therefore referred to as the "Magnificat."

Mary remained with Elisabeth three months, presumably till the birth of Elisabeth's child. Then she returned home.

Luke's choice of legends that centered on Mary rather than, as in Matthew's case, on Joseph, might be significant. The Gentiles knew of goddesses, and their pagan religions often had a strongly feminine cast. If Luke were a Gentile, he would be drawn to the tales of Mary. Matthew, on the other hand, a product of the strongly patriarchal Jewish culture, would automatically deal with Joseph.

Luke's preoccupation with Mary has led to the legend that he knew her personally and learned of the story of Jesus' birth from her in her old age. There is also a tradition to the effect that Luke was an artist and painted a portrait of Mary which was later found in Jerusalem. Such traditions are supported by nothing more than pious belief.

John the Baptist

When Elisabeth's child was born, it was expected he was to be named Zacharias like his father. That Luke should seriously maintain this:

> Luke 1:59. . . . they [kinsmen] *came to circumcise the child; and they called him Zacharias, after the name of his father.*

is an odd departure from Jewish custom. There is no case in the Bible of a child named for a living father, and it is certainly unheard of for pious Jews to do so today. Perhaps this is the kind of lapse one might expect of a Gentile, as Luke is considered to be.

In any case, Elisabeth objected:

> Luke 1:60. *And his mother . . . said, Not so; but he shall be called John.*

Zacharias agreed to this and then intoned a hymn of praise:

> Luke 1:67. And . . . Zacharias . . . prophesied, saying,
> Luke 1:68. Blessed be the Lord God of Israel; for he hath visited and redeemed his people . . .

The first word of this hymn is, in Latin, "Benedictus" and it is by that name that the entire hymn is known.

Zacharias does not appear again in Luke, or anywhere else in the Bible. Some early commentators suggested that the reference by Jesus to Zacharias son of Barachias who was "slain between the temple and the altar" (see page 207) was a reference to the father of John the Baptist. This, however, is almost certainly not so, and the Bible makes no reference whatsoever to the death of John's father.

Caesar Augustus

It is now time for Luke to turn to Mary again and recount the tale of the birth of Jesus. There is no sure indication in what is to follow of the time that has elapsed between the birth of John the

Baptist and the birth of Jesus. Luke merely uses a conventionally indefinite phrase:

Luke 2:1. *And it came to pass in those days . . .*

Of course, if Mary's pregnancy followed hard on the annunciation, which came in the sixth month of Elisabeth's pregnancy, then Jesus had to be born just six months after John the Baptist, assuming both pregnancies to have lasted nine months.

But even if this were so and Jesus were half a year younger than John, in what year were both born?

Matthew says only that Jesus was born "in the days of Herod the king" (see page 121), which sets an extreme time limit between 37 B.C. and 4 B.C. Luke, the Gentile, dates the birth by the Gentile emperor and not by the Jewish king:

Luke 2:1. *And it came to pass in those days, that there went out a decree from Caesar Augustus . . .*

Caesar Augustus was born in 63 B.C., in the very year in which Judea was converted into a Roman province by Pompey (see page 122). His name at birth was Caius Octavius; he was the grandnephew of Julius Caesar, and, eventually, that general's adopted heir. When Julius Caesar was assassinated in 44 B.C., Caius Octavius came to Rome to receive his inheritance and changed his name to Caius Julius Caesar Octavianus. At this period in his life he is best known in history as Octavian.

Octavian was a nineteen-year-old boy, sickly and of unimpressive appearance. The most powerful man in Rome at the time was Mark Antony. For fourteen years the two men fought a civil war against each other, sometimes a hot war of spears and swords, sometimes a cold one of propaganda and maneuver. Octavian was immeasurably the greater man of the two and in 30 B.C. the defeated Mark Antony killed himself. Octavian was then sole and absolute ruler of Rome.

Octavian was Imperator ("Commander") of the army, an old title, but one which came to be associated particularly with him and his successors. In English this has been corrupted to Emperor, so that Octavian became the first Roman Emperor and the government over which he and his successors presided came to be known as the Roman Empire.

In 27 B.C. he was voted the title "Augustus" meaning "undertaken

under favorable auguries" or, which is the same thing, "well-omened."
He is commonly known to history by that name.

The period during which Augustus ruled in Rome and Herod in
Jerusalem—the period during which Jesus must have been born according to Matthew and Luke—was from 27 B.C. and 4 B.C.

In 27 B.C. Augustus closed the Temple of Janus, a move indicating
the coming of peace over the vast area that marked the Roman realm.
This was a notable event, for this had taken place in only four or five
brief periods prior to Augustus' time during all the seven warlike centuries in which the dominion of Rome had gradually spread from a
single city to all the Mediterranean world.

The period of peace that began with Augustus' rule lasted for
centuries (the "pax Romana" or "Roman peace"). The Mediterranean world had never seen so long a period of peace before Augustus'
time, or, for that matter, since.

It is sometimes stated that the beginning of this period of peace
was a particularly appropriate time for Jesus to be born. To those who
accept the divine ordering of human affairs, it seems easy to assume
that matters were deliberately arranged in order that a profound peace
should fall over all the world in preparation for the birth of the
"Prince of Peace."

This, however, is a view that is more romantic than justified. To be
sure, there was peace in the settled regions of the empire (including
Judea), where peace had been conspicuously absent in the preceding
century, and, to be sure, this is not a matter to be lightly dismissed.
The peace, however, was not universal.

All through Augustus' reign and, therefore, all through the period
of Jesus' birth and youth, the Roman boundaries to the north were
aflame. Augustus was pushing the boundaries of the empire to the
Danube and eastward across Germany. For the barbarous tribes south
of the Danube and west of the Elbe, there was no peace.

Cyrenius

The period of Jesus' birth might be narrowed by considering the
reference to the nature of the decree of Caesar Augustus:

> Luke 2:1. . . . . a decree from Caesar Augustus, that all the world
> should be taxed.

Luke 2:2. (*And this taxing was first made when Cyrenius was governor of Syria.*)

Cyrenius was indeed an important Roman official in the time of Augustus. His name was Quirinius, actually, which became "Kyrinios" in Greek and "Cyrenius" in English. The Revised Standard Version restores it to the Latin "Quirinius."

Quirinius was in charge of Roman military affairs in Syria, an office which placed him over the legions in Judea as well, on two different occasions: from 6 to 4 B.C. and from A.D. 6 to 9. All commentators agree that Jesus could not have been born as late as A.D. 6 to 9 and that the incidents surrounding Jesus' birth, if they took place while Quirinius was governor of Syria, had to take place during his first term, from 6 to 4 B.C. This would certainly harmonize Luke's account with Matthew's, at least in this respect.

During Quirinius' second administration, there was (according to Josephus) a census initiated for the purpose of determining some fair basis for the assessment of a special tax.

In ancient times, censuses were generally instituted with either taxation or military enrollment in mind, and this was never popular in either case. Even in the time of David himself, a census was viewed with hostility (see page I-318) and, in post-Exilic times, was looked back upon as having been brought about through nothing less than Satanic inspiration:

1 Chronicles 21:1. *And Satan stood up against Israel, and provoked David to number Israel.*

A Judea which thought of a census with such hostility even when carried through by its great king David was not likely to view with equanimity one that was initiated by a group of Gentile oppressors.

Nevertheless, such a census was an obvious necessity in Quirinius' second administration. Herod Archelaus had just been deposed as ethnarch (see page 138) and now Judea was under direct Roman rule. As long as Judea had been under some native ruler under native laws, Rome might have been willing to have its taxes collected in any fashion that pleased the ruler—provided only he turned over an adequate amount to Rome. Once Rome was in direct charge, however, things would have to be done systematically and the first step would be a census, numbering the people and their possessions.

From our point of view, this is an enlightened measure and one that would work in favor of the common people, for Augustus ruled well and enforced a surprising amount of honesty in provincial government. Unfortunately the purpose of a census and its honest intent could not easily be explained. The Jews (and all the peoples of the east) knew only too well of corrupt governments and gouging tax collectors. The only way in which individuals could save themselves from utter ruin when the tax collector came round was by a combination of cheating and bribery. A census that would expose their actual belongings and place the collector under an obligation to collect a known amount would deprive them of their chance of wiggling their way out of some of the tax.

It is not surprising, then, that there was wild rioting over Judea when the Romans began to carry through their census. Luke even mentions such rioting in Acts:

> Acts 5:37. . . . *Judas of Galilee* [rose up] *in the days of the taxing, and drew away much people after him* . . .

The riots were put down bloodily, of course, and the census was carried through. The memory remained green for decades afterward and it is not surprising that Luke used it as a landmark for the birth of Jesus.

This particular census in Quirinius' second administration is not, however, an accurate landmark. Jesus could not have been born as late as that; he had to be born in Quirinius' first administration and unfortunately we have no records of any census carried through in that time.

It has been suggested that there was indeed a census carried through in 6 B.C. in Quirinius' first administration. At that time, the suggestion has it, Herod ruled over Judea and he might have carried the census through in accordance with Jewish custom. There would then be no disorders and nothing for Josephus to remark upon.

This is conceivable, but it seems most unlikely and no one would dream of suggesting such a thing except for the necessity of justifying the reference in the gospel of St. Luke. Herod was not a popular ruler with the Jewish nationalists. The latter considered him, as an Idumean, to be just as foreign as the Romans. It passes the bounds of belief to suppose that a Herodian census would have been carried through without disorders.

Bethlehem

One might suppose, instead, that Luke made use of the well-remembered census merely as a landmark by which to date the approximate time of birth of Jesus, as Matthew used the star of Bethlehem (see page 128). The Biblical writers are rarely concerned with exact dating, in any case, and find other matters of more importance.

But there is a chance that more was involved. We might argue that Luke was faced with a serious difficulty in telling the tale of Jesus' birth and that he had decided to use the census as a device to get out of that difficulty.

In Mark, the earliest of the gospels, Jesus appears only as Jesus of Nazareth. To Mark, as nearly as we can tell from his gospel, the Messiah was a Galilean by birth, born in Nazareth.

Yet this could not be accepted by Jews learned in the Scriptures. Jesus of Nazareth had to be born in Bethlehem in order to be the Messiah. The prophet Micah was considered to have said so specifically (see page I-653) and the evangelist Matthew accepts that in his gospel (see page 132).

In order to make the birth at Bethlehem (made necessary by theological theory) consistent with the known fact of life at Nazareth, Matthew made Joseph and Mary natives of Bethlehem who migrated to Nazareth not long after Jesus' birth (see page 138).

Luke, however, did not have access to Matthew's version, apparently, and it did not occur to him to make use of so straightforward a device. Instead, he made Joseph and Mary dwellers in Nazareth before the birth of Jesus, and had them travel to Bethlehem just in time to have Jesus born there and then had them return.

That Mary, at least, dwelt in Nazareth, and perhaps had even been born there, seems plain from the fact that Gabriel was sent there to make the annunciation:

> Luke 1:26. . . . *the angel Gabriel was sent from God unto a city of Galilee, named Nazareth,*
> Luke 1:27. *To a virgin* [whose] . . . *name was Mary.*

But if that were so, why should Mary, in her last month of pregnancy, make the difficult and dangerous seventy-mile overland journey to

Bethlehem

Bethlehem? Luke might have said it was done at Gabriel's orders, but he didn't. Instead, with literary economy, he made use of the landmark of Jesus' birth for the additional purpose of having Jesus born at Bethlehem. Once Caesar Augustus had issued his decree commanding the census in advance of taxation:

Luke 2:3. *And all went to be taxed, every one into his own city.*
Luke 2:4. *And Joseph also went up from Galilee, out of the city of Nazareth, into Judaea, unto . . . Bethlehem; (because he was of the house and lineage of David:)*
Luke 2:5. *To be taxed with Mary his espoused wife, being great with child.*

Though this device has much to be said for it from the standpoint of literary economy, it has nothing to be said for it in the way of plausibility. The Romans couldn't possibly have conducted so queer a census as that. Why should they want every person present in the town of his ancestors rather than in the town in which he actually dwelt? Why should they want individuals traveling up and down the length of the land, clogging the roads and interfering with the life of the province? It would even have been a military danger, for the Parthians could find no better time to attack than when Roman troops would find it hard to concentrate because of the thick crisscrossing of civilians on their way to register.

Even if the ancestral town were somehow a piece of essential information, would it not be simpler for each person merely to state what that ancestral town was? And even if, for some reason, a person had to travel to that ancestral town, would it not be sufficient for the head of the household or some agent of his to make the trip? Would a wife have to come along? Particularly one that was in the last month of pregnancy?

No, it is hard to imagine a more complicated tissue of implausibilities and the Romans would certainly arrange no such census.

Those who maintain that there was an earlier census in 6 B.C. or thereabouts, conducted under the auspices of Herod, suggest that one of the reasons this early census went off quietly was precisely because Herod ran things in the Jewish fashion, according to tribes and households. Even if Herod were a popular king (which he wasn't) it is difficult to see how he could have carried through a quiet census by requiring large numbers of people to tramp miles under the dangerous and primitive conditions of travel of the times. All through their history, the Jews had rebelled for far smaller reasons than the declaration of such a requirement.

It is far easier to believe that Luke simply had to explain the birth of Jesus in Bethlehem for theological reasons, when it was well known that he was brought up in Nazareth. And his instinct for drama overcame any feelings he might have had for plausibility.

Judging by results, Luke was right. The implausibility of his story has not prevented it from seizing upon the imagination of the Christian world, and it is this second chapter of the gospel of St. Luke that is the epitome of the story of the Nativity and the inspiration of countless tales and songs and works of art.

Christmas

In Bethlehem, according to Luke's account, Mary gave birth:

> Luke 2:7. *And she* [Mary] *brought forth her firstborn son and wrapped him in swaddling clothes, and laid him in a manger; because there was no room for them in the inn.*

Presumably the inn was full of travelers, as all inns in Judea must have been at that time, if Luke's story of the census is accepted. Every town, after all, would have been receiving its quota of families returning from elsewhere.

There is no indication at all at this point concerning the date of the Nativity. The feast is celebrated, now, by almost all Christian churches on December 25. This is Christmas ("Christ's mass").

But why December 25? No one really knows. To Europeans and North Americans such a date means winter and, in fact, many of our carols depict a wintry scene and so do our paintings. Indeed, so close is the association of winter and snow that each year millions irrationally long for a "white Christmas" though snow means a sharp rise in automobile fatalities.

Yet upon what is such wintry association based? There is no mention of either snow or cold in either Luke or Matthew. In fact, in the verse after the description of the birth, Luke says:

> Luke 2:8. *And there were in the same country shepherds abiding in the field, keeping watch over their flock by night.*

It is customary, since we have the celebration firmly fixed on December 25, to imagine these shepherds as keeping their watch in bitter cold and perhaps in deep snow.

But why? Surely it is much more likely that a night watch would be kept in the summertime when the nights would be mild and, in fact, more comfortable than the scorching heat of the day. For that matter, it is but adding still another dimension to the implausible nature of the census as depicted by Luke if we suppose that all this unnecessary traveling was taking place in the course of a cold winter time.

To be sure, it is a mistake to think of a Palestinian winter as being as cold as one in Germany, Great Britain, or New England. The usual associations of Christmas with snow and ice—even if it *were* on December 25—is purely a local prejudice. It falls in the same class with the manner that medieval artists depicted Mary and Joseph in medieval clothing because they could conceive of no other kind.

Nevertheless, whether December 25 is snowy or mild makes no difference at the moment. The point is that neither Luke nor Matthew give a date of any kind for the Nativity. They give no slightest hint that can be used to deduce a day or even guess at one.

Why, then, December 25? The answer might be found in astronomy and in Roman history.

The noonday Sun is at varying heights in the sky at different seasons of the year because the Earth's axis is tipped by 23 degrees to the plane of Earth's revolution about the Sun. Without going into the astronomy of this in detail, it is sufficient to say that the noonday Sun climbs steadily higher in the sky from December to June, and falls steadily lower from June to December. The steady rise is easily associated with a lengthening day, an eventually warming temperature and quickening of life; the steady decline with a shortening day, an eventually cooling temperature and fading of life.

In primitive times, when the reason for the cycle was not understood in terms of modern astronomy, there was never any certainty that the sinking Sun would ever turn and begin to rise again. Why should it do so, after all, except by the favor of the gods? And that favor might depend entirely upon the proper conduct of a complicated ritual known only to the priests.

It must have been occasion for great gladness each year, then, to observe the decline of the noonday Sun gradually slowing, then coming to a halt and beginning to rise again. The point at which the Sun comes to a halt is the winter "solstice" (from Latin words meaning "sun-halt").

The time of the winter solstice was the occasion for a great feast in honor of what one might call the "birth of the Sun."

In Roman times, a three-day period, later extended to seven days, was devoted to the celebration of the winter solstice. This was the "Saturnalia," named in honor of Saturn, an old Roman god of agriculture.

At the Saturnalia, joy was unrestrained, as befitted a holiday that celebrated a reprieve from death and a return to life. All public business was suspended, in favor of festivals, parties, singing, and gift-giving. It was a season of peace and good will to all men. Even slaves were, for that short period, allowed license that was forbidden at all other times and were treated—temporarily—on a plane of equality with their masters. Naturally, the joy easily turned to the extremes of licentiousness and debauchery, and there were, no doubt, many pious people who deplored the uglier aspects of the festival.

In the Roman calendar—a very poor and erratic one before the time of Julius Caesar—the Saturnalia was celebrated the seventeenth, eighteenth, and nineteenth of December. Once Caesar established a sensible calendar, the winter solstice fell upon December 25 (although in our own calendar, slightly modified since Caesar's time, it comes on December 21).

In the first centuries of the Roman Empire, Christianity had to compete with Mithraism, a form of Sun-worship with its roots in Persia. In Mithraism, the winter solstice was naturally the occasion of a great festival and in A.D. 274, the Roman Emperor, Aurelian, set December 25 as the day of the birth of the Sun. In other words, he lent the Mithraist holiday the official sanction of the government.

The celebration of the winter solstice was a great stumbling block to conversions to Christianity. If Christians held the Saturnalia and the birth of the Sun to be purely pagan then many converts were discouraged. Even if they abandoned belief in the old Roman gods and in Mithras, they wanted the joys of the holiday. (How many people today celebrate the Christmas season with no reference at all to its religious significance and how many would be willing to give up the joy, warmth, and merriment of the season merely because they were not pious Christians?)

But Christianity adapted itself to pagan customs where these, in the judgment of Christian leaders, did not compromise the essential doctrines of the Church. The Bible did not say on which day Jesus was born and there was no dogma that would be affected by one day rather than by another. It might, therefore, be on December 25 as well as on any other.

Once that was settled, converts could join Christianity without giving up their Saturnalian happiness. It was only necessary for them to joyfully greet the birth of the Son rather than the Sun.

If December 25 is Christmas and if it is assumed that Mary became pregnant at the time of the annunciation, then the anniversary of the annunciation must be placed on March 25, nine months before Christmas. And, indeed, March 25 is the day of the Feast of the Annunciation and is called Annunciation Day or, in England, Lady Day, where "Lady" refers to Mary.

Again, if the annunciation came when Elisabeth was six months pregnant, John the Baptist must have been born three months later. June 24 is the day on which his birth is celebrated.

December 25 was gradually accepted through most of the Roman Empire between A.D. 300 and 350. This late period is indicated by the date alone.

There were two general kinds of calendars in use in the ancient Mediterranean world. One is the lunar calendar, which matches the months to the phases of the Moon. It was devised by the Babylonians, who passed it on to the Greeks and the Jews. The other is the solar calendar, which matches the months to the seasons of the year. It was devised by the Egyptians, who passed it on, in Caesar's time, to the Romans, and, by way of Rome, to ourselves.

The lunar calendar does not match the seasons and, in order to keep it from falling out of line, some years must have twelve lunar months and others thirteen, in a rather complex pattern. To people using a solar calendar (as we do) the lunar year is too short when it has twelve months and too long when it has thirteen. A date that is fixed in a lunar calendar slips forward and backward in the solar calendar, although, in the long run, it oscillates about a fixed place.

The holidays established early in Church history made use of the lunar calendar used by the Greeks and Jews. As a result, these holidays shift their day (by our calendar) from year to year. The chief of these days is Easter. It is the prime example of a "movable holiday" and each year we must look at the calendar to see when it might come. All the other movable holidays are tied to Easter and shift with it.

When Christianity spread throughout the Roman Empire and even became the official doctrine of the land, early in the fourth century, it began to make increasing use of the Roman calendar. It became rather complicated to adjust the date of Easter to that calendar. There were serious disagreements among different portions of the Church as to the exact method for doing so, and schisms and heresies arose over the matter.

Those holidays that came into being comparatively late, when Christianity had become official in the empire, made use of the Roman calendar to begin with. Such holiday dates slid back and forth on the lunar calendar but were fixed on solar calendars such as our own. The mere fact that Christmas is celebrated on December 25 every year and that the date never varies on our calendar is enough to show that it was not established as a religious festival until after A.D. 300.

Simeon

Luke goes on to tell of incidents in Jesus' infancy and youth as Matthew does. However, none of the incidents in Luke are to be found in Matthew, and none in Matthew are to be found in Luke. Thus, Luke says nothing at all concerning the flight into Egypt or the slaughter of the innocents. He also says nothing at all about the star of Bethlehem and the three wise men from the east. Similarly, Matthew says nothing at all about the census, the manger, or the shepherds.

According to Luke, when Jesus was presented at the Temple as a first-born son, he was seen by an old man named Simeon. Simeon, who believed he would not die until he saw the Messiah, recognized that Messiah in the infant and said:

> Luke 2:29. *Lord, now lettest thou thy servant depart in peace, according to thy word:*
> Luke 2:30. *For mine eyes have seen thy salvation . . .*

In Latin, Simeon's words begin: "Nunc dimittis servum tuum, Domine," and the whole passage is therefore referred to as the "Nunc Dimittis."

Simeon was an example of those who expected the Messiah but were content to do so quietly and patiently, as opposed to the Zealots who actively searched for a Messiah and were willing to fight upon the slightest suspicion of one.

Another aged habitué of the Temple, a woman, is likewise described as recognizing the infant Jesus as the Messiah:

> Luke 2:36. *And there was one Anna, a prophetess* . . .

Anna is the Greek form of the Hebrew, Hannah (the name of the mother of Samuel).

The Doctors

One tale of Jesus' boyhood is told by Luke, and it is the only tale of Jesus as a boy that is to be found anywhere in the gospels.

At the age of twelve he is taken with his parents when they make their annual trip to Jerusalem at the time of the Passover. When Joseph and Mary leave Jerusalem, they discover Jesus is not with them, and must return in search of him.

> Luke 2:46. *And it came to pass, that after three days they found him in the temple, sitting in the midst of the doctors, both hearing them, and asking them questions.*
> Luke 2:47. *And all that heard him were astonished at his understanding and answers.*

That Jesus was twelve at this time is perhaps no accident. In Judaism, the age of thirteen is taken as the time of coming to religious maturity. It is the time when a young man must take on the responsibility of religious observances. Modern Jews have the ritual of the "bar mitzvah" ("son of the commandments," meaning "one who is responsible for obedience to the commandments"), which each young man goes through on his thirteenth birthday. Prior to that there is a lengthy period of instruction and training in order to fit him for his task.

The ceremony of the bar mitzvah, as at present constituted, seems to be of medieval origin, but no doubt religious education prior to the thirteenth birthday was important in New Testament times. One has a picture of the young Jesus fascinated by the "teachers" (the term used in place of "doctors" in the Revised Standard Version) and eagerly listening to instruction. In modern terms, he was preparing for his bar mitzvah.

This incident in Luke may have been included as a way of refuting those who sneered at the early Christians as followers of an ignorant and unlettered Galilean. Luke attempts to demonstrate here that, even as a child, the intelligence of Jesus and his interest in the Law astonished even the learned men of the Temple.

Tiberius Caesar

But now Luke makes the great jump. He has done with legends of the time before baptism and moves up to the period of time covered by Mark.

> Luke 3:1. Now in the *fifteenth year of the reign of Tiberius Caesar, Pontius Pilate being governor of Judaea, and Herod being tetrarch of Galilee, and his brother Philip tetrarch of Ituraea and of the region of Trachonitis, and Lysanias the tetrarch of Abilene,*
> Luke 3:2. *Annas and Caiaphas being the high priests, the word of God came unto John the son of Zacharias in the wilderness.*

Tiberius Claudius Nero was the stepson of the Emperor Augustus, being the son of Augustus' wife by a previous marriage. He was born in 42 B.C. and during the early years of Augustus' reign he served well as a general guiding the Roman armies against the tribes in the Danubian areas, and against the Germans east of the Rhine.

Augustus had no sons and the two sons of his only daughter had died young. He was therefore forced, rather against his will, to adopt Tiberius as his heir. In A.D. 14, when Augustus died, Tiberius became the second Roman Emperor—that is, Tiberius Caesar.

He reigned for twenty-three years, till A.D. 37. The "fifteenth year" of his reign would be A.D. 28/29.

Of the remaining rulers referred to in these verses, Pontius Pilate, Herod Antipas of Galilee, and Philip of Iturea have been mentioned in connection with Matthew's gospel. Trachonitis, a region north of Iturea proper and south of Damascus, is listed here as part of Philip's territory. Abilene is a district farther north still, lying northeast of Damascus.

Two high priests are listed, Annas and Caiaphas, and this cannot be literally correct. It was Caiaphas who was high priest. However, Annas had been high priest some fifteen years earlier and, as father-in-law of Caiaphas, may still have been honored and influential in the high-priestly circles.

Luke also gives Jesus' age at this period, being the only evangelist to do so:

> Luke 3:23. *And Jesus himself began to be about thirty years of age . . .*

Luke says "about." If this were A.D. 29 and if Jesus were exactly thirty years old, then he would indeed have been born in 1 B.C. And if he were born on December 25 in 1 B.C., then the New Year that would start one week later would be A.D. 1. This is roughly the line of reasoning of Dionysius Exiguus, but it is wrong, because Herod the Great had been dead some four years on December 25, 1 B.C.

Dionysius' mistake, apparently, was to ignore the "about" and to assume that the Biblical writers were more accurate about their dating and chronology than they really were. Jesus would have had to be at least thirty-three years old at the time of his baptism, and perhaps thirty-five.

The Son of Joseph

It is at this point that Luke supplies Jesus with a genealogy, one that runs backward in time rather than forward, as does Matthew's.

> Luke 3:23. . . . *Jesus . . . being (as was supposed) the son of Joseph, which was the son of Heli,*
> Luke 3:24. *Which was the son of Matthat . . .*

The parenthetical phrase "as was supposed" would indicate Luke's acceptance of the virgin birth, unless it was inserted by some pious early copyist of the gospel.

The genealogy traces Jesus' line back not merely to Abraham, the point from which Matthew's genealogy starts (see page 111), but further back still, to the beginning:

> Luke 3:38. *Which was the son of Enos, which was the son of Seth, which was the son of Adam, which was the son of God.*

Matthew, writing from the Jewish standpoint, naturally begins with Abraham. Luke, a Gentile, would not be satisfied to trace Jesus' genealogy only as far back as it remained Jewish. By going back to the beginning, he stressed the universality of Jesus' message, for whereas only Jews were descended from Abraham, all men—Jews and Gentiles alike—were descended from Adam.

Luke lists seventy-five generations in going from Jesus all the way back to Adam, the longest continuous genealogy in the Bible. Nor is Luke as preoccupied with numbers as Matthew was. He makes no effort to divide the genealogy into significant sections. He has fifty-five generations counting back to Abraham in place of Matthew's forty-two.

Luke counts twenty generations from Adam to Abraham, whereas the lists in the fifth and eleventh chapters of Genesis count nineteen. The discrepancy occurs as follows. Luke says:

Luke 3:35. . . . *which was the son of Sala* [Salah],
Luke 3:36. *Which was the son of Cainan, which was the son of Arphaxad* . . .

whereas we find in Genesis:

Genesis 11:12. *And Arphaxad lived five and thirty years, and begat Salah* . . .

In other words, an additional generation has crept in between Salah and Arphaxad, so that the former is the son of the latter in Genesis and the grandson of the latter in Luke. This is undoubtedly a copyist's error, for Cainan is the great-grandson of Adam and occurs also in the appropriate place in Luke's genealogy.

Luke 3:37. . . . *which was the son of Maleleel* [Mahalaleel], *which was the son of Cainan,*
Luke 3:38. *Which was the son of Enos* . . .

So Cainan is counted twice.

From Abraham to David, the genealogies given in Matthew and in Luke agree. Thereafter, they disagree sharply. Matthew follows the descent from David through Solomon, Rehoboam, and the line of Judean kings. Luke follows the descent from David through a son named Nathan:

Luke 3:31. . . . *which was the son of Nathan, which was the son of David* . . .

Nathan was a son just older than Solomon, if the list of sons men-tioned in the Second Book of Samuel are indeed in order of birth:

2 Samuel 5:14. *And these be the names of those that were born unto him* [David] *in Jerusalem; Shammuah, and Shobab, and Nathan, and Solomon* . . .

Luke gives the son of Nathan as Mattatha, and his son as Menan, neither of whom is mentioned elsewhere in the Bible. Indeed, the entire genealogy after Nathan is completely obscure, merely a list of unknown names. Whereas Matthew has virtually every king of Judah listed among the ancestors of Jesus, Luke lists only David himself.

At only one place after David is there even a possibility of coinci-dence. Matthew lists the fifteenth and sixteenth generations after David as being of Shealtiel and Zerubbabel:

Matthew 1:12. *And after they were brought to Babylon, Jechonias* [Jehoiachin] *begat Salathiel* [Shealtiel]; *and Salathiel* [Shealtiel] *begat Zorobabel* [Zerubbabel] . . .

Luke does indeed mention these two names, perhaps because of the prominent role played by Zerubbabel in connection with the return from exile:

Luke 3:27. . . . *which was the son of Zorobabel* [Zerubbabel], *which was the son of Salathiel* [Shealtiel], *which was the son of Neri* . . .

But Matthew follows the Book of Ezra in having Shealtiel the son of Jehoiachin, whereas Luke has him descend from Neri, who is nowhere else mentioned in the Bible. Luke, moreover, has Zerubbabel twenty-two generations after David, rather than Matthew's sixteen.

The two genealogies come together only at Joseph, the husband of Mary. They disagree even in the name of Joseph's father:

Matthew 1:16. *And Jacob begat Joseph the husband of Mary* . . .

Luke 3:23. . . . *Jesus* . . . *the son of Joseph, which was the son of Heli* . . .

Attempts have been made to correlate these wildly differing genealogies by supposing that Matthew was tracing the line of Jesus back
to David through Joseph, while Luke does so through Mary. It is
suggested, for instance, that Joseph was not the "son of Heli" as stated
in Luke 3:23, but actually the son-in-law of Heli, so that Heli was
Mary's father and the rest of the genealogy was Mary's.

This involves no flat contradictions, for the name of Mary's father is
not given directly anywhere in the Bible.

And yet are there grounds for considering Mary to have been descended from David? That she was of Davidic descent is a tradition
that arose early in the history of Christianity. For instance, when Gabriel
is sent to make the annunciation:

> Luke 1:26. . . . *Gabriel was sent* . . .
> Luke 1:27. *To a virgin espoused to a man whose name was Joseph,*
> *of the house of David; and the virgin's name was Mary.*

One might argue that the phrase "of the house of David" referred to Mary rather than to Joseph, or to both.

But the argument is a tenuous one. After all, Mary is described
as a cousin of Elisabeth, who is herself described as a Levite.

Looking at the two genealogies objectively, it is hard not to think of
Matthew's as the more reliable. It includes more names that are to be
found in the Old Testament and it carries the list down the line of
Judean kings, something one would tend to think more appropriate
for a Messiah of Davidic descent.

One might almost think that Luke—a Gentile not acquainted with
Jewish genealogical records—might have invented names to fill in the
generations after David and Nathan.

Judas the brother of James

Luke now goes on with the tales that are also given in Matthew
and Mark. Jesus is tempted by Satan and successfully resists. He
preaches in his home town of Nazareth but is rejected by those who
knew him too well as a youth and will not accept him seriously as a
prophet. He heals the sick and begins to collect disciples.

Luke agrees with Mark in naming the publican disciple Levi (see
page 245). However, in Luke's list of the twelve apostles, Levi is

not mentioned, but Matthew is. This supports the notion that Levi and Matthew are the same person known by two alternate names.

On the other hand, Luke does not mention Lebbaeus Thaddeus by either name and it is this Lebbaeus who might conceivably be Levi the son of Alphaeus that Mark mentions, and therefore the brother of James the son of Alphaeus. In the place of Lebbaeus, Luke includes:

Luke 6:16. *And Judas the brother of James . . .*

This is by no means a reference to Judas Iscariot, for Luke includes him separately, too, as the last of the list, of course.

Luke 6:16. *. . . and Judas Iscariot, which also was the traitor.*

But if there is a second Judas who is the brother of James (presumably the son of Alphaeus), then is this Judas the son of Alphaeus an alternative name for Levi the son of Alphaeus; and is this Judas the publican, Levi, rather than Matthew?

It is hard to tell. The Greek original of Luke 6:16 says simply "Judas of James" and that might be more naturally translated as "Judas son of James" rather than "brother of James." If this Judas is the son of someone named James, then the connection with Levi is lost.

The Centurion

Luke's account of Jesus' life after the baptism is quite similar to that found in Matthew and Mark, the other synoptic gospels, and much of it can, in consequence, be passed over without comment. However, Luke does add or omit items that significantly illustrate the difference in his point of view. He, after all, is taken to be a Gentile, while Mark and Matthew are certainly of Jewish origin.

Thus, Luke includes material that portrays Gentiles favorably. For instance, Luke tells the story of the centurion who asks Jesus to cure his servant. Matthew, in telling that same story, makes no effort to picture the Gentile centurion as anything but a centurion (see page 173).

Luke, however, draws a picture of the centurion as one of touching faith and humility. The centurion does not consider himself worthy to approach Jesus and, instead, sends Jewish elders on his behalf. Yet so worthy is the centurion that the elders (who can't be conceived as being unduly biased in favor of Gentiles) plead for him:

> Luke 7:4. And when they [the elders] came to Jesus, they besought him instantly, saying, That he [the centurion] was worthy . . .
> Luke 7:5. For he loveth our nation, and he hath built us a synagogue.

Luke also demonstrates himself to be sympathetic to women. Thus, in the nativity tale, he concentrates on Mary where Matthew deals primarily with Joseph. Luke portrays a Jesus who can even find room for sympathy toward prostitutes. Thus, when Jesus is dining with a Pharisee:

> Luke 7:37. . . . behold, a woman in the city, which was a sinner, when she knew that Jesus sat at meat in the Pharisee's house . . .
> Luke 7:38. . . . stood at his feet behind him weeping . . .

The Pharisee shows disdain for the woman but Jesus finds her contrition acceptable and her sins forgiven and reads his host a lesson in which the Pharisee comes off rather poorly.

It is immediately on the conclusion of this episode that Luke mentions the women who follow Jesus. This is characteristic of Luke, for the other synoptic gospels mention only the men at this point:

> Luke 8:1. . . . the twelve [apostles] were with him,
> Luke 8:2. And certain women, which had been healed of evil spirits and infirmities, Mary called Magdalene, out of whom went seven devils,
> Luke 8:3. And Joanna the wife of Chuza Herod's steward, and Susanna, and many others . . .

Mary Magdalene is mentioned first and it is sometimes assumed that she was the "woman . . . which was a sinner" of the immediately preceding episode but there is no clear justification for this (see page 238). Neither Joanna nor Susanna is mentioned outside of Luke.

The Good Samaritan

Luke, writing from the Gentile viewpoint, omits those verses in Matthew and Mark which portray Jesus as hostile to non-Jews. Luke does not tell the story of the Canaanite woman who asks that her daughter be cured and who humbly accepts Jesus' designation of Gentiles as "dogs" (see page 172).

And in describing Jesus' sending out of the apostles on their preaching mission, Luke omits the passage in which Jesus forbids them to enter the cities of the Gentiles or Samaritans and declares his own mission to be confined to the Jews (see page 173).

Instead, Luke includes a parable, not found in any of the other gospels, which is among the most popular of all those attributed to Jesus, and which preaches universalism.

The parable is occasioned by the question of a lawyer; that is, a student of the Mosaic Law or a "scribe" as Matthew would call him. He asks of Jesus how one may attain eternal life and Jesus challenges him to answer his own question by citing the Law. The lawyer answers:

> Luke 10:27. . . . *Thou shalt love the Lord thy God with all thy heart, and with all thy soul, and with all thy strength, and with all thy mind; and thy neighbour as thyself.*

The first part of this answer is a quotation from Deuteronomy, one that is held to be a central tenet of Judaism:

> Deuteronomy 6:4. *Hear, O Israel: The Lord our God is one Lord:*
> Deuteronomy 6:5. *And thou shalt love the Lord thy God with all thine heart, and with all thy soul, and with all thy might.*

The last part of the lawyer's quotation is from another section of the Law:

> Leviticus 19:18. *Thou shalt not avenge, nor bear any grudge against the children of thy people, but thou shalt love thy neighbour as thyself . . .*

Jesus approves of the statement, but the lawyer goes on to ask:

> Luke 10:29. . . . *And who is my neighbour?*

The attempt here is to force a nationalist answer, for the remark in Leviticus about loving one's neighbor as one's self, follows immediately after a reference to "the children of thy people." The commandment in Leviticus might therefore be taken as narrowly restricting a man's love to neighbors of his own "people" only.

Jesus might therefore have answered that it was only necessary to love those who were Jews or, a little more broadly, all those, Jews or non-Jews, who worshipped the true God in the approved manner. All others would then be outside the pale of love. (This indeed was what Jesus seemed to be saying in the story of the Canaanite woman in Matthew.)

Jesus does not say this in Luke, however. Instead he tells the famous story of the man (presumably a Jew) who traveled from Jerusalem to Jericho, was beset by thieves and left for dead. A priest and a Levite passed him by, making no effort to help. They were each learned in the Law and undoubtedly knew the verse in Leviticus and were faced with a neighbor (even in the narrow sense of the word) in need. Yet they did nothing.

> Luke 10:33. *But a certain Samaritan . . . came where he was: and when he saw him, he had compassion on him . . .*

The Samaritan saved the man and Jesus asked:

> Luke 10:36. *Which now of these three, thinkest thou, was neighbour unto him that fell among the thieves?*
> Luke 10:37. *And he* [the lawyer] *said, He that shewed mercy on him . . .*

In other words, a man is not a "neighbor" because of what he is but because of what he does. A goodhearted Samaritan is more the neighbor of a Jew, than a hardhearted fellow Jew. And, by extension, one might argue that the parable teaches that all men are neighbors, since all men can do well and have compassion, regardless of nationality. To love one's neighbor is to love all men.

The term "good Samaritan" has been used so often in connection with this parable that one gets the feeling that Samaritans were particularly good people and that it was only to be expected that a Samaritan would help someone in trouble. This loses the point of the story, since to a Jew of the time of Jesus, Samaritans were a hateful and despised people. The hate was returned and it was therefore naturally to be expected that a Samaritan would *not* help a Jew under *any* conditions. The point Jesus was making was that *even* a Samaritan could be a neighbor; how much more so, anyone else.

The flavor of the parable would probably be best captured in modern America, if we had a white southern farmer left for dead, if we then had him ignored by a minister and a sheriff, and saved by a Negro sharecropper. Then the question "Which now of these three . . . was neighbour" would have a sharper point for our time.

The fact that Samaritans could be as narrowly nationalistic as Jews is brought out in Luke, who reports that the Samaritans would not allow Jesus to pass through their territory on his way to Jerusalem, because they would not cooperate with anyone attempting to visit that city so hated by them:

> Luke 9:53. . . . *they* [the Samaritans] *did not receive him* [Jesus], *because his face was as though he would go to Jerusalem.*

Here too Luke seizes the opportunity to display the good will of Jesus as rising above nationalistic considerations, even when he is provoked. James and John, the sons of thunder (see page 247), ask if they ought not to call down a rain of fire on the inhospitable Samaritans, and Jesus answers:

> Luke 9:56. . . . *the Son of man is not come to destroy men's lives, but to save them* . . .

At another point, Luke introduces another tale not found in the other gospels which tends to display a Samaritan in a good light. Jesus cures ten lepers but only one returns to thank him:

> Luke 17:16. . . . *and he was a Samaritan.*
> Luke 17:17. *And Jesus* . . . *said, Were there not ten cleansed? but where are the nine?*
> Luke 17:18. *There are not found that returned to give glory to God, save this stranger.*

Lazarus the Beggar

Luke retains the anti-rich attitude of Matthew (see page 170). He quotes Jesus' remarks about the dangers of wealth:

> Luke 16:13. *No servant can serve two masters* . . . *Ye cannot serve God and mammon.*
>
> . . . .
>
> Luke 18:25. . . . *it is easier for a camel to go through a needle's eye, than for a rich man to enter into the kingdom of God.*

Indeed, Luke goes even beyond Matthew, for he includes a famous parable (found only in Luke) that seems to illustrate this hard view against riches.

> Luke 16:19. *There was a certain rich man* . . .
> Luke 16:20. *And there was a certain beggar named Lazarus, which was laid at his gate, full of sores* . . .

The Latin word for rich is "dives," so that in the Latin version of the Bible, the phrase "rich man" is "homo dives." If the verse is left partly untranslated, it becomes, "There was a certain man, Dives . . ." This is what gives rise to the common misconception that the name of the rich man in this parable was Dives, so that one will speak of the parable of "Dives and Lazarus." Actually, the rich man is not named; he is merely a rich man. As for Lazarus, that is a Greek version of the Hebrew name, Eleazar.

When the beggar dies, however, he goes to heaven:

> Luke 16:22. . . . *the beggar died, and was carried by the angels into Abraham's bosom* . . .

Because of this verse "Abraham's bosom" has entered the English language as synonymous with heaven, but in connection with Lazarus, it means more than that.

The phrase originates out of the dining customs of the period. The Israelites in the time of the kingdoms sat upon chairs at meals, as we do today. Thus, concerning the feast where Saul grew suspicious of David because of the latter's absence, the Bible relates:

> 1 Samuel 20:25. *And the king sat upon his seat, as at other times* . . .

The Greeks, however, (at least among the wealthier classes) had the habit of reclining upon their left elbow on low upholstered couches and eating with the right hand. The custom spread among the better-off of other nations, as a sign of genteel and gracious living. This style of eating gave rise to universally understood metaphors.

A host would put the guest of honor to his immediate right at a meal. If both reclined on their left elbows, the guest's head would now be close to the host's breast. In a manner of speaking, the guest would be "in the host's bosom."

If we use the expression today, when Western eating habits, at all levels of society, include sitting rather than reclining, the expression "in his bosom" gives rise to thoughts of one man cradling the head of another, but that is wrong. It would be better if we translated the phrase into our analogous metaphor today and said, "the beggar died, and was carried by the angels to the right side of Abraham." In short, Lazarus not only went to heaven, but to the post of highest honor, at the right hand of Abraham himself.

As for the rich man, his fate was quite different; he went to hell. What's more, this wasn't the Sheol of the Old Testament, the gray place of infinite nothingness, with the chief punishment that of the absence of God (see page I-173). In Old Testament times, hell, or Sheol, had little to do with punishment. Rewards and punishments were viewed by the Israelites as something that was meted out in this world and not in the next.

However, during the centuries when the Jews were under the domination of outsiders, it seemed too clear that the foreign oppressors were flourishing and the Jews were suffering. The whole problem of good and evil, of reward and suffering, grew tremendously complex, theologically speaking. The Book of Job is an example of the controversy that arose in that respect.

Since to most Jews it was unthinkable that God was unjust, it followed that the apparent injustices of this world would have to be redressed in the world to come. Virtuous men would be rewarded infinitely in heaven, while wicked men would be punished infinitely in hell. This latter view makes itself felt in the last verse in Isaiah, which is part of the post-Exilic "Third Isaiah" (see page I-553). Those who are saved, the verse says:

Isaiah 66:24. . . . *shall go forth, and look upon the carcasses of the men that have transgressed against me: for their worm shall not die, neither shall their fire be quenched . . .*

A contributing factor to the development of the notion of a hell of torture may have been the exposure, in Ptolemaic and Seleucid times, to certain Greek legends. The Greek Hades, generally, was very much like the Israelite Sheol, a gray place of negativeness. A portion of it, Tartarus, was, however, reserved for notable criminals, and there the Greek imagination exhausted itself in imagining ingenious tortures— such as Sisyphus endlessly rolling a rock uphill only to have it roll down again as soon as the top was gained, or thirsty Tantalus forever up to his chin in water which swirled away whenever he stooped to drink.

The less ingenious men of Judea clung to external fire as a means of torture and by New Testament times that was fixed. Thus Mark quotes Jesus as warning men not—

> Mark 9:43. . . . *to go into hell, into the fire that never shall be quenched* . . .

The rich man of the parable of Lazarus the beggar descends into just such a hell:

> Luke 16:22. . . . *the rich man also died, and was buried;*
> Luke 16:23. *And in hell . . . being in torments, . . .*
> Luke 16:24. . . . *he cried . . . , Father Abraham, . . . send Lazarus, that he may dip the tip of his finger in water, and cool my tongue; for I am tormented in this flame.*

Abraham refuses, for there is an impassable gulf between heaven and hell. Moreover, Abraham is described by this parable in Luke as justifying the presence of Lazarus in heaven and the rich man in hell without reference to virtue and wickedness. No sins of the rich man are recalled, merely the fact of his being rich:

> Luke 16:25. *But Abraham said, [to the rich man] Son, remember that thou in thy lifetime receivedst thy good things, and likewise Lazarus evil things: but now he is comforted, and thou art tormented.*

It is this dramatic turnabout, this promise to the poor and downtrodden of the world, that they would have their revenge in the afterworld, that may have helped make this parable particularly popular. Because of its popularity, the term "Lazarus" has come to be applied to diseased beggars. Since the sores mentioned are often presumed to be those of leprosy, the term, particularly in the shortened form "lazar," has come to be synonymous to "leper."

A Far Country

Luke has Jesus relate the parable of the talents (see page 210), though here the units of money are referred to as "pounds." A change is introduced. Instead of, as in Matthew, the mere mention of a man traveling to a far country, the purpose of the journey is given:

Luke 19:12. . . . A *certain nobleman went into a far country to receive for himself a kingdom, and to return.*

. . . .

Luke 19:14. *But his citizens hated him, and sent a message after him, saying, We will not have this man to reign over us.*

Luke 19:15. . . . [But] *he* . . . *returned, having received the kingdom* . . .

In the context of modern times, this would be puzzling. Why should one travel to a far country to receive a kingdom? In New Testament times, however, this was not odd at all, for the far country was Rome.

Around the perimeter of the Roman Empire were a number of puppet kingdoms, each theoretically independent, but all completely under Rome's thumb. No one could succeed to the throne of any of these kingdoms without Rome's permission, and that was not always possible to get without a healthy bribe. And if a claimant hurried to Rome to negotiate such a bribe, it might happen that his subjects at home would send a counter-deputation to plead against it, if the claimant were unpopular.

Just this seems to have happened in the case of Herod Archelaus in 4 B.C., after the death of Herod the Great, and it is to him that the parable seems to refer. Archelaus was confirmed in his rule, but as ethnarch only, not as king, and ten years later, as a result of the persistent pleadings of his subjects, he was deposed.

Herod Antipas

The account of Jesus' climactic week in Jerusalem, as given in Luke, differs little, in general, from the accounts of Matthew and Mark. But Luke is a Gentile and he seems anxious to diminish even further the share of Pilate, the Gentile governor, in the crucifixion of Jesus, and to increase the share of the Jewish secular authorities.

As in Matthew and Mark, Pilate, in Luke, is pictured as unwilling to condemn Jesus, but he declares his belief in Jesus' innocence three times, rather than once as in Matthew or twice as in Mark. Furthermore, in Luke, and in Luke only, Pilate is described as attempting to deny jurisdiction altogether:

> Luke 23:6. . . . *Pilate . . . asked whether the man* [Jesus] *were a Galilaean.*
>
> Luke 23:7. *And as soon as he knew that he belonged unto Herod's jurisdiction, he sent him to Herod, who himself also was at Jerusalem at that time.*

This, of course, is Herod Antipas, tetrarch of Galilee, who was in Jerusalem, presumably, for the Passover season. The trial before Herod comes to nothing, really, because Jesus would not speak in his own behalf. Herod refused to make any judgment:

> Luke 23:11. *And Herod . . . sent him again to Pilate.*

But it would seem that whatever blame falls upon Pilate, in Luke's eyes, falls also upon Herod Antipas.

The Crucifixion

The details of the crucifixion as given by Luke differ in some ways from those given by Matthew and Mark. In Matthew and Mark we have the picture of the "historic Jesus" abandoned and reviled by all, and seeming to die in despair.

In Luke this has largely disappeared and Jesus is pictured as much more clearly the Messiah. He forgives his crucifiers in a noble phrase that is not found in the other gospels:

> Luke 23:34. *Then said Jesus, Father, forgive them; for they know not what they do.*

As in Mark and Matthew, Luke describes three as being crucified at this time, with Jesus on the middle cross between two thieves. Mark says nothing more about this, while Matthew describes even these thieves as reviling Jesus:

> Matthew 27:44. *The thieves also, which were crucified with him, cast the same* [mockery] *in his teeth.*

In Luke, however, Jesus is described as forgiving again. One of the thieves accepts Jesus as Messiah:

Luke 23:42. *And he said unto Jesus, Lord, remember me when thou comest into thy kingdom.*

Luke 23:43. *And Jesus said unto him, Verily I say unto thee, To day shalt thou be with me in paradise.*

This thief is known in tradition as "the good thief" or "the penitent thief." He is not named in the gospels, but tradition supposes his name to be Dismas.

Finally, Luke does not describe Jesus' final despairing cry of "My God, my God, why hast thou forsaken me?" It does not easily fit the Messianic picture, nor can Luke count on his Gentile readers appreciating the subtlety of the application of the psalm whose first phrase that cry is (see page 233). Instead, he has Jesus' last words the much more formal and undramatic:

Luke 23:46. . . . *Jesus . . . said, Father, into thy hands I commend my spirit: and having said thus, he gave up the ghost.*

That too, as it happens, is a quotation from the psalms:

Psalm 31:5. *Into thine hand I commit my spirit: thou hast redeemed me, O Lord God of truth.*

Then follows the tale of the resurrection, told at much greater length and in much more circumstantial detail than in either Matthew or Mark. With that, the gospel of St. Luke ends.

8. JOHN

The Fourth Gospel

The details of Jesus' life, as given in the fourth gospel, are quite
different from those which the first three synoptic gospels have in
common.

There are some who endeavor to accept as correct all four gospels
and who therefore must explain apparent inconsistencies. It is possible
to argue, for instance, that the synoptic gospels deal primarily with
Jesus' preachings to the common people of Galilee and ignore his work
in Jerusalem itself, except for the final climactic week of his life. The
fourth gospel, it could then be suggested, rounds out the picture by
concentrating on Jesus' work in Jerusalem, which it describes as lasting
three years, rather than one week. Jesus' discourses now tend to be long
and argumentative (rather than simple and parable-laden) as would
suit disputes with learned priests and theologians.

On the other hand, it might also be argued that the fourth
gospel was written quite late, for a community that was already
Christian but was involved in doctrinal disputes. Its purpose might
then have been, not to present a realistic picture of Jesus, but rather to
use him as a figure through whom to present the author's theology, as
opposed to the conflicting views of others. It might, from that standpoint, seem that the fourth gospel could be considered a form of
didactic fiction, roughly analogous to the dialogues in which Plato
placed his own philosophy into the mouth of Socrates.

Palestine in the Time of Christ

It is generally agreed that the fourth gospel is later than the others, but by A.D. 150 it seems already to have been known and referred to by Christian writers. Perhaps A.D. 100 might be accepted as a round figure and as a likely date for its composition, though it might be somewhat later still.

If so, the fourth gospel appeared roughly a generation after the destruction of Jerusalem, by which time it was certain that the paths of Judaism and Christianity had diverged irrevocably and that the future of Christianity lay with the Gentile world.

This state of affairs is reflected in the gospel, in which Jesus appears far less as a parochial Jewish prophet and far more as a universal Son of God than in any of the synoptic gospels, far more so, even, than in Luke. And in the fourth gospel, the Jews are treated even less favorably than in Luke.

The Beloved Disciple

As to the authorship of the fourth gospel, that seems to rest with an unnamed individual who is mentioned therein in terms that do not occur in the synoptic gospels. We meet this individual at the last supper, for instance, when Jesus announces that one of the apostles will betray him.

The incident is described in each of the four gospels and in each of the four the response on the part of the apostles is described differently. In Mark, all twelve are troubled:

> Mark 14:19. And they began to be sorrowful, and to say unto him one by one, Is it I? and another said, Is it I?

In Luke, all twelve are troubled, but discuss it among themselves:

> Luke 22:23. And they began to enquire among themselves, which of them it was that should do this thing.

In Matthew, it is Judas Iscariot himself who guiltily rises to the bait:

> Matthew 26:25. Then Judas, which betrayed him, answered and said, Master, is it I? . . .

In the fourth gospel, however, things are not that spontaneous. Jesus is presented as a divine and Godlike figure whom it is far less easy to approach. Since he did not spontaneously reveal the name of the mysterious traitor, it might be that he did not wish to reveal it and that there might therefore be a danger involved in trying to penetrate the secret. Presumably, then, the one to take the risk of inquiring ought to be that disciple who was Jesus' favorite and who might therefore most safely presume on the Master's patience.

John 13:23. *Now there was leaning on Jesus' bosom one of his disciples, whom Jesus loved.*

John 13:24. *Simon Peter therefore beckoned to him, that he should ask who it should be of whom he* [Jesus] *spake.*

We must not assume, of course, that the disciple in question was actually being cradled by Jesus. The phrase "leaning on Jesus' bosom" was merely the common metaphor used to signify that the disciple was seated in the place of honor on Jesus' right (see page 284).

In none of the synoptic gospels is reference made to some particular apostle "whom Jesus loved"; only in the fourth.

The Beloved Disciple is mentioned as witnessing the crucifixion, as being the first apostle to reach the sepulcher from which Jesus had been resurrected, and as recognizing the resurrected Jesus.

Most significantly, he appears at the very end of the gospel when the risen Jesus is giving his final instructions to Peter:

John 21:20. *Then Peter, turning about, seeth the disciple whom Jesus loved following; which also leaned on his breast at supper . . .*

With reference to this, an editorial comment, added a few verses later, reads:

John 21:24. *This is the disciple which testifieth of these things, and wrote these things . . .*

Is this the signature of the Beloved Disciple? Does this mean that the Beloved Disciple actually wrote the fourth gospel as we have it today? Or did someone else write the fourth gospel, after having used the reminiscences of the Beloved Disciple as his source material, and did he then attribute the authorship to that source, considering himself only a secretary? Or was the verse added by a later copyist or commentator who was expressing his own theory that the Beloved Disciple had written the fourth gospel?

It is difficult to see how these questions can ever be answered in such a way as to satisfy everybody. Christian tradition, however, has it that the Beloved Disciple was indeed the author.

It seems odd, perhaps, and even unpleasantly vain, that the Beloved Disciple, if he is the author of the fourth gospel, should so stress his favored position with Jesus each time he mentions himself. But perhaps there is a purpose beyond vanity in this. If the fourth gospel were written to expound a theological viewpoint against strong competing forces, it would be important that the writer stress, as forcefully as he could, his own authority to speak. He was not only one of the apostles, but of all the apostles, Jesus' favorite and the one most likely to be "in the know."

And if the gospel were actually written by a secretary from words or writings of the disciple, it may have been the secretary who kept stressing the favored position of the source for the purpose just given.

John Son of Zebedee

The question next arises as to who the Beloved Disciple might be? To begin with, it seems reasonable to suppose he was one of the apostles, since the Beloved Disciple was at the last supper and, as the synoptic gospels agree, only Jesus and his twelve apostles were at this supper:

> Matthew 26:20. *Now when the even was come, he sat down with the twelve.*
> Matthew 26:21. *And . . . they did eat . . .*

To be sure, however, the fourth gospel, alone of the gospels, does not specifically list the names of the twelve apostles, and does not specifically state that only the apostles joined Jesus at the last supper. Within the context of the fourth gospel, then, the Beloved Disciple might not have been one of the twelve apostles, and several nonapostles have been suggested for the role. Nevertheless, Christian tradition makes the Beloved Disciple one of the apostles.

But which one?

He is the favorite, and it does seem from the synoptic gospels that among the apostles there is an inner group of three, who share more intimately with Jesus the crucial moments of his life. These three,

Peter and the sons of Zebedee, James and John, are described as witnessing the transfiguration, for instance:

> Matthew 17:1. . . . *Jesus taketh Peter, James, and John his brother, and bringeth them up into an high mountain apart,*
> Matthew 17:2. *And was transfigured before them . . .*

The other nine apostles were not vouchsafed this sight.

Again it was Peter, James, and John who were alone with Jesus at the time of the prayer in Gethsemane just before the arrest:

> Matthew 26:37. *And he [Jesus] took with him Peter and the two sons of Zebedee . . .*

One might argue that Jesus would scarcely omit the disciple he loved best from these climactic moments, so that the Beloved Disciple must be one of these three: Peter, James, or John.

Of these three, Peter would seem the almost automatic choice since all the gospels agree that he was the leading apostle who always took the initiative among them. Yet it is precisely Peter who must be eliminated, since on three of the occasions on which the Beloved Disciple is present, Peter is present also, and the two are distinguished as separate individuals. Thus it is Peter who motions to the Beloved Disciple to inquire about the traitor.

This makes it seem that the Beloved Disciple was either James or John, one of the two sons of Zebedee. (Could it be for this reason that the two made so bold as to ask for favored positions with Jesus when the Messianic kingdom was established—see page 196—presuming on his favoritism toward one of them?)

In choosing between James and John, let us return to the final appearance of the Beloved Disciple on the occasion of the resurrected Jesus' last discourse with Peter. Peter turns, sees the Beloved Disciple (see page 293), and asks:

> John 21:21. . . . *and what shall this man do?*
> John 21:22. *Jesus saith unto him, If I will that he tarry till I come, what is that to thee? follow thou me.*

Peter, in other words, is to follow instructions and not worry about the Beloved Disciple. The Beloved Disciple will have his own tasks, which may include anything, even up to and including remaining alive on Earth till the second coming.

The writer of the fourth gospel then goes on to correct a misapprehension, pointing out that Jesus did not say flatly that the Beloved Disciple would not die till the second coming; but that he would not die *if* Jesus chose to arrange it so.

John 21:23. *Then went this saying abroad among the brethren, that that disciple should not die: yet Jesus said not unto him, He shall not die; but, If I will that he tarry till I come, what is that to thee?*

There is important significance here. The early Christians believed that Jesus would soon return and that the kingdom of God would quickly be established. There are verses that would seem to bear them out. Thus, in each of the three synoptic gospels there is repeated what seems to be a definite promise on the part of Jesus to that effect.

Matthew 16:28. *Verily I say unto you, There be some standing here, which shall not taste of death, till they see the Son of man coming in his kingdom.*

Clearly, the Beloved Disciple must have been standing there at the time and if that disciple had an extended lifetime, Jesus' remark must have begun to take on specific meaning. One by one, those who had known and heard Jesus died, but the Beloved Disciple lived on. Surely, then, many must have thought it was he to whom Jesus referred as the someone who "shall not taste of death" till the second coming.

The fourth gospel as the latest-written (seventy years or more after the crucifixion) would have to be less certain than the synoptic gospels on the matter of the imminent second coming. In particular if the Beloved Disciple died without the second coming having taken place, it would be necessary for his secretary or some later commentator to insert a remark to the effect that Jesus *had* made a statement with reference to the Beloved Disciple, but that it had been a conditional and not an absolute one.

(Of course, the reference to some who would not die before the second coming might be taken to refer not to the Beloved Disciple but to some quite obscure person who was standing within earshot of Jesus at the time. This thought probably contributed to the rise of the tale of the so-called "Wandering Jew." This was a Jew who committed some crime or offense against Jesus at the time of the crucifixion and was condemned to wandering the Earth, immortally, until the second coming. Concerning this figure, a vast array of legends has arisen, all of which are entirely without Biblical foundation except for the distant support of this one verse.)

Returning to the Beloved Disciple, however, we can see that this final passage in the fourth gospel can be used to argue that he must have been long-lived. And, indeed, if he wrote the fourth gospel in A.D. 100 or somewhat later, this must be so.

But of the two sons of Zebedee, James was not long-lived. He died a martyr's death not many years after the crucifixion:

> Acts 12:1. *Now about that time Herod the king stretched forth his hands to vex certain of the church.*
>
> Acts 12:2. *And he killed James the brother of John with the sword.*

The leaves John the son of Zebedee, and he is the only one of the apostles concerning whom where is no widely accepted tradition of martyrdom. Rather, legend supposes him to have lived to the age of ninety and beyond.

According to legend, John, in later life, engaged in missionary work in Ephesus, a city on the coast of Asia Minor. During the reign of Domitian (A.D. 81–96), when Christians were persecuted, he retired for safety's sake to the island of Patmos, about fifty miles southwest of Ephesus. After Domitian's death he returned to Ephesus and there died sometime in the reign of Trajan (A.D. 98–117).

If these are indeed the facts and if he were twenty at the time of the crucifixion, John son of Zebedee would have been born A.D. 9 and would have been ninety-one years old in A.D. 100 when the fourth gospel might have been written. That is a great age, but certainly not an impossible one.

Another point in favor of this theory is that John is never mentioned by name in the fourth gospel, so there is no possibility of distinguishing him from the Beloved Disciple. The closest approach comes when some of the disciples are listed among those who witnessed the resurrected Jesus on one occasion:

> John 21:2. . . . *Simon Peter, and Thomas called Didymus, and Nathanael of Cana in Galilee, and the sons of Zebedee, and two other of his disciples.*

And at this point there is no mention of the Beloved Disciple.
There are thus no glaring inconsistencies in supposing the Beloved

Disciple to be John son of Zebedee, and indeed it is the strong tradition of the early Church that this John was the author of the fourth gospel. By A.D. 200 the tradition was universal and it can be traced back to Irenaeus.

His testimony is considered particularly valuable, since he claims to have known Polycarp, a Christian bishop of Asia Minor, who lived from about A.D. 70 to 155 and who, in turn, was supposed to have been a disciple of John himself.

In modern times there have been theories that the John mentioned by Irenaeus as the author of the fourth gospel was some other John, not the son of Zebedee, but the matter is never likely to be settled to the complete satisfaction of everyone. We can say simply that Christian tradition makes John son of Zebedee the author of the fourth gospel and there is no clear and simple way of refuting that tradition. The fourth gospel is therefore called "The Gospel According to St. John."

The Word

The gospel of St. Mark begins with the baptism of Jesus by John the Baptist as the period at which the Holy Spirit entered Jesus. Matthew and Luke begin with the birth of Jesus as that period.

John goes further back still. Whereas in the synoptic gospels Jesus is seen primarily as a human being (although he is the Messiah also), in John, Jesus is seen in much more exalted fashion, as clearly and manifestly divine to all but the villains of the piece. And to stress that point, John begins his gospel with a hymn in praise of "the Word" (or, in Greek "Logos") which carries matters back to the very beginning of time.

John 1:1. *In the beginning was the Word, and the Word was with God, and the Word was God.*

The use of the term "the Word" in its capitalized sense, as an aspect of God, is not found anywhere in the Old Testament, or, for that matter, anywhere in the New Testament except in the gospel of St. John and a couple of other books attributed to the same author.

The term "Logos" is to be found, however, in the writings of the

Greek philosophers, and is used in something of the sense in which it is found in John.

The term dates back to the sixth century B.C., at the time the Kingdom of Judah was coming to an end, and the Jews were being carried off into Babylonian Exile. In that century, a new way of looking at the universe arose among certain scholars on the western coast of Asia Minor.

The first of these was Thales of Miletus, who was born about 640 B.C. (when Manasseh was rounding out his long reign over Judah). He is thought to have first devised the methods of abstract geometry; to have studied electric and magnetic phenomena; to have brought Babylonian astronomy to the Greek world; and to have suggested that water was the fundamental material of the universe.

However, the most important contribution made by Thales and those who studied under him and followed him was the assumption that the universe was not erratic in its workings; and was not at the mercy of impulsive gods or demons who interfered with nature to suit their own whims and who could be swayed by human entreaty or threats. Rather, Thales and his group supposed that the universe ran according to certain fixed rules, which we might term "laws of nature" and that these laws were not forever unknowable but could be worked out by man through observation and reason. This assumption of the rationality and knowability of the universe was established by these Greeks as the foundation of science and it has remained the foundation ever since.

It was not so much that Thales and the rest necessarily denied the existence of gods or the fact that the world was created by superhuman agency. It was just that the gods, in creating the world, did so according to some rational principle and then abided by that principle, without arbitrary interference in the day-to-day workings of the universe.

One of those who followed Thales in this view of the universe was Heraclitus of Ephesus, who taught about 500 B.C. He seems to have used the word "Logos" to represent the rational principle according to which the world was created. (Is it entirely a coincidence that the Logos-permeated gospel of St. John was, according to legend, written in the very city of Ephesus which, in a way, had seen the first introduction of that term?)

Literally, "Logos" means "Word" in English, but the Greek term has implications far beyond the simple significance of "word." "Logos" refers to the whole rational structure of knowledge. We use it in the names of our sciences: "zoology" ("words concerning animals," or, more properly, "the rational structure of knowledge concerning animals"); "geology" ("words concerning the Earth"); "biology" ("words concerning life"); and so on.

As "Logos" came to be used more and more by Greek thinkers, some of them rather mystical, it came to stand not merely for an abstract principle but for a personified entity that had created the world. "Logos" came to be considered a kind of god in its own right; a rational, creative god.

In post-Exilic times, as the Jews came under the influence of Greek philosophy, they felt impelled to try to justify "Logos" in terms of the Jewish God. Often they used a Hebrew word, which we translate as "Wisdom," to represent something like the Greek "Logos." The Wisdom so referred to is not merely worldly learning but, more than that, a kind of inner, spiritual learning that transcends the world of matter.

The use of the term as a substitute for "Logos" was quite apt. As a matter of fact, in the course of the sixth century B.C., the term "philosopher" began to be applied to the Greek scholars and this is a Greek term which can be translated as "lover of wisdom."

It was divine Wisdom, in the eyes of some of the post-Exilic Jewish writers, that created the world and set it upon its rational foundation. Some of the books of the Apocrypha and even some of the later canonical books of the Old Testament contain hymns to Wisdom that almost sound as though it is a formal aspect of God, to be worshipped, rather than a mere abstraction being praised. Its eternal existence is emphasized and in the Book of Proverbs, Wisdom is pictured, at one point, as speaking in the first person and as saying:

> Proverbs 8:22. *The Lord possessed me in the beginning of his way, before his works of old.*
>
> Proverbs 8:23. *I was set up from everlasting, from the beginning, or ever the earth was.*

Ecclesiasticus has a similar passage in which Wisdom is again speaking in the first person:

> Ecclesiasticus 24:9. *He* [God] *created me* [Wisdom] *from the beginning before the world, and I shall never fail.*

In the Wisdom of Solomon, Wisdom is sometimes presented in terms usully reserved for God:

> Wisdom of Solomon 1:6. *For wisdom is a loving spirit; and will not acquit a blasphemer of his words* . . .

The role of Wisdom as the creative aspect of God is also referred to:

> Wisdom of Solomon 7:22. *. . . wisdom . . . is the worker of all things* . . .

There is a reference to Wisdom in the gospel of St. Luke, where Jesus is quoted as saying:

> Luke 11:49. *Therefore also said the wisdom of God, I will send them prophets and apostles* . . .

In Jesus' lifetime, there lived in Alexandria a Jew named Philo (usually called Philo Judaeus, or "Philo the Jew"). He was learned not only in Jewish thought, but in Greek philosophy as well and he labored, in his writings, to explain the former through the words and concepts of the latter.

Philo, writing in Greek, makes use of the term "Logos" rather than "Wisdom" and has it representing the rational and creative aspect of Yahveh. To explain its relationship to God, he speaks of it, metaphorically, as the "image of God" or the "son of God."

John adopts this Philonian view, a view which is particularly fitting, if the gospel were written in Ephesus at the very center of the Greek philosophic tradition and the place where the term "Logos" was first used.

John therefore opens with a hymn to Logos (that might, conceivably, have been adapted from some pagan hymn) which is expressed in such a way as to fit the theological view expressed by the gospel.

There were views concerning Logos which, it seems, John considered incompatible with the true faith.

There were, for instance, philosophers and mystics who tried to separate the notions of God and of Logos. They felt that there was a God who was indeed personified Wisdom, but he was far and remote and unknowable to man. He was pure spirit and had nothing to do with anything material. To these philosophers, this divine, spiritual, and unknowable principle was "Gnosis," which is Greek for "knowledge." Such philosophers are therefore called "Gnostics."

But if Wisdom or Gnosis is remote from matter and unconcerned with it, how did the world come to be created? Here the Gnostics took a turning opposed to that of Thales. It was not a rational principle (divine or otherwise) that created the world, but a sub-divine and evil principle. Where Thales found the world rational and supposed that a rational principle had created it, the Gnostics found the world evil and supposed that an evil principle had created it.

The Greek philosopher Plato had made use of the term "demiourgos" for the creative principle, and this becomes "demiurge" in English. The word means "worker for the people" or, so to speak, "civil servant." It was used in the Greek cities for certain officials who were viewed as serving the public. The Demiurge was looked upon, in other words, as a superhuman civil servant who served mankind by first creating and then governing the world.

To the Gnostics, this Demiurge was an inferior principle who had created an evil world with deliberate malice. What's more, the spiritual essence of man, which was akin to the distant Gnosis, was trapped by the Demiurge in a body which, being made of matter, was evil. For a man to aspire to salvation, it was necessary, somehow, to transcend the evil body and to attain the distant spirituality of Gnosis.

In the early days of Christianity, certain Gnostics adapted their thought to Christianity. Gnosis was still the unknowable, unreachable God. The "God" of the Old Testament, on the other hand, who had created the world, was viewed by the Gnostics as really the Demiurge. It was Yahveh's demonic influence that was responsible for all the evil in the world.

Jesus, on the other hand, was, by the Gnostic view, the Logos, a son or derivative of the spiritual Gnosis. Jesus was himself pure spirit since he could not involve himself with the created matter of the evil Demiurge, but he took on the illusion of a material body in order to help guide men away from the Demiurge of matter to the Gnosis of spirit.

The gospel of St. John sets itself firmly against the Gnostic interpretation. John makes God and Logos equal in all respects. Not only did Logos exist from the very beginning so that Logos was with God, but Logos *was* God.

Furthermore, this God was not a mysterious Gnosis, but was the very God of the Old Testament who had created the world:

John 1:2. *The same [Logos] was in the beginning with God.*
John 1:3. *All things were made by him; and without him was not any thing made that was made.*

and the Logos was the rational, creative aspect of that God.

What's more, this same God of the Old Testament was not merely an entity of matter, while something else was spirit. God was both spirit and matter; God was the "light" toward which men could strive and that was the inner essence of things:

John 1:4. *In him [God/Logos] was life; and the life was the light of men.*
John 1:5. *And the light shineth in darkness* . . .

Nor was Jesus a mere thing of spirit clothed in the illusion of matter. John made it clear that the Logos was to be considered as having been incarnated in a real and actual material body:

John 1:14. *And the Word was made flesh, and dwelt among us* . . .

John the Baptist

The hymn to Logos is interrupted with an emphatic assertion that the Logos is *not* to be interpreted as John the Baptist. In the early decades following the crucifixion there were those who maintained that John the Baptist had been of particular importance and that perhaps he, rather than Jesus, was the Messiah. These may have represented a considerable group even as late as A.D. 100 and they had to be countered.

John 1:6. *There was a man sent from God, whose name was John.*
John 1:7. *The same came for a witness, to bear witness of the Light* . . .
John 1:8. *He was not that Light* . . .

Then, after the conclusion of the hymn to Logos, the fourth gospel quotes John the Baptist himself as denying any pretensions to Messiah-hood:

John 1:19. . . . . *when the Jews sent priests and Levites from Jerusalem to ask him [John the Baptist], Who art thou?*
John 1:20. . . . . *he confessed . . . I am not the Christ.*

The fourth gospel goes still further than that.

The synoptic gospels, written at a time when Christianity was still in its infancy and when it needed allies in its fight against Jewish orthodoxy, seem willing to allow John the Baptist the lesser, but still considerable, role of the incarnated Elijah. The fourth gospel, written at a time when Christianity was a couple of decades stronger, seemed to feel no need for such a compromise:

> John 1:21. And they asked him [John the Baptist], What then? Art thou Elias [Elijah]? And he saith, I am not. Art thou that prophet? And he answered, No.
>
> . . . .
>
> John 1:23. He said, I am the voice of one crying in the wilderness, Make straight the way of the Lord . . .

As for "that prophet" referred to in John 1:21, this is usually thought of as referring to a passage in one of the Deuteronomic discourses attributed to Moses. There, God is quoted as saying:

> Deuteronomy 18:18. I will raise them up a Prophet from among their brethren, like unto thee [Moses], and will put my words in his mouth . . .

It would seem that the Book of Deuteronomy was actually written in the reign of Josiah or shortly before (see page I-195) and it may be that this passage was used to refer to someone contemporary with the Deuteronomist. Josiah may even have been persuaded that the passage referred to one of those who brought him the book after its "discovery" in the Temple, and this may have encouraged him to institute the thorough Yahvist reform that he then carried through.

Nevertheless, by post-Exilic times, this passage seems to have been accepted by the Jews as Messianic in nature, and it was so accepted by the Christians, of course, who saw in it a reference to Jesus. That is why the King James Version capitalizes the word "Prophet" although the Revised Standard Version does not.

John the Baptist is pictured by the fourth gospel as denying an identity with that prophet and as therefore denying Messiah-hood once again.

The Lamb of God

The fourth gospel proceeds, remorselessly, still further. Not only is John quoted as denying the Messiah-hood for himself, but, after baptizing Jesus, he accepts the latter as the Messiah, and proclaims him as such:

> John 1:29. *The next day John seeth Jesus coming unto him, and saith, Behold the Lamb of God, which taketh away the sin of the world.*
>
> John 1:30. *This is he of whom I said, After me cometh a man which is preferred before me . . .*
>
> . . . .
>
> John 1:32. *And John bare record, saying, I saw the Spirit descending from heaven like a dove, and it abode upon him.*
>
> . . . .
>
> John 1:34. *And I saw, and bare record that this is the Son of God.*

In Mark and Luke, there is no reference to any such recognition at all on John's part. In Matthew there is a single verse which refers to John's realization of Jesus' role; for when Jesus comes to be baptized:

> Matthew 3:14. . . . *John forbad him, saying, I have need to be baptized of thee, and comest thou to me?*

Later, however, Matthew, and Luke too, report that John sent disciples to inquire as to whether Jesus were the Messiah, something that would certainly be unnecessary if John had witnessed the Spirit of God descending upon Jesus like a dove. (And certainly the fourth gospel at no time makes mention of any such uncertainties on the part of the Baptist.) The synoptic gospels each report this descent of the Spirit of God but none of the three indicates in any way, then or later, that this descent was witnessed by John, or by anyone besides Jesus.

Indeed, the synoptic gospels show the realization of the Messiah-hood to have developed slowly among Jesus' disciples and, moreover, clearly record Jesus' carefulness in making no specific and open claim to the role. It is only at the very end, before Caiaphas, that he admits he is the Messiah (see page 221) and this, considered by the Jewish authorities to be blasphemy, is at once sufficient to condemn Jesus to death. This view seems, indeed, to be in accord with the historical reality of the times, for to lay claim to Messiah-hood without a proof that would satisfy the authorities was virtually sure death. (Just as in later centuries, to have laid claim to be the new incarnation of Jesus would have paved the way to the stake or, in modern times, to the madhouse.)

In the fourth gospel, however, everyone, from John the Baptist on, is pictured as recognizing Jesus as the Messiah at once. Not only does Jesus not deny the role but he, himself, proclaims it. Thus, when a Samaritan woman speaks to Jesus of the Messiah, Jesus answers quite frankly:

> John 4:26. . . . I that speak unto thee am he.

This open admission of Messiah-hood by Jesus and by others is pictured in the fourth gospel as continuing through a period of three years, in Jerusalem and elsewhere, before Jesus is arrested, condemned, and executed.

From the standpoint of realistic history, this view is quite impossible. However, the gospel is presenting theology and not history, and the theological Jesus, as opposed to the "historical Jesus," is divinity manifest.

In acclaiming Jesus as the Lamb of God, John the Baptist is not only referring to his Messiah-hood but to the actual form that Messiah-hood is to take. He is pictured as recognizing Jesus not as the royal Messiah who will lead the Jews to the ideal kingdom by defeating their enemies with the weapons of war, but rather as the suffering and tortured "servant" of Second Isaiah (see page I-551).

The reference to Jesus as the Lamb of God seems to turn upon a particular verse in one of these suffering servant passages:

> Isaiah 53:7. He [the servant of God] was oppressed, and he was afflicted, yet he opened not his mouth: he is brought as a lamb to the slaughter . . .

Nathanael

The manner in which Jesus collects his disciples is described in the fourth gospel, in quite a different way than in the synoptic gospels. In the synoptic gospels the disciples are selected by Jesus in Galilee; in

John, where Jesus is throughout treated with greater dignity, it is the disciples who come seeking after him.

Thus, John the Baptist acclaims Jesus as the Lamb of God a second time in the presence of two of his disciples and they instantly leave the Baptist and follow Jesus:

John 1:40. *One of the two which heard John* [the Baptist] *speak, and followed him* [Jesus], *was Andrew, Simon Peter's brother.*

The other is not named and he is traditionally assumed to be John son of Zebedee, the Beloved Disciple and the author of the gospel. His modesty is viewed as causing him to refrain from naming himself.

There is no indication in the synoptic gospels that any of the apostles were originally followers of the Baptist. Still, this clearly fits the purpose of the fourth gospel, since it shows that the Baptist's followers, guided by the Baptist himself, clearly prefer Jesus to John, and this further weakens the Baptist party among the evangelist's opponents.

The first two disciples spread the word:

John 1:41. *He* [Andrew] *first findeth his own brother Simon, and saith unto him, We have found the Messias* [Messiah] *. . .*

This quite negates one of the great moments in the synoptic gospels —where Peter confesses his belief in Jesus as the Messiah (see page 194), a confession which turns Jesus toward Jerusalem and the crucifixion. Here, instead, Peter is told at the outset that Jesus is the Messiah and there is no room later in this gospel for any slowly attained realization of this belief by either Peter or any other disciple. The nature of Jesus in the view of the fourth gospel is too exalted to admit of any such slow or gradual realization; the realization must come at once.

Furthermore, the acceptance of these first disciples does not take place in Galilee, but on the site in the Trans-Jordan where John the Baptist was conducting the baptismal rite:

John 1:28. *These things were done . . . beyond Jordan, where John was baptizing.*

And as though to emphasize that fact, Jesus is then described as being on his way to return to Galilee:

John 1:43. *The day following Jesus would go forth into Galilee, and findeth Philip, and saith unto him, Follow me.*

John 1:44. *Now Philip was of Bethsaida, the city of Andrew and Peter.*

Presumably, Philip had been told of the Messiah by Andrew and Peter and he in turn spreads the news still further:

John 1:45. *Philip findeth Nathanael, and saith unto him, We have found him, of whom Moses in the law, and the prophets, did write . . .*

Nathanael is not listed among the apostles in the synoptic gospels; indeed, his name does not occur outside the fourth gospel. On the other hand, Bartholomew, who is listed among the apostles in all three of the synoptic gospels, is not mentioned in John. Since in all three of the synoptic gospels, Bartholomew is named directly after Philip:

Mark 3:18. *And Andrew, and Philip, and Bartholomew . . .*

and since here in John there seems a special relationship between Philip and Nathanael, it is customary to identify Nathanael with Bartholomew. Since Bartholomew means "son of Talmai" and may be a patronymic only, Nathaniel may be the actual given name. The apostle would then be Nathanael Bartholomew ("Nathaniel, son of Talmai").

It may also be that Nathaniel is not one of the twelve disciples but is some disciple outside this inner circle of twelve.

The fourth gospel does not list the twelve apostles at all, the only gospel not to do so. The very word "apostle" does not occur in the fourth gospel. It may well be that John soft-pedals the tradition of the twelve apostles as far as possible, since the analogy there is to the twelve tribes of Israel, an analogy long outmoded by events, at the time the gospel was written.

The Son of Joseph

Philip identifies Jesus clearly and unmistakably, when he reports of him to Nathanael:

John 1:45. *Philip findeth Nathanael, and saith unto him, We have found him, . . . Jesus of Nazareth, the son of Joseph.*

No attempt is made, in this gospel, to refer to the virgin birth at Bethlehem. This is not because John is unaware that among the Jews the birth at Bethlehem was a necessary requirement for a true Messiah, for upon hearing this identification of the Messiah "of whom Moses in the law, and the prophets, did write," Nathanael is at once dubious:

John 1:46. *And Nathanael said unto him* [Philip], *Can there any good thing come out of Nazareth? . . .*

This might have been the contempt of a man of Jerusalem for a Galilean provincial, but it wasn't. Nathanael is himself a Galilean according to John. At one point, where several disciples are listed, John says:

John 21:2. *. . . Simon Peter, and Thomas called Didymus, and Nathanael of Cana in Galilee . . .*

Or Nathanael's remark might simply imply that no prophet ever came out of Galilee, as is stated later in the gospel, when the Pharisees are quoted as saying to one of their own number who spoke in defense of Jesus:

John 7:52. *. . . Art thou also of Galilee? Search, and look: for out of Galilee ariseth no prophet.*

But that isn't so, either. The prophet Jonah (the historical prophet of the time of Jeroboam II, on whom the fable with the whale was later grafted) was from the region, even though it was not called Galilee at the time:

2 Kings 14:25. *. . . Jonah, the son of Amittai, the prophet, which was of Gath-hepher.*

In fact, Gath-hepher was not only in Galilee but it is usually identified with a town only three miles from Nazareth.

Or it might be (as is sometimes suggested) that Nazareth itself had a bad reputation among Galileans generally. Perhaps it was considered a city of fools, like the Gotham of English folk tales. And perhaps this reputation was particularly strong in Nathanael's home town of Cana which was close enough to Nazareth to allow of the kind of neighborly rivalry one gets between Minneapolis and St. Paul, or between Fort Worth and Dallas. There is, however, nothing concrete on which to base such a belief.

It seems most likely that the remark simply refers to the fact that Jews did not expect the Messiah to come from anywhere but Bethlehem. This, too, is stated flatly later in the gospel where the opinions of the people generally are given.

John 7:41. . . . *But some said, Shall Christ come out of Galilee?*
John 7:42. *Hath not the scripture said, That Christ cometh of the seed of David, and out of the town of Bethlehem, where David was?*

It seems logical to suppose that Nathanael, at first hearing that Jesus was of Nazareth, had the same doubt. The evangelist does not bother to counter these doubts by any remark concerning the birth at Bethlehem. Perhaps he felt the birth at Bethlehem was something that concerned only Jews and he intended his own gospel to have a universal importance.

Once Nathanael meets Jesus, he is at once brought over:

John 1:49. *Nathanael . . . saith unto him* [Jesus], *Rabbi, thou art the Son of God; thou art the King of Israel.*

The word "rabbi" used here means "my master" or "my teacher." It is precisely the term of respect one would use for another more learned than himself. In the theocratic society of Judea, it bears somewhat the same aura of respect that the title "professor" does in our own more secular society. Earlier in the chapter, John translates the word. When the first two disciples approach Jesus:

John 1:38. . . . *They said unto him, Rabbi, (which is to say, being interpreted, Master,) where dwellest thou?*

In the other gospels, the King James Version usually gives the Greek equivalent only, so that Jesus is routinely addressed as "Master." Thus, Peter addressing Jesus at the sight of the transfiguration, is quoted as saying:

Mark 9:5. *And Peter . . . said to Jesus, Master, it is good for us to be here . . .*

The equivalent verse in Matthew uses another term of respect, one of more secular tang and perhaps more suitable to the divinity that was gathering about Jesus in the eyes of his disciples:

Matthew 17:4. . . . *Peter . . . said unto Jesus, Lord, it is good for us to be here . . .*

Another form of addresses is "rabboni," meaning "my great master" or "my lord and master." This is used of the resurrected Jesus, by Mary Magdalene:

John 20:16. . . . *She turned herself, and saith unto him, Rabboni; which is to say, Master.*

Cana

Once back in Galilee, Jesus performs his first miracle—one which is found only in John. It takes place at a wedding festival:

Early Journeys of Christ

John 2:1. . . . *there was a marriage in Cana of Galilee; and the mother of Jesus was there:*

John 2:2. *And both Jesus was called, and his disciples, to the marriage.*

Cana, mentioned only in John, is close to Nazareth. It is usually identified with a site about four miles northeast, though some favor a site some nine miles north of Nazareth. It is this town of which Nathanael is a native.

Oddly enough, John's reference to "the mother of Jesus" is characteristic of him. Not only does he not refer to the virgin birth and make Jesus the son of Joseph without qualification, but he never names Mary. His is the only gospel in which Mary is not named; she is referred to only as "the mother of Jesus."

Mary appears in the legends of Jesus' birth and childhood in Matthew and Luke. On one occasion she is mentioned by all three synoptic gospels. This is when she and other members of the family of Jesus try to see him when he is surrounded by his disciples, and Jesus turns them away. That is all.

In John, however, Mary plays a somewhat greater role; and, as is characteristic of John's view of things, she is aware of her son's role and of his ability to work miracles. She tells Jesus that the party is out of wine and instructs the servants to do whatever he tells them to do. Jesus then proceeds to turn water into wine (and, as the gospel carefully explains, into very good wine indeed).

The Jews' Passover

In the synoptic gospels only one visit to Jerusalem is recorded of Jesus, and that takes place in the last week of his life, on the occasion of a Passover.

John, however, records several visits to Jerusalem, including no less than three Passovers. The first Passover visit takes place immediately after the miracle of turning water into wine.

John 2:13. *And the Jews' passover was at hand, and Jesus went up to Jerusalem . . .*

John refers to the festival as "the Jews' passover," for his Gentile audience needed the qualifying adjective to understand what was being spoken of. He is even more carefully explanatory at other times:

John 6:4. *And the passover, a feast of the Jews, was nigh.*

Luke, also writing to a Gentile audience, must also explain:

Luke 22:1. *Now the feast of unleavened bread drew nigh, which is called the Passover.*

Matthew, on the other hand, writing for Jews, feels the need of no explanation:

Matthew 26:2. *Ye know that after two days is the feast of the passover . . .*

A more important point is that John is writing in a time when Christianity has become almost entirely Gentile and completely withdrawn from Judaism and out of sympathy with the Jews.

In the synoptic gospels, it is the Pharisees, Sadducees, and scribes who oppose Jesus on doctrinal points who conspire against him and bring about his crucifixion. It is they who are blamed and not the Jews generally, for it is from the Jews that Jesus' disciples are also drawn.

John, however, seems to feel that party distinctions would be lost on his audience, and usually refers to Jesus' opponents simply as "Jews." Thus, it is the "Jews," rather than the Sadducees of the Temple, who are pictured as questioning John the Baptist:

John 1:19. . . . *the Jews sent priests and Levites from Jerusalem . . .*

And it is the "Jews" rather than the scribes and Pharisees, who question Jesus on the first visit to Jerusalem:

John 2:18. *Then answered the Jews and said unto him* [Jesus], *What sign shewest thou unto us, seeing that thou doest these things?*

Even Jesus' disciples are described as referring to Jesus' opponents simply as "Jews," as though they themselves were not also Jews. Thus, when Jesus planned to go once more into Judea:

John 11:8. *His disciples say unto him, Master, the Jews of late sought to stone thee; and goest thou thither again?*

Then, too, parents whose son had been cured by Jesus deny knowing how the cure came about, and the reason is presented by John as follows:

John 9:22. *These words spake his parents, because they feared the Jews . . .*

although the parents were themselves Jews, of course.

This general reference to Jews in John, where the synoptics speak of specific parties among the Jews, helped rouse antipathy against Jews on the part of Christians in later centuries. It helped give rise to the common oversimplification that "the Jews killed Christ," as though all Jews of Jesus' time were equally responsible and as though all of Jesus' early disciples from Peter to Paul were not themselves Jews.

To be sure, John does on occasion speak of Jews who follow Jesus:

> John 8:31. *Then said Jesus to those Jews which believed on him . . .*

The Temple

On the occasion of this first visit to Jerusalem, John describes Jesus as driving the money-changers from the Temple, placing that event near the beginning of his mission rather than at the end, as in the synoptic gospels. Those who refuse to admit inconsistencies among the gospels are forced to conclude that there were two such episodes, one near the beginning, and one near the end.

The "Jews" (that is, the Sadducee officials of the Temple) are naturally upset over this action of Jesus, and demand some evidence from him that he is indeed acting under divine inspiration.

> John 2:19. *Jesus answered . . . , Destroy this temple, and in three days I will raise it up.*

Jesus is not quoted as making any such statement in the synoptic gospels. In fact, quite the reverse. Mark and Matthew record that a similar statement was *falsely* attributed to Jesus as part of the attempt to condemn him as a blasphemer before Caiaphas.

> Mark 14:57. *And there arose certain, and bare false witness against him, saying,*
> Mark 14:58. *We heard him say, I will destroy this temple that is made with hands, and within three days I will build another made without hands.*

Then, when Jesus was on the cross, he was mocked with this statement:

Mark 15:29. *And they that passed by* [the cross] *railed on him* . . . *saying, Ah, thou that destroyest the temple, and buildest it in three days,*

Mark 15:30. *Save thyself, and come down from the cross.*

But John accepts this as a true saying of Jesus and interprets it as a reference to the resurrection:

John 2:21. *But he* [Jesus] *spake of the temple of his body.*

In connection with this remark concerning the Temple, John mentions the literal-minded retort of the priests—a retort which has been used for chronological purposes:

John 2:20. *Then said the Jews, Forty and six years was this temple in building, and wilt thou rear it up in three days?*

Actually, construction of the Second Temple was begun in 538 B.C. in the reign of Cyrus of Persia and completed in 516 B.C. in the reign of Darius (see page I-449), so that it was only twenty-two years in building.

Herod the Great, however, in his attempt to gain the good will of his subjects, initiated a vast restoration and enlargement of the Temple, one which amounted, virtually, to a rebuilding. This restoration was begun in 19 B.C. and it was not actually completed until A.D. 63—three years before the beginning of the war that was to destroy that same Temple forever. The Temple was eighty-two years in the restoring.

But suppose it had been continuing for forty-six years at the time of Jesus' first Passover visit to Jerusalem and that the priests were saying, in essence, "So far just the temple restoration alone has been proceeding for forty-six years and here you offer to build it from scratch in three days!"

If so, then the year of the visit would be A.D. 27. The next two Passover visits recorded in John would then be in A.D. 28 and 29 and if the last of the three were the one of the crucifixion, that would agree with the chronology as given in Luke in terms of the reign of Tiberius (see page 274).

Nicodemus

Oddly enough, on the first occasion in which John does specify a Pharisee, it is one that he depicts as sympathetic to Jesus (and one who is nowhere mentioned in the synoptic gospels):

> John 3:1. There was a man of the Pharisees, named Nicodemus, a ruler of the Jews:
> John 3:2. The same came to Jesus by night, and said unto him, Rabbi, we know that thou art a teacher come from God . . .

He asked questions of Jesus and listened to the answers which were not given in the form of parables as in the synoptic gospels, but rather in philosophic discourse that Nicodemus found difficult to follow.

Nicodemus was apparently swayed by Jesus' statements, however, for later when the Pharisees planned to put Jesus out of the way for blasphemy, Nicodemus rose and insisted on a fair trial, thus blunting the purpose of Jesus' opponents for the time. (It was Nicodemus who was mockingly asked if he too were from Galilee.)

After the crucifixion, Nicodemus, according to John, took care of Jesus' body, along with Joseph of Arimathea (see page 233), and saw to its proper burial. In early Christian tradition, Nicodemus is supposed to have turned Christian. An apocryphal "Gospel According to Nicodemus" is attributed to him. It dealt with the trial and execution of Jesus, his descent into hell, and his resurrection.

Samaria

Apparently, Jesus' success in attracting followers in Judea attracted the attention of the Pharisees and Jesus thought it best to return to Galilee.

> John 4:3. He left Judaea, and departed again into Galilee.
> John 4:4. And he must needs go through Samaria.

In Matthew and Mark, gospels written for Jewish audiences, Jesus is depicted as sharing the general Jewish hostility to Samaritans. Even

Samaria

in Luke, written for Gentiles and depicting individual Samaritans with sympathy, it is indicated (see page 282) that the Samaritans, generally, oppose Jesus.

Not so in John. Here, in the most Gentile of the gospels, Jesus is depicted as speaking freely to a Samaritan woman (something at which his disciples are shocked) and as offering her salvation on the same basis with Jews. This fits John's thesis that Jesus has come to save all men, and not the Jews alone. If that thesis were not made clear, his gospel would be valueless to his audience.

From the vantage point of a full generation after the destruction of the Temple, John has Jesus point out that the parochialism of both Samaritans (worshipping on Mount Gerizim) and Jews (worshipping on Mount Zion) was soon to have no meaning:

> John 4:21. *Jesus saith unto her, Woman, believe me, the hour cometh, when ye shall neither in this mountain, nor yet at Jerusalem, worship the Father.*

Jesus calmly announces himself as the Messiah, and the Samaritan woman tells others of her people. As is characteristic of John's gospel, the Samaritans at once believe, and accept Jesus not as a Messiah sent to the Jews only, but to all the world (again fitting John's view and his audience).

> John 4:40. . . . *the Samaritans* . . . *besought him* [Jesus] *that he would tarry with them* . . .
> John 4:41. *And many more believed* . . .
> John 4:42. *And said unto the woman, Now we believe* . . . *and know that this is indeed the Christ, the Saviour of the world.*

Once Jesus is back in Galilee, the evangelist mentions in an aside the well-known saying of Jesus that a prophet had no honor in his own country and also later states, again as an aside, the disbelief in Jesus on the part of his close relations:

> John 7:5. *For neither did his* [Jesus'] *brethren believe in him.*

John does not, however, include the account (found in all the synoptic gospels) of Jesus' failure to impress his townsmen at Nazareth. Such a failure would not fit the picture of Jesus as drawn by John.

Jewry

A second trip is then made to Jerusalem, where Jesus heals a crippled man on the Sabbath and gets in trouble with the conservative elements among the Jews for having violated the Sabbath. In the discussion thereafter, John has Jesus implying himself to be the Messiah, and driving the conservative elements into a fury at this seeming blasphemy.

Again, Jesus returns to Galilee as a matter of prudence and there, near the time of a second Passover, performs other miracles, including the feeding of thousands of people by means of five loaves of bread and two fish—the only miracle described in all four gospels.

Jesus remains in Galilee for a time—

John 7:1. . . . *for he would not walk in Jewry, because the Jews sought to kill him.*

The expression "Jewry" is used only three times in the King James Version. Only one of these is in the Old Testament—in the very late Book of Daniel, where the Babylonian king asks Daniel:

Daniel 5:13. . . . *Art thou that Daniel, which art of the children of the captivity of Judah, whom the king my father brought out of Jewry?*

The second occasion is in Luke, where Jesus is accused of sedition before Pilate:

Luke 23:5. . . . *He stirreth up the people, teaching throughout all Jewry . . .*

"Jewry" is an archaic term for Judah or Judea and in the Revised Standard Version, the word is rendered "Judah" in the verse from Daniel, and as "Judea" in the two verses from the gospels.

"Jewry" in modern ears does not have quite the same connotation as Judea. The latter is a geographical term and it was politically distinct from Galilee in Jesus' time. Jesus' priestly enemies were powerful in Judea ("Jewry") but not in Galilee, and Jesus was clearly safer in his home province.

But if "Judea" is clear in its meaning, "Jewry" is so no longer. In modern ears, it sounds rather analogous to the word "Christendom." It seems to cover all the area in which Jews live; it seems indeed to be a way of saying "all the Jews." Place this in conjunction with the following phrase, "because the Jews sought to kill him" (the synoptic gospels would have said, "because the Pharisees sought to kill him"), and the impression is given of the malignant hostility toward Jesus on the part of all the Jews—something that is clearly not the case.

Abraham

But Jesus did return to Jerusalem for a third time, at the time of the Feast of the Tabernacles, and his teachings became ever more bold. Indeed, he finally pronounced himself to be the Messiah in the plainest terms.

John 8:54. *Jesus answered,* . . .

. . . .

John 8:56. *Your father Abraham rejoiced to see my day: and he saw it, and was glad.*

John 8:57. *Then said the Jews unto him, Thou art not yet fifty years old, and hast thou seen Abraham?*

To the Jewish leaders, blasphemy had reached the ultimate, for Jesus was claiming to be not merely the Messiah, but God himself. The deliberate use of the words "I am" in Jesus' climactic answer:

John 8:58. *Jesus said unto them, Verily, verily, I say unto you, Before Abraham was, I am.*

harks back to God's announcement of his own name to Moses:

Exodus 3:14. *And God said unto Moses . . . Thus shalt thou say unto the children of Israel, I AM hath sent me unto you.*

With that, many Jews must have felt perfectly justified in attempting to stone Jesus, for stoning was the traditional method of execution for blasphemers:

Leviticus 24:16. *And he that blasphemeth the name of the Lord, he shall surely be put to death, and all the congregation shall certainly stone him . . .*

Deductions are made concerning Jesus' age from the comment to the effect that Jesus was "not yet fifty years old" and some suppose that he was not far short of fifty at this time. It is even possible to argue that he was forty-six years old by beginning with John's comment that when Jesus spoke of re-erecting the Temple, he was speaking of his own body (see page 315). Therefore, when the Pharisees said it had taken forty-six years to build the Temple, might they not have meant that Jesus was forty-six years old? It is difficult to take this argument seriously, however, for surely, even if Jesus were speaking of his body, the Pharisees weren't, and to use their statement as a basis for deducing Jesus' age is a great deal to ask of a conversation that was supposedly going on at cross-purposes. It seems much more natural to accept Luke's flat statement (see page 275) that Jesus was about thirty years old when he began his mission.

Still, if Jesus were forty-six at the time of his death, and if the crucifixion did take place in A.D. 29, as Luke indicates (see page 274), then Christ must have been born in 17 B.C. There is nothing clearly impossible about this, except that basing it on the comment "Thou art not yet fifty" offers a very thin foundation. The expression might merely be a metaphoric way of saying, "You have not yet attained to years of wisdom," or "You are not even an old man"—and this can be said of a thirty-three-year-old even more forcefully than of a forty-six-year-old.

Jesus goes on to make additional claims to Messiah-hood and divinity. At one point he says:

John 10:11. *I am the good shepherd . . .*

This harks back to a passage in the writings of the prophet Ezekiel in which God is quoted as denouncing the wickedness of the Jewish leaders, who are described metaphorically as wicked shepherds:

Ezekiel 34:2. *Son of man, prophesy against the shepherds of Israel . . . Woe be to the shepherds of Israel that do feed themselves! should not the shepherds feed the flocks?*

Ezekiel goes on to quote God as offering himself to be the shepherd who would save his people:

Ezekiel 34:11. *. . . . I, even I, will both search my sheep, and seek them out.*

Ezekiel 34:12. *As a shepherd seeketh out his flock . . . so will I seek out my sheep . . .*

Then in speaking of the Messianic kingdom, the Messiah is spoken of with the same metaphor:

Ezekiel 34:23. *And I will set up one shepherd over them, and he shall feed them, even my servant David . . .*

In speaking of himself as the good shepherd, then, Jesus is naming himself either the Messiah or God, or both. If the point is not clear, he makes it flatly a little later:

John 10:30. *I and my Father are one.*

and again he narrowly escapes a stoning, and retires to the Trans-Jordan.

Lazarus

It is serious news that now calls Jesus back to Judea for a fourth time as the third and last Passover of John's gospel approaches. A friend was seriously ill.

John 11:1. *Now a certain man was sick, named Lazarus, of Bethany, the town of Mary and her sister Martha.*

. . . .

John 11:3. *Therefore his sisters* [Mary and Martha] *sent unto him, saying, Lord, behold, he whom thou lovest is sick.*

This Lazarus is not mentioned anywhere in the synoptic gospels, which is odd, for the event that is to follow is pictured by John as the very climax of Jesus' miracles on Earth. Yet if it is indeed the climax, why the total silence of the other gospels?

Some have suggested that the story of Lazarus is an allegorical one, intended to show, in concrete form, the power of Jesus' teaching. For that reason, it might be argued, John simply borrowed material for the purpose. The name Lazarus he might have adopted from the beggar in Luke's parable (see page 284), the one who went to heaven while the rich man went to hell.

Why the beggar? Well, when the rich man is in hell, he asks that

Lazarus be sent back to Earth to warn the rich man's five brothers of the torment awaiting them. But Abraham, from heaven, assures the rich man that:

> Luke 16:31. . . . *If they hear not Moses and the prophets, neither will they be persuaded, though one rose from the dead.*

There is thus a connection between Lazarus the beggar, and the notion of being raised from the dead, and the tale, in John, of Lazarus of Bethany who is raised from the dead by Jesus.

There are raisings from the dead in the other gospels. In Luke, for instance, there is the tale of Jesus' raising the dead son of a widow:

> Luke 7:14. . . . *And he [Jesus] said, Young man, I say unto thee, Arise.*
>
> Luke 7:15. *And he that was dead sat up, and began to speak . . .*

The story in Luke is told quickly, however, and is placed near the beginning of Jesus' career. It is no more than on a par with Jesus' other miracles of healing.

In John, however, the analogous story of a raising from the dead is told in much more dramatic detail and is placed at the end of Jesus' career, as a fitting climax to the gathering force of his miracles and self-manifestation.

By the time Jesus reaches Bethany, Lazarus is dead and buried and has remained in the tomb for days. Jesus has the stone blocking the tomb rolled away.

> John 11:43. And . . . *he [Jesus] cried with a loud voice, Lazarus, come forth.*
>
> John 11:44. *And he that was dead came forth . . .*

There are those who suspect that since Lazarus is defined as "he whom thou lovest," that he is none other than the Beloved Disciple and the author of the fourth gospel. It might be possible to argue from that that Lazarus knew the events of the raising firsthand and included them, whereas the other evangelists did not.

This, however, seems weak, for the episode is described as having been public and as having achieved such fame as to be the final straw that determined the Pharisees to have Jesus convicted and executed. How could the synoptic gospels overlook such a thing?

Caiaphas

The Jewish religious leaders see clearly now that if Jesus is not stopped, those who flocked to him in the aftermath of the Lazarus miracle would become uncontrollable. They feared a rebellion and a consequent catastrophe to follow:

> John 11:48. *If we let him* [Jesus] *thus alone, all men will believe on him: and the Romans shall come and take away both our place and nation.*
>
> John 11:49. . . . *Caiaphas* . . . *said unto them* . . .
>
> John 11:50. . . . *it is expedient for us, that one man should die for the people, and that the whole nation perish not.*

This statement of Caiaphas' is to be found only in John, who uses it to fit his own scheme of things. He points out that Caiaphas, who was, after all, high priest, was engaging in unconscious prophecy; that Jesus would indeed die in order that salvation might be brought to all people—but not to the Jews only:

> John 11:52. *And not for that nation only, but that also he* [Jesus] *should gather together in one the children of God that were scattered abroad.*

Of course, by the "children of God that were scattered abroad" one might suppose that John meant the Jews dwelling outside Judea. It is equally possible, however, to suppose it to refer to the Gentiles who lived all over the world and who, by accepting Jesus, would become the "children of God"—the spiritual heirs of Abraham.

If there is doubt here, it is removed by an incident described shortly afterward. Even while the Jewish leaders are planning to have Jesus executed, the first Gentile disciples arrive:

> John 12:20. *And there were certain Greeks among them that came up to worship at the* [Passover] *feast:*
>
> John 12:21. *The same came therefore to Philip* . . . *and desired him, saying, Sir, we would see Jesus.*

Sometimes the word "Greeks" in English translations of the Bible means Jews from Egypt or elsewhere who have Greek as their native language. The original Greek of the New Testament, however, uses slightly different forms to distinguish between men of Jewish birth who speak Greek, and men of Greek birth who had been converted to Judaism. In this case, it seems to be men of Greek birth—converted Gentiles—who are meant.

And they ask to see Jesus. The Gentiles begin to turn toward Jesus, in John's picture of events, just as the Jews are about to turn finally away from him. And it is this decisive turn that marks to Jesus the time of the death and resurrection. The disciples bring word to him that the Greeks wish to see him:

John 12:23. *And Jesus answered them, saying, The hour is come, that the Son of man should be glorified.*

John indicates plainly, then, that the direction of Christianity is toward the Gentile and away from the Jew—as is the theme of his entire gospel, in fact, from the very hymn that opens it:

John 1:11. *He came unto his own, and his own received him not.*
John 1:12. *But as many as received him, to them gave he power to become the sons of God, even to them that believe on his name . . .*

And that, surely, is what John's audience wanted to hear.

The Comforter

John describes the triumphant entry into Jerusalem, though the passage is not as convincing as in the synoptic gospels, where it seems to be the *only* entry.

John does not, however, describe a last supper during Jesus' final night of freedom, or the prayer at Gethsemane. He does not have Jesus pray that the fated cup might be allowed to pass from him (see page 218). That would be not in accord with the divine Jesus pictured by John. Indeed, John has Jesus speak in such a way as to seem to contradict, deliberately, that passage in the synoptic gospels:

John 12:27. *Now is my soul troubled; and what shall I say? Father, save me from this hour: but for this cause came I unto this hour.*

Jesus washes the feet of his disciples (as a lesson in humility, not found in the synoptic gospels) and then continues to deliver self-assured philosophical discourses. During these, he makes statements that helped give rise to thoughts of an imminent second coming among the early Christians. Thus, he tells them, with reference to his forthcoming death:

John 14:2. . . . *I go to prepare a place for you.*
John 14:3. *And . . . I will come again, and receive you unto myself . . .*

This might be interpreted as meaning he would come, unseen, for each disciple, as that disciple lay dying, to lead him to his prepared place in heaven. There was, however, certainly a tendency to assume that this (and other verses in the gospels) implied a return of Christ in glory, and one that was not long delayed either. This return would fulfill the same purposes as the Jews had believed would be fulfilled by the Messiah.

Jesus is quoted as making another promise:

John 14:16. *And I will pray the Father, and he shall give you another Comforter, that he may abide with you for ever;*
John 14:17. *Even the Spirit of truth . . .*

This is usually interpreted as meaning that Christians would be guided by the Holy Spirit once Jesus was taken away from them and that this Spirit would comfort them and guide them aright.

Nevertheless, there were not lacking those among the early Christians who personified the Comforter (or "Paraclete" as the word is in Greek). It seemed to them that Jesus was promising a new and still later Messiah who would take on human appearance, just as Moses was considered to have prophesied Jesus in his reference to a Prophet (see page 304).

Thus, somewhere about A.D. 160 (about half a century after the gospel of St. John had been written) a Christian of Asia Minor named Montanus claimed to be the incarnation of the Comforter.

Montanus was rejected as a false Messiah by the Christian leadership, just as Jesus had been rejected by the Jewish leadership. And just as Jesus slowly gathered disciples who grew in numbers after his death, so did Montanus. The sect of Montanists, puritanical in doctrine, was particularly strong in Carthage and its environs, and among them was Tertullian, the first important Christian leader to write in Latin.

However, Christianity was wider spread than Judaism had been in Jesus' time, and Christianity was not weakened by a catastrophe analogous to the Roman destruction of Judea. Consequently the Montanists were kept in check. Furthermore, they expected an imminent second coming of some sort, and as this did not take place, they slowly withered. Still, some remained until the days of the Moslem conquest of North Africa in the seventh century wiped out Christianity in that region altogether.

Pilate

The story of Jesus' capture and trial is essentially the same in John as in the synoptic gospels, but with an important change in atmosphere. The divine Jesus portrayed by John is by no means the mute and suffering servant pictured by the Second Isaiah and the synoptic gospels. Instead, Jesus is completely self-possessed and in control of events at all times. He goes to his death deliberately.

Thus, he boldly faces those who have come to arrest him and calmly announces his identity even before Judas has a chance to indicate him. And when Pilate asks him if he is the King of the Jews, Jesus questions Pilate in turn and has no difficulty in dominating the exchange:

John 18:34. *Jesus answered him, Sayest thou this thing of thyself, or did others tell it thee of me?*

John 18:35. *Pilate answered, Am I a Jew? Thine own nation and the chief priests have delivered thee unto me: what hast thou done?*

Thus Pilate is clearly forced to confess that he knows nothing of the affair and that he is merely a mouthpiece of the Jewish priesthood. In this way, John, writing for his Gentile audience, does more than any of the synoptic gospels (even Luke) to lift the blame for the crucifixion from the Gentiles and place it on the Jews.

This is made even plainer at a later stage of the trial when Pilate questions Jesus again. Jesus is now silent and Pilate says desperately:

John 19:10. . . . *Speakest thou not unto me? knowest thou not that I have power to crucify thee, and have power to release thee?*

John 19:11. *Jesus answered, Thou couldest have no power at all against me, except it were given thee from above: therefore he that delivered me unto thee hath the greater sin.*

In other words, Pilate is again pictured as a puppet who can do only what he must do, in accordance with the Roman law (or with the will of God). In either case, since he has not been taught the Scriptures, since he knows nothing of the Messiah, and since he has not been exposed to Jesus' preaching, he cannot know what he is doing. The greater sin belongs to those who, knowing of the Scriptures, the Messiah, and Jesus' teaching, nevertheless handed Jesus over to the implacable grinding of Roman law. The expression "he that delivered me" is singular and it may indicate Caiaphas the high priest (though some suggest Judas Iscariot, or even Satan).

If the reader takes the expression to refer to Caiaphas, then here again would be a statement from Jesus that it is the Jewish authority, rather than the Roman authority, that is truly responsible for the crucifixion.

To make this still clearer, John has Pilate show even greater reluctance to carry through the task than even Luke does, and has him yield to the priestly party only after political threats which are not found in the synoptic gospels, but which John's Gentile audience would thoroughly understand:

John 19:12. . . . *the Jews cried out, saying, If thou let this man go, thou art not Caesar's friend: whosoever maketh himself a king speaketh against Caesar.*

In other words, the priestly party is prepared to accuse Pilate of treason if he acquits Jesus. An accusation of treason in the days of the suspicious Tiberius was often equivalent to conviction.

John even has the priests making what the nationalist Jews of the time would consider a treasonable statement to their own cause in their anxiety to enforce the crucifixion. Jesus is mockingly produced to the crowd as the Messianic king:

John 19:15. . . . *Pilate saith unto them, Shall I crucify your King? The chief priest answered, We have no king but Caesar.*

They are thus pictured as denying the Messianic hope altogether and the case against them, as carefully constructed by John, is complete.

The Spear

John's version of the crucifixion differs from that pictured in the synoptic gospels in a number of respects. Jesus bears his own cross. No one is described as having to help him. The humiliating aspects of the crucifixion—including the jeering of the crowd—are omitted. Jesus' mother, Mary, is at the site of the crucifixion (though her presence there is not mentioned in any of the other gospels) and Jesus is sufficiently self-possessed, even on the cross, to place her in the charge of the Beloved Disciple, who is also there.

John, like Luke, omits the last cry of despair (see page 232). Such despair would be unthinkable in the picture of Jesus drawn by John. Instead, John has Jesus merely announce the completion of his mission:

John 19:30. . . . *he said, It is finished: and he bowed his head, and gave up the ghost.*

Certain events following Jesus' death are given in John, but not in the synoptic gospels. John explains that the priests want the crucified individuals (Jesus and the two robbers) down from the cross that very evening, in order not to profane the coming Passover. For that reason, soldiers are sent to break the legs of the crucified men in order that they might be thus killed and taken down. (Actually, however it sounds to us, such leg-breaking seems to be intended as an act of mercy. Those who were crucified might otherwise linger a number of days in gradually increasing torment.)

Jesus, however, had died already, apparently sooner than was expected; sufficiently soon, indeed, to make one soldier suspicious that Jesus might be playing possum:

John 19:33. *But when they* [the soldiers] *came to Jesus, and saw that he was dead already, they brake not his legs:*

John 19:34. *But one of the soldiers with a spear pierced his side, and forthwith came there out blood and water.*

John introduces these items to make a very important theological point; one, apparently, which was disputed by some factions among the early Christians. He therefore emphatically defends the truth of what he has just said:

John 19:35. *And he that saw it bare record, and his record is true: and he knoweth that he saith true, that ye might believe.*

John then goes on to explain the significance of this vehemently defended account of the leg-breaking that did not come to pass and the spear thrust that did:

John 19:36. *For these things were done, that the scripture should be fulfilled, A bone of him shall not be broken.*

John 19:37. *And again another scripture saith, They shall look on him whom they pierced.*

The first quotation is from the Book of Psalms. In one which praises the care of God for those who trust in him, there is the verse:

Psalm 34:20. *He* [the Lord] *keepeth all his* [the righteous one's] *bones; not one of them is broken.*

And in the later, apocalyptic chapters of Zechariah, reference is made to some not clearly defined person who is mistreated:

Zechariah 12:10. . . . *they shall look upon me whom they have pierced, and they shall mourn for him* . . .

But this anxiety to fit the events of Jesus' life into the various utterances found in the Old Testament is not really characteristic of John. He is not Matthew and he is not writing for Matthew's audience.

The reference must be wider still. Jesus was crucified at the Passover festival, and at the beginning of the fourth gospel John the Baptist has referred to Jesus as the "Lamb of God" (see page 305). Well, there is an association of the lamb and Passover.

In God's instructions to Israel on the occasion of the first Passover, on the eve of the Exodus from Egypt, Moses is told:

Exodus 12:3. *Speak ye unto all the congregation of Israel, saying, In the tenth day of this month they shall take to them every man a lamb* . . .

The lamb is to be sacrificed on the eve of Passover and its blood smeared on the doorposts:

Exodus 12:13. . . . *and when I see the blood, I will pass over you, and the plague shall not be upon you* . . .

Later, in the same chapter, a further instruction is given concerning the lamb:

Exodus 12:46. . . . *neither shall ye break a bone thereof.*

This is in accordance with the general rule that all animals sacrificed to God must be in perfect condition and without blemish:

Deuteronomy 17:1. *Thou shalt not sacrifice unto the Lord thy God any bullock, or sheep, wherein is blemish, or any evilfavouredness* . . .

John's analogy seems to be clear. The crucifixion of Jesus on the eve of Passover is a new and greater sacrifice. In place of the unblemished lamb, always a symbol of the pure and innocent, there is the unblemished Lamb of God, the pure and innocent Jesus. Not a bone of Jesus was broken but the blood of Jesus had to be seen in accordance with Exodus 12:13 and 12:46 respectively. Hence the soldiers did not break Jesus' legs and did draw blood with the spear.

The fact that the sacrifice was so much greater—Jesus rather than an ordinary lamb—could be argued as indicating the purpose to be equivalently greater, all mankind rather than the Jews only. This would fit John's scheme of things and would account for the manner in which he insists his account of the spear is true.

Another connotation of this analogy is that a lamb was sometimes used as a sin offering; a sacrifice meant to atone for the sin and clear the sinner before God:

Leviticus 4:27. *And if any one of the common people sin* . . .
. . . .
Leviticus 4:32. *And if he bring a lamb for a sin offering* . . .

Jesus is the unblemished Lamb sacrificed as a sin-offering for all mankind and this gives a further significance to the manner in which John the Baptist first greets Jesus (according to the fourth gospel):

John 1:29. . . . *John seeth Jesus coming unto him, and saith, Behold the Lamb of God, which taketh away the sin of the world.*

Thomas

The story of the resurrection is told by John in greater detail than is found in any of the other gospels. (Apparently, the later the gospel, the more detailed the story of the resurrection.)

The most dramatic account of the initial doubts of the apostles is given here in connection with Thomas:

> John 20:24. *But Thomas, one of the twelve, called Didymus, was not with them when Jesus came.*
>
> John 20:25. *The other disciples therefore said unto him, We have seen the Lord. But he said unto them, Except I shall see in his hands the print of the nails, and put my finger into the print of the nails, and thrust my hand into his side, I will not believe.*

Thomas was granted his desire and accepted the resurrection, but it is this passage which adds the phrase "doubting Thomas" to our language, a phrase that has come to be used for any notorious skeptic.

The surname Didymus means "twin," and it would seem then that "Thomas the Twin" must have had a twin brother or sister. The Bible does not mention any such twin, though legend has been busy (some even maintaining that Thomas was a twin brother of Jesus).

It may be significant that only John uses this surname. Thomas is merely Thomas when he is mentioned in the synoptic gospels. Perhaps the "twin" is not a physical reference at all, but refers to Thomas being "of two minds"; that is, of skeptical tendencies, generally. Perhaps then, "Thomas called Didymus" is merely the evangelist's way of saying "Doubting Thomas."

9. ACTS

THEOPHILUS • MATTHIAS • PENTECOST • TONGUES • PARTHIANS AND MEDES • ANANIAS • GAMALIEL • STEPHEN • PHILIP • SIMON MAGUS • CANDACE • SAUL OF TARSUS • DAMASCUS • BARNABAS • JAMES THE LORD'S BROTHER • LYDDA • CORNELIUS • ANTIOCH • CLAUDIUS CAESAR • HEROD AGRIPPA I • CYPRUS • PAPHOS • PAUL • PAMPHYLIA • PISIDIA • LYCAONIA • ATTALIA • SILAS • TIMOTHY • PHRYGIA AND GALATIA • TROAS • MACEDONIA • PHILIPPI • LYDIA • THESSALONICA • BEREA • ATHENS • EPICUREANS AND STOICS • DIONYSIUS THE AREOPAGITE • CORINTH • AQUILA • GALLIO • EPHESUS • APOLLOS • DIANA OF THE EPHESIANS • MILETUS • RHODES • FELIX • ANTIPATRIS • DRUSILLA • FESTUS • HEROD AGRIPPA II • MYRA • CRETE • MELITA • SYRACUSE • RHEGIUM • ROME

Theophilus

Following the four gospels—the four versions of the life of Jesus—comes a book which is for the most part a straightforward history and is particularly valuable for that reason.

It deals with the slow growth of Christianity during the generation that followed the crucifixion of Jesus—from its beginnings in Jerusalem until its slowly widening influence finally reached Rome itself. In so doing, it indicates the steady shift of Christianity away from its national Jewish foundation to the status of a universal Gentile religion, and the hero of that shift is the apostle Paul.

Although the second half of the book is essentially a biography of Paul, the first half gives some details concerning the other important disciples, so that the book is fairly named "The Acts of the Apostles" (rather than "The Book of Paul").

The author of Acts is generally considered to be the same as that of the third gospel. Acts begins, for instance, with a dedication similar to that which introduces the third gospel (see page 254), and it refers to an earlier book:

Journeys of the Apostles

Acts 1:1. *The former treatise have I made, O Theophilus, of all that Jesus began both to do and teach,*

Acts 1:2. *Until the day in which he was taken up . . .*

This "former treatise" is taken to be the third gospel, and it is universally assumed that Luke (see page 252) wrote that gospel and is also the author of Acts. To be sure, a later hand might have added the dedication to Theophilus in order to make it seem as though the same author had written both the third gospel and Acts, but a careful examination of the style and vocabulary of the two books seems to back up the theory of common authorship.

Indeed, one wonders if Luke and Acts might not originally have formed a single treatise which was divided only when it was decided to gather the various canonical gospels into a group.

The events dealt with in Acts end just prior to the Neronian persecution of Christians in A.D. 64, and some have suggested that the book was written at about that time. Others have favored dates as late as A.D. 100. However, it seems very likely that Acts was written about the same time as Luke and A.D. 80 seems a nice even date for both.

No one knows where Acts was written. The last events recorded take place in Rome, so it might have been written there. If it were written some fifteen years after those events it might well have been composed elsewhere. Some suggest Asia Minor and, in particular, the city of Ephesus. Christian missionary work was especially successful in Ephesus in the first century. Tradition places the composition of other New Testament books there, notably the fourth gospel (see page 297).

Matthias

As Acts begins, the resurrected Jesus is still with his small band of disciples and is giving them his final instructions over a fairly extended period of time:

Acts 1:3. *To whom* [the disciples] *also he* [Jesus] *shewed himself alive . . . , being seen of them forty days . . .*

After this, Jesus was taken up to heaven (the ascension):

Acts 1:9. *. . . while they beheld, he* [Jesus] *was taken up; and a cloud received him out of their sight.*

It was now up to the disciples to continue their work on their own, and their first act was to reconstitute the inner circle of twelve, which had been broken by the defection of Judas Iscariot. The remaining apostles are listed—the fourth list in the New Testament. The other three are in Matthew, Mark, and Luke, respectively; John does not give a list.

> Acts 1:13. . . . *Peter, and James, and John, and Andrew, Philip, and Thomas, Bartholomew, and Matthew, James the son of Alphaeus, and Simon Zelotes, and Judas the brother of James.*

Naturally, Judas Iscariot is omitted, but if we consider these eleven, we find it to include precisely those names listed in Luke, but not precisely those in Matthew and Mark. Only Luke of the three synoptic gospels contains Judas the brother of James as one of the twelve apostles; only Luke identifies Simon as Simon Zelotes. This is an additional piece of evidence in favor of the theory that Luke wrote Acts as well as the third gospel.

Peter arranged to have a new individual selected to take the place of Judas Iscariot in order to bring the number of the inner circle back to the mystical twelve that matched the twelve tribes of Israel. Two were nominated, Joseph Barsabbas and Matthias. To choose between the two, lots were used:

> Acts 1:26. . . . *and the lot fell upon Matthias; and he was numbered with the eleven apostles.*

Neither Joseph Barsabbas nor Matthias are mentioned anywhere else in the New Testament.

But the twelve apostles were by no means the only ones with whom Christianity made its start. Others, in addition, were gathered together in these very early days:

> Acts 1:15. . . . *Peter stood up in the midst of the disciples . . . (the number of names together were about an hundred and twenty,) . . .*

Among them, Acts lists:

> Acts 1:14. . . . *Mary the mother of Jesus, and . . . his brethren.*

This is the last act recorded of Mary in the New Testament. Luke, in common with the other synoptic gospels, had recorded her and Jesus' brothers as having vainly tried to see Jesus (see page 188) and she is never mentioned again. (Her appearance at the crucifixion is to be found only in John.) However, if the evidence of Acts is accepted, she joined the Christian fellowship after her son's death, whatever her doubts might have been in his lifetime.

Pentecost

After the ascension, the second of the three great harvest festivals of Judaism was approaching. This was, in Hebrew, Hag ha-Shabuoth ("feast of weeks") or simply Shabuoth. The significance of the name arises from the manner of determining the time of its observation. That determination was based upon Passover, the first of the harvest festivals:

> Leviticus 23:15. *And ye shall count unto you from the morrow after the sabbath* [of the Passover] *. . . ; seven sabbaths shall be complete:*
> Leviticus 23:16. *Even unto the morrow after the seventh sabbath shall ye number fifty days . . .*

In other words, Shabuoth comes seven weeks and a day after the Passover Sabbath and hence it is the "feast of weeks." The Greek name refers to the number of days that had elapsed; it is "Pentecost" from a Greek word meaning "fiftieth" since it comes on the fiftieth day after Passover. The festival is mentioned by both names in 2 Maccabees:

> 2 Maccabees 12:31. . . . *so they* [certain Jews] *came to Jerusalem, the feast of the weeks approaching.*
> 2 Maccabees 12:32. *And after the feast, called Pentecost, they went forth . . .*

Since the account in Acts makes the ascension take place forty days after the resurrection, which in turn took place the day after the Passover Sabbath, Pentecost must have come ten days after the ascension.

The twelve apostles, still completely Jewish in background and religion, made ready to celebrate the festival:

> Acts 2:1. *And when the day of Pentecost was fully come, they* [the apostles] *were all with one accord in one place.*

Because of what then took place Pentecost remains an important day in the Christian calendar, and is celebrated on the seventh Sunday after Easter.

Tongues

The apostles, gathered to celebrate Pentecost, were overcome by a religious ecstasy, which they attributed to the entry into them of the Holy Spirit—a manifestation promised them by Jesus just before the ascension, for Acts quotes Jesus as saying:

> Acts 1:5. . . . *ye shall be baptized with the Holy Ghost not many days hence.*

The manifestation of the Holy Spirit at Pentecost took the form of ecstatic utterances:

> Acts 2:4. *And they* [the apostles] *were all filled with the Holy Ghost, and began to speak with other tongues, as the Spirit gave them utterance.*

The utterance of incoherent sounds under the influence of religious ecstasy is an effect common to many religions. As an example, the Pythia, the priestess of Apollo at Delphi, gave forth incoherent utterances under the influence of the narcotic leaves she chewed and of the gases that issued from a volcanic vent. These were then interpreted by priests in such a way as to yield the oracles that the Greeks so valued.

This "gift of tongues" or, in Greek, "glossolalia" was a common feature of the ecstatic frenzies of the bands of prophets that were a feature of Israelite religious practices under the judges and the kings. In fact, such ecstatic and incoherent speech was what was usually meant by the term "to prophesy" in the early books of the Bible. The best known case, perhaps, is that of Saul, who, on meeting a band of prophets, caught their fervor (religious ecstasy is contagious) and joined them:

> 1 Samuel 10:10. . . . *a company of prophets met him* [Saul]; *and the Spirit of God came upon him, and he prophesied among them.*

Nor is the "gift of tongues" an ancient phenomenon only. In the emotion-filled gatherings of some Christian sects today, ecstatic events of one sort of another are common. The "Shakers," for instance, a sect that achieved some prominence in nineteenth-century America but is almost extinct today, were so called because they frequently went into convulsions in the course of their prayers and shook as they cried out incoherently. Sects in which exhibitions of the "gift of tongues" is frequent are often referred to as the "Pentecostal Churches" because of the fact that this incident during the apostles' celebration of Pentecost offered them their Biblical justification.

Parthians and Medes

The account in Acts brings the miraculous into this account of the "tongues" spoken by the apostles, by declaring that their utterances were understood by every one who heard them as being spoken in the listeners' native laguage. The audience is described:

> Acts 2:5. *And there were dwelling at Jerusalem Jews, devout men, out of every nation under heaven.*
> . . . .
> Acts 2:9. *Parthians, and Medes, and Elamites, and the dwellers in Mesopotamia, and in Judaea, and Cappadocia, in Pontus, and Asia,*
> Acts 2:10. *Phrygia, and Pamphylia, in Egypt, and in the parts of Libya about Cyrene, and strangers of Rome . . .*
> Acts 2:11. *Cretes and Arabians . . .*

This list of nations represents, for the most part, a systematic sweep from east to west. First are the provinces of the Parthian Empire (then at the peak of its power), the borders of which lay not far to the east of Judea. The Parthians, who were the ruling group within the empire, had, as their native province, the northeastern section of what is now modern Iran, a province just southeast of the Caspian Sea.

Immediately to the west of Parthia proper, was Media, and south of Media was Susiana, the ancient Elam (see page I-455). To the west of Media and Elam was Mesopotamia, the ancient Babylonia. These various provinces made up the main portions of the Parthian Empire, and that brought the listing to Judea itself.

The list moves westward into Asia Minor, where five different regions are named: Cappadocia and Pontus are to be found in the eastern portion of that peninsula, while Asia, Phrygia, and Pamphylia are in the western portion.

Asia is a term which, in modern use, is applied to the entire vast continent of which Asia Minor is part. In Roman times, however, the "province of Asia" referred to the western third of the peninsula only, the area that had once been the kingdom of Pergamum (see page 74). Throughout the Book of Acts, the word "Asia" is to be understood in this sense. As for Phrygia, it had once been an independent kingdom centuries before, but now it was merely a name given to portions of the Asia Minor interior.

At the time of the apostles' Pentecost, all the regions of Asia Minor but Pontus were parts of the Roman Empire. Pontus remained in nominal independence under a puppet king for another generation. In A.D. 63, however, Nero made Pontus into a Roman province outright.

With the regions of Asia Minor northwest of Judea mentioned, the list moves to the southwest, to Egypt and Cyrene, and then to the far west—Rome. Crete and Arabia seem to be added as an afterthought.

While the list is lengthened as though to make extremely impressive the manner in which the apostles spoke (or, at least, were understood) in the language of "every nation under heaven," it might be argued that the list is not as impressive as it seems.

In Roman times, the Greek language had spread widely throughout the east and local native languages had been submerged into a kind of peasant patois. Jews living in those areas learned Greek. As an example, the Jews of Alexandria spoke Greek, not Egyptian.

It followed then that the Jews from Cappadocia, Pontus, Asia, Phrygia, Pamphylia, Egypt, Cyrene, Crete (and from Rome, too), all spoke Greek. Those from the Parthian provinces probably all spoke Aramaic, which was the language of trade and commerce in the regions to the east of the Greek-speaking areas, and which was the native language of Judea itself. In short, if the apostles knew at least some Greek in addition to their native Aramaic (and in those days it is very likely they did), and if, in their ecstasy, they uttered phrases in both languages, then all those who listened to them from the various nations listed, would have understood something. And in this way the account could be accepted without the necessity of a miracle.

Nevertheless, of course, believing Christians accept the incident as miraculous. So did the onlookers, if we accept the account in Acts, for many were converted to the belief in Jesus as Messiah following a speech by Peter:

> Acts 2:41. *Then they that gladly received his [Peter's] word were baptized: and the same day there were added unto them about three thousand souls.*

Ananias

The early Christian community practiced a communism of property:

> Acts 4:32. . . . *they had all things common.*
> . . . .
> Acts 4:34. *Neither was there any among them that lacked: for as many as were possessors of lands or houses sold them, and brought the prices of the things that were sold,*
> Acts 4:35. *And laid them down at the apostles' feet: and distribution was made unto every man according as he had need.*

This idyllic picture of union and selflessness was not, however, without its flaws. Apparently, there were cases where some could not resist holding back at least a little from the common fund, though claiming, falsely, to have delivered the whole.

> Acts 5:1. *But a certain man named Ananias, with Sapphira his wife, sold a possession,*
> Acts 5:2. *And kept back part of the price, his wife also being privy to it, and brought a certain part, and laid it at the apostles' feet.*

Peter saw through the deception and rebuked first Ananias and then Sapphira, accusing each of lying. Each dropped dead upon being rebuked, and Ananias lives on in colloquial speech as a name applied to any liar.

Ananias is the Greek form of the Hebrew name Hananiah. It is an interesting coincidence that, of the fourteen individuals of that name mentioned in the Old Testament, the most considerable is a lying prophet. In the time of Jeremiah, the prophet Hananiah predicted the speedy liberation of the Jews from Babylonian imprisonment. Jeremiah quoted God as threatening Hananiah with death for lying:

Jeremiah 28:17. *So Hananiah the prophet died the same year in the seventh month.*

Gamaliel

That the Christians survived and expanded their influence under Peter was due, at least in part, to a division among the Jewish sects. The aristocratic Sadducees, pro-Roman and opposed to anything that might give rise to political or social unrest, viewed the activities of the apostles with alarm. The religious enthusiasms they aroused, and the atmosphere of revivalist intensity, seemed most dangerous to them.

Acts 5:17. *Then the high priest rose up, and all they that were with him, (which is the sect of the Sadducees,) and were filled with indignation . . .*

More than one attempt was made to imprison the apostles, especially their leader, Peter, and even condemn them to death.

Standing against the Sadducees, however, were the Pharisees. In almost all respects, the religious views of the early Christians were those of the Pharisees. The great dividing line at this time consisted chiefly of the fact that the Christians accepted Jesus as the Messiah and the Pharisees did not. It is quite likely that many of the Pharisees of the time felt that this belief in Jesus was an aberration that would soon die out and that the greater danger within Judaism was the Sadducee sect with whom the Pharisees had been feuding bitterly for about a century and a half.

To defend the apostles against the Sadducee-controlled council, there arose a leader among the Pharisees:

Acts 5:34. *Then stood there up one in the council, a Pharisee, named Gamaliel, a doctor of the law, had in reputation among all the people . . .*

Gamaliel was a grandson of Hillel (see page 145) and carried on the gentle teachings of his renowned grandfather. Gamaliel pointed out that there had been other leaders of popular uprisings in recent decades whose followers had been filled with Messianic hopes and that nothing had come of any of them:

Acts 5:36. For before these days rose up Theudas, boasting himself to be somebody; . . . and all, as many as obeyed him, were scattered, and brought to nought.

Acts 5:37. After this man rose up Judas of Galilee in the days of the taxing . . . : he also perished . . .

Gamaliel pointed out that the Christians would die out too, if their beliefs in Jesus were false, without the council having to take any action, any more than they did in the earlier cases. And if the Christian beliefs were indeed divinely inspired, then any action against them by the council would not only be futile, but also dangerous.

The council was persuaded and the apostles were allowed to continue their work. However, there was no permanent alliance between Christians and Pharisees. The issue of the Messiah-hood of Jesus was insuperable.

Gamaliel led the Pharisees till his death in A.D. 52. A number of his descendants continued to head the shattered Jewish community in Judea after Rome had wiped out all Jewish political power. The last of the line was Gamaliel VI, who died about A.D. 425.

Stephen

The growth of the Christian fellowship was bound to bring problems, and quite early two parties were formed.

One party consisted of Jews of Judea and Galilee, whose language was Aramaic and who carried on their religious observances in the traditional Hebrew. The other party consisted of Jews from outside Judea and Galilee and whose language was Greek, both in their daily lives and their devotions. These two parties can be distinguished on the basis of the language in which they worshipped and are referred to in Acts as Hebrews and Grecians, respectively.

It is understandable that the two groups should misunderstand each other. The Hebrew party could not help but feel that the age-old holy language of Hebrew was the proper one in which to pray and that the holy land of Israel was the proper surrounding in which to pray. To them, the Grecians would naturally seem like foreigners, half corrupted by the Gentiles, speaking a heathen language and tolerant toward pagan ways. The Grecian party, on the other hand, knowing more of the great outside world, would look upon the Hebrews as backward provincials whose narrow outlook was unfitting for the tasks ahead.

Acts 6:1. *And in those days, when the number of the disciples was multiplied, there arose a murmuring of the Grecians against the Hebrews, because their widows were neglected in the daily ministration.*

In other words, the Grecians claimed they were not receiving their fair share of the community income. Since the twelve apostles were all of the Hebrew group there might have been grounds for this complaint.

Had the apostles chosen to override these objections and to maintain a strictly Hebrew stand, the Grecians might have fallen away, and Christianity might have withered.

The apostles did not, however, do this. In a decision which, through hindsight, can be seen to have been statesman-like, they offered the Grecians special representation within the Christian fellowship by allowing them seven leaders who would see to their fair treatment:

Acts 6:5. *And the saying pleased the whole multitude: and they chose Stephen . . . and Philip, and Prochorus, and Nicanor, and Timon, and Parmenas, and Nicolas . . .*

The leader of the Grecian seven was Stephen and he immediately began to be active in missionary labors among his Grecian fellows. Here he met with much opposition:

Acts 6:9. *Then there arose certain of the synagogue, which is called the synagogue of the Libertines, and Cyrenians, and Alexandrians, and of them of Cilicia and of Asia, disputing with Stephen.*

While the Temple was the one place of worship in Jerusalem, there were a number of synagogues in which Jews could gather to discuss the Law, dispute various points, and perhaps carry on their social affairs. It may not have been too different in essence from modern clubs.

Naturally, one would expect Jews of common background to group themselves into a particular synagogue. The Grecians would be happier with others who spoke Greek. Indeed, it might be that those from

Cilicia or Asia, speaking Greek with an Asia Minor accent, would frequent one, while those from Cyrene and Alexandria, speaking with an African accent, would frequent the other. (Cilicia, not mentioned earlier in the Bible, is a region occupying the eastern half of the southern coast of Asia Minor.)

It is not clear whether the "synagogue of the Libertines" represents still a third group, or whether it is the one to which (as the translation in the Jerusalem Bible would have it appear) the Jews of Cyrene and Alexandria belonged.

The word "Libertines," in modern English, refers to those who carry liberty to excess and allow no inhibitions to restrain their unbridled desires. We tend to think of libertines as wicked and lustful, and might consider it quite natural, therefore, for such people to oppose Stephen.

However, "Libertine" has an older meaning; it is applied to a person who has been enslaved but who has been freed, one who is more commonly called in modern terms a "freedman." And, indeed, the Revised Standard Version refers to the "synagog of the Freedmen" rather than to that of the Libertines.

It is thought that the synagogue may have consisted of descendants of Jews who had been taken prisoner by Pompey when he besieged and occupied Jerusalem a century before, and who had later been liberated. They or their descendants may have made their homes in Cyrene and Alexandria, the largest and most flourishing Jewish centers in all the Greek world, and this may have given the name to the synagogue of the Jews of Africa.

Stephen was brought before the council on the charge of blasphemy and, in his defense, he recited the early history of the Jews through the time of Moses, emphasizing the manner in which people in every age had rejected the prophets—even Moses himself—and ending in a furious outcry:

> Acts 7:51. *Ye stiffnecked and uncircumcised in heart and ears, ye do always resist the Holy Ghost; as your fathers did, so do ye.*
>
> Acts 7:52. *Which of the prophets have not your fathers persecuted?* . . .

Such a defense could scarcely win over his audience and, to top that off, Stephen then committed that which seemed clear blasphemy in the view of his audience. He virtually repeated Jesus' statement under similar conditions. Jesus had said:

Matthew 26:64. . . . *Hereafter shall ye see the Son of man sitting on the right hand of power* . . .

referring to Daniel's statement which had been accepted as Messianic (see page I-610).

And Stephen said:

Acts 7:56. . . . *Behold, I see the heavens opened, and the Son of man standing on the right hand of God.*

Stephen was promptly condemned to death by stoning and the sentence was carried through.

This event may have taken place in A.D. 31, two years after the crucifixion, and Stephen ranks as the first Christian martyr. The first man recorded as dying for the new faith, which held Jesus to be the Messiah predicted by the Old Testament prophets, was of the Grecian party. The pendulum was beginning its swing.

Philip

Stephen's death was followed by vigorous action against the Christians in Jerusalem. Many were forced to leave, for safety's sake. Included among these was Philip, the second of the seven leaders of the Grecian party. (He is the only one besides Stephen of whom the Bible has anything more to say than an inclusion in the list of the seven.)

The Philip mentioned here is the second of the two prominent Philips of the New Testament. The first is Philip the apostle, a Galilean and therefore of the Hebrew party. He is mentioned in all four lists of the apostles, including the one in the first chapter of Acts. Except for these listings, he does not appear in the synoptic gospels or in Acts, but is involved in several incidences in the gospel according to St. John.

The second Philip, the one who figures in Acts, is called Philip the evangelist because he preached the gospel outside Judea and won converts. Thus, in the immediate aftermath of Stephen's stoning:

Palestine: The Time of Christ

Acts 8:5. . . . *Philip went down to the city of Samaria, and preached Christ unto them.*

If this verse refers to the city of Samaria that had been the capital of the Northern Kingdom of Israel eight centuries before, that city no longer existed as such. It had been destroyed by the Assyrians and had dragged on thereafter as a small and squalid village until it was finally rebuilt by Herod the Great. He gave it the name of "Sebaste," a Greek word meaning "revered" and taken as the equivalent of the Latin "Augusta," so that that city was named in honor of the emperor, Augustus.

Actually, though, it is not likely that Philip went to Sebaste. The Revised Standard Version translates the verse "Philip went down to a city of Samaria"; some unnamed Samaritan city, in other words.

Apparently, the followers of Jesus had by now been made to feel such heretics by the Jewish authorities, that they found a certain kinship with those other heretics, the Samaritans. The situation is no longer what it was in Jesus' lifetime (as depicted in the gospels) when any approach to the Samaritans on the part of Jesus was a matter for surprise and even disapproval on the part of his disciples.

Now, when Philip began to garner conversions, Peter and John went to Samaria, without apparent hesitation, to complete the conversions and make them official:

Acts 8:17. *Then laid they* [Peter and John] *their hands on them* [the Samaritan converts], *and they received the Holy Ghost.*

In this way, the Samaritans were accepted as Christians in the fullest sense, on a plane of complete equality with Christians of orthodox Jewish origin. This was an important step in the growth of Christianity out of its Jewish swaddling clothes.

Simon Magus

At the time of Philip's arrival, the Samaritans were already impressed with another leader:

Acts 8:9. *But there was a certain man, called Simon, which beforetime in the same city used sorcery, and bewitched the people of Samaria, giving out that himself was some great one.*

Because of this verse, this man is usually identified as Simon the Sorcerer, or Simon Magus (to distinguish him from Simon Peter). We might suppose that he was some healer, preaching much as the apostles did. Such activities are always called divinely inspired by friends, and sorcery by foes. (The Pharisees accused Jesus of sorcery and if their views had won out, he might conceivably have gone down in history as Jesus Magus.)

Simon Magus was himself converted to Christianity by Philip and underwent baptism. When Peter and John arrived as the accepted authorities, by virtue of their rank as apostles, to make such conversion official, Simon attempted to gain equal rights and privileges. Perhaps he felt that as apostolic representative in Samaria, with full powers, he could continue his older activities under a new name and retain whatever worldly power and prestige that had given him. He offered, therefore, to buy the right:

> Acts 8:18. . . . *he* [Simon] *offered them* [Peter and John] *money,*
> Acts 8:19. *Saying, Give me also this power, that on whomsoever I lay hands, he may receive the Holy Ghost.*

It was not after all an uncommon practice to buy religious office. The high priesthood in Jerusalem was bought and sold in Seleucid times (see page 98) and in the times of the Romans; and the practice was undoubtedly common in all religions.

But Simon is roundly rebuked on this occasion by Peter. Nevertheless, the practice of buying religious office has not been unknown in the history of Christianity, and a special name has been given this practice —"simony," from Simon Magus, because of this passage.

The Bible says nothing more about Simon Magus, but he figures largely in the tales transmitted by the early Christian writers. He is supposed to have fallen out of the mainstream of Christianity, to have founded Christian Gnosticism (see page 301), to have continued to use magic and to have opposed Peter and Paul, in later years, by his sorcerers' tricks, with consequences fatal to himself.

The Simonians, a heretical sect that endured for some two centuries, are traced back to Simon Magus. We have only the writings of the early Christians as testimonials to Simonian beliefs and, as can easily be imagined, those testimonials are unfavorable indeed.

Candace

Feeling himself to have completed his task in Samaria, Philip traveled southward to Gaza, which had once been one of the five chief cities of the Philistines in the time of David. There he met a stranger from a far land:

> Acts 8:27. . . . *a man of Ethiopia, an eunuch of great authority under Candace queen of the Ethiopians, who had the charge of all her treasure, and had come to Jerusalem for to worship* . . .

Ethiopia was the name given by the Greeks to the land along the Nile immediately south of Egypt, beyond the river's first cataract. That name is applied nowadays to Abyssinia, which is actually some five hundred miles southeast of the ancient Ethiopia. The region known as Ethiopia to the ancients makes up the northernmost portion of the modern nation of Sudan and might best be termed Nubia.

Philip met, in other words, a Nubian, from the land south of Egypt.

Nubia's earliest history is that of an appendage of Egypt. The Egyptians traded with Nubia and under the strong Egyptian pharaohs, Nubia was conquered and occupied for centuries at a time. Nubia, under pharaonic domination, accepted Egyptian culture and religion but never quite gave up its memory of political independence.

After the disastrous invasions of the Peoples of the Sea (see page I-131), which occurred at the time of the Exodus, Egypt's power shrank permanently, and Nubia broke free. It formed an independent kingdom (still Egyptian in culture and religion) with its capital at Napata, a city on the Nile River about four hundred miles upstream from Egypt's southern boundary.

About 750 B.C. (toward the end of Uzziah's reign in Judah), Nubia came under the rule of a chieftain named Kashta. Under him, Nubia reached the peak of its power and this came just as Egypt was sinking toward a low point. Kashta conquered southern Egypt and established himself as a new pharaoh of what historians call the Twenty-fifth Dynasty. (This is sometimes known as the Ethiopian Dynasty, though Nubian Dynasty would be better.) Kashta's successor, Piankhi, conquered the rest of Egypt in 736 B.C.

This Nubian Dynasty played a significant role in Judean history.

When Sennacherib was laying siege to Jerusalem in 701 B.C., Egypt (in its own self-interest) raised an army against the Assyrian monarch. This army was under the leadership of Taharqa, a prince of the Nubian Dynasty, who, eleven years later, was to ascend the throne of Egypt. He is referred to in 2 Kings as Tirhaka (see page I-384). His campaign against Sennacherib could not be considered as better than a draw, but that was enough to induce the Assyrian (fighting at the end of a long line of communications) to withdraw and attend to pressing needs closer to home. The Nubian Dynasty, therefore, helped in a very material way to preserve Jerusalem.

Sennacherib's successor, Esarhaddon, did better. He reduced Judah to the role of a quiet tributary under Manasseh and then, by 661 B.C., drove the Nubian Dynasty out of Egypt. For twenty years Assyrian garrisons ruled Egypt. Egypt then regained its independence, but under native monarchs. The Nubians never returned.

To make sure that they would not, the native pharaohs of the Twenty-sixth Dynasty established the fort at Elephantine, manned by Jewish mercenaries (see page I-571). These guarded the Nile against incursions by Nubians from the south. Indeed, the Egyptians took the offensive and, about 590 B.C., sacked Napata itself.

From that point on, Nubia remained in isolation (except for a possible Persian raid in 522 B.C.) and slowly declined. Although Nubia continued to cling to the Egyptian religion, Judaism must have penetrated somewhat. Jews from Elephantine may have settled in Nubia or gained converts there. Some of these, whether Jews by birth or conversion, may have undertaken the long trip to Jerusalem to worship at the Temple, as the one true place of worship, just as Moslems today undertake the pilgrimage to Mecca as often as they can.

The eunuch met by Philip was, therefore, a Jew, though whether by birth and descent, or by conversion, the Bible does not say.

In Roman times, Nubia maintained its independence and was ruled by several energetic queens. The Nubian word for queen was rendered by the Greeks as Kandake and by the Romans and ourselves as Candace. This name was applied to all the queens of Nubia at this time.

The most important of these was one who, at the time that Augustus took over Egypt and made it a Roman province, dared invade Egypt. Perhaps she thought that the confusion of the Roman takeover would render Egypt easy pickings.

If so, she was wrong. A Roman army under Gaius Petronius marched southward and sacked Napata in 22 B.C. It would have been Roman policy in the days before Augustus to annex Nubia, but Augustus favored a policy of peace whenever possible. Nubia was evacuated and allowed to retain its independence. It did not attempt any futher adventures northward, however.

A successor of this Candace who had opposed the Romans (a successor also known as Candace) was the "queen of the Ethiopians" of Acts 8:27. She employed a Jewish eunuch as treasurer, and it was this Jewish treasurer of Nubia that Philip met.

The Nubian Jew was reading a passage from Isaiah when Philip met him. Philip interpreted the passage for him in a Messianic sense, applying it to Jesus. The Nubian forthwith asked to be converted and, presumably, carried the Christian message with him to his homeland.

It is interesting that in this case, Peter and John were not there to make the conversion official. The situation was beginning to slip out of the control of apostolic leadership and of the Hebrew party whose power centered in Jerusalem. It was to continue to do so.

Saul of Tarsus

But the greatest Grecian of all was at hand, one who far surpassed Stephen and Philip in his impact upon history. He was a man named Saul, and he began his career as a firm opponent of the followers of Jesus.

Saul was a member of the tribe of Benjamin and had his share of the Jewish stock of nationalist pride, as can be seen from his self-description in his Epistle to the Philippians:

Philippians 3:4. *Circumcised the eighth day, of the stock of Israel, of the tribe of Benjamin, an Hebrew of the Hebrews ...*

It is not surprising that, as a child of a staunch Benjamite family, he was given the name of the greatest Benjamite in history, King Saul. At least King Saul had been the greatest Benjamite till the coming of this new Saul.

Journeys of the Apostles

Yet although Saul describes himself as a "Hebrew of the Hebrews" (that is, not only a Jew but a Jew by birth—the son of Jews) he was not of the Hebrew group of the early Christians for he was not a native of Judea or Galilee. He was born instead in Asia Minor and was, therefore, of the Grecian group:

Acts 21:39. . . . *Paul* [Saul] *said, I am a man which am a Jew of Tarsus, a city in Cilicia, a citizen of no mean city . . .*

Tarsus was indeed the largest city in Cilicia. Its earliest history was probably as a Hittite town. Phoenician traders must have settled there in the great days of Hiram of Tyre (when David and Solomon ruled over Israel) and Greek traders must have arrived there, too. In later centuries, when Greek culture became fashionable, Tarsus always claimed to be a Greek city, but the Phoenician tinge remained strong down into Roman times.

About 850 B.C. Tarsus was captured by the expanding Assyrian Empire, and after Assyria's fall, it continued under the rule of first the Persian kings and then the Seleucids. It always retained considerable self-government, however, and in 171 B.C. it was granted virtual independence by Antiochus IV himself.

The next two centuries saw it at its height, prosperous, cultured, proud of its Greekness, and containing a group of philosophers and an important university as well. The Emperor Augustus, when he was but a teenager, studying on an island in the Aegean Sea, had as his teacher, Athenodorus, a philosopher of Tarsus. It was indeed "no mean city."

After the assassination of Julius Caesar, that general's former lieutenant, Mark Antony, was awarded the east as his sphere of influence and he took up residence in Tarsus.

It was while at Tarsus that Mark Antony called Cleopatra to a conference in order to extract money from wealthy Egypt. Cleopatra came to Tarsus in a ship fitted out to an extreme of luxury and herself deliberately decked out in such a fashion as to entrance the pleasure-loving Roman. She succeeded, and the second most notable event in the history of the city of Tarsus was this initial meeting of Mark Antony and Cleopatra in its harbor.

More important still was a happening that went completely unnoticed in its time. Since Tarsus was an important trading center, it gathered a colony of Jews which grew and prospered. In a particular year which is completely unknown but which we might venture to guess to have been A.D. 10, Saul of Tarsus was born there, and that was indeed the most notable event in the city's history.

Saul's family was apparently of considerable account. They were, for one thing, Roman citizens, and they may have been rich enough to purchase the citizenship. The citizenship was often awarded for some service rendered Rome, but it might also be sold—as has been the case, for instance, with knighthoods in English history. The Bible does not say which was true in the case of Saul's family, but whatever the situation, Saul himself inherited the status and was a citizen by birth.

Roman citizenship was worth having in New Testament times, for it carried not only prestige and status, but certain important privileges as well.

Thus, at one time, when Saul was on the point of being whipped, he took advantage of a Roman citizen's immunity to corporal punishment without trial. He said to the Roman soldier with the whip:

Acts 22:25. . . . *Is it lawful for you to scourge a man that is a Roman, and uncondemned?*

The centurion at once reported this to his captain, who promptly questioned the prisoner:

Acts 22:27. *Then the chief captain came, and said unto him* [Saul], *Tell me, art thou a Roman? He* [Saul] *said, Yea.*

The chief captain proudly announced that he too was a Roman, having paid through the nose for it, and Saul quietly topped him by announcing himself as a citizen by birth:

Acts 22:28. *And the chief captain answered, With a great sum obtained I this freedom. And Paul* [Saul] *said, But I was free born.*

Saul was promptly spared the whipping, saved by his citizenship.

Very little is known of Saul's relatives. He himself seems never to have married and so had no children. He did, however, have at least a sister and a nephew, for they are referred to:

Acts 23:16. . . . *when Paul's* [Saul's] *sister's son heard of their lying in wait, he . . . told Paul* [Saul].

The prosperity of Saul's family might well be further indicated by the fact that they could afford to send their son to Judea for a thorough religious training in Jerusalem itself.

As a result of this, Paul gained a good knowledge of Aramaic (unlike many of the Grecian faction); good enough so that he could not only understand Aramaic commentaries on the Scripture but could actually converse and preach in the language. This bilingual ability gained him considerably more influence with the native population of Judea than he might otherwise have had:

> Acts 21:40. . . . Paul [Saul] . . . beckoned with the hand unto the people. And where there was made a great silence, he spake unto them in the Hebrew tongue [Aramaic] . . .
>
> . . . .
>
> Acts 22:2. (And when they heard that he spake in the Hebrew tongue to them, they kept the more silence . . .

In Jerusalem, Saul attached himself to none other than Gamaliel, the leading Pharisee of the time and the one who had advocated toleration for the Christians (see page 342). Thus, Saul says:

> Acts 22:3. I am . . . a Jew, born in Tarsus . . . yet brought up in this city [Jerusalem] at the feet of Gamaliel, and taught according to the perfect manner of the law of the fathers . . .

And, of course, Saul became a Pharisee in consequence, as he himself admits, for in the same verse in which he describes himself as an Hebrew of the Hebrews, he adds that he is:

> Philippians 3:4. . . . as touching the law, a Pharisee.

In the course of his career, Saul did not scruple to gain the support of the Pharisees by declaring himself to be one of them in philosophy, as opposed to the Sadducee factions. Standing before the council, he shrewdly gained the support of the Pharisee group by saying:

> Acts 23:6. . . . Men and brethren, I am a Pharisee, the son of a Pharisee . . .

Perhaps his family's wealth was not quite sufficient to maintain Saul in idleness throughout his years as a student. He may well have had to, at least in part, "work his way through college" so to speak. If he did so, it was through labor at a craft. He was a working-man as well as a scholar. This craft is referred to when, in his travels, Saul is housed by certain members of the same craft:

Acts 18:3. . . . *because he was of the same craft, he abode with them, and wrought; for by their occupation they were tent-makers.*

This line of work may perhaps more properly be termed that of "weaver," for it is unlikely to have been so specialized as to be limited to tents alone, particularly since he practiced his calling in Greek towns, where there could scarcely have been much call for tents as such. The craft may even have been that of Paul's family generally, for Tarsus was famous for the weaving of cloth made from goat's hair, a cloth known as "cilicium" after the region in which Tarsus was located.

Saul, in his youth, was a thoroughgoing Pharisee and completely opposed to the views of those who believed Jesus to be the Messiah. Presumably, Saul attended the synagogue which was attended by "them of Cilicia and of Asia" (see page 344), for he was himself of Cilicia by birth. No doubt, he disputed with Stephen, and may even have been foremost among those who denounced him. Certainly he was a prominent member of the executing crowd.

The witnesses against Stephen had the duty of casting the first stones, according to the Mosaic Law:

Deuteronomy 17:7. *The hands of the witnesses shall be first upon him* [the condemned] *to put him to death . . .*

The witnesses, in taking care of this duty, discarded their outermost garments in order that their arms might be free to throw.

Acts 7:58. . . . *and the witnesses laid down their clothes at a young man's feet, whose name was Saul . . .*

. . . .

Acts 8:1. *And Saul was consenting unto his* [Stephen's] *death . . .*

This is the first mention of Saul in Acts and quite clearly he must have cast his share of the stones after the witnesses had cast the first.

What's more, Saul led those forces which then instituted a persecution of the Christians:

Acts 8:3. *As for Saul, he made havock of the church, entering into every house and haling men and women committed them to prison.*

In his later life, he refers on a number of occasions to this early period when he persecuted the sect of which he was afterward to be the greatest supporter. He says, for instance, in the Epistle to the Galatians:

Galatians 1:13. *For ye had heard . . . how that beyond measure I persecuted the church of God, and wasted it.*

Damascus

Saul was not content to carry on his zealous hounding of the Christians in Jerusalem, or even in Judea. Apparently the new sect was making its appearance among Jewish congregations in cities outside Judea. Saul wanted authority to travel to such cities and wipe out Christianity there:

Acts 9:1. *And Saul . . . went unto the high priest,*
Acts 9:2. *And desired of him letters to Damascus to the synagogues, that if he found any of this way* [Christians] *. . . he might bring them bound unto Jerusalem.*

In this way, Damascus re-enters the stream of Biblical history. In the time of the kingdoms it had been the capital of a nation that had been an important enemy of Israel, but after its destruction by Assyria in 732 B.C., its importance vanished. It came under the control, successively, of the Assyrians, Chaldeans, and Persians. After the time of Alexander the Great, it was held sometimes by the Ptolemies, sometimes by the Seleucids.

The Romans took it in 64 B.C., but in A.D. 31 they allowed it considerable autonomy under the control of the Arabian kinglet, Aretas —the same one who fought with Herod Antipas over the latter's divorce and remarriage (see page 152) and who now, in Saul's time, was approaching the end of a long, half century reign.

Near Damascus, however, Saul underwent an unusual experience:

Acts 9:3. *. . . as he* [Saul] *. . . came near Damascus . . . there shined round about him a light from heaven:*
Acts 9:4. *And he fell to the earth, and heard a voice saying unto him, Saul, Saul, why persecutest thou me?*

Acts 9:5. *And he* [Saul] *said, Who art thou, Lord? And the Lord said, I am Jesus whom thou persecutest . . .*

Saul was blinded by the vision and had to be led into Damascus, where he remained blind for three days. His sight was then restored at the touch of a Christian disciple in Damascus.

As a result, Saul was converted to Christianity, becoming as fanatical an upholder of the belief as, earlier, he had been fanatical in opposing it. (This is by no means uncommon in conversions.) The year in which this conversion took place is not known; estimates range from A.D. 32 (the year after Stephen's death) to A.D. 36.

Saul at once began to preach Christian doctrine in Damascus, to the surprise of all who knew of his reputation as an anti-Christian fanatic. His successes were apparently great; great enough to cause those Jews who remained unconverted to believe Saul deserved death for blasphemy.

Acts 9:23. *And after that many days were fulfilled, the Jews took counsel to kill him . . .*

Acts does not say how long Saul remained in Damascus beyond the vague "many days." In the Epistle to the Galatians, however, Saul says of this period:

Galatians 1:17. *. . . I went into Arabia, and returned again unto Damascus.*

Galatians 1:18. *Then after three years I went up to Jerusalem . . .*

So we may take it that for three years, Saul pondered the new doctrine (spending some time in quiet introspection in the semidesert region east of Damascus—referred to here as "Arabia"). Gradually he developed his own approach.

Perhaps he might have remained longer in Damascus and its environs, were it not that danger was growing acute. Saul eventually had to go into hiding in order that the indignant Jews of Damascus might not arrest him and place him on trial. In fact, it grew necessary to get him out of the city altogether and this was a rather difficult task.

Acts 9:24. *. . . they* [Saul's enemies] *watched the gates day and night to kill him.*

Acts 9:25. *Then the disciples took him by night, and let him down by the wall in a basket.*

The matter must have been more, however, than a purely doctrinal dispute between Jews and Christians. Damascus may have had a strong contingent of Jews but it was largely a Gentile city and it was under Gentile rule. The Jews could not, of their own authority, have guarded the gates. Apparently Paul's activities also disturbed King Aretas, and it was his soldiers who searched for Saul.

Saul himself, in describing this episode, says:

> 2 Corinthians 11:32. *In Damascus the governor under Aretas the king kept the city of the Damascenes with a garrison, desirous to apprehend me:*
> 2 Corinthians 11:33. *And through a window in a basket was I let down by the wall and escaped his hands.*

Barnabas

Saul returned to Jerusalem now and tried to join the Christian community there. He failed at first, since the disciples were very naturally suspicious of the erstwhile persecutor. Saul needed a sponsor and found one:

> Acts 9:27. *But Barnabas took him* [Saul] *and brought him to the apostles and declared unto them how he* [Saul] *had seen the Lord . . .*

Barnabas was mentioned earlier in Acts in connection with the communism of the early Christian fellowship. In contradistinction to Ananias, who tried to gain the credit of a total contributor to the welfare fund, while secretly holding back some, Barnabas gave all:

> Acts 4:36. *And Joses* [Joseph], *who by the apostles was surnamed Barnabas, (which is, being interpreted, The son of consolation,) a Levite, and of the country of Cyprus,*
> Acts 4:37. *Having land, sold it, and brought the money, and laid it at the apostles' feet.*

It was perhaps this act that caused him to receive the surname of Barnabas, since in those infant days of the community, both the money itself and the appreciation of the feeling of confidence that lay behind the award, must have been consolation indeed.

Barnabas was another of the Grecian group, having been born on the island of Cyprus. He may well have felt a strong feeling of kinship to Saul, for their birthplaces were not very far apart. Cyprus is just off the Cilician seacoast, and the northeastern tip of the island is only about a hundred miles south of Tarsus.

James the Lord's Brother

Acts says little about what Saul did, specifically, after being introduced to the apostles, but Saul himself in his Epistle to the Galatians says:

> Galatians 1:18. . . . *I went up to Jerusalem to see Peter, and abode with him fifteen days.*
> Galatians 1:19. *But other of the apostles saw I none, save James the Lord's brother.*

Paul, in other words, saw the two leading Christians. Peter, as the chief of the original band of twelve apostles, might be considered the nearest worldly representative of the memory of Jesus. It was James "the Lord's brother," however, who seems to have been the actual administrative head of the Jerusalem branch of the fellowship—of the "Mother Church," so to speak.

James was not one of the original apostles. Indeed, on the testimony of the fourth gospel, he was a doubter during Jesus' ministry:

> John 7:5. *For neither did his [Jesus'] brethren believe in him.*

Nevertheless, he apparently came to be a believer by the time of the crucifixion or immediately afterward, for the gathering of the early disciples before the great day of Pentecost included:

> Acts 1:14. . . . *the women, and Mary the mother of Jesus, and . . . his [Jesus'] brethren.*

James's conversion to belief may have come about through a sight of the resurrected Jesus. At least Paul, in his First Epistle to the Corinthians lists him among the witnesses to the resurrection:

> 1 Corinthians 15:5. *And . . . he was seen of Cephas [Peter], then of the twelve:*
> . . . .
> 1 Corinthians 15:7. *After that, he was seen of James; then of all the apostles.*

Presumably, the James mentioned here might be James son of Zebedee or James son of Alphaeus, each one a member of the original band of twelve. However, it is generally accepted that when Acts refers to James, without qualification, they mean Jesus' younger brother. (Again, it should be pointed out that those Christians who accept the belief that Mary, the mother of Jesus, was a perpetual virgin, consider James to be Jesus' cousin or half brother, rather than his brother.)

From Peter and James, Saul, it may be assumed, gathered many details concerning Jesus' ministry and person.

There is always dispute as to whether Saul ever actually saw Jesus in the latter's lifetime. It is not known when Saul arrived in Jerusalem for his education. If he arrived three or four years before his appearance at the stoning of Stephen, as is not at all unlikely, then he would have been in Jerusalem in the hectic week preceding the crucifixion. If he did, it would be almost certain that he would have been among the crowds listening to Jesus' words (and Saul, it might reasonably be assumed, would have been loud in his angry denunciations of Jesus).

And yet even if Saul had been in Jerusalem at that time, and had been among the crowds around Jesus, he might always have been far back and unable to catch a real glimpse. Certainly, if he had met Jesus face to face in the course of the latter's ministry, Saul would have said so in one of his epistles, and he does not.

Most commentators conclude that Saul never actually met Jesus in the flesh, and, if so, the meeting with Peter and James must have been particularly important to Saul. We can well imagine him asking eagerly after the personal memories of these two close associates of the Jesus whom Saul now accepted as the Messiah.

In Jerusalem, Saul continued to preach Christian doctrine ardently and was soon in danger again. The anti-Christian elements must have been particularly resentful over the loss of so valued a member and have chafed at the Christian victory in gaining so notable a defector. Again it was felt that Saul could gain safety only in flight:

> Acts 9:30. . . . . *the brethren . . . brought him* [Saul] *down to Caesarea, and sent him forth to Tarsus.*

This may have been anywhere from A.D. 34 to 38, depending on when it was that Saul's conversion occurred. Saul remained in Tarsus a lengthy time but exactly how lengthy a time can only be deduced from fragmentary evidence. The best guess seems to be from eight to ten years.

Nothing is known concerning this period except that Saul presumably carried on his preaching in Cilicia. He himself says merely:

Galatians 1:21. *Afterwards I came into the regions of Syria and Cilicia;*

Galatians 1:22. *And was unknown by face unto the churches of Judaea . . .*

Galatians 1:23. *But they had heard only, That he which persecuted us in times past now preacheth the faith . . .*

Lydda

The general persecution of the followers of Jesus that had been set off after the stoning of Stephen had by now eased up, and apparently there were groups of Christians in Galilee, as well as in Samaria and Judea:

Acts 9:31. *Then had the churches rest throughout all Judaea and Galilee and Samaria . . .*

Peter, as the spiritual leader of the Christians, felt it safe now to travel through the area, visiting the various groups:

Acts 9:32. . . . *as Peter passed throughout all quarters, he came down also to . . . Lydda.*

Lydda is the Greek form of the Hebrew, Lod, and is a town mentioned only a few times, and then inconsequentially, in the Old Testament. It is on the main road from Jerusalem to the seaport of Joppa, about twenty-two miles from the former and only ten miles from the latter.

Although Lydda was only an unimportant village in Old Testament times, and was to become an unimportant village again after the Jewish rebellion, it was passing through a brief period of consequence in New Testament times. It was large and prosperous and was a respected seat of learning.

Perhaps Lydda's most important claim to fame (aside from this mention in Acts) is that it was the home of a legendary Christian hero who slew a dragon and saved a young lady whom the dragon was about to eat, some time during the period of the Roman Empire. (Oddly enough, this is very like the Greek tale of Perseus and Andromeda—see page I-414—which was supposed to have taken place at Joppa. Could the Christian legend have been borrowed from the Greek?) In any case, the dragon-slaying hero is the St. George who is now considered the patron saint of England.

Lydda exists today as a sizable town of twenty-one thousand in modern Israel.

Cornelius

The most significant event in Peter's journey took place at Caesarea. This was Judea's chief port, about thirty miles north of Joppa. There the Roman power was chiefly concentrated, and there the procurators generally held their seat.

> Acts 10:1. *There was a certain man in Caesarea called Cornelius, a centurion . . .*
> Acts 10:2. *A devout man, and one that feared God . . . gave much alms . . . and prayed to God alway.*

Apparently, although Cornelius was strongly attracted to Jewish doctrine, he was not accepted fully into the Jewish fellowship because he had not yet undergone circumcision, the indispensable initiating rite to Judaism. That this is so is indicated by the fact that when Cornelius hears that Peter is in Joppa and sends for him, Peter hesitates about accepting the invitation. He says:

> Acts 10:28. *. . . Ye know how that it is an unlawful thing for a man that is a Jew to keep company, or come unto one of another nation . . .*

This does not include ordinary contact, of course, but does involve the matter of dining with a Gentile. The complex dietary laws of the Jews are not followed by the Gentiles and for a Jew to dine with a Gentile would cause him to eat food that was ritually unclean and this would be a grave infraction of the Mosaic Law.

Peter, we can well imagine, was torn between two courses. As a good Jew, he was horrified at the thought of eating with a Gentile. On the other hand, as a good Christian, it was quite apparent that a conversion was in the air and a conversion that was too good to turn down lightly. Cornelius is described in Acts as a pious man and he was a Roman soldier. For a Roman soldier to become Christian would be a great victory for the cause and as a centurion, an officer, he could doubtless influence other conversions. Did Peter have a right to toss away such an opportunity lightly—and perhaps even make an enemy of an important soldier in so doing?

The decision was in favor of the centurion despite his status as Gentile, and Acts explains that decision in terms of a vision seen by a Peter in which the Jewish division of food into ritually clean and unclean is abolished. Now Peter could freely eat with a Gentile. And Peter did more:

Acts 10:48. *And he* [Peter] *commanded them to be baptized in the name of the Lord* . . .

This was an important and even crucial step. Until this point, all Christians had taken the Mosaic Law as the basis of their faith. To them Jesus had appeared as the climax and fulfillment of that Law. In Matthew's version of the gospel, Jesus is quoted as saying:

Matthew 5:17. *Think not that I am come to destroy the law* . . . *I am not come to destroy, but to fulfil.*

Those who had accepted Christianity until now, had been Jews either by birth or by conversion, or Samaritans. The Samaritans might be heretics who did not believe in worshipping at Jerusalem but they did accept the Mosaic Law. Even the Nubian eunuch baptized by Philip accepted the Mosaic Law, since he worshipped at the Temple at Jerusalem and no one could do so without being circumcised.

Here, though, Peter had eaten with a heathen who, however devout and well disposed toward Judaism and Christianity, was not circumcised. Furthermore, Peter had allowed a man to become a Christian without having first become a Jew—he had short-circuited the Mosaic Law, so to speak.

This did not sit well with the Christians of Jerusalem:

Acts 11:2. . . . *when Peter was come up to Jerusalem, they that were of the circumcision contended with him,*

Acts 11:3. *Saying, Thou wentest in to men uncircumcised, and didst eat with them.*

Peter explained his side of the matter and Acts makes it appear that this explanation won over the rest:

> Acts 11:18. *When they* [the dissatisfied disciples] *heard these things, they held their peace, and glorified God, saying, Then hath God also to the Gentiles granted repentance unto life.*

But this may not be a fair representation of events. The writer of Acts is Luke, a Gentile, and he presents a pro-Gentile view which would tend to minimize the role of the Hebrew group and soft-pedal their anti-Gentile prejudices. It may well be that Peter was not so easy a victor and that he was forced to back-track by the Hebrew group under James, the brother of Jesus. Thus, in the Epistle to the Galatians, Peter is criticized for weakness:

> Galatians 2:12. *For before that certain* [emissaries] *came from James, he* [Peter] *did eat with the Gentiles: but when they were come, he withdrew and separated himself, fearing them which were of the circumcision.*

Even if Peter backed down, it is scarcely likely that the conversion of Cornelius and his friends was revoked. Perhaps we might speculate that the conversion was allowed to stand provided that those converted submitted to circumcision and to other necessary ritual. And perhaps Peter promised to be more careful in the future. Certainly, no further conversions by Peter are mentioned.

Nevertheless, a Gentile had been converted and Christianity had made its first cautious step beyond the bounds of the Mosaic Law.

Antioch

What was difficult for Peter to do within Judea under the strict eyes of the Jerusalem community of Christians, was easier for those Christians who were far away. Those who had been scattered after the stoning of Stephen had been baptizing, as Philip had done, but sometimes in a carefully limited way:

> Acts 11:19. *Now they which were scattered abroad . . . travelled as far as Phenice* [Phoenicia] *and Cyprus and Antioch, preaching the word to none but unto the Jews only.*

Others, however, did more:

Acts 11:20. *And some of them were men of Cyprus and Cyrene, which, when they were come to Antioch, spake unto the Grecians . . .*

Acts 11:21. . . . *and a great number* [of the Grecians] *believed . . .*

Here the word "Grecians" in 11:20 is clearly intended to be opposed to the "Jews only" of the verse before, so that it can be taken that Greeks, or perhaps Greek-speaking Syrians, were being proselytized and were being converted directly to Christianity.

In Antioch, the church began to take on, for the first time, not only a Grecian, but a Gentile tinge. It is not surprising, then, that it was in Antioch that the followers of Jesus were first really noticed by the Gentiles and were first given a distinct Greek name:

Acts 11:26. . . . *And the disciples were called Christians first in Antioch.*

Antioch, the capital city of the Seleucid king, Antiochus IV, the great villain of the Maccabean revolt, thus became the first major center of Christianity outside Judea, and the birthplace of the word by which the world's dominant religion of today came ever after to be known. The name may have first been applied to the followers of Jesus as a derisive insult shouted out by unconverted Gentile opponents. If so, the call of derision came to be accepted by the disciples as a badge of honor. It is not the only time in history that an insult has been accepted by the insulted and made clean. The name of the modern sect of "Quakers" is an example of that phenomenon too. "Quaker" originated as a term of ridicule.

The developing church at Antioch quickly grew to be of crucial importance. Although Antioch was no longer the capital of a great independent kingdom, it remained a huge and wealthy city of some half million population. In New Testament times, it was the third largest city in the empire, with only Rome itself and Alexandria larger. The church in Antioch was bound to be more prosperous than the churches in Judea, for even Jerusalem, however important it might seem to Biblically minded Jews, was only a provincial town in comparison to a place like Antioch.

As a matter of fact, Antioch remained a great city throughout the

period of the Roman Empire, but it never recovered from an earthquake and a Persian sack in the sixth century A.D. Today it is part of
the modern nation of Turkey, bearing the still-recognizable name of
Antakya and with a population of nearly fifty thousand.

The leaders at Jerusalem, upon hearing reports of growing numbers
of conversions in Antioch, might well have felt uneasy. Were these
conversions, far from their own careful oversight, only of Gentiles who
agreed to be circumcised and uphold the Mosaic Law, or were they
not?

Then, too, we might imagine them wondering whether it was wise
to allow Antioch to go its way uncontrolled. A swelling Christian
community in a city fully three hundred miles north of Jerusalem
might develop traditions of its own and begin to represent a competing center. Internal quarrels between the Christians of different cities
would certainly be bad for Christians as a whole.

The leaders of the Jerusalem church therefore sent Barnabas as
their emissary to Antioch, to serve as a connecting link. Barnabas,
recognizing that the task was more than he could himself carry through,
remembered his old friend, whose fiery spirit, he felt sure, was equal
to any task:

> Acts 11:25. *Then departed Barnabas to Tarsus, for to seek Saul:*
> Acts 11:26. *And when he had found him, he brought him unto*
> *Antioch.*

In this way, Saul was restored to activity after his years of vegetation
in Tarsus.

Claudius Caesar

When, however, was it that Saul came to Antioch? Speculation with
regard to this question is tempting for at this point Acts refers to two
historical events that can be independently dated.

First, there was a famine in Judea:

> Acts 11:27. *And in these days* . . .
> Acts 11:28. . . . *there* . . . [was prophesied] *great dearth through-*
> *out all the world: which came to pass in the days of Claudius*
> *Caesar.*

Tiberius, Rome's second emperor, under whom Jesus had been crucified, died in A.D. 37, about eight years after the crucifixion and perhaps not more than a couple of years after Saul's conversion. Tiberius was followed by his grandnephew, who, under the name Caligula, became Rome's third emperor.

Caligula ruled for four years only, and for at least half this time was quite mad. He is not mentioned in the Bible, but from Josephus we know that in his lunatic desire to be worshipped as a God, he ordered that his statue be set up in the Temple at Jerusalem. The Jews refused vehemently and completely; undoubtedly if Caligula had insisted on erecting such a statue, there would have been a bloody rebellion. Undoubtedly Caligula would have insisted anyway, but before things could come to the final break, the emperor was assassinated in A.D. 41.

He was succeeded by his uncle, Claudius, a much gentler and saner man, though rather weak and not really a successful ruler. However, he did rule for thirteen years, from 41 to 54 A.D., so that merely to say that a famine occurred "in the days of Claudius Caesar" gives unsatisfactory leeway.

To be sure, no famine occurred at this time "throughout all the world" but allowance must be made for Jewish nationalism. The phrase was probably used to mean "throughout all Judea"—that is, throughout all the world that counted.

Josephus does speak of hard times in Judea in A.D. 46–48, but how close is that to the time of Saul's arrival in Antioch? The Biblical phrase "in those days" is not necessarily precise but can be used to signify a very rough contemporaneity. The famine certainly came after Saul's arrival in Antioch, for later he is one of those from Antioch who carries relief to Judea on the occasion of the famine.

The famine, however, may have come fully two or three years after Saul's coming to Antioch.

Herod Agrippa I

A second reference to something that can be used chronologically follows almost at once:

> Acts 12:1. *Now about that time Herod the king stretched forth his hands to vex certain of the church.*
> Acts 12:2. *And he killed James the brother of John with the sword.*

Dominions of Herod Agrippa I

This is not Herod Antipas, or any of the Herods of the gospels, but a new member of the family altogether, one not previously referred to in the Bible. It is Herod Agrippa.

He was born about 10 B.C. and was the son of Aristobulus, who was in turn the son of Herod the Great by his second wife, Mariamne the Maccabean. The little boy received his name in honor of Agrippa, the son-in-law of the Roman emperor, Augustus. Agrippa had died shortly before but he had been a favorite of both the emperor and the Roman people, and a close friend besides of Herod the Great. Through his grandmother, be it noted, Herod Agrippa was of Maccabean descent.

In 6 B.C. Herod Agrippa's father, Aristobulus, and his uncle, Alexander, were executed by Herod. They were the last two adult sprigs of the Maccabean line, and all that were left were three children. There was Herod Agrippa and a younger brother (who was eventually to be known as Herod of Chalcis) and also a sister, Herodias (who was later to be the death of John the Baptist).

In view of Herod the Great's pathologically suspicious nature, it was thought best to take the young Herod Agrippa to Rome. There, as an Eastern princeling, he was treated with every consideration. Indeed, he became quite a favorite with Antonia, sister-in-law of the Emperor Tiberius and mother of the future Emperor Claudius.

As a grown man, Herod Agrippa returned to his homeland, and there he found his sister the wife of Herod Antipas, tetrarch of Galilee. His sister obtained a lucrative position for him in the capital, but Herod Agrippa was a happy-go-lucky man who found that his expenses always outran his income. He soon became too expensive a luxury for his sister, quarreled with Herod Antipas, and had to leave for Rome again in A.D. 36.

In Rome he became friends with the young Caligula, heir to the throne. He became so friendly in fact that the old emperor, Tiberius (as suspicious as Herod the Great), suspected him of conniving to hasten Caligula's accession to the throne. Herod Agrippa was thrown into prison, but within six months Tiberius was dead anyway and Caligula at once liberated his friend.

Caligula made Herod Agrippa king of the realm that had been formerly held by his half uncle, Philip the Tetrarch (see page 136), who had died three years earlier in A.D. 34.

Herod Antipas, who still ruled in Galilee, was annoyed at this elevation of his scapegrace half nephew, and demanded the title of king for himself, too. Herod Agrippa's friendship for the new young emperor, however, was more than enough to counterbalance Antipas' maneuvering and the latter was relieved of his post in A.D. 39 after having ruled for thirty-three years. Galilee was added to Herod Agrippa's dominions and Antipas died soon after in banishment.

When Caligula was assassinated, Herod Agrippa found himself no worse off. His sponsorship by Antonia meant that he had known Claudius, the new emperor, for a long time. Furthermore, the bumbling Claudius found himself uncertain in his initial dealings with the Senate and the smooth and sophisticated Herod Agrippa helped him out. The grateful Claudius appointed Herod Agrippa as king of the entire realm that had once been ruled by Herod the Great. This was in A.D. 41.

For the last time, Judea bore the appearance, at least, of independence and greatness and, indeed, for a short time, the land stood at the peak of prosperity and was materially better off than ever it had been since the days of Solomon. It had no foreign enemies and the danger of war did not threaten. It could relax in profound peace under the benevolent shadow of the Roman Empire as ruled by a weak but well-intentioned emperor.

Herod Agrippa I felt it politic to try to ingratiate himself with his Jewish subjects. He had already gained popularity with them by trying to persuade the mad Caligula not to place the imperial statue in the Temple. Even for a good friend of Caligula that was a rash move and might have been the end of him if Caligula had lived. Caligula died and Herod Agrippa I was safe, but the Jews appreciated the risk he had taken.

Herod Agrippa I scrupulously adhered to all the tenets of Judaism, hoping to make the Jews forget his Idumean origins (for his Maccabean descent was through women while the Idumean descent was through men). This he apparently succeeded in doing for when, during a Passover feast, he wept that he was not a full Jew by birth, the spectators, weeping in sympathy, are supposed to have called out that he *was* a Jew, and their brother.

Clearly, it would be politically profitable for him to display his Jewish zealousness by cracking down on the Christian church which was offending the mainstream of Judaism more than ever by their admission of uncircumcised Gentiles. When James the son of Zebedee was executed, that was the first recorded death of one of the original twelve (barring that of Judas Iscariot).

Herod Agrippa I also imprisoned Peter, who, according to Acts, was miraculously liberated, and who then hastened to a friend's house:

Acts 12:12. . . . *he came to the house of Mary the mother of John, whose surname was Mark . . .*

It is this John Mark who, according to tradition, was the author of the earliest gospel, the second in order in the New Testament (see page 243).

The time in which this persecution took place can be set fairly closely, for Herod Agrippa I had only a short reign, dying suddenly in A.D. 44, in the course of games at Caesarea being held in honor of Claudius. That the Herod referred to in this chapter is indeed Herod Agrippa I is shown by the description (in miraculous terms) of that sudden death:

Acts 12:21. . . . *Herod, arrayed in royal apparel, sat upon his throne . . .*

. . . .

Acts 12:23. And . . . *the angel of the Lord smote him . . . and he . . . gave up the ghost.*

His death was an unparalleled disaster for the Jews. Had he lived another twenty years, as he might have done, his shrewd ability to placate both Jews and Romans might have kept the peace between them and might have established a stable dynasty that would have lasted far beyond his time. The Jewish rebellion might, just possibly, not have come to pass.

As it was, he died leaving a teen-age son, whom Claudius would not trust on the difficult throne of Judea. The land passed under the rule of procurators once more—and under them, Judea chafed more and more until it erupted in the disastrous rebellion of A.D. 66.

For the Christians, on the other hand, Herod Agrippa's sudden death was just as unparalleled a blessing. Had he lived, his strong hand might slowly have beaten down Christianity within his dominions and his influence with the Roman government might have served to see to it that Christianity was suppressed outside Judea, too.

His death made that impossible and, furthermore, by removing the only possible man who could conceivably have prevented the Jewish rebellion, the permanent weakening of Judaism came to pass and on the ruins of Judea, Christianity was able to flourish, grow, and, eventually, conquer Rome and the Western world.

Since Herod Agrippa I reigned from A.D. 41 to 44, it follows that the death of James son of Zebedee took place during this interval, possibly in 43. Perhaps Saul's coming to Antioch also took place about then.

Cyprus

The fact that the daughter church at Antioch was outstripping the mother church at Jerusalem was clear by the time of Herod Agrippa I. The Jerusalem church, plagued by famine and by the heavy hand of

St. Paul's First and Second Journeys

the king, was impoverished, and the church at Antioch, wealthy and secure in comparison, sent relief:

Acts 11:29. . . . *the disciples* [at Antioch], *every man according to his ability, determined to send relief unto the brethren which dwelt in Judaea:*

Acts 11:30. *Which also they did, and sent it to the elders by the hands of Barnabas and Saul.*

The verse which tells of the return to Antioch of Barnabas and Saul, after their mission to Jerusalem, comes immediately after those relating the death of Herod Agrippa I. Perhaps the return to Antioch took place in A.D. 46, when the famine, according to Josephus, was first making its effects seriously felt.

Barnabas and Saul did not go back to Antioch alone:

Acts 12:25. . . . *Barnabas and Saul returned from Jerusalem, . . . and took with them John, whose surname was Mark.*

John Mark was, apparently, a nephew of Barnabas, for he is so referred to in the Epistle to the Colossians:

Colossians 4:10. *Aristarchus my fellowprisoner saluteth you, and Marcus, sister's son to Barnabas . . .*

The vigor of the Antioch church is also indicated by its readiness to engage in missionary activities. Immediately upon the return of Barnabas and Saul, perhaps before A.D. 46 was over, the two were sent across the sea, with John Mark as their assistant.

Acts 13:4. So *they* [Barnabas and Saul] . . . *departed unto Seleucia; and from thence they sailed to Cyprus.*

Acts 13:5. *And when they were at Salamis, they preached the word of God in the synagogues of the Jews: and they had also John to their minister.*

Thus, Saul set forth on what was to be his first missionary voyage. It began in Seleucia, a western suburb of Antioch. Seleucia was on the Mediterranean coast and served as Antioch's seaport. It had been founded in 300 B.C. by Seleucus I (who had also founded Antioch) and it had been named in honor of himself.

Cyprus may have been one of the sites from which the Philistines launched their invasions of Egypt and the Canaanite coast at the time of the Exodus (see page I-201), but it had played no further part in pre-Exilic Jewish history.

Cyprus was early colonized both by Phoenicians and Greeks, though it was politically dominated first by Assyria and then by Persia. After the death of Alexander the Great, Cyprus moved into the orbit of the Ptolemies and remained under rulers of that line for two and a half centuries. It was in this time, undoubtedly, that Jews entered Cyprus in sizable numbers, under the protection of the tolerant Ptolemies. In 58 B.C., Cyprus was annexed by Rome.

Salamis, on the eastern shore of the island, was its chief city in ancient times. It was Greek, and was reputedly settled by colonists from the small Greek island of Salamis near Athens (the Salamis that is famous as the site of the battle at which the Greek fleet defeated the Persians under Xerxes). This tradition may be the result of nothing more than the coincidence of names, however.

Salamis had an important Jewish colony and it was reasonable that the church at Antioch send a mission there. The city was not very far off, only 130 miles by sea. Furthermore, Barnabas was himself a Cypriote Jew and, very possibly, although the Bible does not say so, a native of Salamis. He was, in a sense, returning home. (His reputed tomb is located near the site of that city and also there is the "monastery of St. Barnabas.")

Paphos

Barnabas and Saul then traveled the full width of Cyprus:

Acts 13:6. . . . *they had gone through the isle unto Paphos* . . .

Paphos was best known in ancient times as the site of religious fertility rites in connection with a goddess whom the Greeks identified with Aphrodite (who was therefore sometimes called the "Paphian goddess").

It was second only to Salamis in size among the Cypriote cities. In 15 B.C. it had been virtually destroyed by an earthquake but it had been rebuilt by Augustus and had recovered to the point of serving as the seat of the Roman proconsul, Sergius Paulus, at the time of the missionary voyage of Barnabas and Saul.

Paul

Sergius Paulus, the proconsul, was, apparently, interested in Judaism. He was, perhaps, being instructed in that faith by a Jew attached to his court; a Jew who is described in Acts with a natural lack of sympathy:

> Acts 13:6. . . . *they* [Barnabas and Saul] *found* [in Paphos] *a certain sorceror, a false prophet, a Jew, whose name was Barjesus:*
> Acts 13:8. . . . *the sorcerer . . . withstood them* [Barnabas and Paulus . . .

Sergius Paulus was curious to meet these new men, concerning whom he must have heard reports to the effect that they were preaching a novel and interesting variety of Judaism. Bar-jesus attempted to dissuade the proconsul from this step, since Barnabas and Saul must have seemed, in his eyes, dangerous heretics, and individuals who would compete with him for favor in the eyes of the Roman official.

There may even have been a dispute between them with Sergius Paulus as an interested onlooker and audience:

> Acts 13:8. . . . *the sorcerer . . . withstood them* [Barnabas and Saul], *seeking to turn away the deputy from the faith.*

Saul, however, denounced Bar-jesus and had him miraculously stricken with blindness, thus securing the conversion of the proconsul.

This act is an important turning point in Saul's life. Many Jews in New Testament times had Gentile names, either Greek or Roman. Among the apostles, for instance, there were Andrew and Philip, both excellent Greek names. The seven Grecian leaders (see page 344) all had Greek names; the name "Stephen" means "crown." Sometimes an individual had both a Jewish name and a Gentile name in addition, the latter for use in official dealings with Gentile representatives of the government perhaps. Thus, we have John [Hebrew] Mark [Roman].

The case was the same with Saul, who apparently had a second name for use with Gentiles—Paulus or, in English, Paul. At the time of the confrontation with Bar-jesus, the author of Acts makes the transition from one to the other:

> Acts 13:9. *Then Saul, (who also is called Paul,)* . . . *set his eyes on him* [Bar-jesus] . . .

Up to this point Saul/Paul was called nothing but Saul; after this point he is called nothing but Paul, and it is as Saint Paul that he is known to us.

The transition would seem significant. It comes at a time when Paul (as we shall now call him) was engaged for the first time in converting a Gentile, and in so doing, was opposed by a Jew.

It may even be that Paul was faced with a crucial decision. Sergius Paulus may have been hesitating over conversion to Judaism because of his reluctance to undergo circumcision and undertake the duties and rites (strange to his own culture) of the Mosaic Law. If Paul could require of him faith in Jesus as the Messiah, without circumcision and the Mosaic Law, the conversion might be won.

It was certainly an important conversion since Sergius Paulus was the most important man on the whole island, and would have meant a triumph for Paul. Acts, which throughout tends to minimize the dispute among Christians over the manner of converting Gentiles, does not go into detail here, but the supposition that Sergius Paulus was converted without circumcision (and, what is more important, without the stipulation of later circumcision) is a reasonable one, in the light of later events.

The change from the Hebrew Saul to the Roman Paul may therefore be symbolic of Paul's shift away from the Mosaic Law and toward what we might call the Gentilization of Christianity.

Then, too, the change in name may have been influenced by the name of the proconsul. The Bible does not say that Paul was always the apostle's Roman name from birth, or even from youth. It is never referred to until this point. Could it have been adopted at this point, in honor of Sergius Paulus, or in honor of Paul's victory in securing the conversion of the proconsul? Perhaps so.

Another significance to the change in name may be that now Paul finally felt that he had left his origin behind him. The handicap of having once been a persecutor of Christians had been a heavy one, even after Paul had convinced the disciples of the sincerity of his conversion. When Barnabas had called him to Antioch, he had still had to take a back seat. When the five leaders of the Antioch church are named, Paul is named last:

> Acts 13:1. *Now there were in the church that was at Antioch certain prophets and teachers; as Barnabas, and Simeon . . . and Lucius of Cyrene, and Manaen . . . and Saul.*

(Some have wondered if this Lucius of Cyrene might not be the Luke who wrote the third gospel and Acts, see page 254.)

Again, Paul's activities in the church up to and including the start of this first missionary voyage were only under the sponsorship and continuing protection of Barnabas, as though without the presence of that dedicated Christian, Paul could not maintain himself against the memory in the mind of the fellowship of what he had done at the time of the stoning of Stephen.

Even Paul himself finds forgiveness hard:

> 1 Corinthians 15:9. *For I am the least of the apostles, that am not meet to be called an apostle, because I persecuted the church of God.*

Perhaps, then, Paul felt that the conversion of Sergius Paulus finally tipped the scales in his favor and his early sins had been made up for. The offending Saul could now be wiped away and the newborn and triumphant Christian, Paul, could be put in his place.

Pamphylia

Leaving Paphos, the missionaries crossed the sea again, and here a new change appears, following hard upon the change in name from Saul to Paul.

> Acts 13:13. *Now when Paul and his company loosed from Paphos . . .*

Until this point, whenever Paul and Barnabas had been mentioned together it had always been as "Barnabas and Saul." There is no question but that Barnabas was the older man, the leader, the sponsor, the more considerable.

Now, however, it is "Paul and his company." Paul emerges as the leader and everyone else falls back into subsidiary place. This continues throughout the rest of Acts. It is Paul, Paul, and Paul. When Paul's associates are mentioned they are little more than names that appear and disappear, the details of their comings and goings not being given, while all attention is paid to Paul.

How did this come about? How is it that just at the place of the name change and of the conversion of Sergius Paulus, the apostle became dominant?

We might argue that when Paul and Barnabas were put to the task of wresting Sergius Paulus from the grasp of the Jewish teacher, Bar-jesus, Barnabas flinched away from Paul's suggestion that circumcision be put aside. He fell back, uncertain, and it was Paul who then advanced to combat with Bar-jesus. In taking the initiative at this crucial point, Paul established his ascendancy over Barnabas, an ascendancy Barnabas could never retake.

That this may well be so would appear from Paul's statement in the Epistle to the Galatians. When he is scolding those Christians who clung to the Mosaic Law and who were reluctant to take the chance of eating and otherwise consorting with Gentiles, Paul says:

Galatians 2:13. . . . *Barnabas also was carried away with their dissimulation.*

Barnabas, like Peter, wanted to accept Gentiles, but could not quite bring himself to do so in the face of his early training and the disapproval of the conservatives under James.

Paul and his group reach the coast of Asia Minor:

Acts 13:13. . . . *they came to Perga in Pamphylia* . . .

Pamphylia is the section of the Asia Minor seacoast just to the northwest of Cyprus. To reach Perga, the chief city of Pamphylia, from Paphos in Cyprus, is about a two-hundred-mile sea journey. Pamphylia lay immediately to the west of Cilicia (Paul's home province) and was very like it in culture. In 25 B.C., Pamphylia had been annexed by Rome.

Apparently the quarrel between Paul and other members of the group intensified in the course of this voyage. At least we might assume so from the fact that one important member of the party left and returned home.

Acts 13:13. . . . *and John departing from them returned to Jerusalem.*

It may be that John Mark was simply homesick or ill. Acts gives no reason for the departure. Yet the separation seems to have been viewed with anger by Paul and was the occasion later for a quarrel between Paul and Barnabas, and that would indicate something serious.

It is easy to assume a doctrinal dispute. John Mark was of the Hebrew group of Christians, apparently. If he were indeed the author of the second gospel, we would have to assume that he was conservative with respect to the Mosaic Law, for Mark stresses Jesus' contempt for Samaritans and Gentiles and portrays him in the strict light of Judaism.

Pisidia

From Perga (the capital of Pamphylia, a town situated ten miles north of the coast), Paul traveled northward to a town where there was an important Jewish colony:

Acts 13:14. . . . *when they departed from Perga, they came to Antioch in Pisidia, and went into the synagogue on the sabbath day . . .*

Pisidia was the district just north of Pamphylia. Its chief city had been founded by Seleucus I, who named it Antioch after his father, just as he had named the other city he had founded in Syria. It was the latter which grew into a metropolis and came to be the Antioch meant when that name was used without qualification. The Pisidian capital must be identified as "Antioch in Pisidia." Like Pamphylia, Pisidia became Roman in 25 B.C.

Paul was invited to preach in the synagogue and he promptly told the audience the tale of Jesus, much as Stephen had done in Jerusalem a decade and a half before. Many of the congregation were impressed by the speech, sufficiently so to want to hear more the next Sabbath. The King James Version expresses this in, apparently, a mistranslated manner, for it says:

Acts 13:42. *And when the Jews were gone out of the synagogue, the Gentiles besought that these words might be preached to them the next sabbath.*

This makes it seem that the Gentiles were readier to accept Paul's message than the Jews were, but what would Gentiles be doing in the synagogue?

The Revised Standard Version makes no mention of Gentiles at all but translates the verse as follows: "As they [Paul and Barnabas] went out, the people begged that these things might be told them the next sabbath." The Jerusalem Bible translates it similarly as "As they [Paul and Barnabas] left they were asked to preach on the same theme the following sabbath."

It was not Gentiles that were attracted to Paul's teachings, but some of the congregation, some of the Jews. This is admitted by the King James Version in the very next verse:

> Acts 13:43. *Now when the congregation was broken up, many of the Jews and religious proselytes followed Paul and Barnabas* . . .

The Jewish leaders, however, apparently argued strenuously against the Messianic thesis of Paul, insisting that Jesus could not have represented the fulfillment of the Messianic dream. Their authority swung opinion away from Paul once more.

To Paul, this must have been extremely irritating. He had scored a great victory with the conversion of Sergius Paulus, a Gentile, and now he was experiencing nothing but frustration with the stubborn Jews— his fellow religionists—who, it must have seemed to him, should most naturally have turned to Jesus. Paul, therefore, lost his temper:

> Acts 13:46. *Then Paul and Barnabas waxed bold, and said, It was necessary that the word of God should first have been spoken to you: but seeing ye put it from you, and judge yourselves unworthy of everlasting life, lo, we turn to the Gentiles.*

It is this decision to turn to the Gentiles that caused the translators of the King James Version (perhaps) to drag in, most unjustifiably, the earlier approval of Gentiles of Paul's teachings.

Paul did not turn to the Gentiles exclusively. His ultimatum was for that city alone and in every new city that Paul entered, he always approached the Jews first. But always, when they rejected him, he turned to the Gentiles of that city. What had been perhaps an impulsive act, under the temptation of snagging a rich catch in Paphos, was now becoming a settled policy.

Paul justified this by pointing out a passage in the Second Isaiah, where the suffering servant is said to be intended for more than merely to restore Israel and Judah from exile. The ideal Messianic kingdom is to shed its glory over all the Earth, that Gentiles might admire and, perhaps, undergo conversion:

> Isaiah 49:6. . . . *I will also give thee for a light to the Gentiles, that thou mayest be my salvation unto the end of the earth.*

Apparently Paul was beginning to view himself as that light to the Gentiles of whom Second Isaiah had spoken.

Lycaonia

Despite the winning of converts, Jewish opposition was formidable enough to drive Paul and Barnabas out of Antioch in Pisidia. They headed southeastward some eighty miles:

> Acts 13:51. . . . *and came unto Iconium.*

Iconium was the chief city of the Asia Minor region called Lycaonia, which lay east of Pisidia and north of Cilicia and which, like the latter two, had become Roman in 25 B.C. Of the cities that Paul visited in the first missionary voyage, Iconium survived best. It is the eighth largest city of modern Turkey, under the recognizable name of Konya, and has a population of over 120,000.

Paul and Barnabas preached in Iconium, and the conversions they succeeded in making again roused the dangerous ire of the leading Jews. The missionaries moved again, southward this time:

> Acts 14:6. *They . . . fled unto Lystra and Derbe, cities of Lycaonia . . .*

These cities, fifty and thirty miles, respectively, south of Iconium, are important in history only because of the visits now paid them by Paul.

In Lystra, Paul heals a cripple and the missionaries are promptly hailed as gods by the pagan crowds:

> Acts 14:12. *And they called Barnabas, Jupiter; and Paul, Mercurius, because he was the chief speaker.*

It was common in later Greek myths to tell of trips to Earth by Zeus (Jupiter, in Latin) and Hermes (Mercurius, in Latin, which becomes Mercury in English). The best-known such tale in modern times is that of Philemon and Baucis, a poor old couple, who lived in Asia Minor. When Zeus and Hermes appeared in humble guise, the old couple offered them their bit of hospitality when their neighbors turned the gods away. As a result the neighbors were punished, but the poor hut of Philemon and Baucis was converted into a beautiful temple in which they served as priest and priestess, and they were further granted the boon of ending their life together and remaining united in death.

The tale was told by the Roman poet Ovid a generation earlier and must have been known throughout the Roman world and been of particular interest to those of Asia Minor.

The fact that Barnabas is considered Zeus and Paul Mercury, is often interpreted as meaning that Barnabas presented a distinguished appearance, while Paul did not. In fact, it is common to suppose that Paul was of small stature and unprepossessing appearance, and sickly, too.

Paul himself was given to stressing his own physical shortcomings, perhaps out of modesty, and perhaps as a shrewd, strategic device. Thus, in his Second Epistle to the Corinthians, he describes his opponents as saying:

> 2 Corinthians 10:10. . . . *his* [Paul's] *bodily presence is weak, and his speech contemptible.*

This may be Paul's Socratic irony, which, by deliberately making himself out to be clearly worse than he really is, produces a reaction which makes him seem better than he would otherwise appear. This must be true concerning his reference to his speech, since his speech had to be anything but contemptible, judging from the effects it had.

The very fact that he was called Hermes "because he was the chief speaker" shows this. Indeed, naming Paul Hermes may be taken to be in his favor rather than the reverse. In the visits of Zeus and Hermes to Earth, as told in Greek legends, Zeus, as the chief god, may have felt it beneath his dignity to do much more than look stately and benign, leaving the actual activity to Hermes. Presumably this now was the position with the missionaries. Barnabas, still titular head of the group, but worried about Paul's activities among the

Gentiles, may have withdrawn more and more into a grave silence, while his supposed subordinate, Paul, must have talked with ever-increasing assurance on every occasion.

To be sure, Paul occasionally speaks of some infirmity he has:

2 Corinthians 12:7. *And lest I should be exalted above measure . . . there was given to me a thorn in the flesh, the messenger of Satan to buffet me . . .*

What that "thorn in the flesh" might be is not explicitly stated. Paul seems to dislike talking about it and seems to feel that his listeners know all about it anyway and don't need to have it detailed to them.

It is supposed that it is some sort of recurrent illness, which periodically "buffeted" him, and incapacitated him from work. Thus, he says at one point:

1 Corinthians 2:3. *And I was with you in weakness, and in fear, and in much trembling.*

This may be a metaphorical way of saying he came into the Christian fellowship to preach, not in a vainglorious, self-confident way, but with diffident shyness, afraid to pit himself against those who must know so much more than he. If so, this, too, must be Socratic irony, for there is no trace of diffident shyness in any of the words or acts attributed to Paul, either before or after his conversion.

On the other hand, some interpret this as referring to a sickness, perhaps to the trembling fits induced by recurrent malaria.

It is also suggested by some that Paul suffered from epileptic fits. These would be periodic, of course, and since epilepsy was widely supposed to be caused by demonic possession, Satan could be regarded as buffeting him in the course of these seizures in all literal truth.

Lending this thought some support is Paul's remark in the course of a speech to the Jews of Jerusalem, describing his religious experiences. He said that at one point:

Acts 22:17. . . . *when I was come again to Jerusalem, even while I prayed in the temple, I was in a trance . . .*

Of course, there are many reasons besides epilepsy for trances, but if Paul is considered an epileptic, it becomes possible to argue that what happened near Damascus was a severe epileptic fit that involved a hallucination which Paul interpreted as representing Jesus. If so, epilepsy changed the course of the world in this case at least.

Yet all such arguments concerning Paul's physical appearance and the state of his health rest on very insecure foundations. If, instead, we go by Paul's endless energy, the travelings he endured, the tribulations he surmounted, we can only suppose that he was a man of phenomenal strength and health.

Thus, after Paul had, with difficulty, persuaded the pagans of Lystra not to worship himself and Barnabas as gods, Jews from Antioch in Pisidia and from Iconium roused the people against them and the situation changed at once. From gods they became blasphemers, and Paul was stoned and left for dead. To be stoned until one appears dead is to be battered indeed, yet Paul managed to struggle to his feet and the next day to leave Lystra with Barnabas and to travel to Derbe. No weak and sickly man could have managed that.

Attalia

Paul and Barnabas were now ready to return to Antioch, and from Derbe they might easily have traveled southeastward a hundred and twenty miles or so to the Cilician seacoast and there taken ship for Antioch. They might even have struck farther eastward and visited Paul's home at Tarsus.

Paul did not do this. In fact, he does not appear to have done much in Cilicia in the course of his missionary labors. Could he have completed the job as far as possible during his years in Tarsus before Barnabas called him to Antioch? Or (more likely) was he, like Jesus, a prophet without honor in his own country?

In any case, the missionaries chose, instead, to retrace their steps, visiting again the churches they had founded in the various cities they had visited:

Acts 14:25. *And when they had preached the word in Perga, they went down into Attalia:*

Acts 14:26. *And thence sailed to Antioch . . .*

Attalia was the seaport of Perga. It had been founded by Attalus II of Pergamum and named for its founder. Thus ended Paul's first missionary voyage.

Silas

Paul's report of his activities, particularly of his acceptance of Gentiles directly, without requiring them to undergo the full yoke of the Mosaic Law, was apparently accepted by the church at Antioch:

> Acts 14:27. . . . *they* [Paul and Barnabas] . . . *gathered the church* [at Antioch] *together,* [and] *they rehearsed all that God had done with them, and how he had opened the door of faith unto the Gentiles.*

There was, however, considerable disapproval of this when word reached the Christian elders in Jerusalem. The faction led by James considered the Mosaic Law essential:

> Acts 15:1. *And certain men which came down* [to Antioch] *from Judea . . . said, Except ye be circumcised after the manner of Moses, ye cannot be saved.*

Who these men might have been is not stated, but one of them could have been Peter. In the Epistle to the Galatians, Paul may be referring to this episode, when he said:

> Galatians 2:11. *But when Peter was come to Antioch, I withstood him to the face, because he was to be blamed.*

Paul taunted Peter with having been willing to eat with Gentiles, as in the case of Cornelius (see page 364), yet veering away under pressure from James and his group.

The dispute waxed hot and there seemed real danger of infant Christianity breaking up into two mutually hostile sections. It was decided, therefore, for representatives of the two wings to get together and thrash matters out and come to some general conclusions:

> Acts 15:2. . . . *they* [the Christian leaders at Antioch] *determined that Paul and Barnabas, and certain other of them, should go up to Jerusalem unto the apostles and elders about this question.*

There followed what is termed the Council of Jerusalem, which is supposed to have taken place in A.D. 48. It may be that James took up the extreme Mosaic position, Paul the extreme anti-Mosaic position, while Peter and Barnabas strove for compromise. Thus:

> Acts 15:5. *But there rose up certain of the sect of the Pharisees which believed [in Jesus], saying, That it was needful to circumcise them, and to command them to keep the law of Moses.*

Peter rose, however (perhaps with Paul's sarcastic words in Antioch ringing in his ears), to admit that in the case of Cornelius he himself had accepted an uncircumcised Gentile. He said:

> Acts 15:7. . . . *ye know how that a good while ago God made choice among us, that the Gentiles by my mouth should hear the word of the gospel, and believe.*

That pulled the rug out from under the Mosaic group. Paul recited the achievements of his first missionary voyage, probably describing his actions as following the tradition of Peter. James was forced to capitulate, giving his reason for doing so, too:

> Acts 15:13. . . . *James answered* . . .
> Acts 15:14. *Simeon hath declared how God at the first did visit the Gentiles* . . .

(James refers here to Peter by his full Aramaic name, Simeon, as though the writer of Acts was at pains to demonstrate James's Semitism even through the Greek in which he was writing.)

Nevertheless, James held out for a compromise by insisting on at least four ritual abstentions to which converting Gentiles must agree:

> Acts 15:20. . . . *they [must] abstain from pollutions of idols, and from fornication, and from things strangled, and from blood.*

But they were not to be required to undergo circumcision, or to adhere to the complex dietary laws (not even to abstain from pork, a cause for which martyrs in Maccabean times had willingly died under torture).

It was actually a stunning victory for Paul's view. It may have been on this occasion that Paul (and through him the church at Antioch) was granted equality with the leaders of the church at Jerusalem. Paul refers to such an occasion in the Epistle to the Galatians:

Galatians 2:9. . . . *James, Cephas* [Peter], *and John* . . . *gave to me and Barnabas the right hands of fellowship; that we should go unto the heathen, and they unto the circumcision.*

In this way, two wings of Christianity were indeed formed; a Mosaic wing under James and a Gentile and non-Mosaic wing under Paul. They were not, however, to be at enmity, but with a negotiated truce between them. When Paul and Barnabas returned to Antioch, men of the church at Jerusalem were selected to accompany them, almost as though they were to serve as ambassadors of one wing to the other:

Acts 15:22. *Then pleased it the apostles and elders . . . to send chosen men of their own company to Antioch with Paul and Barnabas; namely, Judas surnamed Barsabas, and Silas . . .*

Judas Barsabas is not mentioned elsewhere than in this chapter, but Silas plays an important later role for he accompanied Paul on later missionary voyages.

Silas, like Paul, may have been a Roman citizen. At least, when both later undergo flogging by the Roman authority, Paul speaks of their citizenship in the plural:

Acts 16:37. . . . *Paul said unto them, They have beaten us* [himself and Silas] *openly uncondemned, being Romans . . .*

If Silas were a Roman citizen, he too might be expected to have a Latin name, equivalent to the Paul of his companion. In Acts, Silas is never referred to by any other name, but in some of the epistles, there is reference to someone of similar name:

1 Thessalonians 1:1. *Paul, and Silvanus, and Timotheus, unto the church of the Thessalonians . . .*

It is usually accepted that Silvanus is the Latin name used by Silas.

Timothy

Some time after the Council of Jerusalem, Paul suggested to Barnabas that they revisit the churches they had founded in Cyprus and Asia Minor. Barnabas agreed and suggested they take John Mark again.

St. Paul's First and Second Journeys

Here, Paul disagreed violently, for he felt that John Mark had deserted them on the first journey:

> Acts 15:39. *And the contention was so sharp between them, that they* [Paul and Barnabas] *departed asunder one from the other . . .*

It may well have been that Paul strongly disapproved of John Mark's tendencies toward the Mosaic view, and may even have distrusted Barnabas' own stand in this matter. He felt the latter to be too ready to compromise with James's group (see page 388). Barnabas, on the other hand, could not so easily condemn his own nephew and may even have resented the fashion in which Paul had gained the upper hand.

In the end, the itinerary was split between Paul and Barnabas:

Acts 15:39. . . . *Barnabas took Mark, and sailed unto Cyprus;*
Acts 15:40. *And Paul chose Silas . . .*
Acts 15:41. *And he went through Syria and Cilicia . . .*

Each, in other words, visited his home territory. With this separation, Barnabas disappears from view and is not further mentioned.

When Paul and Silas reached Lystra in Lycaonia (for Paul merely passed through Cilicia and, presumably, Tarsus, and there is no mention of his preaching there) they picked up a new companion:

Acts 16:1. . . . *a certain disciple was there, named Timotheus, the son of a . . . Jewess [who] . . . believed; but his father was a Greek.*

Apparently Timotheus (Timothy, in English; a name meaning "honoring God") was a third-generation Christian after a fashion, for his mother and grandmother had both been converted in the course of Paul's first missionary visit to Lystra. In Paul's Second Epistle to Timothy, Paul speaks of:

2 Timothy 1:5. . . . *the unfeigned faith . . . which dwelt first in thy grandmother Lois, and thy mother Eunice . . .*

The shaky nature of the truce between Paul's wing of Christianity and that of James was here displayed. Paul wanted to take Timothy along with him on his trip but Timothy was uncircumcised and the Christians of Lystra knew it. Apparently, enough of them were of the Mosaic wing to force Paul into an action of expediency rather than conviction; especially if there were taken further into consideration the view of the unconverted Jews:

Acts 16:4. *Him [Timotheus] would Paul have to go forth with him; and took and circumcised him because of the Jews which were in those quarters . . .*

Phrygia and Galatia

Paul visited the churches he had founded:

Acts 16:6. . . . *they had gone throughout Phrygia and the region of Galatia . . .*

Phrygia and Galatia lay in the very center of Asia Minor, north of Pisidia and Lycaonia. Phrygia did not actually form a distinct political division in Paul's day. It derived its name from a people who had dominated Asia Minor over a thousand years before, at the time of the Trojan War and the Hebrew Exodus from Egypt. It was applied to a region that formed the eastern section of the kingdom of Pergamum during the time of the Seleucids. After 133 B.C., it formed the eastern part of the province of Asia.

Galatia was a comparatively recent formation. It gained its name from the Gauls who invaded Asia Minor about 278 B.C. By 235 B.C. they had been defeated and forced to settle down in peace in central Asia Minor in a region which came to be called Galatia after them. They were quickly hellenized. In 25 B.C., Galatia was made into a Roman province and, as a province, its boundaries were altered from time to time.

Because Galatia, at one time or another, included various districts of inner Asia Minor, the word came to be used in common speech to describe the interior of the peninsula generally.

Troas

Having visited the churches he had already established, Paul headed outward to new pastures. These, however, were not to border on the old ones, and he passed through western Asia Minor without preaching:

> Acts 16:6. . . . they . . . were forbidden of the Holy Ghost to preach the word in Asia,
> Acts 16:7. After they were come to Mysia, they assayed to go into Bithynia: but the Spirit suffered them not.
> Acts 16:8. And they passing by Mysia came down to Troas.

Paul decided not to preach in the cities of the province of Asia but passed through its northwestern section (Mysia) quickly. Nor did he turn aside to preach in Bithynia, a section of Asia Minor which lies to the northeast of Mysia and takes up much of the Black Sea coast of the peninsula. Bithynia, which is separate from the province of Asia, became Roman in 65 B.C.

Finally, Paul reached Troas, that part of Mysia which forms the

northwestern tip of Asia Minor. The name is given to a small peninsula, which bore its name because, twelve centuries before, the city of
Troy had existed there—the city destroyed by the Greeks after the
most famous siege in history.

Troas is a name applied also to a city founded in the vicinity of
the site of ancient Troy. By 300 B.C. it had come to be called
Alexandria Troas (in honor of Alexander the Great), or Troas in
brief. It is to this city rather than to the peninsula that the Biblical
mentions of Troas refer.

It would seem then that having left the churches he had founded,
Paul traveled westward in a great hurry (if we may judge by the manner
in which the journey is compressed into three verses). He must have
traveled with a firm purpose in mind, for he did not veer to either
the left or the right; that is, to preach in either Asia or Bithynia. He
moved, instead, straight into Troas and there found himself six hundred
miles west of Antioch.

Naturally, in the language of the times, this firm purpose driving
Paul onward would be ascribed to the working of the Holy Spirit
forbidding him to preach in either Asia or Bithynia. Some speculate
that this reference to the Spirit is a way of saying that Paul was in
poor health and unable to preach, but there seems no need to indulge
in this supposition. If he were strong enough to travel hundreds of
miles under the arduous conditions of the times, he would be strong
enough to preach. It is easier to suppose that Paul's firm decision, his
strong desire to do what he was planning to do, and nothing else, could
only be interpreted by others, and by himself, too, as the driving force
of the Holy Spirit.

But what was he planning to do? It is tempting to suppose that
when Paul was given official sanction at the Council of Jerusalem to
go to the Gentiles, it occurred to him that he ought to travel to the
very core and fount of Gentile-dom. Why not leave Asia Minor
altogether and penetrate into Europe. The port of Troas was what he
wanted, for from it there would be many ships to take him across the
Aegean and into Macedonia, or even into Greece itself.

Might it not even be that this was his main purpose from the
beginning of his second missionary voyage? That the suggested purpose
to revisit the churches of central Asia Minor was a blind to secure the
blessing of the Antioch community, which might otherwise have
flinched away from too bold a project. Could Paul have confided

these plans to Barnabas, and had Barnabas flinched, too, and was this the true cause of the quarrel between them?

Barnabas, according to this view, lacked the bold vision of Paul, contented himself with the narrow bounds of Cyprus and stepped off the stage of history. Paul went onward without Barnabas, and the future of Christianity went with him.

Macedonia

Once in Troas, Paul lost no time in moving into Europe; a move which the writer of Acts explains in appropriate Biblical terms:

> Acts 16:9. *And a vision appeared to Paul in the night; There stood a man of Macedonia, and prayed him, saying, Come over into Macedonia, and help us.*
>
> Acts 16:10. *And after he had seen the vision, immediately we endeavoured to go into Macedonia . . .*

Macedonia, which in the reign of Alexander the Great had conquered a vast empire, had since 146 B.C. been merely part of the Roman realm. For two centuries it had remained peacefully somnolent under Rome's vast shadow and virtually lacked a history. In the eyes of later generations (but not of contemporaries, of course) it was only Paul's coming that finally brought back Macedonia into significance with respect to the currents of world history.

In Acts 16:10 there is the sudden use of the pronoun "we"—"we endeavoured to go into Macedonia."

The usual conclusion is that Luke, the writer of Acts, is now part of Paul's party. We cannot say, however, how this came to be. The author of the book, with frustrating modesty, never says anything of himself. Was Luke a native of Troas who, like Timothy, was converted and then drawn into the entourage?

In view of the early traditions that he was a Syrian from Antioch, could he have been an emissary from the church at Antioch sent after Paul with messages, or, possibly, to bring back news? Did he overtake Paul in Troas and decide to accompany him?

There is no way of telling from the Biblical account.

Philippi

It was about A.D. 50 that Paul crossed over into Europe:

> Acts 16:11. . . . *loosing from Troas, we came with a straight course to Samothracia, and the next day to Neapolis;*
> Acts 16:12. *And from thence to Philippi* . . .

From Troas to the nearest important seaport of Macedonia was a 125-mile sea journey to the northwest. This was accomplished in two stages, with a stopover at Samothrace, a small island in the northern Aegean Sea (sixty-six square miles in area) which lay approximately midway from point of embarkation to point of destination.

The Macedonian seaport Neapolis ("New Town"), which lay on the northern coast of the Aegean Sea, served the town of Philippi, which lay ten miles inland and was one of the largest of the Macedonian cities. Originally, Philippi had been a Greek settlement called Crenides ("fountains"). In 356 B.C., however, it had been captured by Philip of Macedon and renamed Philippi in his own honor. Its importance to Philip lay in the fact that its possession secured him control of nearby gold mines and Philip used the gold liberally in the subversion of Greek politicians. It was as much Philip's gold as Philip's army that helped the Macedonian gain control of Greece.

Between the time of Philip's capture of the city and Paul's arrival there, only one incident served to bring it into the full glare of history. After the assassination of Julius Caesar, armies led by the assassins Brutus and Cassius faced other armies led by Mark Antony and Octavian. The battle was fought near Philippi in 42 B.C. It was drawn and uncertain at first, but Cassius, prematurely fearful of defeat, killed himself, and thereafter Antony and Octavian won a clear victory.

Through their victory at the battle of Philippi, Antony and Octavian were able to divide the Roman realm between themselves, and, a dozen years later, Octavian defeated Mark Antony, took over sole control, and became the Emperor Augustus.

Lydia

In Philippi, Paul made some conversions:

> Acts 16:14. And *a certain woman named Lydia, a seller of*
> *purple, of the city of Thyatira, which worshipped God, heard us* . . .
> Acts 16:15. And . . . *she was baptized* . . .

Lydia was not in use in ancient times as a feminine name and it
is suggested that the woman was not named Lydia, but that she was
from the region of Lydia and that the verse might better be translated: "And a certain Lydian woman . . ."

Lydia was the name of a kingdom ruling over the western half of
Asia Minor during the period when the Jews were in Babylonian
Exile. From 560 to 546 B.C. it was ruled by Croesus, whose wealth
has become proverbial. In 546 B.C. Croesus was defeated by Cyrus
(see page I-434) and Lydia became part of the Persian Empire. After
the death of Alexander the Great, the region was fought over by his
generals and finally had a rebirth in Greek form as the kingdom of
Pergamum. In 133 B.C., this became Rome's province of Asia, but the
name Lydia could still be applied to the west-central portion of the
province.

The capital of Lydia had been the city of Sardis in west-central
Asia Minor about fifty miles from the Aegean Sea. Thyatira was a
northwestern suburb founded by Seleucus I. It had a thriving trade
in the purple dye that had made the Phoenician city of Tyre famous.
(It was one of the very few dyes known to the ancient world that
would retain its bright color even under the effect of water and
sunlight and it was therefore a most valuable product. Nowadays, of
course, we have any number of synthetic dyes.) The Lydian woman
from Thyatira had brought her trade to a new market and was
probably quite well-to-do as a consequence, for she could afford to put
up Paul's party during their stay in Philippi.

Thus it came about that Paul, who came to Macedonia in search
of new fields for conversion, had as his first convert a woman of Asia
Minor after all.

Paul also found that Gentiles could be persecutors too, and that
it was not only the Jews who were his enemy. The pagans did not,

at that time, distinguish between Jews and Christians and they put into action a law that forbade Jewish proselytization among Greeks. Paul and Silas were brought before the magistrate and the accusation was:

Acts 16:20. . . . *These men, being Jews . . .*
Acts 16:21. . . . *teach customs, which are not lawful for us to receive, neither to observe, being Romans.*

Paul and Silas were flogged and imprisoned for a while and were released, according to the account in Acts, by a miraculous earthquake. Apologies were added when it was discovered they were Roman citizens and had been flogged without a proper trial. No doubt, the claim to citizenship, once verified, would have sufficed for freedom even without the earthquake.

Thessalonica

Paul's party left Philippi after that and traveled westward across Macedonia:

Acts 17:1. *Now when they had passed through Amphipolis and Apollonia, they came to Thessalonica, where was a synagogue of the Jews:*

Amphipolis is a city twenty-five miles southwest of Philippi, and had been founded as an Athenian colony in 436 B.C. when Athens was at the height of its Golden Age. It was captured by Sparta in 424 B.C. and was taken by Philip of Macedon in 357 B.C. In New Testament times it was the seat of the Roman governor of that section of Macedonia, even though it was not actually part of the province but was considered a free city.

Twenty miles farther southwest was Apollonia, a comparatively unimportant town, and forty miles due west of that was Thessalonica.

Thessalonica is located at the northwestern corner of the Aegean Sea. It was originally named Therma, from the Greek word meaning "hot" because of the hot springs in the vicinity. The inlet of the Aegean Sea, at the end of which it was located, was therefore called the Thermaic Gulf.

After the death of Alexander the Great, Cassander, the son of one of his generals, seized control of Macedonia. This was in 316 B.C. and he retained his power until his death twenty years later. He married a half sister of Alexander, a girl named Thessalonica, and in 315 B.C. he built a new city near Therma and named it Thessalonica in her honor.

Because of its advantageous position with respect to trade, Thessalonica grew rapidly and eventually became one of the most important cities in Macedonia. Through all historical vicissitudes, it has remained large and important. After the Turkish conquest of Greece in the fifteenth century, the first syllable dropped away and it became better known as Salonica.

Even today Salonica is a large city. It is, indeed, the second largest city of modern Greece, with a population of 250,000.

Thessalonica was the first Macedonian city in which Paul found a Jewish population large enough to maintain a synagogue. He gained some conversions but (as, very likely, he had anticipated) many more from among the Greeks than from among the Jews. The Jewish leaders, annoyed at this, rioted and claimed that Paul was preaching treason, proclaiming Jesus as a king in opposition to the Roman Emperor. (It was just this view of the matter which had led Pontius Pilate to condemn Jesus to crucifixion.) Paul and Silas found it prudent, therefore, to leave Thessalonica.

Berea

The next move was thirty miles to the westward:

> Acts 17:10. And the brethren immediately sent away Paul and Silas by night unto Berea . . .

In Paul's time, Berea was a large city, on a par with Thessalonica, or even larger. It has declined since but it exists in modern Greece, under the name Verroia, as a sizable town of twenty-five thousand.

It too contained a synagogue and the Jews there are recorded as having been more sympathetic to Paul than were those of Thessalonica. Nevertheless, the Thessalonian Jews sent deputations to Berea to rouse the Jews there to the dangers of this new heresy.

Silas and Timothy remained in Berea for a time, but Paul was sent away.

Athens

This time Paul traveled some two hundred miles southward to the greatest of all the Greek cities, in reputation and glory, if not in size:

Acts 17:15. . . . *they that conducted Paul brought him unto Athens . . .*

In the fifth century B.C., Athens had experienced a Golden Age in art, literature, and philosophy that in some ways has never been surpassed. It was one of a number of small Greek city-states, and Athens, even though one of the largest among them, was no bigger than the state of Rhode Island in area or population.

For a while Athens dominated Greece politically and militarily, but it was defeated in the long and disastrous Peloponnesian War with Sparta, which lasted from 431 to 404 B.C. A century later, Athens led the futile opposition to Philip of Macedon.

But Greek city-states were no longer matches for the larger monarchies that were growing up on all sides. Athens fell farther and farther behind, and although it was saved from destruction time and time again by the universal respect for its great past, it gradually lost all political importance.

For two centuries it retained its self-government and control over its own internal affairs, while under the domination of Macedonia. And after 146 B.C., when Rome established itself as completely dominant over Greece, it nevertheless continued as a free city.

Only once did it waver. In 88 B.C., Mithridates VI of Pontus (a kingdom in northeastern Asia Minor) dared fight against Rome. He won initial victories and swept up all the Roman possessions in the peninsula. Athens, discontented with Roman rule, and misjudging the situation, declared for Mithridates.

However, Rome sent Sulla, one of its competent generals, eastward, and a grim Roman army followed him. Athens tried to resist and withstood a siege but Mithridates did not come to its help and in 86 B.C. Sulla took the city and sacked it. Never again did Athens attempt any independent action of its own.

It settled down to complete submission to the Roman power for as long as that power existed. It remained with its dreams of the past as a quiet "college town" where Romans and Greeks came for an education in philosophy.

While Paul waited in this college town for Silas and Timothy to join him, he disputed with the Jews of the area and stared in horror and revulsion at the beautiful temples and great works of art by which he was surrounded, for all seemed to him but wicked objects given over to idolatry.

Epicureans and Stoics

The Athenian specialty was philosophy. The city had a tradition of absolutely free speech and it welcomed all sorts of views. Various philosophers, then, hearing of a stranger in their midst, one who possessed odd and novel views, sought to know more:

> Acts 17:18. *Then certain philosophers of the Epicureans, and of the Stoicks, encountered him . . .*

The Epicureans and Stoics were two of the important schools of philosophy current in Athens at the time.

The former was founded by Epicurus, who had been born on the Greek island of Samos in 341 B.C. He had established a school in Athens in 306 B.C. and it remained extremely successful until his death in 270 B.C. Epicurus adopted the beliefs of certain earlier Greek philosophers and viewed the universe as made up of tiny particles called atoms. All change, he maintained, consisted of the random breakup and rearrangement of groups of these atoms and there was little room in the Epicurean philosophy for any purposeful direction of man and the universe by gods. The philosophy was essentially atheistic, although the Epicureans were not fanatic about that; they would cheerfully go through rituals they considered meaningless in order to avoid giving unnecessary offense or creating useless trouble for themselves.

In a universe consisting of atoms in random movement, man could be conscious of two things: pleasure and pain. It stood to reason that man should behave in such a way as to enjoy a maximum of pleasure and a minimum of pain. It remained only to decide what was actually a maximum of pleasure. To Epicurus, it seemed that if a little of something gave pleasure, a lot of it did not necessarily give more pleasure. Starvation through undereating was painful, but indigestion through overeating was also painful. The maximum of pleasure came from eating in moderation, and so with other joys of life. Then, too, there were the pleasures of the mind; of learning; of improving discourse; of the emotions of friendship and affection. These pleasures, in the view of Epicurus, were more intensely pleasant and desirable than the ordinary pleasures of the body.

Not all those who followed the Epicurean philosophy were as wise and moderate as Epicurus himself. It was easy to place the pleasures of the body first and hard to set any limit to them. So the word "epicurean" has entered our language as meaning "given to luxury."

So popular did the Epicurean philosophy become in Seleucid times that to the Jews of the period all Greeks seemed Epicurean. Any Jew who abandoned his religion for Greek ways became an "Epicurean" and to this very day, the Jewish term for a Jewish apostate is "Apikoros," a quite recognizable distortion of the old term.

The second famous school of Greek philosophy was founded by Zeno, a Greek (with possibly some Phoenician blood) who was born on the island of Cyprus at about the time of Epicurus' birth.

Zeno, like Epicurus, founded a school in Athens and taught from a place where a porch or corridor was adorned with paintings of scenes from the Trojan War. It was called the "Stoa poikile" ("painted porch") and Zeno's teachings came therefore to be known as "Stoicism" and his followers "Stoics" (or "Stoicks" in the King James Version).

Stoicism recognized a supreme God and seemed to be on the road to a kind of monotheism. It also contended, however, that divine powers might descend upon all sorts of minor gods and even upon those human beings who were deified. In this way, stoics could adjust themselves to prevailing polytheistic practices.

Stoicism saw the necessity of avoiding pain but did not feel that choosing pleasure was necessarily the best way of avoiding pain. One could not always choose pleasure correctly and even if one did, that merely opened the way for a new kind of pain—the pain that arose when a pleasure once enjoyed was lost. Stoics believed in putting one's self beyond both pleasure and pain, by cultivating indifference and lofty detachment of mind, serving justice without emotion. If you desire nothing, you need fear the loss of nothing. All that counted lay within a person. If you are master of yourself, you can be the slave to no one. If you live a life that rigidly follows a stern moral code, you need not fear the agonized uncertainty of day-to-day decisions. To this day, the word "stoic" is used in English to mean "indifferent to pleasure and pain."

At its height, both Epicureanism and Stoicism could produce men of lofty moral fiber and admirable ethical behavior. This was particularly true of Stoicism. Thus, the most famous Stoic of all was the Roman Emperor Marcus Aurelius, who ruled a little over a century after Paul's time and who, although a pagan, had many of the qualities usually associated with a Christian saint.

Dionysius the Areopagite

Apparently Paul's words were sufficiently interesting, or curious, for the philosophers to bring him to a place where as many of the important people of the town could hear him as possible:

> Acts 17:19. And they took him, and brought him unto Areopagus, saying, May we know what this new doctrine . . . is?

The word "Areopagus" means "Hill of Ares" (or "Hill of Mars" in the Latin version) and was the place where the Athenians maintained their chief court. It had been the stronghold of the aristocrats in the days just prior to Athens' greatness, but as Athens grew more and more democratic in the course of its Golden Age, the Areopagus lost more and more of its power. Under Roman domination, the Areopagus regained some of its prestige and served as the instrument through which much of the city's internal affairs were conducted.

If Paul had confined himself merely to preaching matters of ethics and morality he would undoubtedly have received a sympathetic, if patronizing, hearing from the sophisticated and self-consciously superior Athenians. However, when he approached his great theme, the resurrection of Jesus (a theme that fills his epistles) the Athenians could not help but laugh:

> Acts 17:32. And when they heard of the resurrection of the dead, some mocked . . .
>
> . . . .
>
> Acts 17:34. Howbeit certain men clave unto him and believed: among the which was Dionysius the Areopagite . . .

Apparently Dionysius is mentioned because he was a member of Athens' ruling council and, therefore, the most prestigious of Paul's converts there.

This is the only mention of this convert in the Bible and yet later tradition built enormously upon this single verse. Possibly it was unavoidable Greek snobbery to find an Athenian convert particularly important just because he was an Athenian.

By the time a century had passed, the tradition arose that Dionysius the Areopagite had served as the first bishop of Athens.

In the sixth century A.D., the Frankish historian Gregory of Tours spoke of a bishop named Dionysius who had been sent to Gaul about A.D. 250. He became bishop of Paris, was martyred, and was eventually considered the patron saint of France under the French version of his name, Saint Denis. A century later, Gregory's reference was misinterpreted to read that Dionysius was sent to Gaul in A.D. 90 and he was thereupon identified with Dionysius the Areopagite.

And about A.D. 500 some writings appeared in Syria which were attributed to Dionysius the Areopagite. The forgery was patent and clear, for it referred to matters that must have taken place many years after Dionysius' death. The author (who will probably never be known) is referred to as the pseudo-Dionysius. Despite the clumsiness of the forgery, it was accepted as genuine by important church leaders in the east and had great influence over the doctrinal disputes of the day.

Corinth

Upon leaving Athens, Paul traveled some fifty miles westward:

Acts 18:1. *After these things Paul departed from Athens, and came to Corinth.*

Corinth is situated on the narrow peninsula connecting the Peloponnesus (the southernmost peninsula of Greece) with the remainder of the land. Because of this, it has access to the sea on the east and the west and was a great trading center. It was prosperous and wealthy in the days of Greek greatness but it was a trading rival of Athens and therefore fought on the Spartan side in the Peloponnesian War.

After 338 B.C., Corinth was dominated by a Macedonian garrison but it remained prosperous. Indeed, by the time Macedonia was defeated by Rome, and the latter power succeeded to the rule of Greece, Corinth was the most prosperous city on the Greek mainland.

In 149 B.C., however, Macedonia, taking advantage of Roman military preoccupation elsewhere, attempted a revolt. This was quickly crushed, but Roman tempers were short and it seemed to them that the Greek cities had encouraged Macedonia. Deliberately they decided to make an example and sent an army against the richest of them, Corinth.

The city, terrified, hastily surrendered, but that did no good. The Roman commander was out to teach the Greeks a lesson and he did. In 146 B.C. the city was pillaged, its men killed, and its women and children sold into slavery.

For exactly a century Corinth lay in devastated ruins until, in 46 B.C., Julius Caesar had it rebuilt. The new Corinth rose and was flourishing again in Paul's time. It served, indeed, as the capital of the Roman province of Achaea, which included Greece proper.

Corinth had other disasters to contend with in its later history, but it survives to this day as a town of sixteen thousand.

Aquila

In Corinth, Paul remained for a year and a half, and there he settled down to earn his living by means of his craft:

> Acts 18:2. And [Paul] *found a certain Jew named Aquila, born in Pontus, lately come from Italy, with his wife Priscilla; (because that Claudius had commanded all Jews to depart from Rome:) and came unto them.*

It is they who were the tentmakers, or weavers, referred to earlier in this chapter (see page 357).

Apparently Paul arrived in Corinth shortly after Claudius, in a fit of irritation at disorders involving Jews, ordered them all out of Rome. This order, which only held in effect a few years, took place in A.D. 49 and this offers another peg on which to hang the chronology of Paul's voyages.

Gallio

The Corinthian Jews objected strenuously to Paul's activities but, apparently, could do nothing against him under the government then in power. They saw their opportunity, however, when a new governor arrived to begin his term of office. The new governor, they hoped, would sympathize with their point of view.

Acts 18:12. *And when Gallio was the deputy of Achaia, the Jews . . . brought him* [Paul] *to the judgement seat . . .*

Achaia or Achaea (the former is the Greek spelling, the latter the Latin) is the region skirting the northern shore of the Peloponnesus. During the great days of Greece it played only a very minor role, for it was under the thumb of mighty Sparta, just to the south. After the death of Alexander the Great, however, with Sparta long since rendered powerless, the cities of Achaea began to combine for the common defense and formed the "Achaean League." For over a century, the Achaean League preserved a shred of Greek freedom.

It came to an end, however, in 146 B.C. when Corinth was destroyed by the Roman forces. The last bit of Greek independence vanished, but the memory of the Achaean League lingered in the name the Romans gave their Greek province. It was the province of Achaea, or Achaia.

As for the Roman who now came to Corinth to govern the province, he was Junius Annaeus Gallio, though this was only his adopted name, taken after he had been accepted by a well-to-do Roman family. He had been born in Spain and his original name was Marcus Annaeus Novatus.

He was the older brother of Lucius Annaeus Seneca, the most noted Stoic philosopher among the Romans of the early empire, and the tutor of the young man who later became the Emperor Nero.

Gallio's nephew was a young man named Lucan (Marcus Annaeus Lucanus, to be precise) who, later, under Nero, became a poet of considerable reputation.

It is known that Gallio became proconsul of the province of Achaea in A.D. 52 and that fixes the date during which Paul was concluding his stay in Corinth. Gallio listened to the Jewish complaints against Paul with distaste and impatience. To him, it was merely:

> Acts 18:15. . . . *a question of words and names, and of your law* . . .

It was a tedious matter of alien semantics to him, in other words, and he refused to involve himself in it. Paul was therefore safe.

The end of Gallio's life, by the way, was tragic. His younger brother, Seneca the philosopher, and his nephew, Lucan the poet, were both forced to commit suicide a dozen years later during the cruel and tyrannical reign of Nero, simply because they had incurred the emperor's displeasure and the suspicion of involvement in a conspiracy against him. (This was true in the case of Lucan, who turned state's evidence against his fellow conspirators but was condemned anyway.) Upon hearing this news, Gallio committed suicide too.

Ephesus

When Paul finally left Corinth, he took Aquila and Priscilla with him and sailed eastward 250 miles, across the center of the Aegean Sea to the Asia Minor coast:

> Acts 18:19. *And he came to Ephesus, and left them* [Aquila and Priscilla] *there: but he himself entered into the synagogue, and reasoned with the Jews.*

Ephesus was first settled by Greeks, according to tradition, in 1087 B.C., at a time when all of Greece was experiencing a "Dark Age." A group of uncivilized Greek-speaking tribes, the Dorians, had entered Greece a century before and had been ravaging and dominating the land ever since. This was part of the same group of barbarian migrations that flung the Peoples of the Sea against the nations bordering the eastern Mediterranean. The colonization of Ephesus was carried through by Greeks seeking escape from the misery of home.

Indeed, in that period (when the Israelites in Canaan were themselves undergoing similar suffering under Philistine domination) the entire western coast of Asia Minor was colonized by the .Greeks. Ephesus and other cities nearby were colonized by men from Athens and from other regions where the Ionian dialect of Greece was spoken. For that reason, the region around Ephesus was called Ionia.

Under the mild rule of the Lydians in the sixth century B.C., Ionia experienced an amazing cultural growth. It was there that philosophers such as Thales first introduced the basic assumptions of modern science and one of the great Ionian philosophers was Heraclitus of Ephesus (see page 299).

All of Ionia gradually decayed after Persia conquered Lydia, particularly after 500 B.C., when a disastrous revolt of the Ionians against the ruling empire was pitilessly crushed. Ephesus managed to cling to its prosperity more than did the others, however, and, in the centuries after Alexander the Great, it became the most important Greek city in Asia Minor. The prosperity continued under Roman rule, which began in 133 B.C., and Ephesus may not have been far behind Alexandria and Antioch in population and wealth. It survived a sack by Sulla in 84 B.C. and in 6 B.C. it became the capital of the province of Asia.

In Ephesus, Paul disputed with the Jews, but did not remain long. He sailed to Caesarea on the Judean coast:

> Acts 18:22. And when he had landed at Caesarea, and gone up, and saluted the church, he went down to Antioch.

It is usually assumed that by "gone up, and saluted the church" is meant a quick trip to Jerusalem. And thus Paul ended his second missionary journey.

Apollos

It was not long after his return to Antioch that the restless and fiery Paul, who could not seem to endure the settled life of a secure Christian community, left (perhaps in A.D. 54) on his third missionary journey.

> Acts 18:23. . . . after he had spent some time there [in Antioch], he departed, and went over all the country of Galatia and Phrygia in order . . .

Once again he was making the rounds of the churches he had founded in the Asia Minor interior. But meanwhile someone else had arrived in Ephesus, at the western rim of the peninsula:

St. Paul's Third Journey and His Journey to Rome

Acts 18:24. *And a certain Jew named Apollos, born at Alexandria, an eloquent man . . . came to Ephesus.*

Acts 18:25. *. . . knowing only the baptism of John.*

Even now, a quarter century after the death of John the Baptist and of Jesus, there remained a sect that looked back to John the Baptist as their teacher and inspiration, rather than to Jesus.

Nevertheless, since John had preached the imminent coming of a Messiah, the Baptist's disciples seemed readier than other Jews to be converted to Christianity. Some instruction from Aquila and Priscilla (whom Paul had brought to Ephesus from Corinth) quickly brought Apollos into the Christian fold, and he moved on to Corinth to labor there.

Paul himself, in his travels through Asia Minor on this third journey, reached Ephesus and encountered disciples of John the Baptist, who readily submitted to baptism in the name of Jesus.

Paul remained in Ephesus for two to three years, till A.D. 57 perhaps, and under his influence the Christian church there flourished greatly. Indeed, as Jerusalem was the first Christian center, and Antioch the second, so Ephesus became the third. Later Christian tradition elaborated the early history of the church at Ephesus. The apostle John son of Zebedee was supposed to have spent his later life there and written the fourth gospel (see page 297). The Virgin Mary was supposed to have gone there too, and also, Mary Magdalene, and the apostles Andrew and Philip.

Diana of the Ephesians

The growth of the church at Ephesus was not entirely without untoward incident. The most spectacular of these came about as the result of the demagoguery of a silversmith:

Acts 19:24. *. . . . a certain man named Demetrius, a silversmith, which made silver shrines for Diana, brought no small gain unto the craftsmen;*

Acts 19:25. *Whom he called together with the workmen of like occupation . . .*

The reference to Diana is to a goddess to whom Ephesus, at least in part, owed its relative immunity to the vicissitudes of history. It was a respected religious center and its conquerors tended to be in a certain awe of it.

. The religion centered about a fertility goddess of a type familiar in Asia Minor, Syria, and Babylon. The goddess was much like the Ashtaroth so denounced by the Old Testament Yahvists (see page I-232). The rites were orgiastic, though undoubtedly intended, in all seriousness, to encourage the fertility of the soil.

The worship dated back to before the coming of the Greeks to that part of the world and may have centered about the falling of a meteorite originally. Thus, a city official is quoted as saying:

> Acts 19:35. . . . *what man is there that knoweth not how that the city of the Ephesians is a worshipper of the great goddess Diana, and of the image which fell down from Jupiter?*

Meteorites, if seen to fall from the sky, are a natural object of worship for primitive men, who know nothing of astronomy and see them merely as objects hurled down by the sky-god.

If the meteorite was perhaps in the crude shape of a human being (or something that might be imagined to be such a shape) the effect would be all the more impressive. And, in the end, there would not be lacking artisans to hew something that was closer to a recognized form. In New Testament times the goddess worshipped by Ephesus was usually shown as a woman closely draped from the waist down but seeming naked from the waist up and bearing many breasts. These breasts would seem to symbolize the overflowing fertility of the soil which the goddess symbolizes.

The Greeks, finding themselves with this primitive fertility goddess, had to identify her with some more familiar member of the Greek pantheon and they chose Artemis, the goddess of the hunt. It was a remarkably poor choice since the classical Artemis is a chaste and virginal huntress; anything but a many-breasted Earth-mother.

Nevertheless, the choice struck and the many-breasted goddess became "Artemis of the Ephesians" or, in the Roman equivalent, "Diana of the Ephesians."

When Ephesus was under the control of Lydia, a temple was built to Artemis of the Ephesians, under the generous sponsorship of the rich king Croesus. It was called the "Artemision." This temple was burnt down, accidentally, about 400 B.C., but it was quickly rebuilt.

Then, one night in 356 B.C., the Artemision was burnt down again.

This time it was no accident, but was a case of deliberate arson. The culprit was quickly seized and before execution for the crime of sacrilege was passed, he was asked what possible motive he could have had for so senseless an act. He replied that he had done it in order to make his name immortal. Immediately it was decreed that his name be expunged from all records and that no one ever pronounce it. In vain! His name (or some name that purports to be his) is known. It is Herostratus and it is, indeed, immortal. At least it is still remembered over two thousand years later.

Afterward, Greek historians were fond of repeating the story that the night on which the Artemision was burnt down was the very night on which Alexander the Great was born—though in view of the lack of accurate records in those days, it seems doubtful that this interesting coincidence can ever be verified.

Eventually the Artemision was rebuilt, this time under the direction of, among others, an architect who had been in the employ of Alexander the Great himself. The world of Macedonian monarchies was far richer than the earlier world of Greek city-states had been, and the temple was rebuilt on a much larger scale and with much more elaborate ornamentation. Such was its splendor that it came to be considered one of the Seven Wonders of the World.

This Wonder was to endure for seven centuries and it was standing when Paul was in Ephesus. Naturally, the magnificent temple made Ephesus a tourist center and the silversmiths who made trinkets for the tourist trade cleaned up. These silversmiths viewed with the utmost suspicion this Jewish missionary who was convincing more and more men that the great Ephesian goddess was just an idle lump of stone and that the silver trinkets were valueless.

The silversmiths were thrown into fury by the denunciations of Demetrius and in no time at all there was a full-blown riot in the streets:

Acts 19:28. *And when they* [the silversmiths] *heard these sayings, they were full of wrath, and cried out, saying, Great is Diana of the Ephesians.*

Acts 19:29. *And the whole city was filled with confusion . . .*

The city authorities, however, kept the situation in hand, and the riot blew over without real damage.

Miletus

Paul had been intending to visit the churches in Greece again and after the Ephesian riots he left. Perhaps the fact that the church withstood those riots so well led him to feel that he could safely leave it for a time. Or perhaps he felt that his own absence might prevent the recurrence of more dangerous riots.

He spent several months, therefore, in Greece, then, perhaps in A.D. 58, returned to Troas via Macedonia. Again there follows a "we" passage as though Luke had once again joined the party in Troas.

> Acts 20:13. . . . *we went before to ship, and sailed unto Assos* . . .
> Acts 20:14. *And when he [Paul] met with us at Assos, we took him in, and came to Mitylene.*
> Acts 20:15. *And we sailed thence, and came the next day over against Chios; and the next day we arrived at Samos, and tarried at Trogyllium; and the next day we came to Miletus.*

Assos was a town on the southern shore of the Troas peninsula, about twenty miles south of Alexandria Troas. The only incident of note in its history is the fact that Aristotle the philosopher spent three years there studying natural history.

Paul's companions rounded the Troas peninsula by sea, while Paul himself traveled to Assos overland. Paul then boarded the ship and all traveled southward along the Asia Minor west coast, passing three large islands: Lesbos, Chios, and Samos.

Lesbos, the largest of the three (623 square miles) had, as its capital city, Mitylene, located on its eastern shore. The period of Lesbos' greatest prosperity was about 600 B.C. It was then politically strong and contributed great names to music and literature, the greatest being that of the poetess Sappho, whose lyrically phrased praise of girls has given us "Lesbianism" as a word to signify female homosexuality.

Chios and Samos (the former 355 square miles in area, the latter 180) were each firm allies of Athens during the Golden Age of the latter city. Earlier than that, Samos had had a period of power of its own, when its fleet under its pirate-ruler, Polycrates, was the strongest in the eastern Mediterranean. Two great philosophers, Pythagoras and

Epicurus, were Samians by birth. All three islands are now part of the modern kingdom of Greece.

The party, on leaving Samos, remained at Trogyllium overnight; that being the promontory on the Asia Minor coast just south of the eastern edge of Samos. Then they went on to Miletus.

Miletus is on the Asia Minor mainland, about thirty miles south of Ephesus. From 600 to 500 B.C. it was the foremost city of the Greek world. Modern science began in Miletus, for Thales and his pupils, Anaximander and Anaximenes, were natives of that city. Its glories came to an end soon after 500 B.C., after it had led a furious revolt against the Persian Empire. Despite help from Athens (which led to the Persian invasion of Greece) the revolt was crushed, and Miletus as the ringleader was punished with particular severity. It survived, but leadership among the cities of the Asia Minor coast passed to Ephesus.

Miletus always had to fight to keep its harbor open against the tendencies to silt up. In the later centuries of the Roman Empire, the fight was gradually lost. Miletus has been nothing but deserted ruins for many centuries and the same fate, for that matter, has befallen Ephesus, Assos, and Troas.

In Miletus, Paul found himself close to Ephesus but he had no intention of stopping there lest church affairs delay him and keep him from his determination to spend Pentecost in Jerusalem. (Some thirty years had now passed since that first Pentecost.)

He therefore sent for the Ephesian elders and contented himself with giving a farewell address, urging them to selfless labors for the church and concluding with a well-known passage:

Acts 20:35. . . . *remember the words of the Lord Jesus, how he said, It is more blessed to give than to receive.*

As it happens, though, this saying did not come to be recorded in any of the gospels.

Rhodes

The journey southward then continued:

Acts 21:1. . . . *we came with a straight course unto Coos, and the day following unto Rhodes, and from thence unto Patara.*

Coos, or (better) Cos, is a fourth island off the Asia Minor coast and is about forty miles south of Samos. It is 111 square miles in area and was the home of the most important medical school of ancient times. Hippocrates, the "father of medicine," was born in Cos about 460 B.C., while Apelles, the greatest of the painters of antiquity, was born there a century later.

Rhodes, still another island off the west coast of Asia Minor (and the southernmost), is sixty miles southeast of Cos. Rhodes is a considerably larger island, with an area of 545 square miles. The city of Rhodes, on the northeastern tip of the island, was founded in 408 B.C.

After the time of Alexander the Great, Rhodes experienced a period of great prosperity that lasted for a century and a half. In 305-304 B.C., it withstood a long and terrible siege by Demetrius, the son of one of Alexander's generals. In celebration afterward, it erected the most famous great statue of the Greek world, a huge carving of the Sungod. This stood in the harbor, looking out to sea, but it did not, as later legend had it, bestride the harbor, with ships passing between its legs. This statue, the Colossus of Rhodes, was considered one of the Seven Wonders of the World. It stood for less than a century, however, for about 225 B.C. it was overthrown by an earthquake and was never re-erected.

In modern times, Rhodes was Turkish for centuries but was taken by Italy in 1912 and held for a generation. In 1945, after World War II, it and nearby islands were ceded by Italy to Greece.

From Rhodes, Paul and his party went to Patara, a town on the southwestern shore of Asia Minor, fifty miles east of Rhodes. It was the chief seaport of Lycia, a small district of Asia Minor which had managed to retain its nominal independence long after surrounding regions had been annexed to the Roman Empire.

It was not until A.D. 43—about fifteen years before Paul touched down in Patara—that the Emperor Claudius annexed it to the empire and made it part of Pamphylia.

Felix

Paul took another ship at Patara, which carried him to Tyre, and from there he made his way to Jerusalem, stopping at Caesarea to visit Philip the evangelist (see page 346).

In Jerusalem, Paul met with James and other leaders of the church. These, despite the concessions they had made at the Council of Jerusalem a decade earlier, were troubled at reports of the mass conversion of pagans without circumcision and without the requirement of obedience to the Mosaic Law. Even if the Jerusalem leaders were willing to accept this as a matter of practical politics, there were many among the congregation who were not willing at all. The leaders explained to Paul:

> Acts 21:20. . . . *Thou seest, brother, how many thousands of Jews there are which believe; and they are all zealous of the law:*
> Acts 21:21. *And they are informed of thee, that thou teachest all the Jews which are among the Gentiles to forsake Moses . . .*

Actually, it might be argued that Paul only invited Gentiles to become Christians without the Law, while urging Jews to keep the Law, but it could also be argued that if some Christians were free of the Law, other Christians could scarcely be kept to it. James might well have feared that the Christian community at Jerusalem, with their fervent Jewish heritage, on hearing that the Pauline version of Christianity was non-Jewish and even anti-Jewish, might disintegrate, and Christianity would become a Gentile religion altogether. (And this is exactly what did happen in the end.)

Furthermore, the Christian community was working out a record of coexistence with the non-Christian Jews. At least there is no record of James being in trouble with the Jewish authorities after the death of Herod Agrippa I. By proving themselves strict Jews in terms of ritual, the Christians of Jerusalem could perhaps look forward to, first, toleration by the Jews, then the acceptance of Jesus as a prophet at least, and eventually the acceptance of Jesus as the Messiah.

If Christianity came to seem anti-Jewish all such hopes must be gone and the Christians of Jerusalem might even be persecuted, driven out, or hunted down. Paul's very presence in Jerusalem could give rise to this danger. Reports of his missionary activity must have made him notorious as a violator of the Law, and he might be persecuted for this rather than for being a Christian, but the consequences might turn out to be against Christians generally.

James therefore urged Paul to go through an elaborate ritual of purification in the Temple in order to demonstrate his own adherence to the Law. Paul obeyed, but it did not help. He was recognized in

the Temple by some Jews from Asia who might have encountered him
on his missionary journeys, and who might therefore know of his work.
The cry was immediately raised:

> Acts 21:28. . . . Men of Israel, help: This is the man, that teacheth
> all men every where against the people, and the law, and this place
> [the Temple] . . .

Paul was even accused of bringing Gentiles into the Temple and
defiling it in that manner. (There were indeed Gentiles in Paul's
entourage, but he did not bring them into the Temple.)

For a time it seemed that Paul might be lynched, but a Roman
captain and his troop, hearing of the disorders, hurried to the spot and
Paul was taken into protective custody. (The Roman captain's name
is later given as Claudius Lysias.)

With the captain's permission, Paul addressed the crowd in Aramaic
(after speaking to the captain in Greek), recounting the details of his
conversion. The audience grew unruly, however, when Paul began to
talk about his work among the Gentiles.

The captain, puzzled by all this, decided to get down to basics
by questioning Paul under torture, a routine procedure in those days.
Paul, however, saved himself from this by announcing his Roman
citizenship (see page 355).

Paul next faced the Jewish council and escaped from their hands by
announcing himself to be a Pharisee. He maintained that he was being
persecuted for his belief in the doctrine of resurrection—a cardinal
point in Pharisaic doctrine and one that was bitterly opposed by the
Sadducees.

To be sure, Paul's belief in resurrection applied specifically to that
of Jesus after the crucifixion, something the Pharisees did not accept.
However, in the heat of debate, the magic word "resurrection" was
enough to cause the Pharisees in the council to turn upon the Sadducees and opt for Paul's innocence.

Nevertheless, Paul's life remained in danger and somehow Acts does
not mention any part played by the Christians in Jerusalem generally
in all this. Perhaps they were too few in number to make their influence felt or to do anything but make Paul's position worse if they
tried. It is tempting, however, to wonder if perhaps the Jerusalem
Christians might not have been just a little pleased at Paul's troubles.
They might well have considered him a perverter of Christian doctrine
and his troubles might have been viewed as a judgment upon him.

Salvation for Paul came from the Roman captain, Claudius Lysias, who had apparently grown friendly with his prisoner. He decided to get Paul out of Jerusalem and assure his physical safety by sending him to Caesarea to be tried, legally, by the Roman authorities and provided an escort—

Acts 23:24. . . . *that they may . . . bring him* [Paul] *safe unto Felix the governor.*

After the death of Herod Agrippa I, Judea was placed under procurators once more, and each had to deal constantly with bandit leaders claiming to be messiahs and leading rebellions against the authorities.

Indeed, when Claudius Lysias had first taken Paul, he thought his prisoner to be one of these rebels; one who happened to be a Jew from Egypt.

Acts 21:37 . . . *the chief captain . . . said, Canst thou speak Greek?*

Acts 21:38. *Art not thou that Egyptian, which . . . madest an uproar, and leddest out into the wilderness four thousand men that were murderers?*

The first procurator to follow Herod Agrippa I was Cuspius Fadus, and he was succeeded by Tiberius Alexander, a Jewish apostate who was supposed to have been a nephew of Philo Judaeus himself (see page 301). In A.D. 48, about the time of the Council of Jerusalem, Ventidius Cumanus became procurator and governed for four years, through a constant haze of riots and insurrections. In A.D. 52 he was replaced by Antonius Felix, under whom the situation grew steadily worse.

Felix was a freedman (someone who had been born a slave but had been freed) and it was quite unusual for a freedman to become a royal governor. However, under Claudius, freedmen had been given important civil service posts, and one of the most important of these functionaries was Pallas.

This Pallas was not only influential with Claudius, but was also friendly with Claudius' fourth and last wife, Agrippina, who was intriguing for the succession to go to her son, Nero. Felix was the brother of Pallas and it is not surprising therefore that, although a freedman, he should be made procurator of Judea.

In A.D. 54 Agrippina finally won her victory. According to the story, she poisoned Claudius and her son, Nero, succeeded to the throne as the fifth Roman Emperor—a reign most fateful to both Jews and Christians.

Antipatris

Paul was taken out of Jerusalem, which he was never to see again:

Acts 23:31. *Then the soldiers . . . took Paul and brought him by night to Antipatris.*

Antipatris, which is roughly halfway between Jerusalem and Caesarea, is thought to have been built on the site of ancient Aphek, where the Israelite army had been shattered by the Philistines in the time of the high priest Eli (see page I-271).

The city had been built anew by Herod the Great and it had been named Antipatris after the king's father, Antipater the Idumean.

Drusilla

Felix sat in judgment. The Jewish authorities accused Paul of stirring up dissension and profaning the Temple. Paul maintained that he was a Pharisee and again insisted he was being persecuted merely for believing in the Pharisaic doctrine of the resurrection.

Felix listened with considerable interest. He was no Claudius Lysias, and was apparently acquainted with Jewish doctrine, perhaps through his wife.

Acts 24:24. . . . *Felix came with his wife Drusilla, which was a Jewess, . . .* [and] *sent for Paul, and heard him concerning the faith in Christ.*

Drusilla was the youngest of the three daughters of Herod Agrippa I, and was twenty-one years old at this time. She had divorced her previous husband under Felix's pressure and had been forced to marry this Roman Gentile in defiance of Jewish law. Felix lost interest in Christian doctrines, however, when Paul discoursed on its ethical content:

Acts 24:25. *And as he* [Paul] *reasoned of righteousness, temperance, and judgement to come, Felix trembled, and answered, Go thy way . . .*

Felix kept Paul imprisoned for two years, more to prevent disorders in Jerusalem, perhaps, than out of any conviction of Paul's guilt. The terms of the imprisonment were not harsh. At the end of the two years, Pallas, the procurator's brother, had fallen from favor at the court of Nero, and Felix was relieved of his duties. Since this took place, most likely, in A.D. 61, we can place the time of Paul's visit to Jerusalem, his seizure, and his trial at Caesarea, in A.D. 59.

Festus

A new procurator took office:

Acts 24:27. . . . *after two years Porcius Festus came into Felix' room* . . .

The case of Paul was reopened before this new procurator, whose chief aim was to prevent unnecessary trouble with the increasingly troublesome people of the province. He therefore offered to have the apostle tried in Jerusalem. In order to quiet Paul's fears that such a trial might be an unfair one, the procurator offered to preside over it himself.

Paul did not think that Festus would, merely by his presence, insure a fair trial. Indeed, he probably suspected that Festus would be successfully pressured into a conviction, as had been the case with Pontius Pilate thirty-two years before.

Paul, therefore, appealed to the emperor, which was his right as a Roman citizen, and thus made it impossible for the procurator to do anything but send him to Rome.

Herod Agrippa II

Meanwhile, members of the house of Herod were on hand:

Acts 25:13. *And after certain days king Agrippa and Bernice came unto Caesarea to salute Festus.*

The Agrippa referred to here is Herod Agrippa II, the only son of Herod Agrippa I. He was born about A.D. 27, shortly before the crucifixion of Jesus. The young prince was brought up in Rome, where

The Kingdom of Herod Agrippa II

his father was at that time such a favorite with the imperial family. Herod Agrippa was a boy of ten when his father began to rule over sections of Judea, and he was only seventeen when his father died. He was too young for Claudius to be willing to entrust him with the very difficult task of ruling all of Judea and the surrounding territory.

Agrippa's uncle, a younger brother of Herod Agrippa I, was still ruling a small section of land north of Galilee, having been made king there by Claudius in A.D. 41. The area was called Chalcis and Agrippa's uncle was therefore known as Herod of Chalcis.

Herod of Chalcis died in A.D. 48 and a year later Herod Agrippa II was appointed king in his place. In A.D. 53 Nero made him king, in addition, over sections of Galilee and Trans-Jordanian territories. He was the last of the Herodian line to rule anywhere in Jewish territories.

Now, in A.D. 61, Herod Agrippa II was coming to Caesarea from his capital, Tiberias, to convey formal greetings to Festus.

Five years later, he was to be in Jerusalem, when the disorders and fury of the Zealots were mounting toward the suicidal rebellion. Herod Agrippa II counseled patience and moderation but he was (and with justification) scorned as a Roman puppet, and ignored. In the rebellion, he sided with the Romans. In consequence he was able to retire to Rome after the destruction of Jerusalem and to live out the remainder of his life in comfort.

About A.D. 100 Herod Agrippa II, the great-great-grandson of Antipater the Idumean, and the great-great-great-great-great-great-great-grandson of Mattathias, the priest who had sparked the Maccabean rebellion, died. He was the last member of either family to be of any consequence at all.

Bernice, or Berenice, was his sister, the oldest of the three girls born to Herod Agrippa I. (Her youngest sister, Drusilla, had been married to Felix, the previous procurator.) Berenice had been married several times, the first time to her uncle, Herod of Chalcis. She left her third husband, a prince who ruled in Cilicia, to live with her brother at Tiberias. Gossip implied an incestuous relationship, but gossip then, as now, invariably placed the most scandalous possible interpretation on any event.

She too took the Roman side in the rebellion. In fact, she became the mistress of Titus, the young Roman general who finally captured and destroyed Jerusalem in A.D. 70. She went to Rome, along with

Titus and her brother, and remained there the rest of her life. She did not, however, remain Titus' mistress. The Romans were quite anti-Jewish in sentiment at this time and Titus was forced to put her aside. The year of her death is not known.

Paul now had still another hearing before Festus and Agrippa. His defense, couched entirely in Jewish terms, touched Agrippa, who said to Paul:

> Acts 26:28. . . . *Almost thou persuadest me to be a Christian.*

It was agreed that Paul had done nothing deserving of condemnation, but since he had appealed to the emperor, he would have to be allowed to go to Rome.

Myra

Under the guard of a centurion, Paul set sail for Rome, in what amounted to a fourth missionary voyage. Luke, if he is taken to be the author of Acts, was apparently one of the company:

> Acts 27:5. . . . *when we had sailed over the sea of Cilicia and Pamphylia, we came to Myra, a city of Lycia.*

Myra was thirty miles east of Patara, the port at which Paul had disembarked on his way to Jerusalem three years before. It was an important and populous city at the time and one of the chief towns of Lycia, but there is little but ruins left today. Paul's party took another ship and left, and Paul was never to see Asia Minor again.

Crete

And now the journey was beset by bad weather:

> Acts 27:7. . . . *we had . . . scarce . . . come over against Cnidus, the wind not suffering us, we sailed under Crete, over against Salmone;*
> Acts 27:8 And . . . *came unto . . . The fair havens; nigh whereunto was the city of Lasea.*

St. Paul's Third Journey and His Journey to Rome

Cnidus (or Cnidos) is a long promontory on the southwest coast of Asia Minor that juts out just south of the eastern edge of the island of Cos (see page 414). The city of Cnidus was at the tip of the promontory. It played no great role in Greek history, but one of the most famous mathematicians and astronomers of antiquity, Eudoxus, was born there.

Contrary winds did not allow a landing on Cnidus but drove them toward Crete, a hundred twenty miles toward the southwest. This is one of the large islands of the Mediterranean, 3200 square miles in area. It is about 160 miles long from east to west, but only 20 miles, on the average, from north to south.

In very ancient times—long before the time of Abraham, even— Crete was the seat of a high civilization. By 1400 B.C., while the Jews were in Egyptian slavery, Crete was taken by raiders from the Greek mainland and began a slow decline. It could still play an important role in the Trojan War about 1200 B.C., but after that it virtually vanishes from historic annals. All during the centuries in which the Greek cities were great, the Cretan cities were sunk in mutual warfare and banditry. It was a haunt of pirates at various periods when warfare preoccupied other powers and permitted piracy to flourish. In 67 B.C., Rome put an end to that by annexing it.

Paul's ship was driven southward around Cape Salmone at the northeastern tip of the island and came to rest in a harbor midway along the southern shore.

This harbor, Fair Havens, despite its name, was not suitable for any long stay. The captain of the ship therefore tried to make for a second and better harbor, some fifty miles westward along Crete's southern shore. A storm struck and beat the ship wildly along:

Acts 27:16. . . . *running under a certain island which is called Clauda* . . .

This island (called Gavdas nowadays) is a small bit of land some twenty-five miles south of the west end of Crete.

Melita

After most difficult times, the ship and its company was cast ashore on an island:

Acts 28:1. *And when they were escaped, then they knew that the island was called Melita.*

Melita is the island now known as Malta, about ninety-five square miles in area and nearly five hundred miles west of Crete. The island was first colonized by Phoenicians and, in the sixth century B.C., came under the control of Carthage, the greatest of all Phoenician colonies. In 218 B.C., at the very start of the second war between Rome and Carthage, Rome took over control of Malta and it remained part of the Roman realm thereafter.

The bay which the ship was supposed to have entered, near the northern tip of the island, is known as Saint Paul's Bay to this day.

Syracuse

Paul and his party stayed in Malta for three months, during the winter of A.D. 61–62. At the end of that time they left in a ship from Alexandria which had been wintering there.

Acts 28:12. *And landing at Syracuse, we tarried there three days.*

Syracuse was the largest and most notable city on the island of Sicily, which is, itself, not mentioned by name in the Bible. Sicily is the largest island in the Mediterranean, and is just about ten thousand square miles in area. It is about fifty miles north of Malta, and its northern tip is separated from the "toe" of the Italian peninsula by a strait that is, in spots, only two miles wide.

In the eighth century B.C. the eastern portion of Sicily was colonized by Greeks and the western portion by Carthaginians. For five hundred years, Greeks and Carthaginians fought each other on the island, without either being able to drive the other completely out.

It was only in 264 B.C. that the Romans finally reached the island. Their intrusion was the occasion of the first of three wars between Rome and Carthage. At the end of that war, Carthage was finally forced to abandon the island altogether.

The city of Syracuse on the east-central shore of Sicily was the oldest Greek settlement on the island. It was founded, according to tradition, in 734 B.C. (when Ahaz sat on the throne of Judah, and when the Kingdom of Israel had only a dozen years to live).

Syracuse took the lead in fighting the Carthaginians and, on several occasions, reached great heights of power. In 415 B.C., Syracuse had to face the unprovoked attack of a great Athenian fleet. That fleet was completely destroyed and this, more than anything else, helped break Athenian power and lead to the ultimate victory of Sparta over Athens.

In 390 B.C., under Dionysius I, Syracuse was at its peak. It drove Carthage from all but the westernmost tip of the island, and it took over the southern shores of mainland Italy as well. After Dionysius, however, there was a decline and the Carthaginians recovered.

When Rome took over the island after the first war with Carthage, Syracuse was left independent under its king, Hiero II. During his long reign of over half a century, Syracuse was more prosperous than ever, even though it was a Roman puppet. The greatest scientist of antiquity, Archimedes, lived there then.

On the occasion of the second war between Rome and Carthage, it seemed at first that Rome would lose. Syracuse hastily switched to the Carthaginian side and Rome sent out a fleet to occupy it. For three years, Syracuse fought desperately with the help of Archimedes' war weapons. In the end, however, in 212 B.C., Syracuse was taken and Archimedes died during the sack that followed.

After that Syracuse and all the rest of Sicily remained securely Roman, though the island was shaken by slave rebellions now and then.

Rhegium

Paul's party sailed north from Syracuse:

> Acts 28:13. *And from thence we . . . came to Rhegium: and . . . the next day to Puteoli . . .*

At the time that the Greeks were colonizing Sicily, they were also settling along the shores of the southern portion of Italy. On the tip of the "toe" of Italy, just across from Sicily, for instance, they founded the town of Rhegion (or Rhegium, in the Latin spelling) in 720 B.C., according to tradition.

It was ruled by Dionysius I when Syracuse was at the height of its power. Beginning in 280 B.C. the Romans took over the Greek cities in southern Italy one by one. Rhegium was the last to fall, becoming

Roman in 270 B.C. Throughout the Roman period, however, Rhegium retained its Greek language and culture and retained its self-government.

From Rhegium, Paul's party went to Puteoli, a city on Italy's southwestern shore, somewhat north of modern Naples. It was founded by the Greeks in 512 B.C. and taken over by the Romans in 215 B.C. It was a large trading center.

Rome

And so, finally, Paul came to Rome:

Acts 28:16. *And . . . we came to Rome . . .*

In A.D. 62, when Paul arrived in Rome, that city was great and prosperous, the most important city in the world. Nero was just about at the midpoint of his reign, and while he was pleasure-loving, wasteful, and autocratic, the city and the empire continued to be well governed in general.

The Book of Acts says little about the progress of Paul's appeal to the emperor. It records only that he attempted to convert the Jews of Rome to his way of thinking and failed again. After two years of house imprisonment he was freed and the last verse of the book records that he was:

Acts 28:31. *Preaching the kingdom of God . . . with all confidence, no man forbidding him.*

That was A.D. 64.

It is curious that the book ends there, since there was to follow that very year a terrible persecution of the Christians and since there is some evidence that Paul may have set out on his travels even further west. What's more, to carry the story only three years further would have brought it to the reputed year of Paul's death, A.D. 67.

One possibility is that Acts was written in A.D. 64, but this is pretty well discounted. The year of authorship is much more likely to have been something like A.D. 80. A second possibility is that Luke died before he had a chance to complete the book.

Most likely, though, the point chosen for the ending of Acts is deliberate. It represents a high spot.

Thirty-eight years had passed since the crucifixion of Jesus; thirty-three years, perhaps, since Paul's conversion. When Paul began his career, the Christian fellowship consisted of a small group of disciples gathered in Jerusalem, a group in danger of being wiped out by the opposition of the Jewish authorities.

When Paul ended his career, strong, well-organized, and vigorously proselytizing churches dotted Cyprus, Asia Minor, Macedonia, and Greece, and there were Christians even in Rome.

Very much of all this had been accomplished by one remarkable man—he who had been born Saul of Tarsus and who had become Saint Paul. Luke, his friend and physician, may well have wanted to end his biography of Paul at that moment when, having accomplished all this, he was resting secure in Rome, preaching as he wished and "no man forbidding him."

The darkness was soon to close in again, but Luke chose to leave Paul at this sunlit peak.

10. ROMANS

The Epistle to the Romans

Following the Book of Acts in the New Testament are twenty-one letters sent by various apostles to Christians generally, or to various churches or individuals. The majority of these, as many as fourteen according to some traditions, were written by Paul. These letters are referred to as "epistles" (from a Greek word meaning "to send to"). The word is closely related to "apostle" (who is "sent away"). The relationship is the same as that of "missive" to "missionary."

The various epistles include the earliest writings in the New Testament. Some of them may have been written as early as A.D. 50, almost twenty years before even the first of the gospels we now possess reached its present form, and fifty years, perhaps, before the fourth gospel was written.

The Pauline epistles do not appear in the Bible in chronological order. They seem, rather, to be placed in order of length, with the longest first.

The first and longest epistle is listed in the King James Version as "The Epistle of Paul the Apostle to the Romans" but it can be called simply "Romans." Partly because of its length, it contains the most complete exposition of Paul's religious thinking, which is a second reason for placing it first. Then, too, since it is addressed to the Christians of the empire's capital and largest city, the matter of prestige might also have influenced the placing of the epistle.

The letter is not dated in the modern fashion or, for that matter, in any formal fashion at all (nor is any other epistle). We must therefore seek its date (and those of the others) through indirect hints.

St. Paul's First and Second Journeys

Toward the end of the epistle, for instance, Paul tells the business that currently engages him:

> Romans 15:25. *But now I go unto Jerusalem to minister unto the saints.*
>
> Romans 15:26. *For it hath pleased them of Macedonia and Achaia to make a certain contribution for the poor saints which are at Jerusalem.*

This, apparently, is just the situation as it was described in the twentieth chapter of Acts:

> Acts 20:2. . . . *he [Paul] came into Greece,*
>
> Acts 20:3. *And . . . purposed to return through Macedonia.*
>
> . . . .
>
> Acts 20:6. *And . . . sailed away from Philippi . . .*
>
> . . . .
>
> Acts 20:16. . . . *[and] hasted . . . to be at Jerusalem the day of Pentecost.*

Paul was anxious, presumably, to bring the contributions sent by the relatively wealthy churches of Greece and Macedonia to the beset Christians of the mother church in Jerusalem.

This was at the end of Paul's third missionary voyage and if the letter were written while he was still getting ready to make the trip to Jerusalem, it should have been written in 58.

One guess is that at the time of writing, Paul was completing his stay at Corinth where there was a flourishing church which he had established in the course of his second journey. Thus, at the end of Romans, Paul says:

> Romans 16:1. *I commend unto you Phebe our sister, which is a servant of the church which is at Cenchrea.*

Apparently Phebe is the bearer of the letter and this is to serve as her introduction to the Christian leaders in Rome. (She is mentioned as Paul's sister only in a figurative sense, of course.)

Cenchrea is a suburb of Corinth, five miles east of the city proper, on the eastern shore of the isthmus. Presumably, if Phebe is a native of Cenchrea, Paul is himself in the vicinity and, therefore, very likely at Corinth.

However, the sixteenth (and last) chapter of Romans is only questionably part of the original epistle and deductions based on its contents are therefore shaky ones.

Rome

The elaborate address with which Romans starts gives the name of the sender and those who are to receive it:

> Romans 1:1. *Paul, a servant of Jesus Christ, called to be an apostle . . .*
>
> . . . .
>
> Romans 1:7. *To all that be in Rome . . . called to be saints . . .*

At the time the letter was written, Paul had never been to Rome, yet obviously Christianity had reached the city without him. No specific missionary activity on the part of any individual is described in the Bible as having carried the gospel to Rome, but that poses no problem.

There were Jews all over the empire, and there was definitely a colony of them in Rome. Jews from all over the empire, including the city of Rome, traveled to Jerusalem to be present at the Temple during the great feasts, whenever possible, and some of them undoubtedly brought back with them the new doctrines.

Spain

To be sure, Paul intended to visit Rome. Indeed, he hoped to carry the gospel throughout the empire and expressed that hope by projecting a visit to Spain. Jerusalem was in the empire's far east and to plan a visit to Spain in the empire's far west would be to state an intention of traveling throughout the empire:

> Romans 15:24. *Whensoever I take my journey into Spain, I will come to you* [the Romans] . . .

This, and another mention four verses later, is the only place in the Bible where Spain is directly referred to.

To be sure, there was the city of Tartessus, located on the Spanish coast beyond the Strait of Gibraltar (then called the Pillars of Hercules) near the site of modern Cadiz. It was a prosperous trading center, usually identified with the Tarshish mentioned in the Old Testament. King Solomon traded with it (see page I-332) and it is referred to in the Book of 1 Kings as an example of the worldwide spread of his power.

Tartessus, or Tarshish, became proverbial as a kind of "end of the world." After all, it was twenty-five hundred miles west of Jerusalem, and in Biblical times such a distance was almost the equivalent, in modern terms, of a trip to the Moon. Thus, when Jonah decided to run away from God rather than undertake the dangerous task of preaching in Ninevah (see page I-646) he decided to flee as far as possible; to the end of the Earth, in fact.

> Jonah 1:3. . . . *Jonah rose up to flee unto Tarshish from the presence of the Lord* . . .

Tarshish, however, is but very dimly known to us. Spain enters the full light of history only in the sixth century B.C.—at about the time the Jews were being carried off to Babylon.

In that century, both Greeks and Carthaginians were colonizing the Spanish coast and establishing towns. In 480 B.C., Tartessus (Tarshish) was destroyed by the Carthaginians.

After the first war with Rome, Carthage, which had been defeated and driven out of Sicily, turned her attention westward. In 237 B.C. she established her rule over a large section of southeastern Spain. That land was the base of the capable Carthaginian, Hamilcar, whose son, Hannibal, was one of the greatest generals of all time.

Hannibal forced a second war on Rome and nearly defeated her, but Rome endured and by 201 B.C. Carthage was utterly crushed. Rome took over the Carthaginian dominion in Spain, but the takeover was not a peaceful one and chronic warfare against the natives occupied Roman forces for the better part of a century. Indeed, even when Augustus founded the Roman Empire, there were still sections of northern Spain that maintained a stubborn independence of Rome. It was not until 19 B.C. that every bit of the Spanish peninsula could be considered securely Roman.

Paul did not visit Rome as soon as he planned, however, for the trip to Jerusalem which he was ready to undertake at the time of Romans, ended in his imprisonment by Felix (see page 417). It was not until five years after Romans that Paul finally came to Rome and then it was only as a prisoner appealing his case to the emperor.

Whether Paul then went on to Spain is not known. There is a reference in an early writing, dating back to about 95, that Paul reached the "limits of the west," presumably Spain, but such evidence is weak.

Circumcision

Paul deals in Romans with the problem which was paramount in the first decades after Jesus' crucifixion—whether Gentiles converted to Christianity had to be circumcised and observe all the ritual of the Law.

Paul's attitude toward circumcision and the Law was like Jeremiah's attitude toward the Temple (see page I-562). Circumcision, in Paul's view, could not be made use of as a magic talisman to bring automatic salvation to people who were sinful. Nor, by extension, could the absence of circumcision and the Law be considered as losing salvation for people who are otherwise righteous:

Romans 2:25. *For circumcision verily profiteth, if thou keep the law: but if thou be a breaker of the law, thy circumcision is made uncircumcision.*

Romans 2:26. *Therefore if the uncircumcision keep the righteousness of the law, shall not his uncircumcision be counted for circumcision.*

. . . .

Romans 2:29. . . . *he is a Jew, which is one inwardly; and circumcision is that of the heart, in the spirit, and not in the letter . . .*

Furthermore, Paul differentiates between the ritualistic aspects of the Law and its ethical aspects. Even if the Christian is freed from circumcision and other time-honored ritual, he is not freed from its ethics. The name of Christian is not an automatic shield against unrighteousness either:

Romans 6:15. . . . *shall we sin, because we are not under the law, but under grace? God forbid.*

Paul also makes a plea for tolerance.

In most of the churches established in the east, the converted Jews made up the majority at first and they accepted with difficulty, if at all, those converted Gentiles who would not be circumcised. Paul's weight was placed firmly on the side of the Gentile in those cases.

In Rome, however, the Gentile group may well have been the stronger almost from the first. The Emperor Claudius had expelled the Jews from Rome for a brief period about seven years or so before Romans was written. The Christian community in Rome would have had to get along with its Gentile members only. When the Jews returned, those among them who were Christians may have found themselves outsiders in the Church, opposed by those who had had nothing to do with the ritual of the Law and did not want the matter brought up.

Paul, in considering this situation, does not forget he himself is Jewish:

Romans 11:1. *I say then, Hath God cast away his people? God forbid, For I also am an Israelite, of the seed of Abraham, of the tribe of Benjamin.*

He argues that Jews will be converted; that if they show resistance to Christianity at the first, it is part of God's plan to make it easier for Gentiles to be converted. And he seems to plead with the Gentile Christians of Rome to tolerate the Christians of Jewish origin who are scrupulous with respect to such ritualistic matters as the dietary laws:

Romans 14:13. *Let us not therefore judge one another any more . . .*

Romans 14:14. *I know . . . that there is nothing unclean of itself; but to him that esteemeth any thing to be unclean, to him it is unclean.*

Priscilla and Aquila

The last chapter of Romans is very largely a list of names. There is Phebe, who apparently is the bearer of the letter, and then there is mention of over two dozen men and women to whom Paul sends greetings.

It seems unlikely that Paul would know a great many people by name in Rome, a city he had never visited, containing a fellowship with whom he had never dealt directly. There is some suggestion, therefore, that since Romans dealt with matters of interest and importance to Christians generally, and not merely to those of Rome, that copies of it may have been made for use by other churches. It may be, then, that the final chapter of greetings was attached to such a copy rather than to the original letter that made its way to Rome.

It is Ephesians, perhaps, rather than Romans who are being greeted, as might appear from the first to be greeted:

Romans 16:3. *Great Priscilla and Aquila . . .*

Romans 16:4. *Who have for my life laid down their own necks . . .*

Paul had brought Priscilla and Aquila from Corinth to Ephesus at the conclusion of his second missionary voyage (see page 406) and had left them there when he returned to Antioch. When Paul came again to Ephesus in the course of his third missionary journey, Priscilla and Aquila were still there, apparently, for it was during his stay in Ephesus at this time that he wrote epistles to the church at Corinth, and he mentions them there as sending their greetings along with his:

1 Corinthians 16:19. *The churches of Asia salute you. Aquila and Priscilla salute you . . .*

The reference in Romans to Priscilla and Aquila risking their life for Paul may refer to the occasion of the riot of the silversmiths (see page 411). There is no mention of a specific life-saving incident in Acts, but it is not difficult to imagine that Aquila and Priscilla may have done something to protect Paul from the fury of the mob at the risk of their own lives.

Since Romans was written within a year of Paul's leaving Ephesus after the silversmiths' riot, it seems quite likely that Priscilla and Aquila were still there and that the last chapter of greetings is indeed appended to a copy of the epistle which was sent to the Ephesian church.

Rufus

Most of the names in the final chapter of Romans are completely unknown except for their listing here. There is a natural attempt to identify as many of them as possible with those of the same names mentioned elsewhere in the New Testament. Thus, Paul says:

Romans 16:13. *Salute Rufus . . . and his mother . . .*

There is one other Rufus mentioned and that is in Mark. When Jesus is on the way to crucifixion, Mark says:

Mark 15:21. *And they compel one Simon a Cyrenian . . . the father of Alexander and Rufus, to bear his cross.*

Neither Matthew nor Luke, in telling of Simon of Cyrene, mentions his sons. That Mark does so would lead one to suppose that he knows them and expects his readers to know them, so that through them Simon of Cyrene might be identified.

After all, Mark (if he is indeed the author of the second gospel) did accompany Paul on at least part of his first missionary voyage, and might have known various other companions of Paul. If so, the Rufus whom Paul greets at the end of Romans and the Rufus who was the son of Simon of Cyrene may be one and the same.

On the other hand, Luke (if he is indeed the author of the third gospel) seems to have been a much closer associate of Paul than Mark was and he does not mention Rufus in connection with Simon of Cyrene.

And then, Rufus would be a common name. It means "red" and may well have been applied to a good percentage of those who happened to have red hair. It would be quite easy to suppose that Mark's Rufus and Paul's Rufus were two different people.

Jason

With his own greetings out of the way, Paul sends the greetings also of the close co-workers who were with him in Corinth at the time Romans was being written:

> Romans 16:21. *Timotheus my workfellow, and Lucius, and Jason, and Sosipater, my kinsmen, salute you . . .*

Timotheus (a name more familiar, in English, as Timothy) is the young man who joined Paul in Lystra, on the latter's second missionary voyage (see page 391) and who remained a close associate of the apostle for the remainder of Paul's life. Lucius would seem to be the Luke who is considered to be the author of the third gospel and of Acts.

As for Jason, he is usually identified with a man of Thessalonica, who may have offered Paul and Silas the hospitality of his house when the apostle arrived at that city in the course of his second missionary voyage (see page 397). In Thessalonica, Paul and Silas were in considerable danger from a mob and Jason found himself in the midst of a riot:

> Acts 17:5. *But the Jews which believed not . . . set all the city on an uproar and assaulted the house of Jason, and sought to bring them out to the people.*

Jason was dragged before the authorities and had to deposit bail in order to regain his freedom. Paul and Silas were, in the meantime, ushered safely out of the city and to Berea.

In Berea, they apparently gained another convert, Sopater, with whom the Sosipater of Romans 16:21 is usually identified. He is mentioned in Acts toward the close of the third missionary voyage, just after Romans was written. Paul is leaving Greece, and two of those mentioned at the close of Romans are going with him.

> Acts 20:4. *And there accompanied him into Asia Sopater of Berea . . . and Timotheus . . .*

Tertius

Apparently Paul commonly used a secretary to transcribe his words. This can be deduced from the fact that at the end of some epistles, Paul specifically mentions that the signature is his own, placed there by his own hand, as a sign of the authenticity of the letter. The remainder of the letter is therefore to be presumed to be by another's hand, written at Paul's dictation:

> 1 Corinthians 16:21. *The salutation of me Paul with mine own hand.*

This is, of course, not for a moment to be taken as indicating Paul to be illiterate. A learned Jew could not possibly be illiterate. Nevertheless, the use of a secretary leaves one free to think without the disturbance of having to form the words physically as one thinks. Then, too, there is the very practical point that a professional secretary is bound to cultivate a neat and legible handwriting, and it would not reflect on Paul's literacy to suppose that he (like many great men in history) may well have had a poor handwriting.

Romans is the one epistle in which the secretary is named, or, rather, names himself; and adds his own greetings:

> Romans 16:22. *I Tertius, who wrote this epistle, salute you . . .*

Or, it may be, Tertius is the man who made the copy that was sent on to the Ephesians.

Gaius and Erastus

Tertius adds the greetings of still others:

> Romans 16:23. *Gaius mine host . . . saluteth you. Erastus the chamberlain of the city saluteth you . . .*

Gaius is apparently offering Paul and his party the hospitality of his house at this time. If the epistle were indeed written in Corinth, then Gaius is a Corinthian and, indeed, a man of his name is mentioned in Paul's letters to the Corinthians:

1 Corinthians 1:14. . . . *I baptized none of you but Crispus and Gaius.*

Again, if Erastus is a city official, the city in question ought to be Corinth; and indeed in Paul's Second Epistle to Timothy, an Erastus is mentioned:

2 Timothy 4:20. *Erastus abode at Corinth . . .*

as though he were remaining behind in his home town. Thus, a number of points combine to make Corinth more probable as the place at which Romans was written.

11. 1 CORINTHIANS

THE EPISTLES TO THE CORINTHIANS · STEPHANUS · SOSTHENES · APOLLOS · CHARITY · EPHESUS

The Epistles to the Corinthians

Following the Epistle to the Romans are two epistles to the Corinthians which can be referred to as "1 Corinthians" and "2 Corinthians." The first of these is almost the length of Romans, and the second is not much shorter.

The church at Corinth has been founded by Paul about 51, in the course of his second missionary voyage. He had reached Corinth after his unsuccessful stay in Athens (see page 402), and in Corinth he had met Priscilla and Aquila.

He returned to Antioch by way of Ephesus, taking Priscilla and Aquila with him and leaving them at Ephesus while he went on to Antioch. In the course of his third missionary voyage, Paul returned to Ephesus and remained there from 55 to 57. It was during this interval that he wrote 1 Corinthians for he says in it:

1 Corinthians 16:8. . . . *I will tarry at Ephesus until Pentecost.*

This cannot refer to his brief stay at Ephesus at the conclusion of the second missionary voyage for events are referred to in the epistle which must have taken place after that time.

In 1 Corinthians, Paul refers to a still earlier letter he had written to the men of that city:

1 Corinthians 5:9. *I wrote unto you in an epistle not to company with fornicators.*

St. Paul's First and Second Journeys

This early letter (which we might call "o Corinthians") is not, however, necessarily lost. Parts of it may have been combined by later editors with the two epistles we do have.

Stephanus

This very first letter, o Corinthians, which is not preserved separately in the canon, apparently elicited some sort of response, and a letter was brought to Paul in Ephesus by some of the leading men of the Corinthian church. At least Paul alludes to their coming:

1 Corinthians 16:17. *I am glad of the coming of Stephanus and Fortunatus and Achaicus . . .*

There are no other Biblical references to Fortunatus and Achaicus, but the fact that they are Corinthians seems evident from a reference

made by Paul earlier in the epistle to people in Corinth whom he had
personally baptized:

> 1 Corinthians 1:16. . . . *I baptized also the household of Stepha-*
> *nus* . . .

Sosthenes

It was the letter, and perhaps the word of mouth information
brought by these Corinthian emissaries in response to o Corinthians,
that caused Paul to write the letter we know as 1 Corinthians. He
introduces this letter as coming from himself and another:

> 1 Corinthians 1:1. *Paul, called to be an apostle* . . . *and Sosthenes*
> *our brother* . . .

The only other place in the Bible in which a Sosthenes is mentioned
is in connection with Paul's arraignment before Gallio the governor
of Achaea, during the apostle's first stay at Corinth (see page 405).
Gallio refused to rule on the case, maintaining that the matter of
Paul was a problem for the Jews to decide among themselves.

Following this decision:

> Acts 18:17. . . . *all the Greeks took Sosthenes, the chief ruler of*
> *the synagogue, and beat him before the judgment seat* . . .

But there was no reason for the Greeks to beat him after Gallio
had dismissed the case, and the King James translaters seem to
have introduced the word unnecessarily. The Revised Standard Version
has the phrase read: "And they all seized Sosthenes, the ruler of the
synagogue, and beat him in front of the tribunal."

The "they all" might very likely refer to the Jewish conservatives
who had come to the courtroom to hear sentence pronounced against
Paul, and who were disappointed and frustrated over Gallio's action.
They may have turned against their own leader, who, as "prosecutor,"
had mishandled and muffed the case.

Indeed, it might even be argued that the Jews felt that Sosthenes
was "soft on Christianity" and had deliberately refrained from prosecuting Paul with full vigor. At least, there is a tradition that Sosthenes
did turn Christian afterward and eventually joined Paul and was with

him in Ephesus at the time 1 Corinthians was written. If this were so, Sosthenes would be a logical person to add his weight to the epistle, for he would be a Corinthian of note addressing Corinthians.

Apollos

Apparently one piece of news that disturbed Paul was the tale of dissensions and doctrinal disputes within the Corinthian church:

1 Corinthians 1:11. . . . *it hath been declared unto me of you . . . by them which are of the house of Chloe, that there are contentions among you.*

There is no other mention of Chloe in the Bible, but it is possible that Stephanus and the other emissaries met for worship in the house of a woman named Chloe. Perhaps there were other houses in which small groups gathered (the infant church at Corinth could very well have had no formal meeting house) and the emissaries were identified by naming their particular house.

Paul details the nature of the dissensions:

1 Corinthians 1:12. . . . *every one of you saith, I am of Paul; and I of Apollos; and I of Cephas; and I of Christ.*

This might be taken as referring to specific doctrinal difference that had already grown up around the leaders of the church. Cephas (the Aramaic name of which "Peter" is the Latin equivalent—see page 162) might represent the more conservative element of Jewish origin, holding to the Law; while Paul represented the liberal attitude that de-emphasized the importance of ritual.

Those who claimed to follow Christ might be "fundamentalists" who wished to adhere only to the reported sayings of Jesus himself and not to the added teachings of either Peter or Paul.

This leaves Apollos. Apollos had arrived in Ephesus after Paul had left it toward the conclusion of his second missionary journey. He had been a follower of John the Baptist, but Priscilla and Aquila had converted him to Christianity (see page 409).

After Apollos had become a Christian, he decided to go to Greece and work for the cause there:

Acts 18:27. . . . he was disposed to pass into Achaia . . .

. . . .

Acts 19:1. And it came to pass, that, while Apollos was at Corinth . . .

At Corinth, Apollos worked well, for Paul says:

1 Corinthians 3:6. I have planted, Apollos watered . . .

It is because Paul refers in this epistle to Apollos' work in Corinth, which had to come after Paul's first stay in Ephesus, that we know the epistle had to be written during Paul's second, and more extended, stay in that city.

Apollos' work in Corinth was sufficiently effective for him to win a personal following who admired him and considered him as their leader, as opposed to those who spoke of Paul. In what way Apollos' teachings differed from Paul's we don't know. The teachings might not have differed at all and the dispute may have rested on purely personal grounds; one group might have admired Apollos' style of preaching more than Paul's.

At least there seems to have been no animosity between Paul and Apollos. Some time before 1 Corinthians had been written, Apollos must have come back to Ephesus from Corinth and there he and Paul remained friends, for he is always referred to in friendly manner in Paul's letters:

1 Corinthians 16:12. As touching our brother Apollos, I greatly desired him to come unto you . . . he will come when he shall have convenient time.

The friendship remains, for in one of Paul's last letters, he commends Apollos to the care of the one he addresses:

Titus 3:13. Bring Zenas the lawyer and Apollos on their journey diligently, that nothing be wanting unto them.

Charity

Paul recommends unity to the Corinthian church and proceeds to answer questions concerning such things as the role of sex among

Christians. Paul believes sexual abstinence to be most desirable, but marriage is not sinful and is indeed necessary if that is the only way to keep a man from being driven into irregular unions by the whips of desire.

Paul clearly regrets that marriage should be necessary, for he, in common with the Christian fellowship generally, was convinced that the second coming was soon to take place (the new Messianic hope) and that worldly matters would come to an end, anyway:

> 1 Corinthians 7:29. *But this I say, brethren, the time is short . . .*
> . . . .
> 1 Corinthians 7:31. . . . . *the fashion of this world passeth away.*

After dealing with such minor matters as the necessity for a man worshipping with his head uncovered and a woman doing so with her head covered, Paul passes on to the matter of spiritual gifts:

> 1 Corinthians 12:1. *Now concerning spiritual gifts, brethren, I would not have you ignorant.*

The phrase "spiritual gifts" is a translation of the Greek "charisma" which means "gift."

The Greeks had three goddesses that personified all that was delightful and charming. They were known by the related word "Charites" because the desirable qualities of person that made one attractive to others was considered to be a gift of these goddesses.

In Latin, these goddesses were the "Gratiae," which again carries the notion of "gifts" freely given without question of payment (that is "gratis," for which we are "grateful").

The goddesses become in English, the "Graces." A narrow use of the word has come to signify that gift of the Graces which is characterized by smooth and harmonious physical movement. This is "grace" and a person blessed with it is "graceful." More broadly, it can refer to a variety of gifts, and someone who is capable of making such gifts with an air of pleasure is "gracious."

Christians placed emphasis on the graciousness of God. In the old Jewish view, the relationship between God and "his chosen people" was that of a covenant or contract. God would take care of his people in return for their obeying the Law. But Christians now abandoned the Law and argued that in any case no return made by man was adequate as payment for the care taken of him by God. All that man received was the free gift of God without return. Thus, Paul says:

Romans 6:15. . . . *we are not under the law, but under grace.*

Paul lists some of the spiritual gifts awarded men by the grace of God; gifts including wisdom, faith, the working of miracles, prophecy, and the gift of tongues (see page 338). Paul admits all these to be useful gifts, but maintains one gift to be superior to all the rest:

1 Corinthians 13:1. *Though I speak with the tongues of men and of angels, and have not charity, I am become as sounding brass, or a tinkling cymbal.*

1 Corinthians 13:2. *And though I have the gift of prophecy, and understand all mysteries, and all knowledge: and though I have all faith . . . and have not charity, I am nothing.*

But what is charity? The Greek word used by Paul, which is here translated as "charity," is "agape," a word which is usually translated "love." In the Revised Standard Version, in fact, the passage begins: "If I speak in the tongues of men and of angels, but have not love . . ."

The Latin version of the Bible translates "agape" as "caritas" meaning "dear." Something is "dear" if it can be attained at a great price, or if it cannot be obtained even for a great price. If you love something you hold it dear regardless of its intrinsic worth.

For that reason "agape" meaning "love" and "caritas" meaning "holding dear" have much in common. The King James Version uses the closest English analogue of the latter and makes it "charity."

Unfortunately, the translation of "agape" leaves something to be desired in either case. Charity has come to be applied specifically to one aspect of "holding dear"—the ability to hold the poor and unfortunate so dear as to be willing to share one's own wealth and fortune with them. Charity has therefore been narrowed to mean almsgiving and since alms are often given grudgingly and with disdain, and are accepted with humiliation and muffled resentment, the word "charity" has even come to carry a somewhat tainted flavor.

Similarly "love" has come to be applied to that variety of "holding dear" which implies sexual attraction. It becomes almost embarrassing to those who are used to the occurrence of the word "love" in its popular-song sense, to hear Paul praise it. Sometimes there is the impulse to qualify it and translate "agape" as "divine love," "holy love," "spiritual love," or even "Christian love." However, those who experience "agape" even faintly know what Paul means.

As for the remaining spiritual gifts, Paul finds that of prophecy superior to that of tongues; indeed, he seems rather impatient with those possessing the latter gift. To have them too freely encouraged produces pandemonium at service. Paul therefore recommends that they speak only one at a time and even then only when someone with the corresponding gift of interpretation is present. It is interesting that Paul distinguishes between prophecy and tongues, because originally the two were the same (see page I-283).

For the further sake of order at worship, Paul recommends that prophets, too, speak only one at a time and that women not speak at all.

Ephesus

At the end of the epistle, Paul earnestly preaches the doctrine of the resurrection of the body. He points out that if there were no resurrection, then Jesus could not have been resurrected. And if Jesus were not resurrected, all Christian doctrine falls to the ground. And if that is the case what is the purpose of all their efforts? Why should not everyone live for the moment?

1 Corinthians 15:32. *If after the manner of men I have fought with beasts at Ephesus, what advantageth it me, if the dead rise not? let us eat and drink; for to morrow we die.*

The phrase about fighting with beasts may have been meant purely allegorically. Paul may have referred to his labors against the beasts of paganism and sin.

Perhaps, though, there is also something of the literal in it. Can Paul have in mind the rioting sparked by the silversmiths? Were these rioters the beasts? Or might he have considered the possibility of being condemned for blasphemy as an aftermath of the affair and made to undergo a punishment such as facing wild animals in the public arena? We can't tell.

12. 2 CORINTHIANS

TIMOTHEUS · CORINTH · TITUS

Timotheus

The First Epistle to the Corinthians was given, presumably, to Stephanus and the others to take back to Corinth with them. Along with them, however, as a personal emissary, Paul was sending his beloved friend, Timothy; to instruct them in the Pauline doctrine anew:

> 1 Corinthians 4:17. *For this cause have I sent unto you Timotheus, who is my beloved son, . . . who shall bring you into remembrance of my ways, . . . as I teach every where in every church.*

He urges the Corinthians to accept Timothy kindly:

> 1 Corinthians 16:10. *Now if Timotheus come, see that he may be with you without fear . . .*

This sending of Timotheus is recorded in Acts. During Paul's stay in Ephesus in the course of his third missionary voyage, and just before the silversmiths' riot is described, he sends his emissaries:

> Acts 19:22. *So he [Paul] sent into Macedonia . . . Timotheus and Erastus; but he himself stayed in Asia for a season.*

If this Erastus is the same referred to at the end of Romans (see page 438), he is a Corinthian and is going home.

Corinth

Eventually, Paul himself plans to go to Corinth:

St. Paul's First and Second Journeys

1 Corinthians 16:5. *Now I will come unto you, when I shall pass through Macedonia . . .*

1 Corinthians 16:6. *And it may be that I will . . . winter with you.*

This, too, according to Acts, was done, for after the silversmiths' riots:

Acts 20:1. . . . *Paul . . . departed for to go into Macedonia.*

Acts 20:2. *And when he had gone over those parts . . . he came into Greece,*

Acts 20:3. *And there abode three months . . .*

If he abode three months in Corinth specifically, as seems very likely, this would be the second visit to that city mentioned in Acts. It is apparently while en route to Corinth in 57 that 2 Corinthians (or a part of it) was written. Both epistles to the Corinthians were thus written before Romans, which was composed after Paul had reached Corinth and settled down there.

With reference to his journey toward Corinth, Paul says:

> 2 Corinthians 13:1. *This is the third time I am coming to you . . .*

Apparently in between the first and second visits to Corinth which are mentioned in Acts, there was another visit. It is usually suggested that Timothy's mission met with failure and strong opposition on the part of those Corinthians who followed apostles other than Paul (see page 443). It was this which made Paul try a personal visit.

Apparently Paul's flying visit was a failure (and perhaps that was why it was not mentioned in Acts) and on his return he wrote an angry letter:

> 2 Corinthians 2:4. *For out of much affliction and anguish of heart I wrote unto you with many tears . . .*

This letter, written in anguish, is thought to be actually contained in 2 Corinthians as we now have it, making up the last four chapters.

Titus

The angry letter was sent to Corinth by the hand of Titus, a companion of Paul who is never mentioned in Acts, but is spoken of on several occasions in the epistles.

Titus is a Gentile, for in the Epistle to the Galatians, Paul describes his own coming to Jerusalem in 48 to attend the Council of Jerusalem and says:

> Galatians 2:3. . . . *neither Titus, who was with me, being a Greek, was compelled to be circumcised . . .*

Since the central issue facing the council was this very point of Paul's non-circumcision of Gentiles after conversion (see page 388) Paul was making his attitude quite plain in the heart of the territory of the opposition.

It was by this Titus that Paul sent his angry letter to Corinth and made up his mind to let that letter do its work and not go to Corinth again:

2 Corinthians 2:1. *But I determined . . . that I would not come to you in heaviness.*

However, when he left Ephesus after the silversmiths' riot, and traveled westward to Troas, he was worried over the fact that Titus had not returned:

2 Corinthians 2:13. *I had no rest in my spirit, because I found not Titus my brother . . . [so] I went from thence into Macedonia.*

There the news was good. He met Titus, who brought word that the pro-Paul faction at Corinth had won out:

2 Corinthians 7:6. *. . . God . . . comforted us by the coming of Titus;*

2 Corinthians 7:7. *And not by his coming only, but by the consolation wherewith he was comforted in you . . .*

. . . .

2 Corinthians 7:9. *Now I rejoice . . . that ye sorrowed to repentance . . .*

Part of the repentance, apparently, was the punishment of some individual who had offended Paul, perhaps on the occasion of his short second visit, by stubbornly opposing him. The person is not named and the occasion not described, but the punishment is sufficient.

Paul, apparently anxious not to allow his victory to engender such bitterness as to bring about an irrevocable split, urges forbearance. He writes a conciliatory letter (the first nine chapters of 2 Corinthians), again delivered by Titus, and in it he urges moderation, saying of the leader of the anti-Paul faction:

2 Corinthians 2:5. *. . . he hath not grieved me, but in part . . .*
2 Corinthians 2:6. *Sufficient to such a man is the punishment . . .*
2 Corinthians 2:7. *. . . ye ought rather to forgive him, and comfort him . . .*

And, eventually, Paul visited Corinth, sending 2 Corinthians in the course of this trip there, and nothing is said of further dissension.

13. GALATIANS

GALATIA

Galatia

The fourth of the epistles is addressed:

Galatians 1:1. *Paul, an apostle* . . .
Galatians 1:2. *. . . unto the churches of Galatia* . . .

The problem arises at once as to what is meant by "Galatia." Galatia proper was the region settled by the Gauls three centuries before Paul's time (see page 72). This was a relatively small area in north-central Asia Minor. After the Romans took over central and southern Asia Minor a century before Paul's time, the areas known as Lycaonia and Pisidia were combined with Galatia proper and the whole became the Roman "province of Galatia."

The original Galatia can therefore be called "North Galatia" and the Roman additions to it "South Galatia."

On Paul's first missionary journey, he and Barnabas traveled from Pamphylia through Pisidia and Lycaonia ("South Galatia"), then retraced their steps, so that cities such as Lystra, Derbe, and Antioch in Pisidia were probably visited twice.

On Paul's second missionary journey, he and (this time) Silas visited South Galatia:

Acts 16:1. *Then came he to Derbe and Lystra* . . .

Having done so Acts goes on later to say:

Acts 16:6. *. . . . they had gone throughout Phrygia and the region of Galatia* . . .

St. Paul's First and Second Journeys

It is possible that this includes portions of North Galatia, though no city in that region is specifically mentioned.

On Paul's third missionary journey, again it is said:

Acts 18:23. . . . . he departed, and went over all the country of Galatia and Phrygia in order.

Again this may refer to North Galatia.

In short, there are four passages through Galatia mentioned in Acts:

(1) the first half of the first missionary voyage through cities of South Galatia specifically;

(2) the second half of the first missionary voyage through cities of South Galatia specifically,

(3) the second missionary voyage through cities of South Galatia specifically, but possibly also through North Galatia.

(4) the first part of the third missionary voyage, possibly through South Galatia, North Galatia or both.

In Galatians, Paul says:

> Galatians 4:13. *Ye know how through infirmity of the flesh I preached the gospel unto you at the first.*

The usual interpretation is that Paul is referring to a first visit in which he preached while quite ill. And if there was a first visit there must be a second, else why bother to identify the particular visit he is referring to by saying, to paraphrase the verse, "on that first visit when I was sick."

If Paul is addressing the South Galatians, then the two visits may be numbers 1 and 2 above, both having taken place in the course of the first missionary journey, which concluded about 47.

It was then the controversy broke out over the non-circumcision of Gentile converts and the Council of Jerusalem was called to settle the matter. Apparently the conservative view in favor of circumcision was particularly virulent in the Galatian churches. Indeed, during the second missionary voyage when Paul visited Derbe and Lystra (visit number 3 in the list above) and accepted Timotheus as his disciple, he cautiously urged his young friend to accept circumcision (see page 391).

Presumably, there was a strong party in the Galatian churches who denounced Paul's views and denied his authority to grant immunity from circumcision. Galatians is Paul's defense against this and his strong maintenance of his authority.

If Galatians were indeed written soon after the first missionary voyage, then it would have been written from Antioch in 47 and might well be the earliest of Paul's epistles to be preserved and, indeed, possibly the earliest of all the books of the New Testament to achieve written form.

Paul summarizes his early life, indicating the manner in which he was converted to Christianity, and of his labors since. He refers to Peter's coming to Antioch prior to the calling of the council and he refers also to Barnabas who was with him only on the first missionary voyage:

> Galatians 2:11. *But when Peter was come to Antioch, I withstood him to the face . . .*
>
> . . . .

Galatians 2:13. . . . *Barnabas also was carried away with their* [those fearing the conservatives] *dissimulation.*

Paul does not specifically refer to the decision of the Council of Jerusalem (held in 48) which supported his views and which, one might think, ought therefore to be quoted. This backs the possibility of an early date for the epistle.

On the other hand, Paul speaks of reaching a private agreement with James, Cephas [Peter], and John:

Galatians 2:9. . . . *James, Cephas, and John . . . gave to me and Barnabas the right hands of fellowship; that we should go unto the heathen, and they unto the circumcision.*

This might have taken place prior to the first missionary voyage. But it might also have taken place after the council. With Paul's views having won out, James, Peter, and John were merely accepting·the inevitable. And the agreement would be made with both Paul and Barnabas, even though it were after the first missionary journey, for although the two never joined forces again, they had planned to.

Acts 16:36. *And some days after Paul said unto Barnabas, Let us go again and visit our brethren in every city where we have preached . . . and see how they do.*

It was only after the subsequent quarrel concerning John Mark that Paul and Barnabas parted and that Paul went through Asia Minor with Silas instead.

If Paul speaks of a first visit to the Galatians, that might be the first of three, as well as the first of two. Or perhaps visits one and two are considered a single visit since they took place within the limits of a single missionary journey, and visit three, on the second missionary voyage, is counted as the second.

If Galatians were written after the Galatian visit in the course of the second missionary voyage, it might have been written from Corinth, where Paul stayed for an extended period after having passed through Asia Minor. The epistle would then have been written in 51 rather than 47.

If the late date is accepted, one must ask why the Galatian churches did not accept the decision of the Council of Jerusalem. Why were they still so turbulent on the matter of circumcision that Paul had to send a strong letter of rebuke?

As it happens, decisions by the head of organizations are not always accepted by every one in the organization. There might well have been a strong conservative party who rejected the council's decision.

And if Paul does not refer to the council's decision in the epistle to bolster his own view it might well be that he scorned to reply on the authority of James, Peter, and John, but insisted on something more than this. There are several places in Galatians where he goes out of his way to stress his lack of debt to the Galilean apostles.

Thus, he starts off proudly:

> Galatians 1:1. *Paul, an apostle, (not of men, neither by man, but by Jesus Christ, and God the Father . . .*

Furthermore, he insists that he need submit to no other authority, for his doctrine was not something he learned from the other apostles who had known the living Jesus, but something he had learned directly by revelation:

> Galatians 1:12. *For I [Paul] neither received it [his doctrine] of man, neither was I taught it, but by the revelation of Jesus Christ.*

If, however, Paul is addressing the people of North Galatia, then he couldn't possibly have visited them twice until after the first part of his third missionary journey. He might therefore have written Galatians during his stay in Ephesus, shortly before he wrote 1 Corinthians, or even in Corinth in 58, shortly before he wrote Romans. Some commentators prefer this late date because they view the subject matter of Galatians and Romans to be much alike, with Romans a more detailed and thoughtful version.

14. EPHESIANS

Epistle to the Ephesians

Whereas the first four epistles are universally admitted to have been written by Paul, there is a dispute about the fifth, even though in the version that has reached us, Paul's authorship is stated:

> Ephesians 1:1. *Paul, an apostle of Jesus Christ . . . to the saints which are at Ephesus . . .*

Included in the reasons for doubting Paul's authorship are certain differences in style between this epistle and those which are undoubtedly Paul's, and the use of numerous words not characteristic of Paul's other writings. Furthermore, although written to the Ephesians, presumably late in Paul's life, after he had spent some years in the city, it contains no personal greetings.

It is possible, of course, that the letter was not written to the Ephesians specifically, for at least one very early manuscript does not contain the words "at Ephesus" in the first verse. Perhaps it was an epistle meant for churches generally, with copies sent to specific areas with appropriate place names added; and perhaps the one that has survived was the Ephesian copy.

Traditionally, Ephesians was one of a group of epistles written in 62 while Paul was in prison in Rome, but this, too, can be disputed. Even those who agree that the epistle was written in prison may argue, in some cases, that the imprisonment was the one at Caesarea, prior to the voyage to Rome (see page 419), and that the epistle was written in 59. Others even argue for an imprisonment at Ephesus, not mentioned in Acts, at the time of the silversmiths' riot, about 57.

St. Paul's First and Second Journeys

Tychicus

The bearer of the letter, whether a circular one to a number of churches, or indeed a specific one to the Ephesians, was Tychicus.

> Ephesians 6:21. . . . *Tychicus, a beloved brother and faithful minister in the Lord, shall make known to you all things . . .*

In the Book of Acts, Tychicus is mentioned toward the close of the third missionary journey, when Paul was leaving Macedonia for Asia Minor:

> Acts 20:4. *And there accompanied him into Asia Sopater of Berea . . . and of Asia, Tychicus and Trophimus.*

Tychicus, being a native of the province of Asia, may well have been an Ephesian (Ephesus was the capital of the province) and could have been taking the epistle with him on the occasion of a visit home.

Tychicus may have been left behind in Asia Minor after leaving Macedonia with Paul, while the apostle went on to Jerusalem and imprisonment. If so, he rejoined Paul later on, for he is mentioned in several of Paul's later epistles, and could have been the bearer of Ephesians even if it were written as late as 62.

15. PHILIPPIANS

THE EPISTLE TO THE PHILIPPIANS • BISHOPS AND DEACONS • EPAPHRODITUS
• TRUE YOKEFELLOW

The Epistle to the Philippians

This, like Ephesians, is supposed to have been written from prison. Paul alludes to his being in chains:

> Philippians 1:13. . . . *my bonds in Christ are manifest in all the palace . . .*

The phrase "in all the palace" is given in the Revised Standard Version as "throughout the whole praetorian guard." Since the praetorian guard was stationed in Rome, the site of the imprisonment would seem to be fixed there. This is further evidenced by a reference toward the end of the epistle:

> Philippians 4:22. *All the saints salute you, chiefly they that are of Caesar's household.*

Presumably those of Caesar's households are those servants or slaves of the emperor who had been converted to Christianity. Caesar is a common title for the Roman Emperor, in this case, Nero, and this would seem to make it definite that the epistle was written at Rome some time between 62 and 64. (Nero's violent persecution of the Christians after the fire of 64 could scarcely have left any Christians among his own household.)

St. Pauls' First and Second Journeys

Bishops and Deacons

The epistle begins:

> Philippians 1:1. *Paul and Timotheus . . . to all the saints which are at Philippi, with the bishops and deacons.*

Philippi is the Macedonian city which Paul visited in the course of his second missionary voyage (see page 395). It was there that Paul founded a European church for the first time.

The faithful Timotheus is with Paul, but is not apparently under formal imprisonment himself, or, if he is, he is soon to be released, for the apostle hopes to send his friend to Philippi:

> Philippians 2:19. . . . *I trust in the Lord Jesus to send Timotheus shortly unto you . . .*

The reference to bishops and deacons gives us a tantalizing glimpse as to the organization of the early Church, just enough to rouse curiosity, without even beginning to satisfy it.

The first leaders of the church were the apostles themselves, but as the number of Christians increased, other leaders were appointed. It is only natural that these were chosen from among those men preeminent for experience and wisdom. These were most likely to be the older men and they would naturally be called "elders."

Thus, when the dispute arose as to the noncircumcision of Gentile converts:

Acts 15:2. . . . *they* [the church at Antioch] *determined that Paul and Barnabas, and certain other of them, should go up to Jerusalem unto the apostles and elders about this question.*

What's more, elders were regularly appointed in the various churches founded by missionaries:

Acts 14:23. *And when they* [Paul and Barnabas] *ordained elders in every church . . . they commended them to the Lord . . .*

This rule by elders was so universally accepted a matter that the Bible scarcely bothers to mention the matter. Such rule was accepted in secular governments as well as in religious bodies. Sparta was ruled by a body called the "Gerusia" (from a Greek word for "old man") and Rome was ruled by a body called the "Senate" (from a Latin word for "old man").

(It should be mentioned, however, that we need not visualize the elders as necessarily ancient graybeards. In ancient societies, where the average life expectancy was thirty-five at best, anyone over forty qualified as an "elder.")

The Greek word for "elder" is "presbyter" (from another Greek term for "old man"). This was corrupted into "prester" (as in the legendary Prester John) and in English has become "priest."

Paul uses the term "episkopos" (or "episcopus" in the Latin spelling) as a synonym for presbyter. It means "overseer," someone who is in charge and guides the way. "Episcopus" has become, in English, "bishop." The word "deacon" is from the Greek "diakonos" and means "servant." Consequently, when Paul's words are translated as "bishops and deacons" what is really meant are "the elders and their helpers."

After New Testament days the Church developed a complicated hierarchy ("sacred government") of many levels. The basic groupings were in order of decreasing authority: bishops, priests, and deacons. A church in which bishops hold authority over wide areas is "episcopalian" in character. The Roman Catholic Church is episcopalian, as is the Greek Orthodox Church and several Protestant churches, such as the Lutherans and Anglicans. The American analogue of the Anglicans calls itself the Protestant Episcopal Church.

The Presbyterian Church is one in which bishops are not recognized but in which the elders ("presbyters") in each church hold authority on an equal basis.

None of the present significance of bishops, priests, and deacons can safely be read back into the New Testament, however.

Epaphroditus

Apparently, Paul's relationship with the Philippian church was a good one and the letter is an affectionate one of gratitude and of warm exhortation. Indeed, the occasion of the letter is the arrival of a messenger from Philippi with a contribution of money for Paul:

Philippians 4:18. . . . *I am full, having received of Epaphroditus the things which were sent from you . . .*

Furthermore, this was not the only time that the Philippians had contributed to Paul's needs:

Philippians 4:15. . . . *when I departed from Macedonia, no church communicated with me as concerning giving and receiving, but ye only.*

Philippians 4:16. *For even in Thessalonica ye sent once and again unto my necessity.*

While in Rome, Epaphroditus fell sick, but recovered and now was returning to Philippi with Paul's letter:

Philippians 2:27. . . . *he was sick nigh unto death: but God had mercy on him . . .*

Philippians 2:28. *I sent him therefore the more carefully, that, when ye see him again, ye may rejoice . . .*

True Yokefellow

At the end of the epistle, Paul raises the matter of some small dispute between two women of the Philippian church:

> Philippians 4:2. *I beseech Euodias, and beseech Syntyche, that they be of the same mind in the Lord.*
> Philippians 4:3. *And I intreat thee also, true yokefellow, help those women which laboured with me in the gospel* . . .

Nothing further is known of Euodias or Syntyche or what their quarrel was about. However, the phrase "true yokefellow" is of interest. Whom could it mean?

There are some suggestions that it referred to Paul's wife and a number of early commentators on the Bible supposed that Paul had married Lydia, the seller of purple dye whom he met in Philippi and with whom he stayed (see page 396). This does not seem very likely since Paul speaks as though he were unmarried. For in 1 Corinthians, when he reluctantly allows marriage in preference to irregular sexual unions, he wishes that this were not necessary:

> 1 Corinthians 7:7. *For I would that all men were even as I myself* . . .

This would certainly imply that Paul had never had relations with a woman. One might argue, perhaps, that he might have married for companionship, even if sex were out of the question. Indeed, Paul claims the right to do so if he chose:

> 1 Corinthians 9:5. *Have we not power to lead about a sister, a wife, as well as other apostles* . . .

But did he actually do so? It is generally assumed he did not.

But if the "true yokefellow" is not Paul's wife (and the phrase is, in any case, masculine in form in the Greek) it could refer to a close fellow worker in Philippi. A number of names have been suggested—Luke, for instance—but there is no really convincing argument in favor of any of those suggested.

One interesting possibility is that what is intended here is a personal name. The word "yokefellow" is the translation of the Greek

"Syzygos." Could there be a man with that name? Could Paul, by "true Syzygos" mean that Syzygos is well named for he is a Syzygos ("yokefellow," "co-worker") in nature and deed as well as in name. The trouble with that theory is that Syzygos is not known to have been used as a personal name by the Greeks.

The mystery will probably never be solved.

16. COLOSSIANS

COLOSSE * EPAPHRAS * THRONES, DOMINIONS, PRINCIPALITIES, AND POWERS *
LAODICEA * TYCHICUS * ARISTARCHUS * DEMAS

Colosse

The next epistle (apparently also written from Rome in 62) is addressed to a city which Paul had never visited and which is not mentioned in Acts:

> Colossians 1:1. *Paul . . . and Timotheus . . .*
> Colossians 1:2. *To the saints . . . which are at Colosse . . .*

Colosse, or, more properly, Colossae, is a city in the province of Asia, about 125 miles east of Ephesus. In the time of the Persian Empire, it had been a great city on an important trading route. Since the time of Alexander the Great, it had been declining.

Epaphras

If Paul had not himself visited Colossae and founded its church, a close co-worker apparently did so. He speaks of the Colossians knowing the gospel:

> Colossians 1:7. *As ye also learned of Epaphras our dear fellow-servant, who is for you a faithful minister of Christ . . .*

Paul mentions Epaphras again at the close of the epistle as one of those who sent his regards, so that Epaphras must have been with him in Rome. This is made even more explicit at the close of the brief

St. Paul's First and Second Journeys

Epistle to Philemon, which was written about the same time as Colossians. There he says:

> Philemon 1:23. *There salute thee, Epaphras, my fellowprisoner in Christ Jesus . . .*

The term "fellowprisoner" might merely be a metaphorical expression for two individuals who are both completely obedient (and, therefore, slaves) to the Christian doctrine. Or it might mean that Epaphras was not merely with Paul but that he was also in chains.

Thrones, Dominions, Principalities, and Powers

The occasion for the epistle was the news that had come to Paul that the Colossians were falling under the influence of Gnosticism (see page 301). Some of the Colossians were coming to accept mystical doctrines concerning vast heavenly hierarchies of angels, all serving as intermediaries between God and man. Jesus, by this view, would be just another intermediary and perhaps not a particularly important one.

This Paul denounces. He lists the attributes of Jesus, insisting, eloquently, that Jesus is all in all and that nothing can transcend him:

> Colossians 1:15. . . . [Jesus] *is the image of the invisible God . . .*
> Colossians 1:16. *For by him were all things created, that are in heaven, and that are in earth, visible and invisible, whether they be thrones, or dominions, or principalities, or powers: all things were created by him and for him.*

The reference to the thrones, dominions, principalities, and powers are to the names given various levels of angelic intermediaries, each manifesting some mystical attribute of God. Paul warns against such mystical speculations:

> Colossians 2:18. *Let no man beguile you . . .* [into] *worshipping of angels, intruding into those things which he hath not seen, vainly puffed up by his fleshly mind.*

Nevertheless, in the centuries after Paul, mystical thought invaded Christianity and hierarchies of angels were adopted in profusion, although Jesus was recognized as transcending them all. The two highest, seraphim and cherubim, come from the Old Testament, as do the two lowest, archangels and angels. The intermediate levels: thrones, dominions, virtues, powers, and principalities are, however, taken from the Gnostic theories that Paul denounces.

Laodicea

Paul seizes the opportunity to address also the church in nearby Laodicea:

> Colossians 4:16. *And when this epistle is read among you, cause that it be read also in the church of the Laodiceans . . .*

Laodicea was located about ten miles west of Colossae. The town on its site was rebuilt and improved about 250 B.C. by Antiochus II of the Seleucid Empire, who named it after his wife Laodike. It remained Seleucid till 190 B.C. when, after the defeat of Antiochus III by Rome, the region about it was awarded to Rome's ally, Pergamum.

In 133 B.C. it became Roman along with the rest of Pergamum (there-after known as the province of Asia or, simply, Asia).

As Laodice, after its renovation, grew in prosperity, that of the nearby city Colossae declined. Hierapolis, about ten miles north of Laodicea, is also mentioned at the close of the epistle. Speaking of Epaphras, Paul says:

> Colossians 4:13. . . . *he hath a great zeal for you, and them that are in Laodicea, and them in Hierapolis.*

Tychicus

The epistle is to be taken to Colossae by Tychicus the Asian (see page 458).

> Colossians 4:7. *All my state shall Tychicus declare unto you . . .*

A similar statement occurs at the end of Ephesians:

> Ephesians 6:21. . . . *that ye also may know my affairs and how I do, Tychicus . . . shall make known to you all things . . .*

It seems hard to suppose that Tychicus would make two trips to Asia Minor from Rome, if both Ephesians and Colossians were written during the Roman imprisonment. Perhaps there was only one letter, that to the Colossians, and perhaps Ephesians was an epistle written later in time by someone other than Paul in imitation of Colossians. There are certainly similarities between the two, for in Ephesians also is stressed the transcendence of Jesus:

> Ephesians 1:20. . . . *he [God] raised him [Jesus] from the dead, and set him at his own right hand . . .*
> Ephesians 1:21. *Far above all principality, and power, and might, and dominion, and every name that is named, not only in this world, but also in that which is to come:*

Nevertheless, if we were to maintain that there were two letters, both by Paul, we might suppose that he wrote a general letter to be taken from church to church in Asia Minor (the one we now know as Ephesians because the copy to Ephesus had happened to survive) and a more sharply focused one addressed to the Colossians specifically, because they seemed more prone to the Gnostic views than the others.

On his way to Colossae, Tychicus may have delivered copies of Ephesians to various churches, including that at Laodicea.

Thus, when Paul asks the Colossians to have the epistle to them read to the Laodiceans, he adds:

> Colossians 4:16. . . . and . . . ye likewise read the epistle from Laodicea.

This may refer to the copy of Ephesians sent to Colossae from Laodicea.

Aristarchus

Paul sends greetings from those with him:

> Colossians 4:10. Aristarchus my fellowprisoner saluteth you, and Marcus, sister's son to Barnabas . . .

Marcus is presumably John Mark, and if he is now with Paul, the old quarrel (see page 390) seems to have been made up.

Aristarchus, a Macedonian of Jewish background, had been with Paul in Ephesus at the time of the silversmiths' riot and had been, in fact, in considerable danger.

> Acts 19:29. And the whole city was filled with confusion: and having caught Gaius and Aristarchus, men of Macedonia, Paul's companions in travel, they [the rioters] rushed with one accord into the theater.

They were not killed, however, and Aristarchus accompanied Paul to Macedonia and Greece, then back to Asia and, eventually, Jerusalem:

> Acts 20:4. And there accompanied him [Paul] into Asia . . . of the Thessalonians, Aristarchus and Secundus . . .

Later, Aristarchus accompanied Paul on his eventful sea voyage to Rome:

> Acts 27:2. . . . we launched, meaning to sail by the coasts of Asia; . . . Aristarchus, a Macedonian of Thessalonica, being with us.

Demas

With Paul also are Luke and Demas:

Colossians 4:14. *Luke, the beloved physician, and Demas, greet you.*

Demas is mentioned also in the accompanying Epistle to Philemon, which sends greetings from the same group:

Philemon 1:23. *There salute thee Epaphras . . .*
Philemon 1:24. *Marcus, Aristarchus, Demas, Lucas . . .*

Demas is referred to once again in a still later epistle. Apparently Demas could not, in the end, take the hardships of being a Christian and, facing the virtual certainty of cruel martyrdom, forsakes Paul—and possibly Christianity as well. Paul says sadly:

2 Timothy 4:10. *For Demas hath forsaken me, having loved this present world, and is departed unto Thessalonica . . .*

17. 1 THESSALONIANS

Thessalonica

Paul and Silas had visited Thessalonica in the course of Paul's second missionary journey but had not been well received. They had been driven out by members of the Jewish colony, indignant at what seemed to them to be heresy (see page 398). The two missionaries and their company had moved on to Berea in Macedonia, then southward to Athens and Corinth.

Nevertheless, a Christian church had been founded at Thessalonica, made up of men who were of Gentile origin chiefly, and it is these whom Paul addresses:

1 Thessalonians 1:1. *Paul, and Silvanus, and Timotheus, unto the church of the Thessalonians . . .*

The Thessalonian church is apparently vigorous and pious. Paul praises them and explains that he would like to visit them but could not at the moment. He therefore took the step of sending his tried companion, Timotheus, to them:

1 Thessalonians 3:1. *Wherefore when we could no longer forbear, we thought it good to be left at Athens alone;*
1 Thessalonians 3:2. *And sent Timotheus . . . to comfort you . . .*

Timotheus returned with good news concerning the Thessalonians, and Paul now writes to expound on some points of doctrine.

This letter must have been written during Paul's first stay in Corinth,

St. Paul's First and Second Journeys

after he had left Athens, for in Acts we find he was already there when Timotheus returned:

> Acts 18:1. *After these things Paul departed from Athens, and came to Corinth;*

> . . . .

> Acts 18:5. *And when Silas and Timotheus were come from Macedonia, Paul . . . testified to the Jews that Jesus was Christ.*

All are together, in Corinth, and 1 Thessalonians is sent to Thessalonica in the name of all three. It follows that 1 Thessalonians was written about 50 and that it is very likely the earliest of Paul's writings to survive. There is a chance that Galatians was written as early as 47 (see page 455), but this is not considered very likely and most commentators accept 1 Thessalonians as the earliest.

The Trump of God

Apparently the Thessalonian church, mostly Gentile, is unused to
the theological principles developed in Judaism by the Pharisees and is
concerned over the matter of the resurrection and the final judgment.
Paul reassures them and describes the second coming in dramatic
terms:

> 1 Thessalonians 4:16. . . . *the Lord himself shall descend from*
> *heaven with a shout, with the voice of the archangel, and with the*
> *trump of God: and the dead in Christ shall rise first:*
> 1 Thessalonians 4:17. *Then we which are alive and remain shall*
> *be caught up together with them in the clouds, to meet the Lord in*
> *the air.*

The picture of the "voice of the archangel, and . . . the trump of
God" lives with us in the common tradition of the archangel Gabriel
sounding the last trumpet as the final judgment comes. Paul speaks of
this last trumpet in 1 Corinthians, too:

> 1 Corinthians 15:51. . . . *we shall all be changed,*
> 1 Corinthians 15:52. *In a moment, in the twinkling of an eye, at*
> *the last trump . . .*

Nevertheless, Paul does not say it will be Gabriel blowing his horn,
nor is this said anywhere in the Bible.

Paul is convinced that the time of the second coming is not to be
long delayed and certainly the use of "we" in 1 Thessalonians 4:17
points up his conviction that the great day would come in his own
lifetime. Nevertheless, he is careful not to specify exact times:

> 1 Thessalonians 5:1. *But of the times and the seasons, brethren, ye*
> *have no need that I write unto you.*
> 1 Thessalonians 5:2. *For yourselves know perfectly that the day of*
> *the Lord so cometh as a thief in the night.*

18. 2 THESSALONIANS

Man of Sin

The Second Epistle to the Thessalonians must have followed hard upon the first, so it too may be dated 50 and considered to have been written in Corinth.

Apparently Paul's first letter created a disturbing stir. Some of the Thessalonians rejected the possibility of the second coming, since everything seemed to be going so ill and the persecutors seemed so powerful.

Paul therefore strenuously described the day of judgment again, as a time of punishment for those who seemed so triumphant now:

2 Thessalonians 1:7. . . . *the Lord Jesus shall be revealed from heaven with his mighty angels,*

2 Thessalonians 1:8. *In flaming fire taking vengeance on them that know not God, and that obey not the gospel of our Lord Jesus Christ:*

He assures them that the great day is coming, but points out that an essential prelude to that day is the temporary triumph of evil. The very hardness of the times is, in this view, but further evidence of the imminence of the Second Coming:

2 Thessalonians 2:3. . . . *that day shall not come, except there come a falling away first, and that man of sin be revealed . . .*

2 Thessalonians 2:4. *Who opposeth and exalteth himself above all that is called God or that is worshipped . . .*

This is reminiscent of a passage in Daniel referring to the Seleucid persecutor, Antiochus IV:

St. Paul's First and Second Journeys

Daniel 11:36. *And the king shall do according to his will; and he shall exalt himself above every god . . .*

So arises a parallel. As the success of the Maccabees came only after the dark days of Antiochus IV, so would the second coming come after the dark days of the "man of sin." Indeed, Daniel's words might be considered as referring immediately to the Maccabean era and ultimately to the day of judgment.

Paul may be echoing, here, Jewish mystical thought (which may in turn have Babylonian and Persian roots) in which there is a certain symmetry between the beginning and the end of creation. Thus, the heaven and Earth were created, to begin with, through the destruction of Tiamat in the Babylonian myth, or of Leviathan as is hinted in some Biblical verses (see page I-487). At the end of this creation, there is a second creation of a more glorious type still that comes after a second victory over the old enemy.

Ezekiel describes such a last battle between the forces of good and evil in his account of Gog of the land of Magog (see page I-594). Once Gog is destroyed, the ideal kingdom is established.

Jewish legend-makers, in the century before Jesus, gave the name Belial or Beliar (see page I-204) to this final adversary of God. This legend of Beliar may have been based not only on Antiochus IV but also on other great enemies of Jewish nationalism afterward, such as Pompey and Herod the Great.

It is to this final enemy that Paul refers when he says, in a deliberate concatenation of opposites:

2 Corinthians 6:15. *And what concord hath Christ with Belial?* . . .

In the gospels, Jesus is quoted as listing the ills that would come upon the world before the final judgment, and this includes men of evil who pretend to speak in the name of God but do not. They are false Messiahs:

Matthew 24:24. *For there shall arise false Christs* . . .

In the First Epistle of John, such false Christs are referred to as "antichrists" ("opposed to Christ").

1 John 2:18. . . . *ye have heard that antichrist shall come, even now there are many antichrists* . . .

If one speaks of "false Christs" and "antichrists" in the plural, the reference might be to evil people or evil forces generally. Paul, however, uses the singular. He speaks of "that man of sin." It is as though there is an Antichrist, a particular man or force whose business it is to oppose God, win a temporary triumph, and then be smashed into utter defeat.

It would seem quite reasonable to suppose that the single Antichrist was Satan, but this is not specifically stated to be so. The search was on, therefore, at various times in history for some individual human being who might seem to play the role of Antichrist.

Perhaps Paul had in mind Caligula who, in 41, just about a decade before the epistles to the Thessalonians were written, attempted to have himself worshipped as a god within the Temple itself.

However, Caligula had been assassinated before he could quite carry through his evil design, and, in any case, the world still stood. A dozen years or so after the epistles, Nero launched his persecution of the Christians in Rome and then many must have thought that here was

Antichrist at last. Other persecuting emperors—Domitian, Decius, Diocletian—may, in their turn, have seemed to fill the role.

Through the Middle Ages, Christians saw other Christians as antichrist and in the time of the Reformation, accusations flew thickly in both directions. Particular reformers were hailed as antichrist by Catholics; particular popes were awarded the title by Protestants.

As the world went on and the second coming was delayed, despite all these antichrists, the use of the term grew less frequent. Even men who would seem to be perfect examples of Antichrist to their enemies, as, for instance, Lenin or Hitler, were rarely (if at all) hailed with the title.

19. 1 TIMOTHY

Ephesus

Following 2 Thessalonians are three epistles attributed to Paul, which deal largely with practical advice on the management of church affairs and which are therefore often termed the "pastoral epistles."

(The word "pastor" originally meant shepherd, but has come to be used more frequently for priest, who is viewed as a shepherd of souls. The metaphoric view of humans as sheep overseen by religious leaders pictured as shepherds is common in the Bible. The most frequently quoted example is:

Psalm 23:1. *The Lord is my shepherd; I shall not want.*

The first of the pastoral epistles is written to Timotheus (Timothy, in English). It is one of a pair of such epistles and is therefore "the First Epistle to Timothy" or 1 Timothy:

1 Timothy 1:1. *Paul, an apostle of Jesus Christ . . .*
1 Timothy 1:2. *Unto Timothy, my own son in the faith . . .*

This epistle pictures a state of affairs that is rather puzzling. Paul speaks of himself as free and on his travels:

1 Timothy 1:3. . . . *I besought thee to abide still at Ephesus, when I went into Macedonia . . .*

and:

1 Timothy 3:14. *These things write I unto thee, hoping to come to thee shortly . . .*

St. Paul's First and Second Journeys

It seems impossible to fit the situation in 1 Timothy into any period described in Acts and the only alternative (if Paul is indeed the writer of the epistle) is to suppose that the time referred to comes after the conclusion of Acts.

Acts ends in 64 (see page 427), the year in which Nero's persecution of the Christians in Rome took place. It would certainly seem natural to suppose that Paul would have been martyred in the course of that persecution. In the light of 1 Timothy, however, it is usually assumed that Paul was set free, presumably just before the fire at Rome that served as pretext for the persecution.

If Paul then left Rome for the east promptly, he would be out of the city when Nero seized Christians there, fed them to the lions, and made living torches out of them.

According to that view, Timothy, who had remained with Paul throughout his Roman imprisonment, would have accompanied the apostle to Ephesus and stayed there, remaining in charge of the

Ephesian church. According to later tradition, Timothy remained bishop of Ephesus for the remainder of his life, being martyred toward the end of the reign of the Roman emperor, Domitian, during another and more general persecution of Christians.

There are some who argue, however, that the pastoral epistles are not the work of Paul, but of a later writer who tried to give his views on church organization more authority by publishing them as the work of the apostle. This would make it unnecessary to make the troublesome assumption of Paul's liberation from Roman imprisonment in 64. It would also account for the fact that the style, vocabulary, and attitude of the pastoral epistles do not seem typical of Paul.

Hymenaeus

The epistle urges Timothy to deal firmly with heretics who teach false doctrine. Some have drifted away from the faith, says the writer:

> 1 Timothy 1:20. *Of whom is Hymenaeus and Alexander; whom I have delivered unto Satan . . .*

In other words, they have been excommunicated. Probably Hymenaeus and Alexander were Gnostics, for that particular heresy was strong in Asia Minor in the first century.

The excommunication did not serve to bring Hymenaeus back to orthodoxy, for in a Second Epistle to Timothy he is mentioned again, when false teachers are listed:

> 2 Timothy 2:17. . . . *their word will eat as doth a canker: of whom is Hymenaeus . . .*

Alexander, mentioned along with Hymenaeus in 1 Timothy, is mentioned again in 2 Timothy:

> 2 Timothy 4:14. *Alexander the coppersmith did me much evil: the Lord reward him according to his works . . .*

The bulk of 1 Timothy continues with rules for choice of bishops and deacons and with various regulations of churchly life.

20. 2 TIMOTHY

TROAS

Troas

The Second Epistle to Timothy, which begins with verses almost identical with those of the First Epistle, gives additional instructions for church organization. It seems to make allusions to rather wide traveling

St. Paul's First and Second Journeys

after Paul's liberation from his imprisonment at Rome. He mentions Troas, for instance:

2 Timothy 4:13. *The cloke that I left at Troas with Carpus, when thou comest, bring with thee . . .*

He also mentions Miletus:

2 Timothy 4:20. *. . . . Trophimus have I left at Miletum* [Miletus] *sick.*

It was during this period of freedom that Paul is assumed to have written 1 Timothy. His last missionary journey must soon have come to a close, however, for in 2 Timothy he speaks as someone who is condemned to death and is ready to die:

2 Timothy 4:6. *. . . . I am now ready to be offered, and the time of my departure is at hand.*

2 Timothy 4:7. *I have fought a good fight, I have finished my course, I have kept the faith . . .*

The usual assumption is that Paul was imprisoned again and, this time, condemned and executed. The date of his death is given as 67 or 68, toward the end of Nero's reign. It follows that 2 Timothy is Paul's last epistle, if it is genuine.

21. TITUS

CRETE · NICOPOLIS · DALMATIA

Crete

The third of the pastoral epistles is addressed to Titus (see page 450), who is in Crete:

> Titus 1:1. *Paul, a servant of God, and an apostle of Jesus Christ . . .*
> . . . .
> Titus 1:4. *To Titus, mine own son after the common faith . . .*
> Titus 1:5. *For this cause left I thee in Crete, that thou shouldest set in order the things that are wanting . . .*

Paul had sailed into a Cretan harbor on the occasion of his voyage to Rome (see page 424) and it is possible that Titus may have been left behind there at that time. Or Paul and Titus may have visited Crete during the supposed interval between two Roman imprisonments, and Titus may have been left behind on that occasion.

Paul warns Titus against the dangers of heresy and reminds him of the poor reputation of the men of Crete. Paul says:

> Titus 1:12. *One of themselves, even a prophet of their own, said, The Cretians are always liars, evil beasts, slow bellies.*

It is usually taken that the "prophet" being quoted is Epimenides of Knossos, concerning whom there is no hard information at all, only legend. He is supposed to have lived in the seventh century B.C. According to accounts in Roman times, he fell asleep in a cave when a boy and slept for fifty-seven years (the original Rip Van Winkle) and woke to find himself a wizard, living to an age of 150 or, according to some who are anxious to improve still further on a good story, 300.

St. Paul's First and Second Journeys

Nicopolis

The Epistle to Titus seems to have been written while Paul was still at liberty for the apostle says:

> Titus 3:12. . . . *be diligent to come unto me to Nicopolis: for I have determined there to winter.*

The epistle was therefore written before 2 Timothy.

The name "Nicopolis" means "City of Victory" and was a well-omened name used a number of times. The most important Nicopolis in the days of the Roman Empire was, however, one on the western coast of Greece near the promontory of Actium where Augustus (then Octavian, see page 261) had defeated Mark Antony. It was the final battle of the long Roman civil wars and made possible the establishment of the Roman Empire and the general peace that settled over the Mediterranean world for centuries.

Octavian himself founded the city on that site and named it in honor of his victory. Its greatest renown came through the fact that the great Stoic philosopher, Epictetus, came to Nicopolis about a quarter century after Paul's stay, and established a school there.

Dalmatia

Titus is mentioned again in 2 Timothy, Paul's last epistle. He left Crete and was sent on another mission:

> 2 Timothy 4:10. . . . *Demas . . . is departed unto Thessalonica; Crescens to Galatia, Titus unto Dalmatia.*

Dalmatia, mentioned only here in the Bible, is what is now the Yugoslavian coast, on the Adriatic shore opposite Italy. In early Roman times, it was the haunt of troublesome pirates. Rome battled them on a number of occasions and, by 155 B.C., Dalmatia had been forced to submit to Roman overlordship. The Dalmatians revolted on a number of occasions, however, and it was not until A.D. 9 that the land was brought under complete and final control.

22. PHILEMON

Philemon

The shortest epistle attributed to Paul, and the most personal, is one to Philemon, a native of Colossae:

> Philemon 1:1. *Paul, a prisoner of Jesus Christ, and Timothy . . . unto Philemon . . .*
> Philemon 1:2. *And to our beloved Apphia, and Archippus . . . and to the church in thy house . . .*

Philemon was apparently a leader in the Christian community at Colossae, for it was in his home that church meetings were held. Apphia is thought to be his wife and Archippus his son. Archippus is mentioned at the conclusion of Colossians, where Paul tells those he is addressing in that city:

> Colossians 4:17. *And say to Archippus, Take heed to the ministry which thou hast received in the Lord, that thou fulfil it.*

It may have been Archippus, then, that actually led the services at Colossae, and instructed the gathering on doctrinal points.

Onesimus

Indeed, the Epistle to Philemon was written at the same time as Colossians, all are agreed, while Paul was in his first Roman imprisonment. Thus, when Paul sends the Epistle to the Colossians by the hand of Tychicus (see page 469), he sends also another person:

St. Paul's First and Second Journeys

Colossians 4:8. . . . *I have sent [Tychicus] unto you . . .*
Colossians 4:9. *With Onesimus, a faithful and beloved brother, who is one of you . . .*

Onesimus, apparently, was a slave of Philemon. He had run away, taking some valuables of his master with him. Somehow he reached Rome, where he encountered Paul and was converted to Christianity. Paul was now sending him back to his master with the Epistle to Philemon as a personal letter of intercession. Paul says:

Philemon 1:10. *I beseech thee for my son Onesimus . . .*
Philemon 1:11. *Which in time past was to thee unprofitable . . .*

Since Onesimus means "profitable" there is a wry pun here. Paul urges Philemon to receive Onesimus as a fellow Christian and not as merely a returned slave to be punished. Paul even offers to be responsible himself for any financial loss to Philemon:

Philemon 1:15. . . . *thou shouldest receive him for ever;*
Philemon 1:16. *Not now as a servant, but . . . a brother . . .*
. . . .

Philemon 1:18. *If he hath wronged thee, or oweth thee ought,
put that on mine account;*
Philemon 1:19. . . . *I will repay it . . .*

Paul recognizes Christianity as belonging to all, making no distinction
of sex, race, nationality, or conditions of servitude. He says, in a famous
verse:

Galatians 3:28. *There is neither Jew nor Greek, there is neither
bond nor free, there is neither male nor female: for ye are all one in
Christ Jesus.*

Nevertheless, while Paul urges kindness to the slave Onesimus, who is
now Philemon's brother in Christianity, there is no hint anywhere in
Paul that slavery might be wrong and immoral as an institution. Indeed,
Paul even admonishes slaves to obey their masters, so that Christianity,
however novel some of its tenets, was by no means a doctrine of social
revolution:

Ephesians 6:5. *Servants, be obedient to them that are your masters
according to the flesh, with fear and trembling, in singleness of your
heart, as unto Christ . . .*

For that matter, nowhere else in the Bible, either in the Old Testament or the New, is slavery condemned in the abstract. Nor was slavery
denounced by any ancient prophet or philosopher among the Gentiles.
Slavery was so intimately entwined with the social and economic system
of its time that its non-existence was unthinkable. (One wonders if it is
thinkable now only because we have machines to do the work of slaves.)

All that the moral leaders of antiquity could and did do, in and out
of the Bible, was to urge humanity on slaveowners. Thus, Paul
recognizes Philemon's ownership of Onesimus, and sends Onesimus
back into slavery. Even Onesimus' conversion to Christianity makes
him no less a slave and Philemon will be within his legal rights to
punish the slave. Paul can only plead with him to be kind.

23. HEBREWS

The Epistle to the Hebrews

This fairly long epistle is intricately constructed and was originally written in highly polished Greek, so that it seems to be more a carefully written sermon, cast into epistolary form. The author refers to himself on a number of occasions as speaking rather than writing:

> Hebrews 6:9. But, beloved, we are persuaded better things of you, and things that accompany salvation, though we thus speak.

Furthermore, it does not begin as an epistle does, with the formal greetings of the writer or writers to a specifically named person or group being addressed but begins, rather, with a long well-constructed sentence that stretches over four verses:

> Hebrews 1:1. God, who at sundry times and in divers manners spake in time past unto the fathers by the prophets,
> Hebrews 1:2. Hath in these last days spoken unto us by his Son . . .

Who the writer might be, then, is not stated. The King James Version follows the most common tradition by ascribing the epistle to Paul, so that it is headed "The Epistle of Paul the Apostle to the Hebrews."

The most tempting evidence in favor of this is a mention at the end to Paul's other self, Timothy:

> Hebrews 13:23. Know ye that our brother Timothy is set at liberty; with whom, if he come shortly, I will see you.

Journeys of the Apostles

Yet the verse might have been added to bolster the Paul theory, which needs bolstering badly, for there is much against it. The style is much more polished than Paul's is anywhere else. Moreover, the arguments and theology are not characteristic of Paul, and in one or two places run flatly against what he says in other epistles. The line of argument is rather that of an eloquent Jew learned in the Alexandrian philosophy of men such as Philo (see page 301).

It is usually taken for granted nowadays, particularly among Protestant commentators, that Paul did not write the epistle. Who the author might be, if it is not Paul, is not known, of course. Several among the associates of Paul have been considered; as, for example, Silas or Barnabas.

Martin Luther suggested that Apollos may have been the writer and this is a very attractive suggestion. Apollos was an associate of Paul (see page 444) and is described thus:

> Acts 18:24. . . . *a certain Jew named Apollos, born at Alexandria, an eloquent man, and mighty in the scriptures* . . .

This is exactly what one would need to produce Hebrews, and one might almost say that if Apollos were not the author, he ought to be.

To whom is the epistle addressed? What does the general term "To the Hebrews" mean? Does it refer to a specific church? Is it intended for Jews everywhere? Or for Christians of Jewish background?

The one hint is that at the conclusion, the writer sends the greetings of those about him:

> Hebrews 13:24. . . . *They of Italy salute you.*

This might make it seem that the writer is outside Italy and is addressing a group within Italy. Those with the writer who are from Italy would naturally send greetings to their compatriots.

Then, too, the first known use of this epistle was by a Roman Christian named Clement in 96. The epistle existed in that city before it existed anywhere else, perhaps. It may be, then, that the epistle was addressed to Christians of Jewish origin in Rome, and came possibly from Alexandria.

And when was it written? If it had been written by Paul, then the date would probably fall about 64. There are several references to the falling away of men who were previously faithful and the writer exhorts them to remain in the faith, threatening them with divine punishment if they do not:

Hebrews 10:28. *He that despised Moses' law died without mercy under two or three witnesses:*

Hebrews 10:29. *Of how much sorer punishment, suppose ye, shall he be thought worthy, who hath trodden under foot the Son of God . . .*

This might be appropriate for the time of the Neronian persecution in Rome in 64 when it took a great deal of fortitude to remain Christian, and when it was necessary for the author to reassure the faithful and promise a speedy second coming:

Hebrews 10:35. *Cast not away therefore your confidence . . .*
Hebrews 10:36. *For ye have need of patience . . .*
Hebrews 10:37. *For yet a little while, and he that shall come will come, and will not tarry.*

And yet the difficulties of the Neronian persecution would fall on all Christians alike. Why, then, should the epistle exhort, according to its name, and by its whole line of argument, specifically those of Jewish background?

It is possible that the epistle was written after the destruction of the Temple in 70, when general conditions within the Christian fellowship changed radically. To the Christians of Gentile origin, this destruction would not have mattered greatly. It might even have been a source of satisfaction that the Jews who had not accepted Jesus as Messiah had thus been fittingly punished.

To the Christians of Jewish extraction, however, the end of the Temple must have been a terrible blow. Its end would have made sense to them, perhaps, only if it were followed by the establishment, at long last, of the ideal state; if, that is, the second coming had been the climax to which the Temple's destruction had been the prelude.

But the years passed after the Temple's destruction and no second coming took place. Christians of Jewish background may even have felt that the destruction of the Temple could only have been the sign of God's anger at the Christian heresy. The increasing numbers of Christians of Gentile extraction, openly hostile to Jews, might have contributed to their alienation. Conversions to Christianity must largely have ceased among the Jews, and increasing numbers of Christian Jews must have reverted to the older faith, leaving the Church virtually entirely Gentile from 100 onward.

Perhaps, then, Hebrews was written about 80, when Jewish alienation was increasingly obvious and when it seemed to the writer that Jewish defection might gravely damage the Christian cause.

Melchizedek

The bulk of Hebrews, therefore, is an eloquent attempt on the part of the writer to demonstrate, entirely through Old Testament references, that the doctrine of Jesus is superior to that of Moses, and that the old Jewish teachings can only be climaxed and properly brought to its peak in Christianity.

Thus, he endeavors to show Jesus to be the ideal high priest foreshadowed in the very first book of the Bible:

Hebrews 6:20. . . . *Jesus, made an high priest for ever after the order of Melchisedec.*

This refers to an incident that occupies three verses in the Book of Genesis. When Abram [Abraham] and his band are returning from the rescue of Lot from the hands of an invading raiding party, the patriarch passes by Salem (usually taken to be the city eventually known as Jerusalem).

Genesis 14:18. *And Melchizedek king of Salem brought forth bread and wine: and he was the priest of the most high God.*

Melchizedek was both king and priest and this was seized upon before the Exile to justify the priestly functions of the king of Judah at a time when the Temple priesthood was striking hard to reserve those functions for itself (see page I-504). Thus one of the psalms states:

Psalm 110:4. *The Lord hath sworn, and will not repent, Thou art a priest for ever after the order of Melchizedek.*

If this were a coronation psalm, the king of Judah to whom it was addressed would in this fashion be flatteringly addressed as both king and high priest "after the order of Melchizedek."

In post-Exilic times, when the kingship was gone and the priesthood retained full power, the original significance of the psalm was gone. In its place, the psalm gained Messianic significance.

Thus "Melchizedek" means "king of righteousness." And since "Salem" means "peace," Melchizedek as ruler of Salem is "the Prince of Peace" and that is a Messianic title:

Isaiah 9:6. *For unto us a child is born, unto us a son is given:* . . . *and his name shall be called* . . . *The Prince of Peace.*

Furthermore, the verses in Genesis are too brief to give the name of Melchizedek's father or his children. In post-Exilic times, there was gradually ascribed a mystic significance to this and it was taken to mean that Melchizedek had neither father nor son but existed eternally and represented an everlasting priesthood without beginning or end:

Hebrews 7:1. *For this Melchisedec, king of Salem,* . . .
Hebrews 7:2. . . . *which is, King of peace;*
Hebrews 7:3. *Without father, without mother, without descent, having neither beginning of days, nor end of life; but made like unto the Son of God; abideth a priest continually.*

Melchizedek, therefore, seems to be the representative of the Messiah, and may even have been thought by some to have actually been the Messiah, briefly visiting the Earth in order to encounter Abraham.

Abraham apparently recognized the priestly character of Melchizedek for he gave him the usual share of the spoils accorded the priesthood—a tenth (or "tithe").

Genesis 14:20. . . . *And he* [Abram] *gave him* [Melchizedek] *tithes of all.*

The writer of Hebrews comments on this by saying:

Hebrews 7:4. *Now consider how great this man* [Melchizedek] *was, unto whom even the patriarch Abraham gave the tenth of the spoils.*

And if Abraham himself acted the part of submission to Melchizedek, even more so must the Levites—the Jewish priesthood—who are descended from one of Abraham's descendants. If the psalmist's reference concerning "a priest for ever after the order of Melchizedek" is now applied to Jesus, it follows that Jesus' doctrine is superior to that of the Jewish priesthood by reasoning based on the Old Testament itself.

24. JAMES

James

Seven short epistles follow Hebrews, none of which are by Paul, and none of which are addressed to specific churches. Because the problems discussed are also general, they are considered epistles addressed to Christians everywhere. They are therefore called the "general epistles" or "universal epistles." Sometimes they are called the "Catholic epistles" (because "catholic" is from the Greek "katholikos" meaning "universal").

The first of these epistles is attributed to someone named James:

> James 1:1. *James, a servant of God and of the Lord Jesus Christ, to the twelve tribes which are scattered abroad . . .*

It is generally assumed that the James referred to here is James, the brother of Jesus (see page 361), who was the leader of the church in Jerusalem.

According to the Jewish historian Josephus, James was stoned to death in 62. This came at a time after the procurator Festus (see page 419) had ended his term of office and before the new procurator had arrived. The high priest, Ananus II, controlled Jerusalem during this interregnum and found himself facing the increasingly powerful party of the Zealots who, only four years later, were to instigate the disastrous rebellion against Rome.

James, as the leader of the Christians in Jerusalem, must have been abhorrent to the Zealots, not for his doctrines, but for the fact that he represented a pacifist group who urged peaceful submission to Rome. Ananus II attempted to appease the turbulent Zealots by having James

Journeys of the Apostles

executed. When the new procurator, Albinus, arrived, he naturally interpreted this as an anti-Roman move and Ananus II was deposed.

If, then, James were indeed the author of the epistle, it would have had to have been written before 62. Indeed, since the epistle is addressed "to the twelve tribes" as though the problem of Christians of Gentile origin had not yet arisen, and as the dispute over circumcision which led to the Council of Jerusalem is nowhere mentioned, it is sometimes supposed that the epistle was written before 48, the date of the Council. If that were so, James would be the earliest book in the New Testament, earlier than any of Paul's epistles.

However, the book is written in better Greek than one might expect of a relatively unlettered Galilean like James. It might be that the epistle was written about 90, in the time of the persecution by Domitian. It might then have been ascribed to James to give it greater authority.

The substance of the book is largely moralistic, advising its readers on the path of good behavior. It might almost be considered a typical piece of "wisdom literature" (see page I-507). Much the same might be said of the other general epistles.

25. 1 PETER

SYLVANUS · BABYLON

Sylvanus

The next epistle is one of two ascribed to Peter:

1 Peter 1:1. *Peter, an apostle of Jesus Christ, to the strangers scattered throughout Pontus, Galatia, Cappadocia, Asia, and Bithynia . . .*

Much of what this epistle contains sounds very much like Paul, and the region being addressed—Asia Minor—was one that had been proselytized by Paul's unremitting labors.

Peter was a Galilean, who was not very likely to be proficient in Greek, and if he did write this epistle he would very likely have done so through a translater. One is mentioned:

1 Peter 5:12. *By Silvanus, a faithful brother . . . I have written . . .*

The only Sylvanus mentioned elsewhere in the Bible, is the associate of Paul, who was joined with him, for instance, in the writing of the epistles to the Thessalonians:

1 Thessalonians 1:1. *Paul, and Silvanus, and Timotheus, unto the church of the Thessalonians . . .*

This Sylvanus is considered identical with the Silas of Acts, the associate who accompanied Paul on his second missionary journey. If Peter's Sylvanus is identical with Paul's Silas, it would follow that Peter was writing his epistle with the aid of someone well acquainted with Paul's line of thinking. Peter, throughout the New Testament, is made to appear a rather weak personality, and it is not beyond the realm of

Journeys of the Apostles

possibility that in the presence of Silas he might easily be induced to express himself in a Pauline manner.

There are some who suggest that Silas was the real author of the epistle, but if that were so, why was it not ascribed to Paul, rather than to Peter?

Babylon

It might also be argued that the epistle was written long after both Peter and Paul were dead, and that it was merely ascribed to Peter to lend it authority. Thus, at the conclusion of the epistle, the writer sends greetings:

> 1 Peter 5:13. *The church that is at Babylon . . . saluteth you . . .*

Clearly, this cannot be taken literally. There was no church at Babylon, for, indeed, the city no longer existed. But it is an old Biblical device to use the name of a bygone persecutor in order to indicate, discreetly, a present enemy. By Babylon, therefore, is surely meant Rome.

If Peter is the author of the epistle, he is therefore writing from Rome, where he would meet Silas and make use of his services. Later legend does state firmly that Peter went to Rome, helped organize the church there, served as its first bishop, and died a martyr during the persecutions of Nero in 64. (Having received the primacy of the church from Jesus himself Peter passed on this primacy, according to Catholic doctrine, to the successive bishops of Rome that followed him and upon this is based the theory of Papal supremacy.)

If Peter wrote this epistle, then, it would have had to be written before 64. And yet the Bible says nothing directly of Peter's stay in Rome, and Paul, in the epistles written from Roman imprisonment, gives no indication of the presence of Peter there.

Furthermore, it is unlikely that the use of the term Babylon for Rome would occur before 64 or even for some time afterward. In the generation that followed the crucifixion, the chief enemy of the Christians was the Jewish priesthood and it was to Roman officials that Christians turned for protection; to procurators, governors, and even, as in Paul's case (see page 419), to the emperor himself.

The persecutions of 64 may have shaken Christian trust in Rome, but that was only the personal action of Nero, striving to please the Roman populace by putting on a show of zeal in searching for the arsonists who had presumably set the Roman fire. The persecution was confined to the city of Rome and did not last long. The Christians of the eastern provinces, where the large bulk of them were to be found, were not touched.

Then not long after the Neronic persecution, the Jewish rebellion smashed Jewish society and destroyed the Temple. After 70 the Jews of the empire were in no position to try to crush Christianity; they were in desperate danger of being wiped out themselves.

Under the Emperor Domitian, who reigned from 81 to 96, repressive measures were taken against the Jews, with whom the Christians (for the last time) were lumped together. This Domitianic persecution was empire-wide and for the first time the Christians of Asia Minor felt organized repression from the central government. The epistle, addressed to the Christians of Asia Minor, refers to such repression:

1 Peter 4:12. *Beloved, think it not strange concerning the fiery trial which is to try you . . .*

From now on, for two centuries, it is the Roman government that is Christianity's great enemy, and it is now that Rome would become "Babylon." On this basis, it might be argued that 1 Peter is not written by Peter at all, but was written by an unknown person in Domitian's time, a generation after the death of Peter.

26. 2 PETER

Simon Peter

The next epistle is also attributed to Peter:

2 Peter 1:1. *Simon Peter, a servant and an apostle of Jesus Christ, to them that have obtained like precious faith* . . .

This is backed up by a reference to Peter's past life; to his witnessing the transfiguration (see page 195).

2 Peter 1:16. *For we have not followed cunningly devised fables, when we made known unto you the power and coming of our Lord Jesus Christ, but were eyewitnesses of his majesty.*

. . . .

2 Peter 1:18. . . . *when we were with him in the holy mount.*

Nevertheless, from the style and contents, many commentators deduce that it must be of rather late origin. Its writing is related to the Epistle of Jude, which is itself late. Then, too, the epistle mentions Paul's epistles, almost as though they were already collected and considered inspired:

2 Peter 3:15. . . . *the long-suffering of our Lord is salvation; even as our beloved brother Paul . . . hath written unto you;*

2 Peter 3:16. . . . *in all his epistles* . . .

It is possible that 2 Peter, like 1 Peter and James, may date to the Domitianic persecution, and have been written about 90. (Indeed, the book is not mentioned prior to 200 and some commentators suggest that it may even have been written as late as 150.)

Journeys of the Apostles

The Day of the Lord

An indication of the comparative lateness of the epistle may be found in the fact that some Christians must have grown impatient while waiting for a second coming that seemed endlessly delayed. The writer of 2 Peter finds he must exercise his ingenuity to explain the stretched-out delay, after Paul's promise of imminence. He explains:

2 Peter 3:8. . . . *one day is with the Lord as a thousand years, and a thousand years as one day.*

2 Peter 3:9. *The Lord is not slack concerning his promise, as some men count slackness* . . .

The reference here is to a quotation from the psalms:

Psalm 90:4. *For a thousand years in thy sight are but as yesterday when it is past* . . .

In other words, the writer maintains that while the second coming is imminent (since so many authoritative spokesmen have said so) that may mean imminence in God's view of time rather than man's view. And it will come:

2 Peter 3:10. *But the day of the Lord will come as a thief in the night* . . .

27. 1 JOHN

THE WORD

The Word

Three epistles follow which, like Hebrews, do not have the name of the writer in the first verse. However, the style and content are so completely reminiscent of those of the fourth gospel, that it seems certain that whoever wrote the fourth gospel wrote the epistles. Even the characteristic designation of Jesus as the "Word" appears:

> 1 John 1:1. *That which was from the beginning . . . of the Word of life . . .*

The three epistles are therefore ascribed to John son of Zebedee (assuming he wrote the fourth gospel). It would further seem that, like the fourth gospel, these epistles were written in Ephesus about 100. This first and longest of John's three epistles warns against anti-christs (see page 477) and present an exhortation to brotherly love.

Journeys of the Apostles

28. 2 JOHN

The Elder

In the second and third (very short) epistles of John, the author refers to himself merely as an elder or priest:

2 John 1:1. *The elder unto the elect lady and her children . . .*

There have been some speculations that there was a "John the Presbyter" ("John the elder") in Ephesus who is to be distinguished from John the Apostle, and that it was the former who wrote the epistles of John and, therefore, the fourth gospel as well. This depends, however, upon the faintest possible evidence, and is not taken seriously.

As for the elect lady, this may be taken either literally or figuratively. John may be addressing a particular Christian woman, or he may be addressing the Church generally, referring to it in this allegorical manner. In either case, he again exhorts his readers to follow the command of brotherly love.

29. 3 JOHN

Gaius

The third epistle of John begins like the second:

3 John 1:1. *The elder unto the wellbeloved Gaius . . .*

Gaius is some otherwise unknown personage who is treated by John as an ally who will support him against the leader of another faction:

3 John 1:9. *I wrote unto the church: but Diotrephes, who loveth to have the preeminence among them, receiveth us not.*
3 John 1:10. *Wherefore, if I come, I will remember his deeds . . .*

30. JUDE

JUDE • MOSES • ENOCH

Jude

The author of this epistle, the last of the general epistles, identifies himself in the first verse:

Jude 1:1. *Jude, the servant of Jesus Christ, and brother of James, to them that are sanctified* . . .

If this is taken at face value, Jude the brother of James may be identified as another brother of Jesus. Jude is but a short form of Judas and the only pair of brothers named James and Judas in the New Testament, outside this epistle, are among the brothers of Jesus:

Matthew 13:55. *Is not this* [Jesus] *the carpenter's son?* . . . *and his brethren, James, and Joses, and Simon, and Judas?*

But this short epistle is very like the second chapter of 2 Peter, and like 2 Peter, it may well date from the period of Domitian. Since it is unlikely that a brother of Jesus would still be alive at that time, the epistle may be by someone called Judah, a common name, and some later editor added "brother of James" to increase its importance.

Moses

Jude, like 2 Peter, denounces certain heresies. Jude is unusual in that it contains quotes from the apocryphal literature, which it advances as authoritative. Thus, the writer compares the heretics with Satan, since

Journeys of the Apostles

the former slander the true believers as Satan slandered Moses. The writer does not even bother quoting the details of the slander, assuming it to be well known to his readers:

> Jude 1:9. . . . *Michael the archangel, when contending with the devil he disputed about the body of Moses* . . .

This is apparently a reference to "The Assumption of Moses" a book written by some Palestinian Jew during the lifetime of Jesus. It purports to tell of Moses' death, burial, and assumption into heaven. The passage about Michael and the devil is not to be found in the fragmentary copies that remain but from ancient references the matter can be eked out.

It is the devil's task to act as a sort of prosecuting attorney as men's souls are tried. In Moses' case, the devil demanded that he be barred from heaven as a murderer, since he had killed an Egyptian overseer:

> Exodus 2:11. . . . *when Moses was grown . . . he spied an Egyptian smiting an Hebrew* . . .
> Exodus 2:12. *And he looked this way and that way, and when he saw that there was no man, he slew the Egyptian, and hid him in the sand.*

This is another argument for the lateness of Jude, since some time would be expected to pass before so late a writing as "The Assumption of Moses" would begin to gain a cachet of authority.

Enoch

The writer of Jude also quotes from the Book of Enoch, which contains a prophecy of the forthcoming divine punishment of the heretics:

> Jude 1:14. *And Enoch also, the seventh from Adam, prophesied of these, saying, Behold, the Lord cometh with ten thousands of his saints,*
> Jude 1:15. *To execute judgment upon all* . . .

The Book of Enoch, written about 100 B.C., is not accepted as canonical by Jews, Catholics, or Protestants, but Jude apparently considered it inspired. He was even impressed by its supposed antiquity, for he stresses that Enoch is "seventh from Adam"; that is, of the seventh generation after Creation: Adam, Seth, Enos, Cainan, Mahalaleel, Jared, and Enoch.

31. 2 ESDRAS

THE PROPHET ESDRAS * URIEL * THE SODOMITISH SEA * BEHEMOTH AND
LEVIATHAN * THE MESSIAH * THE EAGLE * THE TEN TRIBES * TWO HUNDRED
AND FOUR BOOKS * EGYPT * THE CARMANIANS

The Prophet Esdras

Apocalyptic literature was popular with the Jews of the Greek and
Roman period. Its production did not cease even after the destruction
of the Temple. Indeed, the increase of misery was bound to sharpen the
Messianic longing and the dream that the world would eventually be
set right by divine intervention.

About a generation after that destruction, a Jewish apocalypse was
produced which actually found its way into some versions of the Bible.

In the usual fashion of apocalyptic writing, it was attributed to an
ancient sage—in this case Ezra, the scribe who for a period dominated
Jerusalem after the return from exile some five and a half centuries
before the apocalypse was actually written (see page I-449). Although
quite Jewish in outlook, this apocalypse interested Christians because of
its strong emphasis on Messianic prophecies.

Some unnamed Christian edited the book about 150 and added
what are now its first two chapters. A century later still, another
individual, presumably also Christian, added what are now the final
two chapters.

The mid-portion of the book was originally written in Aramaic, then
translated into Greek. The first two and last two chapters were in
Greek to begin with.

Both Aramaic and Greek versions have vanished. A Latin translation
survived, however, and was included in Catholic versions of the Bible,

Palestine at the Time of the Jewish-Roman War

not as an integral part, but as a kind of appendix to the New Testament. It is therefore included in the Apocrypha, and the King James Version is a translation from the Latin.

Other translations, in various Oriental languages, also survive, however, and the Revised Standard Version draws on these as well as on the Latin.

The apocalypse begins by giving the name of its purported author:

> 2 Esdras 1:1. *The second book of the prophet Esdras* [Ezra] . . .

The first book is, of course, 1 Esdras (see page I-461).

Uriel

The first two chapters of the book, Christian in outlook, describe the manner in which the Jews have consistently failed to heed the prophets. It rejects circumcision, and warns the Jews that they will be forsaken and that others will be chosen in their stead. At times, phraseology very reminiscent of the gospels is chosen.

With the third chapter, however, 2 Esdras begins in its original version, and with it the first of a series of seven visions:

> 2 Esdras 3:1. *In the thirtieth year after the ruin of the city I was in Babylon, and lay troubled upon my bed* . . .
> 2 Esdras 3:2. *For I saw the desolation of Sion, and the wealth of them that dwelt at Babylon.*

On the face of it this would be the thirtieth year after Nebuchadnezzar's destruction of Jerusalem and the Temple, or 556 B.C. This, however, was a century before the true Ezra's time.

Presumably it is the author's way of referring elliptically to the fact that he was writing thirty years after the Roman destruction of Jerusalem and the Temple, or A.D. 100. Perhaps he was on a visit to the city of Rome, then at the peak and pinnacle of its worldly power and luxury, and the contrast between this and ruined Jerusalem was more than he could bear, and it set him to writing the book.

Ezra is pictured as questioning God, wanting to know whether the Babylonians (Romans) were not just as sinful as the Jews, if not more so, and why it was, then, that they should flourish while the

Jews, who at least knew God, even if they were not always perfectly virtuous, were in such misery.

An angel was sent to him to answer his question:

> 2 Esdras 4:1. *And the angel that was sent unto me, whose name was Uriel, gave me an answer* . . .

Uriel ("my light is God") is not to be found in the canonical Old Testament. He is an apocryphal creation, brought to life during the elaborate legends of angels and demons built up in post-Exilic times through Persian influence. Uriel was one of the seven archangels listed in the apocryphal Book of Enoch.

Because of the significance of his name, Milton, in *Paradise Lost* viewed him as the angel who was in particular charge of the sun. The Mohammedans identify Uriel with Israel, the angel in charge of music and the one who will sound the last trump on the day of judgment (the role of Gabriel in Christian legend).

The Sodomitish Sea

Uriel tells Ezra that the human mind is too limited to grasp the purposes of God but that all will become plain in the end, with the day of judgment and the coming of the ideal heavenly state. This is coming soon but only after evil approaches a climax. Then:

> 2 Esdras 5:4. . . . . *the sun shall suddenly shine again in the night, and the moon thrice in the day:*
> 2 Esdras 5:5. *And blood shall drop out of wood, and the stone shall give his voice* . . .
> . . . .
> 2 Esdras 5:7. *And the Sodomitish sea shall cast out fish* . . .

In other words, impossibilities will come to pass, heralding the end of ordered nature. The Sodomitish sea is, of course, the Dead Sea, on the shores of which Sodom had once stood (see page I-71). There are no fish in the salt-filled depths of the Dead Sea so that to find fish teeming there would be as impossible as the sun shining by night, wood bleeding, or stones crying out.

Behemoth and Leviathan

In a second vision Uriel describes more of the impossibilities that will herald the coming of the end. Then, in a third vision, Ezra describes the order of creation as given in the first chapter of Genesis. He adds additional detail, however, in line with the legends that had been added to the Biblical account in Greek times.

> 2 Esdras 6:47. *Upon the fifth day . . .*
>
> . . . .
>
> 2 Esdras 6:49. *Then didst thou ordain two living creatures, the one thou callest Enoch, and the other Leviathan;*
>
> . . . .
>
> 2 Esdras 6:51. *Unto Enoch thou gavest one part . . . wherein are a thousand hills,*
>
> 2 Esdras 6:52. *But unto Leviathan thou gavest the seventh part, namely the moist; and hast kept him to be devoured of whom thou wilt and when.*

The word "Enoch" is more properly "Behemoth" (see page I-485) and it is that which is used in the Revised Standard Version. The existence of these primordial monsters is an example of the colorful legends upon which the rabbis delighted to elaborate. They find their Biblical excuse in a single phrase in the Genesis account of the fifth day:

> Genesis 1:21. *And God created great whales . . .*

The word given here as "whales" is a translation of the Hebrew word "tannin" which is more accurately taken as signifying huge sea creatures generally. Indeed, the Revised Standard Version translates the phrase, "So God created the great sea-monsters . . ."

It is interesting that 2 Esdras refers to the sea as taking up one-seventh of the Earth's surface. The ancient geographers, unable to penetrate far out to sea, had no idea of the true extent of the ocean. Indeed, it was not until the explorations of Captain Cook in the eighteenth century that it was fully borne in on man just how extensive the ocean was; and that it occupied, not 15 percent, but 70 percent of the planetary surface.

The reference to Leviathan being kept "to be devoured of whom thou wilt and when" was in reference to the Rabbinic legend that when the Messiah came and the ideal kingdom was established, the righteous would celebrate at a great feast in which Leviathan would be eaten.

Ezra goes through this account in order to reason that all this magnificent creative endeavor was done for the sake of Israel, and yet (the complaint he makes over and over) Israel has been devastated by the triumphing heathen.

The Messiah

Uriel blames the situation on Adam's original sin in the garden of Eden, and again goes on to describe details of the end of the world. After all the signs have taken place:

> 2 Esdras 7:28. . . . my son Jesus shall be revealed . . . and they that remain shall rejoice within four hundred years.
>
> 2 Esdras 7:29. After these years shall my son Christ die, and all men that have life.

The word "Jesus" is found only in the Latin copy and betrays the hand of the Christian editor. In the Oriental languages, the expression is "my son the Messiah" and it is in that way that the Revised Standard Version gives it.

The Messianic kingdom, in this vision, comes not after the day of judgment, but before. It is the final act of the modern world.

The duration of four hundred years for the Messianic kingdom is found in the Latin translation. One Arabic translation gives a thousand years. Revelation, the completely Christian apocalypse, also speaks of a thousand years as the duration of the Messianic kingdom, with two resurrections, one at the beginning and one at the end of that kingdom:

> Revelation 20:6. . . . he that hath part in the first resurrection . . . shall be priests of God and of Christ, and shall reign with him a thousand years.

It is for this reason that people speak of the "millennium" (Latin for "a thousand years") as a time of ideal bliss. Belief in this doctrine is called "chiliasm" (from a Greek word meaning "a thousand"). Those who believe that the millennium is at hand, and there have been many of these in each generation over the last two thousand years, are called "millennarians" or "chiliasts."

Then, in a fourth vision, Ezra is allowed to see the glories of a heavenly Jerusalem that would eventually succeed the destroyed Earthly one.

The Eagle

The fifth vision is a complicated one after the fashion made popular by the Book of Daniel:

> 2 Esdras 11:1. *Then saw I a dream, and behold, there came up from the sea an eagle, which had twelve feathered wings, and three heads.*

This is later interpreted by Uriel as being the fourth beast in Daniel's vision:

> 2 Esdras 12:11. *The eagle whom thou sawest . . . is the kingdom which was seen in the vision of thy brother Daniel.*
> 2 Esdras 12:12. *But it was not expounded unto him, therefore I declare it unto thee.*

The fourth kingdom is described in Daniel as follows:

> Daniel 7:7. . . . *behold a fourth beast, dreadful and terrible, and strong exceedingly; and it had great iron teeth . . . and it had ten horns.*

To the writer of Daniel, writing in the time of Antiochus IV, this beast represented the Seleucid Empire, and its ten horns were the ten Seleucid kings up to the time of writing. But now the Seleucid Empire was long since gone and it was necessary to reinterpret the beast as the Roman Empire. The twelve wings were the twelve Roman emperors up to the time 2 Esdras was written:

> 2 Esdras 12:14. *In the same shall twelve kings reign, one after another;*
> 2 Esdras 12:15. *Whereof the second . . . shall have more time than any of the twelve.*

2 Esdras 12:16. And this do the twelve wings signify, which thou sawest.

In order to explain this we must take Julius Caesar as the first emperor. He wasn't really, but he was often considered such in ancient times. (Thus, the Roman historian Suetonius wrote a famous and still-existing book called *The Lives of the Twelve Caesars*, about a generation after 2 Esdras was written. It dealt with the first emperors and it too begins with Julius Caesar.)

The twelve are: Julius, Augustus, Tiberius, Caligula, Claudius, Nero, Galba, Otho, Vitellius, Vespasian, Titus, and Domitian. Domitian reigned from 81 to 96 and since there are only twelve wings on the eagle, it would seem that 2 Esdras was composed late in Domitian's reign.

Augustus, the second emperor in the list, reigned forty-one years, far longer than any of the remaining eleven, so that the second did indeed "have more time than any of the twelve." In fact, Augustus' reign was to prove longer than that of any emperor ruling from Rome in the entire history of that empire.

Eventually the three heads of the eagle come into play:

2 Esdras 11:29. . . . there awaked one of the heads . . . namely, it that was in the midst; for that was greater than the two other heads.

. . . .

2 Esdras 11:31. And, behold, the head . . . did eat up the two feathers under the wing that would have reigned.

2 Esdras 11:32. But this head . . . bare rule . . . over all those that dwell in the earth . . .

The three heads are the three emperors of the Flavian Dynasty. The large central one is Vespasian, the two smaller ones on either side, his sons Titus and Domitian. These would be viewed by the writer of 2 Esdras with particular horror, for it was Vespasian and Titus who led the armies against the Jews when they revolted and it was Titus who took and sacked Jerusalem in 70 and destroyed the Temple.

The events referred to in the verses quoted above follow the assassination of Nero when several candidates strove for the vacated throne, with Vespasian winning out. He became emperor in 69 and ruled without dispute for ten years.

In the reign of the third head (Domitian), a new creature entered and rebuked the eagle:

> 2 Esdras 11:37. . . . *a roaring lion chased out of the wood . . .*
> *and said* [to the eagle],
> . . . .
> 2 Esdras 11:39. *Art not thou it that remainest of the four*
> *beasts . . .*
> . . . .
> 2 Esdras 12:3. . . . *and the whole body of the eagle was burnt . . .*

The lion is identified by Uriel:

> 2 Esdras 12:31. *And the lion, whom thou sawest . . . speaking*
> *to the eagle, and rebuking her . . .*
> 2 Esdras 12:32. *This is the anointed . . .*

In other words, the Messiah will come at the end of Domitian's reign and the Roman Empire will be destroyed while the Messianic kingdom will rise in its place.

Of course, this did not happen and, instead, Domitian's reign was followed by that of the five "good emperors" under whom, for eighty years, Rome went through its profoundest period of peace and quiet. Nevertheless, the Messianic longing among the Jews carried them through to one last set of catastrophes.

The revolt in Judea from 66 to 70 had exacerbated relations between Jews and Greeks in Egypt. Eventually, widespread riots led to considerable bloodshed on both sides with the Jews (who were in the minority) eventually getting the worst of it. The Jewish temple in Alexandria was destroyed and thousands of Jews were killed, putting an effective end to what had been the most prosperous, numerous, and intellectually productive Jewish community in the ancient world.

There remained a large colony of Jews in Cyrene to the west of Egypt proper. In 115, during the reign of Trajan, the second emperor to follow Domitian, Messianic fervor (fed by books such as 2 Esdras) led them to revolt and after two years of bitter fighting they were bloodily repressed. The teeming Jewish population of Egypt was brought virtually to an end.

Then in 132, in the reign of Trajan's successor, Hadrian, the remaining Jews of Judea revolted again. They followed the Zealot, Simon Bar-Cocheba, who proclaimed himself a Messiah. It took three years for the revolt to be suppressed and, by that time, Palestinian Jewry had been exterminated.

What Jews remained were scattered in small colonies throughout Roman Europe. They survived, but that is all. Over the course of the next eighteen centuries they were continually oppressed and often slaughtered but not until our own time did they ever again, as a people, take up arms against their enemies.

The reality, as it turned out, was quite the reverse of the visions in 2 Esdras.

The Ten Tribes

In a sixth vision, Ezra sees a man rise from the sea, battle with large numbers and defeat them with fire issuing from his mouth. This is, of course, the Messiah destroying the heathen. But then:

2 Esdras 13:12. *Afterward I saw the same man . . . call unto him another peaceable multitude.*

These are interpreted as follows:

2 Esdras 13:40. *Those are the ten tribes, which were carried away prisoners out of their own land in the time of Osea* [Hoshea] *the king, whom Salmanazer* [Shalmaneser] *the king of Assyria led away captive . . .*

The Jews were still dreaming, eight centuries after the fact, that the men of the Northern Kingdom still existed somewhere as self-aware Israelites. There remained the hope, then and for centuries afterward, that they might even make up a powerful and prosperous kingdom that would someday come to the aid of their oppressed brethren of Judah and Benjamin. They never did, of course, nor could they—for they had long since melted into the populations surrounding them.

Two Hundred and Four Books

In the seventh and final vision, Ezra is commanded to write the books of the Bible. This actually is a reference to an important historic fact. The early books of the Bible did indeed receive their present form during the Exile and immediately afterward. It was the scribes, perhaps under Ezra himself, who prepared the copies and completed the necessary editing of primitive legends, traditional law, and priestly ritual. Ezra may also have been the "Chronicler" who continued the history of Israel from Joshua's time to the rebuilding of the Temple in 1 and 2 Chronicles, Ezra, and Nehemiah (see page I-399).

One of the high points of the Book of Nehemiah is the scene in which Ezra reads the law to the assembled people and expounds upon it:

> Nehemiah 8:5. *And Ezra opened the book in the sight of all the people . . . and . . . all the people stood up:*
>
> . . . .
>
> Nehemiah 8:18. . . . . *day by day, from the first day unto the last day, he read in the book of the law of God . . .*

The remainder of the Bible, past Joshua, was added little by little, with some parts not written (let alone accepted as canonical) before 150 B.C., some three centuries after the time of Ezra. Nevertheless, the writer of 2 Esdras, looking back in time, easily idealized the situation to the point where Ezra is visualized as writing the entire Bible.

To be sure, Ezra isn't looked upon as actually composing the Bible. According to orthodox tradition, the Bible had been written by various pre-Exilic sages such as Moses and Samuel and, according to Rabbinic legends, might very well have pre-existed throughout eternity. Ezra, therefore, merely restored the Bible (according to the view in 2 Esdras) to the condition it was in before the burning of the Temple by Nebuchadnezzar.

> 2 Esdras 14.21. *For thy law is burnt, therefore no man knoweth the things that are done of thee or the works that shall begin.*

Under divine inspiration, Ezra restores the Bible, dictating the entire body of writing to five transcribers over a space of forty days:

> 2 Esdras 14:44. *In forty days they wrote two hundred and four books.*
>
> 2 Esdras 14:45. . . . . . *the Highest spake, saying, The first that thou hast written publish openly . . .*

2 Esdras 14:46. But keep the seventy last, that thou mayest deliver them only to such as be wise among the people . . .

The figure "two hundred and four" given in the Latin version makes no sense. Other versions, accepted by the Revised Standard Version, give the total number of books written as ninety-four and the number to be published openly as twenty-four. This does make sense, for the twenty-four books to be published openly are the twenty-four of the Jewish canon, divided as follows:

(1) Genesis, (2) Exodus, (3) Leviticus, (4) Numbers, (5) Deuteronomy, (6) Joshua, (7) Judges, (8) 1 and 2 Samuel, (9) 1 and 2 Kings, (10) Isaiah, (11) Jeremiah, (12) Ezekiel, (13) the Twelve Minor Prophets, (14) Psalms, (15) Proverbs, (16) Job, (17) Song of Solomon, (18) Ruth, (19) Lamentations, (20) Ecclesiastes, (21) Esther, (22) Daniel, (23) Ezra and Nehemiah, (24) 1 and 2 Chronicles.

The remaining seventy books, which were hidden away from the general view, make up the Apocrypha ("hidden").

This is the actual end of 2 Esdras as originally written.

Egypt

The last two chapters, consisting of prophecies of disaster preceding the last day, seem to have been added in the third century A.D., which would make it the latest passage anywhere in the Bible or Apocrypha. God is quoted as speaking of Egypt, for instance, as follows:

2 Esdras 14:10. Behold, my people is led as a flock to the slaughter: I will not suffer them now to dwell in the land of Egypt:
2 Esdras 14:11. But I will . . . smite Egypt with plagues, as before, and will destroy all the land thereof.

This may be meant allegorically. It is the Christians who are "my people" and by Egypt is actually meant Rome. Nevertheless, the verses may have been inspired by actual events. The Jews were indeed no longer suffered to dwell in the land of Egypt for by 135, the Jews had been virtually wiped out throughout the east (see page 522).

But then in the following century, something that might have looked like retribution was visited upon Egypt and it was smitten with plagues.

In 215 the Emperor Caracalla visited Egypt and put an end to the state support of Alexandria's great Museum. It had been the city's intellectual glory for five centuries, but it was in decay now and so was Rome now that the time of the good emperors had passed.

The situation was even worse according to the tales that have been handed down to us (and which may have been exaggerated). Caracalla was offended with Alexandria for some slights its citizens put upon him. He therefore put the city to the sack, killing thousands.

Then, shortly after 260, in the reign of the Emperor Gallienus, a famine and epidemic swept Egypt. Two thirds of the population of Alexandria are supposed to have died in misery. Perhaps this was going on at the time the last two chapters of 2 Esdras were being written.

The Carmanians

Indeed, the third century saw the Roman Empire plunging into the depths of misery and anarchy. In 235 the Emperor Alexander Severus was murdered, and for fifty years afterward, emperor followed emperor, each struggling with usurpers and suffering assassination in the end, while all the realm fell apart. Christian mystics watching this have been certain that the last days were at hand.

The writer of the end of 2 Esdras describes a vision appropriate to the last days:

> 2 Esdras 15:29. . . . *the nations of the dragons of Arabia shall come out with many chariots . . .*
>
> 2 Esdras 15:30. *Also the Carmanians raging in wrath shall go forth . . .*
>
> . . . .
>
> 2 Esdras 15:43. *And they shall go stedfastly unto Babylon, and make her afraid.*

Naturally, the anarchy and confusion within the Roman Empire offered an unexampled occasion for external enemies to pounce upon her. The most powerful of Rome's enemies lay to the east. The Parthian Empire, which had caused Rome so much trouble in the time of

Herod the Great (see page 123) had declined, but in 226, while Alexander Severus was still on the Roman throne, a new dynasty, the Sassanids, had come to power in the east. The Sassanid Empire carried on warfare against Rome, as earlier the Parthians had done. And since the Sassanids came to power just as Rome was sinking into anarchy they won considerable success every once in a while.

In 240, Shapur I became the Sassanid king and he at once invaded Syria. It is very likely that his hosts from the east represented the "dragons of Arabia." If there is any doubt, the reference to the Carmanians should lay that to rest, for Carmania was a large southern province of the Sassanid Empire.

At the height of his attack, Shapur took Antioch and reached the Mediterranean. Rome painfully retrieved its position, but in 258 Shapur launched a second war against Rome and this time his successes were even greater and Rome's state of dissolution even worse. In 259 Shapur defeated a Roman army in Syria and captured the Roman emperor, Valerian. Surely this sufficed to "make her [Rome] afraid."

The enemy capture of a Roman Emperor for the first time in Rome's history and the dreadful famine in Egypt must have indeed made it seem that the last days were at hand, if the final portion of 2 Esdras was indeed being written at this time.

Shapur, in 260, even invaded Asia Minor, and 2 Esdras contains apocalyptic denunciations of that region, too:

> 2 Esdras 15:46. *And thou, Asia, that art partaker of the hope of Babylon* . . .
> 2 Esdras 15:47. *Woe be unto thee, thou wretch, because thou has made thyself like unto her* . . .

Yet neither did this vision come true. In actual fact, Rome recovered. Shapur was driven back by an Arab leader, named Odenathus. In 268 a capable emperor, Claudius II, came to the Roman throne, and began to win victories. Under his successor, Aurelian, the realm was knit together once more from the fragments into which it had fallen.

Beginning in 284, the Emperor Diocletian undertook a complete reorganization of the empire and under Constantine (who began his reign in 306) the empire turned officially Christian.

32. REVELATION

JOHN * PATMOS * ALPHA AND OMEGA * THE LORD'S DAY * THE SEVEN CHURCHES * NICOLAITANS * THE BOOK OF LIFE * PHILADELPHIA * LAODICEA * THE LAMB * THE FOUR HORSEMEN * AN HUNDRED AND FORTY AND FOUR THOUSAND * EUPHRATES * THE GREAT CITY * THE DRAGON * THE BEAST * THE NUMBER OF THE BEAST * ARMAGEDDON * BABYLON * GOD AND MAGOG * JERUSALEM

John

There are apocalyptic passages in several books of the Old Testament. Isaiah, for instance, contains a "little apocalypse" (see page I-540) and the latter half of Daniel is apocalyptic. However, no book of the Old Testament is entirely apocalyptic, although one such book—2 Esdras (see page 514)—is to be found in the Apocrypha.

During Domitian's time, however, there was written a particularly complex and richly symbolic apocalypse. Its author was a Christian and it was eventually accepted (despite some initial misgivings) as canonical. It now appears as the last book of the New Testament and is the only entirely apocalyptic book in the Bible.

Since "apocalypse" means "unveiling" or "revelation" (of matters, that is, which would otherwise remain forever hidden because they cannot be penetrated by the unaided reason of man) this final book can be called either "The Apocalypse" or "The Revelation." It is called the latter in the King James Version.

The author of Revelation names himself and makes no attempt to place the authorship upon some ancient sage (as is generally done in apocalyptic writing):

Revelation 1:1. *The Revelation of Jesus Christ, which God gave unto him, to shew unto his servants things which must shortly come*

The Seven Churches of Asia Minor

to pass; and he sent and signified it by his angel unto his servant John . . .

That leaves us the question of who John might be. The most common tradition is that the fourth gospel, the three epistles of John, and Revelation are all written by the same person, and that this person is John the apostle; that is, John son of Zebedee. In the Catholic versions of the Bible, the book is accordingly entitled "The Apocalypse of St. John the Apostle."

It is true that the language of the book, while Greek, is filled with Semitic word order and idioms, and is rich in Old Testament allusion in almost every verse. One might almost consider this to prove that the author was a Palestinian Jew who thought in Hebrew or Aramaic and whose Greek had been learned late in life—as one would expect of John the Apostle.

On the other hand, the language might prove nothing one way or the other. It might very well be a self-conscious imitation of the kind of apocalyptic language used by the Palestinian Jewish writers of the previous two centuries. (We have a modern example of this sort of thing in the Book of Mormon, which was written in self-conscious imitation of the style of the King James Version of the Bible.)

Arguing against John the Apostle as writer is the enormous difference in style, vocabulary, and thought between the fourth gospel and Revelation. The two could not be by the same author and if John the apostle wrote the fourth gospel, he could not have written Revelation. Moreover if the writer of Revelation identifies himself as John and is therefore clearly not trying to conceal his identity, why does he not say openly that he is John the apostle, or John the Beloved Disciple? The fact that he does not, makes it seem that he is another John.

The King James Version seems to display caution in this respect for it does not identify John as the apostle, in the name of the book, which it calls: "The Revelation of St. John the Divine." The Revised Standard Version is even more cautious and calls it "The Revelation to John," while the Jerusalem Bible says simply, "The Book of Revelation."

Patmos

The book is undoubtedly the product of someone who, if not a native of the western coast of Asia Minor, is a resident there. The book begins in the form of a letter addressed to the churches of that region:

Revelation 1:4. *John to the seven churches which are in Asia . . .*

Asia here, as everywhere in the New Testament, refers to the western third of the peninsula of Asia Minor, the Roman "province of Asia" of which Ephesus was the capital.

John locates himself specifically near that province:

Revelation 1:9. *I John, who also am your brother, and companion in tribulation, . . . was in the isle that is called Patmos . . .*

Patmos is an island in the Aegean Sea, only about half the size of Manhattan Island, and about seventy miles southwest of Ephesus. Tradition has it that John was there in exile because of the danger of martyrdom if he remained in Ephesus. There seems a hint of this in the reference of John to his being a "brother and companion in tribulation" of those of Asia.

The occasion for Revelation would seem to be similar to the occasions for all apocalyptic writing. The true believers are being oppressed and the forces of evil seem to be triumphing. It becomes necessary to reassure those with fainting hearts that God is not sleeping, that all is working out according to a prearranged plan, that retribution will not be long delayed and that the final day of judgment with the subsequent establishment of the ideal kingdom will be the result of a course of events that is on the point of being initiated:

Revelation 1:3. *Blessed is he that readeth . . . the words of this prophecy . . . for the time is at hand.*

Some have suggested that the specific time of persecution that led to the writing of Revelation was that of Nero. It seems unlikely though that Revelation could be a response to Nero's persecution, short-lived as it was and confined as it was to the city of Rome. It was Domitian's much more general persecution which first visited systematic danger and misery upon the inhabitants of Asia Minor.

It is assumed then that John left Ephesus for Patmos, either in flight from persecution, or possibly carried off to prison there, in Domitian's last years; and that he returned to Ephesus after Domitian's death and the accession of the mild Nerva had put a term to the anti-Christian crisis. Since Domitian was assassinated in 96, Revelation is thought to have been written in 95.

Alpha and Omega

In his preamble, John rhapsodically describes the glory of God:

Revelation 1:7. *Behold, he cometh with clouds; and every eye shall see him, and they also which pierced him: and all kindreds of the earth shall wail because of him . . .*

Revelation 1:8. *I am Alpha and Omega, the beginning and the ending, saith the Lord, which is, and which was, and which is to come . . .*

From the very start of the book one sees how the author composes his symbols out of the very language of the apocalyptic passages of the Old Testament. He is especially fond of Daniel which, up to the time of Revelation itself, was the most successful and respected of the apocalypses, because it was canonical.

Thus, when John says, "Behold, he cometh with clouds," this is harking back to Daniel:

> Daniel 7:13. . . . behold, one like the Son of man came with the clouds of heaven . . .

Then, when he speaks of everyone seeing him, even his enemies ("and they also which pierced him") there is a self-conscious return to the language of Zechariah:

> Zechariah 12:10. . . . they shall look upon me whom they have pierced, and they shall mourn . . .

And in describing the Lord as eternal, the language is that of the Second Isaiah:

> Isaiah 44:6. Thus saith the Lord . . . I am the first and I am the last . . .

John translates Isaiah's remark into the metaphoric reference to the Greek alphabet. Of the twenty-four letters of that alphabet, "alpha" is the first and "omega" the twenty-fourth and last. To say that God is "Alpha and Omega" is therefore equivalent to saying he is "first and last." In modern alphabetical allusion, John might be paraphrased as saying that God is "everything from A to Z."

The Lord's Day

The long vision of Revelation begins at a specific time:

> Revelation 1:10. I was in the Spirit on the Lord's day . . .

There are several possible interpretations of what is meant by "the Lord's day," but the consensus is that it refers to the first day of the week, which we call Sunday. It is the Lord's day because it is the day of the week on which the resurrection took place. It was celebrated at first without prejudice to the seventh day of the week, the Sabbath, and if John is really referring to Sunday when he speaks of the Lord's day, it is the first unmistakable reference in Christian literature to Sunday as a special day.

It was not until Christianity became the official religion of the Roman Empire in the early decades of the fourth century that the

Lord's day took over the full significance of the Sabbath, and that the observance of the seventh day was dropped completely and left entirely to the Jews.

The Seven Churches

John lists the seven churches to which his apocalyptic letters are addressed, and all are in the province of Asia:

> Revelation 1:10. I . . . heard behind me a great voice . . .
> Revelation 1:11. Saying, . . . What thou seest, write in a book, and send it unto the seven churches which are in Asia; unto Ephesus, and unto Smyrna, and unto Pergamos, and unto Thyatira, and unto Sardis, and unto Philadelphia, and unto Laodicea.

Of these seven cities, Ephesus is the best known. It is the capital of the province, is frequently mentioned in Acts, and is the city in which the riot of the silversmiths had taken place and in which Paul had spent considerable time (see page 406).

Thyatira was the city—noted for its dye manufactures—from which came Lydia, the dye-seller whom Paul met in Philippi (see page 396). Laodicea is the city near Colossae to which reference was made in Colossians (see page 468).

The remaining four cities are not mentioned in the Bible in any book other than Revelation.

Smyrna is on the Asia Minor coast about forty miles north of Ephesus. It was an ancient town which invading Greeks took over and colonized as early as 1000 B.C., when David ruled over Israel. By 650 B.C. it was a wealthy and cultured city. But then the Lydians, who had built up a powerful kingdom in the hinterland, took the Greek-speaking Aegean coast. Because Smyrna led the resistance, Alyattes, king of Lydia, ordered the city's destruction.

According to later legend, Alexander the Great, when passing down the coast three centuries later, conceived the notion of re-establishing the city. After his death, his generals, Antigonus and Lysimachus, who temporarily dominated Asia Minor, carried through this dream and about 301 B.C. Smyrna lived again. By Roman times, it had grown almost to rival Ephesus in size and wealth.

In fact, when all the famed ancient cities of the Asia Minor coast

sank into decay and ruin, Smyrna alone continued to flourish. Even
after the Turks captured Asia Minor, Smyrna (now known by the
Turkish name of Izmir) continued as a Greek center, right down into
modern times. After World War I, Greece, which had been on the
victor's side, claimed Smyrna as its own and landed an army in defeated Turkey in 1919. In the war that followed, it was Turkey that
was victorious and the Greek army was driven into the sea. Izmir was
sacked and virtually destroyed and its long Greek history came to an
end. When it was rebuilt yet again it was as a Turkish town and it is
now, with a population of nearly four hundred thousand, the third
largest city in the nation.

Lying forty-five miles east of Smyrna is Sardis, the capital of the
Lydian kingdom which, for a while during the sixth century B.C., included the western half of Asia Minor. In 546 B.C. Lydia came to a
permanent end when it was taken by Cyrus, the Persian conqueror.
Sardis was never to be the capital of an independent kingdom again,
but it remained an important city for centuries. An Athenian expedition burned it in 499 B.C. and that was the occasion that gave rise
to the great Persian war against Greece in the following decades. It
was not until the coming of the Turks that it declined and it was
finally destroyed by Timur (Tamerlane), the Mongol conqueror, in
1402.

Following the destruction of the Persian Empire by Alexander the
Great, a new independent, Greek-speaking nation was founded in
western Asia Minor. Its appearance as an independent nation can be
traced back to 283 B.C. and its capital was the city of Pergamum, some
sixty miles north of Smyrna and about fifteen miles from the coast.

At first, its rulers controlled only a small district about the city, but
under the enlightened sway of its rulers that territory grew and by
230 B.C. became the kingdom of Pergamum (named for its capital)
under King Attalus I.

Pergamum's great enemy was the Seleucid Empire, which was particularly threatening under its conquering king, Antiochus III (see
page 45). Pergamum therefore allied itself with Rome, and when
Rome won its first victories in Asia Minor, Pergamum was rewarded
with large tracts of Seleucid territory.

Under Eumenes II, who reigned from 197 to 160 B.C.—that is, during the period of the Maccabean revolt—Pergamum reached the height

of its prosperity and power. The city had a library second only to that of Alexandria.

Roman power in Asia Minor grew, however, and in 133 B.C., when Pergamum's king, Attalus III, lay dying, he left his kingdom to Rome in his will. He felt that only so could he keep his land from being torn apart by a struggle between various rivals for the throne. He was right and Rome took over with only minor resistance.

The city of Pergamum was no longer the capital of the area, however, for it became the Roman province of Asia and the center of affairs moved to the Greek cities of Ephesus and Smyrna. Pergamum itself began to decline in Mark Antony's time, a generation before the birth of Jesus. Mark Antony, trying to make up to Cleopatra of Egypt for the destruction of some of Alexandria's Library during the small war with Julius Caesar a dozen years before, transferred Pergamum's library to Alexandria. Pergamum still exists today, however, as the town of Bergamo (its name still recognizable) in modern Turkey.

Philadelphia is the smallest of the seven cities and is located about twenty-five miles southeast of Sardis. It was founded about 150 B.C. by Attalus II of Pergamum. He was known as Attalus Philadelphus and the city was named in his own honor. It still exists today as a small Turkish town named Alesehir, which means "red city," so called from the color of its soil.

Seven

John describes a complicated vision of the Son of man to introduce the letters he is sending to each of the seven churches, using terms borrowed chiefly from Daniel. So frequent is the use of the number seven throughout the Book of Revelation that it is usually suspected that the seven churches were chosen not because that was all there were in the province of Asia but because of the mystic qualities of the number itself.

The importance of seven in the Bible appears first in the seven days of the original week (the six days of creation plus the seventh day of rest). That is not the ultimate source, however, for it seems very likely that the first chapter of Genesis was an adaptation of Babylonian creation tales and that the seven-day week was of Babylonian (perhaps ultimately of Sumerian) origin.

The week arose from the accidental astronomical fact that there are seven visible bodies in the sky that move independently against the background of the stars. These are the Sun, the Moon, Mercury, Venus, Mars, Jupiter, and Saturn. The Babylonians found much of mystic importance in the number and motions of these bodies and founded the study of astrology, a pseudo-science that still exists in undiminished importance and influence even in our own supposedly enlightened society.

Each of the seven days of the week is presided over by a planet after which it is named. We still retain relics of that in our own Sunday, Monday (Moon-day), and Saturday (Saturn-day). The other days of the week are named, in English, for Norse deities, but in French, for instance, the planetary system is clear. Tuesday is "mardi" (Mars-day), Wednesday is "mercredi" (Mercury-day), Thursday is "jeudi" (Jove-day), and Friday is "vendredi" (Venus-day).

The seven-day week was all the more useful in that it blended closely into the lunar month, being about a quarter of that period of time. The passage of a week therefore signified a change in the phase of the moon—from new to first quarter, from first quarter to full, from full to third quarter, from third quarter to new again. Indeed, the very word "week" is from an old Teutonic word meaning "change."

The Jews borrowed the week from the Babylonians during the period of exile, and it was then that the Sabbath gained its post-Exilic significance (see page 186). It was then, also, that the number seven became of mystic importance. For the purposes of the writer of Revelation it was a fortunate coincidence that the city of Rome was widely known to have been built on seven hills.

Nicolaitans

The second and third chapters of Revelation are quite prosaic for in them John relays messages from each of seven angels to each of the seven churches in relatively straightforward language. The shortcomings of each church are blamed and their staunchness praised. The original readers for whom the messages are meant understand all the allusions, of course, but modern readers are frustrated because of the lack of background information. Thus, the church at Ephesus is praised but there are some mysterious faults:

Revelation 2:4. *Nevertheless I have somewhat against thee, because thou hast left thy first love.*

Apparently the Ephesian church in certain unspecified ways no longer shows its original enthusiasm. Still, they are praised for rejecting a sect which John views with strong disapproval:

Revelation 2:6. . . . *thou hatest the deeds of the Nicolaitanes, which I also hate.*

Who the Nicolaitans might be and what their doctrines were is not certainly known. It is to be presumed from the name that they followed the teaching of someone called Nicolas.

There is only one Nicolas mentioned in the New Testament, and he was one of the seven men appointed to be leaders of the Grecian party very early in the history of the Church (see page 344):

Acts 6:5. . . . *and they chose Stephen, . . . and Philip, . . . and Nicolas a proselyte of Antioch . . .*

A common guess in past centuries is that the Nicolaitans advocated unrestricted sexual intercourse, that is, "free love." The legend arose that Nicolas, the proselyte of Antioch, taking too literally the communist doctrines of the apostles at the very beginning (see page 341), offered to share his wife with the others. Perhaps this notion arose because Antioch, like other large Gentile cities, had the reputation of being extremely licentious, to the disapproving Jewish and Christian puritans of Roman times.

A hint in this direction is found in the letter to the church at Pergamos. It is warned:

Revelation 2:14. . . . *thou hast there them that hold the doctrine of Balaam, who taught Balac to cast a stumblingblock before the children of Israel . . .*
Revelation 2:15. . . . *also them that hold the doctrine of the Nicolaitanes, which thing I hate.*

The two heresies of Balaam and the Nicolaitans seem to be mentioned as distinct, but perhaps this is the parallelism of Hebrew poetry, where the same thing is mentioned twice in different ways. If so, what is the doctrine of Balaam?

There is a passage in the Book of Numbers that immediately follows the tale of Balaam's oracles (see page I-183) which were intended to be against Israel but which were turned in favor of Israel by God against Balaam's own will:

> Numbers 25:1. *And Israel abode in Shittim, and the people began to commit whoredom with the daughters of Moab.*

It was supposed that Balaam had advised Balak, the king of Moab, to seduce the Israelites in this manner, since such seduction would bring the wrath of God down upon the sinners—to the great benefit of Moab. Thus when the Israelites later took women alive as spoils of war, Moses is quoted as angrily advocating their death and saying:

> Numbers 31:16. *Behold, these caused the children of Israel, through the counsel of Balaam, to commit trespass against the Lord . . . and there was a plague . . .*

Consequently, the name of Balaam was associated with sexual license and this would tie in with Nicolaitanism as a doctrine of release from the severe sexual restrictions demanded by the Law and, for that matter, by Paul's teaching.

Another hint of this is to be found in the message to the church at Thyatira:

> Revelation 2:20. *. . . I have a few things against thee, because thou sufferest that woman Jezebel, which calleth herself a prophetess, to teach and to seduce my servants to commit fornication . . .*

The Book of Life

The church at Sardis gets the negative praise that there are a few worthy among them, and for any that are worthy, the message is:

> Revelation 3:5. *. . . I will not blot out his name out of the book of life . . .*

Originally, the book of life was merely a metaphoric expression signifying the list of living people. It is as though one were enrolled in a great census kept in heaven of all those alive at any time. To die would be to be blotted out of that book. Thus, Moses pleads with God for the Israelites after the incident of the calf of gold (see page

I-151) and says that he himself may as well die if the Israelites are not forgiven:

Exodus 32:32. *Yet now, if thou wilt forgive their sin—; and if not, blot me, I pray thee, out of thy book which thou hast written.*

In post-Exilic times, however, when the doctrine of the resurrection of the body and of a life hereafter was developed, the book of life came to be the list not of those alive in the world, but of those who were to be awarded a life hereafter in heaven. The Book of Daniel, in speaking of the resurrection, says:

Daniel 12:1. . . . *there shall be a time of trouble . . . and at that time thy people shall be delivered, every one that shall be found written in the book.*

Again, in the Book of Psalms, God is asked to visit punishment upon the wicked:

Psalm 69:28. *Let them be blotted out of the book of the living, and not be written with the righteous.*

Philadelphia

Philadelphia is praised:

Revelation 3:8. . . . *thou hast a little strength, and hast kept my word, and hast not denied my name.*

Philadelphia was to live up to this praise over a thousand years later. During a period of three centuries, beginning in 1071, the Turks slowly but inexorably swept over Asia Minor, eradicating Christianity and making it Moslem—a situation that exists to this day. The last city to be taken by the Turks, the last city to remain as a holdout, the one that longest did not deny the name, was Philadelphia. It fell at last in 1390 after an eight-year siege.

In 1682, William Penn was establishing a new colony on the shores of the Delaware River in the New World and was founding a city. He chose the name Philadelphia for two reasons. First, it means, literally, "love of sister (or brother)" so that a city by that name can be called the "city of brotherly love." And secondly, Penn remembered this encomium on Philadelphia in Revelation. Penn founded the city and Philadelphia is now the fourth largest city in the United States, far larger than any of the ancient Philadelphias had ever been.

Laodicea

The church at Laodicea is bitterly condemned, not for being outspokenly opposed to the doctrines favored by John, but for being neutral. John apparently prefers an honest enemy to a doubtful friend:

Revelation 3:15. *I know thy works, that thou art neither cold nor hot: I would thou wert cold or hot.*

Revelation 3:16. *So then because thou art lukewarm, and neither cold nor hot, I will spue thee out of my mouth.*

"Laodicean" has therefore entered the English language as a word meaning "indifferent" or "neutral."

The Lamb

The scene now switches to heaven and all the rest of the Book of Revelation is thickly mystical. John begins by describing God in the midst of the heavenly court with images drawn from Daniel and Ezekiel, and with Isaiah's seraphim (see page I-528) prominently introduced. Amid all these glories there is introduced a book sealed with seven seals. This, presumably, contains the secrets of the future, which cannot be revealed until, one by one, the seals are broken.

The hero who will reveal the contents of the book makes his appearance:

Revelation 5:6. . . . *and, lo, . . . in the midst of the elders, stood a Lamb as it had been slain . . .*

Revelation 5:7. *And he came and took the book out of the right hand of him that sat upon the throne.*

The image of the Messiah as a lamb made into a kind of greater

Passover sacrifice was introduced in the fourth gospel (see page 331). It is explicitly stated in the First Epistle of Peter:

1 Peter 1:18. . . . *ye were . . . redeemed . . .*

1 Peter 1:19. . . . *with the precious blood of Christ, as of a lamb without blemish and without spot . . .*

By the end of the first century, that metaphor had become so well known that the author of Revelation did not have to elaborate on the identity of the Lamb.

The Four Horsemen

One by one the seals of the book are broken and with each of the first four, a horse and rider appeared:

Revelation 6:1. . . . *when the Lamb opened one of the seals . . .*

Revelation 6:2. . . . *behold a white horse: and he that sat on him had a bow; and a crown . . . : and he went forth conquering . . .*

Revelation 6:3. *And when he had opened the second seal . . .*

Revelation 6:4. . . . *there went out another horse that was red: and power was given to him that sat thereon to take peace from the earth . . .*

Revelation 6:5. *And when he had opened the third seal, . . . lo a black horse; and he that sat on him had a pair of balances in his hand.*

Revelation 6:6. *And I heard a voice . . . say, A measure of wheat for a penny . . .*

Revelation 6:7. *And when he had opened the fourth seal, . . .*

Revelation 6:8. . . . *behold a pale horse: and his name that sat on him was Death . . .*

These are the "four horsemen of the apocalypse" representing the variety of evils that were to descend upon the world (specifically upon the Roman Empire, which was viewed by its populace as synonymous with "the world") to mark the beginning of its dissolution and the coming of the Messianic era.

The white horse and its rider seems to represent foreign invasion. At least the bow is the virtual symbol of the Parthian raiders, who since the time of Julius Caesar had been the terror of the east. In the days of Herod the Great, they had occupied Jerusalem, and at no time thereafter were their forces very far to the east.

The red horse and its rider also seem to signify a form of war. It may well represent the bloody disorders of civil war and insurrection.

The black horse and its rider represent famine, for the price offered for a measure of wheat ("a penny") is far higher than normal and is so high in fact that the ordinary populace could not buy enough to live.

The pale horse and its rider are named as "Death," but this is not the kind of death in general that would follow war or famine. That is taken care of by the first three horses. Rather Death represents death by disease, as when we refer to the "Black Death," for instance.

In short, the four horsemen can be most briefly described as War, Revolution, Famine, and Pestilence.

There are many who seek the meaning of the symbolism of Revelation in the events that have happened in the centuries since the book was written. To those, never did the four horsemen ride with such effect as in the days of World War I. Not only was there the bloodiest and most stupidly savage slaughter ever seen, on both western and eastern fronts, but there was a revolution in Russia that affects us even today, a famine in both Germany and Russia immediately after the war, and a world-wide influenza pandemic in 1918 that killed more people than the war did.

Never had War, Revolution, Famine, and Pestilence stalked ghastly over all the world as in the years from 1914 to 1920.

An Hundred and Forty and Four Thousand

When the fifth seal is broken, the souls of the martyrs are revealed waiting for judgment and when the sixth seal is broken, the physical universe begins to crumble. It might seem that now the climax is reached. The seventh seal ought to be broken and the great day of judgment come. However, throughout the Book of Revelation there is a strong reluctance, apparently, to let the climax come. Over and over it is delayed.

The first delay comes at this point, for after the sixth seal is broken, and before the seventh seal can be touched, there is a break:

Revelation 7:1. . . . *I saw four angels . . .*
. . . .
Revelation 7:3. *Saying, Hurt not the earth . . . till we have sealed the servants of our God in their foreheads.*

It was customary in Babylonia from the most ancient times to use seals for identification. These were small cylindrical intaglios which could be rolled upon the soft clay used by the Babylonians for a writing surface. A characteristic picture would appear, serving the place of signature on our own documents.

A slave might be similarly branded (as our cattle are out west) to show indelibly who the master was. A characteristic brand would serve the function of a seal. The picture presented here, then, is of the righteous beings marked somehow (details are not given) with a symbol (again not described) that identifies them as God's slaves to be kept safe through the final disasters.

The number of those to be saved is given specifically:

Revelation 7:4. . . . *I heard the number of them which were sealed . . . an hundred and forty and four thousand of all the tribes of the children of Israel.*

Because of the smallness of the number compared to the total population of the Earth, the notion has arisen that very few are to be saved. On the other hand, the number can't be taken literally.

The twelve tribes of Israel stand, figuratively, for all the righteous. The number 144,000 is twelve times twelve times a thousand, and we must consider the mystic significance of these numbers.

Just as seven probably derives its initial sacred character from the fact that it represents the number of planets in the heavens, so twelve probably derives its sacred character from the fact that there are twelve months in the year. From this is derived the twelve signs of the zodiac and the notion that with twelve one comes full circle. The number 144, which is twelve times twelve, is therefore completeness accentuated. It represents all the righteous (12) of all the tribes (12) and no one is left out.

As for one thousand, that was the largest number which possessed a specific name in ancient times. The Greeks used the word "myrioi" to signify ten thousand, but that is not really a name for a number. It meant "innumerable" originally, which is the sense we use it for when we speak of "a myriad objects." To multiply something by a thousand was to make it as large as one conveniently could in the language of the time. It follows that the number 144,000 does not mean specifically that number but represents an emphatic way of saying, "All the righteous! A large number of them!"

(It should be mentioned that the word "thousand" remained the largest number-word right down into late medieval times. Only then were numbers like "million" invented in Italy.)

Revelation goes on to expand on the mystical completeness of the number by emphasizing that there are to be twelve thousand from each of the twelve tribes, which are given in the following order: Judah, Reuben, Gad, Asher, Naphtali, Manasseh, Simeon, Levi, Issachar, Zebulon, Joseph, and Benjamin.

This is a strange list. Apparently the twelve sons of Jacob should have been listed, but one of the names on the list is Manasseh, the son of Joseph, and a grandson of Jacob. To make room for Manasseh, one of the sons of Jacob would have to be omitted, and the one so omitted is Dan.

This is very likely a mistake on the part of John or of some later copyist. It may be that Man was accidentally written for Dan and that a still later copyist assumed Man to be an abbreviation for Manasseh.

It is, however, difficult for some people to accept something as prosaic as a copyist's error in the Bible, so that significance is sought for even in the most trivial things. Some have suggested, for instance, that Dan was deliberately omitted because Antichrist was to spring from among those of that tribe.

The notion that the tribe of Dan was to give rise to Antichrist can come only from the passage in the Testament of Jacob (see page I-116) which goes:

Genesis 49:17. *Dan shall be a serpent by the way* . . .

It is farfetched to go from this metaphorical description of Dan as a serpent (referring perhaps to the snake as a totemistic symbol of the tribe in primitive times as the lion was for Judah and the wolf for Benjamin) to the post-Exilic identification of the serpent in the garden of Eden with Satan, and thence with Antichrist—but all this is an easy leap for mystics.

These righteous now stand before the Lamb and all their sufferings are washed away in what has become a famous phrase:

Revelation 7:14. . . . *they . . . came out of great tribulation, and have washed their robes, and made them white in the blood of the Lamb.*

Euphrates

And now at last, the seventh seal is broken and one might expect the climax of the vision to approach, but it still doesn't. Instead a new series of seven events begins in the form of seven angels, each of whom blows a trumpet in turn, with gruesome disasters following each trumpet sound. When the fifth angel blows his trumpet, hell itself opens:

Revelation 9:2. . . . *and there arose a smoke out of the pit . . .*
Revelation 9:3. *And there came out of the smoke locusts upon the earth . . .*
. . . .
Revelation 9:7. *And the shapes of the locusts were like unto horses prepared unto battle . . . and their faces were as the faces of men.*

The picture being drawn by John here is clearly inspired by the great terror of the east—the Parthian cavalry, swooping in like a cloud of locusts, dealing their deadly strokes and fading away before they could be properly opposed. The Roman general, Crassus, was defeated in this manner in eastern Syria in 53 B.C. That defeat had never been properly avenged and it was never forgotten.

The characteristic weapons of the Parthian horsemen were their bows, which they could use with great effect. Even when retreating, they could rise in their saddles and shoot, in unison, one rapid volley of arrows back at their pursuers. This "Parthian shot" was often quite effective. It is to such tactics that Revelation may be referring, when they speak of the locusts as:

Revelation 9:10. *And they had tails like unto scorpions, and there were stings in their tails . . .*

When the sixth angel sounds his trumpet, the picture of the Parthian cavalry is continued. The sixth angel is instructed:

> Revelation 9:14. . . . *Loose the four angels which are bound in the great river Euphrates.*

The Euphrates was a boundary in a double sense. First it was the boundary of Israel in the great days of David and Solomon and had been the ideal boundary of Israel ever since. Second, it was the boundary of the Roman realm during most of the days of its empire. The "angels" bound in the Euphrates controlled the enemy hosts on the other side.

The army controlled by these angels of the Euphrates was made to seem unbelievably numerous—an impression made on the awed infantry when they were the object of the sudden onrush of a contingent of horsemen:

> Revelation 9:16. *And the number of the army of the horsemen were two hundred thousand thousand . . .*

This is the number obtained if one makes use of the Greek "myrioi" as a synonym of innumerability, emphasizes it by repetition ("an innumerable, innumerable quantity"), and then doubles it for good measure. If "myrioi" is taken as ten thousand, it becomes two myriad myriad or two hundred thousand thousand, or two hundred million—a number equal to the entire population of the United States.

The Great City

Then before the seventh and final trumpet is sounded there is another digression and the temporary triumph of evil is described.

This temporary triumph represents the persecution of Domitian, then proceeding. The language used in describing this persecution reaches back to the Old Testament, as does everything in Revelation. The oppression of the Church by Rome is therefore cast in the terms Daniel used in describing the oppression of the Temple by the Seleucids:

> Revelation 11:2. . . . *the court which is without the temple . . . is given unto the Gentiles: and the holy city shall they tread under foot forty and two months.*

This is the period of three and a half years during which the Temple was profaned in the time of Antiochus IV. This use of Temple symbolism has been advanced as evidence that the Temple was still standing at the time Revelation was written and that the book was composed, therefore, during Nero's persecution. However, Revelation uses Old Testament symbolism so consistently, that such a deduction doesn't carry conviction. John would speak of the Temple as representing the Church whether the Temple stood or not, and his readers would understand his allegory.

Two prophets are described:

> Revelation 11:3. *And I will give power unto my two witnesses . . .*
> *. . . .*
> Revelation 11:7. *And when they shall have finished their testimony, the beast that ascendeth out of the bottomless pit shall . . . kill them.*
> Revelation 11:8. *And their dead bodies shall lie in the street of the great city . . .*

This continues the allegory, indicating that the Church will be persecuted by the forces of Satan and temporarily be defeated. The particular form of the allegory may, however, be influenced by particular events. Some have suggested that the two witnesses may be Paul and Peter, the apostles martyred, according to tradition, by Nero, who could very well be described as "the beast that ascendeth out of the bottomless pit." In that case, the "great city" would, of course, be Rome.

A later copyist may have felt the great city would have to be Jerusalem and added the phrase:

> Revelation 11:8. . . . *the great city, . . . where also our Lord was crucified.*

The Dragon

Now the seventh trumpet is sounded, but there is still no climax. Instead, a new allegory representing the battle of good and evil is introduced and cast into terms of Babylonian mythology:

Revelation 12:1. *And there appeared a great wonder in heaven;
a woman clothed with the sun, and the moon under her feet, and
upon her head a crown of twelve stars . . .*

In Babylonian mythology, this would be a sun-goddess, the twelve
stars representing the signs of the zodiac through which the Sun passes
each year. To John, it would represent the idealized Israel, the twelve
stars representing the twelve tribes. The woman was in labor and gave
birth to the Messiah:

Revelation 12:5. *And she brought forth a man child, who was to
rule all nations with a rod of iron . . .*

But there was an opponent also in heaven, and this, too, appeared
in Babylonian terms:

Revelation 12:3. *And there appeared another wonder in heaven;
and behold a great red dragon, having seven heads and ten horns,
and seven crowns upon his heads.*

The dragon represents chaos. It is the Babylonian Tiamat or the
Hebrew Leviathan, which had to be defeated in the beginning in
order to allow the ordered universe to be created, and would have to be
defeated again in the end, in order to allow the created universe to
come to an appropriate end. One might expect the mystic number
of seven heads and seven crowns to be carried through to seven horns.
The rather inappropriate number of ten horns harks back to Daniel's
fourth beast, whose ten horns represents the ten Seleucid kings down
to Antiochus IV (see page I-609).

The dragon also represents Satan or Antichrist. He is prepared to
devour the Messiah at the instant of birth, but the Messiah has all
the heavenly hosts on his side:

Revelation 12:7. *And there was war in heaven: Michael and his
angels fought against the dragon; and the dragon fought and his
angels,*
Revelation 12:8. *And prevailed not . . .*
Revelation 12:9. *And the great dragon was cast out, that old
serpent, called the Devil, and Satan . . . and his angels were cast
out with him.*

This reflects the legends that grew up in post-Exilic times under Persian influence. God and Satan led opposing armies in the battle of good versus evil. Only in Revelation, however, does this Persian notion of dualism receive the canonical nod.

Milton, in his epic *Paradise Lost*, begins his description of the fall of Man at the very moment when Satan and his angels (now turned into demons) have been hurled into hell and are slowly recovering their senses after the shock of the fall.

Satan, cast to Earth, and unable to prevail against God, could nevertheless vent his spleen against those righteous men on Earth:

> Revelation 12:17. *And the dragon was wroth with the woman, and went to make war with the remnant of her seed, which keep the commandments of God, and have the testimony of Jesus Christ.*

It is that, of course, which, in the eye of the writer of Revelation, explains all the troubles of the Church.

The Beast

Satan's malevolence sharpens, out of desperation, as the end of the world approaches and he (symbolized as the dragon) passes his powers over to an Earthly entity, represented in the form of Daniel's beast—the well-known allegorical representation of the pagan empires that oppressed the righteous (see page I-609).

> Revelation 13:1. . . . I . . . *saw a beast rise up out of the sea, having seven heads and ten horns . . . and upon his heads the name of blasphemy.*
> Revelation 13:2. . . . *and the dragon gave him his power . . .*
> Revelation 13:3. *And I saw one of his heads as it were wounded to death; and his deadly wound was healed . . .*

The beast (with the usual seven heads and ten horns) is, of course, the Roman Empire, which had initially impinged upon Judean consciousness from across the Mediterranean Sea.

The statement that upon its heads are "the name of blasphemy" refers to the demand that the emperors be worshipped as gods. This emperor-worship was an official state ritual that was little more than a formality designed to bind together the citizens of the empire which were otherwise so diverse in language, custom, and religion. It was a unifying gesture equivalent to our own salute to the flag and recital of the pledge of allegiance.

It was the refusal of Christians to accede to the perfunctory emperor-worshipping ritual that made them suspect, not because of their religion but because of the suspicion that they were traitors to the state. This should not strike us as strange, for there are Christian sects these days who refuse the salute to the flag and the pledge of allegiance, claiming them to be idolatrous acts—and there also exist superpatriots who are offended at this and who take strong action against such sects when in a position to do so.

The healed wound that had killed one of the heads may refer to Nero. Actually, of the twelve Roman Emperors (counting Julius Caesar) who ruled up to the time that Revelation was written, no less than six had died by assassination or suicide: Julius Caesar, Caligula, Nero, Galba, Otho, and Vitellius. Claudius may have been poisoned and Domitian was fated to be assassinated. (Only Augustus, Tiberius, Vespasian, and Titus died undoubtedly of natural causes.)

Nevertheless it was Nero whose death would be most significant to Christians, at least up to the time of Domitian. His suicide would be marked allegorically on the beast. The fact that the Roman Empire survived and that new emperors reigned would be signified by the fact that the wound was healed.

The beast representing the Roman Empire is pictured as being worshipped by all men, but the righteous. Those who worshipped were allowed to live in peace and security; those who refused to worship (the Christians) were persecuted. Just as God sealed those righteous who belonged to him, so did the beast (the Roman Empire) seal those who indulged in emperor-worship and therefore belonged to him:

Revelation 13:15. . . . *as many as would not worship the image of the beast should be killed.*

Revelation 13:16. And he [the beast] *causeth all . . . to receive a mark in their right hand, or in their foreheads:*

Revelation 13:17. And that *no man might buy or sell, save he that had the mark . . .*

The Number of the Beast

Even the Roman Empire is a kind of abstraction and the writer of Revelation zeroes in on a particular man, whom he is reluctant to name—perhaps because if he were to do so, he would be subject to the charge of treason and the punishment of execution. Cautiously he identifies the man in such a way that his more knowledgeable readers will know exactly whom he means and yet the law will not be able to touch him:

> Revelation 13:18. *Here is wisdom. Let him that hath understanding count the number of the beast: for it is the number of a man; and his number is Six hundred threescore and six.*

To understand this we must realize that down through medieval times it was common to use letters of the alphabet to signify numbers. The Jews, Greek, and Romans all did this. We are most familiar with the Roman numerals where I=1, V=5, X=10, L=50, C=100, D=500, and M=1000. It follows that words made up of these letters would also be seen to have a kind of numerical value. If an individual were named Dill McDix, for instance, one could set each letter equal to a number, add them, and reach a total of 2212.

This is hard to do in English since only a few letters of the Latin alphabet are assigned numerical values. In the Greek and Hebrew languages, however, every letter was assigned a numerical value. Naturally, then, all words in Greek or Hebrew would have numerical meaning.

Jewish mystics in Greek and Roman times assumed that the inspired words of the Bible had significance numerically as well as literally and spent much time on the analysis of such numbers. This form of endeavor was called "gematria," a corruption of the Greek "geometria" (and our "geometry").

The "number of the beast" is an example of such gematria, the only significant example in the Bible. Commentators have considered virtually every possible candidate for the beast and the one most frequently mentioned is Nero. If his name is written in the Greek form—Neron—and if his title Caesar is added and if Neron Caesar is written in Hebrew letters, then the total numerical value is indeed 666. If the final "n" is left out, the total is 616, and some old manuscripts of Revelation have 616 rather than 666 as the number of the beast.

And yet Nero seems a poor candidate if the book were written in 95. He had been dead a quarter of a century and his death had brought no great change. Within the year Vespasian had come to the throne and he and his son Titus had given Rome a dozen years of good and humane government.

At the time Revelation was being written, however, Domitian, Vespasian's younger son, was on the throne and his persecution of the Christians was in high gear. It would be natural to refer elliptically to the living, persecuting emperor, and there is probably some way in which Domitian's name and title could be so written as to add up to 666. It may be that he bore a nickname, commonly used by Christians, with a total numerical value of 666, a number which had its own mystic significance, for it fell short of the mystic perfection of 7 three times. For that reason 666 was the acme of imperfection and a suitable number with which to represent Antichrist.

Armageddon

Against the great city ruled by the beast, and his army of men wearing his mark, are the heavenly hosts and the 144,000 righteous ones bearing the seal of God. The victory of the good is certain, for the triumphant song in heaven is:

> Revelation 14:8. . . . *Babylon is fallen, is fallen, that great city . . .*

Babylon is, of course, Rome; and Rome will be destroyed. This destruction is heralded by yet a third set of seven acts of destruction. Seven vials of plagues are emptied upon the earth, one at a time, each bringing its own horrible destruction.

As the hosts of the beast are being remorselessly punished in this manner, the scene is set for the final battle between good and evil:

> Revelation 16:16. *And he* [the beast] *gathered them together into a place called in the Hebrew tongue Armageddon.*

Armageddon is, more properly, "Har-Magedon" or "the Mount of Megiddo." Megiddo, a town just south of the Kishon River and fifty-five miles north of Jerusalem, was indeed the site of two important battles. The first took place in the fifteenth century B.C. when the great Egyptian pharaoh, Thutmose III, defeated a league of Canaanite cities there. This, however, was centuries before the Israelites entered Canaan, and was beyond their historic horizon.

Nearly nine centuries after Thutmose's victory, a battle was fought at Megiddo which was very much in the Jewish view and consciousness. It was between King Josiah of Judah and Pharaoh-nechoh of Egypt in 608 B.C.

> 2 Kings 23:29. . . . *Pharaoh-nechoh king of Egypt went up against the king of Assyria . . . and king Josiah went against him; and he [Pharaoh-nechoh] slew him [Josiah] at Megiddo . . .*

The death of the great reforming king made Megiddo a place that particularly symbolized calamity and disaster. The utter destruction of the hosts of evil there would balance the earlier destruction of good in the person of Josiah.

Babylon

The approach of the end is once again interrupted for still another vision. One of the angels says:

> Revelation 17:1. . . . *Come hither; I will shew unto thee . . . the great whore that sitteth upon many waters:*
> . . . .
> Revelation 17:3. *So he carried me away . . . into the wilderness: and I saw a woman sit upon a scarlet coloured beast, full of the names of blasphemy, having seven heads and ten horns.*
> Revelation 17:4. *And the woman was arrayed in purple and scarlet colour, and decked with gold and precious stones and pearls, . . .*
> Revelation 17:5. *And upon her forehead was a name written . . .* BABYLON THE GREAT . . .

Again, Babylon represents Rome in all its luxury and power. The "many waters" upon which the woman sits is taken from the Old

Testament description of the real Babylon, which was a city of canals. Thus, Jeremiah says:

> Jeremiah 51:12. . . . *the Lord . . . spake against the inhabitants of Babylon.*
> Jeremiah 51:13. *O thou that dwellest upon many waters . . .*

The author of Revelation, unable to resist the Old Testament quotation, must reinterpret it now and does so rather ineptly:

> Revelation 17:15. *And he* [the angel] *saith unto me, The waters which thou sawest, where the whore sitteth, are peoples, and multitudes, and nations, and tongues . . .*

The seven heads of the beast are finally explained in such a way as to make the real identity of "Babylon" unmistakable:

> Revelation 17:9. . . . *The seven heads are seven mountains, on which the woman sitteth.*

The interpretation goes on:

> Revelation 17:10. *And there are seven kings: five are fallen, and one is, and the other is not yet come; and when he cometh, he must continue a short space.*
> Revelation 17:11. *And the beast that was, and is not, even he is the eighth.* . . .

There seems no way of clearly working out this passage in the light of the reign of Domitian, but it can be dealt with, if it were spoken during the reign of Nero or very shortly after. Possibly the writer of Revelation is making use here of a passage of an earlier apocalypse that was indeed prepared in Nero's time, and did it without modifying its figures.

If we go back to Nero's time, we find that he is the sixth emperor (if we count Julius Caesar as the first). In that case, five emperors have "fallen" and "one is" (Nero). The seventh who "must continue a short space" would be Galba, who briefly reigned after Nero's death and was then killed by the praetorian guard, ushering in a short period of anarchy before Vespasian took over.

During this period, it was widely supposed among the common people of the empire that Nero was not really dead but had fled to

safety and would return. There were several "false Neros" who tried
to capitalize on this belief in that year.

It may be Nero, then, that in the view of the earlier apocalypse was
the beast "that was, and is not." When he returned, he would be the
eighth emperor.

But Babylon/Rome is to fall. The final battle of good and evil
(presumably at Armageddon) takes place:

> Revelation 19:20. *And the beast was taken . . . and them that
> worshipped his image. These . . . were cast alive into a lake of
> fire . . .*
> Revelation 19:21. *And the remnant were slain with the sword . . .*

Gog and Magog

Now after the long series of portents, visions, disasters, and symbols,
the end of history has come, and the Messianic age opens. Even that,
however, is not to be truly permanent.

> Revelation 20:1. *And I saw an angel come down from heaven . . .*
> Revelation 20:2. *And he laid hold on the dragon, that old serpent,
> which is the Devil, and Satan, and bound him a thousand years,*
> Revelation 20:3. *. . . and after that he must be loosed a little
> season.*

Why should there be this thousand-year "millennium" (see page
519) to be followed by still another upheaval and an anticlimactic
second battle of good and evil?

There may be a mystic symmetry here. The Earth was created in
six days, followed by a seventh day of rest, according to the first chapter
of Genesis. But for God a day is like a thousand years (see page 505).
Perhaps, then, the Earth's duration is to parallel the week of creation
with a millennium standing for each day.

First the earth will endure six millennia of labor, strife, evil, and sin,
one for each of the six days of creation. Then, for the seventh day of
rest, the Earth will spend one millennium under the Messiah. Only
then, when the Sabbath millennium is over, can the world indeed come
to an end:

> Revelation 20:7. . . . *Satan shall be loosed out of his prison,*
> Revelation 20:8. *And shall go out to deceive the nations* . . .
> *Gog and Magog, to gather them together to battle* . . .

This is an echo of Ezekiel's apocalyptic vision of the last battle:

> Ezekiel 38:2. *Son of man, set thy face against Gog, the land of Magog* . . .

The forces of evil are again defeated and destroyed and now, finally, all is over, even the Sabbath millennium, and the day of judgment is come at last:

> Revelation 20:12. *And I saw the dead, small and great, stand before God; . . . and the dead were judged* . . .

Jerusalem

A second creation, a perfect one, now replaces the old imperfect one:

> Revelation 21:1. *And I saw a new heaven and a new earth: for the first heaven and the first earth were passed away;* . . .
> Revelation 21:2. *And I John saw the holy city, new Jerusalem, coming down from God* . . .

The new Jerusalem is filled with the triumphant symbolism of the number twelve both in its old and new meanings:

> Revelation 21:10. . . . *the holy Jerusalem* . . .
> . . . .
> Revelation 21:12. . . . *had a wall great and high, and had twelve gates . . . and names written thereon, which are the names of the twelve tribes of the children of Israel:*
> . . . .
> Revelation 21:14. *And the wall of the city had twelve foundations, and in them the names of the twelve apostles of the Lamb.*

And when the description of the city in the most glowing possible terms is completed, the writer of the book quotes an angel to remind the reader emphatically that all that is predicted is rapidly to come to pass:

Revelation 22:6. . . . *These sayings are faithful and true: and the Lord God . . . sent his angel to shew . . . the things which must shortly be done.*

Revelation 22:7. *Behold, I come quickly . . .*

And with that assurance—still unfulfilled nearly two thousand years later—the New Testament ends.

DATES OF INTEREST
IN BIBLICAL HISTORY

(Old and New Testament)

NOTE: Many of the dates given in this table are approximate, or controversial.

B.C.

8500 First cities established in Middle East.
5000 Jericho already existing.
4004 Archbishop Ussher's date of creation.
3761 Traditional Jewish date of creation.
3600 Sumerian city-states in existence.
3100 Egypt united under single rule, 1st dynasty founded.
3000 Canaanites enter Canaan.
2700 Assyrian cities come into existence.
2570 Great Pyramid built in Egypt.
2500 Bronze Age reaches Canaan.
2264 Sargon of Agade founds Akkadian Empire.
2050 11th dynasty rules Egypt; 3rd dynasty rules Ur.
2000 Beginning of patriarchal age in Canaan (Abraham).
1971 Sesostris I rules Egypt.
1900 Babylon begins to dominate Tigris-Euphrates valley; Sumerian
         city-states decline.
1730 Hyksos enter Egypt.
1700 Hammurabi rules Babylon.
1650 Israelites in Egypt (Jacob, Joseph).
1570 Hyksos expelled from Egypt.
1500 Assyria becomes independent kingdom.

1490 Thutmose III rules Egypt.

1479 Thutmose III defeats Canaanites at Megiddo.

1475 Mitanni kingdom flourishing.

1450 Tyre founded by colonists from Sidon.

1400 Mycenaean Greeks at height of power.

1397 Amenhotep III rules Egypt, which is at height of its prosperity.

1390 Hittites at height of their power.

1370 Ikhnaton rules Egypt; attempts monotheistic reform; Egyptian power begins to decline; kingdoms of Moab, Ammon, and Edom established.

1290 Rameses II rules Egypt; oppression of the Israelites.

1275 Assyria conquers the Mitanni kingdom, as Assyria enters its first period of strength.

1250 Shalmaneser I rules Assyria.

1235 Tukulti-Ninurta I [Nimrod] rules Assyria.

1223 Merneptah rules Egypt; ancient world convulsed by migrations of peoples.

1211 Death of Merneptah; possibly time of Exodus (Moses).

1200 Hittite kingdom destroyed. Tarshish founded by colonists from Tyre.

1190 Rameses III rules Egypt and defeats Philistines.

1184 Trojan War.

1170 Israelites enter Canaan; Philistines settle coast (Joshua).

1150 Barak and Deborah defeat Sisera; period of judges.

1116 Tiglath-Pileser I rules Assyria.

1100 Gideon defeats Midianites; Greeks begin to settle Asia Minor coast.

1093 Death of Tiglath-Pileser I; Assyria in decline.

1080 Philistines defeat Israelites at Aphek; Shiloh destroyed.

1040 Samuel judges the tribes.

1028 Saul rules Israel.

1013 Philistines defeat Israelites at Mount Gilboa; Saul and Jonathan killed; David rules Judah.

1006 David rules united Israel-Judah.

1000 David establishes capital at Jerusalem; Aramaeans begin infiltration of Syria.

980 David's empire at peak.

973 Death of David; Solomon rules united Israel-Judah.

969 Hiram rules Tyre.
962 Completion of Temple by Solomon.
950 Rezin founds kingdom of Damascus (Syria).
933 Death of Solomon; breakup of Israel-Judah; Jeroboam I rules
        Israel; Rehoboam rules Judah.
928 Shishak of Egypt loots Jerusalem.
917 Abijam rules Judah.
915 Asa rules Judah.
912 Nadab rules Israel.
911 Baasha overthrows Nadab, seizes rule of Israel.
888 Elah rules Israel; overthrown by Zimri.
887 Omri rules Israel; founds Samaria.
883 Asshurnasirpal rules Assyria, which experiences revival.
880 Omri conquers Moab.
875 Ahab rules Israel; Jehoshaphat rules Judah; career of Elijah.
859 Shalmaneser III rules Assyria.
858 Ahab wars with Syrians.
854 Syrian-Israelite coalition holds off Assyria at Karkar.
853 Battle of Ramoth-gilead; death of Ahab; Ahaziah rules Israel.
852 Jehoram rules Israel; career of Elisha.
851 Jehoram (of Judah) rules Judah; J document in written form.
850 Mesha of Moab gains independence.
844 Ahaziah rules Judah.
843 Jehu rebels successfully and rules Israel; Athaliah usurps power
        in Judah; Hazael rules Syria and brings it to height of its
        power.
842 Jehu pays tribute to Assyria.
837 Jehoash rules Judah.
824 Death of Shalmaneser III of Assyria, which enters another period
        of decline.
816 Jehoahaz rules Israel.
814 Carthage founded by colonists from Tyre.
800 Jehoash (of Israel) rules Israel; death of Elisha.
797 Amaziah rules Judah.
785 Jeroboam II rules Israel; Israel at height of its power.
780 Azariah (Uzziah) rules Judah; Judah at height of its power.
760 Amos prophesies.
753 Rome founded.

750 Hosea prophesies; E document in written form.

745 Tiglath-Pileser III (Pul) rules Assyria; its power revives.

744 Death of Jeroboam II; gathering anarchy in Israel.

743 Tiglath-Pileser III conquers Urartu (Ararat).

740 Jotham rules Judah; Isaiah begins prophesying.

738 Pekahiah rules Israel, which is now tributary to Assyria.

737 Pekah rules Israel.

736 Ahaz rules Judah.

734 Pekah attempts to form coalition against Assyria; attacks Judah.

732 Hoshea rules Israel; Tiglath-Pileser III takes Damascus and brings Syrian kingdom to an end.

730 Micah prophesies.

726 Shalmaneser V rules Assyria.

725 Shalmaneser V lays siege to Samaria.

722 Sargon II usurps throne of Assyria and takes Samaria; Israelites carried off into exile; northern kingdom comes to an end.

720 Hezekiah rules Judah.

705 Sennacherib rules Assyria, makes Nineveh his capital.

703 Babylon under Merodach-baladan rebels against Assyria.

701 Sennacherib lays siege to Jerusalem.

700 Deioces founds Median kingdom.

693 Manasseh rules Judah, which is now tributary to Assyria.

681 Sennacherib assassinated; Esarhaddon rules Assyria and brings it to the peak of its power.

671 Esarhaddon invades and controls Egypt.

668 Asshurbanipal rules Assyria; establishes library at Nineveh.

663 Asshurbanipal sacks Thebes, ancient Egyptian capital.

652 Psamtik I rules Egypt, which is now free of Assyria.

640 Asshurbanipal defeats and destroys Elam.

638 Josiah rules Judah.

631 Cyrene founded by colonists from Greece.

630 Zephaniah prophesies.

626 Jeremiah begins to prophesy.

625 Asshurbanipal dies; gathering anarchy in Assyria and Nabopolassar seizes control of Babylonia.

620 Discovery of Book of Deuteronomy in the Temple followed by Yahvist reform in Judah; beginnings of Greek philosophy in Miletus.

615 Nahum prophesies.

612 Nabopolassar takes Nineveh; last Assyrian holdouts at Haran.

610 Necho (Pharaoh-nechoh) rules Egypt.

608 Necho defeats Judah at Megiddo; Josiah killed and Jehoiakim rules Judah; Jeremiah delivers Temple Sermon.

605 Babylonians defeat Necho at Carchemish; Nabopolassar dies; Nebuchadnezzar rules Babylonia and crushes last Assyrian stronghold; Habakkuk prophesies.

597 Judean rebellion crushed by Nebuchadnezzar; first Babylonian Exile; Zedekiah rules Judah.

593 Ezekiel begins to prophesy in captivity; Psamtik II rules Egypt and places Jewish garrison at Elephantine; Astyages rules Media.

588 Apries (Pharaoh-hophra) rules Egypt.

587 Zedekiah rebels against Nebuchadnezzar.

586 Nebuchadnezzar takes Jerusalem and destroys the Temple; second Babylonian Exile; Davidic Dynasty comes to an end; Gedaliah assassinated; Book of Lamentations written.

585 Nebuchadnezzar lays siege to Tyre.

573 Nebuchadnezzar raises siege of Tyre.

569 Aahmes rules Egypt.

568 Nebuchadnezzar invades Egypt unsuccessfully.

562 Death of Nebuchadnezzar; Evil-merodach rules Babylonia; various documents being combined by Jewish scribes in Babylon to form the historical books of the Old Testament.

560 Amel-Marduk assassinated; Nergal-ashur-usur rules Babylonia; Croesus rules Lydia, which is at its peak of power.

556 Nabonidus rules Babylonia; his son, Belshazzar, is co-ruler.

550 Cyrus overthrows Astyages of Media; founds Persian Empire.

546 Cyrus conquers Lydia; brings Lydian kingdom to an end.

540 Second Isaiah prophesies.

538 Cyrus takes Babylon and ends Babylonian kingdom; Jews allowed to return to Judea and first group under Sheshbazzar does so.

530 Death of Cyrus; Cambyses rules Persia.

525 Cambyses invades and conquers Egypt.

521 Darius I rules Persia.

520 Haggai and Zechariah prophesy; Zerubbabel takes over leadership of Jewish returnees.

516 Second Temple dedicated.

509 Rome evicts last king; Republic founded.

500 Obadiah prophesies; Greek cities of Asia Minor revolt against Persia.

490 Persian expedition defeated at Marathon by Athens.

486 Death of Darius I; Xerxes I (Ahasuerus) rules Persia.

480 Persian expedition defeated at Salamis by united Greece; Tarshish destroyed by Carthage.

465 Xerxes I assassinated; Artaxerxes I rules Persia.

460 Malachi prophesies.

459 Ezra in Jerusalem; historical books in final form.

450 Book of Ruth written; Third Isaiah prophesies.

440 Nehemiah in Jerusalem.

437 Walls of Jerusalem completed.

407 Jewish Temple at Elephantine destroyed by Egypt.

400 Books of Chronicles, Ezra, and Nehemiah written; Joel prophesies.

300 Book of Song of Solomon and Book of Jonah written.

275 Apocalyptic portion of Book of Zechariah written.

250 Book of Ecclesiastes written; Book of Proverbs reaches final form; Septuagint in preparation in Alexandria.

180 Book of Ecclesiasticus written.

165 Book of Daniel written.

150 Book of Esther written; Book of Psalms reaches present form.

147 Parthians take Babylonia.

146 Rome annexes Macedonia; sacks Corinth.

145 Death of Alexander Balas and Ptolemy VI; Demetrius II rules Seleucid Empire. Pharisees and Sadducees begin to appear as separate parties.

143 Antiochus VI rules Seleucid Empire.

142 Death of Jonathan; his brother Simon rules over independent Judea.

141 Last Seleucid soldiers leave Jerusalem.

139 Parthians take Demetrius II prisoner.

138 Antiochus VII rules Seleucid Empire; Attalus III rules Pergamum.

134 Simon of Judea assassinated; John Hyrcanus rules Judea.

133 Antiochus VII temporarily occupies Jerusalem. Rome annexes Pergamum, makes it province of Asia.

129 John Hyrcanus conquers Moab and Samaria; destroys Samaritan temple. Antiochus VII dies in battle against Parthians; Demetrius II released and again rules Seleucid Empire.

125 Antiochus VIII rules Seleucid Empire.

104 John Hyrcanus dies; Aristobulus rules Judea and assumes title of king.

103 Alexander Jannaeus rules Judea; Maccabean kingdom at peak; Pharisees in opposition.

100 Book of Jubilees, Prayer of Manasses, Testament of Twelve Patriarchs, Book of Enoch, First Book of Maccabees written.

86 Roman army sacks Athens.

84 Roman army sacks Ephesus.

79 Alexander Jannaeus dies; civil war in Judea; John Hyrcanus II high priest.

75 Book of Wisdom of Solomon written.

67 Antipater of Idumea in virtual control of Judea; Rome annexes Crete and Cyrene.

65 Rome annexes Bithynia in Asia Minor.

64 Rome annexes last remnant of Seleucid Empire.

63 Rome (Pompey) takes Jerusalem; Maccabean kingdom comes to end.

58 Rome annexes Cyprus.

53 Roman army under Crassus defeated by Parthians at Carrhae.

48 Julius Caesar defeats Pompey and controls Rome. Psalms of Solomon written.

44 Julius Caesar assassinated.

42 Octavian and Mark Antony defeat Caesar's assassins at Philippi.

40 Parthians occupy Judea; Antigonus Mattathias high priest.

37 Herod the Great takes Jerusalem and marries Mariamne the Maccabean; Aristobulus III high priest.

35 Herod executes Aristobulus III, last of the Maccabean high priests.

30 Octavian defeats Mark Antony and Cleopatra at Actium; controls Rome.

27 Octavian assumes title of Augustus; inaugurates the Roman Empire.

25 Rome annexes Pamphilia, Pisidia, Lycaonia, and Galatia in Asia Minor.

23 Herod executes Mariamne.

20 Herod starts rebuilding the Temple; Hillel leader of the Pharisees.

7 Herod has his sons by Mariamne executed.

4 Birth of Jesus. Death of Herod the Great; Herod Archelaus rules Judea; Herod Antipas rules Galilee; Herod Philip rules Iturea.

A.D.

1 Herod Philip builds Bethsaida.

6 Herod Archelaus deposed; Judea becomes procuratorial province with capital at Caesarea and Caponius as procurator. Annas high priest.

7 Census in Judea, with consequent disorders.

10 Birth of Saul [Paul]. "Assumption of Moses" written.

14 Augustus dies; Tiberius becomes Roman Emperor; Valerius Gratus becomes Procurator of Judea and deposes Annas.

18 Joseph Caiaphas high priest; Rome annexes Cappadocia in Asia Minor.

20 Herod Antipas founds Tiberias.

26 Pontius Pilate becomes Procurator of Judea.

27 Herod Antipas marries Herodias; John the Baptist begins to preach.

29 John the Baptist imprisoned and executed; Jesus crucified.

30 The Apostles speak with tongues at Pentecost.

34 Stephen is stoned to death; Saul [Paul] persecutes the Christians; death of Herod Philip.

35 Pontius Pilate massacres Samaritans at Mount Gerizim.

36 Pontius Pilate ends term as Procurator of Judea; Marcellus procurator. Caiaphas deposed as high priest; Jonathan high priest.

37 Saul [Paul] converted to Christianity. Tiberius dies; Caligula becomes Roman Emperor; Theophilus high priest.

39 Saul [Paul] escapes from Damascus and makes first appearance in Jerusalem as Christian. Herod Antipas deposed. Caligula attempts to initiate worship of himself in the Temple.

41 Caligula assassinated; Claudius becomes Roman Emperor. All

Judea united under Herod Agrippa I; Death of Philo of Alexandria.

43   James son of Zebedee executed; Peter imprisoned. Church at Antioch flourishes; followers of Jesus first called Christians; Saul [Paul] visits Jerusalem during famine; Rome annexes Lycia in Asia Minor.

44   Death of Herod Agrippa I. Judea again procuratorial province; Cuspius Fadus procurator.

45   Saul [Paul] on first missionary voyage.

46   Tiberius Alexander becomes Procurator of Judea.

48   Council of Jerusalem; Ventidius Cumanus becomes Procurator of Judea.

49   Claudius temporarily evicts Jews from Rome; Paul on second missionary voyage.

50   Paul in Europe; writes Epistles to the Thessalonians.

52   Death of Gamaliel the Pharisee; Paul appears before Gallio, Procurator of Achaia; Antonius Felix becomes Procurator of Judea.

53   Herod Agrippa II rules Galilee; Apollos appears at Ephesus.

54   Paul on third missionary voyage. Claudius dies; Nero becomes Roman Emperor.

55   Paul writes Epistle to the Galatians; imprisoned in Caesarea.

56   Paul writes Epistles to the Corinthians.

58   Paul writes Epistle to the Romans; arrested in Jerusalem.

59   Paul tried before Felix.

61   Porcius Festus becomes Procurator of Judea. Paul preaches before Herod Agrippa II.

62   Paul imprisoned in Rome; writes Epistles to the Ephesians, Philippians, Colossians, and Philemon. Annas high priest; has James the brother of Jesus stoned to death; Lucceius Albinus becomes Procurator of Judea and deposes Annas.

63   Rome annexes Pontus in Asia Minor.

64   Great fire at Rome; Nero persecutes Christians; Peter and Paul executed. (Paul released according to one theory.) Gessius Florus becomes Procurator of Judea.

65   Paul writes First Epistle to Timothy and Epistle to Titus.

66   Jewish rebellion breaks out in Judea and in Alexandria; Vespasian and his son Titus lead Roman armies in Judea.

67 Paul writes Second Epistle to Timothy and is executed; Vespasian conquers Galilee and the historian, Josephus, is taken prisoner.

68 Nero commits suicide; Galba becomes Roman Emperor.

69 Otho and Vitellius are Roman Emperors briefly; Vespasian becomes Roman Emperor.

70 Titus takes Jerusalem, destroys Temple; Gospel of St. Mark written.

71 Vespasian and Titus celebrate joint triumph in Rome; Arch of Titus constructed.

75 Gospel of St. Matthew written.

79 Vespasian dies; Titus becomes Roman Emperor.

80 Gospel of St. Luke and Book of Acts written; Epistle to the Hebrews written.

81 Titus dies; Domitian becomes Roman Emperor.

90 Domitian initiates Christian persecution; epistles of James, Peter, John and Jude written; Jewish rabbis gather at Jamnia to establish Jewish canon.

95 Book of Revelation and Book of 2 Esdras written.

96 Domitian assassinated; Nerva becomes Roman Emperor.

98 Nerva dies; Trajan becomes Roman Emperor. Roman Empire reaches greatest extent.

100 Gospel of St. John written. Letter of Baruch, Epistle of Jeremy, and Martyrdom of Isaiah written. Death of Herod Agrippa II.

115 Jews in Cyrene revolt and are crushed.

117 Trajan dies; Hadrian becomes Roman Emperor.

132 Jews in Judea revolt.

135 Last Jewish stronghold crushed and Jewish history, as a nation, ends for eighteen centuries; Jerusalem renamed Aelia Capitolina and sanctuary to Jupiter is built on the site of the Temple.

150 First two chapters of 2 Esdras written.

226 Parthian kingdom ends. Sassanid Dynasty founds new Persian Empire.

235 Roman Emperor, Alexander Severus, assassinated. Roman Empire sinks into anarchy.

240 Shapur I rules Persia.

259 Shapur I captures Roman Emperor, Valerian, in battle.

260 Famine sweeps Egypt; last two chapters of 2 Esdras written.

268 Roman Empire, under Claudius II, begins recovery.
284 Diocletian becomes Roman Emperor; reorganizes the empire.
303 Constantine I becomes Roman Emperor; begins process of
    making empire Christian.
400 St. Jerome prepares Vulgate (Latin version of the Bible).

INDEX OF BIBLICAL VERSES

Volume One, The Old Testament

Page numbers refer to pages in Volume One and are set in *italics*.

* Main treatment in Volume II.

INDEX OF BIBLICAL VERSES

Volume Two, The New Testament

INDEX OF SUBJECTS

Volume One, The Old Testament

INDEX OF SUBJECTS

Volume Two, The New Testament

1290   INDEX OF SUBJECTS